a Wolters Kluwer busin

GAAP Guide Level A

By Jan R. Williams, Joseph V. Carcello, and Terry L. Neal

Highlights

CCH's *GAAP Guide Level A* analyzes AICPA Accounting Research Bulletins, APB Opinions, and FASB Statements and Interpretations, all of which are contained in Level A of the GAAP hierarchy established by FASB Statement of Accounting Standards No. 162. The book organizes these accounting pronouncements alphabetically by topic under two general areas: generally accepted accounting principles and specialized industry accounting principles. Pronouncements covering the same subject are compiled and incorporated in a single chapter so that the authoritative information is immediately accessible.

2009 Edition

This edition of *GAAP Guide Level A* provides new and expanded coverage in these areas:

- The "About the GAAP Hierarchy" section has been revised to reflect the changes in the GAAP hierarchy promulgated in FAS-162 (The Hierarchy of Generally Accepted Accounting Principles).
- Chapter 4, "Business Combinations," has been revised to incorporate changes required by FAS-141(R) (Business Combinations).

WITHDRAWN THIS VOLUME DOES NOT CIRCULATE

- Chapter 7, "Consolidated Financial Statements," now includes the reporting requirements for noncontrolling interests required by FAS-160 (Noncontrolling Interests in Consolidated Financial Statements).

- Chapter 17, "Financial Instruments," has been revised to reflect amendments to FAS-133 found in FAS-161 (Disclosures about Derivative Instruments and Hedging Activities).

- Chapter 49, "Insurance," has been revised to incorporate the recently-issued FAS-163 (Accounting for Financial Guarantee Insurance Contracts).

In addition to incorporating the new pronouncements identified above, this edition of *GAAP Guide Level A* includes briefs in the form of "Important Notices" throughout the book addressing the following outstanding FASB Exposure Drafts:

- Earnings per Share—An Amendment of FASB Statement No. 128 (Chapter 13, "Earnings per Share")

- Accounting for Transfers of Financial Assets—An Amendment of FASB Statement No. 140 (Chapter 45, "Transfer and Servicing of Financial Assets")

- Not-for-Profit Organizations: Mergers and Acquisitions; and Not-for-Profit Organizations: Goodwill and Other Intangible Assets Acquired in a Merger or Acquisition—An Amendment of FASB Statement No. 142 (Chapter 51, "Not-for-Profit Organizations")

- Consolidated Financial Statements: Purpose and Policy (Chapter 7, "Consolidated Financial Statements")

- Accounting for Hedging Activities—An Amendment of FASB Statement No. 133 (Chapter 17, "Financial Instruments")

- Disclosure of Certain Loss Contingencies—An Amendment of FASB Statement Nos. 5 and 141(R) (Chapter 4, "Business Combinations" and Chapter 8, "Contingencies, Risks, and Uncertainties")

Coverage of the authoritative literature in Levels B, C, and D of the GAAP hierarchy can be found in the companion volume to this *Guide*, the 2009 *GAAP Guide Levels B, C, and D*, which contains incisive analysis of Statements of Position, consensus positions of the EITF, and the FASB Staff Positions.

CCH Learning Center

CCH's goal is to provide you with the clearest, most concise, and up-to-date accounting and auditing information to help further your professional development, as well as a convenient method to help you satisfy your continuing professional education requirements. The CCH Learning Center* offers a complete line of self-study courses covering complex and constantly evolving accounting and auditing issues. We are continually adding new courses to the library to help you stay current on all the latest developments. The CCH Learning Center courses are available 24 hours a day, seven days a week. You'll get immediate exam results and certification. To view our complete accounting and auditing course catalog, go to: **http://cch.learningcenter.com**.

Accounting Research Manager™

Accounting Research Manager is the most comprehensive, up-to-date, and objective online database of financial reporting literature. It includes all authoritative and proposed accounting, auditing, and SEC literature, plus independent, expert-written interpretive guidance.

Our Weekly Summary e-mail newsletter highlights the key developments of the week, giving you the assurance that you have the most current information. It provides links to new FASB, AICPA, SEC, PCAOB, EITF, and IASB authoritative and proposal-stage literature, plus insightful guidance from financial reporting experts.

Our outstanding team of content experts takes pride in updating the system on a daily basis, so you stay as current as possible. You'll learn of newly released literature and deliberations of current financial reporting projects as soon as they occur! Plus, you benefit from their easy-to-understand technical translations.

---

* CCH is registered with the National Association of State Boards of Accountancy (NASBA) as a sponsor of continuing professional education on the National Registry of CPE Sponsors. State boards of accountancy have final authority on the acceptance of individual courses for CPE credit. Complaints regarding registered sponsors may be addressed to the National Registry of CPE Sponsors, 150 Fourth Avenue North, Nashville, TN 37219-2417. Telephone: 615-880-4200.

* CCH is registered with the National Association of State Boards of Accountancy as a Quality Assurance Service (QAS) sponsor of continuing professional education. Participating state boards of accountancy have final authority on the acceptance of individual courses for CPE credit. Complaints regarding QAS program sponsors may be addressed to NASBA, 150 Fourth Avenue North, Suite 700, Nashville, TN 37219-2417. Telephone: 615-880-4200.

With **Accounting Research Manager,** you maximize the efficiency of your research time, while enhancing your results. Learn more about our content, our experts and how you can request a FREE trial by visiting us at **http://www.accountingresearchmanager.com**

10/08

2009

GAAP

GUIDE LEVEL A

Restatement and Analysis of
Current FASB Standards

JAN R. WILLIAMS, Ph.D., CPA

JOSEPH V. CARCELLO, Ph.D., CPA, CMA, CIA

TERRY L. NEAL, Ph.D., CPA

CCH
a Wolters Kluwer business

This publication is designed to provide accurate and authoritative information in regard to the subject matter covered. It is sold with the understanding that the publisher is not engaged in rendering legal, accounting, or other professional services. If legal advice or other professional assistance is required, the services of a competent professional person should be sought.

—From a *Declaration of Principles* jointly adopted by a Committee of the American Bar Association and a Committee of Publishers and Associations

ISBN: 978-0-8080-9218-6

Portions of this work were published in a previous edition.

Printed in the United States of America

Contents

Generally Accepted Accounting Principles

Specialized Industry Accounting Principles

For implementation guidance on the above topics, refer to the *GAAP Guide Level A*'s companion volume, the 2009 *GAAP Guide Levels B, C, and D.* See the Cross-Reference on page CR.01 for specific standards covered in that Guide.

For the most recent activities of the FASB and the AICPA, refer to the *GAAP Update Service* and the *GAAP Library* (www. CCHGroup.com).

Our Peer Review Policy

Thank you for ordering the 2009 *GAAP Guide Level A*. Each year we bring you the best accounting and auditing reference guides. To confirm the technical accuracy and quality control of our materials, CCH voluntarily submitted to a peer review of our publishing system and our publications (see the Peer Review Report on the following page).

In addition to peer review, our publications undergo strict technical and content reviews by qualified practitioners. This ensures that our books meet "real-world" standards and applicability.

Our publications are reviewed every step of the way—from conception to production—to ensure that we bring you the finest guides on the market.

Updated annually, peer reviewed, technically accurate, convenient, and practical—the 2009 *GAAP Guide Level A* shows our commitment to creating books and practice aids you can trust.

Peer Review Statement

Caldwell, Becker, Dervin, Petrick & Co., L.L.P.
CERTIFIED PUBLIC ACCOUNTANTS

July 18, 2006

Executive Board
CCH, a Wolters Kluwer business

We have reviewed the system of quality control for the development and maintenance of GAAP Guide Level A (2007 Edition), of CCH, a Wolters Kluwer business (the company), applicable to non-SEC issuers in effect for the year ended June 30, 2006, and the resultant materials in effect at June 30, 2006. The design of the system, and compliance with it, are the responsibilities of the company. Our responsibility is to express an opinion on the design of the system, and the company's compliance with that system based on our review.

Our review was conducted in accordance with the standards for reviews of quality control materials promulgated by the Peer Review Committee of the Center for Public Company Audit Firms of the American Institute of Certified Public Accountants. In performing our review, we have given consideration to the following general characteristics of a system of quality control. A company's system for the development and maintenance of quality control materials encompasses its organizational structure and the policies and procedures established to provide the users of its materials with reasonable assurance that the quality control materials are reliable aids to assist them in conforming with professional standards in conducting their accounting and auditing practices. The extent of a company's quality control policies and procedures for the development and maintenance of quality control materials and the manner in which they are implemented will depend upon a variety of factors, such as the size and organizational structure of the company and the nature of the materials provided to users. Variance in individual performance and professional interpretation affects the degree of compliance with prescribed quality control policies and procedures. Therefore, adherence to all policies and procedures in every case may not be possible.

Our review and tests were limited to the system of quality control for the development and maintenance of the aforementioned quality control materials of CCH and to the materials themselves and did not extend to the application of these materials by users of the materials nor to the policies and procedures of individual users.

In our opinion, the system of quality control for the development and maintenance of the quality control materials of CCH was suitably designed and was being complied with during the year ended June 30, 2006, to provide users of the materials with reasonable assurance that the materials are reliable aids to assist them in conforming with those professional standards in the United States of America applicable to non-SEC issuers. Also, in our opinion, the quality control materials referred to above are reliable aids at June 30, 2006.

CALDWELL, BECKER, DERVIN, PETRICK & CO., LLP.
CALDWELL, BECKER, DERVIN, PETRICK & CO., L.L.P.

20750 Ventura Boulevard, Suite 140 • Woodland Hills, CA 91364
(818) 704-1040 • FAX (818) 704-5536

Preface

As part of **The Complete *GAAP Library for Business***, the 2009 *GAAP Guide Level A* explains and analyzes promulgated accounting principles in the highest level of the GAAP hierarchy in use today. This edition is current through the issuance of FASB Statement No. 163.

New Pronouncements and Outstanding Exposure Drafts

- FASB Statement 141(R) Business Combinations
- FASB Statement 160 Noncontrolling Interests in Consolidated Financial Statements
- FASB Statement 161 Disclosures about Derivative Instruments and Hedging Activities
- FASB Statement 162 The Hierarchy of Generally Accepted Accounting Principles
- FASB Statement 163 Accounting for Financial Guarantee Insurance Contracts
- FASB Exposure Draft Earnings Per Share—An Amendment of FASB Statement No. 128
- FASB Exposure Draft Not-for-Profit Organizations: Mergers and Acquisitions
- FASB Exposure Draft Not-for-Profit Organizations: Goodwill and Other Intangible Assets Acquired in a Merger or Acquisition—An Amendment of FASB Statement No. 142
- FASB Exposure Draft Accounting for Transfers of Financial Assets—An Amendment of FASB Statement No. 140
- FASB Exposure Draft Consolidated Financial Statements: Purpose and Policy
- FASB Exposure Draft Accounting for Hedging Activities—An Amendment of FASB Statement No. 133
- FASB Exposure Draft Disclosure of Certain Loss Contingencies—An Amendment of FASB Statements Nos. 5 and 141(R)

Also in this edition: **Expanded Cross-Reference** to the Complete Library for Business, which will help you pinpoint guidance by pronouncement.

Coverage of the authoritative literature in Levels B, C, and D of the GAAP hierarchy can be found in the companion volume to this *Guide*, the 2009 *GAAP Guide Levels B, C, and D*, which contains incisive analysis of Statements of Position, consensus positions of the EITF, and FASB Staff Positions.

How to Use the 2009 *GAAP Guide Level A*

The 2009 *GAAP Guide Level A* organizes accounting pronouncements alphabetically by topic under two general areas: generally accepted accounting principles and specialized industry accounting principles. Pronouncements covering the same subject are compiled and incorporated in a single chapter so that the authoritative information is immediately accessible.

Material can be located several ways: The **Cross-Reference** shows the chapter in which a particular pronouncement is discussed. The **Index** provides quick, accurate reference to needed information. In addition, the **Complete GAAP Library** is available on CD-ROM. Researching the *GAAP Guide Level A* and the *GAAP Guide Levels B, C, and D* is now easier than ever.

The *GAAP Guide Level A* is written in clear, comprehensible language. Each pronouncement is discussed in a comprehensive format that makes it easy to understand and apply. Practical illustrations and examples demonstrate and clarify specific accounting principles.

The **Practice Pointers** throughout this edition do just that: they point out in plain English how to apply the standards just discussed.

Observations enrich the discussion by presenting interesting aspects of GAAP, such as conflicts within the authoritative literature. Although no attempt is made to resolve apparent errors and conflicts in the promulgated pronouncements, these items are brought to your attention.

To facilitate research, the *GAAP Guide Level A* includes extensive codification references to pertinent paragraphs of the original pronouncements.

The 2009 *GAAP Guide Level A* meets accounting industry standards overseen by the peer review system. A document covering the peer review of this book is reprinted for your reference.

Acknowledgments

The authors thank James Ulvog for his technical review of new FASB pronouncement material.

Abbreviations

The following abbreviations are used throughout the text to represent accounting and auditing principles:

APB	Accounting Principles Board Opinion
ARB	Accounting Research Bulletin
ASR	Accounting Series Release
CON	FASB Concepts Statements
FAS	FASB Statement of Financial Accounting Standards
FIN	FASB Interpretation
SAS	Statement on Auditing Standards
SOP	AICPA Statement of Position

About the Authors

Jan R. Williams, Ph.D., CPA, is the Pilot Corporation Chair of Excellence and Dean of the College of Business Administration at the University of Tennessee, Knoxville, where he has been on the faculty since 1977. Formerly, he was on the faculties of the University of Georgia and Texas Tech University. He received a Ph.D. in business administration from the University of Arkansas and is a CPA licensed in Arkansas and Tennessee.

Dr. Williams has, for many years, been actively involved in the American Institute of Certified Public Accountants, the Tennessee Society of Certified Public Accountants, and several other professional organizations. Throughout his career, he has taught continuing professional education for CPAs. In 1994, Dr. Williams received the Oustanding Accounting Educator Award from both the Tennessee Society of CPAs and the AICPA. He was president of the American Accounting Association in 1999–2000 and has authored or co-authored five books and more than 70 articles and other publications on issues related to financial reporting and accounting education. Dr. Williams currently serves on the Board of Directors of the AACSB (Association to Advance Collegiate Schools of Business) International.

Joseph V. Carcello, Ph.D., CPA, CMA, CIA, is the Ernst & Young Professor in the Department of Accounting and Information Management at the University of Tennessee. Dr. Carcello also is co-founder and Director of Research for the University's Corporate Governance Center. He has taught continuing professional education courses for two of the Big 4 accounting firms, the AICPA, the Institute of Internal Auditors, the Institute of Management Accountants, and the Tennessee and Florida Societies of CPAs. He has provided consulting services to public companies on revenue recognition and on Section 404 of the Sarbanes-Oxley Act. Dr. Carcello has served the Securities and Exchange Commission as an expert witness.

Dr. Carcello is the co-author of CCH's *GAAS Guide*. He is also the co-author of a funded research study by the Committee of Sponsoring Organizations (COSO) of the Treadway Commission titled *Fraudulent Financial Reporting: 1987–1997, An Analysis of U.S. Public Companies* and of a research monograph, *Fraud-Related SEC Enforcement Actions Against Auditors: 1987–1997*, published by the AICPA's Auditing Standards Board. Dr. Carcello served on COSO's Small Business Controls Guidance Task Force. He currently serves as Vice President–Finance for the American Accounting Association, a member of the Public Company Accounting Oversight Board's (PCAOB) Standing Advisory Group, and a member of the Institute of Internal Auditors' Professional Issues Committee.

Terry L. Neal, Ph.D., CPA, is the Dennis Hendrix Professor in Accounting in the Department of Accounting and Information Management at the University of Tennessee. He also is a Research Fellow at the University of Tennessee's Corporate Governance Center. Dr. Neal currently teaches a graduate course in advanced financial accounting topics, an undergraduate intermediate accounting course, and has taught undergraduate auditing. He has also taught continuing professional education courses for one of the Big 4 accounting firms for several years. Dr. Neal also serves as the director of the Ph.D. program in Accounting and teaches a doctoral seminar in empirical/archival research, with an emphasis on auditing and corporate governance issues.

About the GAAP Hierarchy

The meaning of the term *generally accepted accounting principles* (GAAP) has varied over time. Originally, GAAP referred to accounting policies and procedures that were widely used in practice. As standard-setting bodies and professional organizations became more involved in establishing required or preferred practices, the term came to refer more to the pronouncements issued by particular accounting bodies. Today, many different series of authoritative literature exist, some of which are still in effect but are no longer being issued, like APB Opinions and AICPA Accounting Research Bulletins. Others—such as FASB Statements—continue to be issued by accounting organizations.

To better organize and clarify what is meant by GAAP, SAS-69 (The Meaning of "Present Fairly in Conformity with Generally Accepted Accounting Principles" in the Independent Auditor's Report) established what is commonly referred to as the GAAP hierarchy. The original GAAP hierarchy was amended in 2008 by FAS-162 (The Hierarchy of Generally Accepted Accounting Principles). The purpose of the GAAP hierarchy is to instruct financial statement preparers, auditors, and users of financial statements concerning the relative priority of the different sources of GAAP used by auditors to judge the fairness of presentation in financial statements. Though the GAAP hierarchy originally appeared in the professional auditing literature, its impact goes beyond its importance to auditors: Preparers, users, and others interested in financial statements must understand the sources of GAAP that underlie those statements. The GAAP hierarchy applies to for-profit businesses and non-governmental not-for-profit entities. Separate hierarchies exist for state and local governments and for the federal government.

The *GAAP hierarchy* is structured into four categories of established accounting principles. Because these sources of accounting principles arose over many years and were promulgated by different groups, some conflicts exist among them. The four categories of GAAP correspond to these principles' relative authority. Higher categories carry more weight and must be followed when conflicts arise. When two or more sources of GAAP within a given level of the hierarchy disagree on a particular transaction, the approach that better portrays the substance of the transaction should be followed.

The figure on the following pages displays the four levels of established principles that are supported by authoritative accounting literature, as well as the additional sources of GAAP, and the corresponding CCH coverage. (FAS-162, par. 3)

GAAP Hierarchy   CCH Coverage

CATEGORY A*

- FASB Statements of Financial Accounting Standards (FAS)

  2009 *GAAP Guide Level A*

- FASB Interpretations (FIN)

  2009 *GAAP Guide Level A*

- AICPA APB Opinions (APB) not superseded

  2009 *GAAP Guide Level A*

- AICPA Accounting Research Bulletins (ARB) not superseded

  2009 *GAAP Guide Level A*

- FASB Staff Positions (SFP)

  2009 *GAAP Guide Levels B, C, and D*

- FASB Statement 133 Implementation Issues

  2009 *Financial Instruments*

CATEGORY B*

- FASB Technical Bulletins (FTB)

  2009 *GAAP Guide Levels B, C, and D*

- AICPA Industry Audit and Accounting Guides cleared by FASB

  2008–2009 Engagement Series

- AICPA Statements of Position (SOP) cleared by FASB

  2009 *GAAP Guide Levels B, C, and D*

CATEGORY C*

- Consensus Positions of the Emerging Issues Task Force (EITF)

  2009 *GAAP Guide Levels B, C, and D*

- AICPA Accounting Standards Executive Committee Practice Bulletins cleared by FASB

  2009 *GAAP Guide Levels B, C, and D*

- EITF D-Topics

  2009 *GAAP Guide Levels B, C, and D*

CATEGORY D*

• AICPA Accounting Interpretations (AIN)	2009 *GAAP Guide Levels B, C, and D*
• FASB Implementation Guides (FIG)	2009 *GAAP Guide Levels B, C, and D*
• AICPA Industry Audit and Accounting Guides and Statement of Positions not cleared by FASB	2009 *GAAP Guide Levels B, C, and D*
• Practices widely recognized and prevalent either generally or in the industry	2009 *GAAP Guide Levels B, C, and D*

* All four categories are covered twice-monthly in the *GAAP Update Service*.

If the accounting treatment for a transaction or event is not specified by a pronouncement in Category A, the entity shall consider whether the accounting treatment is specified in another category. If the accounting treatment is specified in another category, the entity shall follow the treatment specified in the highest category in the hierarchy. (FAS-162, par. 4)

If the accounting treatment for a transaction or event is not specified by a pronouncement or established practice in any of the categories in the GAAP hierarchy, the entity shall next consider accounting principles for similar transactions or events within the hierarchy. Next the entity shall consider other accounting literature, including FASB Concepts Statements, AICPA Issues Papers, International Financial Reporting Standards, pronouncements of other professional associations or regulatory agencies, Technical Information Services Inquiries and Replies included in AICPA Technical Practice Aids, and accounting textbooks, handbooks, and articles. The appropriateness of other accounting literature depends on its relevance in the particular circumstances, the specificity of the guidance, and the general recognition of the issuer or author as an authority. (FAS-162, par. 5)

Sarbanes-Oxley Act of 2002

The Sarbanes-Oxley Act was signed into law in the summer of 2002. This legislation is generally viewed as the most far-reaching legislation affecting the accounting profession since the securities laws of the 1930s.

The Sarbanes-Oxley Act applies to SEC registrants and their auditors. The Act does not apply to private companies. The Sarbanes-Oxley Act has 11 sections. These sections address:

1. The Public Company Accounting Oversight Board (PCAOB)

2. Auditor independence

3. Corporate responsibility

4. Enhanced financial disclosures

5. Analyst conflicts of interest

6. Commission resources and authority

7. Studies and reports

8. Corporate and criminal fraud accountability

9. White-collar crime penalty enhancements

10. Corporate tax returns

11. Corporate fraud and accountability

The Sarbanes-Oxley Act is a direct result of the financial reporting frauds at a number of major corporations earlier this decade (e.g., Enron, Global Crossing, Qwest, Adelphia Communications, Tyco, and WorldCom). The outrage in the country to these financial reporting frauds was reflected by the overwhelming votes in favor of Sarbanes-Oxley in both houses of Congress. The Sarbanes-Oxley Act passed the Senate 99-0, and only three votes were cast against it in the House of Representatives.

PUBLIC COMPANY ACCOUNTING OVERSIGHT BOARD

Among the more important provisions of the Sarbanes-Oxley Act is the creation of the Public Company Accounting Oversight Board (PCAOB). The PCAOB is responsible for overseeing all aspects of the public accounting profession related to audits of SEC registrants (hereafter called public companies). Much of the AICPA's self-regulatory efforts are obviated by the creation of the PCAOB.

All accounting firms auditing public companies must register with the PCAOB. The PCAOB is required to establish or adopt auditing, quality control, ethics, and independence standards for auditors of public companies. In addition, the PCAOB conducts inspections of registered public accounting firms. Finally, the PCAOB investigates allegations of substandard performance against auditors of public companies and has the power to discipline accounting firms and individual auditors.

The PCAOB has five full-time members, only two of whom can be licensed CPAs. The SEC will appoint board members after consulting with the Chairman of the Board of Governors of the Federal Reserve System and the Secretary of Treasury. The term of service is five years, and board members are limited to two terms.

The PCAOB's current members are Mark Olson (chairman), Daniel Goelzer, Bill Gradison, Charles Niemeier, and Steve Harris. Mr. Olson previously served as a member of the Federal Reserve Board of Governors and of the Federal Open Market Committee. He also has served as the staff director of the securities subcommittee of the U.S. Senate Committee on Banking, Housing, and Urban Affairs, and served as a partner with Ernst & Young's consulting practice. Mr. Goelzer and Mr. Niemeier are CPAs with experience in public accounting, although they more recently practiced as securities lawyers and have prior experience with the SEC. Mr. Gradison served as a member of the U.S. House of Representatives, as the mayor of Cincinnati, and as president of a health care industry association. Harris previously served as the Staff Director and Chief Counsel to the U.S. Senate Banking, Housing, and Urban Affairs Committee under Senator Sarbanes. Harris was one of the primary drafters of the Sarbanes-Oxley Act.

The accounting and auditing experience of the board members of the PCAOB is limited, so it seems likely that the PCAOB will rely heavily on its professional staff, particularly in setting auditing standards for public companies. The PCAOB's Chief Auditor is Tom Ray. Mr. Ray previously was a partner with KPMG and served as the Director of Audit and Attest Standards for the AICPA. Other professionals in the Office of the Chief Auditor are Jennifer Rand and Greg Scates, both Deputy Chief Auditors with significant experience in the public accounting profession.

The PCAOB assesses and collects a registration fee and an annual fee from each registered public accounting firm. These fees are to be sufficient to recover the costs of both processing registrations and the required annual report that each registered accounting firm is to file with the PCAOB.

Although the PCAOB is charged with promulgating auditing standards, the Sarbanes-Oxley Act specifically requires that these standards include the following provisions:

- Registered public accounting firms must maintain work papers in sufficient detail to support their conclusions in the audit report, and these work papers must be retained for at least seven years.

- The issuance of an audit report must be approved by a concurring or second partner. Each audit report must describe the scope of the auditor's internal control testing. The auditor must include, either in the audit report or in a separate report, the following items: (1) the auditor's findings from the internal control testing, (2) an overall evaluation of the entity's internal control structure and procedures, and (3) a description of any material weaknesses in internal controls.

- Quality control standards related to required internal firm consultations on accounting and auditing questions.

The PCAOB inspects public accounting firms that regularly audit more than 100 public companies on an annual basis. Other public accounting firms that audit at least one public company are inspected no less often than once every three years. Inspections involve reviews of audit engagements and of the firm's quality control system. The PCAOB can report any violation of (1) the Sarbanes-Oxley Act, (2) PCAOB and SEC rules, (3) the firm's own quality control standards, and (4) professional standards to the SEC and each appropriate state regulatory authority.

Registered public accounting firms and their employees are required to cooperate with PCAOB investigations. Firms that fail to cooperate in PCAOB investigations can be suspended or disbarred from being able to audit public companies, as can individual CPAs. Although the PCAOB does not have subpoena power (the PCAOB is specifically designated as a nongovernmental entity), there are procedures for the PCAOB to obtain needed information for an investigation via an SEC-issued subpoena.

Documents and information gathered by the PCAOB in the course of an investigation are not subject to civil discovery. PCAOB sanctions include the ability to suspend or disbar firms or individual CPAs from auditing public companies, as well as monetary penalties as high as $750,000 for individuals and $15 million for firms.

The Sarbanes-Oxley Act amends the Securities Acts of 1933 and 1934 to define as generally accepted accounting principles those principles promulgated by a standards-setting body when the standards-setting body meets a number of requirements set out in the Sarbanes-Oxley Act. The FASB's current structure meets the requirements set out in the Sarbanes-Oxley Act.

The PCAOB's funding and the funding of the accounting standards-setting body (currently the FASB) are recoverable from annual accounting support fees. These annual accounting support fees are assessed against and recoverable from public companies, where the amount of the fee due from each issuer is a function of the issuer's relative market capitalization.

AUDITOR INDEPENDENCE

The Sarbanes-Oxley Act specifically prohibits accounting firms from performing any of the following services for a public company audit client:

- Bookkeeping services

- Financial information systems design and implementation

- Appraisal or valuation services, fairness opinions, or contribution-in-kind reports

- Actuarial services

- Internal audit outsourcing services

- Management or human resources functions

- Broker or dealer, investment adviser, or investment banking services

- Legal services and expert services unrelated to the audit

The provision of any other nonaudit services for an audit client, including tax work, is allowed only if approved in advance by the audit committee. In addition, the audit committee must preapprove audit services.

The Sarbanes-Oxley Act requires that audit partners on audits of public companies be rotated every five years. Also required is a timely report to the audit committee containing the following information: (1) a discussion of critical accounting policies and practices; (2) alternative accounting treatments discussed with management, the ramifications of these alternatives, and the auditor's preferred treatment; and (3) other material communications between the auditor and management (e.g., the management letter, schedule of unadjusted audit differences). Finally, a registered public accounting firm cannot perform an audit of a public company if that company's CEO, CFO, controller, chief accounting officer, or others serving in equivalent positions were employed by the registered public accounting firm and worked on the audit engagement within one year prior to the beginning of the current year's audit.

CORPORATE RESPONSIBILITY

The Sarbanes-Oxley Act specifies that the audit committee is directly responsible for the appointment, compensation, and oversight of the external auditor. The Act also requires that all members of the audit committee be independent. Audit committees are to establish procedures for handling complaints related to accounting, internal controls, and auditing matters, including complaints that may be submitted anonymously. Audit committees are to be given the authority to retain independent counsel and other advisers, if they deem this to be necessary. Finally, each public company must provide the funding that the audit committee believes is necessary to compensate the registered public accounting firm. The Sarbanes-Oxley Act requires the CEO and CFO of each public company to certify, in each annual and quarterly report filed with the SEC, the following conditions:

- The CEO and CFO have reviewed the report;

- To the best of the officers' knowledge, the report does not contain any material omissions or misstatements;

- The financial statements and other financial information included in the report fairly present the entity's financial condition and results of operations;

- The signing officers are responsible for the entity's internal control system, that the internal control system is appropriately designed, that the effectiveness of the internal control system has been evaluated within 90 days of the report, and that the officers' conclusions about the effectiveness of internal controls are included within the report;

- The signing officers have disclosed to their auditors and the audit committee significant deficiencies in the design or operation of the entity's internal control as well as any fraud (even if immaterial) involving management or employees with a significant role in the entity's internal control structure; and

- Whether there have been any significant changes in internal control subsequent to the date of its evaluation.

The Act makes it unlawful for any officer or director, or any other person operating under their direction, to fraudulently influence, coerce, manipulate, or mislead the external auditor in the audit of financial statements.

The Act also requires the CEO and CFO of any issuer restating its financial statements because of material noncompliance with SEC financial reporting requirements to forfeit any bonus or incentive-based or equity-based compensation received within one year of the filing date of the financial statements that are subsequently restated. Profits realized from the sale of securities during this 12-month period also must be forfeited.

ENHANCED FINANCIAL DISCLOSURES

The Sarbanes-Oxley Act requires public companies to reflect all material adjustments to the financial statements identified by the external auditor. As a result of the Sarbanes-Oxley mandate, the SEC issued a Final Rule requiring companies to disclose all material off-balance-sheet transactions, arrangements, and obligations. The SEC now requires companies to explain their off-balance-sheet arrangements in a new, and separately captioned, section of the MD&A. Also, most companies now are required to include a table that presents an overview of certain known contractual obligations. In addition, the Act specifically prohibits misleading pro forma financial information. Pro forma financial information also must be reconciled with what would be required under GAAP.

The Sarbanes-Oxley Act generally prohibits personal loans to executives. In addition, stock transactions by directors, officers, and principal stockholders must be disclosed by the close of the second business day after the date of the stock transaction.

The Act requires internal control reports in each annual report. Management must state that it is responsible for the internal control structure and must provide an assessment of the effectiveness of that structure. Moreover, the external auditor must issue its own opinion on the effectiveness of the company's internal control over financial reporting.

Public companies are required to state whether they have a code of ethics for senior officers and if not, why not. Also, any changes or waivers to the code of ethics for senior officers must be disclosed in a Form 8-K filing. Finally, the issuer must disclose whether the audit committee contains at least one financial expert and if not, why not.

The Act requires the SEC to review the filings of each issuer at least once every three years. Issuers are required to disclose, in plain English, on a rapid and current basis (generally within four business days of the event's occurrence), any material changes in the issuers' financial condition and results of operations.

As a result, items that are required to be disclosed on Form 8-K include:

- Entering into a material definitive agreement not in the ordinary course of business (e.g., business combination agreements).

- Terminating a material definitive agreement not in the ordinary course of business.

- New obligations under the terms of a material direct financial obligation (e.g., a short-term debt obligation arising in other than the ordinary course of business, a long-term debt obligation, and a lease—whether capital or operating), or if the company becomes directly or contingently liable for a material obligation arising from an off-balance sheet arrangement.

- An event that accelerates (e.g., default) or increases a direct financial obligation or an obligation under an off-balance-sheet arrangement.

- Expected costs associated with an exit or disposal plan if the exit or disposal plan meets the criteria of FAS-146 (Accounting for Costs Associated with Exit or Disposal Activities).

- Material asset impairment charges required to be recognized under GAAP.

- A notice of delisting, or a notice of failure to continue to meet listing requirements, received from a national securities exchange (e.g., NYSE) or association (e.g., Nasdaq).

- The sale of equity securities in a transaction that is not registered under the Securities Acts.

- Material modifications to the rights held by any holders of a company's securities.

- A determination by the company that its previously issued financial statements should no longer be relied upon because of an error in the financial statements, including situations wherein the company's auditor indicates that previously issued audit reports should no longer be relied upon.

- If a director resigns from the board or chooses not to stand for reelection because of a disagreement with management, or if a director is removed from the board for cause.

ANALYST CONFLICTS OF INTEREST

The Sarbanes-Oxley Act seeks to increase the objectivity and independence of securities analysts. The Act specifically requires the following:

- Analysts' research reports are no longer subject to clearance or approval by investment bankers.

- Investment bankers are prohibited from providing input into the performance evaluations of research analysts.

- Investment bankers are prohibited from retaliating, or threatening retaliation, against research analysts for reports that may adversely affect investment-banking relationships with existing or prospective clients.

- Structural and institutional safeguards are established to protect research analysts from review, pressure, or oversight by investment bankers.

The Act also requires the disclosure of analyst conflicts of interest in both public appearances and published research reports. When discussing a particular company in a public appearance or research report, the analyst must disclose how much of the company's debt or equity securities the analyst owns. The analyst must disclose whether his or her firm or the analyst personally has received any compensation from the company that is the subject of the research report. If the analyst is recommending a company's securities, the analyst must disclose whether that company is a current client of the analyst's employer or if it has been a client during the past year. The analyst must also disclose whether his or her compensation is tied to investment banking revenues.

COMMISSION RESOURCES AND AUTHORITY

The Act provided substantial incremental funding for the SEC. The SEC used these funds to hire additional professionals to oversee auditors and the public accounting profession.

The Sarbanes-Oxley Act also clarifies the ability of the SEC to censure individuals and to deny, either temporarily or permanently, the ability of individuals to practice before the SEC. These remedies are available to the SEC if an individual:

- Lacks the qualifications needed to represent others.

- Lacks character or integrity.

- Has engaged in unethical or improper professional conduct.

- Has willfully violated, or helped others to willfully violate (i.e., aided and abetted), the securities laws.

The Act defines "improper professional conduct" to include an intentional or knowing violation of applicable professional standards, including a violation attributable to reckless conduct. Improper professional conduct also includes two types of negligent conduct:

1. A single instance of highly unreasonable conduct, leading to a violation of professional standards, when the firm or the

practitioner should have known that heightened scrutiny was warranted; and

2. Repeated instances of unreasonable conduct, leading to a violation of professional standards, which suggests that the individual may lack the competence to practice before the SEC.

STUDIES AND REPORTS

When it was passed, the Act required either the SEC or the General Accounting Office (now known as the Government Accountability Office) (GAO) to conduct five types of studies. These studies involved (1) the consolidation of the public accounting profession, (2) the role of credit rating agencies in the securities markets, (3) violations of securities laws, (4) SEC enforcement actions and restatements of financial statements, and (5) the role and functioning of investment banks in the securities markets.

The GAO studied the effects of the consolidation of the public accounting profession, beginning in the late 1980s, on the securities markets. The study included (1) factors leading to the consolidation of the profession, (2) the impact of this consolidation on capital formation and the securities markets, and (3) solutions to any problems identified, including ways to increase competition and increase the number of accounting firms able to audit large national and multinational companies. The study considered whether the consolidation of the public accounting profession has affected business organizations with regard to higher costs, lower quality, less choice, and lack of auditor independence. The GAO issued this study on July 30, 2003. The GAO found that the Big 4 firms have the potential for significant market power, although there is no evidence to date that competition has been impaired. The GAO failed to find any link between consolidation in the public accounting profession and either audit quality or audit independence. The GAO identified significant barriers to smaller accounting firms joining the ranks of the Big 4 and concluded that market forces are unlikely to expand the ranks of the four largest firms.

The GAO performed a follow-on study of concentration in the audit market that was released in January 2008. The GAO found that the Big 4 firms audit more than 98 percent of the 1,500 public companies with revenues exceeding $1 billion. However, there is evidence that Big 4 firms audit fewer smaller companies today than they did in 2002. The GAO also found that concentration in the market for large company audit services had not reduced quality or fee competitiveness.

The SEC studied the role of credit rating agencies in the securities markets. This study included an examination of threats to the ability of credit rating agencies to accurately assess the risk of issuers. The study also included an examination of barriers to the entry of new credit rating agencies and ways to remove those barriers. The SEC issued this study in January 2003.

As a result of this study, the U.S. Congress passed and President Bush signed, the Credit Rating Agency Reform Act of 2006. The Act amends the 1934 Securities Exchange Act and is designed to both improve the quality of credit ratings and to protect investors by increasing accountability, transparency, and competition in the credit rating industry. The Act creates a voluntary registration and regulatory program, overseen by the SEC, for credit rating agencies that want to be designated as a "nationally recognized statistical rating organization (NRSRO)."

The SEC has issued a rule implementing the Act. Under the SEC's rule, a credit rating agency seeking designation as a NRSRO must meet the following requirements: (1) be in business as a credit rating agency for at least the last three years; and (2) issue credit ratings certified by qualified institutional buyers to one or more of the following groups—financial institutions, brokers, or dealers; insurance companies; corporate issuers; asset-backed securities issuers; and issuers of government or municipal securities. In order to qualify as a credit rating agency, the agency must (1) be engaged in the business of issuing credit ratings through a readily accessible means, for free or a reasonable fee; (2) employ a quantitative methodology, a qualitative methodology, or both, in determining ratings; and (3) receive fees from either issuers, investors, or market participants.

The SEC also studied violations of securities laws between 1998 and 2001. The study investigated the number of public accountants, public accounting firms, investment bankers, investment advisers, brokers, dealers, attorneys, and other securities professionals found to have aided and abetted in the violation of securities laws but who were not sanctioned or disciplined as a primary violator in either an administrative action or a civil proceeding. The SEC also determined the number of such individuals found to have been primary violators of the securities laws. Finally, the SEC categorized the specific securities laws violations, including sanctions imposed on the violators. The SEC issued this study in January 2003. The SEC found that 1,596 securities professionals violated federal securities laws (or aided and abetted others in their violations of such laws) between 1998 and 2001. Public accountants and public accounting firms were *not* among the most frequent violators of federal securities laws. The sections of federal securities law most frequently violated were Section 10(b) of the 1934 Exchange Act and Section 17 (a) of the 1933 Securities Act.

The SEC conducted a study of its enforcement releases and of the financial statement restatements during the five-year period prior to the passage of the Sarbanes-Oxley Act. The focus of this study was on identifying those financial reporting areas most susceptible to fraud, inappropriate manipulation, or inappropriate earnings management. The SEC issued this study in January 2003. The SEC studied enforcement actions issued during the five-year period between July 31, 1997, and July 31, 2002, that were based on improper financial reporting, fraud, audit failure, or auditor independence violations. Improper revenue recognition was the financial reporting area that most frequently involved an enforcement action. There also were a significant number of enforcement actions involving improper expense recognition, including improper capitalization or deferral of expenses, improper use of reserves, and other understatement of expenses. In approximately 75 percent of the cases, the enforcement action was brought against one or more members of senior management. There were 18 enforcement actions brought against auditing firms and 89 enforcement actions were brought against individual auditors. Enforcement actions brought against auditors typically resulted from a lack of evidence, skepticism, and independence.

The GAO conducted a study to determine whether investment banks helped companies manipulate their earnings and obfuscate their true financial condition. The Sarbanes-Oxley Act specifically required the GAO to address the role of investment banks in designing derivative transactions and special-purpose entities for Enron Corporation and the role of investment banks in the swap of fiber-optic capacity by Global Crossing. The GAO issued this study on March 17, 2003. The GAO study found that certain investment banks facilitated complex financial transactions with Enron despite allegedly knowing that the intent of these transactions was to obfuscate Enron's true financial condition. The GAO also found that control groups within financial institutions and bank regulators have increased their review and scrutiny of structured finance transactions in the wake of the problems at Enron and Global Crossing.

CORPORATE AND CRIMINAL FRAUD ACCOUNTABILITY

The Sarbanes-Oxley Act imposes severe criminal penalties for prohibited forms of document destruction and for violations of the securities laws. Prison sentences of up to 20 years can be imposed for the destruction, alteration, or falsification of records in federal investigations and bankruptcy. Auditors must retain their work-papers and other relevant documents related to audit conclusions for seven years. Failure to comply with these SEC rules and regulations can result in prison terms of up to ten years. Finally, an individual who knowingly executes, or attempts to execute, a scheme or artifice to defraud any person relative to the securities laws faces prison sentences of up to 25 years.

The Sarbanes-Oxley Act also changes the bankruptcy laws to specify that debts incurred as a result of violations of the securities laws are not dischargeable in bankruptcy. In addition, the length of time to file a civil suit under the securities laws has been extended to two years after discovering the violation or five years after the violation occurred.

Finally, the Act provides whistleblowers certain protections against retaliation by the public company or its agents. For example, parties who knowingly retaliate against an individual for providing truthful information to a law enforcement officer relative to the commission of any federal offense can be imprisoned for up to ten years.

WHITE-COLLAR CRIME PENALTY ENHANCEMENTS

The Act amends the U.S. Code by increasing the criminal penalties for both mail and wire fraud from five years to 20 years. In addition, the Act imposes criminal penalties on CEOs and CFOs when they certify financial reports that do not comport with the requirements of the Sarbanes-Oxley Act. The penalties are a fine of as much as $1 million and imprisonment for as many as ten years for improper certifications, and a fine of as much as $5 million and imprisonment for as many as 20 years for willfully improper certifications.

CORPORATE TAX RETURNS

The Sarbanes-Oxley Act contains a sense of the Senate, which is not a legal requirement, that CEOs should sign the corporate tax return.

CORPORATE FRAUD AND ACCOUNTABILITY

The Act imposes fines and potential prison terms of up to 20 years for tampering with a record, document, or other object or otherwise impeding an official proceeding. In addition, criminal penalties available under the Securities and Exchange Act of 1934 have been increased.

In some cases, public companies attempt to make large payments to officers, directors, and others when the company is under investigation for possible violations of securities laws. The Act empowers the SEC to petition a federal district court to restrain a public company from making extraordinary payments to officers, directors, and others during the course of the investigation. The proposed payments would be placed in escrow for 45 days, and one extension of this 45-day period could be obtained. If the company is charged with a securities law violation, the contemplated extraordinary payments would continue to be held in escrow until the case was resolved.

The Act makes it easier for the SEC to suspend or permanently prohibit an individual from serving as an officer or director of a public company, if the individual has violated Section 10(b) of the 1934 Securities and Exchange Act or Section 17(a) of the 1933 Securities Act. Previously, the SEC had to bring an action in federal court to bar individuals from serving as an officer or director of a public company.

RECENT DEVELOPMENTS

The Sarbanes-Oxley Act has been subject to frequent criticism, primarily because of the cost and complexity of issuing a management report on the effectiveness of internal control over financial reporting (Section 404a of the Act) and the cost and complexity of having the external auditor issue its own opinion on the effectiveness of the company's internal control over financial reporting (Section 404b). As a result, the SEC has undertaken a number of initiatives.

The SEC extended the effective date of Section 404 for smaller public companies (i.e., non-accelerated filers). For fiscal years ending after December 15, 2007, companies with a market capitalization of below $75 million will have to include in their Form 10-K a management report on the effectiveness of internal control over financial reporting. However, unlike larger public companies, the external auditor will not issue an opinion on the effectiveness of internal control in the first year that these smaller public companies report on internal control. In fiscal years ending after December 15, 2009, the external auditor will issue an opinion on the effectiveness of internal control over financial reporting. In addition, the SEC is currently conducting a study on the costs and benefits of reporting on internal control for smaller public companies.

The SEC also asked the Committee of Sponsoring Organizations of the Treadway Commission (COSO) to develop implementation guidance for applying its internal control framework for smaller public companies. COSO issued this guidance, *Internal Control over Financial Reporting—Guidance for Smaller Public Companies*, in 2006. This document provides implementation guidance for applying COSO's internal control framework in a manner that seeks to maintain the effectiveness of internal control reporting while reducing its cost and complexity.

Finally, the SEC has issued interpretive guidance to management in performing its evaluation of the effectiveness of internal control over financial reporting. In addition, the PCAOB has issued a new standard on auditor reporting on internal control (AS-5) that replaces the PCAOB's original standard (AS-2). Both documents share a number of similarities, including: (1) emphasizing that evaluating internal control should follow a top-down risk-based process, (2) greater reliance on ongoing monitoring as support for management's evaluation and greater reliance on the work of others to support the auditor's opinion, and (3) numerous changes to afford management and the auditor more flexibility in evaluating the design and operating effectiveness of internal controls, which are designed to reduce the cost and burden of internal control reporting.

In early 2006, a small accounting firm and a private special-interest group filed suit in federal court challenging the constitutionality of the PCAOB. The U.S. District Court hearing the case found for the PCAOB, but the plaintiffs are appealing this decision to the U.S. Court of Appeals.

CONCLUSION

Given that SOX has been in effect now for over five years, some trends as a result of the Act seem clear:

- Audit committees are more engaged, are meeting more often, and are taking increasing control of the relation with the external auditor.

- Audit fees have increased, in some cases by a substantial percentage.

- The PCAOB will have a pervasive impact on the practice of public accounting, primarily to-date through its inspection process

- Accounting standards issued by the FASB are likely to be more principles-based, although it appears likely that the FASB will be replaced by the International Accounting Standards Board in the not too distant future.

- Aspects of the Sarbanes-Oxley Act are likely to affect private companies and the auditors that serve these companies, particularly in states with more aggressive regulation.

- Some formerly public companies are likely to go private, at least due in part to the significant compliance burden imposed by Sarbanes-Oxley.

Further consequences of the Sarbanes-Oxley Act will become apparent only with the passage of time.

Generally Accepted
Accounting Principles

CHAPTER 1
ACCOUNTING CHANGES

CONTENTS

OVERVIEW

Accounting changes are broadly classified as (*a*) changes in an
accounting principle, (*b*) changes in an accounting estimate, and
(*c*) changes in the reporting entity (FAS-154, par. 2a). *Corrections of*

errors in previously issued financial statements are not accounting changes but are covered in the same accounting literature because of their similarity. (FAS-154, par. 1).

Two different accounting methods are used within GAAP to account for accounting changes and corrections of errors: (1) current and prospective method, and (2) retroactive restatement method. These methods are not alternatives—the authoritative literature is specific concerning which method is to be used for each type of accounting change or correction of error.

GAAP for accounting changes apply to financial statements prepared in conformity with GAAP and are found in the following authoritative literature:

FAS-111	Rescission of FASB Statement No. 32 and Technical Corrections
FAS-154	Accounting Changes and Error Corrections
FIN-1	Accounting Changes Related to the Cost of Inventory

BACKGROUND

Changes in accounting principle, estimate, and entity are described in the authoritative literature as follows:

- *Change in accounting principle*—Results from the adoption of a generally accepted accounting principle different from the one used previously for financial reporting purposes. The term *principle* includes not only principles and practices, but also methods of applying them (FAS-154, par. 2c).

- *Change in accounting estimate*—Necessary consequence of periodic presentations of financial statements and the many estimates and assumptions that underlie those statements. A change in estimate results in a change in the carrying value of an existing asset or liability or a change in the future accounting treatment of an existing asset or liability (FAS-154, par. 2d).

- *Change in accounting entity*—A special type of change in accounting principle that results when the reporting entity is different from that of previous periods. This type of change is characterized by (a) presenting consolidated or combined financial statements in place of individual company statements, (*b*) changing specific subsidiaries that make up the group of companies for which consolidated financial statements are presented, and (*c*) changing the companies included in combined financial statements (FAS-154, par. 2f).

Corrections of errors are not accounting changes. They are sufficiently similar, however, that the authoritative literature discusses them with accounting changes (FAS-154, par. 1). Errors in financial statements result from mathematical mistakes, mistakes in the application of accounting principles, and the oversight or misuse of facts that existed at the time financial statements were prepared. A change from an unacceptable accounting principle or method to an acceptable one is also considered a correction of an error (FAS-154, par. 2h).

Two approaches for dealing with accounting changes and corrections of errors are included in FAS-154: (1) the current and prospective method, and (2) the retroactive restatement method. In the current and prospective method, the impact of the change is reflected in current and future financial statements without adjustment for prior years. In the retroactive restatement method, prior years' financial statements are restated to include the effect of the change.

The following areas are not considered changes in an accounting principle (FAS-154, par. 5):

- A principle, practice, or method adopted for the first time on new or previously immaterial events or transactions

- A principle, practice, or method adopted or modified because of events or transactions that are clearly different in substance

☛ **PRACTICE POINTER:** A situation that is not mentioned in FAS-154, but generally is not considered a change in accounting principle, is changing from an accelerated depreciation method to the straight-line method at a point in the life of the asset, provided the change is planned at the time the accelerated method is adopted and the policy is applied consistently (FAS-154, footnote 6).

A change in the composition of the elements of cost (material, labor, and overhead) included in inventory is an accounting change that must be justified based on the rule of preferability (FIN-1, par. 5).

The primary source of GAAP for accounting changes and error corrections is FAS-154. FAS-154 applies to all voluntary changes in accounting principle and to changes required by an accounting pronouncement in the unusual instance that the pronouncement does not indicate a specific transition method (FAS-154, par. 1). FAS-154 requires the retrospective application of the new accounting principle to prior periods' financial statements. Retrospective application is defined as the application of a different accounting principle to prior accounting periods as if that principle had always been used or as the adjustment of previously issued financial statements to reflect a change in the reporting entity (FAS-154, par. 2k).

FAS-111 (Rescission of FASB Statement No. 32 and Technical Corrections) provides guidance on the hierarchy of accounting principles set forth in Statement on Auditing Standards (SAS) No. 69 (The Meaning of "Present Fairly in Conformity with Generally Accepted Accounting Principles" in the Independent Auditor's Report). SAS-69 defines four categories of established accounting principles. Sources of accounting principles in higher categories carry more weight and should be followed when conflicts arise. When two sources within the same category provide conflicting guidance, the approach that better portrays the substance of the transaction should be selected. Any voluntary change in accounting principle must be justified on the basis of its preferability (FAS-154, par. 5). An accounting principle in a higher level of the GAAP hierarchy is preferable to a principle in a lower level of the hierarchy. (See the section of this *Guide* titled "About the GAAP Hierarchy" for further information.)

FAS-154 establishes retrospective application as the required method for reporting a change in accounting principle in the absence of explicit transition requirements specified in a newly adopted accounting standard. The standard provides guidance on when retrospective application is impracticable and for reporting a change in accounting principle in that circumstance. Although error corrections are not accounting changes, they have characteristics similar to accounting changes and, thus, they are covered in FAS-154. Error corrections are to be reported by restating previously issued financial statements (FAS-154, par. 1). FAS-154 applies to financial statements of business enterprises and not-for-profit organizations. It also applies to financial summaries of information based on primary financial statements that include an accounting period in which an accounting change or error correction is reflected (FAS-154, par. 3).

FAS-154 provides standards of accounting and reporting, followed by specific disclosure requirements, for four situations: changes in accounting principle, changes in accounting estimate, changes in reporting entity, and corrections of errors in previously issued financial statements.

CHANGES IN ACCOUNTING PRINCIPLE

The following are some common changes in accounting principle:

- A change in the method of pricing inventory, such as LIFO to FIFO or FIFO to LIFO
- A change in the method of accounting for long-term construction-type contracts
- A change in the method of accounting for software development costs.

Financial reporting standards presume that an accounting principle, once adopted, shall not be changed in accounting for events and transactions of the same type. Consistent use of accounting principles from period to period is an important dimension of high-value financial statements that facilitate analysis and enhance comparability (FAS-154, par. 4). A reporting entity shall change an accounting principle only if the change is required by a newly issued accounting pronouncement or the entity can justify the use of a different allowable accounting principle on the basis that it is preferable (FAS-154, par. 5).

An entity making a change in accounting principle will report that change by retrospective application of the new principle to all periods, unless it is impracticable to do so. Retrospective application requires the following three steps (FAS-154, par. 7):

Step 1. The cumulative effect of the change to the new principle on periods prior to those presented shall be reflected in the carrying amount of assets and liabilities as of the beginning of the first period presented.

Step 2. An offsetting adjustment, if any, shall be made to the opening balance of retained earnings for that period.

Step 3. Financial statements for each individual prior period presented are adjusted to reflect the period-specific effects of applying the new principle.

The term "impracticable," as used in FAS-154, means that at least one of the following applies (FAS-154, par. 11):

- After making every reasonable effort to do so, the entity is unable to apply the requirement.
- Retrospective application requires assumptions about management's intent in a prior period that cannot be independently substantiated.

- Retrospective application requires significant estimates, and it is impossible to develop objective information about those estimates that provide evidence of circumstances that existed on the date(s) at which those amounts would be recognized, measured, or disclosed under retrospective application and would have been available when the financial statements for that period were issued.

If the cumulative effect of applying a change in accounting principle to all prior periods can be determined, but it is impracticable to determine the period-specific effects of that change on all prior periods presented, the cumulative effect of the change should be applied to the carrying amounts of assets and liabilities as of the beginning of the earliest period to which the new accounting principle can be applied. The offsetting adjustment, if any, is to the opening balance of retained earnings for that period (FAS-154, par. 8).

If it is impracticable to determine the cumulative effect of applying a change in accounting principle to any prior period, the new principle will be applied as if the change was made prospectively as of the earliest date practicable. A change from the first-in, first-out (FIFO) inventory method to the last-in, first-out (LIFO) inventory method when the effects of having been on LIFO in the past cannot be determined is an example of such a situation (FAS-154, par. 9).

Changing an accounting principle must be supported by a justification on the basis of preferability. The issuance of an accounting pronouncement may require the use of a new accounting principle, interpreting an existing principle, expressing a preference for an accounting principle, or rejecting a specific principle. Any of these may require an entity to change an accounting principle. Such a requirement is sufficient justification for making a change in an accounting principle, provided that the GAAP hierarchy is followed. The burden of justifying other changes in accounting principle rests with the reporting entity making the change (FAS-154, par. 14).

Retrospective application shall ordinarily include only the direct effects of a change in accounting principle, including the income tax effects. If indirect effects are actually incurred and recognized, they shall be reported in the period in which the accounting change is made (FAS-154, par. 10).

A change in accounting principle made in an interim period shall be reported by retrospective application. However, the impracticability exception stated above may not be applied to prechange interim periods of the fiscal year in which the change is made. When retrospective application to prechange interim periods is impractical, the desired change may only be made as of the beginning of a subsequent fiscal year (FAS-154, par. 15).

Publicly traded companies that do not issue separate fourth-quarter reports must disclose in a note to their annual reports any effect of an accounting change made during the fourth quarter (FAS-154, par. 16).

Illustration of the Application of FAS-154— Change in Accounting Principle

Universal Technologies Inc. changes from the LIFO method of inventory valuation to the FIFO method at January 1, 20X7. Universal Technologies had used the LIFO method since its inception on January 1, 20X4. The change in inventory method is preferable.

Sales are $15,000 for each year from 20X4 through 20X7 and selling, general, and administrative expenses are $5,000 in each year. Universal Technologies' effective income tax rate is 30 percent in each year and it has no temporary or permanent income tax differences. Income taxes accrued at the end of each year are paid in cash at the beginning of the next year. Universal Technologies' annual report to shareholders includes three years of income statements and statements of cash flows and two years of balance sheets. (Earnings per share computations are ignored.)

Universal Technologies has determined that the effect of changing from LIFO inventory valuation to FIFO inventory valuation has the following effects on inventory and cost of goods sold for each year from 20X4 through 20X7:

Date	Inventory Determined by		Cost of Sales Determined by	
------	LIFO Method	FIFO Method	LIFO Method	FIFO Method
1/1/20X4	0	0	0	0
12/31/20X4	600	400	4,800	5,000
12/31/20X5	1,000	1,440	5,000	4,360
12/31/20X6	1,200	1,100	5,200	5,740
12/31/20X7	1,600	2,340	5,000	4,160

Universal Technologies' originally reported income statements for 20X4 through 20X6 (using the LIFO inventory method) are:

Income Statement (as originally reported)

	20X6	20X5	20X4
Sales	$15,000	$15,000	$15,000
Cost of goods sold	5,200	5,000	4,800
Selling, general, and administrative expenses	5,000	5,000	5,000
Income before income taxes	4,800	5,000	5,200
Income taxes	1,440	1,500	1,560
Net income	$ 3,360	$ 3,500	$ 3,640

Universal Technologies' income statements showing the retrospective application of the FIFO inventory method (from the LIFO method) are:

Income Statement

	20X7	20X6 As Adjusted (Note A)	20X5 As Adjusted (Note A)
Sales	$15,000	$15,000	$15,000
Cost of goods sold	4,160	5,740	4,360
Selling, general, and administrative expenses	5,000	5,000	5,000
Income before income taxes	5,840	4,260	5,640
Income taxes	1,752	1,278	1,692
Net income	$ 4,088	$ 2,982	$ 3,948

NOTE A: Change in Method of Inventory Valuation   On January 1, 20X7, Universal Technologies Inc. changed from the LIFO inventory valuation method to the FIFO inventory valuation method. The FIFO inventory valuation method was adopted [provide justification for why the FIFO method is preferable to the LIFO method] and the comparative financial statements for 20X6 and 20X5 have been adjusted to apply the FIFO method on a retrospective basis. The following financial statement line items for fiscal years 20X7, 20X6, and 20X5 were affected by the change in accounting principle.

Income Statement—20X7

	As Computed Under LIFO	As Reported Under FIFO	Effect of Change
Cost of goods sold	$5,000	$4,160	$(840)
Income before taxes	$5,000	$5,840	$ 840
Income tax expense	$1,500	$1,752	$ 252
Net income	$3,500	$4,088	$ 588

Income Statement—20X6

	As Originally Reported	As Adjusted	Effect of Change
Cost of goods sold	$5,200	$5,740	$ 540
Income before taxes	$4,800	$4,260	$(540)
Income tax expense	$1,440	$1,278	$(162)
Net income	$3,360	$2,982	$(378)

Income Statement—20X5

	As Originally Reported	As Adjusted	Effect of Change
Cost of goods sold	$5,000	$4,360	$(640)
Income before taxes	$5,000	$5,640	$ 640
Income tax expense	$1,500	$1,692	$ 192
Net income	$3,500	$3,948	$ 448

Balance Sheet—12/31/X7

	As Computed Under FIFO	As Reported Under FIFO	Effect of Change
Cash	$113,900	$113,930	$ 30
Inventory	$ 1,600	$ 2,340	$740
Total assets	$115,500	$116,270	$770
Income tax liability	$ 1,500	$ 1,752	$252
Retained earnings	$ 14,000	$ 14,518	$518

Balance Sheet—12/31/X6

	As Originally Reported	As Adjusted	Effect of Change
Cash	$ 10,740	$110,608	$(132)
Inventory	$ 1,200	$ 1,100	$(100)
Total assets	$111,940	$111,708	$(232)
Income tax liability	$ 1,440	$ 1,278	$(162)
Retained earnings	$ 10,500	$ 10,430	$ (70)

Balance Sheet—12/31/X5

	As Originally Reported	As Adjusted	Effect of Change
Cash	$107,640	$107,700	$ 60
Inventory	$ 1,000	$ 1,440	$440
Total assets	$108,640	$109,140	$500
Income tax liability	$ 1,500	$ 1,692	$192
Retained earnings	$ 7,140	$ 7,448	$308

As a result of the accounting change, retained earnings as of January 1, 20X5 decreased from $3,640, as originally reported using the LIFO method, to $3,500 using the FIFO method.

Statement of Cash Flows—20X7

	As Computed Under LIFO	As Reported Under FIFO	Effect of Change
Net income	$3,500	$ 4,088	$ 588
(Increase) decrease in inventory	$ (400)	$ (1,240)	$ (840)
Increase (decrease) in income tax liability	$ 60	$ 474	$ 414
Net cash provided by operating activities	$3,160	$ 3,322	$ 162
Change in cash	$3,160	$ 3,322	$ 162

Statement of Cash Flows—20X6

	As Originally Reported	As Adjusted	Effect of Change
Net income	$3,360	$2,982	$(378)
(Increase) decrease in inventory	$ (200)	$ 340	$ 540
Increase (decrease) in income tax liability	$ (60)	$ (414)	$(354)
Net cash provided by operating activities	$3,100	$2,908	$(192)
Change in cash	$3,100	$2,908	$(192)

Statement of Cash Flow—20X5

	As Originally Reported	As Adjusted	Effect of Change
Net income	$ 3,500	$ 3,948	$ 448
(Increase) decrease in inventory	$ (400)	$ (1,040)	$ (640)
Increase (decrease) in income tax liability	$ (60)	$ 192	$ 252
Net cash provided by operating activities	$ 3,040	$ 3,100	$ 60
Change in cash	$ 3,040	$ 3,100	$ 60

Disclosure

The following items are required disclosures in the period during which the change in accounting principle is made (FAS-154, par. 17):

- The nature of and reason for the change in principle, including an explanation of why the new principle is preferable.
- The method of applying the change, and:
  - A description of the prior-period information that has been retrospectively adjusted, if any.
  - The effect of the change on income from continuing operations, net income, any other affected financial statement item, and any affected per-share amounts for the current period and any prior periods retrospectively adjusted.
  - The cumulative effect of the change on retained earnings (or other components of equity or net assets in the statement of financial position) as of the beginning of the earliest period presented.
  - If retrospective application to all periods is impracticable, the reasons therefore and a description of the alternative method used to report the change.
- If indirect effects of a change in accounting principle are recognized:
  - A description of the indirect effects, including the amounts that have been recognized in the current period and the related per-share amounts, if applicable.
  - Unless impracticable, the amount of the total recognized indirect effects of the accounting change and the related per-share amounts, if applicable, that are attributable to each prior period presented.

In the fiscal year in which a new accounting principle is adopted, financial information reported for interim periods after the date of adoption will disclose the effect of the change in income from continuing operations, net income, and related per-share amounts, if applicable, for the post-change interim periods (FAS-154, par. 18).

CHANGES IN ACCOUNTING ESTIMATE

A change in accounting estimate is accounted for in the period of change if the change affects only that period, or is accounted for in the period of change and future periods if the change affects both. A change in accounting estimate is not accounted for by restating or retrospectively adjusting amounts reported in financial statements of prior periods or by reporting pro forma amounts for prior periods (FAS-154, par. 19).

Distinguishing between a change in accounting principle and a change in accounting estimate may be difficult. In some cases, a change in estimate is effected by a change in accounting principle, such as when a depreciation method is changed to reflect a change in the estimated future benefits of the asset or the pattern of consumption of those benefits. The change in principle cannot be separated from the effect of the change in accounting estimate. Changes of this type are considered changes in estimate (FAS-154, par. 20). Similar to other changes in accounting principle, a change in accounting estimate that is effected by a change in accounting principle is appropriate only if the new principle is justifiable on the basis that it is preferable (FAS-154, par. 21).

Illustration of Current and Prospective Method

In 20X6, Martin Co. paid $150,000 for a building that was expected to have a ten-year life with an estimated value at the end of that period of $25,000. Straight-line depreciation was used through 20X9. In 20Y0, management's reassessment of the useful lives of all assets resulted in a decision that the useful life would be 15 years from the time of purchase, at which time the estimated value would be approximately $10,000.

The book value of the asset at the time of the change is computed as follows:

Cost	$150,000
Accumulated depreciation [($150,000 − $25,000)/10] × 4	(50,000)
	$100,000

Depreciation for 20Y0 and each of the next 11 years (15 years total − 4 years depreciated to date) is computed and recorded as follows:

Book value at time of change	$100,000
Estimated residual value	(10,000)
Depreciable cost	$ 90,000
Depreciation per year ($90,000/11)	$ 8,182
Entry: Depreciation Expense	8,182
Accumulated Depreciation	8,182

No cumulative effect is recorded. Disclosure is required of the nature of the change and the impact on income ($12,500 − $8,182 = $4,318) as follows:

During 20Y0, management determined that the useful life of the building was longer than originally expected. A change in accounting estimate was recognized to reflect this decision, resulting in an increase in net income of $4,318.

Disclosure

The effect on income from continuing operations, net income, and any related per-share amounts of the current period must be disclosed for a change in estimate that affects several future periods. Disclosure of those effects is not necessary for estimates made each period in the ordinary course of accounting for items, such as uncollectible accounts or inventory obsolescence. Effects of such a change in estimate must be disclosed, however, if the effect is material (FAS-154, par. 22).

When an entity effects a change in estimate by changing an accounting principle, the disclosures required for a change in accounting principles (stated above) are required. If a change in estimate does not have a material effect in the period of change, but is reasonably certain to have a material effect in later periods, a description of the change is required whenever the financial statements of the period of the change are presented (FAS-154, par. 22).

CHANGES IN REPORTING ENTITY

FAS-154 specifies that an accounting change that results in financial statements that are, in effect, those of a different reporting entity must be retrospectively applied so that the specific entities that comprise the reporting entity in the current period are comparable to the specific entities that comprised the reporting entity in previous years. Previously issued interim financial information shall be presented on a retrospective basis with the following exception: the amount of interest cost previously capitalized by applying FAS-58 (Capitalization of Interest Cost in Financial Statements That Include Investments Accounted for by the Equity Method) will not be changed when retrospectively applying the accounting change to the financial statements of prior periods (FAS-154, par. 23).

Disclosure

When there has been a change in reporting entity, the financial statements of the period of change must include a description of the nature of the change and the reason for the change. The effect of the change on income before extraordinary items, net income, other comprehensive income, and any related per-share amounts must be disclosed for all periods presented (FAS-154, par. 24).

CORRECTIONS OF ERRORS IN PREVIOUSLY ISSUED FINANCIAL STATEMENTS

An error in financial statements of prior periods that is discovered after those statements are issued is reported as a prior-period adjustment by restating the prior period financial statements. This requires the following three steps (FAS-154, par. 25):

Step 1. The cumulative effect of the error on periods prior to the period in which the error is discovered and corrected is reflected in the carrying amounts of assets and liabilities as of the beginning of that period.

Step 2. An offsetting adjustment, if any, is made to the opening balance of retained earnings (or other component of equity or net assets in the statement of financial position) for that period.

Step 3. Financial statements for each individual prior period presented are adjusted to reflect correction of the period-specific effects of the error.

☛ **PRACTICE POINTER:** Distinguishing between a *change in accounting estimate* and the *correction of an error* may be difficult and may require significant professional judgment. In the final analysis, the difference comes down to the timing of the availability of the information upon which the change or correction is made. If the information is newly available, the adjustment is a change in accounting estimate. If the information was previously available, but was not used or was misused, the adjustment is a correction of an error. This classification is important because the change in estimate is accounted for prospectively while the correction of an error requires restatement of previously issued financial statements.

Illustration of Correction of Error in Previously Issued Financial Statements

In 20X7 and 20X8, Warren, Inc., inappropriately capitalized $100,000 of period costs as fixed assets in each year. This intentional misstatement was discovered and corrected in 20X9. The period costs inappropriately capitalized as fixed assets were being depreciated on a straight-line basis (with no salvage value) over 10 years. Warren, Inc. accounted for the $100,000 of period costs correctly in 20X9. Warren, Inc.'s effective tax rate is 30 percent, and all income taxes due are paid in full during the year in which they are incurred. Warren, Inc.'s income statements, balance sheets, and statements of retained earnings as originally filed are as follows:

Income Statements (as originally presented)

	20X8	20X7
Revenues	$500,000	$500,000
Cost of goods sold	250,000	250,000
Other expenses (excluding depreciation)	100,000	100,000
Depreciation expense	20,000	10,000
Income before taxes	130,000	140,000
Income tax expense	39,000	42,000
Net income	$ 91,000	$ 98,000

Balance Sheets (as originally presented)

	20X8	20X7
Cash	$119,000	$100,000
Receivables	80,000	60,000
Inventories	80,000	108,000
Income tax refund receivable	—	—
Fixed assets (net)	170,000	90,000
Total assets	$449,000	$358,000
Accounts payable	$ 20,000	$ 20,000
Long-term liabilities	40,000	40,000
Total liabilities	60,000	60,000
Paid-in capital	200,000	200,000
Retained earnings	189,000	98,000
Total stockholders' equity	389,000	298,000
Total liabilities and stockholders' equity	$449,000	$358,000

Statements of Retained Earnings (as originally presented)

	20X8	20X7
Balance, January 1	$98,000	$ —
Net income	91,000	98,000
Balance, December 31	$189,000	$ 98,000

The entry to record this error in 20X9 is as follows:

Accumulated depreciation	30,000	
Retained earnings [($200,000 − $30,000) × .7]	119,000	
Income tax refund receivable	51,000	
Fixed assets		200,000

In 20X9, Warren, Inc. presents income statements and statements of retained earnings for 20X9 and 20X8 and a balance sheet for 20X9. (Warren, Inc.'s statement of cash flows and required disclosures are not presented.)

Income Statements

	20X9	20X8 (as restated)
Revenues	$500,000	$500,000
Cost of goods sold	250,000	250,000
Other expenses (excluding depreciation)	200,000	200,000
	—	—
Depreciation expense		
Income before taxes	50,000	50,000
Income tax expense	15,000	15,000
Net income	$ 35,000	$ 35,000

Statements of Retained Earnings

	20X9	20X8 (as restated)
Balance, January 1	$ 70,000	$ 98,000
Adjustment to correct the error of improper capitalization of period expenses (net of tax)	————	(63,000)*
Adjusted balance, January 1	70,000	35,000
Net income	35,000	35,000
Balance, December 31	$105,000	$70,000

Balance Sheet

	20X9
Cash	$110,000
Receivables	94,000
Inventories	110,000
Income tax refund receivable	51,000
Fixed assets (net)	—
Total assets	$365,000

---

*($10,000−$100,000) × (1−.3)

Balance Sheet (continued)

	20X9
Accounts payable	$20,000
Long-term liabilities	40,000
Total liabilities	60,000
Paid-in capital	200,000
Retained earnings	105,000
Total stockholders' equity	305,000
Total liabilities and stockholders' equity	$365,000

Disclosure

When financial statements have been restated for the correction of an error, the entity must disclose the nature of the error and the fact that previously issued financial statements have been restated. The entity must disclose (FAS-154, par. 26):

- The effect of the correction on each financial statement line item and any per-share amounts affected for each prior period presented.

- The cumulative effect of the change on retained earnings or other appropriate components of equity (or net assets in the statement of financial position) as of the beginning of the earliest period presented.

RELATED CHAPTERS IN 2009 *GAAP GUIDE LEVEL A*

Chapter 2, "Accounting Policies and Standards"
Chapter 13, "Earnings per Share"
Chapter 26, "Interim Financial Reporting"
Chapter 40, "Results of Operations"

RELATED CHAPTERS IN 2009 *GAAP GUIDE LEVELS B, C, AND D*

Chapter 1, "Accounting Changes"
Chapter 2, "Accounting Policies and Standards"
Chapter 13, "Earnings per Share"
Chapter 23, "Interim Financial Reporting"
Chapter 35, "Results of Operations"

RELATED CHAPTERS IN 2009 *INTERNATIONAL ACCOUNTING/FINANCIAL REPORTING STANDARDS GUIDE*

Chapter 5, "Accounting Policies, Changes in Accounting Estimates, and Errors"

Chapter 12, "Earnings per Share"

Chapter 22, "Interim Financial Reporting"

CHAPTER 2
ACCOUNTING POLICIES AND STANDARDS

CONTENTS

OVERVIEW

Accounting policies are important considerations in understanding the content of financial statements. FASB standards require the disclosure of accounting policies as an integral part of financial statements when those statements are intended to present financial position, cash flows, and results of operations in conformity with GAAP.

The following pronouncement is the primary source of promulgated GAAP concerning disclosure of accounting policies:

APB-22   Disclosure of Accounting Policies

> **OBSERVATION:** The GAAP hierarchy for nongovernmental entities (i.e., businesses and not-for-profits), which formerly resided in the auditing literature (SAS-69 as codified in AU 411), has been moved to the accounting literature via the issuance of FAS-162 (The Hierarchy of Generally Accepted Accounting Principles). The FAS-162 hierarchy is explained in the front matter of the 2009 GAAP Guide Level A. The GAAP hierarchy

will be moved to chapter 2 of the GAAP Guide Level A beginning with the 2010 edition.

BACKGROUND

All financial statements that present financial position, cash flows,
and results of operations in accordance with GAAP must include
disclosure of significant accounting policies. This includes financial
statements of not-for-profit entities. Unaudited interim financial
statements that do not include changes in accounting policies since
the end of the preceding year are not required to disclose accounting
policies in those interim statements (APB-22, pars. 8–10).

SIGNIFICANT ACCOUNTING POLICIES

GAAP require a description of all significant accounting policies of a
reporting entity as an integral part of the financial statements. The
preferable presentation of disclosing accounting policies is in the first
footnote of the financial statements, under the caption "Summary of
Significant Accounting Policies." APB-22 (Disclosure of Accounting
Policies) specifically states this preference, but recognizes the need for
flexibility in the matter of formats (APB-22, par. 15).

Examples of areas of accounting for which policies are required
to be disclosed are (APB-22, par. 13):

- Basis of consolidation
- Depreciation methods
- Inventory methods
- Amortization of intangibles
- Recognition of profit on long-term construction contracts
- Recognition of revenue from franchising and leasing operations

DISCLOSURE STANDARDS

Accounting principles and methods of applying them should be
disclosed. Informed professional judgment is necessary to select for
disclosure those principles that materially affect financial position,
cash flows, and results of operations. Accounting principles and
their method of application in the following areas are considered
particularly important (APB-22, par. 12):

- A selection from existing acceptable alternatives

- The areas peculiar to a specific industry in which the entity functions
- Unusual and innovative applications of GAAP

Disclosure of accounting policies should not duplicate information presented elsewhere in the financial statements. In disclosing accounting policies, it may become necessary to refer to items presented elsewhere in the report, such as in the case of a change in an accounting principle that requires specific treatment (APB-22, par. 14).

> ☞ **PRACTICE POINTER:** Many pronouncements require disclosure of information about accounting policies. For example, FAS-95 (Statement of Cash Flows) requires disclosure of the accounting policy for defining the term *cash equivalents*. Because there are so many requirements of this type embedded in the authoritative accounting literature, a financial statement disclosure checklist is a very useful tool to guard against the inadvertent omission of required information.

Illustration of Disclosure of Significant Accounting Policies

Principles of consolidation   The consolidated financial statements include the assets, liabilities, revenues, and expenses of all significant subsidiaries. All significant intercompany transactions have been eliminated in consolidation. Investments in significant companies that are 20% to 50% owned are accounted for by the equity method, which requires the corporation's share of earnings to be included in income. All other investments are carried at market value or amortized cost in conformity with FAS-115 (Accounting for Certain Investments in Debt and Equity Securities).

Cash equivalents   Securities with maturities of three months or less when purchased are treated as cash equivalents in presenting the statement of cash flows.

Accounts receivable   The company grants trade credit to its customers. Receivables are valued at management's estimate of the amount that will ultimately be collected. The allowance for doubtful accounts is based on specific identification of uncollectible accounts and the company's historical collection experience.

Plant assets and depreciation   Plant assets are carried at cost, less accumulated depreciation. Expenditures for replacements are capitalized, and the replaced items are retired. Maintenance and repairs are charged to operations. Gains and losses from the sale of plant assets are included in income. Depreciation is calculated on a straight-line basis utilizing the assets' estimated useful lives, including goodwill. The corporation and its subsidiaries use other depreciation methods (generally accelerated) for tax purposes where appropriate.

Inventories Inventories are stated at the lower of cost or market using the last-in, first-out (LIFO) method for substantially all qualifying domestic inventories and the average cost method for other inventories.

Patents, trademarks, and goodwill Amounts paid for purchased patents and trademarks and for securities of newly acquired subsidiaries in excess of the fair value of the net assets of such subsidiaries are charged to patents, trademarks, and goodwill. Intangible assets with finite useful lives are amortized over those useful lives. Intangible assets with indefinite useful lives are not amortized, but these assets are evaluated, at least annually, for impairment.

Earnings per share Earnings per share is based on the weighted-average number of shares of common stock outstanding in each year. There would have been no material dilutive effect on net income per share for 20X8 or 20X9 if convertible securities had been converted and if outstanding stock options had been exercised.

Pension plans The company has pension plans that cover substantially all employees. Benefits are based primarily on each employee's years of service and average compensation during the last five years of employment. Company policy is to fund annual periodic pension cost to the maximum allowable for federal income tax purposes.

Income taxes Income taxes are accounted for by the asset/liability approach in accordance with FAS-109 (Accounting for Income Taxes). Deferred taxes represent the expected future tax consequences when the reported amounts of assets and liabilities are recovered or paid. They arise from differences between the financial reporting and tax bases of assets and liabilities and are adjusted for changes in tax laws and tax rates when those changes are enacted. The provision for income taxes represents the total of income taxes paid or payable for the current year, plus the change in deferred taxes during the year.

Interest costs Interest related to construction of qualifying assets is capitalized as part of construction costs in accordance with FAS-34 (Capitalization of Interest Cost).

Revenue recognition on long-term contracts The company recognizes revenue on long-term contracts by the percentage-of-completion method of accounting. In accordance with that method, revenue is estimated during each financial reporting period encompassed by the contract based on the degree of completion.

☞ **PRACTICE POINTER:** APB-22 states a preference for all accounting policies to be presented together, and for that presentation to be between the financial statements and their notes or to be the first note. In meeting this requirement, some companies present detailed information in the policy statement that is not directly related to accounting policy. For example, in addition to stating the inventory cost method used, a company also may indicate the dollar breakdown of raw materials, work-in-process, and finished goods. In the author's opinion, this tends to obscure the accounting policy information. A preferable approach is to limit disclosure in the policy statement to information about accounting policy and to present other information in other notes, possibly with cross-references. For example, in the section of the policy statement that states inventory policy, a crossreference to another note covering in detail information about the amount of various types of inventory may be appropriate.

RELATED CHAPTER IN 2009 *GAAP GUIDE* *LEVEL A*

Chapter 1, "Accounting Changes"

RELATED CHAPTERS IN 2009 *GAAP GUIDE* *LEVELS B, C, AND D*

Chapter 1, "Accounting Changes"
Chapter 2, "Accounting Policies and Standards"

RELATED CHAPTER IN 2009 *INTERNATIONAL ACCOUNTING/FINANCIAL REPORTING STANDARDS GUIDE*

Chapter 5, "Accounting Policies, Changes in Accounting Estimates, and Errors"

CHAPTER 3
BALANCE SHEET CLASSIFICATION AND RELATED DISPLAY ISSUES

CONTENTS

OVERVIEW

The distinction between current and noncurrent assets and liabilities in a classified balance sheet is an important feature of financial reporting. There is considerable interest in the liquidity of the reporting enterprise, and the separate classification of current assets and liabilities is an important part of liquidity analysis.

GAAP concerning current assets and current liabilities are found in the following pronouncements:

ARB-43	Chapter 1A, Receivables from Officers, Employees, or Affiliated Companies
	Chapter 3A, Current Assets and Current Liabilities
APB-10	Omnibus Opinion—1966
FAS-6	Classification of Short-Term Obligations Expected to Be Refinanced
FAS-43	Accounting for Compensated Absences

FAS-78	Classification of Obligations That Are Callable by the Creditor
FAS-150	Accounting for Certain Financial Instruments with Characteristics of Both Liabilities and Equity
FIN-8	Classification of a Short-Term Obligation Repaid Prior to Being Replaced by a Long-Term Security
FIN-39	Offsetting of Amounts Related to Certain Contracts
FIN-41	Offsetting of Amounts Related to Certain Repurchase and Reverse Repurchase Agreements

BACKGROUND

In the ordinary course of business there is a continuing circulation of capital within the current assets. For example, a manufacturer expends cash for materials, labor, and factory overhead that are converted into finished inventory. After being sold, inventory usually is converted into trade receivables and, on collection of receivables, is converted back to cash. The average time elapsing between expending the cash and receiving the cash back from the trade receivable is called an *operating cycle*. One year is used as a basis for segregating current assets when more than one operating cycle occurs within a year. When the operating cycle is longer than one year, as with the lumber, tobacco, and distillery businesses, the operating cycle is used for segregating current assets. *In the event that a business clearly has no operating cycle, the one-year rule is used* (ARB-43, Ch. 3A, par. 5).

Frequently, businesses have a *natural business year*, at the end of which the company's activity, inventory, and trade receivables are at their lowest point. This is often the point in time selected as the end of the entity's accounting period for financial reporting purposes.

BASIC DEFINITIONS

Current Assets

Resources that are expected to be realized in cash, sold, or consumed during the next year (or longer operating cycle) are classified as current assets. Current assets are sometimes called circulating or working assets; cash that is restricted as to withdrawal or use for other than current operations is not classified as a current asset (ARB-43, Ch. 3A, par. 6).

The basic types of current assets are cash, cash equivalents, secondary cash resources, receivables, inventories, and prepaid expenses (ARB-43, Ch. 3A, par. 4).

Cash

Includes money in any form, for example, cash on deposit, cash awaiting deposit, and cash funds available for use.

Cash Equivalents

Short-term, highly liquid investments that are (*a*) readily convertible to known amounts of cash and (*b*) so near their maturities that they present insignificant risk of changes in value because of changes in interest rates.

Secondary Cash Resources

The most common type of secondary cash resources is marketable securities.

Receivables

Include accounts receivable, notes receivable, and receivables from officers and employees.

Inventories

Include merchandise, raw materials, work in process, finished goods, operating supplies, and ordinary maintenance material and parts.

Prepaid Expenses

Include prepaid insurance, interest, rents, taxes, advertising, and operating supplies. Prepaid expenses, unlike other current assets, are not expected to be converted into cash; but, if they had not been paid in advance, they would require the use of current assets during the operating cycle.

Current Liabilities

Current liabilities are obligations for which repayment is expected to require the use of current assets or the creation of other current liabilities.

> ☞ **PRACTICE POINTER:** The definition of current liabilities is based on the asset category from which the liability is expected to be retired rather than on a specific period of time. As a practical matter, most current liabilities are those that are expected to be retired during the period of time encompassed by the definition of current assets. Be careful, however, to identify instances where liabilities that are due in the near future should be classified as noncurrent because they will not require the use of current assets. Examples are short-term

obligations expected to be refinanced, and noncurrent liabilities that are near their maturity but that will be paid from noncurrent assets (e.g., bond sinking funds).

There are several basic types of current liabilities (ARB-43, Ch. 3A, par. 7):

Payables from Operations

Include items that have entered the operating cycle, which include trade payables and accrued liabilities such as wages and taxes.

Debt Maturities

Include amounts expected to be liquidated during the current operating cycle, such as short-term notes and the currently maturing portion of long-term debt.

Revenue Received in Advance

Includes collections received in advance of services, for example, prepaid subscriptions and other deferred revenues. This type of current liability is typically liquidated by means other than the payment of cash.

Other Accruals

Include estimates of accrued amounts that are expected to be required to cover expenditures within the year for known obligations (*a*) when the amount can be determined only approximately (provision for accrued bonuses payable) or (*b*) when the specific person(s) to whom payment will be made is (are) unascertainable (provision for warranty of a product) (ARB-43, Ch. 3A, par. 8).

Working Capital and Related Ratios

Working capital is the excess of current assets over current liabilities, and it is often used as a measure of the liquidity of an enterprise (ARB-43, Ch. 3A, par. 3).

Changes in Each Element of Working Capital

The changes in each element of working capital are the increases or decreases in each current asset and current liability over the amounts in the preceding year.

Illustration of Determining Working Capital

	20X8	20X9	Working Capital Increase or (Decrease)
Current Assets:			
Cash	$10,000	$ 15,000	$ 5,000
Accounts receivable, net	25,000	35,000	10,000
Inventory	50,000	60,000	10,000
Prepaid expenses	1,000	500	(500)
Total current assets	$86,000	$110,500	$ 24,500
Current Liabilities:			
Accounts payable	$10,000	$ 15,000	$ (5,000)
Notes payable-current	20,000	15,000	5,000
Accrued expenses	1,000	1,500	(500)
Total current liabilities	$31,000	$ 31,500	$ (500)
Net working capital	$55,000	$ 79,000	
Increase in working capital			$24,000

The *current ratio,* or *working capital ratio,* is a measure of current position and is useful in analyzing short-term credit. The current ratio is computed by dividing the total current assets by the total current liabilities.

Illustration of Current Ratio

	20X8	20X9
Current assets	$86,000	$110,500
Current liabilities	(31,000)	(31,500)
Working capital	$55,000	$79,000
Current ratio	2.8 : 1	3.5 : 1

The *acid-test ratio* (also called the *quick ratio*) is determined by dividing those assets typically closest to cash by total current liabilities. The assets used to calculate this ratio consist of only the most liquid assets, typically cash, receivables, and marketable securities.

> ☛ **PRACTICE POINTER:** Only receivables and securities *convertible into cash* are included; restricted cash and securities are excluded.

Illustration of Acid-Test Ratio

	20X8	20X9
Cash	$10,000	$15,000
Receivables, net	25,000	35,000
Total *quick* assets	$35,000	$50,000
Total current liabilities	$31,000	$31,500
Acid-test ratio	1.1 : 1	1.6 : 1

RECEIVABLES

Accounts receivable are reported in the financial statements at net realizable value. Net realizable value is equal to the gross amount of receivables less an estimated allowance for uncollectible accounts.

Two common procedures of accounting for uncollectible accounts are (*a*) the direct write-off method and (*b*) the allowance method.

Direct Write-Off Method

This method recognizes a bad debt expense only when a specific account is determined to be uncollectible. The conceptual weaknesses of the direct write-off method are:

- Bad debt expense is not *matched* with the related sales.
- Accounts receivable are overstated, because no attempt is made to account for the unknown bad debts included therein.

Ordinarily, the direct write-off method is not considered GAAP, because it results in a mismatching of revenues and expenses (i.e., expenses are recognized in a later period than the revenue to which they relate) and overstates the amount of assets. The method may be acceptable in situations where uncollectible accounts are immaterial in amount.

Allowance Method

The allowance method recognizes an estimate of uncollectible accounts each period, even though the specific individual accounts that will not be collected cannot be identified at that time. Estimates of uncollectible accounts usually are made as a percentage of credit sales or ending receivables. This method is consistent with FAS-5 (Accounting for Contingencies), as explained below.

Under FAS-5, a contingency exists if, at the date of the financial statements, an enterprise does not expect to collect the full amount of its accounts receivable. Under this circumstance, an accrual for a loss contingency must be charged to income, if both of the following conditions exist:

- It is *probable* that as of the date of the financial statements an asset has been impaired or a liability incurred, based on information available before the issuance of the financial statements.

- The amount of the loss can be *estimated reasonably*.

If both of the above conditions are met, an accrual for the estimated amount of uncollectible receivables is made even if the specific uncollectible receivables cannot be identified. An enterprise may base its estimate of uncollectible receivables on its prior experience, the experience of other enterprises in the same industry, the debtor's ability to pay, or an appraisal of current economic conditions. Significant uncertainty may exist in the ultimate collection of receivables if an enterprise is unable to estimate reasonably the amount that is uncollectible. If a significant uncertainty exists in the ultimate collection of the receivables, the installment sales method, cost-recovery method, or some other method of revenue recognition should be used. In the event that both of the above conditions for accrual are not met and a loss contingency is at least *reasonably possible*, certain financial statement disclosures are required by FAS-5.

Illustration of Accounting for Uncollectible Accounts by the Allowance Method

AMB Co. estimates uncollectible accounts at 1% of credit sales. For the current year, credit sales totaled $1,000,000. The year-end balances in accounts receivable and the unadjusted allowance for uncollectible accounts are $250,000 and $15,000, respectively.

The entry to record uncollectible accounts ($1,000,000 × 1% = $10,000) is as follows:

Bad debt expense	10,000	
Allowance for uncollectible accounts		10,000

The balance sheet will include accounts receivable of $250,000, allowance for uncollectible accounts of $25,000 ($15,000 + $10,000), and net accounts receivable of $225,000 ($250,000 − $25,000).

When a specific uncollectible account is written off (e.g., $2,100), the following entry is required:

Allowance for uncollectible accounts	2,100	
Accounts receivable (specific account)		2,100

This entry has no effect on the amount of net accounts receivable, because both the receivables balance and the allowance balance are reduced by the same amount.

If the estimate of uncollectibles had been based on the ending balance of accounts receivable, the same procedure would have been followed, except that the existing balance in the allowance would require consideration. For example, if uncollectible accounts were estimated at 9% of the ending balance in accounts receivable, the bad debt expense for the year would be $7,500, computed as follows:

Required allowance ($250,000 × 9%)	$22,500
Balance before adjustment	(15,000)
Required adjustment	$ 7,500

The balance sheet would include accounts receivable of $250,000, an allowance of $22,500, and a net receivables amount of $227,500.

A variation on the previous method is to "age" accounts receivable, a procedure that provides for recognizing an increasing percentage as uncollectible as accounts become increasingly delinquent. For example, applying this procedure to the $250,000 receivables balance above might result in the following:

	Within 30 Days	30 Days Overdue	60 Days Overdue	Past 60 Days Overdue
Accounts receivable balance	$120,000	$50,000	$50,000	$30,000
Uncollectible %	2%	7%	12%	25%
Uncollectible balance	$ 2,400	$ 3,500	$16,000	$ 7,500

The total uncollectible balance is $19,400, resulting in the recognition of bad debt expense of $4,400, assuming a previous allowance balance of $15,000 ($19,400 − $15,000 = $4,400).

Discounted Notes Receivable

Discounted notes receivable arise when the holder endorses the note (with or without recourse) to a third party and receives a sum of cash. The difference between the amount of cash received by the holder and the maturity value of the note is called the discount. If the note is discounted with recourse, the assignor remains contingently liable for the ultimate payment of the note when it becomes due. If the note is discounted without recourse, the assignor assumes no further liability.

The account "discounted notes receivable" is a contra account, which is deducted from the related receivables for financial statement purposes. The following is the procedure for computing the proceeds of a discounted note:

1. Compute the total maturity value of the note, including interest due at maturity.

2. Compute the discount amount (the maturity value of the note multiplied by the discount rate for the time involved).

3. The difference between the two amounts (1, less 2) equals the proceeds of the note.

Illustration of Discounted Notes Receivable

A $1,000 90-day 10% note is discounted at a bank at 8% when 60 days are remaining to maturity.

Maturity—$1,000 + ($1,000 × .10 × 90/360)	$1,025.00
Discount—$1,025 × .08 × 60/360	(13.67)
Proceeds of note	$1,011.33

Factoring

Factoring is a process by which a company converts its receivables into immediate cash by assigning them to a factor either with or without recourse. *With recourse* means that the assignee can return the receivable to the company and get back the funds paid if the receivable is uncollectible. *Without recourse* means that the assignee assumes the risk of losses on collections. Under factoring arrangements, the customer may or may not be notified.

Pledging

Pledging is the process whereby the company uses existing accounts receivable as collateral for a loan. The company retains title to the receivables but pledges that it will use the proceeds to pay the loan.

CASH SURRENDER VALUE OF LIFE INSURANCE

The proceeds of a life insurance policy usually provide some degree of financial security to one or more beneficiaries named in the policy. Upon death of the insured, the insurance company pays the beneficiary the face amount of the policy, less any outstanding indebtedness.

Insurable Interest

An owner of an insurance contract must have an insurable interest in the insured individual in order for the contract to be valid. An insurable interest in life insurance need only exist at the time the policy is issued, while an insurable interest in property insurance must exist at the time of a loss. An insurable interest is a test of financial relationship. A husband may insure the life of his wife, an employer the life of an employee, a creditor the life of a debtor, and a partner the life of a copartner.

An investment in a life insurance policy is accounted for at the amount that can be realized by the owner of the policy as of the date of its statement of financial position. Generally, the amount that can be realized from a life insurance policy is the amount of its *cash surrender value*. The increase in the cash surrender value of an insurance policy for a particular period is recorded by the owner of the policy and the cash surrender value is included as an asset in its statement of financial position. The insurance expense for the same period is the difference between the total amount of premium paid and the amount of increase in the cash surrender value of the policy.

Illustration of Insurable Interest

An enterprise is the owner and sole beneficiary of a $200,000 life insurance policy on its president. The annual premium is $16,000. The policy is starting its fourth year, and the schedule of cash values indicates that at the end of the fourth year the cash value increases $25 per thousand. The enterprise pays the $16,000 premium, and the journal entry to record the transaction is as follows:

Life insurance expense—officers	11,000	
Cash surrender value—life insurance policy (200 × $25)	5,000	
Cash		16,000

The cash surrender value of a life insurance policy is classified either as a current or noncurrent asset in the policy owner's statement of financial position, depending upon the intentions of the policy owner. If the policy owner intends to surrender the policy to the insurer for its cash value within its normal operating cycle, the cash surrender value is classified as a current asset in the statement of financial position. If there is no intention of collecting the policy's cash value within the normal operating cycle of the policy owner, the cash surrender value is classified as a noncurrent asset in the statement of financial position.

LIABILITY CLASSIFICATION ISSUES

Current Obligations Expected to Be Refinanced

FAS-6 (Classification of Short-Term Obligations Expected to Be Refinanced) and FIN-8 (Classification of a Short-Term Obligation Repaid Prior to Being Replaced by a Long-Term Security) establish GAAP for classifying a short-term obligation that is expected to be refinanced into a long-term liability or stockholders' equity. FAS-6 applies only to those companies that issue classified balance sheets (FAS-6, par. 7).

A short-term obligation can be excluded from current liabilities only if the company intends to refinance it on a long-term basis and the intent is supported by the ability to refinance that is demonstrated in one of the following ways (FAS-6, pars. 9–11):

- A long-term obligation or equity security whose proceeds are used to retire the short-term obligation is issued after the date of the balance sheet but before the issuance of the financial statements.
- Before the issuance of the financial statements, the company has entered into an agreement that enables it to refinance a short-term obligation on a long-term basis. The terms of the agreement must be clear and unambiguous and must contain the following provisions:
  — The agreement may not be canceled by the lender or investor, and it must extend beyond the normal operating cycle of the company.

☛ **PRACTICE POINTER:** If the company has no operating cycle or the operating cycle occurs more than once a year, then the one-year rule is used.

— At the balance sheet date and at its issuance, the company was not in violation, nor was there any information that indicated a violation, of the agreement.

— The lender or investor is expected to be financially capable of honoring the agreement.

The amount of short-term obligation that can be reclassified as non-current cannot exceed the actual proceeds received from the issuance of the new long-term obligation or the amount of available refinancing covered by the established agreement. The amount must be adjusted for any limitations in the agreement that indicate the full amount obtainable will not be available to retire the short-term obligation. In addition, if the agreement indicates that the amount available for refinancing will fluctuate, then the most conservative estimate must be used. If no reasonable estimate can be made, then the agreement does not fulfill the necessary requirements and the full amount of current liabilities must be presented (FAS-6, par. 12).

An enterprise may intend to seek alternative financing sources besides those in the established agreement when the short-term obligation becomes due. If alternative sources do not materialize, however, the company must intend to borrow from the source in the agreement (FAS-6, par. 13).

☛ **PRACTICE POINTER:** If the terms of the agreement allow the prospective lender or investor to set interest rates, collateral requirements, or similar conditions that are unreasonable to the company, the intent to refinance may not exist.

FIN-8 addresses the issue of a short-term obligation that is repaid and is subsequently replaced with a long-term debt obligation or equity securities. Because cash is temporarily required to retire the short-term obligation, the obligation should be classified as a current liability in the balance sheet (FIN-8, par. 3).

Any *rollover agreements* or *revolving credit agreements* must meet the above provisions to enable a company to classify the related shortterm obligations as noncurrent (FAS-6, par. 14). The financial statements must contain a note disclosing the amount excluded from current liabilities and a full description of the financial agreement and new obligations incurred or expected to be incurred or the equity securities issued or expected to be issued (FAS-6, par. 15).

Callable Obligations

FAS-78 (Classification of Obligations That Are Callable by the Creditor) establishes GAAP for the current/noncurrent classification in the debtor's balance sheet of obligations that are payable on demand or callable by the creditor.

FAS-78 is applied to a classified balance sheet to determine whether the obligation should be classified as current or noncurrent for balance sheet purposes. FAS-78 is applied to both classified and unclassified balance sheets to determine the maturity dates of obligations disclosed by notes. For example, an unclassified balance sheet may contain a note disclosure of the maturity dates of obligations, despite the fact that the obligations are not classified in the unclassified balance sheet, or may not be identified separately from other obligations in the unclassified balance sheet (FAS-78, par. 4).

At the debtor's balance sheet date, an obligation may, by its terms, be payable on demand. This includes long-term obligations that are callable because a violation of an objective acceleration clause in a long-term debt agreement may exist at the date of the debtor's balance sheet. Such callable obligations must be classified as a current liability at the debtor's balance sheet date unless (FAS-78, par. 5):

- The creditor has waived the right to demand payment for a period that extends beyond one year (or the debtor's normal operating cycle if longer), or

- The debtor has cured the violation after the balance sheet date, but prior to the issuance date of the financial statements, and the obligation is not callable for a period that extends beyond one year (or the debtor's normal operating cycle if longer).

A long-term debt agreement may provide for a grace period that commences after the occurrence of a violation of an objective acceleration clause. FAS-78 requires that such an obligation be classified as a current liability at the debtor's balance sheet date, unless the two criteria above are met and, in addition, the unexpired grace period extends beyond one year (or the debtor's normal operating cycle if longer) (FAS-78, par. 5).

> **OBSERVATION:** FAS-78, which amends ARB-43, Chapter 3A, requires that an obligation be classified as current or noncurrent, based solely on whether the legal terms of the loan agreement require payment within one year (or the operating cycle if longer).

A creditor may have waived the right to demand payment on a specific obligation for a period that extends beyond one year (or the operating cycle if longer). In this event, the debtor shall classify the obligation as a noncurrent liability.

Acceleration Clauses

An *objective acceleration clause* in a long-term debt agreement is one that contains objective criteria that the creditor must use as the basis for calling part or all of the loan, such as a specified minimum amount of working capital or net worth requirement.

In the event of a violation of an objective acceleration clause, most long-term obligations become immediately callable by the creditor, or become callable after a grace period that is specified in the loan agreement. When this occurs, the creditor can demand payment of part or all of the loan balance, in accordance with the terms of the debt agreement.

A subjective acceleration clause is one that permits the lender to unilaterally accelerate part or all of a long-term obligation. For example, the debt agreement might state that "if, in the opinion of the lender, the borrower experiences recurring losses or liquidity problems, the lender may at its sole discretion accelerate part or all of the loan balance. . . ."

Acceleration clauses are accounted for in the same manner as other loss contingencies. If it is *probable* that the subjective acceleration clause will be exercised by the creditor, the amount of the long-term obligation that is likely to be accelerated shall be classified as a current liability by the debtor. On the other hand, if it is only *reasonably possible* that the subjective acceleration clause will be exercised by the creditor, note disclosure may be all that is required. Finally, if the possibility of subjective acceleration is *remote*, no disclosure may be required.

COMPENSATED ABSENCES

FAS-43 (Accounting for Compensated Absences) establishes GAAP for employees' compensated absences and is concerned only with the proper accrual of the liability for compensated absences rather than the allocation of such costs to interim accounting periods. FAS-43 does not apply to the following (FAS-43, par. 2):

- Severance or termination pay
- Stock or stock options issued to employees
- Deferred compensation
- Postretirement benefits
- Group insurance, disability pay, and other long-term fringe benefits
- Certain sick pay benefits that accumulate

Compensated absences arise from employees' absences from employment because of illness, holiday, vacation, or other reasons. When an employer expects to pay an employee for such compensated absences, a liability for the estimated probable future payments must be accrued if all the following conditions are met (FAS-43, par. 6):

- The employee's right to receive compensation for the future absences is attributable to services already performed by the employee.

- The employee's right to receive the compensation for the future absences is vested, or accumulates.

- It is probable that the compensation will be paid.

- The amount of compensation is reasonably estimable.

The fact that an employer meets the first three conditions and not the fourth condition must be disclosed in the financial statements.

Vested rights are those that have been earned by the employee for services already performed. They are not contingent on any future services by the employee and are an obligation of the employer even if the employee leaves the employer. Rights that accumulate are nonvesting rights to compensated absences that are earned and can be carried forward to succeeding years. Rights that accumulate increase an employee's benefits in one or more years subsequent to the year in which they are earned. An employer does not have to accrue a liability for nonvesting rights to compensated absences that expire at the end of the year in which they are earned, because they do not accumulate (FAS-43, par. 13).

Nonvesting sick pay benefits that accumulate and can be carried forward to succeeding years are given special treatment by FAS-43. If payment of nonvesting accumulating sick pay benefits depends on the future illness of the employee, an employer does not have to accrue a liability for such payments. The reasons cited in FAS-43 for this exception are (*a*) the cost/benefit rule, (*b*) the materiality rule, and (*c*) the reliability of estimating the days an employee will be sick in succeeding years. This exception does not apply in circumstances in which the employer pays the sick pay benefits even though the employee is not actually sick. An employer's general policy for the payment of nonvesting accumulating sick pay benefits should govern the accounting for such payments (FAS-43, par. 7).

> ☞ **PRACTICE POINTER:** One issue that must be resolved in recognizing the expense and liability for compensated absences is the rate of compensation to use—the current rate or the rate expected to apply when the compensated absence is taken by the employee. In situations in which the rate of compensation increases rapidly and/or a long period of time lapses between the time the compensated absence is earned and taken by the employee, the rate of compensation used may be significant. FAS-43 does not provide guidance on this issue. Other authoritative standards may provide some help in making this decision. For example, net periodic pension cost is determined in FAS-87 (Employers' Accounting for Pensions)

based on the projected benefit obligation, which includes expected future increases in compensation. If the difference in the amount of liability for compensated absences, when measured by the current and expected future rates of compensation, is material, the latter more faithfully measures the obligation and expense of the employer.

Once a total amount of liability for compensated absences is determined, the amount expected to require the use of current assets should be classified as a current liability. The remaining balance should be presented as a noncurrent liability.

OFFSETTING ASSETS AND LIABILITIES—GENERAL

Offsetting is the display of a recognized asset and a recognized liability as one net amount in a financial statement. If the amount of the recognized asset is the same as the amount of the recognized liability, then the net or combined amount of both is zero, and, as a result, no amount would appear in the financial statement. If the two amounts are not the same, the net amount of the two items that have been offset is presented in the financial statement and classified in the manner of the larger item.

APB-10 (Omnibus Opinion—1966) discusses the general principle of offsetting in the balance sheet in the context of income tax amounts. APB-10 includes the following statements:

- Offsetting assets and liabilities in the balance sheet is improper except where a right of setoff exists.

- This includes offsetting cash or other assets against a tax liability or other amounts owed to governments that are not, by their terms, designated specifically for the payment of taxes.

- The only exception to this general principle occurs when it is clear that a purchase of securities that are acceptable for the payment of taxes is in substance an advance payment of taxes that are payable in the relatively near future.

The general principle of financial reporting, which holds that offsetting assets and liabilities is improper except where a right of setoff exists, usually is considered in the context of unconditional receivables from and payables to another party. FIN-39 (Offsetting of Amounts Related to Certain Contracts) extends this general principle to *conditional* amounts recognized for contracts under which the amounts to be received or paid or the items to be exchanged depend on future interest rates, future exchange rates, future commodity prices, or other factors.

FIN-39 specifies four criteria that must be met for the right of setoff to exist (FIN-39, par. 5):

1. Each party owes the other party specific amounts.
2. The reporting party has the right to set off the amount payable, by contract or other agreement, with the amount receivable from the other party.
3. The reporting party intends to set off.
4. The right of setoff is enforceable at law.

> **OBSERVATIONS:** The importance of managerial intent is apparent in the third criterion, which states that the reporting party **intends** to set off its payable and receivable. When all of these conditions are met, the reporting entity has a valid right of setoff and may present the net amount of the payable or receivable in the balance sheet.

Generally, debts may be set off if they exist between mutual debtors, each acting in its capacity as both debtor and creditor. State laws and the U.S. Bankruptcy Code may impose restrictions on or prohibitions against the right of set off in bankruptcy under certain circumstances.

Illustration of Offsetting Assets and Liabilities

The offsetting of assets and liabilities is an important issue to consider when determining financial statement presentation of current assets and current liabilities. Any time items are set off, information that would otherwise be available is lost. In addition, important financial statement relationships may be altered when assets and liabilities are set off. Consider the following example:

Current Assets	
Receivable from M Co.	$100
Other assets	400
	$500
Current Liabilities	
Payable to M Co.	$ 75
Other liabilities	175
	$250
Current ratio (500/250)	2:1

Now, consider the same situation, except the $75 payable to M Co. is offset against the $100 receivable from M Co.:

Current Assets

Net receivable from M Co. ($100 − $75)	$25
Other assets	400
	$425
Current Liabilities	
Other liabilities	$175
Current ratio (425/175)	2.4:1

When offsetting is applied, the individual amounts of the receivable and payable are not presented, and only the net amount of $25 is present in the balance sheet. Further, the current ratio is significantly altered by the offsetting activity. This is a simple example, but it illustrates the impact of offsetting, and thus its importance as a financial statement reporting issue.

Many sources of authoritative accounting standards specify accounting treatments that result in offsetting or in a balance sheet presentation that has an effect similar to offsetting. FIN-39 is not intended to modify the accounting treatment in any of those particular circumstances.

The specific sources of GAAP that are covered by this exemption are (FIN-39, par. 7):

- FASB Statements and Interpretations
- APB Opinions
- Accounting Research Bulletins
- FASB Technical Bulletins
- AICPA Accounting Interpretations
- AICPA Audit and Accounting Guides
- AICPA Industry Audit Guides
- AICPA Statements of Position

OFFSETTING IN REPURCHASE AND REVERSE REPURCHASE AGREEMENTS

FIN-41 (Offsetting Amounts Related to Certain Repurchase and Reverse Repurchase Agreements) provides specific guidance as to when payables under repurchase agreements can be offset with receivables under reverse repurchase agreements. These criteria are (FIN-41, par. 3):

1. The agreements are executed with the same counterparty.

2. The agreements have the same settlement date, set forth at inception.

3. The agreements are executed in accordance with a master netting arrangement.

4. The securities under the agreements exist in "book entry" form and can be transferred only by means of entries in the records of the transfer system operator or securities custodian.

5. The agreements will be settled on a securities transfer system that operates in the manner described below, and the enterprise must have associated banking arrangements in place as described below. Cash settlements for securities transferred are made under established banking arrangements that provide that the enterprise will need available cash on deposit only for any net amounts that are due at the end of the business day. It must be *probable* that the associated banking arrangements will provide sufficient *daylight overdraft or other intraday credit* at the settlement date for each of the parties.

6. The enterprise intends to use the same account at the clearing bank (or other financial institution) to settle its receivable (i.e., cash inflow from the reverse purchasing agreement) and its payable (i.e., cash outflow to settle the offsetting repurchase agreement).

If these six criteria are met, the enterprise has the option to offset. That choice must be applied consistently.

The third criterion refers to a "master netting arrangement." A master netting arrangement exists if the reporting entity has multiple contracts, whether for the same type of conditional or exchange contract or for different types of contracts, with a single counterparty that are subject to a contractual agreement that provides for the net settlement of all contracts through a single payment in a single currency in the event of default on or termination of any one contract (FIN-39).

The fourth criterion refers to "book entry" form. FIN-41 sees this as a key element because it provides control over the securities. The controlling record for a "book entry" security is maintained by the transfer system operator. A securities custodian that has a security account with the transfer system operation may maintain "subsidiary" records of "book entry" securities and may transfer the securities within its subsidiary records; however, a security cannot be traded from the account of that custodian to a new custodian without a "book entry" transfer of the security over the securities transfer system. This form of accounting record facilitates repurchase and reverse repurchase agreement transactions on securities transfer systems.

For a transfer system for repurchase and reverse repurchase agreements to meet the fifth criterion, cash transfers must be initiated by the owner of record of the securities notifying its securities custodian to transfer those securities to the counterparty to the arrangement. Under associated banking arrangements, each party to a same-day settlement of both a repurchase agreement and a reverse repurchase agreement would be obligated to pay a gross amount of cash for the securities transferred from its counterparty, but the party would be able to reduce that gross obligation by notifying its securities custodian to transfer other securities to that counterparty the same day (FIN-41, par. 4).

In the fifth criterion, the term *probable* has the same definition as in FAS-5, meaning that a transaction or event is more likely to occur than not. The phrase "daylight overdraft or other intraday credit" refers to the feature of the banking arrangement that permits transactions to be completed during the day when insufficient cash is on deposit, provided there is sufficient cash to cover the net cash requirement at the end of the day.

LIABILITIES AND EQUITY

FAS-150 (Accounting for Certain Financial Instruments with Characteristics of both Liabilities and Equity), more clearly defines the distinction between liabilities and equity. The approach taken is to specifically define liabilities and require that all other financial instruments be classified as equity in the balance sheet. The FASB states that FAS-150 (Accounting for Certain Financial Instruments with Characteristics of Both Liabilities and Equity) is generally consistent with its conceptual framework, specifically FASB Concepts Statement No. 6 (Elements of Financial Statements), which provides definitions of the various elements of the statement of financial position (balance sheet), income statement, and statement of cash flows.

FAS-150 establishes standards for issuers of financial instruments with characteristics of both liabilities and equity related to the classification and measurement of those instruments. It requires the issuer to classify a financial instrument as a liability, or asset in some cases, which was previously classified as equity. The classification standards are generally consistent with the definition of liabilities in FASB Concepts Statement No. 6 and with the FASB's proposal to revise that definition to encompass certain obligations that a reporting entity can or must settle by issuing its own equity shares.

Distinction between Liabilities and Equity

FAS-150 requires an issuer to classify the following instruments as liabilities, or assets in certain circumstances:

- A financial instrument issued in the form of shares that is mandatorily redeemable in that it embodies an unconditional obligation that requires the issuer to redeem the shares by transferring the entity's assets at a specified or determinable date(s) or upon an event that is certain to occur.

- A financial instrument other than an outstanding share that, at its inception, embodies an obligation to repurchase the issuer's equity shares, or is indexed to such an obligation, and that requires or may require the issuer to settle the obligation by transferring assets.

- A financial instrument other than an outstanding share that embodies an unconditional obligation that the issuer must or may settle by issuing a variable number of equity shares if, at inception, the monetary value of the obligation is based solely or predominantly on any of the following:
  — A fixed monetary amount known at inception (e.g., a payable to be settled with a variable number of the issuer's equity shares).
  — Variations in something other than the fair value of the issuer's equity shares (e.g., a financial instrument indexed to the S&P 500 and settleable with a variable number of the issuer's equity shares).
  — Variables inversely related to changes in the fair value of the issuer's equity shares (e.g., a written put option that could be net share settled).

FAS-150 applies to issuers' classification and measurement of freestanding financial instruments, including those that comprise more than one option or forward contract. It does not apply to features that are embedded in a financial instrument that is not a derivative in its entirety. In applying the classification provisions of FAS-150, nonsubstantive or minimal features are to be disregarded.

Required Disclosures

Issuers of financial instruments are required to disclose the nature and terms of the financial instruments and the rights and obligations embodied in those instruments. That disclosure shall include information about any settlement alternatives in the contract and identify the entity that controls the settlement alternatives.

For all outstanding financial instruments within the scope of FAS-150, and the settlement alternative(s), the following information is required to be disclosed by issuers:

- The amount that would be paid, or the number of shares that would be issued and their fair value, determined under the conditions specified in the contract if the settlement were to occur at the reporting date.

- How changes in the fair value of the issuer's equity shares would affect those settlement amounts.

- The maximum amount that the issuer could be required to pay to redeem the instrument by physical settlement, if applicable.

- The maximum number of shares that could be required to be issued, if applicable.

- That a contract does not limit the amount that the issuer could be required to pay or the number of shares that the issuer could be required to issue, if applicable.

- For a forward contract or an option indexed to the issuer's equity shares, the forward price or option strike price, the number of the issuer's shares to which the contract is indexed, and the settlement date(s) of the contract.

Deferred Effective Date

FASB Staff Position (FSP) FAS 150-3 (Effective Date, Disclosures, and Transition for Mandatorily Redeemable Financial Instruments of Certain Nonpublic Entities and Certain Mandatorily Redeemable Noncontrolling Interests Under FASB Statement No. 150) defers indefinitely the effective date of FAS-150 for certain mandatorily redeemable financial instruments of nonpublic entities *that are not registered with the SEC*. FAS-150 is deferred indefinitely for a mandatorily redeemable financial instrument if the instrument is not due on a fixed date for a fixed amount, or if the amount due is not tied to an interest rate index, currency index, or other external index.

In addition, FAS-150's provisions for mandatorily redeemable noncontrolling interests are deferred indefinitely for both public and nonpublic entities under some circumstances. FAS-150's provisions for mandatorily redeemable noncontrolling interests are deferred indefinitely if the interest would not be classified as a liability by the subsidiary (under the "only upon liquidation" exception in FAS-150) but would be classified as a liability by the parent in the consolidated financial statements. In addition, the *measurement* provisions of FAS-150 are deferred indefinitely for mandatorily redeemable noncontrolling interests issued before November 5, 2003. This deferral applies to both the parent company and the subsidiary that issued the noncontrolling interests. The *classification* provisions of FAS-150 are *not* deferred for mandatorily redeemable noncontrolling interests issued before November 5, 2003. The companion book to this *Guide*, the *GAAP Guide Levels B, C, and D* provides additional discussion of FSP FAS 150-3.

FAS-150 should be implemented by reporting the cumulative effect of a change in accounting principle for financial instruments created prior to the issuance date of the standard and still in existence at the beginning of the interim period of adoption. Restatement of prior years' financial statements is not permitted.

Illustration of Applying FAS-150

Mandatorily redeemable financial instruments. Financial instruments issued in the form of shares that embody unconditional obligations of the issuer to redeem the instruments by transferring its assets at a specified or determinable date(s) or upon an event that is certain to occur are required to be classified as liabilities. This includes certain forms of trust-preferred securities and stock that must be redeemed upon the death or termination of the individual who holds them. Although some mandatorily redeemable instruments are issued in the form of shares, those instruments are classified as liabilities under FAS-150 because of the embodied obligation on the part of the issuer to transfer its assets in the future:

Example: Statement of Financial Position

Total assets	$5,000,000
Liabilities other than shares	$4,200,000
Shares subject to mandatory redemption	800,000
Total liabilities	$5,000,000
Notes to Financial Statements	
Shares subject to mandatory redemption:	
Common stock	$600,000
Retained earnings attributed to those shares	200,000
	$800,000

Certain obligations to issue a variable number of shares. FAS-150 requires liability classification if, at inception, the monetary value of an obligation to issue a variable number of shares is based solely or predominantly on any of the following:

- A fixed monetary amount known at inception
- Variations in something other than the fair value of the issuer's equity shares

- Variations inversely related to changes in the fair value of the issuer's equity shares

Example: An entity may receive $500,000 in exchange for a promise to issue a sufficient number of shares of its own stock to be worth $525,000 at a specified future date. The number of shares to be issued to settle the obligation is variable, depending on the number required to meet the $525,000 obligation, and will be determined based on the fair value of the shares at the settlement date. The instrument is classified as a liability under FAS-150.

Freestanding financial instruments. FAS-150 requires certain provisions of FAS-150 to be applied to a freestanding instrument in its entirety:

Example: An issuer has two freestanding instruments with the same counterparty: (1) a contract that combines a written put option at one strike price and a purchased call option at another strike price on its equity shares; and (2) outstanding shares of stock. The primary requirements of FAS-150 are applied to the entire freestanding instrument that includes both a put option and a call option. It is classified as a liability and is measured at fair value. The outstanding shares of stock are not within the scope of FAS-150.

DISCLOSURE STANDARDS

Current assets and current liabilities must be identified clearly in the financial statements, and the basis for determining the stated amounts must be disclosed fully (ARB-43, Ch. 3A, par. 3). The following are the more common disclosures that are required for current assets and current liabilities in the financial statements or in notes thereto:

- Classification of inventories and the method used (e.g., FIFO, LIFO, average cost)
- Restrictions on current assets
- Current portions of long-term obligations
- Description of accounting policies relating to current assets and current liabilities

Accounts receivable and notes receivable from officers, employees, or affiliated companies, if material, must be reported separately in the financial statements (ARB-43, Chapter 1A, par. 5).

RELATED CHAPTERS IN 2009 *GAAP GUIDE* *LEVEL A*

Chapter 8, "Contingencies, Risks, and Uncertainties"
Chapter 9, "Convertible Debt and Debt with Warrants"
Chapter 17, "Financial Instruments"
Chapter 21, "Income Taxes"
Chapter 27, "Inventory"
Chapter 28, "Investments in Debt and Equity Securities"

RELATED CHAPTERS IN 2009 *GAAP GUIDE* *LEVELS B, C, AND D*

Chapter 4, "Balance Sheet Classification and Related Display Issues"
Chapter 11, "Contingencies, Risks, and Uncertainties"
Chapter 12, "Convertible Debt and Debt with Warrants"
Chapter 17, "Financial Instruments"
Chapter 24, "Inventory"
Chapter 25, "Investments in Debt and Equity Securities"

RELATED CHAPTERS IN 2009 *INTERNATIONAL ACCOUNTING/FINANCIAL REPORTING STANDARDS GUIDE*

Chapter 3, "Presentation of Financial Statements"
Chapter 16, "Financial Instruments"
Chapter 20, "Income Taxes"
Chapter 23, "Inventories"
Chapter 24, "Investment Property"
Chapter 28, "Provisions, Contingent Liabilities, and Contingent Assets"

CHAPTER 4
BUSINESS COMBINATIONS

CONTENTS

OVERVIEW

A business combination occurs when two or more entities combine to form a single entity. An *asset combination* results when one company acquires the assets of one or more other companies, or when a new company is formed to acquire the assets of two or more existing companies. In an asset combination, the target companies cease to exist as operating entities and may be liquidated or become investment companies. An *acquisition of stock combination* occurs when one company acquires more than 50% of the outstanding voting common stock of one or more target companies, or when a new company is formed to acquire controlling interest in the outstanding voting common stock of two or more target companies.

Until 2001, two basic methods of accounting existed for business combinations: (1) the purchase method and (2) the pooling-of-interests method. In 2001, the FASB issued FAS-141 (Business Combinations), which eliminated the pooling-of-interests method.

In a purchase method combination, the combined entity reports the assets and liabilities of the target company at fair market value on the date of acquisition. Any excess of the fair market value of the consideration given over the fair market value of the net assets acquired is reported as goodwill. If the fair market value of the consideration given is less than the fair market value of the net assets acquired, the resulting excess of fair value of acquired net assets over the cost of the acquired entity is allocated, on a pro rata basis, against certain assets acquired in the business combination. If any excess over cost remains after reducing certain assets to zero, the remaining excess is recognized as an extraordinary gain. The operating statements for purchase method combinations report combined results only for the period subsequent to the combination.

GAAP for business combinations are found in the following authoritative pronouncements:

FAS-72   Accounting for Certain Acquisitions of Banking or Thrift Institutions

FAS-141	Business Combinations
FAS-142	Goodwill and Other Intangible Assets
FAS-147	Acquisitions of Certain Financial Institutions—An Amendment of FASB Statements No. 72 and 144 and FASB Interpretation No. 9
FIN-9	Applying APB Opinions No. 16 and 17 When a Savings and Loan Association or a Similar Institution Is Acquired in a Business Combination Accounted for by the Purchase Method

2009 TRANSITION GUIDANCE FOR FAS-160

The FASB has recently issued FAS-160, *Noncontrolling Interests in Consolidated Financial Statements, an Amendment of ARB No. 51*, which is effective for fiscal years, and interim periods within those fiscal years, beginning on or after December 15, 2008. Since FAS-160 is not effective for some companies until December 2009, and since early adoption is prohibited, the 2009 *GAAP Guide* does not reflect the requirements of FAS-160. There is a discussion of the requirements of FAS-160 in the Appendix to Chapter 7, "Consolidated Financial Statements." However, any effects of FAS-160 on this chapter have not been reflected in this edition. Therefore, if a company is subject to the requirements of FAS-160, the reader is referred to FAS-160 for these new requirements.

> **OBSERVATION:** FAS-72 (Accounting for Certain Acquisitions of Banking or Thrift Institutions) and FIN-9 (Applying APB Opinions No. 16 and 17 When a Savings and Loan Association or Similar Institution Is Acquired in a Business Combination Accounted for by the Purchase Method) provided guidance on the application of the purchase method to acquisitions of financial institutions. Although FAS-72 and FIN-9 pertained to APB-16 (Business Combinations) and APB-17 (Intangible Assets), they were not superseded by FAS-141 and FAS-142 (Goodwill and Other Intangible Assets), even though both APB-16 and APB-17 were superseded by FAS-141 and FAS-142. This anomaly resulted in acquisitions of financial institutions being accounted for differently from acquisitions of other types of entities. For example, FAS-72 required the recognition of an unidentifiable intangible asset in certain acquisitions and, although this unidentifiable intangible asset is essentially equivalent to goodwill, it continued to be amortized to expense, rather than evaluated for impairment, because FAS-141 and FAS-142 did not supersede FAS-72 and FIN-9. FAS-147 (Acquisitions of Certain Financial Institutions—An Amendment of FASB Statements No. 72 and 144 and FASB Interpretation No. 9) essentially supersedes FAS-72 and FIN-9, except that FAS-72 and FIN-9 continue to apply to transactions between two or more financial institutions that are mutual enterprises.

OBSERVATION: FAS-141(R) (Business Combinations) was issued in December 2007, and is effective for business combinations for which the acquisition date is on or after the beginning of the first annual reporting period beginning on or after December 15, 2008. Since FAS-141(R) is not effective for some companies until December 2009, and since early adoption is prohibited, the body of this chapter will reflect the requirements of FAS-141 prior to its revision in December 2007. However, since FAS-141(R) will be effective for many companies in early 2009, a discussion of the changes in the accounting for business combinations under FAS-141(R) is found in the Appendix to this chapter.

BACKGROUND

For many years, GAAP for business combinations was included in APB-16 and allowed two significantly different methods—the purchase method and the pooling-of-interests method. The purchase method, as the name implies, was based on the assumption that a purchase transaction had occurred (i.e., one entity has purchased the other). This type of transaction was usually executed via the transfer of cash or other assets or through a capital stock transfer. A new cost basis for the assets acquired and the liabilities assumed arose, and goodwill often was established as a result of the business combination. The pooling-of-interests method, on the other hand, was intended for business combinations in which the shareholders of the combining entities became shareholders of a combined company. The essence of a pooling was that the shareholders of the combining companies neither withdrew nor invested assets, but exchanged shares in accordance with a ratio that preserved their interests in the combining companies.

APB-16 was based on an assumption that a business combination was a purchase unless 12 very specific criteria were met, in which case the business combination was a pooling-of-interests. For business combinations initiated after June 30, 2001, the pooling-of-interests method is no longer available and, therefore, that method is not covered in this *Guide* other than for historical reference.

While the primary source of authoritative guidance on business combinations is FAS-141, other pronouncements also address issues related to business combinations. For example:

- FAS-109(Accounting for Income Taxes) requires that a liability or asset be recognized for the deferred tax consequences of differences between the assigned values and the tax bases of the assets and liabilities (other than nondeductible goodwill and leveraged leases) recognized in a purchase business combination.

- FAS-87 (Employers' Accounting for Pensions) requires that assets and liabilities recorded under the purchase method include a liability for the projected benefit obligation in excess of plan assets or an asset for plan assets in excess of the projected benefit obligation, thereby eliminating any previously existing net gain or loss, prior service cost or credit, or transition asset or obligation recognized in accumulated other comprehensive income.

Each of the above issues relating to business combinations is addressed in this chapter.

THE PURCHASE METHOD OF ACCOUNTING FOR BUSINESS COMBINATIONS

Scope

For purposes of applying FAS-141, a business combination occurs when an entity acquires net assets that constitute a business or acquires equity interests of one or more other entities and obtains control over that (or those) other entity (or entities) (FAS-141, par. 9). FAS-141 applies to combinations involving either incorporated or unincorporated entities. Business combinations may take a variety of forms, such as (FAS-141, par. 10):

- One or more entities are merged or become subsidiaries.
- One entity transfers net assets or its owners transfer their interests to another.
- All entities transfer net assets or the owners of those entities transfer their equity interests to a newly formed entity.

The acquisition of some or all of the noncontrolling interests in a subsidiary is not a business combination, although that type of transaction is covered in FAS-141 (FAS-141, par. 11). FAS-141 does not apply to combinations between not-for-profit organizations. Similarly, FAS-141 does not apply to the acquisition of a for-profit organization by a not-for-profit organization (FAS-141, par. 12).

Method of Accounting

All business combinations subject to the requirements of FAS-141 are to be accounted for by the purchase method (FAS-141, par. 13).

The purchase of some or all of the noncontrolling interests in a subsidiary is also required to be accounted for by the purchase method, whether acquired by the parent, the subsidiary itself, or another affiliate (FAS-141, par. 14).

Applying the Purchase Method

Determining the Acquiring Entity

A first step in applying the purchase method is to determine the acquiring entity (FAS-141, par. 15). In a business combination effected through an exchange of equity interests, the entity that issues the equity interests is generally the acquiring entity. Typically the acquiring entity is the larger entity. Often, the combined entity uses the name of the acquiring entity. Circumstances differ, however, and all pertinent facts and circumstances should be considered in determining the acquiring entity (FAS-141, par. 17).

Following are several factors that are particularly important in determining the acquiring entity.

- *The relative voting rights in the combined entity after the combination*—the acquiring entity is the entity whose owners retain or receive the larger portion of the voting rights (FAS-141, par. 17a).

- *The existence of a large minority voting interest when no other owner or organized group of owners has a significant voting interest*—the acquiring entity is typically the combining entity whose single owner or organized group of owners holds the largest minority voting interest in the combined entity (FAS-141, par. 17b).

- *The composition of the governing body of the combined entity*—the acquiring entity is the combining entity whose owners or governing body has the ability to elect or appoint a voting majority of the governing body of the combined entity (FAS-141, par. 17c).

- *The composition of the senior management of the combined entity*—the acquiring entity is the combining entity whose senior management dominates that of the combined entity (FAS-141, par. 17d).

- *The terms of the exchange of equity securities*—the acquiring entity is the combining entity that pays a premium over market value of the equity securities of the other combining entity or entities (FAS-141, par. 17e).

Determining Cost

Determining the cost of the acquisition is similar to determining the cost of assets acquired individually. Cash payment shall be used to measure the cost of an acquired entity. Similarly, the fair value of other assets distributed as consideration and the fair values of liabilities incurred are used to measure the cost of an acquired entity (FAS-141, par. 20).

The fair value of securities traded is generally more clearly evident than the fair value of an acquired entity and, thus, generally should be used to determine cost in a business combination. If the quoted market price is not the fair value of the equity securities, the consideration received shall be estimated even though measuring directly the fair value of net assets received is difficult. Both the net assets received, including goodwill, and the extent of the adjustment of the quoted market price of the shares issued shall be weighed in determining the amount to be recorded. Independent appraisals may be used to aid in determining fair values of securities issues (FAS-141, pars. 22–23).

The cost of an acquired entity includes the direct costs of the business combination, which includes (i.e., is reduced by) costs of registering and issuing equity securities. Indirect and general expenses associated with a business combination should be expensed as incurred (FAS-141, par. 24).

A business combination may include contingent consideration. Cash and other assets distributed, securities issued unconditionally, and amounts of contingent consideration that are determinable at the date of acquisition shall be included in the cost of an acquired entity and recorded at that date. Contingent consideration shall be recorded when the contingency is resolved and consideration is issued or becomes issuable. In general, the issuance of additional securities or distribution of other consideration when contingencies are resolved result in an additional element of cost of an acquired entity (FAS-141, pars. 25–27).

Allocating Cost

An acquiring entity shall allocate the cost of an acquired entity to the assets acquired and liabilities assumed based on their estimated fair values at date of acquisition. Following are general guidelines for the recording of assets acquired and liabilities assumed, except goodwill (FAS-141, par. 37):

- Marketable securities—fair value
- Receivables—present value of amounts to be received
- Inventories (finished goods and merchandise)—estimated selling prices less the costs of disposal and a reasonable profit allowance
- Inventories (work-in-process)—estimated selling prices less the costs to complete, costs of disposal, and reasonable profit margin
- Inventories (raw materials)—current replacement cost
- Plant and equipment (to be used)—current replacement cost
- Plant and equipment (to be sold)—fair value less cost to sell
- Intangible assets—estimated fair values

- Other assets (e.g., land, natural resources, nonmarketable securities)—appraised values
- Accounts and notes payable, long-term debt, and other claims payable—present values of amounts to be paid determined at appropriate current interest rates
- Liability for the projected benefit obligation in excess of plan assets (or vice versa)—amounts determined in accordance with FAS-87 (Employers' Accounting for Pensions)
- Liability for accumulated postretirement benefit obligation in excess of the fair value of plan assets (or vice versa)—amounts determined in accordance with FAS-106 (Employers' Accounting for Postretirement Benefits Other Than Pensions)
- Liabilities and accruals—present values of amounts to be paid determined at appropriate interest rates
- Other liabilities and commitments (e.g., unfavorable leases, contracts)—present value of amounts to be paid determined at appropriate current interest rates

Intangible Assets

An intangible asset shall be recognized as an asset apart from goodwill if it arises from contractual or other legal rights. If this condition is not met, an intangible asset shall be recognized as an asset only if it is separable (i.e., is capable of being sold, transferred, licensed, rented, or exchanged). An assembled workforce cannot be recognized apart from goodwill (FAS-141, par. 39).

Preacquisition Contingencies

The fair value of a preacquisition contingency shall be included in the allocation of the purchase price under the following circumstances (FAS-141, par. 40):

- The fair value of the preacquisition contingency can be determined during the allocation period.
- Information available prior to the end of the of the allocation period indicates that it is probable that an asset exists, a liability has been incurred, or an asset has been impaired at the consummation of the business combination, and the asset or liability can be reasonably estimated.

Goodwill

Any excess of the cost of an acquired entity over the amounts assigned to assets acquired and liabilities assumed is recognized as goodwill. Goodwill so recorded is accounted for in accordance with FAS-142 (FAS-141, par. 43).

Excess of Fair Value over Cost

The sum of the amounts assigned to assets acquired and liabilities assumed may exceed the cost of the acquired entity. That excess shall be allocated as a pro rata reduction of the amounts that otherwise would have been assigned to the acquired assets *except* (*a*) financial assets other than investments accounted for by the equity method, (*b*) assets to be disposed of by sale, (*c*) deferred income taxes, (*d*) prepaid assets related to pension and other postretirement benefit plans, and (*e*) any other current assets. Any excess remaining after reducing to zero the amounts that otherwise would have been assigned to those assets is recognized as an extraordinary gain. That extraordinary gain generally is recognized in the period which the business combination is completed (FAS-141, pars. 44–45).

Financial Statement Disclosure

General Information

Notes to the financial statements shall include the following information in the period in which a business combination that has a material effect on the financial statements is completed (FAS-141, par. 51):

- The name and brief description of the acquired entity and the percentage of voting stock acquired
- The primary reasons for the acquisition
- The period for which the results of operations of the acquired entity are included in the income statement of the combined entity
- The cost of the acquired entity, the number of shares of equity interest issued or issuable, the value assigned to the interests, and the basis for determining that value
- A condensed balance sheet including the amount assigned to each major asset and liability caption of the acquired entity at the acquisition date
- Contingency payments, options, or commitments specified in the acquisition agreement and the accounting treatment of each
- The amount of purchased research and development assets acquired and written off in the period and the location of the write-off in the income statement
- For any purchase price allocation that is not final, that fact and the reasons therefore

Intangible Asset Information

Notes to the financial statements shall include the following information regarding intangible assets and goodwill (FAS-141, par. 52):

- For intangible assets subject to amortization:
  - — Amount assigned to any major intangible asset class
  - — Amount of any significant residual value, in total and by major intangible asset class
  - — Weighted-average amortization period, in total and by major intangible asset class
- For intangible assets not subject to amortization, the total amount assigned and the amounts assigned to any major intangible asset class
- For goodwill:
  - — Total amount of goodwill and the amount that is expected to be deductible for tax purposes.
  - — The amount of goodwill by reportable segment (assuming the entity is required to disclose segment information in accordance with FAS-131 (Disclosures about Segments of an Enterprise and Related Information))

Special Disclosures for Public Companies

Notes to financial statements shall include the following supplemental information on a pro forma basis for the period in which a material business combinations occurs (FAS-141, par. 54):

- Results of operations for the current period as though the combination had been completed at the beginning of the period.
- Results of operations for the comparable prior period as though the combination had been completed at the beginning of that period if comparative financial statements are presented.

These supplemental disclosures must include revenue, income before extraordinary items, net income, and earnings per share (FAS-141, par. 55).

In the period in which an extraordinary gain is recognized related to a business combination, the notes also shall disclose information consistent with paragraph 11 of APB-30 (Reporting the Results of Operations—Reporting the Effects of Disposal of a Segment of a Business, and Extaordinary, Unusual and Infrequently Occurring Events and Transactions) (FAS-141, par. 56).

Interim Financial Statements

The summarized interim financial information of a public enterprise shall disclose the following information if a material business combination is completed during the current year (FAS-141, par. 58):

- The general disclosures described above
- Supplemental pro forma information that discloses the results of operations for the current interim period and the current year to date of the most recent interim statement of financial position presented as though the business combination had been completed at the beginning of the period being reported on
- The nature and amount of any material, nonrecurring items included in the reported pro forma results of operations

PURCHASE METHOD: IMPLEMENTATION GUIDANCE

Types of Purchase Business Combinations

A business combination may be accomplished in one of two ways. The acquiring company may purchase the assets (asset acquisition) of the target company. In this instance, normally the target company is liquidated and only one entity continues. Alternatively, the acquiring company may purchase more than 50% (up to 100%) of the outstanding voting common stock of the target company. In this instance, the financial statements of the two entities are consolidated in accordance with ARB-51 (Consolidated Financial Statements), as amended by FAS-94 (Consolidation of All Majority-Owned Subsidiaries).

In an asset purchase, entries are made to record the assets and assume the liabilities of the target company on the books of the acquiring company. If the purchase price exceeds the fair market value of the net assets, goodwill is recorded in the acquisition entry. If the fair market value of identifiable assets exceeds the purchase price, the resulting excess of fair value of acquired net assets over cost is allocated to reduce all of the acquired assets *except* (*a*) financial assets other than investments accounted for by the equity method, (*b*) assets to be disposed of by sale, (*c*) deferred income taxes, (*d*) prepaid assets related to pension and other postretirement benefit plans, and (*e*) any other current assets (FAS-141, par. 44). If an excess of fair value of acquired net assets over cost remains unallocated, the resulting amount is treated as an extraordinary gain (FAS-141, par. 45).

Illustration of Asset Purchase

On July 1, 20X8, S Company sold all its net assets and business to P Company for $415,000 cash. The following is S Company's balance sheet as of July 1, 20X8:

Balance Sheet

Cash	$ 20,000
Accounts receivable	72,000
Allowance for doubtful accounts	(8,000)
Inventory	120,000
Plant and equipment (net)	260,000
Total assets	$464,000
Accounts payable	$ 60,000
Accrued expenses	5,000
Mortgage payable—plant	120,000
Common stock	200,000
Retained earnings	79,000
Total liabilities and equity	$464,000

Additional Information:

Confirmation of the accounts receivable revealed that $10,000 was uncollectible.

The physical inventory count was $138,000 (fair value).

The fair value of the plant and equipment was $340,000.

The journal entry to record the investment on the books of P Company is:

Cash	$ 20,000	
Accounts receivable	72,000	
Inventory	$138,000	
Plant & equipment	340,000	
Goodwill	40,000	
Allowance for doubtful accounts		$ 10,000
Accounts payable		60,000
Accrued expenses		5,000
Mortgage payable		120,000
Cash		415,000

The computation of goodwill involved in the transaction is:

Computation of Goodwill

Assets	$464,000
Liabilities ($60,000 + $5,000 + $120,000)	(185,000)
Total	$279,000
Additional uncollectibles	(2,000)
Increase in inventory	18,000
Increase in plant and equipment	80,000
Adjusted net assets	$375,000
Cost of purchase	(415,000)
Goodwill	$ 40,000

Had the purchase price been only $350,000, the excess of fair value of acquired net assets over cost would have been computed as follows.

Adjusted net assets	$375,000
Cost of purchase	(350,000)
Excess of fair value of acquired net assets over cost	$ 25,000

The $25,000 of excess of fair value of acquired net assets over cost would be allocated, in this example, to the inventory and plant and equipment account balances (on a pro rata basis).

In an acquisition of stock, entries are made to record the investment in the stock of the investee. An analysis of the difference between the cost of the investment and the underlying book value is required to prepare consolidated financial statements for the parent and subsidiary to reflect the fair market value of the identifiable assets and goodwill as of the date of acquisition. Using data from the previous example, the only entry required to record the combination is:

Investment in S Company	415,000	
Cash		415,000

At the financial statement date, consolidated financial statements will be prepared that combine the assets and liabilities of the parent and subsidiary companies. At that time, the account "Investment in S Company" is eliminated from the statements along with the stockholders' equity in S Company. In addition, the identifiable assets of S Company are adjusted to fair market value and the goodwill of $40,000 is recorded in the consolidated balance sheet. Operating expenses, depreciation, and amortization of the combined entities are adjusted to reflect the revised asset values. In cases in which more than one class of stock is outstanding, the analysis is more complex.

Illustration of Stock Acquisition

For $1,500,000, P Company purchased 90% of the common stock and 50% of the preferred stock of S Company. At the date of acquisition, S Company's stockholders' equity was:

Stockholders' Equity

Common stock, 100,000 shares, $5 par, all authorized, issued, and outstanding	$ 500,000
5%, $100 par value, preferred stock, 10,000 shares, all authorized, issued, and outstanding	1,000,000
Paid-in capital in excess of par value (common)	200,000
Retained earnings	300,000
Total stockholders' equity	$2,000,000

The computation of the goodwill involved in the transaction is:

Computation of Goodwill

Cost of 90% common and 50% preferred	$1,500,000
Less: *Company S equity:*	
Common stock ($500,000 × 90%)	$ 450,000
Preferred stock ($1,000,000 × 50%)	500,000
Paid-in capital ($200,000 × 90%)	180,000
Retained earnings ($300,000 × 90%)	270,000
Total	$1,400,000
Excess of cost over book value (goodwill)	$ 100,000

The journal entry to record the investment is:

Investment in S Company	1,500,000	
Cash		1,500,000

Goodwill is not necessarily the difference between cost and book value of an investment, unless the book value is equal to the fair value of the underlying assets. The underlying assets represented by an investment individually are assigned a fair value at the date of acquisition, and if the assigned fair values are less than the amount of the investment, the difference is goodwill. For consolidation purposes, the acquisition of a stock investment may be considered the purchase price paid for an interest in the underlying net assets of a business.

If any excess of cost over acquired book value is allocated to depreciable assets, the depreciation expense of subsequent periods must be increased to spread the amount of such excess over the remaining life of the assets.

Illustration of Cost-Book Differential Assigned to Plant Assets

Excess cost over book value of $25,000 is assigned (*a*) $5,000 to a parcel of land and (*b*) $20,000 to the building located on the land. The building has a 20-year life, and the following adjusting journal entry is made on the consolidated working papers (assume one full year):

Land	5,000	
Building	20,000	
Investment		25,000
Depreciation	1,000	
Accumulated depreciation		1,000

Since consolidated adjusting journal entries are never posted on the books, these entries must be repeated each year on the worksheet for consolidated statements. In addition, assuming the parent company accounts for the investments using the cost method, a correcting entry must be made for the depreciation for prior years. For example, for the second year, the above entries are made as well as the following entry:

Consolidated retained earnings	1,000	
Accumulated depreciation		1,000

For the third year, the correction would be for $2,000; for the fourth year, $3,000; etc. If the full equity method were used in accounting for the investments in the subsidiary, this correction would not be needed.

Cost Determination

Business combinations accounted for by the purchase method are recorded at cost. Cost is determined as the fair value of the net assets acquired or as the fair value of the consideration given, whichever is more objectively determinable. In exchanges involving cash, the net assets are recorded in the amount of cash disbursed. In exchanges involving the issuance of securities, normally the market value of the securities can be referred to as a basis for recording the acquisition. If the securities given are debt securities, their fair market value can be determined by computing the present value of the debt, discounted at the market rate of interest for the class of debt involved. Any resulting difference between par value and present value of the debt is reflected in the financial statements of the combined entity as discount or premium on the debt, in accordance with APB-21 (Interest on Receivables and Payables).

☞ **PRACTICE POINTER:** The market price of traded securities usually is evidence of fair value. However, the market price of a traded security issued in a business combination may have to be adjusted for the quantity issued, price fluctuations, and issue costs. One way of incorporating these factors into the transaction is to use the average market value before and after the business combination. Independent appraisals of the identifiable assets acquired may also be necessary to determine whether goodwill should be recorded.

Contingent Consideration

The recorded cost of an acquisition is equal to the determinable amount of cash and other net assets that are unconditionally surrendered at the date of acquisition. Contingent consideration is recorded if it is determinable at the date of the acquisition. Other contingent consideration, the amount of which is not determinable at the acquisition date, is disclosed.

Contingent consideration may be on the basis of maintaining or achieving specific earning levels over future periods, or on a security maintaining or achieving a specific market price. When a contingent consideration based on earnings is achieved, the acquiring company records the current fair value of the additional consideration. At this juncture, it is more than likely that the increase in the cost of the acquisition will be in the form of goodwill.

When contingent consideration arises on the basis of maintaining or exceeding a specific market price for the securities issued to consummate the acquisition, the acquiring company will have to issue additional securities or transfer other assets in accordance with the contingency arrangements. The issuance of the additional contingency securities is based on their then-current fair value, but does not increase the overall cost of the acquisition because the recorded cost of the original securities issued is reduced by the same amount. The only item that changes is the total number of shares issued for the acquisition.

Illustration of Contingent Consideration

MRK Company issues 1,000 shares of its common stock to a seller for an acquisition. The market price of the stock, at the date of the sale, is $12 per share, and MRK guarantees that if, at the end of two years, the market price is less than $12 per share, it will issue additional shares to make up any difference. Under the agreed-upon conditions, MRK deposits 500 shares of stock with an independent escrow agent. At the end of the two years, the market price of the stock is $10 per share, and the escrow agent delivers 200 shares to the seller in accordance with the seller's instructions. The remainder of the shares is returned to MRK.

In accordance with FAS-141, MRK records the acquisition at $12,000 ($12 per share × 1,000). MRK records the issuance of the 200 additional shares at the current market price of $10 per share for a total of $2,000, and correspondingly reduces the original stock issued to $10 per share, for a total of $10,000. The total acquisition price remains $12,000, and only the number of shares issued changes from 1,000 to 1,200.

When debt securities are issued in an acquisition and additional debt securities are issued subsequently as contingent consideration, the reduction in value results in the recording of a discount on the debt securities. Discounts arising in this manner are amortized over the life of the securities, commencing from the date the additional securities are issued.

Contingent consideration that provides compensation for services or use of property are accounted for as expenses of the appropriate period upon resolution of the contingency.

Interest or dividends paid or accrued on contingent securities during the contingency period are accounted for in the same manner as the underlying security. Therefore, interest expense or dividend distributions on contingent securities are not recorded until the contingency is resolved. In the event a contingency is resolved that results in the payment of an amount for interest or dividends, that amount is added to the cost of the acquisition at the date of distribution.

Allocating Cost

Acquired assets are recorded at their fair market value. Any excess of the purchase price over the fair market value of identifiable assets acquired less liabilities assumed is recorded as goodwill.

Registration and issue costs of equity securities given in a business combination accounted for by the purchase method are deducted from the fair value of the securities. Any direct costs incurred are treated as consideration and are included as part of the total cost of the acquisition. Liabilities and commitments for expenses of closing a plant that is being acquired are direct costs of the acquisition and are recorded at the present values of amounts to be paid. However, the costs incurred in closing facilities already owned by the acquiring company that duplicate other facilities which are being acquired are not recognized as part of the cost of acquisition. Direct costs include only out-of-pocket costs incurred in effecting the business combination. These include finders' fees and fees paid to outside consultants for accounting and legal services, engineering evaluations, and appraisals. Internal costs incurred in a purchase business combination must be expensed as incurred.

Acquisition of Pension Plan Assets and Liabilities

When a single-employer defined benefit pension plan is acquired as part of a business combination, an excess of the projected benefit obligation over the plan assets is recognized as a liability and an excess of plan assets over the projected benefit obligation is recognized as an asset. The recognition of a new liability or new asset by the purchaser, at the date of a business combination, results in the elimination of any (a) previously existing net gain or loss, (b) prior service cost or credit, and (c) transition asset or obligation recognized in accumulated other comprehensive income (FAS-87, par. 74, as amended by FAS-158, Appendix C, par. C2r). In addition, the effects of an expected plan termination or curtailment are considered by the purchaser in calculating the amount of the projected benefit obligation at the date of a business combination (FAS-87, par. 74).

FAS-106 (Employers' Accounting for Postretirement Benefits Other Than Pensions) has a similar requirement relating to the purchase of assets and liabilities of a postretirement benefit plan other than pensions, and is discussed in the *GAAP Guide Level A* chapter titled "Postemployment and Postretirement Benefits Other Than Pensions."

Different Classes of Capital Stock

In computing a parent's investment in a subsidiary, an important consideration is to isolate those elements of the subsidiary's stockholders' equity to which the parent company is actually entitled. For instance, if the subsidiary had a minority interest, it must be excluded in computing the parent's interest. Other items that must be considered are different classes of stock, dividends in arrears, and liquidating dividends. If another class of stock is participating, it must share in the retained earnings of the subsidiary to the extent of its participation. If another class of stock is cumulative as to dividends, and dividends are in arrears, the amount of dividends in arrears must be deducted from retained earnings before determining the parent's interest in the subsidiary's stockholders' equity.

The following are guidelines for preferred stock issues:

- Nonparticipating and noncumulative preferred stocks require no apportionment of retained earnings.
- Nonparticipating and cumulative preferred stocks require an apportionment only to the extent of any dividends in arrears.
- Participating preferred stock requires an apportionment of retained earnings, under all circumstances. The apportionment is made based on the total dollar amount of the par or stated values of the securities involved.

Illustration of Different Classes of Capital Stock

On January 1, 20X8, for $5,200,000, P Company acquires 80% of the common stock and 60% of the 5% preferred stock of S Company. On the date of acquisition, the stockholders' equity in S Company consisted of:

	Shares	Dollars
Common stock ($1 par)	1,000,000	$1,000,000
5% preferred stock ($100 par) nonparticipating and cumulative	50,000	5,000,000
3% preferred stock ($10 par) fully participating and noncumulative	200,000	2,000,000
Retained earnings		2,000,000

The 5% preferred stock has a liquidating preference value of $105 per share, and dividends of $350,000 are in arrears. The parent's share of the subsidiary's stockholders' equity as of the date of acquisition is determined as follows:

Apportionment of Retained Earnings

Total retained earnings	$2,000,000
Less: Dividends in arrears—Preferred	350,000
Balance	$1,650,000
Less: Liquidating preference dividend $5	250,000
Balance	$1,400,000
Less: 20% minority interest	280,000
Balance to apportion	$1,120,000
3% preferred, 2/3	(746,667)
Balance to P Company	$ 373,333

The 3% preferred stock ($10 par) participates fully with the common stock ($1 par) in the earnings of the company. The apportionment is made based on the total par or stated value dollar amounts of the common and 3% preferred, which are $1,000,000 and $2,000,000, respectively. Therefore, the apportionment of retained earnings after all adjustments is ⅓ to common shareholders and ⅔ to the 3% participating preferred shareholders.

Computation of P's Investment

	Minority Interests 20%	5% Preferred	Participating Preferred	P Company 80%
Common stock	$200,000			$ 800,000
5% preferred		$5,000,000		
3% preferred— participating	————		$2,000,000	
Retained earnings	280,000		746,667	373,333
Dividend— arrears		350,000		
Liquidating dividend	————	250,000		
Totals	$480,000	$5,600,000	$2,746,667	$1,173,333
60% of preferred to P		(3,360,000)		3,360,000
Totals	$480,000	$2,240,000	$2,746,667	$4,533,333
Cost of 80% of common and 60% of preferred				5,200,000
Goodwill				$ 666,667

Acquisition of Stock Directly from Target Company

A stock interest may be acquired directly from the investee. That is, a target company will sell some of its own capital stock to another company. In this event, the amount paid for capital stock is added to the stockholders' equity before determining the acquirer's stock interest.

Illustration of Acquisition of Stock Directly
from Target Company

S Company had 100,000 shares of $1 par capital stock outstanding ($100,000) and $60,000 of retained earnings. On January 1, 20X6, S Company authorized an additional 200,000 shares of capital stock ($1 par) and sold them to P Company for $250,000. Determine P Company's stock interest in S Company.

Computation of S Company's Stockholders' Equity

Common stock ($1 par) (300,000 shares)	$300,000
Paid-in capital—common	50,000
Retained earnings	60,000
Total	$410,000

Computation of P's Investment in S

	Minority Interest 33⅓%	P Company 66⅔%
Common stock	$100,000	$200,000
Paid-in capital	16,667	33,333
Retained earnings	20,000	40,000
Totals	$136,667	$273,333
Cost of P's 66 2/3%		(250,000)
Excess of fair value of acquired net assets over cost		$ 23,333

Step-by-Step Acquisition

A corporation may acquire a target company in more than one transaction. In this case, any goodwill or excess of fair value of acquired net assets over cost involved is computed at the time of each step-by-step transaction. When control is achieved, it is necessary to adjust any earlier step acquisition accounted for by the cost method to the equity method. The result of this treatment is that the parent's portion of the undistributed earnings of the subsidiary for the period prior to achieving control is added to the investment account of the parent.

Illustration of Step-by-Step Acquisition

P Company acquired an interest in S Company in two steps: (1) acquiring 20% of the outstanding common stock for $200,000 and (2) the following year acquiring an additional 60% for $500,000. At the first and second dates of acquisition, the equity book value for S Company was $900,000 and $1,100,000, respectively.

Computation of Excess of Cost over Book Value

First Acquisition:

Cost of 20% acquired	$ 200,000
20% of equity book value of $900,000	(180,000)
Excess of cost over book value (goodwill)	$ 20,000

Second Acquisition:

Cost of 60% acquired	$ 500,000
60% of equity book value of $1,100,000	(660,000)
Excess of fair value of acquired net assets over cost	$(160,000)

As of the date of the second acquisition, P Company adjusts its investment account balance to the amount that would exist if the equity method had been used for the 20% holding, with the following entry:

Investments in S Company	$40,000	
Retained earnings ($200,000 increase in S Company equity × 20%)		$40,000

The above entry may be made on the consolidated worksheet only, but subsequent consolidations would require that it be repeated each year. The simplest arrangement is to record this entry on the parent company's books.

Stock Exchanges—Companies under Common Control

In an exchange of stock between two of its subsidiaries, one or both of which is partially owned, a parent company accounts for its minority interest at historical cost, if the minority shareholders are not a party to the exchange transaction. Under this circumstance, the minority interest remains outstanding and is not affected by the transaction. The acquisition of all or part of a minority interest between companies under common control, regardless of how acquired, is never considered a transfer or exchange by the companies under common control.

The term *business combination* does not apply to the transfer of net assets or the exchange of shares between companies under common control. Therefore, the acquisition of some or all of the stock held by minority shareholders of a subsidiary is not a business combination. The acquisition of some or all of the stock held by minority stockholders of a subsidiary, whether acquired by the parent, the subsidiary itself, or another affiliate, should be accounted for by the purchase method (fair value). Under this circumstance, the minority interest is affected by the transaction and the result is that a new minority interest is created in a different subsidiary.

DISCLOSURE OF CERTAIN LOSS CONTINGENCIES
IMPORTANT NOTICE FOR 2009

As the 2009 *GAAP Guide Level A* goes to press, the FASB has issued an Exposure Draft of a Proposed Statement of Financial Accounting Standards titled "Disclosure of Certain Loss Contingencies—an amendment of FASB Statements No. 5 and 141(R)." The current FASB Technical Plan calls for a final standard to be issued in the fourth quarter of 2008, and would be effective for annual and interim periods ending after December 15, 2008.

The proposed standard would expand the disclosures about loss contingencies within the scope of FAS-5 and FAS-141(R), with limited exceptions. In addition, the proposed standard would: (1) expand the types of loss contingencies that require disclosure, (2) require the disclosure of certain quantitative and qualitative information related to the contingency, and (3) require a tabular reconciliation of recognized loss contingencies. Moreover, the proposed standard provides an exemption from certain disclosure items if making the disclosure would adversely affect the company in a dispute. The proposed standard does not change the criteria for recognizing and measuring contingencies articulated in FAS-5 and FAS-141(R).

The disclosures required under the proposed standard apply to: (1) loss contingencies recognized in a business combination, (2) loss contingencies under FAS-5 where a liability is recognized in the financial statements (i.e., the loss is both probable and reasonably estimable), and (3) loss contingencies under FAS-5 that are not recognized as a liability but where the probability of loss is more than remote. However, even if the probability of loss is remote, disclosure is required if: (1) the contingency is likely to be resolved within one year from the date of the financial statements, and (2) the contingency could have a severe impact on the entity's financial position, results of operations, or cash flows. A severe impact is more than material but less than catastrophic (i.e., bankruptcy) and indicates a significant financially disruptive effect on the normal functioning of the entity. Disclosures related to loss contingencies due to asset impairments would continue to be disclosed in accordance with FAS-5.

The entity is to provide quantitative information about the entity's exposure to loss, including the amount of the claim or assessment. The entity may disclose its best estimate of the possible loss or range of loss if it believes that the claim or assessment is not representative of the entity's exposure. In addition, the proposed standard requires numerous qualitative disclosures, and disclosures related to existing insurance and indemnification agreements. Finally, the entity must provide a tabular reconciliation of the liability for loss contingencies recognized in the statement of financial position from the beginning to the end of the year.

RELATED CHAPTERS IN 2009 *GAAP GUIDE* *LEVEL A*

Chapter 7, "Consolidated Financial Statements"
Chapter 14, "Equity Method"
Chapter 23, "Intangible Assets"

RELATED CHAPTERS IN 2009 *GAAP GUIDE* *LEVELS B, C, AND D*

Chapter 6, "Business Combinations"
Chapter 10, "Consolidated Financial Statements"
Chapter 14, "Equity Method"
Chapter 21, "Intangible Assets"

RELATED CHAPTER IN 2009 *INTERNATIONAL ACCOUNTING/FINANCIAL REPORTING STANDARDS GUIDE*

Chapter 7, "Business Combinations"

APPENDIX: FAS-141(R)

BACKGROUND

In 1996, the FASB added a project on accounting for business combinations to its agenda. The board subsequently decided that the objectives of this project could be best achieved through several phases which each focus on specific issues. The first phase of this project focused on the methods of accounting for business combinations and the accounting for goodwill and other intangible assets. This first phase ended in June 2001 with the concurrent issuance of FAS-141 (Business Combinations) and FAS-142 (Goodwill and Other Intangible Assets). The second phase of the project focused on issues related to the application of the acquisition method of accounting for business combinations and was completed with the issuance of FAS-141(R) (Business Combinations) in December of 2007.

OBJECTIVES

The Board's primary objective in issuing FAS-141(R) was to improve the completeness, relevance, and comparability of financial information about business combinations provided in financial statements. FAS-141(R) achieves this objective by expanding the scope of business combinations that must apply the acquisition method to include business combinations that (1) do not involve transfer of consideration, (2) involve mutual entities, and (3) are achieved in stages (step acquisitions). A secondary objective of FAS-141(R) was to develop a single, high-quality accounting standard that could be used for both international and domestic financial reporting. Thus, this second phase of the business combinations project was conducted jointly with the International Accounting Standards Board (IASB).

FAS-141(R)

Scope

FAS-141(R) applies to any transaction or event in which an acquirer obtains control of one or more businesses. This includes combinations that are achieved without any consideration being transferred as well as to combinations involving mutual entities. FAS-141(R) does not apply to (FAS-141(R), par. 2):

- The formation of a joint venture.
- The acquisition of an asset or a group of assets that does not constitute a business.
- A combination between entities or businesses under common control.
- A combination between not-for-profit organizations or the acquisition of a for-profit business by a not-for-profit organization.

The Acquisition Method

All business combinations subject to the requirements of FAS-141(R) are to be accounted for by the acquisition method (which FAS-141 called the purchase method). Application of the acquisition method requires the following (FAS-141(R), par. 7):

- Identifying the acquirer
- Determining the acquisition date
- Recognizing and measuring the identifiable assets acquired, the liabilities assumed, and any noncontrolling interests in the acquiree
- Recognizing and measuring goodwill or a gain from a bargain purchase.

Identifying the Acquirer

FAS-141(R) defines the acquirer as the entity that obtains control of one or more businesses in the business combination. Under current GAAP, FAS-141 provides guidance to be used in identifying the acquirer. However, FAS-141(R) requires the identification of the acquirer to be initially based on the guidance in ARB-51 (Consolidated Financial Statements), as amended by FAS-160 (Noncontrolling Interests in Consolidated Financial Statements, an amendment of ARB No. 51). If the guidance in the amended ARB-51 does not clearly indicate which of the combining entities is the acquirer, then the additional guidance carried forward from FAS-141 and included in FAS-141(R) must be applied (FAS-141(R), par. 9).

FAS-141(R) also provides additional guidance for identifying the acquirer in a business combination in which a variable interest entity is acquired. The acquirer is always the primary beneficiary of the variable interest entity. Determination of which party, if any, is the primary beneficiary of the entity shall be based on the guidance in FIN-46 (Consolidation of Variable Interest Entities), not on the guidance in ARB-51 nor on the additional guidance provided in FAS-141(R) (FAS-141(R), par. 9).

Determining the Acquisition Date

The acquirer must identify the acquisition date as the date on which it obtains control of the acquiree (FAS-141(R), par. 10). This is usually the date on which the acquirer legally transfers the consideration for the combination, although in certain instances the acquirer may obtain control on an earlier or later date (FAS-141(R), par. 11).

Recognizing and Measuring the Identifiable Assets Acquired, the Liabilities Assumed, and Any Noncontrolling Interests in the Acquiree

Recognition Principle   The acquirer must recognize, as of the acquisition date, the identifiable assets acquired, the liabilities assumed, and any noncontrolling interests in the acquireee separately from goodwill (FAS-141(R), par. 12). To be recognized under the acquisition method, the assets acquired and liabilities assumed must meet the definitions of assets and liabilities in FASB Concepts Statement No. 6 (Elements of Financial Statements), at the acquisition date. For example, expected future costs for which the acquirer is not obligated at the acquisition date, such as relocation of acquiree's employees, are not liabilities at the acquisition date and, therefore, are not recognized when applying the acquisition method (FAS-141(R), par. 13).

In some cases, the appropriate accounting treatment for a particular asset or liability depends on how the asset or liability has been classified or designated by the entity. FAS-141(R) requires the acquirer, at the acquisition date, to classify or designate the identifiable assets acquired and liabilities assumed as necessary to permit the subsequent application of other relevant GAAP. Some examples of these classifications and designations include (FAS-141(R), par. 18):

- Classification of particular investments in securities as trading, available for sale, or held to maturity in accordance with FAS-115 (Accounting for Certain Investments in Debt and Equity Securities).

- Designation of a derivative instrument as a hedging instrument in accordance with FAS-133 (Accounting for Derivative Instruments and Hedging Activities).

- Assessment of whether an embedded derivative is required to be separated from the host contract in accordance with FAS-133.

Measurement Principle The acquirer is required to measure the identifiable assets acquired, the liabilities assumed, and any non-controlling interests in the acquiree at their acquisition-date fair values (FAS-141(R), par. 20). The acquirer will not recognize a separate valuation allowance for an asset that has related uncertainty regarding cash flows, because the effects of the cash flow uncertainty are included in the fair value measure (FAS-141(R), par. A57). In some cases, the acquirer may not intend to use a particular acquired asset, or may intend to use the asset in a way other than its highest and best use. Nevertheless, the acquirer must measure the asset at fair value reflecting its highest and best use in accordance with FAS-157 (Fair Value Measurements), both initially and for purposes of subsequent impairment testing (FAS-141(R), par. A59). This includes research and development assets acquired in a business combination that under current GAAP are expensed at the acquisition date, but under FAS-141(R) must be measured and recognized at their acquisition-date fair values.

Exception to the Recognition Principle An exception to the recognition principle is made for assets and liabilities arising from contingencies. The acquirer *does not apply* the guidance in FAS-5 (Accounting for Contingencies) in determining which assets and liabilities arising from contingencies to recognize as of the acquisition date. Rather, FAS-141(R) requires the acquirer to recognize as of the acquisition date all of the assets acquired and liabilities assumed that arise from *contractual contingencies*, measured at their acquisition-date fair values (FAS-141(R), par. 24a). For *non-contractual contingencies* the acquirer must assess whether it is *more likely than not* that as of the acquisition date the contingency gives rise to an asset or liability as defined in Concepts Statement No. 6, and will recognize the asset or liability at its acquisition-date fair value if that definition is met. If that definition is not met, the acquirer must account for the non-contractual contingency in accordance with other GAAP, including FAS-5, as appropriate (FAS-141(R), par. 24b).

Exceptions to both the Recognition and Measurement Principles Deferred tax assets and liabilities arising from the assets acquired and liabilities assumed in a business combination are to be recognized in accordance with FAS-109 (Accounting for Income Taxes) (FAS-141(R), par. 26). The acquirer shall also recognize a liability (or asset, if any) related to the acquiree's employee benefit plans in accordance with other relevant GAAP (FAS-141(R), par. 28).

The acquiree may in some cases contractually indemnify the acquirer for the outcome of an asset or liability arising from a contingency. As a result, the acquirer obtains an indemnification asset, which shall be recognized at the same time the acquirer recognizes the indemnified item, measured on the same basis as the indemnified item (FAS-141(R), par. 29).

Exceptions to the Measurement Principle   As part of a business combination, an acquirer may reacquire a right that it had previously granted to the acquiree. This may include, for example, the right to use the acquirer's trade name under a franchise agreement or a right to use certain of the acquirer's technology. A reacquired right is an identifiable intangible asset that is recognized by the acquirer separately from goodwill. The determination of the acquisition-date fair value of the reacquired right is based on the remaining term of the contract to which the reacquired right relates, even if market participants would consider potential contractual renewals in determining its fair value (FAS-141(R), par. 31).

An acquirer may also recognize a liability or an equity instrument related to the replacement of an acquiree's share-based payment awards with share-based payment awards of the acquirer. In this case, the acquirer must measure the liability or equity instrument in accordance with FAS-123(R) (Share-Based Payment) (FAS-141(R), par. 32).

*Recognizing and Measuring Goodwill or a Gain from
a Bargain Purchase*

Goodwill   The acquirer shall recognize goodwill as of the acquisition date, measured as the excess of (a) over (b) below (FAS-141(R), par. 34):

1. The aggregate of:
    a. The consideration transferred, which is usually the acquisition-date fair value.
    b. The fair value of any noncontrolling interests in the acquiree
    c. In a business combination achieved in stages, the acquisition-date fair value of the acquirer's previously held equity interest in the acquiree
2. The net of the acquisition-date amounts of the identifiable assets acquired and the liabilities assumed

In a business combination involving two mutual entities, the acquisition-date fair value of the acquiree's equity interests may be more readily measurable than the acquisition-date fair value of the acquirer's equity interests. If so, the acquirer shall use the acquisition-date fair value of the acquiree's equity interests in determining the amount of goodwill to be recognized. In a business combination in which no consideration is transferred, the acquirer must use a valuation technique to determine the acquisition-date fair value of the acquirer's interest in the acquiree. The value derived from this valuation technique is then used in place of the acquisition-date fair value of the consideration transferred when determining the amount of goodwill to be recognized (FAS-141(R), par. 35).

Gain from a Bargain Purchase   Occasionally, an acquirer will make a bargain purchase, which is a business combination in which the amount of net assets acquired exceeds the value of the consideration transferred plus the fair value of any noncontrolling interests in the acquiree plus the fair value of the acquirer's previously held equity interest in the acquiree. Under current GAAP, the amount of the bargain is treated as "negative goodwill" and is allocated across certain assets as a reduction of their recognition amount, which results in these assets being recognized at less than their acquisition-date fair value. However, FAS-141(R) requires the acquired assets and assumed liabilities to be recorded at their acquisition-date fair values with limited exceptions. This requirement replaces the cost allocation approach in FAS-141 and results in the acquired assets and assumed liabilities being recognized at their fair value, while the amount of the bargain is recognized by the acquirer in earnings on the acquisition date (FAS-141(R), par. 36).

However, before recognizing a gain from a bargain purchase, the acquirer is required by FAS-141(R) to reassess whether it has correctly identified all of the acquired assets and assumed liabilities, and to recognize any additional assets or liabilities that are discovered during this review. The acquirer must also review the procedures it used to measure the following amounts as of the acquisition date (FAS-141(R), par. 38):

1. The identifiable assets acquired and liabilities assumed

2. The noncontrolling interests in the acquiree, if any

3. For a business combination achieved in stages, the acquirer's previously held equity interest in the acquiree

4. The consideration transferred

Consideration Transferred   The consideration transferred in a business combination must be measured at fair value, and equals the sum of the acquisition-date fair values of the assets transferred by the acquirer, the liabilities incurred by the acquirer to former owners of the acquiree, and the equity interests issued by the acquirer. The consideration transferred may include assets and liabilities of the acquirer that have acquisition-date fair value that differ from their carrying amounts. If so, the acquirer must remeasure the transferred assets and liabilities to their fair values as of the acquisition date and recognize a gain or loss in earnings, unless the transferred assets and liabilities remain with the combined entity after the combination. In that case, the acquirer will continue to measure the transferred assets and liabilities at their carrying amounts immediately prior to the acquisition date and not recognize any gain or loss in earnings, since the acquirer controls the assets and liabilities both before and after the business combination (FAS-141(R), par. 39–40).

In some business combinations, the acquirer has an obligation to make additional payments based on the occurrence of future events (often called "contingent consideration"). Any such obligation must be recognized by the acquirer at its acquisition-date fair value as a part of the total consideration transferred (FAS-141(R), par. 41). Another type of consideration is share-based payment awards which are awarded by the acquirer to replace awards held by employees of the acquiree. If the acquirer is obligated to issue these awards as a replacement for the acquiree's awards, then at least some, if not all, of the fair value of the acquirer's replacement awards are included in the amount of consideration transferred in the business combination (FAS-141(R), par. 43). However, if the acquirer is not obligated to replace the acquiree awards but chooses to do so anyway, then all of the fair-value-based measure of the replacement awards must be recognized as compensation expense by the acquirer in the post-combination financial statements (FAS-141(R), par. 44).

Additional Guidance for Applying the Acquisition Method to Particular Types of Business Combinations

A Business Combination Achieved in Stages   An acquirer may obtain control over another business in which it already owns a minority equity interest. FAS-141(R) refers to this as a *business combination achieved in stages*, but also as a step acquisition. In these cases, the acquirer must remeasure its previously held equity interest in the acquiree to reflect its acquisition-date fair value, with any resulting gain or loss recognized in earnings. The acquirer must also reclassify any changes in the value of its equity interest in the acquiree that it had recognized in previous reporting periods in other comprehensive income and include that amount in the calculation of gain or loss as of the acquisition date (FAS-141(R), par. 48).

A Business Combination Achieved without a Transfer of Consideration   As a result of the broader scope of FAS-141(R), the acquisition method of accounting for business combinations applies to those combinations that are achieved without a transfer of consideration by the acquirer. Examples of such combinations include (FAS-141(R), par. 49):

1.   The acquiree repurchases a sufficient number of its own shares for an existing investor (the acquirer) to obtain control.

2.   Minority veto rights lapse that previously kept the acquirer from controlling an acquiree in which the acquirer held a majority voting interest.

3. The acquirer and acquiree agree to combine their businesses by contract alone

Measurement Period

In some business combinations, the end of the reporting period occurs before the acquirer can complete the initial accounting for the combination. In these cases, the acquirer must report provisional amounts in its financial statements for those items for which the accounting is incomplete. FAS-141(R) provides a measurement period that allows the acquirer to obtain additional information that is needed to complete the accounting for the combination. This includes the information necessary to identify and measure the following as of the acquisition date (FAS-141(R), par. 52):

1. The identifiable assets acquired, liabilities assumed, and any noncontrolling interests in the acquiree
2. The consideration transferred for the acquiree
3. In a business combination achieved in stages, the equity interest in the acquiree previously held by the acquirer
4. The resulting goodwill recognized for the business combination or the gain recognized on a bargain purchase

If during the measurement period the acquirer obtains new information about facts and circumstances that existed at the acquisition date that, if known, would have affected the measurement of amounts recognized as of that date, the acquirer must retrospectively adjust the provisional amounts that were recognized at the acquisition date. Further, the acquirer must recognize additional assets or liabilities if it obtains new information about facts or circumstances that existed as of the acquisition date and that, if known, would have resulted in the recognition of those assets and liabilities as of that date. The measurement period must not exceed one year and will end as soon as the acquirer receives the information it was seeking or learns that additional information is not obtainable (FAS-141(R), par. 51).

Measurement period adjustments are not included in earnings, but rather are recognized as an offset to goodwill. For example, if an acquirer recognizes an increase in the provisional amount recognized for an identifiable asset, there must be a corresponding decrease in goodwill. Adjustments made by the acquirer during the measurement period must be recognized as if the accounting for the business combination had been completed at the acquisition date. Thus, the acquirer must revise comparative information for prior periods in the financial statements as needed. After the measurement period ends, the accounting for a business combination shall only be revised by the acquirer to correct an error in accordance with FAS-154 (Accounting Changes and Error Corrections) (FAS-141(R), par. 54–56).

Determining What Is Part of the Business Combination Transaction

In some cases, the acquirer and the acquiree may have preexisting or additional business arrangements that must be separated from the business combination. When applying the acquisition method to account for a business combination, the acquirer must recognize only the consideration transferred for the acquiree and the assets acquired and liabilities assumed in the exchange for the acquiree. All separate transactions must be accounted for in accordance with the relevant GAAP.

Transactions entered into before the business combination by the acquirer or primarily for the benefit of the acquirer or the combined entity, rather than primarily for the benefit of the acquiree, are likely to be separate transactions and not part of the business combination transaction. The following are examples of separate transactions that shall not be included as part of the business combination (FAS-141(R), par. 58):

1. A transaction that in effect settles preexisting relationships between the acquirer and acquiree

2. A transaction that compensates employees or former owners of the acquiree for future services

3. A transaction that reimburses the acquiree or its former owners for paying the acquirer's acquisition-related costs

Under current GAAP, direct acquisition costs are included as part of the purchase price that is allocated to the assets acquired and liabilities assumed. In contrast, FAS-141(R) requires the acquirer to recognize acquisition-related costs as expenses in the periods in which the costs are incurred and the services are received. The costs to issue debt and equity securities are to be recognized in accordance with other relevant GAAP (FAS-141(R), par. 59).

Subsequent Measurement and Accounting

In general, the assets acquired, liabilities assumed or incurred, and equity instruments issued in a business combination shall be subsequently measured and accounted for by the acquirer in accordance with other applicable GAAP. However, FAS-141(R) provides specific guidance for the subsequent measurement and accounting for the following assets acquired, liabilities assumed or incurred, and equity instruments issued in a combination (FAS-141(R), par. 60):

- Reacquired rights
- Assets and liabilities arising from contingencies recognized as of the acquisition date
- Indemnification assets
- Contingent consideration

Reaquired Rights

A reacquired right recognized as an intangible asset as of the acquisition date must be amortized over the remaining contractual period of the contract in which the right was granted (FAS-141(R), par. 61).

Assets and Liabilities Arising from Contingencies

An asset or liability arising from a contingency recognized as of the acquisition date, that would be in the scope of FAS-5 if not acquired or assumed in a business combination, shall continue to be recognized by the acquirer at its acquisition-date fair value unless new information is obtained about the possible outcome of the contingency. When new information is obtained, the acquirer must evaluate that information and measure an asset at the *lower* of its acquisition-date fair value or the best estimate of its future settlement amount, while a liability is measured at the *higher* of its acquisition-date fair value or the amount that would be recognized under FAS-5 (FAS-141(R), par. 62). An asset or liability arising from a contingency shall only be derecognized by the acquirer when the contingency is resolved.

Indemnification Assets

The acquirer must subsequently measure an indemnification asset on the same basis as the indemnified liability or asset. If the indemnification asset is not measured at its fair value, the collectibility of the asset must be assessed. Indemnification assets shall only be derecognized by the acquirer when it collects the asset, sells it, or otherwise loses the right to it (FAS-141(R), par. 64).

Contingent Consideration

Some changes in the fair value of contingent consideration are measurement period adjustments and are accounted for in accordance with paragraphs 51–55 of FAS-141(R). However, other changes in the fair value of contingent consideration result from events that occur after the acquisition date such as meetings a specified earnings target or reaching a specified share price. These changes are not measurement period adjustments, and the acquirer must account for them as follows (FAS-141(R), par. 65):

1. Contingent consideration classified as equity shall not be remeasured and its subsequent settlement shall be accounted for within equity

2. Contingent consideration classified as an asset or a liability is remeasured to fair value at each reporting date until the contingency is resolved. The changes in fair value are recognized in earnings unless the contingency involves a hedging instrument which is required by FAS-133 to recognize the changes in other comprehensive income

Financial Statement Disclosures

General Information

The acquirer shall disclose the following information for each business combination that transpires during the current reporting period (FAS-141(R), par. 68):

*   The name and a description of the acquiree
*   The acquisition date
*   The percentage of voting stock acquired
*   The primary reasons for the acquisition
*   The acquisition-date fair value of the total consideration transferred and of each class of consideration transferred (e.g., cash, equity interests, liabilities incurred)
*   The amounts recognized as of the acquisition date for each major class of assets acquired and liabilities assumed
*   The fair value of any noncontrolling interests in the acquiree at the acquisition date, including a description of how the fair value of the noncontrolling interests was measured
*   For acquired receivables not subject to the requirements of SOP 03-3
    (*Accounting for Certain Loans or Debt Securities Acquired in a Transfer*):
    — The fair value of the receivables
    — The gross contractual amounts receivable

— The best estimate at the acquisition date of the expected uncollectible amount of the receivables

- In a bargain purchase:
  — The amount of gain recognized and the line item in the income statement in which the gain is recognized
  — A description of the reasons why the transaction resulted in a gain

- In a business combination achieved in stages:
  — The acquisition-date fair value of the equity interest in the acquiree held by the acquirer immediately before the acquisition date
  — The amount of gain or loss recognized as a result of remeasuring to fair value the equity interest in the acquiree held by the acquirer before the business combination, and the line item in the income statement in which that gain or loss is recognized

Contingencies

The acquirer shall disclose the following information regarding contingencies:

- For contingent consideration arrangements (FAS-141(R), par. 68g):
  — The amount recognized as of the acquisition date
  — A description of the arrangement and the basis for determining the amount of the payment
  — An estimate of the range of outcomes (undiscounted) or, if a range cannot be estimated, that fact and the reasons why a range cannot be estimated

- For assets and liabilities arising from contingencies (FAS-141(R), par. 68j):
  — The amounts recognized at the acquisition date or an explanation of why no amount was recognized
  — The nature of recognized and unrecognized contingencies
  — An estimate of the range of outcomes (undiscounted) for contingencies or, if a range cannot be estimated, that fact and the reasons why a range cannot be estimated

Goodwill

The acquirer shall disclose the following information regarding goodwill (FAS-141(R), par. 68):

- A qualitative description of the factors that make up for the goodwill recognized. For example:
  — Expected synergies from combining the operations of the acquiree and the acquirer
  — Intangible assets that do not qualify for separate recognition
- The amount of goodwill that is expected to be deductible for tax purposes
- The amount of goodwill by reportable segment (assuming the entity is required to disclose segment information in accordance with FAS-131, *Disclosures about Segments of an Enterprise and Related Information*)

Transactions Recognized Separately from the Business Combination

The acquirer shall disclose the following information regarding transactions that are not part of the exchange for the acquiree, but rather are accounted for separately from the business combination (FAS-141(R), pars. 68m–68n):

- A description of each transaction
- How the acquirer accounted for each transaction
- The amounts recognized for each transaction and the line item in the financial statements in which each amount is recognized
- The method used to determine the settlement amount when the transaction is the effective settlement of a preexisting relationship
- The amount of acquisition-related costs, including the amount recognized as an expense and the line item(s) in the income statement in which those expenses are recognized
- The amount of issuance costs that are not recognized as an expense and a description of how they are recognized

Special Disclosures for Public Companies

If the acquirer is a public company, it shall disclose the following information (FAS-141(R), par. 68r):

- The amounts of revenue and earnings of the acquiree since the acquisition date included in the consolidated income statement for the reporting period

- The revenue and earnings of the combined entity for the current reporting period as though the acquisition date for all business combinations that occurred during the year had been as of the beginning of the annual reporting period (*supplemental pro forma information*)
- If comparative financial statements are presented, the revenue and earnings of the combined entity for the comparable prior reporting period as though the acquisition date for all business combinations that occurred during the current year had occurred as of the beginning of the comparable prior annual reporting period (*supplemental pro forma information*)

ACQUISITION METHOD: IMPLEMENTATION GUIDANCE

Types of Business Combinations

A business combination may be accomplished in one of two ways. The acquiring company may purchase the assets (asset acquisition) of the target company. In this instance, normally the target company is liquidated and only one entity continues. Alternatively, the acquiring company may purchase more than 50% (up to 100%) of the outstanding voting common stock of the target company. In this instance, the financial statements of the two entities are consolidated in accordance with ARB-51 (Consolidated Financial Statements), as amended by FAS-160 (Noncontrolling Interests in Consolidated Financial Statements, an amendment of ARB No. 51).

Asset Acquisition

In an asset acquisition, entries are made to record the assets and assume the liabilities of the target company on the books of the acquiring company. These assets and liabilities are recorded at their acquisition-date fair values, with limited exceptions. If the purchase price exceeds the fair market value of the net assets, goodwill is recorded in the acquisition entry. If the fair market value of identifiable assets exceeds the purchase price, the resulting excess of fair value of acquired net assets over cost is recognized as a gain in earnings on the acquisition date (FAS-141(R), par. 36).

Illustration of Asset Acquisition

On July 1, 20X8, S Company sold all its net assets and business to P Company for $430,000 cash. The following is S Company's balance sheet as of July 1, 20X8:

Balance Sheet

Cash	$ 20,000
Accounts receivable	72,000
Allowance for doubtful accounts	(8,000)
Inventory	120,000
Plant and equipment (net)	260,000
Total assets	$464,000
Accounts payable	$ 60,000
Accrued expenses	5,000
Mortgage payable—plant	120,000
Common stock	200,000
Retained earnings	79,000
Total liabilities and equity	$464,000

Additional Information:

Confirmation of the accounts receivable revealed that $10,000 was uncollectible.

The physical inventory count was $138,000 (fair value).

The fair value of the plant and equipment was $340,000.

S Company has in-process research and development costs that have a fair value of $15,000.

The journal entry to record the investment on the books of P Company is:

Cash	$20,000	
Accounts receivable	62,000	
Inventory	138,000	
Plant & equipment	340,000	
In-process R&D	15,000	
Goodwill	40,000	
Accounts payable		$ 60,000
Accrued expenses		5,000
Mortgage payable		120,000
Cash		430,000

The computation of goodwill involved in the transaction is:

Computation of Goodwill

Assets (book value)	$ 464,000
Liabilities ($60,000 + $5,000 + $120,000)	(185,000)
Total net assets (book value)	$ 279,000
Adjustments to fair value:	
Additional uncollectibles	(2,000)
Increase in inventory	18,000
Increase in plant and equipment	80,000
In-process R&D	15,000
Adjusted net assets (fair value)	$ 390,000
Consideration transferred	$ 430,000
Adjusted net assets (fair value)	(390,000)
Goodwill	$ 40,000

Had the purchase price been only $365,000, the excess of fair value of acquired net assets over consideration transferred would have been computed as follows.

Adjusted net assets (fair value)	$ 390,000
Consideration transferred	(365,000)
Excess of fair value of acquired net assets over consideration transferred	$ 25,000

The $25,000 excess of fair value of acquired net assets over consideration transferred represents the "bargain" for this business combination that the acquirer must recognize in earnings as a gain on the acquisition date. The journal entry to record the investment on the books of P Company is:

Cash	$20,000	
Accounts receivable	62,000	
Inventory	138,000	
Plant & equipement	340,000	
In-process R&D	15,000	
Accounts payable		$ 60,000
Accrued expenses		5,000
Mortgage payable		120,000
Cash		365,000
Gain on bargain purchase		25,000

Stock Acquisition

In an acquisition of stock, entries are made to record the investment in the stock of the investee. An analysis of the difference between the underlying book value and the sum of the consideration transferred plus fair value of any noncontrolling interests is required to prepare consolidated financial statements for the parent and subsidiary to reflect the fair market value of the identifiable assets and goodwill as of the date of acquisition. Using data from the previous example in which the consideration transferred was $430,000, the only entry required to record the combination is:

Investment in S Company	$430,000	
Cash		$430,000

At the financial statement date, consolidated financial statements will be prepared that combine the assets and liabilities of the parent and subsidiary companies. At that time, the account "Investment in S Company" is eliminated from the statements along with the stock-holders' equity in S Company. In addition, the identifiable assets of S Company are adjusted to fair market value and the goodwill of $40,000 is recorded in the consolidated balance sheet. Operating expenses, depreciation, and amortization of the combined entities are adjusted to reflect the revised asset values.

In a stock acquisition in which the acquirer purchases less than 100% of the outstanding voting common stock of the target company, the acquirer must recognize any noncontrolling interests at its fair value as of the acquisition date. Measuring the noncontrolling interests at its fair value results in the recognition of goodwill attributable to the noncontrolling interests in addition to the goodwill attributable to the acquirer. In the case of a bargain purchase, the recognition of the noncontrolling interests at its acquisition-date fair value may not result in any goodwill being recognized, but rather may reduce the amount of the bargain reported by the acquirer in its current income statement.

Illustration of Stock Acquisition

On July 1, 20X8, P Company acquires 90% of the equity interests of S Company for $540,000 cash. The following is S Company's balance sheet as of July 1, 20X8:

Balance Sheet

Cash	$ 40,000
Accounts receivable	65,000

Allowance for doubtful accounts	(5,000)
Inventory	175,000
Plant and equipment (net)	210,000
Total assets	$485,000

Accounts payable	$ 85,000
Accrued expenses	15,000
Common stock	260,000
Retained earnings	125,000
Total liabilities and equity	$485,000

Additional Information:

Confirmation of the accounts receivable revealed that $10,000 was uncollectible.

The physical inventory count was $230,000 (fair value).

The fair value of the plant and equipment was $275,000.

The fair value of the 10% noncontrolling interests in S Company is $60,000.

The journal entry to record the investment on the books of P Company is:

Investment in S Company	$540,000	
Cash		$540,000

P Company would record its acquisition of S Company in its consolidated financial statements as follows:

Cash	$40,000	
Accounts receivable	55,000	
Inventory	230,000	
Plant & equipment	275,000	
Goodwill	100,000	
Accounts payable		$ 85,000
Accrued expenses		15,000
Cash		540,000
Equity—noncontrolling interests in S Company		60,000

The computation of goodwill involved in the transaction is:

Computation of Goodwill

Assets (book value)	$ 485,000
Liabilities ($85,000 + $15,000)	(100,000)
Total net assets (book value)	$ 385,000

Adjustments to fair value:

Additional uncollectibles	(5,000)
Increase in inventory	55,000
Increase in plant and equipment	65,000
Adjusted net assets (fair value)	$ 500,000

Consideration transferred	$ 540,000
Fair value of noncontrolling interests in S Company	60,000
Adjusted net assets (fair value)	(500,000)
Goodwill	$ 100,000

Assume the former owners of S Company had to dispose of their investments in S Company by a specified date and didn't have time to market S Company to multiple potential buyers. Therefore, the purchase price paid by P Company for its 90% ownership was only $425,000. In this case, the amount of gain on this bargain purchase that would be recognized by P Company in its income statement on the acquisition date is computed as follows.

Adjusted net assets (fair value)	$ 500,000
Consideration transferred	(425,000)
Fair value of noncontrolling interests in S Company	(60,000)
Excess of fair value of acquired net assets over consideration transferred plus noncontrolling interests	$ 15,000

The $15,000 excess of fair value of acquired net assets over consideration transferred plus noncontrolling interests represents the "bargain" for this business combination that the acquirer must recognize in earnings as a gain on the acquisition date. P Company would record its acquisition of S Company in its consolidated financial statements as follows:

Cash	$40,000	
Accounts receivable	55,000	
Inventory	230,000	
Plant & equipment	275,000	
Accounts payable		$ 85,000
Accrued expenses		15,000
Cash		425,000
Equity—noncontrolling interests in S Company		60,000
Gain on bargain purchase		15,000

EFFECTIVE DATE

FAS-141(R) must be applied prospectively to business combinations for which the acquisition date is on or after the beginning of the first annual reporting period beginning on or after December 15, 2008. Earlier adoption is prohibited.

TRANSITION

Assets and liabilities that were recognized related to business combinations that occurred prior to the application of FAS-141(R) shall not be adjusted upon application of this Statement. Also, an entity that has not yet applied FAS-142 in its entirety shall apply that Statement in its entirety at the same time that it applies FAS-141 (R). Finally, an entity, such as a mutual entity, that has had one or more business combinations that were accounted for using the purchase method, but that has not yet applied FAS-141 and FAS-147 (Acquisitions of Certain Financial Institutions), shall apply the transition guidance provided in paragraphs A130 through A134 of FAS-141(R).

CHAPTER 5
CASH FLOW STATEMENT

CONTENTS

OVERVIEW

A statement of cash flows is required as part of a complete set of financial statements prepared in conformity with GAAP for all business enterprises. Within that statement, cash receipts and payments are classified as operating, investing, and financing activities, which are presented in a manner to reconcile the change in cash from the beginning to the end of the period.

GAAP for the presentation of the cash flow statement are included in the following pronouncements:

FAS-95	Statement of Cash Flows
FAS-102	Statement of Cash Flows—Exemption of Certain Enterprises and Classification of Cash Flows from Certain Securities Acquired for Resale
FAS-104	Statement of Cash Flows—Net Reporting of Certain Cash Receipts and Cash Payments and Classification of Cash Flows from Hedging Transactions
FAS-145	Recission of FASB Statements No. 4, 44, and 64, Amendment of FASB Statement No. 13, and Technical Corrections

BACKGROUND

Information in a statement of cash flows, when used in conjunction with information available in other financial statements and related disclosures, is expected to be helpful to investors, creditors, and other users to:

- Assess the enterprise's ability to generate positive future net cash flows

- Assess the enterprise's ability to meet its obligations, pay dividends, and satisfy its needs for external financing

- Assess the reasons for differences between net income and associated cash receipts and payments

- Assess the effects on an enterprise's financial position of both its cash and noncash investing and financing transactions

FAS-95 (Statement of Cash Flows) requires that a *statement of cash flows* be included as part of a full set of general financial statements that are externally issued by any business enterprise. All business enterprises are required to comply with the provision of FAS-95. FAS-95 subsequently was amended by FAS-102 (Statement of Cash Flows—Exemption of Certain Enterprises and Classification of Cash Flows from Certain Securities Acquired for Sale) and FAS-104 (Statement of Cash Flows—Net Reporting of Certain Cash Receipts and Cash Payments and Classification of Cash Flows from Hedging Transactions).

FAS-102 was issued to provide exemptions from the provisions of FAS-95 to (*a*) certain employee benefit plans that report their financial information in accordance with FAS-35 (Accounting and Reporting by

Defined Benefit Pension Plans) and (*b*) highly liquid investment companies that meet certain conditions (FAS-102, pars. 5–6).

FAS-102 also provides that cash receipts and cash payments resulting from transactions in certain securities, other assets, and loans acquired specifically for resale must be classified as *operating cash flows* in a statement of cash flows (FAS-102, par. 8).

FAS-104 amends FAS-95 to permit banks, savings institutions, and credit unions to report net cash flows from certain transactions instead of gross cash flows required by the provisions of FAS-95 (FAS-104, par. 7a). FAS-104 also amends FAS-95 by allowing an enterprise that meets certain conditions to classify the cash flow of a hedging transaction and the cash flow of its related hedged item in the same category of cash flow (operating activity, investing activity, or financing activity) (FAS-104, par. 7b).

STATEMENT OF CASH FLOWS—GENERAL

A statement of cash flows specifies the amount of net cash provided or used by an enterprise during a period from (*a*) operating activities, (*b*) investing activities, and (*c*) financing activities. The statement of cash flows indicates the net effect of these cash flows on the enterprise's cash and cash equivalents. A reconciliation of beginning and ending cash and cash equivalents is included in the statement of cash flows. FAS-95 also requires that the statement of cash flows contain separate related disclosures about all investing and financing activities of an enterprise that affect its financial position, but do not directly affect its cash flows during the period (FAS-95, par. 6). Descriptive terms such as *cash* or *cash and cash equivalents* are required in the statement of cash flows, whereas ambiguous terms such as *funds* are inappropriate (FAS-95, par. 7).

Cash Equivalents

Under FAS-95, cash equivalents are short-term, highly liquid investments that are (*a*) readily convertible to known amounts of cash and (*b*) so near their maturities that they present insignificant risk of changes in value because of changes in interest rates. As a general rule, only investments with original maturities of three months or less qualify as cash equivalents (FAS-95, par. 8). Examples of items commonly considered to be cash equivalents include Treasury bills, commercial paper, money market funds, and federal funds that are sold (FAS-95, par. 9).

☞ **PRACTICE POINTER:** An enterprise must disclose its policy for determining which items are treated as cash equivalents. Any change in that policy is accounted for as a change in accounting principle and is effected by restating financial statements of earlier years that are presented for comparative purposes (FAS-95, par. 10). FAS-95 does not specify the accounting treatment of amounts in bank accounts that are unavailable for immediate withdrawal, such as compensating balances in the bank account of a borrower. Logically, these amounts should be treated as cash, with disclosure of any material restrictions on withdrawal.

Gross and Net Cash Flows

As a general rule, FAS-95 requires an enterprise to report the gross amounts of its cash receipts and cash payments in the statement of cash flows. For example, outlays for acquisitions of property, plant, and equipment should be reported separately from proceeds from the sale of these assets. Similarly, proceeds from borrowing are reported separately from repayments. The gross amounts of cash receipts and cash payments usually are presumed to be more relevant than net amounts. It may be sufficient in some circumstances, however, to report the net amounts of certain assets and liabilities instead of their gross amounts (FAS-95, par. 11).

The net changes during a period may be reported for those assets and liabilities in which turnover is quick, amounts are large, and maturities are short (FAS-95, par. 12). These include cash receipts and cash payments pertaining to (*a*) investments (other than cash equivalents), (*b*) loans receivable, and (*c*) debt, provided the original maturity of the asset or liability is three months or less (FAS-95, par. 13).

FAS-104 permits banks, savings institutions, and credit unions to report net amounts for (*a*) deposits placed with other financial institutions and withdrawals of deposits, (*b*) time deposits accepted and repayments of deposits, and (*c*) loans made to customers and principal collections of loans (FAS-104, par. 7a).

Classification of Cash Receipts and Cash Payments

Under FAS-95, an enterprise is required to classify its cash receipts and cash payments into operating activities, investing activities, or financing activities (FAS-95, par. 14).

Operating Activities   Include all transactions and other events that are not defined as investing or financing activities. Operating activities generally involve producing and delivering goods and providing services (i.e., transactions that enter into the determination of net income) (FAS-95, par. 21).

Cash inflows:

- Cash receipts from sales of goods or services, including receipts from collection or sale of accounts receivable and short-term and long-term notes arising from such sales

- Cash receipts from returns on loans, other debt instruments of other entities, and equity securities
- All other cash receipts not classified as investing or financing activities

Cash outflows:

- Cash payments for materials for manufacture or goods for resale, including principal payments on accounts payable and short-term and long-term notes to suppliers
- Cash payments to other suppliers and employers for other goods and services
- Cash payments to governments for taxes, duties, fines, and other fees or penalties
- Cash payments to lenders and others for interest
- All other cash payments not classified as investing or financing activities

Investing Activities   Include making and collecting loans and acquiring and disposing of debt or equity instruments and property, plant, and equipment and other productive assets; that is, assets held for or used in the production of goods or services by the enterprise (other than materials that are part of the enterprise's inventory) (FAS-95, par. 15). Acquiring and disposing of certain loans or other debt or equity instruments that are acquired specifically for resale are excluded from investing activities (FAS-102, par. 10).

Cash inflows:

- Receipts from collections or sales of loans and of others' debt instruments
- Receipts from sales of equity instruments of other enterprises and from returns of investments in those instruments
- Receipts from sales of property, plant, and equipment and other productive assets

Cash outflows:

- Payments for loans made by the enterprise and to acquire debt instruments of other entities
- Payments to acquire equity instruments in other enterprises
- Payments at the time of purchase or soon thereafter to acquire property, plant, and equipment and other productive assets

Financing Activities Include obtaining resources from owners and providing them with a return on, and return of, their investment; borrowing money and repaying amounts borrowed, or otherwise settling the obligation; and obtaining and paying for other resources obtained from creditors on long-term credit (FAS-95, par. 18).

Cash inflows:

- Proceeds from issuing equity instruments
- Proceeds from issuing bonds, mortgages, notes, and other short-term or long-term borrowing

Cash outflows:

- Payments of dividends or other distributions to owners, including outlays to reacquire the enterprise's equity instruments
- Repayments of amounts borrowed
- Other principal payments to creditors that have extended long-term credit

☛ **PRACTICE POINTER:** Classify cash received from sales of inventory to customers as cash from operating activities, whether received at the time of sale or collected at some other time, on open account or on a note (short-term, long-term, or installment). Similarly, classify cash paid to suppliers for inventory as cash used for operating activities, whether paid at the time of purchase or paid at some other time, on open account or on a note (short-term, long-term, or installment).

☛ **PRACTICE POINTER:** FAS-123(R) (Share-Based Payment), amends FAS-95 to require that excess tax benefits be reported as a financing cash inflow rather than as a reduction in taxes paid.

A cash receipt or a cash payment that can qualify for more than one cash flow activity is appropriately classified as the activity that is likely to be the predominant source of cash flows for that item. For example, the acquisition and sale of equipment used by an enterprise or rented to others generally are investing activities. If the intention of an enterprise is to use or rent the equipment for a short period of time and then sell it, however, the cash receipts and cash payments associated with the acquisition or production of the equipment and the subsequent sale are considered cash flows from operating activities (FAS-95, par. 24).

☛ **PRACTICE POINTER:** Take care in classifying certain cash flows. The FASB has indicated how to classify certain items that might fit logically in more than one of the major categories of the statement of cash flows. Following are examples of these items:

Interest paid Presented as an operating activity, despite the fact that dividends paid are presented as a financing activity.

Interest and dividends received Presented as an operating activity, despite their close association with other activities presented as investing activities.

Gains and losses on asset and liability transactions (e.g., sale of plant assets, extinguishment of debt) Presented as investing and financing activities, although the gain/loss was included in net income.

Income taxes Presented entirely as an operating activity, despite the fact that gains and losses that may affect income taxes are presented as investing and financing activities.

As a general rule, each cash receipt or cash payment is required to be classified according to its source (operating, investing, or financing) without regard to whether it arose as a hedge of another item. However, FAS-104, as amended by FAS-133 (Accounting for Derivative Instruments and Hedging Activities), indicates that the cash flows from derivative instruments that are accounted for as fair-value or cash-flow hedges under FAS-133 may be classified in the same category as the cash flow of the related hedged item, provided that the enterprise (a) discloses this accounting policy and (b) reports the gain or loss on the hedging instrument in the same accounting period as the offsetting gain or loss on the hedged item (FAS-104, par. 7).

FAS-102 provides that cash receipts and cash payments must be classified as operating cash flows in a statement of cash flows when such cash receipts and cash payments result from the acquisition or sale of (a) securities and other assets that are acquired specifically for resale and carried at market value in a trading account and (b) loans that are acquired specifically for resale and carried at market value or the lower of cost or market value (FAS-102, par. 8). The cash receipts and cash payments from the sale of loans originally acquired as investments, however, are classified as investing cash flows in a statement of cash flows, regardless of any subsequent change in the purpose of holding those loans (FAS-102, par. 9).

Foreign Currency Cash Flows

An enterprise with foreign currency translations or foreign operations shall report, in its statement of cash flows, the reporting currency equivalent of foreign currency cash flows using the exchange rates in effect at the time of the cash flows. An appropriately weighted average exchange rate for the period may be used in lieu of the actual currency rates at the dates of the cash flows, provided that the results are substantially the same. The effect of exchange rate changes on cash balances held in foreign currencies is reported in the statement of cash flows as a separate part of the reconciliation of the change in cash and cash equivalents during the period (FAS-95, par. 25).

Exemption for Certain Employee Benefit Plans

FAS-102 provides an exemption from the provisions of FAS-95 for
(a) defined benefit pension plans that present their financial information in accordance with FAS-35 (Accounting and Reporting by
Defined Benefit Pension Plans) and (b) other employee benefit plans
that present their financial information similar to that required by
FAS-35, including those employee benefit plans that present their
plan investments at fair value. Thus, these employee benefit pension
plans are not required to include a statement of cash flows in their
financial presentations. However, FAS-102 encourages all employee
benefit pension plans to include a statement of cash flows as part of
their financial presentation in those circumstances in which such a
statement would provide relevant information concerning a plan's
ability to meet its future obligations (FAS-102, par. 5).

Exemption for Certain Investment Companies

FAS-102 was issued to provide for certain exemptions from the provisions of FAS-95. One of these exemptions provides that certain
investment-type entities that meet all of the conditions specified
in FAS-102 are not required to include a statement of cash flows as
part of their complete financial presentation in accordance
with GAAP. The entities entitled to this exemption are as follows
(FAS-102, par. 6):

- Investment companies that are subject to the registration and
  regulatory requirements of the Investment Company Act of
  1940 (1940 Act)
- Investment enterprises that have essentially the same characteristics as investment companies subject to the 1940 Act
- Common trust funds, variable annuity accounts, or similar
  funds maintained by a bank, insurance company, or other enterprise in its capacity as a trustee, administrator, or guardian
  for the collective investment and reinvestment of moneys

Under FAS-102, the investment-type entities specified above are
not required to include a statement of cash flows in their financial
presentations, provided that they meet all of the following conditions (FAS-102, par. 7):

- Substantially all investments owned by the enterprise were
  highly liquid during the period covered by the financial statements (highly liquid investments include, but are not limited
  to, marketable securities and other assets that can be sold
  through existing markets).
- Substantially all of the investments owned by the enterprise
  are carried at market value including securities for which

market value is calculated by the use of matrix pricing techniques (described in the AICPA Industry Audit and Accounting Guide titled *Audits of Investment Companies*). Securities that do not meet this condition are those for which (*a*) market value is not readily ascertainable and (*b*) fair value must be determined in good faith by the board of directors of the enterprise.

- Based on average debt outstanding during the period, the enterprise had little or no debt in relation to average total assets. For purposes of FAS-102, average debt outstanding generally may exclude obligations from (*a*) redemption of shares by the enterprise, (*b*) unsettled purchases of securities or similar assets, or (*c*) written covered options.

- The enterprise provides a statement of changes in net assets.

CONTENT AND FORM OF STATEMENT OF CASH FLOWS

A statement of cash flows shall disclose separately the amount of net cash provided or used during a period from an enterprise's (*a*) operating activities, (*b*) investing activities, and (*c*) financing activities. The effect of the total amount of net cash provided or used during a period from all sources (operating, investing, and financing) on an enterprise's cash and cash equivalents shall be clearly disclosed in a manner that reconciles beginning and ending cash and cash equivalents (FAS-95, par. 26).

In reporting cash flows from *operating activities* in the statement of cash flows, FAS-95 encourages but does not require an enterprise to use the *direct method* (FAS-95, par. 27). Enterprises that do not use the direct method to report their cash flows from operating activities may use the *indirect method* (also referred to as the reconciliation method). The amount of cash flows from operating activities is the same whether calculated and presented by the direct or indirect method. There is no difference in reporting the cash flows from investing and financing activities, regardless of whether the direct or indirect method is used to report cash flows from operations.

Direct Method

A presentation of a statement of cash flows by the direct method reflects the gross amounts of the principal components of cash receipts and cash payments from operating activities, such as cash received from customers and cash paid to suppliers and employees. Using the direct method, the amount of net cash provided by or used in operating activities during the period is equal to the difference between the total amount of gross cash receipts and the total amount of gross cash payments arising from operating activities.

FAS-95 requires enterprises using the direct method of reporting the amount of net cash flow provided from or used by operating activities to present separately, at a minimum, in their statement of cash flows, the following principal components of operating cash receipts and operating cash payments (FAS-95, par. 27):

- Cash collected from customers, including lessees, licensees, and other similar receipts
- Interest and dividends received
- Any other operating cash receipts
- Cash paid to employees and other suppliers of goods or services including suppliers of insurance, advertising, and other similar cash payments
- Any other operating cash payments, including interest paid, income taxes paid, and other similar cash payments

☛ **PRACTICE POINTER:** An enterprise may use an alternate method of computation to arrive at the amounts shown in a statement of cash flows. For example, when preparing a direct method statement of cash flows, an enterprise may make an alternate computation to determine the amount of cash received from customers; i.e., it may start with total sales for the period and adjust that figure for the difference between beginning and ending accounts receivable.

The provisions of FAS-95 encourage, but do not require, an enterprise to include in its statement of cash flows other meaningful details pertaining to its cash receipts and cash payments from operating activities. For example, a retailer or manufacturer might decide to subdivide cash paid to employees and suppliers into cash payments for costs of inventory and cash payments for selling, general, and administrative expenses (FAS-95, par. 27).

OBSERVATION: The use of the direct method is encouraged by FAS-95 because it reflects the gross amounts of the principal components of cash receipts and cash payments from operating activities, while the indirect method does not. This presentation is more compatible with the manner of presenting cash flows from financing and investing activities than is the indirect method. Despite the FASB's preference for the direct method, the predominant method used in practice is the indirect method.

Indirect Method

Enterprises that choose not to provide information about major classes of operating cash receipts and cash payments by the direct method, as encouraged by FAS-95, can indirectly determine and report the same amount of net cash flow from operating activities by reconciling net income to net cash flow from operating activities (the indirect or reconciliation method). The adjustments necessary to reconcile net income to net cash flow are made to net income to remove (*a*) the effects of all deferrals of past operating cash receipts and cash payments, such as changes during the period in inventory, deferred income and the like, (*b*) the effects of all accruals of expected future operating cash receipts and cash payments, such as changes during the period in receivables and payables, and (*c*) the effects of all items classified as investing or financing cash flows, such as gains or losses on sales of property, plant, and equipment and discontinued operations (investing activities), and gains or losses on extinguishment of debt (financing activities) (FAS-95, par. 28).

Reconciliation of Net Income to Net Cash Flow

Regardless of whether an enterprise uses the direct or indirect method of reporting net cash flow from *operating* activities, FAS-95 requires that a reconciliation of net income to net cash flow be provided in conjunction with the statement of cash flows. The reconciliation of net income to net cash flow from operating activities provides information about the net effects of operating transactions and other events that affect net income and operating cash flows in different periods. This reconciliation separately reflects all major classes of reconciling items. For example, major classes of deferrals of past operating cash receipts and payments and accruals of expected future operating cash receipts and payments, including at a minimum changes during the period in receivables and payables pertaining to *operating* activities, are reported separately. Enterprises are encouraged to further break down those categories they consider meaningful. For example, changes in trade receivables for an enterprise's sale of goods or services might be reported separately from changes in other operating receivables (FAS-95, par. 29).

If an enterprise uses the direct method, the reconciliation of net income to net cash flow from operating activities is provided in a separate schedule accompanying the statement of cash flows (FAS-95, par. 30).

If an enterprise uses the indirect method, the reconciliation may be *either* included within and as part of the statement of cash flows *or* provided in a separate schedule, with the statement of cash flows reporting only the net cash flow from operating activities. If the reconciliation is included within and as part of the statement of cash flows, all adjustments to net income to determine net cash flow from operating activities shall be clearly identified as reconciling items (FAS-95, par. 30).

Regardless of whether the direct or the indirect method is used to report net cash flow from operating activities, FAS-95 requires the separate disclosure of the amounts of interest paid (net of amounts capitalized) and income taxes paid during the period (FAS-95, par. 29). These disclosures usually are in the operating activities section of the statement if the direct method is used and in a note if the indirect method is used.

Noncash Investing and Financing Activities

Disclosures in conjunction with the statement of cash flows must contain information about all investing and financing activities of an enterprise during a period that affect recognized assets or liabilities but that do not result in cash receipts or cash payments. These disclosures may be either narrative or summarized in a schedule, and they shall clearly relate the cash and noncash aspects of transactions involving similar items. Examples of noncash investing and financing transactions include:

- Converting debt to equity
- Acquiring assets by assuming directly related liabilities (e.g., capital leases, purchasing a building by incurring a mortgage to the seller)
- Exchanging noncash assets or liabilities for other noncash assets or liabilities

Only the cash portion of a part-cash, part-noncash transaction is reported in the body of the statement of cash flows (FAS-95, par. 32).

Cash Flow per Share

An enterprise is prohibited from reporting any amount representing cash flow per share in its financial statements (FAS-95, par. 33).

FINANCIAL INSTITUTIONS

FAS-102 primarily affects the statements of cash flows of financial institutions. Cash receipts and payments associated with securities that are carried in *trading accounts* by banks, brokers, and dealers in securities are classified as cash flows from operating activities. In addition, cash inflows and outflows associated with securities classified as trading securities (see FAS-115 [Accounting for Certain Investments in Debt or Equity Securities]) must be shown as operating cash flows (FAS-145, par. 9g). On the other hand, if securities are acquired for investment purposes, the related cash receipts and cash payments are classified as cash flows from investing activities. Loans are given similar treatment. The cash receipts and cash payments associated with mortgage loans that are held for resale by a bank or mortgage broker are classified as cash flows from operating activities. If the mortgage loans are held for investment purposes, however, the related cash receipts and cash payments are classified as cash flows from investing activities (FAS-102, pars. 8–9).

Instead of reporting gross amounts of cash flows in their statements of cash flows, as would be required by FAS-95, banks, savings institutions, and credit unions are permitted by FAS-104 to report *net* amounts of cash flows that result from (*a*) deposits and deposit withdrawals with other financial institutions, (*b*) time deposits accepted and repayments of deposits, and (*c*) loans to customers and principal collections of loans (FAS-104, par. 7). Thus, an enterprise has the following choices in reporting cash flows in its statement of cash flows:

- To report the gross amount of all cash receipts and disbursements
- To report the net cash flows in the limited situations allowed by FAS-95, such as loans with maturities of three months or less, and to report gross amounts for all other transactions
- If the enterprise is a bank, savings institution, or credit union, to report net cash flows in the limited situations allowed by FAS-104, such as time deposits, and to report gross amounts for all other transactions
- If the enterprise is a bank, savings institution, or credit union, to report net cash flows in the situations allowed by FAS-95 and also those allowed by FAS-104, and to report gross amounts for all other transactions

If a consolidated enterprise includes a bank, savings institution, or credit union that uses net cash reporting as allowed by FAS-104, the statement of cash flows of the consolidated enterprise must report separately (*a*) the net cash flows of the financial institution and (*b*) the gross cash receipts and cash payments of other members of the consolidated enterprise, including subsidiaries of a financial institution that are not themselves financial institutions (FAS-104, par. 7).

> **OBSERVATION:** The above provision requires separate reporting of net cash flows and gross cash flows in a consolidated statement, if the net cash flows are allowed by FAS-104. It would seem desirable, along similar lines, to require separate reporting of net cash flows and gross cash flows, if the net cash flows are allowed by the exceptions contained in FAS-95, such as loans with maturities of three months or less. However, neither FAS-95 nor FAS-104 expressly requires separate reporting in these situations.

Illustration of Procedures for Preparing a Statement of Cash Flows

Following are Holcomb Company's balance sheets for the year ending December 31, 20X8 and the quarter ending March 31, 20X9, as well as the income statement for the three months ending March 31, 20X9.

Balance Sheet

	December 31, 20X8	March 31, 20X9
Cash	$ 25,300	$ 87,400
Marketable securities	16,500	7,300
Accounts receivable, net	24,320	49,320
Inventory	31,090	48,590
Total current assets	97,210	192,610
Land	40,000	18,700
Building	250,000	250,000
Equipment	—	81,500
Accumulated depreciation	(15,000)	(16,250)
Investment in 30% owned company	61,220	67,100
Other assets	15,100	15,100
Total	$448,530	$608,760
Accounts payable	$ 21,220	$ 17,330
Dividend payable	—	8,000
Income taxes payable	—	34,616
Total current liabilities	21,220	59,946
Other liabilities	186,000	186,000
Bonds payable	50,000	115,000
Discount on bonds payable	(2,300)	(2,150)
Deferred income taxes	510	846
Preferred stock ($2 par)	30,000	—
Common stock ($1 par)	80,000	110,000
Dividends declared	—	(8,000)
Retained earnings	83,100	147,118
Total	$448,530	$608,760

Income Statement

	For the Three Months Ended March 31, 20X9
Sales	$242,807
Gain on sale of marketable investments	2,400
Equity in earnings of 30% owned company	5,880
Gain on condemnation of land	10,700
Total revenues and gains	261,787
Cost of sales	138,407
General and administrative expenses	22,010
Depreciation	1,250
Interest expense	1,150
Income taxes	34,952
	197,769
Net income	$ 64,018

The following information has been identified:

(1) In January 20X9, the company sold marketable securities for cash of $11,600. These securities had been held for several months.

(2) The preferred stock is convertible into common stock at a rate of one share of preferred for three shares of common.

(3) In February 20X9, land was condemned. An award of $32,000 in cash was received in March.

(4) During February 20X9, the company purchased equipment for cash.

(5) During March 20X9, bonds were issued by the company at par for cash.

(6) The investment in the 30% owned company included $3,220 attributable to goodwill at December 31, 20X8.

Worksheet for Preparing the Statement of Cash Flows for the Quarter Ended March 31, 20X9

Real Accounts	Balances 12/31/X8	Changes Debit	Changes Credit	Balances 3/31/X9
Debits:				
Cash	$ 25,300	(n) $62,100		$87,400
Marketable Securities	16,500		(f) 9,200	7,300
Accounts Receivable, Net	24,320	(a) 25,000		49,320
Inventory	31,090	(b) 17,500		48,590
Land	40,000		(g) 21,300	18,700
Building	250,000			250,000

Real Accounts	Balances 12/31/X8		Changes Debit		Changes Credit	Balances 3/31/X9
Equipment	0	(h)	81,500			81,500
Investment in 30% Owned Company	61,220	(j)	5,880			67,100
Other Assets	15,100					15,100
Discount on Bonds Payable	2,300			(e)	150	2,150
Dividends Declared	0	(m)	8,000			8,000
	465,830					635,160
Credits:						
Accumulated Depreciation	15,000			(d)	1,250	16,250
Accounts Payable	21,220	(b)	3,890			17,330
Dividend Payable	0			(m)	8,000	8,000
Income Taxes Payable	0			(i)	34,616	34,616
Other Liabilities	186,000					186,000
Bonds Payable	50,000			(k)	65,000	115,000
Deferred Income Taxes	510			(i)	336	846
Preferred Stock	30,000	(l)	30,000			0
Common Stock	80,000			(l)	30,000	110,000
Retained Earnings	83,100				64,018 ←	147,118
	465,830		233,870		233,870	635,160

Nominal Accounts						
Sales				(a)	242,807	
Gain on Sale of Marketable Securities				(f)	2,400	
Equity in Earnings of 30% Owned Company				(j)	5,880	
Gain on Condemnation of Land				(g)	10,700	
Cost of Sales		(b)	138,407			
General and Administrative Expenses		(c)	22,010			
Depreciation		(d)	1,250			
Interest Expense		(e)	1,150			
Income Taxes		(i)	34,952			
			197,769		261,787	
			64,018 ─			
			261,787		261,787	

	Balances 12/31/X8	Changes Debit	Changes Credit	Balances 3/31/X9
Cash Flow Categories				
Operating Activities:				
Cash Collected from Customers	(a) 217,807			
Cash Paid for Goods to Be Sold			(b) 159,797	
Cash Flow Categories				
Cash Paid for General and Administrative Expenses	(c) 22,010			
Cash Paid for Interest			(e) 1,000	
Investing Activities				
Cash Received from Sale of Marketable Securities	(f) 11,600			
Cash Received from Land Condemnation	(g) 32,000			
Cash Paid for Purchase of Equipment			(h) 81,500	
Financing Activities				
Cash Received from Sale of Bonds Payable	(k) 65,000			
	326,407	264,307		
Increase in Cash			(n) 62,100	
	326,407	326,407		

Explanation of Worksheet Entries

(a)	Sales	$242,807
	Less increase in receivables	(25,000)
	Cash collected from customers	$217,807
(b)	Cost of sales	$138,407
	Plus increase in inventory	17,500
	Plus decrease in accounts payable	3,890
	Cash paid for goods to be sold	$159,797
(c)	G&A expenses	$ 22,010
	No adjustments	—
	Cash paid for G&A expenses	$ 22,010

(d) $1,250 reconciliation of depreciation expense and change in accumulated depreciation. No statement of cash flow effects.

(e) Interest expense $ 1,150

Less decrease in discount on bonds payable   (150)

Cash paid for interest $ 1,000

(f) Decrease in marketable securities $ 9,200

Plus gain on sale of marketable securities   2,400

Cash received from sale of marketable securities $ 11,600

(g) Decrease in land $ 21,300

Plus gain on condemnation of land   10,700

Cash received from land condemnation $ 32,000

(h) Increase in equipment account ($81,500) also cash paid for equipment.

(i) Reconciliation of income tax expense ($34,952) to income tax payable ($34,616) and increase in deferred income tax ($336). No statement of cash flow effect.

(j) Reconciliation of $5,880 equity in earnings of 30% owned company (income statement) to change in inventory in 30% owned company. No statement of cash flow effects.

(k) Increase in bonds payable account $ 65,000

No adjustment   —

Cash received from sale of bonds payable $ 65,000

(l) Noncash transaction to record retirement of preferred stock and issuance of common stock at $30,000. No statement of cash flow effects, but disclosure is required.

(m) Reconciliation of $8,000 dividends declared to increase in dividends payable. No statement of cash flow effects but disclosure is required.

(n) Reconciliation of $62,100 increase in cash to net of all sources (increases) and uses (decreases) in cash.

Holcomb Company
Statement of Cash Flows (Direct Method)
for the Three Months Ended March 31, 20X9

Cash Flows from Operating Activities

Cash Received from Customers		$217,807
Cash Paid for Goods to be Sold	$ 159,797	
Cash Paid for General and Administrative Expenses	22,010	
Cash Paid for Interest	1,000	
Cash Disbursed for Operating Activities		182,807
Net Cash Provided by Operating Activities		$ 35,000

Cash Flows from Investing Activities

Proceeds from Sale of Marketable Securities	$ 11,600	
Proceeds from Condemnation of Land	32,000	
Purchases of Equipment	(81,500)	
Net Cash Used in Investing Activities		(37,900)

Cash Flows from Financing Activities

Proceeds of Long-Term Debt	65,000
Net Increase in Cash	$ 62,100
Cash, January 1, 20X9	25,300
Cash, March 31, 20X9	$ 87,400

Reconciliation of Net Income to
Net Cash Provided by
Operating Activities:

Net Income	$64,018

Adjustments to Reconcile Net Income to Net Cash Provided by Operating Activities:

Depreciation Expense	1,250
Bond Discount Amortization	150
Increase in Deferred Income Tax	336
Gain on Sale of Marketable Securities	(2,400)
Equity in Earnings of Investee	(5,880)
Gain on Sale of Land	(10,700)
Accounts Receivable Increase	(25,000)
Inventory Increase	(17,500)
Accounts Payable Decrease	(3,890)
Income Taxes Payable Increase	34,616
Net Cash Provided by Operating Activities	$ 35,000

Schedule of Noncash Financing Activities

Retirement of Preferred Stock by Conversion to Common Stock	$ 30,000
Declaration of Cash Dividends to be Paid	$ 8,000

Holcomb Company
Statement of Cash Flows (Indirect Method)
for the Three Months Ended March 31, 20X9

Cash Flows from Operating Activities

Net Income	$64,018
Adjustments to Reconcile Net Income to Net Cash Provided by Operating Activities:	
Depreciation Expense	1,250
Bond Discount Amortization	150
Increase in Deferred Income Tax	336
Gain on Sale of Marketable Securities	(2,400)
Equity in Earnings of Investee	(5,880)
Gain on Sale of Land	(10,700)
Accounts Receivable Increase	(25,000)
Inventory Increase	(17,500)
Accounts Payable Decrease	(3,890)
Income Taxes Payable Increase	34,616
Net Cash Provided by Operating Activities	$ 35,000

Cash Flows from Investing Activities

Proceeds from Sale of Marketable Securities	$ 11,600	
Proceeds from Condemnation of Land	32,000	
Purchases of Equipment	(81,500)	
Net Cash Used in Investing Activities		(37,900)

Cash Flows from Financing Activities

Proceeds of Long-Term Debt	65,000
Net Increase in Cash	$ 62,100
Cash, January 1, 20X9	25,300
Cash, March 31, 20X9	$ 87,400

Schedule of Noncash Financing Activities

Retirement of Preferred Stock by Conversion to Common Stock	$ 30,000
Declaration of Cash Dividends to be Paid	$ 8,000

RELATED CHAPTER IN 2009 *GAAP GUIDE* *LEVEL A*

Chapter 40, "Results of Operations"

RELATED CHAPTERS IN 2009 *GAAP GUIDE* *LEVELS B, C, AND D*

Chapter 8, "Cash Flow Statement"
Chapter 35, "Results of Operations"

RELATED CHAPTERS IN 2009 *INTERNATIONAL ACCOUNTING/FINANCIAL REPORTING STANDARDS GUIDE*

Chapter 3, "Presentation of Financial Statements"
Chapter 8, "Cash Flow Statements"

CHAPTER 6
COMPUTER SOFTWARE

CONTENTS

OVERVIEW

Accounting for computer software is a relatively recent development
that has resulted in significant accounting issues, particularly when
that software is developed internally. Similar to research and development costs and start-up costs of a new entity, computer software
costs are elusive and often difficult to identify and measure. A major
issue for internally developed software is the distinction between

costs that should be expensed immediately and those that should be capitalized and amortized over some period in the future.

The limited accounting standards available in the area of computer software are in the following sources:

FAS-86   Accounting for the Costs of Computer Software to Be Sold, Leased, or Otherwise Marketed

FIN-6   Applicability of FASB Statement No. 2 to Computer Software

> **OBSERVATION:** This *Guide* includes coverage of accounting literature in Level A of the FAS-162 GAAP hierarchy. Important authoritative literature is included in lower levels of the hierarchy. This is particularly true in the case of accounting for computer software. The reader is encouraged to reference Chapter 10 of the *GAAP Guide Levels B, C, and D,* and in particular SOP 97-2, 98-1, and 98-9, which are covered in that chapter.

2009 TRANSITION GUIDANCE FOR FAS-141(R) AND FAS-160

The FASB has recently issued FAS-141(R), *Business Combinations,* which is effective for business combinations for which the acquisition date is on or after the beginning of the first annual reporting period beginning on or after December 15, 2008. The FASB has also issued FAS-160, *Noncontrolling Interests in Consolidated Financial Statements, an Amendment of ARB No. 51,* which is effective for fiscal years, and interim periods within those fiscal years, beginning on or after December 15, 2008. Because these standards are not effective for some companies until December 2009, and because early adoption is prohibited, the 2009 *GAAP Guide* reflects the requirements of FAS-141 prior to its revision in December 2007 and does not reflect the requirements of FAS-160. There is a discussion of the changes in the accounting for business combinations under FAS-141(R) in the Appendix to Chapter 4, "Business Combinations." Similarly, the Appendix to Chapter 7, "Consolidated Financial Statements," includes a discussion of the requirements of FAS-160. However, any effects of FAS-141(R) and/or FAS-160 in this chapter have not been reflected in this edition. Therefore, if a company is subject to the requirements of FAS-141(R) and/or FAS-160, the reader is referred to FAS-141(R) and FAS-160 for these new requirements.

BACKGROUND

The role of computer software in our economy has increased rapidly over the past 20 years and its role is likely to continue to grow in the future. Some entities develop computer software for sale to other parties. These entities need guidance on recognizing revenue from the sale of computer software. Entities that sell computer software also need guidance on accounting for the costs of such software development.

Other entities do not sell computer software, but they use software internally in the operation of their businesses. Such software may be purchased externally or developed internally. These entities need guidance on accounting for the costs of computer software used in the operation of their businesses, particularly the software that is developed internally.

FAS-86 (Accounting for the Costs of Computer Software to Be Sold, Leased, or Otherwise Marketed) provides guidance on accounting for the costs of developing computer software for those entities that plan to sell that software. Generally, accounting for such software parallels accounting for research and development costs. To the point of establishing technological feasibility, costs are expensed as incurred. Once technological feasibility is established, it is evident that the particular software can be produced in accordance with design specifications. After that point, all costs incurred in developing the computer software product should be capitalized.

FIN-2 (Imputing Interest on Debt Arrangements Make under the Federal Bankruptcy Act) specifies that the development costs of a computer system that improves an enterprise's administrative and selling procedures are not considered R&D costs. Costs incurred for internally developed computer software products that are used in the enterprise's own R&D activities, however, are considered R&D and should be accounted for accordingly.

COMPUTER SOFTWARE TO BE SOLD, LEASED, OR OTHERWISE MARKETED

FAS-86 applies to those costs incurred in purchasing or internally developing and producing computer software products that are sold, leased, or otherwise marketed by an enterprise. The costs covered by FAS-86 may be incurred (*a*) for separate computer software products or (*b*) for integral parts of computer software products or processes. FAS-86 does *not* cover those costs incurred for computer software that is (*a*) produced by an enterprise for others under a contractual arrangement or (*b*) created for the internal use of an enterprise (FAS-86, par. 2).

Under FAS-86, the terms *computer software product, software product,* and *product* are used interchangeably to mean either (*a*) a computer software program, (*b*) a group of programs, or (*c*) a product enhancement. A product enhancement represents improvement to an existing product that significantly improves the marketability or extends the estimated useful life of the original product. A product enhancement almost always involves a new design or redesign of the original computer software product (FAS-86, par. 2).

The primary activities that are involved in the creation of a computer software product are the (a) planning function, (b) design function, and (c) production function. The planning function of a computer software product generally includes preliminary product specifications and design and the development of production and financial plans for the product. In addition, the planning function should include a marketing analysis and a marketing plan for the product. The planning function should generate sufficient documentation and detail information for an enterprise to make a determination of the overall feasibility of the proposed computer software product.

The design function of a computer software product includes the product design and the detail program design. The production of a product master generally involves coding, testing, and the development of training materials. Coding is the process in which the requirements of the detail program design are converted into a computer language. Testing includes the steps necessary to determine whether the computer software product works in accordance with its design specifications and documentation.

Computer Software Costs

FAS-86 specifies that all costs incurred in establishing the technological feasibility of a computer software product that is to be sold, leased, or otherwise marketed by an enterprise are research and development costs, which must be accounted for as required by FAS-2 (Accounting for Research and Development Costs). Thus, until technological feasibility is established in accordance with FAS-86, all costs incurred through the purchase or internal development and production of a computer software product that is to be sold, leased, or otherwise marketed are accounted for as R&D costs and expensed in the period incurred (FAS-86, par. 3).

The development costs of a computer system that improves an enterprise's administrative or selling procedures are not considered R&D costs. All costs incurred for internally developed computer software products used in an enterprise's own R&D activities, however, should be charged to expense when incurred, because the alternative future use test does not apply to such costs (FIN-6, par. 8).

Production costs incurred for integral parts of a computer software product or process are expensed, unless (a) technological feasibility has been established for the computer software product or process and (b) all research and development activities have been completed for the other components of the computer software product or process (FAS-86, par. 5).

Technological Feasibility

Technological feasibility is established upon completion of all of the activities that are necessary to substantiate that the computer software product can be produced in accordance with its design specifications, including functions, features, and technical performance requirements. Thus, all planning, designing, coding, and testing activities that are required to substantiate that the computer software product can be produced to meet its design specifications must have been completed before technological feasibility is established (FAS-86, par. 4).

Under FAS-86, the method of establishing the technological feasibility of a computer software product depends on whether the process of creating the computer software product includes a detail program design or not. The minimum requirements for establishing the technological feasibility of a computer software product are discussed below (FAS-86, par. 4).

Including Detail Program Design

If the process of creating the computer software product includes a detail program design, the following criteria establish the technological feasibility of a computer software product (FAS-86, par. 4a):

- An enterprise must complete the product design and detail program design for the computer software product and establish that it has available the necessary skills, hardware, and software technology to produce the product.

- An enterprise must substantiate the completeness of the program design and its consistency with the product design by documenting and tracing the detail program design to the product specifications.

- An enterprise must identify the high-risk development issues in the computer software product through review of the detail program design; if any uncertainties relating to the highrisk development issues are discovered, they must be resolved through coding and testing. High-risk development issues that may be encountered in the production of a computer software product may include novel, unique, or unproven functions and features, and/or technological innovations.

Not Including Detail Program Design

If the process of creating the computer software product *does not* include a detail program design, the following criteria establish the technological feasibility of a computer software product (FAS-86, par. 4b):

- An enterprise must complete a product design and a working model of the computer software product.

- An enterprise must substantiate the completeness of the working model and its consistency with the product design by testing the model.

Computer Software Costs That Must Be Capitalized

After technological feasibility has been established, FAS-86 specifies that all costs incurred for a computer software product that is sold, leased, or otherwise marketed by an enterprise shall be capitalized. Thus, the costs of producing product masters for a computer software product, including costs for coding and testing, are capitalized, but only after technological feasibility has been established (FAS-86, par. 5).

Production costs for computer software that is to be used as an integral part of a product or process are capitalized, but only after (*a*) technological feasibility has been established for the software and (*b*) all R&D activities for the other components of the product or process have been completed.

Capitalization of computer software costs is discontinued when the computer software product is available to be sold, leased, or otherwise marketed. Costs for maintenance and customer support are charged to expense when incurred or when the related revenue is recognized, whichever occurs first (FAS-86, par. 6).

> **OBSERVATION:** Under FAS-86, the amount of costs that an enterprise is required to capitalize depends primarily on its choice of production methods. Thus, an enterprise may control the amount of computer software costs that it capitalizes by establishing technological feasibility at a designated time during the production process.

Amortization of Capitalized Computer Software Costs

Amortization of capitalized computer software costs, on a product-by-product basis, begins when the product is available to be sold, leased, or otherwise marketed. Periodic amortization, on a product-by-product basis, is equal to the greater of (*a*) the amount computed by the straight-line method over the estimated useful life of the product or (*b*) the amount computed by using the ratio that current gross revenues bear to total estimated gross revenues (including current gross revenues) (FAS-86, par. 8).

Inventory Costs

Inventory costs are capitalized on a unit-specific basis and charged to cost of sales when the related revenue from the sale of those units is recognized. Inventory costs include duplicate copies of the computer software product made from the product master, documentation, training materials, and the costs incurred for packaging the product for distribution (FAS-86, par. 9).

Periodic Evaluation of Capitalized Computer Software Costs

Unamortized computer software costs that have been capitalized previously in accordance with FAS-86 are reported at net realizable value on an enterprise's balance sheet. Net realizable value is determined on a product-by-product basis and is equal to the estimated future gross revenues of a specific product, less estimated future costs of completing and disposing of that specific product, including the costs of performing maintenance and customer support on a product-by-product basis as required by the terms of the sale.

The excess of any unamortized computer software costs over its related net realizable value at a balance sheet date shall be written down. The amount of write-down is charged to periodic income. Capitalized costs that have been written down as a charge to income shall not be capitalized again or restored in any future period (FAS-86, par. 10).

Financial Statement Disclosure

The total amount of unamortized computer software costs that is included in each balance sheet presented shall be disclosed in the financial statements. The total amount of computer software costs charged to expense shall be disclosed for each income statement presented. The total amount of computer software costs charged to expense shall include amortization expense and amounts written down to net realizable value (FAS-86, par. 11).

All computer software costs that are classified as R&D costs shall be accounted for in accordance with FAS-2. These costs may include the costs of planning, product design, detail program design, and the costs incurred in establishing technological feasibility of a computer software product (FAS-86, par. 12).

RELATED CHAPTERS IN 2009 *GAAP GUIDE LEVEL A*

Chapter 12, "Development Stage Enterprises"
Chapter 23, "Intangible Assets"
Chapter 39, "Research and Development"

RELATED CHAPTERS IN 2009 *GAAP GUIDE LEVELS B, C, AND D*

Chapter 9, "Computer Software"
Chapter 21, "Intangible Assets"
Chapter 34, "Research and Development"

RELATED CHAPTER IN 2009 *INTERNATIONAL ACCOUNTING/FINANCIAL REPORTING STANDARDS GUIDE*

Chapter 21, "Intangible Assets"

CHAPTER 7
CONSOLIDATED FINANCIAL STATEMENTS

CONTENTS

OVERVIEW

Consolidated financial statements represent the results of operations, statement of cash flows, and financial position of a single entity, even though multiple, separate legal entities are involved. Consolidated financial statements are presumed to present more meaningful information than separate financial statements and must be used in substantially all cases in which a parent directly or indirectly controls the majority voting interest (over 50%) of a subsidiary. Consolidated financial statements should not be used in those circumstances in which there is significant doubt concerning the parent's ability to control the subsidiary.

The promulgated accounting standards and reporting principles for consolidated financial statements, combined financial statements, and comparative financial statements are:

ARB-43	Chapter 1A, Rules Adopted by Membership
	Chapter 2A, Comparative Financial Statements
ARB-51	Consolidated Financial Statements (as amended)
FAS-94	Consolidation of All Majority-Owned Subsidiaries
FIN-46(R)	Consolidation of Variable Interest Entities

2009 TRANSITION GUIDANCE FOR FAS-141(R)

The FASB has recently issued FAS-141(R), *Business Combinations*, which is effective for business combinations for which the acquisition date is on or after the beginning of the first annual reporting period beginning on or after December 15, 2008. Since FAS-141(R) is not effective for some companies until December 2009, and since early adoption is prohibited, the 2009 *GAAP Guide* reflects the requirements of FAS-141 prior to its revision in December 2007. There is a discussion of the changes in the accounting for business combinations under FAS-141(R) in the Appendix to Chapter 4, "Business Combinations." However, any effects of FAS-141(R) on this chapter have not been reflected in this edition. Therefore, if a company is subject to the requirements of FAS-141(R), the reader is referred to FAS-141(R) for these new requirements.

> **OBSERVATION:** FAS-160 (Noncontrolling Interests in Consolidated Financial Statements: an amendment of ARB No. 51) was issued in December 2007, and is effective for fiscal years, and interim periods within those fiscal years, beginning on or after December 15, 2008. Since FAS-160 is not effective for some companies until December 2009, and since early adoption is prohibited, the body of this chapter will reflect the requirements of ARB-51 prior to its amending by FAS-160. However, since FAS-160 will be effective for many companies in early 2009, a discussion of the changes in the accounting for noncontrolling interests in consolidated financial statements under FAS-160 is found in the Appendix to this chapter.

BACKGROUND

ARB-43, Chapter 1A (Rules Adopted by Membership), contains six rules that were adopted by the Professional Organization of Certified

Public Accountants in 1934. The third rule deals with consolidated financial statements and requires that a subsidiary company's retained earnings created prior to the date of its acquisition cannot be considered part of the consolidated retained earnings of the parent company and its subsidiaries. Furthermore, any dividends declared out of such retained earnings cannot be included in the net income of the parent company.

ARB-43, Chapter 2A (Comparative Financial Statements), discusses the desirability of presenting comparative financial statements in annual reports, because such a presentation is likely to provide much more information than noncomparative statements.

ARB-51 (Consolidated Financial Statements), as amended by FAS-94 (Consolidation of All Majority-Owned Subsidiaries) and interpreted by FIN-46 (Consolidation of Variable Interest Activities), is the main source of GAAP relating to consolidated financial statements. Under ARB-51, a consolidated financial statement represents the results of operations, statement of cash flows, and financial position of a single entity. FAS-94 amended ARB-51 to require, with few exceptions, a parent company to consolidate all of its majority-owned subsidiaries. FIN-46 requires a company to consolidate the assets, liabilities, revenues, and expenses of a variable interest entity if the company has a controlling financial interest in that entity.

Retained earnings of a subsidiary at the date of acquisition are not treated as part of consolidated retained earnings (ARB-51, par. 9). The retained earnings, other capital accounts, and contributed capital at the date of acquisition represent the book value that is eliminated in preparing consolidated statements.

A parent company should not exclude a majority-owned subsidiary from consolidation because it has a different fiscal year. For consolidation purposes, a subsidiary usually can prepare financial statements that correspond with its parent's fiscal period. If a subsidiary's fiscal year is within three months or less of its parent's fiscal year, it is acceptable to use those fiscal-year financial statements for consolidation purposes, provided that adequate disclosure is made of any material events occurring within the intervening period (ARB-51, par. 4).

MAJORITY-OWNED SUBSIDIARIES

ARB-51, as amended by FAS-94 and FAS-144 (Accounting for the Impairment or Disposal of Long-Lived Assets), requires that all investments in which a parent company has a controlling financial interest represented by the direct or indirect ownership of a majority voting interest (more than 50%) be consolidated, except those in which significant doubt exists regarding the parent's ability to control the subsidiary. For example, a subsidiary in legal reorganization or bankruptcy is controlled by the receiver or trustee and not by the parent company (FAS-94, par. 13).

> ☞ **PRACTICE POINTER:** In determining whether consolidated financial statements are required in a particular situation, a reasonable starting point is to assume that if majority ownership exists, consolidation is appropriate. For that point, consider those rare circumstances in which a majority ownership interest does exist but consolidation would not be appropriate. However, such circumstances are clearly intended to be exceptions to a policy of consolidation in most situations of majority ownership.

FAS-94 amends Chapter 12 of ARB-43 by superseding paragraphs 8 and 9 (Consolidation of Foreign Subsidiaries), which had permitted the exclusion from consolidation of majority-owned foreign subsidiaries because of foreign currency and/or exchange restrictions. FAS-94 requires that the exchange restrictions or other governmental controls in a foreign subsidiary be so severe that they "cast significant doubt on the parent's ability to control the subsidiary." This amendment narrows the exception for a majority-owned foreign subsidiary from one that permits exclusion from consolidation of any or all foreign subsidiaries to one that effectively eliminates distinctions between foreign and domestic subsidiaries (FAS-94, par. 9). Thus, a majority-owned subsidiary must be consolidated unless significant doubt exists regarding the parent's control of the subsidiary. FAS-52 (Foreign Currency Translation) contains special rules for translating foreign currency financial statements of foreign subsidiaries that operate in countries with highly inflationary economies.

FAS-94 amends APB-18 (The Equity Method of Accounting for Investments in Common Stock) by removing the requirement of APB-18 to report unconsolidated majority-owned subsidiaries by the equity method. In addition, FAS-94 eliminates the provisions of APB-18 applying to "parent-company financial statements prepared for issuance to stockholders as the financial statements of the primary reporting entity" (FAS-94, par. 15).

> ☞ **PRACTICE POINTER:** FAS-94 comes close to requiring that all majority-owned subsidiaries be consolidated. A limited exception is a situation where control does not rest with the majority owner, as when a subsidiary is in legal reorganization or bankruptcy. APB-18, on the other hand, is amended by FAS-94 to eliminate the requirement that unconsolidated subsidiaries be accounted for by the equity method. In the rare instance indicated above, where (majority-owned) subsidiaries are not consolidated, the authoritative literature apparently does not specify a particular method of accounting, although the equity method may be judged the appropriate method to use in the circumstances.

ACCOUNTING AND REPORTING ON SUBSIDIARIES

The common stock or net assets of a subsidiary may be purchased (*a*) for book value, (*b*) in excess of book value, and (*c*) for less than book value. If purchased for more than book value, there may be resulting goodwill; if purchased for less than book value, the excess amounts assigned to assets acquired and liabilities assumed over the cost of the acquired entity are allocated to all of the assets acquired, with certain limited exceptions. If any excess remains after reducing all of the permitted assets to zero, the remaining excess is recognized as an extraordinary gain (FAS-141, pars. 44–45).

When a subsidiary's common stock is acquired by the purchase method in more than one transaction, each purchase should be determined on a step-by-step basis and consolidation usually is not made until control (more than 50%) is achieved. In the year that control is achieved, the percentage amount of net income from the purchased subsidiary will probably vary (ARB-51, par. 10). ARB-51 suggests two methods for the inclusion of income from a subsidiary in periods in which there are several purchases. The preferable method usually is to include the subsidiary in the consolidation as if it had been acquired at the beginning of the period, and to deduct at the bottom of the consolidated income statement the net income of the subsidiary that does not accrue to the parent (ARB-51, par. 11).

> **OBSERVATION:** Apparently, when this method is being used, all the revenue and expense accounts of the subsidiary remain in the consolidated income statement, since only the net income that the parent is not entitled to is deducted from the consolidated net income at the bottom of the statement.

The other method that ARB-51 suggests is to include in the parent's consolidated income statement only the subsidiary's revenue and expenses subsequent to the date that control was obtained (ARB-51, par. 11).

CONSOLIDATION ISSUES

Combined Financial Statements

Consolidated financial statements usually are justified on the basis that one of the consolidating entities exercises control over the affiliated group. When there is no such control, combined financial statements may be used to accomplish the same results. For example, a group of companies controlled by an individual shareholder, or a group of unconsolidated subsidiaries that could otherwise not be consolidated, should utilize combined financial statements. Combined financial statements are prepared on the same basis as consolidated financial statements, except that no company in the group has a controlling interest in the other (ARB-51, pars. 22–23).

Comparative Financial Statements

Comparative financial statements reveal much more information than noncomparative statements and furnish useful data about differences in the results of operations for the periods involved or in the financial position at the comparison dates (ARB-43, Ch. 2A, par. 1).

Consistency is a major factor in creating comparability. Prior-year amounts and classifications must be, in fact, comparable with the current period presented, and exceptions must be disclosed clearly (ARB-43, Ch. 2A, par. 2).

Consolidation versus Equity Method

The income and balance sheet effects of intercompany transactions are eliminated in equity method adjustments as well as in the financial statements of consolidated entities (ARB-51, par. 6). In consolidated financial statements, the details of all entities to the consolidation are reported in full. In the equity method, the investment is shown as a single amount in the investor balance sheet, and earnings or losses generally are shown as a single amount in the income statement. This is the reason the equity method is frequently referred to as *one-line consolidation.*

> ☛ **PRACTICE POINTER:** While their impact on reporting income is the same, the equity method and consolidation differ in the extent of detail each reflects in the financial statements. The authoritative literature clearly states that the equity method is not necessarily an appropriate alternative to consolidation, or vice versa. Generally, consolidation is appropriate where majority interest exists, and the equity method is appropriate where the investor has the ability to exert significant influence over the investee but lacks majority ownership.

Consolidated Work Papers and Intercompany Transactions

The preparation of consolidated financial statements is facilitated by the preparation of a consolidated statements worksheet. Traditionally, this worksheet was prepared by hand and the adjustments and eliminations required for consolidation were not posted to the books of the individual companies. Computerization of accounting processes, including the preparation of worksheets to assist in the preparation of consolidated financial statements, has modernized this process and all eliminations and adjustments are posted.

Following is a brief discussion of some of the most frequently encountered intercompany transactions.

Sales and Purchases

The gross amount of all intercompany sales and/or purchases is eliminated on the consolidated work papers. When the adjustment has already been made in the trial balance for ending inventory, the eliminating entry is made by debiting sales and crediting cost of sales. When no adjustment has been made for ending inventory, the eliminating entry is made by crediting the purchases account. In this latter case, a more straightforward approach is to make an adjusting entry establishing the cost of sales and then eliminating intercompany sales by crediting cost of sales.

Receivables and Payables

Intercompany receivables and payables include:

- Accounts receivable and accounts payable.
- Advances to and from affiliates.
- Notes receivable and notes payable.
- Interest receivable and interest payable.

The gross amounts of all intercompany receivables and payables are eliminated on the consolidated work papers. Care must be exercised when a receivable is discounted with one of the consolidated companies (no contingent liability). If the balance sheet reflects a discounted receivable with another affiliate, the amount must be eliminated by a debit to discounted receivables and a credit to receivables. If one affiliate discounts a receivable to another affiliate, who in turn discounts it to an outsider, a real contingent liability still exists, and must be shown on the consolidated balance sheet.

Unrealized Profits in Inventory

Regardless of any minority interests, all (100%) of any intercompany profit in ending inventory is eliminated on the consolidated workpapers. In addition, the cost of sales account must be adjusted for intercompany profit in beginning inventory arising from intercompany transactions in the previous year. If the adjustment for intercompany profits in inventories is not made, consolidated net income will be incorrect and consolidated ending inventory will be overstated.

Illustration of Profit in Inventory

P Company purchased $200,000 and $250,000 of merchandise in 20X8 and 20X9, respectively, from its subsidiary S at 25% above cost. As of December 31, 20X8, and 20X9, P had on hand $25,000 and $30,000 of merchandise purchased from S. The following is the computation of intercompany profits:

Computation of Intercompany Profits

Beginning inventory	$25,000	=	125%
Cost to S	(20,000)	=	(100%)
Intercompany profit	$ 5,000		25%
Ending inventory	$30,000	=	125%
Cost to S	(24,000)	=	(100%)
Intercompany profit	$ 6,000		25%

The adjustment is different for a consolidated balance sheet than for a consolidated income statement and balance sheet. If intercompany profit adjustments have not been recorded in equity method entries on P Company's books, for a consolidated balance sheet only the elimination entry is:

Retained earnings	6,000	
Inventory		6,000

Assuming no equity method adjustments are made, and a perpetual inventory system is used, for a consolidated income statement and balance sheet the following adjustments are necessary:

Sales	250,000	
Costs of sales		250,000
To eliminate intercompany sales.		
Consolidated retained earnings	5,000	
Cost of sales		5,000
To reverse consolidated adjustment of 12/31/X8.		
Cost of sales	6,000	
Inventory		6,000
To eliminate intercompany profit in ending inventory.		

The adjustment to consolidated retained earnings is necessary because the intercompany profit was eliminated on the prior year's consolidated work papers. (Consolidated adjustments and eliminations are not posted to the books of the individual companies. Therefore, the beginning inventory for P still reflected the prior year's intercompany inventory profits from S.)

If merchandise containing an intercompany inventory profit is reduced from the purchase price to market value and the reduction is equal to, or more than, the actual intercompany inventory profit, no deferral of profit entry is required in consolidation. For example, if merchandise costing one affiliate $10,000 is sold to another affiliate for $12,000, who reduces it to market value of $11,000, the consolidated work paper adjustment for unrealized intercompany inventory profits should be only $1,000.

Minority interests do not affect the adjustment for unrealized intercompany profits in inventories. Consolidated net income and minority interests in the net income of a subsidiary are affected by the adjustment, however, because the reduction or increase in beginning or ending inventory of a partially owned subsidiary does affect the determination of net income.

Unrealized intercompany losses in inventory are accounted for in the same manner as unrealized profits, except that they have the opposite effect. Profits or losses on sales and/or purchases prior to an affiliation are not recognized as a consolidated adjustment.

Unrealized Profits in Long-Lived Assets

Regardless of any minority interests, all (100%) of any intercompany profits on the sale and/or purchase of long-lived assets between affiliates is eliminated on the consolidated workpapers.

When one affiliate constructs or sells a long-lived asset to another affiliate at a profit, the profit is eliminated on the consolidated workpapers. As with unrealized intercompany profits or losses in inventory, minority interests do not affect any consolidated adjustment for profits in intercompany sales of long-lived assets between affiliates. Net income of the subsidiary involved in the intercompany profit on a long-lived asset is affected by the adjustment, however, which in turn affects consolidated net income and minority interests.

If a nondepreciable asset is involved in an intercompany profit on a long-lived asset, the profit is eliminated by a debit to either retained earnings, in the case of an adjusted consolidated balance sheet, or to gain on sale, in the case of a consolidated income statement.

Depreciable assets require the same adjustment for intercompany profit as nondepreciable long-lived assets, and an adjustment must also be made for any depreciation recorded on the intercompany profit.

Illustration of Profit in Long-Lived Assets

S Company, an 80%-owned subsidiary, sells to P Company for $100,000 a piece of machinery that cost $80,000. The sale was made on July 1, 20X8, and consolidated statements are being prepared for December 31, 20X8. P

Company depreciates machinery over ten years on a straight-line basis and records one-half year's depreciation on the purchased machinery.

The first entry eliminates the $20,000 of intercompany profit, as follows:

Gain on sale of machinery	20,000	
Machinery		20,000

Since P Company has recorded one-half year's depreciation on the machinery, the following additional entry is made:

Accumulated depreciation	1,000	
Depreciation expense		1,000

Because consolidated eliminations and adjustments are never posted to any books, additional entries are required in the following year. Assuming that intercompany profit adjustments were not made under the equity method on P Company's books, the following eliminations are needed:

Retained earnings—P Company	16,000	
Retained earnings—S Company	4,000	
Machinery		20,000

To eliminate intercompany profit on prior year's sale of machinery.

Accumulated depreciation	3,000	
Retained earnings—P Company		800
Retained earnings—S Company		200
Depreciation expense		2,000

To eliminate the $2,000 depreciation expense on intercompany profit on the sale of machinery and to eliminate the $1,000 depreciation expense for prior year's depreciation.

If the intercompany sale had been made from P Company to S Company, the retained earnings adjustments would have been made only to P Company's accounts.

The process of eliminating the depreciation expense on the intercompany profit on the sale of long-lived assets continues until the asset is fully depreciated. Thereafter, until the asset is disposed of or retired, adjustments are needed to the machinery and accumulated depreciation accounts. In the example, the following entry would be made every year on the consolidated work papers after the asset is fully depreciated and before it is disposed of or retired.

Accumulated depreciation	20,000	
Machinery		20,000

An affiliate that makes an intercompany profit on the sale of long-lived assets to another affiliate may pay income taxes on the gain. This occurs usually when the affiliated group does not file consolidated tax returns and the gain cannot be avoided for tax purposes. In such cases, the intercompany profit on the sale should be reduced by the related tax effects in computing the consolidated adjusting entry.

Intercompany Bondholdings

Intercompany bonds purchased by an affiliate are treated in the year of acquisition as though they have been retired. Any gain or loss is recognized in the consolidated income statement for the year of acquisition.

The amount of gain or loss on an intercompany bond purchase is the difference between the unamortized bond premium or discount on the books of the issuer and the amount of any purchase discount or premium.

An intercompany gain or loss on bonds does not occur when an affiliate makes the purchase directly from the affiliated issuer, because the selling price will be exactly equal to the cost.

Illustration of Intercompany Bonds

An affiliate purchases $20,000 face value 6% bonds from an affiliated issuer for $19,500.

On the affiliated investor's books the following entry is made:

Investment in bonds	19,500	
Cash		19,500

On the affiliated issuer's books the entry is:

Cash	19,500	
Discount on bonds payable	500	
Bonds payable		20,000

The consolidated elimination is:

Bonds payable	20,000	
Discount on bonds payable		500
Investment in bonds		19,500

An intercompany gain or loss on bonds does not occur when the purchase price is exactly the same as the carrying value on the books of the affiliated issuer.

The following conditions must exist for an affiliated investor to realize a gain or loss on intercompany bondholdings:

- The bonds are already outstanding.
- The bonds are purchased from outside the affiliated group.
- The price paid is different from the carrying value of the affiliated issuer.

Illustration of Intercompany Bonds with Gain/Loss

Company S acquires $50,000 of face amount 6% bonds from an outsider. These bonds were part of an original issue of $300,000 made by the parent of Company S. The purchase price was $45,000, and the bonds mature in four years and nine months (57 months). Interest is payable on June 30 and December 31, and the purchase was made on March 31.

The journal entry on the books of Company S to record the purchase is:

Investment in bonds	45,000	
Accrued interest receivable	750	
Cash		45,750

On the consolidated workpapers at the end of the year, the following entries are made:

Investment in bonds	5,000	
Gain on intercompany bondholdings		5,000

To adjust the investment in bonds to face amount and record the gain.

Bonds payable—Co. P	50,000	
Investment in bonds—Co. S		50,000

To eliminate intercompany bondholdings.

Interest income—Co. S	2,250	
Interest expense—Co. P		2,250

To eliminate intercompany interest on bonds that was actually paid.

Interest income—Co. S	788	
Investment in bonds		788

To eliminate amortization of $5,000 discount on bonds recorded on Co. S's books. (9/57 of $5,000 = $788)

Accrued interest payable	1,500	
Accrued interest receivable		1,500

To eliminate accrued interest payable on
Dec. 31 by Co. P, and the accrued interest
receivable on Dec. 31 by Co. S.

This example contains all the possible adjustments except for an issuer's premium or discount. Assume the following additional information on the original issue:

Face amount	$300,000
Issued at 96	288,000
Date of issue	1/1/X1
Maturity date	1/1/Y0

Company S had purchased its $50,000 face amount when the issue had four years and nine months left to maturity.

On the parent company's books, this discount is being amortized over the life of the bond issue at the rate of $1,200 per year ($12,000 discount divided by 10 years). An adjustment is made on the consolidated workpapers to eliminate the portion of the unamortized bond discount existing at the date of purchase that is applicable to the $50,000 face amount purchased by Company S.

Total discount on issue	$12,000
1/6 applicable to Co. S's purchase	$ 2,000
Amount of discount per month	$ 16.67
($2,000 divided by 120 months)	
Four years and nine months equal	$ 950
57 months × $16.67	

The amount of unamortized bond discount on Co. P's books applicable to the $50,000 purchase made by Company S was $950 at the date of purchase. This $950 would have entered into the computation of the gain or loss on intercompany bondholdings. In the example, the gain or loss on intercompany bondholdings of $5,000 would have been reduced by $950 ($4,050) and the following additional consolidated elimination would have been made:

Gain or loss on intercompany bondholdings	950	
Unamortized bond discount		950

In addition, the amortization on the intercompany portion of the bond discount would be reversed in the consolidated worksheet (9 months x $16.67):

Unamortized bond discount	150	
Interest expense		150

Intercompany Dividends

Intercompany dividends are eliminated on the consolidated work-papers. Consolidated retained earnings should reflect the accumulated earnings of the consolidated group arising since acquisition that have not been distributed to the shareholders of, or capitalized by, the parent company. In the event that a subsidiary capitalizes earnings arising since acquisition by means of a stock dividend, or otherwise, a transfer to paid-in capital is not required in consolidating (ARB-51, par. 18).

Intercompany Stockholdings

Shares of the parent held by a subsidiary should not be treated as outstanding stock in the consolidated balance sheet. Such shares are treated as "treasury stock" on the consolidated balance sheet and subtracted from consolidated stockholders' equity.

Income Tax Considerations

Income taxes are deferred on any intercompany profits where the asset still exists within the consolidated group (ARB-51, par. 17). If consolidated tax returns are filed, however, no adjustment need be made for deferred income taxes, because intercompany profits are eliminated in computing the consolidated tax liability.

Minority Interests

Consolidated financial statements are prepared primarily for the benefit of creditors and shareholders.

Minority interests in net income are deducted to arrive at consolidated net income. Minority interests are theoretically limited to the extent of their equity capital, however, and losses in excess of minority interest equity capital are charged against the majority interest. Subsequently, when the losses reverse, the majority interests should be credited with the amount of minority interest losses previously absorbed before credit is made to the minority interests (ARB-51, par. 15).

Disclosure

The consolidation policy should be disclosed fully on the financial statements or in footnotes thereto (ARB-51, par. 5).

Disclosure of Minority Interests

The *parent company theory* is used in practice almost exclusively for disclosing minority interests in a consolidated balance sheet. Under the parent company theory, minority interests are *not* considered part of stockholders' equity and are disclosed in the consolidated balance sheet between the liability section and the stockholders' equity section. Whereas minority interests are insignificant and do not warrant a separate classification in the consolidated balance sheet, some enterprises have seen fit to disclose minority interests among other liabilities. Minority interests in consolidated net income are shown as a deduction in arriving at consolidated net income.

Under the *entity theory,* minority interests are disclosed within and as part of the consolidated stockholders' equity section of the consolidated balance sheet. Although the entity theory has much more theoretical support, it is seldom used in practice.

Illustration of Computing Minority Interest and Consolidated Net Income

Computing minority interests in a complex father-son-grandson affiliation may be demonstrated by using the following diagram (dollar amounts are income figures for the separate entities):

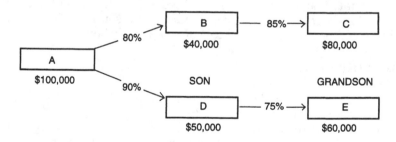

The computations of minority interests and consolidated net income follow:

	E	D	C	B	A
Net income	$60,000	$50,000	$80,000	$40,000	$100,000
75% to D	(45,000)	45,000			
		$95,000			
90% to A		(85,500)			85,500
85% to B			(68,000)	68,000	
				$108,000	
80% to A				(86,400)	86,400

| Minority interests | $15,000 | $9,500 | $12,000 | $21,600 |

Consolidated net income $271,900

In a situation in which a subsidiary owns shares of the parent company, consolidated net income may be found algebraically, as the following depicts:

Company	Unconsolidated Income (excluding income from investees)	
A	$40,000	A, the parent, owns 80% of B
B	20,000	B owns 70% of C
C	10,000	C owns 20% of A

Let A = A's *consolidated basis* net income
     B = B's *consolidated basis* net income
     C = C's *consolidated basis* net income

The figures and relationships can be put into algebraic form so as to compute *consolidated net income.*

$$A = 40,000 + 0.8B$$
$$B = 20,000 + 0.7C$$
$$C = 10,000 + 0.2A$$

Solving for A, we have:

$$A = 40,000 + 0.8(20,000 + 0.7C)$$
$$A = 40,000 + 16,000 + 0.56C$$
$$A = 56,000 + 0.56C$$
$$A = 56,000 + 0.56(10,000 + 0.2A)$$
$$A = 56,000 + 5,600 + 0.112A$$
$$0.888A = 61,600$$
$$A = 69,369$$

Company A's income on an equity basis, which equals consolidated income, is determined by multiplying by the 80% interest outstanding (i.e., the remaining 20% is held within the consolidated entity):

$69,369 \times 0.8 = \$55,495$ consolidated net income

The minority interests in the two subsidiaries are determined as follows:

$$C = \$10,000 + 0.2(\$69,369)$$
$$= \$23,874$$

$$Minority\ interest\ share\ of\ C = 0.3(\$23,874)$$
$$= \$7,162$$
$$B = \$20,000 + 0.7(\$23,874)$$
$$= \$36,712$$
$$Minority\ interest\ share\ of\ B = 0.2(\$36,712)$$
$$= \$7,342$$

VARIABLE INTEREST ENTITIES

FIN-46 (revised December 2003) interprets ARB-51 and addresses consolidation by business enterprises of variable interest entities that have certain specified characteristics. If a business enterprise has a controlling financial interest in a variable interest entity, the assets, liabilities, and results of activities of that entity should be included in the consolidated financial statements of the business enterprise.

> **OBSERVATION:** FIN-46(R) was issued because transactions involving variable interest entities have become increasingly common, and the authoritative accounting literature related to these transactions is fragmented and incomplete.

FIN-46(R) is intended to clarify the application of ARB-51 to certain entities in which equity investors do not have the typical characteristics of a controlling financial interest or do not have sufficient equity at risk for the entity to finance its activities without additional subordinated financial support, even if that additional subordinated financial support is provided by the entity's equity investors. ARB-51 indicates that consolidated financial statements usually are required for a fair presentation when one of the companies in the group directly or indirectly has a controlling financial interest in the other companies. ARB-51 goes on to say that the usual condition for a controlling financial interest is a majority voting interest. For certain types of entities, however, application of the majority voting interest requirement may not identify the party with a controlling interest because the control may be achieved through arrangements that do not involve voting interests (FIN-46(R), par. 1).

Key Definitions

Variable interest in a variable interest entity refers to a contractual, ownership, or other pecuniary interest in an entity that changes with changes in the fair value of the entity's net assets excluding variable interests. Equity interests with or without voting rights are considered variable interests if the entity is a variable interest entity, only to the extent that the investment is at risk (FIN-46(R), par. 2). In FIN-46(R), *entity* is used to refer to any legal structure used to conduct activities or hold assets. This includes corporations, partnerships, limited liability companies, grantor trusts, and other trusts (FIN-46(R), par. 3).

> ☞ **PRACTICE POINTER:** Examples of variable interests in a variable interest entity often include (1) equity investments that are at risk, (2) investments in subordinated beneficial interests, (3) investments in subordinated debt instruments, (4) guarantees, (5) written put options, (6) forward purchase and sale contracts, (7) derivatives and total return swaps that reduce the exposure of the entity to risks that cause variability, and (8) leases with a residual value guarantee and options to acquire leased assets at the lease's termination at specified prices (FIN-46(R), Appendix B).
>
> Fees paid to a decision maker could be a variable interest, but if *all* of the following conditions are met, such fees would *not* be considered a variable interest: (1) the fees represent fair compensation for the services provided; (2) the fees are not subordinate to other operating liabilities; (3) in circumstances other than the first two, the decision maker (and its related parties) do not hold interests that would result in the decision maker absorbing more than a trivial amount of expected losses or receiving more than a trivial amount of expected returns; and (4) the decision maker can be terminated (i.e., is subject to substantive kick-out rights) (FIN-46(R), Appendix B19). Substantive kick-out rights have two features: (1) the decision maker can be terminated by a simple majority vote of interests held by parties other than the decision maker (and its related parties) and (2) there are no substantial barriers to the exercise of the kick-out rights (examples of such barriers include financial penalties for terminating the decision maker and a lack of an adequate number of qualified replacements) (FIN-46(R), Appendix B20).

Scope

FIN-46(R) applies to all entities except (1) not-for-profit (NFP) organizations, unless the NFP organization is used by a business enterprise to circumvent the provisions of FIN-46(R); (2) pension, other postretirement, and other postemployment benefit plans subject to the provisions of FAS-87, FAS-106, and FAS-112; (3) transferors to qualifying and grandfathered, special-purpose entities under the provisions of FAS-140; and (4) separate accounts for life insurance enterprises. Investment companies subject to SEC regulation S-X, Rule 6-03(c)(1) should not consolidate an entity unless that entity is also subject to the same SEC regulation. In addition to the transferor not consolidating a qualifying, or grandfathered, special-purpose entity, no other entity should consolidate a qualifying, or grandfathered, special-purpose entity unless the other entity has the unilateral ability to cause the special-purpose entity to liquidate or to change in such a way that it would no longer be a qualifying, or grandfathered, special-purpose entity (FIN-46(R), par. 4).

In addition to the above exceptions contained in the original FIN-46, FIN-46 as revised added three more exceptions. These exceptions pertain to situations in which the data needed to apply FIN-46(R) is unavailable, where the entity to be evaluated qualifies as a *business*, and where the entity to be evaluated is a governmental organization (FIN-46(R), par. 4).

FIN-46(R) does not have to be applied to variable interest entities (or potential variable interest entities) created before December 31, 2003, if the reporting enterprise does not have the necessary information to (1) determine whether the entity is a variable interest entity, (2) determine whether the enterprise is the primary beneficiary of the variable interest entity, and (3) apply the consolidation provisions of FIN-46(R) to a variable interest entity where the enterprise is the primary beneficiary. However, this exception is available only to those enterprises that lack the necessary information to apply FIN-46(R) after making an *exhaustive effort* to obtain the needed information, and the exception lasts only as long as the needed information cannot be obtained (FIN 46(R), par. 4g).

> ☞ **PRACTICE POINTER:** The FASB does not define what it means by an *exhaustive effort*. Therefore, companies and their auditors should exercise significant judgment in claiming a scope exception to FIN-46(R) under this provision.

In most circumstances, an entity that qualifies as a *business* does not have to be evaluated by a reporting enterprise to determine whether it is a variable interest entity (FIN-46(R), par. 4h). For the purpose of this exception to the requirements of FIN-46(R), the FASB defines a business as a self-sustaining set of activities and assets conducted and managed for the purpose of providing a return to investors. A business must have inputs (e.g., assets and employees), processes applied to those inputs (e.g., business strategies and operations), and outputs that generate revenues. A business must have all the inputs and processes needed for it to conduct normal operations, which entail generating revenues by providing outputs to customers (FIN-46(R), Appendix C). However, if *one or more* of the following conditions exist, an entity that qualifies as a business must be evaluated by the reporting enterprise to determine whether the consolidation criteria of FIN-46(R) apply (FIN-46(R), par. 4h):

- The reporting enterprise (or its related parties) designed or redesigned the entity (with the exception of operating joint ventures under joint control and franchisees).

- Substantially all of the entity's activities involve or are conducted on behalf of the reporting enterprise (or its related parties).

- The reporting enterprise (and its related parties) provide more than half of the entity's equity, subordinated debt, and other forms of subordinated financial support.

- The entity's primary activities are securitizations, asset-backed financings, or single-lessee leasing arrangements.

The consolidation criteria of FIN-46(R) generally are not applicable to governmental organizations or financing entities established by a governmental organization. The exception to this rule is if the governmental organization is used by a business enterprise to circumvent the provisions of FIN-46(R).

Finally, the provisions of FIN-46(R) are deferred for investment companies that *are not* subject to SEC Regulation S-X, Rule 6-03(c)(1), but rather are accounting for their investments in accordance with the AICPA Audit and Accounting Guide, *Audits of Investment Companies*. The deferral of the effective date of FIN-46(R) does not apply to investments made after March 27, 2002, if held by an investment company that is not a separate legal entity, unless those investments were acquired under the terms of an irrevocable binding commitment that existed prior to March 28, 2002. Investment companies that fall under this deferral provision are exempt from the transitional disclosure provisions of FIN-46(R), described later (FIN-46(R), par. 36).

Consolidation Criteria

An entity is subject to consolidation if *at least one* of the following three conditions exists, as a result of the manner in which the entity was originally structured (FIN-46(R), par. 5):

1. The total equity investment at risk is not sufficient to permit the entity to finance its activities without additional subordinated financial support from any party, including equity holders (FIN-46(R), par. 5a). The total equity investment at risk:
    a. Includes only equity investments in the entity that participate significantly in profits and losses, even if those investments have no voting rights.
    b. Does *not* include equity interests that the entity issued in exchange for subordinated interests in other variable interest entities.
    c. Does *not* include amounts provided to the equity investor directly or indirectly by the entity or by other parties involved with the entity unless the provider is a parent,

subsidiary, or affiliate of the investor that is required to be included in the same set of consolidated financial statements as the investor.

   d. Does *not* include amounts financed for the equity investor directly by the entity or by other parties involved with the entity unless that party is a parent, subsidiary, or affiliate of the investor that is required to be included in the same set of consolidated financial statements as the investor.

2. As a group, the holders of the equity investment at risk *lack any one* of the following characteristics of a controlling financial interest (FIN-46(R), par. 5b):

   a. The direct or indirect ability to make decisions about an entity's activities that have a significant effect on the success of the entity through voting rights or similar rights. (The investors do not have that ability through voting rights or similar rights if no owners hold voting rights or similar rights.)

   b. The obligation to absorb the expected losses of the entity. (The investors do not have that obligation if they are directly or indirectly protected from the expected losses or are guaranteed a return by the entity itself or by other parties involved with the entity.)

   c. The right to receive the expected residual returns of the entity. (The investors do not have that right if their returns are capped by the entity's governing documents or by arrangements with other variable interest holders or with the entity.)

3. Equity investors are considered to lack the direct or indirect ability to make decisions about an entity's activities if (FIN-46 (R), par. 5c):

   a. The voting rights of some investors are not proportional to their rights to receive returns or absorb losses. In applying this requirement, the enterprise is to consider each party's obligations to absorb losses or receive returns related to all of each party's interests in the entity, not only to the equity investment at risk.

   b. Most of the entity's activities involve or are conducted for an investor that has disproportionately few voting rights.

A *variable interest entity* is an entity subject to FIN-46(R). *Variable interests* are the investments or other interests that will absorb portions of a variable interest entity's expected losses or receive portions of the entity's expected residual returns. The initial determination of whether an entity is a variable interest entity is made when an enterprise becomes involved with the entity, based on the circumstances on that date and including future changes that are required in existing governing documents and contractual arrangements (FIN-46(R), par. 6). The initial determination of whether an entity is a variable interest entity is reconsidered only if one or more of the following occurs (FIN-46(R), par. 7):

- The entity's governing documents or the contractual arrangements among the parties involved change and the change affects the characteristics or the adequacy of the entity's equity investment at risk.

- The equity investment or a portion thereof is returned to equity investors, and other interests become exposed to expected losses.

- The entity undertakes additional activities or acquires additional assets—beyond those envisioned when the entity was formed or at the most recent reconsideration event—that increase the entity's expected losses.

- An additional at-risk equity investment is received by the entity, or the entity's activities are changed in a manner as to reduce its expected losses.

> ☞ **PRACTICE POINTER:** A troubled debt restructuring (see the discussion of FAS-15 in the chapter of this *Guide* titled "Troubled Debt Restructuring") does not require an enterprise to reconsider whether the entity involved is a variable interest entity (FIN-46 (R), par. 7).

Expected Losses and Expected Residual Returns

Expected losses (expected residual returns) are a function of expected negative (positive) variability in the fair value of the entity's net assets, excluding variable interests (FIN-46(R), par. 8).

> ☞ **PRACTICE POINTER:** Variable interests held by the potential variable interest entity are excluded in computing expected losses (expected residual returns) because a variable interest is expected to absorb volatility and expected losses, rather than to create them (FIN-46(R), par. D26).

An equity investment at risk of less than 10% of the entity's total assets is considered insufficient to permit the entity to finance its activities without subordinated financial support in addition to the equity investment, unless the equity investment can be demonstrated to be sufficient. FIN-46(R) establishes a hierarchy for evaluating the sufficiency of the equity investment: a qualitative assessment first; then a quantitative assessment if a conclusion about the adequacy of the equity investment at risk cannot be made after diligent effort; and finally, if neither analysis taken alone is conclusive, both the qualitative and quantitative analyses should be considered (FIN-46(R), par. 9). The two qualitative factors that should be considered are whether (1) the entity has demonstrated that it can finance its activities without additional subordinated financial support (FIN-46(R), par. 9a) and (2) the entity has at least as much equity invested as other entities that hold only similar assets of similar quality in similar amounts and operate with no additional subordinated financial support (FIN-46 (R), par. 9b). If the adequacy of the equity investment at risk cannot be determined based on the qualitative assessment, the one quantitative factor that should be considered is whether the amount of equity invested in the entity exceeds the estimate of the entity's expected losses based on reasonable quantitative evidence (FIN-46(R), par. 9c).

Some entities may require an equity investment at risk of greater than 10% of their assets to finance their activities, especially if they are involved in high-risk activities, hold high-risk assets, or have exposure to risks that are not reflected in the reported amounts of the entities' assets or liabilities (FIN-46(R), par. 10).

Variable Interests and Interests in Specified Assets

A variable interest in specified assets of a variable interest entity is deemed to be a variable interest in the entity only if the fair value of the specified assets is more than half of the total fair value of the entity's assets or if the holder has another variable interest in the entity as a whole. The expected losses and expected residual returns applicable to variable interests in specified assets of a variable interest entity are deemed to be expected losses and expected residual returns of the entity only if that variable interest is deemed to be a variable interest in the entity. Expected losses related to variable interests in specified assets are not considered part of the expected losses of the entity for purposes of determining the adequacy of the equity at risk or identifying the primary beneficiary in the entity unless the specified assets constitute a majority of the assets of the entity (FIN-46(R), par. 12).

An enterprise with a variable interest in specified assets of a variable interest entity shall treat a portion of the entity as a separate variable interest entity if the specified assets are essentially the only source of payment for specified liabilities or specified other interests. This requirement does not apply unless the entity has been determined to be a variable interest entity (FIN-46(R), par. 13).

Consolidation Policy

An enterprise shall consolidate a variable interest entity if that enterprise has a variable interest (or combination thereof) that will absorb a majority of the entity's expected losses, receive a majority of the entity's expected residual returns, or both. An entity shall consider the rights and obligations conveyed by its variable interests and the relationship of its variable interests with those of other parties to determine whether its variable interests will absorb a majority of a variable interest entity's expected losses, receive a majority of the entity's expected residual returns, or both (FIN-46(R), par. 14).

> ☞ **PRACTICE POINTER:** If one entity will absorb the majority of the variable interest entity's expected losses and another entity will receive a majority of the variable interest entity's expected returns, the entity absorbing the majority of the variable interest entity's expected losses should consolidate the entity (FIN-46(R), par. 14).

The entity that consolidates a variable interest entity is called the *primary beneficiary* of that entity. This determination is made at the time the enterprise becomes involved with the entity. The primary beneficiary shall reconsider its initial decision to consolidate a variable interest entity if either of the following occurs:

- There is a reallocation of the obligation to absorb expected losses and the right to receive expected residual returns between the primary beneficiary and other unrelated parties.

- The primary beneficiary sells or otherwise disposes of all or part of its variable interest to unrelated parties.

A holder of a variable interest that is not the primary beneficiary shall reconsider whether it is the primary beneficiary if the enterprise acquires additional variable interests in the entity (FIN-46(R), par. 15).

> ☞ **PRACTICE POINTER:** A related party includes not only those entities meeting the FAS-57 (Related Party Transactions) requirement but also those parties acting as de facto agents for the entity holding the variable interest. Examples of de facto agents of the enterprise include (1) a party that is dependent on the enterprise for the financing of its operations; (2) a party whose interest in the variable interest entity results from a contribution or loan from the enterprise; (3) an officer, director, or employee of the enterprise; and (4) a party that cannot sell, transfer, or encumber its interest in the entity without the approval of the enterprise (FIN-46(R), par. 16). If two or more related parties would qualify as the primary beneficiary if their interests were combined, then the party within the related party group that is most closely associated with the variable interest entity is the primary beneficiary. Significant judgment must be exercised in making this determination (FIN-46(R), par. 17).

Initial Measurement

Generally, the primary beneficiary of a variable interest entity shall initially measure the assets, liabilities, and noncontrolling interests of a newly consolidated entity at their fair values when the enterprise first becomes the primary beneficiary, which also is the date on which the enterprise would report the entity in its consolidated financial statements (FIN-46(R), par. 18).

The primary beneficiary of a variable interest entity that is under common control with the variable interest entity shall initially measure the assets, liabilities, and noncontrolling interests of a variable interest entity at the amounts at which they are carried in the accounts of the enterprise that controls the variable interest entity (FIN-46(R), par. 19).

The primary beneficiary of a variable interest entity shall initially measure assets and liabilities that it has transferred to that entity at the same amounts at which the assets and liabilities would have been measured had they not been transferred. No gain or loss is recognized on the transfer (FIN-46(R), par. 20).

> ☛ **PRACTICE POINTER:** This provision applies to transfers at, after, or shortly before the enterprise became the primary beneficiary (FIN-46(R), par. 20).

The excess, if any, of the fair value of the newly consolidated assets and the reported amounts of assets transferred by the primary beneficiary over the sum of the fair value of the consideration paid, the reported amount of any previously held interest, and the fair value of newly consolidated liabilities and noncontrolling interests are allocated and reported as a pro rata adjustment to the amounts that would have been assigned to all of the newly consolidated assets as specified in FAS-141 (Business Combinations). Any excess of the sum of the fair value of the consideration paid, the reported amount of any previously held interests, and the fair value of the newly consolidated liabilities and noncontrolling interests over the fair value of the newly consolidated identifiable assets and the reported amount of identifiable assets transferred by the primary beneficiary to the variable interest entity is reported as goodwill in the period in which the enterprise becomes the primary beneficiary if the variable interest entity is a business; otherwise it is reported as an extraordinary loss (FIN-46(R), par. 21).

Accounting after Initial Measurement

The principles of consolidated financial statements in ARB-51 apply to the primary beneficiaries' accounting for consolidated variable interest entities. After initial measurement, accounting shall be as if the entity were consolidated based on voting interests. Any specialized accounting requirements applicable to the type of business of the variable interest entity shall be applied as they would for a consolidated subsidiary. Intercompany balances and transactions are eliminated. Fees and other sources of income or expense between a primary beneficiary and a consolidated variable interest entity are eliminated against the related expense or income of the variable interest entity. The effect of this elimination on net income or expense of the variable interest entity is attributed to the primary beneficiary in the consolidated financial statements (FIN-46(R), par. 22).

Disclosure Requirements

The primary beneficiary shall disclose the following (in addition to the disclosures required by other standards) (FIN-46(R), par. 23):

- The nature, purpose, size, and activities of the variable interest entity
- The carrying amount and classification of consolidated assets that are collateral for the variable interest entity's obligations
- The lack of recourse if creditors of a consolidated variable interest entity have no recourse to the general credit of the primary beneficiary

An enterprise that holds a significant variable interest in a variable interest entity but is not the primary beneficiary shall disclose the following (FIN-46(R), par. 24):

- The nature of its involvement with the variable interest entity and when that involvement began
- The nature, purpose, size, and activities of the variable interest entity
- The enterprise's maximum exposure to loss as a result of its involvement with the variable interest entity

An enterprise that does not apply FIN-46(R) because the enterprise, after exhaustive effort, does not have the information necessary to (1) determine whether the entity is a variable interest entity, (2) determine whether the enterprise is the primary beneficiary of the variable interest entity, and (3) apply the consolidation provisions of FIN-46(R) to a variable interest entity where the enterprise is the primary beneficiary must make additional disclosures. These disclosures are (FIN-46(R), par. 26):

- The number of entities to which FIN-46(R) is not being applied and why the necessary information is not available.

- The nature, purpose, entity activities, size (if available), and the relation between the enterprise and entity or entities to which FIN-46(R) is not applied.

- The maximum amount of loss to which the reporting enterprise is exposed because of its involvement with the entity or entities.

- For all periods presented, the amount of income, expense, purchases, sales, or other activity measures, between the reporting enterprise and the entity or entities. This information does not have to be disclosed for prior periods if it is unavailable.

Illustration of the Application of FIN-46(R) to a Synthetic Lease

Crispy Doughnuts has entered into a synthetic lease transaction to acquire a corporate headquarters building. The benefit of a synthetic lease is that the lessee is viewed as the owner of the property for tax purposes and therefore receives the tax depreciation deduction, whereas the lease is treated as an operating lease for financial reporting purposes.

Crispy Doughnuts seeks to acquire a five-story office building in Norwalk, Connecticut. The cost of the property is $25 million and the lease term is six years. The lease on the facility will begin on 1/1/20X6.

Leasing America is a variable interest entity established for the purpose of acquiring the property needed by Crispy Doughnuts and leasing it to Crispy Doughnuts. Leasing America is financed with (1) funding of $20,000,000 in junior notes from Provident Capital; (2) funding of $3,000,000 in senior notes from TB&B Corp.; and (3) $2,000,000 of equity investment in ownership certificates issued by Leasing America. The equity investors are substantive operating companies, no single investor holds a majority of the equity stake, and the equity investors control Leasing America through possession of voting rights.

Because Leasing America is a newly formed entity, it does not have an operating history that demonstrates its ability to finance its activities without additional subordinated financial support. Also, Crispy Doughnuts is unable to determine whether Leasing America has as much equity invested as other entities that hold similar assets of similar quality in similar amounts. These two factors prevent Crispy Doughnuts from making a qualitative assessment of the sufficiency of Leasing America's equity investment.

Crispy Doughnuts is viewed as the owner of the property for tax purposes and the lease is structured to qualify as an operating lease under FAS-13 (Accounting for Leases). The monthly lease payment will equal the interest payments due on the notes plus a yield on the equity investors' capital investment. However, the present value of the lease payments will be less than 90% of the fair value of the leased property.

At the lease term's expiration, Crispy Doughnuts is required to remarket the building for Leasing America. Crispy Doughnuts is required to use the sales proceeds to retire the principal outstanding on the notes and to repay the holders of the equity investment. In addition, any deficiency in the sales proceeds will be absorbed by Leasing America and any excess sales proceeds will be remitted to Leasing America.

Crispy Doughnuts estimates cash flows from selling the property, with associated probabilities, as follows: $10 million (10%), $13 million (15%), $15 million (30%), $18 million (40%), and $24 million (5%).

The appropriate discount rate (the interest rate on risk-free investments for six years) is 6%.

Crispy Doughnuts will be required to consolidate Leasing America if at least one of three conditions exist: (1) the total equity investment at risk in Leasing America is insufficient to permit Leasing America to finance its activities without additional subordinated financial support, (2) the holders of the equity investment in Leasing America lack one or more of the three characteristics of a controlling financial interest, and (3) the equity investors lack the direct or indirect ability to make decisions about the entity's activities.

The holders of the equity investment in Leasing America have voting rights, the obligation to absorb losses if they occur, and the right to receive residual returns if they occur. Therefore, the equity investors in Leasing America do not lack any of the three characteristics of a controlling financial interest.

Because Crispy Doughnuts cannot perform a qualitative assessment of the sufficiency of Leasing America's equity investment, whether Crispy Doughnuts will have to consolidate Leasing America depends on a quantitative assessment of the sufficiency of Leasing America's equity investment at risk. The quantitative assessment is whether the amount of equity invested in Leasing America exceeds the estimate of the entity's expected losses based on reasonable quantitative evidence.

Crispy Doughnuts would calculate expected losses as follows:

Computation of Expected Cash Flows

Estimated Cash Flows	Probability (%)	Expected Cash Flows	Present Value Interest Factor (6%, 6 Yrs.)	Fair Value
$10,000,000	10	$1,000,000	.704961	$ 704,961
13,000,000	15	1,950,000	.704961	1,374,673
15,000,000	30	4,500,000	.704961	3,172,322
18,000,000	40	7,200,000	.704961	5,075,716
24,000,000	5	1,200,000	.704961	845,953
	100%	$15,850,000		$11,173,625

Computation of Expected Losses

Estimated Cash Flows	Expected Cash Flows	Difference Estimated (Losses) Residual Returns	Probability (%)	Expected Losses Based on Expected Cash Flows	Present Value Interest Factor (6%, 6 Yrs.)	Expected Losses Based on Fair Value
$10,000,000	$15,850,000	$(5,850,000)	10	(585,000)	.704961	$(412,402)
13,000,000	15,850,000	(2,850,000)	15	(427,500)	.704961	(301,371)
15,000,000	15,850,000	(850,000)	30	(255,000)	.704961	(179,765)
18,000,000	15,850,000	2,150,000	40	Considered in computing expected residual returns		
24,000,000	15,850,000	8,150,000	5			
			100%	$(1,267,500)		$(893,537)

It might appear that Crispy Doughnuts has to consolidate its investment in Leasing America because the equity investment in Leasing America, $2,000,000, is less than 10% of Leasing America's total assets ($25,000,000). However, as computed above, the amount of equity invested in Leasing America, $2,000,000, exceeds the estimate of Leasing America's losses, $893,537 (assuming reasonable quantitative evidence is available to estimate these losses). Therefore, Crispy Doughnuts does not have to consolidate Leasing America under the provisions of FIN-46(R).

RELATED CHAPTERS IN 2009 *GAAP GUIDE LEVEL A*

Chapter 4, "Business Combinations"
Chapter 14, "Equity Method"
Chapter 18, "Foreign Operations and Exchange"
Chapter 20, "Impairment of Long-Lived Assets"
Chapter 44, "Stockholders' Equity"

RELATED CHAPTERS IN 2009 *GAAP GUIDE LEVELS B, C, AND D*

Chapter 6, "Business Combinations"
Chapter 10, "Consolidated Financial Statements"
Chapter 14, "Equity Method"
Chapter 18, "Foreign Operations and Exchange"
Chapter 19, "Impairment of Long-Lived Assets"
Chapter 39, "Stockholders' Equity"

RELATED CHAPTER IN 2009 *INTERNATIONAL ACCOUNTING/FINANCIAL REPORTING STANDARDS GUIDE*

Chapter 10, "Consolidated Financial Statements"

APPENDIX: FAS-160

BACKGROUND

In December 2007, the FASB issued FAS-160 (Noncontrolling Interests in Consolidated Financial Statements: an amendment of ARB No. 51). FAS-160 amends certain of ARB-51's consolidation procedures to make them consistent with the requirements of FAS-141(R), which was issued at the same time as FAS-160. FAS-160 applies to all entities, other than not-for-profit organizations, that prepare consolidated financial statements. Not-for-profit organizations must continue to apply the guidance in ARB-51, before the amendments made by FAS-160, until the Board issues additional guidance.

OBJECTIVES

The Board's primary objective in issuing FAS-160 was to improve the relevance, comparability, and transparency of financial information provided in consolidated financial statements. FAS-160 achieves this objective by establishing accounting and reporting standards that ensure consistency in the reporting and disclosure of noncontrolling interests in consolidated financial statements, including the deconsolidation of a subsidiary. A secondary objective of FAS-160 was to converge the accounting for and reporting of noncontrolling interests in consolidated financial statements with the requirements of international financial reporting standards. This objective was achieved with the concurrent issuance by the IASB of IAS-27 (Consolidated and Separate Financial Statements), which was issued at the same time as FAS-160.

AMENDMENTS TO ARB-51

FAS-160 amends ARB-51 in the following five areas:

1. Nature and classification of the noncontrolling interest in the consolidated statement of financial position
2. Attributing net income and comprehensive income to the parent and the noncontrolling interest
3. Changes in a parent's ownership interest in a subsidiary

4. Deconsolidation of a subsidiary

5. Disclosures

Nature of Classification of the Noncontrolling Interest in the Consolidated Statement of Financial Position

FAS-160 defines a noncontrolling interest as a portion of equity in a subsidiary that is not attributable to a parent company, and thus clarifies a noncontrolling interest in a subsidiary as part of the equity of the consolidated group (FAS-160, par. 25). Furthermore, FAS-160 limits a noncontrolling interest to a parent's ownership of a financial instrument issued by a subsidiary that is classified as equity in the subsidiary's financial statements. A financial instrument that is classified as a liability in the subsidiary's financial statements based on the guidance in other standards does not represent an ownership interest and, therefore, is not a noncontrolling interest (FAS-160, par. 27).

Prior to FAS-160, there was limited guidance related to the classification and reporting of noncontrolling interests. This resulted in considerable diversity in practice with noncontrolling interests reported either as liabilities or in the mezzanine section between liabilities and equity. FAS-160 eliminates this diversity and improves comparability by requiring a noncontrolling interest to be reported in the consolidated statement of financial position within equity, separately from the parent's equity (FAS-160, par. 26).

Attributing Net Income and Comprehensive Income to the Parent and the Noncontrolling Interest

FAS-160 requires revenues, expenses, gains, losses, net income or loss, and other comprehensive income attributable to the noncontrolling interest to be included in the amount reported in consolidated net income (FAS-160 par. 29). Prior to FAS-160, these amounts were usually reported as an expense or other deduction in arriving at consolidated net income. FAS-160 also requires the amounts of consolidated net income attributable to the parent and to the noncontrolling interest to be disclosed on the face of the consolidated statement of income.

FAS-160 modifies how a subsidiary's losses are attributed to the parent and the noncontrolling interest in the unusual case in which losses attributable to the parent and the noncontrolling interest exceed their interests in the subsidiary's equity. Prior to FAS-160 such excess losses attributable to the noncontrolling interest were charged against the parent. However, per FAS-160, such excess losses attributable to the parent and the noncontrolling interest are charged to those interests, respectively. In other words, the noncontrolling interest must continue to be attributed its share of losses even if doing so results in a deficit noncontrolling interest balance (FAS-160, par. 31).

Changes in a Parent's Ownership Interest in a Subsidiary

FAS-160 establishes a single method of accounting for changes in a parent's ownership interest in a subsidiary when the parent retains its controlling financial interest in the subsidiary. Such a change in the parent's ownership interest in a subsidiary could include (FAS-160, par. 32):

- the parent purchases additional ownership interests in its subsidiary,
- the parent sells some of its ownership interests in its subsidiary,
- the subsidiary reacquires some of its ownership interests, or
- the subsidiary issues additional ownership interests.

FAS-160 clarifies that changes in a parent's ownership while retaining a controlling financial interest in the subsidiary must be accounted for as equity transactions, and, therefore, no gain or loss shall be recognized in consolidated net income or comprehensive income. Note that prior to FAS-160, a decrease in a parent's ownership could be accounted for as either an equity transaction or as a transaction with a gain or loss recognized in the income statement. Per FAS-160, the noncontrolling interest carrying amount is required to be adjusted to reflect the change in its ownership interest in the subsidiary, and any difference between the fair value of the consideration received or paid and the amount by which the noncontrolling interest is adjusted must be recognized in the equity attributable to the parent (FAS-160, par. 33). Similarly, if a change in a parent's ownership interest occurs in a subsidiary that has accumulated other comprehensive income, the carrying amount of accumulated other comprehensive income shall be adjusted to reflect the change in ownership interest with a corresponding charge or credit to the equity attributable to the parent (FAS-160, par. 34).

Illustration of Changes in a Parent's Ownership Interest in a Subsidiary

Example 1

Subsidiary A has 50,000 shares of common stock outstanding, all of which are owned by its parent, ABC Co. The carrying amount of Subsidiary A's equity is $800,000. ABC Co. sells 10,000 of its shares in Subsidiary A to an unrelated entity for $200,000 in cash, reducing its ownership interest from 100 percent to 80 percent. That transaction is accounted for by recognizing a noncontrolling interest in the amount of $160,000 ($800,000 × 20 percent). The $40,000 excess of the cash received ($200,000) over the adjustment to the carrying amount of the noncontrolling interest ($160,000) is recognized as an increase in additional paid-in capital attributable to ABC Co. The sale of Subsidiary A's shares by ABC Co. is accounted for as an equity transaction in the consolidated financial statements as follows:

Cash	$200,000	
Noncontrolling interest		$ 160,000
Additional paid-in capital (ABC Co.)		40,000

Example 2

Subsidiary A has 50,000 shares of common stock outstanding. Of those shares, 45,000 are owned by its parent, ABC Co., and 5,000 are owned by other shareholders (a noncontrolling interest in Subsidiary A). The carrying amount of Subsidiary A's equity is $1,200,000. Of that amount, $1,080,000 is attrlbutable to ABC Co., and $120,000 is a noncontrolling interest in Subsidiary A. Subsidiary A issues 10,000 previously unissued shares to a third party for $480,000 in cash, reducing ABC Co.'s ownership interest in Subsidiary A from 90 percent to 75 percent (45,000 shares owned by ABC Co. / 60,000 issued shares).

Even though the percentage of ABC Co.'s ownership interest in Subsidiary A is reduced when Subsidiary A issues additional shares to a third party, ABC Co.'s investment in Subsidiary A increases to $1,260,000, calculated as 75 percent of Subsidiary A's equity of $1,680,000 ($1,200,000 + $480,000). Therefore, ABC Co. recognizes a $180,000 increase in its investment in Subsidiary A ($1,260,000 − $1,080,000) and a corresponding increase in its additional paid-in capital (that is, the additional paid-in capital attributable to ABC Co.). In addition, the noncontrolling interest is increased to $420,000, calculated as 25 percent of $1,680,000. The sale of additional shares by Subsidiary A is accounted for as an equity transaction in the consolidated financial statements as follows:

Cash	$480,000	
Noncontrolling interest		$ 300,000
Additional paid-in capital (ABC Co.)		180,000

Example 3

Subsidiary A has 50,000 shares of common stock outstanding. Of those shares, 40,000 are owned by its parent, ABC Co., and 10,000 are owned by other shareholders (a noncontrolling interest in Subsidiary A). The carrying amount of the noncontrolling interest is $240,000, which includes $20,000 of accumulated other comprehensive income. ABC Co. pays $150,000 in cash to purchase 5,000 shares held by the noncontrolling shareholders (50 percent of the noncontrolling interest), increasing its ownership interest from 80 percent to 90 percent. That transaction is recognized by reducing the carrying amount of the noncontrolling interest by $120,000 ($240,000 × 50 percent). The $30,000 excess of the cash paid ($150,000) over the adjustment to the carrying amount of the noncontrolling interest ($120,000) is recognized as a decrease in additional paid-in capital attributable to ABC Co. In addition, ABC Co.'s share of accumulated other comprehensive income is increased by $10,000 ($20,000 × 50 percent) through a corresponding decrease in additional paid-in capital attributable to ABC Co. The purchase of shares from the noncontrolling shareholders is accounted for as an equity transaction in the consolidated financial statements as follows:

Noncontrolling interest	$120,000	
Additional paid-in capital (ABC Co.)	40,000	
Accumulated other comprehensive income (ABC Co.)		$ 150,000
Cash		10,000

Deconsolidation of a Subsidiary

FAS-160 requires a parent to deconsolidate a subsidiary as of the date the parent ceases to have a controlling financial interest in the subsidiary. For example, the following events would result in the deconsolidation of a subsidiary (FAS-160, par. 35):

- A parent sells some or all of its ownership interest in the subsidiary, and as a result, the parent no longer has a controlling financial interest in the subsidiary

- A contractual agreement expires, and the parent's control of the subsidiary is dependent on that agreement

- The subsidiary issues additional shares, thereby reducing the parent's ownership interest in the subsidiary to a point that does not result in the parent having a controlling financial interest

- The subsidiary becomes under the control of a government, court, administrator, or regulator

When deconsolidating a subsidiary, the parent shall measure any noncontrolling interest it retains in the former subsidiary at its fair value and recognize a gain or loss in net income attributable to the parent, measured as the difference between:

1. The aggregate of:
   a. The fair value of any consideration received
   b. The fair value of any retained noncontrolling investment in the former subsidiary at the date the subsidiary is deconsolidated
   c. The carrying amount of any noncontrolling interest in the former subsidiary held by any party other than the former parent (including any accumulated other comprehensive income attributable to the noncontrolling interest) at the date the subsidiary is deconsolidated
2. The carrying amount of the former subsidiary's assets and liabilities

---

Illustration of Gain or Loss on the Deconsolidation of a Subsidiary

Sub Co. has 10,000 shares of common stock outstanding. Of those shares, 8,000 are owned by its parent, ABC Co., and 2,000 are owned by other shareholders (a noncontrolling interest in Sub Co.). The carrying amount of Sub Co.'s equity is $1,000,000. ABC Co. sells 4,000 of its shares in Sub Co. to an unrelated entity for $600,000 in cash, reducing its ownership interest from 80 percent to 40 percent. Therefore, ABC Co. no longer has a controlling interest in Sub Co., and would recognize a gain of $400,000 on the deconsolidation of Sub Co., calculated as follows:

Fair value of consideration received	$600,000
Fair value of retained noncontrolling investment in Sub Co.	600,000
Carrying amount of noncontrolling interest in Sub Co. held by parties other than ABC Co.	200,000
	$1,400,000
Less: carrying amount of Sub Co.'s net assets	− 1,000,000
Gain on deconsolidation of Sub Co.	$400,000

Note that FAS-160 does not apply to the deconsolidation of a subsidiary through a nonreciprocal transfer to owners, such as a spinoff. In this case, the guidance provided in APB-29 (Accounting for Nonmonetary Transactions) applies (FAS-160, par. 36).

Disclosures

FAS-160 requires expanded disclosures in the consolidated financial statements that clearly identify and distinguish between the interests of the parent and the interests of the noncontrolling owners of a subsidiary. A parent with one or more less-than-wholly-owned subsidiaries shall disclose for each reporting period (FAS-160, par. 38):

- Separately, on the face of the consolidated financial statements, the amounts of consolidated net income and consolidated comprehensive income, including the amounts of each that are attributable to the parent and the noncontrolling interest

- Either in the notes or on the face of the consolidated income statement, amounts attributable to the parent for the following, if reported in the consolidated financial statements:
  — Income from continuing operations
  — Discontinued operations
  — Extraordinary items

- Either in the consolidated statement of changes in equity, if presented, or in the notes to the consolidated financial statements, a reconciliation at the beginning and the end of the period of the carrying amount of total equity (net assets), including the amounts attributable to the parent and to the noncontrolling interest. The reconciliation must separately disclose:
  — Net income
  — Transactions with owners acting in their capacity as owners, showing separately contributions from and distributions to owners
  — Each component of other comprehensive income

- In the notes to the consolidated financial statements, a separate schedule that shows the effects of any changes in a parent's ownership interest in a subsidiary on the equity attributable to the parent

If a subsidiary is deconsolidated, the parent is required to disclose (FAS-160, par. 39):

- The amount of any gain or loss recognized

- The portion of any gain or loss related to the remeasurement of any retained investment in the former subsidiary to its fair value

- The caption in the income statement in which the gain or loss is recognized unless separately presented on the face of the income statement

EFFECTIVE DATE

FAS-160 is effective for fiscal years, and interim periods within those fiscal years, beginning on or after December 15, 2008. Earlier adoption is prohibited. The effective date is the same as that for FAS-141(R).

TRANSITION

FAS-160 shall be applied prospectively as of the beginning of the fiscal year in which the statement is initially applied, except for the requirements for presentation and disclosure. The presentation and disclosure requirements are required to be applied retrospectively for all periods presented, as follows (FAS-160, par. 5):

- The noncontrolling interest must be reclassified to equity
- Consolidated net income must be adjusted to include the net income attributed to the noncontrolling interest
- Consolidated comprehensive income must be adjusted to include the comprehensive income attributable to the noncontrolling interest
- The additional disclosures required by paragraphs 38 and 39 of FAS-160, as discussed above, must be provided

CHAPTER 8
CONTINGENCIES, RISKS,
AND UNCERTAINTIES

CONTENTS

OVERVIEW

Accounting for contingencies is an important feature of the preparation of financial statements in accordance with GAAP, because of the many uncertainties that may exist at the end of each accounting period. Standards governing accounting for loss contingencies require accrual and/or note disclosure when specified recognition and disclosure criteria are met. Gain contingencies generally are not recognized in financial statements but may be disclosed.

GAAP concerning accounting for contingencies are provided in the following pronouncements:

FAS-5	Accounting for Contingencies
FAS-141	Business Combinations
FIN-14	Reasonable Estimation of the Amount of a Loss
FIN-45	Guarantor's Accounting and Disclosure Requirements for Guarantees, Including Indirect Guarantees of Indebtedness of Others

> **OBSERVATION:**   AICPA Statement of Position (SOP) 94-6 (Disclosure of Certain Significant Risks and Uncertainties) is closely related to the requirements of FAS-5 (Accounting for Contingencies). Although many SOPs are specialized in their application, SOP 94-6 has broad applicability and care should be taken not to overlook its reporting requirements in the following four areas:
>
> 1. Nature of an entity's operations
> 2. Use of certain information in the preparation of financial statements
> 3. Certain significant estimates
> 4. Current vulnerability to concentrations
>
> SOP 94-6 is covered in the *GAAP Guide Levels B, C, and D,* which includes a wide variety of FASB, AICPA, and EITF authoritative literature not included in the *GAAP Guide Level A.*

2009 TRANSITION GUIDANCE FOR FAS-141(R) AND FAS-160

The FASB has recently issued FAS-141(R), *Business Combinations,* which is effective for business combinations for which the acquisition date is on or after the beginning of the first annual reporting period beginning on or after December 15, 2008. The FASB has also issued FAS-160, *Noncontrolling Interests in Consolidated Financial*

Statements, an Amendment of ARB No. 51, which is effective for fiscal years, and interim periods within those fiscal years, beginning on or after December 15, 2008. Because these standards are not effective for some companies until December 2009, and because early adoption is prohibited, the 2009 *GAAP Guide* reflects the requirements of FAS-141 prior to its revision in December 2007 and does not reflect the requirements of FAS-160. There is a discussion of the changes in the accounting for business combinations under FAS-141(R) in the Appendix to Chapter 4, "Business Combinations." Similarly, the Appendix to Chapter 7, "Consolidated Financial Statements," includes a discussion of the requirements of FAS-160. However, any effects of FAS-141(R) and/or FAS-160 in this chapter have not been reflected in this edition. Therefore, if a company is subject to the requirements of FAS-141(R) and/or FAS-160, the reader is referred to FAS-141(R) and FAS-160 for these new requirements.

BACKGROUND

A *contingency* is an existing condition, situation, or set of circumstances involving uncertainty that may, through one or more related future events, result in the acquisition or loss of an asset or the incurrence or avoidance of a liability, usually with the concurrence of a gain or loss. The resulting gain or loss is referred to as a *gain contingency* or a *loss contingency.*

The existence of a loss contingency may be established on or before the date of the financial statements, or after the date of the financial statements but prior to the issuance date of the financial statements. After a loss contingency is established, the probability of its developing into an actual loss must be evaluated. Accounting for a loss contingency is based upon the degree of probability that one or more future events will occur that will confirm that a loss has already occurred. Gain contingencies are ordinarily not recorded until they are actually realized, although note disclosure in the financial statements may be necessary.

Loss contingencies may arise from the risk of exposure resulting from items such as the following (FAS-5, par. 4):

- Collectibility of receivables
- Property loss by fire, explosion, or other hazards
- Expropriation of assets
- Pending or threatened litigation, claims, or assessments
- Product warranties or defects
- Catastrophic losses of property

☞ **PRACTICE POINTER:** Not all uncertainties in the accounting process are *contingencies*, as that term is used in FAS 5. Many estimates that are inherent in the financial reporting process are **not** contingencies, and the authoritative literature covered in this section does **not** apply. For example, depreciable assets have a reasonably estimated life, and depreciation expense is used to allocate the cost of the asset systematically over its estimated useful life.

OBSERVATION: FAS-5 does not apply to accounting for income taxes because FIN-48 addresses the uncertainty associated with income taxes.

LOSS CONTINGENCIES

Classification

A loss contingency will develop into an actual loss only upon the occurrence of one or more future events, whose likelihood of occurring may vary significantly. The likelihood that future events will confirm a loss must be classified as (*a*) probable (likely to occur), (*b*) reasonably possible (between *probable* and *remote*), or (*c*) remote (slight chance of occurring) (FAS-5, par. 3).

The accounting treatment for loss contingencies flows logically from the three ranges of probability described in the previous paragraph. Figure 8-1 provides the general structure of accounting that is required.

Accounting and Reporting

Depending upon whether a loss contingency is classified as probable, reasonably possible, or remote, it should be (*a*) accrued as a charge to income as of the date of the financial statements, (*b*) disclosed by note to the financial statements, or (*c*) neither accrued nor disclosed.

The following two conditions must be met for a *loss contingency* to be accrued as a charge to income as of the date of the financial statements (FAS-5, par. 8):

1. It is *probable* that as of the date of the financial statements an asset has been impaired or a liability incurred, based on information available before the actual issuance date of the financial statements.

It is implicit in this condition that it must be probable that one or more future events will occur to confirm the loss.

2. The amount of loss can be estimated reasonably.

☞ **PRACTICE POINTER:** If a loss contingency is classified as *probable* and only a range of possible loss (similar to a minimum–maximum) can be established, then the **minimum** amount in the range is accrued, unless some other amount within the range appears to be a better estimate (FIN-14, par. 3). The range of possible loss must also be disclosed.

Loss contingencies that are accrued ordinarily require note disclosure so that the financial statements are not misleading. This disclosure ordinarily consists of the nature of the contingency and, in some circumstances, the amount accrued (FAS-5, par. 9).

Illustration of Accrued Contingent Liability

Following is a pro forma illustration of disclosure of a loss contingency for which the probability of future events confirming a loss is high and for which an amount can be reasonably estimated:

> During 20X8, the Company became aware of past circumstances (describe nature of contingency) that management believes are likely to require recognition of a loss(es) in future year(s). While the exact amount of this (these) loss(es) is not known, a reasonable estimate, based on information currently available, is $XXX. This amount has been recognized as a loss in the current year and appears as a contingent liability (provide title) in the 20X8 statement of financial position. Recognition of this loss had the impact of reducing net income and earnings per share by $XX and $XX, respectively, in 20X8.

If one or both conditions for the accrual of a loss contingency are not met and the probability of loss is considered either *probable* or *reasonably possible*, financial statement disclosure of the loss contingency is required. The disclosure shall contain a description of the nature of the loss contingency and the range of possible loss, or include a statement that an estimate of the loss cannot be made (FAS-5, par. 10).

Figure 8-1:   Probability That Future Event(s) Will Confirm Loss

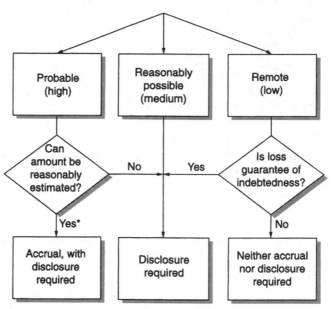

* Includes estimation of a range of loss, in which case the minimum amount is accrued and the amount of the range is disclosed.

Litigation, Claims, or Assessments

If both conditions for the accrual of a loss contingency are met, an accrual for the estimated amount of pending or threatened litigation and actual or possible claims or assessments is required. Some of the factors that should be considered in determining whether the conditions for accrual have been met are the (*a*) nature of the litigation, claim, or assessment, (*b*) progress of the case, including progress after the date of the financial statements but before the issuance date of the financial statements, (*c*) opinions of legal counsel, and (*d*) management's intended response to the litigation, claim, or assessment (FAS-5, par. 36).

Illustration of Disclosed Loss Contingency

Following is a pro forma illustration of disclosure of a loss contingency for which the probability of future events confirming the loss is reasonably possible and for which the outcome is sufficiently uncertain that accrual is not appropriate:

> During 20X8, a suit was filed against the company by a former employee alleging that the company engaged in discriminatory employment practices. The suit requests damages of $1,000,000. Management has indicated its plans to vigorously contest this suit and believes that the loss, if any, resulting from the suit will not have a material impact on the company's financial position, results of operations, or cash flows in future years.

Allowance for Uncollectible Receivables

For the purposes of GAAP, accounts receivable must be reported at their net realizable value. Net realizable value is equal to the total amount of the receivables less an estimated allowance for uncollectible accounts.

Under FAS-5, an accrual for a loss contingency must be charged to income if both of the following conditions are met:

- It is *probable* that as of the date of the financial statements an enterprise does not expect to collect the full amount of its accounts receivable, based on information available before the actual issuance of the financial statements.

- The amount of loss contingency (uncollectible receivables) can be *reasonably estimated*.

If both of these conditions are met, an accrual for the estimated amount of uncollectible receivables must be made even if the uncollectible receivables cannot be identified specifically (FAS-5, par. 22). An enterprise may base its estimate of uncollectible receivables on its prior experience, the experience of other enterprises in the same industry, the debtor's ability to pay, and/or an appraisal of current economic conditions (FAS-5, par. 23).

> ☛ **PRACTICE POINTER:** A significant uncertainty exists in the ultimate collection of accounts receivable if an enterprise is unable to estimate reasonably the amount of its uncollectible receivables. If a significant uncertainty does exist in the collection of the receivables, use the installment sales method, cost-recovery method, or some other method of revenue recognition (APB-10, par. 12).

Product or Service Warranty Obligation

A product or service warranty obligation is a contingency under the provisions of FAS-5, because of the potential claims that may result from the warranty. If both of the conditions for the accrual of a loss contingency are met, an accrual for the estimated amount of a warranty obligation must be made even if the warranty obligation cannot be identified specifically. An enterprise may base its estimate of a warranty obligation on its prior experience, the experience of other enterprises in the same industry, and/or an appraisal of current economic conditions. If an enterprise is unable to estimate reasonably the amount of its warranty obligation and the range of possible loss is wide, significant uncertainty exists as to whether a sale should be recorded (FAS-5, par. 25). If a significant uncertainty does exist in estimating a warranty obligation, a sale shall not be recorded and the installment sales method, cost-recovery method, or some other method of revenue recognition shall be used (APB-10, par. 12).

Loss Contingencies Arising after the Date of the Financial Statements

A loss contingency that is classified as *probable* or *reasonably possible*, that occurs after the balance sheet date but before the issuance date of the financial statements, may have to be disclosed to avoid misleading financial statements. If professional judgment deems this type of disclosure necessary, the disclosure shall contain a description of the nature of the loss contingency and the range of possible loss, or include a statement that no estimate of the loss can be made. It may be desirable to disclose this type of loss contingency by supplementing the historical financial statements with pro forma statements reflecting the loss as if it occurred at the date of the financial statements (FAS-5, par. 11).

☛ **PRACTICE POINTER:** Disclosing loss contingencies that arise after the date of the financial statements may require either adjustment to the financial statements or note disclosure, depending on the nature of the loss contingency. If the subsequent event confirms or provides additional information on a condition that existed at the financial statement date, make an adjustment to the financial statements. Otherwise, disclose the loss contingency, which, in some cases, may be made best by presenting pro forma restated financial information as a part of the note disclosure.

Unasserted Claims or Assessments

An *unasserted claim* is one that has not been asserted by the claimant because the claimant has no knowledge of the existing claim or has not elected to assert the existing claim. If it is *probable* that an unasserted claim will be asserted by the claimant and it is *probable* or *reasonably possible* that an unfavorable outcome will result, the unasserted claim must be disclosed in the financial statements. If these conditions are not met, however, disclosure is not required for unasserted claims or assessments in which the potential claimant apparently has no knowledge of the claim's existence (FAS-5, par. 38).

Disclosure of Noninsured Property

An enterprise may be underinsured or not insured at all against the risk of future loss or damage to its property by fire, explosion, or other hazard. The fact that an enterprise's property is underinsured or not insured at all constitutes an existing uncertainty as defined by FAS-5. The absence of insurance does not mean, however, that an asset has been impaired or a liability incurred as of the date of the financial statements (FAS-5, par. 28). Therefore, FAS-5 does not require financial statement disclosure of noninsurance or underinsurance of possible losses, but specifically states that it does not discourage this practice (FAS-5, par. 103).

> ☛ **PRACTICE POINTER:** The removal of insurance does not, in and of itself, mean that a loss has already been incurred and that a contingent liability should be recorded. While the uninsured enterprise assumes greater risk than an insured one, a contingent loss results from a past event and the removal of insurance does not qualify for such an event.

Appropriations of Retained Earnings

FAS-5 does not prohibit an enterprise from appropriating specific amounts of retained earnings for potential loss contingencies. The amount of appropriated retained earnings, however, must be reported within the stockholders' equity section of the balance sheet and clearly identified as an appropriation of retained earnings. In addition, the following rules must be observed (FAS-5, par. 15):

- No costs or losses shall be charged against the appropriated retained earnings and no part of the appropriated retained earnings may be transferred to income or in any way used to affect the determination of net income for any period.
- The appropriated retained earnings shall be restored intact to retained earnings when the appropriation is no longer considered necessary.

Preacquisition Contingencies

All preacquisition contingencies arising in a purchase business combination other than certain tax-related contingencies are to be included in the purchase price determination (FAS-141, par. 40). Tax-related contingencies that exist at the acquisition date (e.g., the potential tax effects of temporary differences and carryforwards, income tax uncertainties related to the tax basis of an acquired asset or liability) are accounted for in accordance with the provisions of FAS-109 (Accounting for Income Taxes) (FAS-141, footnote 13).

The fair value of the preacquisition contingency is used in allocating the purchase price to individual assets and liabilities if the preacquisition contingency's fair value can be determined during the *allocation period* (FAS-141, par. 40a). The *allocation period* is the period that is required by the purchaser to identify and quantify the acquired assets and assumed liabilities for the purpose of allocating the total cost of the acquisition in accordance with FAS-141 (Business Combinations). The allocation period should not typically exceed one year from when the business combination is consummated (FAS-141, par. F1).

If the preacquisition contingency's fair value cannot be determined during the allocation period, an estimated dollar amount is assigned to the preacquisition contingency in allocating the purchase price to individual assets and liabilities if:

- Prior to the end of the allocation period information becomes available that indicates that it is probable that an asset existed, a liability has been incurred, or an asset was impaired at the time the business combination was consummated, and

- The amount of the asset or liability can be reasonably estimated (FAS-141, par. 40b).

An adjustment to the recorded amount of the preacquisition contingency that occurs after the allocation period is included in the determination of net income in the period in which the adjustment occurs (FAS-141, par. 41).

GAIN CONTINGENCIES

Gain contingencies may be disclosed in the financial statements by note, but should not be reflected in income, because doing so may result in recognizing revenue prior to its realization. Care should be exercised in disclosing gain contingencies to avoid misleading implications as to the recognition of revenue prior to its realization (FAS-5, par. 17).

ACCOUNTING FOR GUARANTEES

Guarantees are a relatively common business transaction. Examples include (1) the guarantee of the indebtedness of another party, (2) obligations of commercial banks under "standby letters of credit," and (3) guarantees to repurchase receivables that have been sold. The FASB has observed differences in how companies inter-pret the need for issuers of guarantees to recognize a liability and the disclosures required by issuers of guarantees. FIN-45 (Guarantor's Accounting and Disclosure Requirements for Guarantees, Including Indirect Guarantees of Indebtedness of Others) intends to clarify both of these issues. It carries forward without reconsideration the guidance provided by FIN-34 (Disclo-sure of Indirect Guarantees of Indebtedness of Others) related to indirect guarantees of the indebtedness of others (FIN-45, par. 1).

FIN-45 does not specify the subsequent accounting for guaran-tees that have been recognized. If a guarantee represents a deriva-tive financial instrument, appropriate accounting is in conformity with FAS-133 (Accounting for Derivative Instruments and Hedging Activities). If the guarantee does not qualify for derivative account-ing, guidance is provided by FAS-5 (FIN-45, par. 2).

FIN-45 applies to guarantees that have any of the following char-acteristics:

- Contracts that contingently require the guarantor to make pay-ments (in cash, financial instruments, other assets, shares of its stock, or provision of services) to the guaranteed party based on changes in the *underlying* that is related to an asset, liability, or an equity security of the guaranteed party (FIN-45, par. 3a). (FAS-133 uses the term *underlying* to denote a specified interest rate, security price, commodity price, foreign exchange rate, index of price or rate, or other variable. An underlying may be a price or rate of an asset or liability but is not the asset or liability itself.)

- Contracts that require the guarantor to make payments to the guaranteed party based on another entity's failure to perform under an obligating agreement (FIN-45, par. 3b).

- Indemnification agreements that contingently require the indemnifying party to make payments to the indemnified party based on changes in an underlying that is related to an asset, liability, or equity security of the indemnified party (FIN-45, par. 3c).

- Indirect guarantees of the indebtedness of others (FIN-45, par. 3d).

Commercial letters of credit or other loan commitments that are commonly thought of as guarantees of funding are not included in the scope of FIN-45 because they do not meet the characteristics of guarantees as previously stated. Similarly, the scope of FIN-45 does not include indemnifications or guarantees based on an entity's own future performance (FIN-45, par. 4).

The provisions of FIN-45 related to recognizing a liability do *not* apply to the following, but the disclosure requirements of FIN-45 do apply in these circumstances (FIN-45, par. 7):

- Product warranties
- Guarantees that are accounted for as derivatives
- Guarantees that represent contingent consideration in a business combination
- Guarantees for which the guarantor's obligation would be reported by an equity item (i.e., rather than a liability)
- An original lessee's guarantee of lease payments when the lessee remains secondarily liable in conjunction with being relieved from being the primary obligor under a lease restructuring
- Guarantee issued between either parents and their subsidiaries or corporations under common control
- A parent's guarantee of a subsidiary's debt to a third party, and a subsidiary's guarantee of the debt owed to a third party by either its parent or another subsidiary of the parent

Disclosure of Guarantees

FIN-45 clarified that a guarantor is required to disclose the following information (FIN-45, par. 13):

- The nature of the guarantee, including the approximate term of the guarantee, how it arose, and the events or circumstances that would require the guarantor to perform under the guarantee
- The maximum potential amount of future payments under the guarantee
- The carrying amount of the liability, if any, for the guarantor's obligations under the guarantee
- The nature and extent of any recourse provisions or available collateral that would enable the guarantor to recover the amounts paid under the guarantee

For product warranties, the guarantor is required to disclose its accounting policy and method of determining its liability under the warranty rather than disclosing the maximum potential amount for future payments under the guarantee. In addition, a tabular reconciliation of the changes in the guarantor's product warranty liability for the reporting period is required (FIN-45, par. 14).

The FASB states that the previous practice of reporting only the nature and amount of guarantees does not provide the level of useful information that is now required by FIN-45.

Recognition of a Guarantee Liability

In addition clarifying the disclosure required for guarantee liabilities, FIN-45 clarifies that a guarantor is required to recognize, at the inception of a guarantee, a liability for the obligations it has under-taken, including its ongoing obligations to perform under the terms of a guarantee in the event the specified triggering events or conditions occur. The initial recording of the liability should be the fair value of the guarantee at its inception (FIN-45, pars. 8–9).

When a liability due to the issuance of a guarantee is recorded, the nature of the offsetting debit depends on the nature of the original transaction giving rise to the guarantee (FIN-45, par. 11). If the guarantee is issued in a standalone transaction *for consideration*, cash or a receivable would be debited. If the guarantee is issued in a standalone transaction to an unrelated party *for no consideration*, an expense would be debited. If the guarantee is issued as part of a sale of assets, a product, or a business, the consideration received in the sale would be allocated between the guarantee and the assets, product, or business sold. If the guarantee relates to the formation of a partially owned business or joint venture, the offsetting debit would increase the value of the investment account. If a lessee provides a guarantee of the lease property's residual value in an operating lease, the offsetting debit is to prepaid rent.

The FASB states that currently many entities may not be recognizing liabilities for a guarantee because (1) the recognition requirements in FAS-5 related to loss contingencies have not been met at the inception of the guarantee and (2) the premium for the guarantee was not separately identified because it was embedded in purchase or sales agreements, service contracts, joint venture agreements, or other commercial agreements (FIN-45, par. 9). FIN-45 indicates that an entity is to record the fair value of a guarantee at inception, even if it is *not* probable that payments will be required under the guarantee (FIN-45, par. 9). The Interpretation also indicates that where the premium for the guarantee is not separately identified it must be estimated. The party issuing the guarantee should consider what the premium would be if the guarantee had been issued on a standalone basis in a transaction with an unrelated party as a practical expedient (FIN-45, par. 9b).

Indirect Guarantees

Indirect guarantees arise under an agreement that obligates one entity to transfer funds to a second entity upon the occurrence of specified events under conditions whereby the funds become legally available to the creditors of the second entity and those creditors may enforce the second entity's claim against the first entity under the agreement (FIN-45, par. 17). Although the risk of loss may be remote, indirect guarantees of the indebtedness of others must be disclosed in the financial statements (FAS-5, par. 12).

DISCLOSURE OF CERTAIN LOSS CONTINGENCIES
IMPORTANT NOTICE FOR 2009

As the 2009 *GAAP Guide Level A* goes to press, the FASB has issued an Exposure Draft of a Proposed Statement of Financial Accounting Standards titled "Disclosure of Certain Loss Contingencies—an amendment of FASB Statements No. 5 and 141(R)." The current FASB Technical Plan calls for a final standard to be issued in the fourth quarter of 2008, and would be effective for annual and interim periods ending after December 15, 2008.

The proposed standard would expand the disclosures about loss contingencies within the scope of FAS-5 and FAS-141(R), with limited exceptions. In addition, the proposed standard would: (1) expand the types of loss contingencies that require disclosure, (2) require the disclosure of certain quantitative and qualitative information related to the contingency, and (3) require a tabular reconciliation of recognized loss contingencies. Moreover, the proposed standard provides an exemption from certain disclosure items if making the disclosure would adversely affect the company in a dispute. The proposed standard does not change the criteria for recognizing and measuring contingencies articulated in FAS-5 and FAS-141(R).

The disclosures required under the proposed standard apply to: (1) loss contingencies recognized in a business combination, (2) loss contingencies under FAS-5 where a liability is recognized in the financial statements (i.e., the loss is both probable and reasonably estimable), and (3) loss contingencies under FAS-5 that are not recognized as a liability but where the probability of loss is more than remote. However, even if the probability of loss is remote, disclosure is required if: (1) the contingency is likely to be resolved within one year from the date of the financial statements, and (2) the contingency could have a severe impact on the entity's financial position, results of operations, or cash flows. A severe impact is more than material but less than catastrophic (i.e., bankruptcy) and indicates a significant financially disruptive effect on the normal functioning of the entity. Disclosures related to loss contingencies due to asset impairments would continue to be disclosed in accordance with FAS-5.

The entity is to provide quantitative information about the entity's exposure to loss, including the amount of the claim or assessment. The entity may disclose its best estimate of the possible loss or range of loss if it believes that the claim or assessment is not representative of the entity's exposure. In addition, the proposed standard requires numerous qualitative disclosures, and disclosures related to existing insurance and indemnification agreements. Finally, the entity must provide a tabular reconciliation of the liability for loss contingencies recognized in the statement of financial position from the beginning to the end of the year.

RELATED CHAPTERS IN 2009 *GAAP GUIDE LEVEL A*

Chapter 3, "Balance Sheet Classification and Related Display Issues"
Chapter 4, "Business Combinations"
Chapter 21, "Income Taxes"
Chapter 41, "Revenue Recognition"

RELATED CHAPTERS IN 2009 *GAAP GUIDE LEVELS B, C, AND D*

Chapter 4, "Balance Sheet Classification and Related Display Issues"
Chapter 6, "Business Combinations"
Chapter 11, "Contingencies, Risks, and Uncertainties"
Chapter 20, "Income Taxes"
Chapter 36, "Revenue Recognition"

RELATED CHAPTERS IN 2009 *INTERNATIONAL ACCOUNTING/FINANCIAL REPORTING STANDARDS GUIDE*

Chapter 3, "Presentation of Financial Statements"
Chapter 7, "Business Combinations"
Chapter 20, "Income Taxes"
Chapter 28, "Provisions, Contingent Liabilities, and Contingent Assets"
Chapter 30, "Revenue"

CHAPTER 9
CONVERTIBLE DEBT AND DEBT
WITH WARRANTS

CONTENTS

OVERVIEW

Debt may be issued with a conversion feature or a feature that permits the separate purchase of other securities, usually common stock of the issuing company. These "hybrid" debt/equity securities generally derive some portion of their value from the equity component (i.e., the conversion feature or the separate purchase option) that is included in the issue price. The significant accounting question that arises is the recognition, if any, of the equity feature when a hybrid security is issued. That treatment, in turn, affects the subsequent accounting when the conversion feature or separate purchase option is exercised.

GAAP in the area of convertible debt and debt issued with purchase options are included in the following pronouncements:

APB-14   Accounting for Convertible Debt and Debt Issued with Stock Purchase Warrants

FAS-84   Induced Conversions of Convertible Debt

BACKGROUND

Convertible debt is convertible into the common stock of the issuer or an affiliated enterprise. Common characteristics of convertible debt are (APB-14, par. 3):

- The interest rate is lower than the interest rate on an equivalent, but not convertible, security.

- The initial conversion price is greater than the market value of the underlying security.

- The conversion price does not change (except pursuant to certain antidilutive considerations).

- The security usually is callable by the issuer.

- The debt usually is subordinate to the nonconvertible debt of the issuer.

Conversion of the convertible debt requires the holders to relinquish their status as debtholders to become stockholders.

Debt also may be issued with detachable purchase warrants that usually permit the holders to purchase shares of common stock at a set price for a specified period. The holders of the detachable warrants are not required to relinquish their status as debtholders to become stockholders.

CONVERTIBLE DEBT

Issuance

Under current GAAP, when convertible debt is issued, no portion of the proceeds is accounted for as attributable to the conversion feature. At that time, the debt issue is treated entirely as debt and no formal accounting recognition is assigned to the value inherent in the conversion feature. In reaching this conclusion, APB-14 (Accounting for Convertible Debt and Debt Issued with Stock Purchase Warrants) placed greater weight on the inseparability of the debt and the conversion feature, and less weight on practical problems of valuing the conversion feature (APB-14, par. 12).

OBSERVATION: In considering alternative methods of accounting for convertible debt, some felt that the value of the equity component (conversion feature) should be recognized at the time the convertible debt is issued; others felt that it should be given formal recognition not at that time, but later when conversion occurs. APB-14 concluded that the most important reason for accounting for convertible debt solely as debt at the time of issuance is the inseparability of the debt and conversion option. The holder must give up rights as a debtholder to become a stockholder. The alternatives are mutually exclusive.

Illustration of Convertible Bond Issuance

Alpha Company issues $1,000,000 of convertible bonds at 98% of par value. Each $1,000 bond is convertible into 10 shares of the company's common stock. The bond issue is recorded as if there were no conversion feature, as follows:

Cash ($1,000,000 × 98%)	980,000	
Discount on bonds payable	20,000	
Bonds payable		1,000,000

Disclosure of the features of the bond, including the conversion option, is required. The entry above, however, is the same as it would be had the bonds not been convertible.

Conversion

When a convertible debt security with an inseparable conversion feature is converted into equity securities of the debtor in accordance with the original conversion terms, the convertible debt security is surrendered by the holder and the debt is retired by the debtor. The issuer substitutes equity for debt in its balance sheet. The following is an illustration of such a transaction.

Illustration of Convertible Debt Security
Converted into Equity Security

Blue Corporation has outstanding $20,000,000 of 8% convertible bonds, with an unamortized bond premium balance of $800,000. Each $1,000 bond is convertible into ten shares of Blue Corporation's $5 par value common stock. On April 1, 20X8, all of the convertible bonds were converted by the bondholders.

8% convertible bonds payable	20,000,000	
Unamortized bond premium	800,000	
Common stock ($5 par × 200,000)		1,000,000
Capital in excess of par (common stock)		19,800,000

Under current accounting practice, no gain or loss is recognized on the conversion of convertible bonds to common stock if the conversion is made in accordance with the original conversion terms.

Generally, convertible debt is issued in anticipation that it will be converted into equity securities, and that the issuer will not have to pay the face amount of the debt at its maturity date. Although most convertible debt issues provide for the issuance of common equity shares upon conversion, the terms of a convertible debt security may provide for the issuance of preferred or other type of equity security upon conversion. When an enterprise converts debt to common equity shares, the liability for the debt is eliminated and the number of common equity shares outstanding is increased, which may affect the computation of earnings per share (EPS). When debt is converted to common equity shares, the pretax net income of the enterprise also increases by the amount of interest expense that was previously paid on the convertible debt.

> ☞ **PRACTICE POINTER:** Convertible debt generally is converted by a holder when the market value of its underlying equity securities into which the debt can be converted exceeds the face amount of the debt. If a convertible bondholder does not convert, the issuer may exercise the call provision in the debt to force conversion.

Convertible debt usually is not converted when the market value of its underlying equity securities is less than the face amount of the debt. Under this circumstance, the issuer may (*a*) exercise the call provision in the debt and pay the bondholders the face amount of the convertible debt, (*b*) offer the bondholders an inducement to convert that exceeds the original conversion terms, or (*c*) not pay off the debt until the scheduled maturity date (APB-14, par. 4).

Induced Conversion

FAS-84 (Induced Conversions of Convertible Debt) applies to conversions of convertible debt in which the original conversion terms are changed by the debtor to encourage the holder of the convertible debt to convert to equity securities of the debtor. Changes in the original conversion terms may include (*a*) the reduction of the original conversion price to increase the number of shares of equity securities received by the bondholder, (*b*) the issuance of warrants or other securities, or (*c*) the payment of cash or some other type of consideration (FAS-84, par. 2).

FAS-84 applies only to induced conversions that (*a*) are exercisable for a limited period of time and (*b*) include the issuance of no less than the number of shares of equity securities required by the original conversion terms for each convertible bond converted. Thus, for each convertible bond that is converted, the debtor must issue, at a minimum, the amount of equity securities required by the original conversion terms (FAS-84, par. 2).

> ☞ **PRACTICE POINTER:** FAS-84 applies only to those induced conversions that are offered for a "limited period of time." This phrase is not explicitly defined by the standard, however.
>
> Example 1 of Appendix A of FAS-84 appears to indicate that 60 days is a "limited period of time." Example 2 indicates that 30 days is considered a limited period of time. However, paragraph 32 of FAS-84 seems to indicate that a "limited period of time" may even be longer than 60 days.

In an induced conversion of convertible debt under FAS-84, a debtor does not recognize any gain or loss on the amount of equity securities that are required to be issued under the original conversion terms for each convertible bond converted. However, the fair value of any equity securities or other consideration paid or issued by the debtor that exceeds the amount of equity securities required to be issued for each convertible bond converted under the original conversion terms is recognized as current expense on the date the inducement offer is accepted by the bondholder (FAS-84, par. 3).

If the additional inducement consists of equity securities, the market value of such securities is credited to capital stock, and if necessary to capital in excess of par, with an offsetting debit to debt conversion expense. If the additional inducement consists of assets other than the debtor's equity securities, the market value of such assets is credited with an offsetting debit to debt conversion expense.

The fair value of the securities or other consideration is measured as of the date the inducement offer is accepted by the debtholder. This usually is the date the debtholder converts the debt into equity securities or enters into a binding agreement to do so (FAS-84, par. 4).

> ☞ **PRACTICE POINTER:** If individual bondholders accepted an inducement offer on many different days during the "limited period of time" allowed by FAS-84, a separate computation of the fair value of the incremental consideration would be required if the fair value of the debtor's common stock changes from day to day.

Illustration of Induced Conversion

Black Corporation has outstanding 100 10% convertible bonds, issued at par value and due on December 31, 20X8. Each $1,000 bond is convertible into 20 shares of Black Corporation $1 par value common stock. To induce bond-holders to convert to its common stock, Black Corporation increases the conversion rate from 20 shares per $1,000 bond to 25 shares per $1,000 bond. This offer was made by Black Corporation for a limited period of 60 days commencing March 1, 20X9.

On April 1, when the market price of Black's common stock was $60, one bondholder tendered a $1,000 convertible bond for conversion. Under FAS-84, the amount of incremental consideration is equal to the fair value of the additional five shares of Black Corporation's common stock on April 1. Thus, the amount of incremental consideration is $300 (5 shares × $60 per share).

The journal entry to record the transaction is:

Convertible bonds payable	1,000	
Debt conversion expense	300	
Common stock ($1 par value) ($1 × 25 shares)		25
Capital in excess of par (common stock)		1,275

The incremental consideration paid or issued by a debtor may also be calculated as the difference between (a) the fair value of the equity securities and/or other consideration required to be issued under the original terms of the conversion privilege and (b) the fair value of the equity securities and/or other consideration that is actually issued.

Market value of securities based on inducement (25 × $60)	$1,500
Market value of securities based on original terms (20 × $60)	(1,200)
Fair value of incremental consideration	$ 300

OBSERVATION: There is a significant difference between extinguishment accounting and conversion accounting. As a rule, gain or loss is recognized in extinguishment accounting, while no gain or loss is recognized in conversion accounting. Extinguishment accounting results in the **extinguishment** of a debt, while conversion accounting results in the issuance of equity securities and the **retirement** of a debt. Although FAS-84 refers to both extinguishment and conversion accounting, it does not distinguish between the two.

OBSERVATION: When an enterprise gives up **assets** or increases its **liabilities** to induce the conversion of its convertible debt to its equity securities, there is little question that a cost is incurred. Some doubt exists, however, about whether an enterprise incurs a cost when it gives up its own **equity securities** as an inducement for the conversion of convertible debt. The FASB's Conceptual Framework states that expenses represent outflows or other using up of assets or incurrences of liabilities (or a combination of both) during a period. There is no outflow or other using up of assets or incurrence of liabilities when, as a conversion inducement, an enterprise issues its equity securities and records their fair market value as debt conversion expense. FAS-84 appears to contradict the fact that the issuance of capital stock is a capital transaction, and under current accounting practice described in APB-9 (Reporting the Results of Operations), capital transactions do not enter into the income determination of an enterprise.

DEBT WITH DETACHABLE PURCHASE WARRANTS

Issuance

In contrast to accounting for convertible debt, when detachable purchase warrants are issued in conjunction with debt, APB-14 requires that separate amounts attributable to the debt and the purchase warrants be computed and accounting recognition be given to each component. The allocation to the two components of the hybrid debt/equity security is based on the relative market values of the two securities at the time of issuance (APB-14, par. 16). This conclusion is based primarily on the fact that the options available to the debtholder are *not* mutually exclusive—bondholders can become stockholders and retain their status as bondholders.

Illustration of Issuance of Debt with Detachable Warrants

Xeta Corporation issues 100 $100-par-value, 5% bonds with a detachable common stock warrant to purchase one share of Xeta's common stock at a specified price. At the time of issuance, the quoted market price of the bonds was $97, and the stock warrants were quoted at $2 each. The proceeds of the sale to Xeta Corporation were $9,900. The transaction is accounted for as follows:

Cash	9,900	
Discount on 5% bonds payable (100 × $3)	300	
5% bonds payable		10,000
Paid-in capital (stock warrants) (100 × $2)		200

The bonds and warrants are recorded separately at their market values:

Bonds: $10,000 × 97% = $9,700, recorded at $10,000 par value, less $300 discount

Warrants: 100 × $2 = $200

Exercise of Warrants

Once a separate purchase feature, such as a detachable stock purchase warrant, is issued, it usually is traded separately from its related convertible debt security. The separate purchase feature has its own market price, and conversion requires (*a*) the surrender of the purchase option and (*b*) the payment of any other consideration required by the terms of the warrant.

Under current accounting practice (APB-14), when a separate purchase feature is exercised in accordance with the original purchase terms, no gain or loss is recognized on the transaction. The amount previously credited to paid-in capital for the purchase feature at issuance is eliminated, the amount of cash received, if any, is recorded, and the par value of the capital stock issued and the appropriate amount of capital stock in excess of par is recorded. The following is an illustration of such a transaction.

Illustration of Exercise of Separate Purchase Feature

Ace Corporation previously issued debt securities with detachable stock purchase warrants. A credit of $10 for each warrant was recorded in paid-in capital at the date of issuance, representing the relative market value of each warrant. There was no discount or premium on the issuance of the related debt with detachable stock purchase warrants. Each stock purchase warrant permitted the purchase of 50 shares of Ace's $1 par value common stock, upon the payment of $200 and the surrender of the warrant. Assuming that one warrant was exercised, the journal entry would be:

Cash	200	
Paid-in capital (stock warrants)	10	
Capital stock ($1 par value)		50
Capital in excess of par (common stock)		160

The conversion of a separate conversion feature, such as a detachable stock purchase warrant, is accounted for solely as an equity transaction, and no gain or loss is recorded.

☛ **PRACTICE POINTER:** The accounting described in this section applies to "detachable" stock purchase warrants and other similar instruments, meaning that the stock purchase warrant can be exercised without affecting the other security from which it is detachable. Occasionally, a stock purchase warrant is encountered that is inseparable from another security (i.e., a nondetachable stock purchase warrant), and the related security must be surrendered to effect the stock purchase. In this case, although the name may imply otherwise, the stock purchase warrant effectively is part of a convertible security and should be accounted for as such.

OBSERVATION: APB-14 recognized that it is not practical to discuss all possible types of debt with conversion features and debt issued with purchase warrants, or debt issued with a combination of the two. It states that securities not explicitly dealt with in APB-14 should be accounted for in accordance with the substance of the transaction in a manner consistent with APB-14 (APB-14, par. 18).

RELATED CHAPTERS IN 2009 *GAAP GUIDE* LEVEL A

Chapter 3, "Balance Sheet Classification and Related Display Issues"
Chapter 13, "Earnings per Share"
Chapter 44, "Stockholders' Equity"

RELATED CHAPTERS IN 2009 *GAAP GUIDE* LEVELS B, C, AND D

Chapter 4, "Balance Sheet Classification and Related Display Issues"
Chapter 12, "Convertible Debt and Debt with Warrants"
Chapter 13, "Earnings per Share"
Chapter 39, "Stockholders' Equity"

RELATED CHAPTERS IN 2009 *INTERNATIONAL ACCOUNTING/FINANCIAL REPORTING STANDARDS GUIDE*

Chapter 3, "Presentation of Financial Statements"
Chapter 12, "Earnings per Share"
Chapter 16, "Financial Instruments"

CHAPTER 10
DEFERRED COMPENSATION
CONTRACTS

CONTENTS

OVERVIEW

Deferred compensation contracts are accounted for individually on an accrual basis. Such contracts ordinarily include certain requirements such as continued employment for a specified period of time, availability for consulting services, and agreements not to compete after retirement. The estimated amounts to be paid under each contract are accrued in a systematic and rational manner over the period of active employment from the initiation of the contract, unless it is evident that future services expected to be received by the employer are commensurate with the payments or a portion of the payments to be made. If elements of both current and future services are present, only the portion applicable to the current services is accrued.

GAAP for deferred compensation contracts are found in the following pronouncements:

APB-12   Omnibus Opinion—1967 (Deferred Compensation Contracts)

FAS-106   Employers' Accounting for Postretirement Benefits Other Than Pensions

BACKGROUND

The main source of GAAP for deferred compensation contracts is APB-12 (Omnibus Opinion—1967), paragraphs 6 through 8, as amended by FAS-106 (Employers' Accounting for Postretirement Benefits Other Than Pensions). If individual deferred compensation contracts, as a group, are tantamount to a pension plan, they are accounted for in accordance with the GAAP for pension plans, discussed in this *Guide* in the chapter titled "Pension Plans."

If individual deferred compensation contracts are, as a group, tantamount to a plan for postretirement benefits other than pensions, they are accounted for in accordance with the GAAP on postretirement benefits, discussed in this *Guide* in the chapter titled "Postemployment and Postretirement Benefits Other Than Pensions."

> **OBSERVATION:** Professional judgment is required to determine whether individual contracts are tantamount to a pension or postretirement plan.

ACCOUNTING STANDARDS

According to APB-12, deferred compensation contracts shall be accounted for on an individual basis for each employee. If a deferred compensation contract is based on current and future employment, only the amounts attributable to the current portion of employment are accrued (APB-12, par. 6).

If a deferred compensation contract contains benefits payable for the life of a beneficiary, the total liability is based on the beneficiary's life expectancy or on the estimated cost of an annuity contract that would provide sufficient funds to pay the required benefits (APB-12, par. 7).

The total liability for deferred compensation contracts is determined by the terms of each individual contract. The amount of the periodic accrual, computed from the first day of the employment contract, must total no less than the then present value of the benefits provided for in the contract. The periodic accruals are made systematically over the active term of employment (FAS-106, par. 13).

Illustration of Calculating Deferred Compensation

A deferred compensation contract provides for the payment of $50,000 per year for five years, beginning one year after the end of the employee's ten year contract. A 10% interest rate is appropriate.

The present value for the five $50,000 payments at the end of ten years is determined as follows:

Present value of $50,000 in five years	$ 31,045
Present value of $50,000 in four years	34,150
Present value of $50,000 in three years	37,565
Present value of $50,000 in two years	41,320
Present value of $50,000 in one year	45,455
Total present value of benefits at end of employment	$189,535

In order to have available the funds required to pay the benefits in accordance with the contract, $189,535 must be accumulated over ten years. To find the amount of the annual accrual that earning 10% interest will total $189,535 at the end of ten years, the following formula for the value of an annuity due may be used:

$$\$189,535 \quad = \quad R\,(17.531^*)$$
$$R \quad = \quad \$10,811$$

*Amount of an annuity due at 10% for 10 periods

FAS-106 amends APB-12 with regard to the method of accruing an employer's obligation under deferred compensation contracts that are not tantamount to a plan for pension or other postretirement benefits. FAS-106 requires the employer to make periodic accruals, so that the cost of the deferred compensation is attributed to the appropriate years of an employee's service, in accordance with the terms of the contract between the employer and that employee (FAS-106, par. 13).

> ☛ **PRACTICE POINTER:** The employer must make the attribution in a systematic and rational manner. By the time an employee becomes fully eligible for the deferred compensation specified in the contract, the accrued amount should equal the then present value of the expected future payments of deferred compensation.

Illustrations of Accruals Required by FAS-106

Example 1: *Employee must remain in service for a number of years to be eligible for the deferred compensation.*

A deferred compensation contract with a newly hired employee provides for a payment of $100,000 upon termination of employment, provided the employee remains in service for at least four years.

The employer makes annual accruals during each of the first four years of this employee's service, to recognize the portion of deferred compensation cost attributable to each of these years. To make these annual accruals, the employer starts by making reasonable assumptions about (a) the employee's anticipated retirement date and (b) the discount rate for making computations of present value.

If the employer assumes that the employee will remain in service for a total of nine years (including five years after becoming fully eligible for the deferred compensation), and the discount rate is 8%, the present value of the $100,000 deferred compensation at the end of the fourth year will be $68,058 (present value of $100,000 payable at the end of five years at 8% discount).

Accruals are made for each of the first four years, so that the balance in the accrued liability account at the end of the fourth year will be $68,058. The simplest way to accomplish this is on a straight-line basis, as follows:

Accrued amount anticipated at end of fourth year	$68,058
Annual accrual during each of first four years (1/4 of $68,058)	$17,015

This computation results in the recognition of $17,015 deferred compensation cost during each of the first four years of the employee's service. The balance in the accrued liability account at the end of the fourth year, when the employee is eligible to terminate and collect the deferred compensation, is $68,058, the present value of the $100,000 deferred compensation payable five years later. (The five years represent the anticipated total service of nine years, less the four years already served.)

Next, assume the employee remains in service throughout the fifth year and is still expected to complete the nine-year term originally anticipated. The accrued liability is adjusted as of the end of the fifth year to reflect the present value of the deferred compensation, which is $73,503 (present value of $100,000 payable at the end of four years at 8% discount).

The cost recognized for the fifth year will therefore be $5,445, determined as follows:

Accrued amount at end of fifth year	$ 73,503
Accrued amount at end of fourth year	(68,058)
Cost recognized in fifth year	$ 5,445

Example 2: *Employee is eligible in the same year the contract is signed.*

An employee is hired on January 1, 20X8. The contract provides for a payment of $20,000 upon termination of employment, provided the employee remains in service for at least six months. The employer anticipates that the employee will remain in service for three years. The assumed discount rate is 8%.

The employee is still in service at the end of calendar year 20X8. Having completed at least six months of service, the employee is eligible to terminate and collect the deferred compensation. The accrual as of December 31, 20X8, is $17,147, the present value of $20,000 payable at the end of two years at 8% discount. (The two years represent the originally anticipated service of three years, less the one year of 20X8 already served.) The entire amount of the accrual is recognized as a deferred compensation cost in 20X8, since the employee achieved full eligibility by the end of the year.

If the employee remains in service throughout 20X9 and all assumptions remain unchanged, the amount of the accrued liability as of December 31, 20X9, is adjusted to $18,519, the present value of $20,000 at the end of one year at 8% discount.

The cost recognized in 20X9 is therefore $1,372, determined as follows:

Accrued amount at end of 20X9	$18,519
Accrued amount at end of 20X8	(17,147)
Cost recognized in 20X9	$ 1,372

RELATED CHAPTERS IN 2009 *GAAP GUIDE* LEVEL A

Chapter 33, "Pension Plans"
Chapter 34, "Postemployment and Postretirement Benefits Other Than Pensions"

RELATED CHAPTERS IN 2009 *GAAP GUIDE* LEVELS B, C, AND D

Chapter 29, "Pension Plans—Employers"
Chapter 32, "Postemployment and Postretirement Benefits Other Than Pensions"

RELATED CHAPTER IN 2009 *INTERNATIONAL ACCOUNTING/FINANCIAL REPORTING STANDARDS GUIDE*

Chapter 13, "Employee Benefits"

CHAPTER 11
DEPRECIABLE ASSETS AND DEPRECIATION

CONTENTS

OVERVIEW

Recognition of depreciation is required in general-purpose financial statements that present financial position, cash flows, and results of operations. Depreciation is an area where a variety of methods are available in practice.

GAAP in the area of depreciable assets and depreciation are established in the following pronouncements:

ARB-43	Chapter 9A, Depreciation and High Costs Chapter 9C, Emergency Facilities
APB-6	Paragraph 17, Depreciation on Appreciation
APB-12	Paragraphs 4 and 5, Disclosure of Depreciable Assets and Depreciation
FAS-109	Accounting for Income Taxes
FAS-143	Accounting for Asset Retirement Obligations
FIN-47	Accounting for Conditional Asset Retirement Obligations: An Interpretation of FAS-143

BACKGROUND

Fixed assets, also referred to as *property, plant, and equipment*, or *plant assets*, are used in production, distribution, and services by all enterprises. Examples include land, buildings, furniture, fixtures, machinery, equipment, and vehicles. The nature of the assets employed by a particular enterprise is determined by the nature of its activities.

Fixed assets have two primary characteristics:

1. They are acquired for use in operations and enter into the revenue-generating stream indirectly. They are held primarily for use, not for sale.
2. They have relatively long lives.

GAAP generally require fixed assets to be recorded at their cost, which is written off periodically, or depreciated, in a systematic and rational manner. Commonly used depreciation methods include straight-line, units of production, sum-of-the-years'-digits, and declining balance, although other methods may meet the criteria of *systematic* and *rational*.

PRINCIPLES OF ACCOUNTING FOR DEPRECIABLE ASSETS

Asset Cost

The basis of accounting for depreciable fixed assets is cost, and all normal expenditures of readying an asset for use are capitalized. However, unnecessary expenditures that do not add to the utility of the asset are charged to expense. For example, an expenditure for repairing a piece of equipment that was damaged during shipment should be charged to expense.

Razing and removal costs (less salvage value) of structures located on land purchased as a building site are added to the cost of the land. Land itself is never depreciated.

> **OBSERVATION:** Promulgated GAAP (ARB-43, Ch. 9A, par. 7) require that assets be recorded at cost, except in the case of quasi-reorganizations (corporate readjustments) in which it is permissible to write up or write down assets to market values (APB-6, par. 17).
>
> When price-level accounting methods are used as supplemental statements, the distortion of assets and related depreciation resulting from inflation is somewhat ameliorated.

Salvage Value

Salvage or *residual value* is an estimate of the amount that will be realized at the end of the useful life of a depreciable asset through sale or other disposal. Frequently, depreciable assets have little or no salvage value at the end of their estimated useful life and, if immaterial, the amount(s) may be ignored.

Estimated Useful Life

The *estimated useful life* of a depreciable asset is the period over which services are expected to be rendered by the asset (ARB-43, Ch. 9C, par. 5). An asset's estimated useful life may differ from company to company or industry to industry. A company's maintenance policy may affect the longevity of a depreciable asset.

> **OBSERVATION:** Total utility of an asset, expressed in time, is called the *physical life*. The utility of an asset to a specific owner, expressed in time, is called the *service life*.

Valuation of Assets

Under specific circumstances, assets may be valued in the following ways:

Historical Cost

The amount paid at the date of acquisition, including all normal expenditures of readying an asset for use.

Replacement Cost

The amount that it would cost to replace an asset. Frequently, replacement cost is the same as fair value.

Fair Market Value

The price at which a illing seller would sell to a willing buyer, neither of them being under any compulsion to buy or to sell.

Present Value

The value today of something due in the future.

General Price-Level Restatement

The value of an asset restated in terms of current purchasing power.

Leasehold Improvements

Leased assets may provide the lessee (i.e., party acquiring use of the assets) with many of the benefits of ownership. The lessee may invest in improvements on leased assets to enhance their usefulness. These investments are referred to as *leasehold improvements*.

Leasehold improvements frequently are made to property for which the lease extends over a relatively long period. For example, improvements to a leased building might range from relatively in-expensive improvements to extensive remodeling to prepare the leased asset for the intended use of the lessee.

Leasehold improvements are established in a separate account at cost and amortized over the shorter of the life of the improvement or the length of the lease. Amortization or depreciation policy is usually the same as similar expenditures for owned assets. If no similar assets are owned, amortization or depreciation must employ a method that is systematic and rational (as discussed above) and based on reasonable assumptions.

> ☞ **PRACTICE POINTER:** Leasehold improvements generally should be depreciated over the estimated useful lives of the improvements or the remaining lease term, whichever is less. For example, if the lessee constructs a street, curbs, and lighting on land leased for 15 years, those improvements should

be depreciated over their estimated useful lives or 15 years, whichever is less. The method of depreciation (most likely straight-line) should generally be that of similar assets (i.e., streets, curbs, lighting) that the company has installed on owned land. Because improvements will revert to the lessor at the end of the lease term, the period of depreciation should not exceed the term of the lease.

Some leases contain renewal options, and a number of entities (particularly retailers) have depreciated leasehold improvements over the remaining lease term plus the term of the renewal period (assuming that this period is less than the estimated economic life of the leasehold improvement). The SEC addressed the appropriateness of this accounting treatment in a letter from the Chief Accountant's office to the AICPA in February 2005. Leasehold improvements should only be depreciated over a term that includes the renewal option period when the exercise of the renewal option is "reasonably assured" per FAS-13. Under FAS-13, a renewal option is only "reasonably assured" if the rent available at renewal is sufficiently less than the property's fair rental value as to reasonably assure that the renewal option will be exercised. Many public companies were routinely including the renewal option period in determining the depreciable live of the leasehold improvement, even if the renewal rental amount was not below fair value. The SEC's clarification of its position on this issue has led to a large number of restatements being filed. In addition, companies should disclose the depreciation (amortization) period of material leasehold improvements and the relationship of this period to the initial lease term.

Some lessors provide incentives or allowances under operating leases to fund leasehold improvements. These incentives or allowances are to be accounted for as leasehold improvements and depreciated as discussed above. The proper accounting treatment for incentives or allowances received from lessors is discussed in Chapter 29, "Leases."

Self-Constructed Depreciable Assets

When a business constructs a depreciable asset for its own use, the following procedure is appropriate:

1. All *direct costs* are included in the total cost of the asset.

2. *Fixed overhead costs* are not included unless they are increased by the construction of the asset.

3. *Interest costs* may or may not be capitalized as part of construction cost of the fixed assets.

> **OBSERVATION:** Interest costs that are material must be capitalized on certain qualifying assets under the provisions of

FAS-34 (Capitalization of Interest Cost). (See in this *Guide* the chapter titled "Interest Costs Capitalized.")

Illustration of Self-Constructed Depreciable Assets

A company takes advantage of excess capacity to construct its own machinery. Costs associated with the construction are as follows:

Direct material	$100,000
Direct labor	50,000
Overhead —Variable	25,000
—Fixed	35,000
	$210,000

The machinery has an estimated useful life of five years, with an expected salvage value of 10% of its cost.

The cost of the machine is $175,000, which includes all of the scheduled costs above except fixed overhead. Because fixed overhead is unaffected by the construction of the machinery, to capitalize fixed overhead as part of the cost would relieve operations of expenses that should be charged to them.

The amount subject to depreciation is computed as follows:

$$175,000 - .10 (\$175,000) = \$157,500$$

Write-Up of Assets to Appraisal Values

GAAP generally prohibit the write-up of fixed assets to market or appraisal values. At the same time, however, GAAP state that if fixed assets are written up to market or appraisal values, depreciation should be based on the written-up amounts (APB-6, par. 17).

Improvement of Depreciable Assets

Expenditures that increase the capacity or operating efficiency or extend the useful life of an asset, if they are substantial, are capitalized. Minor expenditures usually are treated as period costs even though they may have the characteristics of capital expenditures. When the cost of improvements is substantial or when there is a change in the estimated useful life of an asset, depreciation charges for future periods are revised based on the new book value and the new estimated remaining useful life.

The revision of an asset's estimated useful life is measured prospectively and accounted for in the current and future periods. No adjustment is made to prior depreciation.

Illustration of Improvement of Depreciable Assets

A machine that originally cost $100,000 was being depreciated (no salvage value) over ten years, using the straight-line method. At the beginning of the fifth year, $20,000 was expended, which improved the operating efficiency of the machine and extended its useful life two years.

Original cost	$100,000
Less: Four years' depreciation	(40,000)
Book value	$ 60,000
New expenditures	20,000
New depreciable base	$ 80,000
Divided by: Useful life (6 + 2) in years	8
Amount of annual depreciation	$ 10,000

Impairment of Assets

In certain specified circumstances, depreciable assets are subject to a write-down of their recorded amount to reflect an impairment of value. This procedure generally is followed only when unusual circumstances indicate that the value of the asset is below its recorded amount or carrying value.

Specific procedures for identifying assets subject to write-down for impairment, as well as standards for measuring the amount of the write-down, are included in FAS-144 (Accounting for the Impairment or Disposal of Long-Lived Assets) and covered in the chapter of this *Guide* titled "Impairment of Long-Lived Assets."

DEPRECIATION

Types of Depreciation

Physical depreciation is related to a depreciable asset's wear and deterioration over a period.

Functional depreciation arises from obsolescence or inadequacy of the asset to perform efficiently. Obsolescence may arise when there is no further demand for the product that the depreciable asset produces or from the availability of a new depreciable asset that can perform the same function for substantially less cost.

Depreciation Methods

The goal of depreciation methods is to provide for a reasonable, consistent matching of revenue and expense by allocating the cost of the depreciable asset systematically over its estimated useful life.

The accumulation of depreciation in the books is accomplished by using a contra account, called accumulated depreciation or allowance for depreciation.

The amount subject to depreciation—*depreciable base*—is the difference between cost and estimate of residual or salvage value.

Straight-Line Method

Straight-line depreciation is determined by the formula:

$$\frac{\text{Cost less salvage valve}}{\text{Estimated useful life in years}}$$

The straight-line method of depreciation is appropriate when the asset use is expected to be relatively even over its estimated useful life or there is no discernible pattern of decline in service potential.

Illustration of Straight-Line Method of Depreciation

A machine with an invoice price of $500,000 has an expected useful life of eight years. Costs to transport, install, and test the machine were $25,000. The salvage value of the machine at the end of its eight-year life is estimated to be $50,000.

Straight-line depreciation is the same each year. It is computed by adding the $25,000 costs to prepare the asset for its intended use to the $500,000 invoice price, reducing that amount by the estimated salvage value of $50,000, and dividing by the estimated years of useful life:

$$\frac{(\$500,000 + \$25,000) - \$50,000}{8 \text{ years}} = \$59,375$$

Units-of-Production Method

The *units-of-production method* relates depreciation to the estimated production capability of an asset and is expressed in a rate per unit or hour. The formula is:

$$\frac{\text{Cost less salvage valve}}{\text{Estimated units or hours}}$$

Illustration of Units-of-Production Method of Depreciation

A machine is purchased at a cost of $850,000 and has a salvage value of $100,000. It is estimated that the machine has a useful life of 75,000 hours.

$$\frac{\$850,000 - \$100,000}{75,000} = \$10 \text{ per hour depreciation}$$

In an accounting period during which the machine was used 12,500 hours, depreciation would be $125,000 (12,500 × $10).

The units-of-production method is used in situations in which the usage of the depreciable asset varies considerably from period to period, and in those circumstances in which the service life is more a function of use than passage of time.

Sum-of-the-Years'-Digits Method

The *sum-of-the-years'-digits method* is an accelerated method of depreciation that provides higher depreciation expense in the early years and lower charges in later years.

To find the sum of the years' digits, the digit of each year is progressively numbered and then added up. For example, the sum of the years' digits for a five-year life would be:

$$5 + 4 + 3 + 2 + 1 = 15$$

The sum of the years' digits becomes the denominator, and the digit of the highest year becomes the first numerator. For example, the first year's depreciation for a five-year life would be 5/15 of the depreciable base of the asset, the second year's depreciation would be 4/15, and so on.

When dealing with an asset with a long life, it is helpful to use the following formula for finding the sum of the years' digits, S, where N is the number of years in the asset's life.

$$S = N \left(\frac{N+1}{2}\right)$$

To find the sum of the years' digits for an asset with a 50-year life:

$$S = 50 \left(\frac{50+1}{2}\right)$$

$$S = 50(25\ 1/2)$$
$$S = 1,275$$

Illustration of Sum-of-the-Years'-Digits Method of Depreciation

Assume that an asset costing $11,000 has a salvage value of $1,000 and an estimated useful life of four years.

The first step is to determine the depreciable base:

Cost of asset	$11,000
Less: Salvage value	1,000
Depreciable base	$10,000

The sum of the years' digits for four years is: $4 + 3 + 2 + 1 = 10$

The first year's depreciation is 4/10, the second year's 3/10, the third year's 2/10, and the fourth year's 1/10, as follows:

4/10 of $10,000	=	$ 4,000
3/10 of $10,000	=	3,000
2/10 of $10,000	=	2,000
1/10 of $10,000	=	1,000
Total depreciation		$10,000

Declining-Balance Methods

A frequently used accelerated method is the *double-declining-balance method*, although other alternative (lower than double) methods are acceptable. Under double-declining balance, depreciation is computed at double the straight-line rate and this percentage is applied to the remaining book value. No allowance is made for salvage until the book value (cost less accumulated depreciation) reaches estimated salvage value. At that time, depreciation recognition ceases.

Illustration of Double-Declining-Balance Method of Depreciation

An asset costing $10,000 has an estimated useful life of ten years. Using the double-declining-balance method, depreciation expense is computed as follows.

First, the regular straight-line method percentage is determined, which in this case is 10% (ten-year life). This amount is doubled to 20% and applied each year to the remaining book value, as follows:

Year	Percentage	Remaining book value	Depreciation expense
1	20	$10,000	$2,000
2	20	8,000	1,600
3	20	6,400	1,280
4	20	5,120	1,024
5	20	4,096	819
6	20	3,277	655
7	20	2,622	524
8	20	2,098	420
9	20	1,678	336
10	20	1,342	268
Salvage value		1,074	

In this example, a book value (i.e., portion of cost not depreciated) of $1,074 remains after recognizing ten years of depreciation. Should the asset remain in service, depreciation would continue to be recognized until the asset is no longer used or the book value approaches zero. Should the salvage value be a greater amount (e.g., $1,500), depreciation would cease to be recognized when a total of $8,500 is reached ($10,000 cost − $8,500 accumulated depreciation = $1,500 book value). In the above example, under this assumption, only $178 of depreciation would be recognized in the ninth year, leaving a book value of $1,500. No depreciation would be recognized in the tenth year.

Had the preceding illustration been 150% of declining balance, the rate would have been 15% of the remaining book value (i.e., 150% of 10%). The declining-balance method meets the requirements of being systematic and rational. If the expected productivity or revenue-earning power of the asset is relatively greater during the early years of its life, or where maintenance charges tend to increase during later years, the declining-balance method may provide the most satisfactory allocation of cost (FAS-109, par. 288).

Partial-Year Depreciation

When an asset is placed in service during the year, the depreciation expense is taken only for the portion of the year that the asset is used.

For example, if an asset (of a company on a calendar-year basis) is placed in service on July 1, only six months' depreciation is taken.

Alternatively, a company may adopt a simplifying assumption concerning partial-year depreciation which, applied consistently, usually is considered a reasonable approximation of depreciation computed to the nearest month. For example, the following policies are sometimes encountered:

- A half year of depreciation in the year of purchase and in the year of disposal
- A full year of depreciation taken in the year of purchase and none taken in the year of sale (or the opposite)

These policies are particularly appropriate when a large number of fixed assets are placed in service and removed from service on a constant basis.

Illustration of Partial-Year Depreciation

A calendar-year company purchased a machine on March 7. The machine cost $64,000, and at the end of its expected five-year life it will have a salvage value of $10,000.

Depreciation on a monthly basis is calculated as follows:

$$\frac{\$64,000 - \$10,000}{5 \text{ years}} = \$10,800$$

$$\frac{\$10,800}{12 \text{ months}} = \$900 \text{ per month}$$

Depreciation for the year of purchase under three different policies is as follows:

Policy	Depreciation for Year of Purchase
Computed to nearest full month	10 months × $900 = $9,000
Full year's depreciation in year of purchase; none in last year of asset's useful life	$10,800
Half year's depreciation in first and last years of asset's life	$10,800 × 1/2 = $5,400

Other Types of Depreciation

GAAP require that depreciation be determined in a manner that systematically and rationally allocates the cost of an asset over its estimated useful life. Straight-line, units-of-production, sum-of-the-years'-digits, and declining-depreciation methods are considered acceptable, provided they are based on reasonable estimates of useful life and salvage value. Other methods that are used less frequently are:

Replacement Depreciation

The original cost is carried on the books, and the replacement cost is charged to expense in the period the replacement occurs.

Retirement Depreciation

The cost of the asset is charged to expense in the period it is retired.

Present-Value Depreciation

Depreciation is computed so that the return on the investment of the asset remains constant over the period involved.

> ☞ **PRACTICE POINTER:** For financial accounting purposes, companies should not use depreciation guidelines or other tax regulations issued by the IRS, but should estimate useful lives and calculate depreciation expense according to generally accepted procedures. Only when the difference between a GAAP depreciation method and a tax depreciation method is immaterial is the latter acceptable in financial statements. When fixed asset write-offs for tax purposes differ from depreciation for financial accounting purposes, deferred income taxes are recognized.

In periods of inflation, depreciation charges based on historical cost of the original fixed asset may not reflect current price levels, and hence may not be an appropriate matching of revenues and expenses for the current period. In 1953, promulgated GAAP (ARB-43, Ch. 9A, par. 6) took the position that it was acceptable to provide an appropriation of retained earnings for replacement of fixed assets, but not acceptable to depart from the traditional cost method in the treatment of depreciation, because a radical departure from the generally accepted procedures would create too much confusion in the minds of the users of financial statements. Although inflation has become quite serious from time to time, depreciation based on historical cost remains the official, promulgated accounting principle.

DEPLETION

Depletion is the process of allocating the cost of a natural resource over its estimated useful life in a manner similar to depreciation. An estimate is made of the amount of natural resources to be extracted, in units or tons, barrels, or any other measurement. The estimate of total recoverable units is then divided into the total cost of the depletable asset, to arrive at a depletion rate per unit. Estimated costs to restore the property should be added, and estimated residual value should be subtracted. The annual depletion expense is the rate per unit times the number of units extracted during the fiscal year. If at any time there is a revision of the estimated number of units that are expected to be extracted, a new unit rate is computed. The cost of the natural resource property is reduced each year by the amount of the depletion expense for the year. This process is similar to the units-of-production depreciation method explained earlier.

DISCLOSURE

Accumulated depreciation and depletion are deducted from the assets to which they relate. The following disclosures of depreciable assets and depreciation are required in the financial statements or notes thereto (APB-12, par. 5):

- Depreciation expense for the period
- Balances of major classes of depreciable assets by nature or function
- Accumulated depreciation allowances by classes or in total
- The methods used, by major classes, in computing depreciation

> ☞ **PRACTICE POINTER:** Practice varies on whether these disclosures are made in the aggregate for all categories of depreciable assets or separately for each category. Presentation in the aggregate seems to be the dominant practice, despite the fact that separate disclosure provides more useful information.

> **OBSERVATIONS:** GAAP (APB-12, par. 5) require that the above disclosures be made in the financial statements or in the notes. In addition, FAS-154 (Accounting Changes and Error Corrections) requires disclosure of the effect of a change from one depreciation method to another (FAS-154, par. 22).

ASSET RETIREMENT OBLIGATIONS

FAS-143 (Accounting for Asset Retirement Obligations) requires accounting recognition and measurement of a liability for an asset retirement obligation and associated asset retirement costs. It was issued to narrow areas of differences in the way that companies previously accounted for obligations related to the retirement of long-lived assets, some of which recognized liabilities as they were incurred, while others did not recognize liabilities until the asset was retired. Also, practices varied in terms of how asset retirement obligations were measured and presented in financial statements.

Scope

FAS-143 applies to all entities, including rate-regulated entities that meet the criteria for applying FAS-71 (Accounting for the Effects of Certain Types of Regulation). It applies to all legal obligations associated with the retirement of tangible long-lived assets that result from an acquisition, construction, or development. A legal obligation is defined as an obligation that a party is required to settle as a result of an existing or enacted law, statue, ordinance, or written or oral contract, or by legal construction of a contract under the doctrine of promissory estoppel (FAS-143, pars. 2, 19).

FAS-143 does not apply to obligations that arise solely from a plan to dispose of a long-lived asset as defined in FAS-144 (Accounting for the Impairment or Disposal of Long-Lived Assets). FAS-143 does not apply to obligations of a lessee in connection with leased property (FAS-143, pars. 2, 18).

Initial Recognition and Measurement

Recognition of a liability for the fair value of an asset retirement obligation is required in the period in which it is incurred, if a reasonable estimate of fair value can be made. If such an estimate cannot be made in the period the obligation is incurred, the liability shall be recognized when a reasonable estimate of fair value can be made.

> **OBSERVATIONS:** The FASB indicates that this requirement is consistent with the definition of a liability in CON-6 (Elements of Financial Statements), which states that liabilities are probable future sacrifices of economic benefits arising from present obligations of a particular entity to transfer assets or provide services to other entities in the future as a result of past transactions or events. The term "probable," in CON-5 (Recognition and Measurement in Financial Statements of Business Enterprises), is used with its general meaning and refers to that which can be reasonably expected or believed

on the basis of available evidence or logic, but is neither certain nor proved. It is intended to reflect the fact that business and other economic activities occur in an environment in which few outcomes are certain. This is in contrast to the use of the word "probable" in FAS-5 (Accounting for Contingencies), which requires a high degree of expectation.

The fair value of a liability for an asset retirement obligation will typically be determined using an expected present value technique. Cash flows shall be discounted using a credit-adjusted risk-free rate. This results in the effect of an entity's credit standing affecting the discount rate rather than affecting expected cash flows (FAS-157, par. E23b).

The obligation may be incurred over more than one financial reporting period if the events that lead to the obligation occur over more than one period. An incremental liability incurred in a subsequent reporting period shall be considered an additional layer of the original liability, with each layer measured at fair value and combined with the original layer(s) (FAS-143, par. 10).

Accounting Subsequent to Initial Recognition

When the initial liability is recognized, the asset cost is increased by the amount equal to the same amount as the liability. That cost shall subsequently be allocated to expense using a systematic and rational method over the asset's useful life. This process does not preclude the entity from capitalizing an amount of asset retirement cost and allocating an equal amount to expense in the same accounting period (FAS-143, par. 11).

In applying the provisions of FAS-144 in asset impairment situations, the carrying amount of the asset being tested for impairment shall include the amounts of capitalized asset retirement costs. Estimates of future cash flows related to the liability for an asset retirement obligation that has been recognized in the financial statements shall be excluded from the undiscounted cash flows used to test the asset for recoverability and from the discounted cash flows used to measure the asset's fair value. If the fair value of the asset is based on a quoted market price and that price considers the costs that will be incurred in retiring the asset, the quoted market price shall be increased by the fair value of the asset retirement obligation when measuring the amount of impairment (FAS-143, par. 12).

In subsequent periods, changes in the liability for an asset retirement obligation resulting from the passage of time and revisions to either the timing or amount of the original estimate of undiscounted cash flows shall be recognized. In so doing, changes due to the passage of time shall first be incorporated before measuring changes resulting from a revision of either the timing or the amount of estimated cash flows (FAS-143, par. 13). Changes in the liability due to the passage of time shall be measured by applying an interest method of allocation to the liability at the beginning of the period using the credit-adjusted risk-free interest rate that existed when the liability was initially measured. That amount shall be recognized as an increase in the carrying amount of the liability and the expense shown as an operating item in the income statement (referred to as accretion expense) (FAS-143, par. 14). Changes resulting from revisions in the amount and/or timing of the original estimate of undiscounted cash flows shall be recognized as an increase or decrease in the carrying amount of the liability and the related asset retirement cost capitalized. Upward revisions shall be discounted using the current credit-adjusted risk-free rate. Downward revisions shall be discounted using the credit-adjusted risk-free rate that existed when the original liability was recognized. When the asset cost changes as a result of revisions to estimated cash flows, the amount of the asset retirement cost allocated to expense in the period of change and subsequent periods, as appropriate, shall be adjusted (FAS-143, par. 15).

Illustration of Accounting for an Asset Retirement Obligation— Obligation Incurred in a Single Reporting Period

This example illustrates (*a*) initial measurement of a liability for an asset retirement obligation using an expected present value technique, (*b*) subsequent measurement assuming that there are no changes in expected cash flows, and (*c*) settlement of the asset retirement obligation (ARO liability) at the end of its term.

Ocaxet Inc. completes construction of and places into service an offshore oil platform on January 1, 20X8. The entity is legally required to dismantle and remove the platform at the end of its useful life, which is estimated to be five years. Ocaxet Inc. develops the following estimates of costs to dismantle and remove the platform.

Labor costs are based on current, relevant marketplace wages and Ocaxet Inc. estimates the probability of a range of cash flow estimates as follows:

Cash Flow Estimate	Estimated Probability	Expected Cash Flows
$ 125,000	20%	$ 25,000
150,000	60	90,000
200,000	20	40,000
		$ 155,000

Ocaxet Inc. estimates allocated overhead and equipment charges to be 70% of labor costs.

Ocaxet Inc. understands that the contractor typically adds a markup on labor and allocated internal costs to provide a profit margin on the job and estimates this markup rate to be 15%. Ocaxet Inc. also estimates the market risk premium to be 5% of the estimated inflation-adjusted cash flows. The risk-free rate of interest is 4%, and Ocaxet Inc. adjusts that rate by 3% to reflect the effect of its credit standing. Thus, the credit-adjusted risk-free rate used to compute expected present value is 7%. Ocaxet Inc. also assumes an annual inflation rate of 3.5% annually over the five-year period.

Initial measurement of the ARO liability at January 1, 20X8:

	Expected Cash Flows
Expected labor costs	$ 155,000
Allocated overhead and equipment charges (.70 × $155,000)	108,500
Contractor's markup [.15 × ($155,000 + $108,500)]	39,525
Expected cash outflows before inflation adjustment	303,025
Inflation factor (1.035^5)	1.1877
Expected cash flows adjusted for inflation	359,903
Market-risk premium (.05 × $359,903)	17,995
Expected cash flows adjusted for market risk	$377,898
Expected present value using credit-adjusted risk-free rate of 7% for 5 years [(1/(1 + .07^5) × $377,898]	$269,436

On December 31, 20Y2, Ocaxet Inc. settles its asset retirement obligation by using its internal workforce at a cost of $357,000. Assuming no changes during the five-year period in the cash flows used to estimate the obligation, the entity would recognize a gain of $20,898 on settlement of the obligation:

Labor	$210,000
Allocated overhead and equipment charges (70% of labor)	147,000
Total costs incurred	357,000
ARO liability	377,898
Gain on settlement of obligation	$ 20,898

Interest Method of Allocation

Year	Liability Balance 1/1	Accretion (7%)	Liability Balance 12/31
20X8	269,436	18,861	288,297
20X9	288,297	20,181	308,478
20Y0	308,478	21,593	330,071
20Y1	330,071	23,105	353,176
20Y2	353,176	24,722	377,898

Schedule of Expenses

Year-End	Accretion Expense	Depreciation Expense*	Total Expense
20X8	18,861	53,887	72,748
20X9	20,181	53,887	74,068
20Y0	21,593	53,887	75,480
20Y1	23,105	53,887	76,992
20Y2	24,722	53,887	78,609

*Assume straight-line deprecation ($269,436/5)

Journal Entries:

January 1, 20X8:

Long-lived asset (asset retirement cost)	269,436	
ARO liability		269,436
To record the initial fair value of the ARO liability		

December 31, 20X8–20Y2:

Depreciation expense (asset retirement cost)	53,887	
Accumulated depreciation		53,887
To record straight-line depreciation on the asset retirement cost		
Accretion expense	Per schedule	
ARO liability		Per schedule
To record accretion expense on the ARO liability		

December 31, 20Y2:

ARO liability	377,898	
Wages payable		210,000
Allocated overhead and equipment charges		147,000
Gain on settlement of ARO liability		20,898
To record settlement of the ARO liability		

Illustration of Accounting for an Asset Retirement Obligation— Obligation Incurred over Multiple Reporting Periods

This example highlights the recognition and measurement provisions for an ARO liability that is incurred over more than one reporting period.

Asem Inc. places a nuclear utility plant into service on December 31, 20X8. The entity is legally required to decommission the plant at the end of its useful life, which is estimated to be ten years.

The following schedule reflects the expected cash flows and respective credit-adjusted risk-free rates used to measure each portion of the liability through December 31, 20Y0, at which time the plant is 90% contaminated:

Date	Expected Cash Flows	Credit-Adjusted Risk-Free Rate
12/31/X8	$30,000	8.0%
12/31/X9	2,250	7.3
12/31/Y0	2,775	7.7

On December 31, 20Y0, Asem Inc. increases by 10% its estimate of expected cash flows that were used to measure those portions of the liability recognized on December 31, 20X8, and December 31, 20X9. Because the change results in an upward revision to the expected cash flows, the incremental estimated cash flow is discounted at the current credit-adjusted risk-free rate of 7.7%. As a result, the total incremental cash flows of $6,000 [($30,000 + $2,250) × 10%) + $2,775] are discounted at the then current credit-adjusted risk-free rate of 7.7% and recorded as a liability on December 31, 20Y0.

	Date Incurred		
	12/31/X8	12/31/X9	12/31/Y0
Initial measurement of the ARO liability:			
Expected labor cost	$30,000	$2,250	$2,775
Credit-adjusted risk-free rate	8.0%	7.3%	7.7%
Discount period in years	10	9	8
Expected present value	$13,896	$1,193	$1,533

Measurement of incremental expected cash flows occurring on 12/31/Y0:

Increase in expected cash flows of 10% [($30,000 + 2,250) × 10%]	$3,225
Credit-adjusted risk-free rate at December 31, 2010	7.7%
Discount period remaining in years	8
Expected present value [$3,225 × (1/(1.077^8)]	$1,782

Carrying Amount of Liability Incurred in 20X8

Year	Liability Balance 1/1	Accretion (8.0%)	New Liability	Liability Balance 12/31
20X8			13,896	13,896
20X9	13,896	1,112		15,008
20Y0	15,008	1,201		16,209

Carrying Amount of Liability Incurred in 20X9

Year	Liability Balance 1/1	Accretion (7.3%)	New Liability	Liability Balance 12/31
20X9			$1,193	$1,193
20Y0	$1,193	$87		1,280

Carrying Amount of Liability Incurred in 20Y0
Plus Effect of Change in Expected Cash Flows

Year	Liability Balance 1/1	Accretion (7.7%)	Change in Cash Flow Estimate	New Liability	Liability Balance 12/31
20Y0			$1,782	$1,533	$3,315

Carrying Amount of Total Liability

Year	Liability Balance 1/1	Accretion	Change in Cash Flow Estimate	New Liability	Liability Balance 12/31
20X8				$13,896	$13,896
20X9	$13,896	$1,112		1,193	16,201
20Y0	16,201	1,288	$1,782	1,533	20,804

Journal Entries:

December 31, 20X8:

Long-lived asset (asset retirement cost)   13,896
      ARO liability   13,896
To record the initial fair value of the ARO liability incurred in this period

December 31, 20X9:

Depreciation expense ($13,896/10)   1,390
      Accumulated depreciation   1,390
To record straight-line depreciation on the asset retirement cost

Accretion expense   1,112
      ARO liability   1,112
To record accretion expense on the ARO liability

Long-lived asset (asset retirement cost)   1,193
      ARO liability   1,193
To record the initial fair value of the ARO liability incurred in
    this period

December 31, 20Y0:

Depreciation expense [($13,896/10) + ($1,193/9)]   1,523
      Accumulated depreciation   1,523
To record straight-line depreciation on the asset retirement cost

Accretion expense   1,288
      ARO liability   1,288
To record accretion expense on the ARO liability

Long-lived asset (asset retirement cost)   1,782
      ARO liability   1,782
To record the change in liability resulting from a revision in
    expected cash flows

Long-lived asset (asset retirement cost)   1,533
      ARO liability   1,533
To record the initial fair value of the ARO liability incurred in this period

---

CONDITIONAL ASSET RETIREMENT OBLIGATIONS

FIN-47 (Accounting for Conditional Asset Retirement Obligations —An Interpretation of FAS-143), provides guidance on measuring the liability associated with an asset retirement obligation when there is uncertainty associated with the timing or method of the asset retirement. Although FAS-143 requires entities to recognize the fair value of an asset retirement obligation in the period in which the obligation is incurred, differences in practice have arisen because of differences in interpretation as to when a reasonable estimate of fair value can be made. In particular, although an entity may be legally required to retire a fixed asset, there may be uncertainties associated with the timing and/or method of the asset retirement. The timing and/or method may be conditional on a future event, and the entity may or may not control this future event. Some entities recognize a liability at the time the asset retirement obligation is incurred, and consider the uncertainties associated with the timing and/or method of retiring the asset in estimating the liability's fair value. Other entities only recognize a liability when the date and method of asset retirement are essentially fixed. FIN-47 is designed to reduce these differences in practice.

Interpretive Guidance

An asset can be retired by, among other ways, sale, abandonment, recycling, and disposal (FIN-47, par. 2). A liability exists if an entity has a legal obligation to retire a fixed asset, even if the timing and/or method of retiring the asset is conditional on a future event. That is, the obligation to retire the asset is unconditional, even though the timing and/or method of retiring the asset may be uncertain. Because a liability exists, that liability should be recognized if its fair value can be reasonably estimated (FIN-47, par. 3).

An asset retirement obligation is reasonably estimable if (1) the purchase price of the asset reflects the costs associated with the legally mandated obligation to retire the fixed asset, (2) the entity could transfer the asset retirement obligation to another party because an active market for such transfers exists, and (3) enough information exists to apply an expected present value technique (FIN-47, par. 4). In many instances, the fair value of the asset retirement obligation will not be transparent in the purchase price, nor will an active market for the transfer of the obligation exist. Therefore, very commonly, the fair value of an asset retirement obligation is determined using an expected present value technique.

Assuming the use of an expected present value technique, the fair value of an asset retirement obligation is reasonably estimable if either of two conditions exists (FIN-47, par. 5):

1. The settlement date and the method of settlement have been determined by the party that created the legal obligation (e.g., the legislative, executive, or private body that created the law, regulation, or contract giving rise to the legal obligation).

☞ **PRACTICE POINTER:**   The only uncertainty remaining if the date and method of settlement have been determined is whether the entity will be required to retire the asset by the party that created the legal obligation. The entity will either be required to retire the asset or it will not. If no information exists as to which outcome is more likely, the entity is to assign a 50% probability to each outcome (FIN-47, footnote 5).

2. Information is available that enables the entity to estimate the settlement date or range of possible settlement dates, and to assign probabilities to these potential settlement dates, and estimate the settlement method or potential settlement alternatives, and to assign probabilities to these potential settlement methods. This information should be developed from the entity's past practice, industry practice, the intent of management, and the asset's economic life.

☞ **PRACTICE POINTER:**   In some cases the entity still may be able to arrive at a reasonable estimate of the fair value of the asset retirement obligation even if the entity cannot assign probabilities to the potential settlement dates or methods of settlement. For example, the potential settlement dates may be close in time to each other and the alternative settlement methods may involve similar cash outflows. In this instance, differences in the assigned probabilities would not have a material effect on the computed fair value of the asset retirement obligation (FIN-47, footnote 8).

Notwithstanding the above guidance, there will be some instances where although a legal obligation to retire the asset exists (i.e., a liability exists), the liability will not be recognized because the entity cannot reasonably estimate the fair value of the liability. A liability must be recorded in a latter period, however, when information becomes available to estimate the fair value of the liability. And, if a liability is not recognized because it cannot be reasonably estimated, the entity must disclose that fact and must disclose the reasons the fair value of the liability cannot be reasonably estimated (FIN-47, par. 6).

Illustration of Accounting for a Conditional Asset Retirement Obligation

A company constructs manufacturing, distribution, and sales facilities that contain a building material that is non-toxic in its present state, but which is toxic if disposed of without following special procedures. There is no legal requirement to dispose of the building material. If any building is destroyed or substantially remodeled, however, the entity must follow legally mandated disposal procedures for the toxic material.

The company is able to estimate dates on which it is likely to destroy (raze) or substantially remodel each building, the methods that are likely to be used, and the associated probabilities. Therefore, at the date that each building is constructed, the company is able to estimate the asset retirement obligation using an expected present value technique. The recorded value of each building would be increased by the estimated present value of the asset retirement obligation, and a liability for the asset retirement obligation would be recognized as well.

Disclosure

Following are disclosures required about asset retirement obligations:

- General description of the asset retirement obligation and the associated long-lived asset
- Fair value of assets that are legally restricted for purposes of settling asset retirement obligations
- A reconciliation of the beginning and ending carrying amounts of asset retirement obligations showing separately:
  — Liabilities incurred in the current period
  — Liabilities settled in the current period
  — Accretion expense
  — Revisions in estimated cash flows where there is a significant change in the current period

If the fair value of an asset retirement obligation cannot be reasonably estimated, that fact and the reasons should be disclosed (FAS-143, par. 22).

RELATED CHAPTERS IN 2009 *GAAP GUIDE LEVEL A*

Chapter 1, "Accounting Changes"
Chapter 2, "Accounting Policies and Standards"
Chapter 16, "Fair Value"
Chapter 20, "Impairment of Long-Lived Assets"
Chapter 21, "Income Taxes"
Chapter 23, "Intangible Assets"
Chapter 24, "Interest Costs Capitalized"
Chapter 29, "Leases"
Chapter 32, "Nonmonetary Transactions"
Chapter 37, "Real Estate Transactions"

RELATED CHAPTERS IN 2009 *GAAP GUIDE* *LEVELS B, C, AND D*

Chapter 1, "Accounting Changes"
Chapter 2, "Accounting Policies and Standards"
Chapter 7, "Capitalization and Expense Recognition Concepts"
Chapter 16, "Fair Value"
Chapter 19, "Impairment of Long-Lived Assets"
Chapter 20, "Income Taxes"
Chapter 21, "Intangible Assets"
Chapter 26, "Leases"
Chapter 28, "Nonmonetary Transactions"
Chapter 33, "Real Estate Transactions"

RELATED CHAPTERS IN 2009 *INTERNATIONAL ACCOUNTING/FINANCIAL REPORTING STANDARDS GUIDE*

Chapter 2, "Framework for the Preparation and Presentation of Financial Statements"
Chapter 5, "Accounting Policies, Changes in Accounting Estimates, and Errors"
Chapter 6, "Borrowing Costs"
Chapter 9, "Changing Prices and Hyperinflationary Economies"
Chapter 16, "Financial Instruments"
Chapter 19, "Impairment of Assets"
Chapter 20, "Income Taxes"
Chapter 21, "Intangible Assets"
Chapter 25, "Leases"
Chapter 26, "Non-Current Assets Held for Sale and Discontinued Operations"
Chapter 27, "Property, Plant, and Equipment"

CHAPTER 12
DEVELOPMENT STAGE ENTERPRISES

CONTENTS

OVERVIEW

A development stage company is one for which principal operations have not commenced or principal operations have generated an insignificant amount of revenue. GAAP require that these entities issue the same financial statements as other enterprises and include additional disclosures.

GAAP for development stage companies are established in the following pronouncements:

FAS-7   Accounting and Reporting by Development Stage Enterprises

FIN-7   Applying FASB Statement No. 7 in Financial Statements of Established Operating Enterprises

BACKGROUND

A development stage company devotes most of its activities to establishing a new business. Planned principal activities have not commenced, or have commenced and have not yet produced significant revenue (FAS-7, par. 8). Typical development stage activities include raising capital, building production facilities, acquiring operating assets, training personnel, developing markets, and starting production.

> ☞ **PRACTICE POINTER:** FAS-7 (Accounting and Reporting by Development Stage Enterprises) does not provide guidance on what constitutes "significant" revenue; therefore, use judgment to determine whether a company is a development stage enterprise. An enterprise involved in the following activities can be said to be in the development stage (FAS-7, par. 9):
>
> - Financial planning
> - Raising capital
> - Exploring for natural resources
> - Developing natural resources
> - Research and development
> - Establishing sources of supply
> - Acquiring property, plant, equipment, and other operating assets
> - Training personnel
> - Developing markets
>
> Once the company's primary attention is turned to routine, ongoing activities, it ceases to be a development stage enterprise. The point at which an enterprise ceases to be in the development stage is a matter of judgment and must be evaluated on a case-by-case basis.

ACCOUNTING AND REPORTING STANDARDS

A development stage company issues the same basic financial statements as any other enterprise, and such statements should be prepared in conformity with GAAP. Accordingly, capitalized or deferred costs are subject to the same assessment of realizability as for an operating enterprise (FAS-7, par. 10).

In the case of a subsidiary or a similar type of enterprise, the determination of expensing or capitalizing costs is made within the context of the entity presenting the financial statements. Thus, it would be possible to expense an item in the financial statements of a subsidiary and capitalize the same expense in the financial statements of the parent company. For example, if a subsidiary purchases a machine that will be used only for research and development, it would expense the cost of the item in the year of acquisition. The parent company could capitalize the same machine, however, if in its normal course of business such a machine has an alternative future use elsewhere in the company (FIN-7, par. 4).

A development stage company that is a subsidiary may change an accounting method to conform to the requirements of FAS-7. In this situation, the effect would be reflected generally in the established operating enterprise's consolidated financial statements that include the subsidiary (FIN-7, par. 5).

> **OBSERVATION:** Some observers have taken the position that development stage companies should be permitted to apply standards that are different from those of established operating enterprises. For example, because significant revenue has yet to be generated, some believe that operating costs during a start-up period would be capitalized rather than expensed and amortized over the early years of operations. This was a common practice before FAS-7 was issued. The FASB took a position contrary to this view when it required development stage enterprises to present financial statements based on the same GAAP as established operating enterprises, with additional disclosures during the development stage.

DISCLOSURE STANDARDS

FAS-7 concentrates on establishing reporting and disclosure requirements for development stage companies. The required financial statements and additional information, summarized in Table 12-1, are as follows (FAS-7, par. 11):

- A balance sheet, presenting accumulated losses as "deficit accumulated during the development stage"
- An income statement, including revenues and expenses for each period being presented and also a cumulative total of both amounts from the company's inception. This provision also applies to dormant companies that have been reactivated at the development stage. In such cases, the totals begin from the time that development stage activities are initiated.
- A statement of cash flows, showing cumulative totals of cash inflows and cash outflows from the company's inception and amounts for the current period
- A statement of stockholders' equity, containing the following information:
  — The date and number of shares of stock (or other securities) issued for cash or other consideration and the dollar amount assigned
  — For each issuance of capital stock involving noncash consideration, a description of the nature of the consideration and the basis for its valuation

> ☞ **PRACTICE POINTER:** A company can combine separate transactions of equity securities, provided that the same type of securities, consideration per equity unit, and type of consideration are involved and the transactions are made in the same fiscal period.

Modification of the statement of stockholders' equity may be required for a combined group of companies that form a development stage company or for an unincorporated development stage entity.

> **OBSERVATION:**   GAAP do not indicate the types of modifications that might be necessary. Therefore, judgment must be exercised in the preparation of financial statements of development stage enterprises.

- The financial statements are to be identified as those of a development stage company and contain a description of the proposed business activities (FAS-7, par. 12).
- The financial statements for the first year that the company is no longer in the development stage shall indicate that in the prior year it was in the development stage. If the company includes prior years for comparative purposes, the cumulative amounts specified in 2 and 3 are not required (FAS-7, par. 13).

Table 12-1: Disclosure Requirements for Development Stage Companies

Category of Disclosure	Additional Information Required
Balance sheet	Accumulated losses during development stage, identified as "deficit accumulated during the development stage"
Income statement	Cumulative totals of revenues and expenses from the company's inception
Statement of cash flows	Cumulative totals of cash inflows and cash outflows from the company's inception
Statement of stockholders' equity	Date and number of shares of stock issued for cash and other consideration and dollar amounts assigned; nature of consideration and basis for valuation for each issuance of capital stock for non-cash consideration
Notes to financial statements	Identification of enterprise as development stage and proposed line of business

---

RELATED CHAPTERS IN 2009 *GAAP GUIDE LEVEL A*

Chapter 23, "Intangible Assets"
Chapter 39, "Research and Development"
Chapter 44, "Stockholders' Equity"

RELATED CHAPTERS IN 2009 *GAAP GUIDE LEVELS B, C, AND D*

Chapter 21, "Intangible Assets"
Chapter 34, "Research and Development"
Chapter 39, "Stockholders' Equity"

RELATED CHAPTER IN 2009 *INTERNATIONAL ACCOUNTING/FINANCIAL REPORTING STANDARDS GUIDE*

Chapter 21, "Intangible Assets"

CHAPTER 13
EARNINGS PER SHARE

CONTENTS

OVERVIEW

Earnings per share (EPS) is an important measure of corporate performance for investors and other users of financial statements. EPS figures are required to be presented in the income statement of publicly held companies and are presented in a manner consistent with the captions included in the income statement. Certain securities, such as convertible bonds, preferred stock, and stock options, permit their holders to become common stockholders or add to the number of shares of common stock already held. When potential reduction, called *dilution*, of EPS figures is inherent in a company's capital structure, a dual presentation of EPS is required—basic and diluted EPS.

GAAP governing the calculation and presentation of EPS information in financial statements are found in the following pronouncements:

FAS-128   Earnings per Share

2009 TRANSITION GUIDANCE FOR FAS-141(R) AND FAS-160

The FASB has recently issued FAS-141(R), *Business Combinations*, which is effective for business combinations for which the acquisition date is on or after the beginning of the first annual reporting period beginning on or after December 15, 2008. The FASB has also issued FAS-160, *Noncontrolling Interests in Consolidated Financial Statements, an Amendment of ARB No. 51*, which is effective for fiscal years, and interim periods within those fiscal years, beginning on or after December 15, 2008. Because these standards are not effective for some companies until December 2009, and because early adoption is prohibited, the 2009 *GAAP Guide* reflects the requirements of FAS-141 prior to its revision in December 2007 and does not reflect the requirements of FAS-160. There is a discussion of the changes in the accounting for business combinations under FAS-141(R) in the Appendix to Chapter 4, "Business Combinations." Similarly, the Appendix to Chapter 7, "Consolidated Financial Statements," includes a discussion of the requirements of FAS-160. However, any effects of FAS-141(R) and/or FAS-160 in this chapter have not been reflected in this edition. Therefore, if a company is subject to the requirements of FAS-141(R) and/or FAS-160, the reader is referred to FAS-141(R) and FAS-160 for these new requirements.

BACKGROUND

EPS figures are used to evaluate the past operating performance of a business in forming an opinion concerning its potential and in making investment decisions. EPS figures are commonly presented in prospectuses, proxy material, and financial reports to shareholders. They are also used in the compilation of business earnings data for the press, statistical services, and other publications. They generally are believed to be of value to investors in weighing the significance of a corporation's current net income and of changes in its net income from period to period in relation to the shares the investor holds or may acquire.

In 1969, the AICPA issued APB-15 (Earnings per Share), which required companies with complex capital structures to make a dual presentation of earnings per share (EPS)—primary and fully diluted. Companies with simple capital structures were required to make a single EPS presentation. By 1971, 102 interpretations of APB-15 had been issued. Given the importance of EPS figures, the primary objective of APB-15 and its many interpretations was to standardize the calculation and presentation of EPS so that figures would be computed on a consistent basis and presented in the most meaningful manner. An important dimension of APB-15 was the inclusion of common stock equivalents in the determination of primary EPS. This accounts for much of the uniqueness of U.S. GAAP when compared with practices in other parts of the world.

In 1993, the International Accounting Standards Committee (IASC) issued a draft on EPS for public comment. In recognition of the widespread importance of EPS, this proposed international standard was intended to begin a common approach to the determination and presentation of EPS that would permit global comparisons. The FASB simultaneously pursued a project that would help achieve international harmonization by requiring EPS be computed in a manner similar to that in the proposed IASC standard. FAS-128 (Earnings per Share) was issued at the same time as IASC-33 (Earnings per Share) and includes provisions that are substantially the same.

FAS-128 applies to entities with publicly held common stock or potential common stock (e.g., financial instruments or contracts that could result in the issuance of additional shares). It simplified the standards in APB-15 (Earnings per Share) for computing EPS by replacing primary earnings per share with basic EPS and by altering the calculation of diluted EPS, which replaces fully diluted EPS.

FAS-128 superseded APB-15 and its 102 interpretations. It also amended several other accounting pronouncements that make reference to primary and fully diluted EPS.

SIMPLE AND COMPLEX CAPITAL STRUCTURES

FAS-128 applies to all entities that have issued common stock or potential common stock that trades in a public market (i.e., in a stock exchange or in an over-the-counter market, including securities that trade only locally or regionally). *Potential common stock* consists of other securities and contractual arrangements that may result in the issuance of common stock in the future, such as (FAS-128, par. 6):

- Options
- Warrants
- Convertible securities
- Contingent stock agreements

Additional guidance on the applicability of FAS-128 includes the following (FAS-128, par. 6):

- The standard applies in situations in which an entity has made a filing, or is in the process of making a filing, with a regulatory agency in anticipation of selling securities in the future.
- The standard does *not* require the presentation of EPS by investment companies or in financial statements of wholly owned subsidiaries.
- The standard applies to entities that are not required to present EPS but choose to do so.

For purposes of presenting earnings per share, a distinction is made between enterprises with a simple capital structure and those with a complex capital structure.

Simple Capital Structures

A simple capital structure is one that consists of capital stock and includes no potential for dilution via conversions, exercise of options, or other arrangements that would increase the number of shares outstanding. For organizations with simple capital structures, the presentation of EPS using assumed income numbers and 50,000 shares of common stock outstanding in the income statement would appear as follows:

	20X9	20X8
Income before extraordinary item	$175,000	$160,000

Extraordinary item (describe)	15,000	—
Net income	$190,000	$160,000
Earnings per common share:		
Income before extraordinary item	$ 3.50	$ 3.20
Extraordinary item	.30	—
Net income per share	$ 3.80	$ 3.20

Complex Capital Structures

For organizations with complex capital structures, two EPS figures are presented with equal prominence on the face of the income statement. The captions for the two EPS figures are "Earnings per common share" and "Earnings per common share—assuming dilution" (or other similar descriptions).

The first of these captions is referred to as *basic EPS* and the second as *diluted EPS*. The difference between basic EPS and diluted EPS is that basic EPS considers only outstanding common stock, whereas diluted EPS incorporates the potential dilution from all potentially dilutive securities that would have reduced EPS.

Based on the information presented in the previous section and assuming 60,000 shares of stock outstanding for basic EPS and 75,000 for diluted EPS, EPS for a complex capital structure might appear as follows:

	20X9	20X8
Earnings per common share		
Income before extraordinary item	$ 2.92	$ 2.67
Extraordinary item	.25	—
Net income	$ 3.17	$ 2.67
Earnings per share assuming dilution		
Income before extraordinary item	$ 2.33	$ 2.13
Extraordinary item	.20	—
Net income	$ 2.53	$ 2.13

CALCULATING EPS

Objectives and General Guidance

The objectives and general approach for measuring basic and diluted EPS are presented in Table 13-1:

Table 13-1: Basic EPS vs. Diluted EPS

	Basic EPS	Diluted EPS
Objective	To measure the performance of an entity over the reporting period based on its outstanding common stock	To measure the performance of an entity over the reporting period based on its outstanding common stock and after giving effect to all dilutive potential common-shares that were outstanding during the period
Computation	Income attributable to common stock ÷ Weighted average number of common shares outstanding	(Income attributable to common stock + Adjustments for changes in income [loss] that are consistent with the issuance of dilutive potential common shares) ÷ (Weighted average number of common shares outstanding + Dilutive potential common shares)

Additional guidelines for determining *basic EPS* are as follows (FAS-128, pars. 8–10):

- Shares issued and acquired (e.g., treasury stock) during the period are weighted for the portion of the period they were outstanding.

- The amount of income (or loss) attributable to common stock is reduced (or increased) by dividends declared on preferred stock (whether or not paid) and by dividends on cumulative preferred stock (whether or not declared or paid).

- Contingently issuable shares (i.e., shares that are issuable for little or no cash consideration upon the satisfaction of certain conditions) are treated as outstanding and included in computing basic EPS as of the date that the conditions required for their issuance have been satisfied.

Additional guidelines for computing *diluted EPS* are as follows (FAS-128, pars. 11–12):

- The denominator is similar to that for basic EPS, except that dilutive potential common shares are added.

- Numerator adjustments are required that are consistent with the assumed issuance of dilutive potential common shares. For example, if shares issuable upon conversion of a convertible bond are added to the denominator, the after-tax interest savings is added to the numerator.

- The denominator of diluted EPS is based on the most advantageous conversion rate or exercise price from the standpoint of the security holder (i.e., the maximum number of shares that would be issued).

- Once EPS figures have been published, they are not retroactively restated for subsequent conversions or changes in the market price of the common stock.

Illustration of Determining Weighted-Average Shares

Common stock outstanding, 1/1/20X9	200,000 shares
Preferred stock (convertible into 2 shares of common stock) outstanding, 1/1/20X9	50,000 shares
Convertible debentures (convertible into 100 shares of common stock for each $1,000 bond)	$100,000

On March 31, ABC reacquired 5,000 shares of its own common stock.
On May 1, 20,000 shares of ABC preferred stock were converted into common stock.
On July 1, $50,000 of ABC convertible debentures was converted into common stock.
On September 30, ABC reacquired 5,000 shares of its common stock.

Computation of Weighted-Average Shares

1. Common stock outstanding, 1/1/x9   200,000
2. Common stock reacquired, 3/31/x9 ($5,000 \times {}^{9}/_{12}$)   (3,750)
3. Conversion of preferred stock on 5/1/x9 ($20,000 \times 2 \times {}^{8}/_{12}$)   26,667
4. Conversion of convertible debentures on 7/1/X9 ($50 \times 100 \times {}^{6}/_{12}$)   2,500
5. Common stock reacquired on 9/30/x9 ($5,000 \times {}^{3}/_{12}$)   <u>(1,250)</u>

      Total weighted average shares, 20x9   <u>224,167</u>

1. **Common stock outstanding** Because the 200,000 shares of common stock were outstanding for the entire year, all the shares are included in the weighted average shares.

2. **Common stock reacquired** On March 31, 20X9, 5,000 shares were reacquired, which means that 9/12 of the year they were not outstanding. Since the 5,000 shares are already included in the 200,000 shares

(1. above), that portion which was not outstanding during the full year must be deducted. Thus, 9/12 of the 5,000 shares, or 3,750 shares, are excluded from the computations, which means that only 196,250 of the 200,000 shares were outstanding for the full year.

3. **Conversion of preferred**   On May 1, 20X9, 20,000 shares of the preferred were converted into common stock. Since the conversion rate is 2 for 1, an additional 40,000 shares were outstanding from May 1 to the end of the year. Thus, 8/12 of the 40,000 shares, or 26,667 shares, are included in the weighted average shares outstanding for the year.

4. **Conversion of convertible debentures**   On July 1, 20X9, $50,000 of the convertible debentures were converted into common stock. The conversion rate is 100 shares for each $1,000 bond, which means that the $50,000 converted consisted of fifty $1,000 bonds, or 5,000 shares of common stock. Since the conversion was on July 1, only 6/12 of the 5,000 shares, or 2,500 shares, are included in the weighted average shares outstanding for the year.

5. **Common stock reacquired**   5,000 additional shares out of the 200,000 shares outstanding at the beginning of the year were reacquired on September 30, which means that for 3/12 of the year they were not outstanding. Thus, 3/12 of 5,000 shares, or 1,250 shares, must be excluded from the computation of weighted average shares outstanding for the year.

Stock splits or stock dividends (or reverse splits or dividends) are retroactively recognized in all periods presented in the financial statements. A stock split or stock dividend is recognized if it occurs after the close of the period but before issuance of the financial statements. If this situation occurs, it must be disclosed in the statements. Also, the dividends per share must be reported in terms of the equivalent number of shares outstanding at the time the dividend is declared.

Antidilution

The term *antidilution* refers to increases in EPS or decreases in loss per share. Diluted EPS computed in accordance with FAS-128 is intended to be a conservative measure of performance and, accordingly, is intended to reflect the potential reduction in EPS resulting from issuance of additional common shares. Thus, potential issuances that would increase EPS or reduce loss per share generally are excluded from the calculation.

Illustration of Antidilution

A company reports net income of $100,000 and has 50,000 shares of outstanding common stock. Basic EPS is $2.00 ($100,000/50,000 shares). The same company has 15,000 shares of potential common stock.

Situation 1

Assume the numerator adjustment for the potential common shares is $15,000. Including these potential common shares, EPS is computed as follows:

$$\frac{\$100,000 + \$15,000}{50,000 + 15,000} = \frac{\$115,000}{65,000} = \$1.77 \text{ per share}$$

In this situation, the potential common shares are *dilutive* (i.e., they reduce EPS), and diluted EPS is $1.77.

Situation 2

Assume the numerator adjustment for the potential common shares is $50,000. Including these potential common shares, EPS is computed as follows:

$$\frac{\$100,000 + \$50,000}{50,000 + 15,000} = \frac{\$150,000}{65,000} = \$2.31 \text{ per share}$$

In this situation, the potential common shares are *antidilutive* (i.e., they increase EPS), and would not be included in diluted EPS.

In applying the antidilution provisions of FAS-128, the following guidelines are important (FAS-128, pars. 13–16):

- In determining whether potential common shares are dilutive or antidilutive, each issue or series of issues of potential common shares is considered separately.

- In cases in which multiple issuances of potential common shares exist, one may be dilutive on its own but antidilutive when combined with other potential common shares. To reflect maximum dilution, each issue or series of issues of potential common shares is considered in sequence, starting with the most dilutive and moving to the least dilutive.

- An entity may report more than one income figure in its income statement (e.g., income from continuing operations, income before extraordinary item or income before accounting change, as well as net income). For purposes of determining whether potential common stock is dilutive, the diagram in Figure 13-1 shows which income figure should be used.

Once an issue or series of issues of potential common shares is determined to be *dilutive* using the appropriate income figure in Exhibit I, that issue or series of issues is considered to be outstanding in computing diluted EPS on all income amounts, even if it is antidilutive in one or more of those amounts. Similarly, once an issue or series of issues of potential common shares is determined to be *antidilutive* using the appropriate income figure in Figure 13-1, that issue or series of issues is omitted in computing diluted EPS on all income amounts, even if it would have been dilutive in one or more of those amounts.

Options and Warrants

The dilutive effect of options and warrants generally is determined by the *treasury stock method* (FAS-128, pars. 17–19). That method involves three interrelated steps, as follows:

Step 1: Exercise is assumed to have taken place and common shares are assumed to have been issued.

Step 2: The proceeds from the issuance of common stock are assumed to have been used to purchase treasury stock at the average market price for the period.

Step 3: The incremental shares issued (i.e., shares sold in Step 1 reduced by share repurchased in Step 2) are added to the denominator of the diluted EPS computation.

Figure 13-1: Control Income Figure for Judging Dilution

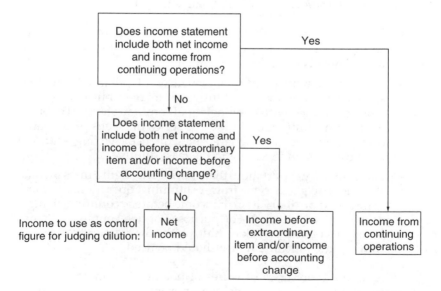

Illustration of Application of the Treasury Stock Method

By dividing its $100,000 net income by 100,000 shares of outstanding common stock, a company determines its basic EPS to be $1. In addition, options are outstanding that permit the purchase of 10,000 shares of common stock at $25. The average market price of the stock is $40. The treasury stock method is applied as follows:

Step 1: 10,000 shares sold at $25: 10,000 × $25 = $250,000 in proceeds

Step 2: $250,000 used to purchase treasury stock at $40: $250,000 / $40 = 6,250

Step 3: Net increase in outstanding shares: 10,000 − 6,250 = 3,750

Diluted EPS is computed as follows:

$$\frac{\$100,000}{100,000 + 3,750} = \frac{\$100,000}{103,750} = \$.96$$

Under this method, options and warrants will have a dilutive effect on EPS when the average market price of the stock (used for assumed repurchase in Step 2) exceeds the issuance price (used for assumed sale in Step 1), because of an assumed net increase in the number of outstanding shares. In this situation, options and warrants are described as "in the money." When options and warrants are outstanding for only part of the period, the amount determined by applying the treasury stock method is weighted for the part of the period the options and warrants were outstanding.

The rationale behind the treasury stock method is that any number of shares of common stock that could have been purchased on the open market with the exercised price funds from the options or similar instruments are not additional outstanding stock and have no dilutive effect on EPS.

☞ **PRACTICE POINTER:** A shortcut method of calculating the net increase in the number of outstanding shares of common stock by the treasury stock method is as follows:

$$\text{Incremental shares outstanding} = \frac{M - E}{M} \times \text{Number of shares obtainable}$$

where M = the market price and E = the exercise price

For example, assume a company has 10,000 options outstanding that permit the purchase of 1 share of common stock each at $16. The average market price is $25. Applying the three-step process of the treasury stock method indicates a net increase of 3,600 shares:

1. Proceeds = 10,000 × $16 = $160,000
2. Repurchase of shares = $160,000/25 = 6,400 shares
3. Net increase = 10,000 – 6,400 = 3,600 shares

The short-cut calculation is as follows:

$$\frac{\$25 - \$16}{\$25} \times \$10,000 = 3,600$$

When the market price of common stock rises significantly during the year, computation of the weighted average on a quarterly basis is preferred.

Illustration of Computation of Incremental Shares for Stock Options and Similar Instruments

A company has 10,000 stock options outstanding, which are exercisable at $60 each. Given the following market prices, determine the incremental shares by quarters, and the number of shares that are included in diluted EPS.

	Quarters			
	1	2	3	4
Average market price	56	64	70	68
Ending market price	60	68	72	64

Determining the incremental shares by quarters for diluted EPS follows:

1st quarter: no calculation* = 0

$$2\text{nd quarter:} 10,000 - \frac{100,000 + \$60}{\$64} = 625$$

$$3\text{rd quarter:} 10,000 - \frac{100,000 + \$60}{\$70} = 1,429$$

$$4\text{nd quarter:} 10,000 - \frac{100,000 + \$60}{\$68} = 1,176$$

Total incremental shares = 3,230

Divided by 4 quarters = 808

*The exercise price of $60 is higher than the average market price.

The total is divided by four quarters because four quarters entered into the computation. The 808 shares must be included in the computation of diluted EPS.

Share-Based Payment Arrangements and Awards of Share Options and Nonvested Shares

Fixed awards and nonvested stock to be issued to an employee under a stock-based compensation plan are considered options for purposes of computing diluted EPS. Guidelines for including these arrangements in diluted EPS are (FAS-128, pars. 20–23):

- They are considered to be outstanding as of the grant date, even though their exercise may be contingent upon vesting.
- They are included even if the employee may not receive the stock until some future date.
- Their impact is determined by applying the treasury stock method, and they are included only if their impact is dilutive.

In applying the treasury stock method, an important determination is the amount of proceeds due the issuing entity. FAS-128 identifies three components of the amount of proceeds from stock-based compensation arrangements:

1. The amount, if any, the employee must pay
2. The amount of compensation cost attributed to future services and not yet recognized
3. The amount of current and deferred tax benefits, if any, that would be credited to additional paid-in capital upon exercise of the options

These paragraphs make several other important observations. First, if stock-based compensation arrangements are payable in common stock or in cash at the discretion of either the employee or the employer, the determination of whether they are potential common shares is based on the provisions of paragraph 29 (covered below). Second, if the plan permits the employee to choose between types of equity instruments, diluted EPS is computed based on the terms used in the computation of compensation expense for the period. Finally, performance awards and targeted stock price options are subject to FAS-128's provisions on contingently issuable shares (covered below).

Illustration of Application of Treasury Stock Method to a Share-Based Payment Arrangement

Entity H adopted a share option plan on January 1, 20X8, and granted 500,000 at-the-money share options with an exercise price of $25. On that date, the fair value of each share option granted was $16.33. All share options vest at the end of five years (cliff vesting). At the grant date, Entity H assumes an annual forfeiture rate of 2% and therefore expects to receive the requisite service for 451,960 [500,000 × (.98^5)] share options. Employees forfeited 8,000 stock options ratably during 20X8. Thus, the weighted average number of share options outstanding in 20X8 equaled 496,000 [(500,000 + 492,000)/2]. The average stock price during 20X8 is $40, and there are 15,000,000 weighted-average common shares outstanding for the year. Net income for the period is $50,000,000 (inclusive of share-based compensation). Entity H's tax rate is 35%.

Entity H has sufficient previously recognized excess tax benefits in additional paid-in capital from prior share-based payment arrangements to offset any write-off of deferred tax assets associated with its grant of share options on January 1, 20X8. All share options are the type that upon exercise give rise to deductible compensation cost for income tax purposes.

Computation of Basic EPS for the Year Ended 12/31/20X8:

Net income	$ 50,000,000
Weighted-average common shares outstanding	15,000,000
Basic earnings per share	$ 3.333

Computation of average unrecognized compensation cost in 20X8:

Beginning of period:

Unrecognized compensation cost (500,000 × $16.33)		$ 8,165,000

End of period:

Beginning unrecognized compensation cost	$8,165,000	
Annual compensation cost recognized during 20×8, based on estimated forfeitures [(451,960 × $16.33) / 3]	(2,460,169)	
Annual compensation cost not recognized during the period related to outstanding options at 12/31/20×8, for which service is not expected to be rendered [(492,000 − 451,960) × $16.33) / 3]	(217,951)	
Total compensation cost of actual forfeited options (8,000 × $16.33)	(130,640)	
Total unrecognized compensation cost at end of period, based on actual forfeitures		5,356,240

Average total unrecognized compensation,
based on actual forfeitures
[(8,165,000 + 5,356,240) / 2] $ 6,760,620

Computation of tax benefit:

Total compensation cost of average
outstanding options (496,000 × $16.33) $ 8,099,680

Intrinsic value of average outstanding options
for the year ended 12/31/20X8
[496,000 × ($40 − $25)]   (7,440,000)

Excess of total compensation cost over
estimated tax deduction   659,680

Tax benefit deficiency ($659,680 ×.35) $ 230,888

Computation of assumed proceeds for diluted earnings per share:

Amount employees would pay if the
weighted-average number of options
outstanding were exercised using the
average exercise price (496,000 × $25) $ 12,400,000

Average unrecognized compensation cost in
20×8 (see above calculation)   6,760,620

Tax benefit deficiency that would be offset in
paid-in capital (see above calculation)   (230,888)

Assumed proceeds $ 18,929,732

Assumed repurchase of shares:

Repurchase shares at average market price
during the year ($18,929,732 / $40)   473,243

Incremental shares (496,000 − 473,243)   22,757

Computation of Diluted EPS for the Year Ended 12/31/20X8:

Net income $ 50,000,000

Weighted-average common shares
outstanding   15,000,000

Incremental shares   22,757

Total shares outstanding   15,022,757

Diluted earnings per share $ 3.328

Written Put Options and Purchased Options

Certain contracts may require an entity to repurchase its own stock. Examples are written put options and forward purchase contracts other than forward purchase contracts accounted for as a liability under FAS-150 (Accounting for Certain Financial Instruments with Characteristics of both Liabilities and Equity) (FAS-150, par. C1). These contracts are reflected in the calculation of diluted EPS if their effect is dilutive when the *reverse treasury stock method* is applied. As the name implies, that method is the reverse of the treasury stock method for requirements to repurchase, rather than issue, shares of common stock in stock option plans (FAS-128, par. 24).

The steps in the reverse treasury stock method are analogous to those in the treasury stock method:

Step 1: It is assumed that enough common shares were issued at the average market price to raise enough proceeds to satisfy the contract.

Step 2: The proceeds are assumed to be used to buy back the shares required in the contract.

Step 3: The increase in number of shares (i.e., shares sold in Step 1 reduced by the shares purchased in Step 2) are added to the denominator of the diluted EPS computation.

Applying the reverse treasury stock method will result in dilution of EPS if the options are "in the money" (i.e., the exercise price is above the average market price).

Illustration of the Reverse Treasury Stock Method

Ranalli's Lawn Service International (RLSI) has sold 10,000 put options at an exercise price of $40 per option. The average market price of RLSI's common stock during 20X8 is $25 per share. RLSI would apply the reverse treasury stock method as follows:

Step 1: RLSI needs to raise $400,000 (10,000 × $40) to satisfy its obligation under the put contract. In order to raise $400,000, RLSI nees to sell 16,000 shares of common stock, given the average market price per share of its stock during 20X8 ($400,000 / $25 = 16,000 shares).

Step 2: It is assumed that the $400,000 will be used to buy back the 10,000 shares, at $40 per share, per the terms of the put options written by RLSI.

Step 3: The 6,000 increase in the number of shares outstanding (16,000 shares issued from Step 1 minus the 10,000 shares repurchased from Step 2) are added to the denominator in calculating diluted EPS.

Contracts held by an entity on its own stock (e.g., purchased put options and purchased call options) are not included in the determination of diluted EPS, because to do so would be antidilutive due to the reduced number of outstanding shares (FAS-128, par. 25).

Convertible Securities

Incorporating the dilutive effect of convertible securities into EPS figures requires application of the *if-converted method* (FAS-128, pars. 26–28). The method derives its name from the underlying assumption that both the numerator and the denominator of the EPS calculation are restated to what they would have been if the convertible security had already been converted into common stock for the period. This usually requires the numerator to be adjusted for the amount of the preferred dividend (convertible preferred stock) or the interest expense (convertible debt instrument).

Specific guidelines for applying the if-converted method are as follows:

- For convertible preferred stock, the amount of the preferred dividend deducted in determining income attributable to common stockholders is added back in the numerator.

- For convertible debt securities, the numerator is adjusted for the following:
  — Interest charges applicable to the security are added back to the numerator.
  — To the extent nondiscretionary adjustments based on income would have been computed differently if the interest on convertible debt had never been recognized, the numerator is adjusted appropriately (e.g., for profit-sharing and royalty arrangements).
  — The above adjustments are made net-of-tax.

- Convertible preferred stock and convertible debt are treated as having been converted at the beginning of the period or at the time of issuance, if later.

- Conversion is not assumed if the effect is antidilutive. (This effect occurs when the preferred dividend per common share or the interest net of tax and nondiscretionary adjustments per common share exceeds basic EPS.)

Illustration of the If-Converted Method

A company had $100,000 of net income for the year and 100,000 shares of common stock outstanding. Consider the following two independent situations:

Situation 1

25,000 shares of 6%, $10 par-value convertible preferred stock are outstanding, and are convertible into 25,000 shares of common stock.

Basic EPS :
$$\frac{\$100,000 - \$15,000}{100,000 \text{ shares}} = \frac{\$85,000}{100,000} = \$.85$$

*Preferred dividend = 25,000 shares × $10 par × .06

Diluted EPS :
$$\frac{\$100,000 - \$15,000 + \$15,000}{100,000 + 25,000 \text{ shares}} = \frac{\$100,000}{125,000} = \$.80$$

Explanation: The $15,000 preferred dividend is deducted to determine basic EPS. To determine diluted EPS, the preferred dividend is added back to the numerator, and the 25,000 equivalent common shares are added to the denominator. This reduces EPS from $.85 to $.80.

Situation 2

100 convertible bonds, 10%, 1,000 par value, are outstanding, and each is convertible into 150 shares of common stock. The income tax rate is 35%, and interest already has been deducted in determining net income.

Basic EPS :
$$\frac{\$100,000}{100,000 \text{ shares}} = \$1.00$$

Diluted EPS :
$$\frac{\$100,000 + \$6,500}{100,000 + (100 \times 150) \text{ shares}} = \frac{\$106,500}{115,000} = \$.93$$

*After-tax interest: (100 bonds × $1,000 par × .10) × (1−.35)

Explanation: Basic EPS is calculated based on $100,000 of net income and 100,000 shares of common stock outstanding. To include the dilutive effect of the convertible bonds in diluted EPS, the after-tax effect of the interest is added to the numerator (i.e., interest that would have been avoided and the accompanying increase in income taxes), and the equivalent number of common shares (150 per bond) is added to the denominator. The impact is a reduction in EPS from $1.00 to $.93.

Contracts Subject to Settlement in Stock or Cash

Entities may issue a contract that allows either the entity or the holder to elect settlement in either common stock or cash. The impact of this type of arrangement on EPS is determined on the basis of the facts available each period. Usually it will be assumed that the contract will be settled in common stock if the effect of that assumption is more dilutive than an assumption that the contract will be settled in cash. If past experience or stated policy provides a reasonable basis for assuming that the contract will be settled in cash, however, the assumption that it will be settled in common stock may be overcome.

A contract that is reported as an asset or liability in the financial statements may require an adjustment to the numerator for any change in income or loss that would have taken place if the contract had been reported as an equity instrument. This is similar to the numerator adjustment for a convertible security presented earlier (i.e., the if-converted method) (FAS-128, par. 29).

Contingently Issuable Shares

Contingently issuable shares are shares that must be issued upon the satisfaction of certain conditions. They are considered outstanding and are included in diluted EPS as follows (FAS-128, par. 30):

- *All conditions for issuance satisfied by the end of the period*—Contingently issuable shares are included as of the beginning of the period in which the conditions were satisfied, or as of the date of the contingent stock agreement, if later.

- *All conditions for issuance not satisfied by the end of the period*—The number of contingently issuable shares included in diluted EPS is based on the number of shares, if any, that would be issuable if the end of the reporting period were the end of the contingency period.

In applying these procedures, the following guidance is provided (FAS-128, pars. 31–35):

Condition for Issuance of Stock	Treatment of Contingent Issuance in Diluted EPS, If Dilutive
Attainment or maintenance of a specified level of earnings, and that amount has been attained	Additional shares that would be issued, based on current earnings, are included in diluted EPS.
Future market price of stock	Additional shares that would be issued, based on the current market price, are included in diluted EPS.

Condition for Issuance of Stock	Treatment of Contingent Issuance in Diluted EPS, If Dilutive
Future earnings and market price of stock	Additional shares that would be issued, based on both current earnings and current market price of stock, are included in diluted EPS only if both conditions are met.
Condition other than earnings and/or market price of stock	Additional shares that would be issued under an assumption that the current status will remain unchanged are included in diluted EPS.
Other contingently issuable potential common shares (e.g., contingently issuable convertible securities)	Additional shares that would be issuable under current conditions based on appropriate sections of FAS-128 for options and warrants, convertible securities, and contracts that may be settled in stock or cash are included in diluted EPS.

INCOME STATEMENT PRESENTATION AND DISCLOSURE

Entities with simple capital structures (i.e., without potential common shares) and entities with complex capital structures (i.e., with potential common shares) are required to present EPS on the face of the income statement as follows (FAS-128, par. 36):

- *Simple capital structure*—basic EPS on income from continuing operations (or income before extraordinary item and/or change in accounting) and net income
- *Complex capital structure*—basic and diluted EPS (with equal prominence) on income from continuing operations (or income before extraordinary item and/or change in accounting) and net income

An entity that reports discontinued operations, an extraordinary item, or a cumulative effect of an accounting change shall include basic and diluted EPS on these items either on the face of the income statement or in related notes. If an entity chooses to present EPS figures on other items, those figures must be in notes to the financial statements, along with an indication of whether the EPS figures are pretax or net-of-tax (FAS-128, par. 37).

Several other guidelines for the presentation of EPS figures are as follows (FAS-128, pars. 38–39):

- EPS figures are required for all periods for which an income statement (or summary of earnings) is presented.

- If diluted EPS is presented for one period, it must be presented for all periods presented, even if it is the same as basic EPS for one or more periods.

- The terms "basic EPS" and "diluted EPS" are used in FAS-128, but are not required to be used in financial statements. Alternative titles, such as "earnings per common share" and "earnings per common share—assuming dilution" are acceptable.

In addition to specifying the EPS content on the face of the financial statement, FAS-128 also requires the following disclosures (FAS-128, par. 40):

- A reconciliation of the numerators and denominators used to compute basic and diluted EPS for income from continuing operations (or income before extraordinary item and/or cumulative effect of accounting change or net income, as appropriate)

- The amount of preferred dividend deducted in arriving at the amount of income attributable to common stockholders

- Potential common stock that was not included in the calculation of diluted EPS because it is antidilutive in the current period

- Description of any transaction that occurred after the end of the most recent period that would have materially affected the number of common shares outstanding or potential common shares if the transaction had occurred before the end of the reporting period

☛ **PRACTICE POINTER:** Normally, antidilutive potential common stock is omitted in determining diluted EPS. In applying the specific provisions of FAS-128, however, there are some instances in which potential common stock that is antidilutive is required to be included. There are also instances in which potential common stock that appears to be dilutive must be excluded. Take care to include or exclude the potential common stock in determining diluted EPS, even though doing this may seem counter-intuitive to the assumptions and intent underlying diluted EPS.

Two situations in which this is the case are as follows:

Including Antidilution

If the income statement includes more than one income figure [e.g., income (loss) from continuing operations, income (loss) before extraordinary item, net income (loss)], the one that appears first in the income statement is the benchmark number for determining whether potential common stock is included. If the potential diluter dilutes that income figure, it is included in determining diluted EPS for both or all three income figures, even though it may be antidilutive in the second or third income figure presented. For example, a company may report income as follows:

Income before extraordinary item	$100,000
Extraordinary loss	(125,000)
Net loss	($25,000)

Stock options that would dilute EPS on income before extraordinary item are outstanding. Because the market price of the stock exceeds the exercise price of the options, these options are dilutive and are included in computing earnings per share.

In this case, the stock options are considered to be potential common stock in determining earnings (loss) per share on *both* income before extraordinary item and net loss, even though they are dilutive in the first figure and antidilutive in the second.

Excluding Dilution

Where multiple convertible securities exist, test them for dilution in their order of dilutive effect, beginning with the most dilutive and proceeding to the least dilutive. EPS adjusted for previously considered convertible securities becomes the basis for judging the potential of each convertible security in the order considered.

For example, assume a company has basic EPS of $1.00 and has two convertible bond issues outstanding. These two convertibles have ratios of numerator adjustment (interest net of tax) to denominator adjustment (number of shares) as follows:

Bonds A	$.90
Bonds B	$.95

Bonds A are more dilutive than Bonds B ($.90 is less than $.95), so they are considered first. Assume that including Bonds A reduces EPS from $1.00 to $.97. The $.95 figure for Bonds B is compared with $.97, determined to be further dilutive, and included in determining diluted EPS. On the other hand, if including Bonds A had reduced EPS from $1.00 to $.85, Bonds B would have been judged antidilutive and excluded from the determination of diluted EPS, even though they would have been dilutive if considered alone.

Illustration of Basic and Diluted EPS

In 20X8, Stahl, Inc., a public company, had 52,500 shares of common stock outstanding at January 1, sold 10,500 shares on March 1, and repurchased 2,000 shares on November 1. Net income for the year was $375,000, and the appropriate income tax rate was 35%. Stahl's common stock sold for an average of $25 during the year and ended the year at $28.

Other financial instruments in the company's capital structure are as follows:

- Preferred stock—10,000 shares outstanding, $50 par, 6% dividend (cumulative)
- Stock options—15,000 options to purchase one share each of common stock stock at $20 each
- Convertible bonds—$200,000 par, 10%, convertible into 20 shares of common stock per $1,000 bond

Basic and diluted EPS are determined as follows:

Preliminary Calculations

Weighted-average number of common shares outstanding

Jan. 1	52,500 × 2 months	=	105,000
	10,500		
March 1	63,000 × 8 months	=	504,000
	(2000)		
Nov. 1	61,000 × $\frac{2 \text{ months}}{12}$	=	$\frac{122,000}{731,000}$
	731,000 / 12 months	=	60,917

Alternatively, the weighted-average can be calculated as follows:

Jan. 1	Outstanding	=	52,500
March 1	10,500 × $10/_{12}$	=	8,750
Nov. 1	2,000 × $2/_{12}$	=	$\frac{(333)}{60,917}$

Preferred dividend

$$10,000 \text{ shares} \times \$50 \text{ par value} \times .06 = \$30,000$$

Treasury stock method applied to stock options

Sale of common stock	15,000 shares × $20	=	$300,000
Repurchase of common stock	$300,000 / $25	=	12,000
Net increase in outstanding shares	15,000 − 12,000	=	3,000

Alternatively, the effect of applying the treasury stock method may be computed as follows:

$$(25 - 20) / 25 \times 15,000 \qquad = \qquad 3,000$$

If-converted method applied to convertible bonds

Numerator increase	$200,000 × .10 × (1 − .35)	=	$13,000
Denominator increase	20 shares × 200 bonds	=	4,000
Dilutive effect	$13,000 / 4,000 shares	=	3.25

Basic and Diluted EPS

Numerator	Net income	$375,000c	
	Preferred income	(30,000)	
		$345,000	Basic
	Impact of potential common shares:		
	Convertible bonds	13,000	
		$358,000	Diluted
Denominator	Weighted-average outstanding shares	60,917	Basic
	Impact of potential common shares:		
	Convertible bonds	4,000	
	Stock options	3,000	
		67,917	Diluted
Basic EPS	$345,00/60,917	= $5.66	
Diluted EPS	$358,000/67,917	= $5.27	

EARNINGS PER SHARE
IMPORTANT NOTICE FOR 2009

As the 2009 *GAAP Guide Level A* goes to press, the FASB has issued an Exposure Draft of a Proposed Statement of Financial Accounting Standards titled "Earnings per Share." This proposed standard would amend FAS-128 (Earnings per Share). The proposed standard was covered in the *GAAP Update Service*, Vol. 4, Issue 5 (March 15, 2004), and a revised version of the proposed standard was covered in the *GAAP Update Service*, Vol. 5, Issue 24 (December 30, 2005). The current FASB Technical Plan calls for a third exposure draft to be issued in 2008.

At the current time, the proposed standard includes mandatorily convertible instruments in basic EPS only if the holders of these instruments could participate in current period earnings with common stockholders. That is, if holders of the mandatorily convertible instrument could receive consideration above the specified contractual amount as a result of a distribution to common stockholders, then these instruments would be included in the computation of basic EPS.

Instruments that give the holder the right to share in current period earnings with common stockholders should be included in the denominator of the EPS calculation. Examples of these instruments are: (1) instruments exercisable at little, if any, cost to the holder; and (2) participating securities whose fair value changes are not included in current period income or that are not measured at fair value.

The proposed standard also would alter the computational guidance for calculating the number of incremental shares included in diluted earnings per share when the treasury stock method is applied. The dilutive effect of options and warrants should be reflected by applying the treasury stock method for the year-to-date period independently of any interim computation. Options and warrants will have a dilutive effect only when the average market price of the common stock for the year-to-date period exceeds the exercise price of the options and warrants. In addition, the carrying amount of a liability extinguished through the issuance of additional shares is to be treated as proceeds in computing the number of incremental shares issued under the treasury stock method.

The proposed standard requires that shares that would be issued upon conversion of a mandatorily convertible security be included in the computation of basic and diluted earnings per share from the date the securities become mandatorily convertible. In addition, when an entity has issued a contract that may be settled either in shares or in cash at the entity's option, the entity should presume that the contract will be settled in shares if the effect is dilutive. Also, the proposed standard treats contingently issuable shares as outstanding in computing diluted EPS from the beginning of the period in which the conditions for the issuance of additional shares are met or, if later, the date of the contingent share arrangement.

Additional shares issuable upon conversion of an instrument that is recorded at fair value with changes in fair value included in current period earnings is *not* included in the denominator of the diluted EPS computation. The change in fair value included in earnings sufficiently reflects the dilutive effect of these instruments.

RELATED CHAPTERS IN 2009 *GAAP GUIDE LEVEL A*

Chapter 1, "Accounting Changes"
Chapter 9, "Convertible Debt and Debt with Warrants"
Chapter 17, "Financial Instruments"
Chapter 40, "Results of Operations"
Chapter 44, "Stockholders' Equity"

RELATED CHAPTERS IN 2009 *GAAP GUIDE LEVELS B, C, AND D*

Chapter 1, "Accounting Changes"
Chapter 12, "Convertible Debt and Debt with Warrants"
Chapter 13, "Earnings per Share"
Chapter 17, "Financial Instruments"
Chapter 35, "Results of Operations"
Chapter 39, "Stockholders' Equity"

RELATED CHAPTERS IN 2009 *INTERNATIONAL ACCOUNTING/FINANCIAL REPORTING STANDARDS GUIDE*

Chapter 3, "Presentation of Financial Statements"
Chapter 5, "Accounting Policies, Changes in Accounting Estimates, and Errors"
Chapter 12, "Earnings per Share"
Chapter 16, "Financial Instruments"

CHAPTER 14
EQUITY METHOD

CONTENTS

OVERVIEW

The equity method of accounting for investments in common stock is appropriate if an investment enables the investor to influence the operating or financial decisions of the investee. In these circumstances, the investor has a degree of responsibility for the return on its investment, and it is appropriate to include in the investor's results of operations its share of the earnings or losses of the investee. The equity method is not intended as a substitute for consolidated financial statements when the conditions for consolidation are present.

The following pronouncements are the sources of promulgated GAAP concerning the equity method:

APB-18   The Equity Method of Accounting for Investments in Common Stock

FAS-94   Consolidation of All Majority-Owned Subsidiaries

FIN-35   Criteria for Applying the Equity Method of Accounting for Investments in Common Stock

2009 TRANSITION GUIDANCE FOR FAS-141(R) AND FAS-160

The FASB has recently issued FAS-141(R), *Business Combinations*, which is effective for business combinations for which the acquisition date is on or after the beginning of the first annual reporting period beginning on or after December 15, 2008. The FASB has also issued FAS-160, *Noncontrolling Interests in Consolidated Financial Statements, an Amendment of ARB No. 51*, which is effective for fiscal years, and interim periods within those fiscal years, beginning on or after December 15, 2008. Because these standards are not effective for some companies until December 2009, and because early adoption is prohibited, the 2009 *GAAP Guide* reflects the requirements of FAS-141 prior to its revision in December 2007 and does not reflect the requirements of FAS-160. There is a discussion of the changes in the accounting for business combinations under FAS-141(R) in the Appendix to Chapter 4, "Business Combinations." Similarly, the Appendix to Chapter 7, "Consolidated Financial Statements," includes a discussion of the requirements of FAS-160. However, any effects of FAS-141(R) and/or FAS-160 in this chapter have not been reflected in this edition. Therefore, if a company is subject to the requirements of FAS-141(R) and/or FAS-160, the reader is referred to FAS-141(R) and FAS-160 for these new requirements.

BACKGROUND

Domestic and foreign investments in common stock and corporate joint ventures shall be presented in financial statements on the *equity basis* by an investor whose investment in the voting stock and other factors give it the ability to *exercise significant influence over the operating and financial policies* of the investment.

The equity method of accounting is not required in accounting for unconsolidated majority-owned subsidiaries in consolidated financial statements (FAS-94, par. 15).

Under the equity method of accounting for investments in common stock, net income during a period includes the investor's proportionate share of the net income reported by the investee for the periods subsequent to acquisition. *The effect of this treatment is that net income for the period and stockholders' equity at the end of the period are the same as if the companies had been consolidated.* Any dividends received are treated as adjustments of the amount of the investment under the equity basis.

When appropriate, investors use the equity method to account for investments in common stock, corporate joint ventures, and in other common stock investments (domestic and foreign) in which ownership is less than a majority interest.

PRESUMPTION OF SIGNIFICANT INFLUENCE

Evidence that the investor has significant influence over the investee includes the following (APB-18, par. 17):

- Investor has representation on the board of directors of the investee.

- Investor participates in the policy-making process of the investee.

- Material intercompany transactions occur between the investor and the investee.

- There is an interchange of managerial personnel between the investor and the investee.

- Technological dependency of the investee on the investor exists.

- There exists significant extent of ownership of the investor in relation to the concentration of other shareholders.

Absent evidence to the contrary, an investment (directly or indirectly) of less than 20% of the voting stock of an investee is presumed to indicate lack of significant influence, and the use of the equity method or consolidated statements is not required.

Absent evidence to the contrary, *an investment (directly or indirectly) of 20% or more of the voting stock of an investee is presumed to indicate the ability to exercise significant influence, and the equity method is required for a fair presentation* (APB-18, par. 17).

☞ **PRACTICE POINTER:** There is a presumption in APB-18 (The Equity Method of Accounting for Investments in Common Stock) that significant influence does not exist in an investment of less than 20%. However, APB-18 makes clear that this presumption may be overcome by evidence to the contrary. Thus, significant influence over the operating and financial policies of an investment of less than 20% can occur. The 20% cut-off is intended to be a guideline, subject to individual judgment, rather than a rigid rule.

For example, an investor might own only 15% of the voting common stock of an investee, be responsible for a substantial amount of the sales of the investee, and be represented on the investee's board of directors. In this case, the equity method may be the appropriate method of accounting by the investor, even though the investor holds only 15% of the voting stock.

Even with an investment of 20% or more, evidence may exist to demonstrate that the investor cannot exercise significant influence over the operating and financial policies of the investee. Thus, the presumption of significant influence in investments of 20% or more may be overcome by sufficient evidence.

The 20% ownership is based on current outstanding securities that have voting privilege. Potential ownership and voting privileges should be disregarded (APB-18, par. 18).

The following conditions may indicate that an investor is *unable* to exercise significant influence over the operating and financial policies of an investee:

- The investee opposes the investment (e.g., files a lawsuit, complains to government regulatory authorities), challenging the ability of the investee to exercise significant influence (FIN-35, par. 4a).

- An agreement is executed between the investee and the investor that indicates that significant influence does not exist (FIN-35, par. 4b).

> **OBSERVATION:** These types of agreements generally are referred to as *standstill agreements* and frequently are used to settle disputes between an investor and an investee. They may contain information as to whether the investor can or cannot exercise significant influence over the investee. The following are some typical provisions of a standstill agreement:
>
> - The investee agrees to use its best efforts to obtain representation for the investor on its board of directors.
> - The investor agrees not to seek representation on the investee's board of directors.
> - The investee may agree to cooperate with the investor.
> - The investor may agree to limit its ownership in the investee.
> - The investor may agree not to exercise its significant influence over the investee.
> - The investee may acknowledge or refute the investor's ability to exercise significant influence.
>
> If a standstill agreement contains provisions indicating that the investor has given up some significant rights as a shareholder, the agreement is regarded, under FIN-35 (Criteria for Applying the Equity Method of Accounting for Investments in Common Stock), as a factor in determining that the equity method should not be used.

- Significant influence is exercised by a small group of shareholders other than the investor representing majority ownership of the investee (FIN-35, par. 4c).

- The investor attempts, but cannot obtain, the financial information that is necessary to apply the equity method (FIN-35, par. 4d).

☞ **PRACTICE POINTER:** The *Codification of Statements on Auditing Standards* (AU 332.57(f)(3)) states that "Management's inability to obtain information from an investee may suggest that it does not have the ability to significantly influence the investee."

- The investor attempts and fails to obtain representation on the investee's board of directors (FIN-35, par. 4e).

OBSERVATION: FIN-35 implies that the investor must actually try to obtain financial information or representation on the investee's board. It seems logical that the same effect should result in the event that the investor had prior knowledge that it would fail in these attempts and, therefore, did not even attempt them.

Many other factors, not listed above, may affect an investor's ability to exercise significant influence over the operating and financial policies of an investee. An investor must evaluate all existing circumstances to determine whether factors exist that overcome the presumption of significant influence in an investment of 20% or more of an investee.

OBSERVATION: On the other hand, an investor must also evaluate existing circumstances in an investment of less than 20% of an investee. The presumption that significant influence does not exist in an investment of less than 20% may be overcome by factors that indicate that significant influence does exist.

If there is not enough evidence to reach a definitive conclusion at the time that the investment is made, it may be advisable to wait until more evidence becomes available.

Change in Significant Influence

Because of the purchase or sale of investment shares, and for other reasons that may affect the assessment of the ability to significantly influence the investee, an investor may be required to change to or from the equity method. The following procedures are applied in the following circumstances (APB-18, par. 19):

- If an investment in voting stock falls below the 20% level, or other factors indicate that the investor can no longer exercise significant influence, the presumption is that the investor has lost the ability to exercise significant influence and control, in which case the equity method should be discontinued. The carrying amount at the date of discontinuance becomes the cost of the investment. Subsequent dividends are accounted for in current income from the date the equity method was discontinued.

- An investor who, because of other factors, obtains significant influence or who acquires more than 20% ownership in an investee after having had less than 20% *must retroactively adjust its accounts to the equity method based on a step-by-step acquisition of an investment*. In this event, at the date of each step in the acquisition, the carrying value of the investment is compared with the underlying net assets of the investee to determine the existence of differences between investment cost and the underlying book value of the investee's net assets. Such differential is amortized as an addition to or a deduction from investment income.

☛ **PRACTICE POINTER:** In applying the equity method on a step-by-step basis, use the actual percentage of common stock owned in past periods, even if at that time the investment did *not* qualify for equity-method accounting. For example, assume that a company owned 10% of the common stock of an investee in 20X8 and 20X9, increased its ownership to 15% for 20Y0, and again increased its ownership to 24% in 20Y1, at which time the company adopted the equity method. The step-by-step restatement would include 10% of income for 20X8 and 20X9 and 15% of income for 20Y0, even though those ownership percentages did not justify the use of the equity method during those years.

APPLYING THE EQUITY METHOD

Under the equity method, the original investment is recorded at cost and is adjusted periodically to recognize the investor's share of earnings or losses after the date of acquisition. *Dividends received reduce the basis of the investment.* Continuing operating losses from the investment may indicate the need for an adjustment in the basis of the investment in excess of those recognized by the application of the equity method.

An investor's share of earnings or losses from its investment usually is shown as a *single amount* (called a *one-line consolidation*) in the income statement. The following procedures are appropriate in applying the equity method (APB-18, par. 19):

1. Intercompany profits and losses are eliminated by reducing the investment balance and the income from investee for the investor's share of the unrealized intercompany profits and losses.

2. The investment is shown in the investor's balance sheet as a single amount and earnings or losses are shown as a single amount (one-line consolidation) in the income statement, *except for the investor's share of (a) extraordinary items and (b) prior-period adjustments, which are shown separately.*

3. Capital transactions of the investee that affect the investor's share of stockholders' equity are accounted for as if the investee were consolidated.

4. Gain or loss is recognized when an investor sells the common stock investment, *equal to the difference between the selling price and the carrying amount of the investment at the time of sale.*

5. If the investee's financial reports are not timely enough for an investor to apply the equity method currently, the investor may use the most recent available financial statements, and the lag in time created should be consistent from period to period.

6. Other than temporary declines, a loss in value of an investment should be recognized in the books of the investor.

7. When the investee has losses, applying the equity method decreases the basis of the investment. The investment account generally is not reduced below zero, at which point the use of the equity method is discontinued, unless the investor has guaranteed obligations of the investee or is committed to provide financial support. The investor resumes the equity method when the investee subsequently reports net income and the net income exceeds the investor's share of any net losses that were not recognized during the period of discontinuance.

8. Dividends for cumulative preferred stock of the investee are deducted before the investor's share of earnings or losses is computed, whether the dividend was declared or not.

9. The investor's shares of earnings or losses from an investment accounted for by the equity method are based on the outstanding shares of the investee without regard to common stock equivalents (APB-18, par. 18).

☛ **PRACTICE POINTER:** As a result of FAS-142 (Goodwill and Other Intangible Assets) any difference between the underlying equity in net assets of the investee and the cost of the investment is *no longer amortized.* However, equity method goodwill is tested for impairment, no less frequently than on an annual basis. Moreover, an impairment in the value of an equity method investment that is other than temporary should be recognized currently in income (FAS-142, par. 40).

Illustration of Equity Method

On December 31, 20X8, LKM Corporation acquired a 30% interest in Nerox Company for $260,000. Total stockholders' equity on the date of acquisition consisted of capital stock (common $1 par) of $500,000 and retained earnings of $250,000. During 20X9, Nerox Company had net income of $90,000 and paid a $40,000 dividend. LKM has an income tax rate of 35%.

Entries to record the investment, the dividends and net income of the investee are as follows:

Investment in Nerox	260,000	
Cash		260,000
Cash ($40,000 × 30%)	12,000	
Investment in Nerox		12,000
Investment in Nerox	27,000	
Income from investee		27,000
Income tax expense	5,250	
Deferred income taxes		5,250

The deferred income tax is determined as follows:

$$(\$27,000 - \$12,000) \times 35\% = \$5,250$$

On December 31, 20X9, the investment account on the balance sheet would show $275,000 ($260,000 − $12,000 + $27,000) and the income statement would show $27,000 as income from investee. Income tax expense and deferred income tax liability would increase by $5,250. Also, at December 31, 20X9, LKM Corporation would have to test the equity method goodwill for impairment using the FAS-142 guidance (see the chapter titled "Business Combinations" of this *Guide*). The equity method goodwill at acquisition is determined as follows:

$$(\$260,000 - 30\% (\$500,000 + \$250,000)) = \$35,000$$

Assume that the equity method goodwill is not impaired as of December 31, 20X9.

The balance in the investment account equals the investment percentage multiplied by the stockholders' equity of the investee, adjusted for any unamortized goodwill. This reconciliation for the above example is as follows:

Stockholders' equity, beginning of 20X9	$750,000
Add: 20X9 net income	90,000
Deduct: 20X9 dividends	(40,000)
Stockholders' equity, end of 20X9	$800,000
Ownership percentage	30%
Pro rata share of stockholders' equity	$240,000

Investment balance, end of 20X9	$275,000
Less: Equity method goodwill	(35,000)
Investment balance adjusted for equity method goodwill	$240,000

Illustration of Step Acquisition

Roper, Inc. owned common stock in Purple Tiger Co. from 20X8 to 20Y1 as follows: 20X8 and 20X9—10%; 20Y0—17%; 20Y1—25%. Purple Tiger has no preferred stock outstanding. Roper, Inc. carries the investment at cost, which approximates market value.

As part of the audit of the 20Y1 financial statements, the decision was made to change to the equity method for the investment in Purple Tiger Co. The net income and dividends paid by Purple Tiger Co. from 20X8 to 20Y1 were as follows:

	Net Income	Dividends Paid
20X8	$72,500	$30,000
20X9	65,000	35,000
20Y1	68,800	38,000
20Y2	85,000	40,000

Dividends received have been properly recorded for 20X8–20Y1 as dividend revenue. All investments were made in amounts approximating the underlying book value acquired.

The general journal entry to record Roper, Inc.'s change from the cost to the equity method, ignoring income taxes, is as follows:

Dividend income	10,000	
Investment in Purple Tiger, Co.	23,736	
($46,696 – 22,960)		
Equity in income of Purple Tiger Co.		21,250
Retained earnings		12,486
($25,446 –12,960)		

Analysis of net income and dividends:

	Net Income	Roper Share	Dividends	Roper Share
20X8	$72,500 × 10% =	$ 7,250	$30,000 × 10% =	$ 3,000
20X9	65,000 × 10% =	6,500	35,000 × 10% =	3,500
20Y0	68,800 × 17% =	11,696	38,000 × 17% =	6,460
		25,446		12,960
20Y1	85,000 × 25% =	21,250	40,000 × 25% =	10,000
		$46,696		$22,960

Joint Ventures

A *joint venture* is an entity that is owned, operated, and jointly controlled by a group of investors. A joint venture might be organized as a partnership or a corporation, or be unincorporated (each investor holding an undivided interest).

Technically, APB-18 applies only to corporate joint ventures. If the criteria for applying the equity method are met, investments in corporate joint ventures must use the equity method. In 1979, the AICPA Accounting Standards Executive Committee (AcSEC) published an Issues Paper titled *Joint Venture Accounting*, which made several recommendations regarding accounting for joint ventures:

- The equity method should be applied to investments in unincorporated joint ventures subject to joint control.

- Majority interests in unincorporated joint ventures should be consolidated.

- Investments in joint ventures not subject to joint control should be accounted for by proportionate consolidation.

- Additional supplementary disclosures regarding the assets, liabilities, and results of operations are required for all material investments in unincorporated joint ventures.

Income Taxes

Applying the equity method results in the recognition of income based on the undistributed earnings of the investee. If the investee is not an S corporation, the investor has no tax liability for equity method income until those earnings are distributed. Thus, application of the equity method gives rise to temporary differences that should be considered when deferred tax assets and liabilities are measured.

Intercompany Profits and Losses

If transactions between an investor and an investee result in assets that contain unrealized profits from intercompany sales, both the investment account and the income from investee account must be adjusted to eliminate the intercompany profits. These adjustments also give rise to deferred tax adjustments.

Illustration of Elimination of Intercompany Profits

An equity method investor sells inventory "downstream" to an investee. At the end of the year, $50,000 of profit remains in inventory from intercompany sales. The investor has a 40% interest in the voting stock of the investee, and the income tax rate is 30%. The entry for the elimination of intercompany profits is made as follows:

Income from investee ($50,000 × 40%)	20,000	
Deferred tax asset ($20,000 × 30%)	6,000	
Investment in investee		20,000
Income tax expense		6,000

If the intercompany sales were "upstream" (i.e., from the investee to the investor), the elimination entry would be as follows:

Income from investee [$20,000 × (1 −.30)]	14,000	
Deferred tax asset	6,000	
Inventory		20,000

DISCLOSURE STANDARDS

Disclosure must be made for investments accounted for by the equity method and include (APB-18, par. 20):

- The name of the investment
- The percentage of ownership
- The accounting policies of the investor in accounting for the investment
- The difference between the carrying value of the investment and the underlying equity in the net assets, and the accounting treatment of such difference
- The quoted market price of the investment, except if it is a subsidiary
- If material, a summary of the assets, liabilities, and results of operations presented as a footnote or as separate statements
- The material effect on the investor of any convertible securities of the investee

If the equity method is not used for an investment of 20% or more of the voting stock, disclosure of the reason is required. Conversely, if the equity method is used for an investment of less than 20%, disclosure of the reason is required.

☞ **PRACTICE POINTER:** In evaluating the extent of disclosure, the investor must weigh the significance of the investment in relation to its financial position and results of operations.

RELATED CHAPTERS IN 2009 *GAAP GUIDE LEVEL A*

Chapter 4, "Business Combinations"
Chapter 7, "Consolidated Financial Statements"
Chapter 17, "Financial Instruments"
Chapter 21, "Income Taxes"
Chapter 28, "Investments in Debt and Equity Securities"

RELATED CHAPTERS IN 2009 *GAAP GUIDE LEVELS B, C, AND D*

Chapter 6, "Business Combinations"
Chapter 10, "Consolidated Financial Statements"
Chapter 14, "Equity Method"
Chapter 17, "Financial Instruments"
Chapter 20, "Income Taxes"
Chapter 25, "Investments in Debt and Equity Securities"

RELATED CHAPTERS IN 2009 *INTERNATIONAL ACCOUNTING/FINANCIAL REPORTING STANDARDS GUIDE*

Chapter 7, "Business Combinations"
Chapter 10, "Consolidated Financial Statements"
Chapter 14, "The Equity Method"
Chapter 16, "Financial Instruments"
Chapter 20, "Income Taxes"
Chapter 24, "Investment Property"

CHAPTER 15
EXTINGUISHMENT OF DEBT

CONTENTS

OVERVIEW

An *extinguishment of debt* is the reacquisition of debt, or removal of debt from the balance sheet, prior to or at the maturity date of that debt. Gain or loss on the extinguishment is the difference between the total reacquisition cost of the debt to the debtor and the net carrying amount of the debt on the debtor's books at the date of extinguishment.

GAAP for the extinguishment of debt are found in the following authoritative pronouncements:

APB-26	Early Extinguishment of Debt
FAS-22	Changes in the Provisions of Lease Agreements Resulting from Refundings of Tax-Exempt Debt
FAS-140	Accounting for Transfers and Servicing of Financial Assets and Extinguishments of Liabilities
FAS-145	Rescission of FASB Statements No. 4, 44, and 64, Amendment of FASB Statement No. 13, and Technical Corrections

The authoritative literature carefully defines when debt has been extinguished and generally requires any gain or loss on extinguishments of debt to be included in the determination of net income in the period of the extinguishment transaction.

BACKGROUND

Prior to the establishment of GAAP for extinguishment of debt, differences in practice existed with regard to the recognition of gains and losses from refunding of debt issues. APB-26 (Early Extinguishment of Debt) was issued to narrow these differences in practice by requiring that gains and losses from early extinguishment of debt be included in net income of the period of extinguishment.

In May 2002, the FASB issued FAS-145 (Rescission of FASB Statements No. 4, 44, and 64, Amendment of FASB Statement No. 13, and Technical Corrections). The rescission of FAS-4 (Reporting Gains and Losses from Extinguishment of Debt) and FAS-64 (Extinguishments of Debt Made to Satisfy Sinking-Fund Requirements) eliminates the former requirement that gains and losses from the extinguishments of debt be presented as an extraordinary item, net of related income taxes, on the face of the income statement.

WHEN DEBT IS EXTINGUISHED

According to FAS-125 (Accounting for Transfers and Servicing of Financial Assets and Extinguishments of Liabilities), debt is extinguished and should be derecognized in the debtor's financial statements only in the following circumstances (FAS-140, par. 16):

- The debtor pays the creditor and is relieved of its obligations for the liability. This includes (a) the transfer of cash, other financial assets, goods, or services or (b) the debtor's reacquisition of its outstanding debt securities, whether the securities are cancelled or held as treasury bonds.

- The debtor is legally released from being the primary obligor under the liability, either judicially or by the creditor. If a third party assumes nonrecourse debt in conjunction with the sale of an asset that serves as sole collateral for that debt, the sale and related assumption effectively accomplish a legal release of the seller-debtor for purposes of applying FAS-140 (Accounting for Transfers and Servicing of Financial Assets and Extinguishments of Liabilities).

When a refunding is desired because of lower interest rates or some other reason, the old debt issue may not be callable for several years. This is the usual circumstance for an advance refunding. In an advance refunding, a new debt issue is sold to replace the old debt issue that cannot be called. The proceeds from the sale of the new debt issue are used to purchase high grade investments, which are placed in an escrow account. The earnings from the investments in the escrow account are used to pay the interest and/or principal payments on the existing debt, up to the date that the existing debt can be called. On the call date of the existing debt, whatever remains in the escrow account is used to pay the call premium, if any, and all remaining principal and interest due on the existing debt. This process is frequently referred to as an in-substance defeasance. An insubstance defeasance is *not* considered an extinguishment of debt.

ACCOUNTING FOR EXTINGUISHMENTS OF DEBT

Under APB-26, all extinguishments of debt are basically alike, and accounting for such transactions is the same, regardless of the method used to achieve the extinguishment (APB-26, par. 19). Therefore, in terms of gain or loss recognition, there is no difference in accounting for an extinguishment of debt by (a) cash purchase, (b) exchange of stock for debt, (c) exchange of debt for debt, or (d) any other method.

Gain or loss on the extinguishment of debt is the difference between the reacquisition price and the net carrying amount of the debt on the date of the extinguishment (APB-26, par. 20).

Reacquisition Price

This is the amount paid for the extinguishment. It includes call premium and any other costs of reacquiring the portion of the debt being extinguished (APB-26, par. 3). When extinguishment is achieved through the exchange of securities, the reacquisition price is the total present value of the new securities being issued.

Net Carrying Amount

This is the amount due at the maturity of the debt, adjusted for any unamortized premium or discount and any other costs of issuance (legal, accounting, underwriter's fees, etc.) (APB-26, par. 3).

REFUNDING OF TAX-EXEMPT DEBT

If a change in a lease occurs as a result of a refunding by the lessor of tax-exempt debt and (a) the lessee receives the economic advantages of the refunding and (b) the revised lease qualifies and is classified either as a capital lease by the lessee or as a direct financing lease by the lessor, the change in the lease shall be accounted for on the basis of whether or not an extinguishment of debt has occurred, as follows (FAS-22, par. 12):

- Accounted for as an extinguishment of debt:
  - — The lessee adjusts the lease obligation to the present value of the future minimum lease payments under the revised agreement, using the effective interest rate of the new lease agreement. Any gain or loss shall be treated as a gain or loss on an early extinguishment of debt.
  - — The lessor adjusts the balance of the minimum lease payments receivable and the gross investment in the lease (if affected) for the difference between the present values of the old and new or revised agreement. Any gain or loss shall be recognized in the current period.

- Not accounted for as an extinguishment of debt:
  - — The lessee accrues any costs connected with the refunding that it is obligated to reimburse to the lessor. The interest method is used to amortize the costs over the period from the date of the refunding to the call date of the debt to be refunded.
  - — The lessor recognizes as revenue any reimbursements to be received from the lessee for costs paid related to the debt to be refunded over the period from the date of the refunding to the call date of the debt to be refunded.

INCOME STATEMENT CLASSIFICATION OF DEBT EXTINGUISHMENT

FAS-145 requires that gains or losses on debt extinguishments be evaluated for proper income statement classification in the same manner as all other business transactions and events. That is, if the two criteria for extraordinary item treatment specified in APB-30 (Reporting the Results of Operations—Reporting the Effects of Disposal of a Segment of a Business, and Extraordinary, Unusual and Infrequently Occurring Events and Transactions) are met—the transaction or event is unusual in nature and infrequent in occurrence—the gain or loss on the debt extinguishments would be treated as an extraordinary item (FAS-145, par. A5). If the two criteria in APB-30 are not met, the gain or loss on debt extinguishments would be considered in computing income before discontinued operations, extraordinary items, and cumulative effect of a change in accounting principle.

OBSERVATION: The FASB recognizes that the application of APB-30 to debt extinguishments will seldom, if ever, result in gains or losses from debt extinguishments being accounted for as extraordinary items. However, the Board pointed out that APB-30 requires separate disclosure (not net of tax) of gains or losses from transactions that are *either* unusual in nature or infrequent in occurrence. Therefore, although gains or losses from debt extinguishments may seldom qualify for extraordinary item treatment, such gains or losses usually will be disclosed separately on the face of the income statement as a component of income from continuing operations (FAS-145, Par. A5).

Illustration of Reacquisition Loss on Extinguishment

On December 31, 20X8, a corporation decides to retire $500,000 of an original issue of $1,000,000 8% debentures, which were sold on December 31, 20X3, for $98 per $100 par-value bond and are callable at $101 per bond. Legal and other expenses for issuing the debentures were $30,000. Both the original discount and the issue costs are being amortized over the 10-year life of the issue by the straight-line method.

Amount of original expenses of issue	$30,000
Amount of original discount (2% of $1,000,000)	$20,000
Amount of premium paid for redemption (debentures callable at 101, 1% of $500,000)	$ 5,000
Date of issue	12/31/20X3
Date of maturity	12/31/20Y3
Date of redemption	12/31/20X8

Because that the original expenses of $30,000 are being amortized over the ten year life of the issue and five years have elapsed since the issue date, half of these expenses have been amortized, leaving a balance of $15,000 at the date of reacquisition. Only half of the outstanding debentures are being retired, however, which leaves $7,500 to account for in the computation of gain or loss.

The original discount of $20,000 (debentures sold at $98) is handled the same as the legal and other expenses. Because half of the discount has already been amortized, leaving a $10,000 balance at the date of redemption, and because only half of the issue is being reacquired, $5,000 must be included into the computation of gain or loss.

Based on the above information, the loss on reacquisition is computed as follows:

Reacquisition price:		
$500,000 × 101%		$505,000
Net carrying amount:		
Face value	$500,000	
Discount	(5,000)	
Legal and other expenses	(7,500)	
		(487,500)
Loss on reacquisition		$ 17,500

The general journal entry to record the reacquisition of the bonds is as follows:

Bond payable	500,000	
Loss of retirement of bonds payable	17,500	
Discount on bonds payable		5,000
Deferred legal and other expenses		7,500
Cash		$505,000

RELATED CHAPTERS IN 2009 *GAAP GUIDE* LEVEL A

Chapter 9, "Convertible Debt and Debt with Warrants"
Chapter 17, "Financial Instruments"
Chapter 29, "Leases"
Chapter 40, "Results of Operations"
Chapter 46, "Troubled Debt Restructuring"

RELATED CHAPTERS IN 2009 *GAAP GUIDE* LEVELS B, C, AND D

Chapter 12, "Convertible Debt and Debt with Warrants"
Chapter 15, "Extinguishment of Debt"
Chapter 17, "Financial Instruments"
Chapter 26, "Leases"
Chapter 35, "Results of Operations"
Chapter 41, "Troubled Debt Restructuring"

RELATED CHAPTERS IN 2009 *INTERNATIONAL ACCOUNTING/FINANCIAL REPORTING STANDARDS GUIDE*

Chapter 3, "Presentation of Financial Statements"
Chapter 16, "Financial Instruments"
Chapter 25, "Leases"

CHAPTER 16
FAIR VALUE

CONTENTS

OVERVIEW

The early years of the 21st century have introduced a new era in which fair value measurement is gradually replacing historical cost as the primary measurement approach for certain assets and liabilities. Evidence suggests that fair value measurement and reporting will be extended to a wide range of balance sheet items as experience with developing and auditing fair value information becomes more widespread.

To date, the FASB has issued two primary standards on fair value: FAS-157 (Fair Value Measurements) and FAS-159 (The Fair Value Option for Financial Assets and Financial Liabilities). In addition, fair value is currently required in accounting for a wide range of financial instruments under other FASB standards. This chapter presents a broad overview of fair value, focusing primarily on the following standards:

FAS-89	Financial Reporting and Changing Prices
FAS-157	Fair Value Measurement
FAS-159	The Fair Value Option for Financial Assets and Financial Liabilities

FAS-33 (Financial Reporting and Changing Prices) was issued in 1979 during a period of the highest inflation in the United States in recent history. That standard, which was subsequently superseded by FAS-89 of the same title, required companies that met a specified size criterion to report supplemental information on current value basis. FAS-89 was later eliminated as a requirement owing to a reduction in inflation and the belief that the information required was of limited value to users of financial statements. The 2009 *GAAP Guide Level A* retains coverage of FAS-89 as an appendix to this chapter because it is technically still in effect, although application of it is on a voluntary basis and rarely, if ever, implemented.

BACKGROUND

For many years, historical cost was the primary basis by which assets and liabilities were accounted. The advantage of historical cost over alternative measurement methods was primarily due to its objectivity. That is, the cost of an item at its origin (i.e., its historical cost) to the reporting entity was generally believed to be more readily determined by objective means than were other measures of value, such as current replacement cost, current exit or sales price, or fair value. Notable exceptions were situations in which the historical cost exceeded the current value of an item, leading to the application of the lower of cost or market for inventories and some investments. More recently, however, standards have been developed that require an assessment of the impairment of value where evidence suggests that an item's current worth is less than its recorded amount.

FAIR VALUE MEASUREMENT

FAS-157 (Fair Value Measurements) defines fair value, establishes a framework for measuring fair value in generally accepted accounting principles, and expands disclosures about fair value measurements. The standard applies in situations where other accounting pronouncements either permit or require fair value measurements. FAS-157 does not require any new fair value measurements.

Changes in practice that will result from applying FAS-157 relate to the definition of fair value, the methods used to measure fair value, and the expanded disclosure about fair value measurements that will be required.

The FASB believes that the changes in practice that result from the application of FAS-157 will improve financial reporting by increasing both consistency and comparability in fair value measurements. The expanded disclosures required about the use of fair value to measure assets and liabilities should provide financial statement users with better information about the extent to which fair value is used to measure recognized assets and liabilities, the inputs used to develop the measurements of fair value, and the effects of certain measurements on earnings (or changes in net assets) for the period.

FAS-157 is effective for financial statements issued for fiscal years beginning after November 15, 2007, and for interim periods within those fiscal years. Earlier application is encouraged, provided that the reporting entity has not already issued financial statements for that fiscal year, including interim periods within that fiscal year. Generally, the provisions of FAS-157 are to be applied prospectively as of the beginning of the fiscal year in which the statement is initially applied with exceptions for certain financial instruments; in such cases, retrospective application is required.

> **OBSERVATION:** The FASB issued FSP 157-2 in February 2008 providing for a partial delay in the effective date of FAS-157. The effective date of FAS-157 is deferred until fiscal years beginning after November 15, 2008, and for interim periods within those fiscal years, for nonfinancial assets and nonfinancial liabilities. No deferral is granted if (1) the nonfinancial asset or nonfinancial liability is recognized and disclosed at fair value in the financial statements on a recurring basis, or (2) the entity has already issued interim or annual financial statements applying FAS-157's provisions to nonfinancial assets and nonfinancial liabilities.

Scope

FAS-157 applies in situations where other accounting pronouncements require or permit fair value measurements with the following exceptions:

- FAS-157 does not apply under accounting pronouncements that address share-based payment transactions, such as FAS-123(R) (Share-Based Payment) and its related interpretative pronouncements.

- FAS-157 does not eliminate the practicability exceptions to fair value measurements that are included in accounting pronouncements within the scope of FAS-157.

In addition, FAS-157 does not apply under accounting pronouncements that require or permit measurements that are similar to fair value but that are not intended to measure fair value. Examples are accounting pronouncements that permit measurements that are based on vendor-specific objective evidence of fair value, such as SOP 97-2 (Software Revenue Recognition) and ARB-43, Chapter 4, *Inventory Pricing* (FAS-157, pars. 2–3).

Measurement

Fair value is the price that would be received to sell an asset or paid to transfer a liability in an orderly transaction between market participants at the measurement date.

A fair value measurement is for a particular asset or liability and, therefore, the measurement should consider attributes specific to the asset or liability. For example, it should consider the condition and/or location of the asset or liability and any restrictions on the sale or use of the asset at the measurement date affecting the asset or liability's fair value. The asset or liability may be a standalone asset or liability or a group of assets or liabilities, depending on its unit of account. The unit of account determines what is being measured by reference to the level at which the asset or liability is aggregated for purposes of applying other accounting pronouncements.

Fair value measurement assumes that the asset or liability is exchanged in an orderly transaction between market participants to sell the asset or transfer the liability at the measurement date. The term "orderly transaction" refers to a transaction that assumes exposure to the market for a period prior to the measurement date to allow for market activities that are usual and customary for transactions involving such assets or liabilities. It is not a forced transaction. The objective of a fair value measurement is to determine the price that would be received to sell the asset or paid to transfer the liability at the measurement date (referred to as the exit price) (FAS-157, pars. 5–7).

☞ **PRACTICE POINTER:** The Securities and Exchange Commission's Division of Corporate Finance indicates that actual market prices are relevant in determining fair value even when the market is less liquid than its historical norm (i.e., reduced trading volume). However, actual market prices should not be used in determining fair value if they reflect a forced liquidation or distress sale.

Principal or Most Advantageous Market

A fair value measurement assumes that the transaction to sell the asset or transfer the liability occurs in the principal market for the asset or liability or, in the absence of a principal market, the most advantageous market for the asset or liability. The principal market is the market in which the reporting entity would sell the asset or transfer the liability with the greatest volume and level of activity for the asset or liability. The most advantageous market is the market in which the reporting entity would sell the asset or transfer the liability at a price that maximizes the amount that would be received for the asset or minimizes the amount that would be paid to transfer the liability (FAS-157, par. 8).

OBSERVATION: Assuming a principal market (i.e., market with the greatest volume of activity for the asset or liability), fair value is determined by reference to the price in that market even if the price in another market is more advantageous for the company.

The price in the principal or most advantageous market used to measure the fair value of the asset or liability should not be adjusted for transaction costs. Transaction costs represent the incremental direct costs to sell the asset or transfer the liability in the principal or most advantageous market for the asset or liability. These costs are not an attribute of the asset or liability. Transaction costs do not include the costs that would be incurred to transport the asset or liability to its principal or most advantageous market. The price in the principal or most advantageous market used to measure the fair value of the asset or liability shall be adjusted for the costs that would be incurred to transport the asset or liability to its principal or most advantageous market (FAS-157, par. 9).

Illustration of Determining the Highest and Best Use of an Asset

Hogan Company (Hogan) has recently acquired land in a business combination. The land hosts a manufacturing facility. Similar parcels of land have recently been sold and converted to residential use. Hogan determines that it could sell its land for residential use. The fair value of the manufacturing operation is $2.5 million. It would cost Hogan $500,000 to demolish the manufacturing operation and to otherwise convert the land to a vacant site suitable for residential development. The value of a vacant site if sold for such a development is $2.7 million. The fair value of the land if used to host the manufacturing operation (i.e., in-use value), $2.5 million, exceeds the fair value of the land if readied and sold for residential development (i.e., in-exchange value), $2.2 million (i.e., $2.7 million − 0.5 million). Therefore, the highest and best use of the land is its in-use value, $2.5 million.

Market Participants

Market participants are buyers and sellers in the principal or most advantageous market for the asset or liability that meet the following criteria:

- They are independent of the reporting entity.
- They are knowledgeable, having a reasonable understanding about the asset or liability and the transaction based on all available information.
- They are able to transact for the asset or liability.
- They are willing to transact for the asset or liability (i.e., willing, but not forced or otherwise compelled to do so).

The fair value of the asset or liability is determined based on the assumptions market participants would use in pricing the asset or liability. In developing the assumptions, the reporting entity is not required to identify specific market participants. Rather, it should identify characteristics that distinguish market participants generally, considering factors specific to the asset or liability, the principal or most advantageous market for the asset or liability, and market participants with whom the reporting entity would transact in that market (FAS-157, pars. 10–11).

Application to Assets

A fair value measurement assumes the highest and best use of the asset by market participants, considering the use of the asset that is physically possible, legally permissible, and financially feasible at the measurement date. The highest and best use of the asset determines the valuation premise that is used to measure the fair value of the asset.

In-Use Assets The highest and best use of the asset is in use if the asset would provide maximum value to market participants principally in combination with other assets as a group. In this instance, the fair value of the asset is determined based on the price that would be received in a current transaction to sell the asset assuming that the asset would be used with other assets as a group and that the assets would be available to market participants.

In-Exchange Assets The highest and best use of an asset is in-exchange if the asset would provide maximum value to market participants principally on a standalone basis. In this instance, the fair value of the asset is measured using an in-exchange valuation premise. The fair value is determined based on the price that would be received in a current transaction to sell the asset standalone (FAS-157, pars. 12–14).

Application to Liabilities

Fair value measurement assumes that the liability is transferred to a market participant at the measurement date and that the nonperformance risk related to the liability is the same before and after its transfer. Nonperformance risk refers to the risk that the obligation will not be fulfilled and affects the value at which the liability is transferred. The fair value of the liability shall reflect the nonperformance risk relating to that liability. The credit risk of the reporting entity is one factor in determining the nonperformance risk (FAS-157, par. 15).

Fair Value at Initial Recognition

When an asset is acquired or a liability assumed in an exchange, the transaction price represents the price paid to acquire the asset or received to assume the liability. In contrast, the fair value of the asset or liability represents the price that would be received to sell the asset or paid to transfer the liability (i.e., an exit price).

In many cases, the transaction price equals the exit price and, therefore, represents the fair value of the asset or liability at initial recognition. In determining whether a transaction price represents the fair value of the asset or liability at initial recognition, the reporting entity must consider factors specific to the transaction and to the specific asset or liability. Examples of situations in which the transaction price might not represent the fair value of an asset or liability at initial recognition are when:

- The transaction is between related parties.

- The transaction occurs under duress or the seller is forced to accept the price in the transaction.

- The unit of account represented by the transaction price is different from the unit of account of the asset or liability measured at fair value (e.g., the asset is one element in the transaction that includes multiple elements).

- The market in which the transaction occurs is different from the market in which the reporting entity would sell the asset or transfer the liability. (FAS-157, pars. 16–17.)

Illustration of Using Observable Market Inputs in the Most Advantageous Market

Daves Incorporated (Daves) owns 50,000 shares of the common stock of Fauver Company (Fauver). The stock of Fauver is traded on two different markets, A and B. The price of Fauver on A is $17 per share and transaction costs are $2. The price of Fauver on B is $16 per share and transaction costs are $0.50. Neither market is the principal market for Fauver. Because neither market is the principal market, fair value is determined using the market that maximizes the amount that would be received after considering transaction costs. The net amount received on Market A would be $15 and it would be $15.50 on Market B. Therefore, the fair value of Fauver stock is determined using the price in that market—$16. Note that although transaction costs are considered in determining the most advantageous market, these costs are not considered in determining the fair value of the asset.

Valuation Techniques

Valuation techniques are classified in FAS-157 in three categories: (1) market approach; (2) income approach; and (3) cost approach. Following are brief descriptions of each approach.

Market approach   The market approach uses prices and other relevant information generated by market transactions involving identical or comparable assets or liabilities. These approaches often use market multiples derived from a set of comparables. Multiples might lie in ranges with a different multiple for each comparable. The selection of where within the range the appropriate multiple falls requires judgment. Matrix pricing is a valuation technique that is consistent with the market approach.

Income approach   The income approach uses valuation techniques to convert future amounts to a single present amount. The measurement is based on the value indicated by current market expectations about those future amounts. Examples include present value techniques, option pricing models, such as the Black-Scholes-Merton formula, and a binomial model.

Cost approach   The cost approach is based on the amount that currently would be required to replace the service capacity of an asset (sometimes referred to as current replacement cost). The price that would be received from the asset is determined on the basis of the cost to a buyer to acquire or construct a substitute asset of comparable utility, adjusted for obsolescence.

Valuation techniques that are appropriate in the circumstances and for which sufficient data are available shall be used to measure fair value. A combination of valuation techniques may be appropriate, and valuation techniques used to measure fair value shall be applied consistently. A change in the valuation technique or its application is appropriate if the change results in a measurement that is equally or more representative of fair value in the circumstance. Revisions from a change in the valuation technique or its application are accounted for as changes in accounting estimate in accordance with FAS-154 (Accounting Changes and Error Corrections).

The term "inputs" refers to the assumptions that market participants use in pricing the asset or liability. Observable inputs reflect the assumptions market participants would use in pricing the asset or liability based on market data obtained from sources independent of the reporting entity. Unobservable inputs reflect the reporting entity's own assumptions about the assumptions market participants would use in pricing the asset or liability developed on the basis of the best information available in the circumstances. Valuation techniques should maximize the use of observable inputs and minimize the use of unobservable inputs (FAS-157, pars. 18–21).

Illustration of Use of Multiple Techniques to Estimate Fair Value

Cochran Incorporated (Cochran) completes a business acquisition on July 1, 20X8. Among the assets acquired is an internally developed, custom software program that is licensed to external customers. Cochran must estimate the fair value of this software program in assigning the purchase price to the individual assets and liabilities acquired. Cochran determines that the asset has a higher value in use than in exchange. Cochran cannot determine the fair value of the asset using a market approach because transactions for comparable software assets are not available given the customized nature of the software. Cochran estimates the fair value of the software using both the income and cost approach. Cochran applies the income approach by determining the present value of expected license fees over the software's useful life; the estimated fair value using this approach is $7 million. The cost of writing a substitute software program of comparable utility is $5 million. Because the software program was developed using proprietary information, Cochran concludes that it is not possible to directly replace the existing program. Therefore, Cochran estimates the fair value of the software program as $7 million.

Fair Value Hierarchy

FAS-157 develops a fair value hierarchy that is intended to increase consistency and comparability in fair value measurements and related disclosures. This hierarchy prioritizes the inputs to valuation techniques used to measure fair value into three levels: Level 1 (highest priority), Level 2, and Level 3 (lowest priority):

1. **Quoted Market Prices in Active Markets (Level 1):**
   a. Level 1 inputs are quoted market prices in active markets for identical assets or liabilities that are accessible at the measurement date.
   b. An active market for the asset or liability is a market in which transactions for the asset or liability occur with sufficient frequency and volume to provide pricing information on an ongoing basis.
   c. A quoted market price in an active market provides the most reliable evidence of fair value and should be used whenever available.

2. **Other Than Quoted Market Inputs (Level 2):**
   a. Level 2 inputs are from other than quoted market prices included in Level 1 that are observable for the asset or liability, either directly or indirectly.
   b. Level 2 inputs include the following:
      (1) Quoted market prices of similar assets or liabilities in active markets;
      (2) Quoted market prices for identical or similar assets or liabilities in markets that are not active;
      (3) Inputs other than quoted prices that are observable for the asset or liability (e.g., interest rates and yield curves observable at commonly quoted intervals, volatilities, prepayment speeds, loss severities, credit risks, and default rates); and
      (4) Inputs that are derived principally from or corroborated by observable market data by correlation or other means.

3. **Unobservable Inputs (Level 3):**
    a. Level 3 inputs are unobservable and shall be used to measure fair value to the extent that observable inputs are not available.
    b. Unobservable inputs are allowed in situations where there is little, if any, market activity for the asset or liability at the measurement date.
    c. Unobservable inputs reflect the reporting entity's own assumptions about the assumptions that market participants would use in pricing the asset or liability.
    d. Unobservable inputs shall be developed based on the best information available under the circumstances. The entity is not required to consider all possible efforts to obtain information about market participant assumptions, but the entity shall not ignore information about market participant assumptions that is reasonably available without undue cost and effort.

If a fair value measurement is based on bid and ask prices, the price within the bid-ask spread that is most representative of fair value in the circumstances shall be used to measure fair value (FAS-157, pars. 22–31).

Illustration of Using a Level 2 Input to Estimate Fair Value

King Company (King) acquires a recently developed and unoccupied office building. King needs to estimate the fair value of the building in assigning the purchase price to the individual assets and liabilities acquired. As the building is new and has not yet been occupied, King cannot determine the fair value of the building using a Level 1 input—a quoted price in an active market for the identical asset. However, it can determine a fair value for the building using a Level 2 input. King determines the price per square foot received in rent for similar buildings in similar locations based on actual transactions. Using this price per square foot, King can determine the likely rental income the building will generate and thereby estimate the fair value of the building using an income approach.

Disclosures

For assets and liabilities that are measured at fair value on a *recurring basis* in periods subsequent to initial recognition, the reporting entity shall disclose information that enables users of the financial statements to assess the inputs used to develop the fair value measurements. For recurring fair value measurement using significant unobservable inputs (Level 3), the effect of the measurements on earnings (or changes in net assets) for the period shall be disclosed. To meet these requirements, for each interim and annual period separately for each major category of assets and liabilities, the following information is required:

- The fair value measurements at the reporting date.
- The level within the fair value hierarchy in which the fair value measurements in their entirety fall, segregating fair value measurements using quoted prices in active markets (Level 1), significant other observable inputs (Level 2), and significant unobservable inputs (Level 3).
- For fair value measurements using significant unobservable inputs (Level 3), a reconciliation as of the beginning and ending balances, separately presenting changes during the period from each of the following:
  - Total gains or losses for the period (realized and unrealized), segregating those gains or losses included in earnings (or changes in net assets) and a description of where those gains or losses included in earnings (or changes in net assets) are reported in the statement of income (or activities);
  - Purchases, sales, issuances, and settlements; and
  - Transfers in and/or out of Level 3.
- The amount of the total gains or losses for the period included in earnings (or changes in net assets) that are attributable to the change in unrealized gains or losses relating to those assets and liabilities still held at the reporting date and a description of where those unrealized gains or losses are reported in the statement of income (or activities).
- In annual periods only, the valuation technique(s) used to measure fair value and a discussion of changes in valuation techniques, if any, that have occurred during the period.

For assets and liabilities that are measured at fair value on a *nonrecurring basis* in periods subsequent to initial recognition, the reporting entity shall disclose information that enables users of its financial statements to assess the inputs used to develop those measurements. To meet this objective, the reporting entity shall disclose the following for each interim and annual period by major category of assets and liabilities:

- The fair value measurements recorded during the period and the reasons for the measurements.

- The level within the fair value hierarchy in which the fair value measurements in their entirety fall, segregating fair value measurements using quoted prices in active markets for identical assets or liabilities (Level 1), significant other observable inputs (Level 2), and significant unobservable inputs (Level 3).

- For fair value measurement using significant unobservable inputs (Level 3), a description of the inputs and the information used to develop the inputs.

- In annual periods only, the valuation technique(s) used to measure fair value and a discussion of any change in the valuation technique(s) used to measure similar assets and/or liabilities in prior periods.

The quantitative disclosures required by FAS-157 are required to be presented using a tabular format. FAS-157 encourages entities to combine the fair value information disclosed under FAS-157 with the fair value information required to be disclosed under other accounting pronouncements, if practicable (FAS-157, pars. 32–35).

> **OBSERVATION:** For public companies, if the fair value of a material amount of assets or liabilities are determined using unobservable inputs the company needs to disclose in its Management Discussion & Analysis (MD&A): (1) how the fair values were determined, and (2) how the fair value of assets and liabilities, and changes to these amounts, affected or could affect the company's results of operations, liquidity, and capital resources. In addition, when the fair value of a material amount of assets or liabilities are based on unobservable inputs, the company should consider disclosing in the MD&A:
>
> - The percentage of assets and liabilities measured using unobservable inputs to the total of assets and liabilities measured at fair value.
> - The dollar amount of any material change (increase or decrease) in assets and liabilities measured using Level 3 inputs rather than Level 1 or 2 inputs, or assets and liabilities measured using Level 1 or 2 inputs rather than Level 3 inputs, and the reasons for such changes.
>   — If a material amount of assets or liabilities, formerly valued using Level 1 or 2 inputs, are changed to being measured using Level 3 inputs during the period: (1) disclose the significant inputs no longer deemed observable, and (2) any material gain or loss on these assets and liabilities recognized during the period.
> - For assets or liabilities measured using Level 3 inputs, disclose, if material: (1) whether realized and unrealized gains and losses affected results of operations, liquidity, and capital resources, (2) the reason for any material change (increase or decrease) in fair value, (3) whether you believe fair values

differ materially from the amount expected to be realized at settlement or maturity including the reasons and support for this view.

• The nature and types of assets supporting asset-backed securities, the years the securities were issued and the credit ratings of the securities, including changes or potential changes in these securities.

Also, regardless of whether fair values are determined using Level 1, 2, or 3 inputs, the company should consider disclosing in the MD&A:

• For material assets and liabilities, a general description of the valuation techniques or models used, and any changes to the valuation techniques or models during the period, why the change was made, and the quantitative effect of the change.

• If material, discuss how and how much relevant market indices were used in determining fair value.

• The company's approach to validating techniques and models (e.g., how often the technique or model is calibrated, whether the company back-tests, etc.).

• The sensitivity of fair value estimates for material assets and liabilities to changes in significant inputs to the valuation technique or model. Providing a range of values around the fair value estimate can be helpful. The company should disclose those inputs that are the key drivers of variability.

Effective Date and Transition

FAS-157 is effective for financial statements for fiscal years beginning after November 15, 2007, and for interim periods within those fiscal years. Earlier application is encouraged, provided that the reporting entity has not already issued financial statements for that fiscal year, including for any interim periods within that fiscal year.

FAS-157 is to be applied prospectively as of the beginning of the fiscal year in which the statement is initially applied except as indicated below. The statement is to be applied retrospectively to the following financial instruments as of the beginning of the fiscal year in which the statement is initially applied:

• A position in a financial instrument that trades in an active market held by a broker-dealer or investment company within the scope of the AICPA Audit and Accounting Guides for those industries which was measured at fair value using a blockage factor prior to initial application of FAS-157.

- A financial instrument that was measured at fair value at initial recognition under FAS-133 (Accounting for Derivative Instruments and Hedging Activities), using the transaction price in accordance with the guidance in EITF Issue No. 02-3, "Issues Involved in Accounting for Derivative Contracts Held for Trading Purposes and Contracts Involved in Energy Trading and Risk Management Activities," prior to initial application of FAS-157.

- A hybrid financial instrument that was measured at fair value at initial recognition under FAS-133 using the transaction price in accordance with FAS-133 guidance added by FAS-155 (Accounting for Certain Hybrid Financial Instruments) prior to initial application of FAS-157.

When FAS-157 is first applied, the difference between the carrying amount and the fair values of those instruments listed above shall be recognized as a cumulative effect adjustment to the beginning balance of retained earnings (or other appropriate components of equity or net assets in the statement of position) for that fiscal year, presented separately. The disclosure requirements of FAS-154 for a change in accounting principle do not apply.

The disclosure requirements outlined above shall be applied in the first interim period of the fiscal year in which FAS-157 is initially applied. The disclosure requirements of FAS-157 need not be applied for financial statements for periods presented prior to initial application of FAS-157 (FAS-157, pars. 36–39).

FAS-157 and its related appendices are among the most extensive of any FASB standard issued to date. Appendices include material in the following areas:

- Implementation guidance (Appendix A);
- Present value techniques (Appendix B);
- Background information and basis for conclusions (Appendix C); and
- References to APB and FASB Pronouncements (Appendix D).

FAIR VALUE OPTION FOR FINANCIAL ASSETS AND LIABILITIES

FAS-159 (The Fair Value Option for Financial Assets and Financial Liabilities) provides companies with an option to report selected financial assets and liabilities at fair value. The standard, which includes an amendment to FAS-115 (Accounting for Certain Investments in Debt and Equity Securities), reduces both the complexity in accounting for financial instruments and the volatility in earnings caused by measuring related assets and liabilities differently. FAS-159 establishes presentation and disclosure requirements that are designed to facilitate comparisons between companies that choose different measurement attributes for similar types of assets and liabilities.

FAS-159 requires companies to provide additional information that is intended to help investors and other users of financial statements to more easily understand the effects on reported earnings of the company's choice to use fair value. It also requires companies to display the fair value of those assets and liabilities for which the company has chosen to use fair value in the primary financial statements.

FAS-159 is effective for fiscal years beginning after November 15, 2007. Early adoption is permitted as of the beginning of the previous fiscal year provided that the entity makes the choice in the first 120 days of that fiscal year and also elects to apply FAS-157 (Fair Value Measurements).

FAS-159 permits all entities to elect to measure eligible items at fair value. This is hereafter referred to as the "fair value option." Under the new standard, a business entity shall report unrealized gains and losses at each subsequent reporting date. Upfront costs and fees related to items for which the fair value option is elected are recognized in earnings as incurred and are not deferred.

Eligibility

The following items are eligible to be accounted for by FAS-159:

- A recognized financial asset or liability (with certain specified exceptions).
- A firm commitment that would otherwise not be recognized at inception and that involves only financial instruments.
- A written loan commitment.
- The rights and obligations under an insurance contract that is not a financial instrument but whose terms permit the insurer to settle by paying a third party to provide those goods or services.
- The rights and obligations under a warranty that is not a financial instrument but whose terms permit the warrantor to settle by paying a third party to provide those goods or services.
- A host of financial instruments resulting from the separation of an embedded nonfinancial derivative instrument from a nonfinancial hybrid instrument under FAS-133 (Accounting for Derivative Instruments and Hedging Activities) (FAS-159, par. 7).

On the other hand, the following are *not* eligible for FAS-159 accounting:

- An investment in a subsidiary that the entity is required to consolidate.
- An interest in a variable interest entity that the entity is required to consolidate.
- Employers' and plans' obligations for pension benefits, other postretirement benefits, postemployment benefits, employee stock options and stock purchase plans, and other forms of deferred compensation.
- Financial assets and financial liabilities recognized under leases.
- Deposit liabilities, withdrawable on demand, of banks, savings and loan associations, credit unions, and other similar depository institutions.
- Financial instruments that, in whole or in part, are classified by the issuer as a component of stockholders' equity (FAS-159, par. 8).

Election Dates

The choice of whether to elect the fair value option is made on each eligible item's election date, which is when one of the following occurs:

- The entity first recognizes the eligible item.
- The entity enters into an eligible firm commitment.
- Financial assets that have been reported at fair value with unrealized gains and losses included in earnings because of specialized accounting principles cease to qualify for that specialized accounting.
- The accounting treatment for an investment in another entity changes because (1) the investment becomes subject to the equity method of accounting; or (2) the investor ceases to consolidate a subsidiary or variable interest entity but retains an interest.
- An event that requires an eligible item to be measured at fair value at the time of the event but does not require fair value measurement at each subsequent reporting date (excluding the recognition of impairment under lower-of-cost-or-market accounting or other-than-temporary impairment).

Some additional events that require the remeasurement of eligible items at fair value, initial recognition of eligible items, or both, and thereby create an election date for the fair value option are (1) business combinations; (2) consolidation or deconsolidation of a subsidiary or variable interest entity; and (3) significant modifications of debt (FAS-159, pars. 9–10).

Applying FAS-159

The fair value option may be elected for a single eligible item without electing it for other identical items with the following exceptions:

- If multiple advances are made to one borrower pursuant to a single contract, and the individual advances lose their identity as a part of a larger loan balance, the fair value option must be applied only to the larger balance and not to each advance individually.

- If the fair value option is applied to an investment that would otherwise be accounted for by the equity method, it is applied to all of the investor's financial interests in the same entity that are eligible items.

- If the fair value option is applied to an eligible insurance or reinsurance contract, it shall be applied to all claims and obligations under the contract.

- If the fair value option is elected for an insurance contract for which integrated or unintegrated contract features or coverages are issued, the fair value option must also be applied to those features or coverages (FAS-159, par. 12).

The fair value option is not required to be applied to all instruments issued or acquired in a single transaction. A financial instrument that is legally a single contract may not be separated into parts for the purposes of applying the fair value option. In contrast, a loan syndication arrangement may result in multiple loans to the same borrower by different lenders, each of which is a separate instrument for which the fair value option may be elected or not elected. An investor in an equity security may elect the fair value option for its entire investment in that security, including any fractional shares issued by the investee (FAS-159, par. 13).

In the statement of financial position, entities shall report assets and liabilities that are presented by the fair value option in a manner that separates those reported fair values from the carrying amounts of similar assets and liabilities measured using another measurement attribute in either of the following ways:

- Present the aggregate of fair value and non-fair-value amounts in the same line item and parenthetically disclose the amount measured at fair value included in that aggregate amount; or
- Present two separate line items to display fair value and non-fair-value carrying amounts (FAS-159, par. 15).

In the statement of cash flows, receipts and cash payments related to items measured at fair value are classified according to their nature and purpose as required by FAS-95 (Statement of Cash Flows), as amended (FAS-159, par. 16).

Disclosure Requirements

FAS-159 includes extensive disclosures in the financial statements. The primary objectives of these disclosures are to facilitate comparisons between (1) entities that choose different measurement attributes for similar assets and liabilities; and (2) assets and liabilities in the financial statements of an entity that selects different measurement attributes for similar assets and liabilities.

As of each date for which a statement of financial position is presented, the following information is required to be disclosed:

1. Management's reason for electing a fair value option for each eligible item or for a group of eligible items
2. If the fair value option is elected for some, but not all, eligible items within a group:
    a. A description of those items and the reason for partial election
    b. Information to enable users to understand how the group of similar items relates to individual line items on the statement of financial position
3. For each line item in the statement of financial position that includes an item or items for which the fair value option has been elected:
    a. Information to enable users to understand how each line item in the statement of financial position relates to major categories of assets and liabilities presented in accordance with FAS-157's fair value disclosure requirements
    b. The aggregate carrying amount of items included in each line item in the statement of financial position that are not eligible for the fair value option
4. The difference between the aggregate fair value and the aggregate unpaid principal balance of:

    a. Loans and long-term receivables that have contractual principal amounts and for which the fair value option has been elected

    b. Long-term debt instruments that have contractual principal amounts and for which the fair value option has been elected

5. For loans held as assets for which the fair value option has been elected:

    a. The aggregate fair value of loans that are 90 days or more past due

    b. If the entity's policy is to recognize interest income separately from other changes in fair value, the aggregate fair value of loans in nonaccrual status

    c. The difference between the aggregate fair value and the aggregate unpaid principal balance for loans that are 90 days or more past due, in nonaccrual status, or both

6. For investments that would have been accounted for under the equity method if the entity had not chosen the fair value option, the information required by APB-18 (The Equity Method of Accounting for Investments in Common Stock) with certain specified exclusions (FAS-159, par. 18).

For each period for which an interim or annual income statement is presented, the following information is required:

1. For each line item in the statement of financial position, the amounts of gains and losses from fair value changes included in earnings during the period and in which line item in the income statement those items are reported

2. A description of how interest and dividends are measured and where they are reported in the income statement

3. For loans and other receivable held as assets:

    a. The estimated amount of gains or losses included in earnings during the period attributable to changes in instrument-specific credit risk

    b. How the gains or losses attributed to changes in instrument-specific credit risk were determined

4. For liabilities with fair values that have been significantly affected during the reporting period by changes in the instrument-specific credit risk:

    a. The estimated amount of gains and losses from fair value changes included in earnings that are attributed to changes in the instrument-specific credit risk

    b. Qualitative information about the reasons for those changes

c. How the gains and losses attributed to changes in instrument-specific credit risk were determined (FAS-159, par. 19)

Other disclosure requirements are as follows:

1. In annual periods only, an entity shall disclose the methods and significant assumptions used to estimate the fair value of items for which the fair value option has been elected.
2. If an entity elects the fair value option at the time of the events described in paragraphs 9(d) or 9(e) of FAS-159 (see explanation below), the following information is required:
    a. Qualitative information about the nature of the event
    b. Quantitative information by line item in the statement of financial position indicating which line items in the income statement include the effect on earnings of initially electing the fair value option for an item (FAS-159, par. 21–22).

Paragraphs 9(d) and 9(e) permit the fair value option to be elected when the accounting treatment of an investment changes because of either of the following: the investment becomes subject to the equity method of accounting; or the investor ceases to consolidate a subsidiary or variable interest entity but retains an interest. Paragraph 10 of FAS-159 also indicates that a business combination, consolidation or deconsolidation of a subsidiary, and significant modifications of debt are options that would trigger this disclosure.

Applying FAS-159 to Not-for-Profit Organizations

The following modifications are required in applying FAS-159 to not-for-profit organizations:

- References throughout FAS-159 to the income statement are replaced with references to the statement of activities, statement of changes in net assets, or statement of operations. Similarly, references to earnings are replaced with references to changes in net assets.
- Health care organizations subject to the AICPA Audit and Accounting Guide, *Health Care Organizations*, shall report unrealized gains and losses on items for which the fair value option has been elected within the performance indicator or a part of discontinued operations, as appropriate.
- Certain disclosure requirements (presented in paragraph 19 of FAS-159) apply not only with respect to the effect on performance indicators or other measures of operations, if presented, but also with respect to the effect on the change in each

of the net asset classes (unrestricted, temporarily restricted, and permanently restricted), as appropriate (FAS-159, par. 23).

Effective Date and Early Adoption

FAS-159 is effective as of the beginning of each reporting entity's first fiscal year that begins after November 15, 2007. FAS-159 shall not be applied retrospectively to fiscal years beginning prior to the effective date, except as permitted if the entity chooses early adoption.

At the effective date, an entity may elect the fair value option for eligible items that exist at that date. The effect of the first remeasurement to fair value is reported as a cumulative-effect adjustment to the opening balance of retained earnings. A not-for-profit organization shall report the cumulative-effect adjustment as a separate line item within the change in the appropriate net asset class or classes in its statement of activities, outside any performance indicator or other intermediate measure of operations.

The differences between the carrying amount and the fair value of eligible items for which the fair value option is elected at the effective date are removed from the statement of financial position and included in the cumulative-effect adjustment. These differences include, but are not limited to:

- Unamortized deferred costs, fees, premiums, and discounts.
- Valuation allowances.
- Accrued interest, which would be reported as part of the fair value of the eligible item.

Available-for-sale and held-to-maturity securities held at the effective date are eligible for the fair value option at that date. If the fair value option is elected, the cumulative unrealized gains or losses at that date are included in the cumulative-effect adjustment. The amount of unrealized gains and losses reclassified from accumulated other comprehensive income (available-for-sale securities) and for the amount of unrealized gains and losses that was previously unrecognized (held-to-maturity securities) are separately reported.

If the fair value option is adopted for a held-to-maturity or available-for-sale security, that security shall be reported as a trading security under FAS-115, but the accounting for a transfer to the trading category in FAS-115 does not apply. Electing the fair value option for an existing held-to-maturity security does not call into question the intent to hold other debt securities to maturity in the future.

If FAS-157 is adopted at the same time as FAS-159, any change in an existing eligible item's recorded fair value at the effective date due to the application of FAS-157 is included in the cumulative-effect adjustment if the fair value option was elected for that item.

An entity may elect FAS-159 early, including applying the fair value option to existing eligible items, as of the beginning of a fiscal year that begins on or before November 1, 2007, subject to the following limitations:

- The choice is made within 120 days of the beginning of the fiscal year of adoption.

- The entity also adopts all of the requirements of FAS-157 at its early adoption date.

- At the time the entity chooses to adopt FAS-159 early, the entity has not yet issued financial statements for any interim period of the fiscal year that includes the early adoption date.

- The choices to apply or not apply the fair value option to eligible items existing at the early adoption date are retroactive to the early adoption date.

- For eligible items with an election date occurring after the early adoption date but before the date of the entity's choice to apply early, the election for those items is retroactive to their election date.

- All other requirements that would normally apply as of the required effective date also apply as of the early adoption date (FAS-159, pars. 24–30).

RELATED CHAPTERS IN 2009 *GAAP GUIDE LEVEL A*

Chapter 5, "Cash Flow Statement"
Chapter 17, "Financial Instruments"
Chapter 20, "Impairment of Long-Lived Assets"
Chapter 25, "Interest on Receivables and Payables"
Chapter 28, "Investments in Debt and Equity Securities"
Chapter 38, "Related Party Disclosures"
Chapter 45, "Transfer and Servicing of Financial Assets"
Chapter 51, "Not-for-Profit Organizations"

RELATED CHAPTERS IN 2009 *GAAP GUIDE LEVELS B, C, AND D*

Chapter 17, "Financial Instruments"
Chapter 19, "Impairment of Long-Lived Assets"
Chapter 25, "Investments in Debt and Equity Securities"
Chapter 40, "Transfer of Financial Assets"

RELATED CHAPTERS IN 2009 *INTERNATIONAL ACCOUNTING/FINANCIAL REPORTING STANDARDS GUIDE*

Chapter 8, "Cash Flow Statements"
Chapter 16, "Financial Instruments"
Chapter 19, "Impairment of Assets"
Chapter 24, "Investment Property"
Chapter 29, "Related Party Disclosures"

APPENDIX: REPORTING CHANGING PRICES UNDER FAS-89

Financial statements prepared in conformity with GAAP are based on the assumption of a stable monetary unit. That is, the assumption is made that the monetary unit used to convert all financial statement items into a common denominator (i.e., dollars) does not vary sufficiently over time so that distortions in the financial statements are material. In addition, financial statements prepared in conformity with GAAP are primarily based on historical cost (i.e., the characteristic of most financial statement items that is measured and presented is the historical cost of the item).

Over the years, two approaches have been proposed and procedures developed to compensate for changes in the monetary unit and changes in the value of assets and liabilities after their acquisition—current value accounting and general price-level accounting. Current value accounting substitutes a measure of current value for historical cost as the primary measurement upon which the elements of financial statements are based. General price-level accounting adheres to historical cost but substitutes a current value of the dollar for historical dollars through the use of price indexes. Neither current value accounting nor general price-level accounting is required at the present time. In FAS-89 (Financial Reporting and Changing Prices), the FASB has developed disclosure standards that are optional for dealing with the problem of the impact of changing prices on financial statements.

BACKGROUND

FAS-33 (Financial Reporting and Changing Prices) (superseded by FAS-89), issued in 1979, required certain large enterprises to disclose the effects of changing prices via a series of supplemental disclosures. Several later FASB Statements and Technical Bulletins provided additional guidance on this matter.

FAS-89 subsequently specified that such disclosures are encouraged, but not required (FAS-89, par. 3). An appendix to FAS-89 provides guidelines on the disclosure of the effects of changing prices. These guidelines are substantially the same as prior FASB pronouncements, except that the guidelines are not mandatory.

REPORTING UNDER FAS-89

Net Monetary Position

Assets and liabilities are identified as monetary items if their amounts are fixed or determinable without reference to future prices of specific goods and services. Cash, accounts and notes receivable in cash, and accounts and notes payable in cash are examples of monetary items (FAS-89, par. 44).

Monetary items lose or gain general purchasing power during inflation or deflation as a result of changes in the general price-level index (FAS-89, par. 41). For example, a holder of a $10,000 promissory note executed ten years ago and due today will receive exactly $10,000 today, in spite of the fact that $10,000 in cash today is worth less than $10,000 was worth ten years ago.

Assets and liabilities that are not fixed in terms of the monetary unit are called nonmonetary items. Inventories, investment in common stocks, property, plant, and equipment, and deferred charges are examples of nonmonetary items (FAS-89, par. 41). A nonmonetary asset or liability is affected (a) by the rise or fall of the general price-level index and (b) by the increase or decrease of the fair value of the nonmonetary item. Holders of nonmonetary items lose or gain with the rise or fall of the general price-level index if the nonmonetary item does not rise or fall in proportion to the change in the price-level index. For example, the purchaser of 10,000 shares of common stock ten years ago was subject (a) to the decrease in purchasing power of the dollar and (b) to the change in the fair value of the stock. Only if the decrease in purchasing power exactly offsets an increase in the price of the stock is the purchaser in the same economic position today as ten years ago.

The difference between monetary assets and monetary liabilities at any specific date is the net monetary position. The net monetary position may be either positive (monetary assets exceed monetary liabilities) or negative (monetary liabilities exceed monetary assets).

In periods in which the general price level is rising (inflation), it is advantageous for a business to maintain a net negative (liability) monetary position. The opposite is true during periods in which the general price level is falling (deflation). In periods of inflation, a business that has a net negative monetary position will experience general price-level gains, because it can pay its liabilities in a fixed number of dollars that are declining in value over time. In contrast, in periods of inflation, a business that has a net positive (asset) monetary position will experience general price-level losses because it holds more monetary assets than liabilities and the value of the dollar is declining.

☛ **PRACTICE POINTER:** Some assets and liabilities have characteristics of both monetary and nonmonetary items.

Convertible debt, for example, is monetary in terms of its fixed obligation, but nonmonetary in terms of its conversion feature. Whether an item is monetary or nonmonetary is determined as of the balance sheet date. Therefore, if convertible debt has not been converted as of that date, classify it as a monetary item. Additionally, classify a bond receivable held for speculation as nonmonetary, because the amount that will be received when the bond is sold is no longer fixed in amount, as it would be if the same bond were held to maturity. FAS-89 (pars. 96–108) contains a table that reflects the monetary/nonmonetary classification of most assets and liabilities.

Current Cost Accounting

Current cost accounting is a method of measuring and reporting assets and expenses associated with the use or sale of assets at their current cost or lower recoverable amount at the balance sheet date or at the date of use or sale. Current cost/constant purchasing power accounting is a method of accounting based on measures of current cost of lower recoverable amounts in units of currency that each have the same general purchasing power. For operations for which the U.S. dollar is the functional currency, the general purchasing power of the dollar is used. For operations for which the functional currency is other than the U.S. dollar, the general purchasing power of either (*a*) the dollar or (*b*) the functional currency is used (FAS-89, par. 44).

Determining Current Costs

Current cost is the current cost to purchase or reproduce a specific asset. Current reproduction cost must contain an allocation for current overhead costs (direct costing is not permitted).

The current cost of inventory owned by an enterprise is the current cost to purchase or reproduce that specific inventory. The current cost of property, plant, and equipment owned by an enterprise is the current cost of acquiring an asset that will perform or produce in a manner similar to the owned asset (FAS-89, pars. 17 and 18).

An enterprise may obtain its current cost information internally or externally, including independent appraisals, and may apply the information to a single item or to groups of items. An enterprise is expected to select the types of current cost information that are most appropriate for its particular circumstances. The following types and sources of current cost information may be utilized by an enterprise (FAS-89, par. 19):

- Current invoice prices

- Vendor firms' price lists, quotations, or estimates
- Standard manufacturing costs that reflect current costs
- Unit pricing, which is a method of determining current cost for assets, such as buildings, by applying a unit price per square foot of space to the total square footage in the building
- Revision of historical cost by the use of indexation, based on:
  — Externally generated price indexes for the goods or services being restated, or
  — Internally generated indexes for the goods or services being restated

Depreciation Methods

Depreciation methods, useful lives, and salvage values used for current cost purposes are generally the same as those used for historical cost purposes. If historical cost computations already include an allowance for changing prices, then a different method may be used for current cost purposes. However, any material differences shall be disclosed in the explanatory notes to the supplementary information (FAS-89, par. 22).

Recoverable Amounts

Recoverable amounts may be determined by reference to net realizable values or values in use. They reflect write-downs during a current period, from the current cost amount to a lower recoverable amount. These reductions reflect a permanent decline in the value of inventory, or property, plant, and equipment.

Net Realizable Value

Net realizable value is the expected amount of net cash or other net equivalent to be received from the sale of an asset in the regular course of business. Net realizable value is used only if the specific asset is about to be sold (FAS-89, par. 29).

Value in Use

Value in use is the total present value of all future cash inflows that are expected to be received from the use of an asset. Value in use is used only if there is no immediate intention to sell or otherwise dispose of the asset. Value in use is estimated by taking into consideration an appropriate discount rate that includes an allowance for the risk involved in the circumstances (FAS-89, par. 44).

Income Tax Expense

Income tax expense and the provision for deferred taxes, if any, are not restated in terms of current cost and are presented in the supplementary information at their historical cost. Disclosure is required in the supplementary information to the effect that income tax expense for the current period is presented at its historical cost.

Minimum Supplementary Information under FAS-89

Under FAS-89, an enterprise is encouraged to disclose certain minimum supplementary information for each of its five most recent years. In addition, if income from continuing operations as shown in the primary financial statements differs significantly from income from continuing operations determined on a current cost/constant purchasing power basis, certain additional disclosures relating to the components of income from continuing operations for the current year also should be disclosed (FAS-89, par. 11).

The minimum supplementary information encouraged by FAS-89 is disclosed in average-for-the-year units of constant purchasing power. The Consumer Price Index for All Urban Consumers (CPI-U) is used to restate the current cost of an item in average-for-the-year units of constant purchasing power. Alternatively, an enterprise may disclose the minimum supplementary information in dollars having a purchasing power equal to that of dollars of the base period used in calculating the CPI-U. The level of the CPI-U used for each of the five most recent years should be disclosed (FAS-89, par. 8).

An enterprise is encouraged to disclose the following minimum supplementary information for the five most recent years (FAS-89, par. 7):

- Net sales and other operating revenue
- Income from continuing operations on a current cost basis
- Purchasing power gain or loss on net monetary items
- Increase or decrease in the current cost or lower recoverable amount of inventory and property, plant, and equipment, net of inflation
- Aggregate foreign currency translation adjustment on a current cost basis, if applicable
- Net assets at the end of each fiscal year on a current cost basis
- Income per common share from continuing operations on a current cost basis
- Cash dividends declared per common share

- Market price per common share at year-end
- Average level of the CPI-U for each year

Each of the above disclosures included in the five-year summary of selected financial data is discussed below.

Net Sales and Other Operating Revenue

Net sales and other operating revenue for each of the five most recent years is restated in average-for-the-year units of constant purchasing power using the CPI-U.

Income from Continuing Operations on a Current Cost Basis

Income from continuing operations on a current cost basis for each of the five most recent years is computed in accordance with FAS-89 and then restated in average-for-the-year units of constant purchasing power using the CPI-U. For purposes of the minimum supplementary information, only certain items that are included in income from continuing operations in the primary financial statements have to be adjusted to compute income from continuing operations on a current cost basis. Under FAS-89, these items are adjusted to compare income from continuing operations on a current basis (FAS-89, par. 32):

- *Cost of goods sold* Determined on a current cost basis or lower recoverable amount at the date of a sale or at the date on which resources are used on or committed to a specific contract
- *Depreciation, depletion, and amortization* Determined based on the average current cost of the assets' service potentials or lower recoverable amounts during the period of use
- *Gain or loss on the sale, retirement, or write-down of inventory, property, plant, and equipment* Equal to the difference between the value of the consideration received or the written-down amount and the current cost or lower recoverable amount of the item prior to its sale, retirement, or write-down

All other revenue, expenses, gains, and losses that are included in the primary financial statements are not adjusted in computing income from continuing operations on a current cost basis.

Income tax expense that is included in the primary financial statements is not adjusted in computing income from continuing operations on a current cost basis (FAS-89, par. 33). Disclosure must be made in the minimum supplementary information to the effect that income tax expense for the current period is presented at its historical cost.

Purchasing Power Gain or Loss on Net Monetary Items

The purchasing power gain or loss on net monetary items for each of the five most recent years is computed and then restated in average-for-the-year units of constant purchasing power using the CPI-U. The purchasing power gain or loss on net monetary items is determined by restating in units of constant purchasing power the opening and closing balances of, and transactions in, monetary assets and monetary liabilities (FAS-89, par. 40).

Increase or Decrease in Inventory, Property, Plant, and Equipment at Current Costs

The increase or decrease in current costs for inventory and property, plant, and equipment for each of the five most recent years must be restated in average-for-the-year units of constant purchasing power using the CPI-U. The increase or decrease in the current cost amounts represents the difference between the measures of the assets at their entry dates for the year and at their exit dates for the year. The entry date is the beginning of the year or the date of acquisition, whichever is applicable. The exit date is the end of the year or the date of use, sale, or commitment to a specific contract, whichever is applicable (FAS-89, par. 34).

The increase or decrease in the current cost amounts of inventory, property, plant, and equipment for the five-year summary is reported after the effects of each year's general inflation. The increase or decrease in the current cost amounts for the current year is reported both before and after the effects of general inflation (FAS-89, par. 35).

Aggregate Foreign Currency Translation Adjustment (if Applicable)

The aggregate foreign currency translation adjustment (if applicable) for each of the five most recent years is computed on a current cost basis and then restated in average-for-the-year units of constant purchasing power using the CPI-U.

Current cost information for operations measured in a foreign functional currency is measured either (a) after translation and based on the CPI-U (the translate-restate method) or (b) before translation and based on a broad measure of the change in the general purchasing power of the functional currency (the restate-translate method). In this event, the same method must be used for all operations measured in foreign functional currencies and for all periods presented. Appendix A of FAS-89 contains illustrative calculations of current cost/constant purchasing power information (FAS-89, par. 37).

Net Assets at End of Each Fiscal Year

For purposes of the minimum supplementary information required by FAS-89, net assets at the end of each fiscal year are equal to all of the net assets appearing in the basic historical cost financial statements except that inventories, property, plant, and equipment are included at their current costs or at a lower recoverable amount. (Total net assets at historical cost less inventories, property, plant, and equipment at historical cost, plus inventories, property, plant, and equipment at current costs or lower recoverable amounts, equals net assets as encouraged by FAS-89.) The amount computed for net assets at end of each fiscal year is then restated in average-for-the-year units of constant purchasing power using the CPI-U (FAS-89, par. 27).

When comprehensive restatement of financial statements is made in lieu of the minimum supplementary information, net assets for the five-year summary of selected financial data may be reported at the same amount shown in the comprehensive restated financial statements (FAS-89, par. 28).

Income per Common Share from Continuing Operations on a
Current Cost Basis

Income per common share from continuing operations for each of the five most recent years is computed and then restated in average-for-the-year units of constant purchasing power using the CPI-U. Income per common share from continuing operations on a current cost basis is found by dividing the outstanding number of shares of common stock into the total restated income from continuing operations on a current cost basis.

Cash Dividends Declared per Common Share

Cash dividends declared per common share for each of the five most recent years are restated in average-for-the-year units of constant purchasing power using the CPI-U.

Market Price per Common Share at Year-End

Market price per common share at year-end for each of the five most recent years is restated in average-for-the-year units of constant purchasing power using the CPI-U.

Average Level of CPI-U

The average level of CPI-U for each of the five most recent years is disclosed in a note to the minimum supplementary information. If an enterprise presents comprehensive current cost/constant purchasing power financial statements measured in year-end units of purchasing power, the year-end level of the CPI-U for each of the five most recent years is disclosed (FAS-89, par. 8).

Explanatory Disclosures

An enterprise shall provide an explanation of the disclosures encouraged by FAS-89 and a discussion of their significance in the circumstances of the enterprise. These explanatory statements should be detailed sufficiently so that a user who possesses reasonable business acumen will be able to understand the information presented (FAS-89, par. 10).

Additional Disclosures for the Current Year

If income from continuing operations as shown in the primary financial statements differs significantly from income from continuing operations determined on a current cost/constant purchasing power basis, certain other disclosures for the current year are encouraged by FAS-89 in addition to the minimum supplementary information.

Income from continuing operations for the current year on a current cost basis is computed in accordance with FAS-89 and then restated in average-for-the-year units of constant purchasing power using the CPI-U. The information for income from continuing operations for the current year on a current cost basis is presented in either a *statement format* or a *reconciliation format*, which discloses all adjustments between the supplementary information and the basic historical cost financial statements (see illustrations in Appendix A of FAS-89). The same categories of revenue and expense that appear in the basic historical cost financial statements are used for the presentation of income from continuing operations for the current year on a current cost basis. Account classifications may be combined if they are not individually significant for restating purposes, or if the restated amounts are approximately the same as the historical cost amounts (FAS-89, par. 12).

Income from continuing operations for the current year on a current cost basis does not include (*a*) the purchasing power gain or loss on net monetary items; (*b*) the increase or decrease in the current cost or lower recoverable amount of inventory and property, plant, and equipment, net of inflation; and (c) the translation adjustment (if applicable). However, an enterprise may include this information after the presentation of income from continuing operations for the current year on a current cost basis (see illustrations in Appendix A of FAS-89) (FAS-89, par. 12).

Only certain items that are included in income from continuing operations in the primary financial statements have to be adjusted to compute income from continuing operations for the current year on a current cost basis. Under FAS-89, these items are (FAS-89, par. 32):

- *Cost of goods sold* Determined on a current cost basis or lower recoverable amount at the date of sale or at the date on which resources are used on or committed to a specific contract

- *Depreciation, depletion, and amortization* Determined based on the average current cost of the assets' service potentials or lower recoverable amounts during the period of use

- *Gain or loss on the sale, retirement, or write-down of inventory, property, plant, and equipment* Equal to the difference between the value of the consideration received or the written down amount and the current cost or lower recoverable amount of the item prior to its sale, retirement, or write-down

Other revenues, expenses, gains, and losses that are included in the primary financial statements are not adjusted and may be measured at amounts included in those statements.

Income tax expense that is included in the primary financial statements is not adjusted in computing income from continuing operations for the current year on a current cost basis (FAS-89, par. 33). Disclosure must be made in the minimum supplementary information to the effect that income tax expense for the current period is presented at its historical cost.

Disclosure must also include (FAS-89, par. 13):

- Separate amounts for the current cost or lower recoverable amount at the end of the current year of (a) inventory and (b) property, plant, and equipment (see illustrations in Appendix A of FAS-89).

- The increase or decrease in current cost or lower recoverable amount before and after adjusting for the effects of inflation of (a) inventory and (b) property, plant, and equipment.

- The principal types and sources of information used to calculate current costs for the current year.

- The differences, if any, in depreciation methods, useful lives, and salvage values used in (a) the primary financial statements and (b) the disclosure of current cost information for the current year.

Specialized Assets

Timberlands, growing timber, mineral ore bodies, proved oil and gas reserves, income-producing real estate, and motion picture films are classified as specialized assets. Specialized assets are considered unique, and the determination of their current costs frequently is difficult, if not impossible. For example, the current cost of an existing oil field may be difficult to determine because the oil field is one of a kind and cannot be duplicated. Yet, the definition of current cost is the current cost to purchase or reproduce the specific asset, and the current cost of property that is owned is the current cost of acquiring an asset that will perform or produce in a manner similar to that of the owned property.

FAS-89 provides special rules for determining the current costs of specialized assets. As a substitute for the current cost amounts and related expenses, the historical cost amounts of specialized assets may be adjusted for changes in specific prices by the use of a broad index of general purchasing power (FAS-89, par. 25).

> **OBSERVATION:** FAS-89 provides additional guidance on reporting the effects of changing prices on timber assets and mineral resource assets, but does not provide similar guidance for other types of specialized assets.

Timber Assets

In the event an enterprise estimates the current cost of growing timber and timber harvested by adjusting historical costs for changes in specific prices, the historical costs may include either (a) only costs that are capitalized in the primary financial statements or (b) all direct costs of reforestation and forest management, even if such costs are not capitalized in the primary financial statements. Reforestation and forest management costs include planting, fertilization, fire protection, property taxes, and nursery stock (FAS-89, par. 26).

Mineral Resource Assets

The requirements for determining the current cost amounts for mineral resource assets are flexible because there is no generally accepted approach for measuring the current cost of finding mineral reserves. In determining the current cost amounts of mineral resource assets, FAS-89 permits the use of specific price indexes applied to historical costs, market buying prices, and other statistical data to determine current replacement costs. FAS-89 encourages the disclosure of the types of data or information that are used to determine current cost amounts (FAS-89, par. 23).

FAS-89 contains the following definitions relating to mineral resource assets (FAS-89, par. 44):

> **Mineral resource assets** Assets that are directly associated with and derive value from all minerals extracted from the earth. Such minerals include oil and gas, ores containing ferrous and non-ferrous metals, coal, shale, geothermal steam, sulphur, salt, stone, phosphate, sand, and gravel. Mineral resource assets include mineral interests in properties, completed and uncompleted wells, and related equipment and facilities, and other facilities required for purposes of extraction (FAS-19, Financial Accounting and Reporting by Oil and Gas Producing Companies, par. 11). The definition does not cover support equipment, because that equipment is included in the property, plant, and equipment for which current cost measurements are required by this appendix.

> **Proved mineral reserves** In extractive industries other than oil and gas, the estimated quantities of commercially recoverable reserves that, based on geological, geophysical, and engineering data, can be demonstrated with a reasonably high degree of certainty to be recoverable in the future from known mineral deposits by either primary or improved recovery methods.

> **Probable mineral reserves** In extractive industries other than oil and gas, the estimated quantities of commercially recoverable reserves that are less well defined than proved.

For enterprises that own significant mineral reserves, the following information on owned mineral reserves, excluding oil and gas, is encouraged to be disclosed for each of the five most recent years (FAS-89, par. 14):

- The estimated amount of proved or of proved and probable mineral reserves on hand at the end of the year. A date during the year may be used, but the date must be disclosed.

- The estimated quantity of each significant mineral product that is commercially recoverable from the mineral reserves in (1) above. The estimated quantity may be expressed in percentages or in physical units.

- The quantities of each significant mineral produced during the year. The quantity of each significant mineral produced by milling or similar processes also must be disclosed.

- The quantity of mineral reserves (proved or proved and probable) purchased or sold in place during the year.

- The average market price of each significant mineral product. If transferred within the enterprise, the equivalent market price prior to further use should be disclosed.

In classifying and detailing the above information, current industry practices should prevail.

The following procedures shall be used in determining the quantities of mineral reserves that should be reported (FAS-89, par. 15):

- In consolidated financial statements, 100% of the quantities of mineral reserves attributable to both the parent company and all consolidated subsidiaries shall be reported regardless of whether a subsidiary is partially or wholly owned.

- In a proportionately consolidated investment, an investor shall include only its proportionate share of the investor's mineral reserves.

- Mineral reserve quantities attributable to an investment accounted for by the equity method shall not be included at all. If significant, however, the mineral reserve quantities should be reported separately by the investor.

RELATED CHAPTER IN 2009 *INTERNATIONAL ACCOUNTING/FINANCIAL REPORTING STANDARDS GUIDE*

Chapter 9, "Changing Prices and Hyperinflationary Economies"

CHAPTER 17
FINANCIAL INSTRUMENTS

CONTENTS

OVERVIEW

The term *financial instrument* is extremely broad and encompasses a wide variety of transactions. A financial instrument is cash, an ownership interest in another entity, or a contract that imposes a contractual obligation on one entity and conveys a corresponding right to a second entity to require delivery (receipt) or exchange of a financial instrument (FAS-107, par. 3). Accounting principles for financial instruments are contained in numerous pronouncements. This chapter focuses on principles governing only the most active areas related to financial instruments—accounting for derivative instruments (including hybrid instruments with an embdedded derivative), offsetting of assets and liabilities arising from derivative transactions, and fair value disclosures for all financial instruments. GAAP established by the FASB for financial instruments are contained in the following:

FAS-107	Disclosures about Fair Value of Financial Instruments
FAS-126	Exemption from Certain Required Disclosures about Financial Instruments for Certain Nonpublic Entities
FAS-133	Accounting for Derivative Instruments and Hedging Activities
FAS-137	Deferral of the Effective Date of FASB Statement No. 133

FAS-138	Accounting for Certain Derivative Instruments and Certain Hedging Activities
FAS-149	Amendment of FASB Statement No. 133 on Derivative Instruments and Hedging Activities
FAS-155	Accounting for Certain Hybrid Financial Instruments: an amendment of FASB Statements No. 133 and 140
FIN-39	Offsetting of Amounts Related to Certain Contracts

Other chapters within this *Guide* discuss pronouncements that specifically address other types of financial instruments. For ease of reference, the table below summarizes current accounting pronouncements related to financial instruments and the specific chapters containing relevant discussions.

Pronouncement	*Title*	*Location*
APB-14	Accounting for Convertible Debt and Debt Issued with Stock Purchase Warrants	Chapter 9, Convertible Debt and Debt with Warrants
		Chapter 44, Stockholders' Equity
APB-21	Interest on Receivables and Payables	Chapter 25, Interest on Receivables and Payables
APB-26	Early Extinguishments of Debt	Chapter 15, Extinguishment of Debt
FAS-15	Accounting by Debtors and Creditors for Troubled Debt Restructurings	Chapter 46, Troubled Debt Restructuring
FAS-65	Accounting for Certain Mortgage Banking Activities	Chapter 50, Mortgage Banking
FAS-78	Classification of Obligations That Are Callable by the Creditor	Chapter 3, Balance Sheet Classification and Related Display Issues
FAS-84	Induced Conversions of Convertible Debt	Chapter 9, Convertible Debt and Debt with Warrants

Pronouncement	Title	Location
FAS-91	Accounting for Nonrefundable Fees and Costs Associated with Originating or Acquiring Loans and Initial Direct Costs of Leases	Chapter 29, Leases Chapter 47, Banking and Thrift Institutions Chapter 49, Insurance Chapter 50, Mortgage Banking
FAS-114	Accounting by Creditors for Impairment of a Loan	Chapter 46, Troubled Debt Restructuring Chapter 20, Impairment of Long-Lived Assets
FAS-115	Accounting for Certain Investments in Debt and Equity Securities	Chapter 28, Investments in Debt and Equity Securities
FAS-118	Accounting by Creditors for Impairment of a Loan—Income Recognition and Disclosures	Chapter 20, Impairment of Long-Lived Assets
FAS-129	Disclosure of Information about Capital Structure	Chapter 44, Stockholders' Equity
FAS-134	Accounting for Mortgage-Backed Securities Retained after the Securitization of Mortgage Loans Held for Sale by a Mortgage Banking Enterprise	Chapter 50, Mortgage Banking
FAS-140	Accounting for Transfers and Servicing of Financial Assets and Extinguishments of Debt	Chapter 45, Transfer and Servicing of Financial Assets
FAS-150	Accounting for Certain Financial Instrument with Characteristics of both Liabilities and Equity	Chapter 3, Balance Sheet Classification and Related Display Issues

Pronouncement	Title	Location
FIN-8	Classification of a Short-Term Obligation Repaid Prior to Being Replaced by a Long-Term Security	Chapter 3, Balance Sheet Classification and Related Display Issues
FIN-39	Offsetting of Amounts Related to Certain Contracts	Chapter 3, Balance Sheet Classification and Related Display Issues
FIN-41	Offsetting of Amounts Related to Certain Repurchase and Reverse Repurchase Agreements	Chapter 3, Balance Sheet Classification and Related Display Issues
FIN-45	Guarantor's Accounting and Disclosure Requirements for Guarantees, Including Indirect Guarantees of Indebtedness of Others	Chapter 8, Contingencies, Risks, and Uncertainties
FIN-46(R)	Consolidation of Variable Interest Entities	Chapter 7, Consolidated Financial Instruments
		Chapter 45, Transfer and Servicing of Financial Assets

2009 TRANSITION GUIDANCE FOR FAS-141(R) AND FAS-160

The FASB has recently issued FAS-141(R), *Business Combinations,* which is effective for business combinations for which the acquisition date is on or after the beginning of the first annual reporting period beginning on or after December 15, 2008. The FASB has also issued FAS-160, *Noncontrolling Interests in Consolidated Financial Statements, an Amendment of ARB No. 51,* which is effective for fiscal years, and interim periods within those fiscal years, beginning on or after December 15, 2008. Because these standards are not effective for some companies until December 2009, and because early adoption is prohibited, the 2009 *GAAP Guide* reflects the requirements of FAS-141 prior to its revision in December 2007 and does not reflect the requirements of FAS-160. There is a discussion of the changes in the accounting for business combinations under FAS-141(R) in the Appendix to Chapter 4, "Business Combinations." Similarly, the Appendix to Chapter 7, "Consolidated Financial Statements" includes a discussion of the requirements of FAS-160. However, any effects of FAS-141(R) and/or FAS-160 on this chapter have not been reflected in this edition. Therefore, if a company is subject to the requirements of FAS-141(R) and/or FAS-160, the reader is referred to FAS-141(R) and FAS-160 for these new requirements.

> **OBSERVATION:** The accounting for financial instruments has become increasingly complex in recent years. In addition to the pronouncements in the table above, which are within the highest level of GAAP, significant guidance for financial instruments also is contained in EITF Issues, FASB Staff Implementation Guides, FASB Staff Positions (FSPs), and other literature. Readers should refer to the *GAAP Guide Levels B, C, and D* for additional information regarding other accounting pronouncements related to financial instruments. Readers also should refer to CCH's *Financial Instruments* for comprehensive accounting guidance for each major type of financial instrument or transaction. Practitioners who encounter these areas should seek the assistance of experts in analyzing the applicable accounting literature.

> **OBSERVATION:** FAS-161 (Disclosures about Derivative Instruments and Hedging Activities, an Amendment of FASB Statement No. 133) was issued in March 2008, and is effective for financial statements issued for fiscal years and interim periods beginning after November 15, 2008. Because FAS-161 will not be mandatory for all companies until November 2009, the body of this chapter will reflect the requirements of FAS-133 prior to its amending by FAS-161. However, since entities are permitted early adoption of FAS-161 and since many companies will be affected in early 2009, a discussion of the changes in the disclosure requirements for derivative instruments and hedging activities upon the adoption of FAS-161 is found in the Appendix to this chapter.

BACKGROUND

Significant financial innovation and the rapid development of complex financial instruments prompted the FASB to undertake an involved and lengthy project to develop a set of accounting standards for financial instruments in 1986. Many financial instruments were described as *off-balance-sheet* instruments because they failed to meet one or more of the criteria for recognition. Before addressing the difficult recognition and measurement issues associated with financial instruments, the FASB developed standards to improve disclosures surrounding financial instruments. Initially, the FASB issued two broad pronouncements for financial instrument disclosures: FAS-105 (Disclosure of Information about Financial Instruments with Off-Balance-Sheet Risk and Financial Instruments with Concentrations of Credit Risk), issued in 1990, and FAS-107 (Disclosures about Fair Value of Financial Instruments), issued in 1991. Additionally, the FASB issued FAS-119 (Disclosure about Derivative Financial Instruments and Fair Value of Financial Instruments) in 1994.

The FASB issued several pronouncements in the early and mid-1990s that addressed the recognition and measurement of financial instruments, including FAS-114 (Accounting by Creditors for Impairment of a Loan), FAS-115 (Accounting for Certain Investments in Debt and Equity Securities), FAS-118 (Accounting by Creditors for Impairment of a Loan—Income Recognition and Disclosures), and FAS-125, which was later replaced by FAS-140 (Accounting for Transfers and Servicing of Financial Assets and Extinguishments of Liabilities). A significant milestone in the FASB's financial instrument project was reached in 1998 with the issuance of FAS-133 (Accounting for Derivative Instruments and Hedging Activities). FAS-133 was the result of extensive discussion and debate by the FASB on the subject of accounting for derivative instruments; it overhauled the fragmented preexisting accounting model for derivative instruments by establishing recognition and measurement standards for all derivatives, regardless of their use, based on fair value. FAS-133 replaced FAS-105, FAS-119, and amended FAS-107 as well as various other pronouncements.

ACCOUNTING FOR DERIVATIVE INSTRUMENTS AND HEDGING ACTIVITIES

FAS-133 (Accounting for Derivative Instruments and Hedging Activities) was issued in June 1998 and was originally effective for fiscal periods (both years and quarters) beginning after June 15, 1999. This effective date was delayed one year to June 15, 2000, by FAS-137. FAS-133 subsequently was amended by FAS-138 (Accounting for Certain Derivative Instruments and Certain Hedging Activities), primarily to ease implementation difficulties for a large number of the entities required to apply the standard. FAS-149 (Amendment of Statement 133 on Derivative Instruments and Hedging Activities), issued in 2003, further amended FAS-133 to clarify the definition of a derivative and to incorporate certain implementation guidance. FAS-155 further amends FAS-133 and provides guidance in accounting for hybrid financial instruments with an embedded derivative.

FAS-133, as amended, establishes accounting and reporting standards for derivative instruments, including derivative instruments that are embedded in other contracts, and hedging activities. FAS-133 is based on the following fundamental principles (FAS-133, par. 3):

- Derivative instruments represent rights or obligations that meet the definitions of assets and liabilities and, therefore, should be reported in the financial statements.

- Fair value is the most relevant measure for financial instruments and the only relevant measure for derivative instruments.

- Only items that are assets or liabilities should be reported as such in the financial statements.

- Special accounting for items designated as being hedged should be provided only for qualifying items. One aspect of qualification is an assessment of the expectation of effective offsetting changes in fair value or cash flows during the term of the hedge for the risk being hedged.

Definition of a Derivative and Scope Issues

A derivative instrument is defined as a financial instrument or other contract with all of the following characteristics:

- It has (1) one or more underlyings and (2) one or more notional amounts or payment provisions, or both. (An *underlying* is a specified interest rate, security price, commodity price, foreign exchange rate, index of prices or rates or other variable including the occurrence or nonoccurrence of a specified event. A *notional amount* is a number of currency units, shares, bushels, pounds, or other unit specified in the contract.) The interaction of the underlying and notional amount determine the amount of the settlement and, in some cases, whether or not a settlement is required;

- It requires no initial investment or an initial investment that is smaller than would be required for other types of contracts that would be expected to have a similar response to changes in market factors; and

- Its terms require or permit net settlement, it can be readily settled net by a means outside the contract, or it provides for delivery of an asset that puts the recipient in a position not substantially different from net settlement (FAS-133, pars. 6–9).

FAS-133 contains a number of exceptions to the definition of a derivative. Some of the scope exceptions were granted because the FASB recognized established accounting models already existed for certain instruments that would meet the definition of a derivative.

Other scope exceptions were granted in order to simplify application of the standard. The following is a partial list of those scope exceptions (FAS-133, pars. 10–11):

- "Regular-way" security trades (i.e., security trades that require delivery of an existing security within a timeframe established by regulations in the marketplace or exchange in which the transaction is executed), if they cannot be net settled; purchases and sales of "when-issued" securities or other securities that do not yet exist that meet certain specified conditions; and all security trades that are required to be recognized on a trade-date basis by other GAAP

- Normal purchases and normal sales (i.e., contracts that provide for the purchase or sale of something other than a financial instrument or derivative instrument that will be delivered in quantities expected to be used or sold by the reporting entity over a reasonable period in the normal course of business)

- Certain insurance contracts

- Certain financial guarantee contracts

- Certain contracts that are not traded on an exchange

- Derivatives that serve as impediments to sales accounting

- Investments in life insurance (in specific circumstances)

- Certain investment contracts (in specific circumstances)

- Loan commitments for origination of any type of loan that are held by a potential borrower

- Loan commitments issued to originate mortgage loans that will be classified as held for investment under FAS-65 (however, loan commitments issued to originate mortgage loans that will be classified as held for sale under FAS-65 are subject to FAS-133)

- Contracts issued or held by the reporting entity that are both indexed to the entity's own stock and classified in stockholders' equity

- Contracts issued by the entity in connection with stock-based compensation arrangements (should be analyzed to determine if subject to FAS-133)

- Contracts issued as contingent consideration in business combinations

- Forward purchase contracts for the reporting entity's shares that require physical settlement that are covered by paragraphs 21 and 22 of FAS-150

A contract that qualifies for a scope exception under FAS-133 should be accounted for in accordance with relevant GAAP.

☞ **PRACTICE POINTER:** The definition of a derivative and the scope exceptions in FAS-133 are complicated and highly interpretive. Practitioners encountering complex instruments that may be subject to FAS-133 should seek the advice of experts in the area of accounting for derivatives.

Embedded Derivatives

Contracts that do not in their entirety meet the definition of a derivative instrument (e.g., bonds, insurance policies, leases) may contain embedded derivative instruments as a result of implicit or explicit terms that affect some or all of the cash flows or the value of other exchanges required by the contract in a manner that makes them similar to a derivative instrument.

FAS-155 extends the requirements of FAS-133 to interests in securitized financial assets (eliminating the FAS-133 exemption that previously applied to securitizations). That is, an entity must now evaluate whether an interest in securitized financial assets contains an embedded derivative (FAS-155, par. 2b). Prior to FAS-155, this analysis was not required for interests in securitized financial assets. In addition, FAS-155 clarifies that concentrations of credit risk are not embedded derivatives (FAS-155, par. 4b). In addition, changes in the expected cash flows of a securitized interest due to changes in the creditworthiness of the assets or liabilities that underlie the interest do not represent an embedded derivative.

FAS-155 indicates that interest-only and principal-only strips are not subject to the provisions of FAS-133 if the interest-only or principal-only strips represent the rights to receive only a specified proportion of the contractual interest cash flows or contractual principal cash flows of a particular debt instrument and do not include any terms not in the original debt instrument. This exemption applies if some portion of the interest or principal cash flows are stripped to provide compensation to either a servicer or to the entity that stripped the debt instrument. However, this exemption from FAS-133 does not apply if a portion of the interest or principal cash flows are stripped to guarantee payments, to pay for servicing in excess of adequate compensation, or for any other purpose (FAS-155, par. 4a).

☞ **PRACTICE POINTER:** FAS-155 repeals the guidance in Implementation Issue D1 that permitted entities to not evaluate whether a securitized interest contained an embedded derivative (FAS-155, par. A2).

Other than the limited exemption provided above, a holder of an interest in a securitized financial asset must determine whether the interest represents a freestanding derivative or whether it contains an embedded derivative. The analysis requires the entity to understand the contractual terms of the interest in the securitized financial assets. The entity must analyze the nature and amounts of assets, liabilities, and other financial instruments that comprise the entire securitization transaction. The holder of an interest in securitized financial assets must understand the interest's payoff structure and its payment priority to determine whether the instrument contains an embedded derivative (FAS-155, par. 4b). Prior to FAS-155, FAS-133 required an embedded derivative to be separated from the host contract and accounted for as a derivative instrument assuming the following conditions are met (FAS-133, par. 12):

- The economic characteristics and risks of the embedded derivative instrument are not clearly and closely related to the economic characteristics of the host contract.

- The hybrid instrument that embodies the embedded derivative instrument and the host contract is not remeasured at fair value under otherwise applicable generally accepted accounting principles.

- A separate instrument with the same terms as the embedded instrument would be a derivative subject to the requirements of FAS-133. However, this criterion is not met if the separate instrument with the same terms as the embedded derivative instrument would be classified in stockholders' equity absent the provisions in FAS-150.

☛ **PRACTICE POINTER:** FAS-133 contains implementation guidance and illustrations related to the assessment of whether an embedded derivative is considered clearly and closely related to a host contract. For a more in-depth discussion of the application of FAS-133 and related interpretations to instruments with embedded derivatives, see CCH's *Financial Instruments*.

Under FAS-155, entities are permitted, but not required, to irrevocably elect to measure financial instruments with an embedded derivative at fair value. Rather than bifurcating the instrument, as previously required under FAS-133, with the embedded derivative accounted for at fair value and the host contract accounted for separately under whatever GAAP requirements pertain to that instrument, the entire instrument can be accounted for at fair value. However, a hybrid financial instrument that is not bifurcated between the embedded derivative and the underlying host, but rather is accounted for as one combined instrument at fair value, *cannot* be designated as a hedging instrument under FAS-133 (FAS-155, par. 4C).

The hybrid financial instrument can be either an asset or a liability, and it can either have been issued by or acquired by the entity. The election as to whether to record a hybrid financial instrument at fair value can be made on an instrument-by-instrument basis. Once an entity chooses to measure a hybrid financial instrument at fair value, it cannot change this measurement basis for that particular instrument in the future. Changes in the fair value of the hybrid financial instrument are recognized in earnings as they occur (FAS-155, par. 4C).

An entity that chooses to measure a hybrid financial instrument at fair value must support the decision with concurrent documentation. Alternatively, an entity can have a policy to automatically elect to measure hybrid financial instruments at fair value, but any such preexisting policy must be documented (FAS-155, par. 4C).

At the inception of a hybrid financial instrument, the transaction price and the instrument's fair value would normally be the same. However, in some circumstances, the transaction price may differ from the instrument's fair value. In these situations, the difference between the transaction price and fair value can only be recognized in earnings if the entity chooses the fair value election and if fair value is determined by a quoted market price in an active market, comparison to other observable current market transactions, and a valuation technique that uses observable market data (FAS-155, par. 4d).

Entities may have some hybrid financial instruments measured at fair value under the FAS-155 election (or due to FAS-133's practicability exception) and other hybrid financial instruments measured using another measurement attribute. Hybrid financial instruments with different measurement bases must be separately grouped and presented on the balance sheet. The entity can include separate line items on the balance sheet for the fair-value/non-fair-value carrying amounts or combine the amounts, with parenthetical disclosure, on the face of the balance sheet, of the fair value amount included in the combined total (FAS-155, par. 4e).

Entities that choose to measure hybrid financial instruments at fair value under the FAS-155 election (or due to FAS-133's practicability exception) must provide information to allow users to understand the effect of changes in fair value on earnings (FAS-155, par. 4e).

☞ **PRACTICE POINTER:** Entities are not required to measure the dollar difference on earnings from accounting for a hybrid financial instrument in its entirety at fair value rather than on a bifurcated basis (FAS-155, par. A32). Rather, the entity must provide a more general description of the effect on earnings of changes in fair value.

Recognition and Measurement of Derivatives

FAS-133 requires the recognition of all derivatives (both assets and liabilities) in the statement of financial position and the recognition of their measurement at fair value. In accordance with FAS-133, each derivative instrument is classified in one of the following four categories: (1) no hedge designation, (2) fair value hedge, (3) cash flow hedge, and (4) foreign currency hedge. Changes in the fair value of derivative instruments in each category are accounted for as indicated in the following table (FAS-133, par. 18):

Derivative Designation	*Accounting for Changes in Fair Value*
No hedge designation	Included in current income
Fair value hedge	Included in current net income (with the offsetting gain or loss on the hedged item attributable to the risk being hedged)
Cash flow hedge	Included in other comprehensive income (outside net income)
Foreign currency hedge of a net investment in a foreign operation	Included in comprehensive income (outside of net income) as part of the cumulative translation adjustment

Derivatives Designated in Hedging Relationships

Fair Value Hedges

Certain instruments are designated as hedging the exposure to changes in the fair value of an asset or liability or an identified portion thereof that is attributed to a particular risk. A fair value hedge must meet all of the following criteria (FAS-133, par. 20, as amended by FAS-149):

- At the inception of the hedge, there is formal documentation of the hedging relationship and the entity's risk management objective and strategy for undertaking the hedge. This must include identification of (*a*) the hedged instrument, (*b*) the hedged item, (*c*) the nature of the risk being hedged, and (*d*) how the hedging instrument's effectiveness in offsetting the exposure to changes in the fair value of the hedged item will be assessed.

- Both at the inception of the hedge and on an ongoing basis, the hedging relationship is expected to be highly effective in achieving offsetting changes in fair value attributed to the hedged risk during the period that the hedge is designated. An assessment is required whenever financial statements or earnings are reported, and at least every three months.

- If a written option is designated as hedging a recognized asset or liability or an unrecognized firm commitment, the combination of the hedged item and the written option provides at least as much potential for gains as the exposure to losses from changes in the combined fair values.

An asset or liability is eligible for designation as a hedged item in a fair value hedge if all of the following criteria are met (FAS-133, par. 21):

- The hedged item is specifically identified as either all or a specified portion of a recognized asset or a recognized liability or an unrecognized firm commitment. The hedged item is a single asset or liability (or specified portion thereof) or is a portfolio of similar assets or a portfolio of similar liabilities (or a specified portion thereof).

- The hedged item presents an exposure to changes in fair value attributable to the hedged risk that could affect reported earnings. (The reference to affecting reported earnings does not apply to an entity that does not report earnings as a separate caption in a statement of financial performance, such as a not-for-profit organization.)

- The hedged item is not *(a)* an asset or liability that is remeasured with the changes in fair value attributable to the hedged risk reported currently in earnings, *(b)* an investment accounted for by the equity method, *(c)* a minority interest in one or more consolidated subsidiaries, *(d)* an equity investment in a consolidated subsidiary, *(e)* a firm commitment either to enter into a business combination or to acquire or dispose of a subsidiary, a minority interest, or an equity method investee, or *(f)* an equity instrument issued by the entity and classified as stockholders' equity in the statement of financial position.

- If the hedged item is all or a portion of a debt security that is classified as held-to-maturity by FAS-115 (Accounting for Certain Investments in Debt and Equity Securities), the designated risk being hedged is the risk of changes in its fair value attributable to credit risk, foreign exchange risk, or both. If the hedged item is an option component of a held-to-maturity security that permits its prepayment, the designated risk being hedged is the risk of changes in the entire fair value of that option component.

- If the hedged item is a nonfinancial asset or liability other than a recognized loan servicing right or a nonfinancial firm commitment with financial components, the designated risk being hedged is the risk of changes in the fair value of the entire hedged asset or liability.

- If the hedged item is a financial asset or liability, a recognized loan servicing right, or a nonfinancial firm commitment with financial components, the designated risk being hedged is (a) the risk of changes in the overall fair value of the entire hedged item, (b) the risk of changes in its fair value attributable to changes in the designated benchmark interest rate (i.e., interest rate risk), (c) the risk of changes in its fair value attributable to changes in the related foreign currency exchange risk (i.e., foreign exchange risk), or (d) the risk of changes in its fair value attributable to both changes in the obligor's creditworthiness and changes in spread over the benchmark interest rate with respect to the hedged item's credit section at inception (i.e., credit risk).

Changes in the fair value of derivative instruments that qualify as fair value hedges are recognized currently in earnings. The gain or loss on the hedged item attributable to the hedged risk adjusts the carrying amount of the hedged item and is recognized currently in earnings (FAS-133, par. 22).

> **OBSERVATION:** Although FAS-133 generally requires accounting for derivative instruments at fair value, those qualifying as fair value hedges are the only types of hedges for which the change in value is included currently in determining net income. This accounting distinguishes fair value hedges from cash flow hedges and foreign currency hedges and can be expected to result in some volatility in reported income.

An entity shall discontinue prospectively accounting for a fair value hedge if *any* of the following occurs (FAS-133, par. 25):

- Any criterion of a fair value hedge, or hedged item, is no longer met.

- The derivative expires, or is sold, terminated, or exercised.

- The entity removes the designation of the fair value hedge.

An asset or liability that is designated as a fair value hedge is subject to the applicable GAAP requirement for assessment of impairment (asset) or recognition of an increased obligation (liability) (FAS-133, par. 27).

Cash Flow Hedges

A derivative instrument may be designated as hedging the exposure to variability in expected future cash flows attributed to a particular risk. That exposure may be associated with an existing recognized asset or liability (e.g., variable rate debt) or a forecasted transaction (e.g., a forecasted purchase or sale). Designated hedging instruments and hedged items or transactions qualify for cash flow hedge accounting if all of the following criteria are met (FAS-133, par. 28):

- At the inception of the hedge, there is formal documentation of the hedging relationship and the entity's risk management objective and strategy for undertaking the hedge. This must include identification of *(a)* the hedging instrument, *(b)* the hedged transaction, *(c)* the nature of the risk being hedged, and *(d)* how the hedging instrument's effectiveness hedges the risk to the hedged transaction's variability in cash flows attributable to the hedged risk will be assessed.

- Both at the inception of the hedge and on an ongoing basis, the hedging relationship is expected to be highly effective in achieving offsetting cash flows attributable to the hedged risk during the term of the hedge. An assessment is required when financial statements or earnings are reported, and at least every three months.

- If a written option is designated as hedging the variability in cash flows for a recognized asset or liability, the combination of the hedged item and the written option provides at least as much potential for favorable cash flows as the exposure to unfavorable cash flows.

- If a hedging instrument is used to modify the interest receipts or payments associated with a recognized financial asset or liability from one variable rate to another variable rate, the hedging instrument must be a link between an existing designated asset with variable cash flows and an existing designated liability with variable cash flows and must be highly effective in achieving offsetting cash flows.

A forecasted transaction is eligible for designation as a hedged transaction in a cash flow hedge if all of the following additional criteria are met (FAS-133, par. 29):

- The forecasted transaction is specifically identified as a single transaction or a group of individual transactions. If a group, the individual transactions within the group must share the same risk exposure that is being hedged.

- The occurrence of the forecasted transaction is probable.

- The forecasted transaction is with a party external to the reporting entity.

- The forecasted transaction is not the acquisition of an asset or incurrence of a liability that will subsequently be remeasured with changes in fair value attributed to the hedged risk reported currently in earnings.

- If the variable cash flows of the forecasted transaction relate to a debt security that is classified as held-to-maturity under FAS-115, the risk being hedged is the risk of changes in its cash flows attributable to credit risk, foreign exchange risk, or both.

- The forecasted transaction does not involve a business combination subject to the provisions of FAS-141 (Business Combinations) and is not a transaction involving (a) a parent company's interest in consolidated subsidiaries, (b) a minority interest in a consolidated subsidiary, (c) an equity-method investment, or (d) an entity's own equity instruments.

- If the hedged transaction is the forecasted purchase or sale of a nonfinancial asset, the designated risk being hedged is (a) the risk of changes in the functional-currency-equivalent cash flows attributable to changes in the related foreign currency exchange rates, or (b) the risk of changes in the cash flows relating to all changes in the purchase price or sales price of the asset, regardless of whether that price and the related cash flows are stated in the entity's functional currency or a foreign currency.

- If the hedged transaction is the forecasted purchase or sale of a financial asset or liability, the interest payments on that financial asset or liability, or the variable cash inflow or outflow of an existing financial asset or liability, the designated risk being hedged is (a) the overall risk of changes in the hedged cash flows related to the asset or liability, (b) the risk of changes in its cash flows attributable to changes in the designated benchmark interest rates, (c) the risk of changes in the functional-currency-equivalent cash flows attributable to changes in the related foreign currency exchange rates, or (d) the risk of changes in cash flows attributable to default, changes in the obligor's creditworthiness, and changes in the spread over the benchmark interest rate.

The effective portion of the gain or loss (i.e., change in fair value) on a derivative designated as a cash flow hedge is reported in other comprehensive income (outside net income). The ineffective portion is reported in earnings. Amounts in accumulated other comprehensive income are reclassified into earnings (net income) in the same period in which the hedged forecasted transaction affects earnings (FAS-133, par. 30).

> **OBSERVATION:**   Changes in the fair value of cash flow hedges are not included currently in determining net income as they are with fair value hedges. Rather, they are included in "other comprehensive income," outside the determination of net income.

An entity shall discontinue prospectively accounting for cash flow hedges as specified above if *any* of the following occurs (FAS-133, par. 32):

- Any criterion for a cash flow hedge, or the hedged forecasted transaction is no longer met.

- The derivative expires, or is sold, terminated, or exercised.

- The entity removes the designation of the cash flow hedge.

If cash flow hedge accounting is discontinued, the accumulated amount in other comprehensive income remains and is reclassified into earnings when the hedged forecasted transaction affects earnings. Existing GAAP for impairment of an asset or recognition of an increased liability apply to the asset or liability that gives rise to the variable cash flows that were designated in the cash flow hedge (FAS-133, par. 34).

Foreign Currency Hedges

If the hedged item is denominated in a foreign currency, FAS-133 indicates that an entity may designate the following types of hedges as hedges of foreign currency exposure:

- A fair value hedge of an unrecognized firm commitment or a recognized asset or liability (including an available-for-sale security)

- A cash flow hedge of a forecasted transaction, an unrecognized firm commitment, the forecasted functional-currency equivalent cash flows associated with a recognized asset or liability, or a forecasted intercompany transaction

- A hedge of a net investment in a foreign operation

Foreign currency fair value hedges and cash flows hedges are generally subject to the fair value and cash flow hedge accounting requirements, respectively, covered earlier.

The change in fair value of a derivative instrument that qualifies as a hedge of net investment of a foreign operation is reported in other comprehensive income (outside net income) as part of the cumulative translation adjustment in accordance with FAS-52 (Foreign Currency Translation) (FAS-133, par. 42).

> **OBSERVATION:** Foreign currency hedges build on the standards for fair value and cash flow hedges presented earlier, and (for foreign currency hedges of net investments in foreign operations) on accounting for the cumulative translation adjustment requirements of FAS-52 (Foreign Currency Translation). If a foreign currency hedge satisfies the FAS-133 criteria as a fair value or cash flow hedge, it is treated accordingly. If the foreign currency hedge is a hedge of net investment in a foreign operation, it is treated as a part of the cumulative translation adjustment. In this latter case, changes in fair value are included in other comprehensive income (much like a cash flow hedge), and are included in the cumulative translation adjustment rather than separately disclosed.

Required Disclosures

General

For instruments that qualify as hedging instruments, the following disclosures are required (FAS-133, par. 44):

- Objectives for holding or issuing the instruments
- The context needed to understand these objectives
- The entity's strategies for achieving these objectives
- Distinction concerning the above between derivative instruments designated as fair value hedging instruments, cash flow hedging instruments, hedges of the foreign currency exposure of a net investment in a foreign operation, and all other derivatives
- The entity's risk management policy for each type of hedge, including a description of the items or transactions for which risks are hedged
- For instruments not designated as hedging instruments, the purpose of the derivative activity

Fair Value Hedges

The following disclosures are required for derivative instruments, as well as nonderivative instruments that may give rise to foreign currency transaction gains or losses under FAS-52, that have been designated and qualify as fair value hedging instruments (FAS-133, par. 45a):

- The net gain or loss recognized in earnings during the period representing:
  — The amount of the hedges' ineffectiveness.
  — The component of the derivative instruments' gain or loss, if any, excluded from the assessment of hedge effectiveness.
  — A description of where the net gain or loss is reported in the statement of income or other statement of financial performance.

- The amount of net gain or loss recognized in earnings when a hedged firm commitment no longer qualifies as a fair value hedge.

Cash Flow Hedges

The following disclosures are required for derivatives that have been designated and qualify as cash flow hedging instruments and the related hedged transactions (FAS-133, par. 45b):

- The net gain or loss recognized in earnings during the reporting period representing:
  — The amount of the hedges' ineffectiveness.
  — The component of the derivative instruments' gain or loss, if any, excluded from the assessment of hedge effectiveness.
  — A description of where the net gain or loss is reported in the statement of income or other statement of financial performance.

- A description of the transactions or other events that will result in the reclassification into earnings of gains or losses that are reported in accumulated other comprehensive income and the estimated net amount of the existing gains or losses at the reporting date that is expected to be reclassified into earnings within the next 12 months.

- The maximum length of time over which the entity is hedging its exposure to the variability in future cash flows for forecasted transactions excluding those forecasted transactions related to the payment of variable interest on existing financial instruments.

- The amount of gains and losses reclassified into earnings as a result of the discontinuance of cash flow hedges, because it is probable that the original forecasted transactions will not occur by the end of the originally specified time period.

Hedges of a Net Investment in a Foreign Operation

For derivative instruments, as well as nonderivative instruments that may give rise to foreign currency transaction gains or losses under FAS-52, that have been designated and qualify as hedging instruments for hedges of the foreign currency exposure of a net investment in a foreign operation. The net amount of gains and losses included in the cumulative translation adjustment during the reporting period must be disclosed (FAS-133, par. 45c).

Reporting Cash Flows of Derivative Instruments That Contain Financing Elements

An instrument accounted for as a derivative under FAS-133 that at its inception includes off-market terms, requires an up-front cash payment, or both, contains a financing element. If a significant financing element is present at inception, other than a financing element inherently included in an at-the-market derivative instrument with no prepayments, then the borrower shall report all cash inflows and outflows associated with that derivative instrument as a financing activity as described in FAS-95 (Statement of Cash Flows) (FAS-133, par. 45A).

Reporting Changes in Components of Comprehensive Income

Changes in components of comprehensive income are the following:

- Within other comprehensive income, entities must display a separate classification of the net gain or loss on derivative instruments designated and qualifying as cash flow hedging instruments that are reported in comprehensive income (FAS-133, par. 46)

- As part of the disclosure of accumulated other comprehensive income in accordance with FAS-130 (Reporting Comprehensive Income), entities must disclose the beginning and ending accumulated derivative gain or loss, the related net change associated with current period hedging transactions, and the net amount of any reclassification into earnings (FAS-133, par. 47)

OFFSETTING DERIVATIVE ASSETS AND LIABILITIES

FIN-39 specifies that offsetting of assets and liabilities in the balance sheet is improper except when the right of setoff exists. FIN-39 establishes four criteria that must be satisfied to in turn establish a valid right of setoff. Generally, for an asset and liability to be offset and displayed as a net position, all four criteria of FIN-39 must be satisfied:

1. Each party owes the other party determinable amounts.
2. The reporting party has the right to set off the amount payable, by contract or other agreement, with the amount receivable.
3. The reporting entity intends to net settle.
4. The right of setoff is enforceable at law.

The chapter in this *Guide* titled "Balance Sheet Classification and Related Display Issues" discusses the provisions of FIN-39 in greater detail.

An exception to the general rule in FIN-39 exists for derivative contracts executed with the same counterparty under a master netting agreement. A master netting agreement is a contractual agreement entered into by two parties to multiple contracts that provides for the net settlement of all contracts covered by the agreement in the event of default under any one contract. For such derivative contracts, assets and liabilities may be offset and presented as a net amount even if the reporting entity does not meet the requirement in FIN-39 that the reporting entity has the intent to net settle. Offsetting derivative assets and liabilities under this exception is an election and the reporting entity must apply the election consistently.

DISCLOSURE OF INFORMATION ABOUT
FAIR VALUE OF FINANCIAL INSTRUMENTS

Definitions and Scope

FAS-107 (Disclosures about Fair Value of Financial Instruments) defines the term "financial instrument" as cash, evidence of an ownership interest in an entity, or a contract that both (FAS-107, par. 3):

*   Imposes on one entity a contractual obligation (1) to deliver cash or another financial instrument to a second entity or (2) to exchange other financial instruments on potentially unfavorable terms with the second entity
*   Conveys to the second entity a contractual right (1) to receive cash or another financial instrument from the first entity or (2) to exchange other financial instruments on potentially favorable terms with the first entity

The term *fair value* is defined as the price that would be received to sell the instrument in an orderly transaction between market participants at the measurement date (FAS-157, par. 5).

FAS-107 requires disclosure of fair value information about financial instruments, whether or not those instruments are recognized in the financial statements, with certain exceptions. It applies to all entities. It does not change requirements for recognition, measurement, or classification of financial instruments in financial statements (FAS-107, par. 7).

General Disclosure Requirements

FAS-107 establishes specific disclosure requirements and certain procedures that must be followed in estimating the fair value of financial instruments, as follows:

- An entity shall disclose, either in the body of the financial statements or in the accompanying notes, the fair value of financial instruments for which it is practicable to estimate that value. An entity also shall disclose the method(s) and significant assumptions used to estimate the fair value of financial instruments. For financial instruments recognized at fair value in the statement of financial position, the disclosure requirements of FAS-157 (Fair Value Measurements) also apply (FAS-107, par. 10).

> **OBSERVATION:** FAS-133 adds a note to FAS-107 that indicates that fair value information disclosed in the notes shall be presented with the related carrying value in a form that makes it clear whether the fair value and the carrying value represent assets or liabilities and how the carrying amounts relate to information reported in the statement of financial position. If disclosure of fair value information is in more than one note, one of the notes must include a summary table that contains cross-referenced locations(s) of the remaining disclosures (FAS-107, par. 10, as amended by FAS-133).

- In estimating the fair value of deposit liabilities, a financial entity shall not take into account the value of its long-term relationships with depositors, commonly known as core deposit intangibles, which are separate intangible assets, not financial instruments. For deposit liabilities with no defined maturities, the fair value to be disclosed is the amount payable on demand at the reporting date. FAS-107 does not prohibit an entity from disclosing separately the estimated fair value of any of its nonfinancial intangible and tangible assets and nonfinancial liabilities (FAS-107, par. 12).

- For trade receivables and payables, no disclosure is required under FAS-107 when the carrying amount approximates fair value (FAS-107, par. 13).

- In disclosing the fair value of a financial instrument, amounts of instruments shall not be netted, even if the instruments are of the same class or otherwise related except as permitted by FIN-39 (Offsetting of Amounts Related to Certain Contracts) and FIN-41 (Offsetting of Amounts Related to Certain Repurchase and Reverse Repurchase Agreements) (FAS-133, par. 531c).

- If it is not practicable for an entity to estimate the fair value of a financial instrument, or a class of financial instruments, the entity shall disclose information pertinent to estimating the fair value, such as the carrying amount, effective interest rate, and maturity, and provide an explanation of why it is not practicable to estimate fair value (FAS-107, par. 14).

Disclosures about Concentrations of Credit Risk

An entity shall disclose all significant credit risks from all financial instruments. Group concentrations of credit risk exist if a number of counterparties are engaged in similar activities and have similar economic characteristics that would cause their ability to meet contractual obligations to be affected in a similar way by changes in economic or other conditions. Following is information required to be disclosed about each significant concentration of credit risk (FAS-133, par. 531):

- Information about the shared activity, region, or economic characteristic that identifies the concentration

- The maximum amount of loss due to credit risk (i.e., the loss that would result to parties to the financial instrument if the parties failed completely to perform and any security proved to be of no value)

- The entity's policy of requiring collateral to support financial instruments subject to credit risk, information about the entity's access to the collateral, and the nature and a brief description of collateral

- The entity's policy of entering into master netting arrangements to mitigate credit risk of financial instruments, information about the arrangements for which the entity is a party, and a description of the terms of those agreements.

Encouraged Disclosures about Market Risk of All Financial Instruments

Entities are encouraged, but not required, to disclose quantitative information about the market risks of financial instruments that are consistent with the way it manages or adjusts those risks (FAS-107, par. 15(c), as amended by FAS-133).

Methods of disclosure are expected to vary among reporting entities. Possible ways of disclosing this information include (FAS-107, par. 15D, as amended by FAS-133):

- Details about current positions and activity during the period

- The hypothetical effects on comprehensive income or net income of possible changes in market value

- A gap analysis of interest rate repricing or maturity dates

- The duration of the financial instruments

- The entity's value at risk from derivatives and from other positions at the end of the reporting period and the average value of the risk during the period.

Situations Not Covered by FAS-107

While FAS-107 is intended to require disclosure of fair value information about a wide spectrum of financial instruments, a number of instruments and other items are exempt. These exemptions fall into three categories (FAS-107, par. 8):

1. Items subject to reporting and disclosure requirements of other authoritative pronouncements (e.g., pensions, extinguished debt, insurance contracts other than financial guarantees and investment contracts, leases, and equity method investments). FAS-107 does not change existing disclosure requirements for these items.

2. Other items explained in terms of certain definitional problems that the FASB was unable to resolve at the time (e.g., insurance contracts other than those mentioned above, lease contracts, warranty obligations, and unconditional purchase obligations that may have both financial and nonfinancial components) (FAS-107, par. 74). The FASB believes that definitional and valuation difficulties for these contracts and obligations require further consideration before decisions can be made about the appropriateness of fair value disclosure requirements.

3. The FAS-107 disclosures are intended to apply only to financial assets and liabilities, thereby excluding items such as minority interests in consolidated subsidiaries and an entity's own equity instruments included in stockholders' equity.

Optional Disclosures for Nonpublic Entities

FAS-126 makes the fair value disclosures of FAS-107 optional for entities meeting the following criteria (FAS-126, par. 2; FAS-133, par. 537):

- The entity is a nonpublic entity.

- The entity is small enough that it comes under the size criterion of less than $100 million of total assets on the date of the financial statements.

- The entity has no instrument that, in whole or in part, is accounted for as a derivative under FAS-133, other than commitments related to the origination of mortgage loans to be held for sale, during the reporting period.

> **OBSERVATION:** Public accountants serving smaller nonpublic entities convinced the FASB that the practicability provisions of FAS-107 were useful in reducing the costs of compliance, but a cost is still incurred simply to document compliance, even if the fair value information is deemed to be not practicable.
>
> The FASB observed that smaller nonpublic entities are less likely than larger entities to engage in complex financial transactions. These smaller entities' financial assets tend to consist of traded securities, investments in other closely held entities, and balances with related parties. Their financial liabilities tend to be trade payables and variable-rate and fixed-rate loans. The FASB also observed that the types of financial instruments commonly held by smaller nonpublic entities, such as trade receivables and payables and variablerate instruments, already are carried at amounts that approximate fair value, or that information about fair values already is required by other authoritative pronouncements, such as FAS-115 (Accounting for Certain Investments in Debt and Equity Securities) and FAS-124 (Accounting for Certain Investments Held by Not-for-Profit Organizations). Taken together, these mutually reinforcing observations led the FASB to conclude that the FAS-107 disclosure requirements should be optional for smaller nonpublic companies.

Estimating Fair Value

One of the greatest challenges in applying FAS-107 is estimating the fair value of financial instruments. FAS-157 establishes a framework for measuring fair value and discusses alternative valuation techniques that can be used to measure fair value.

> ☞ **PRACTICE POINTER:** An important dimension of FAS-107 is the latitude that entities have in deciding whether applying procedures to measure fair value is "practicable." *Practicable* means that an entity can estimate fair value without incurring excessive costs. It is a dynamic concept—what is practicable in one year may not be in another. Cost considerations are important in judging practicability and may affect the precision of the estimate, leading to determination of fair value for a class of financial instruments, an entire portfolio (rather than individual instruments), or a subset of a portfolio. Whatever is practicable to determine must be disclosed. The burden of this decision rests on the reporting entity and its auditor; if the decision is made that determining fair value is not practicable, reasons for not disclosing the information must be given. The explanation will normally be found in notes to the financial statement (FAS-107, par. 15).

FINANCIAL INSTRUMENTS
IMPORTANT NOTICE FOR 2009

As the 2009 *GAAP Guide Level A* goes to press, the FASB has outstanding an Exposure Draft of a Statement of Financial Accounting Standards (Accounting for Hedging Activities—an amendment of FASB Statement No. 133) that may have an important impact on the preparation of financial statements in the future.

The proposed standard addresses certain difficulties that exist in practice regarding the accounting for hedging activities. These difficulties include quantitatively assessing the effectiveness of hedging relationships, measuring ineffectiveness in a cash flow hedge, and measuring the change in value of a hedged item attributable to the hedged risk in a fair value hedge. Some of the proposed changes are as follows:

- With two exceptions, an entity will not be permitted to designate individual risks as the hedged risk in a fair value or cash flow hedge. The exceptions are (1) interest rate risk related to its own issued debt, if hedged at inception, and (2) foreign currency exchange risk.

- The shortcut method and critical terms matching will be eliminated.

- The effectiveness threshold necessary to apply hedge accounting will be modified from *highly effective* to *reasonably* effective.

- An evaluation of hedge effectiveness will be required at inception, but afterward would only be required if circumstances suggest that the hedging relationship may no longer be reasonably effective.

- The assessment of hedge effectiveness may be *qualitative* in nature, unless a *quantitative* assessment is more efficient.

The proposed effective date of the Exposure Draft is stated as for fiscal years beginning after June 15, 2009, and interim periods within those fiscal years. The current FASB agenda indicates a final standard is expected in the fourth quarter of 2008.

RELATED CHAPTERS IN 2009 *GAAP GUIDE LEVEL A*

Chapter 3, "Balance Sheet Classification and Related Display Issues"
Chapter 8, "Contingencies, Risks, and Uncertainties"
Chapter 9, "Convertible Debt and Debt with Warrants"
Chapter 15, "Extinguishment of Debt"
Chapter 18, "Foreign Operations and Exchange"
Chapter 25, "Interest on Receivables and Payables"
Chapter 28, "Investments in Debt and Equity Securities"
Chapter 44, "Stockholders' Equity"
Chapter 45, "Transfer and Servicing of Financial Assets"
Chapter 46, "Troubled Debt Restructuring"
Chapter 47, "Banking and Thrift Institutions"
Chapter 50, "Mortgage Banking"

RELATED CHAPTERS IN 2009 *GAAP GUIDE LEVELS B, C, AND D*

Chapter 4, "Balance Sheet Classification and Related Display Issues"
Chapter 11, "Contingencies, Risks, and Uncertainties"
Chapter 12, "Convertible Debt and Debt with Warrants"

Chapter 15, "Extinguishment of Debt"
Chapter 17, "Financial Instruments"
Chapter 18, "Foreign Operations and Exchange"
Chapter 22, "Interest on Receivables and Payables"
Chapter 25, "Investments in Debt and Equity Securities"
Chapter 39, "Stockholders' Equity"
Chapter 40, "Transfer and Servicing of Financial Assets"
Chapter 41, "Troubled Debt Restructuring"

RELATED CHAPTER IN 2009 *INTERNATIONAL ACCOUNTING/FINANCIAL REPORTING STANDARDS GUIDE*

Chapter 16, "Financial Instruments"

APPENDIX: FAS-161

BACKGROUND

In March 2008, the FASB issued FAS-161 (Disclosures about Derivative Instruments and Hedging Activities: an amendment of FASB Statement No. 133) as a response to constituents' concerns that the existing disclosure requirements in FAS-133 do not provide sufficient information about how derivative and hedging activities affect an entity's financial position, financial performance, and cash flows. FAS-161 applies to all entities, including not-for-profit organizations, defined benefit pension plans, and mutual fund companies.

OBJECTIVES

The Board's primary objective in issuing FAS-161 was to provide users of financial statements with an enhanced understanding of:

- How and why an entity uses derivative instruments
- How derivative instruments and related hedged items are accounted for
- How derivative instruments and related hedged items affect an entity's financial position, financial performance, and cash flows

FAS-161 achieves this objective by expanding the requirements for qualitative disclosures about an entity's objectives and strategies for using derivative instruments. FAS-161 also establishes requirements for quantitative disclosures about fair value amounts of derivative instruments and gains and losses on derivative instruments, as well as disclosures about credit-risk-related contingent features in derivative agreements.

AMENDMENTS TO FAS-133

Qualitative Disclosures

FAS-133 already requires an entity to make qualitative disclosures about its objectives and strategies for using derivative instruments, with such information provided by accounting designation (e.g., fair value hedge, cash flow hedge, etc.). FAS-161 expands on these disclosures and requires an entity to also provide qualitative information about these instruments in the context of each instrument's primary underlying risk exposure (e.g., interest rate, credit, foreign exchange rate, etc.). FAS-161 also requires an entity to distinguish those derivative instruments that are used for risk management purposes and those that are used for other purposes, and to provide information that would allow users of its financial statements to understand the volume of its derivative activity (FAS-161, par. 44).

Quantitative Disclosures

FAS-161 requires the following quantitative disclosures to be made for all derivative instruments and nonderivative instruments that qualify as hedging instruments (FAS-161, par. 44C):

- The location and fair value amounts of derivative instruments reported in the statement of financial position
  - Fair value shall be presented on a gross basis even when the derivative instruments qualify for net presentation in accordance with FIN-39 (Offsetting of Amounts Related to Certain Contracts)
  - Fair value amounts shall be presented as separate asset and liability values segregated between derivatives that are designated and qualify as hedging instruments and those that are not. Within these two broad categories, fair values amounts shall be presented separately by type of derivative contract (e.g., interest rate contracts, foreign exchange contracts, commodity contracts, etc.)
  - The disclosure shall identify the line item(s) in the statement of financial position in which the fair value amounts are included

- The location and amount of gains and losses on derivative instruments and related hedged items reported in the statement of financial performance, or when applicable the statement of financial position (e.g., gains and losses initially recognized in other comprehensive income). Gains and losses must be presented separately for:
  - Fair value hedges and related hedged items
  - The effective portion of gains and losses in cash flow hedges and net investment hedges that was recognized in other comprehensive income during the current period

— The effective portion of gains and losses in cash flow hedges and net investment hedges recorded in accumulated other comprehensive income during the term of the hedging relationship and reclassified into earnings during the current period

— The portion of gains and losses in cash flow hedges and net investment hedges representing:

• The amount of the hedges' ineffectiveness

• The amount, if any, excluded from the assessment of hedge effectiveness

— Derivative instruments not designated or qualifying as hedging instruments

The quantitative disclosures listed above must be presented in tabular format except for the information required for fair value hedges and their related hedged items, which can be disclosed in either a tabular or nontabular format.

Disclosures about Credit-Risk-Related Contingent Features

Derivative instruments often include contingent features that can result in an immediate payment to a counterparty or a posting of additional collateral on an agreement that is in a liability position. FAS-161 requires disclosures about credit-risk-related contingent features that could affect an entity's liquidity. Specifically, an entity must disclose (FAS-161, par. 44D):

• The existence and nature of credit-risk-related contingent features and the circumstances that would trigger these features in derivative instruments that are in a net liability position at the end of the reporting period

• The aggregate fair value amounts of derivative instruments that contain credit-risk-related contingent features and are in a net liability position at the end of the reporting period

• The aggregate fair value of assets already posted as collateral at the end of the reporting period and:

— The aggregate fair value of additional assets that would be required to be posted as collateral if the contingent features were triggered

— The aggregate fair value of assets needed to settle the instruments immediately if the contingent features were triggered

Cross-Referencing to Other Footnotes

Disclosures about derivative instruments are typically scattered throughout multiple footnotes to the financial statements, which can make them difficult to understand and follow. FAS-161 requires an entity to cross-reference from the derivative footnote to any other footnotes in which derivative-related information is disclosed (FAS-161, par. 44E).

EFFECTIVE DATE

FAS-161 is effective for financial statements issued for fiscal years and interim periods beginning after November 15, 2008. Earlier adoption is encouraged.

TRANSITION

FAS-161 encourages but does not require disclosures for earlier periods presented for comparative purposes at initial adoption. In years following initial adoption, FAS-161 requires comparative disclosures only for periods subsequent to initial adoption.

CHAPTER 18
FOREIGN OPERATIONS AND EXCHANGE

CONTENTS

OVERVIEW

There are two major areas of foreign operations:

1. Translation of foreign currency financial statements for purposes of consolidation, combination, or reporting on the equity method (one-line consolidation)
2. Accounting and reporting of foreign currency transactions, including forward exchange contracts

GAAP for foreign operations and exchange are found in the following pronouncements:

FAS-52 Foreign Currency Translation

FIN-37 Accounting for Translation Adjustments upon Sale of Part of an Investment in a Foreign Entity

BACKGROUND

Business transactions and foreign operations that are recorded in a foreign currency must be restated in U.S. dollars in accordance with generally accepted accounting principles.

Transactions occur at various dates and exchange rates tend to fluctuate considerably. Before an attempt is made to translate the records of a foreign operation, the records should be in conformity with GAAP. In addition, if the foreign statements have any accounts stated in a currency other than their own, they must be converted into the foreign statement's currency before translation into U.S. dollars or any other reporting currency.

A brief summary of FAS-52 (Foreign Currency Translation) follows:

- Foreign currency financial statements must be in conformity with GAAP before they are translated.

- Assets, liabilities, and operations of an entity must be expressed in the functional currency of the entity. The functional currency of an entity is the currency of the primary economic environment in which the entity operates.

- The current rate of exchange is used to translate the assets and liabilities of a foreign entity from its functional currency into the reporting currency.

— The weighted-average exchange rate for the period is used to translate revenue, expenses, and gains and losses of a foreign entity from its functional currency to the reporting currency.

— The current rate of exchange is used to translate changes in financial position other than those items found in the income statement, which are translated at the weighted average exchange rate for the period.

- Gain or loss on the translation of foreign currency financial statements is not recognized in current net income but is reported as a separate component of stockholders' equity. If remeasurement from the recording currency to the functional currency is necessary prior to translation, however, gain or loss on remeasurement is recognized in current net income.

- The amounts accumulated in the separate component of stockholders' equity are realized on the sale or substantially complete liquidation of the investment in the foreign entity.

- The financial statements of a foreign entity in a country that has had cumulative inflation of approximately 100% or more over a three-year period (highly inflationary) must be remeasured into the functional currency of the reporting entity.

- A foreign currency transaction is one that requires settlement in a currency other than the functional currency of the reporting entity.

- Gains or losses from foreign currency transactions are recognized in current net income, except for:

  — Gain or loss on a designated and effective economic hedge of a net investment in a foreign entity

  — Gain or loss on certain long-term intercompany foreign currency transactions

  — Gain or loss on a designated and effective economic hedge of a firm, identifiable, foreign currency commitment that meets certain conditions

- Taxable foreign exchange gains or losses that do not appear in the same period in taxable income and either (a) financial accounting income (books) or (b) a separate component of stockholders' equity (books) are temporary differences for which deferred taxes must be provided in accordance with existing GAAP.

- Certain specific disclosures are required by FAS-52.

OBSERVATION: FAS-133 (Accounting for Derivative Instruments and Hedging Activities) addresses accounting for free-standing foreign currency derivatives and certain foreign currency derivatives embedded in other instruments. FAS-52 does not address accounting for derivative instruments.

TRANSLATION OBJECTIVES

FAS-52 establishes accounting and reporting standards for (*a*) foreign currency transactions and (*b*) translation of foreign currency financial statements that are included by consolidation, combination, or the equity method in a parent company's financial statements. Foreign financial statements must conform to U.S. generally accepted accounting principles before they can be translated into dollars (FAS-52, par. 4).

An important objective in translating foreign currency is to preserve the financial results and relationships that are expressed in the foreign currency. This is accomplished by using the *functional currency* of the foreign entity. The functional currency is then translated into the *reporting currency* of the reporting entity. FAS-52 assumes that the reporting currency for an enterprise is U.S. dollars. The reporting currency may be a currency other than U.S. dollars, however.

> **OBSERVATION:** Perhaps the ultimate objective of translating foreign transactions and financial statements is to produce the same results that each individual underlying transaction would have produced on the date it occurred, if it had then been recorded in the reporting currency.

FUNCTIONAL CURRENCY

FAS-52 requires that the assets, liabilities, and operations of an entity be measured in terms of the functional currency of that entity. The functional currency is the currency of the primary economic environment in which an entity generates and expends cash. The functional currency generally is the currency of the country in which the entity is located (FAS-52, par. 5).

> **OBSERVATION:** In some instances, two levels of translation are required. For example, if a foreign entity's books of record are kept in Euros and the functional currency is the British pound, the books of record are remeasured into British pounds before the financial statements are translated into the currency of the reporting entity. Any translation gain or loss from Euros to British pounds is included in the remeasured net income. If the functional currency of the foreign entity is the Euro, only translation to the reporting currency is necessary. If the functional currency of the foreign entity is that of the reporting entity, only remeasurement from Euros to the reporting currency is required.

For the purposes of determining functional currency under FAS-52, foreign operations may be separated into two models.

The first model is the self-contained foreign operation, located in a particular country, whose daily operations are not dependent on the economic environment of the parent's functional currency. This type of foreign operation primarily generates and expends local currency; the net cash flows that it produces in local currency may be reinvested, or converted and distributed to its parent company. The functional currency for this type of foreign operation is its local (domestic) currency (FAS-52, par. 6).

The second model of foreign operation usually is a direct and integral component or extension of the parent company's operation. Financing usually is in U.S. dollars and frequently is supplied by the parent. The purchase and sale of assets usually are made in U.S. dollars. In other words, the daily operations of this type of foreign operation are dependent on the economic environment of the parent's currency. In addition, the changes in the foreign operation's individual assets and liabilities directly affect the cash flow of the parent company. The functional currency for this type of foreign operation is the U.S. dollar (FAS-52, par. 6).

In the event that the facts in a given situation do not clearly identify the functional currency, the determination rests on the judgment of management. The FASB has developed guidelines based on certain indicators, discussed below, that should be considered in determining the functional currency of a foreign operation (FAS-52, par. 42).

Cash Flow Indicators

The foreign operation's cash flows are mostly in foreign currency that does not directly affect the parent company's cash flows. Under these circumstances, the functional currency is the local currency.

The foreign operation's cash flows directly affect the parent company's cash flows on a current basis and usually are available for remittance through intercompany account settlement. Under these circumstances, the functional currency is the parent company's currency.

Sales Price Indicators

The foreign operation's sales prices for its products are primarily determined (on a short-term basis) by local competition or local government regulation, and not by exchange rate changes. Under these circumstances, the functional currency is the local currency.

The foreign operation's sales prices for its products are mostly responsive (on a short-term basis) to exchange rate changes, such as worldwide competition and prices. Under these circumstances, the functional currency is the parent company's currency.

Sales Market Indicators

The foreign operation has an active local sales market for its products, although there also may be significant amounts of exports. Under these circumstances, the functional currency is the local currency.

The foreign operation's sales market is mostly in the parent's country, or sales contracts are mostly made in the parent company's currency. Under these circumstances, the functional currency is the parent company's currency.

Expense Indicators

The foreign operation's costs of production (e.g., labor or material) or service are mostly local costs, although there also may be imports from other countries. Under these circumstances, the functional currency is the local currency.

The foreign operation's costs of production or service, on a continuing basis, are primarily costs for components obtained from the parent's country. Under these circumstances, the functional currency is the parent company's currency.

Financing Indicators

Financing for the foreign operation is in local currency, and funds generated by the foreign operation are sufficient to service debt obligations. Under these circumstances, the functional currency is the local currency.

Financing for the foreign operation is provided by the parent company or is obtained in U.S. dollars. Funds generated by the foreign operation are insufficient to service its debt. Under these circumstances, the functional currency is the parent company's currency.

Intercompany Transactions

There is little interrelationship between the operations of the foreign entity and the parent company, except for competitive advantages, such as trademarks, patents, etc. Intercompany transactions are of a low volume. Under these circumstances, the functional currency is the local currency.

There is an extensive interrelationship between the operations of the foreign entity and the parent company. Intercompany transactions are numerous. Under these circumstances, the functional currency is the parent company's currency.

The functional currency of a foreign entity must be used consistently from one fiscal year to another, unless significant changes in economic facts and circumstances dictate a change (FAS-52, par. 9).

☛ **PRACTICE POINTER:** Once an entity determines its functional currency, the entity should not change that determination unless significant changes in economic facts and circumstances indicate that the functional currency has changed (FAS-52, par. 45). If there is a change in the functional currency of a foreign entity, that change is accounted for as a change in accounting estimate. Thus, the change is accounted for in the period of the change and/or future periods (prospectively).

If a change in functional currency occurs, do not remove the translation adjustments for prior periods from the separate component of stockholders' equity. Thus, the translated amounts of nonmonetary assets at the end of the period prior to the change in functional currency become the accounting basis for subsequent periods (FAS-52, par. 46).

REMEASURING FINANCIAL STATEMENTS TO THE FUNCTIONAL CURRENCY

The following is a brief review of the translation provisions of FAS-52 for the remeasurement process from the recording currency to the functional currency, prior to translation from the functional currency to the reporting currency. (For further explanation, see the observation under the "Functional Currency" section, above.)

Two categories of exchange rates are used in remeasuring financial statements. Historical exchange rates are those that existed at the time of the transaction, and the current exchange rate is the rate that is current at the date of remeasurement.

Monetary assets and liabilities are those that are fixed in amount, such as cash, accounts receivable, and most liabilities. Monetary assets and liabilities are translated at the current rate of exchange. All other assets, liabilities, and stockholders' equity are remeasured by reference to the following four money price exchanges based on the type of market and time:

1. *Past purchase exchange*—the historical or acquisition cost, because it is based on the actual past purchase price

2. *Current purchase exchange*—the replacement cost, because it is measured by the current purchase price of a similar resource

3. *Current sale exchange*—the market price, because it is based on the current selling price of the resource

4. *Future exchange*—the present value of future net money receipts, discounted cash flow, or the discounted net realizable value, because it is based on a future resource

All other assets, liabilities, and stockholders' equity are remeasured based on the four money price exchanges, as follows:

- Accounts based on past purchase exchanges (historical or acquisition cost) are remeasured at historical exchange rates.
- Accounts based on current purchase, current sale, and future exchanges are remeasured at the current exchange rate.

Revenue and expense transactions are remeasured at the average exchange rate for the period, except those expenses related to assets and liabilities, which are remeasured at historical exchange rates. For example, depreciation and amortization are remeasured at historical exchange rates, the rate that existed at the time the underlying related asset was acquired.

The following is a list of assets, liabilities, and stockholders' equity items and their corresponding remeasurement rates under FAS-52:

	Remeasurement Rates	
	Current	*Historical*
Cash (in almost all forms)	X	
Marketable securities—at cost		X
Marketable securities—at market	X	
Accounts and notes receivable	X	
Allowance for receivables	X	
Inventories—at cost		X
Inventories—at market, net realizable value, selling price	X	
Inventories—under fixed contract price	X	
Prepaid expenses		X
Refundable deposits	X	
Advances to subsidiaries	X	
Fixed assets		X
Accumulated depreciation		X
Cash surrender value—life insurance	X	
Intangible assets (all)		X
Accounts and notes payable	X	
Accrued expenses	X	
Accrued losses on firm commitments	X	
Taxes payable	X	
All long-term liabilities	X	
Unamortized premium or discount on long-term liabilities	X	
Obligations under warranties	X	
Deferred income		X
Capital stock		X
Retained earnings		X
Minority interests		X

Revenue and expenses not related to any balance sheet items are remeasured at the average currency exchange rate for the period. The average may be based on a daily, weekly, monthly, or quarterly basis or on the weighted-average rate for the period, which will probably result in a more meaningful conversion. Revenue and expense items that are related to a balance sheet account, such as deferred income, depreciation, and beginning and ending inventories, are remeasured at the same exchange rate as the related balance sheet item.

In remeasuring the lower-of-cost-or-market rule, the remeasured historical cost is compared to the remeasured market, and whichever is lower in functional currency is used. This may require a write-down in the functional currency from cost to market, which was not required in the foreign currency financial statements. On the other hand, if market was used on the foreign statements and in remeasuring to the functional currency market exceeds historical cost, the write-down to market on the foreign statements will have to be reversed before remeasuring, which would then be done at the historical rate. Once inventory has been written down to market in remeasured functional currency statements, the resulting carrying amount is used in future translations until the inventory is sold or a further write-down is necessary. This same procedure is used for assets, other than inventory, that may have to be written down from historical cost.

> **OBSERVATION:** The reason for the above procedure in applying the lower-of-cost-or-market rule in remeasuring foreign financial statements is that exchange gains and losses are a consequence of remeasurement and not of applying the lower-of-cost-or-market rule. This means that remeasured market is equal to replacement cost (market) in the foreign currency remeasured at the current exchange rate, except that:
>
> • Remeasured market cannot exceed net realizable value in foreign currency translated at the current exchange rate.
> • Remeasured market cannot be less than (1) above, reduced by an approximate normal profit translated at the current exchange rate.

For remeasurement purposes, the current exchange rate is the one in effect as of the balance sheet date of the foreign statements. Therefore, if the parent company's financial statements are at a date different from the date(s) of its foreign operation(s), the exchange rate in effect at the date of the foreign subsidiary's balance sheet is used for remeasurement and translation purposes.

Any translation adjustment arising from the remeasurement process is included in remeasured net income. In other words, any gain or loss resulting from the remeasurement process that is required by FAS-52 is included in net income in the remeasured financial statements (FAS-52, par. 47).

After the foreign entity's financial statements are remeasured in the functional currency, they are ready for translation. If the functional currency of a foreign entity is the U.S dollar and the reporting currency of the parent is also the U.S. dollar, there will be no translation adjustment.

TRANSLATION OF FOREIGN OPERATIONS—HIGHLY INFLATIONARY ECONOMIES

FAS-52 defines a highly inflationary economy as one in which the cumulative inflation over a three-year consecutive period approximates 100%. In other words, the inflation rate in an economy must be rising at the rate of about 30 to 35% per year for three consecutive years to be classified as highly inflationary.

For the purposes of FAS-52, a foreign entity in a highly inflationary economy does not have a functional currency. The functional currency of the reporting entity is used as the functional currency of the foreign entity in a highly inflationary economy. Thus, the financial statements for a foreign entity in a highly inflationary economy are remeasured into the functional currency of the reporting entity. The remeasurement process required by FAS-52 is the same as that required for a foreign entity's financial statements that are not expressed in the functional currency (FAS-52, par. 11).

> **OBSERVATION:** Apparently, exchange adjustments resulting from the remeasurement process for foreign entities in highly inflationary economies are included in the determination of remeasured net income, rather than reported as a separate component of stockholders' equity. Paragraph 11 of FAS-52 is not clear on this point, but does state that the remeasurement process must be done in accordance with paragraph 10.

The International Monetary Fund (IMF) publishes monthly statistics on international inflation rates. After the financial statements of a foreign entity in a highly inflationary economy are expressed in the functional currency of the reporting entity, they are ready for translation. Since the financial statements are now expressed in the reporting currency, however, there will be no translation adjustment.

TRANSLATION OF FOREIGN CURRENCY STATEMENTS

Foreign currency financial statements must be in conformity with GAAP before they are translated into the functional currency of the reporting entity. FAS-52 covers the translation of financial statements from one functional currency to another for the purposes of consolidation, combination, or the equity method of accounting. Translation of financial statements for any other purpose is beyond the scope of FAS-52 (FAS-52, par. 2).

> **OBSERVATION:** If the functional currency of a foreign operation is the same as that of its parent, there is no need for translation. A translation adjustment occurs only if the foreign operation's functional currency is a functional currency different from that of its parent.

The translation of foreign currency financial statements to the functional currency of the reporting entity does not produce realized exchange gains or losses. Instead, the gains or losses are considered unrealized and are recorded and reported as a separate component of stockholders' equity (FAS-52, par. 13).

> **OBSERVATION:** Paragraph 12 of FAS-52 states, "All elements of financial statements shall be translated by using a current exchange rate." This statement is potentially misleading because common stock, paid-in capital, donated capital, retained earnings, and similar items are not translated at the current exchange rate. Translation of these elements of the financial statements is made as follows:
>
> *Capital accounts* are translated at their historical exchange rates when the capital stock was issued, or at the historical exchange rate when the capital stock was acquired.
>
> *Retained earnings* are translated at the translated amount at the end of the prior period, plus the translated amount of net income for the current period, less the translated amount of any dividends declared during the current period.

Assets and liabilities are translated from the foreign entity's functional currency to the reporting entity's functional currency using the current exchange rate at the balance sheet date of the foreign entity (FAS-52, par. 12). If a current exchange rate is not available at the balance sheet date of the foreign entity being translated, the first exchange rate available after the balance sheet date is used (FAS-52, par. 26).

Revenue, expenses, and gains and losses are translated from the foreign entity's functional currency to produce the approximate results that would have occurred if each transaction had been translated using the exchange rate in effect on the date that the transaction was recognized. Since the separate translation of every transaction is impractical, an appropriate weighted-average exchange rate for the period should be used (FAS-52, par. 12).

Gains or losses on the translation of foreign currency financial statements for the purposes of consolidation, combination, or reporting on the equity method are not included in current net income. All adjustments resulting from the translation of foreign currency financial statements are recorded and reported as a separate component of stockholders' equity. Thus, these adjustments are treated as unrealized gains and losses, similar to unrealized gains and losses of available-for-sale securities (FAS-115 [Accounting for Certain Investments in Debt and Equity Securities]).

To summarize, the translation process embodied in FAS-52 includes the following steps:

1. Financial statements must be in conformity with U.S. GAAP prior to translation.

2. The functional currency of the foreign entity is determined.

3. The financial statements are expressed in the functional currency of the foreign entity. Remeasurement of the financial statements into the functional currency may be necessary. Gains or losses from remeasurement are included in remeasured current net income.

4. If the foreign entity operates in a country with a highly inflationary economy, its financial statements are remeasured into the functional currency of the reporting entity.

5. The functional currency financial statements of the foreign entity are translated into the functional currency of the reporting entity using the current rate of exchange method. Gains or losses from translation are not included in current net income.

Illustration of Foreign Currency Translation When Euro Is Functional Currency

On December 31, 20X8, Gardial Inc. (a U.S. company) created a 100%-owned subsidiary in Prague, investing $15,000,000 in equity at that time when the direct exchange rate was $1.20. Gardial used this investment to purchase $13,200,000 of fixed assets on that date. The direct exchange rates were $1.30 at December 31, 20X9, and $1.25 for 20X9 as an average. No dividends were declared or paid in 20X9.

During 20Y0, the dollar strengthened so that the direct exchange rate at December 31, 20Y0, was $1.26. The average rate for 20Y0 was $1.28. Cash dividends of €1,000 were declared and paid on November 29, 20Y0, when the direct exchange rate was $1.27.

Assume that (1) the subsidiary is a self-contained foreign operation that uses the euro as its functional currency, (2) the statements have already been adjusted so that they conform to U.S. GAAP, (3) all intercompany adjustments have been made, and (4) all sales, costs, and expenses occurred evenly throughout the year.

All Current Translation Method

Euro Is Recording and Functional Currency
U.S. Dollar Is Reporting Currency

(in thousands)	For the Year Ended 12/31/20X9				For the Year Ended 12/31/20Y0			
	Euros	Exchange Code	Rate	U.S. Dollars	Euros	Exchange Code	Rate	U.S. Dollars
Income Statement								
Revenues	€ 12,000	A	$1.25	$ 15,000	€ 15,000	A	$1.28	$ 19,200
Cost of sales	(8,000)	A	$1.25	(10,000)	(10,500)	A	$1.28	(13,440)
Operating expenses	(2,000)	A	$1.25	(2,500)	(1,700)	A	$1.28	(2,176)
Depreciation expense	(500)	A	$1.25	(625)	(500)	A	$1.28	(640)
Net income	€ 1,500			$ 1,875	€ 2,300			$ 2,944
Retained Earnings Statement								
Balance, January 1	€ -			$ -	€ 1,500	A	$1.28	$ 1,875
Net income	1,500	A	$1.25	1,875	2,300			2,944
Dividends	-			-	(1,000)	H	$1.27	(1,270)
Balance, December 31	€ 1,500			$ 1,875	€ 2,800			$ 3,549
Balance Sheet								
Assets								
Cash	€ 3,000	C	$1.30	$ 3,900	€ 3,000	C	$1.26	$ 3,780
Accounts Receivable, net	1,000	C	$1.30	1,300	1,500	C	$1.26	1,890
Inventory	2,000	C	$1.30	2,600	3,500	C	$1.26	4,410
Fixed Assets	11,000	C	$1.30	14,300	11,000	C	$1.26	13,860
Accumulated Depreciation	(500)	C	$1.30	(650)	(1,000)	C	$1.26	(1,260)
Total assets	€ 16,500			$ 21,450	€ 18,000			$ 22,680

For the Year Ended 12/31/20X9

(in thousands)

	Euros	Exchange Code	Rate	U.S. Dollars
Liabilities and Equity				
Accounts payable	€ 2,500	C	$1.30	$ 3,250
Common stock	12,500	H	$1.20	15,000
Retained earnings	1,500			1,875
AOCI—Cumulative Unrealized Translation Adjustment:				
Prior years				-
Current year				1,325
Total liabilities and equity	€ 16,500			$ 21,450

Code: A = Average rate, C = Current rate, H = Historical rate

Calculation of Translation Adjustment Amount:

	Euros	Diff. between end rate and applicable rate	U.S. Dollars
Net asset (equity) position at 1/1	€ 12,500	.10 (1.30 - 1.20)	$ 1,250
Plus: Net income	1,500	.05 (1.25 - 1.20)	75
Less: Dividends	-		-
Net asset (equity) position at 12/31	€ 14,000		
Unrealized Translation Gain/(Loss)			$ 1,325

For the Year Ended 12/31/20Y0

	Euros	Exchange Code	Rate	U.S. Dollars
Liabilities and Equity				
Accounts payable	€ 2,700	C	$1.26	$ 3,402
Common stock	12,500	H	$1.20	15,000
Retained earnings	2,800			3,549
AOCI—Cumulative Unrealized Translation Adjustment:				
Prior years				1,325
Current year				(596)
Total liabilities and equity	€ 18,000			$ 22,680

Calculation of Translation Adjustment Amount:

	Euros	Diff. between end rate and applicable rate	U.S. Dollars
Net asset (equity) position at 1/1	€ 14,000	-.04 (1.26 - 1.30)	$ (560)
Plus: Net income	2,300	-.02 (1.26 - 1.28)	(46)
Less: Dividends	(1,000)	-.01 (1.26 - 1.27)	10
Net asset (equity) position at 12/31	€ 15,300		
Unrealized Translation Gain/(Loss)			$ (596)

Illustration of Foreign Currency Translation When U.S. Dollar Is Functional Currency

Assume the same monetary facts as in the previous illustration. In addition, all ending inventory existing on December 31, 20X9, was purchased when the exchange rate was $1.29, and all ending inventory existing on December 31, 20Y0, was purchased when the exchange rate was $1.27. Also, the ending inventory cost was always below market. All fixed assets were acquired in prior years when the direct exchange rate was $1.20, and no fixed assets were retired in 20X9 or 20Y0.

Also assume that (1) the subsidiary is a direct and integral component of the parent company's operation and uses the U.S. dollar as its functional currency, (2) the statements have already been adjusted so that they conform to U.S. GAAP, (3) all intercompany adjustments have been made, and (4) all sales, costs, and expenses occurred evenly throughout the year.

Monetary/Nonmonetary Translation Method

Euro Is Recording Currency
U.S. Dollar Is Reporting and Functional Currency

(in thousands)	For the Year Ended 12/31/20X9				For the Year Ended 12/31/20Y0			
	Euros	Exchange Code	Rate	U.S. Dollars	Euros	Exchange Code	Rate	U.S. Dollars
Income Statement								
Revenues	€ 12,000	A	$1.25	$ 15,000	€ 15,000	A	$1.28	$ 19,200
Cost of sales:								
Beginning inventory	10,000	A	$1.25	12,500	2,000	H	$1.29	2,580
+ Purchases	-				12,000	A	$1.28	15,360
- Ending inventory	(2,000)	H	$1.29	(2,580)	(3,500)	H	$1.27	(4,445)
= Cost of sales	€ (8,000)			$ (9,920)	€ (10,500)			$ (13,495)
Operating expenses	(2,000)	A	$1.25	(2,500)	(1,700)	A	$1.28	(2,176)
Depreciation expense	(500)	H	$1.20	(600)	(500)	H	$1.20	(600)
Translation exchange gain (loss)				150				(76)
Net income	€ 1,500			$ 2,130	€ 2,300			$ 2,853
Retained Earnings Statement								
Balance, January 1	€ -			$ -	€ 1,500			$ 2,130
Net income	1,500			2,130	2,300			2,853
Dividends	-			-	(1,000)	H	$1.27	(1,270)
Balance, December 31	€ 1,500			$ 2,130	€ 2,800			$ 3,713
Balance Sheet								
Assets								
Cash	€ 3,000	C	$1.30	$ 3,900	€ 3,000	C	$1.26	$ 3,780
Accounts Receivable	1,000	C	$1.30	1,300	1,500	C	$1.26	1,890
Inventory	2,000	H	$1.29	2,580	3,500	H	$1.27	4,445
Fixed Assets	11,000	H	$1.20	13,200	11,000	H	$1.20	13,200
Accumulated Depreciation	(500)	H	$1.20	(600)	(1,000)	H	$1.20	(1,200)
Total assets	€ 16,500			$ 20,380	€ 18,000			$ 22,115

For the Year Ended 12/31/20X9

(in thousands) Liabilities and Equity	Euros	Exchange Code	Rate	U.S. Dollars
Accounts payable	€ 2,500	C	$1.30	$ 3,250
Common stock	12,500	H	$1.20	15,000
Retained earnings	1,500			2,130
Total liabilities and equity	€ 16,500			$ 20,380

Code: A = Average rate, C = Current rate, H = Historical rate (Note that historical rates will vary for different items)

Analysis of Monetary Items:

Monetary Items (in Euros)

	Assets	Liabilities	Net
Monetary items, 1/1	€ 1,500	€ -	€ 1,500
Sales	12,000		12,000
Purchases		10,000	(10,000)
Operating expenses		2,000	(2,000)
Payment of liabilities	(9,500)	(9,500)	-
Dividend payment			-
Monetary items, 12/31	€ 4,000	€ 2,500	€ 1,500

Calculation of Translation Gain (Loss):

		Diff. between end rate & applicable rate	
Monetary assets at 1/1 (less any dividends)	€ 1,500	0.1 (1.30 - 1.20)	$ 150
Dividends (paid out of monetary assets)	-		-
Monetary liabilities at 1/1			
Sales	12,000	0.05 (1.30 - 1.25)	600
Purchases	(10,000)	0.05 (1.30 - 1.25)	(500)
Operating expenses	(2,000)	0.05 (1.30 - 1.25)	(100)
Translation Gain (Loss) from Remeasurement			$ 150

*Difference between rate at dividend declaration date and beginning rate

For the Year Ended 12/31/20Y0

(in thousands) Liabilities and Equity	Euros	Exchange Code	Rate	U.S. Dollars
Accounts payable	€ 2,700	C	$1.26	$ 3,402
Common stock	12,500	H	$1.20	15,000
Retained earnings	2,800			3,713
Total liabilities and equity	€ 18,000			$ 22,115

Analysis of Monetary Items:

Monetary Items (in Euros)

	Assets	Liabilities	Net
Monetary items, 1/1	€ 4,000	€ 2,500	€ 1,500
Sales	15,000		15,000
Purchases		12,000	(12,000)
Operating expenses		1,700	(1,700)
Payment of liabilities	(13,500)	(13,500)	-
Dividend payment	(1,000)		(1,000)
Monetary items, 12/31	€ 4,500	€ 2,700	€ 1,800

Calculation of Translation Gain (Loss):

		Diff. between end rate & applicable rate	
Monetary assets at 1/1 (less any dividends)	€ 3,000	-0.04 (1.26 - 1.30)	$ (120)
Dividends (paid out of monetary assets)	1,000	-0.03 (1.27 - 1.30)*	(30)
Monetary liabilities at 1/1	(2,500)	-0.04 (1.26 - 1.30)	100
Sales	15,000	-0.02 (1.26 - 1.28)	(300)
Purchases	(12,000)	-0.02 (1.26 - 1.28)	240
Operating expenses	(1,700)	-0.02 (1.26 - 1.28)	34
Translation Gain (Loss) from Remeasurement			$ (76)

> **OBSERVATION:** Total assets and total equity are both slightly higher under the Current Translation Method than under the Monetary/Nonmonetary Translation Method. This difference is the result of using historical exchange rates for inventory and fixed assets rather than the current rate. Thus, under certain circumstances, these two methods can produce significantly different reporting results.

REALIZATION OF SEPARATE COMPONENT OF STOCKHOLDERS' EQUITY

Upon part, complete, or substantially complete sale or upon complete liquidation of an investment in a foreign entity, a *pro rata* portion of the accumulated translation adjustments attributable to that foreign entity, which has been recorded as a separate component of stockholders' equity, is included in determining the gain or loss on the sale or other disposition of that foreign investment (FIN-37, par. 2). Thus, if an enterprise sells a 50% ownership interest in a foreign investment, 50% of the accumulated translation adjustments related to that foreign investment is included in determining the gain or loss on the sale of the interest.

> **OBSERVATION:** Any required provision for the permanent impairment of a foreign investment is determined before translation and consolidation (FAS-52, par. 118). Apparently, this means that the amounts accumulated in the separate component of stockholders' equity for a specific foreign investment are not included in determining whether the investment has become permanently impaired.

FOREIGN CURRENCY TRANSACTIONS

A foreign currency transaction is one that requires settlement in a currency other than the functional currency of the reporting entity. Generally, gains and losses on foreign currency transactions are recognized in current net income (FAS-52, par. 15). The following transactions, however, may require different treatment:

- Gain or loss resulting from a foreign currency transaction that is designated as an economic hedge of a net investment in a foreign entity
- Gain or loss resulting from intercompany foreign currency transactions of a capital nature or long-term financing nature, between an investor and investee where the investee entity is consolidated, combined, or accounted for by the equity method by the investor
- Forward exchange contracts

If the exchange rate changes between the time a purchase or sale is contracted for and the time actual payment is made, a foreign exchange gain or loss results.

Illustration of Foreign Currency Transaction

Alex Co. purchased goods for 100,000 pesos when the exchange rate was 10 pesos to a dollar. The journal entry in dollars is:

Purchases	10,000	
Accounts payable		10,000

Assuming that when the goods are paid for, the exchange rate is 12:1, the journal entry in dollars is:

Accounts payable	10,000	
Cash		8,333
Foreign exchange gain		1,667

At a 12:1 exchange rate, the $8,333 can purchase 100,000 pesos. The difference between the $8,333 and the original recorded liability of $10,000 is a foreign exchange gain. If payment is made when the exchange rate is less than 10 pesos to a dollar, a foreign exchange loss would result.

For example, if the exchange rate when the payment is made in only eight pesos to one dollar, a loss of $2,500 would result because $12,500 would be required to satisfy the payable of 100,000 pesos. In this case, the entry to record the payment would be:

Accounts payable	10,000	
Foreign exchange loss	2,500	
Cash		12,500

A foreign exchange gain or loss is computed at each balance sheet date on all recorded foreign transactions that have not been settled. The difference between the exchange rate that could have been used to settle the transaction at the date it occurred, and the exchange rate that can be used to settle the transaction at a subsequent balance sheet date, is the gain or loss recognized in current net income. Generally, the current exchange rate is the rate that is used to settle a transaction on the date it occurs, or on a subsequent balance sheet date (FAS-52, par. 16).

Deferred Foreign Currency Transactions

Certain gains and losses on forward exchange contracts and certain types of foreign currency transactions are not included in current net income but are either (*a*) reported in the separate component of stockholders' equity, along with translation adjustments, or (*b*) included in the overall gain or loss of the related foreign currency transaction. These deferred gains and losses may be classified as follows (FAS-52, par. 20):

- Gain or loss on a designated and effective economic hedge of a net investment in a foreign entity
- Gain or loss on certain long-term intercompany foreign currency transactions
- Gain or loss on a designated and effective economic hedge of a firm, identifiable, foreign currency commitment

The accounting required by FAS-52 commences with the designation date of the transaction (FAS-52, par. 21).

> **OBSERVATION:** As an example of a foreign currency transaction intended to be an economic hedge of a net investment in a foreign entity, take the case of a U.S. parent company with a net investment in a Greek subsidiary that borrows Greek currency in the amount of its net investment in the Greek subsidiary.
>
> The U.S. company designates the loan as an economic hedge of its net investment in the Greek subsidiary. In other words, the U.S. parent computes its net investment in the foreign currency of its foreign subsidiary and then borrows the same amount of foreign currency as the amount of its net investment. In this event, if the net investment in the foreign subsidiary declines because of a change in exchange rates, the change is made up in the foreign currency loan. The U.S. company can buy a larger amount of the subsidiary's foreign currency with fewer U.S. dollars. When the net investment in the foreign subsidiary and the loan in the foreign currency of the foreign subsidiary are both translated into U.S. dollars, the change in the net investment in the foreign subsidiary (an asset) should be approximately equal to the change in the foreign currency loan, except for taxes, if any. Thus, the foreign currency loan acts as a hedge against any increase or decrease in the net foreign investment that is attributable to a change in the exchange rate.
>
> FAS-52 requires that both translated amounts be recorded and reported in a separate component of stockholders' equity. If the translated amount of the foreign currency loan (after taxes, if any) exceeds the translated amount of the net investment in the foreign subsidiary that was hedged, however, the gain or loss that is allocable to the excess must be included in net income, and not recorded and reported as a separate component of stockholders' equity.

Gains or losses on intercompany foreign currency transactions of a capital or long-term nature are not included in current net income, but are reported in the separate component of stockholders' equity, along with translation adjustments. The entities involved in the intercompany foreign currency transactions reported in this manner must be consolidated, combined, or accounted for by the equity method. Gain or loss on intercompany foreign currency transactions that are not of a permanent nature are included in net income (FAS-52, par. 20).

Accounting for a gain or loss on a foreign currency transaction that is intended to hedge an identifiable foreign currency commitment is addressed by FAS-133 (Accounting for Derivative Instruments and Hedging Activities). An example is an agreement to purchase or sell equipment.

Deferred Taxes

FAS-52 requires that deferred taxes be recognized on taxable foreign currency transactions and taxable translation adjustments of foreign currency financial statements, regardless of whether the exchange gain or loss is charged to current net income or recorded and reported as a separate component of stockholders' equity. Thus, all taxable foreign exchange gains or losses that do not appear in the same period in taxable income and either (*a*) financial accounting income or (*b*) the separate component of stockholders' equity are temporary differences, for which deferred taxes must be provided (FAS-52, par. 22). The amount of the deferred taxes should be determined in accordance with existing GAAP (FAS-52, par. 23).

> **OBSERVATION:** Historically, there has been a presumption in GAAP that all undistributed earnings of a subsidiary (domestic or foreign) would eventually be transferred to the parent company. Hence, GAAP have always considered undistributed income from foreign and domestic subsidiaries to be a temporary difference, requiring a provision for deferred income taxes. FAS-109 (Accounting for Income Taxes) does not require deferred taxes to be provided for the excess of the book basis over the tax basis of an investment in a foreign subsidiary, if the excess is considered to be relatively permanent. An important reason that such an excess might exist is undistributed income from foreign subsidiaries. Paragraph 31 of FAS-109 states:
>
>> A deferred tax liability is not recognized for the following types of temporary differences, unless it is apparent that those temporary differences will reverse in the foreseeable future:
>>
>>> a. An excess of the amount for financial reporting over the tax basis of an investment in a foreign subsidiary or

> a foreign corporate joint venture as defined in APB-18 (The Equity Method of Accounting for Investments in Common Stock) that is essentially permanent in duration.
>
> In the basis for conclusions of FAS-109, the FASB states that the hypothetical nature of the tax allocation calculations for undistributed income from foreign subsidiaries "introduces significant implementation issues." Thus, tax allocation is not required for undistributed income of foreign subsidiaries that is essentially permanent in nature or for any other difference between the book basis and tax basis of investments of permanent nature.

Intraperiod income tax allocation is also required in the preparation of financial statements. The total income tax expense for a period should be allocated properly to (*a*) income before extraordinary items, (*b*) extraordinary items, (*c*) adjustments of prior periods, and (*d*) direct entries to other stockholders' equity accounts. Therefore, the portion of income tax expense for a period that is attributable to items in the separate component of stockholders' equity is allocated to the separate component of stockholders' equity, and does not appear as an increase or decrease of income tax expense for the period. In other words, deferred taxes related to items in the separate component of stockholders' equity account are charged or credited to the separate component of stockholders' equity account (FAS-52, par. 24). The illustration at the end of the chapter demonstrates this concept.

> **OBSERVATION:** All aspects of income tax allocation are complicated, and these provisions of FAS-52 require careful application to the specific facts of each situation. In particular, intercompany transactions of a long-term nature and the discontinuation of a foreign operation may present peculiar problems.

Elimination of Intercompany Profits

The exchange rate to be used to eliminate intercompany profits is the rate that existed on the date of the intercompany transaction. The use of approximations and/or averages is permitted as long as they are reasonable (FAS-52, par. 25).

> **OBSERVATION:** Intercompany profits occur on the date of sale or transfer. Thus, the exchange rate on the date of sale or transfer is used to determine the amount of intercompany profit to be eliminated.

EXCHANGE RATES

The balance sheet date of the foreign entity that is consolidated, combined, or accounted for by the equity method is used for translation purposes, if different from the balance sheet date of the reporting entity. Thus, the current exchange rate for the translation of foreign currency financial statements is the rate in effect on the balance sheet date of the foreign entity that is being translated (FAS-52, par. 28). If a current exchange rate is not available at the foreign entity's balance sheet date, the first exchange rate available after the balance sheet date is used. The current rate used for the above translations is the rate applicable to currency conversion for the purpose of dividend remittances (FAS-52, par. 27).

Conditions may exist when it will be prudent to exclude a foreign entity from financial statements that are consolidated, combined, or accounted for by the equity method. Disruption of a foreign operation caused by internal strife or severe exchange restrictions may make it impossible to compute meaningful exchange rates. Under these circumstances, it is best to include earnings of a foreign operation only to the extent that cash has been received in unrestricted funds. Adequate disclosure should be made of any foreign subsidiary or investment that is excluded from the financial statements of the parent or investor. This may be accomplished by separate supplemental statements or a summary describing the important facts and information.

Financial Statement Disclosure

The aggregate transaction gain or loss that is included in determining net income for the period, including gain or loss on forward exchange contracts, shall be disclosed in the financial statements or notes thereto (FAS-52, par. 30).

> **OBSERVATION:** Transaction gains or losses on derivative instruments must comply with the disclosure requirements of FAS-133 (Accounting for Derivative Instruments and Hedging Activities).

An analysis of the changes in the separate component of stockholders' equity account for cumulative translation adjustments for the period shall be disclosed in either (*a*) a separate financial statement or (*b*) notes to the financial statements, or (*c*) be included as part of a stockholders' equity or a similar statement. The following is the minimum information that must be disclosed in the analysis (FAS-52, par. 31):

- Beginning and ending cumulative balances
- The aggregate increase or decrease for the period from translation adjustments and gains and losses from (*a*) hedges of a net investment in a foreign entity and (*b*) long-term intercompany transactions (FAS-133 specifies additional disclosures for instruments designated as hedges of the foreign currency exposure of a net investment in a foreign operation.)
- The amount of income taxes for the period allocated to translation adjustments
- The amount of translation adjustment transferred to net income during the period as a result of a sale or complete or substantially complete liquidation of a foreign investment

Disclosure of exchange rate changes and related effects on foreign currency transactions that occur subsequent to the balance sheet date should be disclosed, if the effects are material. No adjustment should be made to the financial statements for exchange rate changes that occur subsequent to the balance sheet date (FAS-52, par. 32).

Illustration of How an Enterprise Determines the Beginning Balance of the Separate Component of Stockholders' Equity

	Beginning of the Year			Beginning of the Year		
	Functional currency	FAS-52 exchange rates	U.S. dollars	Functional currency	Current exchange rates	U.S. dollars
Current Assets						
Cash	F 1,000	C*1.25	$ 800	F 1,000	C 1.25	$ 800
Accounts receivable	4,000	C 1.25	3,200	4,000	C 1.25	3,200
Inventory	10,000	H†2.00	5,000	10,000	C 1.25	8,000
Total	F15,000		$ 9,000	F15,000		$12,000
Property, plant, & equipment	F75,000	H 1.50	$50,000	F75,000	C 1.25	$60,000
Total assets	F90,000		$59,000	F90,000		$72,000
Current Liabilities	F20,000	C 1.25	$16,000	F20,000	C 1.25	$16,000
Deferred income taxes	5,000	H 2.00	2,500	5,000	C 1.25	4,000
Long-term obligations	20,000	C 1.25	16,000	20,000	C 1.25	16,000
Total liabilities	F45,000		$34,500	F45,000		$36,000
Net assets (equals stockholders' equity)	F45,000		$24,500	F45,000		$36,000

Computation of the Beginning Balance of the Separate Component of Stockholders' Equity

Net assets at beginning of the year at current exchange rate	$36,000
Net assets at beginning of the year at FAS-52 rates	($24,500)
Beginning balance of separate component of stockholders' equity	$11,500

*C = Current exchange rate. †H = Historical exchange rate.

RELATED CHAPTERS IN 2009 *GAAP GUIDE LEVEL A*

Chapter 7, "Consolidated Financial Statements"
Chapter 14, "Equity Method"
Chapter 21, "Income Taxes"

RELATED CHAPTERS IN 2009 *GAAP GUIDE LEVELS B, C, AND D*

Chapter 10, "Consolidated Financial Statements"
Chapter 14, "Equity Method"
Chapter 18, "Foreign Operations and Exchange"
Chapter 20, "Income Taxes"

RELATED CHAPTER IN 2009 *INTERNATIONAL ACCOUNTING/FINANCIAL REPORTING STANDARDS GUIDE*

Chapter 17, "Foreign Currency Translation"

CHAPTER 19
GOVERNMENT CONTRACTS

CONTENTS

OVERVIEW

Government contracts often include certain unique features, such as being based on the costs incurred by the contractor (i.e., cost-plus-fixed-fee) and being subject to renegotiation and termination.

GAAP for government contracts are found in the following pronouncements:

ARB-43	Chapter 11, Government Contracts
	A. Cost-Plus-Fixed-Fee Contracts
	B. Renegotiation
	C. Terminated War and Defense Contracts
FAS-131	Disclosures about Segments of an Enterprise and Related Information

BACKGROUND

Government contracts are usually performed under a cost-plus-fixed-fee arrangement, which provides for possible renegotiation if the contracting officer for the government believes that excess profits were made by the contractor. These contracts may also provide that the government may terminate the contract at its convenience.

COST-PLUS-FIXED-FEE CONTRACTS

Cost-plus-fixed-fee (CPFF) contracts generally require the government to pay a fixed fee in addition to all costs involved in fulfilling the contract. The contract may include the manufacture of a product or only the performance of services, and the government may or may not withhold a specified percentage of the interim payments until completion of the entire contract. Furthermore, CPFF contracts usually are cancellable by the government. When such contracts are terminated, the contractor is entitled to reimbursement for all costs, plus an equitable portion of the fixed fee (ARB-43, Ch. 11C, par. 13).

One of the main problems in accounting for CPFF contracts is determining when profits should be recognized. As a general rule, profits are not recognized until the right to full payment becomes unconditional, which is usually when the product has been delivered and accepted or the services have been fully rendered (completed-contract method).

When CPFF contracts extend over several years, however, the percentage-of-completion method is acceptable, provided that costs and profits can be reasonably estimated and realization of the contract is reasonably assured (ARB-43, Ch. 11A, par. 13).

Illustration of Percentage-of-Completion on CPFF Contract

A company enters into a contract with the government that calls for a 20% profit on costs. The percentage-of-completion method is appropriate because costs and profits can be reasonably estimated.

Accumulated costs through the end of the third year of the contract totaled $1,200,000. Profits recognized in the first and second years of the contract were $100,000 and $75,000, respectively.

Profit recognized in the third year of the contract is computed as follows:

Accumulated costs to date	$1,200,000
CPFF percentage	20%
Estimated profit to date	$ 240,000
Profits recognized in previous years ($100,000 + $75,000)	(175,000)
Profit recognized in third year	$ 65,000

☞ **PRACTICE POINTER:**   When CPFF contracts involve the manufacture and delivery of products, the reimbursable costs and
fees ordinarily are included in appropriate sales or other revenue accounts. When CPFF contracts involve only services, only
the fees ordinarily should be included in revenues.

An advance payment by the government may not be offset as a
payment on account, unless it is expected to be applied as such with
reasonable certainty. In the event that an advance is offset, it must be
disclosed clearly (ARB-43, Ch. 11A, par. 5).

A distinction should be made in the balance sheet between un-
billed costs and fees and billed amounts (ARB-43, Ch. 11A, par. 4).

RENEGOTIATION

Renegotiation involves the adjustment of the original selling price or
contract. Since the government makes renegotiation adjustments an
integral part of a contract, a provision for such probable adjustments
is necessary. A provision for renegotiation is based on the contractor's
past experience or on the general experience of the particular
industry, and it is shown in the income statement as a reduction of
the related sales or income. If a reasonable estimate cannot be made,
that fact should be disclosed in the financial statements or accompanying notes. The provision for renegotiation is reported as a liability
in the balance sheet (ARB-43, Ch. 11B, par. 4). Classification as a
current liability is appropriate if the criteria established in ARB-43,
Chapter 3A (Current Assets and Current Liabilities) are met.

☞ **PRACTICE POINTER:**   In those unusual cases in which collection is not reasonably assured, it may be preferable to employ
the installment-sale or cost-recovery method in accounting for a
government contract.

When a provision for renegotiation is made in a particular
year and the subsequent final adjustment differs materially,
show the difference in the income statement of the year of
final determination.

Disclosure

When a significant portion of a company's business is derived from
government contracts, such disclosure should be made in the financial statements or notes thereto, indicating the uncertainties involved
and the possibility of renegotiation in excess of the amount provided.
In addition, the basis of determining the provision for renegotiation should be disclosed (prior experience, industry experience,

etc.) (ARB-43, Ch. 11B, par. 5). Disclosure is required if 10% or more of an enterprise's revenue is derived from sales to the federal government, a state government, a local government, or a foreign government (FAS-131, par. 39).

TERMINATED WAR AND DEFENSE CONTRACTS

ARB-43, Chapter 11C (Terminated War and Defense Contracts), deals with both fixed-price and CPFF contracts. It addresses the problems involved in the termination of a government contract by the government; it does not cover terminations resulting from default of the contractor (ARB-43, Ch. 11C, par. 1).

The determination of profit or loss on a terminated government contract is made as of the effective date of termination. This is the date that the contractor accrues the right to receive payment on that portion of the contract that has been terminated (ARB-43, Ch. 11C, par. 3).

Although most government contracts provide for a minimum profit percentage formula in the event agreement cannot be reached, the amount of profit to be reported in the case of termination for the convenience of the government is the difference between all allowable costs incurred and the amount of the termination claim (ARB-43, Ch. 11C, pars. 16–17).

If a reasonable estimate of the termination claim for reporting purposes cannot be made, full disclosure of this fact should be made by note to the financial statements, which should describe the uncertainties involved (ARB-43, Ch. 11C, par. 4).

Termination claims are classified as current assets if the criteria in ARB-43, Chapter 3A are met. Prior to the termination notice, advances received are deducted from termination claims receivable for reporting purposes. Loans received on the security of the contract or termination claim are shown separately as current liabilities (ARB-43, Ch. 11C, par. 6).

The cost of items included in the termination claim that are subsequently reacquired by the contractor is recorded as a new purchase, and the amount is applied as a reduction of the termination claim. These types of reductions from the termination claim generally are referred to as *disposal credits* (ARB-43, Ch. 11C, par. 8).

Disclosure

Material amounts of termination claims are classified separately from other receivables in the financial statements (ARB-43, Ch. 11C, par. 5).

Termination claims are stated at the amount estimated as collectible, and adequate provision or disclosure should be made for items of a controversial nature (ARB-43, Ch. 11C, par. 19).

RELATED CHAPTERS IN 2009 *GAAP GUIDE*
LEVEL A

Chapter 3, "Balance Sheet Classification and Related Display Issues"
Chapter 42, "Segment Reporting"

RELATED CHAPTERS IN 2009 *GAAP GUIDE*
LEVELS B, C, AND D

Chapter 4, "Balance Sheet Classification and Related Display Issues"
Chapter 37, "Segment Reporting"

RELATED CHAPTERS IN 2009 *INTERNATIONAL ACCOUNTING/FINANCIAL REPORTING STANDARDS GUIDE*

Chapter 3, "Presentation of Financial Statements"
Chapter 18, "Government Grants and Government Assistance"
Chapter 31, "Segment Reporting"

CHAPTER 20
IMPAIRMENT OF LONG-LIVED ASSETS

CONTENTS

OVERVIEW

Impairment of a long-lived asset exists when the asset's fair value is less than its carrying amount, which is defined as cost less accumulated depreciation and is often referred to as book value. Recognition of an impairment loss is required in this circumstance, because the carrying amount will not be recovered in the future. This general principle underlies accounting for impairment losses of all long-lived assets, but it is applied differently for those assets that are expected to be held and used and for assets to be disposed of by sale or otherwise.

GAAP for recognizing impairment losses of long-lived assets and the disposal of long-lived assets are found in the following authoritative pronouncement.

FAS-144   Accounting for the Impairment or Disposal of Long-Lived Assets

BACKGROUND

Long-lived assets, such as plant and equipment and intangibles, as well as other similar assets, are initially recorded at cost, which is usually the fair value of the asset at its date of acquisition. For most assets, cost is subsequently reduced by depreciation or amortization as the asset's cost is gradually transferred to the income statement in a manner that allocates the cost as an expense over the useful life of the asset. This process is commonly referred to as "matching," and is an important element in the determination of periodic net income. This process focuses primarily on the determination of income rather than the valuation of the asset. In fact, the resulting carrying amount or book value of the asset, which is included in the balance sheet, is not intended to represent the current or fair value of the asset, but is best thought of as that portion of the historical cost of the asset that is awaiting allocation to income in future periods.

Historically, the practice of systematically allocating the cost of a long-lived asset to expense as a part of determining net income was modified in some circumstances in which the value of the asset was believed to be impaired, and was generally defined as its future value being less than its carrying amount. A loss was recognized for the amount of this excess, although this practice was not consistently followed; nor were standards for measuring the amount of the impairment loss well established prior to the issuance of FAS-121 (Accounting for the Impairment of Long-Lived Assets and for Long-Lived Assets to Be Disposed Of). This GAAP standard was developed for when an impairment loss should be recognized, and specified measurement and presentation principles for the recognition of impairment losses for assets in two categories: (1) to be held and used and (2) to be disposed of.

FAS-144 (Accounting for the Impairment or Disposal of Long-Lived Assets) was issued later to replace FAS-121 in order to standardize practices regarding assets to be sold or otherwise disposed of. Under FAS-121 and APB-30 (Reporting the Results of Operations— Reporting the Effects of Disposal of a Segment of a Business, and Extraordinary, Unusual and Infrequently Occurring Events and Transactions), an inconsistency existed between the accounting for impaired assets and for assets to be disposed of. The primary difference between FAS-121 and FAS-144 is the elimination of this inconsistency. Thus, FAS-144 replaces FAS-121 and amends APB-30. FAS-144 essentially carries forward the standards of FAS-121 with regard to assets to be held and used and extends the APB-30 standards for disposal of a segment of a business to any component of an entity that has been disposed of or is classified as held for sale (FAS-144, par. 2).

FAS-144 applies to long-lived assets (i.e., plant or fixed assets), to intangible assets being amortized, and to long-lived assets to be disposed of. FAS-144's scope includes capital leases of lessees, long-lived assets of lessors under operating leases, proved oil and gas properties accounted for under the successful efforts method, and long-term prepaid assets (FAS-144, par. 3). FAS-144 applies to all entities. It does *not* apply to the following types of assets (FAS-144, par. 5):

- Goodwill
- Intangible assets not being amortized that are to be held and used
- Financial instruments, including cost- or equity-method investments
- Deferred policy acquisition costs
- Deferred tax assets
- Unproved oil and gas properties under the successful efforts method

Certain FASB Standards establish separate standards of accounting for specific long-lived assets in specialized situations. FAS-144 does not change those standards. Specifically, assets whose accounting is prescribed in the following pronouncements are *not* changed by FAS-144 (FAS-144, par. 5):

- FAS-50 (Financial Reporting in the Record and Music Industry)
- FAS-63 (Financial Reporting by Broadcasters)
- FAS-86 (Accounting for the Costs of Computer Software to Be Sold, Leased, or Otherwise Marketed)
- FAS-90 (Regulated Enterprises—Accounting for Abandonments and Disallowances of Plant Costs)

LONG-LIVED ASSETS TO BE HELD AND USED

Impairment is defined in FAS-144 as the condition that exists when the carrying amount of a long-lived asset exceeds its fair value. An impairment loss is recognized only if the carrying amount of a long-lived asset is not recoverable and exceeds its fair value. This circumstance exits if the carrying amount of the asset in question exceeds the sum of the undiscounted cash flows expected to result from the use and eventual disposition of the asset. The impairment loss is measured as the amount by which the carrying amount of a long-lived asset exceeds its fair value (FAS-144, par. 7).

Testing Assets for Recoverability

A long-lived asset must be tested for recoverability when events or changes in circumstances indicate that the carrying amount of the asset may not be recoverable. Examples of such events or changes in circumstances are (FAS-144, par. 8):

- A significant decrease in the market price of a long-lived asset.
- A significant adverse change in the extent or manner in which a long-lived asset is used, or in its physical condition.
- A significant adverse change in legal factors or in the business climate that could affect the value of a long-lived asset.
- An accumulation of costs significantly in excess of the amount originally expected for the acquisition or construction of a long-lived asset.
- A current period operating or cash flow loss, combined with a history of operating or cash flow losses or a projection or forecast that demonstrates continuing losses associated with the use of a long-lived asset.
- A current expectation that it is more likely than not that a long-lived asset will be sold or otherwise disposed of significantly before the end of its previously estimated useful life.

Testing a long-lived asset for recoverability may require a review of depreciation estimates and method as required by FAS-154 (Accounting Changes and Error Corrections) or the amortization period required by FAS-142 (Goodwill and Other Intangible Assets). Any revision in the remaining useful life of a long-lived asset resulting from that review shall be considered in developing the estimates of future cash flows that are used to test the asset for recoverability (FAS-144, par. 9).

> ☞ **PRACTICE POINTER:** The approach identified in FAS-144 requires the investigation of potential impairments on an **exception basis.** The requirement to compare undiscounted future cash flows with the carrying amount of the asset represents a "trigger mechanism" to assist in identifying those assets that require further analysis. In explaining its conclusions, the FASB states that an asset must be tested for recoverability only if there is reason to believe that the asset is impaired.

Grouping Assets

For purposes of recognizing and measuring an impairment loss, a long-lived asset shall be grouped with other assets and liabilities at the lowest level for which identifiable cash flows are largely independent of the cash flows of other assets and liabilities. In limited circumstances, a long-lived asset may not have identifiable cash flows that are largely independent on the cash flows of other assets and liabilities. In this situation, the asset group for the long-lived asset that is being evaluated for an impairment loss includes all assets and liabilities of the entity. An example of this circumstance is a corporate headquarters facility (FAS-144, pars. 10–11).

When fair value is estimated on the basis of the present value of expected future cash flows, assets should be grouped at the lowest level for which there are identifiable cash flows that are largely independent of the cash flows of other groups of assets. For example, assume a company has four long-lived assets identified as A, B, C, and D. Evidence suggests that the value of Asset A is impaired. If the cash flows of the four assets can be separately identified, those associated with Asset A alone are used to measure the fair value of that asset. On the other hand, if the cash flows of Assets A and B are intermingled such that separate identification of cash flows of each asset is impossible, the joint cash flows of these two assets must be considered in measuring the fair value of Assets A and B combined, even though evidence does not suggest that the value of Asset B is impaired.

☞ **PRACTICE POINTER:** As the level of aggregation of assets in applying FAS-144 goes up, the likelihood that a loss will be recognized goes down. This is because when assets are aggregated, the impairment loss that may exist within one asset is offset by the excess of fair value over carrying amount for the other assets that are part of the aggregation. For example, if impairment appears to exist for Asset A, and if Asset A can be valued independently, a loss is recognized. On the other hand, if the fair value of Asset A cannot be determined independently of Assets B and C, the excess of fair value over carrying amount of these two assets must be overcome by the impairment loss of Asset A before a loss is recognized. When assets are aggregated in applying FAS-144, it is reasonable to conclude that some— perhaps many—impairment losses are never recognized, because they are offset against the fair value in excess of carrying amount of other assets.

Goodwill is included in an asset group to be tested for impairment under FAS-144 only if the asset group is or includes a reporting unit. A reporting unit is defined in FAS-142 as one level below an operating segment. FAS-142 requires goodwill to be tested for impairment at the reporting unit level. Goodwill shall not be included in a lower-level asset group that includes only part of a reporting unit. Estimates of future cash flows used to test that lower-level asset group for recoverability shall not be adjusted for the effect of excluding goodwill from the group (FAS-144, par. 12).

Other than goodwill, the carrying amounts of any assets and liabilities not covered by FAS-144 that are included in an asset group shall be adjusted in accordance with other applicable generally accepted accounting principles prior to testing the asset group for recoverability (FAS-144, par. 13).

An impairment loss for an asset group reduces only the carrying amounts of long-lived asset or assets of the group. The loss is allocated to the long-lived assets of the group on a pro rata basis using the relative carrying amounts of the assets, except that the loss allocated to an individual long-lived asset of the group shall not reduce the carrying amount of that asset below its fair value whenever that fair value is determinable without undue cost and effort (FAS-144, par. 14).

New Cost Basis

When an impairment loss is recognized, the adjusted carrying amount of the long-lived asset becomes its new cost basis. This basis is used to depreciate the asset over its remaining useful life. Restoration of previously recognized impairment losses is prohibited, even though circumstances subsequent to the loss recognition indicate that the earlier carrying amount of the asset is recoverable (FAS-144, par. 15).

Estimating Future Cash Flows

Estimates of future cash flows used to test the recoverability of a long-lived asset shall include only the future cash flows that are directly associated with, and that are expected to arise, as a direct result of using and eventually disposing of the asset. Estimates of future cash flows used to test recoverability shall incorporate the entity's own assumptions about its use of the asset and shall consider all available evidence (FAS-144, pars. 16–17).

Estimates of future cash flows used to test recoverability shall be made for the remaining useful life of the asset to the entity. The remaining useful life, where recoverability is evaluated at an asset group level, is based on the remaining useful life of the primary asset in the group. The primary asset is the asset group's most significant cash-flow-generating tangible asset being depreciated or intangible asset being amortized. These estimates are based on the existing service potential of the asset to the entity. Estimates of future cash flows used to test the recoverability of a long-lived asset that is in use, including a long-lived asset for which development is substantially complete, are based on the existing service potential of the asset at the date it is tested. This encompasses its remaining useful life, cash flow generating capacity and, for tangible assets, physical output capacity. Those estimates include cash flows associated with future expenditures necessary to maintain the existing service potential of a long-lived asset, including those that replace the service potential of a component part of a long-lived asset. Those estimates exclude cash flows associated with future capital expenditures that would increase the potential of a long-lived asset (FAS-144, pars. 18–19).

Estimates of future cash flows used to test the recoverability of a long-lived asset that is under development shall be based on the expected service potential of the asset when it is substantially complete, including cash flows associated with all future expenditures necessary to develop a long-lived asset and including interest payments that will be capitalized as part of the cost of the asset (FAS-144, par. 20).

Fair Value

Fair value is best estimated using an expected present value technique. This is especially true when the long-lived assets have uncertainties as to both timing and amount (FAS-157, par. E24b).

Illustration of Recognizing an Impairment Loss on Assets to Be Held and Used

Zeta Company has machinery for which circumstances indicate a potential impairment in value. The machinery cost $100,000 and has accumulated depreciation of $35,000, resulting in a carrying amount of $65,000. The first step is to determine how the undiscounted future cash flows compare with $65,000. Assuming that those cash flows are estimated to be $50,000, an impairment loss is evident. The next step is to determine the fair value of the asset by the appropriate method (i.e., quoted market price, estimate based on similar assets, estimate based on an appropriate valuation technique). If the fair value is determined to be $40,000, the result is an impairment loss of $25,000, computed as follows:

Asset cost	$100,000
Less: Accumulated depreciation	35,000
Carrying amount	$ 65,000
Less: Fair value	40,000
Impairment loss	$ 25,000

An impairment loss of $25,000 is recognized, and $40,000 is now considered the cost of the asset for future accounting and depreciation purposes.

Notice that the undiscounted future cash flow of $50,000 is used only to identify the need to measure the amount of the impairment loss. That amount is not used directly to determine the amount of the loss, although it may be useful if the fair value is determined by estimating the present value of future cash flows.

LONG-LIVED ASSETS TO BE DISPOSED OF

In addition to covering assets to be held and used, FAS-144 also specifies accounting standards for assets to be disposed of. Assets to be disposed of other than by sale (e.g., by abandonment or in an exchange for a similar productive asset) shall continue to be classified as held and used until disposition. An asset to be abandoned is considered disposed of when it ceases to be used. If an entity commits to a plan to abandon a long-lived asset before the end of its estimated useful life, depreciation estimates shall be revised in accordance with FAS-154 to reflect the use of the asset over a shorter useful life than originally expected. A temporarily idle asset is not considered abandoned. An asset to be exchanged for a similar productive asset is considered disposed of when it is exchanged. Similarly, an asset that is to be distributed to owners in a spin-off is considered to have been disposed of when it is distributed (FAS-144, pars. 27–29).

Disposal by Sale

A long-lived asset to be sold is classified as held for sale in the period in which all of the following criteria are met (FAS-144, par. 30):

- Management commits to a plan to sell the asset or asset group.
- The asset (asset group) is available for immediate sale in its present condition.
- An active program to locate a buyer has been initiated.
- The sale of the asset (asset group) is probable, and transfer of the asset (asset group) is expected to qualify for recognition as a completed sale within one year. FAS-144 provides certain exceptions to this one-year requirement (par. 31).
- The asset (asset group) is being actively marketed for sale at a price that is reasonable in relation to its fair value.
- Actions required to complete the plan indicate that it is unlikely that significant changes in the plan will be made or that the plan will be withdrawn.

A long-lived asset (asset group) that is newly acquired and that will be held for sale rather than for use should be classified as held for sale as of the acquisition date only if the sale is expected within one year and the other requirements stated in the previous paragraph that are not met are probable of being met within a short period from the acquisition date (FAS-144, par. 32).

> ☛ **PRACTICE POINTER:** FAS-144 indicates that in applying this requirement, the term "short period" should be interpreted as within three months.

If the criteria for considering an asset as held for sale are met after the financial statement date, but before the financial statements are issued, that asset shall be treated as held and used in the financial statements. Information concerning the intent to sell the asset is required to be presented in notes to the financial statements (FAS-144, par. 33).

A long-lived asset (asset group) classified as held for sale shall be measured at the lower of its carrying amount or fair value less cost to sell. If the asset (asset group) is newly acquired, the carrying amount of the asset (asset group) shall be based on its fair value less cost to sell at the acquisition date. A long-lived asset shall not be depreciated once it is classified as held for sale (FAS-144, par. 34).

Costs to sell are the incremental direct costs to transact a sale. These are the costs that result directly from and are essential to a sale transaction and that would not have been incurred if the decision to sell had not been made. These costs include:

- Broker commissions
- Legal and title transfer fees
- Closing costs that must be incurred before legal title can be transferred

Figure 20-1: Impairment of Assets Held and Used

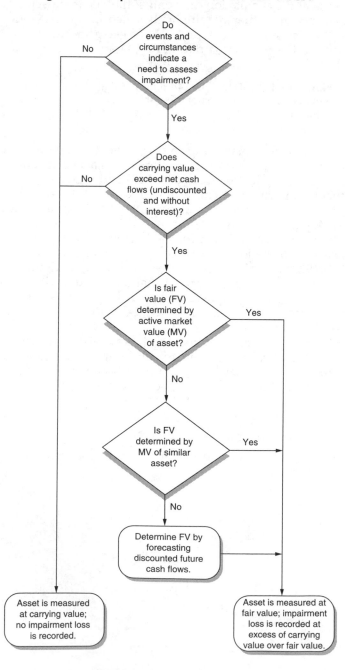

These costs exclude expected future losses associated with the operations of the asset (asset group) while it is classified as held for sale (FAS-144, par. 35).

A loss shall be recognized for any initial or subsequent write-down to fair value less cost to sell. A gain shall be recognized for any subsequent increase in fair value less cost to sell, but not in excess of the cumulative loss previously recognized. The loss or gain shall adjust only the carrying amount of a long-lived asset, whether classified as held for sale individually, or as part of a disposal group (FAS-144, par. 37).

Illustration of Impairment of Asset to Be Disposed Of

Wampler, Inc. has a piece of specialized machinery that is no longer efficiently usable for its operations as a result of technological advances that require replacement. The machine cost Wampler $500,000 and has an accumulated depreciation (based on double-declining balance) of $275,000. The specialized market for this asset is limited, and some potential buyers are expected to require the updated machinery that Wampler desires. For that reason, estimates of the selling price and the cost to sell, including solicitation and execution of a sales agreement, are $185,000 and $25,000, respectively. Wampler should record an impairment loss in the current period, as follows:

Asset cost		$500,000
Accumulated depreciation		(275,000)
Asset carrying amount		$225,000
Less: Estimated selling price	$185,000	
Cost to sell	(25,000)	(160,000)
Impairment loss		$ 65,000

Changes in a Plan to Sell

Circumstances may arise that cause an entity to decide not to sell a long-lived asset (asset group) that was previously classified as held for sale. In this instance the asset (asset group) should be reclassified as to be held and used. An asset (asset group) that is so reclassified should be measured individually at the lower of (1) its carrying amount before the asset (asset group) was classified as held for sale, adjusted for any depreciation or amortization expense that would have been recognized had the asset (asset group) been continuously classified as held and used, or (2) the fair value at the date of the decision not to sell the asset (FAS-144, par. 38). Any adjustment required by this process is included as an element of income from continuing operations in the period of the decision to not sell the asset (FAS-144, par. 39).

FAS-144 REPORTING REQUIREMENTS

Assets Held and Used

An impairment loss on long-lived assets to be held and used shall be included in income from continuing operations before income taxes in the income statement of a business enterprise and in income from continuing operations in the statement of activities of a not-for-profit organization (FAS-144, par. 25).

The following information shall be disclosed in the period in which an impairment loss on an asset to be held and used is recognized (FAS-144, par. 26):

- Description of the impaired long-lived asset and the facts and circumstances leading to the impairment.
- The amount of the impairment loss and the caption of the income statement or statement of activities that includes the loss.
- The method(s) of determining fair value.
- If applicable, the segment in which the impaired long-lived asset is reported under FAS-131 (Disclosures about Segments of an Enterprise and Related Information).

Assets to Be Disposed Of

The results of operations of a component of an entity that has either been disposed of or is classified as held for sale shall be reported in discontinued operations if both of the following conditions are met: (1) The operations and cash flows of the component have been eliminated from the ongoing operations of the entity as a result of the disposal transaction and (2) the entity will have no significant continuing involvement in the operations of the component after the disposal transaction. Discontinued Operations is presented in the income statement following the caption, Income from Continuing Operations (FAS-144, par. 42).

Illustration of Presentation of Discontinued Operations

Note: This illustration uses assumed numbers (in thousands of dollars) for purposes of illustrating how discontinued operations is presented in the income statement.

Income from continuing operations before income taxes	10,000	
Income taxes	3,500	
Income from continuing operations		6,500
Discontinued operations (Note X)		
Loss from operations of discontinued component ABC, including loss on disposal	3,000	
Income tax benefit*	1,050	
Loss on discontinued operations		1,950
Net income		4,550

*Separate disclosure of a gain or loss on disposal is required, either on the face of the income statement or in a related note (FAS-144, par. 43).

Adjustments to amounts previously reported in discontinued operations that are directly related to the disposal of a component of an entity in a period are classified in the current period as discontinued operations. The nature and amount of such adjustment shall be disclosed (FAS-144, par. 44).

A gain or loss recognized on the sale of a long-lived asset that is not a component of an entity shall be included in income from continuing operations before income taxes in the income statement of a business enterprise and in income from continuing operations of a not-for-profit organization (FAS-144, par. 45).

The following information is required in notes to the financial statements when a long-lived asset has been sold or is classified as held for sale (FAS-144, par. 47):

- Description of the facts and circumstances leading to the expected disposal, the expected manner and timing of that disposal, and the carrying amount(s) of the major classes of assets and liabilities included as part of the disposal group.
- The gain or loss recognized on the initial, or subsequent, write-down to fair value and, if not separately presented on the face of the income statement, the location in the income statement of the gain or loss.
- If applicable, the amounts of revenue and pretax profit or loss reported in discontinued operations.
- If applicable, the segment in which the long-lived asset is reported under FAS-131 (Disclosures about Segments of an Enterprise and Related Information).

RELATED CHAPTERS IN 2009 *GAAP GUIDE* LEVEL A

Chapter 1, "Accounting Changes"
Chapter 11, "Depreciable Assets and Depreciation"
Chapter 16, "Fair Value"
Chapter 23, "Intangible Assets"
Chapter 40, "Results of Operations"

RELATED CHAPTERS IN 2009 *GAAP GUIDE* LEVELS B, C, AND D

Chapter 1, "Accounting Changes"
Chapter 7, "Capitalization and Expense Recognition Concepts"
Chapter 19, "Impairment of Long-Lived Assets"
Chapter 21, "Intangible Assets"
Chapter 35, "Results of Operations"

RELATED CHAPTERS IN 2009 *INTERNATIONAL ACCOUNTING/FINANCIAL REPORTING STANDARDS GUIDE*

Chapter 5, "Accounting Policies, Changes in Accounting
            Estimates, and Errors"
Chapter 16, "Financial Instruments"
Chapter 19, "Impairment of Assets"
Chapter 21, "Intangible Assets"
Chapter 26, "Non-Current Assets Held for Sale and Discontinued
            Operations"
Chapter 27, "Property, Plant, and Equipment"

CHAPTER 21
INCOME TAXES

CONTENTS

OVERVIEW

The tax consequences of many transactions recognized in the financial statements are included in determining income taxes currently payable in the same accounting period. Sometimes, however, tax laws differ from the recognition and measurement requirements of financial reporting standards. Differences arise between the tax bases of assets or liabilities and their reported amounts in the financial statements. These differences are called *temporary differences* and they give rise to deferred tax assets and liabilities.

Temporary differences ordinarily reverse when the related asset is recovered or the related liability is settled. A *deferred tax liability* or *deferred tax asset* represents the increase or decrease in taxes payable or refundable in future years as a result of temporary differences and carryforwards at the end of the current year.

The objectives of accounting for income taxes are to recognize:

- The amount of taxes payable or refundable for the current year.

- The deferred tax liabilities and assets that result from future tax consequences of events that have been recognized in the enterprise's financial statements or tax returns.

GAAP for accounting for income taxes are in the following pronouncements:

APB-2	Accounting for the "Investment Credit"
APB-4	Accounting for the "Investment Credit"
APB-10	Paragraph 6, Tax Allocation Accounts—Discounting Paragraph 7, Offsetting Securities against Taxes Payable
APB-23	Accounting for Income Taxes—Special Areas
FAS-37	Balance Sheet Classification of Deferred Income Taxes
FAS-109	Accounting for Income Taxes
FIN-18	Accounting for Income Taxes in Interim Periods

2009 TRANSITION GUIDANCE FOR
FAS-141(R) AND FAS-160

The FASB has recently issued FAS-141(R), *Business Combinations*, which is effective for business combinations for which the acquisition date is on or after the beginning of the first annual reporting period beginning on or after December 15, 2008. The FASB has also issued FAS-160, *Noncontrolling Interests in Consolidated Financial Statements, an Amendment of ARB No. 51*, which is effective for fiscal years, and interim periods within those fiscal years, beginning on or after December 15, 2008. Because these standards are not effective for some companies until December 2009, and because early adoption is prohibited, the 2009 *GAAP Guide* reflects the requirements of FAS-141 prior to its revision in December 2007 and does not reflect the requirements of FAS-160. There is a discussion of the changes in the accounting for business combinations under FAS-141(R) in the Appendix to Chapter 4, "Business Combinations." Similarly, the Appendix to Chapter 7, "Consolidated Financial Statements," includes a discussion of the requirements of FAS-160. However, any effects of FAS-141(R) and/or FAS-160 in this chapter have not been reflected in this edition. Therefore, if a company is subject to the requirements of FAS-141(R) and/or FAS-160, the reader is referred to FAS-141(R) and FAS-160 for these new requirements.

BACKGROUND

FAS-109 (Accounting for Income Taxes) superseded FAS-96 and addresses financial accounting and reporting for income taxes. FAS-109 changed accounting for income taxes from the deferred method, required by APB-11 (Accounting for Income Taxes), to the asset/liability method, commonly referred to as simply the *liability method*.

The *deferred method* placed primary emphasis on the matching of revenues and expenses. Income tax expense was determined by applying the current income tax rate to pretax accounting income. Any difference between the resulting expense and the amount of income taxes payable was an adjustment to deferred income taxes. The deferred method focused first on the income statement, and adjustments to balance sheet elements were determined by the measurement of income tax expense.

The *asset/liability method* places primary emphasis on the valuation of current and deferred tax assets and liabilities. The amount of income tax expense recognized for a period is the amount of income taxes currently payable or refundable, plus or minus the change in aggregate deferred tax assets and liabilities. The method focuses first on the balance sheet, and the amount of income tax expense is determined by changes in the elements of the balance sheet.

THE ASSET/LIABILITY METHOD

FAS-109 requires income taxes to be accounted for by the asset/ liability method. Its main effects on financial statements include the following:

- Emphasis is on the recognition and measurement of deferred tax assets and liabilities. Deferred income tax expense is determined residually (i.e., as the difference between the beginning and required ending balances in deferred tax assets and liabilities for the period).

- Deferred tax asset and liability amounts are remeasured when tax rates change to approximate more closely the amounts at which those assets and liabilities will be realized or settled.

- Deferred tax assets are recognized for operating loss and other carryforwards. Deferred tax assets are subject to reduction by a valuation allowance if evidence indicates that it is *more likely than not* that some or all of the deferred tax assets will not be realized. Determining this valuation allowance is similar to accounting for reductions in receivables to net realizable value.

* Disclosure requirements result in the presentation of a significant amount of information in the notes to the financial statements.

GENERAL PROVISIONS OF FAS-109

Scope

FAS-109 requires what traditionally has been referred to as "comprehensive income tax allocation," as opposed to partial allocation or nonallocation. This means that the income tax effects of all revenues, expenses, gains, losses, and other events that create differences between the tax bases of assets and liabilities and their amounts for financial reporting are required to be recognized (FAS-109, par. 3).

FAS-109 is applicable to (FAS-109, par. 4):

* Domestic federal income taxes and foreign, state, and local taxes based on income, based on the provisions in FIN-48.

* An enterprise's domestic and foreign operations that are consolidated, combined, or accounted for by the equity method. FIN-48 provides guidance for determining the tax bases of assets and liabilities for financial reporting purposes.

* Foreign enterprises in preparing financial statements in accordance with U.S. GAAP.

Three important financial statement issues are specifically set aside and not covered by FAS-109 (FAS-109, par. 5):

1. Accounting for the investment tax credit (ITC)
2. Accounting for income taxes in interim periods
3. Discounting deferred income taxes

Accounting for the ITC and accounting for income taxes in interim periods are covered by existing authoritative pronouncements, which FAS-109 does not affect. Accounting for the ITC is covered in APB-2 (Accounting for the "Investment Credit") and APB-4 (Accounting for the "Investment Credit"), and accounting for income taxes in interim periods is discussed in APB-28 (Interim Financial Reporting) and FIN-18 (Accounting for Income Taxes in Interim Periods). The issue of discounting deferred income taxes is beyond the scope of FAS-109.

Basic Principles of the Asset/Liability Method

The objectives of accounting for income taxes are identified in terms of elements of the balance sheet (FAS-109, par. 6):

- To recognize the amount of taxes currently payable or refundable, based on the provisions of FIN-48. FIN-48 provides guidance for determining the tax bases of assets and liabilities for financial reporting purposes.

- To recognize the deferred tax assets and liabilities for the future tax consequences of events that have been recognized in the financial statements or in tax returns

This emphasis on the balance sheet is consistent with the liability method of accounting for income taxes incorporated in FAS-109.

Four basic principles are particularly important in understanding the liability method and the procedures that are developed in FAS-109 for accounting for income taxes. Each of the following basic principles focuses on the elements of the balance sheet relating to income taxes (FAS-109, par. 8):

1. Recognize a *tax liability or asset* for the amount of taxes currently payable or refundable, based on the provisions of FIN-48.

2. Recognize a *deferred tax liability or asset* for the estimated future tax effects of temporary differences or carryforwards. FIN-48 provides guidance for determining the tax bases of assets and liabilities for financial reporting purposes.

3. Measure *current* and *deferred tax assets* and *liabilities* based on provisions of enacted tax laws.

4. Reduce the amount of any deferred *tax assets* by a valuation allowance, if necessary, based on available evidence.

The following are exceptions to the four basic principles (FAS-109, par. 9):

- Certain exceptions to the requirements for recognition of deferred tax assets and liabilities for the areas addressed by APB-23 (Accounting for Income Taxes—Special Areas) as amended by FAS-109, paragraphs 31 through 34, notably the investments in foreign subsidiaries and joint ventures

- Special transitional procedures for temporary differences related to deposits in statutory reserve funds by U.S. steamship enterprises

- Accounting for leveraged leases as required by FAS-13 (Accounting for Leases) and FIN-21 (Accounting for Leases in a Business Combination)

- Prohibition of the recognition of a deferred tax liability or asset related to goodwill for which amortization is not deductible for tax purposes
- Accounting for income taxes under ARB-51 (Consolidated Financial Statements)
- Prohibition of the recognition of a deferred tax liability or asset for differences related to assets and liabilities accounted for under FAS-52 (Foreign Currency Translation)

Temporary Differences

Deferred tax assets and liabilities that result from temporary differences are based on the assumption that assets and liabilities in an entity's balance sheet eventually will be realized or settled at their recorded amounts (FAS-109, par. 11).

The following major categories of temporary differences refer to events that result in differences between the tax bases of assets and liabilities and their reported amounts in the financial statements (FAS-109, par. 11):

- Revenues or gains that are taxable after they are recognized in accounting income (e.g., receivables from installment sales)
- Expenses or losses that are deductible for tax purposes after they are recognized in accounting income (e.g., a product warranty liability)
- Revenues or gains that are taxable before they are recognized in accounting income (e.g., subscriptions received in advance)
- Expenses or losses that are deductible for tax purposes before they are recognized in accounting income (e.g., depreciation expense)

Other less common examples of temporary differences are:

- Investment tax credits accounted for by the deferred method.
- Business combinations accounted for by the purchase method.

Taxable and Deductible Temporary Differences

An important distinction in applying the procedures required to account for income taxes by the asset/liability method under FAS-109 is the difference between *taxable* and *deductible* temporary differences. A *taxable temporary difference* is one that will result in the payment of income taxes in the future when the temporary difference reverses. A *deductible temporary difference* is one that will result in reduced income taxes in future years when the temporary difference reverses (FAS-109, par. 13). Taxable temporary differences give rise to deferred tax liabilities; deductible temporary differences give rise to deferred tax assets. Table 21-1 further illustrates this important difference between taxable and deductible temporary differences.

The expanded definition of *temporary differences* in FAS-109 includes some items that do not appear in the company's balance sheet. For example, a company may expense organization costs when they are incurred but recognize them as a tax deduction in a later year. Between the two events, no balance-sheet item exists for this type of temporary difference (FAS-109, par. 15).

The identification of temporary differences may require significant professional judgment. Similar items may be temporary differences in one instance and not in another. For example, the excess of the cash surrender value of life insurance over premiums paid is a temporary difference and results in deferred taxes if the cash surrender value is expected to be recovered by surrendering the policy, but it is not a temporary difference and does not result in deferred taxes if the asset is expected to be recovered upon the death of the insured (FAS-109, par. 14). Management intent and professional judgment are important factors in making the appropriate determination of the nature of assets and liabilities of this type.

☛ **PRACTICE POINTER:** Developing a system for identifying and tracking the amounts of all temporary differences and carryforwards is an important implementation issue for FAS-109. Theoretically, differences should be identified by comparing items and amounts in the entity's balance sheets for accounting purposes and for tax purposes. Many companies do not maintain tax-basis balance sheets, though this may be the most logical way to identify and track temporary differences in relatively complex situations in which FAS-109 is applied.

Table 21-1: Examples of Taxable and Deductible Temporary Differences

Nature of Temporary Difference	Explanation	Deferred Tax
Taxable Temporary Differences		
Depreciable assets	Use of modified accelerated cost recovery system (MACRS) for tax purposes and straight-line for accounting purposes makes the tax basis of the asset less than the accounting basis	Liability, to be paid as MACRS deduction becomes less than straight-line depreciation

Installment sale receivable	Sales recognized for accounting purposes at transaction date and deferred for tax purposes until collection, resulting in a difference between the tax and accounting basis of the installment receivable	Liability, to be paid when the sale is recognized for tax purposes

Deductible Temporary Differences

Warranty liability	Expense recognized on accrual basis for accounting purposes and on cash basis for tax purposes, resulting in a liability that is recognized for financial reporting purposes but has a zero basis for tax purposes	Asset, to be recovered when deduction is recognized for tax purposes
Accounts receivable/ allowance for doubtful accounts	Expense recognized on an accrual basis for accounting purposes and deferred for tax purposes	Asset, to be recovered when uncollectible account is written off for tax purposes

FAS-109 carries forward the APB-11 concept of *permanent differences*, although that term is not used. FAS-109 points out that certain differences between the tax basis and the accounting basis of assets and liabilities will not result in taxable or deductible amounts in future years, and no deferred tax asset or liability should be recognized (FAS-109, par. 14).

Recognizing and Measuring Deferred Tax Assets and Liabilities

The emphasis placed on the balance sheet by the asset/liability method of accounting for income taxes is evident from the focus on the recognition of deferred tax liabilities and assets. The change in these liabilities and assets is combined with the income taxes currently payable or refundable to determine income tax expense (FAS-109, par. 16).

Five steps are required to complete the annual computation of deferred tax liabilities and assets (FAS-109, par. 17):

1. Identify the types and amounts of existing temporary differences and the nature and amount of each type of operating loss and tax credit carryforward and the remaining length of the carryforward period.

2. Measure the total deferred tax liability for taxable temporary differences using the applicable tax rate.

3. Measure the total deferred tax asset for deductible temporary differences and operating loss carryforwards using the applicable tax rate.

4. Measure deferred tax assets for each type of tax credit carryforward.

5. Reduce deferred tax assets by a valuation allowance if it is more likely than not that some or all of the deferred tax assets will not be realized.

Valuation Allowance and Tax-Planning Strategies

Determining the need for and calculating the amount of the valuation allowance requires the following steps at the end of each accounting period (FAS-109, par. 21):

1. Determine the amount of the deferred tax asset recognized on each deductible temporary difference, operating loss, and tax credit carryforward. (These are not offset by the deferred tax liability on taxable temporary differences.)

2. Assess the sources of future taxable income which may be available to recognize the deductible differences and carryforwards by considering the following:
   a. Taxable income in prior carryback year(s) if carryback is permitted under tax law
   b. Future reversals of existing taxable temporary differences
   c. Tax planning strategies that would make income available at appropriate times in the future that would otherwise not be available
   d. Future taxable income exclusive of reversing differences and carryforwards

☞ **PRACTICE POINTER:** The four sources of income are organized differently here than in FAS-109 in order to emphasize the implementation of the standard. In identifying income to support the recognition of deferred tax assets (and thereby supporting a case that an allowance is not required), a logical approach is to consider sources of income in order from the most objective to the least objective. Income in prior carryback years is most objective, followed by the income from the reversal of taxable temporary differences, income resulting from tax planning strategies, and finally, future income from other sources.

3. Based on all available evidence, make a judgment concerning the realizability of the deferred tax asset.

4. Record the amount of the valuation allowance, or change in the valuation allowance (the example below assumes that the allowance is being recorded for the first time or is being increased for $100,000).

Income tax expense $100,000

    Allowance to reduce
      deferred tax asset to
      lower recoverable value $100,000

OBSERVATION: FAS-109 relaxes the criteria for recognizing deferred tax assets by requiring the recognition of deferred tax assets for all deductible temporary differences and all operating loss and tax credit carryforwards. An important adjunct to this provision, however, is the requirement to determine the need for, and amount of, a valuation allowance to reduce the deferred tax asset to its realizable value. The valuation allowance aspects of FAS-109 require significant judgment on the part of accountants and auditors of financial statements. A valuation allowance is required if it is more likely than not that some or all of the deferred tax assets will not be realized. *More likely than not* is defined as a likelihood of more than 50%.

Applicable Tax Rate

Reference to the applicable tax rate is made in the four steps identified above. The *applicable tax rate* is that rate expected to apply to taxable income in the periods in which the deferred tax liability or asset is expected to be settled or realized based on enacted tax law. If the entity's taxable income is low enough to make the graduated tax rates a significant factor, the entity uses the average graduated tax rate applicable to the amount of estimated annual taxable income in the periods in which the deferred tax liability or asset is expected to be settled or realized (FAS-109, par. 18). For example, if a company has taxable temporary differences of $20,000 that are expected to reverse in a year when no other income is expected, the applicable tax rate under current tax law is 15% and the deferred tax liability is:

$$\$20,000 \times 15\% \quad = \quad \$3,000$$

If the taxable temporary differences total $60,000, graduated tax rates become a factor (the tax rate changes at $50,000); deferred taxes are $10,000:

$$\$50,000 \times 15\% = \$ 7,500$$
$$\$10,000 \times 25\% = \underline{2,500}$$
$$\underline{\$10,000}$$

The average applicable tax rate is 16.67%.

$$\$10,000/\$60,000 = 16.67\%$$

☛ **PRACTICE POINTER:** Determining the applicable tax rate may be a very simple task, or it may require careful analysis and professional judgment. When an entity has been consistently profitable at sufficiently high levels that graduated tax rates are not a significant factor, use the single flat tax rate at which all income is used to compute the amount of deferred taxes on cumulative temporary differences. If a company experiences intermittent tax loss and tax income years, or if the company is consistently profitable at a level low enough that the graduated tax rates are a significant factor, greater judgment is required to determine the applicable tax rate under FAS-109.

Deferred tax assets and liabilities are remeasured at the end of each accounting period and adjusted for changes in the amounts of cumulative temporary differences and for changes in the applicable income tax rate, as well as for other changes in the tax law (FAS-109, par. 27). As a result of this procedure, the deferred tax provision is a combination of two elements:

1. The change in deferred taxes because of the change in the amounts of temporary differences
2. The change in deferred taxes because of a change in the tax rate caused by new enacted rates or a change in the applicability of graduated tax rates (or other changes in the tax law)

Treating the change in income tax rates in this manner is consistent with accounting for a change in estimate under FAS-154 (Accounting Changes and Error Corrections).

Tax Planning Strategies

Consideration of tax planning strategies is also required by FAS-109. Tax planning strategies are an important part of determining the need for, and the amount of, the valuation allowance for deferred tax assets. FAS-109 describes tax-planning strategies as actions that (FAS-109, par. 22):

• Are prudent and feasible

- The entity might not ordinarily take, but *would* take to prevent an operating loss or tax credit carryforward from expiring before it is used
- Would result in the realization of deferred tax assets

Examples include actions the entity could take to accelerate taxable income to utilize expiring carryforwards, to change the character of taxable or deductible amounts from ordinary income or loss to capital gain or loss, and to switch from tax-exempt to taxable investments.

Negative Evidence

If negative evidence is present, such as cumulative losses in recent years, it is difficult to conclude that a valuation allowance is not necessary. Other examples of negative evidence are (FAS-109, par. 23):

- A history of operating loss or tax credit carryforwards expiring before they are used
- Losses expected in early future years
- Unsettled circumstances that, if unfavorably resolved, would adversely affect future operations and profit levels on a continuing basis in future years
- A carryback or carryforward period that is so brief that it significantly limits the probability of realizing deferred tax assets

Positive Evidence

Positive evidence supports a conclusion that a valuation allowance is *not required*. Examples of positive evidence are (FAS-109, par. 24):

- Existing contracts or firm sales backlog that will produce more than enough taxable income to realize the deferred tax asset based on existing sales prices and cost structures
- An excess of appreciated asset value over the tax basis of the entity's net assets in an amount sufficient to realize the deferred tax asset
- A strong earnings history exclusive of the loss that created the future deductible amount, coupled with evidence indicating that the loss is an aberration rather than a continuing condition

☞ **PRACTICE POINTER:** Projecting the reversal of temporary differences for each future year individually is commonly referred to as "scheduling." Does FAS-109 require scheduling? On the one hand, the requirement to recognize deferred tax assets and liabilities for all taxable and deductible temporary differences, as well as for all carryforwards, seems to diminish or eliminate the need to schedule. Also, using a flat tax rate in determining the amount of deferred tax assets and liabilities, as described earlier, diminishes the need to schedule individual future years. On the other hand, scheduling may help determine the need for, and amount of, a valuation allowance, including the consideration of tax-planning strategies. To determine the availability of taxable income in the appropriate years—to take advantage of deferred tax assets and to make the judgments concerning the valuation allowance—projecting taxable income from known or estimated sources by year may still be important.

Professional judgment is required in considering the relative impact of negative and positive evidence to determine the need for, and amount of, the valuation allowance for deferred tax assets. The weight given the effect of negative and positive evidence should be commensurate with the extent to which it can be objectively verified. The more negative evidence exists, the more positive evidence is needed to conclude that a valuation allowance is not required (FAS-109, par. 25).

The effect of a change in the valuation allowance that results from a change in circumstances, which in turn causes a change in judgment about the realizability of the related deferred tax asset, is included in income from continuing operations with limited exceptions (FAS-109, par. 26).

SPECIALIZED APPLICATIONS OF FAS-109

Several specialized applications of FAS-109 are summarized briefly below.

Change in Tax Status

An enterprise's tax status may change from nontaxable to taxable or taxable to nontaxable. A deferred tax liability or asset shall be recognized for temporary differences at the date that a nontaxable enterprise becomes a taxable enterprise. A deferred tax liability or asset shall be eliminated at the date an enterprise becomes a nontaxable enterprise (FAS-109, par. 28).

Regulated Enterprises

Regulated enterprises are *not* exempt from the requirements of FAS-109. Specifically, FAS-109 (FAS-109, par. 29):

- Prohibits net-of-tax accounting and reporting
- Requires recognition of a deferred tax liability for tax benefits that flow through to customers when temporary differences originate and for the equity component of the allowance for funds used during construction
- Requires adjustment of a deferred tax liability or asset for an enacted change in tax laws or rates

If as a result of an action by a regulator, it is probable that the future increase or decrease in taxes payable for items (2) and (3) above will be restored from or returned to customers through future rates, an asset or a liability is recognized for that probable future revenue or reduction in future revenue in accordance with FAS-71 (Accounting for the Effects of Certain Types of Regulation). That asset or liability is a temporary difference for which a deferred tax liability or asset is required.

Business Combinations

A deferred tax asset or liability is recognized for differences between the assigned values (i.e., allocated portion of historical cost) and the tax bases of assets and liabilities resulting from a business combination (in contrast to the recording of these items on a net-of-tax basis, as required by APB-11). If a valuation allowance is recognized for the deferred tax asset for an acquired entity's deductible temporary differences, operating loss, or tax credit carryforward at the acquisition date, the tax benefits for those items that are first recognized in financial statements after the acquisition date are applied in the following order (FAS-109, par. 30):

1. Reduce to zero any goodwill related to the acquisition.
2. Reduce to zero other noncurrent intangible assets related to the acquisition.
3. Reduce income tax expense.

APB-23 and U.S. Steamship Enterprises

A deferred tax liability is not recognized for the following temporary differences, unless it becomes apparent that they will reverse in the foreseeable future (FAS-109, par. 31):

- An excess of the amount for financial reporting over the tax basis of an investment in a foreign subsidiary or a foreign corporate joint venture as defined in APB-18 (The Equity Method of Accounting for Investments in Common Stock) that is essentially permanent in nature
- For a domestic subsidiary or a domestic corporate joint venture that is essentially permanent in duration, undistributed earnings that arose in fiscal years beginning on or before December 15, 1992
- "Bad debt reserves" for tax purposes of U.S. savings and loan associations and other qualified thrifts that arose in tax years beginning before December 31, 1987
- Policyholders' surplus of stock life insurance companies that arose in fiscal years beginning on or before December 15, 1992

A deferred tax liability is recognized for the following types of taxable temporary differences (FAS-109, par. 32):

- An excess of the amount of accounting basis over the tax basis of an investment in a domestic subsidiary that arises in fiscal years beginning after December 15, 1992
- An excess of the amount for accounting purposes over the tax basis of an investment in a 50%-or-less-owned investee except as provided in FAS-109 for a foreign corporate joint venture that is essentially permanent in nature
- "Bad debt reserves" for tax purposes of U.S. savings and loan associations and other qualified thrifts that arise in tax years beginning after December 31, 1987

Whether an excess of the amount for accounting purposes over the tax basis of an investment in a more-than-50%-owned domestic subsidiary is a taxable temporary difference must be assessed. It is not a taxable temporary difference if the tax law provides a means by which the reported amount of that investment can be recovered taxfree and the enterprise expects that it will ultimately use that means (FAS-109, par. 33).

A deferred tax asset is recognized for an excess of the tax basis over the amount for accounting purposes of an investment in a subsidiary or corporate joint venture that is essentially permanent in duration only if it is apparent that the temporary difference will reverse in the foreseeable future (FAS-109, par. 34).

Intraperiod Tax Allocation

Income tax expense or benefit for the year shall be allocated among continuing operations, discontinued operations, extraordinary items, and items charged or credited directly to shareholders' equity. The amount allocated to continuing operations is the tax effect of the pretax income or loss from continuing operations that occurred during the year, plus or minus income tax effects of:

- Changes in circumstances that cause a change in judgment about the realization of deferred tax assets
- Changes in tax laws or rates
- Changes in tax status
- Tax deductible dividends paid to shareholders, except for dividends paid on unallocated shares held by an employee stock ownership plan (ESOP)

The remainder is allocated to items other than continuing operations (FAS-109, par. 35).

The tax effects of the following items are charged or credited directly to the related components of stockholders' equity (FAS-109, par. 36):

- Adjustments of the opening balance of retained earnings for certain changes in accounting principles or to correct an error
- Gains and losses included in comprehensive income but excluded from net income
- An increase or decrease in contributed capital
- Expenses for employee stock options recognized differently for accounting and tax purposes
- Dividends that are paid on unallocated shares held by an ESOP and that are charged to retained earnings
- Deductible temporary differences and carryforwards that existed at the date of a quasi-reorganization

Generally, the tax benefit of an operating loss carryforward or carryback is reported in the same manner as the source of the income or loss in the current year, and not in the same manner as (*a*) the source of the operating loss carryforward or taxes paid in a prior year or (*b*) the source of expected future income that will result in realization of deferred tax assets for an operating loss carryforward from the current year. Exceptions to this general rule are:

- Tax effects of deductible temporary differences and carryforwards that existed at the date of a purchase business combination and for which a tax benefit is recognized initially in subsequent years in accordance with FAS-109, par. 30

- Tax effects of deductible temporary differences and carryforwards that are allocated to shareholders' equity in accordance with FAS-109, par. 36 (See previous list.)

If there is only one item other than continuing operations, the portion of income tax expense or benefit that remains after the allocation to continuing operations is allocated to that item. If there are two or more items, the amount that remains after the allocation to continuing operations is allocated among those other items in proportion to their individual effects on income tax expense or benefit for the year (FAS-109, par. 38).

Quasi-Reorganizations

The tax benefits of deductible temporary differences and carryforwards as of the date of a quasi-reorganization ordinarily are reported as a direct addition to contributed capital if the tax benefits are recognized in subsequent years. The only exception is for enterprises that previously adopted FAS-96 (Accounting for Income Taxes) and affected a quasi-reorganization involving only the elimination of a deficit in retained earnings by a noncurrent reduction in contributed capital prior to adopting FAS-109. For those enterprises, subsequent recognition of the tax benefit of prior deductible temporary differences and carryforwards is included in income, reported as required by FAS-109, and then reclassified from retained earnings to contributed capital (FAS-109, par. 39).

Separate Financial Statements of a Subsidiary

The allocation of income taxes among the members of a group of entities that file a consolidated tax return must be based on a method that is systematic, rational, and consistent with the broad principles established in FAS-109, although FAS-109 does not require a single allocation method. A method that allocates current and deferred taxes to members of the group by applying FAS-109 to each member as if it were a separate taxpayer meets those criteria. Examples of methods that are *not* consistent with the broad principles of FAS-109 include (FAS-109, par. 40):

- A method that allocates only current taxes payable to a member of the group that has taxable temporary differences
- A method that allocates deferred taxes to a member of the group using a method fundamentally different from the asset and liability method

- A method that allocates no current or deferred tax expense to a member of the group that has taxable income because the consolidated group has no current or deferred tax expense

Miscellaneous Topics

The following pronouncements are essentially unchanged by FAS-109:

- APB-10, paragraph 6
- APB-10, paragraph 7
- APB-23
- FIN-18

APB-10 (Omnibus Opinion—1966) indicates that deferred taxes should not be discounted (paragraph 6), and that offsetting of assets and liabilities (including tax assets and liabilities) is prohibited unless a legal right of setoff exists (paragraph 7).

APB-23, covered earlier in this chapter, indicates several situations in which deferred taxes are not recognized for certain temporary differences unless it becomes apparent that those differences will reverse in the foreseeable future.

FIN-18 provides guidance in accounting for income taxes in interim periods in accordance with the provisions of APB-28. APB-28 generally requires an estimated annual effective tax rate to be used to determine the interim period income tax provision.

> **OBSERVATION:** The special applications of FAS-109 discussed in this section illustrate the pervasive nature of accounting for income taxes. Income tax considerations affect many parts of the financial statements and many kinds of business transactions. This dimension of accounting for income taxes makes FAS-109 a very important pronouncement and accounts, at least partially, for the long and difficult process of making the transition from the deferred method under APB-11 to the asset/liability method under FAS-109.

FINANCIAL STATEMENT PRESENTATION AND DISCLOSURE ISSUES

FAS-109 requires deferred tax assets and liabilities to be presented in a classified balance sheet in current and noncurrent categories. The following policies are included for applying this requirement (FAS-109, pars. 41–42):

- If the temporary difference giving rise to the deferred tax asset or liability is reflected in a balance sheet asset or liability, the classification of the deferred tax is governed by that related asset or liability. For example, the temporary difference for depreciable assets is classified as noncurrent because the related asset (i.e., property, plant and equipment) is noncurrent.

- If the deferred tax does not relate to an underlying asset or liability on the balance sheet, classification is based on the expected timing of reversal. For example, if organization costs are expensed when incurred for accounting purposes but deferred and deducted later for tax purposes, there is no related balance sheet asset or liability. (FAS-37, par. 19)

- For a particular taxpaying component of an enterprise and within a particular tax jurisdiction (e.g., federal and state), all current deferred tax liabilities and assets are offset and presented as a single amount; the same procedure is followed for all noncurrent deferred tax liabilities and assets. Deferred tax liabilities and assets that are attributable to different taxpaying components of the enterprise or to different tax jurisdictions are *not* offset.

> **OBSERVATION:** The classification of deferred tax assets and liabilities as current or noncurrent based on the underlying asset is conceptually inferior to classifying them based on the expected timing of the receipt or payment of taxes. The latter approach is conceptually stronger in terms of the intent of the current/noncurrent classification—namely, to isolate as current those assets and liabilities expected to have cash flow consequences in the near future. Classifying a deferred tax asset or liability based on the underlying asset or liability appears to have been part of an effort by the FASB to reduce complexity and eliminate, to the extent possible, procedures that would require scheduling of taxable income for individual future years in determining the amounts of deferred tax assets and liabilities and their classifications.

Disclosures

The following components of the net deferred tax liability or asset recognized in an enterprise's balance sheet must be disclosed (FAS-109, par. 43):

- The total of all deferred tax liabilities for taxable temporary differences

- The total of all deferred tax assets for deductible temporary differences and loss and tax credit carryforwards
- The total valuation allowance recognized for deferred tax assets
- The net change during the year in the total valuation allowance

Earlier, several exceptions were identified under APB-23 for which deferred taxes are not recognized. Whenever a deferred tax liability is not recognized because of those exceptions, the following information is required to be disclosed (FAS-109, par. 44):

- A description of the types of temporary differences for which a deferred tax liability has not been recognized and the types of events that would cause those temporary differences to become taxable
- The cumulative amount of each type of temporary difference
- The amount of the unrecognized deferred tax liability for temporary differences related to investments in foreign subsidiaries and foreign corporate joint ventures that are essentially permanent in duration if determination of that liability is practicable, or a statement that determination is not practicable
- The amount of the deferred tax liability for temporary differences other than those in item (3) above that is not recognized based on exceptions granted by APB-23

Disclosure of significant components of income tax expense attributable to continuing operations for each year presented is required in the financial statements or related notes (FAS-109, par. 45):

- Current tax expense or benefit
- Deferred tax expense or benefit
- Investment tax credit
- Government grants (to the extent recognized as reductions in income tax expense)
- Tax benefits of operating loss carryforwards
- Tax expense that results from allocating tax benefits (*a*) directly to contributed capital or (*b*) to reduce goodwill or other non-current intangible assets of an acquired entity
- Adjustments to a deferred tax liability or asset for enacted changes in tax laws or rates or for a change in the tax status of the enterprise

- Adjustments of the beginning balance of the valuation allowance because of a change in circumstances that causes a change in judgment about the realizability of the related deferred tax asset in the future

> **OBSERVATION:** The effect of two unique features of the asset/liability method can be seen in the disclosure requirements listed above. Item (7) requires disclosure of the amount of the adjustment to deferred tax assets and liabilities for enacted changes in tax laws or rates. Item (8) requires disclosure of the amount of the adjustment of the beginning balance of the valuation allowance on deferred tax assets made as a result of a change in judgment about the realizability of that item.

The amount of income tax expense or benefit allocated to continuing operations and amounts separately allocated to other items shall be disclosed for each year for which those items are presented.

Several distinctions are made in the disclosures required by public enterprises and those required by nonpublic enterprises. The two most significant ones are summarized as follows (FAS-109, pars. 43–47):

	Public/Nonpublic Company Disclosures	
	Public	*Nonpublic*
Temporary Differences and Carryforwards	Approximation of tax effect of each type	Description of types
Statutory Reconciliation	Reconciliation in percentages or dollars	Description of major reconciling items

Companies with operating loss and tax credit carryforwards must disclose the amount and expiration dates. Disclosure is also required for any portion of the valuation allowance for deferred tax assets for which subsequently recognized tax benefits will be allocated (*a*) to reduce goodwill or other noncurrent intangible assets of an acquired entity or (*b*) directly to contributed equity (FAS-109, par. 48).

An entity that is a member of a group that files a consolidated tax return shall disclose the following in its separately issued financial statements (FAS-109, par. 49):

- The aggregate amount of current and deferred tax expense for each statement of earnings presented and the amount of any tax-related balances due to or from affiliates as of the date of each statement of financial position presented

• The principal provisions of the method by which the consolidated amount of current and deferred tax expense is allocated to members of the group and the nature and effect of any changes in that method during the year

---

Illustration of Major Provisions of FAS-109

This illustration considers Power Company for three consecutive years, with the objective of preparing the year-end income tax accrual and income tax information for the company's financial statements. Power Company's first year of operations is 20X8. During that year, the company reported $160,000 of pretax accounting income. Permanent and temporary differences are combined with pretax financial income to derive taxable income, as follows:

Pretax financial income	$160,000
Permanent difference:	
Iterest on municipal securities	(5,000)
Pretax financial income subject to tax	$155,000
Temporary differences:	
Depreciation	(28,000)
Warranties	10,000
Revenue received in advance	7,000
Taxable income	$144,000

The $5,000 interest on municipal securities represents nontaxable income, and the $28,000 depreciation temporary difference represents the excess of accelerated write-off for tax purposes over straight-line depreciation for financial reporting purposes. Warranties are expensed at the time of sale on an estimated basis, but are deductible for income tax purposes only when paid. In 20X8, $10,000 more was accrued than paid. Revenue received in advance is taxable at the time received, but is deferred for financial reporting purposes until earned. In 20X8, $7,000 was received that was not earned by year-end. Depreciation is a *taxable temporary difference* that reduces current tax payable and gives rise to deferred tax liability. The warranties and revenue received in advance are *deductible temporary differences* that increase current tax payable and give rise to deferred tax assets.

Exhibit A presents analyses that facilitate the preparation of the year-end tax accrual, as well as information for the financial statements. Similar analyses are used for each of the three years in this Illustration. The analysis in the upper portion of Exhibit A "rolls forward" the amount of the temporary differences from the beginning to the end of the year. Because 20X8 is the first year for Power Company, the beginning balances are all zero. The change column includes the amounts used in the earlier calculation to determine taxable income from pretax accounting income. The numbers without parentheses are deductible temporary differences; those in parentheses are taxable temporary differences. The company is in a net taxable temporary difference position at the end of the year because the net amount of temporary differences is $(11,000), due to the large amount of the depreciation difference.

EXHIBIT A: Analysis of Cumulative Temporary Differences and Deferred Taxes, 20X8

Cumulative Temporary Differences (TD)

	Beginning Balance 20X8	Change	Ending Balance 20X8
Deductible TD:			
Warranties	0	$ 10,000	$ 10,000
Revenue received in advance	0	7,000	7,000
(Taxable) TD:			
Depreciation	0	(28,000)	(28,000)
	0	$(11,000)	$(11,000)

Deferred Income Taxes

	Beginning Balance @—%	Ending Balance @34%	Change	Classification Current	Classification Non-current
Assets:					
Warranties	0	$ 3,400	$ 3,400		$ 3,400
Revenue received in advance	0	2,380	2,380	$2,380	
(Liabilities):					
Depreciation	0	(9,520)	(9,520)		(9,520)
	0	$(3,740)	$(3,740)	$2,380	$(6,120)

The lower portion of Exhibit A converts these temporary differences to amounts of deferred income taxes based on those differences. Again, the beginning balances are all zero and the ending balances are computed at 34%, the assumed income tax rate for 20X8 in this Illustration. The amounts in parentheses are deferred tax liabilities, based on taxable temporary differences. The numbers without parentheses are deferred tax assets, based on deductible temporary differences.

The classification columns on the lower right side of Exhibit A separate the ending balances into current and noncurrent for balance sheet classification purposes. This distinction is based on the asset or liability (if one exists) underlying the temporary difference. If no such asset or liability exists, classification is based on the timing of the expected cash flow. In this case, the warranty period is assumed to be five years, so the related temporary difference is noncurrent, as is depreciation, because of the noncurrent classification of the underlying plant assets. The revenue received in advance is expected to be earned in the coming period, and thus is a current asset.

The December 31, 20X8, entry to record the income tax accrual for Power Company is as follows:

Dec. 31, 20X8

Income tax expense ($48,960 + $3,740)	$52,700	
Deferred income tax—Current	2,380	
Income tax payable ($144,000 × 34%)		$48,960
Deferred income tax—Noncurrent		6,120

Notice that the amounts of deferred income taxes—current and noncurrent—are taken from the lower analysis in Exhibit A. The income tax payable is determined by multiplying the $144,000 taxable income by the 34% tax rate. An important point to understand is that income tax expense is determined last: It is the net of the other three numbers and can be computed only after the remaining elements of the entry have been determined.

An important step to complete before moving to 20X9 is a proof of the numbers obtained, commonly referred to as a *statutory rate reconciliation*. For 20X8, this calculation is as follows:

Pretax financial income @ statutory rate ($160,000 × 34%)	$54,400
Less: Permanent differences ($5,000 × 34%)	(1,700)
Income tax expense	$52,700

Effects of these calculations on the balance sheet and income statement will be considered after all three years of analysis are completed.

Power Company's second year of operations is 20X9, in which pretax financial income is $150,000. Municipal interest is $12,000 and temporary differences for depreciation and warranties are $(35,000) and $12,000, respectively. Of the revenue received in advance in 20X8, $5,000 is earned and an additional $9,000 is received in 20X9 that is expected to be earned in 20Y0. A new temporary difference is the litigation loss that results from the $10,000 accrual on an estimated basis for accounting purposes. This loss will be deductible for tax purposes when the suit is settled, which is expected to occur in 20Y0.

Taxable income for 20X9 is determined as follows:

Pretax financial income	$150,000
Permanent difference:	
Interest on municipal securities	(12,000)
Pretax financial income subject to tax	$138,000
Temporary differences:	
Depreciation	(35,000)
Warranties	12,000
Revenue received in advance ($9,000 – $5,000)	4,000
Litigation loss	10,000
Taxable income	$129,000

Exhibit B includes a 20X9 analysis similar to the 20X8 analysis in Exhibit A. During 20X9, new tax legislation increases the income tax rate for 20X9 and all future years to 40%. The amounts in 20X9 simply are moved forward from the end of 20X8. In the lower portion of Exhibit B, the change column is calculated by determining the change required to move the beginning balance to the desired ending balance. The litigation loss is classified as current because of its expected settlement in 20Y0, when it will be deductible for income tax purposes.

The entry to record income taxes at the end of 20X9 is as follows:

Dec. 31, 20X9

Income tax expense	55,860	
($51,600 + $4,260)		
Deferred income tax—Current	6,020	
($8,400 – $2,380)		
Income tax payable		51,600
($129,000 × 40%)		
Deferred income tax—Noncurrent		10,280
($16,400 – $6,120)		

Notice that the debits and credits to deferred income tax—current and noncurrent, respectively—are calculated as the changes in those accounts. It is not necessary to deal with that consideration in 20X8 because it was the company's first year. The desired ending balances of current and noncurrent deferred income taxes from Exhibit B are compared with the balances from Exhibit A and the differences are debited or credited into the deferred tax accounts, as appropriate, to produce the desired ending balances. For example, deferred income tax—noncurrent must have a credit (liability) balance of $16,400 at the end of 20X9. The account began with a credit balance of $6,120, requiring a credit of $10,280 in the year-end tax accrual. Similarly, the required debit (asset) balance for deferred income taxes—current is $8,400; with a debit balance of $2,380 at the end of 20X8, the adjustment is $6,020 ($8,400 – $2,380). This illustrates the basic approach of the liability method of accounting for income taxes: The desired balance sheet figures are determined first and the expense is recognized in the amount required to meet the balance sheet objective.

EXHIBIT B: Analysis of Cumulative Temporary Differences and Deferred Taxes, 20X9

Cumulative Temporary Differences (TD)

	Beginning Balance 20X9	Change	Ending Balance 20X9
Deductible TD:			
Warranties	$ 10,000	$12,000	$ 22,000
Revenue received in advance	7,000	4,000	11,000
Litigation	0	10,000	10,000
(Taxable) TD:			
Depreciation	(28,000)	(35,000)	(63,000)
	$(11,000)	$ (9,000)	$(20,000)

Deferred Income Taxes

	Beginning Balance @34%	Ending Balance @40%	Change	Classification Current	Classification Non-current
Assets:					
Warranties	$ 3,400	$ 8,800	$ 5,400		$ 8,800
Revenue received in advance	2,380	4,400	2,020	$4,400	
Litigation loss	0	4,000	4,000	4,000	
(Liabilities):					
Depreciation	(9,520)	(25,200)	(15,680)		(25,200)
	$(3,740)	$ (8,000)	$ (4,260)	$8,400	$(16,400)

The statutory rate reconciliation has an additional component in 20X9, because of the tax rate change from 34% to 40%. This change has the effect of increasing deferred taxes and, therefore, tax expense, as indicated in the following reconciliation:

Pretax financial income at statutory rate ($150,000 × 40%)	$ 60,000
Less: Permanent differences ($12,000 × 40%)	(4,800)
Plus: Tax increase on beginning cumulative	
temporary differences [$11,000 × (40% –34%)]	660
Income tax expense	$ 55,860

Notice that the adjustment for the tax increase is calculated only for the beginning balance of cumulative temporary differences. The temporary differences originating in 20X9 have already been taxed at 40%. As indicated earlier, the balance sheet and income statement presentation of deferred tax information will be considered after the analysis for 20Y0.

During the third year of this Illustration, Power Company's activities took a significant downturn. Because of negative economic trends and a loss of several important contracts, the company reported a pretax financial *loss* of $275,000.

An analysis of the pretax financial loss, permanent and temporary differences, and the amount of loss for tax purposes are analyzed as follows:

Pretax financial (loss)	$(275,000)
Permanent difference:	
Interest on municipal securities	(15,000)
Pretax financial (loss) subject to tax	$(290,000)
Temporary differences:	
Depreciation	(40,000)
Warranties	18,000
Revenue received in advance ($15,000 – $10,000)	5,000
Litigation loss	(10,000)
Taxable (loss)	$(317,000)

This analysis is similar to those for 20X8 and 20X9, except for the negative amount entered as pretax financial loss. Revenue of $10,000 received in advance that was previously taxed was recognized in accounting income and an additional $15,000 was received that was deferred for accounting purposes, but taxed currently. The litigation of 20X9 was completed and the $10,000 loss was deducted for tax purposes.

Notice that the loss for tax purposes is $317,000. Assume that Power Company decides to carry back the loss to the extent possible and receive a refund for income taxes paid in the carryback period. Under current tax law, the loss can be carried back only two years, the entire life of Power Company. The amount of the refund to be received is $100,560:

20X8: $144,000 × 34%	=	$ 48,960
20X9: $129,000 × 40%	=	51,600
		$100,560

The determination of deferred tax balances in Exhibit C is similar to those in the two previous exhibits with modifications necessary to include the loss carryforward of $44,000, which is determined by subtracting the amount of loss that is carried back from the total loss for tax purposes for 20Y0:

$$\$317,000 - (\$144,000 + \$129,000) = \$44,000$$

EXHIBIT C: Analysis of Cumulative Temporary Differences and Deferred Taxes, 20Y0

Cumulative Temporary Differences (TD)

	Beginning Balance 20Y0	Change	Ending Balance 20Y0
Deductible TD:			
Warranties	$ 22,000	$ 18,000	$ 40,000
Revenue received in advance	11,000	5,000	16,000
Litigation	10,000	(10,000)	0
(Taxable) TD:			
Depreciation	(63,000)	(40,000)	(103,000)
Loss Carryforward:			
20Y0 Loss*	0	44,000	44,000
	$(20,000)	$ 17,000	$ (3,000)

Deferred Income Taxes

	Beginning Balance @40%	Ending Balance @40%	Change	Classification Current	Classification Non-current
Assets:					
Warranties	$ 8,800	$16,000	$ 7,200		$16,000
Revenue received in advance	4,400	6,400	2,000	$6,400	
Litigation loss	4,000	0	(4,000)		
Loss carryforward	0	17,600	17,600		17,600
(Liabilities):					
Depreciation	(25,200)	(41,200)	(16,000)		(41,200)
	$(8,000)	$(1,200)	$6,800	$6,400	$(7,600)

* [$317,000 − ($144,000 + $129,000)]

Notice that a category for the loss carryforward has been added to the analysis at the top of Exhibit C and the $44,000 loss carryforward in 20Y0 has been included. The loss carryforward gives rise to a deferred tax asset, as indicated in the analysis at the bottom of Exhibit C. This item is classified as noncurrent on the assumption that, given the large loss encountered by Power Company in 20Y0, it will be several years before the company returns to profitable operations and is able to recognize the benefit of the loss carryforward. That item is treated in the same manner as a deductible temporary difference for purposes of determining deferred tax assets and liabilities.

☛ **PRACTICE POINTER:** Accumulating the information required to implement FAS-109 is facilitated by preparing a workpaper like those in Exhibits A, B, and C. Such a workpaper includes the following major components:

- A record of the cumulative temporary differences and carryforwards, including:
  — Separation of temporary differences into taxable and deductible categories
  — Beginning balances, the increase or decrease in the cumulative temporary differences, and the ending balances
- A record of cumulative amounts of carryforwards identified by year
- A record of deferred income taxes, including:
  — Separate classifications of deferred tax liabilities and assets
  — Beginning balances, ending balances, and the resulting changes in deferred taxes for the year
  — The classification of the ending balances of deferred tax assets and liabilities into current and noncurrent balance sheet categories

The journal entry to record income taxes at the end of 20Y0 is as follows:

Dec. 31, 20Y0

Receivable for past income taxes		
[($144,000 × 34%) + ($129,000 × 40%)] $100,560		
Deferred income tax—Noncurrent		
($16,400 − $7,600)	8,800	
Deferred income tax—Current		
($8,400 − $6,400)		$ 2,000
Income tax benefit ($100,560 + $6,800)		107,360

As shown in the two right-hand columns of Exhibits B and C, the balances of both deferred income taxes—current (debit) and deferred income taxes—noncurrent (credit) declined from 20X9 to 20Y0. The two most significant differences are the reversal of the temporary difference from the litigation loss and the inclusion of the loss carryforward, both of which are relatively large amounts.

In the journal entry above, income tax expense has been replaced by the account income tax benefit, which indicates the positive impact (loss reduction) of using the 20Y0 loss to receive the refund of 20X8 and 20X9 income taxes and to offset income taxes that would otherwise have to be paid after 20Y0.

The 20Y0 statutory rate reconciliation can now be prepared as follows:

Pretax financial (loss) at statutory rate [($275,000) × 40%]	$(110,000)
Less: Permanent differences ($15,000 × 40%)	(6,000)
Plus: Loss carryback at 34% [$144,000 × (40% − 34%)]	8,640
Income tax (benefit)	$(107,360)

The last item in the reconciliation, identified as "loss carryback at 34%," is required because the 20X8 part of the carryback was determined at 34%, the 20X8 income tax rate, rather than the current (20Y0) rate of 40%.

Now that the three-year analysis of the cumulative temporary differences and the loss carryforward, the related deferred tax assets and liabilities, and the year-end journal entries to record income taxes is completed, attention should be focused on the amounts that will be presented in the balance sheet and income statement. That information is presented in Exhibit D. For each year, a portion of deferred taxes appears in the current asset section of the balance sheet. This amount represents the net amount of deferred taxes on temporary differences on assets and liabilities that are classified as current in the balance sheet. In addition, in 20Y0, a current asset is presented for the $100,560 receivable of 20X8 and 20X9 taxes resulting from the 20Y0 carryback. For 20X8 and 20X9, a current liability is presented for income taxes payable—$48,960 and $51,600 in 20X8 and 20X9, respectively.

Among noncurrent liabilities, each year includes a deferred tax amount that represents deferred taxes resulting from temporary differences classified as noncurrent, and from the loss carryforward. The amount of noncurrent deferred taxes declines between 20X9 and 20Y0 because of the loss carryforward, which partially offsets the large deferred tax liability related to the depreciation temporary difference for the first time in 20Y0.

The income statement presentation for each year displays pretax financial income (loss), followed by income tax expense (benefit), separated into current and deferred components. In 20X8 and 20X9, income tax expense reduces the amount of net income reported, as would be expected given the profitability reported by the company in those years. In 20Y0, however, the benefit of the carryback and carryforward results in a reduction in the amount of loss that would otherwise have been reported because of the refund of past taxes and the anticipation of reduced taxes in the future, when the carryforward is realized.

To examine the accounting procedures required when a valuation allowance is established for deferred tax assets, return to Exhibit C. Assume that, after careful consideration, management determines it is more likely than not that 25% of the deferred tax assets will not be realized. This requires a valuation allowance of $10,000, determined as follows, based on the information from Exhibit C:

EXHIBIT D: Financial Statement Presentation of Income Taxes, 20X8–20Y0

Balance Sheet

	20X8	20X9	20Y0
Current assets:			
Receivable for past income taxes			$ 100,560
Deferred income taxes	$ 2,380	$ 8,400	6,400
Current liabilities:			
Income taxes payable	48,960	51,600	
Noncurrent liabilities:			
Deferred income taxes	6,120	16,400	7,600

Income Statement

	20X8	20X9	20Y0
Income (loss):			
Before income tax	$160,000	$150,000	$(275,000)
Income tax expense (benefit):			
Current	48,960	51,600	(100,560)
Deferred	3,740	4,260	(6,800)
	52,700	55,860	(107,360)
Net income (loss)	$107,300	$ 94,140	$(167,640)

Current deferred tax assets:			
Revenue received in advance			$ 6,400
Noncurrent deferred tax assets:			
Warranties		$16,000	
Loss carryforward		17,600	33,600
			$40,000
Valuation allowance: 25% × $40,000			$10,000

Allocation to current/noncurrent:

Current: ($6,400/$40,000) × $10,000	$ 1,600
Noncurrent: ($33,600/$40,000) × $10,000	8,400
	$10,000

This allocation results in a $1,600 reduction in the current deferred tax asset and a $8,400 addition to the net noncurrent deferred tax liability. In the following comparative analysis, the impact of the valuation allowance is determined as indicated in the right-hand column, and is compared with the figures presented earlier without a valuation allowance in the left-hand column.

	Without Valuation Allowance	With Valuation Allowance
Current deferred tax asset	$ 6,400	$ 6,400
Less: Allowance	0	(1,600)
	$ 6,400	$ 4,800
Noncurrent deferred tax liability:		
Asset component	$33,600	$ 33,600
Less: Allowance	0	(8,400)
	$33,600	$ 25,200
Liability component	(41,200)	(41,200)
	$ (7,600)	$(16,000)
Total deferred tax	$ (1,200)	$(11,200)

The difference between the totals in the two columns is $10,000, exactly the amount of the valuation allowance.

The journal entry to record income taxes at the end of 20Y0 under these revised assumptions, and including the valuation allowance, is as follows:

Dec. 31, 20Y0

Receivable for past income taxes	$100,560	
[($144,000 × 34%) + ($129,000 × 40%)]		
Deferred income tax—Noncurrent	8,800	
($16,400 – $7,600)		
Allowance to reduce deferred tax assets		$10,000
to lower recoverable value		
Deferred income tax—Current		2,000
($8,400 – $6,400)		
Income tax benefit		97,360
($100,560 + $6,800 – $10,000)		

The statutory rate reconciliation for 20Y0, including the recognition of the valuation allowance, is as follows:

Pretax financial income (loss) at statutory rate	
[($275,000) × 40%]	$(110,000)
Less: Permanent differences ($15,000 × 40%)	(6,000)
Plus: Loss carryback at 34% [$144,000 × (40%–34%)]	8,640
Increase in valuation allowance	10,000
Income tax (benefit)	$ (97,360)

The valuation allowance is evaluated at the end of each year, considering positive and negative evidence about whether the asset will be realized. At that time, the allowance will either be increased or reduced; reduction could result in the complete elimination of the allowance if positive evidence indicates that the value of the deferred tax assets is no longer impaired and the allowance is no longer required.

UNCERTAIN TAX POSITIONS

FIN-48 interprets FAS-109 and recognizes that the ultimate deductibility of positions taken on tax returns is often uncertain. FIN-48 provides guidance on when tax positions claimed by an entity can be recognized (recognition) and guidance on the dollar amount at which those positions are recorded (measurement). Differences between tax positions taken in a tax return and recognized in accordance with FIN-48 will generally result in an increase in income taxes currently payable or a reduction in an income tax refund receivable or an increase in a deferred tax liability or a decrease in a deferred tax asset.

Scope

Because income taxes primarily affect business enterprises, FIN-48 is most applicable to for-profit businesses. However, FIN-48 also applies, assuming income taxes are an issue, to not-for-profit entities and pass-through entities (e.g., real estate investment trusts and investment companies) (FIN-48, par. 1).

FIN-48 applies to any tax position that is within the purview of FAS-109 (FIN-48, par. 3). A tax position is a position taken in a tax return already filed or to be filed in the future and that affects the determination of current or deferred income tax assets or liabilities (in either annual or quarterly financial statements). The effects of a tax position can result in either a permanent reduction in taxes payable or a reduction in the deferral of taxes payable to a future period, or can increase the realizability of deferred tax assets. Examples of tax positions include shifting income from one tax jurisdiction to another, the inclusion and characterization of income, and the recognition of deductions (FIN-48, par. 4).

Recognition

The definition of the appropriate unit of account for analyzing uncertain tax positions is judgmental. In exercising this judgment, the entity should consider both how it prepares and supports its tax return, as well as the likely approach taken by the relevant taxing authority in defining the unit of account for the entity (FIN-48, par. 5).

The entity should initially recognize the effects on the financial statements of a tax position when it is more likely than not (i.e., greater than a 50% likelihood) that the claimed tax position will be upheld by the relevant taxing authority, including any appeals or litigation. The evaluation of whether the tax position is more likely than not to be upheld should be based on the technical merits of the position (FIN-48, par. 6). In making this evaluation, the entity should:

- Consider the facts, circumstances, and information that exist at the reporting date (FIN-48, par. 6).

- Presume that the tax position will be evaluated by the relevant taxing authority, and that this authority will have full knowledge of the facts and circumstances surrounding the position (FIN-48, par. 7a).

- Evaluate the technical merits of a tax position based on tax legislation, statutes, and related legislative intent (implementing regulations and rulings and case law) (FIN-48, par. 7b).

- Consider each tax position on its own—that is, do not consider the possibility of offset or aggregation (FIN-48, par. 7c).

The benefits associated with tax positions that are not more-likely-than-not to be upheld are not recognized in the financial statements. Rather, a liability for the additional tax that taxing authorities are likely to assess is recognized in the financial statements.

Measurement

Before the financial statement effects of a tax position are recognized, the entity must conclude that it is more-likely-than-not that the tax position will be upheld by the relevant taxing authority. For each tax position, the entity is to consider the possible dollar amounts that might be realized upon settlement with the appropriate taxing authority (i.e., there is an implicit assumption that the tax return will be audited and that all tax positions will be evaluated). The entity is to estimate the probabilities associated with each possible settlement of the tax position. The amount recognized in the financial statements is the largest amount where the probability of ultimate receipt exceeds 50% (FIN-48, par. 8).

☞ **PRACTICE POINTER:** Very few tax disputes are litigated and even fewer are litigated to the court of "last resort." Therefore, assuming the tax position is more-likely-than-not to be upheld, the amount recognized related to the tax position is often the amount that the entity would settle for in a negotiation with taxing authorities (FIN-48, par. A3).

Effect of FIN-48 on Evaluation of Deferred Tax Assets

To realize a deferred tax asset, an entity must have taxable income in the future. Some entities plan to use one or more tax-planning strategies to provide taxable income in the future. FIN-48 is to be applied in evaluating the amount of any future taxable income as a result of using a tax-planning strategy (FIN-48, par. 9).

> ☞ **PRACTICE POINTER:**   To the extent that future taxable income as a result of applying a tax-planning strategy is not more-likely-than-not to be realized, the entity may have to increase the valuation allowance associated with any recognized deferred tax asset.

Subsequent Recognition

A tax position may not be more-likely-than-not to be upheld at the time the position is initially taken, but circumstances may change in the future such that the tax position becomes more-likely-than-not to be upheld. The financial statement effects of the tax position are to be recognized in the first interim period that any of the following conditions occur: (1) it is now more-likely-than-not that the tax position will be upheld by the relevant taxing authority, (2) the entity has negotiated a settlement of the tax position with the taxing authority, or (3) the statute of limitations for the taxing authority to challenge the claimed tax position has expired (FIN-48, par. 10).

Any such change in the evaluation of the realizability of a tax position should result from the receipt of new information, not from a new evaluation of information that existed at the time the tax position was originally taken (FIN-48, par. 12).

Derecognition

If circumstances change and an unrecognized tax position is no longer more-likely-than-not to be recognized, the financial statement effects of the tax position are to be derecognized in the first period when this change occurs. An entity cannot use a valuation allowance account as a substitute for derecognizing the financial statement effects of the tax position (FIN-48, par. 11).

Treatment of Interest and Penalties

Most taxing authorities require interest to be paid on an underpayment of income taxes. If a tax position is deemed not more-likely-than-not to be realized, the entity should begin accruing interest from the first period where the relevant taxing authority would begin to impose interest. Interest is computed by applying the relevant statutory tax rate to the difference between the tax position taken in the income tax return and the tax position recognized per the provisions of FIN-48 (i.e., essentially the difference between the tax position taken in the tax return and the tax position that is likely to be eventually upheld by the relevant taxing authority) (FIN-48, par. 15).

An entity may take a tax position in its return that does not even meet the minimum statutory threshold for the avoidance of penalties. In this case, the entity should recognize an expense for the amount of the statutory penalty in the period in which the tax position is taken. If circumstances change and the more-likely-than-not threshold is met, a settlement with the taxing authorities is reached, or the statute of limitations for examining prior tax returns lapses, than previously recognized interest and penalties should be derecognized (FIN-48, par. 16).

The recognition of interest that result from the application of FIN-48 can be treated as either income tax expense or interest expense, and penalties can be treated as either income tax expense or in another expense classification. The entity is given discretion in categorizing interest and penalties under FIN-48. However, the categorization of interest and penalties must be consistently applied (FIN-48, par. 19). In addition, the entity must disclose its policy on how it treats interest and penalties in its financial statements (FIN-48, par. 20).

Financial Statement Classification

An unrecognized tax benefit exists for the difference between a position taken on a tax return and the amount recognized under the provisions of FIN-48. Essentially, tax positions that are unlikely to be upheld are not recognized in the financial statements and are labeled as unrecognized tax benefits. An unrecognized tax position creates a liability for financial reporting purposes (or reduces an income tax refund receivable or a net operating loss carryforward). The liability reflects the fact that an entity is paying a taxing authority less (based on the filed tax return) than is likely to eventually be owed because certain tax positions are unlikely to be upheld. A liability associated with an unrecognized tax position is to be shown as a current liability if the entity expects to pay cash within one year or within the operating cycle, if longer (FIN-48, par. 17).

The application of FIN-48 also may affect the recognition of deferred tax assets and liabilities. Prior to the issuance of FIN-48, taxable and deductible temporary differences resulted from the difference between the book basis of assets and liabilities and the tax basis of those same assets and liabilities, based on the tax treatment used in the tax return. Post FIN-48, taxable and deductible temporary differences result from the difference between the book basis of assets and liabilities and the tax basis of those same assets and liabilities. Taxable and deductible temporary differences, formerly based on the tax treatment used in the tax return, are based on the tax treatment that is likely to ultimately be upheld by the relevant taxing authorities (FIN-48, par. 18).

Disclosure Requirements

A table reconciling the total amounts of unrecognized tax benefits from the beginning to the end of the year must be included for each annual reporting period. At a minimum, this table must include (FIN-48, par. 21a):

- The gross amounts of increases and decreases in unrecognized tax benefits as a result of tax positions taken in the current and prior periods. An unrecognized tax benefit results from a tax position claimed on a tax return that is not given financial statement effect because it is not more-likely-than-not that the tax position will be upheld by taxing authorities.

- The gross amounts of decreases in unrecognized tax benefits resulting from settlements with taxing authorities.

- The gross amounts of decreases in unrecognized tax benefits resulting from a lapse in the statute of limitations.

In addition to the above, the entity must disclose the total amount of unrecognized tax benefits that would affect the entity's tax rate if they were recognized and the total amount of interest and penalties included in the income statement and the balance sheet (FIN-48, pars. b–c). Moreover, if the entity has any unrecognized tax benefits where the amount of these unrecognized benefits may significantly increase or decrease over the next year, the entity must disclose (FIN-48, par. 21d):

- A description of the uncertainty.
- A description of the event that could change the amount of unrecognized tax benefits.
- An estimate of the amount by which the unrecognized tax benefit may change (range) or a statement that an estimate of this range cannot be developed.

The entity also must disclose the tax years that are still subject to examination by the taxing authorities (FIN-48, par. 21e).

Effective Date

FIN-48 is effective for fiscal years beginning after December 15, 2006. An entity can apply FIN-48 earlier (i.e., as of the beginning of the entity's fiscal year). However, if an entity wants to apply FIN-48 early, it can not have already issued any financial statements for the fiscal year, including financial statements for interim periods (FIN-48, par. 22).

> **OBSERVATION:** The FASB issued FSP FIN 48-2 in February 2008 providing for a partial delay in the effective date of FIN-48. The effective date of FIN-48 is deferred until fiscal years beginning after December 15, 2007, for *nonpublic* companies. No deferral is granted if: (1) the nonpublic company's financial statements are included in the consolidated financial statements of a public company, or (2) the nonpublic company has already issued a full set of annual financial statements applying FIN-48.

Transition Provisions

All tax positions of an entity are to be evaluated at the time FIN-48 is initially applied. To the extent that one or more tax positions do not meet the more-likely-than-not criteria, the current or deferred tax asset or liability already recognized is to be derecognized. The off-setting entry is a cumulative effect adjustment to the opening balance of retained earnings (FIN-48, par. 23). The cumulative effect on retained earnings, if any, must be disclosed in the balance sheet in the year of adoption of FIN-48 (FIN-48, par. 24).

Illustration of FIN-48—Measuring Benefit of a Tax Position

Hust and Jacony Inc. have taken a tax position that results in a $80 million tax benefit. Hust and Jacony conclude that it is more-likely-than-not (more than a 50% likelihood) that its claimed tax position will be upheld by the relevant taxing authority and, as such, the benefit associated with the tax position should be recognized. However, Hust and Jacoby believe that it may not receive the full $80 million tax benefit. In determining the amount of tax benefit to record in its financial statements, Hust and Jacoby estimate potential outcomes and the probabilities associated with those outcomes. Hust and Jacoby develop the following schedule:

Estimated Outcome	Individual Probability	Cumulative Probability
$80 million	10%	10%
60 million	15%	25%
50 million	40%	65%
40 million	20%	85%
20 million	15%	100%

Hust and Jacoby would record a benefit associated with this tax position of $50 million because this is the largest benefit that has more than a 50% cumulative probability of being received.

Illustration of FIN-48—Measurement when Uncertainty Exists Surrounding the Timing of Tax Deductibility

Neel and Neal Inc. (N&N) purchase a separately identifiable intangible asset for $4.5 million on 1-1-X7. The intangible asset has an indefinite life for financial reporting purposes and is therefore not being amortized. The tax treatment related to the timing of the deductibility of the intangible asset is ambiguous—there is some support for an immediate expensing of the intangible asset, but other sources suggest that the intangible is to be amortized over 15 years. N&N deduct the entire cost of the intangible asset in 20X7 for tax purposes.

N&N conclude that realization of the tax benefit associated with deducting the cost of the intangible asset is more-likely-than-not and, therefore, a tax benefit is to be recognized in the financial statements. The only uncertainty is whether the entire tax benefit is recognizable in 20X7 or ratably over the next 15 years.

N&N estimates that it has a 35% likelihood of being able to deduct the entire cost of the intangible asset in 20X7. If immediate expensing is not allowed, deductibility through periodic amortization over the next 15 years would be allowed. The tax benefit that is more than 50% likely of being realized is associated with amortization over 15 years (the probability of immediate expensing being supported is only 35%). Therefore, the tax benefit is the tax savings associated with a $300,000 ($4.5 million ÷ 15 years) in 20X7.

N&N would recognize the following on its 12-31-X7 financial statements:

- A deferred tax liability related for the tax effects of the difference between the book basis of the intangible asset ($4.5 million) and the tax basis of the intangible asset ($4.2 million) (The tax basis of the intangible asset is computed based on the provisions of FIN-48, not on the amount deducted in the tax return.)
- An income tax liability for the tax effects of the difference between the deduction claimed on the tax return ($4.5 million) and the appropriate deduction determined based on the provisions of FIN-48 ($300 thousand)

In addition, N&N must evaluate whether to accrue interest and penalties because the amount claimed on the tax return exceeds the amount that is supportable under the provisions of FIN-48 (i.e., the amount that has a greater than 50% likelihood of being ultimately realized).

RELATED CHAPTERS IN 2009 *GAAP GUIDE* *LEVEL A*

Chapter 7, "Consolidated Financial Statements"
Chapter 8, "Contingencies, Risks, and Uncertainties"
Chapter 11, "Depreciable Assets and Depreciation"
Chapter 22, "Installment Sales"
Chapter 26, "Interim Financial Reporting"
Chapter 29, "Leases"
Chapter 40, "Results of Operations"
Chapter 44, "Stockholders' Equity"

RELATED CHAPTERS IN 2009 *GAAP GUIDE* *LEVELS B, C, AND D*

Chapter 7, "Capitalization and Expense Recognition Concepts"
Chapter 10, "Consolidated Financial Statements"
Chapter 11, "Contingencies, Risks, and Uncertainties"
Chapter 20, "Income Taxes"
Chapter 23, "Interim Financial Reporting"
Chapter 26, "Leases"
Chapter 35, "Results of Operations"
Chapter 39, "Stockholders' Equity"

RELATED CHAPTERS IN 2009 *INTERNATIONAL ACCOUNTING/FINANCIAL REPORTING STANDARDS GUIDE*

Chapter 10, "Consolidated Financial Statements"
Chapter 20, "Income Taxes"
Chapter 22, "Interim Financial Reporting"
Chapter 25, "Leases"
Chapter 27, "Property, Plant, and Equipment"
Chapter 28, "Provisions, Contingent Liabilities, and Contingent Assets"

CHAPTER 22
INSTALLMENT SALES

CONTENTS

OVERVIEW

The installment sales method of accounting defers the recognition of gross profit on installment sales until cash is collected. It is commonly used for income tax purposes, but is acceptable for purposes of financial reporting in limited situations.

GAAP for the installment sales method are found in the following pronouncements:

ARB-43	Chapter 1, Prior Opinions A. Rules Adopted by Membership
APB-10	Paragraph 12, Omnibus Opinion—1966 (Installment Method of Accounting)

BACKGROUND

The installment sales method is acceptable only under unusual circumstances in which collectibility cannot be reasonably estimated or assured. The doubtfulness of collectibility can be caused by the length of an extended collection period or because no basis for estimating the probability of collection can be established. In such cases, a company may consider using either the installment sales method or the even more conservative cost recovery method (APB-10, par. 12).

INSTALLMENT SALES METHOD

Under the installment sales method of accounting, gross profit is recognized only to the extent that cash has been collected. Each payment collected consists of *part* recovery of cost and *part* gross profit, in the same ratio that these two elements existed in the original sale.

> ☛ **PRACTICE POINTER:** Because gross profit ratios are different for many products and departments and may vary from year to year, keep a separate record of sales by year, product line, and department. Keep separate accounts and records for receivables, realized gross profit, unrealized gross profit, and repossessions for each category of product.

Generally, the seller will protect its interest in an installment sale by retaining title to the goods through a conditional sales contract, lease, mortgage, or trustee. In the event of a default on an installment sales contract, the related account receivable and unrealized gross profit are written off. In many cases of default, the goods are repossessed by the seller. The loss (or gain) on a default of an installment sales contract is determined as follows:

$$\text{Loss (or Gain)} = \begin{bmatrix} \text{balance of} \\ \text{account} \\ \text{receivable} \end{bmatrix} \text{less} \begin{bmatrix} \text{unrealized} \\ \text{gross} \\ \text{profit} \end{bmatrix} \text{less} \begin{bmatrix} \text{inventory carrying} \\ \text{amount of} \\ \text{repossessed} \\ \text{merchandise} \\ \text{(if any)} \end{bmatrix}$$

When goods are repossessed, one of the major problems is determining the value of these inventory goods. Some of the methods of determining their value include:

- Fair market value
- Unrecovered cost (results in no gain or loss)
- Resale value less reconditioning costs plus a normal profit (net realizable value)
- No value—a good method when no other method is appropriate, particularly when the actual value is minor

> ☛ **PRACTICE POINTER:** Care should be taken in valuing repossessed goods at unrecovered cost because a loss that should be recorded may be overlooked.

Illustration of Installment Sales Method

A furniture dealer sells for $1000 a chair that cost $700. The gross profit percentage for this sale is 30%. Under the installment sales method, the dealer would recognize 70% of each payment as a recovery of cost and 30% as realized gross profit.

The entries to record the initial sale, assuming the use of a perpetual inventory system and no down payment, are:

Accounts receivable—installment sales	1,000	
Installment sales		1,000
Cost of installment sales	700	
Inventory		700

At the end of the accounting period, the company closes out the installment sales account and the cost of installment sales to unrealized gross profit on installment sales account, which in this example is $300. The entry is:

Installment sales	1,000	
Cost of installment sales		700
Unrealized gross profit on installment sales		300

In the period that the company collects $400, the entries are:

Cash	400	
Accounts receivable—installment sales		400
Unrealized gross profit on installment sales	120	
Realized gross profit on installment sales		120

The $400 collected includes $280 recovery of cost and $120 of realized gross profit on installment sales (a 70%/30% relationship).

If the first payment of $400 was the only payment the company received and the goods were not repossessed, the journal entry to record the default and loss would be:

Unrealized gross profit	180	
Loss on installment sales	420	
Accounts receivable—installment sales		600

If the goods were repossessed and had an inventory value of $250, the journal entry would be:

Unrealized gross profit	180	
Loss on installment sales	170	
Inventory	250	
Accounts receivable—installment sales		600

COST RECOVERY METHOD

The cost recovery method is used in very unusual situations in which recovery of cost is undeterminable or extremely questionable. The procedure is simply that all cost is recovered before any profit is recognized. Once all cost has been recovered, any other collections are recognized as profit. The only expenses remaining to be charged against such revenue are those relating to the collection process.

Illustration of Cost Recovery Method

If a company sells for $100 an item that cost $40 and receives no down payment, the first $20 collected, regardless of the year collected, is considered recovery of half the cost. The next $20 collected is recovery of the balance of the cost, regardless of the year collected. The remaining $60 (all gross profit) is recognized as income when received. The only additional expenses that are charged against the remaining $60 are those directly related to the collection process.

DEFERRED INCOME TAXES

The installment sales method is generally acceptable for income tax purposes, because the government attempts to collect taxes when the taxpayer has the cash available rather than basing collection on a theoretical analysis of accounting principles. The use of installment accounting for tax purposes and the accrual method for financial reporting purposes often results in a temporary difference and creates a deferred tax liability.

DISCLOSURE

Accounts receivable on installment sales are shown separately in the balance sheet. They are classified as current assets in accordance with the normal operating cycle of the entity, which may extend for more than one year. The amounts maturing each period for each class of installment receivable should also be disclosed.

Unrealized gross profit is presented in the balance sheet as a separate caption, usually as a contra account to the related installment receivable.

RELATED CHAPTER IN 2009 *GAAP GUIDE LEVEL A*

Chapter 41, "Revenue Recognition"

RELATED CHAPTER IN 2009 *GAAP GUIDE LEVELS B, C, AND D*

Chapter 36, "Revenue Recognition"

RELATED CHAPTER IN 2009 *INTERNATIONAL ACCOUNTING/FINANCIAL REPORTING STANDARDS GUIDE*

Chapter 30, "Revenue"

CHAPTER 23
INTANGIBLE ASSETS

CONTENTS

OVERVIEW

Intangible assets are long-lived assets used in the production of goods and services. They are similar to property, plant, and equipment except for their lack of physical properties. Examples of intangible assets include copyrights, patents, trademarks, and goodwill. Intangible assets with finite lives are subject to amortization over their estimated useful lives. Assets with indefinite useful lives are not amortized. Each period these assets are tested annually for impairment and also to determine whether the assumption of an indefinite useful life is still valid. If the asset's life is determined to have become limited, it is amortized prospectively over its remaining useful life.

The following pronouncements contain GAAP for intangible assets:

FAS-72   Accounting for Certain Acquisitions of Banking or Thrift Institutions

FAS-141   Business Combinations

FAS-142   Goodwill and Other Intangible Assets

FAS-147   Acquisitions of Certain Financial Institutions—An Amendment of FASB Statements No. 72 and 144 and FASB Interpretation No. 9

FIN-9   Applying APB Opinions No. 16 and 17 When a Savings and Loan Association or a Similar Institution Is Acquired in a Business Combination Accounted for by the Purchase Method

> **OBSERVATION:** Although FIN-9 relates directly to APB-16 and APB-17, it is not superseded by FAS-141, which supersedes APB-16, or by FAS-142, which supersedes APB-17. FAS-147 amends FAS-72 and FIN-9 so that these standards now apply only to acquisitions between two or more mutual enterprises that are financial institutions. However, FAS-141(R) supersedes FIN-9.

2009 TRANSITION GUIDANCE FOR FAS-141(R) AND FAS-160

The FASB has recently issued FAS-141(R), *Business Combinations,* which is effective for business combinations for which the acquisition date is on or after the beginning of the first annual reporting period beginning on or after December 15, 2008. The FASB has also issued FAS-160, *Noncontrolling Interests in Consolidated Financial Statements, an Amendment of ARB No. 51*, which is effective for fiscal years, and interim periods within those fiscal years, beginning on or after December 15, 2008. Because these standards are not effective for some companies until December 2009, and because early adoption is prohibited, the 2009 *GAAP Guide* reflects the requirements of FAS-141 prior to its revision in December 2007 and does not reflect the requirements of FAS-160. There is a discussion of the changes in the accounting for business combinations under FAS-141(R) in the Appendix to Chapter 4, "Business Combinations." Similarly, the Appendix to Chapter 7, "Consolidated Financial Statements," includes a discussion of the requirements of FAS-160. However, any effects of FAS-141(R) and/or FAS-160 in this chapter have not been reflected in this edition. Therefore, if a company is subject to the requirements of FAS-141(R) and/or FAS-160, the reader is referred to FAS-141(R) and FAS-160 for these new requirements.

BACKGROUND

The term *intangible asset* refers to non-financial assets that lack physical substance and that provide the entity with various benefits. Intangible assets differ considerably in their characteristics, useful lives, and relationship to operations of an enterprise.

For many years, accounting for intangible assets was determined by APB-17 (Intangible Assets). That standard was replaced in 2001 by FAS-142 (Goodwill and Other Intangible Assets). APB-17 required all intangible assets to be amortized over their estimated useful lives or a maximum period of 40 years, if no life could be reasonably estimated. As explained in the following section of this chapter, FAS-142 requires the separation of intangible assets into two categories—those with finite useful lives, which are amortized, and those with indefinite useful lives, which are not amortized.

The following are some of the basic principles upon which accounting for intangible assets in accordance with FAS-142 is based.

Identifiability

Patents, copyrights, franchises, trademarks, and other similar intangible assets that can be specifically identified with reasonably descriptive names. Other types of intangible assets lack specific identification, the most common being goodwill.

Manner of Acquisition

Intangible assets may be purchased or developed internally and may be acquired singly, in groups, or in business combinations.

Determinate or Indeterminate Life

Patents, copyrights, and most franchises are examples of intangible assets with determinate lives, established by law or by contract. Other intangible assets, such as secret processes and goodwill, have no established term of existence, and the expected period of benefit may be indeterminate at the time of acquisition.

Transferability

The rights to a patent, copyright, or franchise can be identified separately and bought or sold. Goodwill, on the other hand, is inseparable from a business and is transferable only as an inseparable intangible asset of an enterprise.

Cost of Intangibles

A company records as assets the costs of intangible assets acquired from other enterprises or individuals. The cost of an intangible asset is measured by (*a*) the amount of cash disbursed or the fair value of other assets distributed, (*b*) the present value of amounts to be paid for liabilities incurred, and (*c*) the fair value of consideration received for stock issued.

ACCOUNTING FOR GOODWILL AND OTHER INTANGIBLE ASSETS BY FAS-142

Scope

FAS-142 covers the following aspects of accounting and reporting for intangible assets:

- Intangible assets acquired individually or with a group of assets other than in a business combination
- Intangible assets, including goodwill recognized in accordance with FAS-141 (Business Combinations), subsequent to their acquisition (FAS-142, par. 4)

Intangible assets acquired in a business combination are covered in FAS-141. FAS-141 supersedes APB-17, but it carries forward unchanged the provisions of APB-17 related to internally developed intangible assets.

FAS-142 does not change accounting that is prescribed in the following pronouncements (FAS-142, par. 8, as amended by FAS-145, par. 9m):

- FAS-2 (Accounting for Research and Development Costs)
- FAS-19 (Financial Accounting and Reporting by Oil and Gas Producing Companies)
- FAS-50 (Financial Reporting in the Record and Music Industry)
- FAS-61 (Accounting for Title Plant)
- FAS-63 (Financial Reporting by Broadcasters)
- FAS-71 (Accounting for the Effects of Certain Types of Regulation)
- FAS-72 (Accounting for Certain Acquisitions of Banking or Thrift Institutions)
- FAS-86 (Accounting for the Cost of Computer Software to Be Sold, Leased, or Otherwise Marketed)
- FAS-109 (Accounting for Income Taxes)
- FAS-140 (Accounting for Transfers and Servicing of Financial Assets and Extinguishments of Liabilities)
- FIN-4 (Applicability of FASB Statement No. 2 to Business Combinations Accounted for by the Purchase Method)
- FIN-9 (Applying APB Opinion No. 16 and 17, When a Savings and Loan Association or Similar Institution Is Acquired in a Business Combination Accounted for by the Purchase Method)

Initial Recognition and Measurement

Intangible assets that are acquired individually or as part of a group of assets, other than those acquired in a business combination, are initially recorded at their fair value. The cost of a group of assets acquired in a transaction is allocated to the individual assets based on their relative fair values. Goodwill does not arise in such a transaction. Intangible assets that are acquired in a business combination are accounted for in accordance with FAS-141 (FAS-142, par. 9).

The costs of intangible assets that are developed internally as well as the costs of maintaining or restoring intangible assets that have indeterminate lives or that are inherent in a continuing business and related to the entity as a whole, are expensed as incurred (FAS-142, par. 10).

Accounting Subsequent to Acquisition

Intangible Assets Subject to Amortization

Intangible assets with finite useful lives are amortized over those lives. Intangible assets with indefinite useful lives are not amortized. Guidelines for determining the useful lives of intangible assets are:

- The expected use of the asset by the entity
- The expected useful life of another asset or group of assets to which the useful life of the asset in question may relate
- Legal, regulatory, or contractual provisions that may limit the asset's useful life
- Legal, regulatory, or contractual provisions that enable renewal or extension of the useful life without significant cost
- The effects of obsolescence, demand, competition, and other economic factors
- The level of maintenance expenditures required to obtain the expected future cash flows from the asset (FAS-142, par. 11)

As asset for which no legal, regulatory, contractual, competitive, economic, or other factors limit the useful life is considered to have an indefinite, but not infinite, useful life (FAS-142, par. 11).

> ☛ **PRACTICE POINTER:** Since FAS-142 was issued, there has been uncertainty as to whether customer-related intangible assets have an indefinite life (and therefore are not amortized) or whether they have a limited life (and are subject to yearly amortization). The SEC staff has indicated that assuming an indefinite life for customer-related intangible assets should be done very rarely. The SEC views customer-related intangible assets as having a limited life because every business typically experiences a normal customer "churn" rate. In addition, customer-related intangible assets reflect relationships between customers and the entity's personnel, and the entity's personnel are subject to turnover.
>
> Among the factors that an entity should consider in determining the useful life of a customer-related intangible asset are (1) the normal customer churn rate, (2) the relative cost or penalty faced by the customer if the relationship is terminated, and (3) alternative suppliers of the product or service provided by the entity—greater competition makes it easier for customers to switch suppliers.
>
> In initially assigning a value to a customer-related intangible asset, the entity should consider what value the outside market would place on the intangible asset. This market-determined value is a better indication of the economic value of the customer-related intangible asset than a value determined exclusively using entity-specific assumptions.

The cost of a recognized intangible asset, less its residual value to the reporting entity, should be amortized over its useful life unless that life is determined to be indefinite.

The remaining amortization period, for those assets being amortized, should be reviewed at each reporting period (FAS-142, pars. 12–14). If the life is finite, but the precise length of that life is not known, the best estimate of the assets useful life shall be used for amortization purposes. The method of amortization shall be the pattern in which the economic benefits are consumed or otherwise used up. If that pattern cannot be reliably determined, the straight-line method shall be used. An intangible asset should not be written off in the period of acquisition unless it is determined to be impaired during that period (FAS-142, par. 12).

An intangible asset that is subject to amortization shall be reviewed for impairment in accordance with FAS-144 (Accounting for the Impairment or Disposal of Long-Lived Assets).

> ☛ **PRACTICE POINTER:**   An entity acquires a copyright that has a remaining legal life of 40 years. The entity expects to receive cash flows from the copyright for the next 20 years. The copyright will be amortized over the next 20 years, in a manner consistent with the benefits received from the copyright. The copyright will be reviewed for impairment using the provisions of FAS-144.

Intangible Assets Not Subject to Amortization

If an intangible asset is determined to have an indefinite useful life, it shall not be amortized until its useful life is determined to be no longer indefinite. An assessment of the useful life of an intangible asset that is not being amortized is required each reporting period to determine whether events and circumstances continue to support an indefinite useful life. If such an asset is determined to have a finite useful life, the asset shall be tested for impairment (FAS-142, par. 16). The FAS-142 impairment test requires a comparison of the intangible asset's fair value with its carrying amount. If the asset's fair value is below its carrying amount, the intangible asset is written down to its carrying amount (FAS-142, par. 17). The fair value of an intangible asset is the amount that the asset would sell for in a transaction between willing parties (i.e., in other than a forced or liquidation sale) (FAS-142, par. 23). In future periods, the asset is then amortized prospectively over its estimated remaining useful life and accounted for in the same way as other intangible assets subject to amortization (FAS-142, par. 16). In subsequent periods, the asset is tested for impairment in accordance with FAS-144.

All intangible assets not subject to amortization (those with indefinite useful lives) shall be tested for impairment annually, or more frequently if events and circumstances indicate that the asset may be impaired. If impaired, an impairment loss is recognized in an amount equal to the excess of the asset's carrying value over its fair value. After such a loss is recognized, the adjusted carrying amount of the asset is its new accounting basis. Subsequent reversal of a previously recognized impairment loss is prohibited (FAS-142, par. 17).

> **OBSERVATION:** The remaining useful life of an intangible asset subject to amortization is reviewed each reporting period, as is the continuing status of intangible assets viewed to have an indefinite life. Conversely, unless certain events or circumstances suggest otherwise, the impairment status of intangible assets are only tested on an annual basis.

> ☞ **PRACTICE POINTER:** An entity has the rights to a broadcast license that can be renewed indefinitely. Based on a review of the relevant facts and circumstances, it appears likely that the entity will continue to renew its license for the foreseeable future and that the license will continue to have economic value and will generate positive cash flows for the entity holding the license. The cost of the broadcast license will not be amortized because the expected useful life of the license is indefinite. The broadcast license will be reviewed for impairment using the provisions of paragraph 17 of FAS-142.

> ☞ **PRACTICE POINTER:** An entity acquired a trademark associated with a product in 20X8. At acquisition, based on the relevant facts and circumstances, the trademarked product appeared to have an indefinite life. Therefore, the cost of the trademark was not amortized. In 20Y1, the entity decided to phase out production of the trademarked product over a period of five years. Since the trademark no longer has an indefinite life, it would be reviewed for impairment using the provisions of paragraph 17 of FAS-142. The carrying amount of the trademark, after any necessary impairment-related adjustment, would be amortized over the next five years. During each of the next five years, the trademark would be reviewed for impairment using the provisions of FAS-144 (since the intangible asset is now subject to periodic amortization).

Accounting for Goodwill

Goodwill is not amortized and is tested for impairment at a level of reporting referred to as a reporting unit (FAS-142, par. 18). A reporting unit is an operating segment or one level below an operating segment (referred to as a component) as defined in FAS-131 (Disclosures about Segments of an Enterprise and Related Information). A component of an operating segment is a reporting unit if the component constitutes a business for which discrete financial information is available and segment management regularly reviews the operating results of that component. Two or more components of an operating segment shall be aggregated and treated as a single reporting unit if the components have similar operating characteristics. An operating segment is deemed to be a reporting unit if (1) all of its components are similar, (2) none of its components is a reporting unit, or (3) if it comprises only a single component (FAS-142, par. 30).

Evaluation of goodwill for impairment involves two steps (FAS-142, pars. 19–20):

Step 1: Identify potential impairment by comparing the fair value of a reporting unit with its carrying amount, including goodwill.

Step 2: Measure the amount of goodwill loss by comparing the implied fair value of the reporting unit goodwill with the carrying amount of that goodwill and recognize a loss by the excess of the latter over the former.

The implied fair value of goodwill is determined in the same way that goodwill is recognized in a business combination. The entity allocates the fair value of a reporting unit to all the assets and liabilities of that unit as if the reporting unit had been acquired in a business combination and the fair value of the reporting unit was the price paid to acquire that unit. The excess of the fair value of the unit over the amounts assigned to its other assets and its liabilities is the implied fair value of goodwill. That process is performed only for purposes of testing goodwill for impairment. The entity shall neither write up nor write down a recognized asset or liability, nor should it recognize a previously unrecognized intangible asset as a result of the allocation process (FAS-142, par. 21).

If the determination of the amount of loss due to the impairment of goodwill is not complete when the financial statements are issued and a goodwill impairment loss is considered probable and can be reasonably estimated, the best estimate of that loss shall be recognized in the financial statements (FAS-142, par. 22).

Fair Value Measurements

The fair value of an asset or liability is the amount at which that asset or liability could be bought or incurred, or sold or settled, in a current transaction—other than a forced liquidation—between willing parties. Quoted market prices are the best evidence of fair value. If quoted market prices are not available, an estimate of fair value should be based on the best information available. This may involve prices of similar assets and liabilities and the use of other valuation techniques, such as a present value technique. An estimate of fair value may be based on multiples of earnings or revenue or another similar performance measure if that technique is consistent with the objectives of measuring fair value (FAS-142, pars. 23–25).

Testing for Impairment

Goodwill is tested for impairment on an annual basis, or more frequently if events and circumstances change (FAS-142, par. 26). Examples of such events and circumstances are (FAS-142, par. 28):

- A significant adverse change in legal factors or in the business climate
- An adverse action or assessment by a regulator
- Unanticipated competition
- Loss of key personnel
- An expectation that a reporting unit or a significant portion of a reporting unit will be sold or otherwise disposed of
- Recognition of a goodwill loss in the financial statements of a subsidiary that is a component of a reporting unit

A determination of fair value of reporting unit may be carried forward from one year to the next if all of the following criteria are met (FAS-142, par. 27):

- The assets and liabilities that make up the reporting unit have not changed significantly since the most recent fair value determination.
- The most recent fair value determination resulted in an amount that exceeded the carrying amount of the reporting unit by a substantial amount.
- Based on an analysis of events and circumstances that have changed since the most recent fair value determination, the likelihood that a current fair value determination would be less than the current carrying amount of the reporting unit is remote.

Assigning Assets and Liabilities to Reporting Units

For purposes of testing goodwill impairment, acquired assets and assumed liabilities are assigned to a reporting unit if both of the following criteria are met:

- The asset will be employed in, or the liability relates to, the operations of a reporting unit.
- The asset or liability will be considered in determining the fair value of the reporting unit.

Assets and liabilities may be employed in the operations of more than one reporting unit. The method used to determine the amount of such assets and liabilities to be assigned to a reporting unit must be reasonable and supported, and applied consistently (FAS-142, pars. 32–33).

Assigning Goodwill to Reporting Units

For purposes of testing goodwill for impairment, all goodwill that is acquired in a business combination must be assigned to one or more reporting units as of the acquisition date. Goodwill is assigned to reporting units on the basis of expected benefits from the synergies of the combination, even though other assets or liabilities of the acquired entity may not be assigned to those reporting units. Goodwill may be divided among multiple reporting units, and the method of allocating goodwill must be reasonable and supportable, and applied consistently (FAS-142, par. 34).

Subsidiary Goodwill

Goodwill recognized by a public or nonpublic subsidiary in its separate financial statements prepared in accordance with GAAP shall be accounted for in accordance with FAS-142. Such subsidiary goodwill shall be tested for impairment in accordance with FAS-142 using the subsidiary's reporting unit. If a goodwill impairment loss is recognized at the subsidiary level, goodwill of the reporting unit(s), at which the subsidiary resides, must be tested for impairment if the event that gave rise to the loss at the subsidiary level would more likely than not reduce the fair value of the reporting unit below its carrying amount (FAS-142, par. 37).

Disposal of a Reporting Unit

When a reporting unit is to be disposed of in its entirety, goodwill of that unit shall be included in the carrying amount of the reporting unit in determining any gain or loss on disposal. When a portion of a reporting unit that constitutes a business is to be disposed of, goodwill associated with that business shall be included in the carrying amount of the business in determining the gain or loss on disposal. The amount of goodwill included is based on the relative fair value of the business to be disposed of and the portion of the reporting unit that will be retained (FAS-142, par. 39).

Financial Statement Presentation and Disclosure

At a minimum, all intangible assets shall be combined and presented as a separate line item in the statement of financial position (balance sheet). This is not intended to preclude separate presentation of individual intangible assets or classes of intangible assets. Amortization expense and impairment losses on intangible assets are required to be presented in the income statement as separate items within continuing operations. An impairment loss is not recognized as a change in accounting principle (FAS-142, par. 42).

The aggregate amount of goodwill shall be presented as a separate line item in the statement of financial position. The aggregate amount of goodwill impairment losses shall be presented as a separate line item in the income statement before the amount of income from continuing operations, unless the goodwill impairment is associated with discontinued operations, in which case the impairment loss is presented within discontinued operations (FAS-142, par. 43).

In the period of acquisition, the following information is required for intangible assets acquired, whether acquired individually or with a group of assets (FAS-142, par. 44):

- For intangible assets subject to amortization:
  - The total amount assigned and the amount assigned to any major intangible asset class
  - The amount of any significant residual value, in total and by major intangible asset class
  - The weighted-average amortization period in total and by major intangible asset class

- For intangible assets not subject to amortization, the total amount assigned and the amount assigned to any major intangible asset class.

- The amount of research and development assets acquired and written off in the period, and the line item in the income statement in which the amounts written off are aggregated.

The following information is required in the financial statements or related notes for each period for which a statement of financial position (balance sheet) is presented (FAS-142, par. 45):

- The gross carrying amount and accumulated amortization, in total and by major intangible asset class
- The aggregate amortization expense for the period
- The estimated aggregate amortization expense for each of the five succeeding years

- For intangible assets not subject to amortization, the total carrying amount and the carrying amount for each major intangible asset class

- Changes in the carrying amount of goodwill during the period, including the aggregate amount of goodwill acquired, the aggregate amount of impairment losses recognized, and the amount of goodwill included in the gain or loss on disposal of all or a portion of a reporting unit

For each impairment loss recognized related to an intangible asset, the following information is required to be disclosed (FAS-142, par. 46):

- A description of the impaired intangible asset, and the facts and circumstances leading to the impairment

- The amount of the impairment loss and the method of determining fair value

- The caption in the income statement (or the statement of activities) in which the impairment loss is aggregated

- The segment in which the impaired intangible asset is reported under FAS-131, if applicable

For each goodwill impairment loss recognized, the following information is required to be disclosed (FAS-142, par. 47):

- A description of the facts and circumstances leading to the impairment

Figure 23-1: Summary of Accounting for Intangible Assets by FAS-142

Part I: At point of acquisition

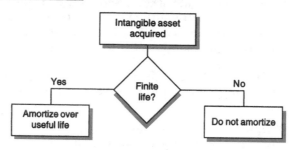

Part II: Subsequent to point of acquisition

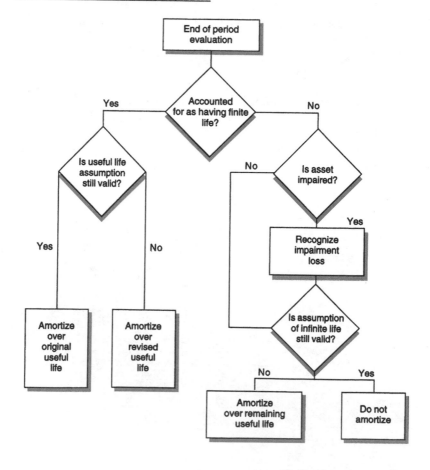

- The amount of the impairment loss and the method of determining the fair value of the associated reporting unit
- If a recognized impairment loss is an estimate that has not yet been finalized, that fact and the reasons therefore and, in subsequent years, the nature and amount of any significant adjustments made to the initial estimate of the impairment loss

MUTUAL AND NOT-FOR-PROFIT ENTERPRISES

FAS-142 shall not be applied to previously r ecognized goodwill and intangible assets acquired in a business combination between two or more mutual enterprises acquired in a combination between not-for-profit organizations or arising from the acquisition of a for-profit business by a not-for-profit organization until interpretive guidance related to the purchase method to those transactions is issued at a future date. These transactions shall continue to be accounted for in accordance with APB-17 (FAS-142, par. 48c).

RELATED CHAPTERS IN 2009 *GAAP GUIDE* *LEVEL A*

Chapter 4, "Business Combinations"
Chapter 11, "Depreciable Assets and Depreciation"
Chapter 12, "Development Stage Enterprises"
Chapter 14, "Equity Method"
Chapter 20, "Impairment of Long-Lived Assets"
Chapter 39, "Research and Development"
Chapter 42, "Segment Reporting"
Chapter 47, "Banking and Thrift Institutions"

RELATED CHAPTERS IN 2009 *GAAP GUIDE* *LEVELS B, C, AND D*

Chapter 6, "Business Combinations"
Chapter 7, "Capitalization and Expense Recognition Concepts"
Chapter 14, "Equity Method"
Chapter 19, "Impairment of Long-Lived Assets"
Chapter 21, "Intangible Assets"
Chapter 34, "Research and Development"
Chapter 37, "Segment Reporting"

RELATED CHAPTERS IN 2009 *INTERNATIONAL ACCOUNTING/FINANCIAL REPORTING STANDARDS GUIDE*

Chapter 7, "Business Combinations"
Chapter 14, "The Equity Method"
Chapter 19, "Impairment of Assets"
Chapter 21, "Intangible Assets"
Chapter 27, "Property, Plant, and Equipment"
Chapter 31, "Segment Reporting"

CHAPTER 24
INTEREST COSTS CAPITALIZED

CONTENTS

OVERVIEW

Under certain conditions, interest is capitalized as part of the acquisition cost of an asset. Interest is capitalized only during the period of time required to complete and prepare the asset for its intended use, which may be either *sale or use within the business*. Capitalization of interest is based on the principle that a better measure of acquisition cost is achieved when certain interest costs are capitalized. This results in a better matching of revenue and costs in future periods.

Promulgated GAAP for the capitalization of interest costs are found in the following pronouncements:

FAS-34   Capitalization of Interest Cost

FAS-42   Determining Materiality for Capitalization of Interest Cost

FAS-58   Capitalization of Interest Cost in Financial Statements That Include Investments Accounted for by the Equity Method

FAS-62   Capitalization of Interest Cost in Situations Involving Certain Tax-Exempt Borrowings and Certain Gifts and Grants

FIN-33   Applying FASB Statement No. 34 to Oil and Gas Producing Operations Accounted for by the Full Cost Method

BACKGROUND

The basis of accounting for depreciable fixed assets is cost, including all normal expenditures of readying an asset for use are capitalized as part of acquisition cost. Unnecessary expenditures that do not add to the utility of the asset should be charged to expense.

FAS-34 (Capitalization of Interest Cost) covers the promulgated GAAP on the capitalization of interest costs on certain qualifying assets that are undergoing activities to prepare them for their intended use. FAS-42 (Determining Materiality for Capitalization of Interest Cost) amends FAS-34 and requires that the same materiality tests applied by regular GAAP be applied to the materiality of capitalizing interest cost.

FAS-58 (Capitalization of Interest Cost in Financial Statements That Include Investments Accounted for by the Equity Method) extends the provisions of FAS-34 to provide for capitalization of interest cost on equity funds, loans, and advances made by investors to certain investees that are accounted for by the equity method as described by APB-18 (The Equity Method of Accounting for Investments in Common Stock).

FAS-62 (Capitalization of Interest Cost in Situations Involving Certain Tax-Exempt Borrowings and Certain Gifts and Grants)

amends FAS-34 to provide special treatment in capitalizing interest costs on qualifying assets that are acquired with (*a*) the proceeds of tax-exempt borrowings and (*b*) gifts or grants that are restricted for the sole purpose of acquiring a specific asset.

> **OBSERVATION:** The basis of capitalizing certain interest costs is that the cost of an asset should include all costs necessary to bring the asset to the condition and location for its intended use. The requirements of FAS-34 to capitalize interest cost may result in a lack of comparability among reporting entities, depending on their method of financing major asset acquisitions. For example, Company A and Company B both acquire an identical asset for $10 million that requires three years to complete for its intended use. Company A pays cash, and at the end of three years, the total cost of the asset is $10 million. In addition, assume that Company A also had net income of $2 million a year for each of the three years and had no interest expense. Assume also that Company B had $1.5 million net income for each of the three years after deducting $500,000 of interest expense per year. If Company B qualifies for capitalized interest costs under FAS-34, it would reflect $2 million per year net income and not show any interest expense. On the balance sheet of Company B at the end of three years, the identical asset would appear at a cost of $11.5 million. Future depreciation charges will vary between the two companies by a total of $1.5 million. Although the interest cost may be necessary to Company B, it does not add to the utility of the asset.

QUALIFYING ASSETS

Acquisition Period

Interest cost must be capitalized for all assets that require an *acquisition period* to get them ready for their intended use. *Acquisition period* is defined as the period commencing with the first expenditure for a qualifying asset and ending when the asset is substantially complete and ready for its intended use. Thus, before interest costs can be capitalized, expenditures must have been made for the qualifying asset, providing an investment base on which to compute interest, and activities that are required to get the asset ready for its intended use must actually be in progress (FAS-34, par. 8).

FAS-42 was issued to reaffirm that the usual rules of materiality embodied in GAAP must be followed in determining the materiality for the capitalization of interest costs. One of the purposes of FAS-42 was to eliminate language in FAS-34 that implies capitalization of interest costs can be avoided in certain circumstances. Thus, in applying the provisions of FAS-34, all the usual materiality tests used in applying other promulgated GAAP should also be used in determining the materiality for capitalization of interest costs (FAS-42, par. 2).

Intended Use

Capitalization of interest cost is applicable for assets that require an acquisition period to prepare them for their intended use. Assets to which capitalized interest must be allocated include both (1) assets acquired for a company's own use and (2) assets acquired for sale in the ordinary course of business (FAS-34, par. 9). Thus, inventory items that require a long time to produce, such as a real estate development, qualify for capitalization of interest costs. However, interest costs are not capitalized for inventories that are routinely produced in large quantities on a repetitive basis (FAS-34, par. 10).

> **OBSERVATION:** The FASB concluded that the benefit of capitalizing interest costs on inventories that are routinely produced in large quantities does not justify the cost. Thus, interest costs should not be capitalized for inventories that are routinely produced in large quantities.

Capitalization of interest cost is not permitted (*a*) for assets that are ready for their intended use or that are actually being used in the earning activities of a business and (*b*) for assets that are not being used in the earning activities of a business and that are not undergoing the activities required to get them ready for use (FAS-34, par. 10).

COMPUTING INTEREST COST TO BE CAPITALIZED

The amount of interest cost that may be capitalized for any accounting period may not exceed the actual interest cost (from any source) that is incurred by an enterprise during that same accounting period (FAS-34, par. 15). In addition to interest paid and/or accrued on debt instruments, interest imputed in accordance with APB-21 (Interest on Receivables and Payables) and interest recognized on capital leases in accordance with FAS-13 (Accounting for Leases) are available for capitalization. FAS-34 specifically prohibits imputing interest costs on any equity funds. In consolidated financial statements, this limitation on the maximum amount of interest cost that may be capitalized in a period should be applied on a consolidated basis.

> **OBSERVATION:** Footnote 4 to paragraph 16 of FAS-87 (Employers' Accounting for Pensions) states that, "The interest cost component of net periodic pension cost shall not be considered to be interest for purposes of applying FASB Statement No. 34, Capitalization of Interest Cost."
> Similarly, footnote 8 to paragraph 22 of FAS-106 (Employers' Accounting for Postretirement Benefits Other Than Pensions) states that, "The interest cost component of postretirement benefit cost shall not be considered interest for purposes of

applying FASB Statement No. 34, Capitalization of Interest Cost."

☛ **PRACTICE POINTER:** A logical starting point for applying FAS-34 and related pronouncements is to determine the total amount of interest that was incurred and that is available for capitalization as a cost of a qualifying asset. If a company incurs little or no qualifying interest on debt instruments, interest imputed in accordance with APB-21, or interest on capital leases, the requirement to capitalize interest may not be effective, even though the company may have invested in assets that would otherwise require interest capitalization.

Average Accumulated Investment

To compute the amount of interest cost to be capitalized for a particular accounting period, the average accumulated investment in a qualifying asset during that period must be determined. To determine the average accumulated investment, each expenditure must be *weighted* for the time it was outstanding during the particular accounting period.

Illustration of Computing Average Accumulated Investment

In the acquisition of a qualifying asset, a calendar year company expends $225,000 on January 1, 20X8; $360,000 on March 1, 20X8; and $180,000 on November 1, 20X8. The average accumulated investment for 20X8 is computed as follows:

Amount of Expenditure	Period from Expenditure to End of Year	Average Investment
$225,000	12 months (12/12)	$225,000
360,000	10 months (10/12)	300,000
180,000	2 months (2/12)	30,000
$765,000		$555,000

Identification of Interest Rates

If a specific borrowing is made to acquire the qualifying asset, the interest rate incurred on that borrowing may be used to determine the amount of interest costs to be capitalized. That interest rate is applied to the average accumulated investment for the period to calculate the amount of capitalized interest cost on the qualifying asset. Capitalized interest cost on average accumulated investments in excess of the amount of the specific borrowing is calculated by the use of the weighted-average interest rate incurred on other borrowings outstanding during the period (FAS-34, par. 13).

If no specific borrowing is made to acquire the qualifying asset, the weighted-average interest rate incurred on other borrowings outstanding during the period is used to determine the amount of interest cost to be capitalized. The weighted-average interest rate is applied to the average accumulated investment for the period to calculate the amount of capitalized interest cost on the qualifying asset. Judgment may be required to identify and select the appropriate specific borrowings that should be used in determining the weighted-average interest rate. The objective should be to obtain a reasonable cost of financing for the qualifying asset that could have been avoided if the asset had not been acquired (FAS-34, par. 14).

> ☛ **PRACTICE POINTER:** In determining the weighted average interest rate for purposes of capitalizing interest, take care not to overlook interest that is available for capitalization even though it has another specific purpose. For example, a company might have interest on mortgage debt on buildings and plant assets. Unless that interest already is being capitalized into a different asset under FAS-34, it is available for capitalization despite the fact that it was incurred specifically to finance the acquisition of a different asset.

Progress payments received from the buyer of a qualifying asset are deducted in the computation of the average amount of accumulated expenditures during a period. Nonetheless, the determination of the average amount of accumulated expenditures for a period may be reasonably estimated (FAS-34, par 16).

Illustration of Calculating Weighted-Average Interest Rate

A company has the following three debt issues outstanding during a year in which interest must be capitalized as part of the cost of a plant assets:

$1,000,000 par value, 8% interest rate
$1,500,000 par value, 9% interest rate
$1,200,000 par value, 10% interest rate

The weighted-average interest rate is computed as follows:

$1,000,000 × 8%	=	$ 80,000
1,500,000 × 9%	=	135,000
1,800,000 × 10%	=	180,000
$4,300,000	=	$395,000

$395,000/$4,300,000 = 9.19%

Interest available for capitalization is $395,000. Assuming none of the debt issues relates directly to the asset for which interest is being capitalized, interest is charged to the cost of the asset at a 9.19% interest rate applied to the average investment made on the asset during the year. If, instead, one of the debt issues relates directly to the asset for which interest is being capitalized, interest may be charged at the interest rate applicable to that debt issue on the investment equal to the amount of that debt. Interest on any remaining investment is calculated at the weighted-average interest rate for the remaining debt.

Capitalization Period

The interest capitalization period starts when three conditions are met (FAS-34, par. 17):

1. Expenditures have occurred.

2. Activities necessary to prepare the asset (including administrative activities before construction) have begun.

3. Interest cost has been incurred.

Interest is not capitalized during delays or interruptions initially by the entity, except for brief interruptions, that occur during the acquisition or development stage of the qualifying asset. However, interest continues to be capitalized during externally imposed delays or interruptions (e.g., strikes) (FAS-34, par. 17).

When the qualifying asset is substantially complete and ready for its intended use, the capitalization of interest ceases. The qualifying asset may be completed in independent parts (i.e., the parts can be used separately from the rest of the project, like units in a condominium) or in dependent parts (i.e., parts that, although complete, cannot be used until other parts are finished, like subassemblies of a machine). Interest capitalization ceases for an independent part when it is substantially complete and ready for its intended use. For dependent parts of a qualifying asset, however, interest capitalization does not stop until all dependent parts are substantially complete and ready for their intended use (FAS-34, par. 18).

SPECIAL APPLICATIONS

Equity Method Investments

Under the provisions of FAS-58, an investor's qualifying assets, for the purposes of capitalizing interest costs under FAS-34, include equity funds, loans, and advances made to investees accounted for by the equity method (FAS-58, par. 5). Thus, an investor must capitalize interest costs on such qualifying assets if, during that period, the investee is undergoing activities necessary to start its planned principal operations and such activities include the use of funds to acquire qualifying assets for its operations. The investor does not capitalize any interest costs on or after the date that the investee actually begins its planned principal operations (FAS-58, par. 6).

> ☞ **PRACTICE POINTER:** The term *planned principal operations* has the same meaning as used in FAS-7 (Accounting and Reporting for Development Stage Enterprises). Under the provisions of FAS-7, a development stage company is one that devotes substantially all of its efforts to establishing a new business and (*a*) planned principal operations have not commenced or (*b*) planned principal operations have commenced, but there has been no significant revenue therefrom.

For the purposes of FAS-58, the term *investor* means both the parent company and all consolidated subsidiaries (FAS-58, par. 3). Thus, all qualifying assets of a parent company and its consolidated subsidiaries that appear in the consolidated balance sheet are subject to the interest capitalization provisions of FAS-34 (as amended). FAS-58 expressly states that it does not affect the accounting or reporting of capitalized interest cost in an investee's separate financial statements (FAS-58, par. 4).

Capitalized interest costs on an investment accounted for by the equity method are included in the carrying amount of the investment (FAS-58, par. 7). Up to the date on which the planned principal operations of the investee begin, the investor's carrying amount of the investment, which includes capitalized interest costs (if any), may exceed the underlying equity in the investment. If the investor cannot relate the excess carrying amount of the investment to specific identifiable assets of the investee, the difference is considered goodwill (APB-18, par. 19(n)).

Any interest cost capitalized under the provisions of FAS-58 is not changed in restating financial statements of prior periods. Thus, if an unconsolidated investee is subsequently consolidated in the investor's financial statements as a result of increased ownership or a voluntary change by the reporting entity, interest costs capitalized in accordance with FAS-58 are not changed if restatement of financial statements is necessary (FAS-58, par. 8).

Tax-Exempt Borrowings and Gifts and Grants

Under the provisions of FAS-34, capitalized interest cost for a qualifying asset is determined by applying either a specific interest rate or a weighted-average interest rate to the average accumulated expenditures during a particular period for the qualifying asset. An underlying premise in FAS-34 is that borrowings usually cannot be identified with specific qualifying assets. The financing policies of most enterprises are planned to meet general funding objectives, and the identification of specific borrowings with specific assets is considered highly subjective.

FAS-62 concludes that different circumstances are involved in the acquisition of a qualifying asset with tax-exempt borrowings, such as industrial revenue bonds and pollution control bonds. The tax-exempt borrowings, temporary interest income on unused funds, and construction expenditures for the qualifying asset are so integrated that they must be accounted for as a single transaction (FAS-62, par. 2). Thus, FAS-62 amends FAS-34 to provide for the capitalization of interest cost for any portion of a qualifying asset that is acquired with tax-exempt borrowings, as follows (FAS-62, par. 4):

Capitalization Period

Interest cost is capitalized from the date of the tax-exempt borrowings to the date that the qualifying asset is ready for its intended use (FAS-62, par. 7).

Amount of Capitalized Interest Cost

The amount of capitalized interest cost allowable under FAS-62 is equal to the total actual interest cost on the tax-exempt borrowing, less any interest income earned on temporary investments of the tax exempt funds. The net cost of interest on the tax-exempt borrowing is capitalized and added to the acquisition cost of the related qualifying asset (FAS-62, par. 4).

External Restriction Requirement

FAS-62 applies only when the qualifying asset is financed by tax-exempt borrowing, in which the use of the borrowed funds is restricted to acquiring the assets or servicing the related debt. The restriction must be *external*, that is, imposed by law, contract, or other authority outside the enterprise that borrows the funds.

FAS-62 does not permit the capitalization of interest cost on any portion of a qualifying asset that is acquired with a gift or grant that is restricted to the acquisition of the specified qualifying asset. Restricted interest income on temporary investment of funds is considered an addition to the restricted gift or grant (FAS-62, par. 5).

> **OBSERVATION:** FAS-62 concludes that no interest cost should be capitalized on qualifying assets acquired by restricted gifts

or grants, because there is no economic cost of financing involved in acquiring an asset with a gift or grant. In addition, any interest earned on temporary investment of funds from a gift or grant is, in substance, part of the gift or grant.

Full Cost Method in Extractive Industries

FIN-33 covers the application of FAS-34 to oil and gas producing activities that are being accounted for by the full cost method.

Unproved properties and major developments that represent unusually significant investments are assets which qualify for capitalization of interest costs, if the following conditions are met (FIN-33, par. 2):

- Exploration or development activities are in progress.
- The assets are not currently being depreciated, depleted, or amortized.

Other assets that qualify for capitalization of interest costs are significant properties or projects within a nonproducing cost center on which exploration or development activities are in progress (FAS-34, par. 11).

All assets that are currently being depreciated, depleted, or amortized are considered in use in the earning activities of the business and do not qualify for capitalization of interest costs (FAS-34, par. 10).

Disposition of Capitalized Interest

If capitalized interest costs are added to the overall cost of an asset, the total cost of the asset, including capitalized interest, may exceed the net realizable or other lower value of the asset that is required by GAAP. In this event, FAS-34 requires that the provision to reduce the asset cost to the lower value required by GAAP be increased. Thus, the total asset cost, including capitalized interest, less the provision, will equal the lower value for the asset that is required by GAAP (FAS-34, par. 19).

Capitalized interest costs become an integral part of the acquisition costs of an asset and should be accounted for as such in the event of disposal of the asset (FAS-34, par. 20).

DISCLOSURE REQUIREMENTS

The total amount of interest costs incurred and charged to expense during the period and the amount of interest costs, if any, which has been capitalized during the period, should be disclosed in the financial statements or notes thereto (FAS-34, par. 21).

Illustration of the Application of FAS-34

On January 1, 20X8, Poll Powerhouse borrowed $300,000 from its bank at an annual rate of 12%. The principal amount plus interest is due on January 1, 20Y0. The funds from this loan are specifically designated for the construction of a new plant facility. On February 1, 20X8, Poll paid $15,000 for architects' fees and for fees for filing a project application with the state government.

On March 1, 20X8, Poll received state approval for the project and began construction. The following summarizes the costs incurred on this project.

20X8

February 1 (architects' and filing fees)	$ 15,000
April 1	150,000
September 1	60,000

20X9

January 1	1,000
March 1	360,000
November 1	180,000
Total Project Cost	$766,000

The $1,000 is a miscellaneous cost and was expensed in 20X9, since it was determined by Poll to be immaterial.

The following schedule summarizes the additional borrowings of Poll as of December 31, 20X9:

Borrowing Date	Amount	Maturity Date	Annual Interest Rate
Mar. 1, 20X8	$1,000,000	Feb. 28, 20Y0	13%
Oct. 1, 20X9	$ 500,000	Sept. 30, 20Y1	14%

From February 1, 20X9, to March 31, 20X9, a major strike of construction workers occurred, halting all construction activity during this period.

In August 20X9, Poll voluntarily halted construction for the entire month because the chief executive officer did not want construction to continue without her supervision during her scheduled vacation.

Calculation of Interest

Poll's new plant facility is a qualifying asset under the provisions of FAS-34 and is subject to interest capitalization. The interest capitalization period begins on the first date that an expenditure is made by Poll, which was for architects' fees, February 1, 20X8.

To compute the interest capitalization for 20X8, the average accumulated expenditures for 20X8 are first calculated as follows:

Amount of Expenditure	Period from Expenditure to End of Year	Average Investment
$ 15,000	11 months (11/12)	$ 13,750
150,000	9 months (9/12)	112,500
60,000	4 months (4/12)	20,000
$225,000		$146,250

Next, the average investment amounts are multiplied by the interest rate on the borrowing (12%). This rate is used because Poll has specifically associated the borrowing with the construction of the new plant facility, and the average accumulated investment ($146,250) do not exceed the amount of the borrowing ($300,000). Therefore, the interest capitalized for 20X8 is computed as follows:

Average accumulated investment	$146,250
Interest rate	12%
Capitalizable interest cost—20X8	$ 17,550

Since Poll incurred $144,333 of interest costs [($300,000 × 12%) + ($1,000,000 × 13% × 10/12)], the full $17,550 must be capitalized.

The investment in the asset for 20X8 ($225,000 + $17,550 capitalized interest = $242,550) is included as part of the base to compute 20X9 capitalizable interest cost. One further adjustment is necessary to calculate the average accumulated expenditures for 20X9. The plant facility was completed on December 31, 20X9, but there were two interruptions in construction in 20X9. Interest is capitalized during delays or interruptions that are externally imposed, or during delays inherent in acquiring the qualifying asset. However, interest is not capitalized during delays or interruptions that are caused internally by an enterprise, unless they are brief. Thus, in this problem, interest capitalization continues during the externally imposed strike. However, interest capitalization ceases during August 20X9, because the CEO's vacation is a voluntary interruption.

The average accumulated investment for 20X9 is computed as follows:

Amount of Expenditure	Period from Expenditure to End of Year, Less One Month of Interruption	Average Investment
$242,550	11 months (11/12)	$222,338
360,000	9 months (9/12)	270,000
180,000	2 months (2/12)	30,000
$782,550		$522,338

Note: The $180,000 was expended on November 1, 20X9, after the interruption, so no adjustment need be made to the average expenditure of $30,000 for the interruption.

The $1,000 miscellaneous cost is not included, since Poll decided that this amount was immaterial and expensed it.

If the average accumulated investment for the qualifying asset exceeds the amount of the specific borrowing made to construct the asset, the capitalization rate applicable to the excess is the weighted-average interest rate incurred on other borrowings. In this problem, the computation of the excess investment over the original loan amount is as follows:

Average investment through December 31, 20X9	$522,338
Less: Amount of original loan	300,000
Excess investment	$222,338

Thus, in 20X9, interest on $222,338 of the $522,338 average investment is capitalized using the weighted-average borrowing rate, whereas interest on the balance of $300,000 is capitalized using the interest rate on the original loan made specifically to acquire the qualifying asset. The weighted-average rate on the other borrowings is computed as follows:

Amount	Weighted Amount	Rate	Annual Interest
$1,000,000	$1,000,000	13%	$130,000
500,000	125,000 (3 mos.)	14%	$ 17,500
$1,500,000	$1,125,000		$147,500

$$\frac{\$147,500}{\$1,125,000} = 13.11\% \text{ weighted-average interest rate.}$$

The interest cost to be capitalized for 20X9 is computed as follows:

$300,000	×	12.00%	=	$36,000
222,338	×	13.11%	=	29,149
$522,338				$65,149

Since Poll incurred $183,500 [($300,000 × 12%) + ($1,000,000 × 13%) + ($500,000 × 14% × 3/12)] of interest, the full $65,149 is capitalizable as part of the acquisition cost of the asset in 20X9.

The total interest capitalized on the asset is $82,699 ($17,550 in 20X8 plus $65,149 in 20X9). The total asset cost at the end of 20X9 is as follows:

Expenditures other than interest	$765,000
Interest cost capitalized	$ 82,699
	$847,699

OBSERVATION: In this illustration, interest capitalized in 20X9 was based on an investment amount from 20X8 that included the amount of interest capitalized in 20X8. The authors have not found specific authoritative guidance that supports the inclusion of previously capitalized interest in the investment base, but believes this is consistent with the inclusion of interest in other situations and is logical in the circumstances.

RELATED CHAPTERS IN 2009 *GAAP GUIDE* *LEVEL A*

Chapter 11, "Depreciable Assets and Depreciation"
Chapter 14, "Equity Method"
Chapter 25, "Interest on Receivables and Payables"
Chapter 29, "Leases"
Chapter 52, "Oil and Gas"

RELATED CHAPTERS IN 2009 *GAAP GUIDE* *LEVELS B, C, AND D*

Chapter 7, "Capitalization and Expense Recognition Concepts"
Chapter 22, "Interest on Receivables and Payables"
Chapter 26, "Leases"

RELATED CHAPTERS IN 2009 *INTERNATIONAL* *ACCOUNTING/FINANCIAL REPORTING* *STANDARDS GUIDE*

Chapter 6, "Borrowing Costs"
Chapter 14, "Equity Method"
Chapter 18, "Government Grants and Government Assistance"
Chapter 25, "Leases"
Chapter 27, "Property, Plant, and Equipment"
Chapter 35, "Mineral Resources"

CHAPTER 25
INTEREST ON RECEIVABLES
AND PAYABLES

CONTENTS

OVERVIEW

Business transactions may involve the exchange of cash or other assets for a note or other instrument. When the interest rate on the instrument is consistent with the market rate at the time of the transaction, the face amount of the instrument is assumed to be equal to the value of the other asset(s) exchanged. An interest rate that is different from the prevailing market rate, however, implies that the face amount of the instrument may not equal the value of the other asset(s) exchanged. In this case, it may be necessary to impute interest that is not stated as part of the instrument, or to recognize interest at a rate other than that stated in the instrument.

GAAP in the area of recognizing interest on receivables and payables are found in the following pronouncement:

APB-21 Interest on Receivables and Payables

BACKGROUND

APB-21 (Interest on Receivables and Payables) is the main source of GAAP on imputing interest on receivables and payables. However, APB-21 excludes receivables and payables under the following conditions (APB-21, par. 3):

- They arise in the ordinary course of business and are due in approximately one year or less.

- Their repayment will be applied to the purchase price of the property, goods, or services to which they relate rather than requiring a transfer of cash.

- They represent security or retainage deposits.

- They arise in the ordinary course of business of a lending institution.

- They arise from transactions between a parent and its subsidiaries, or between subsidiaries of a common parent.

- Their interest rate is determined by a governmental agency.

Receivables and payables that are not specifically excluded from the provisions of APB-21 and that are contractual rights to receive or pay money at a fixed or determinable date must be recorded at their present value if (*a*) the interest rate is not stated or (*b*) the stated interest rate is unreasonable (APB-21, par. 12).

> **OBSERVATION:** This is an application of the basic principle of substance over form in that the substance of the instrument (interest-bearing), rather than the form of the instrument (noninterest-bearing or bearing interest at an unreasonable rate), becomes the basis for recording.

CIRCUMSTANCES REQUIRING IMPUTED INTEREST

A note issued or received in a noncash transaction contains two elements to be valued: (1) the principal amount for the property, goods, or services exchanged and (2) an interest factor for the use of funds over the period of the note. These types of notes must be recorded at their present value. Any difference between the face amount of the note and its present value is a discount or premium that is amortized over the life of the note.

☛ **PRACTICE POINTER:** The interest rate on a note that results from a business transaction entered into at arm's length is generally presumed to be fair. If no interest is stated or if the interest stated appears unreasonable, however, record the substance of the transaction. Further, if rights or privileges are attached to the note, evaluate them separately.

For example, a beer distributor lends $5,000 for two years at no interest to a customer who wishes to purchase bar equipment. There is a tacit agreement that the customer will buy the distributor's products. In this event, a present value must be established for the note receivable, and the difference between the face of the note ($5,000) and its present value must be considered an additional cost of doing business for the beer distributor.

Circumstances requiring interest to be imputed as specified in APB-21 are summarized in Figure 25-1.

The present value techniques used in APB-21 should not be applied to estimates of a contractual property or other obligations that are assumed in connection with a sale of property, goods, or services such as an estimated warranty for product performance.

OBSERVATION: Interest that is imputed on certain receivables and payables in accordance with APB-21 is eligible for capitalization under the provisions of FAS-34 (see the chapter in this *Guide* titled "Interest Costs Capitalized").

APPLYING APB-21 PRINCIPLES

Determining Present Value

There is no predetermined formula for determining an appropriate interest rate. *However, the objective is to approximate what the rate would have been, using the same terms and conditions, if it had been negotiated by an independent lender.* The following factors should be considered (APB-21, par. 13):

- Credit rating of the borrower
- Restrictive covenants or collateral involved
- Prevailing market rates
- Rate at which the debtor can borrow funds

The appropriate interest rate depends on a combination of the above factors.

☛ **PRACTICE POINTER:** In determining an appropriate interest rate for purposes of imputing interest for the purchaser in a

Figure 25-1: Circumstances Indicating a Need to Impute Interest

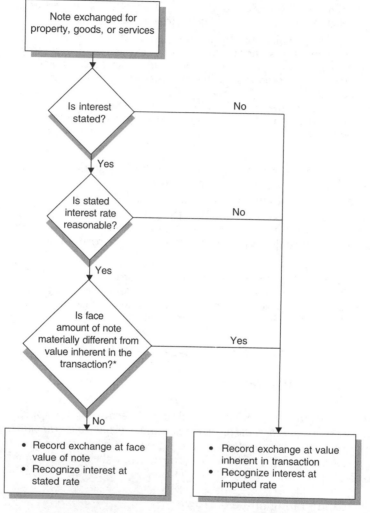

* Value inherent in transaction is the fair value of the property, goods, or services or the market value of the note, whichever is more readily determinable.

transaction, a starting point might be the most recent borrowing rate. The more recent the borrowing, the more appropriate that rate may be. Even if the borrowing rate is recent, however, give consideration to the impact that the additional debt from the earlier borrowing would likely have on the company's next borrowing. The size of the transaction for which interest is being imputed relative to other outstanding debt also may be an important factor in determining an appropriate rate.

Discount and Premium

The difference between the present value and the face amount of the receivable or the payable represents the amount of premium or discount. A discount exists if the present value of the total cash flow of the note (face amount plus stated interest), using the appropriate rate of interest, is *less* than the face amount of the note. A premium exists if the present value of the total proceeds of the note (face amount plus stated interest), using the appropriate rate of interest, is *more* than the face amount of the note.

The premium or discount is amortized over the life of the note, using a constant rate on any outstanding balance. This method is called the *interest method* and illustrated at the end of this chapter (APB-21, par. 15).

The premium or discount that arises from the use of present values on cash and noncash transactions is inseparable from the related asset or liability. Therefore, premiums and discounts are added to or deducted from their related asset or liability in the balance sheet. Discounts or premiums resulting from imputing interest are not classified as deferred charges or credits (APB-21, par. 16).

Disclosure

A description of the receivable or payable, the effective interest rate, and the face amount of the note should be disclosed in the financial statements or notes thereto. Issue costs are reported separately in the balance sheet as deferred charges (APB-21, par. 16).

Illustration of Interest Imputed and Accounted for on a Noninterest-Bearing Note

A manufacturer sells a machine for $10,000 and accepts a $10,000 note receivable bearing no interest for five years; 10% is an appropriate interest rate. The initial journal entry would be:

Note receivable	10,000.00	
Sales (present value at 10%)		6,209.00
Unamortized discount on note		3,791.00

The manufacturer records the note at its face amount but records the sale at the present value of the note because that is the value of the note today. The difference between the face amount of the note and its present value is recorded as *unamortized discount on note*.

The *interest method* is used to produce a constant rate, which is applied to any outstanding balance. In the above example, the present value of $6,209 was recorded for the $10,000 sale using the appropriate interest rate of 10% for the five-year term of the note. The difference between the $10,000 sale and its present value of $6,209 is $3,791, which was recorded as unamortized discount on note. The 10% rate, when applied to each annual outstanding balance for the same five years, will result in amortization of the discount on the note, as follows:

		Amortization of Discount on the Note
Original balance	$ 6,209.00	$3,791.00
Year 1, 10%	620.90	(620.90)
Remaining balance	$ 6,829.90	$3,170.10
Year 2, 10%	682.99	(682.99)
Remaining balance	$ 7,512.89	$2,487.11
Year 3, 10%	751.29	(751.29)
Remaining balance	$ 8,264.18	$1,735.82
Year 4, 10%	826.42	(826.42)
Remaining balance	$ 9,090.60	$ 909.40
Year 5, to clear accounts	909.40	(909.40)
Remaining balance	$10,000.00	$ -0-

Following are the journal entries to record imputed interest at the end of each year and the final collection of the note.

End of 1st year:

Unamortized discount on note	620.90	
Interest income		620.90

End of 2nd year:

Unamortized discount on note	682.99	
Interest income		682.99

End of 3rd year:

Unamortized discount on note	751.29	
Interest income		751.29

End of 4th year:

Unamortized discount on note	826.42	
Interest income		826.42

End of 5th year:

Unamortized discount on note	909.40	
Interest income		909.40
Cash	10,000.00	
Note receivable		10,000.00

Illustration of Recording a Note with an Unreasonable Rate of Interest

A company purchases a $10,000 machine and issues for payment a $10,000 four-year note bearing 2% compound interest per year; 10% is considered an appropriate rate of interest. The entire amount due, including all interest, is payable at the maturity date of the note. The initial journal entry is:

Machine (present value of $10,824 @		
10% for 4 periods)	7,393	
Unamortized discount on note	3,431	
Note payable		10,000
Deferred interest payable		824

First year:

Interest expense	739	
Unamortized discount on note		
(10% on $7,393)		739

Second year:

Interest expense	813	
Unamortized discount on note		
[10% on ($7,393 + $739)]		813

Third year:

Interest expense	895	
Unamortized discount on note		
[10% on ($7,393 + $739 + $813)]		895

Fourth year:

Interest expense	984	
Unamortized discount on note		
[10% on ($7,393 + $739 + $813 + $895)]		984

In the fourth year, when the note and the 2% interest are paid, the following journal entry is made:

Note payable	$10,000	
Deferred interest payable	824	
Cash		$10,824

The future amount of the note is $10,824 ($10,000 × 1.0824, which compounds the 2% for four periods). The company records a note payable ($10,000) and the deferred interest ($824). The machine is recorded at the present value of this amount ($7,393), determined by discounting the $10,824 at 10% (the reasonable interest rate) for four years. This is because today the $10,824 is worth only $7,393, which is the amount at which the sale is recorded. The difference between the total amount due in four years ($10,824) and its present value ($7,393) is deferred interest ($3,431) for the use of the seller's funds and is amortized by the interest method over the term of the note.

RELATED CHAPTERS IN 2009 *GAAP GUIDE* LEVEL A

Chapter 11, "Depreciable Assets and Depreciation"
Chapter 24, "Interest Costs Capitalized"

RELATED CHAPTER IN 2009 *GAAP GUIDE* LEVELS B, C, AND D

Chapter 7, "Capitalization and Expense Recognition Concepts"

RELATED CHAPTERS IN 2009 *INTERNATIONAL ACCOUNTING/FINANCIAL REPORTING STANDARDS GUIDE*

Chapter 6, "Borrowing Costs"
Chapter 27, "Property, Plant, and Equipment"

CHAPTER 26
INTERIM FINANCIAL REPORTING

CONTENTS

OVERVIEW

Interim financial reports may be issued quarterly, monthly, or at other intervals, and may include complete financial statements or summarized data. In addition, they usually include the current interim period and a cumulative year-to-date period, or last twelve months to date, with comparative reports on the corresponding periods of the immediately preceding fiscal year.

GAAP for interim financial statements are found primarily in the following pronouncement:

APB-28   Interim Financial Reporting

BACKGROUND

The majority of GAAP have been developed with annual financial reporting in mind. These reporting standards generally are also applicable to interim financial reports. Some problems exist, however, in attempting to apply GAAP intended primarily for annual reporting purposes to financial reporting for shorter periods of time.

Two opposing approaches explain the relationship between interim financial reports and annual financial reports. The *discrete* approach, sometimes called the *independent* approach, views an interim period in the same way as an annual period. Within this approach accounting principles for an annual period are equally appropriate for periods of differing lengths of time and are applied in the same manner. Opposite that view is the *integral* approach, sometimes called the *dependent* approach, which views an interim period as a component, or *integral* part, of the annual period rather than a separate or discrete period. Within this approach, the purpose of interim financial reporting is to provide information over the course of the annual period that helps anticipate annual results.

APB-28 (Interim Financial Reporting) endorses aspects of both the discrete and integral approaches, but generally favors the *integral*, or *dependent*, approach to financial reporting for interim periods. Accordingly, certain procedures that are used in reporting for annual periods are modified in reporting for interim periods.

☞ **PRACTICE POINTER:**   Take care in preparing and reviewing interim financial statements *not* to assume that GAAP appropriate for *annual* financial statements are appropriate for *interim* statements. Examples where GAAP differ are the determination of cost of goods sold where a LIFO inventory layer has been eroded in an early interim period, accounting for income taxes on a cumulative year-to-date basis, and the determination of the materiality of items in interim financial statements.

ACCOUNTING AND REPORTING IN INTERIM PERIODS

Each interim period should be viewed as an integral part of the annual period. An important objective of interim reporting is for the user of the information to become progressively better informed about annual information as time passes. Accounting principles and reporting practices generally are those of the latest annual reports of the entity, with limited exceptions, such as a change in an accounting principle (APB-28, par. 10). A change in an accounting principle during an interim period is discussed in the chapter titled "Accounting Changes."

Revenues are recognized as earned on the same basis as fiscal periods (APB-28, par. 11).

As closely as possible, product costs are determined as those for the fiscal period with some exceptions for inventory valuation, as follows (APB-28, pars. 13–14):

- Companies using the gross profit method to determine interim inventory costs, or other methods different from those used for annual inventory valuation, should disclose the method used at the interim date and any significant adjustments that result from reconciliation(s) with the annual physical inventory.

- A liquidation of a base-period LIFO inventory at an interim date that is expected to be recovered by the end of the annual period is valued at the expected cost of replacement. Cost of sales for the interim period includes the expected cost of replacement and not the cost of the base-period LIFO inventory.

- Inventory losses from market declines are included in the interim period in which they occur, and gains in subsequent interim periods are recognized in such interim periods but cannot exceed the losses included in prior interim periods. (*Temporary* market declines that are expected to be made up by the end of the annual period need not be recognized in interim periods.)

- Inventory and product costs computed by the use of a standard cost accounting system are determined by the same procedures used at the end of a fiscal year. Variances from standard costs that are expected to be made up by the end of the fiscal year need not be included in interim-period statements.

Other costs and expenses are charged or allocated to produce a fair presentation of the results of operations, cash flows, and financial position for all interim periods. The following apply in accounting for other costs and expenses:

- A general rule in preparing interim-period financial statements is that costs and expenses that clearly benefit more than one period are allocated to the periods affected. This procedure should be applied consistently (APB-28, par. 16).

- Companies that have material seasonal revenue variations must take care to avoid the possibility that interim-period financial statements become misleading. Disclosure of such variations should be made in the interim-period financial statements. In addition, it is desirable to disclose results for a full year, ending with the current interim period (APB-28, par. 18).

- Unusual and infrequent transactions that are material and not designated as extraordinary items, such as the effects of a disposal of a segment of business, are reported separately in the interim periods in which they occur (APB-28, par. 21).

- All other pertinent information, such as accounting changes, contingencies, seasonal results, and business combinations, is disclosed to provide the necessary information for the proper understanding of the interim financial statements (APB-28, pars. 21–23).

Interim reports should not contain arbitrary amounts of costs or expenses. Estimates should be reasonable and based on all available information applied consistently from period to period (APB-28, par. 17). An effective tax rate is used for determining the income tax provision in interim periods, applied on a cumulative year-to-date basis (APB-28, par. 19). Income taxes for interim-period reports are discussed in the *GAAP Guide* chapter titled "Income Taxes."

Illustration of Quarterly Income Tax Calculation

Valentine, Inc. reports pretax income for the first two quarters of 20X9 as follows: January–March, $500,000; April–June, $450,000. At the end of the first quarter, management estimates that its effective annual income tax rate will be 40%. At the end of the second quarter, this estimate had been revised to 38%.

Income tax expense for the first quarter is calculated as follows:

$$\$500,000 \times 40\% = \$200,000$$

Income tax expense for the second quarter is determined by applying the revised estimate of the effective annual income tax rate to the cumulative pretax income to date and subtracting the amount recognized as income tax expense in the first quarter:

$$[(\$500,000 + \$450,000) \times 38\%] - \$200,000 = \$161,000$$

This same process is followed for the remaining quarters of the year: cumulative income to date × the estimated annual income tax rate – previous quarters' tax expense = current quarter expense.

Material contingencies and other uncertainties that exist at an interim date are disclosed in interim reports in the same manner as that required for annual reports. These interim-date contingencies and uncertainties should be evaluated in relation to the annual report. The disclosure for such items must be repeated in every interim and annual report until the contingency is resolved or becomes immaterial (APB-28, par. 22).

SUMMARIZED INTERIM FINANCIAL INFORMATION

Publicly traded companies reporting summarized financial information at interim dates should include the following (APB-28, par. 30):

- Gross revenues, provision for income taxes, extraordinary items, effects of changes in accounting principles, and net income
- Basic and diluted earnings-per-share data
- Material seasonal variations of revenues, costs, or expenses
- Significant changes in estimates or provisions for income taxes
- Disposal of a segment of a business and extraordinary, unusual, or infrequently occurring items
- Contingent items
- Changes in accounting principles or estimates
- Significant changes in financial position
- Information about fair value recognized in the statement of position per FAS-157 (Fair Value Measurements).

☛ **PRACTICE POINTER:**   To satisfy the above disclosure requirements, companies may present abbreviated financial statements, separate information items, or both. For example, a company may present an abbreviated income statement and selected information items from the balance sheet and statement of cash flows. Another company will present abbreviated versions of all three financial statements. In all approaches, companies typically omit most of the detailed note disclosures that are required in annual financial statements.

When summarized financial information is reported regularly on a quarterly basis, the above information should be furnished for the current quarter, the current year-to-date or the last twelve months to date, with comparable information for the preceding year (APB-28, par. 30). (The illustration at the end of this chapter suggests a format for this information.)

☛ **PRACTICE POINTER:**   Summarized interim financial statements based on these minimum disclosures *do not* constitute a fair presentation of financial position and results of operations in conformity with GAAP. Care should be taken that statements do not imply that interim information is in accordance with GAAP, unless it is (which is rarely the case).

In the event that fourth-quarter results are not issued separately, the annual report should include disclosures for the fourth quarter on the aggregate effect of material year-end adjustments and infrequently occurring items, extraordinary items, and disposal of business segments that occurred in the fourth quarter (APB-28, par. 31).

Illustration of Format for Presenting
Interim Financial Information

When quarterly information is regularly reported by publicly held companies, APB-28 requires (1) minimum disclosure of specific information items for the current quarter and comparable information for the same quarter of the previous year and (2) current year-to-date or twelve-months-to-date information and comparable information for the same period of the previous year.

The following is a suggested format, using illustrative dates and numbers, for the presentation of this information:

Hypothetical Company
Interim Financial Information
For Quarter Ending June 30, 20X8, and Comparable Periods
(in thousands)

	Current Quarter		Twelve-Months-to-Date	
	3 months ending 6/30/20X8	*3 months ending 6/30/20X7*	*Year ending 6/30/20X8*	*Year ending 6/30/20X7*
[Information item]	$50	$40	$425	$575

RELATED CHAPTERS IN 2009 *GAAP GUIDE* *LEVEL A*

Chapter 1, "Accounting Changes"
Chapter 21, "Income Taxes"
Chapter 27, "Inventory"
Chapter 40, "Results of Operations"
Chapter 42, "Segment Reporting"

RELATED CHAPTERS IN 2009 *GAAP GUIDE* *LEVELS B, C, AND D*

Chapter 1, "Accounting Changes"
Chapter 20, "Income Taxes"
Chapter 23, "Interim Financial Reporting"
Chapter 24, "Inventory"
Chapter 35, "Results of Operations"
Chapter 37, "Segment Reporting"

RELATED CHAPTERS IN 2009 *INTERNATIONAL ACCOUNTING/FINANCIAL REPORTING STANDARDS GUIDE*

Chapter 5, "Accounting Policies, Changes in Accounting
      Estimates, and Errors"
Chapter 20, "Income Taxes"
Chapter 22, "Interim Financial Reporting"
Chapter 23, "Inventories"
Chapter 31, "Segment Reporting"

CHAPTER 27
INVENTORY

CONTENTS

OVERVIEW

The preparation of financial statements requires careful determination of an appropriate dollar amount of inventory. Usually, that amount is presented as a current asset in the balance sheet and is a direct determinant of cost of goods sold in the income statement; as such, it has a significant impact on the amount of net income. When the matching principle is applied in determining net income, the valuation of inventories is of primary importance.

GAAP for the measurement of inventories are found in the following pronouncements:

ARB-43	Chapter 4, Inventory Pricing
APB-28	Interim Financial Reporting
FAS-2	Accounting for Research and Development Costs
FAS-151	Inventory Costs, An Amendment of ARB No. 43, Chapter 4
FIN-1	Accounting Changes Related to the Cost of Inventory

2009 TRANSITION GUIDANCE FOR
FAS-141(R) AND FAS-160

The FASB has recently issued FAS-141(R), *Business Combinations*, which is effective for business combinations for which the acquisition date is on or after the beginning of the first annual reporting period beginning on or after December 15, 2008. The FASB has also issued FAS-160, *Noncontrolling Interests in Consolidated Financial Statements, an Amendment of ARB No. 51*, which is effective for fiscal years, and interim periods within those fiscal years, beginning on or after December 15, 2008. Because these standards are not effective for some companies until December 2009, and because early adoption is prohibited, the 2009 *GAAP Guide* reflects the requirements of FAS-141 prior to its revision in December 2007 and does not reflect the requirements of FAS-160. There is a discussion of the changes in the accounting for business combinations under FAS-141(R) in the Appendix to Chapter 4, "Business Combinations." Similarly, the Appendix to Chapter 7, "Consolidated Financial Statements," includes a discussion of the requirements of FAS-160. However, any effects of FAS-141(R) and/or FAS-160 in this chapter have not been reflected in this edition. Therefore, if a company is subject to the requirements of FAS-141(R) and/or FAS-160, the reader is referred to FAS-141(R) and FAS-160 for these new requirements.

BACKGROUND

Inventories of goods must periodically be compiled, measured, and recorded in the books of accounts of a business. Inventory usually is classified as (*a*) finished goods, (*b*) work in process, or (*c*) raw materials (ARB-43, Ch. 4, Statement 1). Inventories exclude long-term assets that are subject to depreciation.

> **OBSERVATION:** Inventories are normally classified as current assets. However, when there are excessive quantities that may not reasonably be expected to be used or sold within the normal operating cycle of a business, we believe that excess inventory should be classified as noncurrent.

The basis of accounting for inventories is cost, which is the price paid or consideration given to acquire the asset. In inventory accounting, cost is the sum of the expenditures and charges, direct and indirect, in bringing goods to their existing condition or location (ARB-43, Ch. 4, Statement 3).

While the principle of measuring inventory at cost can be easily stated, the application of the principle, particularly to work-in-process items and finished goods, is difficult because of the problem involved in allocating various costs and charges. For example, idle factory expense, excessive spoilage, double freight, and rehandling costs can be so abnormal that they may have to be charged to the current period, rather than be treated as elements of inventory cost. Selling expenses are not part of inventory costs. *The exclusion of all overhead from inventory costs* (direct or variable costing) *is an unacceptable accounting procedure* (ARB-43, Ch. 4, par. 5).

INVENTORY SYSTEMS

Periodic System

Inventory is determined by a physical count as of a specific date. As long as the count is made frequently enough for reporting purposes, it is not necessary to maintain extensive inventory records. The inventory shown in the balance sheet is determined by the physical count and is priced in accordance with the inventory costing method used. The net change between the beginning and ending inventories enters into the computation of the cost of goods sold.

Perpetual System

In a perpetual system, inventory records are maintained and updated continuously as items are purchased and sold. The system has the advantage of providing inventory information on a timely basis but requires the maintenance of a full set of inventory records. Theoretically, physical counts are not necessary, but they are normally taken to verify the inventory records. GAAP require that a physical check of perpetual inventory records be made periodically.

LOWER OF COST OR MARKET

When the utility of the goods in the ordinary course of business is no longer as great as their cost, a departure from the cost principle of measuring the inventory is required. Whether the cause is obsolescence, physical deterioration, changes in price levels, or any other, the difference should be recognized by a charge to income in the current period. This usually is accomplished by stating the goods at a lower level designated as market (lower of cost or market principle) (ARB-43, Ch. 4, Statement 5).

In the phrase *lower of cost or market,* the term *market* means current replacement cost, whether by purchase or by reproduction, *but is limited to the following maximum and minimum amounts* (ARB-43, Ch. 4, Statement 6):

- *Maximum:* the estimated selling price less any costs of completion and disposal, referred to as net realizable value
- *Minimum:* net realizable value, less an allowance for normal profit

The purpose of reducing inventory to the lower of cost or market is to reflect fairly the income of the period. When market is lower than cost, the purposes of the maximum and minimum limitations are:

- The maximum prevents a loss in future periods by at least valuing the inventory at its estimated selling price less costs of completion and disposal.
- The minimum prevents any future periods from realizing any more than a normal profit.

Illustration of How Maximum and Minimum Constraints Impact Lower-of-Cost-or-Market Determination

Item	Cost	Replacement Cost	(1) Selling Price	(2) Cost of Completion	(1 – 2) Maximum*	(3) Normal Profit	[(1 – 2) – 3] Minimum
1	$20.50	$ 19.00	$ 25.00	$ 1.00	$ 24.00	$ 6.00	$ 18.00
2	26.00	20.00	30.00	2.00	28.00	7.00	21.00
3	10.00	12.00	15.00	1.00	14.00	3.00	11.00
4	40.00	55.00	60.00	6.00	54.00	4.00	50.00
	$96.50	$106.00	$130.00	$10.00	$120.00	$20.00	$100.00

*The maximum is equal to the realizable value.

Applying the lower of cost or market to the above four items individually results in the following amounts:

Item 1	$19.00	Item 3	$10.00
Item 2	$21.00	Item 4	$40.00

The lower of cost or market principle may be applied to a single item, a category, or the total inventory, provided that the method most clearly reflects periodic income (ARB-43, Ch. 4, Statement 7). The basic principle of consistency must be applied in the valuation of inventory, and the method should be disclosed in the financial statements (ARB-43, Ch. 4, Statement 8).

The write-down of inventory to market usually is reflected in cost of goods sold, unless the amount is unusually material, in which case the loss should be identified separately in the income statement (ARB-43, Ch. 4, par. 14).

In the event that a significant change occurs in the measurement of inventory, disclosure of the nature of the change and, if material, the effect on income should be made in the financial statements.

Exceptional cases, such as precious metals having a fixed determinable monetary value with no substantial cost of marketing, may be stated at such monetary value. When inventory is stated at a value in excess of cost, this fact should be disclosed fully in the financial statements (ARB-43, Ch. 4, Statement 9).

To apply this exception to other types of inventory, there must be: (*a*) immediate marketability at quoted prices, (*b*) inability to determine approximate costs, and (*c*) interchangeability of units.

> **OBSERVATION:** FAS-133 (Accounting for Derivative Instruments and Hedging Activities) states that if inventory has been the hedged item in a fair value hedge, the inventory's cost basis used in determining the lower-of-cost-or-market shall include the effects of adjusting its carrying amount as a result of recording the gain or loss on the hedged item. FAS-133 is covered in the chapter of this *Guide* titled "Financial Instruments."

INVENTORY COST METHODS

For inventory purposes, cost may be determined by specific identification or by the association of the flow of cost factors—first-in, first out (FIFO), last-in, first-out (LIFO), and average cost.

In selecting an inventory cost method, an important objective is the selection of the method that under the circumstances most clearly reflects periodic income. When similar goods are purchased at different times, it may not be possible or practical to identify and match the specific costs of the item sold. Frequently, the identity of goods and their specific related costs are lost between the time of acquisition and the time of use or sale. This has resulted in the general acceptance of several assumptions with respect to the flow of cost factors to provide practical bases for the measurement of periodic income (ARB-43, Ch. 4, Statement 4).

First-In, First-Out Method (FIFO)

The FIFO method of identifying inventory is based on the assumption that costs are charged against revenue in the order in which they occur. The inventory remaining on hand is presumed to consist of the most recent costs.

Theoretically, FIFO approximates the results that would be obtained by the specific identification method if items were sold in the order in which they were purchased.

Last-In, First-Out Method (LIFO)

The LIFO method matches the most recent costs incurred with current revenue, leaving the first cost incurred to be included as inventory. LIFO requires that records be maintained as to the base-year layer and additional layers that may be created or used up. An additional LIFO layer is created in any year in which the quantity of ending inventory is more than the beginning inventory and is priced at the earliest or average costs of the year in which it was created.

When the quantity of ending inventory is less than the beginning inventory, one or more LIFO layers may be used up. Once a LIFO layer is used up, any future new LIFO layer is priced at the cost of the year in which it is created, and not by reinstating a prior LIFO layer cost.

In addition to the disclosure of significant accounting policies required by APB-22 (Disclosure of Accounting Policies) and of composition of inventories (ARB-43, Ch. 4, Statement 8), a business using the LIFO method of reporting inventory must disclose the following, if it reports to the SEC:

- Current replacement value of the LIFO inventories at each balance sheet date presented

- The effect on the results of operations for any reduction of a LIFO layer

☛ **PRACTICE POINTER:** Although using the LIFO inventory method is sometimes justified on the basis of a superior matching of current revenues and current costs, the primary catalysts for using it are its acceptance for income tax purposes and the lower taxable income that it produces. Income tax law requires a company that uses LIFO for tax purposes to also use LIFO for financial reporting purposes. In changing from another inventory cost method to the LIFO method for financial reporting purposes, the company must present a justification. Changing an accounting method for financial reporting purposes because of its preferability for tax purposes generally is not acceptable. Therefore, changing to LIFO usually is justified by reasons such as higher quality earnings that result from matching current revenues with current costs, and bringing the company into conformity with normal industry practice.

Weighted-Average Method

The weighted-average method of inventory valuation assumes that costs are charged against revenue based on an average of the number of units acquired at each price level. The resulting average price is applied to the ending inventory to find the total ending inventory value. The weighted average is determined by dividing the total costs of the inventory available, including any beginning inventory, by the total number of units.

Illustration of Application of FIFO, LIFO, and the Weighted-Average Methods of Inventory Valuation

Assume the following facts:

Units Purchased During the Year

Date	Units	Cost per Unit	Total Cost
January 15	10,000	$5.10	$ 51,000
March 20	20,000	5.20	104,000
May 10	50,000	5.00	250,000
June 8	30,000	5.40	162,000
October 12	5,000	5.30	26,500
December 21	5,000	5.50	27,500
Totals	120,000		$621,000

Beginning inventory consisted of 10,000 units at $5.

Ending inventory consisted of 14,000 units.

Under *FIFO*, the first units in stock are the first units out, which means that the ending inventory is of the units purchased last. Since the ending inventory is 14,000 units and December purchases were only 5,000 units, go back to October purchases for another 5,000 units and to June purchases for another 4,000 units, as follows:

December purchases	5,000 units @ $5.50	=	$27,500
October purchases	5,000 units @ 5.30	=	26,500
From June purchases	4,000 units @ 5.40	=	21,600
Ending inventory using FIFO	14,000 units		$75,600

Under *LIFO*, the last units in stock are the first units out, which means that the ending inventory is composed of the units purchased first. Using LIFO, go back to the earliest inventory to start the calculations. The earliest inventory available is the *beginning inventory* of 10,000 units at $5, but the ending inventory is 14,000 units. Thus, go to the next earliest purchase, which is January, and use 4,000 units at the January price to complete the ending inventory valuation, as follows:

Beginning inventory	10,000 units @	$5.00	=	$50,000
From January purchase	4,000 units @	5.10	=	20,400
Ending inventory using LIFO	14,000 units			$70,400

Under the *weighted-average* method, multiply the weighted-average cost per unit by the 14,000 units in the ending inventory, thus:

	Units	Cost per Unit	Total Cost
Beginning inventory	10,000	$ 5.00	$ 50,000
Purchases:			
January 15	10,000	5.10	51,000
March 20	20,000	5.20	104,000
May 10	50,000	5.00	250,000
June 8	30,000	5.40	162,000
October 12	5,000	5.30	26,500
December 21	5,000	5.50	27,500
Totals	130,000		$ 671,000

Weighted average	=	Total costs divided by total units
	=	$671,000 divided by 130,000
	=	$5.1615 per unit
Ending inventory	=	14,000 × $5.1615 per unit = $72,261

Comparison of the Three Methods

Ending inventory, FIFO	$75,600
Ending inventory, LIFO	70,400
Ending inventory, weighted average	72,261

In periods of inflation, the FIFO method produces the highest ending inventory, resulting in the lowest cost of goods sold and the highest gross profit. LIFO produces the lowest ending inventory, resulting in the highest cost of goods sold and the lowest gross profit. The weighted-average method yields results between those of LIFO and FIFO.

Moving-Average Method

The moving-average method can be used only with a perpetual inventory. The cost per unit is recomputed after every addition to the inventory.

Illustration of Moving-Average Method

	Total Units	Total Cost	Unit Cost
Beginning inventory	1,000	$ 5,000	$5.00
Sales of 200 units	800	4,000	5.00
Purchase of 1,200 @ $6	2,000	11,200*	5.60
Sales of 1,000 units	1,000	5,600	5.60
Purchase of 1,000 @ $5	2,000	10,600**	5.30

*$4,000 + (1,200 @ $6) = $11,200;$11,200/2,000 units = $5,60/unit

**$5,600 + (1,000 @ $5) = $10,600;$10,600/2,000 units = $5,30/unit

Note: Only purchases change the unit price; sales are taken out at the prior moving-average unit cost.

Under the moving-average method, the ending inventory is costed at the last moving-average unit cost for the period.

Dollar-Value LIFO Method

A variation of the conventional LIFO method is the dollar-value LIFO method. Under the regular LIFO method, units of inventory are priced at unit prices. Under the dollar-value LIFO method, the base-year inventory is priced in dollars; for inventories of all subsequent years, price indices are used, with the base year as 100.

Illustration of Dollar-Value LIFO Method

Year	Inventory at Base-Year Prices	Price Index	LIFO Inventory Amount
1	$100,000	100	$100,000
2	20,000	105	21,000
3	10,000	110	11,000
4	20,000	120	24,000
5	20,000	125	25,000
Totals	$170,000		$181,000

Retail Inventory Method

Because of the great variety and quantity of inventory in some types of businesses, the reversed markup procedure of inventory pricing, such as the retail inventory method, may be both practical and appropriate.

The retail inventory method requires the maintenance of records of purchases at both cost and selling price. A ratio of cost to retail is calculated and applied to the ending inventory at retail to compute the approximate cost.

Illustration of Basic Retail Inventory Method

	Cost	Retail
Inventory, at beginning of period	$ 100,000	$ 150,000
Purchases during the period	1,100,000	1,850,000
Totals (ratio of cost to retail 60%)	$1,200,000	$2,000,000
Sales during the period		(1,800,000)
Estimated ending inventory at retail		$ 200,000
Estimated ending inventory at cost (60% × $200,000)		$ 120,000

Physical inventories measured by the retail method should be taken periodically as a check on the accuracy of the estimated inventories.

Original selling prices may be modified, thus necessitating an understanding of the following terminology:

- *Original retail*—the first selling price at which goods are offered for sale
- *Markup*—the selling price raised above the original selling price
- *Markdown*—the selling price lowered below the original selling price
- *Markup cancellation*—markup selling price decreased, but not below the original selling price
- *Markdown cancellation*—markdown selling price increased, but not above the original selling price
- *Net markup*—markup less markup cancellation
- *Net markdown*—markdown less markdown cancellation

- *Markon*—difference between the cost and the original selling price, plus any net markups

---

Illustration of Markups and Markdowns

Original cost	$100
Original selling price ($50 markon)	$150
Markup	50
Original selling price plus markup	200
Markup cancellation	(25)
Original selling price plus net markup	175
Markdown (consists of $25 markup cancellation and a $25 markdown)	(50)
Original selling price less markdown	125
Markdown	(25)
Original selling price less markdown	100
Markdown cancellation	25
Original selling price less net markdown	125
Markup (consists of a $25 markdown cancellation and a $25 markup)	50
Original selling price plus net markup	$175

Theoretically, the last selling price consists of:

$50	markup
(25)	markup cancellation
(25)	markup cancellation
(25)	markdown
(25)	markdown
25	markdown cancellation
25	markdown cancellation
25	markup
$25	net plus change

Now the goods are priced at the original selling price plus a net markup of $25, or a total of $175.

The purpose of the conventional retail inventory method is to produce an inventory valuation closely approximating what would be obtained by taking a physical inventory and pricing the goods at the lower of cost or market.

The basic assumption of the retail inventory method is that there exists an equal distribution of goods (high-cost ratio and low-cost ratio) between sales, beginning inventory, and ending inventory. In instances in which this basic premise does not prevail, cost ratios should be determined by departments or small units. This requires keeping separate sales, purchases, markups, markdowns, and beginning and ending inventories by departments.

Lower-of-Cost-or-Market Application

To approximate the lower of cost or market in the computations, *markdowns and markdown cancellations are excluded in calculating the ratio of cost to retail and are added to the retail inventory after the ratio is determined.*

In calculating the cost-to-retail ratio, any adjustment to the retail value will necessarily affect the ratio and the resulting cost figure. Adjustments that decrease the denominator of the ratio increase the ratio and the value for ending inventory at cost, increasing gross profit. In the interest of conservatism, as well as for other reasons, adjustments that decrease the retail figure should be avoided. Markups, which increase the denominator, however, are included *net* of cancellations.

Net markdowns (markdowns less markdown cancellations) are an example of adjustments that decrease the denominator. Including them in the retail figure violates the lower-of-cost-or-market rule. As shown below, net markdowns are not included in the calculation of the ratio but *are* included in the determination of ending inventory after computing the ratio. The rationale for this is that the cost-to-retail ratio is presumed to be based on normal conditions, and markdown is not a normal condition. When *applying* the ratio, however, to conform to the lower-of-cost-or-market rule, the retail value must be reduced by the amount of the markdowns.

Employee discounts apply only to goods sold, not those remaining on hand. A sale at less than normal retail price to an employee does not represent a valid reduction to lower of cost or market, nor does it represent a valid adjustment of the cost-to-retail ratio or the value of the ending inventory. Therefore, employee discounts should not enter into any of the calculations, but are deducted from retail in the same way as markdowns after the computation of the cost-to-retail ratio.

Inventory spoilage and shrinkage affect the ending inventory figure but do not enter into the cost-to-retail ratio calculation. When arriving at the final figure for inventory at cost, the amount of shrinkage is deducted either at cost or at retail depending upon whether shrinkage is stated at cost or at retail.

Illustration of Retail Method/Lower-of-Cost-or-Market Application

	Cost	Retail
Inventory, at beginning of period	$ 200,000	$ 300,000
Purchases	550,000	800,000
Transportation-in	50,000	
Markups		100,000
Markup cancellations		20,000
Markdowns		70,000
Markdown cancellations		10,000

The calculations are as follows:

	Cost	Retail
Inventory, at beginning of period	$200,000	$ 300,000
Purchases	550,000	800,000
Transportation-in	50,000	
Markups		100,000
Markup cancellations		(20,000)
Totals (ratio of cost to retail 67.8%)	$800,000	$1,180,000
Markdowns		(70,000)
Markdown cancellations		10,000
Total goods at retail		$1,120,000
Less: Sales during the period		(860,000)
Inventory, ending (at retail)		$ 260,000
Inventory, ending (67.8% × $260,000)*		$ 176,280

*At estimated lower cost or market

LIFO Application

The LIFO method of evaluating inventory can be estimated via the retail inventory method by using procedures somewhat different from the conventional retail method. Basically, two differences have to be taken into consideration:

1. Because the LIFO method produces a valuation approximating cost, and the conventional retail method produces a valuation approximating the lower of cost or market, to apply the LIFO concept to the conventional retail method it is necessary to include all markdowns as well as markups in determining the ratio of cost to retail.

2. With the LIFO method, the quantity of inventory on hand is from the earliest purchases during the year or from prior years' LIFO layers. The cost-to-retail ratio considers the current relationship between cost and selling price. Therefore, the beginning inventory is omitted from the cost-to-retail ratio, because it may cause a distortion.

Illustration of Retail Method/LIFO Application

Information from the previous example is restated on a LIFO basis, as follows:

	Cost	Retail
Inventory, beginning of period	omitted	omitted
Purchases	$550,000	$ 800,000
Transportation-in	50,000	
Markups		100,000
Markup cancellations		(20,000)
Markdowns		(70,000)
Markdown cancellations		10,000
Totals (ratio of cost to retail 73.2%)	$600,000	$ 820,000
Add: Inventory, beginning of period		300,000
Total goods at retail		$1,120,000
Less: Sales during period		(860,000)
Inventory, ending of period (at retail)		$ 260,000

Because the $260,000 ending LIFO inventory (at retail) is less than the $300,000 beginning LIFO inventory (at retail), a prior LIFO layer was partially depleted:

	Retail
Beginning inventory	$300,000
Ending inventory	(260,000)
LIFO layer depleted	$ 40,000

The $40,000 difference is multiplied by the beginning inventory cost-to-retail ratio ($200,000/$300,000 = 66.7%) and then subtracted from the beginning inventory at cost, as follows:

	Cost
Beginning inventory	$200,000
$40,000 × 66.7%	(26,680)
Ending inventory (at cost)	$173,320

If the ending LIFO inventory (at retail) had been greater than the beginning LIFO inventory (at retail), a new LIFO layer would have been created which would have been costed at the new cost-to-retail ratio (73.2%).

MISCELLANEOUS INVENTORY ISSUES

Title to Goods

Legal title to merchandise usually determines whether or not it is included in the inventory of an enterprise. Title to goods passes from the seller to the buyer in any manner and on any conditions explicitly agreed on by the parties. If no conditions are explicitly agreed on, title to goods passes from the seller to the buyer at the time and place at which the seller completes its performance with reference to the physical delivery of the goods. Title passes to the buyer at the time and place of shipment if the seller is required only to send the goods. If the contract requires delivery at destination, however, title passes when the goods are tendered at the destination.

Commonly encountered terms are F.O.B. *(free on board) Destination* and F.O.B. *Shipping Point.* In the former case, the seller is responsible for the goods during shipment; title passes when the goods are received by the buyer. In the latter case, the buyer is responsible for the goods during shipment; title passes when the goods leave the seller's location.

Abnormal Facility and Other Costs

Accounting for abnormal amounts of idle facility expense, freight, handling costs, and spoilage was one of the narrow differences that existed between the standards of the FASB and the IASB that the FASB decided to address by issuing FAS-151 (Inventory Costs—An Amendment of ARB No. 43, Chapter 4). ARB-43, Chapter 4, stated that these costs may be "so abnormal" that they should be expensed currently. The term "so abnormal" was not defined, however, which could lead to a lack of comparability of financial reporting, if interpreted differently by preparers of financial statements.

As amended, the basic principle for accounting for inventory according to ARB-43, Chapter 4, is that inventories are to be accounted for at cost, meaning acquisition and production costs. Although this principle may be easily stated, it is difficult to apply because of the variety of considerations inherent in the allocation of costs and charges. Guidelines for applying the principles in ARB-43, Chapter 4, as amended, can be summarized as follow (FAS-151, par. 2):

- Variable production overhead costs are allocated to each unit of production on the basis of the actual use of the production facilities.

- The allocation of fixed production overheads to the costs of conversion is based on the normal capacity of the production facilities.

- "Normal capacity" refers to a range of production levels and is the production expected to be achieved over a number of periods or seasons under normal circumstances, taking into account the loss of capacity resulting from planned maintenance.

- Some variation in production levels from period to period is expected and establishes the range of normal production. This range will vary based on business-related and industry-related factors.

- Judgment is required to determine when a production level is abnormally low (i.e., outside the range of expected variation in production).

- Examples of factors that might be anticipated to cause an abnormally low production level include significantly reduced demand, labor and materials shortages, and unplanned facilities or equipment downtime.

- The actual level of production may be used if it approximates normal capacity.

- In periods of abnormally high production, the amount of fixed overhead allocated to each unit of production is decreased so that inventories are not measured above cost. The amount of fixed overhead allocated to each unit of production is not increased as a consequence of abnormally low production or an idle plant.

Unallocated overhead costs are recognized as an expense in the period in which they are incurred. Other costs, such as abnormal handling costs, are treated as a current period expense, as are general and administrative costs, except for the portion that clearly relates to production and constitutes a part of inventory costs. Selling expenses are not included in inventory costs. The exclusion of all overhead costs from inventory costs is not an accepted accounting procedure (FAS-151, par. 2).

☞ **PRACTICE POINTER:** The exercise of judgment in individual situations involves a consideration of the adequacy of the procedures of the cost accounting system in use, the soundness of the principles on which that system is based, and the consistency of the application of those principles.

The provisions of FAS-151 are to be applied prospectively to costs incurred during fiscal years beginning after June, 15, 2005. Earlier application is permitted for inventory costs incurred during fiscal years beginning after the date FAS-151 was issued (November 2004) (FAS-151, par. 5).

Standard Costs

The use of standard costs is a management tool that identifies favorable or unfavorable variances from predetermined estimates established by past performance or time and motion studies. Inventory valuation by the use of standard costs is acceptable, if adjusted at reasonable intervals to reflect the approximate costs computed under one of the recognized methods, and adequate disclosure is made in the financial statements.

At the end of the reporting period, the physical inventory is costed at LIFO, FIFO, or some other generally accepted method. Any variation between this result and the carrying value of the inventory at standard cost must be closed out to cost of goods sold and ending inventory such that the reported figure represents that which the generally accepted method would yield.

Relative Sales Value Costing

Determining the relative sales cost of inventory items is used when costs cannot be determined individually. Joint products, lump-sum purchase of assets (basket purchase), and large assets that are subdivided (real estate tracts) are examples of items that would be costed by their relative sales value.

Illustration of Relative Sales Value Costing

ABC Company purchases inventory consisting of four large pieces of machinery for $100,000. At the time of purchase, an appraisal discloses the following fair values:

Machine #1	$ 12,000
Machine #2	28,000
Machine #3	40,000
Machine #4	30,000
Total	$110,000

The cost of each machine is an allocated amount, based on relative fair values, as follows:

Machine #1	12/110 × $100,000	=	$ 10,909
Machine #2	28/110 × $100,000	=	25,455
Machine #3	40/110 × $100,000	=	36,364
Machine #4	30/110 × $100,000	=	27,272
Total cost allocated			$100,000

Alternatively, a percentage of total cost to the appraised value can be computed: $100,000/$110,000 = 90.91%. That percentage is then applied to the value of each item to determine its cost. For example, cost for Machine 1 is $12,000 × 90.91% = $10,909.

Firm Purchase Commitments

Losses on firm purchase commitments for inventory goods are measured in the same manner as inventory losses and, if material, recognized in the accounts and disclosed separately in the income statement (ARB-43, Ch. 4, Statement 10).

The recognition of losses, which are expected to arise from firm, noncancelable commitments and which arise from the decline in the utility of a cost expenditure, should be disclosed in the current period income statement. In addition, all significant firm purchase commitments must be disclosed in the financial statements or in footnotes, whether or not any losses are recognized.

Discontinued Operations

Inventories used in a component of a business entity should be written down to their fair value less cost to sell and the amount of write-down included as part of the gain or loss recognized on the disposal of the component of the business entity (FAS-144, pars. 37 and 41). Such a write-down, however, should not be attributable to any inventory adjustment that should have been recognized prior to the measurement date of the loss on disposal. In this event, the loss on the write-down is included in the operating results of the component of the business entity in accordance with FAS-144 (Accounting for the Impairment or Disposal of Long-Lived Assets) (FAS-144, par. 43).

Interim Financial Reporting

Generally, the same principles and methods are used to value inventories for interim financial statements as are used for annual reports. For practical purposes, however, APB-28 specifies certain exceptions (APB-28, par. 14):

- An estimated gross profit frequently is used to determine the cost of goods sold during an interim period. This is acceptable for GAAP, as long as periodic physical inventories are taken to adjust the gross profit percentage used. Companies using the gross profit method for interim financial statements should disclose that fact and any significant adjustments that may occur in amounts determined by a physical count.

- When the LIFO method is used for interim financial statements and a LIFO layer is depleted, in part or in whole, that is expected to be replaced before the end of the fiscal period, it is acceptable to use the expected cost of replacement for the depleted LIFO inventory in determining cost of goods sold for the interim period.

- Inventory losses from market declines, other than those expected to be recovered before the end of the fiscal year, are included in the results of operations of the interim period in which the loss occurs. Subsequent gains from market price recovery in later interim periods are included in the results of operation in which the gain occurs, but only to the extent of the previously recognized losses.

- Standard costs are acceptable in determining inventory valuations for interim financial reporting. Unplanned or unanticipated purchase price, volume, or capacity variances should be included in the results of operations of the interim period in which they occur. Anticipated and planned purchase price, volume, or capacity variances that are expected to be recovered by the end of the fiscal year are deferred at interim dates. In general, the same procedures for standard costs used at the end of the fiscal year should be used for interim financial reporting.

☞ **PRACTICE POINTER:** Although all four of these procedures are acceptable in interim financial statements, they are not considered GAAP for purposes of annual financial statements. Some may result in material differences in the amount of net income (e.g., using the replacement cost for erosion of a LIFO layer in an early interim period), and care should be taken that a similar procedure is not used in annual financial statements.

Business Combinations

GAAP pertaining to the valuation of inventory acquired as the result of a business combination are contained in FAS-141 (Business Combinations).

Inventory acquired in a business combination is valued as follows (FAS-141, par. 37c):

- *Raw materials*—current replacement cost
- *Finished goods*—estimated selling price less costs of disposal and a reasonable profit for the selling effort
- *Work in process*—estimated selling price for finished goods, less costs to complete and dispose, and a reasonable profit for the completion and selling effort

Terminated Contracts

When inventory is acquired for a specific customer contract that is subsequently terminated for any purpose, the carrying value of such inventory should be adjusted to reflect any loss in value.

Research and Development

FAS-2 (Accounting for Research and Development Costs) contains GAAP relevant to inventory expense allocation. Inventories of supplies used in research and development activities are charged to expense unless they clearly have an alternative use or can be used in future research and development projects.

When research and development activities consume goods, supplies, or materials from other sources within an organization, the carrying value of such inventory is charged to research and development expense. Goods produced by research and development activities that may be used in the regular inventory of the organization may be transferred physically to regular inventory, at which time a credit in the amount of the costs assigned to the goods should be made to research and development.

Intercompany Profits

Regardless of any minority interest, all intercompany profits in inventory are eliminated for consolidated financial statements and investments in common stocks accounted for by the equity method.

Long-Term Construction-Type Contracts

The construction in progress account used in both the completed-contract and percentage-of-completion methods of accounting for long-term construction-type contracts is an inventory account.

Income Taxes

Inventories accounted differently for financial accounting and tax purposes may create temporary differences for which the recognition of deferred taxes may be necessary.

Accounting Change

An accounting change involving inventories in interim or annual reports necessitates accounting for the cumulative effect of the change and/or restatement of prior-period reports, including certain required pro forma information in accordance with FAS-154 (Accounting Changes and Error Corrections).

Nonmonetary Exchanges

A nonmonetary exchange of inventory held for sale in the ordinary course of business for similar property to be held for the same purpose does not complete the earnings process and no gain or loss is recognized. The inventory received in the nonmonetary exchange should be recorded at the book value of the inventory surrendered, unless cash is also involved in the transaction, in accordance with APB-29 (Accounting for Nonmonetary Transactions).

Inventory Profits

Profits from the sale of inventory, whose cost and selling price have increased significantly since acquisition, may include *ghost profits* or *inventory profits*. These profits are abnormal, because the cost to replace the inventory has increased significantly and the normal gross profit on the inventory is considerably less than the gross profit containing the ghost or inventory profits.

During periods of rapid inflation, a significant portion of reported net income of a business may actually be ghost or inventory profits. The use of the LIFO method for pricing inventories may offset part or all of any ghost or inventory profits, because current purchases or production costs are matched against current revenue, leaving the earliest inventory on hand.

Certain publicly held companies are encouraged by the SEC to disclose in a supplemental statement the current replacement cost for cost of goods sold, inventories, and resulting ghost or inventory profits.

DISCLOSURE

The general disclosure requirements for inventories are:

- A description of accounting principles used and the methods of applying those principles (APB-22, par. 12).
- Any accounting principles or methods that are peculiar to a particular industry (APB-22, par. 12).
- Classification of inventories (ARB-43, Ch. 4, Statement 8).
- Basis of pricing inventories (ARB-43, Ch. 4, Statement 8).

Businesses that depend on a limited number of sources for raw material or inventory or upon precarious sources (labor problems, foreign governments, etc.) should disclose the pertinent facts in their financial statements or footnotes thereto.

RELATED CHAPTERS IN 2009 *GAAP GUIDE*
LEVEL A

Chapter 1, "Accounting Changes"
Chapter 2, "Accounting Policies and Standards"
Chapter 3, "Balance Sheet Classification and Related Display Issues"
Chapter 4, "Business Combinations"
Chapter 7, "Consolidated Financial Statements"
Chapter 16, "Fair Value"
Chapter 24, "Interest Costs Capitalized"
Chapter 26, "Interim Financial Reporting"
Chapter 30, "Long-Term Construction Contracts"
Chapter 32, "Nonmonetary Transactions"
Chapter 40, "Results of Operations"

RELATED CHAPTERS IN 2009 *GAAP GUIDE*
LEVELS B, C, AND D

Chapter 1, "Accounting Changes"
Chapter 2, "Accounting Policies and Standards"

Chapter 4, "Balance Sheet Classification and Related Display Issues"
Chapter 6, "Business Combinations"
Chapter 10, "Consolidated Financial Statements"
Chapter 16, "Fair Value"
Chapter 23, "Interim Financial Reporting"
Chapter 24, "Inventory"
Chapter 27, "Long-Term Construction Contracts"
Chapter 28, "Nonmonetary Transactions"
Chapter 35, "Results of Operations"

RELATED CHAPTERS IN 2009 *INTERNATIONAL ACCOUNTING/FINANCIAL REPORTING STANDARDS GUIDE*

Chapter 3, "Presentation of Financial Statements"
Chapter 5, "Accounting Policies, Changes in Accounting Estimates, and Errors"
Chapter 6, "Borrowing Costs"
Chapter 7, "Business Combinations"
Chapter 9, "Changing Prices and Hyperinflationary Economies"
Chapter 10, "Consolidated Financial Statements"
Chapter 11, "Construction Contracts"
Chapter 22, "Interim Financial Reporting"

CHAPTER 28
INVESTMENTS IN DEBT AND
EQUITY SECURITIES

CONTENTS

OVERVIEW

The primary issue in accounting and reporting for debt and equity investments is the appropriate use of market value. GAAP for many investments are included in the following pronouncements:

FAS-115 Accounting for Certain Investments in Debt and Equity Securities

FAS-130   Reporting Comprehensive Income

FAS-159   The Fair Value Option for Financial Assets and Financial Liabilities

FAS-115 (Accounting for Certain Investments in Debt and Equity Securities) addresses accounting and reporting for (*a*) investments in equity securities that have readily determinable fair values and (*b*) all investments in debt securities. It requires that these securities be classified in three categories and given specific accounting treatments, as follows:

Classification	*Accounting Treatment*

Held-to-maturity
    Debt securities with the intent
    and ability to hold to maturity
	Amortized cost

Trading securities
    Debt and equity securities
    bought and held primarily
    for sale in the near term
	Fair value, with unrealized
	holding gains and losses
	included in earnings

Available-for-sale
    Debt and equity securities not
    classified as held-to-maturity
    or trading
	Fair value, with unrealized
	holding gains and losses
	excluded from earnings
	and reported as a separate
	component of shareholders'
	equity

> **OBSERVATION:** FAS-159 (The Fair Value Option for Financial Assets and Financial Liabilities) permits companies to account for a variety of financial instruments by the fair value method. To the extent to which an entity selects the fair value method for investments that would otherwise have been accounted for under FAS-115, the following applies: An enterprise shall report its investments in available-for-sale securities and trading securities separately from similar assets that are subsequently measured using another measurement attribute on the face of the statement of financial position. Two options are available for presenting this information: (1) the aggregate of those measured by fair value and those measured by non-fair-value amounts are presented in the same line item and the amount of fair value included in the aggregate amount is parenthetically disclosed; (2) two separate line items are presented, one for the fair value amount and one for the non-fair-value amount. FAS-159 is covered in Chapter 16, "Fair Value," in *GAAP Guide Level A*.

BACKGROUND

FAS-115 defines *debt securities* and *equity securities* as follows:

Debt Security

A *debt security* is any security that represents a creditor relationship with an enterprise. It includes preferred stock that must be redeemed by the issuing enterprise or that is redeemable at the option of the investor. It also includes a collateralized mortgage obligation that is issued in equity form but is required to be accounted for as a non-equity instrument, regardless of how that instrument is classified in the issuer's statement of financial position. Other examples of debt securities are the following:

- U.S. Treasury securities
- U.S. government agency securities
- Municipal securities
- Corporate bonds
- Convertible debt
- Commercial paper
- All securitized debt instruments, such as collateralized mortgage obligations and real estate mortgage investment conduits
- Interest-only and principal-only strips

The following items are *not* debt securities:

- Option contracts
- Financial futures contracts
- Forward contracts
- Lease contracts
- Trade accounts receivable arising from sales on credit by industrial or commercial enterprises
- Loans receivable arising from consumer, commercial, and real estate lending activities of financial institutions

These last two items are examples of receivables that do not meet the definition of *security* unless they have been securitized, in which case they *do* meet the definition.

Equity Security

An *equity security* is any security representing an ownership interest in an enterprise (e.g., common, preferred, or other capital stock) or the right to acquire or dispose of an ownership interest in an enterprise at fixed or determinable prices (e.g., warrants, rights, call options, and put options).

ACCOUNTING FOR INVESTMENTS BY FAS-115

Scope

FAS-115 establishes standards of financial accounting and reporting for (*a*) investments in equity securities that have readily determinable fair values and (*b*) all investments in debt securities. Following are guidelines for the determination of fair value (FAS-115, par. 3):

- Fair value of an equity security is readily determinable if sales prices and bid-and-asked quotations are currently available on a securities exchange registered with the Securities and Exchange Commission or in the over-the-counter market, assuming the over-the-counter securities are publicly reported by the National Association of Securities Dealers Automated Quotations system or by the National Quotation Bureau. Restricted stock (i.e., equity securities whose sale is restricted by governmental or contractual requirement) does not have a readily determinable fair value.

- Fair value of an equity security traded only on a foreign market is considered readily determinable if that foreign market is of a breadth and scope comparable to one of the U.S. markets referred to above.

- Fair value of an investment in a mutual fund is readily determinable if the fair value per share is determined and published and is the basis for current transactions.

FAS-115 does not apply to the following (FAS-115, par. 4):

- Investments in equity securities that, absent the election of the fair value option under FAS-159, are required to be accounted for by the equity method.
- Investments in consolidated subsidiaries.
- Enterprises whose specialized accounting practices include accounting for substantially all investments in debt and equity securities at market or fair value, with changes in value recognized in earnings or in the change in net assets.
- Investments in derivative instruments subject to the guidance in FAS-133 (Accounting for Derivative Instruments

and Hedging Activities). If a derivative instrument is embedded into an investment security, the host instrument (i.e., the investment security itself) remains subject to FAS-115.

- Not-for-profit organizations; guidance in accounting for investments for not-for-profit organizations is provided in FAS-124 (Accounting for Certain Investments Held by Not-for-Profit Organizations).

Classifications of Debt and Equity Securities

FAS-115 requires that an enterprise classify all debt securities and selected equity securities into one of three categories: (1) held-to-maturity, (2) trading, or (3) available-for-sale. The enterprise should reassess the classification at each reporting date (FAS-115, par. 6).

☞ **PRACTICE POINTER:** FAS-115 provides little guidance on how management should determine the appropriate classification of debt and equity investments. Classification is based primarily on management's intent for holding a particular investment:

- Trading securities (both debt and equity) provide a source of ready cash when needed, with the hope of gain from holding the investment for a short period of time.
- Held-to-maturity investments (debt only) are positively intended to be retained until maturity.
- Available-for-sale investments (both debt and equity) rest somewhere between these extremes.

Management's past patterns of practices with regard to securities are an important consideration in determining appropriate classification, as are projections of cash requirements that may imply a need to liquidate investments.

Held-to-Maturity Securities

The *held-to-maturity* category is limited to debt securities. They are measured at amortized cost in the statement of financial position only if the reporting enterprise has the intent and ability to hold them to maturity (FAS-115, par. 7). In certain circumstances, a company may change its intent concerning securities originally classified as held-to-maturity, resulting in their sale or reclassification, without calling into question the company's intent to hold other securities to maturity. FAS-115 identifies the following circumstances in which the sale or transfer of held-to-maturity investments is not considered to be inconsistent with their original classification (FAS-115, par. 8):

- Significant deterioration in the issuer's creditworthiness
- Change in tax law that eliminates or reduces the tax-exempt status of interest on the debt security
- A major business combination or major disposition that necessitates the sale or transfer of the security to maintain the enterprise's existing interest rate risk position or credit risk policy
- A change in statutory or regulatory requirements significantly modifying either what constitutes a permissible investment or the maximum level of investments in certain kinds of securities
- A significant increase by the regulator in the industry's capital requirements that causes a need to downsize by selling held-to-maturity securities
- A significant increase in the risk weights of debt securities used for regulatory risk-based capital purposes
- Other events that are isolated, nonrecurring, and unusual and that could not have been reasonably anticipated by the enterprise

A debt security is not classified as held-to-maturity if the investing enterprise intends to hold the security for only an indefinite period. A debt security is not appropriately classified as held-to-maturity, for example, if it is available for sale in response to the following circumstances (FAS-115, par. 9):

- Changes in market interest rates and related changes in the security's prepayment risk
- Need for liquidity
- Changes in the availability of and the yield on alternative investments
- Changes in funding sources and terms
- Changes in foreign currency risk

FAS-159 includes certain options to record held-to-maturity securities at fair value. Doing so does not challenge the intent to hold to maturity (see Chapter 16, "Fair Value") (FAS-159, pars. 28–29).

Trading Securities

The *trading securities* category includes both debt securities and equity securities with readily determinable fair values. They are measured at fair value in the statement of financial position. Trading securities (FAS-115, par. 12):

- Are bought and held primarily for purposes of selling them in the near term.
- Reflect active and frequent buying and selling.
- Generally are used with the objective of generating profits on short-term differences in price.

Available-for-Sale Securities

The *available-for-sale* category of debt securities includes those debt securities that are not classified in either the held-to-maturity category or the trading category (FAS-115, par. 12).

Standards of Accounting and Reporting Subsequent to Classification

After debt and equity investments are classified as held-to-maturity, trading, and available-for-sale, three important accounting issues must be addressed: (1) reporting changes in fair value, (2) transfers between categories, and (3) impairment of securities.

Reporting Changes in Fair Value

Investments in debt and equity securities classified as trading and available-for-sale are required to be carried at fair value in the statement of financial position. Unrealized holding gains and losses represent the net change in fair value of a security, *excluding*:

- Dividend or interest income recognized but not yet received.
- Any write-downs for permanent impairment.

Unrealized holding gains and losses are accounted for as follows (FAS-115, par. 13):

- *Trading*—included in earnings.
- *Available-for-sale*—excluded from earnings and reported in other comprehensive income until realized.

☞ **PRACTICE POINTER:** The accumulated amount of unrealized holding gains and losses on available-for-sale investments that is included in stockholders' equity is *not* a direct adjustment to retained earnings. It is a separate component of stockholders' equity—a positive amount (credit balance) for accumulated unrealized gains and a negative amount (debit balance) for accumulated unrealized losses. Adjust this account each time the portfolio of available-for-sale investments is revalued (e.g., at the end of each accounting period) as an element of comprehensive income. Recognize the accumulated unrealized gain or loss for a particular security as an element of net income when that security is sold and recognize it in income at that time.

Dividend and interest income, including amortization of premium and discount arising at acquisition, are included in earnings for all three categories of investments. Also, realized gains and losses for securities classified as available-for-sale and held-to-maturity are reported in earnings (FAS-115, par. 14).

Transfers between Categories

Transfers of securities between categories of investments are accounted for at fair value with an unrealized holding gain or loss treated as indicated in the following summarization (FAS-115, par. 15):

Transfer*		
From	To	Accounting Treatment
T	A or H	Unrealized holding gain or loss was already recognized in earnings during prior period(s) and is not reversed.
A or H	T	Unrealized holding gain or loss at the date of transfer is immediately recognized in earnings.
H	A	Unrealized holding gain or loss at the date of transfer is reported in other comprehensive income (FAS-130, par. 33(b)).
A	H	Unrealized holding gain or loss continues to be reported in a separate component of shareholders' equity and is amortized over the remaining life of the security as an adjustment of yield.

*T = Trading; A = Available-for-sale; H = Held-to-maturity

Given the criteria for classification of debt securities in the held-to-maturity category, transfers from that category should be rare. Also, because of the securities' nature, transfers to or from trading are rare (FAS-115, par. 15).

Impairment of Securities

For individual securities classified as either available-for-sale or held-to-maturity, when fair value declines below amortized cost an enterprise should determine whether the decline is temporary or permanent. If the decline in fair value is other than temporary, the following standards apply (FAS-115, par. 16):

- The cost basis of the individual security is written down to fair value as a new cost basis.

- The amount of the write-down is included in current earnings (i.e., accounted for as a realized loss).

- The new cost basis is not changed for subsequent recoveries in fair value; subsequent increases in fair value of available-for-sale securities are included in other comprehensive income; any subsequent decreases in fair value, if temporary, are also included in other comprehensive income [FAS-130, par. 33(d)].

> ☛ **PRACTICE POINTER:** Professional judgment is required to determine whether a decline in fair value of an available-for-sale investment is temporary or other than temporary. A starting point is to judge whether the decline in value results from company-specific events, industry developments, general economic conditions, or other reasons. Once the general reason for the decline is identified, further judgments are required as to whether those causal events are likely to reverse and, if so, whether that reversal is likely to result in a recovery of the fair value of the investment. To help make these judgments, consider how similar circumstances have affected other debt and equity securities.

Financial Statement Presentation and Disclosures

Financial statement presentation of debt and equity investment activities subject to FAS-115 are summarized as follows:

- In the statement of financial position [FAS-135, par. 4t(2)]:
  - *Trading securities, held-to-maturity, and available-for-sale securities*—Current or noncurrent, subject to provisions of ARB-43, Chapter 3A (Current Assets and Current Liabilities)
  - Investments in available-for-sale securities and trading securities that are measured at fair value and non-fair value amounts are reported separately, either as two line items or via parenthetical disclosure of the fair value amount.

- In the statement of cash flows (FAS-115, par. 18, as amended by FAS-159, par. C5b):

  — *Trading securities*—Cash flows from purchases, sales, and maturities classified based on the nature and purpose for which the securities were purchased

  — *Held-to-maturity and available-for-sale*—Cash flows from purchases, sales, and maturities classified as investing activities and reported gross for each classification

☛ **PRACTICE POINTER:** For available-for-sale and held-to-maturity investments, the usual classification in the statement of financial position would be noncurrent, inasmuch as those securities that are held primarily for *liquidity purposes* should be in the trading category. In certain circumstances, however, these investments may qualify for inclusion among current assets. For example, when held-to-maturity (debt) investments are within one year of maturity, they are expected to provide near-term cash and would be classified appropriately as current assets. Similarly, management intent concerning available-for-sale securities that have been held for a period of time may qualify those securities for classification as current, whereas in the past they would have been considered noncurrent.

Treating cash flows from trading securities in the operating category in the statement of cash flows is consistent with the fact that trading securities involve active and frequent buying and selling, and are used generally with the objective of generating profits. Classifying cash flows from held-to-maturity and available-for-sale securities as investing cash flows is consistent with the longer-term nature of those investments.

FAS-115 (as amended by FAS-133) disclosure requirements are as follows:

Required disclosures, by major security type at the date of each statement of financial position presented, for available-for-sale securities are as follows [FAS-133, par. 534(e)]:

- Aggregate fair value
- Total gains for securities with net gains in accumulated other comprehensive income
- Total losses for securities with net losses in accumulated other comprehensive income

Required disclosures, by major security type at the date of each statement of financial position presented, for held-to-maturity securities are as follows [FAS-133, par. 534(e)]:

- Aggregate fair value
- Gross unrecognized holding gains

- Gross unrecognized holding losses
- Net carrying amount
- Gross gains and losses in accumulated other comprehensive income for derivatives that hedged the forecasted acquisition of held-to-maturity securities

  In complying with this requirement, financial institutions shall include the following major types of securities, although additional types may also be included as appropriate:
  — Equity securities
  — Debt securities issued by the U.S. Treasury and other U.S. government corporations and agencies
  — Debt securities issued by states of the United States and political subdivisions of the states
  — Debt securities issued by foreign governments
  — Corporate debt securities
  — Mortgage-backed securities
  — Other debt securities (FAS-115, par. 19)

- Contractual maturities as of the date of the most recent statement of financial position (FAS-115, par. 20). [In complying with this requirement, financial institutions shall disclose the fair value and amortized cost of debt securities in at least four maturity groupings:
  — Within one year
  — One to five years
  — Five to ten years
  — After ten years]

For each period for which the results of operations are presented, the following disclosures are required [FAS-115, par. 21 and FAS-133, par. 534(g)]:

- Proceeds from the sale of available-for-sale securities and the gross realized gains and losses included in earnings
- The basis on which cost of a security sold or the amount reclassified out of accumulated other comprehensive income into earnings was determined (i.e., specific identification, average cost, or other)
- Gross gains and losses from transfers of securities from the available-for-sale category to the trading category that are included in earnings
- Amount of the net unrealized holding gain or loss on available-for-sale securities for the period that has been included in accumulated other comprehensive income, and the amount of gains

and losses reclassified out of accumulated other comprehensive income during the period

- Portion of trading gains and losses for the period pertaining to those trading securities still held at the balance sheet date

For each period for which results of operations are presented, the following information is required for held-to-maturity securities that are sold or transferred into another category [FAS-115, par. 22 and FAS-133, par. 534(h)]:

- The net carrying amount of the sold or transferred security
- The net gain or loss in accumulated other comprehensive income for any derivative that hedged the forecasted acquisition of the held-to-maturity security
- The related realized or unrealized gain or loss
- The circumstances leading to the decision to sell or transfer the security

☛ **PRACTICE POINTER:** If a company has more than one category of debt and equity investments, an efficient way to make many of the required disclosures is to prepare a table: Use columns for investment type (e.g., trading, available-for-sale, and/or held-to-maturity) and rows for the specific information items (e.g., aggregate fair value, unrealized holding gains and losses). This approach not only saves space, but is relatively easy for users of the financial statements to read and understand. If a company has only one category of investments, presentation of information may be more efficient in paragraph form.

Illustration of General Application of FAS-115

To illustrate the general application of FAS-115, consider the case of Marble Co., which invests in two securities on January 1, 20X5, as follows:

Debt investment—$100,000 par value, 9% Paper Co. bonds priced to yield 10%, maturity date 12/31/X9

Equity investment—5,000 shares of Plastic Co. $1 par value common stock at $30 per share

FAS-115 is applied to each investment from the date of purchase. Assume that the debt investment pays interest annually and matures five years from purchase. The purchase price of the two securities is as follows:

Paper Co. bonds:

Present value of interest payments ($100,000 × 9% × 3.79079*)	$ 34,117
Present value of maturity value ($100,000 × .62092**)	62,092
	$ 96,209

Plastic Co. common stock:

5,000 shares @ $30 per share	$150,000
Total	$246,209

The discount on the Paper Co. bonds is amortized over the five-year period to maturity by the effective-interest method, as follows:

	(A) Interest Income	(B) Cash Rec'd	(C) Discount Amortization	(D) Remaining Discount	(E) Carrying Amount
1/1/X5	—	—	—	$3,791	$96,209
12/31/X5	$9,621	$9,000	$621	3,170	96,830
12/31/X6	9,683	9,000	683	2,487	97,513
12/31/X7	9,751	9,000	751	1,736	98,264
12/31/X8	9,826	9,000	826	910	99,090
12/31/X9	9,910	9,000	910	—	100,000

*Present value of annuity at 10%, compounded annually, five periods.
**Present value of one at 10%, five periods.

(A) Previous carrying amount (E) × 10%
(B) $100,000 × 9%
(C) [(A) − (B)]
(D) [Previous-year (D)] − [Current-year (C)]
(E) $100,000 − (D)

Market values for the investments are as follows:

	12/31/X5	12/31/X6
Paper Co. bond	$ 98,000	$ 97,500
Plastic Co. common	155,000	152,000
	$253,000	$249,500

Trading Securities

Assume that Marble Co. classifies the investments described above as trading securities. The securities are initially recorded at cost when they are purchased; discount is amortized on the bond investments to state interest income properly; interest and dividend income are recorded as they are received; and the securities are adjusted to market value at the end of the year with the unrealized gain or loss recognized in income. Assuming dividends of $4 per share are received on October 31, 20X5, on the Plastic Co. common, entries to record all events for 20X5 are as follows:

1/1/X5	Investments (trading)	96,209	
	Cash		96,209
	Purchase of bonds as trading investment.		
1/1/X5	Investments (trading)	150,000	
	Cash		150,000
	Purchase of common as trading investment.		
10/31/X5	Cash (5,000 shares @ $4)	20,000	
	Dividend income		20,000
	Dividends received on common stock investment.		
12/31/X5	Investments (trading)	621	
	Cash	9,000	
	Interest income		9,621
	Interest received and amortization of discount on bond investment.		
12/31/X5	Investments (trading)	6,170	
	Unrealized gain on investments		6,170
	Market value adjustment for trading investments.		

The $6,170 unrealized gain is determined as follows:

Market value of trading securities at 12/31/X5 ($98,000 + $155,000)	$253,000
Carrying amount of trading securities at 12/31/X5 ($96,830 + $150,000)	(246,830)
Unrealized gain	$ 6,170

FAS-115 requires the presentation of trading securities in the balance sheet as current assets and cash flows from trading securities to be classified as operating activities in the statement of cash flows. Those presentations are illustrated later in this example.

Continuing the example into 20X6, assume that the Plastic Co. common pays a $3 per share dividend on October 31. Entries for 20X6 are as follows:

10/31/X6	Cash (5,000 × $3)	15,000	
	Dividend income		15,000
	Dividend received on trading investment.		

12/31/X6	Investments (trading)	683	
	Cash	9,000	
	Interest income		9,683
	Interest and amortization of discount on bond investment.		
12/31/X6	Unrealized loss on investments	4,183	
	Investments (trading)		4,183
	Market value adjustment for trading investments.		

The market value adjustment is determined as follows:

Market value at 12/31/X6 ($97,500 + $152,000)	$249,500
Carrying amount at 12/31/X6 ($98,683 + $155,000)	(253,683)
Unrealized loss	$ 4,183

The carrying amount of the bond investment is the 12/31/X5 market value, adjusted for the discount amortization ($98,000 + $683).

The financial statement presentation for 20X5 and 20X6 for the trading securities is illustrated as follows:

	20X5	20X6
Balance Sheet:		
Current assets: Trading investments	$253,000	$249,500
Income Statement:		
Interest income	$ 9,621	$ 9,683
Dividend income	20,000	15,000
Unrealized gain (loss) on investments	6,170	(4,183)
Statement of Cash Flows:		
Operating activities:		
Dividends	$ 20,000	$ 15,000
Interest	9,000	9,000
Purchase of investment	246,209	—

Available-for-Sale

Now assume that these same investments are classified by management as available-for-sale. All entries for 20X4 and 20X5 are the same, except as follows:

- The investments account is subtitled "available-for-sale" rather than "trading."
- The year-end market value adjustment is not recognized in income, but rather is accumulated and presented in other comprehensive income.

The final entries for 20X5 and 20X6 are as follows:

12/31/X5	Investments (available-for-sale)	6,170	
	Accumulated unrealized gains/ losses on investments		6,170
	Market value adjustment for available-for-sale investments.		
12/31/X6	Accumulated unrealized gains/losses on investments	4,183	
	Investments (available-for-sale)		4,183
	Market value adjustment for available-for-sale investments.		

In 20X6, the accumulated unrealized gains/losses on investments account is used to accumulate the net unrealized gains and losses over the two years. That account has a positive (credit) balance of $6,170 at the end of 20X5; it has a positive (credit) balance of $1,987 ($6,170 – $4,183) at the end of 20X6. FAS-115 indicates that available-for-sale securities may be classified in the balance sheet as either current or noncurrent. Assuming currently marketable investments, that decision would be made primarily on the basis of managerial intent. Cash flows from the purchase and sale of available-for-sale securities are classified in the statement of cash flows as investing activities.

The financial statement presentation for 20X5 and 20X6 for the available-for-sale securities is as follows:

	20X5	20X6
Balance Sheet:		
Assets: Available-for-sale investments	$253,000	$249,500
Stockholders' equity: Other comprehensive income	6,170	1,987
Income Statement:		
Interest income	9,621	9,683
Dividend income	20,000	15,000
Statement of Cash Flows:		
Operating activities:		
Dividends	$ 20,000	$ 15,000
Interest	9,000	9,000
Investing activities:		
Purchase of investments	$246,209	—

Held-to-Maturity

Now assume that the bond investment used in the previous illustrations is classified as held-to-maturity. (The stock investment is not included in the continuation of the illustration, because the held-to-maturity classification is available for debt investments only.)

The entries relative to the purchase of the bond investment and the receipt of interest and amortization of discount are also appropriate for the held-to-maturity classification, assuming the investment account is properly identified as held-to-maturity. No entry is made, however, to recognize the change in market value of the investment at the end of each year, because the method of accounting for the held-to-maturity securities is amortized cost. Held-to-maturity investments ordinarily would be classified in the balance sheet as noncurrent, except when the maturity date is within the period used to identify current assets (e.g., one year). Cash flows from transactions involving held-to-maturity investments are classified as investing activities in the statement of cash flows.

The financial statement presentation for the held-to-maturity investment for 20X5 and 20X6 is as follows:

	20X5	20X6
Balance Sheet:		
Assets: Held-to-maturity investments	$96,830	$97,513
Income Statement:		
Interest income	$ 9,621	$9,683
Statement of Cash Flows:		
Operating activities:		
Interest	$ 9,000	$9,000
Investing activities:		
Purchase of investments	$96,209	—

RELATED CHAPTERS IN 2009 *GAAP GUIDE LEVEL A*

Chapter 3, "Balance Sheet Classification and Related Display Issues"

Chapter 7, "Consolidated Financial Statements"

Chapter 14, "Equity Method"

Chapter 16, "Fair Value"

Chapter 17, "Financial Instruments"

Chapter 18, "Foreign Operations and Exchange"

Chapter 40, "Results of Operations"

Chapter 50, "Mortgage Banking"

Chapter 51, "Not-for-Profit Organizations"

RELATED CHAPTERS IN 2009 *GAAP GUIDE LEVELS B, C, AND D*

Chapter 4, "Balance Sheet Classification and Related Display Issues"

Chapter 10, "Consolidated Financial Statements"

Chapter 14, "Equity Method"

Chapter 17, "Financial Instruments"

Chapter 18, "Foreign Operations and Exchange"

Chapter 25, "Investments in Debt and Equity Securities"

Chapter 35, "Results of Operations"

RELATED CHAPTERS IN 2009 *INTERNATIONAL ACCOUNTING/FINANCIAL REPORTING STANDARDS GUIDE*

Chapter 3, "Presentation of Financial Statements"

Chapter 10, "Consolidated Financial Statements"

Chapter 14, "The Equity Method"

Chapter 16, "Financial Instruments"

Chapter 17, "Foreign Currency Translation"

Chapter 24, "Investment Property"

CHAPTER 29
LEASES

CONTENTS

OVERVIEW

A *lease* is an agreement that conveys the right to use property, usually for a specified period. Leases typically involve two parties:

the owner of the property (lessor) and the party contracting to use the property (lessee). Because of certain tax, cash flow, and other advantages, leases have become an important alternative to the outright purchase of property by which companies (lessees) acquire the resources needed to operate.

Leases include agreements that, while not nominally referred to as leases, have the characteristic of transferring the right to use property (e.g., heat supply contracts), and agreements that transfer the right to use property even though the contractor may be required to provide substantial services in connection with the operation or maintenance of the assets (FAS-13, par. 1).

The term *lease*, as used in promulgated GAAP, does *not* include the following (FAS-13, par. 1):

- Agreements that are contracts for services that do not transfer the right to use property from one contracting party to another
- Agreements that concern the right to explore for or exploit natural resources such as oil, gas, minerals, and timber
- Agreements that represent licensing agreements for items such as motion picture films, plays, manuscripts, patents, and copyrights

A central accounting issue associated with leases is the identification of those leases that are treated appropriately as sales of the property by lessors and as purchases of the property by lessees (*capital leases*). Those leases that are not identified as capital leases are called *operating leases* and are not treated as sales by lessors and as purchases by lessees. Rather, they are treated on a prospective basis as a series of cash flows from the lessee to the lessor.

GAAP for leases include the largest number of authoritative accounting pronouncements of any single subject in accounting literature. Pronouncements that follow FAS-13 (Accounting for Leases) explain, interpret, or amend that pronouncement in a variety of ways; many of them arose as a result of attempts to implement FAS-13. Following are pronouncements that collectively establish promulgated GAAP for lease accounting:

FAS-13	Accounting for Leases
FAS-22	Changes in the Provisions of Lease Agreements Resulting from Refundings of Tax-Exempt Debt
FAS-23	Inception of the Lease
FAS-27	Classification of Renewals or Extensions of Existing Sales-Type or Direct Financing Leases
FAS-28	Accounting for Sales with Leasebacks
FAS-29	Determining Contingent Rentals

FAS-91	Accounting for Nonrefundable Fees and Costs Associated with Originating or Acquiring Loans and Initial Direct Costs of Leases
FAS-98	Accounting for Leases:

- Sale-Leaseback Transactions Involving Real Estate
- Sales-Type Leases of Real Estate
- Definition of the Lease Term
- Initial Direct Costs of Direct Financing Leases

FAS-145	Rescission of FASB Statements No. 4, 44, and 64, Amendment of FASB Statement No. 13, and Technical Corrections
FIN-19	Lessee Guarantee of the Residual Value of Leased Property
FIN-21	Accounting for Leases in a Business Combination
FIN-23	Leases of Certain Property Owned by a Governmental Unit or Authority
FIN-24	Leases Involving Only Part of a Building
FIN-26	Accounting for Purchase of a Leased Asset by the Lessee during the Term of the Lease
FIN-27	Accounting for a Loss on a Sublease

Following is a brief overview of the nine Statements of Financial Accounting Standards included in the promulgated GAAP for leases.

FAS-13 defines a lease as an agreement that conveys the right to use assets (tangible or intangible) for a stated period. A lease that transfers substantially all the benefits and risks inherent in the ownership of property is called a *capital lease*. Such a lease is accounted for by the lessee as the acquisition of an asset and the incurrence of a liability. The lessor accounts for such a lease as a sale (sales-type lease) or financing (direct financing lease). All other leases are referred to as *operating leases*.

FAS-22 addresses an inconsistency between FAS-13 and APB-26 (Early Extinguishment of Debt) arising from refundings of tax-exempt debt, including advance refundings that are accounted for as early extinguishments of debt. FAS-22 is covered in more detail later in this chapter.

FAS-23 amends FAS-13 to specify that, if the leased property is yet to be constructed or acquired by the lessor at the inception of the lease, the lessor's criterion pertaining to "no important uncertainties of unreimbursable costs yet to be incurred by the lessor" is applied at the date that construction of the property is completed or the property is acquired. FAS-23 amends FAS-13 to specify that any increases in the minimum lease payments that have occurred during the preacquisition or preconstruction period as a result of an escalation clause are to be considered in determining the fair value of the leased property at the inception of the lease. FAS-23 also amends FAS-13 to limit the amount that can be recorded by the lessor for the residual value of leased property to an amount not greater than the estimate as of the inception of the lease. FAS-23 is discussed more fully throughout this chapter.

FAS-27 modifies FAS-13 to require a lessor to classify a renewal or an extension of a sales-type or direct financing lease as a sales-type lease if the lease would otherwise qualify as a sales-type lease and the renewal or extension occurs at or near the end of the lease term. Otherwise, FAS-13 prohibits the classification of a renewal or extension of a sales-type or direct financing lease as a sales-type lease at any other time during the lease term.

FAS-28 amends FAS-13 to specify the appropriate accounting for sale-leaseback transactions depending on the percentage amount of the property that the seller-lessee leases back (substantially all of the property, a minor portion of the property, or more than a minor portion of the property but less than substantially all) and whether the lease is classified as a capital lease or an operating lease.

FAS-29 amends FAS-13 to provide a new definition for *contingent rentals* as those that cannot be determined at the inception of the lease because they depend on future factors or events. Rental payments based on future sales volume, future machine hours, future interest rates, and future price indexes are examples of contingent rentals. Contingent rentals can either increase or decrease lease payments.

FAS-91 establishes accounting and reporting standards for nonrefundable fees and costs associated with lending, committing to lend, or purchasing a loan or group of loans. Under FAS-91, direct loan origination fees and costs, including initial direct costs incurred by a lessor in negotiating and consummating a lease, are offset against each other and the net amount is deferred and recognized over the life of the loan as an adjustment to the yield on the loan. The provisions of FAS-91 apply to all types of loans, including debt securities, and to all types of lenders, including banks, thrift institutions, insurance companies, mortgage bankers, and other financial and nonfinancial institutions. However, FAS-91 does not apply to nonrefundable fees and costs that are associated with originating or acquiring loans which are carried at market value.

FAS-98 amends FAS-13 to establish a new definition of *penalty* and *lease term* for all leasing transactions. FAS-98 specifies the appropriate accounting for a seller-lessee in a sale-leaseback transaction involving real estate, including real estate with equipment, such as manufacturing facilities, power plants, furnished office buildings, etc. FAS-98 establishes the appropriate accounting for a sale-leaseback transaction in which property improvements or integral equipment is sold to a purchaser-lessor and leased back by the seller-lessee who retains the ownership of the underlying land. FAS-98 also provides the appropriate accounting for sale-leaseback transactions involving real estate with equipment that include separate sale and leaseback agreements for the real estate and the equipment (*a*) with the same entity or related parties and (*b*) that are consummated at or near the same time, suggesting that they were negotiated as a package.

FAS-145 amends FAS-13 to eliminate certain inconsistencies between how sale-leaseback transactions are accounted for under FAS-98 or FAS-28 and how certain lease modifications, where the modification results in the lease transaction being similar to a sale-leaseback, have been accounted for under FAS-13.

BACKGROUND

Some lease agreements are such that an asset and a related liability should be reported on the balance sheet of the lessee enterprise. The distinction is one of *substance over form* when the transaction actually *transfers substantially all the benefits and risks inherent in the ownership of the property.*

Established in GAAP are criteria to determine whether a lease transaction is in substance a transfer of the incidents of ownership. If, *at its inception*, a lease meets one or more of the following four criteria, the lease is classified as a capital lease (FAS-13, par. 7):

1. By the end of the lease term, ownership of the leased property is transferred to the lessee.

2. The lease contains a bargain purchase option.

3. The lease term is substantially (75% or more) equal to the estimated useful life of the leased property.

4. At the inception of the lease, the present value of the minimum lease payments, with certain adjustments, is 90% or more of the fair value of the leased property.

These criteria are examined in more detail later in this chapter.

TERMINOLOGY

The authoritative literature includes many terms that are important for an understanding of lease accounting. Several of these terms are explained below.

Capital Lease

A capital lease transfers the benefits and risks inherent in the ownership of the property to the lessee, who accounts for the lease as an acquisition of an asset and the incurrence of a liability (FAS-13, par. 6a).

Sales-Type Lease

A sales-type lease is a type of capital lease that results in a manufacturer's or dealer's profit or loss to the lessor and transfers substantially all the benefits and risks inherent in the ownership of the leased property to the lessee; in addition, (*a*) the minimum lease payments are reasonably predictable of collection and (*b*) no important uncertainties exist regarding costs to be incurred by the lessor under the terms of the lease (FAS-13, par. 6b).

In a sales-type lease, the *fair value* of the leased property at the inception of the lease differs from the cost or carrying amount because a manufacturer's or dealer's profit or loss exists. Fair value usually is the *normal selling price* of the property.

Direct Financing Lease

A direct financing lease is a type of capital lease that does *not* result in a manufacturer's or dealer's profit or loss to the lessor, but does transfer substantially all the benefits and risks inherent in the ownership of the leased property to the lessee; in addition, (*a*) the minimum lease payments are reasonably predictable of collection and (*b*) no important uncertainties exist regarding costs to be incurred by the lessor under the terms of the lease (FAS-13, par. 6b).

Separately identifying sales-type and direct financing leases is an accounting issue for the lessor only, who accounts for the two types of capital leases differently, as described later in this chapter. Both types of leases transfer substantially all the benefits and risks inherent in the ownership of the leased property to the lessee, who records the transaction as a *capital lease*.

Fair Value

Fair value is the price for which the leased property could be sold between unrelated parties in an arm's-length transaction at the measurement date (FAS-13, par. 5c, as amended by FAS-157, par. E4a).

For the manufacturer or dealer, fair value usually is the normal selling price less trade or volume discounts. Fair value may be less than the normal selling price, however, and sometimes less than the cost of the property.

For others, fair value usually is cost less trade or volume discounts. Fair value may be less than cost, however, especially in circumstances in which a long period elapses between the acquisition of the property by the lessor and the inception of a lease.

Fair Rental

Fair rental is the rental rate for similar property under similar lease terms and conditions.

Related Parties

Related parties are one or more entities subject to the significant influence over the operating and financial policies of another entity (FAS-13, par. 5a).

Executory Costs

Executory costs are items such as insurance, maintenance, and taxes paid in connection with the leased property (FAS-13, par. 7d).

Bargain Purchase Option

A bargain purchase option is a lessee's option to purchase the leased property at a sufficiently low price that makes the exercise of the option relatively certain (FAS-13, par. 5d).

Bargain Renewal Option

A bargain renewal option is a lessee's option to renew the lease at a sufficiently low rental that makes the exercise of the option relatively certain (FAS-13, par. 5e).

Estimated Economic Life

Estimated economic life is the estimated remaining useful life of the property for the purpose for which it was intended, regardless of the term of the lease (FAS-13, par. 5g).

Estimated Residual Value

Estimated residual value is the estimated fair value of the leased property at the end of the lease term. The estimated residual value shall not exceed the amount estimated at the inception of the lease except for the effect of any increases that result during the construction or preacquisition period, because of escalation provisions in the lease (FAS-13, par. 5h).

Unguaranteed Residual Value

Unguaranteed residual value is the estimated fair value of the leased property at the end of the lease term that is not guaranteed by either the lessee or a third party unrelated to the lessor. A guarantee by a third party related to the lessee is considered a lessee guarantee (FAS-13, par. 5i).

Lessee's Incremental Borrowing Rate

The lessee's incremental borrowing rate is the rate of interest that the lessee would have had to pay at the inception of the lease to borrow the funds, on similar terms, to purchase the leased property (FAS-13, par. 5l).

Inception of Lease

The inception of the lease is the date of the lease agreement *or* the date of a written commitment signed by the parties involved that sets forth the principal provisions of the lease transaction. A written commitment that does not contain all of the principal provisions of the lease transaction does not establish the inception date (FAS-23, par. 6).

Interest Rate Implicit in the Lease

The interest rate implicit in the lease is the rate that, when applied to certain items (enumerated below), results in an aggregate present value equal to the fair value of the leased property at the beginning of the lease term, less any investment credit expected to be realized and retained by the lessor. The discount rate is applied to (a) the minimum lease payments, excluding executory costs such as insurance, maintenance, and taxes (including any profit thereon) that are paid by the lessor and (b) the estimated fair value of the property at the end of the lease term, exclusive of any portion guaranteed by either the lessee or a third party unrelated to the lessor (unguaranteed residual value) (FAS-13, par. 5k).

Initial Direct Costs

The definition of *initial direct costs* is as follows (FAS-91, par. 24):

> *Initial direct costs.** Only those costs incurred by the lessor that are (a) costs to originate a lease incurred in transactions with independent third parties that (i) result directly from and are essential to acquire that lease and (ii) would not have been incurred had that leasing transaction not occurred and (b) certain costs directly related to specified

activities performed by the lessor for that lease. Those activities are: evaluating the prospective lessee's financial condition; evaluating and recording guarantees, collateral, and other security arrangements; negotiating lease terms; preparing and processing lease documents; and closing the transaction. The costs directly related to those activities shall include only that portion of the employees' total compensation and payroll-related fringe benefits directly related to time spent performing those activities for that lease and other costs related to those activities that would not have been incurred but for that lease. Initial direct costs shall not include costs related to activities performed by the lessor for advertising, soliciting potential lessees, servicing existing leases, and other ancillary activities related to establishing and monitoring credit policies, supervision, and administration. Initial direct costs shall not include administrative costs, rent, depreciation, any other occupancy and equipment costs, and employees' compensation and fringe benefits related to activities described in the previous sentence, unsuccessful origination efforts, and idle time.

---

*Initial direct cost shall be offset by nonrefundable fees that are yield adjustments as prescribed in FAS-91.

In determining the net amount of initial direct costs in a leasing transaction under FAS-13, a lessor shall apply the provisions of FAS-91 relating to loan origination fees, commitment fees, and direct loan origination costs of completed loans. Initial direct costs are accounted for by lessors as part of the investment in a direct financing lease.

> **OBSERVATION:** The recognition of a portion of the unearned income at the inception of a lease transaction to offset initial direct costs is not permitted (FAS-91, par. 23).

Contingent Rentals

Contingent rentals are those that cannot be determined at the inception of the lease because they depend on future factors or events. Rental payments based on future sales volume, future machine hours, future interest rates, and future price indexes are examples of contingent rentals. Contingent rentals can either increase or decrease lease payments (FAS-29, par. 11).

Increases in minimum lease payments that occur during the preacquisition or construction period as a result of an escalation clause in the lease are not considered contingent rentals (FAS-29, par. 11).

Lease Term

The lease term includes all of the following (FAS-98, par. 22a):

- Any fixed noncancelable term
- Any period covered by a bargain renewal option
- Any period in which penalties are imposed in an amount that at the inception of the lease reasonably assures the renewal of the lease by the lessee
- Any period covered by ordinary renewal options during which a guarantee by the lessee of the lessor's debt that is directly or indirectly related to the leased property is expected to be in effect or a loan from the lessee to the lessor that is directly or indirectly related to the leased property is expected to be outstanding

   Note: The phrase *indirectly related to the leased property* is used to cover situations that in substance are guarantees of the lessor's debt or loans to the lessor by the lessee that are related to the leased property, but are structured in such a manner that they do not represent a direct guarantee or loan.
- Any period covered by ordinary renewal options preceding the date on which a bargain purchase option is exercisable
- Any period representing renewals or extensions of the lease at the lessor's option

A lease term does not extend beyond the date a bargain purchase option becomes exercisable.

Noncancelable Lease Term

A noncancelable lease term is a provision in a lease agreement that specifies that the lease may be canceled only (*a*) on some remote contingency, (*b*) with permission of the lessor, or (*c*) if the lessee enters into a new lease with the same lessor (FAS-98, par. 22a).

Penalty

The term *penalty* refers to any outside factor or provision of the lease agreement that does or can impose on the lessee the requirement to disburse cash, incur or assume a liability, perform services, surrender or transfer an asset or rights to an asset or otherwise forego an economic benefit, or suffer an economic detriment (FAS-98, par. 22b).

MINIMUM LEASE PAYMENTS

Normal minimum lease payments for the lessee include (FAS-13, par. 5j):

- The minimum rent called for during the lease term
- Any payment or guarantee that the lessee must make or is required to make concerning the leased property at the end of the lease term (residual value), including:
  — Any amount stated to purchase the leased property
  — Any amount stated to make up any deficiency from a specified minimum
  — Any amount payable for failure to renew or extend the lease at the expiration of the lease term

When a lease contains a *bargain purchase option*, the minimum lease payments include only (*a*) the *minimum rental payments over the lease term* and (*b*) *the payment required to exercise the bargain purchase option.*

The following are excluded in determining minimum lease payments (FAS-13, par. 5j):

- A guarantee by the lessee to pay the lessor's debt on the leased property
- The lessee's obligation (separate from the rental payments) to pay executory costs (insurance, taxes, etc.) in connection with the leased property
- Contingent rentals (FAS-29, par. 10)

> **OBSERVATION:** FIN-19 (Lessee Guarantee of the Residual Value of Leased Property) clarifies certain guarantees of the residual value of leased property made by a lessee, as follows:
>
> - A guarantee by a lessee to make up a residual value deficiency caused by damage, extraordinary wear and tear, or excessive usage is similar to a contingent rental, since the amount is not determinable at the inception of the lease. Therefore, this type of lessee guarantee does not constitute a lessee guarantee of residual value for purposes of computing the lessee's minimum lease payments (FIN-19, par. 3).
> - A lessee's guarantee to make up a residual value deficiency at the end of a lease term is limited to the specified maximum deficiency called for by the lease (FIN-19, par. 4).
> - Unless the lessor explicitly releases the lessee, a guarantee of residual value by an unrelated third party for the benefit of the lessor does not release the obligation of the lessee. Therefore, such a guarantee by an unrelated third party shall not be used to reduce the lessee's minimum lease pay-

ments. Costs incurred in connection with a guarantee by an unrelated third party are considered executory costs and are not included in computing the lessee's minimum lease payments (FIN-19, par. 5).

The minimum lease payments to a lessor are the sum of (FAS-13, par. 5j):

- The minimum lease payments under the lease terms
- Any guarantee by a third party, unrelated to the lessee and lessor, of the residual value or rental payments beyond the lease term, providing such guarantor is financially capable of discharging the potential obligation

LEASE CLASSIFICATION

Lessees

If one or more of the following four criteria is present at the inception of a lease, it is classified as a capital lease by the lessee (FAS-13, par. 7):

1. Ownership of the property is transferred to the lessee by the end of the lease term.
2. The lease contains a bargain purchase option.
3. The lease term, at inception, is substantially (75% or more) equal to the estimated economic life of the leased property, including earlier years of use. (*Exception:* This criterion cannot be used for a lease that begins within the last 25% of the original estimated economic life of the leased property. *Example:* A jet aircraft that has an estimated economic life of 25 years is leased for five successive five-year leases. If the first four five-year leases were classified as operating leases, the last five-year lease cannot be classified as a capital lease, because the lease would commence within the last 25% of the estimated economic life of the property and would fall under this exception.)
4. The present value of the minimum lease payments at the beginning of the lease term, excluding executory costs and profits thereon to be paid by the lessor, is 90% or more of the fair value of the property at the inception of the lease, less any investment tax credit retained and expected to be realized by the lessor. (*Exception:* This criterion cannot be used for a lease that begins within the last 25% of the original estimated economic life of the leased property.)

A lessee's incremental borrowing rate is used to determine the present value of the minimum lease payments, except that the lessor's implicit rate of interest is used if it is known and it is lower (FAS-13, par. 7d).

> ☞ **PRACTICE POINTER:** While the criteria for identifying a capital lease appear very specific, significant professional judgment must be exercised in implementing them. For example:
>
> - Except in the simplest cases, determining the lease term may involve judgment.
> - Several of the criteria include terms that require judgment when they are applied to a specific lease. These include "bargain purchase option," "estimated useful life of the property," and "fair value of the property."
> - The lease term and the present value of minimum lease payments criteria are not available for leases that begin within the last 25% of the asset's estimated useful life, which is subject to judgment.
> - Determining the minimum lease payments for the lessee may require use of that party's incremental borrowing rate, which may involve judgment.

Lessors

If, at inception, a lease meets any one (or more) of the four criteria indicating that substantially all the benefits and risks of ownership have been transferred to the lessee, and it *meets both the following conditions,* the lease is classified by the lessor as a sales-type or direct financing lease, whichever is appropriate:

- *Collection of the minimum lease payments is reasonably predictable.* A receivable resulting from a lease subject to an estimate of uncollectibility based on experience is not precluded from being classified as either a sales-type or a direct financing lease (FAS-98, par. 22f).
- *No important uncertainties exist for unreimbursable costs yet to be incurred by the lessor under the lease.* Important uncertainties include extensive warranties and material commitments beyond normal practice. *Executory costs,* such as insurance, maintenance, and taxes, are not considered important uncertainties (FAS-13, par. 8b).

  Note: In the event the leased property is not acquired or constructed before the inception of the lease, this condition is not applied until such time as the leased property is acquired or constructed by the lessor (FAS-23, par. 7).

In applying the fourth basic capitalization criterion—the present value of the lease equals or exceeds 90% of the fair value of the property—a *lessor* computes the present value of the minimum lease payments, using the interest rate *implicit in the lease* (FAS-13, par. 7d).

A lease involving real estate is not classified by the lessor as a sales-type lease unless the title to the leased property is transferred to the lessee at or shortly after the end of the lease term (FAS-98, par. 22c).

Classification of a lease as a capital or operating lease is summarized in Figure 29-1.

CHANGING A PROVISION OF A LEASE

If a change in a provision of a lease results in a different lease classification at the inception of the lease because it meets different criteria, a new lease agreement is created that must be reclassified according to its different criteria. Renewal, extension, or a new lease under which the lessee continues to use the same property is not considered a change in a lease provision (FAS-13, par. 9).

Any action that extends the lease term, except to void a residual guarantee, or a penalty for failure to renew the lease at the end of the lease term, is considered a new lease agreement that is classified according to the different criteria (FAS-13, par. 9).

Changes in estimates or circumstances do not cause a reclassification.

Refunding of Tax-Exempt Debt

If a change in a lease occurs as a result of a refunding by the lessor of tax-exempt debt and (*a*) the lessee receives the economic advantages of the refunding and (*b*) the revised lease qualifies and is classified either as a capital lease by the lessee or as a direct financing lease by the lessor, the change in the lease shall be accounted for on the basis of whether or not an extinguishment of debt has occurred, as follows (FAS-22, par. 12):

- Accounted for as an extinguishment of debt:
  - The lessee adjusts the lease obligation to the present value of the future minimum lease payments under the revised agreement, using the effective interest rate of the new lease agreement. Any gain or loss is treated as a gain or loss on an early extinguishment of debt.
  - The lessor adjusts the balance of the minimum lease payments receivable and the gross investment in the lease (if affected) for the difference between the present values of the old and new or revised agreement. Any gain or loss is recognized in the current period.

Figure 29-1: Classification of a Lease as a Capital or Operating Lease

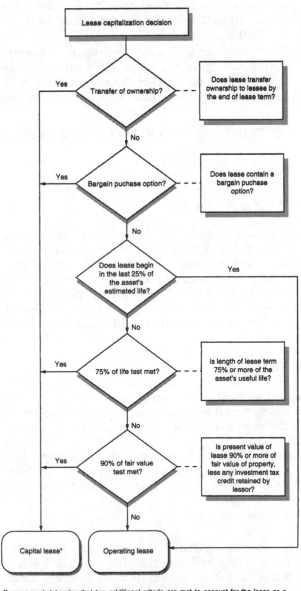

*Lessor must determine that two additional criteria are met to account for the lease as a capital lease:

1. Collection of minimum lease payments is reasonably predictable.
2. No important uncertainties exist for unreimbursable costs to be incurred by the lessor.

- Not accounted for as an extinguishment of debt:
  - — The lessee accrues any costs connected with the refunding that are obligated to be reimbursed to the lessor. The interest method is used to amortize the costs over the period from the date of the refunding to the call date of the debt to be refunded.
  - — The lessor recognizes as revenue any reimbursements to be received from the lessee for costs paid related to the debt to be refunded over the period from the date of the refunding to the call date of the debt to be refunded.

ACCOUNTING AND REPORTING BY LESSEES

Capital Leases

Initial Recording

The lessee records a capital lease as an asset and a corresponding liability. The initial recording value of a lease is the *lesser* of the fair value of the leased property or the present value of the minimum lease payments, excluding any portion representing executory costs and profit thereon to be paid by the lessor. Fair value is determined as of the inception of the lease, and the present value of the minimum lease payments is computed at the beginning of the lease term. The inception of the lease and the beginning of the lease term are not necessarily the same dates (FAS-13, par. 10).

Because the lessee's minimum lease payments *exclude* a lessee's obligation to pay executory costs, executory costs paid by the lessee are expensed as paid or appropriately accrued. If such costs are included in the rental payments and are not identified separately (which is the most likely case), an estimate of the amount is necessary (FAS-13, par. 10).

A lessee's incremental borrowing rate is used to determine the present value of the minimum lease payments unless the lessor's implicit rate of interest is known and is lower (FAS-13, par. 7d).

Leases with Escalation Clauses

In lease agreements or written commitments in which the leased property is to be acquired or constructed by the lessor, there may be a provision for the escalation of the minimum lease payments during the construction or preacquisition period. Usually, the escalation is based on increased costs of acquisition or construction of the leased property. A provision to escalate the minimum lease payments during the construction or preacquisition period can also be based on other measures of cost or value, including general price-level changes or changes in the consumer price index.

The relationship between the total amount of minimum lease payments and the fair value of a lease is such that when one increases so does the other. For example, assume that the total minimum lease payments of a particular lease are $100,000 payable in five equal annual installments, and the fair value of the same lease is $350,000. If the minimum lease payments are increased 20% to $120,000, it is likely that the fair value of the lease will increase correspondingly, because the lease is then worth more to an investor.

FAS-23 requires that increases in the minimum lease payments that occur during the preacquisition or construction period as a result of an escalation clause be considered in determining the fair value of the leased property at the inception of the lease for the purposes of the initial recording of the lease transaction by the lessee, or where fair value is used as a basis of allocation (FAS-23, par. 8).

The initial recording value of a lease transaction by the lessee, which is required by FAS-13, is the lesser of the fair value of the leased property or the present value of the minimum lease payments. FAS-23 changes the lessee's determination of fair value for leases that contain escalation clauses from the fair value on the inception date to a fair value amount that includes the effect of any increases which have occurred as a result of the escalation clause. The changes embodied in FAS-23 are intended to create lease classifications that more closely reflect the substance of a lease transaction.

> **OBSERVATION:** The question arises as to when leases of this type should be recorded on the books of the lessee. FAS-23 appears to indicate that the initial recording should be made only after the effects of the escalation clause on the fair value of the leased property are determined. Otherwise, FAS-23 is silent in all respects as to when the lease transaction should be recorded. In the case of significant amounts of leases, it appears illogical to wait several years to record the transaction. If this is the only viable alternative, however, full disclosure of all pertinent facts pertaining to the lease agreement or commitment should be made in a prominent footnote.
>
> The other alternative is to record these types of lease transactions immediately at the inception of the lease, utilizing whatever information is available and subsequently adjusting the recorded amounts when the effects of the escalation clauses are known. This alternative does not appear to be viable because of the difficulties mentioned in the following paragraphs.
>
> The last-enumerated criterion in FAS-13 for capitalizing a lease is when the present value of the minimum lease payments is 90% or more of the fair value of the leased property at the inception of the lease. When this criterion is considered for capitalizing a lease in conjunction with the alternative of recording lease transactions covered by FAS-23 at the inception of the lease and then subsequently adjusting the recorded amounts when the effects of the escalation clauses become known, the

following problems arise, which are not addressed by either FAS-13 or FAS-23.

- If we assume that FAS-23 requires that the fair value of leases with escalation clauses be determined at a future date, what fair value should be used to determine whether the lease is or is not a capital lease in accordance with the criterion of whether the present value of the minimum lease payments is 90% or more of the fair value of the leased property at the inception of the lease?

- What if a lease of this type is capitalized in accordance with the criterion that the present value of the minimum lease payments is 90% or more of the fair value at inception of the lease, and subsequently, as a result of the escalation clause, the present value becomes less than 90% of the fair value, so that the lease should not have been capitalized?

- Suppose a lease with an escalation clause is properly classified as an operating lease at inception of the lease and subsequently, as a result of the escalation clause, the lease qualifies as a capital lease.

The above are just a few of the complications that could arise in applying the provisions of FAS-23 to lease transactions.

FAS-23 also permits increases in the estimated residual value (see definition) that occur as a result of escalation provisions in leases in which the leased property is to be acquired or constructed by the lessor. For example, if the estimated residual value is 10% of the fair value at the inception of a lease and during the construction or preacquisition period of the leased property the effects of the escalation clause increase the fair value, then the estimated residual value also is allowed to increase above the amount that was estimated at the date of the inception of the lease (FAS-23, par. 9).

Amortization

The asset recorded under a capital lease is amortized in a manner consistent with the lessee's normal depreciation policy for other owned assets. The period for amortization is either (*a*) the estimated economic life or (*b*) the lease term, depending on which criterion was used to classify the lease. If the criterion used is either of the first two criteria (ownership of the property is transferred to the lessee by the end of the lease term or the lease contains a bargain purchase option), the asset is amortized over its estimated economic life. In all other cases, the asset is amortized over the lease term. Any *estimated residual value* is deducted from the asset to determine the amortizable base (FAS-13, par. 11).

☛ **PRACTICE POINTER:** Determining the appropriate amortization period for capital leases is an important issue where the lease term is significantly less than the expected useful life of the asset. A simple rule of thumb is simply to determine which party to the lease is expected to have use of the property during the period between the end of the lease period and the end of the expected life of the asset. If the lease is capitalized by the first or second capitalization criteria (transfer of title and bargain purchase option), the underlying assumption is that the lessee will become the legal owner of the asset by the end of the lease term and will have use of it for the remainder of the asset's expected life. Thus, the estimated life of the asset is the logical period of amortization. On the other hand, an assumption of the transfer of legal title does not underlie the lease if it is capitalized because of the third or fourth criteria (lease term and the present value of minimum lease payments). In either of these circumstances, the lease term is the logical period for amortization of the leased asset. Generally, if the same lease satisfies one or both of the first two criteria and one or both of the second criteria, use the expected life of the asset as the period of amortization.

Interest Expense: Interest Method

The interest method, sometimes referred to as the *effective interest method*, is used to produce a constant rate of interest on the remaining lease liability. A portion of each minimum lease payment is allocated to interest expense and/or amortization, and the balance is applied to reduce the lease liability. Any *residual guarantee(s)* by the lessee or penalty payments are automatically taken into consideration by using the interest method and will result in a balance at the end of the lease term equal to the amount of the guarantee or penalty payments at that date (FAS-13, par. 12).

Illustration of Interest Method

Jones Company leases a tractor-trailer for $8,000 per year on a noncancelable five-year lease. The yearly lease payment is due at the beginning of the year. Jones guarantees to the lessor that the tractor-trailer will have a residual value of at least $5,000 at the end of the lease term.
Assume that a 12% interest rate is used.

Present value of $8,000 payments for five years at 12% =		$32,299*
Present value of $5,000 guaranteed residual value in five years at 12%	=	2,837**
Total asset and lease obligation		$35,136

---

*$8,000 × 4.03735
**$5,000 × .56743

A schedule of interest expense, amortization, and reduction of the lease obligation of $35,136 to the $5,000 residual guarantee using the interest method follows:

Book Value Lease Obligation Beginning of Year	Rental Payment/ Reduction in Lease Obligation	Outstanding Balance During Year	Interest @ 12%	Book Value Lease Obligation End of Year
$35,136	$8,000	$27,136	$3,256	$30,392
30,392	8,000	22,392	2,687	25,079
25,079	8,000	17,079	2,049	19,129
19,129	8,000	11,129	1,335	12,464
12,464	8,000	4,464	536	5,000

Change in Lease Terms

If a guarantee or penalty is rendered inoperative because of a renewal or other extension of the *lease term*, or if a new lease is consummated in which the lessee continues to lease the same property, an adjustment must be made to the asset and lease obligation for the difference between the present values of the old and the revised agreements. In these cases, the present value of the future minimum lease payments under the new or revised agreement is computed using the original rate of interest on the initial lease (FAS-13, par. 12).

Other lease changes are accounted for as follows (FAS-13, par. 14):

- If a lease change results in revised minimum lease payments, but also is classified as a capital lease, an adjustment is made to the asset and lease obligation for the difference between the present values of the old and the new or revised agreement. The present value of the future minimum lease payments under the new or revised agreement is computed using the original rate of interest used on the initial lease.

- A capital lease may be modified in such a way that the new lease agreement is treated as an operating lease. FAS-13 required that the lease asset and obligation (liability) be removed from the accounts and any resulting gain or loss be recognized in determining current period income. The new lease agreement was accounted for as an operating lease (FAS-13, par. 14a).

  The FASB concluded that the economic effects of the above transaction are similar to those of a sale-leaseback. However, FAS-13 does not require sale-leaseback accounting. FAS-145 requires sale-leaseback accounting, under the provisions of

FAS-98 or FAS-28, when a capital lease is modified such that the revised lease agreement is classified as an operating lease. FAS-98 (Accounting for Leases: Sale-Leaseback Transactions Involving Real Estate; Sales-Type Leases of Real Estate; Definition of the Lease Term; Initial Direct Costs of Direct Financing Leases) provides guidance on sale-leaseback transactions involving real estate; FAS-28 (Accounting for Sales with Lease-backs) provides guidance on all other types of saleleaseback transactions (FAS-145, par. 8).

- A renewal, extension, or new lease under which the lessee continues to use the same property, except when a guarantee or penalty is rendered inoperative (see above), is accounted for as follows:

  — *Renewal or extension classified as a capital lease:* An adjustment is made for the difference between the original and revised present values, using the original discount rate.

  — *Renewal or extension classified as an operating lease:* The existing lease continues to be accounted for as a capital lease to the end of its lease term, and the renewal or extension is accounted for as an operating lease.

When leased property under a capital lease is purchased by the lessee, it is accounted for as a renewal or extension of a capital lease. Thus, any difference between the carrying amount and the purchase price on the date of purchase is treated as an adjustment of the carrying amount of the property (FIN-26, par. 5).

Termination of a Lease

Gain or loss, if any, is recognized on the termination of a capital lease, and the asset and lease liability is removed from the books (FAS-13, par. 14).

Illustration of Capital Lease (Lessee)

Paine Corporation leases a computer under a noncancelable five-year lease for annual rental payments of $10,000. The yearly lease payment is due at the beginning of the year. The fair value of the computer at the inception of the lease is $40,373, and the incremental borrowing rate of Paine is 10%. There are no executory costs. The annual rent of $10,000 is considered a fair rental as opposed to a bargain rental. The estimated economic life of the computer is ten years.

Classification of Lease

A review is made of the criteria involved in the provisions of the lease to determine its classification.

1. Criterion (1) is not met, because there is no transfer of the ownership of the leased property before the end of the lease term.

2. Criterion (2) is not met, because the lease does not contain a bargain purchase option.

3. Criterion (3) is not met, because the lease term (five years) is not equal to 75% or more of the estimated economic life (10 years) of the leased property. (**Note:** There are no other provisions affecting the lease term other than the five-year noncancelable term.)

4. Criterion (4) is met, because the present value ($41,699) of the minimum lease payments, excluding executory costs and profits thereon paid by the lessor, is 90% or more of the fair value ($40,373 × .9 = $36,336) of the leased property. [**Note:** The present value of the lease is $41,699, computed as follows: $10,000 × 4.16987, the present value factor for an annuity due, 5 periods, 10%.]

Paine Corporation should record the transaction as a capital lease.

Accounting for the Lease

The initial recording value of the leased property, at the beginning of the lease term, is the lesser of the fair value of the leased property or the present value of the minimum lease payments, excluding any portion that represents executory costs and profit thereon to be paid by the lessor.

The discount rate used by the lessee to find the present value of the minimum lease payments is its incremental borrowing rate of 10%, unless the lessee has knowledge of the lessor's implicit interest rate in the lease, and that rate is lower.

The lessor's interest rate implicit in the lease in this example is 12%. As a rule, the interest rate implicit in the lease is equal to the discount rate that, when applied to the minimum lease payments of $10,000 per year for five years and, if any, the unguaranteed residual value of the leased property, results in a present value equal to the fair value of the leased property at the inception of the lease. (For simplicity, this definition excludes any unusual factors that a lessor might recognize in determining its rate of return.)

This means that Paine must use its incremental borrowing rate of 10% to discount the minimum lease payments to their present value, which is $41,699.

The initial recording value of the leased property is the lesser of the fair value of the leased property at inception or the present value of the minimum lease payments using the lower interest rate. Therefore, the $40,373 fair value is less than the minimum lease payments of $41,699 (computed by using the lower incremental borrowing rate) and is used to initially record the lease, as follows:

| Lease property, capital leases | 40,373 | |
| Obligations, capital leases | | 40,373 |

Amortization by Lessee

The asset(s) recorded under a capital lease is amortized in a manner consistent with the lessee's normal depreciation policy for other owned assets. The period for amortization is either (*a*) the estimated economic life or (*b*) the lease term, depending on which criterion was used to classify the lease. If the criterion used to classify the lease as a capital lease was either criterion (1) (ownership of the property is transferred to the lessee by the end of the lease term) or criterion (2) (lease contains a bargain purchase option), the asset is amortized over its economic life. In all other cases, the asset is amortized over the lease term. Any residual value is deducted from the asset to determine the amortizable base.

Because the Paine Corporation's lease qualified under criterion (4) (present value of the minimum lease payments, excluding executory costs and profit thereon paid by the lessor, is 90% or more of the fair value of the leased property), the amortization period is over the lease term.

A schedule of amortization, interest expense, and lease obligation payments for Paine Corporation's computer lease, using the interest method, follows:

Book Value Lease Obligation Beginning of Year	Rental Payment/ Reduction in Lease Obligation	Outstanding Balance During Year	Interest @ 12%	Book Value Lease Obligation End of Year
$40,373	$10,000	$30,373	$3,645	$34,018
34,018	10,000	24,018	2,882	26,900
26,900	10,000	16,900	2,028	18,928
18,928	10,000	8,928	1,072	10,000
10,000	10,000	-0-	-0-	-0-

Note: The interest rate used is 12%, which is the interest rate implicit in the lease.

Operating Leases

Leases that do not qualify as capital leases in accordance with the provisions of FAS-13 are classified as operating leases. The cost of property covering an operating lease is included in the lessor's balance sheet as property, plant, and equipment. FAS-13 requires that rental income and expense relating to an operating lease be recognized over the periods in which the lessee derives benefit from the physical usage of the leased property. Thus, rental expense is recognized over the lease term on a straight-line basis, unless some other systematic and rational basis is more representative of the time pattern in which the benefits of the leased property are derived by the lessee (FAS-13, par. 15).

> ☞ **PRACTICE POINTER:** Use care when implementing accounting standards for sales-type leases involving real estate. FAS-98 amended FAS-13 to require that the lessor shall not classify a lease involving real estate as a sales-type lease unless title to the leased property is transferred to the lessee at or shortly after the end of the lease term. As a result, a lessor may be required to classify a lease involving real estate as an operating lease, instead of a sales-type lease, because the lease agreement does not provide for the transfer of the leased property to the lessee by the end of the lease term. In this event, the lessor must recognize a loss at the inception of an operating lease involving real estate if the fair value of the leased property is less than its cost or carrying amount, whichever is applicable. The amount of loss is equal to the difference between the fair value of the leased property and its cost or carrying amount at the inception of the lease.

Contingent Rental Expense

Some operating lease agreements provide for rental increases or decreases based on one or more future conditions, such as future sales volume, future machine hours, future interest rates, or future price indexes. These types of rental increases or decreases are classified as *contingent rentals*. Contingent rentals are defined as those that cannot be determined at the inception of the lease because they depend on future conditions or events. A lessee's contingent rental payments are deducted as an expense in the period in which they arise (FAS-29, par. 11).

Scheduled Rent Increases or Decreases

To accommodate the lessee, a lessor may structure an operating lease agreement to provide for smaller rental payments in the early years of the lease and higher rental payments toward the end of the lease. *Example:* A six-year operating lease agreement may provide for rental payments of $1,000 per month for the first two years; $1,500 per month for the next two years; and $2,000 per month for the last two years; for a total rental payment of $108,000 for the six years. Under this circumstance, FAS-13 requires that the $108,000 total rental payments be amortized over the six-year lease term on a straight-line basis. The monthly amortization for the first two years of the lease term is

$1,500, even though only $1,000 per month is paid by the lessee under the terms of the lease (FAS-13, par. 15).

> **OBSERVATION:** A reasonable argument can be made that in the early years of the above type of lease agreement, the lessee receives not only the use of the leased property, but also the temporary use of cash, equal to the excess of the fair rental value of the leased property over the actual rental payments. Theoretically, to recognize the economic substance of this lease transaction, both the lessee and the lessor should record imputed interest on the difference between the actual amount of rental payments and the computed amount of level rental payments. FAS-13, however, precludes the use of the time value of money as a factor in recognizing rentals under operating leases.

Leasehold Improvements

In a letter dated February 7, 2005, from the Chief Accountant of the SEC to the AICPA, the SEC staff stated its belief that leasehold improvements in an operating lease should be amortized by the lessee over the shorter of the economic life of the improvement or the lease term. An assumption of lease renewal where a renewal option exists is appropriate only when the renewal has been determined to be "reasonably assured," as that term is contemplated in FAS-13.

The SEC staff further indicated that leasehold improvements made by a lessee that are funded by landlord incentives or allowances under an operating lease should be recorded by the lessee as leasehold improvement assets and should be amortized over a term consistent with the above-stated guidance. The incentives should be recorded as deferred rent and amortized as reductions to lease expense over the lease term. The SEC staff indicates that it is inappropriate to net the deferred rent against the leasehold improvements. Further, the statement of cash flows should reflect cash received from the lessor that is accounted for as a lease incentive within operating activities and the acquisition of leasehold improvements for cash within investing activities.

Rent Holidays

In the same February 2005 letter, the SEC staff indicated that rent holidays in an operating lease should be recognized by the lessee on a straight-line basis over the lease term (including any rent holiday period), unless another systematic and rational allocation is more representative of the time pattern in which leased property is physically employed.

Financial Statement Disclosure

General Disclosure

A general description of the lessee's leasing arrangements, including (*a*) basis of contingent rental payments; (*b*) terms of renewals, purchase options, and escalation clauses; and (*c*) restrictions imposed by lease agreements, such as additional debt, dividends, and leasing limitations, must be disclosed (FAS-13, par. 16).

Capital Leases

Assets, accumulated amortization, and liabilities from capital leases are reported separately in the balance sheet and classified as current or noncurrent in the same manner as other assets and liabilities (FAS-13, par. 13).

Current amortization charges to income must be disclosed clearly, along with additional information (FAS-13, par. 16):

- Gross assets as of each balance sheet date presented, in aggregate and by major property categories (this information may be combined with comparable owned assets)
- Minimum future lease payments in total and for each of the next five years, showing deductions for executory costs, including any profit thereon, and the amount of imputed interest to reduce the net minimum lease payments to present values
- Minimum sublease income due in future periods under noncancelable subleases
- Total contingent rentals actually incurred for each period for which an income statement is presented

Operating Leases

The following financial statement disclosure is required for all operating leases of lessees having noncancelable lease terms in excess of one year (FAS-13, par. 16):

- Minimum future rental payments in total and for each of the next five years
- Minimum sublease income due in future periods under noncancelable subleases
- Schedule of total rental expense showing the composition by minimum rentals, contingent rentals, and sublease income

(excluding leases with terms of a month or less that were not renewed)

Following is an illustration of a lessee's financial statement disclosure (using assumed numbers).

Illustration of Lessee's Financial Statement Disclosure

Lessee's Balance Sheet
(in thousands)

	December 31	
	20X6	*20X5*
Assets:		
Leased property:		
Capital leases, less accumulated		
amortization (Note:_____)	$ 2,200	$ 1,600
Liabilities:		
Current:		
Obligations under capital leases		
(Note:_____)	$ 365	$ 340
Noncurrent:		
Obligations under capital leases		
(Note:_____)	$ 1,368	$ 1,260

Capital Leases
Gross Assets and
Accumulated Amortization
(in thousands)

	December 31	
	20X6	*20X5*
Type of Property		
Manufacturing plants	$ 1,500	$ 1,100
Retail stores	1,200	840
Other	300	210
Total	$ 3,000	$ 2,150
Less: Accumulated amortization	800	550
Capital leases, net	$ 2,200	$ 1,600

Capital Leases
Minimum Future Lease
Payments and Present Values of the
Net Minimum Lease Payments
(in thousands)

Year Ended
December 31

20X7	$ 406
20X8	1,232
20X9	160
20Y0	125
20Y1	100
After 20Y1	450
Total minimum lease payments	$ 2,473
Less: Executory costs (estimated)	250
Net minimum lease payments	$ 2,223
Less: Imputed interest	490
Present value of net minimum lease payments	$ 1,733

In addition to the foregoing statements and schedules, footnotes describing minimum sublease income and contingent rentals should be included, if required.

Operating Leases
Schedule of Minimum Future Rental Payments
(in thousands)

Year Ended
December 31

20X7	$ 815
20X8	2,400
20X9	320
20Y0	250
20Y1	200
After 20Y0	900
Total minimum future rental payments	$ 4,885

In addition to the above information on operating leases, a note should be included describing minimum sublease income due in the future under noncancelable subleases.

Operating Leases
Composition of Total Rental Expense
(in thousands)

	December 31	
	20X6	*20X5*
Minimum rentals	$1,100	$1,050
Contingent rentals	100	125
Less: Sublease rental income	(200)	(150)
Total rental expense, net	$1,000	$1,025

Note: The above schedule of total rental expense excludes leases with terms of one month or less that were not renewed.

In addition to the foregoing information on capital and operating leases, a footnote describing the general disclosure policy for the lessee's leases should be included, containing (a) general leasing arrangements, (b) basis of contingent rental payments, (c) terms of renewals, purchase options, and escalation clauses, and (d) restrictions imposed by lease agreements, such as additional debt, dividends, and leasing limitations.

ACCOUNTING AND REPORTING BY LESSORS

Leases are classified for the lessor as either (a) sales-type, (b) direct financing, or (c) operating. Both sales-type and direct financing are forms of capital leases.

Sales-type leases usually are used by sellers of property to increase the marketability of expensive assets. The occurrence of a manufacturer's or dealer's profit or loss generally is present in a sales-type lease.

Direct financing leases do not give rise to a manufacturer's or dealer's profit or loss, and the fair value usually is the cost or the carrying amount of the property.

Capital Leases

Recording Sales-Type Leases

The lessor's *gross investment* in the lease is the sum of (a) the minimum lease payments to be received less any executory costs and profit thereon to be paid by the lessor and (*b*) any unguaranteed residual value accruing to the benefit of the lessor (this is the estimated fair value of the leased property at the end of the lease term, which is not guaranteed). (**Note:** If the residual value is guaranteed, it is included in the minimum lease payments) (FAS-13, par. 17a).

The estimated residual value used to compute the unguaranteed residual value accruing to the benefit of the lessor shall not exceed the amount estimated at the inception of the lease (FAS-13, par. 17d).

Using the interest rate implicit in the lease, the lessor's gross investment in the lease is discounted to its present value. The present value of the lessor's gross investment in the lease represents the sales price of the property that is included in income for the period. (**Note:** When using the interest rate implicit in the lease, the present value will always be equal to the fair value) (FAS-13, par. 17c).

The cost or carrying amount of the property sold plus any initial direct costs (costs incurred by the lessor to negotiate and consummate the lease, such as legal fees and commissions), less the present value of the unguaranteed residual value (if any) accruing to the benefit of the lessor is charged against income in the period in which the corresponding sale is recorded (FAS-13, par. 17c).

The difference between the lessor's gross investment in the lease and the sales price of the property is recorded as unearned income, which is amortized to income over the lease term by the interest method. The unearned income is included in the balance sheet as a deduction from the related gross investment, which results in the net investment in the lease (FAS-13, par. 17b).

A lease involving real estate is not classified by the lessor as a sales-type lease unless the title to the leased property is transferred to the lessee at or shortly after the end of the lease term (FAS-98, par. 22c).

Recording Direct Financing Leases

The lessor's *gross investment* in the lease is computed, which is equal to the sum of (*a*) the minimum lease payments to be received by the lessor, less any executory costs and profit thereon to be paid by the lessor, and (*b*) any unguaranteed residual value accruing to the benefit of the lessor (this is the estimated fair value of the lease property at the end of the lease term, which is not guaranteed). If the residual value is guaranteed, it is included in the minimum lease payments (FAS-98, par. 22h).

Under FAS-91, loan origination fees and direct loan origination costs, including initial direct costs incurred by the lessor in negotiating and consummating the lease, are offset against each other and the resulting net amount is deferred and recognized over the life of the loan as an adjustment to the yield on the loan (FAS-91, par. 5).

The difference between the lessor's gross investment in the lease and the cost or carrying amount of the leased property, if different, is recorded as unearned income, which is amortized to income over the lease term by the interest method. The unearned income is included in the balance sheet as a deduction from the related gross investment, which results in the net investment in the lease (FAS-98, par. 22i).

> **OBSERVATION:** The practice of recognizing a portion of the unearned income at the inception of the lease to offset initial direct costs is no longer acceptable (FAS-91, par 5).

Balance Sheet Classification

The resulting net investment in both sales-type and direct financing leases is subject to the same treatment as other assets in classifying as current or noncurrent (FAS-98, par. 22i).

Annual Review of Residual Values

The unguaranteed residual values of both sales-type and direct financing leases should be reviewed at least annually to determine whether a decline, other than temporary, has occurred in their estimated values. If a decline is not temporary, the accounting for the transaction should be revised using the new estimate, and the resulting loss should be recognized in the period that the change is made. *Upward adjustments are not allowed* (FAS-13, pars. 17d, 18d).

Accounting for Lease Changes

The definition of *lease term* includes any periods in which penalties are imposed in an amount that reasonably assures the renewal of the lease by the lessee. The definition of *minimum lease payments* includes any payments or guarantees that the lessee is required to make concerning the leased property, including any amount (*a*) to purchase the leased property, (*b*) to make up any deficiency from a specified minimum, and (*c*) for failure to renew or extend the lease at the expiration of the lease term. Guarantees and penalties such as these usually are canceled and become inoperative in the event the lease is renewed or extended or a new lease for the same property is consummated.

If a sales-type or direct financing lease contains a residual guarantee or a penalty for failure to renew and is rendered inoperative as a result of a lease renewal or other extension of the lease term, or if a new lease is consummated in which the lessee continues to lease the same property, an adjustment must be made to the unearned income account for the difference between the present values of the old and the revised agreements. The present value of the future minimum lease payments under the new agreement is computed by using the original rate of interest used for the initial lease (FAS-13, par. 17e).

In sales-type and direct financing leases that do not contain residual guarantees or penalties for failure to renew, an adjustment is made to account for lease changes, renewals, or other extensions, including a new lease in which the lessee continues to lease the same property. If the classification of the lease remains unchanged or is classified as a direct financing lease and the amount of the remaining minimum lease payments is changed, an adjustment is made to unearned income to account for the difference between the present values of the old and the new agreements (FAS-13, par. 17f). If a new classification results in a sales-type lease, it is classified and treated as a direct financing lease, unless the transaction occurs within the last few months of the original lease, in which case it is classified as a sales-type lease (FAS-27, par. 6).

If the classification of a lease is changed to an operating lease, the accounting treatment depends upon whether the operating lease starts immediately or at the end of the existing lease. If the operating lease starts immediately, the remaining net investment is eliminated from the accounts and the leased property is recorded as an asset using the lower of (*a*) original cost, (*b*) present fair value, or (*c*) present carrying amount. The difference between the remaining net investment and the new recorded value of the asset is charged to income in the period of change (FAS-13, par. 17f).

If the operating lease starts at the end of the existing lease, the existing lease continues to be accounted for as a sales-type or direct financing lease until the new operating lease commences, at which time the accounting treatment is the same as if the operating lease started immediately. Renewals and extensions usually commence at the end of the original sales-type or direct financing lease. Under these circumstances there should not be any remaining investment to eliminate from the books and the leased property is not recorded as an asset (FAS-13, par. 17f).

Termination of a Lease

Termination of a lease is recognized in the income of the period in which the termination occurs by the following journal entries (FAS-13, par. 17f):

- The remaining net investment is eliminated from the accounts.
- The leased property is recorded as an asset using the lower of the (*a*) original cost, (*b*) present fair value, or (*c*) present carrying amount.

Operating Leases

Leases that do not qualify as capital leases in accordance with the provisions of FAS-13 are classified as operating leases. The cost of the property leased to the lessee is included in the lessor's balance sheet as property, plant, and equipment. The lessor's income statement will normally include the expenses of the leased property (unless it is a net lease), such as depreciation, maintenance, taxes, insurance, and other related items. Material initial direct costs (those directly related to the negotiation and consummation of the lease) are deferred and allocated to income over the lease term (FAS-13, pars. 19a, 19c).

FAS-13 requires that rental income from an operating lease be amortized over the periods in which the lessor's benefits in the leased property are depleted. Thus, rental income is amortized over the lease term on a straight-line basis, unless some other systematic and rational basis is more representative of the time pattern in which the benefits of the leased property are depleted (FAS-13, par. 19b).

FAS-98 amended FAS-13 to require that a lease involving real estate not be classified by the lessor as a sales-type lease unless title to the leased property is transferred to the lessee at or shortly after the end of the lease term. As a result, an enterprise may be required to classify a lease involving real estate as an operating lease, instead of a sales-type lease, because the lease agreement does not provide for the transfer of the leased property to the lessee by the end of the lease term. In this event, the lessor recognizes a loss at the inception of an operating lease involving real estate if the fair value of the leased property is less than its cost or carrying amount, whichever is applicable. The amount of loss is equal to the difference between the fair value of the leased property and its cost or carrying amount at the inception of the lease (FAS-98, par. 22c).

Contingent Rental Income

Contingent rental income is defined as that which cannot be determined at the inception of the lease because it depends on future conditions or events. A lessor's contingent rental income is accrued in the period in which it arises (FAS-29, par. 13).

Lease Sale or Assignment to Third Parties

Sale or assignment of a sales-type or a direct financing lease does not negate the original accounting treatment. The transfer of minimum lease payments under a sales-type or direct financing lease are accounted for in accordance with FAS-140 (Accounting for Transfers and

Servicing of Financial Assets and Extinguishments of Liabilities). The accounting for transfers of residual values depends on whether the residual value is guaranteed. If the residual value is guaranteed, its transfer is accounted for in accordance with FAS-140. Transfers of unguaranteed residual values are not subject to the guidance in FAS-140 (FAS-140, par. 352).

Frequently, a sale of property *subject to an operating lease* is complicated by some type of indemnification agreement by the seller. The seller may guarantee that the property will remain leased or may agree to reacquire the property if the tenant does not pay the specified rent. These types of transactions cannot be accounted for as a sale because of the substantial risk assumed by the seller. The principle of *substance over form* must be applied to such situations and treated accordingly. Examples of *substantial risk* on the part of the seller are (FAS-13, par. 21):

- Agreements to reacquire the property or lease.
- Agreements to substitute another existing lease.
- Agreements to use "best efforts" to secure a replacement buyer or lessee.

Examples of *nonsubstantial risk* situations on the part of the seller are (FAS-13, par. 21):

- Execution of a remarketing agreement that includes a fee for the seller.
- Situations in which the seller does not give priority to the re-leasing or other disposition of the property owned by a third party.

If a sale to a third-party purchaser is not recorded as a sale because of the substantial risk factor assumed by the seller, it is accounted for as a *borrowing*. The proceeds from the "sale" are recorded as an obligation on the books of the seller. Rental payments made by the lessee under the operating lease are recorded as revenue to the seller, even if the rentals are paid to the third party. Each rental payment shall consist of imputed interest, and the balance of the payment shall be applied as a reduction of the obligation. Any sale or assignment of lease payments under an operating lease is accounted for as a borrowing (FAS-13, par. 22).

Financial Statement Disclosure

The following financial statement disclosure is required by lessors whose *significant business activity is leasing* (not including *leveraged* leasing):

General Disclosures

General disclosures for leases of lessors: a general description of the lessor's leasing arrangements (FAS-13, par. 23c).

Capital Leases

For sales-type and direct financing leases (FAS-13, par. 23a; FAS-91, par. 25d):

- A schedule of the components of the *net investment* in leases, as of each balance sheet date, including:
  - Future minimum lease payments, with separate deductions for executory costs and the allowance for uncollectibles
  - Unguaranteed residual values accruing to the benefit of the lessor
  - Initial direct costs (direct financing leases only)
  - Unearned income
- A schedule of the minimum lease payments, in total and for the next five years
- Contingent rentals included in income

Operating Leases

For operating leases (FAS-13, par. 23b):

- A schedule of the investment in property on operating leases, and property held for lease, by major categories, less accumulated depreciation, as of each balance sheet presented
- A schedule of future minimum rentals on noncancelable operating leases, in total and for each of the next five years
- The amount of contingent rentals included in each income statement presented

Following is an illustration of a lessor's disclosure (using assumed numbers).

Illustration of Lessor's Financial Statement Disclosure

Lessor's Balance Sheet
(in thousands)

	December 31	
	20X6	20X5
Assets:		
Current assets:		
Net investment in sales-type and direct financing leases (Note:)	$ 208	$ 200
Noncurrent assets:		
Net investment in sales-type and direct financing leases (Note:)	$ 972	$ 830
Property on operating leases and property held for leases (net of accumulated depreciation of $450 and $400 for 20X6 and 20X5, respectively) (Note:)	$1,800	$1,600

Schedule of Components—Net Investment in
Leases Sales-Type and Direct
Financing Leases
(in thousands)

	20X6	20X5
Total minimum lease payments receivable	$1,450	$1,250
Less: Estimated executory costs, including profit thereon	150	125
Minimum lease payments	$1,300	$1,125
Less: Allowance for uncollectibles	65	60
Net minimum lease payments receivable	$1,235	$1,065
Add: Estimated unguaranteed residual values of leased properties	240	215
	$1,475	$1,280
Less: Unearned income	295	250
Net investment in sales-type and direct financing leases	$1,180	$1,030

A footnote should be included for contingent rentals.

Schedule of Minimum Lease Payments
(in thousands)

Year Ended
December 31

20X7	$ 260
20X8	195
20X9	156
20Y0	132
20Y1	125
After 20Y1	432
Total minimum lease payments receivable, net of executory costs	$1,300

Schedule of Investment in Property
on Operating Leases and Property Held
for Lease (by Major Class Categories)
(in thousands)

Data-processing equipment	$ 900
Transportation equipment	700
Construction equipment	400
Other	200
Total	$2,200
Less: Accumulated depreciation	400
Net investment	$1,800

Schedule of Future Minimum Rentals
on Noncancelable Operating Leases
(in thousands)

Year Ended
December 31

20X7	$ 200
20X8	175
20X9	165
20Y0	125
20Y1	110
After 20Y1	200
Total future minimum rentals	$ 975

A footnote should be included for contingent rentals.

LEASES INVOLVING REAL ESTATE

Leases involving real estate are categorized as follows (FAS-13, par. 24):

- Land only
- Land and building(s)
- Land, building(s), and equipment
- Only part of a building(s)

Review of Classification of Leases by Lessees

A review of the classifications of leases by lessees is necessary because accounting for leases involving real estate depends primarily on the criteria for classifying leases.

If one or more of the following four criteria are present at the inception of a lease, it is classified as a capital lease by the lessee:

1. Ownership of the property is transferred to the lessee by the end of the lease term.
2. The lease contains a bargain purchase option.
3. The lease term, at inception, is substantially (75% or more) equal to the estimated economic life of the leased property, including earlier years of use. (*Exception*: This criterion cannot be used for a lease that begins within the last 25% of the original estimated economic life of the leased property.)
4. The present value of the minimum lease payments at the beginning of the lease term, excluding executory costs and profits thereon to be paid by the lessor, is 90% or more of the fair value of the property at the inception of the lease, less any investment tax credit retained and expected to be realized by the lessor. (*Exception*: This criterion cannot be used for a lease that begins within the last 25% of the original estimated economic life of the leased property.)

These criteria are referred to by number in the following discussion.

Leases Involving Land Only

A *lessee* accounts for a lease involving land only as a capital lease if either criterion 1 or criterion 2 is met. All other leases involving land only are classified as operating leases by the lessee.

A *lessor* classifies a lease involving land only as a sales-type lease and accounts for the transaction as a sale under the provisions of FAS-66, if the lease gives rise to a manufacturer's or dealer's profit (or loss) and criterion 1 is met. A lessor classifies a lease involving land only as a direct financing lease or a leveraged lease, whichever is applicable, if the lease does not give rise to a manufacturer's or dealer's profit (or loss), criterion 1 is met, and (*a*) the collection of the minimum lease payments is reasonably predictable and (*b*) no important uncertainties exist regarding costs yet to be incurred by the lessor under the lease. A lessor classifies a lease involving land only as a direct financing lease, a leveraged lease, or an operating lease, whichever is applicable, if criterion 2 is met, and (*a*) the collection of the minimum lease payments is reasonably predictable and (*b*) no important uncertainties exist regarding costs yet to be incurred by the lessor under the lease. All other leases involving land only are classified as operating leases by the lessor (FAS-98, par. 22k).

☛ **PRACTICE POINTER:** The criteria for recognition of a sale under FAS-66 are quite similar to the additional criteria that must be met by lessors under FAS-13 in order for the lease to qualify as a capital lease. That is, under FAS-66, two criteria must be met in order for profit to be recognized in full at the time of the sale: (1) the sales price is reasonably predictable of collection and (2) the lessor of the land is not obligated to perform significant activities under the terms of the lease (FAS-66, par. 3). Collectibility is assessed by evaluating the adequacy of the lessee's initial and continuing investment (FAS-66, par. 4). For land to be developed within (after) two years of the sale, the lessee's initial investment should be at least 20% (25%) of the land's sales value (FAS-66, par. 54). The lessee's continuing investment must be at least an amount equal to the level annual payment required to liquidate the unpaid balance (both interest and principal) over no more than 20 years for a lease involving land (FAS-66, par. 12).

Leases Involving Land and Building(s)

Leases involving land and building(s) may be categorized as follows:

- Leases that meet criterion 1 or criterion 2
- Leases in which the fair value of the land is less than 25% of the total fair value of the leased property at the inception of the lease
- Leases in which the fair value of the land is 25% or more of the total fair value of the leased property at the inception of the lease

Leases That Meet Criterion 1 or Criterion 2

Leases that meet either criterion 1 or criterion 2 are accounted for as follows:

- *Lessee* The present value of the minimum lease payments, less executory costs and profits thereon (to be paid by the lessor), is allocated between the land and building(s) in proportion to their fair value at the inception of the lease. The present value assigned to the building(s) is amortized in accordance with the lessee's normal depreciation policy (FAS-13, par. 26a).

- *Lessor* If a lease gives rise to a manufacturer's or dealer's profit (or loss) and criterion 1 is met, a lessor classifies a lease involving land and building(s) as a sales-type lease and accounts for the transaction as a sale under the provisions of FAS-66. If a lease does not give rise to a manufacturer's or dealer's profit (or loss) and criterion 1 is met, a lessor classifies a lease involving land and building(s) as a direct financing lease or a leveraged lease, whichever is applicable, providing that (*a*) collection of the minimum lease payments are reasonably predictable and (*b*) no important uncertainties exist regarding costs yet to be incurred by the lessor under the lease (FAS-98, par. 22I).

  If a lease gives rise to a manufacturer's or dealer's profit (or loss) and criterion 2 is met, a lessor classifies a lease involving land and building(s) as an operating lease. If the lease does not give rise to a manufacturer's or dealer's profit (or loss) and criterion 2 is met, a lessor classifies a lease involving land and building(s) as a direct financing lease or a leveraged lease, whichever is applicable, providing that (*a*) collection of the minimum lease payments is reasonably predictable and (*b*) no important uncertainties exist regarding costs yet to be incurred by the lessor under the lease (FAS-98, par. 22I).

  All other leases involving land and building(s) are classified as operating leases by the lessor.

Fair Value of the Land Is Less Than 25% of the Total Fair Value of the Leased Property at the Inception of the Lease

When applying criteria 3 and 4, both the lessee and the lessor consider the land and building(s) as a single unit, and the estimated economic life of the building(s) is the estimated economic life of the single unit. This type of lease is accounted for as follows:

- *Lessee* The land and building(s) are accounted for as a single capitalized asset and amortized in accordance with the lessee's normal depreciation policy over the lease term if either criterion 3 or criterion 4 is met (FAS-13, par. 26b).

- *Lessor*   If a lease gives rise to a manufacturer's or dealer's profit (or loss) and criterion 3 or criterion 4 is met, a lessor classifies a lease involving land and building(s), in which the fair value of the land is less than 25% of the total fair value of the leased property at the inception of the lease as an operating lease. If the lease does not give rise to a manufacturer's or dealer's profit (or loss) and criterion 3 or criterion 4 is met, a lessor classifies a lease involving land and building(s) in which the fair value of the land is less than 25% of the total fair value of the leased property at the inception of the lease as a direct financing lease or a leveraged lease, whichever is applicable, providing that (*a*) collection of the minimum lease payments is reasonably predictable and (*b*) no important uncertainties exist regarding costs yet to be incurred by the lessor under the lease. All other leases involving land and building(s) are classified as operating leases by the lessor (FAS-98, par. 22m).

Fair Value of the Land Is 25% or More of the Total Fair Value of the Leased Property at the Inception of the Lease

When applying criteria 3 and 4, both the lessee and the lessor shall consider the land and building(s) separately. To determine the separate values of the land and building(s), the lessee's incremental borrowing rate is applied to the fair value of the land to determine the annual minimum lease payments applicable to the land. The balance of the minimum lease payments remaining is attributed to the building(s). This type of lease is accounted for as follows (FAS-13, par. 26b):

- *Lessee*   The building(s) portion is accounted for as a capital lease and amortized in accordance with the lessee's normal depreciation policy over the lease term if the building(s) portion meets either criterion 3 or criterion 4. The land portion is accounted for separately as an operating lease.
- *Lessor*   If a lease gives rise to a manufacturer's or dealer's profit (or loss) and criterion 3 or criterion 4 is met, a lessor classifies a lease involving land and building(s) in which the fair value of the land is 25% or more of the total fair value of the leased property at the inception of the lease as an operating lease. If the lease does not give rise to a manufacturer's or dealer's profit (or loss) and criterion 3 or 4 is met, a lessor shall classify the building(s) portion of a lease in which the fair value of the land is 25% or more of the total fair value of the leased property at the inception of the lease as a direct financing lease or a leveraged lease, whichever is applicable, providing that (*a*) collection of the minimum lease payments is reasonably predictable and (*b*) no important uncertainties exist regarding costs yet to be incurred by the lessor under the lease. The land portion is accounted for separately as an operating lease.

All other leases involving land and building(s) are classified as operating leases by the lessor.

Leases Involving Land, Building(s), and Equipment

Equipment values, if material, should not be commingled with real estate values in leases. The minimum lease payments attributed to the equipment shall, if necessary, be estimated appropriately and stated separately. The criteria for the classification of leases are applied separately to the equipment to determine proper accountability (FAS-13, par. 27).

Leases Involving Only Part of a Building(s)

If the cost and fair value of a lease involving only part of a building(s) can be determined objectively, the lease classification and accounting are the same as for any other land and building(s) lease. An independent appraisal of the leased property or replacement cost can be made as a basis for the objective determination of fair value (FIN-24, par. 6). In the event that cost and fair value cannot be determined objectively, leases involving only part of a building(s) are classified and accounted for as follows (FAS-13, par. 28):

Lessee

The lessee classifies the lease only in accordance with criterion 3 as follows: The lease term, at inception, is substantially (75% or more) equal to the estimated economic life of the leased property, including earlier years of use. (*Exception*: This particular criterion cannot be used for a lease that begins within the last 25% of the original estimated economic life of the leased property.)

In applying the above criterion, the estimated economic life of the building(s) in which the leased premises are located is used.

In the event the above criterion is met, the leased property is capitalized as a single unit and amortized in accordance with the lessee's normal depreciation policy over the lease term. In all other cases, the lease is classified as an operating lease.

Lessor

In all cases in which the cost and fair value are indeterminable, the lessor accounts for the lease as an operating lease.

SALE-LEASEBACK TRANSACTIONS

A sale-leaseback is a transaction in which an owner sells property and then leases back part or all of the same property. Such an owner is referred to as the seller-lessee. The purchaser-lessor is the party who purchases the property and leases back the same property to the seller-lessee. Sale-leaseback transactions involving real estate are addressed in FAS-98. All other sale-leaseback transactions are covered by FAS-28.

Non-Real Estate

Profit or loss on the sale is the amount that would have been recognized on the sale by the seller-lessee, assuming there was no leaseback (FAS-28, par. 3).

Recognition of profit or loss from the sale-leaseback by the seller-lessee is determined by the degree of rights in the remaining use of the property the seller-lessee retains, as follows:

- Substantially all
- Minor
- More than minor but less than substantially all

Substantially All or Minor

Under the terms of the lease, the seller-lessee may have a *minor* portion or *substantially all* of the rights to the remaining use of the property. This is determined by the present value of a total *reasonable rental* for the rights to the remaining use of the property retained by the seller-lessee. The seller-lessee has transferred *substantially all* of the rights to the remaining use of the property to the purchaser-lessor if the present value of the total *reasonable rental* under the terms of the lease is 10% or less of the fair value of the property sold at the inception of the lease. The seller-lessee has transferred a *minor* portion of the remaining rights to the purchaser-lessor if the terms of the leaseback include the entire property sold and qualify as a capital lease under FAS-13 (FAS-28, par. 3a).

> **OBSERVATION:** FAS-28 does not define *reasonable rental* or *fair value*. FAS-13, however, defines *fair value* as the price the leased property could be sold for between unrelated parties in an arm's length transaction. FAS-13 defines *fair rental* as the rental rate for similar property under similar lease terms and conditions.

Whether the lease is recorded as a capital lease or an operating lease, any profit or loss on the sale by the seller-lessee must be deferred and amortized as follows:

- *Capital lease* For a capital lease, the deferred profit or loss on the sale is amortized in proportion to the amortization of the leased property.
- *Operating lease* For an operating lease, the deferred profit or loss on the sale is amortized in proportion to the gross rental charged to expense over the lease term.

Whether a capital lease or an operating lease, if the leased asset is land only, the amortization of the deferred profit or loss on the sale must be on a straight-line basis over the lease term.

If the seller-lessee retains the rights to a *minor* portion of the remaining use in the property, the seller-lessee accounts for the sale and leaseback as two independent transactions based on their separate terms. The lease must provide for a reasonable amount of rent, however, considering prevailing market conditions at the inception of the lease. The seller-lessee must increase or decrease the profit or loss on the sale by an amount, if any, which brings the total rental for the leased property to a reasonable amount. Any amount created by this adjustment is amortized, as follows:

- *Capital lease* For a capital lease, the deferred or accrued amount is amortized in proportion to the amortization of the leased property.
- *Operating lease* For an operating lease, the deferred or accrued amount is amortized in proportion to the gross rental charged to expense over the lease term.

Whether a capital lease or an operating lease, if the leased asset is land only, the amortization of the deferred or accrued amount must be on a straight-line basis over the lease term.

☛ **PRACTICE POINTER:** If the total rental on the lease is less than a reasonable amount compared to prevailing market conditions at the inception of the lease, increase a profit on the sale and decrease a loss on the sale.

For an operating lease, the journal entry is a debit to prepaid rent and a credit to profit or loss. Amortize the prepaid rent in an amount that increases the periodic rental expense over the lease term to a reasonable amount. Conversely, if the total rental on the lease is more than a reasonable amount compared to prevailing market conditions at the inception of the lease, decrease a profit on the sale and increase a loss on the sale. The journal entry is a debit to profit or loss and a credit to deferred rent. Amortize the deferred rent in an amount that decreases the periodic rental expense over the lease term to a reasonable amount.

For a capital lease, make no debit to prepaid rent or credit to deferred rent. Instead, the debit or credit increases or decreases the amount that is recorded for the leased property. Then, amortize the leased property in the usual manner.

More Than Minor but Less Than Substantially All

If the seller-lessee retains the rights to more than minor but less than substantially all of the remaining use in the property, the seller-lessee shall recognize any excess profit (not losses) determined at the date of sale as follows (FAS-28, par. 3b):

- *Capital lease* The excess profit (if any) on a sale-leaseback transaction is equal to the amount of profit that exceeds the seller-lessee's recorded amount of the property as determined under the provisions of FAS-13 (the lesser of the fair value of the leased property or the present value of the minimum lease payments). For example, if the seller-lessee's recorded amount of the sale-leaseback property is $100,000 as determined under the provisions of FAS-13, and the amount of profit on the sale-leaseback transaction is $120,000, the excess profit that is recognized by the seller-lessee is $20,000. The balance of the profit ($100,000) is deferred and amortized in proportion to the amortization of the leased property.

- *Operating lease* The excess profit (if any) on a sale-leaseback transaction is equal to the amount of profit that exceeds the present value of the minimum lease payments over the term of the lease. The amount of profit on the sale-leaseback transaction that is not recognized at the date of the sale is deferred and amortized over the lease term in proportion to the gross rentals charged to expense.

Whether a capital lease or an operating lease, if the leased property is land only, the amortization of the deferred profit (if any) must be on a straight-line basis over the lease term.

Real Estate

Standards of accounting for sale-leaseback transactions involving real estate include transactions including real estate with equipment, such as a manufacturing facility, power plant, and an office building with furniture and fixtures. A sale-leaseback transaction involving real estate with equipment includes any sale-leaseback transaction in which the equipment and the real estate are sold and leased back as a package without regard to the relative value of the equipment and real estate elements of the transaction.

Criteria for Sale-Leaseback Accounting

Sale-leaseback accounting shall be used by a lessor-lessee only if the transaction meets all of the following criteria:

- The leaseback is a normal leaseback (see discussion below).
- Payment terms and provisions adequately demonstrate the buyer-lessor's initial and continuing investment in the property.
- Payment terms and provisions transfer all of the other risks and rewards of ownership as demonstrated by the absence of any continuing involvement by the seller-lessee.

A *normal leaseback* is one in which the seller-lessee actively uses the property in consideration for payment of rent, including contingent rentals that are based on the future operations of the seller-lessee. The phrase "actively uses the property" refers to the use of the property during the lease term in the seller-lessee's trade or business, provided that subleasing of the property is minor. The term "minor" means that the present value of the sublease is not more than 10% of the fair value of the asset sold. Active use of the property may involve providing services where the occupancy of the property is generally transient or short-term and is integral to the ancillary services being provided. Ancillary services may include, but are not limited to, housekeeping inventory control, entertainment, bookkeeping, and food services. For example, the use of property by a seller-lessee engaged in the hotel or bonded warehouse business or the operation of a golf course or parking lot is considered active use.

Terms of the Sale-Leaseback Transaction

Terms of the sale-leaseback transaction that are substantially different from terms that an independent third-party would accept represent an exchange of some stated or unstated rights or privileges. Those rights or privileges are considered in evaluating the seller-lessor's continuing involvement (described below). Those terms or conditions include, but are not limited to, the sales price, interest rate, and other terms of any loan from the seller-lessee to the buyer-lessor. The fair value of the property used in making that evaluation is based on objective evidence, such as an independent third-party appraisal or recent sales of comparable property.

Continuing Involvement

A sale-leaseback transaction that does not qualify for sale-leaseback accounting because of continuing involvement by the seller-lessee other than a normal leaseback shall account for the transaction by the deposit method or the financing method, whichever is appropriate. Two examples of continuing involvement that are frequently found in sale-leaseback transactions are:

- The seller-lessee has an obligation or an option to repurchase the property so that the buyer-lessor can compel the seller-lessee to repurchase the property.
- The seller-lessee guarantees the buyer-lessor's investment or a return on that investment for a limited or extended period of time.

Other provisions or conditions that represent guarantees and that do not transfer all of the risks of ownership and that constitute continuing involvement for purposes of these standards include:

- The seller-lessee is required to pay the buyer-lessor at the end of the lease term a decline in the fair value of the property below the estimated residual value on some basis other than excess wear and tear of the property.
- The seller-lessee provides nonrecourse financing to the buyer-lessor for any portion of the sales proceeds or provides recourse financing in which the only recourse is to the leased asset.
- The seller-lessee is not relieved of the obligation under any existing debt related to the property.
- The seller-lessee provides collateral on behalf of the buyer-lessor other than the property directly involved in the sale-leaseback transcation, the seller-lessee or a related party guarantees the buyer-lessor's debt, or a related party to the seller-lessee guarantees a return of or on the buyer-lessor's investment.
- The seller-lessee's rental payment is contingent on some predetermined or determinable level of future operations by the buyer-lessor.

Examples of provisions or conditions that are considered continuing involvement for purposes of determining proper accounting for sale-leaseback transactions of real estate are as follows:

- The seller-lessee enters into a sale-leaseback transaction involving property improvements or integral equipment without leasing the underlying land to the buyer-lessor.
- The buyer-lessor is obligated to share with the seller-lessee any portion of the appreciation on the property.

- Any other provision or circumstance that allows the seller-lessee to participate in any future profits of the buyer-lessor or the appreciation of the leased property.

Financial Statement Presentation

In addition to disclosure requirements presented earlier for leases in general, the financial statements of a seller-lessee shall include a description of the terms of sale-leaseback transactions, including future commitments, obligations, provisions, or circumstances that require or result in the seller-lessee's continuing involvement.

The financial statements of a seller-lessee that has accounted for a sale-leaseback transaction by the deposit method or as a financing shall disclose the following information:

- The obligation for future minimum lease payments as of the date of the latest balance sheet presented in the aggregate and for each of the five succeeding fiscal years.

- The total minimum sublease rentals, if any, to be received in the future under noncancelable subleases in the aggregate for each of the five succeeding fiscal years.

> **OBSERVATION:** Additional guidance concerning profit recognition and sale-leaseback transactions involving real estate can be found in this *Guide* in the chapter "Real Estate Transactions."

LEASE MODIFICATIONS

Under the provisions of FAS-13, a capital lease may be modified in such a way that the new lease agreement is treated as an operating lease. FAS-13 requires that the lease asset and obligation (liability) be removed from the accounts and any resulting gain or loss be recognized in determining current period income. The new lease agreement is accounted for as an operating lease.

The FASB concluded that the economic effects of the above transaction are similar to those of a sale-leaseback accounting, under the provisions of FAS-98 or FAS-28, when a capital lease is modified such that the revised lease agreement is classified as an operating lease. FAS-98 (Accounting for Leases: Sale-Leaseback Transactions Involving Real Estate; Sales-Type Leases of Real Estate; Definition of the Lease Term; Initial Direct Costs of Direct Financing Leases) provides guidance on sale-leaseback transactions involving real estate; FAS-28 (Accounting for Sales with Leasebacks) provides guidance on all other types of sale-leaseback transactions.

OTHER LEASE ACCOUNTING ISSUES

Wrap Lease Transactions

In a wrap lease transaction, a lessor leases equipment to a lessee and obtains nonrecourse financing from a financial institution using the lease receivable and the asset as collateral. The lessor sells the asset subject to the lease and the nonrecourse financing to a third-party investor and then leases the asset back. Thus, the original lessor remains the principal lessor, who continues to service the lease. The transaction with the third-party investor may or may not occur at the same time that the original lease is executed with the original equipment user. As a matter of fact, it is not unusual in a wrap lease transaction for the subsequent nonrecourse financing or sale to a third party to occur up to six months after the original lease agreement is executed.

In exchange for the sale of the asset to a third-party investor, the lessor may receive a combination of cash, a note, an interest in the residual value of the leased asset, and certain other rights or contingent rights, such as the right to remarket the asset at the end of the lease term. Depending on the terms of the specific transaction, (a) the lessor may or may not be liable for the leaseback payments if the primary lessee defaults, (b) the lessor may or may not receive a fee for servicing the lease, (c) payments under the leaseback may or may not approximate collections under the note, and (d) the terms of the leaseback may or may not correspond with the terms of the original equipment lease.

A wrap lease transaction consists primarily of a sale-leaseback of property and is accounted for as such under FAS-13 or FAS-98, whichever is applicable. If the property involved in a wrap lease transaction is other than real estate, the provisions of FAS-13, as amended by FAS-28, must be followed. On the other hand, if the property involved is real estate, the provisions of FAS-98 must be observed in accounting for the sale-leaseback transaction.

Under sale-leaseback accounting, the sale portion of a sale-leaseback transaction is recorded as a sale by the seller-lessee. The property sold and all of its related liabilities are eliminated from the seller-lessee's balance sheet. Gain or loss on the sale portion of the sale-leaseback transaction is recognized by the seller-lessee in accordance with paragraph 33 of FAS-13, as amended by FAS-28. The lease portion of the sale-leaseback transaction should be classified as a capital lease or an operating lease in accordance with paragraph 6 of FAS-13 and accounted for by the seller-lessee in accordance with paragraph 33 of FAS-13 (FAS-28, par. 3).

The purchaser-lessor records a sale-leaseback transaction as a purchase and a direct financing lease if the lease portion of the sale-leaseback meets the criteria of a capital lease under FAS-13.

Otherwise, the purchaser-lessor records the transaction as a purchase and an operating lease (FAS-13, par. 34).

The main difference in accounting for a sale-leaseback under FAS-13 and FAS-98 is that under the provisions of FAS-98, the sale portion of the sale-leaseback must meet all of the criteria for sales recognition under the provisions of FAS-66. FAS-98 prohibits a lease involving real estate from being classified as a sales-type lease unless the lease agreement provides for the title of the leased property to be transferred to the lessee at or shortly after the end of the lease term.

In reporting a wrap lease transaction, an enterprise's statement of financial position should include (a) the amount of the retained residual interest in the leased property, (b) the amount of the gross sublease receivable, (c) the amount of the nonrecourse third-party debt, (d) the amount of the leaseback obligation, and (e) the amount of the note receivable from the investor.

Illustration of Wrap Lease Transactions

Assume that a lessor leases an asset with an undepreciated cost of $1,000 to a lessee for five years at $19.12 a month. The residual value of the leased asset at the end of the lease term is estimated to be $164.53 and the interest rate implicit in the lease is 10%. The lessor would classify the lease as a direct financing lease under the provisions of FAS-13 and record the following journal entry:

Lease receivable (60 × $19.12)	1,147.20	
Residual value of leased asset	164.53	
Asset		1,000.00
Unearned income—lease receivable		247.20
Unearned income—residual		64.53

Note: For financial reporting purposes, FAS-13 requires that the lease receivable and residual value of the leased asset be combined and reported as the gross investment in the lease. In addition, the unearned income amounts must also be combined.

Using the lease receivable and the asset as collateral, the lessor enters into a nonrecourse financing arrangement with a financial institution for $900.00 (the present value of the $19.12 monthly lease payment for 60 months discounted at 10%) at a rate of 10%. The lessor would record the following journal entry to reflect the liability for the nonrecourse debt:

Cash	900.00	
Nonrecourse debt		900.00

The lessor then sells the asset subject to the lease and the nonrecourse debt to a group of equity partners and leases the asset back for five years at

$19.12 a month (for simplicity, assume that the lease, the nonrecourse financing, and the sale to the equity partners occur at the same time). The lessor is now the lessee-sublessor and remains the obligor with the financial institution that financed the nonrecourse debt. In return for the asset, the lessor receives the following:

1. Cash of $50, representing the sale of 50% of the residual value of the leased asset
2. An additional $103.66 in cash, representing the transfer of tax benefits
3. A note receivable for $900.00 bearing interest at 10% with 60 monthly payments of $19.12 (60 payments at $19.12 represent a gross note of $1,147.20 and unearned income of $247.20)
4. The right to receive a fee of $82.27 for remarketing the asset at the end of the initial lease term (the present value of an $82.27 payment 60 months in the future discounted at 10% equals $50.00)
5. In addition, the lessor retains a 50% interest in the proceeds of the residual value of the leased asset at the end of the lease term

Subleases and Similar Transactions

Unless the original lease agreement is replaced by a new agreement, the original lessor continues to account for the lease as before (FAS-13, par. 36).

A termination of a lease is recognized by a lessor in the income of the period in which termination occurs, as follows (FAS-13, par. 37):

- The remaining net investment is eliminated from the accounts.
- The leased property is recorded as an asset using the lower of the (*a*) original cost, (*b*) present value at termination, or (*c*) present carrying amount at termination.

When an original lessee subleases property, the new lessee is either (1) substituted under the *original* lease agreement (paragraph 35b of FAS-13) or (2) substituted through a *new* lease agreement (paragraph 35c of FAS-13). In either case, the original lessee is relieved of the primary obligation under the original lease. FAS-145, through its replacement of paragraph 38 of FAS-13, indicates that the accounting for the termination of the original lease agreement depends on whether the original lease was for property other than real estate or whether it was for real estate.

If the original lease was a capital lease for property other than real estate, the termination of the lease agreement is accounted for as follows (FAS-145, par. 9c[a]):

- Remove the asset and liability pertaining to the capital lease from the books.

- Recognize a gain or loss for the difference between the lease asset and lease liability, and consider any consideration received or paid upon lease termination in computing the gain or loss.

- If the original lessee remains secondarily liable, recognize this guarantee obligation under the provisions specified in FAS-140 (Accounting for Transfers and Servicing of Financial Assets and Extinguishments of Liabilities).

If the original lease was a capital lease for real estate, the termination of the lease agreement is accounted for as follows (FAS-145, par. 9c[b]).

- The lease asset and liability are to be removed from the books if the FAS-66 (Accounting for Sales of Real Estate) criteria for sale recognition are met.

- If the FAS-66 sales criteria are met, treatment of (1) the lease asset and liability, (2) any consideration received or paid, and (3) any guarantees are all accounted for as immediately above (the same as if the original lease was a capital lease for property other than real estate).

- Any gain should be recognized by the full accrual method if the FAS-66 criteria for the use of this method are met; otherwise, gain should be recognized using one of the other revenue recognition methods discussed in FAS-66 (installment, cost recovery, deposit, or reduced-profit methods).

- Any loss is recognized immediately.

Finally, the original lessee is to recognize its guarantee obligation (per FAS-140) if it remains secondarily liable on a lease that was originally classified as an operating lease (FAS-145, par. 9c[c]).

When a lessee subleases leased property, the original lease continues and a simultaneous new lease is created in which the lessee becomes a sublessor. The results are that the original lessee is both a lessee in the original lease and, at the same time, a sublessor in the new lease. In situations like this, the original lease continues to be accounted for as if nothing happened, but the new lease is classified and accounted for separately.

If an original lessee is not relieved of the primary obligation under an original lease, the transaction is accounted for by the original lessee-sublessor as follows (FAS-13, par. 39):

- If the criterion for the original lease was criterion (1) (ownership of the property is transferred before the end of the lease term) or (2) (lease contains a bargain purchase option), the new lease is classified based on its own new criteria. If the new lease qualifies for capitalization, it is accounted for as a sales-type or a direct financing lease, whichever is appropriate, and the unamortized balance of the asset under the original lease is treated as the cost of the leased property to the sublessor (original lessee).

In the event that the new lease does not qualify for capitalization, it is treated as an operating lease.

- If the criterion for the original lease was criterion (3) (lease term is substantially—75% or more—equal to the estimated economic life of the leased property at the inception of the lease) or (4) (present value of the minimum lease payments—excluding executory costs—is 90% or more of the fair value at inception), the new lease is capitalized only if it meets criterion (3) and (*a*) the collection of the minimum lease payments is reasonably predictable and (*b*) no important uncertainties exist regarding costs yet to be incurred by the lessor under the lease. If the new lease meets the criteria above, it is accounted for as a direct financing lease, with the amortized balance of the asset under the original lease as the cost of the leased property.

  If the new lease does not meet the specific conditions above, it is accounted for as an operating lease.

In any event, if the original lease is an operating lease, the sublease also is accounted for as an operating lease (FAS-13, par. 39c).

Even though the sublessor (original lessee) remains primarily obligated under an original lease, a loss may be recognized on a sublease. The loss is measured as the difference between the unamortized cost of the leased property (net carrying amount) and the present value of the minimum lease payments which will be received under the terms of the sublease (FIN-27, par. 2).

> **OBSERVATION:** FIN-27 (Accounting for a Loss on a Sublease) is silent as to recognition of any gain on subleases in which the sublessor (original lessee) remains primarily obligated under the original lease. FAS-13, paragraph 39, however, implies that **both** gain and loss may be recognized on sales-type and direct financing leases.

FAS-144 supersedes the discussion in APB-30 and FIN-27 on the accounting treatment of long-term leases (including related sublease revenue) terminated as part of the disposal of a component of a business entity. FAS-144 requires that the assets in the component of the business entity being disposed of be carried at the lower of the asset's carrying amount or fair value less cost to sell. Although explicit guidance on this topic no longer appears in the literature, the authors believe that the fair value of the component of the business entity to be disposed of will be (implicitly) reduced by the present value of future rental receipts to be paid on the original lease in excess of the present value of future rental receipts that will be collected on the operating sublease.

Leases Involving Governmental Units

Leases with governmental units usually lack fair values, have indeterminable economic lives, and cannot provide for transfer of ownership. These special provisions usually prevent their classification as any other than operating leases (FAS-13, par. 28).

Leases involving governmental units, however, are subject to the same criteria as any other lease unless all of the following conditions exist; and in that event, these leases are classified as operating leases (FIN-23, par. 8):

- A governmental unit or authority owns the leased property.

- The leased property is operated by or on behalf of a governmental unit or authority and is part of a larger facility, such as an airport.

- The leased property cannot be moved to another location because it is a permanent structure or part of a permanent structure.

- Any governmental unit or authority can terminate the lease agreement at any time under the terms of the lease agreement, existing statutes, or regulations.

- Ownership is not transferred to the lessee and the lessee cannot purchase the leased property.

- Equivalent property in the same area as the leased property cannot be purchased or leased from anyone else.

Related Party Leases

Except in cases in which the substance of a lease transaction indicates clearly that the terms and conditions have been significantly influenced by the related parties, related party leases are classified and accounted for as if the parties were unrelated (FAS-13, par. 29).

It is important to note that, generally, a subsidiary whose principal business activity is leasing property to its parent must be consolidated with the parent's financial statements (FAS-13, par. 31).

> **OBSERVATION:** Specific financial statement disclosures pertaining to related parties are required by FAS-57 (Related Party Disclosures).

Leveraged Leases

A lessee classifies and accounts for *leveraged* leases in the same manner as *nonleveraged* leases. *Only a lessor* must classify and account for leveraged leases in the specific manner prescribed herein (FAS-13, par. 41).

FAS-13 defines a *leveraged lease* as a lease having all the following characteristics (FAS-13, par. 42):

- A leveraged lease meets the definition of a *direct financing lease* as follows:

    A direct financing lease is a lease that does not result in a manufacturer's or dealer's profit or loss because the fair value of the leased property at the inception of the lease is the same as the cost or carrying amount. In a direct financing lease, substantially all the benefits and risks inherent in the ownership of the leased property are transferred to the lessee. In addition, the following requirements must be met:
    - The minimum lease payments are reasonably predictable of collection.
    - No important uncertainties exist regarding costs to be incurred by the lessor under the terms of the lease.

- It involves at least three parties: (*a*) a lessee, (*b*) a lessor, and (*c*) a long-term creditor. (**Note:** The lessor is sometimes referred to as the *equity participant.*)

- The financing is sufficient to provide the lessor with substantial leverage in the transaction and is nonrecourse as to the general credit of the lessor.

- Once the lessor's net investment is completed, it declines in the early years and rises in later years before being liquidated. These fluctuations in the lessor's net investment can occur more than once in the lease term.

> ☛ **PRACTICE POINTER:** Leveraged leases are complex contracts that meet very specific criteria. Accounting for leveraged leases is unique in certain ways (e.g., offsetting assets and liabilities) and, therefore, determining whether a given lease is a leveraged lease is particularly important. A lease must meet *all* of the following specific criteria (taken from the definition of a leveraged lease) to be accounted for as a leveraged lease:
>
> 1. The lease is a direct financing lease.
> 2. The lease involves three parties rather than the normal two.
> 3. The lease provides the lessor with substantial leverage.
> 4. The pattern of the lessor's investment declines then rises.

Only when all four of these criteria are met is the lease subject to leveraged lease accounting.

If the investment tax credit is accounted for as provided herein and a lease meets the preceding definition, it is classified and accounted for as a leveraged lease (FAS-13, par. 42).

The initial and continuing investment of the lessor in a leveraged lease is recorded *net* of the nonrecourse debt, as follows (FAS-13, par. 43):

- Rentals receivable, net of that portion applicable to principal and interest on the nonrecourse debt
- A receivable for the amount of the investment tax credit to be realized on the transaction
- The estimated residual value of the leased property
- Unearned and deferred income consisting of (*a*) the estimated pretax lease income or loss, after deducting initial direct costs of negotiating and consummating the lease transaction, that remains to be allocated to income over the lease term and (*b*) the investment tax credit that remains to be allocated to income over the lease term

The investment in a leveraged lease, less applicable deferred taxes, represents the lessor's net investment for purposes of computing periodic net income from the leveraged lease (FAS-13, par. 43). The following method is used to compute periodic net income (FAS-13, par. 44):

- A projected cash flow analysis is prepared for the lease term.
- The rate of return on net investment in the years it is positive is computed (usually by trial and error).
- Every year the net investment is increased or decreased by the difference between the net cash flow and the amount of income recognized, if any.

The amount of net income that is recognized each year consists of (FAS-13, par. 44):

- Pretax lease income or loss (allocated from the unearned income portion of the net investment)
- Investment tax credit (allocated from the deferred income portion of the net investment)
- The tax effect of the pretax lease income or loss recognized (which is reflected in tax expense for the year)

Any tax effect on the difference between pretax accounting income or loss and taxable income or loss is charged or credited to deferred taxes.

All the important assumptions affecting the estimated net income from the leveraged lease, including any estimated residual values, should be reviewed at least annually.

If, at the inception or at any time during the lease, the projected net cash receipts over the initial or remaining lease term are less than the lessor's initial or current investment, the resulting loss is immediately recognized (FAS-13, par. 45).

Upward adjustments of the estimated residual value are not permitted (FAS-13, par. 46).

The lessor's financial statement disclosure for leveraged leases shall include the amount of deferred taxes stated separately. When leveraged leasing is a significant part of the lessor's business activity, a schedule of the components of the net investment in leveraged leases shall be disclosed fully in the footnotes to the financial statements (FAS-13, par. 47).

Lessor's Existing Asset in a Leveraged Lease

Only a direct financing lease may qualify as a leveraged lease (FAS-13, par. 42a). One of the requirements of a direct financing lease is that it may not result in a manufacturer's or dealer's profit or loss. It is difficult for an existing asset of a lessor to qualify for leveraged lease accounting because the carrying amount (cost less accumulated depreciation) of an asset previously placed in service is not likely to be the same as its fair value. An existing asset of a lessor may qualify for leveraged lease accounting, however, if its carrying amount is equal to its fair value, without any write-down or other adjustment to its fair value.

Business Combinations

A business combination, in itself (FIN-21, pars. 13–14), does not affect the classification of a lease. If as a result of a business combination, however, a lease is revised or modified to the extent that under FAS-13 it is considered a new agreement, it is reclassified based on its revision or modification. Ordinarily, a lease retains its previous classification under FAS-13 and is accounted for in the same manner as it was prior to the combination.

The acquiring company in a business combination accounts for a leveraged lease by assigning a fair value (present value, net of tax) to the net investment in a leveraged lease based on the remaining future cash flows with appropriate recognition for any future estimated tax effects. After the fair value (present value, net of tax) of the net investment is determined, it is allocated to net rentals receivable, estimated residual value, and unearned income. Thereafter, a company accounts for the leveraged lease by allocating the periodic cash flow between the net investment and the lease income (FIN-21, par. 16).

In a business combination in which an acquired lease has not been conformed to FAS-13, the acquiring company classifies such a lease to conform retroactively to FAS-13 (FIN-21, par. 17).

RELATED CHAPTERS IN 2009 *GAAP GUIDE* *LEVEL A*

Chapter 3, "Balance Sheet Classification and Related Display Issues"
Chapter 4, "Business Combinations"
Chapter 7, "Consolidated Financial Statements"
Chapter 11, "Depreciable Assets and Depreciation"
Chapter 15, "Extinguishments of Debt"
Chapter 16, "Fair Value"
Chapter 23, "Intangible Assets"
Chapter 31, "Long-Term Obligations"
Chapter 37, "Real Estate Transactions"
Chapter 38, "Related Party Disclosures"
Chapter 45, "Transfer and Servicing of Financial Assets"

RELATED CHAPTERS IN 2009 *GAAP GUIDE* *LEVELS B, C, AND D*

Chapter 4, "Balance Sheet Classification and Related Display Issues"
Chapter 6, "Business Combinations"
Chapter 10, "Consolidated Financial Statements"
Chapter 15, "Extinguishments of Debt"
Chapter 26, "Leases"
Chapter 33, "Real Estate Transactions"
Chapter 40, "Transfer and Servicing of Financial Assets"

RELATED CHAPTERS IN 2009 *INTERNATIONAL ACCOUNTING/FINANCIAL REPORTING STANDARDS GUIDE*

Chapter 3, "Presentation of Financial Statements"
Chapter 7, "Business Combinations"
Chapter 10, "Consolidated Financial Statements"

Chapter 16, "Financial Instruments"
Chapter 21, "Intangible Assets"
Chapter 25, "Leases"
Chapter 27, "Property, Plant, Equipment"
Chapter 29, "Related Party Disclosures"

CHAPTER 30
LONG-TERM CONSTRUCTION CONTRACTS

CONTENTS

OVERVIEW

Long-term construction contracts present a difficult financial reporting problem, primarily because of their large dollar amounts and their relatively long duration (i.e., they span more than one accounting period, sometimes beginning and ending several years apart). GAAP, in the area of revenue recognition for long-term construction contracts, deal with this situation by permitting two methods—the *percentage-of-completion method* and the *completed-contract method*—although the two are not alternatives for the same situation. The percentage-of-completion method is required in situations in which reliable estimates of the degree of completion are possible, in which case a pro rata portion of the income from the contract is recognized in each accounting period covered by the contract. In those rare situations where reliable estimates are not possible, the completed-contract method is used, in which income is deferred until the end of the contract period.

GAAP for long-term construction contracts are found in the following pronouncement:

ARB-45   Long-Term Construction-Type Contracts

BACKGROUND

Because of the length of time involved in long-term construction contracts, a problem exists as to when income should be recognized. The completed-contract method and the percentage-of-completion method generally are followed to account for these long-term contracts.

> **OBSERVATION:** The specialized accounting and auditing practices for construction contractors appear in the AICPA Industry Audit and Accounting Guide titled "Construction Contractors." Specialized accounting practices also appear in the AICPA SOP 81-1 (Accounting for Performance of Construction-Type and Certain Production-Type Contracts).
>
> The "Construction Contractors" guide and SOP 81-1 were issued concurrently in 1981 and supersede the previous Audit Guide ("Audits of Construction Contractors") issued in 1965. The "Construction Contractors" guide primarily focuses on the construction industry, whereas SOP 81-1 makes recommendations on accounting issues that apply to a broad range of contracting activities.
>
> The percentage-of-completion method is required when the estimated cost to complete the contract and the extent of progress made on the contract are reasonably determinable. When estimates are not possible or are unreliable, the completed-contract method is required. SOP 81-1 is covered in *GAAP Guide Levels B, C, and D.*

COMPLETED-CONTRACT METHOD

The completed-contract method recognizes income only on completion or substantial completion of the contract. *A contract is regarded as substantially complete if the remaining costs are insignificant* (ARB-45, par. 9).

Any excess of accumulated costs over related billings is reflected in the balance sheet as a current asset; any excess of accumulated billings over related costs is reflected as a current liability. In the case of more than one contract, the accumulated costs or liabilities should be stated separately on the balance sheet. The preferred terminology for the balance sheet presentation is *(Costs) (Billings) of uncompleted contracts in excess of related (billings) (costs)* (ARB-45, par. 12).

In some cases, it is preferable to allocate general and administrative expenses to contract costs rather than to period income. In years in which no contracts are completed, a better matching of costs and revenues is achieved by carrying general expense as a charge to the contract. If a contractor has many jobs, however, it is more appropriate to charge these expenses to current periods (ARB-45, par. 10).

Although income is not recognized until completion of the contract, a provision for an expected loss should be recognized when it becomes evident that a loss will occur. (ARB-45, par. 11).

Illustration of the Completed-Contract Method

A construction company has a balance in its construction-in-progress account of $500,000, representing the costs incurred to date on a project. While the project was initially expected to be profitable, management now expects a loss on the project at completion of $75,000. At the time of this determination, the following entry should be made:

Estimated loss on construction project	75,000	
Construction in progress		75,000

This entry reduces the construction (inventory) account by $75,000 and recognizes the loss in income of the period in which the determination of the loss is estimable. Assuming the estimate of the loss is accurate, future costs will be charged to the construction account as incurred and the balance in that account will equal the revenue on the contract.

The primary advantage of the completed-contract method is that it is based on final results rather than on estimates. The primary disadvantage of this method is that it does not reflect current performances when the period of the contract extends over more than one accounting period (ARB-45, pars. 13–14).

Accounting for the Completed-Contract Method

The following are important points in accounting for contracts under the completed-contract method:

1. Overhead and direct costs are charged to a construction-in-progress account (an asset).
2. Billings and/or cash received are charged to advances on the construction-in-progress account (a liability).
3. At completion of the contract, gross profit or loss is recognized as follows:

   Contract price − total costs = gross profit or loss

4. At balance sheet dates that occur during the contract period, the excess of either the construction-in-progress account or the advances account over the other is classified as a current asset or a current liability. It is a *current* asset or a *current* liability because of the *normal operating cycle concept.*

5. Expected losses are recognized in full in the year they are identified. An expected loss on the total contract is determined by:
    a. Adding estimated costs to complete to the recorded costs to date to arrive at total contract costs
    b. Adding to advances any additional revenue expected to arrive at total contract revenue
    c. Subtracting b from a to arrive at total estimated loss on contract

PERCENTAGE-OF-COMPLETION METHOD

Revenues generally are recognized when (a) the earning process is complete or virtually complete and (b) an exchange has taken place.

Accounting for long-term construction contracts by the percentage-of-completion method is a modification of the general practice of realization at the point of sale. Realization is based on the evidence that the ultimate proceeds are available and the consensus that the result is a better measure of periodic income (matching-of-revenue-and-cost principle).

The principal merits of the percentage-of-completion method are the reflection of the status of the uncompleted contracts and the periodic recognition of the income currently rather than irregularly as contracts are completed. The principal disadvantage of this method is the necessity of relying on estimates of the ultimate costs (ARB-45, pars. 7–8).

The percentage-of-completion method recognizes income as work progresses on the contract. The method is based on an estimate of the income earned to date, less income recognized in earlier periods. Estimates of the degree of completion usually are based on one of the following (ARB-45, par. 4):

- The relationship of costs incurred to date to expected total costs for the contract
- Other measures of progress toward completion, such as engineering estimates

During the early stages of a contract, all or a portion of items such as material and subcontract costs may be excluded if it appears that the results would produce a more meaningful allocation of periodic income (ARB-45, par. 4).

When current estimates of the total contract costs indicate a loss, a provision for the loss on the entire contract should be made. When a loss is indicated on a total contract that is part of a related group of contracts, however, the group may be treated as a unit in determining the necessity of providing for losses (ARB-45, par. 6).

☞ **PRACTICE POINTER:** Income to be recognized under the percentage-of-completion method at various stages ordinarily should not be measured by interim billings.

Accounting for the Percentage-of-Completion Method

The following are important points in accounting for contracts under the percentage-of-completion method:

- Journal entries and balance sheet treatment are the same as for the completed-contract method, *except* that the amount of estimated gross profit earned in each period is recorded by charging the construction-in-progress account and crediting realized gross profit.
- Gross profit or loss is recognized in each period by the following formula:

$$\left[\begin{array}{c} \text{percentage} \\ \text{of} \\ \text{completion} \end{array} \times \begin{array}{c} \text{total estimated} \\ \text{gross profit or} \\ \text{loss} \end{array} \right] - \begin{array}{c} \text{gross profit} \\ \text{recognized to} \\ \text{date} \end{array} = \begin{array}{c} \text{current period} \\ \text{realized gross} \\ \text{profit} \end{array}$$

- An estimated loss on the total contract is recognized immediately in the year it is discovered. Any gross profit (or loss) reported in prior years, however, must be added (or deducted) from the total estimated loss.

☛ **PRACTICE POINTER:** The completed-contract and percentage-of-completion methods are *not* intended to be alternative methods of accounting for the same contract. Each is appropriate in certain circumstances, but do *not* consider them *equally appropriate in the same circumstances.* Where reasonable estimates of the percentage of completion are possible, the percentage-of-completion method constitutes GAAP and should be used. On the other hand, if reasonable estimates of the percentage are *not* possible, the completed-contract method constitutes GAAP and should be used.

Illustration of Accounting for the Completed-Contract and Percentage-of-Completion Methods

The following data pertain to a $2,000,000 long-term construction contract:

	20X5	*20X6*	*20X7*
Costs incurred during the year	$ 500,000	$700,000	$ 300,000
Year-end estimated costs to complete	1,000,000	300,000	—
Billing during the year	400,000	700,000	900,000
Collections during the year	200,000	500,000	1,200,000

The journal entries for both the completed-contract method and the percentage-of-completion method for the three years are as follows, assuming the degree of completion is determined based on costs incurred:

20X5	Completed Contract		% of Completion	
Construction in progress	500,000		500,000	
Cash or liability		500,000		500,000
Accounts receivable	400,000		400,000	
Advance billings		400,000		400,000
Cash	200,000		200,000	
Accounts receivable		200,000		200,000
Construction in progress	no entry		166,667	
Realized gross profit (P&L)				166,667

20X6	Completed Contract		% of Completion	
Construction in progress	700,000		700,000	
Cash or liability		700,000		700,000
Accounts receivable	700,000		700,000	
Advance billings		700,000		700,000
Cash	500,000		500,000	
Accounts receivable		500,000		500,000
Construction in progress	no entry		233,333	
Realized gross profit (P&L)				233,333

20X7	Completed Contract		% of Completion	
Construction in progress	300,000		300,000	
Cash or liability		300,000		300,000
Accounts receivable	900,000		900,000	
Advance billings		900,000		900,000
Cash	1,200,000		1,200,000	
Accounts receivable		1,200,000		1,200,000
Construction in progress	no entry		100,000	
Realized gross profit (P&L)				100,000
Advance billings	2,000,000		2,000,000	
Construction in progress		1,500,000		2,000,000
Realized gross profit (P&L)		500,000		—

Computation of Realized Gross Profit

20X5

$$\frac{\$500,000}{\$1,500,000} \times \$500,000^* - 0 \qquad\qquad = \$166,667$$

20X6

$$\frac{\$1,200,000}{\$1,500,000} \times \$500,000 - \$166,667 \qquad = \$233,333$$

20X7

$$\frac{\$1,500,000}{\$1,500,000} \times \$500,000 - (\$166,667 + \$233,333) = \$100,000$$

Total gross profit

$$\underline{\underline{\$500,000^*}}$$

---

*$2,000,000 - ($500,000 + $1,000,000) = $500,000

At the end of each year during which the contract is in progress, the excess of the construction-in-progress account over the advance billings account is presented as a current asset:

20X5: ($500,000 + $166,667) − $400,000 = $266,667

20X6: ($500,00 + $166,667 + $700,00 + $233,333)
     − ($400,000 + $700,00) = $500,000

In this illustration, the estimated gross profit of $500,000 was the actual gross profit on the contract. If changes in the estimated cost to complete the contract had been appropriate at the end of 20X5 and/or 20X6, or if the actual costs to complete had been determined to be different when the contract was completed in 20X7, those changes would have been incorporated into revised estimates during the contract period. For example, if at the end of 20X6 the costs to complete were estimated to be $400,000 instead of $300,000, the 20X6 gross profit of $133,333 would have been determined as follows:

$$\left(\frac{\$1,200,000}{\$1,600,000^*}\right) \times (2,000,000 - \$1,6000,000) = \$300,000$$

$$\$300,000 - \$166,667 = \$133,333$$

---

*$500,000 (20X5) + $700,000 (20X6) + $400,000 (20X6 estimated) = $1,600,000

RELATED CHAPTERS IN 2009 *GAAP GUIDE LEVEL A*

Chapter 2, "Accounting Policies and Standards"
Chapter 19, "Government Contracts"
Chapter 27, "Inventory"
Chapter 41, "Revenue Recognition"

RELATED CHAPTERS IN 2009 *GAAP GUIDE LEVELS B, C, AND D*

Chapter 2, "Accounting Policies and Standards"
Chapter 24, "Inventory"
Chapter 27, "Long-Term Construction Contracts"
Chapter 36, "Revenue Recognition"

RELATED CHAPTERS IN 2009 *INTERNATIONAL ACCOUNTING/FINANCIAL REPORTING STANDARDS GUIDE*

Chapter 5, "Accounting Policies, Changes in Accounting Estimates, and Errors"
Chapter 11, "Construction Contracts"
Chapter 18, "Government Grants and Government Assistance"
Chapter 23, "Inventories"
Chapter 30, "Revenue"

CHAPTER 31
LONG-TERM OBLIGATIONS

CONTENTS

OVERVIEW

The authoritative accounting literature contains disclosure requirements for many types of long-term obligations. These include unrecorded obligations (e.g., unrecorded unconditional purchase obligations), as well as recorded obligations (e.g., recorded purchase obligations, debt maturities, required stock redemptions).

The general source of GAAP for disclosure of long-term obligations is the following pronouncement:

FAS-47   Disclosure of Long-Term Obligations

Other pronouncements cover disclosure requirements for specific types of obligations (e.g., FAS-13 [Accounting for Leases]).

For unrecorded unconditional purchase obligations, FAS-47 (Disclosure of Long-Term Obligations) requires disclosure of the nature and terms of the obligation, amounts of the obligation at the latest balance sheet date, and for each of the next five years, a description of any variable portion of the obligation and amounts purchased under the obligation for each period for which an income statement is presented. Similar disclosures are required for recorded obligations, including purchase obligations, debt maturities, and capital stock redemption requirements.

BACKGROUND

Enterprises and/or individuals frequently acquire assets or liabilities by written contract. A contract may contain unconditional rights and obligations or conditional rights and obligations. A right or obligation is unconditional when only the passage of time is necessary for it to mature. A conditional right or obligation is one that matures only on the occurrence of one or more events that are specified in the contract.

If a significant period elapses between the execution and subsequent performance of a contract, a problem may arise as to when, if at all, the assets and/or liabilities created by the contract should be recognized by the contracting parties. Under existing accounting practices, assets and/or liabilities that are created by a contract may not be recognized at all, or may be either recognized in the accounts or disclosed in a note to the financial statements.

Under existing accounting principles, exchanges between enterprises or individuals usually are recorded when the transfer of resources, services, and/or obligations occurs. Unfulfilled purchase commitments for the future exchange of resources, services, and/or obligations, however, are not recorded until the commitment is at least partially fulfilled by one of the contracting parties. Exceptions to the general rule for unfulfilled purchase commitments are certain leases and losses on firm noncancelable purchase commitments, which are recorded under existing accounting principles.

> ☛ **PRACTICE POINTER:** The disclosure of certain contractual rights or obligations is sometimes confused with the disclosure of a contingency. The disclosure of a contingency is necessary only when a contingent *gain* or *loss* exists in accordance with the provisions of FAS-5 (Accounting for Contingencies). If there is no contingent *gain* or *loss*, disclosure is not required. On the other hand, the disclosure of information on certain contractual rights or obligations may be required by GAAP to avoid financial statements that are misleading.
>
> A situation may arise in which the disclosure of a contractual obligation is required by GAAP and—at the same time—a *loss contingency* may exist involving the same contractual obligation. In this event, disclose the information concerning both the obligation and the contingency in accordance with GAAP.

PURCHASE OBLIGATIONS

Unconditional Purchase Obligations

For the purposes of FAS-47, an *unconditional purchase obligation* is one in which one party is required to transfer funds to another party in return for future delivery of specified quantities of goods or services at specified prices.

> **OBSERVATION:** In contrast, an unconditional purchase obligation to transfer assets other than funds to another party in return for specified quantities of goods or services at specified prices is not considered an unconditional obligation and, apparently, would not be covered by FAS-47.

For FAS-47 disclosure requirements to apply, an unconditional purchase obligation must be associated with the financing arrangements (*a*) for the facilities that will provide the contracted goods or services or (*b*) relating to the costs of the contracted goods or services (such as carrying costs). Unconditional purchase obligations that have a remaining term of one year or less are excluded from the provisions of FAS-47. An unconditional purchase obligation qualifies for disclosure even though it is cancelable because of (FAS-47, par. 6):

- A remote contingency
- Permission of the other party
- A replacement agreement between the same parties
- A provision for a penalty payment in an amount that reasonably assures the continuation of the agreement

The provisions in FAS-47 dealing with unrecorded purchase obligations are primarily directed to take-or-pay contracts and throughput contracts.

> **OBSERVATION:** In a *take-or-pay contract*, a buyer agrees to pay certain periodic amounts for certain products or services. The buyer must make the specified periodic payments, even though it does not take delivery of the products or services.
>
> In a *throughput contract*, one party agrees to pay certain periodic amounts to another party for the transportation or processing of a product. The periodic payments must be made, even though the minimum quantities specified in the agreement in each period have not been sent to the other party for transporting or processing.

In take-or-pay contracts and throughput contracts, the periodic payments are unconditional and are not dependent on the occurrence of a specified event or the fulfillment of a condition.

Disclosure of Unrecorded Unconditional Purchase Obligations

FAS-47 does not change GAAP in terms of the recording of liabilities in conjunction with unconditional purchase obligations or other similar obligations. It does, however, require disclosure of information for unrecorded unconditional purchase obligations that are (*a*) substantially noncancelable, (*b*) associated with the financing arrangements for the facilities that will provide the contracted goods or services or related to the costs of the contracted goods or services (such as carrying costs), and (*c*) for a remaining term in excess of one year. The following information is to be disclosed (FAS-47, par. 7):

- A description of the nature and term of the obligation
- The total determinable amount of unrecorded unconditional purchase obligations as of the latest balance sheet date, and the total determinable amount of unrecorded unconditional purchase obligations for each of the five years after the latest balance sheet date
- A description of the nature of any variable component of the unrecorded unconditional purchase obligations
- For each income statement presented, the amounts actually purchased under the unconditional purchase obligations

> **OBSERVATION:** An unconditional obligation may consist of a determinable portion and a variable portion. The determinable portion is quantified and disclosed in accordance with item (2) above. The variable portion need not be quantified, but the nature of such amounts must be disclosed in accordance with item (3) above.

Similar or related obligations may be combined and disclosures are not required if the aggregate commitment of all unrecorded unconditional purchase obligations is immaterial.

FAS-13 (Accounting for Leases) requires the disclosure of certain minimum lease payments. Minimum lease payments that are not required to be disclosed in accordance with FAS-13, however, must be disclosed if they meet the requirements for disclosure outlined in FAS-47 (FAS-47, par. 6).

> **OBSERVATION:** Apparently, FAS-47 requires the disclosure of certain leases that were specifically excluded from FAS-13, if such leases are (a) substantially noncancelable, (b) part of the financing arrangements for the facilities that will provide

specified goods or services, or related to the costs of the specified goods or services, and (c) for a remaining term in excess of one year. The following types of leases and similar agreements were expressly excluded from FAS-13 and may require disclosure under the provisions of FAS-47:

1. Natural resource leases, including oil, gas, minerals, and timber
2. Leases involving services only
3. Licensing agreements, including motion picture films, plays, manuscripts, patents, and copyrights

Furthermore, despite the similarity to take-or-pay contracts, "nuclear fuel heat supply contracts" are specifically included in FAS-13 as leases and therefore are not covered by FAS-47.

FAS-47 does not require, but does encourage, the disclosure of the present value of the total determinable amounts of unrecorded unconditional purchase obligations for each of the five years after the latest balance sheet date (item 2 above). In computing the present value of an obligation, the discount rate usually is the effective interest rate at the inception of the borrowings that (a) financed the project or (b) are associated with the unrecorded unconditional purchase obligations. If it is not practical to determine the discount rate, or if there are no borrowings associated with the obligations, the discount rate is the purchaser's incremental borrowing rate. The purchaser's incremental borrowing rate is the rate the purchaser would have incurred at the inception of the obligation to borrow funds, on similar terms, to discharge the unconditional purchase obligation (FAS-47, par. 8).

DISCLOSURE OF RECORDED OBLIGATIONS

In addition to requiring disclosure of information about unrecorded purchase obligations as described above, FAS-47 also requires disclosure of similar information for a variety of recorded obligations. The following specific disclosures must be made as of the date of the latest balance sheet presented (FAS-47, par. 10):

- *Unconditional Purchase Obligations* For each of the five years immediately following the latest balance sheet date, the amount of payments for recorded unconditional purchase obligations that meet FAS-47 disclosure provisions must be disclosed. In addition, all amounts due after the fifth year shall be disclosed in a caption labeled "subsequent years." The disclosure provisions of FAS-47 require that an unconditional purchase obligation (a) be substantially noncancelable, (b) have a remaining term in excess of one year, and (c) be associated with the financing arrangements for facilities that will provide the contracted goods or services or relating to the costs of the contracted goods or services (see Illustration of Take-or-Pay, Throughput, and Similar Contracts, below).

- *Debt Payments*   For each of the five years immediately following the latest balance sheet date, the combined total of maturities and sinking fund requirements for all long-term borrowings must be disclosed (see Illustration of Maturities and Sinking Fund Requirements below).

- *Capital Stock Redemptions*   For each of the five years immediately following the latest balance sheet date, the total of required redemptions (separately or combined) for all classes of capital stock that are redeemable at determinable prices on determinable dates must be disclosed (see Illustration of Redemption of Capital Stock below). This requirement was carried forward into FAS-129 (Disclosure of Information about Capital Structure) unchanged.

☛ **PRACTICE POINTER:** The requirement to disclose the payments due in each of the next five years on recorded obligations is sometimes overlooked, according to several studies of disclosure deficiencies in financial statements. This may be because FAS-47 is erroneously thought of as requiring disclosure only for unrecorded obligations. While it does cover unrecorded obligations, it also applies to recorded obligations.

Illustration of Take-or-Pay, Throughput, and Similar Contracts

During 20X5, Memphis Company entered into a long-term contract to purchase all of the widgets produced by a supplier. The contract expires in 20Y3, and Memphis Company must make minimum annual payments to the supplier, whether or not it takes delivery of the widgets. The minimum total payments for each of the five and later years succeeding December 31, 20X5, are as follows:

Year	Total Payments (in thousands)
20X6	$ 4,000
20X7	12,000
20X8	14,000
20X9	10,000
20Y0	12,000
Subsequent years	28,000
Total	80,000
Less: Imputed interest	(30,000)
Present value of payments	$50,000

Illustration of Maturities and Sinking Fund Requirements

Maturities of long-term debt and sinking fund requirements on long-term debt for each of the five years* succeeding December 31, 20X5, are as follows:

Year	Long-Term Debt and Sinking Fund Requirements
20X6	$ 50,000
20X7	50,000
20X8	100,000
20X9	100,000
20Y0	50,000

*FAS-47 does *not* require the disclosure of the above information for periods subsequent to the fifth year.

Illustration of Redemption of Capital Stock

Mandatory redemption requirements for all classes of capital stock for each of the five years* succeeding December 31, 20X5, are as follows:

Year	4% Preferred	7% Preferred
20X6	$ 200,000	$ 400,000
20X7	200,000	400,000
20X8	200,000	400,000
20X9	none	400,000
20Y0	none	400,000

*FAS-47 does *not* require the disclosure of the above information for periods subsequent to the fifth year.

☛ **PRACTICE POINTER:** When disclosing unconditional obligations, much like operating leases, take care that the financial statements present both sides of the transaction. Thus, when recording an obligation, including a capital lease, both the asset (i.e., benefit) and the liability (i.e., obligation) are disclosed. Disclosure under FAS-47 applies only to the obligation side of the contract.

Paragraph 7a of FAS-47, which requires a statement about the nature and term of the obligation, may be the appropriate place for an enterprise to describe the associated benefits, if any. The last sentence of paragraph 19, Appendix A, of FAS-47 states, "The lack of explicit requirements to disclose associated benefits does not preclude an enterprise from describing those benefits."

OBSERVATION: FAS-47 contains specific disclosure requirements for recorded and unrecorded take-or-pay and throughput contracts. Both of these types of contracts are considered unconditional obligations under the provisions of FAS-47. However, a take-or-pay or throughput contract may, in substance, be a product financing arrangement. A product financing arrangement may also require unconditional periodic payments that are not dependent on the occurrence of a specified event or the fulfillment of a specified condition. Product financing arrangements are covered in this *Guide* in the chapter titled "Product Financing Arrangements."

RELATED CHAPTERS IN 2009 *GAAP GUIDE* LEVEL A

Chapter 8, "Contingencies, Risks, and Uncertainties"

Chapter 9, "Convertible Debt and Debt with Warrants"

Chapter 29, "Leases"

Chapter 35, "Product Financing Arrangements"

RELATED CHAPTERS IN 2009 *GAAP GUIDE* LEVELS B, C, AND D

Chapter 11, "Contingencies, Risks, and Uncertainties"

Chapter 12, "Convertible Debt and Debt with Warrants"

Chapter 26, "Leases"

Chapter 27, "Long-Term Construction Contracts"

RELATED CHAPTERS IN 2009 *INTERNATIONAL ACCOUNTING/FINANCIAL REPORTING STANDARDS GUIDE*

Chapter 11, "Construction Contracts"

Chapter 25, "Leases"

Chapter 28, "Provisions, Contingent Liabilities, and Contingent Assets"

CHAPTER 32
NONMONETARY TRANSACTIONS

CONTENTS

OVERVIEW

As a general rule, GAAP require that both monetary and nonmonetary exchanges be recorded based on the fair value inherent in the transaction. Certain exceptions exist, however, for nonmonetary transactions. Different accounting bases may be required for these transactions, depending on the unique characteristics of the exchange transaction.

GAAP for nonmonetary transactions are found in the following pronouncements:

APB-29	Accounting for Nonmonetary Transactions
FAS-153	Exchange of Nonmonetary Assets
FIN-30	Accounting for Involuntary Conversions of Nonmonetary Assets to Monetary Assets

BACKGROUND

Business transactions usually involve cash or monetary assets or liabilities that are exchanged for goods or services. These are identified as monetary transactions. Monetary assets or liabilities are fixed in terms of currency and usually are contractual claims to fixed amounts of money. Examples of monetary assets and liabilities are cash, accounts and notes receivable, and accounts and notes payable.

Some business transactions involve the exchange or transfer of nonmonetary assets or liabilities that are not fixed in terms of currency. These are identified as *nonmonetary transactions*. Nonmonetary assets and liabilities are those other than monetary assets and liabilities. Examples are inventory, investments in common stock, property, plant, and equipment, liability for advance rent collected, and common stock.

> ☛ **PRACTICE POINTER:** Under certain circumstances, management's intent may affect the monetary/nonmonetary classification of an asset or liability. For example, a marketable bond being held to maturity qualifies as a monetary asset because its face amount is fixed in terms of currency. If the same bond were being held for speculation, however, it would be classified as a nonmonetary asset, because the amount that would be received when sold would not be determinable and therefore not fixed in terms of currency.

ACCOUNTING FOR NONMONETARY EXCHANGES AND TRANSACTIONS

An *exchange* is a reciprocal transfer between an enterprise and another entity that results in the enterprise's acquiring assets or services or satisfying liabilities by surrendering other assets or services or incurring other obligations. A reciprocal transfer of a nonmonetary asset is considered an exchange only if the transferor has no substantial continuing involvement in the transferred asset such that the usual risks and rewards of ownership of the asset are transferred (FAS-153, par. 2).

A *nonreciprocal transfer* is a transfer of assets or services in one direction, either from an enterprise to its owners or another entity, or from owners or another entity to the enterprise (APB-29, par. 3). Examples of nonreciprocal transfers are:

- Declaration and distribution of a dividend
- Acquisition of treasury stock
- Sale of capital stock
- Conversion of convertible debt
- Charitable contributions

Basic Principle

In general, APB-29 requires that accounting for nonmonetary transactions should be based on the fair values of the assets or services
involved, which is the same basis that ordinarily would be used for
monetary transactions. The cost of a nonmonetary asset acquired in
exchange for another nonmonetary asset is the fair value of the asset
surrendered to obtain it. A gain or loss is recognized in the exchange.
The fair value of the asset received should be used to measure the
cost if that amount is more clearly evident than the fair value of the
asset surrendered. Similarly, a transfer of a nonmonetary asset to a
stockholder or to another entity in a nonreciprocal transfer is
recorded at the fair value of the asset transferred, and a gain or
loss is recognized on the disposition of the asset (APB-29, par. 18).

Fair value is determined by referring to estimated realizable
values in cash transactions of the same or similar assets, quoted
market prices, independent appraisals, estimated fair values of
assets or services received in exchange, and other available evidence.
If one of the parties in a nonmonetary transaction could have elected
to receive cash instead of the nonmonetary asset, the amount of cash
that could have been received may be evidence of the fair value of the
nonmonetary assets exchanged (APB-29, par. 25).

Fair value should be regarded as not determinable if major uncertainties exist about the realizability of the value that would be
assigned to an asset received in a nonmonetary transaction. If the
fair value of either the asset surrendered or the asset received is not
determinable within reasonable limits, the recorded amount of the
nonmonetary asset transferred from the enterprise may be the only
available measure of the transaction (APB-29, par. 26).

FAS-153 Amendments to APB-29

FAS-153 amends APB-29 to require that exchanges of nonmonetary
assets be recorded at fair value unless the transaction lacks commercial substance.

> **OBSERVATION:** The FASB has a couple of motives for amend-
> ing APB-29 by issuing FAS-153. First, FAS-153 increases the
> comparability of cross-border financial reporting. The statement
> narrows the areas of difference between generally accepted
> accounting principles in the U.S. and the International Financial
> Reporting Standards (IFRS) of the International Accounting
> Standards Board (IASB). Second, under APB-29 it often was
> difficult to determine whether an exchange of assets involved
> similar productive assets, which then called for the exchange to
> be accounted for at book value, not at fair value.

If one of the parties in a nonmonetary transaction could have elected to receive cash instead of the nonmonetary asset, the amount of cash that could have been received may be evidence of the fair value of the nonmonetary assets exchanged (FAS-157, par. E2a).

APB-29 involves accounting for the transfer of nonmonetary assets in a reciprocal transfer between an entity and another party. FAS-153 indicates that any reciprocal transfer only qualifies as an exchange if the transferor has no substantial continuing involvement with the assets transferred. The risks and rewards of ownership must be transferred for an exchange transaction to take place.

FAS-153 reiterates APB-29's conclusion that exchanges of nonmonetary assets generally are to be accounted for at fair value. There are three circumstances, however, when an exchange is to be recorded based on the book value (less any reduction for impairment) of the net asset transferred. These are when:

- The fair value of the asset transferred or received is not determinable.

- The exchange is to facilitate a sale to a customer and it involves the exchange of a product held for sale in the ordinary course of business for another product to be sold in the same line of business.

- The exchange transaction lacks commercial substance. (FAS-153, par. 2c)

An exchange has commercial substance if the entity's future cash flows are expected to change as a result of the transaction. An entity's future cash flows are expected to change if either (1) the amount, timing, or uncertainty of the future cash flows from the asset received differs significantly from the amount, timing, or uncertainty of the future cash flows from the asset transferred or (2) there is a significant difference between the entity-specific value of the asset received and the entity-specific value of the asset transferred. An asset's entity-specific value is its value to a particular entity, given the entity's intended use for that asset, rather than the asset's value as determined by the marketplace (FAS-153, par. 2d).

FAS-153 indicates that an exchange would not have commercial substance if such substance were based solely on cash flows as a result of achieving certain tax benefits, if the tax benefits arise solely from achieving a certain financial reporting result.

Gain or Loss

Gain or loss, when applicable, is recognized in nonmonetary transactions. A difference in the gain or loss for tax purposes and that recognized for accounting purposes may constitute a temporary difference in income tax provision (APB-29, par. 27).

The process of determining the appropriate amount of gain or loss, if any, to be recognized in nonmonetary exchanges in accordance with APB-29, as amended by FAS-153, is summarized in Figure 32-1.

Illustration of the Major Provisions of APB-29

In all of the following cases, an enterprise is giving up nonmonetary Asset A, which has a recorded amount of $10,000.

Case 1: Asset A is exchanged for dissimilar nonmonetary Asset B, which is valued at $12,000. Entry to record:

Asset B	12,000	
Asset A		10,000
Gain on exchange		2,000

Explanation: Nonmonetary transaction is recorded at fair value and any gain or loss is recognized.

Case 2: Asset A is exchanged for similar productive (nonmonetary) Asset C, which is valued at $9,500. Entry to record:

Asset C	9,500	
Loss on exchange	500	
Asset A		10,000

Explanation: Exchange of similar assets is recorded at fair value; loss is recognized.

Case 3: Asset A is exchanged for similar productive (nonmonetary) Asset D, which is valued at $15,000. Entry to record:

Asset D	15,000	
Asset A		10,000
Gain on exchange		5,000

Explanation: Exchange of similar assets is recorded at fair value; gain is recognized.

Case 4: Asset A is exchanged for a similar productive (nonmonetary) Asset E, which is valued at $13,000; the transaction lacks commercial substance because it does not significantly alter future cash flows. Entry to record:

Asset E	10,000	
Asset A		10,000

Explanation: Exchange of similar assets is recorded at book value of asset surrendered because the transaction lacks commercial substance.

Case 5: Asset A is exchanged for a similar productive (nonmonetary) Asset F in a transaction that has commercial substance, but for which the fair value of neither asset can be reasonably determined. Entry to record:

Asset F	10,000	
Asset A		10,000

Explanation: Because fair value cannot be reasonably determined for either Asset A or Asset F, the acquired asset is recorded at the book value of the asset surrendered.

Figure 32-1: Accounting for Nonmonetary Exchanges

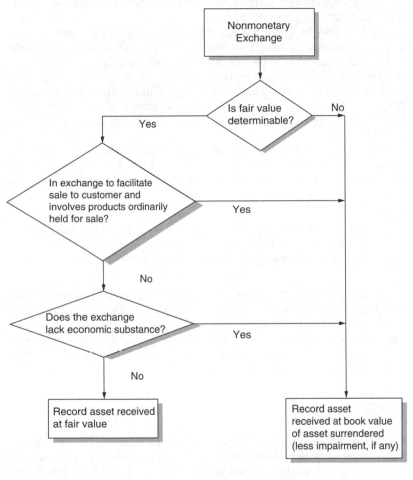

Involuntary Conversion of Nonmonetary Assets to Monetary Assets

When a nonmonetary asset is involuntarily converted to a monetary asset, a monetary transaction results, and FIN-30 (Accounting for Involuntary Conversions of Nonmonetary Assets to Monetary Assets) requires that a gain or loss be recognized in the period of conversion (FIN-30, par. 2). The gain or loss is the difference between the carrying amount of the nonmonetary asset and the proceeds from the conversion.

Examples of involuntary conversion are the total or partial destruction of property through fire or other catastrophe, theft of property, or condemnation of property by a governmental authority (eminent domain proceedings).

Gain or loss from an involuntary conversion of a nonmonetary asset to a monetary asset is classified as part of continuing operations, extraordinary items, disposal of a segment, etc., according to the particular circumstances (FIN-30, par. 4). In addition, a gain or loss recognized for tax purposes in a period different from that for financial accounting purposes creates a temporary difference, for which recognition of deferred taxes may be necessary (FIN-30, par. 5).

The involuntary conversion of a LIFO inventory layer at an interim reporting date does not have to be recognized if the proceeds are reinvested in replacement inventory by the end of the fiscal year (FIN-30, par. 11).

> **OBSERVATION:** This is the same treatment afforded a temporary liquidation at interim dates of a LIFO inventory layer that is expected to be replaced by the end of the annual period.

In the event the proceeds from an involuntary conversion of a LIFO inventory layer are not reinvested in replacement inventory by the end of the fiscal year, gain for financial accounting purposes need not be recognized, providing the taxpayer does not recognize such gains for income tax reporting purposes and provided that replacement is intended but not yet made by year-end (FIN-30, par. 11).

Disclosure

Disclosure of the nature of the nonmonetary transaction, the basis of accounting for assets transferred, and gains or losses recognized are required in the financial statements for the period in which the transaction occurs (APB-29, par. 28).

RELATED CHAPTERS IN 2009 *GAAP GUIDE*
LEVEL A

Chapter 11, "Depreciable Assets and Depreciation"
Chapter 20, "Impairment of Long-Lived Assets"
Chapter 27, "Inventory"
Chapter 28, "Investments in Debt and Equity Securities"
Chapter 40, "Results of Operations"

RELATED CHAPTERS IN 2009 *GAAP GUIDE LEVELS B, C, AND D*

Chapter 7, "Capitalization and Expense Recognition Concepts"
Chapter 19, "Impairment of Long-Lived Assets"
Chapter 24, "Inventory"
Chapter 25, "Investments in Debt and Equity Securities"
Chapter 28, "Nonmonetary Transactions"
Chapter 35, "Results of Operations"

RELATED CHAPTERS IN 2009 *INTERNATIONAL ACCOUNTING/FINANCIAL REPORTING STANDARDS GUIDE*

Chapter 19, "Impairment of Assets"
Chapter 23, "Inventories"
Chapter 24, "Investment Property"
Chapter 27, "Property, Plant, and Equipment"

CHAPTER 33
PENSION PLANS

CONTENTS

OVERVIEW

GAAP for employers' accounting for pension plans emphasizes the determination of annual pension expense (identified as net periodic pension cost) and the presentation of the funded status of the pension plan. If the pension plan is overfunded, an asset is recognized in the sponsoring employer's statement of financial position; if the plan is underfunded, a liability is recognized. Net periodic pension cost has often been viewed as a single homogeneous amount, but it is actually made up of several components that reflect different aspects of the employer's financial arrangements, as well as the cost of benefits earned by employees.

In applying principles of accrual accounting for pension plans, the FASB emphasizes three fundamental features:

1. *Delayed income statement recognition*—changes in the pension obligation and changes in the value of pension assets are recognized on the balance sheet as they occur, through changes in the pension asset and/or liability; however, on the income statement these changes are not recognized as they occur, but rather systematically and gradually over subsequent periods. Items recognized on the balance sheet immediately but deferred for income statement recognition are included in accumulated other comprehensive income.

2. *Net cost*—the recognized consequences of events and transactions affecting a pension plan are reported as a single net amount in the employer's financial statements. This approach results in the aggregation of items that would be presented separately for any other part of the employer's operations: the compensation cost of benefits, the interest cost resulting from deferred payment of those benefits, and the results of investing pension assets.

3. *Offsetting*—pension assets and liabilities are shown net in the employer's statement of financial position, even though the liability has not been settled. The assets may still be controlled and substantial risks and rewards associated with both are clearly borne by the employer.

Employers sometimes cancel (settle) or reduce (curtail) a pension plan. A *settlement of a pension plan* is an irrevocable action that relieves the employer (or the plan) of primary responsibility for an obligation and eliminates significant risks related to the obligation and the assets used to effect the settlement. Examples of transactions that constitute a settlement include (*a*) making lump-sum cash payments to plan participants in exchange for their rights to receive specified pension benefits and (*b*) purchasing nonparticipating annuity contracts to cover vested benefits.

A *curtailment* is a significant reduction in, or an elimination of, defined benefit accruals for present employees' future services. Examples of curtailments are (*a*) termination of employees' services earlier than expected, which may or may not involve closing a facility or discontinuing a segment of a business, and (*b*) termination or suspension of a plan so that employees do not earn additional defined benefits for future services.

GAAP for accounting for pensions, including settlements and curtailments, by employers are located in the following pronouncement:

FAS-87	Employers' Accounting for Pensions
FAS-88	Employers' Accounting for Settlements and Curtailments of Defined Benefit Pension Plans and for Termination Benefits
FAS-132 (Revised 2003)	Employers' Disclosures about Pensions and Other Postretirement Benefits
FAS-158	Employers' Accounting for Defined Benefit Pension and Other Postretirement Plans

2009 TRANSITION GUIDANCE FOR FAS-141(R) AND FAS-160

The FASB has recently issued FAS-141(R), *Business Combinations,* which is effective for business combinations for which the acquisition date is on or after the beginning of the first annual reporting period beginning on or after December 15, 2008. The FASB has also issued FAS-160, *Noncontrolling Interests in Consolidated Financial Statements, an Amendment of ARB No. 51,* which is effective for fiscal years, and interim periods within those fiscal years, beginning on or after December 15, 2008. Because these standards are not effective for some companies until December 2009, and because early adoption is prohibited, the 2009 *GAAP Guide* reflects the requirements of FAS-141 prior to its revision in December 2007 and does not reflect the requirements of FAS-160. There is a discussion of the changes in the accounting for business combinations under FAS-141(R) in the Appendix to Chapter 4, "Business Combinations." Similarly, the Appendix to Chapter 7, "Consolidated Financial Statements," includes a discussion of the requirements of FAS-160. However, any effects of FAS-141(R) and/or FAS-160 in this chapter have not been reflected in this edition. Therefore, if a company is subject to the requirements of FAS-141(R) and/or FAS-160, the reader is referred to FAS-141(R) and FAS-160 for these new requirements.

BACKGROUND

Employment is based on an explicit or implicit exchange agreement. The employee agrees to provide services for the employer in exchange for a current wage, a pension benefit, and frequently other benefits such as death, dental, disability. Although pension benefits and some other benefits are not paid currently, they represent deferred compensation that must be accounted for as part of the employee's total compensation package.

Pension benefits usually are paid to retired employees or their survivors on a periodic basis, but may be paid in a single lump sum. Other benefits, such as death and disability, may also be provided through a pension plan. Most pension plans also provide benefits upon early retirement or termination of service.

A pension plan may be contributory or noncontributory; that is, the employees may be required to contribute to the plan (contributory), or the entire cost of the plan may be borne by the employer (noncontributory). A pension plan may be funded or unfunded; that is, the employees and/or the employer may make cash contributions to a pension plan trustee (funded), or the employer may make only credit entries on its books reflecting the pension liability under the plan (unfunded).

> **OBSERVATION:** A qualified pension plan under the Employee Retirement Income Security Act (ERISA) has to be funded. Every year the plan actuary must determine the minimum funding for the defined benefit pension plan. If the plan fails to meet the minimum funding requirement, a penalty tax is imposed on the employer on the funding deficiency.

Although interest cost on the pension liability and the expected return on a pension plan's assets will increase or decrease net periodic pension cost, they are considered financial costs rather than employee compensation costs. Financial costs can be controlled by the manner in which the employer provides financing for the pension plan. An employer can eliminate interest cost by funding the plan completely or by purchasing annuity contracts to settle all pension obligations. The return on plan assets can be increased by the contribution of more assets to the pension fund.

Pension Plan Accounting

The assets of a pension plan usually are kept in a trust account, segregated from the assets of the employer. The employer makes periodic contributions to the pension trust account and, if the plan is contributory, so do employees. The plan assets are invested in stocks, bonds, real estate, and other types of investments. Plan assets are increased by contributions and earnings and gains on investments and are decreased by losses on investments, payment of pension benefits, and administrative expenses. The employer usually cannot withdraw plan assets placed in a trust account. An exception arises, however, when the plan assets exceed the pension obligation and the plan is terminated. In this event, the pension plan agreement may permit the employer to withdraw the excess amount of plan assets, providing that all other existing pension plan obligations have been satisfied by the employer. Under GAAP, pension plan assets that are not effectively restricted for the payment of pension benefits or segregated in a trust are not considered pension plan assets.

Accounting and reporting for a pension plan (defined benefit plan) as a separate reporting entity are covered by FAS-35 (Accounting and Reporting by Defined Benefit Pension Plans).

Deferred Compensation Plan

A deferred compensation plan is a contractual agreement that specifies that a portion of the employee's compensation will be set aside and paid in future periods as retirement benefits. FAS-87 (Employers' Accounting for Pensions) covers deferred compensation plans that are in substance pension plans.

Postemployment and postretirement benefits generally are considered a form of deferred compensation to an employee because an employer provides these types of benefits in exchange for an employee's services. Thus, these benefits must be measured properly and recognized in the financial statements and, if the amount is material, financial statement disclosure may be required.

> **OBSERVATION:** For a discussion of postemployment and postretirement benefits and their disclosure requirements, see the chapters titled "Deferred Compensation Contracts" and "Postemployment and Postretirement Benefits Other Than Pensions."

OVERVIEW OF FAS-87

Scope and Applicability

Most of the provisions of FAS-87 address *defined benefit pension plans* of single employers. A defined benefit pension plan is one that contains a pension benefit formula, which generally describes the amount of pension benefit that each employee will receive for services performed during a specified period of employment (FAS-87, par. 11). The amount of the employer's periodic contribution to a defined benefit pension plan is based on the total pension benefits (projected to employees' normal retirement dates) that could be earned by all eligible participants.

In contrast, a *defined contribution pension plan* does not contain a pension benefit formula, but generally specifies the periodic amount that the employer must contribute to the pension plan and how that amount will be allocated to the eligible employees who perform services during that same period. Each periodic employer contribution is allocated among separate accounts maintained for each employee, and pension benefits are based solely on the amount available in each employee's account at the time of his or her retirement.

For the purposes of FAS-87, any plan that is not a defined contribution pension plan is considered a defined benefit pension plan (see definition of *defined benefit pension plan* in Appendix D of FAS-87).

FAS-87 requires that its provisions be applied to any arrangement, expressed or implied, that is similar in substance to a pension plan, regardless of its form or method of financing. Thus, a pension plan arrangement does not have to be in writing if the existence of a pension plan is implied by company policy. A qualified plan, however, has to be in writing under ERISA, as well as for federal and state tax purposes. Frequently, defined contribution pension plans provide for some method of determining defined benefits for employees, as may be the case with some *target benefit* plans. A target benefit plan is a defined contribution plan. The benefit defined in the document is only for the purpose of determining the contribution to be allocated to each participant's account. It is not intended to promise any benefit in the future. If, in substance, a plan does provide defined benefits for employees, it is accounted for as a defined benefit pension plan.

Actuarial Assumptions

Actuarial assumptions are factors used to calculate the estimated cost of pension plan benefits. Employee mortality, employee turnover, retirement age, administrative expenses of the pension plan, interest earned on plan assets, and the date on which a benefit becomes fully vested are some of the more important actuarial assumptions (FAS-87, par. 39).

Under FAS-87, each significant actuarial assumption must reflect the best estimate for that particular assumption. In the absence of evidence to the contrary, all actuarial assumptions are made on the basis that the pension plan will continue in existence (going-concern concept) (FAS-87, par. 43).

Discount rates used in actuarial valuations reflect the rates at which the pension benefits could be settled effectively. In selecting appropriate interest rates, employers should refer to current information on rates used in annuity contracts that could be purchased to settle pension obligations, including annuity rates published by the Pension Benefit Guaranty Corporation (PBGC), or the rates of return on high-quality fixed-income investments that are expected to be available through the maturity dates of the pension benefits (FAS-87, par. 44).

The chosen discount rate should produce a liability amount that would generate the necessary future cash flows to pay pension benefits as they become due, if such amount was invested at the financial statement date in a portfolio of high-quality fixed-income investments. This liability amount is theoretically equal to the market value of a portfolio of high-quality zero coupon bonds, where each bond matches the amount and maturity of future payments due under the pension plan. However, reinvestment risk exists to the extent that the pension plan's assets include interest-bearing debt instruments (rather than only zero coupon bonds) and to the extent that plan investments have a maturity date less than some of the anticipated pension payments. In such cases, the assumed discount (interest) rate needs to consider expected reinvestment rates extrapolated using the existing yield curve at the financial statement date. The discount rate should be reevaluated at each measurement (financial statement) date (FAS-87, par. 44A, as amended by FAS-158, par. C2n).

☛ **PRACTICE POINTER:**   The discount rate used to determine the pension liability and the interest cost component of net periodic pension cost should change in accordance with changes in market interest rates—if interest rates rise the discount rate should increase, if interest rates fall the discount rate should decline. In addition, the determination of the discount rate is separate from the determination of the expected return on plan assets.

An actuarial gain or loss is the difference between an actuarial assumption and actual experience. Under FAS-87, actuarial gains and losses that are not included in determining net periodic pension cost in the year in which they arise are included in other comprehensive income, and they may be included as a component of net periodic pension cost in subsequent periods if certain criteria are met (FAS-87, par. 29).

☛ **PRACTICE POINTER:**   In accounting for pension plans—particularly defined benefit plans—the CPA relies heavily on the expertise of actuaries. Actuaries are educated in mathematics, modeling, and other areas that permit them to deal with the many uncertainties required to make estimates related to an enterprise's pension plan that are necessary for both funding and financial reporting. Actuarial assumptions are one area where the CPA is particularly vulnerable, because of the significant impact that different actuarial assumptions may have on the elements of the financial statements. Essentially, the CPA's responsibility is to be generally familiar with the actuary's work and to approach the results of the actuary's work with the professional skepticism that is typical of the CPA's work in many areas. The guidance in CCH's *GAAS Guide* AU Section 336 "Using the Work of a Specialist" is particularly germane when the CPA needs to rely on the work of an actuary.

Pension Plan Assets

The resources of a pension plan may be converted into (*a*) plan assets that are invested to provide pension benefits for the participants of the plan, such as stocks, bonds, and other investments (FAS-87, par. 19) or (*b*) plan assets that are used in the operation of the plan, such as real estate, furniture, and fixtures (FAS-87, par. 51). Plan assets must be segregated in a trust or otherwise effectively restricted so that the employer cannot use them for other purposes. Under FAS-87, plan assets do not include amounts accrued by an employer as net periodic pension cost, but not yet paid to the pension plan. Plan assets may include securities of the employer if they are freely transferable (FAS-87, par. 19).

Pension plan assets that are held as investments to provide pension benefits are measured at fair value (FAS-87, par. 23). (Additional guidance on determining fair values can be found in the "Fair Value" chapter of this *Guide*.) Pension plan assets that are used in the operation of the plan are measured at cost, less accumulated depreciation or amortization (FAS-87, par. 51). All plan assets are measured as of the date of the financial statements or, if used consistently from year to year, as of a date not more than three months prior to that date (FAS-87, par. 52).

> **OBSERVATION:** FAS-158 requires pension plan assets and liabilities to be measured as of the financial statement date. This provision of FAS-158 is effective for fiscal years ending after December 15, 2008.

For the purposes of FAS-87, plan liabilities that are incurred, other than for pension benefits, may be considered reductions of plan assets (Appendix D of FAS-87, under definition of "Plan Assets").

Recording Pension Events

Under FAS-87, as amended by FAS-158, an enterprise makes three primary types of entries in its records each accounting period:

1. To record net periodic pension cost
2. To record funding of the pension plan
3. To recognize the funded status of the pension plan

Illustration of Basic Entries to Record Pension Events

Maddux Co. determines its net periodic pension cost to be $10,000 for 20X7, its first year of operation. An equal amount is funded by transferring cash to the insurance company that administers the plan. The fair value of Maddux's pension plan assets equals the pension liability at year end. The applicable tax rate is 35%. The entries to record these events areas follow:

Net periodic pension cost	10,000	
Deferred tax asset	3,500	
Deferred tax benefit—net income		3,500
Liability for pension benefits		10,000
Liability for pension benefits	10,000	
Cash		10,000

In this case, the fair value of the pension plan assets and liabilities are equal so there is no need for a third journal entry, to recognize a pension plan asset (overfunded plan) or a pension plan liability (underfunded plan).

As this illustration shows, the transfer of cash to the plan administrator is treated as a retirement of the pension liability. Most of the provisions of FAS-87 pertain to the computation of the amount to be recorded in the first journal entry type in the above illustration as net periodic pension cost. This computation requires numerous worksheet calculations, which are illustrated throughout FAS-87.

Pension Plan Terminology

Key terms that are important for an understanding of accounting for pensions in accordance with FAS-87 are discussed below.

Projected Benefit Obligation

Projected benefit obligation is the actuarial present value, as of a specified date, of the total cost of all employees' vested and nonvested pension benefits that have been attributed by the pension benefit formula to services performed by employees to that date.

The projected benefit obligation includes the actuarial present value of all pension benefits (vested and nonvested) attributed by the pension benefit formula, *including consideration of future employee compensation levels* (FAS-87, Appendix D). Vested benefits are pension benefits that an employee has an irrevocable right to receive at a date specified in the pension agreement, even if the employee does not continue to work for the employer (FAS-87, Appendix D). In the event a pension plan is discontinued, a vested benefit obligation remains a liability of the employer.

Payments of pension benefits decrease both the projected benefit obligation and the fair value of plan assets, while contributions to a plan decrease cash and the financial statement liability.

The projected benefit obligation does not appear on the books of the employer, but the difference between the projected benefit obligation and the fair value of the pension plan's assets (i.e., the funded status of the plan) is recognized as a pension plan asset or liability. In addtion, the employer maintains a worksheet record of the projected benefit obligation.

Accumulated Benefit Obligation

Accumulated benefit obligation is an alternative measure of the pension obligation; it is calculated like the projected benefit obligation, except that current or past compensation levels instead of future compensation levels are used to determine pension benefits (FAS-87, Appendix D). In the event a pension plan is discontinued, the balance of any unfunded accumulated benefit obligation remains a liability of the employer.

> **OBSERVATION:** Basically, there are two types of pension benefit formulas: pay-related benefit and nonpay-related benefit. For a nonpay-related benefit formula, the accumulated benefit obligation and the projected benefit obligation are the same.

Fair Value of Plan Assets

Fair value of plan assets are determined in accordance with the guidance in FAS-157 (Fair Value Measurements). (Additional guidance on determining fair values can be found in the "Fair Value" chapter of this *Guide*.) The fair value of pension plan investments should be reduced by brokerage commissions and other selling costs if these are likely to be significant (FAS-87, par. 49). Plan assets that are used in the operation of the pension plan (building, equipment, furniture, fixtures, etc.) are valued at cost less accumulated depreciation or amortization (FAS-87, par. 51).

Pension plan assets are recorded on the books of the pension plan. However, an employer maintains worksheet records of the cost and fair value of all pension plan assets.

Funded Status of Plan

For the employer's accounting purposes, *funded status of plan* is the difference between the projected benefit obligation and the fair value of plan assets as of a given date (FAS-87, Appendix B). If the projected benefit obligation exceeds the fair value of the plan assets, a pension plan liability exists. If the fair value of plan assets exceeds the projected benefit obligation, a pension plan asset exists. FAS-158 requires that the employer recognize a pension plan asset or liability in its statement of financial position.

Prior Service Cost or Credit

Unrecognized prior service cost is the cost of retroactive benefits granted in a plan amendment. Upon the initial adoption of a pension plan or through a plan amendment, certain employees may be granted pension benefits for services performed in prior periods. These retroactive pension benefits are referred to as *prior service costs,* and usually are granted by the employer with the expectation that they will produce future economic benefits, such as reducing employee turnover, improving employee productivity, and minimizing the need to increase future employee compensation. If retroactive benefits are granted in a plan amendment the employer debits other comprehensive income and credits the liability for pension benefits. In addition, an employer is required to amortize any prior service cost in equal amounts over the future periods of active employees who are expected to receive the benefits (FAS-87, par. 24). The amortization of prior service cost is included as a component of net periodic pension cost.

An employer can amend a pension plan to reduce pension benefits. This results in a prior service credit and is recorded by reducing the liability for pension benefits and increasing other comprehensive income. Any prior service credit is first applied to reduce any prior service cost remaining in accumulated other comprehensive income. Any balance remaining is amortized as a component of net periodic pension cost in a similar manner to the amortization of prior service cost (FAS-87, par. 28 as amended by FAS-158, par. C2e).

An employer does not establish a general ledger account for prior service cost—rather any increase in this amount directly affects other comprehensive income and the liability for pension benefits, but the employer does maintain worksheet records of such amounts.

Gain or Loss

Gain or loss results in a change in either plan assets or the projected benefit obligation as a result of actual results that differ from expectations or changes in actuarial assumptions. For example, gains or losses arise from the difference between (a) the actual and expected amount of projected benefit obligation at the end of a period and/or (b) the actual and expected amount of the fair value of pension plan assets at the end of the period. Gains and losses are recognized by adjusting other comprehensive income and the liability for pension benefits. In addition, gains and losses may be recognized as a component of net periodic benefit cost in subsequent periods if certain criteria are met (FAS-87, par. 29).

A gain or loss that, as of the beginning of the year, exceeds 10% of the greater of (a) the projected benefit obligation or (b) the market-related value of plan assets is subject to recognition. Recognition for the year is equal to the amount of the gain or loss in excess of 10% of the greater of the projected benefit obligation or the value of plan assets, divided by the average remaining service period of active employees expected to receive benefits under the plan. This frequently is referred to as the *corridor test* in applying FAS-87 (FAS-87, par. 32). The gain or loss that is subject to the corridor test is included in the balance of accumulated other comprehensive income and, if recognized, is removed from accumulated other comprehensive income (through recognition in other comprehensive income in the current period) with the offsetting entry affecting net periodic pension cost.

An employer does not establish general ledger accounts for pension gains and losses. Rather, any changes in these amounts directly affect other comprehensive income and the liability for pension benefits; however, the employer does maintain worksheet records of such amounts.

Transition Obligation (or Transition Asset) at Date of Initial Application of FAS-87

The *transition obligation or transition asset at date of initial application of FAS-87* is the difference between the projected benefit obligation and the fair value of plan assets, plus previously recognized unfunded accrued pension cost or minus previously recognized prepaid pension cost at the time FAS-87 was adopted. This transition obligation or transition asset represents the difference between the funded status of a plan (projected benefit obligation less the fair value of plan assets) and the total amount of accrued or prepaid pension cost existing on the books of the employer as of the date of the initial application of FAS-87 (FAS-87, par. 77).

The transition obligation or transition asset as of the date of initial application of FAS-87 is amortized on a straight-line basis over the average remaining service period of employees expected to receive benefits under the plan, except that (a) if the amortization period is less than 15 years, the employer may elect to use 15 years, and (b) if the plan is composed of all or substantially all inactive participants, the employer shall use those participants' average remaining life expectancy as the amortization period (FAS-87, par. 77).

The amount of the employer's transition obligation or transition asset is included in the projected benefit obligation as of the date of the employer's initial application of FAS-87. However, an employer does not record its transition obligation or transition asset on its books as of the date of the initial application of FAS-87, but maintains a worksheet record of such amount.

The unamortized portion of the transition obligation or asset is included in accumulated other comprehensive income at the time that FAS-158 is adopted. As this amount is amortized, accumulated other comprehensive income is increased (through an increase in other comprehensive income in the current period) and net periodic pension cost is increased.

NET PERIODIC PENSION COST

The employer's *net periodic pension cost* represents the net amount of pension cost for a specified period that is charged against income. Under FAS-87, the components of net periodic pension cost are (a) service cost, (b) interest cost on the projected benefit obligation, (c) actual return on plan assets, (d) amortization of prior service cost or credit (if any), (e) recognition of gain or loss (if required by FAS-87), and (f) amortization of any transition obligation or asset that remains and that is included in accumulated other comprehensive income (FAS-87, par. 20, as amended by FAS-158, par. C2b).

All of the components of net periodic pension cost are not necessarily recognized in determining income in the year when they arise. For example, the total prior service cost that results from a plan amendment is determined in the period in which it arises. Under the provisions of FAS-87, however, the employer recognizes cost in equal amounts over the future service periods of each active employee who is expected to receive the benefits of the plan amendment that gave rise to the prior service cost (FAS-87, par. 24).

Net periodic pension cost is estimated in advance at the beginning of a period based on actuarial assumptions relating to (a) the discount rate on the projected benefit obligation, (b) the expected long-term rate of return on pension plan assets, and (c) the average remaining service periods of active employees covered by the pension plan. At the end of the period, adjustments are made to account for the differences (actuarial gains or losses), if any, between the estimated and actual amounts (FAS-87, par. 29).

The actuarial assumptions used to calculate the previous year's net periodic pension cost are used to calculate that cost in subsequent interim financial statements, unless more current valuations of plan assets and obligations are available or a significant event has occurred, such as a plan amendment, which usually would require new valuations (FAS-87, par. 52).

The following illustration shows how the different components of net periodic pension cost are estimated.

Illustration of Computing Net Periodic Pension Cost

Service cost component	$2,000
Interest cost component	3,000
Return on plan assets	(2,500)
Amortization of prior service cost	1,000
Amortization of (gain) or loss	1,000
Amortization of transition obligation (asset)	1,500
Total net periodic pension cost	$6,000

For simplicity, an assumption is made that there are no differences (actuarial gains or losses) between the estimated and actual amounts at the end of the period, and that the employer made no contributions to the pension fund during the period.

		Beginning of period	End of period
(a)	Projected benefit obligation	$(115,000)	$(120,000)
(b)	Fair value of plan assets	65,000	67,500
(c)	Funded status of plan	$ (50,000)	$ (52,500)
(d)	Prior service cost	10,000	9,000
(e)	(Gain) or loss	5,000	4,000
(f)	Transition obligation or asset at date of initial application of FAS-87	35,000	33,500
(g)	Balance in accumulated other comprehensive income related to the pension plan	$ (50,000)	$ (46,500)
(h)	Reduction in net income during the period related to the pension plan		$ (6,000)

The following journal entries are recorded to record the initial funded status of the pension plan (at the adoption of FAS-158) and to recognize net periodic pension cost during the year (and to transfer amounts out of accumulated other comprehensive income) (tax effects are not considered):

Accumulated other comprehensive income	50,000	
Liability for pension benefits		50,000
Net periodic pension cost	2,500	
Liability for pension benefits		2,500
Net periodic benefit cost	3,500	
Other comprehensive income		3,500

The following explains the changes in the accounts that were affected by the net periodic pension cost accrual.

(a) *Projected benefit obligation* An increase in the projected benefit obligation of $5,000, representing the service cost component of $2,000 and interest cost component of $3,000 for the period. The projected benefit obligation is not recorded in the employer's books, but is important information in accounting for pension cost.

(b) *Fair value of plan assets* The $2,500 increase in the fair value of plan assets, between the beginning and end of the period, represents the increase in the fair value of plan assets for the period. The fair value of plan assets is not recorded in the employer's books, but is important information in accounting for pension cost.

(c) *Funded status of plan* The $2,500 decrease in the funded status of the plan, between the beginning and end of the period, is the difference between the $5,000 increase in the projected benefit obligation for the period and the $2,500 increase in the fair value of plan assets for the period.

(d) *Prior service cost* The $1,000 decrease in prior service cost, between the beginning and end of the period, is the amount of amortization of prior service cost that has been recognized by the employer as a component of net periodic pension cost.

Prior service cost is not recorded on the books of the employer, but worksheet records are maintained for such amounts. Thus, the employer reduces the worksheet balance of the unrecognized prior service cost by $1,000. However, prior service cost is included in accumulated other comprehensive income until it is recognized as a component of net periodic pension cost.

(e) *Gain or loss* The $1,000 decrease in the gain or loss (actuarial gain or loss), between the beginning and end of the period, is the amount of amortization that has been recognized by the employer as a component of net periodic pension cost.

Gain or loss (actuarial gain or loss) is not recorded on the books of the employer, but worksheet records are maintained for such amounts. Thus, the employer reduces the worksheet balance of the unrecognized net gain or loss by $1,000. As above, the gain or loss is included in accumulated other comprehensive income until it is recognized as a component of net periodic pension cost.

(f) *Transition obligation or transition asset at date of initial application of FAS-87* The $1,500 decrease in the transition obligation, between the beginning and the end of the period, is the amount of amortization that has been recognized by the employer as a component of net periodic pension cost for the period.

The transition obligation or asset is not recorded on the books of the employer, but worksheet records are maintained for such amounts. Thus, the employer reduces the worksheet balance of the unrecognized net obligation or net asset by $1,500. As above, the transition obligation or asset is included in accumulated other comprehensive income until it is recognized as a component of net periodic pension cost.

(g) *Balance in accumulated other comprehensive income related to the pension plan* At the beginning of the year, the entire unfunded status of the pension plan is due to amounts for prior service cost, gain or loss, and transition obligation that have not yet been recognized as a component of net periodic benefit cost. By the end of the year, the balance in accumulated other comprehensive income is reduced to $46,500 because $3,500 of these amounts were included in net periodic pension cost during the year.

(h) *Reduction in net income during the period related to the pension plan* Net income is reduced during the year by the amount of net periodic pension cost, $6,000. The unfunded status of the pension plan, $52,500, now comprises two components: amounts for prior service cost, gain or loss, and transition obligations that have not yet been recognized as a component of net periodic benefit cost equal $46,500. The remaining $6,000 represents the pension cost for the period, none of which has been funded (i.e., the employer made no contributions to the plan during the period).

Service Cost Component

In a defined benefit pension plan, FAS-87 requires that a pension benefit formula be used to determine the amount of pension benefit earned by each employee for services performed during a specified period. Under FAS-87, attribution is the process of assigning pension benefits or cost to periods of employee service, in accordance with the pension benefit formula (FAS-87, par. 21).

The service cost component of net periodic pension cost is defined as the actuarial present value of pension benefits attributed by the pension benefit formula to employee service during a specified period (FAS-87, par. 21). For example, a pension benefit formula may state that an employee shall receive, at the retirement age stated in the plan, a pension benefit of $20 per month for life, for each year of service. To compute the total future value of the pension benefit for the year, the monthly benefit is multiplied by the number of months in the employee's life expectancy at retirement age. This number of months is determined by reference to mortality tables. The actuarial present value of all employees' future pension benefits that are earned during a period is computed and included as the service cost component of the net periodic pension cost for the same period (FAS-87, par. 40).

If the terms of the pension benefit formula provide for benefits based on estimated future compensation levels of employees, estimates of those future compensation levels are used to determine the service cost component of net periodic pension cost. For example, if the pension benefit formula states that an employee's benefit for a period is equal to 1% of his or her final pay, an estimate of the employee's final pay is used to calculate the benefit for the period. Assumed compensation levels should reflect the best estimate of the future compensation levels of the employee involved and be consistent with assumed discount rates to the extent that they both incorporate expectation of the same future economic conditions (FAS-87, par. 202). Thus, future compensation levels in final-pay plans or career-average-pay plans are reflected in the service cost component of net periodic pension cost. Assumed compensation levels also shall reflect changes because of general price levels, productivity, seniority, promotion, and other factors (FAS-87, par. 46).

Changes resulting from a plan amendment that has become effective and automatic benefit changes specified by the terms of the pension plan, such as cost-of-living increases, are included in the determination of service cost for a period (FAS-87, par. 48).

An employer's substantive commitment to make future plan amendments in recognition of employees' prior services may indicate pension benefits in excess of those reflected in the existing pension benefit formula. Such a commitment may be evidenced by a history of regular increases in nonpay-related benefits, benefits under a career-average pay plan, or other evidence. In this event, FAS-87 requires that the pension plan be accounted for based on the employer's substantive commitment, and that appropriate disclosure be made in the employer's financial statements (FAS-87, par. 41).

A plan's pension benefit formula might provide no benefits for the first 19 years of an employee's service and a vested benefit of $1,000 per month for life in the 20th year of an employee's service. This benefit pattern is no different than providing a benefit of $50 per month for 20 years and requiring 20 years before the benefits vest. If a pension plan benefit formula attributes all or a disproportionate portion of total pension benefits to later years, the employee's *total projected benefit* is calculated and used as the basis of assigning the total pension benefits under the plan. In this event, the employee's total projected benefit is assumed to accumulate in proportion to the ratio of the total completed years of service to date to the total completed years of service as of the date the benefit becomes fully vested (FAS-87, par. 42). An employee's total projected benefit from a pension plan is the actuarial present value of the total cost of pension benefits that the employee is likely to receive under the plan. If the pension benefit formula is based on future compensation, future compensation is used in calculating the employee's total projected benefit.

> **OBSERVATION:** Under current pension law, the longest a single employer can make an employee wait before receiving vested benefits is five years. For a multiemployer plan, the longest period is ten years.

In the event a pension benefit formula does not indicate the manner in which a specific benefit relates to specific services performed by an employee, the benefit shall be assumed to accumulate as follows (FAS-87, par. 42):

- *If the benefit is includable in vested benefits*   The benefit is accumulated in proportion to the ratio of total completed years of service to date to the total completed years of service as of the date the benefit becomes fully vested.

A vested benefit is a benefit that an employee has an irrevocable right to receive. For example, an employee is entitled to receive a vested benefit whether or not he or she continues to work for the employer.

- *If the benefit is not includable in vested benefits* The benefit is accumulated in proportion to the ratio of completed years of service to date to the total projected years of service. (An example of a benefit that is not includable in vested benefits is a death or disability benefit that is payable only if death or disability occurs during the employee's active service.)

Interest Cost Component

The two factors used to determine the actuarial present value of a future pension benefit are (1) the probability that the benefit will be paid to the employee (through the use of actuarial assumptions) and (2) the time value of money (through the use of discounts for interest cost). The probability that a pension benefit will be paid is based on actuarial assumptions such as employee mortality, employee turnover, and the date the benefits become vested. An employer's liability for a retirement fund of $56,520 that is due in ten years is not equal to a present liability of $56,520. At an 8% discount rate the $56,520 has a present value of only $26,179. The $26,179 increases each year by the employer's interest cost of 8%, and in ten years grows to $56,520, if the 8% interest rate does not change.

FAS-87 requires an employer to recognize, as a component of net periodic pension cost, the interest cost on the projected benefit obligation. The interest cost is equal to the increase in the amount of the projected benefit obligation because of the passage of time (FAS-87, par. 22).

> **OBSERVATION:** FAS-87 specifies that the interest cost component of net periodic pension cost shall **not** be considered to be interest for the purposes of applying the provisions of FAS-34 (Capitalization of Interest Cost).

Actual Return on Plan Assets Component

The actual return on plan assets is equal to the difference between the fair value of plan assets at the beginning and end of a period, adjusted for employer and employee contributions (if a contributory plan) and pension benefit payments made during the period (FAS-87, par. 23). *Fair value* is the amount that a pension plan could reasonably be expected to receive from a current sale of an investment in an orderly, nonforced transaction (FAS-157, par. 5 and 7). Plan assets that are used in the operation of the pension plan (building, equipment, furniture, fixtures, etc.) are valued at cost, less accumulated depreciation or amortization (FAS-87, par. 51).

A return on plan assets decreases the employer's cost of providing pension benefits to its employees, while a loss increases pension cost. Net periodic pension income can result from a significantly high return on pension plan assets during a period.

FAS-87 requires an employer to recognize, as a component of net periodic pension cost, the actual return (or loss) on pension plan assets (FAS-87, par. 16).

Amortization of Prior Service Cost or Credit Component

Upon the initial adoption of a pension plan or as the result of a plan amendment, employees may be granted pension benefits for services performed in prior periods. These retroactive pension benefits are assumed to have been granted by the employer in the expectation that they will produce future economic benefits, such as reducing employee turnover, improving employee productivity, and minimizing the need for increasing future employee compensation. The cost of pension benefits that are granted retroactively to employees for services performed in prior periods is referred to as *prior service cost* (FAS-87, par. 24).

Under FAS-87, only a portion of the total amount of prior service cost arising in a period, including retroactive benefits that are granted to retirees, is included in net periodic pension cost. FAS-87 requires that the total prior service cost arising in a period from an adoption or amendment of a plan be amortized in equal amounts over the future service periods of *active* employees who are expected to receive the retroactive benefits (FAS-87, par. 25).

> ☞ **PRACTICE POINTER:** Because retirees are not expected to render future services, the cost of their retroactive benefits cannot be recognized over their remaining service periods. FAS-87 requires that the total prior service cost arising from a plan adoption or amendment, including the cost attributed to the benefits of retirees, shall be amortized in equal amounts over the future service periods of only the active employees who are expected to receive benefits.

If substantially all of the participants of a pension plan are inactive, the prior service cost attributed to the benefits of the inactive participants shall be amortized over the remaining life expectancy of those participants (FAS-87, par. 25).

> **OBSERVATION:** The last sentence of paragraph 25 of FAS-87 addresses the method of amortizing that portion of the cost of retroactive plan amendments that affect benefits of inactive participants of a plan composed of substantially all inactive participants, but does not address the method of amortizing the portion of the cost of the same retroactive plan amendments that affect benefits of the active participants of the same plan. Two alternatives appear to be available. The first is that the cost of the active participants' benefits is charged to income of the

period of the plan amendment. The second is that the cost of the **active** participants' benefits is amortized in the same manner as if the plan were not composed of substantially all inactive participants. In this event, the cost attributed to the retroactive benefits of the **active** participants of a plan composed of substantially all **inactive** participants is amortized in equal amounts over the future service periods of each active employee who is expected to receive the retroactive benefits.

FAS-87 permits the consistent use of an alternative approach that more rapidly amortizes the amount of prior service cost. For example, straight-line amortization of prior service cost over the average future service period of active employees who are expected to receive benefits under the plan is acceptable. If an alternative method is used to amortize prior service cost, it must be disclosed in the financial statements (FAS-87, par. 26).

Some companies have a history of increasing pension benefits through regular plan amendments. In these cases, the period in which an employer expects to realize the economic benefits from retroactive pension benefits that were previously granted will be shorter than the entire remaining future service period of all active employees. Under this circumstance, FAS-87 requires that a more rapid rate of amortization be applied to the remaining balance of the prior service cost to reflect the earlier realization of the employer's economic benefits and to allocate properly the cost to the periods benefited (FAS-87, par. 27).

An amendment to a pension plan usually increases the cost of employees' pension benefits and increases the amount of the projected benefit obligation. However, a pension plan amendment may decrease the cost of employees' pension benefits, which results in a decrease in the amount of the projected benefit obligation and is referred to as a prior service credit. Any decrease resulting from a pension plan amendment shall be applied to reduce the balance of any existing prior service cost in accumulated other comprehensive income and any excess shall be amortized on the same basis as increases in prior service cost (FAS-87, par. 28).

Gains and Losses Component

Gains and losses are changes in the amount of either the projected benefit obligation or pension plan assets, resulting from the differences between estimates or assumptions used and actual experience. Thus, a gain or loss can result from the difference between (*a*) the expected and actual amounts of the projected benefit obligation at the end of a period and/or (*b*) the expected and actual amounts of the fair value of pension plan assets at the end of a period. Technically, both of these types of gains and losses are considered *actuarial gains and losses*. Under FAS-87, however, a gain or loss resulting from a change in the projected benefit obligation is referred to as an *actuarial gain or loss*, while a gain or loss resulting from a change in the fair value of pension plan assets is referred to as a *net asset gain or loss*. For the purposes of FAS-87, the sources of these gains and losses are not distinguished separately, and they include amounts that have been realized as well as amounts that are unrealized (FAS-87, par. 29).

Under FAS-87, the gains and losses component of net periodic pension cost consists of (*a*) the difference between the expected and actual returns on pension plan assets (net asset gain or loss) and (*b*) if required, amortization of any net gain or loss from previous periods and included in accumulated other comprehensive income (FAS-87, par. 16, as amended by FAS-158, par. C2h, and FAS-87, par. 34).

As discussed in a previous section, the actual return on pension plan assets is equal to the difference between the fair value of pension plan assets at the beginning and end of a period, adjusted for any contributions and pension benefit payments made during that period. Fair value is the amount that a pension plan could reasonably be expected to receive from a current sale of an investment in an orderly, nonforced transaction (FAS-157, par. 5 and 7).

The expected return on pension plan assets during the period is computed by multiplying the *market-related value* of plan assets by the *expected long-term rate of return*. The expected long-term rate of return is an actuarial assumption of the expected long-term rate of return that will be earned on plan assets during the period. Under FAS-87, the current rate of return earned on plan assets and the likely reinvestment rate of return should be considered in estimating the long-term rate of return on plan assets. The expected long-term rate of return on plan assets should reflect the average rate of earnings expected on plan investments (FAS-87, par. 45).

To reduce the volatility of changes in the fair value of pension plan assets and the resulting effect on net periodic pension cost, FAS-87 requires the use of a market-related value for plan assets to compute the expected return on such assets during a period. Market-related value is used only to compute the expected return on pension plan assets for the period (expected return = market-related value × expected long-term rate of return) (FAS-87, par. 30).

Under FAS-87, the market-related value of a plan asset can be either (*a*) the actual fair value of the pension plan asset or (*b*) a calculated value that recognizes, in a systematic and rational manner, the changes in the actual fair value of the pension plan asset over a period of not more than five years (FAS-87, par. 30). Thus, in computing the market-related value of a pension plan asset, an enterprise may use actual fair value or a calculated value based on a five-year moving average of the changes in the actual fair value of the pension plan asset. In this event, the calculated market-related value would include only 20% of the total changes in the actual fair value of the pension plan asset that have occurred during the past five years. For example, if the actual fair value of a plan asset at the end of each of the last six years was $8,000, $10,000, $12,000, $14,000, $16,000, and $13,000, the net gain for the most recent five years is $5,000 ($2,000 + $2,000 + $2,000 + $2,000 − $3,000 = $5,000). In this event, only 20% of the $5,000 gain ($1,000) is included in computing the calculated market-related value of the pension plan asset for the current year.

The difference between the actual fair value of a pension plan asset and its calculated market-related value is the amount of net gain or loss from previous years that has not yet been recognized in the calculated market-related value.

Market-related value may be computed differently for each class of plan assets, but the method of computing it must be applied consistently from year to year for each class of plan assets. For example, fair value may be used for bonds and other fixed income investments, and a calculated market-related value for stocks and other equities (FAS-87, par. 30).

Illustration of Computing Market-Related Value

For computing the market-related value of a particular class of plan assets as of the end of each period, an employer uses a calculated value that includes 20% of the gains and losses on the plan assets that have occurred over the last five years. The total market-related value of this particular class of plan assets at the beginning of calendar year 20X5 was $100,000. The total fair value of the plan assets was $120,000 at the beginning of 20X5 and $130,000 at the end of 20X5. Actual gains and losses for the past five years as of the beginning of 20X5 were: 20X0 $10,000; 20X1 $(8,000); 20X2 $12,000; 20X3 $10,000; 20X4 $(4,000); the result is a net gain of $20,000 for these five years. Employer's contributions to the plan for 20X5 are estimated at $2,000 and benefit payments expected to be paid from the plan in 20X5 are also $2,000. The expected long-term rate of return on plan assets for 20X5 is 10%. The computation of the estimated market-related value as of December 31, 20X5, for this particular class of plan assets is determined as follows:

Market-related value at the beginning of period	$100,000
Add:	
Expected return on assets for 20X5 (market-related value, multiplied by expected long-term rate of return ($100,000 × 10%)	10,000
20% of the net gain or loss for the last five years (20% × $20,000)	4,000
Employer's contribution	2,000
Benefit payments made from plan	(2,000)
Estimated market-related value, Dec. 31, 20X5	$114,000
(Note:_____)	

Note: The difference between the fair value ($130,000) and market-related value ($114,000) of plan assets at the end of 20X5 is $16,000. This difference represents the amount of net gain from the five years to the beginning of 20X5 that has not yet been recognized in the market-related value of plan assets.

The expected return on plan assets is based on market-related values, which do not include all of the net asset gains and losses from previous years (unless market-related values are equal to fair values). Thus, net asset gains and losses may include both (*a*) gains and losses of previous years that have been included in market-related value and (*b*) gains and losses of previous years that have not yet been included in market-related value (FAS-87, par. 31).

As mentioned above, FAS-87 does not require the recognition of any gains and losses as components of net periodic pension cost of the period in which they arise, except to the extent that the net asset gain or loss for the period offsets or supplements the actual return of pension plan assets for the period. However, gains and losses are recognized as a component of other comprehensive income as they occur. In subsequent years, however, all gains and losses, except those which have not yet been recognized in the market-related values of pension plan assets, are subject to certain minimum amortization provisions of FAS-87. Gains and losses that are amortized as a component of net periodic pension cost are removed from the beginning balance of accumulated other comprehensive income.

FAS-87 requires recognition of net gains or losses based on beginning-of-the-year balances. A net gain or loss that, as of the beginning of the year, exceeds 10% of (*a*) the projected benefit obligation or (*b*) the market-related value of plan assets, whichever is greater, is subject to recognition. The minimum recognition for the year is calculated by dividing the average remaining service period of active employees who are expected to receive benefits under the plan into the amount of net gain or loss that, as of the beginning of the year, exceeds 10 % of (*a*) the projected benefit obligation or (*b*) the market-related value of plan assets, whichever is greater. If substantially all of a plan's participants are inactive, however, the average remaining life expectancy of the inactive participants is divided into the excess net gain or loss subject to amortization. The computation of the minimum amortization required by FAS-87 is made each year based on beginning-of-the-year balances of unrecognized net gains or losses (FAS-87, par. 32).

In lieu of the minimum amortization of net gains and losses specified by FAS-87, an employer may use an alternative method provided that the method (*a*) is systematic and applied consistently, (*b*) is applied to both gains and losses similarly, (*c*) reduces the unamortized balance included in accumulated other comprehensive income by an amount greater than the amount that would result from the minimum amortization method provided by FAS-87, and (*d*) is disclosed in the financial statements (FAS-87, par. 33).

Illustration of Gains and Losses Component of
Net Periodic Pension Cost

ABC Corporation has a remaining transition obligation of $400 on January 1, 20X5. ABC Corp. amortized $40 of this transition obligation in 20X5. The net asset (gain) or loss for 20X5, resulting from changes in actuarial assumptions, was a loss of $400, which was recognized in other comprehensive income. The market-related value of pension plan assets at the beginning of 20X6 is $1,600 and the average remaining service life of active employees is ten years.

The expected net periodic pension cost for 20X6 is $340, determined as follows: the sum of service cost $200, interest cost $240 (10%), amortization of unrecognized net asset loss $20, and amortization of the transition obligation $40, less a 10% expected return on plan assets of $160 (expected return = market-related value of plan assets of $1,600 × expected long-term rate of return of 10%). No contributions were made to the pension plan in 20X6.

		Actual 12/31/X5	Expected 12/31/X6	Actual 12/31/X6
(a)	Projected benefit obligation	$(2,400)	$(2,840)	$(2,900)
(b)	Fair value of plan assets	1,640	1,800	1,750
	Funded status of plan	$ (760)	$(1,040)	$(1,150)
	Prior service cost	0	0	0
	Net (gain) or loss	400	380	490
	Transition obligation existing at 12/31/X5	360	320	320

(a) The difference between the actual projected benefit obligation for 20X5 and the expected projected benefit obligation for 20X6 is $440, which consists of the expected service cost of $200, and the expected interest cost of $240. However, the actual projected benefit for 20X6 increased $500 over the actual projected benefit for 20X5. The difference between the expected increase in the projected benefit obligation of $440 and the actual increase of $500 represents a $60 actuarial loss. The $60 loss occurred because the actuarial assumptions used were different from actual experience.

The $40 amortization of the transition obligation does not affect the projected benefit obligation because the full amount of the transition obligation was recognized in the projected benefit obligation as of the date of the initial application of FAS-87.

(b) The difference between the actual fair value of plan assets for 20X5 and the expected fair value of plan assets for 20X6 is $160, which represents the 10% expected return on plan assets (market-related value of plan assets of $1,600 × 10%). However, the actual fair value of plan assets for 20X6 of $1,750 increased only $110 over the actual fair value of plan assets of $1,640 for 20X5. The difference between the expected increase in the fair value of plan assets of $160 and the actual increase of $110 represents a $50 net asset loss for the period. The loss occurred because the actual rate of return on pension plan assets was less than the expected rate of return.

Cost Components of Net Periodic Pension Cost for 20X6

FAS-87, as amended by FAS-132 (Employers' Disclosures about Pensions and Other Postretirement Benefits) (revised 2003), requires financial statement disclosure of the amount of net periodic pension cost for the period. The disclosure shall indicate separately the service cost component, the interest cost component, the expected return on plan assets for the period, the amortization of the transition obligation or asset, gains and losses recognized, prior service cost recognized, and gain or loss recognized due to a settlement or curtailment (FAS-132, par. 5d).

Service cost	$200
Interest cost	240
Expected return on plan assets	(160)
Amortization of transition obligation	40
Amortization of prior service cost	0
Recognized net actuarial loss	20
Net periodic pension cost	$340

Note: A net asset gain or loss is not recognized in income in the period in which it arises (FAS-87, par. 29). In this case, the net asset loss is $50—the difference between the expected return on plan assets, $160, and the actual return on plan assets, $110. The expected return on plan assets is included as a component of net periodic pension cost. Recognition of the net asset loss is deferred to future periods. However, the net asset gain or loss is included as a component of other comprehensive income.

Computation of the Amortization of the Net Gain or Loss for 20X6

Net (gain) or loss 1/1/X6	$400
Add asset gain or subtract asset loss not yet recognized in market-related values at 1/1 [difference between fair value of plan assets ($1,640) and market-related value ($1,600)]	40
Net (gain) or loss subject to the minimum amortization provisions of FAS-87	440
10% of the greater of the projected benefit obligation or market-related value at 1/1	(240)
Net (gain) or loss subject to amortization	$200
Amortization for 20X6 (over the ten-year average remaining service life of active employees)	$ 20

Note: The net (gain) or loss at 1/1 must be adjusted to exclude asset gains and losses not yet reflected in market-related values, because gains and losses are not required to be amortized (FAS-87, par. 31).

Note: The $60 loss that occurred in 20X6 as a result of the difference be-
tween the expected and actual projected benefit obligation for 20X6,
and the $50 loss that occurred in 20X6 as a result of the difference
between the expected and actual fair value of plan assets for 20X6, will
become subject to the minimum amortization provisions of FAS-87 as
of 1/1/X7. The computation of the amount of net (gain) or loss as of 1/1/
X7, is as follows:

Net asset (gain) or loss 1/1/X6		$400
Less: Amortization for 20X6		20
Net asset (gain) or loss 12/31/X6		380
Add: Actuarial net (gain) or loss for 20X6	$60	
Net asset (gain) or loss for 20X6	50	110
Net (gain) or loss as of 1/1/X7		$ 490

Amortization of the Transition Obligation or Transition Asset (as of the Date of Initial Application of FAS-87)

The *funded status* of a pension plan for employer accounting purposes is
equal to the difference between the projected benefit obligation and the
fair value of pension plan assets. The funded status indicates whether
the employer has underfunded or overfunded the pension plan.

The transition obligation or transition asset of a pension plan is
determined by the employer as of the date of its financial statements
of the beginning of the year in which FAS-87 is first applied. The transition obligation or transition asset is equal to the difference between
the projected benefit obligation and fair value of pension plan assets,
plus previously recognized unfunded accrued pension cost or less
previously recognized prepaid pension cost. In the event there is no
accrued or prepaid pension cost on the employer's statement of financial position as of the date of transition to FAS-87, the funded status of
the pension plan and the unrecognized net obligation or net asset are
exactly equal (FAS-87, par. 77).

A transition obligation or asset is amortized by the employer on
a straight-line basis over the average remaining service period of
employees expected to receive benefits under the plan, as of the date
of initial application of FAS-87, except under the following circumstances (FAS-87, par. 77):

- If the amortization period is less than 15 years, an employer
  may elect to use 15 years.

- If the plan is composed of all or substantially all inactive participants, the employer shall use those participants' average
  remaining life expectancy as the amortization period.

The above amortization method is also used to recognize, as of the date of the initial application of FAS-87, any unrecognized net obligation or net asset of a defined contribution pension plan.

RECOGNITION OF FUNDED STATUS OF PENSION PLAN

As a result of FAS-158, an employer is required to recognize the overfunded or underfunded status of a defined benefit pension plan as an asset or a liability in its statement of financial position. If the fair value of a pension plan's assets exceeds the plan's projected benefit obligation the plan is overfunded and an asset is recognized. If the plan's projected benefit obligation exceeds the fair value of the plan's assets the plan is underfunded and a liability is recognized (FAS-87, par. 35, as amended by FAS-158, par. C2j). When the funded status of the pension plan is first recognized in the statement of financial position, the offsetting entry is to accumulated other comprehensive income (net of tax). The recognition of a pension plan asset or liability may result in temporary differences under FAS-109 (Accounting for Income Taxes). Deferred tax effects are to be recognized for these temporary differences as a component of income tax expense or benefit in the year in which the differences arise, and allocated to various financial statement components (FAS-87, par. 37, as amended by FAS-158, par. C2l).

Asset and liability gains and losses, and prior service costs or credits, that occur in periods after recognition of the funded status of the plan and that are not immediately included as a component of net periodic pension cost are included in other comprehensive income. As gains and losses, prior service costs and credits, and the transition asset or obligation are included in net periodic pension cost they are recognized as an adjustment to other comprehensive income (FAS-87, par. 38, as amended by FAS-158, par. C2m).

Illustration of Recognition of Overfunded or Underfunded Status

Ditkowsky & Sons Inc. applies the requirements of FAS-158 at the end of its fiscal year ending December 31, 20X6. Ditkowsky measures plan assets and liabilities at its financial statement date. The following information applies to Ditkowsky's pension plan at 12/31/X6 and 12/31/X7.

	12/31/X6 *(in thousands)*	12/31/X7 *(in thousands)*
Projected benefit obligation	$(3,200)	$(3,700)
Plan assets at fair value	4,100	4,700
Funded status	900	1,000
Items not yet recognized as a component of net periodic pension cost:		

Transition obligation	100	50
Prior service cost	180	160
Net gain	(1,240)	(1,410)
Total	(960)	(1,200)

Under the prior provisions of FAS-87, Ditkowsky reported an accrued pension cost (liability) of $60,000, representing the excess of past net periodic pension cost over past contributions. Ditkowsky's applicable tax rate is 30%.

At December 31, 20X6, Ditkowsky recognizes an asset for the overfunded status of its pension plan. Accumulated other comprehensive income, net of tax, is adjusted for the net transition obligation, prior service cost, and net gain that have not yet been included as part of net periodic pension cost. The journal entry made by Ditkowsky at 12/31/X6 is (in thousands):

Pension plan asset	900	
Accrued pension cost	60	
Deferred tax obligation—accumulated other comprehensive income	288	
Deferred tax liability		288
Accumulated other comprehensive income		960

The disclosures required by FAS-158 at 12/31/X6 require Ditkowsky to disclose the incremental effect on individual line items in the statement of financial position of applying FAS-158. These are (in thousands): (1) an increase in the overfunded pension plan asset account of $900; (2) an increase in total assets of $900; (3) a decrease in accrued pension cost of $60, an increase in deferred income tax liability of $288; (4) an increase in total liabilities of $228 ($288 − $60); (5) an increase in accumulated other comprehensive income of $672 ($960 − $288); and (6) an increase in total stockholders' equity of $672.

During 20X7 Ditkowsky will (1) recognize a pension liability and net periodic benefit cost, net of tax, for the service cost, interest cost, and expected return on plan assets; (2) adjust other comprehensive income, net of tax, to recognize the amortization of the transition obligation in net periodic benefit cost; (3) adjust other comprehensive income, net of tax, to recognize the amortization of the prior service cost in net periodic benefit cost; (4) adjust other comprehensive income, net of tax, to recognize the amortization of the net gain (amortization is required because it exceeds the greater of 10% of the projected benefit obligation or the market-related value of plan assets) in net periodic benefit cost; and (5) recognize a pension asset for the additional net gain occurring during the year, and a corresponding increase in other comprehensive income, net of tax.

The components of net periodic benefit cost for Ditkowsky for the year ended December 31, 20X7, are as follows (in thousands):

Service cost	$400
Interest cost	160
Expected return on plan assets	(450)
Amortization of the transition obligation	50

Amortization of prior service cost	20
Amortization of the net (gain) loss	(40)
Net periodic benefit cost	$140

The actual return on plan assets during 20X7 is $600,000, and because the expected return on plan assets is $450,000, there is an unexpected gain of $150,000 during the year. In addition, there is an actuarial gain during the year of $60,000. The unexpected gain on pension plan assets of $150,000, when combined with the actuarial gain of $60,000, minus the $40,000 gain amortized during the year, results in an increase in the net gain account of $170,000 during the year. Ditkowsky made no contributions to the pension plan during the year.

Ditkowsky will make the following journal entries during 20X7 in applying FAS-158 (in thousands):

To recognize a pension liability and net periodic benefit cost for the service cost, interest cost, and expected return on plan assets, net of tax.

Net periodic benefit cost ($400 + $160 − $450)	110	
Deferred tax asset	33	
Deferred tax benefit—net income		33
Liability for pension benefits		110

To recognize net periodic benefit cost and a corresponding increase in other comprehensive income, net of tax, for amortization of the transition obligation:

Net periodic benefit cost	50	
Deferred tax benefit—other comprehensive income	15	
Deferred tax benefit—net income		15
Other comprehensive income		50

To recognize net periodic benefit cost and a corresponding increase in other comprehensive income, net of tax, for amortization of prior service cost:

Net periodic benefit cost	20	
Deferred tax benefit—other comprehensive income	6	
Deferred tax benefit—net income		6
Other comprehensive income		20

To recognize net periodic benefit cost and a corresponding decrease in other comprehensive income, net of tax, for amortization of the net gain:

Other comprehensive income	40	
Deferred tax benefit—net income	12	
Deferred tax benefit—other comprehensive income		12
Net periodic benefit cost		40

To recognize a pension asset for the additional net gain during the year and a corresponding increase in other comprehensive income, net of tax:

Pension plan asset [($1,410 − $1,240) + $40]	210	
Deferred tax obligation—other comprehensive income	63	
Deferred tax liability		63
Other comprehensive income		210

All pension plans that are overfunded should be aggregated and a noncurrent asset presented in the statement of financial position. All pension plans that are underfunded should be aggregated and a liability presented in the statement of financial position. The liability is current to the extent that the actuarial present value of benefits to be paid within the next year, or operating cycle if longer, exceeds the fair value of plan assets. This determination is to be made on a plan-by-plan basis. Otherwise, the liability is noncurrent (FAS-87, par. 36, as amended by FAS-158, par. C2k). The employer should not reduce a liability resulting from an underfunded pension plan because another pension plan is overfunded (FAS-87, par. 55, as amended by FAS-158, par. C2q).

MISCELLANEOUS CONSIDERATIONS

Measurement Dates

All pension plan assets that are held as investments to provide pension benefits are measured generally at their fair values as of the date of the financial statements. There are two exceptions to this general rule. If a subsidiary sponsors a pension plan and the subsidiary has a different year end than its parent, the fair value of the subsidiary's pension plan assets is measured at the date of the subsidiary's financial statements. If an investee, accounted for using the equity method, sponsors a pension plan and the investee has a different year-end than the investor, the fair value of the investee's pension plan assets is measured at the date of the investee's financial statements (FAS-87, par. 52, as amended by FAS-158, par. C2p).

> **OBSERVATION:** The requirement to measure the fair value of pension plan assets at the financial statement date is not effective until fiscal years ending after December 15, 2008. Prior to this date, and consistent with the existing requirements of FAS-87, an entity can measure the fair value of pension plan assets at year end or using a date within three months of year-end.

Unless more current amounts are available for both the obligation and plan assets, the funded status of the pension plan reported in interim financial statements shall be the same amount as reported by the employer in its previous year-end statement of financial position, adjusted for subsequent accruals of service cost, interest cost, return on plan assets, contributions, and benefit payments (FAS-87, par. 52, as amended by FAS-158, par. C2p).

The same assumptions used to calculate the previous year-end net periodic pension cost are used to calculate the net periodic pension cost in subsequent interim financial statements, unless more current valuations of plan assets and obligations are available or a significant event has occurred, such as a plan amendment that usually would require new valuations (FAS-87, par. 53).

Financial Statement Disclosure

The disclosure requirements that were originally included in FAS-87 (as well as in other pronouncements concerning pension and other postretirement benefits that are covered in other chapters) were replaced by the disclosure requirements of FAS-132 (Employers' Disclosures about Pensions and Other Postretirement Benefits) and again by FAS-132 (revised 2003), as subsequently amended by FAS-158. In addition to simplifying and streamlining disclosures about pensions, FAS-132 (revised 2003) consolidates the disclosures about pensions, settlement and curtailment of pension plans, and retirement benefits other than pensions into a single set of requirements.

FAS-132 (revised 2003) retains virtually all of the disclosure requirements of FAS-132 and requires additional disclosures in response to concerns expressed by users of financial statements. The incremental disclosures required by FAS-132 (revised 2003) relate to types of plan assets, investment strategy, measurement dates, plan obligations, cash flows, and components of net periodic benefit cost recognized in interim periods. FAS-132 (revised 2003) retains reduced disclosures for nonpublic entities and includes reduced disclosures for certain added requirements for nonpublic companies. The required information should be presented separately for pension plans and other postretirement plans.

> **OBSERVATION:** The FASB states that it believes the increased disclosures FAS-132 (revised 2003) are consistent with its conceptual framework and the mandate to provide information about economic resources of an enterprise, claims to those resources, and the effects of transactions, events, and circumstances that change those resources and claims to them. The FASB further states that the preparation of financial statements in accordance with generally accepted accounting principles already requires the preparation of much of the additional information required by FAS-132 (revised 2003) and that, although some additional effort and cost may be required, most of the information is already available. The incremental costs required

to compile, analyze, and audit the additional disclosures required by FAS-132 (revised 2003) are believed to be modest in contrast to the benefits to be derived from the information by users of financial statements.

Disclosures about Pension Plans and Other Postretirement Plans

Paragraph 5 of FAS-132 (revised 2003) (as amended by FAS-158, par. E1) requires the following information to be provided for each period for which an income statement is presented:

- Reconciliation of beginning and ending balances of the benefit obligation showing separately the effects of service cost, interest cost, contributions by plan participants, actuarial gains and losses, changes in foreign currency exchange rates, benefits paid, plan amendments, business combinations, divestitures, curtailments, settlements, and special termination benefits

- Reconciliation of beginning and ending balances of the fair value of plan assets, showing separately the effects of actual return on plan assets, changes in foreign currency exchange rates, contributions by the employer, contributions by plan participants, benefits paid, business combinations, divestitures, and settlements

- Funded status of the plan, and the amounts recognized in the statement of financial position, with separate disclosure of assets, current liabilities, and noncurrent liabilities

- Information about plan assets:
  — For each major category of plan assets, the percentage of the fair value of total plan assets held as of the financial statement date
  — Narrative description of investment policies and strategies
  — Narrative description of the basis used to determine the overall expected long-term rate-of-return-on-asset assumption
  — Additional asset categories and additional information about specific assets within a category are encouraged if they are expected to be useful in understanding the risks associated with each asset category and its expected long-term rate of return
  — The amount and timing of any plan assets expected to be returned to the employer (plan sponsor) over the next year, or operating cycle if longer

- For defined benefit pension plans, the accumulated benefit obligation

- The benefits expected to be paid in each of the next five fiscal years and in the aggregate for the five fiscal years thereafter

- The employer's best estimate of contributions expected to be paid to the plan during the next fiscal year beginning after the date of the latest statement of financial position

- The amount of net periodic benefit cost recognized, showing separately the service cost component, the interest cost component, the expected return on plan assets, the transition asset or obligation component, the gain or loss component, the prior service cost or credit component, and amount of gains or losses recognized due to a plan settlement or curtailment

- The net gain or loss and prior service cost or credit included in other comprehensive income during the period

- The net gain or loss, prior service cost or credit, and transition asset or obligation included in net periodic benefit cost during the period and removed from accumulated other comprehensive income via an entry to other comprehensive income

- Amounts included in accumulated other comprehensive income and not yet recognized as a component of net periodic benefit cost, separately showing the net gain or loss, net prior service cost or credit, and net transition asset or obligation

- Amounts included in accumulated other comprehensive income and expected to be included as a component of net periodic benefit cost in the next fiscal year, separately showing the net gain or loss, net prior service cost or credit, and net transition asset or liability to be recognized

- On a weighted-average basis, the following assumptions: assumed discount rates, rates of compensation increase, and expected long-term rates of return on plan assets

- Assumed health care cost trend rates for the next year used to determine expected cost of benefits covered by the plan, and a general description of the direction and pattern of change in the assumed trend rates thereafter

- The effect of a one-percentage increase and a one-percentage decrease in the assumed health care cost trend rates on the aggregate of the service and interest cost components of net periodic postretirement health care benefit costs and the accumulated postretirement benefit obligation for health care benefits

- Amounts and types of securities of the employer and related parties included in the plan assets, the approximate future annual benefits of plan participants covered by insurance contracts issued by the employer or related parties, and any significant transactions between the employer or related parties and the plan during the period

- Any alternative method used to amortize prior service amounts or net gains and losses
- Any substantive commitments used as the basis for accounting for the benefit obligation
- The cost of providing special or contractual termination benefits recognized during the period and a description of the nature of the event
- Explanation of any significant change in the benefit obligation or plan assets not otherwise apparent from the other disclosures required by FAS-132(R)

Disclosures by Employers with Two or More Plans

Employers with two or more plans shall aggregate information for all defined benefit pension plans and for all other defined benefit postretirement plans unless disaggregating in groups is considered to provide more useful information. Disclosures about pension plans with assets in excess of the accumulated benefit obligation generally may be aggregated with disclosures about pension plans with accumulated obligations in excess of assets. The same is true for other postretirement benefit plans. If aggregate disclosures are presented, the following information is required:

- The aggregate benefit obligation and aggregate fair value of plan assets for plans with benefit obligations in excess of plan assets
- The aggregate pension accumulated benefit obligation and aggregate fair values of plan assets for pension plans with accumulated benefit obligations in excess of plan assets (FAS-132(R), par. 6, as amended by FAS-158, par. E1).

Reduced Disclosures for Nonpublic Companies

Under FAS-132(R), a nonpublic entity is not required to present the complete set of information identified earlier as being required for public entities. The required disclosures for a nonpublic entity are as follows (FAS-132(R), par. 8, as amended by FAS-158, par. E11):

- The benefit obligation, fair value of plan assets, and funded status of the plan.
- Employer contributions, participant contributions, and benefits paid.

- Information about plan assets:
  — For each major category of plan assets (e.g., equity securities, debt securities, real estate), the percentage of the fair value of total plan asset held as of the measurement date used for each statement of financial position presented.
  — A narrative description of investment policies and strategies.
  — A narrative description of the basis used to determine the overall expected long-term rate-of-return-on-assets assumption.
  — Disclosure of additional asset categories and additional information about specific assets within a category is encouraged if that information is expected to be useful in understanding the risks associated with each asset category and the overall expected long-term rate of return on assets.

- For defined benefit pension plans, the accumulated benefit obligation.

- The benefits expected to be paid in each of the next five fiscal years, and in the aggregate for the five fiscal years thereafter.

- The employer's best estimate of contributions expected to be paid to the plan during the next fiscal year.

- The amounts recognized in the statements of financial position.

- The amount of net periodic benefit cost recognized, showing separately the service cost component, the interest cost component, the expected return on plan assets, the gain or loss component, the prior service cost or credit component, the transition asset or obligation component, and gain and loss from settlements or curtailments.

- On a weighted-average basis, the following assumptions used in the accounting for the plan: discount rates, rates of compensation increase, and expected long-term rates of return on plan assets.

- The assumed health care trend rates for the year used to measure the expected cost of benefits covered by the plan, and a general description of the direction and pattern of change in the assumed trend rates thereafter, and the ultimate trend rates and when those rates are expected to be achieved.

- If applicable, the amounts and types of securities of the employer and related parties included in plan assets, the approximate amount of future annual benefits of plan participants covered by insurance contracts issued by the employer or related parties, and any significant transactions between the employers and related parties and the plan during the period.

- The nature and effect of significant nonroutine events, such as amendments, combinations, divestitures, curtailments, and settlements.

A nonpublic entity that has more than one defined benefit pension plan or more than one other defined benefit postretirement plan shall provide the required information separately for pension plans and other postretirement benefit plans.

Disclosures in Interim Financial Reports

A publicly traded entity shall disclose the following information in its financial statements that include an income statement:

- The amount of net periodic benefit cost recognized for each period for which an income statement is presented with separate disclosure of the components of net periodic benefit cost
- The total amount of the employee's contributions paid, or expected to be paid, during the current year if significantly different from amounts previously disclosed pursuant to paragraph 5(g) of FAS-132

A nonpublic entity shall disclose in interim periods for which a complete set of financial statements are presented the total amount of the employer's contributions paid and expected to be paid if significantly different from paragraph 8(f) of FAS-132. Paragraph 8(f) of FAS-132 requires disclosure of the employer's best estimate of contributions expected to be paid to the plan during the next fiscal year beginning after the date of the latest statement of financial position presented.

Employers with Two or More Pension Plans

If an employer sponsors more than one defined benefit pension plan, the provisions of FAS-87 are applied separately to each plan. An employer shall not apply the assets of one plan to reduce or eliminate the underfunding of another plan, unless the employer clearly has the right to do so (FAS-87, par. 55).

Annuity Contracts

All or part of an employer's obligation to provide pension plan benefits to individuals may be transferred effectively to an insurance company by the purchase of annuity contracts. An annuity contract is an irrevocable agreement in which an insurance company unconditionally agrees to provide specific periodic payments, or a lump-sum payment to another party, in return for a specified premium. Thus, by use of an annuity contract, an employer can effectively transfer to an insurance company its legal obligation to provide specific employee pension plan benefits. For the purposes of FAS-87, an annuity contract is not considered an annuity contract if the insurance company is a captive insurer or there is reasonable doubt that the insurance company will meet its obligation. A captive insurer is one that does business primarily with the employer and its related parties (FAS-87, par. 57).

An annuity contract may be participating or nonparticipating. In a participating annuity contract, the insurance company's investing activities with the funds received for the annuity contract generally are shared, in the form of dividends, with the purchaser (the employer or the pension fund). An annuity contract is not considered an annuity contract, for the purposes of FAS-87, unless all the risks and rewards associated with the assets and obligations assumed by the insurance company are actually transferred to the insurance company by the employer (FAS-87, par. 57).

The cost incurred for currently earned benefits under an annuity contract is the cost of those benefits, except for the cost of participating rights of participating annuity contracts, which must be accounted for separately (see below). Thus, the service cost component of net periodic pension cost for the current period is the cost incurred for nonparticipating annuity contracts that cover all currently earned benefits (FAS-87, par. 58). Pension benefits not covered by annuity contracts are accounted for in accordance with the provisions of FAS-87 that address accounting for the cost of pension benefits not covered by annuity contracts (FAS-87, par. 59).

The projected benefit obligation and the accumulated benefit obligation do not include the cost of benefits covered by annuity contracts. Except for the cost of participation rights (see below), pension plan assets do not include the cost of any annuity contracts (FAS-87, par. 60).

The difference in cost between a nonparticipating annuity contract and a participating annuity contract usually is attributable to the cost of the participation right. The cost of a participation right, at the date of its purchase, is recognized as a pension plan asset. In subsequent periods, a participation right is included in plan assets at its fair value, if fair value is reasonably determinable. If fair value is not reasonably determinable, a participation right is included in plan assets at its amortized cost and systematically amortized over the expected dividend period stated in the contract. In this event, amortized cost may not exceed the net realizable value of the participation right (FAS-87, par. 61).

Other Contracts with Insurance Companies

The purchase of insurance contracts that are, in substance, annuity contracts, is accounted for in accordance with the provisions of

FAS-87 (see previous section). The purchase of other types of insurance contracts shall be accounted for as pension plan assets and reported at fair value. The best evidence of fair value for some insurance contracts may be their contract values. Under FAS-87, the cash surrender value or conversion value of an insurance contract is presumed to be its fair value (FAS-87, par. 62).

Multiemployer Plans

A multiemployer plan is a pension plan to which two or more unrelated employers make contributions, usually pursuant to one or more collective-bargaining agreements. In a multiemployer pension plan, assets contributed by one employer are not segregated in separate accounts or restricted to provide benefits only to employees of that employer. Thus, assets contributed by one employer in a multiemployer plan may be used to provide benefits to employees of other participating employers (FAS-87, par. 67).

The net periodic pension cost of an employer participating in a multiemployer plan is the amount of the required contribution for the period. An employer participating in a multiemployer plan shall also recognize as a liability any of its contributions that are due and unpaid (FAS-87, par. 68).

> **OBSERVATION:** A withdrawal from a multiemployer pension plan may result in a loss contingency if the withdrawing employer has a potential liability to the plan for a portion of its unfunded benefit obligation. Under FAS-87, if it is probable or reasonably possible that the loss contingency will develop into an actual loss, the withdrawing employer shall account for the loss contingency in accordance with the provisions of FAS-5 (Accounting for Contingencies) (FAS-87, par. 70).

An employer participating in a multiemployer plan shall disclose the following information (FAS-132, par. 10):

- The amount of contributions to multiemployer plans during the period—amounts contributed to pension and postretirement benefit plans do not have to be disaggregated

- A description of any changes in pension or postretirement benefit plans that would affect comparability, including a discussion of the nature and effects of the change —examples include a change in the rate of employer contributions, business combinations, and divestitures

Multiple-Employer Plans

Some pension plans to which two or more unrelated employers contribute are not multiemployer plans, but are groups of single-employer plans combined to allow participating employers to pool assets for investment purposes and to reduce the cost of plan administration. Under FAS-87, multiple-employer plans are considered single-employer plans and each employer's accounting shall be based on its respective interest in the plan (FAS-87, par. 71).

Non-U.S. Pension Plans

FAS-87 does not make any special provision for non-U.S. pension plans. In some foreign countries, it is customary or required for an employer to provide benefits for employees in the event of a voluntary or involuntary severance of employment. In this event, if the substance of the arrangement is a pension plan, it is subject to the provisions of FAS-87 (for example, benefits are paid for substantially all terminations) (FAS-87, par. 73).

Business Combinations

The total cost of a business combination accounted for by the purchase method must be allocated to the individual assets acquired and liabilities assumed (FAS-141 (Business Combinations)). Each identifiable asset is assigned a cost equal to its fair value. Liabilities are accounted for at the present value of the amount that will eventually be paid and, if certain criteria are met, appropriate consideration should be given to contingent assets and liabilities (FAS-141, pars. 40 and 41 (Business Combinations)).

When a single-employer defined benefit pension plan is acquired as part of a business combination accounted for by the purchase method, an excess of the projected benefit obligation over the plan assets is recognized as a liability and an excess of plan assets over the projected benefit obligation is recognized as an asset. The recognition of a new liability or new asset by the purchaser, at the date of a business combination accounted for by the purchase method, results in the elimination of any (a) previously existing net gain or loss, (b) prior service cost or credit, and (c) transition asset or obligation recognized in accumulated other comprehensive income.

The effects of an expected plan termination or curtailment shall be considered by the purchaser in calculating the amount of the projected benefit obligation at the date of a business combination accounted for by the purchase method (FAS-87, par. 74, as amended by FAS-158, par. C2r).

FAS-158 Effective Dates, Transition, and Disclosure

The requirement to recognize the funded status of a pension plan in the statement of financial position is effective for public companies for fiscal years ending after December 15, 2006 (FAS-158, par. 12). An employer without publicly traded equity securities is required to recognize the funded status of a pension plan in fiscal years ending after June 15, 2007. Earlier application is encouraged, but early application applies to all of the employer's benefit plans (FAS-158, par. 13). If a nonpublic employer does not apply the recognition provisions early, the following disclosures are required in financial statements dated between December 15, 2006, and June 16, 2007: (1) a brief description of FAS-158, (2) the date that FAS-158 must be adopted and, if the entity plans to adopt any earlier, that date (FAS-158, par. 14).

The requirement that pension plan assets be measured at the financial statement date, rather than on any date within three months of the employer's year end, is effective for fiscal years ending after December 15, 2008 (FAS-158, par. 15).

The requirement to recognize the funded status of a pension plan is as of the end of the first fiscal year that FAS-158 applies. Net gains and losses, prior service cost or credit, transition net asset or obligation that have not yet been included in net periodic pension cost are recognized as a component of accumulated other comprehensive income (FAS-158, par. 16). In the first year that the recognition provisions are applied, the employer must disclose the effects of applying FAS-158 on individual line items in the statement of financial position (FAS-158, par. 20).

Two transition options exist for transitioning from a measurement date for plan assets that is within three months of the financial statement date to measuring all plan assets on the financial statement date. Under the first option, the employer would remeasure plan assets and liabilities as of the beginning of the first year that the measurement date provisions apply (e.g., January 1, 2008, for a company with a calendar year-end). The net periodic benefit cost (exclusive of any curtailment or settlement gain or loss) that applies to the period between the previous measurement date (e.g., September 30, 2007) and the beginning of the year that the measurement date provisions apply (e.g., January 1, 2008) is recognized as a separate adjustment of the beginning balance of retained earnings, net of tax. Any curtailment or settlement gain or loss between the previous measurement date and the beginning of the fiscal year that the measurement date provisions apply is recognized in income in that previous period and not as part of the adjustment to the beginning balance of retained earnings. Finally, any other changes in the fair value of plan assets or in the projected benefit obligation between the previous measurement date and the beginning of the fiscal year that the measurement date provisions apply (e.g., gains or losses) is recognized as an adjustment to the beginning balance of accumulated other comprehensive income, net of tax (FAS-158, par. 18).

The second transition option does not require the employer to remeasure plan assets and liabilities as of the beginning of the fiscal year that the measurement date provisions apply. The employer would continue to use the value of plan assets and liabilities determined at the end of the previous year, which could have been measured up to three months before the end of the year. The employer would determine net periodic pension cost between the previous measurement date (e.g., September 30, 2007) and the end of the fiscal year that the measurement date provisions apply (e.g., December 31, 2008) and allocate this cost proportionately to the two periods (3/15th as an adjustment to the beginning balance of retained earnings, and 12/15th to net periodic pension cost in 2008). Any curtailment or settlement gain or loss between the previous measurement date and the beginning of the fiscal year that the measurement date provisions apply is recognized in income in that previous period and not as part of the adjustment to the beginning balance of retained earnings. Finally, any other changes in the fair value of plan assets or in the projected benefit obligation between the previous measurement date and the end of the fiscal year that the measurement date provisions apply (e.g., gains or losses) is recognized in other comprehensive income, net of tax, in the year that the measurement date provisions of FAS-158 are first applied (FAS-158, par. 19).

In the year that the measurement date provisions are first applied, the separate adjustment of retained earnings and accumulated other comprehensive income from applying the standard is disclosed (FAS-158, par. 21).

Illustration of Change in Measurement Date, Plan Assets and Liabilities Not Remeasured at Beginning of Year

Black and Turner, Inc., operates on a calendar year and prior to FAS-158 had measured its pension plan assets and liabilities at September 30th. In accordance with FAS-158, Black and Turner measures its pension plan assets and liabilities at 12/31/08 rather than at 9/30/08. FAS-158 provides two transition alternatives: (1) pension plan assets and liabilities can be remeasured at the beginning of the fiscal year that the measurement provisions of FAS-158 are applied or (2) pension plan assets and liabilities can continue to be valued as they were at the beginning of the fiscal year (i.e., as of September 30th of 2007). Black and Turner choose the latter approach. The applicable tax rate is 50%.

Black and Turner's valuation of applicable pension accounts at 9/30/07 and 12/31/08 is as follows.

	9/30/07 (in thousands)	12/31/08 (in thousands)
Projected benefit obligation	$(4,800)	$(5,250)
Plan assets at fair value	3,300	3,500
Funded status	(1,500)	(1,750)

Items not yet recognized as a
  component of net periodic benefit
  cost:

Prior service cost	$600	$415
Net loss	400	380
Total	1,000	795

Black and Turner rely on actuarial valuation in determining net periodic pension cost between October 1, 2007, and December 31, 2008. Net periodic pension cost is allocated between an adjustment to the beginning balance of retained earnings and an amount to be recognized in the 2008 income statement. This allocation is as follows:

	15-Month Total	Allocated to 9/30/07–12/31/07	Allocated to 2008
Net periodic pension cost:			
Service cost	$195		
Interest cost	225		
Expected return on plan assets	(150)		
Total service cost, interest cost, and expected return on plan assets	270	$54	$216
Amortization of prior service cost	185	37	148
Amortization of net loss	0		
Total amortization	185	37	148
Net periodic pension cost	$455	$91	$364

(Note: The net loss was not amortized because its beginning balance was less than 10% of the larger of the beginning projected benefit obligation or market-related value of plan assets.)

The actual return on pension plan assets is $200,000 and the expected return is $150,000, so Black and Turner experienced a $50,000 gain. In addition, Black and Turner experienced an actuarial loss of $30,000 during the year. The $50,000 excess return on pension plan assets, when combined with the $30,000 actuarial loss, results in the net loss account decreasing by $20,000 during the year. No contributions to the pension plan were made during the year.

Black and Turner would make the following journal entries during 2008 (in thousands):

Adjust the beginning of the year balances in retained earnings, accumulated other comprehensive income, pension liability, and deferred tax accounts for 20% (3/15th) of net periodic benefit cost from October 1, 2007, through December 31, 2008:

Retained earnings	91	
Deferred tax assets ($54 × .50)	27	
Deferred tax benefit—other comprehensive income ($37 × .50)	18.50	
Deferred tax benefit—retained earnings		45.50
Accumulated other comprehensive income		37
Liability for pension benefits		54

Recognize net periodic benefit cost for 2008:

Net periodic pension cost	364	
Deferred tax assets ($216 × .50)	108	
Deferred tax benefit—other comprehensive income ($148 × .50)	74	
Deferred tax benefit—net income		182
Other comprehensive income		148
Liability for pension benefits		216

Recognize the entire gain occurring between 10/1/07 and 12/31/08 in 2008:

Liability for pension benefits ($400 − $380)	20	
Deferred tax obligation—other comprehensive income (20 × .5)	10	
Deferred tax liability		10
Other comprehensive income		20

DEFINED CONTRIBUTION PENSION PLANS

A defined contribution pension plan provides for employers' contributions that are defined in the plan, but does not contain any provision for defined pension benefits for employees. Thus, a defined contribution pension plan does not contain a defined benefit pension formula. Based on the amount of the employer's defined contributions, however, pension benefits are provided in return for services performed by employees (FAS-87, par. 63).

Under FAS-87, a defined contribution pension plan provides for individual accounts for each plan participant and contains the terms that specify how contributions are determined for each participant's individual account. Each periodic employer contribution is allocated to each participant's individual account in accordance with the terms of the plan, and pension benefits are based solely on the amount available in each participant's account at the time of his or her retirement. The amount available in each participant's account at the time of his or her retirement is the total of the amounts contributed by the employer, plus the returns earned on investments of those contributions, and forfeitures of other participants' benefits that have been allocated to the participant's account, less any allocated administrative expenses (FAS-87, par. 63).

Under FAS-87, the net periodic pension cost of a defined contribution pension plan is the amount of contributions made or due in a period on behalf of participants who performed services during that same period. Contributions for periods after an individual retires or terminates shall be estimated and accrued during periods in which the individual performs services (FAS-87, par. 64).

The amount of the unrecognized net obligation of a defined contribution pension plan, at the date of initial application of FAS-87, is amortized on a straight-line basis over the average remaining service period of employees expected to receive benefits under the plan, except (*a*) if the amortization period is less than 15 years, the employer may elect to use 15 years, and (*b*) if the plan is composed of all or substantially all inactive participants, the employer shall use those participants' average remaining life expectancy as the amortization period (FAS-87, par. 77).

An employer who sponsors one or more defined contribution pension plans shall disclose the amount of cost recognized for defined contribution pension and other postretirement benefit plans during the period. This disclosure shall include the nature and effect of any significant changes during the period affecting comparability—examples include a change in the rate of employer contributions, business combinations, or divestitures (FAS-132, par. 9).

SETTLEMENTS AND CURTAILMENTS

In connection with the operation of a defined benefit pension plan, FAS-87 (Employers' Accounting for Pensions) provides for the delayed recognition of actuarial gains and losses, prior service costs, and the net obligation or asset that arises at the date of the initial application of FAS-87. As a result, at any given date, an employer's pension plan records may reflect a balance of a (*a*) net gain or loss, (*b*) prior service cost, and/or (*c*) net transition obligation or net asset. These amounts are included in accumulated other comprehensive income until they are recognized as a component of net periodic pension cost. Part or all of these amounts may be recognized in a settlement or curtailment of a pension plan.

In a settlement of a defined benefit pension plan, the employer or the pension plan is released irrevocably from its primary responsibility for all or part of its pension plan obligation, and all significant risks relating to the settlement are eliminated. For example, through the purchase of nonparticipating annuity contracts or cash payments to some or all of the plan participants in exchange for their pension benefits, an employer may be released irrevocably from the pension plan obligation related to the benefits involved in the exchange. After the settlement of a pension plan, an employer may continue to provide pension benefits in the same pension plan or a new plan.

In a curtailment of a defined benefit pension plan, some of the future pension benefits for present employees are reduced, generally resulting in a net decrease (gain) or increase (loss) in the projected benefit obligation. For example, if employees are terminated as a result of a plan curtailment, some or all of their pension benefits based on future compensation levels may cease to be an obligation of the employer or pension plan. In this event, the projected benefit obligation is decreased (a gain) by the amount of the pension benefits that are no longer an obligation of the plan. On the other hand, if terminated employees who are eligible for subsidized early retirement benefits accept the benefits at a date earlier than expected, there is an increase (loss) in the projected benefit obligation. Gain or loss on a plan curtailment is based on the net decrease (gain) or increase (loss) in the projected benefit obligation.

An employer may have to recognize an additional loss that is not included in the gain or loss on a plan curtailment, but is recognized as part of the total effects of a plan curtailment. This loss is equal to the amount of decrease in the unrecognized prior service cost of the pension benefits that are reduced by the plan curtailment. A separate loss computation is necessary for the prior service cost of each plan amendment.

The pension benefits that are reduced or eliminated in a plan curtailment may have been granted to some or all of the employees who were working for the employer as of the date of the initial application of FAS-87 (Employers' Accounting for Pensions). For this reason, any transition *net obligation* that arose at the date of the initial application of FAS-87 and that remains unamortized at the date of the plan curtailment is also treated as a separate prior service cost.

A pension plan settlement and a pension plan curtailment may occur simultaneously or separately. If the expected years of future service for some employees are reduced but the pension plan continues in existence, a curtailment has occurred, but not a settlement. If an employer settles all or a portion of its pension obligation and continues to provide defined benefits to employees for future services, either in the same plan or in a successor plan, a settlement has occurred, but not a curtailment. If an employer terminates its defined benefit pension plan without replacing it with another defined benefit pension plan, and settles its present pension plan obligation in full, a curtailment and settlement has occurred. Under these circumstances, it makes no difference whether or not some or all of the employees continue to work for the employer.

Employers frequently offer termination benefits as part of an overall plan to reduce employment levels, to increase productivity, or generally to decrease payroll costs. To induce certain groups of employees to terminate employment, many employers offer attractive termination benefits. This is particularly true for those employees who are close to, or have reached, the early retirement age specified in the employer's existing pension plan. Termination benefits may consist of periodic future payments, lump-sum payments, or a combination of both. The payment of termination benefits may be made from a new or existing employee benefit plan, from the employer's existing assets, or from a combination of these sources.

Under FAS-88 (Employers' Accounting for Settlements and Curtailments of Defined Benefit Pension Plans and for Termination Benefits), termination benefits are classified either as *special* or *contractual*. Special termination benefits are those that are offered to employees for a short period of time in connection with their termination of employment. Contractual termination benefits are those that are required by the terms of an existing plan or agreement and are provided only on the occurrence of a specified event, such as early retirement or the closing of a facility.

FAS-88 requires that the cost of termination benefits be recognized by an employer as a loss and a corresponding liability. The recognition date depends on whether the benefits are special or contractual.

Before applying the provisions of FAS-88, an employer should bring its defined benefit pension plan records up to date, preferably as of the day before the curtailment and/or settlement of the plan. The effects of the pending curtailment and/or settlement are ignored in the updating process and all computations including the net periodic pension cost accrual are consistent with prior periods. The updating process includes the measurement of the fair value of pension plan assets and the computation of the net periodic pension cost accrual.

SETTLEMENTS OF DEFINED BENEFIT PENSION PLANS

Under FAS-88, a settlement of a defined benefit pension plan is an irrevocable transaction that (*a*) releases the employer or the pension plan from its primary responsibility for the payment of all or a portion of the pension plan obligation and (*b*) eliminates all of the significant risks associated with the assets and obligations used to effectuate the settlement (FAS-88, par. 3). A settlement of a defined benefit pension plan does not require that the plan be completely terminated (FAS-88, par. 26).

All or a part of an employer's obligation to provide pension plan benefits to individuals may be transferred effectively to an insurance company by the purchase of annuity contracts. An annuity contract is an irrevocable agreement in which an insurance company unconditionally agrees to provide specific periodic payments or a lump sum payment to another party in return for a specified premium. For the purposes of FAS-87 and FAS-88, this definition of an annuity contract is not met if the insurance company is a *captive insurer* or there is reasonable doubt that the insurance company will meet its obligation. A captive insurer is one that does business primarily with the employer and its related parties (FAS-88, par. 5).

An annuity contract may be participating or nonparticipating. In a participating annuity contract, the insurance company's investing returns are shared generally, in the form of dividends, with the purchaser of the contract (the employer or the pension fund). An annuity contract is not considered an annuity contract unless all the risks and rewards associated with the assets and obligations assumed by the insurance company are actually transferred to the insurance company by the employer (FAS-88, par. 5).

Gain or loss on a plan settlement is based on pension plan records that have been updated as of the day before the settlement. Under FAS-88, the maximum gain or loss on a settlement of a defined benefit pension plan is equal to the total balance of (*a*) any net gain or loss that remains in accumulated other comprehensive income the date of the plan settlement and (*b*) any transition asset that arose at the date of the initial application of FAS-87 that remains in accumulated other comprehensive income (FAS-88, par. 9, as amended by FAS-158, par. C6a).

If the total pension plan obligation is settled by the employer, the maximum gain or loss is recognized. If part of the pension benefit obligation is settled, the employer must recognize a pro rata portion of the maximum gain or loss, equal to the percentage reduction in the projected benefit obligation, unless the transaction qualifies as a "small settlement" (discussed below). Thus, if 40% of the pension plan obligation is settled, 40% of the maximum gain or loss on the settlement is recognized, and if 100% of the pension benefit obligation is settled, 100% of the maximum gain or loss is recognized (FAS-88, par. 9).

If the employer purchases a participating annuity contract to settle a pension obligation, the cost of the contract must be allocated between the cost of the pure annuity feature and the cost of the participation right. The amount of cost allocated to the participation rights reduces gain (but not loss) that would otherwise be recognized on a plan settlement. However, the participation rights do not affect the determination of the amount of loss that is recognized on a plan settlement (FAS-88, par. 10).

Reporting Gain or Loss on a Plan Settlement

Gain or loss on a plan settlement is reported as an ordinary gain or loss, unless it meets the criteria of an extraordinary item as specified in APB-30 (Reporting the Results of Operations) (FAS-88, par. 48).

Small Settlements for the Year

Part or all of a pension plan's obligation to an employee may be settled by the payment of cash or the purchase of an annuity contract.

The cost of a cash settlement of a pension plan obligation is the amount of cash paid to the employee. The cost of a settlement of a pension plan obligation involving a nonparticipating annuity contract is the cost of the contract. The cost of a settlement involving a participating annuity contract is the cost of the contract less the amount attributed to the participation rights (FAS-88, par. 11).

If the total cost of all plan settlements for the year is small or insignificant, gain or loss recognition may not be required. FAS-88 provides that an employer is not required, but is permitted, to recognize the gain or loss on all plan settlements for the year if the cost of all such settlements does not exceed the sum of the service cost and interest cost components of the net periodic pension cost for the current year. Once an accounting policy is adopted for small or insignificant settlements, it must be applied consistently from year to year. Thus, an employer that initially elects nonrecognition of gain or loss on all small settlements during a year must continue that same accounting policy from year to year (FAS-88, par. 11).

> ☞ **PRACTICE POINTER:** If the total cost of all plan settlements for the year is small or insignificant, the employer has discretion to decide whether or not to recognize gain or loss, provided only that the accounting policy is followed consistently from year to year.

CURTAILMENT OF DEFINED BENEFIT PENSION PLANS

Under FAS-88, a curtailment of a defined benefit pension plan results from an event in which (*a*) the expected years of future service arising from a prior plan amendment are *significantly* reduced for present employees who are entitled to receive pension benefits from that prior plan amendment or (*b*) the accrual of defined pension benefits is eliminated for some or all of the future services of a *significant* number of employees (FAS-88, par. 6).

The total effects of a plan curtailment consist of (1) the decrease (loss) in the prior service cost (or unrecognized transition obligation) remaining in accumulated other comprehensive income that results from the significant reduction of the expected years of future service for present employees (see (*a*) above), and (2) the net decrease (gain) or increase (loss) in the projected benefit obligation that results from the elimination of the accrual of defined pension benefits for some or all of the future services of a significant number of employees (see (*b*) above). Each of these two components that comprise the total effects of a plan curtailment are discussed separately below (FAS-88, par. 12–13, as amended by FAS-158, par. C6b and c).

Decrease (Loss) in Prior Service Cost

Retroactive pension benefits are sometimes granted by an employer, upon adoption of a plan or through a plan amendment, based on employees' services in prior periods. The costs of these retroactive pension benefits are referred to as prior service costs. Retroactive pension benefits are granted by an employer in expectation of future economic benefits, such as reduced employee turnover and higher productivity. FAS-87 requires that the prior service cost relating to a specific plan amendment be amortized in equal amounts over the expected years of future service of each active employee who is expected to receive benefits from the plan amendment. Periodic amortization for each expected year of future service is calculated by dividing the total expected years of future service into the total amount of unrecognized prior service cost. The total amount of prior service cost represents the total cost of pension benefits that have been granted under the provisions of the plan amendment. If the expected years of future service are reduced as a result of a plan curtailment, the related prior service cost also must be reduced and recognized as a loss by the employer.

The expected years of future service for present employees may be reduced significantly by the termination or suspension of pension benefits for future services so that employees are no longer allowed to earn additional benefits. In addition, the termination of some of the present employees earlier than expected may also result in a significant reduction in their total expected years of future service. As a result of the significant reduction in the expected years of future service, a loss is incurred by the employer in the amount of the decrease in the balance of the related unamortized unrecognized prior service cost at the date of the plan curtailment. To compute the loss, the percentage reduction in the total remaining expected years of future service at the date of the plan curtailment first must be calculated (number of expected years of future service that are reduced, divided by the total number of remaining expected years of future service before reduction). To determine the amount of the loss, the balance of the related prior service cost amount at the date of the plan curtailment is multiplied by the percentage reduction in the total number of expected years of future service. For example, if the total remaining expected years of future service at the date of the plan curtailment is 1,000, and the number of years of future service that is reduced is 400, the percentage reduction is 40%. The balance of the related prior service cost at the date of the plan curtailment is reduced by 40%, which represents the loss that the employer must recognize as part of the total effects of the plan curtailment.

For the purposes of FAS-88, the balance of any transition *net obligation* that arose at the date of the initial application of FAS-87, which is included in accumulated other comprehensive income at the date of a subsequent plan curtailment, also is treated as a separate prior service cost amount (FAS-88, par. 12, as amended by FAS-158, par. C6, b). Thus, if the expected years of future service are reduced significantly for those employees employed at the date of the initial application of FAS-87, a separate loss must be calculated and recognized by the employer. This loss equals the amount by which the *transition obligation* included in accumulated other comprehensive income is reduced when multiplied by the percentage reduction resulting from the expected years of future service that are significantly reduced for those employees who were employed at the date of the initial application of FAS-87.

The total of all decreases (losses) in prior service costs and/or transition net obligation is included in the total effects of a plan curtailment, but is not included in the gain or loss on the plan curtailment (FAS-88, par. 40).

The following steps are necessary to compute each decrease (loss) in the balance of the prior service cost amount at the date of a plan curtailment arising from a significant reduction in the expected years of employees' future service:

Step 1:   Compute the percentage reduction in the total remaining expected years of future service, at the date of the plan curtailment, resulting from the expected years of future service that are significantly reduced. For example, if the expected years of future service that are reduced are 600 and the total remaining expected years of future service at the date of the plan curtailment is 1,000, the percentage reduction is 60%.

Step 2:   Multiply the balance of the prior service cost included in accumulated comprehensive income (or transition obligation) of each plan amendment affected by the plan curtailment by the percentage calculated in Step 1. The result is the amount of loss that the employer must recognize as part of the total effects of the plan curtailment. The balance of the prior service cost amount (or transition obligation) is also reduced by the same amount.

(From a practical standpoint, the dollar amount of amortization for each expected year of future service can be multiplied by the total number of expected years of future service that is reduced.)

Step 3: The amount of loss recognized on the decrease in the balance of the prior service cost amount (or transition obligation) is not part of the gain or loss on the plan curtailment (FAS-88, par. 40), but is included in the total effects of the plan curtailment.

Illustration of Computation of Expected Years of Future Service and Loss from the Decrease in Prior Service Cost Resulting from the Expected Years of Future Service That Are Significantly Reduced by a Plan Curtailment

Company X had 50 employees who were expected to receive pension benefits under a new pension plan amendment, which became effective January 1, 20X5. In the computation of the expected years of future service for each employee who was entitled to receive benefits under the new plan amendment, the company assumed that five employees would either quit or retire each year during the next ten years. The total amount of prior service cost arising from the new pension plan amendment was $27,500.

Employee Number	Expected Years of Future Service	X5	X6	X7	X8	X9	Y0	Y1	Y2	Y3	Y4
1–5	5	5									
6–10	10	5	5								
11–15	15	5	5	5							
16–20	20	5	5	5	5						
21–25	25	5	5	5	5	5					
26–30	30	5	5	5	5	5	5				
31–35	35	5	5	5	5	5	5	5			
36–40	40	5	5	5	5	5	5	5	5		
41–45	45	5	5	5	5	5	5	5	5	5	
46–50	50	5	5	5	5	5	5	5	5	5	5
Service years rendered	275	50	45	40	35	30	25	20	15	10	5
Amortization fraction		50/275	45/275	40/275	35/275	30/275	25/275	20/275	15/275	10/275	5/275

Amortization for each expected year of future service equals $100 ($27,500 prior service cost divided by 275 years of expected future service).

Assume, at the beginning of X7, that 15 employees are terminated, resulting in a reduction of 90 years (given) of expected future service. The percentage reduction of expected future service years is 50%, determined as follows:

Expected years of future service, beginning of X7, before terminations (275, less amortization of 50 for X5 and 45 for X6)	180
Reduction due to terminations (given)	90
Percentage reduction: 90/180	50%

The remaining balance of prior service cost relating to the new plan amendment at the beginning of year 3 was $18,000 (180 remaining years of expected future service multiplied by the $100 amortization rate per year). Thus, the pension plan curtailment, relating to the expected years of future service that were significantly reduced by the termination of 15 employees, results in a loss of $9,000 (50% of $18,000).

Decrease (Gain) or Increase (Loss) in the Projected Benefit Obligation

A plan curtailment may result in a net decrease (gain) or net increase (loss) in the projected benefit obligation. For example, if employees are terminated as a result of a plan curtailment, some or all of their pension benefits based on future compensation levels may cease to be an obligation of the employer or pension plan. In this event, the projected benefit obligation is decreased (a gain) by the amount of the benefits that are no longer an obligation of the plan. On the other hand, if terminated employees who are eligible for subsidized early retirement benefits accept those benefits at an earlier date than expected, there usually is an increase (loss) in the projected benefit obligation. Gain or loss on a plan curtailment is based on the net decrease (gain) or increase (loss) in the projected benefit obligation (FAS-88, par. 13).

A plan curtailment may result from the closing of a facility or the disposal of a discontinued business segment. If the event that results in the plan curtailment is related to the disposal of a discontinued business segment, gain or loss on the plan curtailment must be included in the total gain or loss on the disposal of the discontinued business segment (FAS-88, par. 16).

The following steps are necessary to compute the gain or loss on a plan curtailment:

Step 1:   Determine the total net gain (decrease) or net loss (increase) in the projected benefit obligation resulting from the plan curtailment. Do not include any increase (loss) in the projected benefit obligation that arises in connection with termination benefits (FAS-88, par. 13).

Step 2:   Determine whether a net gain or net loss exists. Combine the remaining balance of any unrecognized *net obligation* that arose at the date of the initial application of FAS-87 and remains in accumulated other comprehensive income at the date of the plan curtailment, with the balance of any unrecognized net gain or loss that arose after the initial application of FAS-87 and also remains unamortized at the date of the plan curtailment. (**Note:** The remaining balance of any transition obligation that arose at the date of the initial application of FAS-87 and remains in accumulated other comprehensive income at the date of the plan curtailment is treated as part of prior service cost.) (FAS-88, par. 12, as amended by FAS-158, par. C6b).

The amount of gain or loss on the plan curtailment is recognized as follows:

- *If the change in the projected benefit obligation is a net gain (Step 1) and there is a net gain included in accumulated other comprehensive income (Step 2)* Curtailment gain is recognized in the amount of the net gain in the projected benefit obligation. (The unrecognized net gain computed in Step 2 is not used.)

- *If the change in the projected benefit obligation is a net gain (Step 1) and there is an unrecognized net loss (Step 2)* If the net gain in the projected benefit obligation does not exceed the net loss included in accumulated other comprehensive income, no curtailment gain or loss is recognized. If the net gain exceeds the net loss included in accumulated other comprehensive income, curtailment gain is recognized in the amount of the excess of the net gain in the projected benefit obligation over the net loss included in accumulated other comprehensive income.

- *If the change in the projected benefit obligation is a net loss (Step 1) and there is a net gain included in accumulated other comprehensive income (Step 2)* If the net loss in the projected benefit obligation does not exceed the net gain, no curtailment gain or loss is recognized. If the net loss exceeds the net gain included in accumulated other comprehensive income, curtailment loss is recognized in the amount of the excess of the net loss in the projected benefit obligation over the net gain in accumulated other comprehensive income.

- *If the change in the projected benefit obligation is a net loss (Step 1) and there is a net loss in accumulated other comprehensive income (Step 2)* Curtailment loss is recognized in the amount of the net loss in the projected benefit obligation. (The unrecognized net loss computed in Step 2 is not used.)

Recognition of the Total Effects of a Plan Curtailment

The total effects of a plan curtailment consist of (*a*) the decrease (loss) in the prior service cost amount and/or transition net obligation, resulting from the significant reduction of the expected years of future service for present employees, and (*b*) the net decrease (gain) or increase (loss) in the projected benefit obligation that results from the elimination of the accrual of defined pension benefits for some or all of the future services of a significant number of employees.

If the total effects of a plan curtailment result in a loss, the loss is recognized when it is *probable* that the curtailment will occur and the effects of the curtailment can be *reasonably estimated*. If the total effects of a plan curtailment result in a gain, the gain is recognized only when the related employees terminate or the plan suspension or amendment is adopted (FAS-88, par. 14).

Reporting Total Effects of a Plan Curtailment

Gain or loss on the total effects of a pension plan curtailment is reported as an ordinary gain or loss, unless it meets the criteria of an extraordinary item as specified by APB-30 (FAS-88, par. 48).

TERMINATION BENEFITS

Under FAS-88, termination benefits are classified as either *special* or *contractual*. Special termination benefits are those that are offered to employees for a short period in connection with the termination of their employment. Contractual termination benefits are those that are required by the terms of an existing plan or agreement and that are provided only on the occurrence of a specified event, such as early retirement or the closing of a facility (FAS-88, par. 15).

FAS-88 requires the recognition of the cost of termination benefits as a loss and corresponding liability. The recognition date depends on whether the benefits are special or contractual.

Special Termination Benefits

The recognition date on which the employer records the loss and corresponding liability for special termination benefits occurs when (a) the employees accept the offer of the special termination benefits and (b) the amount of the cost of the benefits can be reasonably estimated (FAS-88, par. 15).

Contractual Termination Benefits

The recognition date on which the employer records the loss and corresponding liability for contractual termination benefits occurs when (a) it is probable that employees will be entitled to the benefits and (b) the amount of the cost of the benefits can be estimated reasonably (FAS-88, par. 15).

Reporting a Loss on Termination Benefits

A loss on termination benefits is reported as an ordinary loss, unless it meets the criteria of an extraordinary item as specified in APB-30 (FAS-88, par. 48).

DISPOSAL OF AN IDENTIFIABLE BUSINESS SEGMENT

Under APB-30, severance pay, additional pension costs, and employee relocation expenses are all costs directly associated with the decision to dispose of an identifiable business segment and are properly includable in the total gain or loss on disposal. Gains and losses resulting from the application of FAS-88 that are directly related to the disposal of an identifiable business segment are accounted for in accordance with APB-30 (FAS-88, par. 16).

FINANCIAL STATEMENT DISCLOSURE

The disclosure requirements for settlements and curtailments of plans are incorporated into a general set of disclosure requirements for all pension and other postretirement plans. They are covered earlier in this chapter.

Illustration of Curtailment and Settlement of a Pension Plan

The updated records of a defined benefit pension plan reflect the following:

Vested benefits	$ (30,000)
Nonvested benefits	(50,000)
Accumulated benefit obligation	$ (80,000)
Effects on benefits as a result of considering future compensation levels	(20,000)
Projected benefit obligation	$(100,000)
Fair value of plan assets	95,000
Funded status of plan, recognized as a liability on the balance sheet per the provisions of FAS-158	$ (5,000)
Prior service cost	1,000
Net (gain) or loss	(1,000)
Transition net obligation or (net asset) at date of initial application of FAS-87	2,000

Assume that the above plan is completely terminated without a successor plan. Under this circumstance, the effects on benefits as a result of considering future compensation levels are no longer an obligation of the employer or the plan, since all of the plan participants have been terminated. Assume also that the total projected benefit obligation was settled by the purchase of non-participating annuity contracts for $80,000, and the excess plan assets in the amount of $15,000 were withdrawn by the employer.

Computation of the total effects of a plan curtailment The total effects of a plan curtailment consist of (*a*) the total loss resulting from the decreases in the balances of any unamortized unrecognized prior service costs and/or the transition net obligation included in accumulated other comprehensive income relating to the expected years of future service that were significantly reduced for present employees and (*b*) the net decrease (gain) or increase (loss) in the projected benefit obligation resulting from the elimination of the accrual of defined pension benefits for some or all of the future services of a significant number of employees.

The loss resulting from the decrease in the balance of any prior service costs (or transition net obligation) is computed as follows:

Step 1.   The percentage reduction, if any, in the balances of any prior service cost and/or the transition net obligation must be calculated (each loss must be computed separately, unless the pension plan is completely terminated). In the above illustration, the percentage reduction resulting from the significant reduction in the expected years of future service is 100%, because the plan is completely terminated. As a result, no separate computation is necessary.

Step 2.   Multiply the balance of the prior service cost and transition net obligation by its percentage reduction, if any. In the above illustration, the balance of the prior service cost of $1,000 is multiplied by 100%, and the balance of the transition net obligation of $2,000 is multiplied by 100%; the sum of the resulting amounts is a total loss of $3,000.

Step 3.   The $3,000 computed in Step 2 is treated as an effect of the plan curtailment, not as part of the gain or loss on the plan curtailment.

The net decrease (gain) or increase (loss) in the projected benefit obligation is computed as follows:

Step 4.   Calculate the net decrease (gain) or net increase (loss) in the projected benefit obligation resulting from the plan curtailment. Do not include any increase (loss) in the projected benefit obligation that arose in connection with termination benefits (FAS-88, par. 13, footnote 4). In the above illustration, the effects on benefits as a result of considering future compensation levels of $20,000 are no longer an obligation of the employer or the plan. This results in a $20,000 net decrease (gain) in the projected benefit obligation, because there are no other decreases or increases.

Step 5.   Compute the total of (*a*) the balance of any net gain or loss that remains in accumulated other comprehensive income at the date of the plan curtailment and (*b*) the balance of any transition net asset that remains in accumulated other comprehensive income at the date of the plan curtailment. In the above illustration, the total is a gain of $1,000 (net gain of $1,000 and no net asset).

Step 6.   Compute the gain or loss on the plan curtailment, as follows:

- If Step 4 (projected benefit obligation) is a gain and Step 5 is also a gain, curtailment gain is recognized in the amount of Step 4 (the amount of gain in Step 5 is ignored).

- If Step 4 (projected benefit obligation) is a loss and Step 5 is also a loss, curtailment loss is recognized in the amount of Step 4 (the amount of loss in Step 5 is ignored).

- If Step 4 (projected benefit obligation) is a gain and Step 5 is a loss, curtailment gain is recognized in the amount by which the gain in Step 4 exceeds the loss in Step 5. If Step 5 exceeds Step 4, no gain or loss is recognized.

- If Step 4 (projected benefit obligation) is a loss and Step 5 is a gain, curtailment loss is recognized in the amount by which the loss in Step 4 exceeds the gain in Step 5. If Step 5 exceeds Step 4, no gain or loss is recognized.

In the above illustration, the net decrease (gain) in the projected benefit obligation was $20,000 (Step 4) and the total net gain or loss is a gain of $1,000 (Step 5). Since both steps result in a gain, a gain on the plan curtailment in the amount of Step 4 is recognized, which is $20,000.

Settlement gain or loss   As in Step 5 above, compute the total of (*a*) the balance of any net gain or loss that remains in accumulated other comprehensive income at the date of the plan settlement and (*b*) the balance of any transition net asset that remains in accumulated other comprehensive income at the date of the plan settlement.

If part of the pension obligation is settled, the employer must recognize a pro rata portion of the maximum gain or loss, equal to the total of the net gain or loss and/or the transition net asset multiplied by the percentage reduction in the projected benefit obligation. In the above illustration, there was a net gain of $1,000 and no transition net asset. Since the pension plan was terminated, the pension obligation completely settled, and the decrease in the projected benefit obligation was 100%, the pro rata portion that must be recognized is 100%, or $1,000. Thus, the gain on the settlement of the pension plan is $1,000.

Summary   The loss on the decrease in the prior service cost amount and transition net obligation is $3,000, which was computed in Step 3. This loss is reported as a "Loss on Effects of Curtailment of Pension Plan." The net gain on the decrease in the projected benefit obligation is $20,000, which was computed in Step 6. This gain is reported as a "Gain on the Curtailment of Pension Plan." The "Gain on the Settlement of Pension Plan" is $1,000, which was computed separately above. Thus, the net gain on the pension plan curtailment and settlement was $18,000 ($3,000 loss, $20,000 gain, and $1,000 gain).

Journal entry The journal entry and suggested financial statement presentation of the net gain on pension plan curtailment and settlement of $18,000 is as follows:

Cash (excess plan assets)	15,000	
Liability for pension benefits	3,000	
Gain from termination of pension plan		18,000

Suggested financial statement presentation:

Gain on curtailment of pension plan	$20,000
Loss on effects of curtailment of pension plan	(3,000)
Total effects of plan curtailment	$17,000
Gain on settlement of pension plan	1,000
Net gain on pension plan curtailment and settlement	$18,000

RELATED CHAPTERS IN 2009 *GAAP GUIDE* LEVEL A

Chapter 4, "Business Combinations"
Chapter 10, "Deferred Compensation Contracts"
Chapter 16, "Fair Value"
Chapter 24, "Interest Costs Capitalized"
Chapter 26, "Interim Financial Reporting"
Chapter 34, "Postemployment and Postretirement Benefits Other Than Pensions"
Chapter 40, "Results of Operations"
Chapter 53, "Pension Plans"

RELATED CHAPTERS IN 2009 *GAAP GUIDE* LEVELS B, C, AND D

Chapter 6, "Business Combinations"
Chapter 23, "Interim Financial Reporting"
Chapter 29, "Pension Plans—Employers"
Chapter 30, "Pension Plans—Settlements and Curtailments"
Chapter 32, "Postemployment and Postretirement Benefits Other Than Pensions"
Chapter 35, "Results of Operations"

RELATED CHAPTERS IN 2009 *INTERNATIONAL ACCOUNTING/FINANCIAL REPORTING STANDARDS GUIDE*

Chapter 7, "Business Combinations"
Chapter 13, "Employee Benefits"
Chapter 16, "Financial Instruments"
Chapter 22, "Interim Financial Reporting"

CHAPTER 34
POSTEMPLOYMENT AND POSTRETIREMENT BENEFITS OTHER THAN PENSIONS

CONTENTS

OVERVIEW

FAS-106 (Employers'Accounting for Postretirement Benefits Other Than Pensions) requires the accrual of postretirement benefits in a manner similar to the recognition of net periodic pension cost under FAS-87 (Employers' Accounting for Pensions). The provisions of FAS-106 are similar in most respects to those of FAS-87 and differ only where there are compelling reasons for different treatments.

Similar to FAS-87, FAS-106 incorporates the following features in the required accounting for postretirement benefits:

- *Delayed income statement recognition*—certain changes in the obligation for postretirement benefits and in the value of plan assets are recognized on the balance sheet as they occur, through changes in the postretirement benefit asset and/or liability; however, on the income statement these changes are not recognized as they occur, but rather systematically and gradually over subsequent periods. Items recognized on the balance sheet immediately but deferred for income statement recognition are included in accumulated other comprehensive income.

- *Net cost*—the recognized consequences of events and transactions affecting a postretirement benefit plan are reported as a single amount in the employers' financial statements. That amount includes at least three types of events or transactions that might otherwise be reported separately—exchanging a promise of deferred compensation for current employee services, the interest cost arising from the passage of time until those benefits are paid, and the returns from the investment in plan assets if the plan is funded.

- *Offsetting*—plan assets (assets that have been segregated and restricted for the payment of postretirement benefits) offset the accumulated postretirement benefit obligation in determining amounts in the employer's statement of financial position. Also, the return on plan assets reduces postretirement benefit cost in the employer's statement of income. That reduction is reflected, even though the obligation has not been settled and the investment in the assets may be largely controlled by the employer, and substantial risks and rewards associated with both the obligation and the assets are borne by the employer.

The FASB also has established accounting standards for employers that provide benefits for former or inactive employees after employment, but before retirement (*postemployment benefits*). FAS-112 (Employers' Accounting for Postemployment Benefits) requires employers to recognize the obligation to provide postemployment benefits in accordance with FAS-43 (Accounting for Compensated Absences) if the criteria for accrual established in that pronouncement are met. If the FAS-43 criteria are not met, the employer should account for postemployment benefits when it is probable that a liability has been incurred and the amount of that liability can be reasonably estimated, in accordance with FAS-5 (Accounting for Contingencies).

GAAP for postemployment and postretirement benefits are found in the following pronouncements:

APB-12   Omnibus Opinion—1967

FAS-106   Employers' Accounting for Postretirement Benefits Other Than Pensions

FAS-112   Employers' Accounting for Postemployment Benefits

FAS-132   Employers' Disclosures about Pensions and Other Postretirement Benefits (revised 2003)

FAS-158   Employers' Accounting for Defined Benefit Pension and Other Postretirement Plans

2009 TRANSITION GUIDANCE FOR FAS-141(R) AND FAS-160

The FASB has recently issued FAS-141(R), *Business Combinations,* which is effective for business combinations for which the acquisition date is on or after the beginning of the first annual reporting period beginning on or after December 15, 2008. The FASB has also issued FAS-160, *Noncontrolling Interests in Consolidated Financial Statements, an Amendment of ARB No. 51,* which is effective for fiscal years, and interim periods within those fiscal years, beginning on or after December 15, 2008. Because these standards are not effective for some companies until December 2009, and because early adoption is prohibited, the 2009 *GAAP Guide* reflects the requirements of FAS-141 prior to its revision in December 2007 and does not reflect the requirements of FAS-160. There is a discussion of the changes in the accounting for business combinations under FAS-141(R) in the Appendix to Chapter 4, "Business Combinations." Similarly, the Appendix to Chapter 7, "Consolidated Financial Statements," includes a discussion of the requirements of FAS-160. However, any effects of FAS-141(R) and/or FAS-160 in this chapter have not been reflected in this edition. Therefore, if a company is subject to the requirements of FAS-141(R) and/or FAS-160, the reader is referred to FAS-141(R) and FAS-160 for these new requirements.

BACKGROUND

FAS-106, issued in December 1990, establishes employers' accounting for postretirement benefits other than pensions. Disclosure standards for both pensions and postretirement benefits are provided in FAS-132.

For convenient discussion, this chapter uses the term *postretirement benefits* to mean postretirement benefits other than pensions. Practice sometimes uses the abbreviation "OPEB" (other postretirement employee benefits) with the same meaning.

GAAP ACCORDING TO FAS-106

FAS-106 establishes *accounting* standards for employers with postretirement benefit plans. *Postretirement benefits* consist of all forms of benefits other than retirement income provided by an employer to retired workers, their beneficiaries, and their dependents (FAS-106, par. 6). The term does not include benefits paid after employment but before retirement, such as layoff benefits. Postemployment benefits are covered by FAS-112, which is the subject of a later section in this chapter.

Postretirement benefit payments may begin immediately on employees' termination of service or may be deferred until retired employees reach a specified age. Benefits such as health care, tuition assistance, or legal services are provided to retirees as the need arises. Other benefits, such as life insurance, are provided on the occurrence of specified events (FAS-106, par. 7).

A *postretirement benefit plan* is one in which an employer agrees to provide certain postretirement benefits to current and former employees after they retire. A postretirement benefit plan may be *contributory* (employees may be required to contribute to the plan) or *noncontributory* (the entire cost of the plan is borne by the employer).

A postretirement benefit plan may be *funded* or *unfunded*—that is, the employees and/or the employer may make cash contributions to a postretirement benefit plan trustee (i.e., funded), or the employer may make only credit entries on its books reflecting the postretirement benefit liability under the plan and pay all benefits from its general assets (i.e., unfunded).

General Approach of FAS-106—Deferred Compensation

According to FAS-106, postretirement benefits are a type of *deferred compensation* that is accounted for as part of an employee's total compensation package. A *deferred compensation plan* is an agreement specifying that a portion of an employee's compensation will be set aside and paid in future periods. FAS-106 requires employers to account for postretirement benefit plans on the accrual basis.

Comparison of FAS-106 to FAS-87 and FAS-88

Although there are some important differences, many provisions of FAS-106 are similar to the accounting and reporting requirements for pension accounting established by FAS-87 and FAS-88 (Employers' Accounting for Settlements and Curtailments of Defined Benefit Pension Plans and for Termination Benefits).

In accounting for postretirement benefits under FAS-106, an employer makes at least two types of journal entries to record its cost of these benefits—one to record the annual expense and related liability and a second to record the payment or funding of the liability, if any.

Illustration of Basic Entries for Recording Postretirement Benefits

Assuming a company determines its annual expense for postretirement benefits is $10,000 and funds that amount, the following entries are made (assume a 30% tax rate):

1.	Net periodic postretirement benefit cost	10,000	
	Deferred tax asset	3,000	
	Deferred tax benefit—net income		3,000
	Liability for postretirement benefits		10,000
	(To accrue postretirement benefit cost of $10,000 for a specific period.)		
2.	Liability for postretirement benefits	10,000	
	Cash		10,000
	(To record cash contribution to postretirement plan trust or to pay benefits of $10,000.)		

These entries are similar to those required for pension accounting under FAS-87, except for differences in the titles of the accounts.

Most of the provisions of FAS-87 and FAS-106 pertain to the computation of the amount to be recorded in journal entry type (1) above. This computation requires numerous worksheet calculations, which are illustrated throughout FAS-87 and FAS-106.

Use of Reasonable Approximations

FAS-106 allows an employer to use estimates, averages, or computational shortcuts, provided that the employer reasonably expects that the results will not be materially different from those which would have been reached by a fully detailed application of the provisions of FAS-106 (FAS-106, par. 15).

Scope and Applicability of FAS-106

The applicability of FAS-106 is discussed in terms of five areas:

1. Types of benefits
2. Types of beneficiaries

3. General rather than selective coverage of employees
4. Source and form of payment
5. Nature of the employer's undertaking

Types of Benefits

FAS-106 applies to an employer's undertaking to provide various types of nonpension benefits to employees after they retire. The benefits may commence immediately upon termination of the employee's active service, or may be deferred until the retired employee reaches a specified age.

The benefits include health care, life insurance outside of a pension plan, tuition assistance, day care, legal services, housing subsidies, and other types of postretirement benefits (FAS-106, par. 6). However, FAS-106 does not apply to pension or life insurance benefits provided by a pension plan. The GAAP for pensions and life insurance benefits provided by pension plans are established by FAS-87 and FAS-88 (FAS-106, par. 11).

If an employer has established a plan to provide benefits to active employees as well as to retired employees, FAS-106 requires the employer to divide the plan into two parts for accounting purposes; one part covering benefits to active employees and the other part covering benefits to retired employees. The employer should use the accounting standards of FAS-106 only for the part covering benefits to retired employees (FAS-106, par. 10).

Types of Beneficiaries

The beneficiaries may be retired employees, disabled employees, any other former employees who are expected to receive benefits, or retirees' beneficiaries and covered dependents, pursuant to the terms of an employer's undertaking to provide such benefits. The beneficiaries may also be individuals who (*a*) have ceased permanent active employment because of disability, (*b*) have not yet completed formal procedures for retirement, or (*c*) are carried on nonretired status under the disability provisions of the plan so that they can continue accumulating credit for pensions or other postretirement benefits (FAS-106, pars. 6, 137).

General Rather Than Selective Coverage of Employees

The plan should cover employees in general, rather than selected individual employees. An employer's practice of providing postretirement benefits to selected employees under individual contracts with specific terms determined on an individual basis does not constitute a postretirement benefit plan under FAS-106. FAS-106 does apply to contracts with individual employees if these contracts, taken together, are equivalent to a plan covering employees in general (FAS-106, par. 9).

> **OBSERVATION:** An employer's commitment to selected individual employees is accrued in accordance with the terms of the individual contracts (see the *Guide* chapter titled "Deferred Compensation Contracts"). Professional judgment is required whenever contracts with individual employees may be equivalent to a general plan. FAS-106 provides no guidance on how to make the determination.

Source and Form of Payment

A plan is covered by FAS-106 if it provides reimbursement or direct payment to providers for the cost of specified services as the need for those services arises, or if it provides lump sum benefits, such as death benefits. The plan may be either funded or unfunded (FAS-106, par. 6 and par. 8).

> **OBSERVATION:** If the plan is funded, the assets of a postretirement benefit plan usually are kept in a trust account, segregated from the assets of the employer. Contributions to the postretirement benefit plan trust account are made periodically by the employer and, if the plan is contributory, by the employees. The plan assets may be invested in stocks, bonds, real estate, and other types of investments. Plan assets are increased by earnings, gains on investments, and contributions by the employer (and employees if the plan is contributory), and are decreased by losses on investments and the payment of benefits and any related administrative expenses.

Nature of the Employer's Undertaking

FAS-106 applies to any arrangement that is in substance a plan for providing postretirement benefits, regardless of its form (FAS-106, par. 8).

> **OBSERVATION:** When it is not clear that a plan exists, professional judgment is required in determining whether a plan exists "in substance." FAS-106 provides little guidance on this issue.

FAS-106 applies not only to written plans, but also to unwritten plans if the existence of these plans can be perceived based on (*a*) the employer's practice of paying benefits or (*b*) the employer's oral representations to current or former employees. Once an employer pays benefits or promises to pay benefits, FAS-106 presumes that the employer has undertaken to provide future benefits as indicated by the past payments or promises, unless there is evidence to the contrary (FAS-106, par. 8).

> **OBSERVATION:** To indicate the existence of a plan, it appears that the employer's oral representations (a) should refer to a plan that is general in its scope and (b) should be communicated to current or former employees in general, or to individual employees as representatives of the employees in general.

One issue is whether FAS-106 applies only to legally enforceable obligations, or to a broader range of commitments including those that cannot be legally enforced.

> **OBSERVATION:**   The Employee Retirement Income Security Act (ERISA) gives substantial legal protection to the expectations of employees under pension plans, but does not give the same level of protection to employee expectations of nonpension benefits. Courts have upheld the right of employers to terminate or curtail benefits under non-pension plans, unless the employers have entered into legally binding commitments to maintain benefits, such as collective bargaining agreements.

The "Basis for Conclusions" in FAS-106 explains in more detail the type of employer's obligation that is covered by FAS-106. Although the "Basis for Conclusions" is not part of the formal pronouncement, it provides significant guidance and states that an employer's undertaking comes within the scope of FAS-106 if the undertaking is a *liability* under CON-6 (Elements of Financial Statements).

The "Basis for Conclusions" in FAS-106 relies on CON-6 for the proposition that an obligation can qualify as a liability whether or not the obligation is legally enforceable. The test is whether the obligation "is effectively binding on the employer because of past practices, social or moral sanctions, or customs." FAS-106 concludes that an employer, by paying benefits or promising to do so, incurs a liability to be accounted for under FAS-106, in the absence of evidence to the contrary.

> **OBSERVATION:**
> * Accountants should obtain expert advice before (a) advising employers on the applicability of FAS-106 to existing plans, (b) advising employers on the structuring of new plans or the restructuring of existing plans if the structure of the plan may determine whether the plan is within the scope of FAS-106, or (c) auditing the financial statements of an employer if there is a serious question as to whether the employer's plan is within the scope of FAS-106.
> * If a plan is covered by FAS-106, the next question is whether the plan is a defined benefit plan or a defined contribution plan. FAS-106 prescribes significantly different accounting and reporting requirements for these two categories. FAS-106 deals primarily with defined benefit plans. For the distinctive accounting and reporting requirements applicable to defined contribution plans, see the section titled "Defined Contribution Plans" in this chapter. When considering the structuring or restructuring of a plan, the employer and its advisors should consider whether the plan is covered by FAS-106 and, if so, whether the plan is governed by the accounting and reporting requirements for defined benefit plans or for defined contribution plans.

SINGLE-EMPLOYER DEFINED BENEFIT POSTRETIREMENT PLANS

FAS-106 deals primarily with an employer's accounting for a single-employer plan that provides defined benefits. FAS-106 also briefly covers multiemployer plans, multiple-employer plans, and defined contribution plans. Each is discussed later in this chapter.

> **OBSERVATION:** The accounting and reporting requirements for defined contribution plans differ significantly from those for defined benefit plans. If a plan has some characteristics of each type, FAS-106 calls for careful analysis of the substance of the plan. The difference in the accounting and reporting requirements, depending on whether the plan is a defined benefit plan or a defined contribution plan, may be a significant factor to be considered by employers attempting to structure or restructure their plans.

In a defined benefit plan, the benefit may be defined in terms of a specified monetary amount (such as a life insurance benefit), or a specified type of benefit (such as all or a percentage of the cost of specified surgical procedures). The benefits may be subject to a maximum (or *cap*), either per individual employee or for the plan as a whole, or the employer may agree to pay the full amount of benefits without regard to any maximum amount (FAS-106, par. 17).

The employee's entitlement to benefits is expressed in the benefit formula, which specifies the years of service to be rendered, age to be attained while in service, or a combination of both, which must be met for an employee to be eligible to receive benefits under the plan. The benefit formula may also define the beginning of the period of service during which the employee earns credit toward eligibility, as well as the levels of benefits earned for specific periods of service (FAS-106, par. 18).

The total amount of benefits depends not only on the benefit formula but also on actuarial factors, such as the longevity of the retired employee (and the longevity of the retiree's beneficiaries and covered dependents), and the occurrence of specific events entitling the individuals to benefits (such as illnesses) (FAS-106, par. 20).

Because of these factors, the employer cannot precisely calculate the amount of benefits to be paid in the future to any retired employee (or to the retiree's beneficiaries and covered dependents). The FASB is satisfied, however, that employers can make reasonable estimates useful for accounting purposes.

Accumulated Postretirement Benefit Obligation

FAS-106 requires the employer to accrue the accumulated postretirement benefit obligation. Once an employee has attained full eligibility, the amount of this obligation is the same as the employee's *expected* postretirement benefit obligation. Until then, the *accumulated* amount is the portion of the expected amount attributed to employee service rendered to a particular date (FAS-106, par. 21).

The accumulated and the expected amounts represent the actuarial present value of the anticipated benefits. Measurement of these amounts is based on assumptions regarding such items as the expected cost of providing future benefits and any cost-sharing provisions under which the employee, the government, or others will absorb part of these costs. If the benefits or cost-sharing provisions are related to the employee's salary progression, the calculation of benefits and cost-sharing reflects the anticipated impact of this progression (FAS-106, par. 20).

> **OBSERVATION:**   FAS-106 differs from the accounting for pensions in FAS-87 in this respect, because FAS-87 does not anticipate salary progression in determining the accumulated pension benefit obligation.

Illustration of Relationship between Expected and Accumulated Postretirement Benefit Obligations

A plan provides postretirement health care benefits to all employees who render at least ten years of service and attain age 65 while in service. A 60-year-old employee, hired at age 45, is expected to terminate employment at the end of the year in which the employee attains age 67 and is expected to live to age 77. A discount rate of 8% is assumed.

At December 31, 20X5, the employer estimates the expected amount and timing of benefit payments for that employee as follows:

Age	Expected Future Claims	Present Value at Age 60	Present Value at Age 65
68	$ 2,322	$ 1,255	$ 1,843
69	2,564	1,283	1,885
70	2,850	1,320	1,940
71	3,154	1,353	1,988
72	3,488	1,385	2,035
73	3,868	1,422	2,090
74	4,274	1,455	2,138
75	4,734	1,492	2,193
76	5,240	1,530	2,247
77	7,798	2,108	3,097
	$40,292	$14,603	$21,456

At December 31, 20X5, when the employee's age is 60, the *expected* postretirement benefit obligation is $14,603, and the *accumulated* postretirement benefit obligation is $10,952 (15/20 of $14,603 because the employee has worked 15 of the 20 years needed to attain age 65 while in service and thus become fully eligible for benefits).

Assuming no changes in health care costs or other circumstances, the obligations at later dates are as follows:

- December 31, 20Y0 (age 65), the expected and the accumulated postretirement benefit obligations are both $21,456. These amounts are the same, because the employee is fully eligible.
- December 31, 20Y1 (age 66), the expected and the accumulated postretirement benefit obligations are both $23,172 ($21,456 the previous year, plus interest at 8% for 1 year).

Measurement of Cost and Obligations

In discussing the measurement of cost and obligations of single-employer defined benefit plans, FAS-106 addresses the following issues:

- Accounting for the substantive plan
- Assumptions
- Attribution

Accounting for the Substantive Plan

According to FAS-106, the accounting and reporting should reflect the substantive plan; that is, the plan as understood by the employer and the employees. Generally, the substantive plan is accurately reflected in writing. The employer's past practice or communications of intended future changes, however, may indicate that the substantive plan differs from the written plan (FAS-106, par. 23).

> ☞ **PRACTICE POINTER:** If an independent auditor is faced with a situation in which the substantive plan appears to be different from the written plan, the auditor should (a) seek expert advice, (b) consult with the highest levels of the employer's management, and (c) fully document the matter in the audit files.

FAS-106 discusses the following areas in which the substantive plan may differ from the written plan:

- Cost sharing
- Benefit changes
- Plan amendments

Cost Sharing

In general, the employer's cost-sharing policy is regarded as part of the substantive plan if (*a*) the employer has maintained a consistent level of cost-sharing with retirees, (*b*) the employer consistently has increased or decreased the share of the cost contributed by employees or retirees, or (*c*) the employer has the ability to change the cost-sharing provisions at a specified time or when certain conditions exist, and has communicated to plan participants its intent to make such changes (FAS-106, par. 24).

An employer's past practice regarding cost sharing, however, is not regarded as the substantive plan if (FAS-106, par. 25):

- The cost sharing was accompanied by offsetting changes in other benefits or compensation.

- The employer was subjected to significant costs, such as work stoppages, to carry out that policy.

Along similar lines, an employer's communication of its intent to change the cost-sharing provisions is not regarded as the substantive plan if (FAS-106, par. 25):

- The plan participants would be unwilling to accept the change without adverse results to the employer's operations.

- The plan participants would insist on other modifications of the plan, that would offset the change in cost sharing, to accept the proposed change.

In estimating the amount of contributions to be received by the plan from active or retired employees, the employer should consider any relevant substantive plan provisions, such as the employer's past practice of consistently changing the contribution rates. If the employer is obliged to return contributions to employees who do not become eligible for benefits (together with interest, if applicable), the estimated amount of this obligation is (*a*) included in the employer's total benefit obligation and (*b*) factored into calculations of the contributions needed by the plan (FAS-106, par. 27).

Benefit Changes

The measurement of the obligation under the plan includes automatic benefit changes specified by the plan. An example is a plan that promises to pay a benefit in kind, such as health care benefits, instead of a defined dollar amount. The obligation to pay the benefit automatically changes in amount when the cost of the benefit changes (FAS-106, par. 28).

Plan Amendments

Measurement also includes plan amendments as soon as they have been contractually agreed upon, even if some or all of the provisions become effective in later periods (FAS-106, par. 28).

> **OBSERVATION:** Even if a plan amendment has not been contractually agreed upon, it appears that an employer should reflect the amendment if it can be regarded as a change in the substantive plan. In general, a substantive plan may differ from the written plan in either of two cases: (1) when the employer has communicated its intention to adopt the amendment and certain conditions are met or (2) when the employer has engaged in consistent past practice.

Assumptions

An employer has to make numerous assumptions to apply FAS-106. Each assumption should reflect the best estimate of the future event to which it relates, without regard to the estimates involved in making other assumptions. FAS-106 describes this as an explicit approach to assumptions (FAS-106, par. 29).

> **OBSERVATION:** The FASB finds the use of **explicit** assumptions preferable to **implicit** assumptions, under which the reliability of assumptions would be judged in the aggregate, not individually (FAS-106, par. 181).

All assumptions should be based on the expectation that the plan will continue in the absence of evidence that it will not continue (FAS-106, par. 30). Some of the assumptions discussed in FAS-106 apply generally to all types of benefits, while other assumptions are unique to health care benefits.

FAS-106 discusses the following general assumptions:

- Time value of money (discount rates)
- Expected long-term rate of return on plan assets
- Future compensation levels
- Other general assumptions

Time Value of Money (Discount Rates)

One of the essential assumptions relates to discount rates. Assumed discount rates are used in measuring the expected and accumulated postretirement benefit obligations and the service cost and interest cost components of net periodic postretirement benefit cost. Assumed discount rates should reflect the time value of money at the measurement date, as indicated by rates of return on high-quality fixed-income investments currently available with cash flows corresponding to the anticipated needs of the plan. If the employer could possibly settle its obligation under the plan by purchasing insurance (for example, nonparticipating life insurance contracts to provide death benefits), the interest rates inherent in the potential settlement amount are relevant to the employer's determination of assumed discount rates (FAS-106, par. 31).

The chosen discount rate should produce a liability amount that would generate the necessary future cash flows to pay postretirement benefits as they become due if such amount was invested at the financial statement date in a portfolio of high-quality fixed-income investments. This liability amount is theoretically equal to the market value of a portfolio of high-quality zero coupon bonds, where each bond matches the amount and maturity of future payments due under the postretirement benefit plan. However, reinvestment risk exists to the extent that the plan's assets include interest-bearing debt instruments (rather than only zero coupon bonds) and to the extent that plan investments have a maturity date that is sooner than some of the anticipated postretirement benefit payments. In such cases, the assumed discount (interest) rate needs to consider expected reinvestment rates extrapolated using the existing yield curve at the financial statement date. The discount rate should be reevaluated at each measurement (financial statement) date (FAS-106, par. 31A, as amended by FAS-158, par. D2c).

> ☞ **PRACTICE POINTER:** The discount rate used to determine the postretirement benefit liability and the interest cost component of net periodic postretirement benefit cost should change in accordance with changes in market interest rates: if interest rates rise, the discount rate should increase; if interest rates fall, the discount rate should decline. In addition, the determination of the discount rate is separate from the determination of the expected return on plan assets.

Expected Long-Term Rate of Return on Plan Assets

Assumptions are also required in determining the expected long-term rate of return on plan assets. In general, plan assets are investments that have been segregated and restricted, usually in a trust, for the exclusive purpose of paying postretirement benefits.

The expected long-term rate of return on plan assets should reflect the anticipated average rate of earnings on existing plan assets and those expected to be contributed during the period (FAS-106, par. 32).

> **OBSERVATION:** This factor is used, together with the *market-related value* of plan assets, in computing the *expected return* on plan assets. The difference between the actual return and the expected return on plan assets is defined in FAS-106 as "plan asset gain or loss," discussed later.

If the return on plan assets is taxable to the trust or other fund under the plan, the expected long-term rate of return shall be reduced to reflect the related income taxes expected to be paid (FAS-106, par. 32).

When estimating the rate of return on plan assets, the employer should consider the rate of return on (*a*) assets currently invested and (*b*) assets that will be reinvested. If the income from plan assets is taxable, the anticipated amount of taxes should be deducted to produce a net-of-tax rate of return. If a plan is unfunded or has no assets that qualify as plan assets under FAS-106, the employer has no basis or need to calculate an expected long-term rate of return on plan assets (FAS-106, par. 32).

Future Compensation Levels

If the benefit formula provides for varying amounts of postretirement benefits based on the compensation levels of employees, the employer has to make further assumptions about the impact of anticipated future compensation levels on the cost of benefits and the obligation to pay them (FAS-106, par. 33).

Estimates of future compensation are based on anticipated compensation of individual employees, including future changes arising from general price levels, productivity, seniority, promotion, and other factors. All assumptions should be consistent with regard to general factors such as future rates of inflation. The assumptions should also include any indirect effects related to salary progression, such as the impact of inflation-based adjustments to the maximum benefit provided under the plan (FAS-106, par. 33).

Other General Assumptions

Other general assumptions involved in applying FAS-106 include the following:

- Participation rates for contributory plans
- The probability of payment (such as turnover of employees, dependency status, and mortality)

> ☞ **PRACTICE POINTER:** As is the case in pension accounting, the CPA is not expected to be an expert in actuarial science. In fact, accounting for pensions and other retirement benefits is an area where the CPA relies heavily on the expertise of actuaries. However, the CPA still must have a general understanding of the work of the actuary, including the reasonableness of the underlying assumptions the actuary is using to prepare information that may have a significant impact on an enterprise's funding of benefit plans, as well as its financial statements.

Assumptions Unique to Postretirement Health Care Benefits

Most postretirement benefit plans include health care benefits. Measurement of an employer's postretirement health care obligation requires the use of special types of assumptions that will affect the amount and timing of future benefit payments for postretirement health care, in addition to the general assumptions required by all postretirement benefit plans.

FAS-106 discusses the following assumptions unique to postretirement health care benefits:

- Per capita claims cost
- Assumptions about trends in health care costs

Per Capita Claims Cost

An employer should estimate the net incurred claims cost at each age at which a participant is expected to receive benefits. To estimate this net cost, the employer first estimates the assumed per capita gross claims cost at each age, and then subtracts the effects of (*a*) Medicare and other reimbursements from third parties and (*b*) cost-sharing provisions that cause the participant to collect less than 100% of the claim. If plan participants are required to make contributions to the plan during their active service, the actuarial present value of the participants' future contributions should be subtracted from the actuarial present value of the assumed net incurred claims costs (FAS-106, par. 35).

The *assumed per capita claims cost* is the annual cost of benefits from the time at which an individual's coverage begins, for the remainder of that person's life (or until coverage ends, when sooner). The annual benefit cost is based on the best possible estimate of the expected future cost of benefits covered by the plan that reflects age and other appropriate factors such as gender and geographical location. If the employer incurs significant costs in administering the plan, these costs should also be considered part of the assumed per capita claims cost (FAS-106, par. 36).

If an employer does not have a reliable basis for estimating the assumed per capita claims cost by age, the employer may base its estimate on other reliable information. For example, the estimate may be based on the claims costs that have actually been incurred for employees of all ages, adjusted by factors to reflect health care cost trends, age of the covered population, and cost sharing (FAS-106, par. 38).

A number of assumptions are based on the estimated effects of inflation. The employer should use consistent methods of estimating inflation, whether the assumption relates to discount rates, compensation levels, or health care cost trend rates.

If the history of the plan is reliable enough to provide a basis for future estimates, the past and present claims data of the plan are considered in calculating the assumed per capita claims cost. If the plan does not provide any reliable data, the employer may base its estimates on other employers' claims information, as assembled by insurance companies, actuarial firms, or employee benefits consulting firms (FAS-106, par. 38).

> **OBSERVATION:** The independent auditor should verify that any outside information comes from reliable and independent sources, and that the audit files fully identify these sources.

The estimates derived from the experience of other employers should, however, be adjusted to reflect the demographics of the specific employer and the benefits available under its plan, to the extent they differ from those of the other employers. Relevant factors include, for example, health care utilization patterns, expected geographical locations of retirees and their dependents, and significant differences among the nature and types of benefits covered (FAS-106, par. 38).

Assumptions about Trends in Health Care Cost Rates

Assumptions about the trend in health care cost rates represent the expected annual rate of change in the cost of health care benefits currently provided under the plan (because of factors other than changes in the demographics of participants) for each year from the measurement date until the payment of benefits. The trend rates are based on past and current cost trends, reflecting such factors as health care cost inflation, changes in utilization or delivery patterns, technological advances, and changes in the health status of plan participants. Examples include the possible future use of technology that is now being developed, or the reduction of the need for benefits resulting from participation in wellness programs (FAS-106, par. 39).

Different cost trend rates may be required for different types of services. For example, the cost trend rate for hospital care may differ from that for dental care. Further, the cost trend rates may fluctuate at different rates during different projected periods in the future. For example, there may be a rapid short-term increase, with a subsequent leveling off in the longer term.

Absent information to the contrary, the employer should assume that governmental benefits will continue as provided by existing law, and that benefits from other providers will continue in accordance with their existing plans. Future changes in the law are not anticipated (FAS-106, par. 40).

Attribution

Once the expected postretirement benefit obligation for an employee has been determined, an equal amount of that obligation is attributed to each year of service in the attribution period, unless the benefit formula of the plan is frontloaded and thus necessitates attribution on a different basis (FAS-106, par. 43).

The attribution period starts when the employee begins earning credit toward postretirement benefits. This generally occurs on the date of hire, but may be at a later date if the benefit formula requires a significant waiting period before the employee can earn credit. In any event, the attribution period ends when the employee reaches full eligibility for benefits. Thus, the cost of providing the benefits is attributed to the period during which the employee builds up full eligibility. The employer does not attribute any of the service cost to any period after the employee has achieved full eligibility (FAS-106, par. 44).

Illustration of Attribution Period

Under the postretirement benefit plan of Company Q, employees qualify by rendering at least five years of service and reaching age 65 while in service. The company hires an employee at age 61. Assume the expected postretirement benefit obligation for this employee is $10,000.

The attribution period is five years. (Note that the employee will not become eligible at age 65, because the employee will not yet have completed five years of service.) For each of the first five years of service, the annual service cost will be $2,000 (1/5 of $10,000). No service cost will be attributed after the first five years, even if the employee remains in service.

Illustration of Attribution under a Frontloaded Plan

A "frontloaded" plan is one in which a disproportionate share of the benefit obligation is attributed to the early years of an employee's service.

A life insurance plan provides postretirement death benefits of $200,000 for 10 years of service after age 45 and additional death benefits of $10,000 for each year of service thereafter until age 65. (The maximum benefit is therefore $300,000, consisting of the basic $200,000 plus 10 additional years @ $10,000.)

In this situation, the benefit obligation is attributed to periods corresponding to the benefit formula, as follows:

- The actuarial present value of a death benefit of $20,000 (1/10 of $200,000) is attributed to each of the first 10 years of service after age 45.

- The actuarial present value of an additional $10,000 death benefit is attributed to each year of service thereafter until age 65.

RECOGNITION OF NET PERIODIC POSTRETIREMENT BENEFIT COST

The amount of net periodic postretirement benefit cost is derived from the net change in the amount of the accumulated postretirement benefit obligation, after ignoring those components of the net change that do not pertain to the cost of benefits (FAS-106, par. 45).

The net periodic postretirement benefit cost recognized for a period consists of the following components (FAS-106, par. 46, as amended by FAS-158, par. D2e):

- Service cost
- Interest cost
- Actual return on plan assets, if any
- Amortization of prior service cost or credit included in accumulated other comprehensive income
- Gain or loss (to the extent recognized)
- Amortization of the transition obligation or asset at the date of initial application of FAS-106 (if the full amount was not immediately recognized upon adoption of FAS-106) and still remaining in accumulated other comprehensive income

> **OBSERVATION:** The employer makes one entry to accrue the net periodic postretirement benefit cost, the amount of which is the total of the components listed above, determined by worksheet calculations.

Illustration of Basic Transactions and Adjustments

Company A's date of transition to FAS-106 was the beginning of Year 1. At that time, the accumulated postretirement benefit obligation was $300,000. The plan was unfunded.

At the end of Year 1, Company A paid $65,000 of postretirement benefits. Service cost attributed to Year 1 was $60,000. The assumed discount rate was 10%.

Worksheets as of the end of Year 1 are as follows:

	Postretirement Benefit Cost	Accumulated Postretirement Benefit Obligation	Transition Obligation
Beginning of year	$ NA	$(300,000)	$300,000
Recognition of components of net periodic post-retirement benefit cost:			
Service cost	(60,000)	(60,000)	
Interest cost[a]	(30,000)	(30,000)	
Amortization of transition obligation[b]	(15,000)		(15,000)
	$(105,000)	(90,000)	(15,000)

Benefit payments	65,000	
Net change	(25,000)	(15,000)
End of year	$(325,000)	$285,000

(a) 10% (assumed discount rate) of $300,000 (accumulated postretirement obligation at beginning of year)

(b) 20-year straight-line amortization of transition obligation (discussed later in this chapter)

The amounts on this worksheet are reflected in the reconciliation of the funded status of the plan with the amounts shown on the statement of financial position, as follows:

	Beginning of Year 1	Net Change	End of Year 1
Accumulated postretirement benefit obligation	$(300,000)	$(25,000)	$(325,000)
Plan assets at fair value	-0-		-0-
Funded status—Recognized as a liability on the balance sheet[(a)]	(300,000)	(25,000)	(325,000)
Transition obligation included in other comprehensive income	300,000	(15,000)	285,000

(a) The liability for postretirement benefits is $300,000 at the beginning of Year 1. It increases during Year 1 by the amount that service cost, interest cost, and expected return on plan assets exceed the cash contributions during the year ($90,000 − $65,000).

Basic Transactions and Adjustments

Service Cost Component

The *service cost component* of net periodic postretirement benefit cost is defined by FAS-106 as the portion of the expected postretirement benefit obligation attributed to employee service during a specified period, based on the actuarial present value of the expected obligation (FAS-106, par. 47).

A *defined benefit* postretirement benefit plan contains a benefit formula that defines the benefit an employee will receive for services performed during a specified period (service cost). FAS-106 requires that the terms of the benefit formula be used to determine the amount of postretirement benefit earned by each employee for services performed during a specified period. Under FAS-106, attribution is the process of assigning postretirement benefits or cost to periods of employee service, in accordance with the postretirement benefit formula.

Interest Cost Component

FAS-106 requires an employer to recognize as a component of net periodic postretirement benefit cost the interest cost on the accumulated postretirement benefit obligation. The interest cost is equal to the increase in the amount of the obligation because of the passage of time, measured at a rate equal to the assumed discount rate. FAS-106 specifies that the interest cost component of net periodic postretirement benefit cost is not considered interest expense for purposes of applying FAS-34 (Capitalization of Interest Cost) (FAS-106, par. 48).

Actual Return on Plan Assets Component

If a plan is funded, one component of periodic postretirement benefit cost is the actual return on plan assets. The amount of the actual return on plan assets is equal to the difference between the fair value of plan assets at the beginning and end of a period, adjusted for employer contributions, employee contributions (if the plan is contributory) and postretirement benefits paid during the period.

Fair value is the amount that reasonably could be expected to result from a current sale of an investment between a willing buyer and a willing seller, that is, a sale other than a forced liquidation. Plan assets that are used in the operation of the postretirement benefit plan (e.g., building, equipment, furniture, fixtures) are valued at cost less accumulated depreciation or amortization. The actual return on plan assets is shown net of tax expense if the fund holding the plan assets is a taxable entity (FAS-106, par. 49).

A return on plan assets decreases the employer's cost of providing postretirement benefits to its employees, while a loss on plan assets increases postretirement benefit cost. Net periodic postretirement benefit income can result from a significantly high return on plan assets during a period.

Illustration of Actual Return on Plan Assets

An employer may determine its actual gain or loss on plan assets as follows:

Plan assets, beginning of year, at fair value	$ 200,000
Add: Amounts contributed to plan	750,000

Less: Benefit payments from plan	(650,000)
	300,000
Less: Plan assets, end of year, at fair value	340,000
Actual (return) loss on plan assets	$ (40,000)

OBSERVATION: Actual return on plan assets is one of the components of net periodic postretirement benefit cost. As discussed later in this chapter, FAS-106, as amended by FAS-132, requires this component to be disclosed in the notes to the financial statements. Another component of net postretirement benefit cost is gains and losses (discussed later in this chapter). The "gains and losses" component includes, among other items, "plan asset gains and losses," defined as the difference between the actual return and the expected return on plan assets.

The following example illustrates the combined effect on net periodic postretirement benefit cost of (a) actual return on plan assets and (b) plan asset gains and losses: If the actual return on plan assets is $1,000,000 and the expected return is $700,000, the plan asset gain is the $300,000 difference between the actual return and the expected return. This $300,000 plan asset gain is part of the "gains and losses" component of net periodic postretirement benefit cost, while the $1,000,000 actual return on plan assets is another component. The combined effect is a net decrease of $700,000 in net periodic postretirement benefit cost, the result of offsetting the $300,000 plan asset gain against the $1,000,000 actual return. This $700,000 is equal to the expected return on plan assets. The total amount of net periodic postretirement benefit cost will include the $700,000 as well as other components, including service cost, interest cost, etc. The $300,000 plan asset gain will be taken into account in computing in future years (a) the expected return on plan assets and (b) amortization of deferred gains and losses. (See discussion and illustration later in this chapter.)

Amortization of Prior Service Cost or Credit Component

When a postretirement benefit plan is initially adopted or amended, employees may be granted benefits for services performed in prior periods. The cost of postretirement benefits that are granted retroactively to employees is referred to as *prior service cost* (FAS-106, par. 50).

Under FAS-106, only a portion of the total amount of prior service cost arising in a period is included in net periodic postretirement benefit cost. FAS-106 requires that the total prior service cost arising in a period from the adoption or amendment of a plan be amortized in a systematic manner. *Amortization* of prior service cost is a component of net periodic postretirement benefit cost (FAS-106, par. 50).

Initiation of a plan, or amendment that improves benefits in an existing plan   When an employer initiates a plan or adopts an amendment that improves the benefits in an existing plan, the amount of prior service cost is the amount of increase in the accumulated postretirement benefit obligation that can be attributed to service of employees in prior periods (FAS-106, par. 50).

Methods of amortizing prior service cost   FAS-106 provides a number of rules regarding the amortization of prior service cost, as follows:

- General rule
- Special rule if all or most employees are fully eligible
- Simplified computation
- Accelerated amortization

Illustration of Plan Amendment Increasing Benefits

At the beginning of Year 2, Company A amended its plan, causing the accumulated postretirement benefit obligation to increase by $84,000. Active plan participants had an average of 12 remaining years of service before reaching full eligibility for benefits.

At the end of Year 2, the employer paid $60,000 in benefits. Service cost was $50,000.

The worksheets as of the end of Year 2 are as follows:

	Postretirement Benefit Cost	Accumulated Postretirement Benefit Obligation	Transition Obligation	Prior Service Cost
Beginning of year	NA	$(325,000)	$285,000	$ -0-
Plan amendment		(84,000)		84,000
Recognition of components of net periodic postretirement benefit cost:				
Service cost	(50,000)	(50,000)		
Interest cost[a]	(40,900)	(40,900)		
Amortization of transition obligation[b]	(15,000)		(15,000)	
Amortization of prior service cost[c]	(7,000)			(7,000)
	(112,900)	(174,900)	(15,000)	77,000
Benefit payments		60,000		
Net change		(114,900)	(15,000)	77,000
End of year[d]		$(439,900)	$270,000	$77,000

(a) 10% (assumed discount rate) of $325,000 (accumulated postretirement benefit obligation at beginning of year), plus 10% of $84,000 (increase in obligation by plan amendment)

(b) 20-year amortization of original $300,000 transition obligation

(c) Straight-line amortization of prior service cost, based on average remaining years of service (12 years) of active plan participants before reaching full eligibility

(d) The liability on the balance sheet at the end of year 2 ($439,900) equals the liability at the beginning of the year ($325,000) increased by the plan amendment ($84,000) and by the excess of service cost, interest cost, and expected return on plan assets ($90,900) over cash contributions ($60,000) during the year.

Analysis of postretirement benefit accounts:

	End of Year 1	Net Change	End of Year 2
Accumulated postretirement benefit obligation	$(325,000)	$(114,900)	$(439,900)
Plan assets at fair value	-0-		-0-
Funded status—Recognized as a liability on the balance sheet	(325,000)	(114,900)	(439,900)
Prior service cost	-0-	77,000	77,000
Transition obligation	285,000	(15,000)	270,000

- *General rule*: The general rule requires amortization of prior service cost in equal installments during each employee's remaining years of service until that employee reaches full eligibility under the new or amended plan (FAS-106, par. 51).

- *Special rule if all or most employees are fully eligible*: If all or almost all employees are already fully eligible for benefits when the plan is initiated or amended, the employer amortizes prior service cost over the remaining life expectancy of those employees (FAS-106, par. 52).

- *Simplified computation*: FAS-106 allows a simplified form of computation, provided it amortizes prior service cost more quickly than the methods described above. For example, instead of basing its amortization on the period during which each individual employee reaches full eligibility, an employer may amortize prior service cost over the *average* remaining years of service of all active plan participants until they reach full eligibility (FAS-106, par. 53).

- *Accelerated amortization*: An enterprise uses an accelerated method of amortization if a history of plan amendments and other evidence indicates that the employer's economic benefits from the initiation or amendment of the plan will be exhausted before the employees reach full eligibility for postretirement benefits. In this situation, amortization should reflect the period during which the employer expects to receive economic benefits from the existence of the plan (FAS-106, par. 54).

Plan amendments that reduce obligation   If a plan amendment reduces the accumulated postretirement obligation, the reduction (a negative prior service cost) is recognized as a credit to other comprehensive income. The prior service credit is amortized in accordance with the above rules after it is applied (*a*) to reduce any existing (positive) prior service cost included in accumulated other comprehensive income and (*b*) to reduce any transition obligation included in accumulated other comprehensive income (FAS-106, par. 55, as amended by FAS-158, par. D2, h).

Gain or Loss Component

The approach to gains and losses in FAS-106 is similar to that in FAS-87. Gains or losses consist of certain types of changes in (*a*) the accumulated postretirement benefit obligation and (*b*) the plan assets. The changes may result from either (*a*) experience different from that assumed or (*b*) changes in assumptions (FAS-106, par. 56).

Gains and losses include amounts that have been realized (for example, the sale of a security) and amounts that have not been realized (for example, changes in the market value of plan assets) (FAS-106, par. 56). Gains or losses that are not recognized immediately are included in other comprehensive income in the year they occur.

Elements of the gain or loss component   The gain or loss component of net periodic postretirement benefit cost is the combination of three elements (FAS-106, par. 62):

1. Plan asset gains and losses during the period
2. Other gains and losses immediately realized
3. Amortization of deferred gains and losses from previous periods and included in accumulated other comprehensive income

☛ **PRACTICE POINTER:**   The gain or loss component of net postretirement benefit cost does not include the actual return on plan assets during the period, which is another component of net periodic postretirement benefit cost, discussed earlier in this chapter.

The gain or loss component does include, among other items, the difference between the actual return and the expected return on plan assets, since this difference falls within the general concept of gains and losses according to FAS-106—

changes resulting from experience different from that assumed or from changes in assumptions.

Plan asset gains and losses   Plan asset gains and losses are the difference between the actual return (including earnings and holding gains/losses) and the expected return for the same period (FAS-106, par. 57).

The computation of plan asset gains and losses starts with determining the expected return on plan assets, which is computed by multiplying the following two items: (1) the expected long-term rate of return on plan assets and (2) the market-related value of plan assets. Plan asset gains and losses include both changes reflected in the market-related value of plan assets and changes not yet reflected in the market-related value of plan assets (FAS-106, par. 58).

The market-related value may be either fair market value or a calculation that recognizes changes in fair market value systematically over a period of five years or less. The employer may use different methods of calculating market-related value for different categories of assets, but each category must be treated consistently during successive periods (FAS-106, par. 57). FAS-106 requires plan asset gains and losses during the period to be included as a component of net periodic postretirement benefit cost.

> **OBSERVATION:** Plan asset gains and losses (excluding amounts not yet reflected in the market-related value of plan assets) are taken into account in computing the future expected return on plan assets. This year's plan asset gains and losses will therefore be reflected, in the computation of the expected return on plan assets, in future years' net periodic postretirement benefit cost. Plan asset gains and losses (excluding amounts not yet reflected in the market-related value of plan assets) are also taken into account in computing amortization of net gains and losses included in accumulated other comprehensive income.

Other gains and losses immediately realized   Immediate recognition of other types of gains and losses is required in some situations and permitted in others.

An employer recognizes an immediate gain or loss if it decides to deviate temporarily from its substantive plan, either by (*a*) forgiving a retrospective adjustment of the current or prior years' cost-sharing provisions as they relate to benefit costs already incurred by retirees or (*b*) otherwise changing the employer's share of benefit costs incurred in the current or prior periods (FAS-106, par. 61).

If immediate recognition of gains and losses is not required, an employer may elect to use a method that consistently recognizes gains and losses immediately, provided: (*a*) any gain that does not offset a loss previously recognized in income must first offset any transition obligation included in accumulated other comprehensive income and (*b*) any loss that does not offset a gain previously recognized in income must first offset any transition asset included in accumulated other comprehensive income (FAS-106, par. 60, as amended by FAS-158, par. D2).

Amortization of deferred gains and losses from previous periods Any gains and losses not recognized immediately as a component of net periodic benefit cost are immediately recognized in other comprehensive income. FAS-106 establishes a special formula to determine (*a*) whether an employer is required to amortize gains and losses included in accumulated other comprehensive income and (*b*) if amortization is required, the minimum amount of periodic amortization. FAS-106 allows other methods instead of those provided by the formula, if certain qualifications are met.

FAS-106 requires amortization of net gains and losses included in accumulated other comprehensive income if the beginning-of-year balance of net unrecognized gain or loss (with a modification noted below) is more than a base figure used for comparison purposes (FAS-106, par. 59).

The base figure is 10% of the greater of the accumulated postretirement benefit obligation or the market-related value of plan assets as of the beginning of the year (FAS-106, par. 59).

For purposes of this comparison, the gain or loss included in accumulated other comprehensive income is modified, so as to exclude any plan asset gains or losses that have not yet been reflected in market-related value.

> ☛ **PRACTICE POINTER:** If gains or losses included in accumulated other comprehensive income are not greater than the base figure, they come within the 10% "corridor" and the employer need not recognize them. This procedure is similar to the corridor test for recognizing gains and losses on pensions in accordance with FAS-87.

If amortization is required under the formula, the amount to be amortized is the difference between the beginning-of-year balance of net gain or loss (adjusted to exclude any plan asset gains or losses that have not yet been reflected in the market-related value) and the base figure.

The minimum amortization is the amount to be amortized, determined as above, divided by the average remaining service period of active plan participants. If all or almost all of the plan's participants are inactive, divide instead by the average remaining life expectancy of the inactive participants (FAS-106, par. 59).

Instead of using the minimum amortization method, an employer may use any other systematic method of amortization, provided that (*a*) the amortization for each period is at least as much as the amount determined by the minimum amortization method, (*b*) the method is used consistently, (*c*) the method applies consistently to gains and losses, and (*d*) the method is disclosed (FAS-106, par. 60).

Illustration of Gains and Losses

At the beginning of 20X5, Company L prepared the following projection of changes during that year:

	Postretire-ment Benefit Cost	Cash	Transition Obligation	Net Loss	Liability for Postretire-ment Benefit Plan	MEMO ACCT Accumulated Postretire-ment Benefit Obligation	MEMO ACCT Plan Assets
Beginning of year	NA	NA	$2,700,000		$302,500	($2,596,500)	($3,625,000)	($1,028,500)
Recognition of components of net periodic post-retirement benefit cost:							
Service cost	180,000					(180,000)	
Interest cost	326,250					(326,250)	
Amortization of transition obligation	150,000		(150,000)				
Amortization of unrecognized net loss							
Expected return on plan assets[(a)]	(96,850)						96,850
Assets contribu-ted to plan		(956,250)					956,250
Benefit payments from plan						450,000	(450,000)
Net expense or net change	559,400	(956,250)	(150,000)			(546,850)	(56,250)	603,100
End of year— projected	NA	NA	$2,550,000		$302,500	($2,049,650)	($3,681,250)	$1,631,600

(a)   See Schedule 1.

As of the end of 20X5, Company L prepared the following worksheet and supporting schedules to reflect actual changes during the year:

	Projected 12/31/X5	Net Gain (Loss)	Actual 12/31/X5
Accumulated postre-tirement benefit obligation	$(3,681,250)	$ 118,630[b]	$(3,562,620)
Plan assets at fair value	1,631,600	(110,180)[c]	1,521,420
Funded status—liability	(2,049,650)	8,450	(2,041,200)
Net (gain) loss	302,500	(8,450)	294,050
Transition obligation	2,550,000	—	2,550,000

(b) Liability at year-end was $118,630 less than projected, because of changes in assumptions not detailed here.

(c) See Schedule 1.

Net Periodic Postretirement Benefit Cost

Service cost	$180,000
Interest cost	326,250
Expected return on plan assets[d]	(96,850)
Amortization of transition obligation	150,000
Net periodic postretirement benefit cost	$559,400

(d) See Schedule 3.

Schedule 1—Plan Assets

Expected long-term rate of return on plan assets	10%
Beginning balance, market-related value[f]	$ 968,500
Contributions to plan (end of year)	956,250
Benefits paid by plan	(450,000)
Expected return on plan assets	96,850
	1,571,600
20% of each of last five years' asset gains (losses)	(7,036)
Ending balance, market-related value	$ 1,564,564
Beginning balance, fair value of plan assets	$ 1,028,500
Contributions to plan	956,250

Benefits paid	(450,000)
Actual return (loss) on plan assets[(g)]	(13,330)
Ending balance, fair value of plan assets	$ 1,521,420
Deferred asset gain (loss) for year[(h)]	$ (110,180)
Gain (loss) not included in ending balance market-related value[(i)]	$ (43,144)

(f)   This example adds 20% of each of the last five years' gains or losses.
(g)   See Schedule 3.
(h)   (Actual return on plan assets) – (expected return on plan assets). **Note:** The term *deferred asset gain (loss) for year* follows the terminology in the illustrations attached to FAS-106, although the text of FAS-106 refers to the same item as *plan asset gains and losses*.
(i)   (Ending balance, fair value of plan assets) – (ending balance, market-related value of plan assets).

Schedule 2—Amortization of Unrecognized Net Gain or Loss

10% of beginning balance of accumulated postretirement benefit obligation	$ 362,500
10% of beginning balance of market-related value of plan assets[(j)]	96,850
Greater of the above	$ 362,500
Unrecognized net (gain) loss at beginning of year	$ 302,500
Asset gain (loss) not included in beginning balance of market-related value[(k)] ($1,028,500 – $968,500)	60,000
Amount subject to amortization	$ 362,500
Amount in excess of the corridor subject to amortization	None
Required amortization	None

(j)   See Schedule 1.
(k)   See Schedule 1.

Schedule 3—Actual Return or Loss on Plan Assets

Plan assets at fair value, beginning of year	$1,028,500
Plus: Assets contributed to plan	956,250
Less: Benefit payments from plan	(450,000)
	1,534,750
Less: Plan assets at fair value, end of year	(1,521,420)
Actual (return) loss on plan assets	$ 13,330

Amortization of Transition Obligation/Asset Component

The final component of net periodic postretirement benefit cost is amortization of the transition obligation or asset at the date of initial application of FAS-106 that remains in accumulated other comprehensive income. At the beginning of the fiscal year in which FAS-106 is first applied, the funded status of the plan was computed by comparing the difference between (1) the accumulated postretirement benefit obligation and (2) the fair value of plan assets plus any recognized accrued postretirement benefit cost less any recognized prepaid postretirement benefit cost. The resulting difference, either a transition asset or transition obligation, can either be recognized immediately in net income or on a delayed basis as a component of net periodic postretirement benefit cost (FAS-106, par. 110).

If delayed recognition is chosen, the transition asset or obligation is generally recognized over the average remaining service period of active plan participants (FAS-106, par. 112). However, there are a number of exceptions to this general requirement:

- If the average remaining service period of active plan participants is less than 20 years, the transition asset or obligation can be amortized over 20 years.

- If all or almost all of the plan's participants are inactive, the transition asset or obligation can be amortized over the average remaining life expectancy of these plan participants.

- Amortization of the transition obligation (not transition asset) must be accelerated if cumulative benefit payments subsequent to the transition date exceed cumulative postretirement benefit cost accrued subsequent to the transition date. Additional amortization of the transition obligation is recognized to the extent that cumulative benefit payments exceed cumulative accrued postretirement benefit cost. Cumulative benefit payments include any payments related to a plan settlement and cumulative benefit payments are to be reduced by: (1) plan assets and (2) any recognized accrued postretirement benefit obligation, both measured as of the transition date.

RECOGNITION OF FUNDED STATUS OF POSTRETIREMENT BENEFIT PLANS

As a result of FAS-158, an employer is required to recognize the overfunded or underfunded status of a defined postretirement benefit plan as an asset or a liability in its statement of financial position. If the fair value of a postretirement benefit plan's assets exceeds the plan's accumulated postretirement benefit obligation, the plan is overfunded and an asset is recognized. If the plan's accumulated postretirement benefit obligation exceeds the fair value of the plan's assets, the plan is underfunded and a liability is recognized (FAS-106, par. 44A, as amended by FAS-158, par. D2d). When the funded status of the postretirement benefit plan is first recognized in the statement of financial position, the offsetting entry is to accumulated other comprehensive income (net of tax). The recognition of a postretirement benefit plan asset or liability may result in temporary differences under FAS-109 (Accounting for Income Taxes). Deferred tax effects are to be recognized for these temporary differences as a component of income tax expense or benefit in the year in which the differences arise, and allocated to various financial statement components.

Asset and liability gains and losses as well as prior service costs or credits that occur in periods after recognition of the funded status of the plan and that are not immediately included as a component of net periodic postretirement benefit cost are included in other comprehensive income. As gains and losses, prior service costs and credits, and the transition asset or obligation are included in net periodic postretirement benefit cost, they are recognized as an adjustment to other comprehensive income.

All postretirement benefit plans that are overfunded should be aggregated, and a noncurrent asset presented in the statement of financial position. All postretirement benefit plans that are underfunded should be aggregated, and a liability presented in the statement of financial position. The liability is current to the extent that the actuarial present value of benefits to be paid within the next year, or operating cycle if longer, exceeds the fair value of plan assets. This determination is to be made on a plan-by-plan basis. Otherwise, the liability is noncurrent (FAS-106, par. 44B, as amended by FAS-158, par. D2d).

☛ **PRACTICE POINTER:**   See Chapter 33, "Pension Plans," for examples of journal entries when applying FAS-158.

MEASUREMENT OF PLAN ASSETS

Plan assets generally are stocks, bonds, and other investments. Such assets may include the participation rights in participating insurance contracts, but not other rights in insurance contracts. The employer's own securities may be included as plan assets, but only if they are transferable and otherwise meet the conditions under FAS-106 (FAS-106, par. 63).

Plan assets are increased by various means, including the employer's contributions, employees' contributions if the plan is contributory, and earnings from investing the contributed amounts. Plan assets are decreased by benefit payments, income taxes, and other expenses (FAS-106, par. 63).

All plan assets should be segregated and restricted for paying postretirement benefits. Usually, the assets are in a trust. Plan assets may be withdrawn only for the stated purposes of the plan. In limited circumstances, the plan may permit withdrawal when the plan's assets exceed its obligations and the employer has taken appropriate steps to satisfy existing obligations (FAS-106, par. 64).

If assets are not segregated or restricted effectively in some other way, they are not plan assets even though the employer intends to use them for paying postretirement benefits. Contributions that are accrued but not yet paid into the plan are not regarded as plan assets (FAS-106, par. 64).

For purposes of disclosure, FAS-106 requires the employer to use fair value as the measurement for all plan investments, including equity or debt securities, real estate, and other items (FAS-106, par. 65). Fair value is determined in accordance with the guidance in FAS-157 (Fair Value Measurements). (Additional guidance on determining fair values can be found in the "Fair Value" chapter of this *Guide*.)

Plan assets used in plan operations, such as buildings, equipment, furniture and fixtures, and leasehold improvements, are measured at cost less accumulated depreciation or amortization (FAS-106, par. 66).

Insurance Contracts

Benefits covered by insurance contracts (defined below) are excluded from the accumulated postretirement benefit obligation. Insurance contracts are also excluded from plan assets, except for the amounts attributable to participation rights in participating insurance contracts.

Definition of Insurance Contracts

FAS-106 defines an *insurance contract* as a contract in which the insurance company unconditionally undertakes a legal obligation to provide specified benefits to specific individuals in return for a fixed premium. The contract must be irrevocable and must involve the transfer of significant risk from the employer (or the plan) to the insurance company. A contract does not qualify as an insurance contract if (*a*) the insurance company is a *captive insurer* doing business primarily with the employer and related parties or (*b*) there is any reasonable doubt that the insurance company will meet its obligations under the contract (FAS-106, par. 67).

Participating Insurance Contracts

Some contracts are *participating insurance contracts,* in which the purchaser (either the plan or the employer) participates in the experience of the insurance company. The purchaser's participation generally takes the form of a dividend that effectively reduces the cost of the plan. If, however, the employer's participation is so great that the employer retains all or most of the risks and rewards of the plan, the contract is not regarded as an insurance contract for purposes of FAS-106 (FAS-106, par. 68).

The purchase price of a participating contract ordinarily is higher than the price of a similar contract without the participation right. The difference between the price with and without the participation right is considered to be the cost of the participation right. The employer should regard this cost as an asset when purchased. At subsequent dates, the employer measures the participation right at its fair value if fair value can be estimated reasonably. Otherwise, the participation right is measured at its amortized cost, but this amount should not exceed the participation right's net realizable value. The cost is amortized systematically over the expected dividend period (FAS-106, par. 69).

Cost of Insurance

Insurance contracts, such as life insurance contracts, may be purchased during a period to cover postretirement benefits attributed to service by employees in the same period. In this situation, the cost of the benefits equals the cost of purchasing the insurance (after adjusting for the cost of any participation rights included in the contract) (FAS-106, par. 70).

Accordingly, if all postretirement benefits attributed to service by employees in the current period are covered by nonparticipating insurance contracts purchased during the same period, the cost of the benefits equals the cost of purchasing the insurance. If the benefits are only partially covered by nonparticipating insurance contracts, the uninsured portion of the benefits is accounted for in the same way as benefits under uninsured plans (FAS-106, par. 70).

Insurance Company Not Fully Bound

If the insurance company does not unconditionally undertake a legal obligation to pay specified benefits to specific individuals, the arrangement does not qualify as an insurance contract for purposes of FAS-106. The arrangement is accounted for as an investment at fair value (FAS-106, par. 71).

Fair value is presumed to equal the cash surrender value or conversion value, if any. In some cases, the best estimate of fair value is the contract value.

MEASUREMENT DATE

All postretirement benefit plan assets that are held as investments to provide postretirement benefits are generally measured at their fair values as of the date of the financial statements. There are two exceptions to this general rule. First, if a subsidiary sponsors a postretirement benefit plan and the subsidiary has a different year-end than its parent, the fair value of the subsidiary's postretirement benefit plan assets is measured at the date of the subsidiary's financial statements. Second, if an investee, accounted for using the equity method, sponsors a postretirement benefit plan and the investee has a different year-end than the investor, the fair value of the investee's postretirement benefit plan assets is measured at the date of the investee's financial statements (FAS-106, par. 72, as amended by FAS-158, par. D2n).

> **OBSERVATION:** The requirement to measure the fair value of postretirement benefit plan assets at the financial statement date is not effective until fiscal years ending after December 15, 2008. Prior to this date, and consistent with the existing requirements of FAS-106, an entity can measure the fair value of postretirement benefit plan assets at year-end or using a date within three months of year-end.

Unless more current amounts are available for both the obligation and plan assets, the funded status of the postretirement benefit plan reported in interim financial statements shall be the same amount as reported by the employer in its previous year-end statement of financial position, adjusted for subsequent accruals of service cost, interest cost, and return on plan assets, contributions, and benefit payments (FAS-106, par. 73, as amended by FAS-158, par. D2o).

DISCLOSURES

The disclosure requirements of FAS-106 were replaced by FAS-132 (R), and amended by FAS-158 and consolidated with the disclosure of information about pensions. They are covered in the chapter titled "Pension Plans" in this *Guide*.

EMPLOYERS WITH TWO OR MORE PLANS

FAS-106 deals with the questions of measurement and disclosure separately for an employer with two or more plans and for employers with one plan.

Aggregate Measurement

FAS-106 generally requires an employer with two or more plans to measure each plan separately. An employer may measure its plans as an aggregate rather than as separate plans, however, if the plans meet the following criteria (FAS-106, pars. 75 and 76):

- The plans provide postretirement health care benefits
- The plans provide either of the following:
  — Different benefits to the same group of employees
  — The same benefits to different groups of employees

- The plans are unfunded (without any plan assets)
- The employer aggregates all of its plans that meet the preceding three tests.

An employer may make a separate aggregation of plans providing welfare benefits (that is, postretirement benefits other than health care), if requirements (2) through (4) above are met. However, a plan that has plan assets should not be aggregated with other plans, but should be measured separately (FAS-106, par. 76).

MULTIEMPLOYER PLANS

A *multiemployer plan* is one to which two or more unrelated employers contribute. Multiemployer plans generally result from *collective bargaining agreements*, and are administered by a joint board of trustees representing management and labor of all contributing employers. Sometimes these plans are called *joint trusts*, *Taft–Hartley*, or *union plans*. An employer may participate in a number of plans; for example, the employees may belong to a number of unions. Numerous employers may participate in a multiemployer plan. Often the employers are in the same industry, but sometimes the employers are in different industries, and the only common element among the employers is that their employees belong to the same labor union (FAS-106, par. 80).

The assets contributed by one employer may be used to provide benefits to employees of other employers, since the assets contributed by one employer are not segregated from those contributed by other employers. Even though the plan provides defined benefits to employees of all the employers, the plan typically requires a defined contribution from each participating employer, but the amount of an employer's obligation may be changed by events affecting other participating employers and their employees (FAS-106, par. 79).

A multiemployer plan can exist even without the involvement of a labor union. For example, a national not-for-profit organization may organize a multiemployer plan for itself and its local chapters.

Accounting for Multiemployer Plans

Distinctive accounting requirements apply to an employer that participates in a multiemployer plan. The employer recognizes as net postretirement benefit cost the contribution required for the period, including cash and the fair value of noncash contributions. The employer recognizes as a liability any unpaid contributions required for the period (FAS-106, par. 81).

> **OBSERVATION:**
> - This accounting resembles that required for the single employer that has a *defined contribution plan* (see section titled "Defined Contribution Plans").
> - By participating in a multiemployer plan, an employer that has a *defined benefit plan* accounts for it essentially as if it were a *defined contribution plan.* The financing of the plan is, in effect, off-balance-sheet.

The following disclosures are required for multiemployer plans, separate from disclosures for any single-employer plan (FAS-132, par. 10):

- The amount of contributions to multiemployer plans during the period.

- A description of the nature and effect of any changes affecting comparability (e.g., a change in the rate of employer contributions, a business combination, or a divestiture).

> ☛ **PRACTICE POINTER:** The total contributions made to multiemployer plans may be disclosed without separately disclosing the amount attributable to pensions and other postretirement benefits.

Withdrawal from Multiemployer Plans

When an employer withdraws from a multiemployer plan, the employer may be contractually liable to pay into the plan a portion of its unfunded accumulated postretirement benefit obligation.

> **OBSERVATION:** Contractual obligations are the only ones facing the employer that withdraws from a multiemployer **postretirement** benefit plan. In contrast, an employer that withdraws from a multiemployer **pension** plan is subject not only to contractual obligations, but also to statutory obligations under the Multiemployer Pension Plan Amendments Act of 1980.

An employer should apply FAS-5 if withdrawal from the plan is probable or reasonably possible, and the employer will incur an obligation as a result (FAS-132, par. 11).

Obligation under "Maintenance of Benefits" Clause

An employer should also apply FAS-5 if it is probable or reasonably possible that the employer's contribution to the multiemployer plan will increase during the remainder of the contract period under a "maintenance of benefits" clause, to make up for a shortfall in the funding of the plan to assure the full level of benefits described in the plan (FAS-106, par. 83).

MULTIPLE-EMPLOYER PLANS

A multiple-employer plan is distinct from a multiemployer plan. In a *multiple-employer* plan, individual employers combine their single-employer plans for pooling assets for investment purposes, or for reducing the costs of administration. The participating employers may have different benefit formulas; each employer's contributions to the plan are based on that employer's benefit formula. These plans generally are not the result of collective bargaining agreements.

Each employer should account for its interest in a multiple-employer plan as if that interest were a single-employer plan (FAS-106, par. 84).

> **OBSERVATION:** If an employer is a participant in a multiple-employer plan, the employer should consider disclosing this fact, as well as the other information included in the required disclosures about single-employer plans.

PLANS OUTSIDE THE UNITED STATES

FAS-106 applies to plans outside as well as inside the United States. If the accumulated postretirement obligation of the plans outside the United States is significant in proportion to the total of all the employer's postretirement benefit plans, the employer should make separate disclosure of the plans outside the United States. Otherwise, the employer may make combined disclosure of plans outside and inside the United States (FAS-106, par. 85 and par. 381).

> **OBSERVATION:** FAS-106 does not define *outside the United States*. The following factors, among others, may be relevant: (a) where all or most of the employees and beneficiaries are located and (b) which country's law governs the relationships among employees, beneficiaries, and the employer.

BUSINESS COMBINATIONS

If an employer sponsors a single-employer defined benefit post-retirement plan, and the employer is acquired in a business combination treated as a purchase, the allocation of the purchase price must reflect the existence of the plan, once FAS-106 is adopted. To do this, the allocation should reflect either (*a*) a liability (for the excess of the accumulated postretirement benefit obligation over the plan assets) or (*b*) an asset (for the excess of the plan assets over the accumulated postretirement benefit obligation) (FAS-106, par. 86).

For purposes of this allocation, plan assets are measured at fair value. The accumulated postretirement benefit obligation is measured based on the benefits attributable to employee service rendered to the acquired employer before consummation of the business combination. This amount should be adjusted to reflect (*a*) any changes in assumptions based on the purchaser's assessment of future events and (*b*) any changes the purchaser makes in the substantive plan (FAS-106, par. 86).

Benefit Improvements Attributed to Prior Service

If benefits of an existing plan are improved in connection with a business combination treated as a purchase, and all or part of the improvement is attributable to employee service prior to the consummation date of the purchase, the accounting depends on whether the improvement was a condition of the purchase agreement.

If the improvement was a condition of the agreement, the improvement should be accounted for as part of the purchase agreement, and not as prior service cost, even though all or part of the improvement is attributable to prior service. On the other hand, if the improvement was not a condition of the agreement, the improvement should be accounted for as prior service cost to the extent the improvement is attributable to prior service (FAS-106, par. 87).

Termination or Curtailment

If a postretirement benefit plan is likely to be terminated or curtailed when an employer is acquired in a business combination accounted for as a purchase, the effect of the anticipated termination or curtailment should be taken into account in measuring the accumulated postretirement benefit obligation at the time of acquisition (FAS-106, par. 87).

Anticipate Additional Liabilities Only If Certain or Probable

In connection with a purchase-type acquisition, the purchaser should anticipate additional liabilities only if their occurrence is either (*a*) certain (for example, when the additional liability is a condition of the acquisition agreement) or (*b*) probable (as indicated by the circumstances).

> **OBSERVATION:** The "Basis for Conclusions" indicates that, in the context of purchase-type acquisitions, an enterprise participating in a **multiemployer** plan should not recognize additional liabilities to the plan, unless specific conditions exist that make additional liabilities probable. The FASB was not convinced that an obligation for future contributions to a multiemployer plan ordinarily exists, or that an employer should recognize any contractual withdrawal liability unless withdrawal is probable.

Elimination of Unrecognized Items

When an employer applies the preceding provisions for business combinations, the result will be the elimination of the following preexisting items of the acquired employer:

- Net gain or loss included in accumulated other comprehensive income

- Prior service cost or credit included in accumulated other comprehensive income

- Transition obligation or transition asset included in accumulated other comprehensive income (FAS-106, par. 88, as amended by FAS-158, par. D2p).

After the acquisition, the difference between the amount contributed and the net periodic postretirement benefit cost will reduce the liability or asset recognized at the time of the acquisition, to the extent the net obligation assumed or the net asset acquired is taken into account in determining the amount of contributions to the plan (FAS-106, par. 88).

SETTLEMENT AND CURTAILMENT OF A POSTRETIREMENT BENEFIT OBLIGATION

According to FAS-106, a *settlement* is a transaction that has the following characteristics (FAS-106, par. 90):

- Is an irrevocable action
- Relieves the employer (or the plan) of primary responsibility for the postretirement benefit obligation
- Eliminates significant risks related to the obligation and the assets used to put the settlement into effect

Settlements take place, for example, in the following situations (FAS-106, par. 90):

- The employer makes lump-sum cash payments to plan participants, buying their rights to receive future specified postretirement benefits.

- The employer purchases long-term nonparticipating insurance contracts to cover the accumulated postretirement benefit obligation for some or all of the participants in the plan (but the insurance company cannot be under the employer's control).

Settlements do *not* take place, however, in the following situations (FAS-106, par. 91):

- The employer purchases an insurance contract from an insurance company controlled by the employer. This does not qualify as a settlement because the employer is still exposed to risk through its relationship with the insurance company.

- The employer invests in high-quality fixed-income securities with principal and income payment dates similar to the estimated due dates of benefits. This does not qualify as a settlement because (a) the investment decision can be revoked, (b) the purchase of the securities does not relieve the employer or the plan of primary responsibility for the postretirement benefit obligation, and (c) the purchase of the securities does not eliminate significant risks related to the postretirement benefit obligation.

Accounting for a Plan Settlement

Maximum Gain or Loss

When a postretirement benefit obligation is settled, the maximum gain or loss to be recognized in income is the gain or loss plus any transition asset included in accumulated other comprehensive income. This maximum gain or loss includes any gain or loss resulting from the remeasurement of plan assets and of the accumulated postretirement benefit obligation at the time of settlement (FAS-106, par. 92, as amended by FAS-158, par. D2q).

Settlement Gain or Loss When Entire Obligation Is Settled

If an employer settles the entire accumulated postretirement benefit obligation, a further distinction is made depending on whether the maximum amount subject to recognition is a gain or a loss.

If the maximum amount is a gain, the amount of this gain first reduces any transition obligation remaining in accumulated other comprehensive income and any excess gain is recognized in income. If the maximum amount is a loss, the full amount of this loss is recognized in income (FAS-106, par. 93, as amended by FAS-158, par. D2r).

Settlement Gain or Loss When Only Part of Obligation Is Settled

If an employer settles only part of the accumulated postretirement benefit obligation, the employer recognizes in income a pro rata portion of the amount of gain or loss that would have been recognized if the entire obligation had been settled. The pro rata portion equals the percentage by which the partial settlement reduces the accumulated postretirement benefit obligation (FAS-106, par. 93).

Participating Insurance

If an employer settles the obligation by purchasing a participating insurance contract, the cost of the participation right is deducted from the maximum gain but not from the maximum loss, before the employer determines the amount to be recognized in income (FAS-106, par. 94).

Settlements at Lower Cost Than Current Cost of Service and Interest

FAS-106 defines the *cost of a settlement* as follows (FAS-106, par. 95):

- If the settlement is for cash, its cost is the amount of cash paid to plan participants.

- If the settlement uses nonparticipating insurance contracts, its cost is the cost of the contracts.

- If the settlement uses participating insurance contracts, its cost is the cost of the contracts, less the amount attributed to participation rights.

If the cost of all settlements during a year is no more than the combined amount of service cost and interest cost components of net postretirement benefit cost for the same year, FAS-106 permits but does not require the employer to recognize gain or loss for those settlements. The employer should apply a consistent policy each year (FAS-106, par. 95).

Accounting for a Plan Curtailment

A *curtailment* is an event that either (*a*) significantly reduces the expected years of future service of active plan participants or (*b*) eliminates the accrual of defined benefits for some or all of the future services of a significant number of active plan participants. The following events are examples of curtailments (FAS-106, par. 96):

- Termination of employees' services earlier than anticipated. (This may or may not relate to the closing of a facility or the discontinuation of a segment of the employer's business.)

- Termination or suspension of a plan, so that employees no longer earn additional benefits for future service. (If the plan is suspended, future service may be counted toward eligibility for benefits accumulated based on past service.)

Gain and Loss Recognition

Under the general provisions of FAS-106 for plans that continue without curtailment, the employer should recognize prior service cost on an amortized basis, on the theory that the employer receives economic benefits from the future services of employees covered by the plan.

When a plan is curtailed, the employer's expectation of receiving benefits from future services of its employees is reduced. Accordingly, curtailment requires the employer to recognize as a loss all or part of the remaining balance of prior service cost included in accumulated other comprehensive income. In this context, prior service cost includes the cost of plan amendments and any transition obligation remaining in accumulated other comprehensive income (FAS-106, par. 97, as amended by FAS-158, par. D2s).

Curtailment Resulting from Termination of Employees

If a curtailment occurs as the result of the termination of a significant number of employees who were plan participants, the curtailment loss consists of the following components (FAS-106, par. 97, as amended by FAS-158, par. D2s):

- The portion of the remaining prior service cost included in accumlated other comprehensive income (relating to this and any prior plan amendment) attributable to the previously estimated number of remaining future years of service of all terminated employees, **plus**

- The portion of the remaining transition obligation included in accumulated other comprehensive income attributable to the previously estimated number of remaining future years of service, but only of the terminated employees who were participants in the plan at the date of transition to FAS-106.

Curtailment Resulting from Terminating Accrual of Additional Benefits for Future Services

If a curtailment results from terminating the accrual of additional benefits for the future services of a significant number of employees, the curtailment loss consists of the following components (FAS-106, par. 97, as amended by FAS-158, par. D2s):

- *The **pro rata** amount of the remaining prior service cost included in accumulated other comprehensive income*—This amount is based on the portion of the remaining expected years of service in the amortization period that originally was attributable to the employees (a) who were plan participants at the date of the plan amendment and (b) whose future accrual of benefits has been terminated, **plus**

- *The **pro rata** amount of the remaining transition obligation included in accumulated other comprehensive income*—This amount is based on the portion of the remaining years of service of all participants who were active at the date of transition to FAS-106, that originally was attributable to the remaining expected future years of service of the employees whose future accrual of benefits has been terminated.

Changes in Accumulated Postretirement Benefit Obligation

A curtailment may cause a gain by decreasing the accumulated post-retirement benefit obligation, or a loss by increasing that obligation.

If a curtailment decreases the accumulated obligation, the gain from this decrease is first used to offset any net loss included in accumulated other comprehensive income and the excess is a curtailment gain. If a curtailment increases the accumulated obligation, the loss from this increase is first used to offset any net gain included in accumulated other comprehensive income and the excess is a curtailment loss. In this context, any remaining transition asset is regarded as a net gain, and is combined with the net gain or loss included in accumulated other comprehensive income (FAS-106, par. 98, as amended by FAS-158, par. D2t).

If a curtailment produces a net loss as the combined effect of the above calculations regarding prior service cost and the accumulated postretirement benefit obligation, this combined net loss is recognized in income when it is *probable* that a curtailment will occur and the net effect of the curtailment is reasonably estimable. If the sum of these effects results in a net gain, however, the net gain is recognized in income when the affected employees terminate or the plan suspension or amendment is adopted (FAS-106, par. 99).

Illustration of Curtailment

Company B reduced its workforce, including a significant number of employees who had been accumulating benefits under the postretirement benefit plan. An analysis of the terminated employees revealed:

1. At the time of curtailment, the terminated employees represented 22% of the *remaining years of expected service* of all employees who had been plan participants at the employer's date of transition.

2. At the time of curtailment, the terminated employees represented 18% of the *remaining years of service prior to full eligibility* of all employees who had been plan participants at the date of a prior plan amendment.

Company B's worksheet computation of the curtailment gain or loss is as follows:

	Before Curtailment	*Curtailment*	*After Curtailment*
Accumulated postretire-ment benefit obligation	$(514,000)	$108,000	$(406,000)
Plan assets at fair value	146,000		146,000
Funded status	(368,000)	108,000	(260,000)
Net gain	(89,150)		(89,150)
Prior service cost[a]	66,000	(11,880)	54,120
Transition obligation[b]	390,000	(85,800)	304,200

(a) Effect of curtailment is 18% of $66,000 (prior service cost).
(b) Effect of curtailment is 22% of $390,000 (transition obligation).

Relationship of Settlements and Curtailments to Other Events

An event may be either a settlement, or a curtailment, or both at the same time (FAS-106, par. 100).

A curtailment occurs, but not a settlement, if the expected future benefits are eliminated for some plan participants (for example, because their employment is terminated), but the plan continues to exist, to pay benefits, to invest assets, and to receive contributions.

A settlement occurs, but not a curtailment, if an employer purchases nonparticipating insurance contracts to cover the accumulated postretirement benefit obligation, while continuing to provide defined benefits for future service (either in the same plan or in a successor plan).

A termination, or in effect both a settlement and curtailment, occurs if an employer settles its obligation and terminates the plan without establishing a successor defined benefit plan to take its place. This occurs whether the employees continue to work for the employer or not.

Illustration of Partial Settlement and Full Curtailment Resulting from Sale of Line of Business

Company C sold a line of business to Company D. Company C has a separate postretirement benefit plan that provides benefits to retirees of the division that is sold. In connection with the sale:

1. Company C terminated all employees of the sold division (a full curtailment).
2. Company D hired most of the employees.
3. Company D assumed the accumulated postretirement benefit obligation of $160,000 for postretirement benefits related to the former employees of Company C hired by Company D, and Company C retained the obligation for its current retirees (a partial settlement).
4. The plan trustee transferred $200,000 of plan assets to Company D, consisting of $160,000 for the settlement of the accumulated postretirement benefit obligation and $40,000 as an excess contribution.
5. Company C determined that its gain on the sale of the division was $600,000, before considering any of the effects of the sale on the postretirement benefit plan.

Company C's accounting policy is to determine the effects of a curtailment before determining the effects of a settlement when both events occur simultaneously.

For Company C, the net loss from the curtailment is $456,000, which is recognized with the $600,000 gain resulting from the disposal of the division. The effect of the curtailment is determined as follows:

	Before Curtailment	Curtailment-Related Effects Resulting from Sale	After Curtailment
Accumulated postretirement benefit obligation	$(514,000)	$ (20,000)[a]	$(534,000)
Plan assets at fair value	220,000		220,000
Funded status	(294,000)	(20,000)	(314,000)
Net gain	(99,150)	20,000[a]	(79,150)
Prior service cost	66,000	(66,000)[b]	—
Transition obligation	390,000	(390,000)[c]	—

(a) Loss from earlier-than-expected retirement of fully eligible employees (not detailed here)
(b) 100% (reduction in remaining years for service to full eligibility) of the unrecognized prior service cost
(c) 100% (reduction in remaining years for service to full eligibility) of the unrecognized transition obligation

The $16,255 loss related to the settlement and transfer of plan assets that is recognized with the gain from the sale is determined as follows:

	After Curtailment	Settlement and Transfer of Plan Assets	After Settlement
Accumulated postretirement benefit obligation	$(534,000)	$160,000	$(374,000)
Plan assets at fair value	220,000	(200,000)	20,000
Funded status	(314,000)	(40,000)	(354,000)
Net gain	(79,150)	23,745[d]	(55,405)
Prior service cost	—	—	—
Transition obligation	—	—	—
Computation of loss on settlement and transfer	$(393,150)	$ (16,255)	$(409,405)

(d) The unrecognized net gain is computed as follows:

Step 1. Compute the percentage of the accumulated postretirement benefit obligation settled to the total accumulated postretirement benefit obligation ($160,000/$534,000 = 30%).

Step 2. Maximum gain is measured as the transition asset, plus any net gain included in other comprehensive income ($79,150 + $0 = $79,150).

Step 3. The settlement gain is 30% of $79,150 = $23,745.

MEASUREMENT OF THE EFFECTS OF TERMINATION BENEFITS

If an employer offers postretirement benefits as special termination benefits that are not required by any preexisting contract, the employer recognizes a liability and a loss when the employees accept the offer and the amount is reasonably estimable. If the employer is contractually obliged to provide postretirement benefits as termination benefits, the employer recognizes a liability and a loss when it is probable that benefits will be paid and the amount is reasonably estimable (FAS-106, par. 101).

If an employer offers special or contractual termination benefits and curtails the postretirement benefit plan at the same time, FAS-106 requires the employer to account separately for the termination benefits and the curtailment (FAS-106, par. 101).

The amount of the liability and loss to be recognized when employees accept an offer of termination benefits in the form of postretirement benefits is determined by taking the following steps (FAS-106, par. 102):

Step 1.   Determine the accumulated postretirement benefit obligation for those employees (without including any special termination benefits), on the assumption that (a) any of those employees who are not yet fully eligible for benefits will terminate as soon as they become fully eligible, and (b) any of those employees who are fully eligible will retire immediately.

Step 2.   Adjust the accumulated postretirement benefit obligation as computed in Step 1 to reflect the special termination benefits.

Step 3.   Subtract the amount in Step 1 from the amount in Step 2.

DEFINED CONTRIBUTION PLANS

A *defined contribution plan* provides an individual account for each participant, and specifies how to determine the amount to be contributed to each individual's account. The plan does not specify the amount of postretirement benefits to be received by any individual. This amount is determined by the amount of contributions, the return on the investment of the amount contributed, and any forfeitures of the benefits of other plan participants that are allocated to the individual's account (FAS-106, par. 104).

Accounting for Contributions

A defined contribution plan may require the employer to contribute to the plan only for periods in which an employee renders services, or the employer may be required to continue making payments for periods after the employee retires or terminates employment. To the extent an employer's contribution is made in the same period as the employee renders services, the employer's net periodic postretirement benefit cost equals the amount of contributions required for that period. If the plan requires the employer to continue contributions after the employee retires or terminates, the employer should make accruals during the employee's service period of the estimated amount of contributions to be made after the employee's retirement or termination (FAS-106, par. 105).

Disclosure

The disclosure requirements for defined contribution plans are consolidated with disclosure requirements for both pension and other postretirement plans. They are covered in the chapter titled "Pension Plans" in this *Guide*.

POSTEMPLOYMENT BENEFITS

FAS-112 specifies GAAP for postemployment benefits and generally applies to benefits provided to former or inactive employees, their beneficiaries, and covered dependents after employment, but before retirement. Benefits may be provided in cash or in kind and may be paid as a result of a disability, layoff, death, or other event. Benefits may be paid immediately upon cessation of active employment, or over a specified period of time.

Postemployment benefits that meet the following conditions of FAS-43 shall be accounted for in accordance with that Statement (FAS-112, par. 6):

- The employer's obligation relating to employees' rights to receive compensation for future compensated absences is attributable to employees' services already rendered.
- The obligation relates to rights that vest or accumulate.
- Payment of the compensation is probable.
- The amount can be estimated reasonably.

Postemployment benefits that are covered by FAS-112 but do not meet the above criteria of FAS-43 are accounted for in accordance with FAS-5. FAS-5 requires recognition of a loss contingency, including a liability for postemployment benefits, when the following conditions are met (FAS-112, par. 6):

- Information available prior to issuance of the financial statements indicates that it is probable that an asset has been impaired or a liability incurred at the date of the financial statements.
- The amount of loss can be reasonably estimated.

If an obligation for postemployment benefits is not accrued in accordance with either FAS-43 or FAS-5 only because the amount cannot be estimated, the financial statements shall disclose that fact (FAS-112, par. 7).

RELATED CHAPTERS IN 2009 *GAAP GUIDE* LEVEL A

Chapter 4, "Business Combinations"
Chapter 10, "Deferred Compensation Contracts"
Chapter 16, "Fair Value"
Chapter 24, "Interest Costs Capitalized"
Chapter 33, "Pension Plans"
Chapter 40, "Results of Operations"

RELATED CHAPTERS IN 2009 *GAAP GUIDE* LEVELS B, C, AND D

Chapter 6, "Business Combinations"
Chapter 29, "Pension Plans—Employers"
Chapter 30, "Pension Plans—Settlements and Curtailments"
Chapter 32, "Postemployment and Postretirement Benefits Other Than Pensions"
Chapter 35, "Results of Operations"

RELATED CHAPTERS IN 2009 *INTERNATIONAL ACCOUNTING/FINANCIAL REPORTING STANDARDS GUIDE*

Chapter 7, "Business Combinations"
Chapter 13, "Employee Benefits"
Chapter 16, "Financial Instruments"

CHAPTER 35
PRODUCT FINANCING ARRANGEMENTS

CONTENTS

OVERVIEW

A *product financing arrangement* is a transaction in which an enterprise sells and agrees to repurchase inventory at a purchase price equal to the original sale price plus carrying and financing costs, or other similar transaction. In certain circumstances, a transaction labeled a *sale* is, in substance, a product financing arrangement and should be treated as such.

GAAP for product financing arrangements are included in the following pronouncement:

FAS-49   Accounting for Product Financing Arrangements

BACKGROUND

Product financing arrangements usually provide for one entity to obtain inventory or product for another entity (the sponsor), which agrees to purchase the inventory or product at specific prices over a specific period. The agreed-upon prices usually include financing and holding costs. The following are examples of common types of product financing arrangements (FAS-49, par. 3):

- A sponsor sells inventory or product to another entity and in a related arrangement agrees to buy the inventory or product back.

- An entity agrees to purchase a product or inventory for a sponsor, who, in a related arrangement, agrees to buy the product or inventory from the first entity.

- A sponsor, by arrangement, controls the product or inventory purchased or held by another entity.

In all of the above examples of product financing arrangements, the sponsor agrees to purchase, over a specified period, the product or inventory from the other entity at prearranged prices. The substance of a product financing arrangement, regardless of its legal form, is that of a financing arrangement rather than a sale or purchase by the sponsor.

> ☛ **PRACTICE POINTER:** Distinguishing a product financing arrangement from the outright sale of products may require careful professional judgment. Usually it will require an analysis and consideration of two related transactions rather than a single transaction. For example, if a sponsor sells inventory or product to another entity and in a separate agreement contracts to buy the inventory or product back, the initial transaction may appear to be a sale. Only when the two transactions (i.e., the "sale" and the later repurchase) are combined is the true substance of the transaction apparent. In applying GAAP for product financing arrangements, an important dimension is the follow-through analysis and understanding of the subsequent transaction.

Other factors that may be present in a product financing arrangement are (FAS-49, par. 4):

- The entity that provides the financing arrangement to the sponsor is an existing trust, nonbusiness entity or credit grantor, or was formed for the sole purpose of providing the financing arrangement to the sponsor.

- Small quantities of the product involved in the financing arrangement may be sold by the financing entity, but most of the product is ultimately used or sold by the sponsor.

- The product is stored on the sponsor's premises.

- The sponsor guarantees the debt of the other entity.

For purposes of FAS-49 (Accounting for Product Financing Arrangements), unmined or unharvested natural resources and financial instruments are not considered products. Thus, they are not covered by the provisions of FAS-49 (FAS-49, par. 5).

> **OBSERVATION:** No mention is made in FAS-49 as to how a product financing arrangement involving unmined or unharvested natural resources should be accounted for. For example, X Company enters into a financing arrangement with Y Company wherein Y Company acquires 10,000 acres of unharvested

timberlands for the sole benefit of X Company. X Company guarantees the bank loan that was necessary to acquire the timberlands and agrees to purchase the processed timber from Y Company at specified prices over a specified period. The specified prices include (a) the cost of the timber, (b) processing costs, (c) interest costs on the bank loan, and (d) a handling fee. Only the standing timber was purchased and not the land.

It appears that the provisions of FAS-49 are appropriate for this type of transaction, but FAS-49 does not expressly cover this situation.

In a product financing arrangement, the specified prices that the sponsor must pay cannot be subject to change except for fluctuations because of finance and holding costs. The specified prices may be stated or determinable by reference to the substance of the arrangement, such as (*a*) resale price guarantees or (*b*) options that, in substance, compel or require the sponsor to purchase the product. In addition, the cost of the product and related costs to the other entity must be covered substantially by the specified prices that the seller must pay for the product. Related costs include interest, holding costs, and other fees charged by the other entity (FAS-49, par. 5).

ACCOUNTING FOR PRODUCT FINANCING ARRANGEMENTS

An arrangement that contains the characteristics of a product financing arrangement is accounted for by the sponsor of the arrangement as follows (FAS-49, par. 8):

- If an entity buys a product from a sponsor and in a related arrangement agrees to sell the product, or a processed product containing the original product, back to the sponsor, no sale is recorded and the product remains an asset on the sponsor's books. Also, the sponsor records a liability in the amount of the proceeds received from the other entity under the provisions of the product financing arrangement.

- If an entity buys a product for a sponsor's benefit and the sponsor agrees, in a related arrangement, to buy the product, or a processed product containing the original product, back from the other entity, an asset and the related liability are recorded by the sponsor at the time the other entity acquires the product.

Excluding processing costs, the difference between (*a*) the regular product cost the sponsor would have paid if there were no product financing arrangement and (*b*) the cost the sponsor actually pays under the terms of the product financing arrangement is accounted for by the sponsor as financing and holding costs. These financing and holding costs are recorded on the books of the sponsor in accordance with its regular accounting policies for such costs, even though the costs are incurred and paid directly by the other entity (FAS-49, par. 9).

Separately identified interest costs that the sponsor pays as part of the specified prices may qualify for interest capitalization under FAS-34 (Capitalization of Interest Cost). If not, the separately identified interest costs actually paid by the sponsor are included in the total interest costs incurred during the period (FAS-49, par. 9).

Illustration of Accounting for Product Financing Arrangements

Assume that each of the following situations meets the definition of a product financing arrangement (PFA) in accordance with FAS-49. In each situation, Walsh is the sponsor and Foster is the purchaser. Following are the appropriate journal entries for Walsh.

Case 1: Walsh sells inventory costing $800 to Foster for $1,000 and agrees to repurchase the same inventory for $1,050 in 30 days.

Cash (or receivable)	1,000	
Due to Foster under PFA		1,000
Inventory under PFA	800	
Inventory		800

Case 2: Walsh arranges for Foster to purchase inventory costing $1,000 from a third party and agrees to purchase that inventory from Foster for $1,050 in 30 days.

Inventory under PFA	1,000	
Due to Foster under PFA		1,000

Case 3: Walsh sells inventory costing $700 to Foster for $800 and agrees to a resale price of $1,000 to outside parties.

Cash (or receivable)	800	
Due to Foster under PFA		800
Inventory under PFA	700	
Inventory		700

Case 4: Walsh arranges for Foster to acquire inventory from an outside party for $750 and guarantees the resale price to outside parties for $850.

Inventory under PFA	750	
Due to Foster under PFA		750

RELATED CHAPTER IN 2009 *GAAP GUIDE*
LEVEL A

Chapter 31, "Long-Term Obligations"

CHAPTER 36
PROPERTY TAXES

CONTENTS

OVERVIEW

GAAP for real and personal property taxes are found in the following pronouncement:

    ARB-43   Chapter 10A, Real and Personal Property Taxes

Generally, the basis for recognizing expense for property taxes is monthly accrual on the taxpayers' books over the fiscal period of the taxing authority for which the taxes are levied. At the end of the accounting period, the financial statements will show the appropriate accrual or prepayment.

> **OBSERVATION:** Accounting Research Bulletins were not intended to be officially promulgated GAAP at the time they were adopted by the Committee on Accounting Procedure. Instead, they reflected the views of the members and were intended as general guidance. ARBs were elevated to the status of GAAP by the Accounting Principles Board. As a result, obsolete and sometimes inappropriate material from ARBs now constitute GAAP. Moreover, ARBs were developed in an era in which the emphasis was primarily on revenue and expense reporting. That viewpoint contrasts with the asset-liability viewpoint of today. The asset–liability perspective of the FASB Concepts Statements suggests that a liability be measured for real and personal property taxes at the end of each reporting year. The amount of expense is the difference between two liability amounts.

BACKGROUND

FASB Concepts Statements (CONs) constitute the FASB's conceptual framework. In CON-6 (Elements of Financial Statements), *liabilities* are defined as probable future sacrifices of economic benefits arising from present obligations of a particular entity to transfer assets or provide services to other entities in the future as a result of past transactions or events. A liability has three essential characteristics:

1. It embodies a present duty or responsibility to one or more other entities that entails settlement by probable future transfer of assets at a specified or determinable date, on occurrence of a specific event, or on demand.

2. The duty or responsibility obligates a particular entity, leaving it little or no discretion to avoid the future sacrifice.

3. The transaction or other event obligating the entity has already happened.

Unlike excise tax, income tax, and Social Security tax, which are directly related to particular business events, real and personal property taxes are based on an assessed valuation of property as of a given date, as determined by law. For this reason, the legal liability for such taxes generally is considered to accrue when a specific event occurs, rather than over a period of time. Following are several dates that have been suggested as the point in time in which property taxes legally accrue (ARB-43, Ch. 10A, par. 2):

*   Assessment date
*   Beginning of the taxing authority's fiscal year
*   End of the taxing authority's fiscal year
*   Date on which the tax becomes a lien on the property
*   Date the tax is levied
*   Date(s) the tax is payable
*   Date the tax becomes delinquent
*   Tax period appearing on a tax bill

The date most widely accepted as obligating the entity is the date of assessment of the taxes by the appropriate taxing authority.

ACCOUNTING AND REPORTING STANDARDS

Although many states have different laws or precedents as to when the legal liability accrues for real and personal property taxes, the general rule is that it accrues on the date the taxes are assessed (ARB-43, Ch. 10A, par. 4). The exact amount of tax may not be known on the assessment date, however, and a reasonable estimate must be made. The inability to determine the exact amount of real and personal property taxes is not an acceptable reason for not recognizing an existing tax liability (ARB-43, Ch. 10A, par. 9).

In those cases in which the accrued amount is subject to a great deal of uncertainty, the liability should be described as estimated. Whether the amount of the accrued tax liability for real and personal property taxes is known or estimated, it should be reported as a current liability in the balance sheet (ARB-43, Ch. 10A, par. 16).

A monthly accrual over the fiscal period of the taxing authority is considered the most acceptable basis for recording real and personal property taxes. This results in the appropriate accrual or prepayment at any closing date (ARB-43, Ch. 10A, par. 14). An adjustment to the estimated tax liability of a prior year is made when the exact amount is determined. This adjustment is made in the income statement of the period in which the exact amount is determined, either as an adjustment to the current year's provision or as a separate item on the income statement (ARB-43, Ch. 10A, par. 11).

In most circumstances, however, real and personal property taxes are considered an expense of doing business and are reported in the appropriate income statement (*a*) as an operating expense, (*b*) as a deduction from income, or (*c*) allocated to several expense accounts, such as manufacturing overhead and general and administrative expenses. As a general rule, real and personal property taxes should not be combined with income taxes (ARB-43, Ch. 10A, pars. 17–18).

☛ **PRACTICE POINTER:** In interim financial reports, estimate the end-of-period liability in order to estimate the expense for the year. Reflect adjustments to the amount of the estimate in the interim period during which the adjustment becomes known.

Property taxes on property held for resale to customers or under construction are typically capitalized.

OBSERVATION: The promulgated GAAP do not describe the criteria for capitalizing or not capitalizing real estate taxes.

Illustration of Accounting and Reporting Standards for Property Taxes

On October 1, 20X5, the City assesses $12,000 of property taxes on Wilson, Inc., for the fiscal year, October 1, 20X5–September 30, 20X6. Wilson records the assessment as follows:

<u>Oct. 1, 20X5</u>

Deferred property taxes	12,000	
Property taxes payable		12,000

At December 31, 20X5, the end of Wilson's financial reporting year, Wilson adjusts the deferred property taxes account by recognizing three months of expense, as follows:

<u>Dec. 31, 20X5</u>

Property tax expense	3,000	
Deferred property taxes		3,000

At February 1, 20X6, Wilson pays the property taxes and makes the following entry:

<u>Feb. 1, 20X6</u>

Property taxes payable	12,000	
Cash		12,000

Throughout, or at the end of 20X6, the remaining nine months of property taxes are recognized as expense:

<u>Various dates, 20X6</u>

Property tax expense	9,000	
Deferred property taxes		9,000

RELATED CHAPTERS IN 2009 *GAAP GUIDE*
LEVEL A

Chapter 3, "Balance Sheet Classification and Related Display Issues"
Chapter 21, "Income Taxes"
Chapter 26, "Interim Financial Reporting"

RELATED CHAPTERS IN 2009 *GAAP GUIDE*
LEVELS B, C, AND D

Chapter 4, "Balance Sheet Classification and Related Display Issues"
Chapter 20, "Income Taxes"
Chapter 23, "Interim Financial Reporting"

CHAPTER 37
REAL ESTATE TRANSACTIONS

CONTENTS

OVERVIEW

A significant financial reporting issue encountered in accounting for real estate transactions is the timing of revenue recognition. Promulgated GAAP address this important issue by classifying real estate transactions into the following three categories:

1. Real estate sales, except retail land sales
2. Sale-leasebacks involving real estate
3. Retail land sales

The authoritative literature also establishes standards for the acquisition, development, construction, and selling and rental costs related to real estate projects. In addition, they cover accounting for initial rental operations and include rules for ascertaining when a real estate project is substantially completed and available for occupancy.

The following pronouncements include standards of financial reporting for these types of real estate transactions:

FAS-66	Accounting for Sales of Real Estate
FAS-67	Accounting for Costs and Initial Rental Operations of Real Estate Projects
FAS-98	Accounting for Leases:

- Sale-Leaseback Transactions Involving Real Estate
- Sales-Type Leases of Real Estate
- Definition of the Lease Term
- Initial Direct Costs of Direct Financing

FAS-152	Accounting for Real Estate Time-Sharing Transactions— An Amendment of FASB Statements No. 66 and 67
FAS-154	Accounting Changes and Error Corrections
FIN-43	Real Estate Sales

BACKGROUND

The matching principle requires that revenue and related costs be recognized simultaneously in determining net income for a specific period. If revenue is deferred to a future period, the associated costs of that revenue are also deferred. Frequently, it may be necessary to estimate revenue and/or costs to achieve a proper matching.

GAAP require that the realization of revenue be recognized in the accounting period in which the earning process is substantially completed and an exchange has taken place. In addition, revenue usually is recognized at the amount established by the parties to the exchange, except for transactions in which collection of the receivable is not reasonably assured. In the event that collection of the receivable is not reasonably assured, the installment method or cost-recovery method may be used (APB-10 [Omnibus Opinion—1966]). Alternatively, collections may be recorded properly as deposits in the event that considerable uncertainty exists as to their eventual collectibility.

FAS-66 (Accounting for Sales of Real Estate) and FAS-98 (Accounting for Leases) address the recognition of revenue from real estate sales. FAS-98 specifically addresses sale-leaseback transactions involving real estate, and FAS-66 contains many of the specialized accounting and reporting principles and practices that were originally published in the following AICPA publications:

- Industry Accounting Guide (Accounting for Profit Recognition on Sales of Real Estate)

- Industry Accounting Guide (Accounting for Retail Land Sales)

- SOP 75-6 (Questions Concerning Profit Recognition of Sales of Real Estate)

- SOP 78-4 (Application of the Deposit, Installment, and Cost Recovery Methods in Accounting for Sales of Real Estate)

FAS-66 does not include those portions of the Industry Accounting Guide titled "Accounting for Retail Land Sales," which cover costs of real estate projects. These costs are covered in FAS-67 (Accounting for Costs and Initial Rental Operations of Real Estate Projects).

FAS-66 establishes GAAP for the recognition of revenue on all real estate transactions for any type of accounting entity. It provides separate criteria for the recognition of revenue on (*a*) all real estate transactions except retail land sales and (*b*) retail land sales. The following items are expressly excluded from the provisions of FAS-66:

- Exchanges of real estate for other real estate

- Sales and leasebacks

FAS-98 contains financial accounting and reporting standards that establish:

- A new definition of *lease term* for all leasing transactions.

- The appropriate accounting for a seller-lessee in a sale-lease-back transaction involving real estate, including real estate with equipment, such as manufacturing facilities, power plants, and furnished office buildings.

- The appropriate accounting for a sale-leaseback transaction in which property improvements or integral equipment is sold to a purchaser-lessor and leased back by the seller-lessee who retains the ownership of the underlying land. (The term *property improvements or integral equipment* refers to any physical structure or equipment attached to the real estate, or other parts thereof, that cannot be removed and used separately without incurring significant cost.)

- The appropriate accounting for sale-leaseback transactions involving real estate with equipment that include separate sale and leaseback agreements for the real estate and the equipment (*a*) with the same entity or related parties and (*b*) consummated at or near the same time, suggesting that they were negotiated as a package.

Sale-leaseback transactions are addressed by FAS-28 (Accounting for Sales with Leasebacks) and FAS-13 (Accounting for Leases), except for sale-leaseback transactions involving real estate, which are addressed by FAS-98. A *sale-leaseback* transaction is one in which an owner sells property and then leases that same property back again from the purchaser. The parties to a sale-leaseback transaction are the *seller-lessee* and the *purchaser-lessor*.

If the lease portion of a sale-leaseback transaction meets the criteria for capitalization under FAS-13, the purchaser-lessor records the acquisition of the property as a purchase and the lease as a direct financing lease. If the lease portion of a sale-leaseback transaction does not meet the criteria for capitalization under FAS-13, the purchaser-lessor records the acquisition of the property as a purchase and the lease as an operating lease.

The seller-lessee accounts for the lease in a sale-leaseback transaction based on the portion of the property that is leased back. Under FAS-28, a seller-lessee can lease back (*a*) a minor portion of the property, (*b*) substantially all of the property, or (*c*) somewhere between more than a minor portion of the property and less than substantially all of the property.

Before the issuance of FAS-98, some enterprises recorded a sale of real estate in a sale-leaseback transaction ignoring the provisions of the sale-leaseback agreement, while other enterprises considered the provisions of the sale-leaseback agreement in evaluating whether the sale recognition criteria of FAS-66 were met. This difference in recording resulted from different interpretations of paragraph 40 of FAS-66. Paragraph 40 of FAS-66 required that the *amount* of profit recognized on a sale-leaseback transaction be determined at the date of the sale in accordance with the provisions of FAS-66, but the amount of profit determined in this manner was to be accounted for in accordance with the provisions of FAS-13 and FAS-28. FAS-98 solves this problem by requiring that a sale-leaseback involving real estate, including real estate with equipment, be accounted for as a sale only if it qualifies as a sale under the provisions of FAS-66 and the seller makes active use of the leased property during the lease term.

Under FAS-66, a real estate sale must be consummated before it qualifies as a sale. Consummation of a real estate sale usually requires the seller to transfer title to the buyer. Before the issuance of FAS-98, FAS-13, as amended by FAS-26 (Profit Recognition on Sales-Type Leases of Real Estate), provided that a sale of real estate could be recognized in a sales-type lease even if the title were never transferred. This resulted in a conflict between FAS-66 and FAS-13, which FAS-98 eliminates by prohibiting leases involving real estate from being classified as sales-type leases, under the provisions of FAS-13, unless the lease agreement provides for the title to the property to be transferred to the lessee at or shortly after the end of the lease term.

Under FAS-13, as amended by FAS-98, the lease term may be affected if the lessee provides financing to the lessor and the loan is considered a *guarantee of the lessor's debt*. The lease term may also be affected by the interpretation of the term *economic penalty*. The lease term includes all periods covered by ordinary renewal options during which a guarantee by the lessee of the lessor's debt directly or indirectly related to the leased property is expected to be in effect or a loan from the lessee to the lessor related to the leased property is expected to be outstanding. The lease term also includes all periods for which failure to renew the lease imposes a penalty on the lessee in an amount that makes renewal appear to be reasonably assured. The term *penalty* is defined by FAS-98 as "any requirement that is imposed or can be imposed on the lessee by the lease agreement or by factors outside the lease agreement to disburse cash, incur or assume a liability, perform services, surrender or transfer an asset or rights to an asset or otherwise forego an economic benefit, or suffer an economic detriment" (FAS-98, par. 22b).

FAS-67 (Accounting for Costs and Initial Rental Operations of Real Estate Projects) contains the specialized accounting and reporting principles and practices that were originally published in the following AICPA publications:

- SOP 78-3 Accounting for Costs to Sell and Rent, and Initial Rental Operations of Real Estate Projects
- SOP 80-3 Accounting for Real Estate Acquisition, Development, and Construction Costs

In addition, FAS-67 includes those portions of the Industry Accounting Guide titled "Accounting for Retail Land Sales" that relate to costs of real estate projects.

The following items are expressly *excluded* from the provisions of FAS-67:

- Real estate projects that are not for sale or rent and are developed by an entity for its own use; this includes real estate reported in consolidated financial statements that was developed by one affiliated member of the group for use in the operations of another member of the group
- Initial direct costs of leases, including sales-type leases
- Direct costs that are related to commercial activities such as manufacturing, merchandising, or service-oriented activities
- Real estate rental periods of less than one month in duration

Real estate acquisition costs may be classified as (*a*) preacquisition costs and (*b*) postacquisition costs. Preacquisition costs are those that are incurred prior to the acquisition of the property, such as appraisals, surveys, legal fees, travel expenses, and costs to acquire options to purchase the property. Postacquisition costs are those that are incurred after the property has been acquired, such as development and construction costs. Postacquisition costs may be classified further as (*a*) direct costs, (*b*) indirect costs, (*c*) costs of amenities, and (*d*) incidental operational costs.

Direct costs are those that can be directly identified with the real estate project. Indirect costs may or may not be related to a specific real estate project. Indirect costs of several real estate projects may be allocated to each project on a reasonable allocation basis. Incidental operations of a real estate project occur during the development stage of the project and are intended to reduce the cost of the real estate project. Incidental operations do not include activities that result in a profit or return on the use of the real property.

Capitalized costs of a real estate project are allocated to the individual components within the project. The allocation usually is accomplished by the specific identification method, if the individual components within the project can be identified specifically. If specific identification is not possible, capitalized land cost and all other common costs, including common costs of amenities, are allocated based on the relative fair value of each land parcel benefited prior to any construction. Capitalized construction costs are allocated based on the relative sales value of each individual component within the real estate project. Individual components of a real estate project may consist of lots, acres, or some other identifiable unit.

Costs incurred to sell real estate projects may be accounted for as (*a*) project costs, (*b*) prepaid expenses, or (*c*) period costs, according to the accounting periods that are benefited.

Costs to rent real estate projects under operating leases are either chargeable to future periods or chargeable to the current period, according to whether their recovery is reasonably expected from future rental revenue.

FAS-66 and FAS-98 combined include standards of financial reporting for real estate transactions in the three categories: real estate sales, sales-leasebacks involving real estate, and retail land sales. As interpreted by FIN-43 (Real Estate Sales), FAS-66 is applicable for the recognition of profit on all real estate sales transactions without regard to the nature of the seller's business. FIN-43 also clarifies that the phrase "all real estate sales" includes sales of real estate with property improvements or integral equipment that cannot be removed and used separately from the real estate without incurring significant costs (FIN-43, par. 2).

RECOGNITION OF SALES

Real Estate Sales (Except Retail Land Sales)

In a real estate sale, a significant portion of the sales price usually is represented by a long-term receivable, which is not backed by the full faith and credit of the buyer. Usually, the seller can recover the property only in the event of default by the buyer. Another unusual facet of real estate sales is the seller's possible continuing involvement in the property. For instance, the seller may be legally bound to make certain improvements to the property or to adjacent property.

To ensure the collection of the long-term receivable, which usually is part of a real estate transaction, FAS-66 requires minimum down payments for all real estate sales before a seller is permitted to recognize a profit. FAS-66 emphasizes the timing of the recognition of profits but does not cover other aspects of real estate accounting.

Real estate transactions that are *not* considered "retail land sales" include the following:

- Sales of homes, buildings, and parcels of land
- Sales of lots to builders
- Sales of corporate stock or a partnership interest in which the substance of the transaction is actually a sale of real estate
- Sales of options to acquire real estate
- Sales of time-sharing interests in real estate

As stated above, sales of time-sharing interests in real estate are to be accounted for as nonretail land sales. In addition, FAS-66 states that SOP 04-2 (Accounting for Real Estate Time-Sharing Transactions) provides additional guidance on accounting for time-share transactions (FAS-152, par. 3).

For a seller to report the total profit on a sale of real estate (other than a retail land sale) by the full accrual method, FAS-66 requires that the transaction meet specific criteria, as follows (FAS-66, par. 5):

- A sale must be completed (consummated).
- The buyer's initial and continuing payments (investment) must be adequate.

- The seller's receivable is not subject to future subordination, except to (*a*) a primary lien on the property existing at the date of sale or (*b*) a future loan or an existing permanent loan commitment the proceeds of which must first be applied to the payment of the seller's receivable.
- All of the benefits and risks of ownership in the property are substantially transferred to the buyer by the seller.
- The seller does not have a substantial continued involvement with the property after the sale.

If a sale of real estate, other than a retail land sale, meets all of the above criteria, the seller must recognize the entire profit on the sale in accordance with the full accrual method of accounting. If a real estate sale fails to meet all of the above criteria, profit on the sale is recognized by (*a*) the deposit method, (*b*) the installment sales method, (*c*) the cost-recovery method, (*d*) the reduced profit method, or (*e*) the percentage-of-completion method. The method that is used is determined by the specific circumstances of each real estate sale.

When a Real Estate Sale Is Consummated

FAS-66 contains four criteria that must be met for a sale of real estate to be considered "consummated" (FAS-66, par. 6):

1. The contracting parties are legally bound by the contract.
2. All consideration required by the terms of the contract has been paid.
3. If the seller is responsible by the terms of the contract to obtain permanent financing for the buyer, the seller must have arranged for such financing.
4. The seller has performed all of the acts required by the contract to earn the revenue.

As a general rule, the above criteria are met at the time of, or after, the closing of the real estate sale. These criteria rarely are met before closing or at the time a sales agreement is executed.

An exception to the "consummation rule" may occur if, after the date of sale, the seller has continued involvement with the property to construct office buildings, condominiums, shopping centers, or other similar improvements on the land that take a long time to complete. As will be discussed later, FAS-66 permits some profit recognition under certain circumstances even if the seller has this type of substantial continued involvement with the property.

Buyer's Initial and Continuing Investment

In determining whether the buyer's minimum initial investment is adequate under the provisions of FAS-66, the *sales value* of the property—not the stated sales price in the contract—is used. The *sales value* is defined as the stated sales price of the property, increased or decreased for other considerations included in the sale that clearly represent greater or smaller proceeds to the seller on the sale. Thus, any payments made by the buyer that are not included in the stated sales price in the contract and that represent additional proceeds to the seller are included as part of the buyer's minimum investment. These additional proceeds enter into the determination of both the buyer's minimum investment and the sales value of the property. Examples of additional proceeds to the seller are (*a*) the exercise price of a real estate option to purchase the property, (*b*) management fees, (*c*) points to obtain financing, (*d*) prepaid interest and principal payments, (*e*) payments by the buyer to third parties that reduce previously existing indebtedness on the property, and (*f*) any payments made by the buyer to the seller that will be applied at a future date against amounts due the seller (FAS-66, par. 7a). However, payments by the buyer to third parties for improvements to the property or payments that are not verifiable are not considered as additional proceeds to the seller (FAS-66, par. 10).

Decreases in the stated sales price that are necessary to arrive at the sales value of the property may include, but are not limited to, the following (FAS-66, par. 7b):

- The amount of discount, if any, necessary to reduce the buyer's receivable to its present value. Thus, if the buyer's receivable does not bear interest or if the rate of interest is less than the prevailing rate, a discount would be required to reduce it to its present value according to APB-21 (Interest on Receivables and Payables).

- The present value of services that the seller agrees to perform without compensation or, if the seller agrees to perform services at less than prevailing rates, the difference between (*a*) the present value of the services at prevailing rates and (*b*) the present value of the agreed-upon compensation.

Illustration of Computation of Sales Value

XYZ, Inc. agrees to build improvements for ABC Company for a total price of $1,750,000. The improvements are to be built on land leased by ABC from a third party. The payments on the land lease are $18,000 per year, payable monthly in advance, and the lease term is for 45 years. ABC Company will pay for the improvements as follows:

Cash down payment	$ 250,000
10% unsecured note payable in five annual payments of $20,000 plus interest	100,000
Primary loan from insurance company secured by improvements to the property, payable in equal monthly payments over 28 years at 8 1/2% interest	1,400,000
Total stated sales price of improvements	$1,750,000

The computation of the *sales value*, as required by FAS-66, is as follows:

Present value of land lease payments for 28 years, payable $1,500 monthly, discounted at 8 1/2% interest	$ 193,361
Primary loan from insurance company	1,400,000
Total equivalent primary debt	$1,593,361
Unsecured note from buyer to seller	100,000
Cash down payment	250,000
Sales value*	$1,943,361

*The adequacy of the buyer's minimum initial investment in the property is based on the *sales value* of the property and not on the stated sales price.

The effects of an underlying land lease must also be included in computing the sales value of the property. If a seller sells a buyer improvements that are to be built on property subject to an underlying land lease, the present value of the lease payments must be included in the sales value of the property. The present value of the lease payments is computed over the actual term of the primary indebtedness of the improvements, if any, or over the usual term of primary indebtedness for the type of improvements involved. The present value of the land lease payments is tantamount to additional indebtedness on the property (FAS-66, Appendix C). If the land lease is not subordinated, the discount rate to determine the present value of the land lease payments should be comparable to interest rates on primary debt of the same nature. If the land lease is subordinated, however, a higher discount rate comparable to secondary debt of the same nature should be used (FAS-66, footnote 15).

If a land lease exists between the buyer and a third party, its effects on the sales value of the property are used only to determine the adequacy of the buyer's initial investment. When the seller of the improvements is also the lessor of the land lease, however, the computation of the profit on the sale of the improvements is also affected. Because it is impossible to separate the profits on the improvements from the profits on the underlying lease, FAS-66 requires a special computation limiting the amount of profit that can be recognized. The amount of profit that can be recognized on the improvements is equal to the sales value of the property, less the cost of improvements and the cost of the land. However, the present value of the lease payments in the sales value may not exceed the actual cost of the land (FAS-66, par. 39).

The result of limiting the amount of profit that can be recognized on the sale of improvements is to defer any residual profit on the land from being recognized until the land is sold or the future rental payments actually are received (FAS-66, par. 39).

If a land lease between a buyer and a seller of improvements on the land is for a term of less than 20 years or does not substantially cover the economic life of the improvements being made to the property, the transaction should be accounted for as a single lease of land and improvements (FAS-66, par. 38).

The buyer's minimum initial investment must be made in cash or cash equivalency at or before the time of sale. A buyer's note does not qualify for the minimum initial investment unless payment of the note is unconditionally guaranteed by an irrevocable letter of credit from an established unrelated lending institution. A permanent loan commitment by an independent third party to replace a loan made by the seller is not included in the buyer's initial investment. Any funds that have been loaned or will be loaned, directly or indirectly, to the buyer by the seller are deducted from the buyer's initial investment (down payment) to determine whether the required minimum has been met. For the purposes of this provision, the seller must be exposed to a potential loss as a result of the funds loaned to the buyer. For example, if a buyer made an initial cash investment of $200,000 in a real estate transaction, $25,000 of which was a loan from the seller, the buyer's minimum initial investment under the provisions of FAS-66 would be $175,000. However, if an unrelated banking institution unconditionally guaranteed the timely repayment of the $25,000 to the seller, the entire $200,000 would be eligible as the buyer's initial investment (FAS-66, pars. 9–10).

A direct relationship exists between the amount of a buyer's first investment (down payment) and the probability that the seller eventually will collect the balance due. The larger the down payment, the more likely it is that the buyer will pay the balance due. A reasonable basis for establishing the amount of a buyer's initial investment is the prevailing practices of independent lending institutions. Thus, the difference between the amount of primary mortgage an independent lending institution would lend on a particular parcel of real estate and the sales value of the property is a realistic guide to figure the amount of the buyer's initial investment (FAS-66, par. 11).

To apply the full accrual method of accounting to a real estate transaction (other than a retail land sale), FAS-66 provides that the minimum initial investment (down payment) of the buyer should be the *greater* of 1 or 2 below:

1. The percentage of the sales value of the property as indicated
    in the following (FAS-66, par. 53a):

Minimum
Down Payment
(% of Sales Value)

	Minimum Down Payment (% of Sales Value)
Land:	
Held for commercial, industrial, or residential development to commence within two years after sale	20%
Held for commercial, industrial, or residential development after two years	25%
Commercial and Industrial Property:	
Office and industrial buildings, shopping centers, etc.:	
Properties subject to lease on a long-term lease basis to parties having satisfactory credit rating; cash flow currently sufficient to service all indebtedness	10%
Single tenancy properties sold to a user having a satisfactory credit rating	15%
All other	20%
Other Income-Producing Properties (hotels, motels, marinas, mobile home parks, etc.):	
Cash flow currently sufficient to service all indebtedness	15%
Start-up situations or current deficiencies in cash flow	25%
Multi-Family Residential Property:	
Primary residence:	
Cash flow currently sufficient to service all indebtedness	10%
Start-up situations or current deficiencies in cash flow	15%
Secondary or recreational residence:	
Cash flow currently sufficient to service all indebtedness	15%
Start-up situations or current deficiencies in cash flow	25%
Single Family Residential Property (including condominium or cooperative housing):	
Primary residence of the buyer	5%*
Secondary or recreational residence	10%*

*If collectibility of the remaining portion of the sales price cannot be supported
by reliable evidence of collection experience, a higher down payment is called for and
should not be less than 60% of the difference between the sales value and the financing
available from loans guaranteed by regulatory bodies, such as FHA or VA, or from
independent financial institutions. This 60% test applies when independent first-mort-
gage financing is not utilized and the seller takes a receivable from the buyer for the
difference between the sales value and the initial investment. When independent first-
mortgage financing is utilized, the adequacy of the initial investment on sales of single
family residential property should be determined in accordance with FAS-66.

2. The *lesser* of the following (FAS-66, par. 53b):

   a. The difference between the sales value of the property and 115% of the maximum permanent mortgage loan or commitment on the property recently obtained from a primary independent lending institution, or

   b. Twenty-five percent (25%) of the sales value of the property

---

Illustration of Determination of Buyer's Minimum Initial Investment in Accordance with FAS-66

The sales value of property being sold is $200,000, and the maximum permanent mortgage loan recently placed on the property from an independent lending institution is $150,000. The property being sold is commercial land, which will be developed by the buyer within two years after the date of sale. For the full accrual method of accounting to be applied to this real estate transaction, FAS-66 provides that the minimum initial investment (down payment) of the buyer should be the greater of (1) or (2) below:

1. The percentage of the sales value of the property as indicated on the table is $40,000 (20% of $200,000).

2. a. The difference between the sales value of the property and 115% of the recently placed permanent mortgage loan is $27,500 (115% of $150,000 = $172,500 and the difference between $200,000 [sales value] and $172,500 is $27,500).

   b. 25% of the sales value ($200,000) is $50,000.

   The lesser of 2a ($27,500) and 2b ($50,000) = $27,500.
   The greater of 2a ($27,500) and 1 ($40,000) = $40,000.

   Thus, the minimum down payment of the buyer is $40,000.

☛ **PRACTICE POINTER:** Even if the buyer makes the required minimum initial investment, make a separate assessment to determine the collectibility of the receivable. In other words, there must be reasonable assurance that the receivable will be collected after the seller receives the minimum initial investment; if there is not, do not record the sale by the full accrual method. The buyer must make the minimum initial investment, and the seller must be reasonably assured that the balance of the sales price will be collected, before the real estate sale is recorded and any profits are recognized. The assessment of the receivable by the seller should include credit reports on the buyer and an evaluation of the adequacy of the cash flow from the property.

In addition to an adequate initial investment, FAS-66 requires that the buyer maintain a continuing investment in the property by increasing his or her investment each year. The buyer's total indebtedness for the purchase price of the property must be reduced each year in equal amounts, which will extinguish the entire indebtedness (interest and principal) over a specified maximum period. The specified maximum period for land transactions is 20 years. The specified maximum period for all other real estate transactions is no more than that offered by independent financial institutions at the time of sale for first mortgages (FAS-66, par. 12).

The buyer's commitment to pay the full amount of his or her indebtedness to the seller becomes doubtful if the total indebtedness is not to be paid within the specified maximum period.

A buyer's payments on his or her indebtedness must be in cash or cash equivalency. Funds provided directly or indirectly by the seller cannot be considered in determining the buyer's continuing investment in the property (FAS-66, par. 12).

Release Provisions

Real estate agreements involving land frequently provide for the periodic release of part of the land to the buyer. The buyer obtains the released land free of any liens. The conditions for the release usually require the buyer to have previously paid sufficient funds to cover the sales price of the released land, and often an additional sum is required to effectuate the release. In these types of transactions involving released land, the requirements for a buyer's initial and continuing investment must be determined based on the sales value of property not released or not subject to release (FAS-66, par. 13). In other words, for a seller to recognize profit at the time of sale, a buyer's investment must be enough to pay any amounts for the release of land and still meet the specified initial and continued investment required by the provisions of FAS-66 (FAS-66, par. 14). If the buyer's initial and continuing investment is not sufficient, then each release of land should be treated as a separate sale and profit recognized at that time (FAS-66, par. 15).

Future Subordination

If, at the time of sale, a seller's receivable is subject to future subordination, other than (*a*) to a primary (first mortgage) lien on the property existing at the date of sale or (*b*) to a future loan or existing permanent loan commitment the proceeds of which must first be applied to the payment of the seller's receivable, no profit should be recognized, because the effect of future subordination on the collectibility of a receivable cannot be evaluated reasonably. The cost-recovery method should be used to recognize profit at the time of sale if the seller's receivable is subject to future subordination, other than the exceptions (*a*) and (*b*) noted above (FAS-66, par. 17).

Nontransfer of Ownership and Seller's Continued Involvement

Real estate transactions must be analyzed carefully to determine their economic substance. Frequently, the economic substance of a real estate sale is no more than a management fee arrangement or an indication that the risks and benefits of ownership have not really been transferred in the agreement. Accounting for a real estate transaction can become quite complicated because of the many types of continuing relations that can exist between a buyer and a seller. The substance of the real estate transaction should dictate the accounting method that should be used.

> ☛ **PRACTICE POINTER:** As a general rule, before a profit is recognized, a sale must occur, collectibility of the receivable must be reasonably assured, and the seller must perform all of the acts required by the contract to earn the revenue. Profit also may be recognized—at the time of the sale—on contracts that provide for the continued involvement of the seller if the maximum potential loss of the seller is expressly limited and defined by the terms of the contract. In this event, recognize the total profit on the sale, less the maximum potential loss that could occur because of the seller's involvement, at the time of the sale.

Two important factors in evaluating the economic substance of a real estate sale are (1) the transfer of the usual risks and rewards of ownership in the property and (2) the full performance by the seller of all acts required by the contract to earn the revenue. Generally, both of these factors must be accomplished before full profit can be recognized on the sale of real estate. The more common types of real estate transactions and how they should be accounted for are discussed in the following paragraphs.

Profit Recognition Other Than Full Accrual Basis

If a sale of real estate, other than a retail land sale, meets all of the FAS-66 criteria discussed earlier, the seller must recognize the entire profit on the sale in accordance with the full accrual basis of accounting.

When one (or more) of the FAS-66 criteria are not met in a real estate sale, an alternative method of recognizing revenue from the sale must be used. The alternative method selected may be required by FAS-66 or may be a matter of professional judgment. The four accounting methods recommended by FAS-66 are (1) the deposit method, (2) the cost-recovery method, (3) the installment sales method, and (4) the reduced profit method.

Deposit Accounting The uncertainty about the collectibility of the sales price in a real estate transaction may be so great that the effective date of the sale is deferred and any cash received by the seller is accounted for as a deposit. However, cash received that is designated by contract as nonrefundable interest may be applied as an offset to existing carrying charges on the property, such as property taxes and interest, instead of being accounted for as a deposit (FAS-66, par. 65).

All cash received, except that appropriately used as an offset to the carrying charges of the property, must be reflected in the seller's balance sheet as a liability (deposit on a contract for the sale of real estate). No change is made in accounting for the property subject to the contract and its related mortgage debt, if any. However, the seller's financial statements should disclose that these items are subject to a sales contract. Depreciation expense should continue as a period cost, in spite of the fact that the property has been sold legally. Until the requirements of FAS-66 are met for profit recognition, the seller does not report a sale and continues to report all cash received (including interest received) either as a deposit or, in the case of nonrefundable interest, as an offset to the carrying charges of the property involved (FAS-66, par. 65). If the buyer forfeits a nonrefundable deposit, or defaults on the contract, the seller should reduce the deposit account appropriately and include such amounts in income of the period (FAS-66, par. 66).

Cost Recovery Method If a seller's receivable is subject to subordination that cannot be reasonably evaluated, or if uncertainty exists as to the recovery of the seller's cost on default by the buyer, the cost recovery method should be used. Even if cost has been recovered by the seller but additional collections are highly doubtful, the cost-recovery method is appropriate. Frequently, the cost recovery method is used initially for transactions that would also qualify for the installment sales method.

> **OBSERVATION:** Both the cost recovery method and the installment sales method defer the recognitions on the sale until collections actually are received.

Under the cost recovery method, all collections (including interest received) are applied first to the recovery of the cost of the property; only after full cost has been received is any profit recognized (FAS-66, par. 62). The only expenses remaining to be charged against the profit are those relating to the collection process. When the cost recovery method is used, the total sales value is included in the income statement for the period in which the sale is made (FAS-66, par. 63). From the total sales value in the income statement, the total cost of the sale and the deferred gross profit on the sale are deducted. On the balance sheet, the deferred gross profit is reflected as a reduction of the related receivable. Until full cost is recovered, principal payments received are applied to reduce the related receivable, and interest payments received are added to the deferred gross profit. At any given time, the related receivable, less the deferred gross profit, equals the remaining cost that must be recovered. After all cost is recovered, subsequent collections reduce the deferred gross profit and appear as a separate item of revenue on the income statement.

Installment Sales Method   Promulgated GAAP prohibit accounting for sales by installment accounting except under exceptional circumstances in which collectibility cannot be assured or estimated reasonably. Collectibility can be in doubt because of the length of an extended collection period or because no basis of estimation can be established.

> ☞ **PRACTICE POINTER:** The installment sales method frequently is more appropriate for real estate transactions in which collectibility of the receivable from the buyer cannot be reasonably assured because defaults on loans secured by real estate usually result in the recovery of the property sold.

Under the installment sales method of accounting, each payment collected consists of part recovery of cost and part recovery of gross profit, in the same ratio that these two elements existed in the original sale. In a real estate transaction, the original sale is equal to the sales value of the property. Thus, under the installment sales method, profit is recognized on cash payments made by the buyer to the holder of the primary debt assumed and on cash payments to the seller. The profit recognized on the cash payments is based on the percentage of total profit to total sales value (FAS-66, par. 56).

Illustration of Installment Sales Method

Jones Company sells real property to Smith for $2,000,000. Smith will assume an existing $1,200,000 first mortgage and pay $300,000 in cash as a down payment. The $500,000 balance will be in the form of a 12% second mortgage to Jones Company payable in equal payments of principal and interest over a ten-year period. The cost of the property to Jones is $1,200,000.

Computation of Sales Value and Gross Profit

Cash	$ 300,000
Second mortgage	500,000
First mortgage	1,200,000
Total sales value (which is the same as the stated sales price)	$2,000,000
Less: Cost of property sold	1,200,000

Total gross profit on sale	$ 800,000
Gross profit percentage ($800,000/$2,000,000)	40.0%
Profit to be recognized on down payment (40% of $300,000)	$ 120,000

Assuming that the $300,000 down payment is not sufficient to meet the requirements of full profit recognition on the sale, Jones recognizes $120,000 gross profit at the time of sale. Several months later Smith makes a cash payment of $100,000 on the first mortgage and $50,000 on the second mortgage. The amount of gross profit that Jones recognizes on these payments would be as follows:

Payment on first mortgage	$100,000
Payment on second mortgage	50,000
Total cash payments	$150,000
Gross profit realized (40% of $150,000)	$ 60,000

Even though Jones does not receive any cash on Smith's payment on the first mortgage, gross profit is still realized because the gross profit percentage was based on the total sales value, which included the first mortgage liability.

When the installment sales method is used, the total sales value is included in the income statement of the period in which the sale is made. From the total sales value in the income statement, the total cost of the sale and the deferred gross profit are deducted (FAS-66, par. 59). On the balance sheet, the deferred gross profit on the sale is deducted from the related receivable. As cash payments are received, the portion allocated to realized gross profit is presented as a separate item of revenue on the income statement and deferred gross profit is reduced by the same amount. At any given time, the related receivable, less the deferred gross profit, represents the remaining cost of the property sold (FAS-66, par. 58). Since realized gross profit is recognized as a portion of each cash collection, a percentage relationship will always exist between the long-term receivable and its related deferred gross profit. This percentage relationship will be the same as the gross profit ratio on the initial sales value.

Reduced Profit Method   The buyer's receivable is discounted to the present value of the lowest level of annual payments required by the sales contract. The discount period is the maximum allowed under the provisions of FAS-66, and all lump-sum payments are excluded in the calculation. The discount rate cannot be less than that stated in the sales contract, if any, or than the prevailing interest rate in accordance with existing GAAP (APB-21). The buyer's receivable discounted as described above is used in determining the profit on the sale of real estate and usually results in a "reduced profit" from that which would be obtained under normal accounting procedures. Lump-sum and other payments are recognized as profit when the seller receives them (FAS-66, par. 68).

Change to Full Accrual Method   After the cost-recovery method or the installment sales method is adopted for a real estate transaction, the receivable should be evaluated periodically for collectibility. When it becomes apparent that the seller's receivable is reasonably assured of being collected, the seller should change to the full accrual accounting method. The change is a change in accounting estimate. When the change to the full accrual accounting method is made, any remaining deferred gross profit is recognized in full in the period in which the change is made (FAS-66, pars. 61, 64). If the change creates a material effect on the seller's financial statements, full disclosure of the effects and the reason for the change should be appropriately made in the financial statements or footnotes thereto.

Profit Recognition When Sale Is Not Consummated

If a real estate sale has not been consummated in accordance with the provisions of FAS-66, the deposit method of accounting is used until the sale is consummated (FAS-66, par. 20).

As mentioned previously, an exception to the "consummation rule" occurs if the terms of the contract require the seller to sell a parcel of land and also construct on the same parcel a building that takes an extended period to complete. In other words, the seller is still involved with the property after the sale because he or she must construct the building. In most jurisdictions a "certificate of occupancy" must be obtained, indicating that the building or other structure has been constructed in accordance with the local building regulations and is ready for occupancy. Thus, a certificate of occupancy usually is necessary to consummate the real estate transaction. However, FAS-66 contains a special provision for profit recognition when a sale of real estate requires the seller to develop the property in the future. If the seller has contracted (*a*) for future development of the land; (*b*) to construct buildings, amenities, or other facilities on the land; or (*c*) to provide offsite improvements, partial recognition of profit may be made if future costs of development can be estimated reasonably at the time of sale (FAS-66, par. 20). In this event, profit can be recognized for any work performed and finished by the seller when (*a*) the sale of the land is consummated and (*b*) the initial and continuing investments of the buyer are adequate. In other words, if the sale of the land meets the first two criteria for the use of the full accrual method of accounting, any profit allocable to (*a*) the work performed before the sale of the land and (*b*) the sale of the land can be recognized by the percentage of-completion method. Thus, the total profit on the sale may be allocated to work performed before the sale of the land and before future construction and development work. The allocation of the total profit is based on the estimated costs for each activity using a uniform rate of gross profit for all activities. If significant uncertainties exist or if costs and profits cannot be reasonably estimated, however, the completed contract method should be used (FAS-66, pars. 41–42).

If a buyer has the right to defer until completion payments due for developmental and construction work, or if the buyer is financially unable to pay these amounts as they come due, care should be exercised in recognizing any profits until completion or satisfactory payment.

The terms of a real estate transaction accounted for by the deposit method may indicate that the carrying amount of the property involved is more than the sales value in the contract and that a loss has been incurred. Because the seller is using the deposit method, no sale is recorded and thus no loss. However, the information indicates an impairment of an asset that should be appropriately recorded by the seller in the period of discovery by a charge to income and the creation of a valuation allowance account for the property involved (FAS-66, par. 21).

Profit Recognition When Buyer's Investment Is Inadequate

If all of the criteria for the full accrual method of accounting are met except that the buyer's initial investment is inadequate, the seller accounts for the sale by the installment sales method, provided the seller is reasonably assured of recovering the cost of the property if the buyer defaults. If the seller is not reasonably assured of recovering the cost of the property, or if cost recovery has been made but future collections are uncertain, the seller uses the cost-recovery method or the deposit method to account for the sale (FAS-66, par. 22).

If all of the criteria for the full accrual method of accounting are met except that the buyer's continuing investment is inadequate, the seller shall account for the sale by the reduced profit method, provided the buyer's periodic payments cover both of the following items (FAS-66, par. 23):

- Amortization of principal and interest based on the maximum primary mortgage that could be obtained on the property
- Interest, at an appropriate rate, on the excess amount, if any, of the total actual debt on the property over the maximum primary mortgage that could be obtained on the property

If both of the above conditions are not met, the seller shall not use the reduced profit method. Instead, the seller should account for the sale by either the installment sales method or the cost-recovery method, whichever is more appropriate under the specific circumstances (FAS-66, par. 23).

Profit Recognition—Subordinated Receivable

As mentioned previously, the cost-recovery method is used to recognize profit at the time of sale if the seller's receivable is subject to future subordination (FAS-66, par. 24).

This restriction does not apply in the following circumstances (FAS-66, par. 17):

- A receivable is subordinate to a first mortgage on the property existing at the time of sale.

- A future loan, including an existing permanent loan commitment, is provided for by the terms of the sale, and the proceeds of the loan will be applied first to the payment of the seller's receivable.

Profit Recognition—Seller's Continued Involvement

In some real estate transactions the seller does not transfer the benefits and risks of ownership to the buyer, or the seller maintains a substantial continued involvement with the property after the date of sale. These types of real estate transactions require careful examination to determine the appropriate method of accounting to be applied.

In legal form a real estate transaction may be a sale, but if in substance the contract is a profit-sharing, financing, or leasing arrangement, no sale or profit is recognized. If a real estate contract contains any of the following provisions, it should be accounted for as a profit-sharing, financing, or leasing arrangement:

- The return of the buyer's investment in the property is guaranteed by the seller (FAS-66, par. 28).
- The buyer can compel the seller to repurchase the property (FAS-66, par. 26).
- An option or obligation exists for the seller to repurchase the property (FAS-66, par. 26).
- The seller is required to operate the property at its own risk for an extended period (FAS-66, par. 29).
- The seller, as general partner, holds a receivable from the limited partnership as a result of a real estate sale. The collection of

the receivable depends on the successful operation of the limited partnership by the general partner, who is also the seller and holder of the receivable (FAS-66, par. 27).

- The seller guarantees a specific return on the buyer's investment for an extended period of time (FAS-66, par. 28).

- The sale includes a leaseback to the seller of all or part of the property (FAS-66, par. 23).

In real estate transactions in which the seller guarantees for a limited period (*a*) to return the buyer's investment or (*b*) to give the buyer a specific rate of return, the seller shall account for the sale by the deposit method of accounting. After the operations of the property become profitable, the seller may recognize profit based on performance. After the limited period has expired and all of the criteria for the full accrual method of accounting are met in accordance with FAS-66, the seller may recognize in full any remaining profit on the sale of real estate.

Initiating and Supporting Operations   As part of a real estate transaction, the seller may be required to initiate or support the operations of the property for a stated period of time or until a certain level of operations has been achieved. In other words, the seller may agree to operate the property for a certain period or until a certain level of rental income has been reached.

Even if there is no agreement, there is a presumption that a seller has an obligation to initiate and support operations of the property he or she has sold in any of the following circumstances (FAS-66, par. 27 and footnote 10):

- The seller sells to a limited partnership an interest in property in which he or she is a general partner.

- The seller retains an equity interest in the property sold by the seller.

- A management contract between the buyer and seller provides for compensation that is significantly higher or lower than comparable prevailing rates and that cannot be terminated by either the buyer or the seller.

- The collection of the receivable from the sale held by the seller is dependent on the operations of the property and represents a significant portion of the sales price. A *significant receivable* is defined as one in excess of 15% of the maximum primary financing that could have been obtained from an established lending institution.

If the seller has agreed to the initiating and supporting operations for a limited period, the seller may recognize profit on the sale based on the performance of the required services. The measurement of performance shall be related to the cost incurred to date and the total estimated costs to be incurred for the services. However, profit recognition may not start until there is reasonable assurance that estimated future rent receipts will cover (*a*) all operating costs, (*b*) debt service, and (*c*) any payments due the seller under the terms of the contract. For this purpose, the estimated future rent receipts shall not exceed the greater of (*a*) leases actually executed or (*b*) two-thirds of the estimated future rent receipts. The difference between the estimated future rent receipts and the greater of (*a*) or (*b*) shall be reserved as a safety factor (FAS-66, par. 29).

If the sales contract does not specify the period for which the seller must initiate and support operations of the property, a two-year period shall be presumed. The two-year period shall commence at the time of initial rental, unless rent receipts cover all operating cost, debt service, and other commitments before the end of the two-year period (FAS-66, par. 30).

Services without Compensation   As part of the contract for the sale of real estate, the seller may be required to perform services related to the property sold without compensation or at a reduced rate. In determining profit to be recognized at the time of sale, a value should be placed on such services at the prevailing rates and deducted from the sales price of the property sold. The value of the compensation should then be recognized over the period in which the services are to be performed by the seller (FAS-66, par. 31).

Sale of Real Estate Options   Proceeds from the sale of real estate options shall be accounted for by the deposit method. If the option is not exercised by its expiration date, the seller of the option shall recognize profit at that time. If an option is sold by the owner of the land and subsequently exercised, the proceeds from the sale of the option are included in determining the sales value of the property sold (FAS-66, par. 32 and footnote 11).

Sales of Partial Interests in Property   A seller may continue to be involved in property sold by retaining an interest in the property and by giving the buyer preference as to profits, cash flow, return on investment, or some other similar arrangement. In this event, if the transaction is in substance a sale, the seller shall recognize profit to the extent that the sale proceeds, including receivables, exceed the seller's total cost in the property (FAS-66, par. 36).

A seller may retain a partial interest in the property sold, such as an undivided interest or some other form of equity. If a seller sells a partial interest in real estate property and the sale meets all of the criteria for the full accrual method, except for the seller's continued involvement related to the partial interest in the property, the seller shall recognize the proportionate share of the profit that is attributable to the outside interests in the property. If the seller controls the buyer, however, profit on the sale shall not be recognized until realized from transactions with outside individuals, or through the sale of the property to outside parties (FAS-66, par. 34).

A seller may sell single-family units or time-sharing interests in a condominium project. If the units or interests are sold individually, the seller shall recognize profit on the sales by the percentage-of completion method, provided all of the following conditions are met (FAS-66, par. 37):

- Construction has progressed beyond the preliminary stage, which means that the engineering and design work, execution of construction contracts, site clearance and preparation, and excavation or completion of the building foundation have all been completed.

- The buyer cannot obtain a refund, except for nondelivery.

- The property will not revert to rental property, as evidenced by the number of units or interests that have been sold. In determining the sufficiency of the number of units or interests sold, reference shall be made to local and state laws, the provisions of the condominium or time-sharing contract, and the terms of the financing agreements.

- Total sales and costs can be estimated reasonably in accordance with the percentage-of-completion method of accounting.

- Sales prices are collectible.

Until all of the above conditions are met, the seller shall account for the sales proceeds from the single-family units or time-sharing interests by the deposit method of accounting (FAS-66, par. 37).

Disclosures FAS-66 does not contain any specific disclosure requirements for the sale of real estate, other than retail land sales. However, professional judgment may require that a significant sale of real estate be disclosed appropriately in the financial statements.

If interest is imputed on a receivable arising out of a real estate sale, certain disclosures are required by APB-21. In addition, if commitments or contingencies arise in a real estate sale, disclosure may be required by FAS-5 (Accounting for Contingencies).

Sale-Leasebacks Involving Real Estate

Under FAS-98, the sale portion of a sale-leaseback transaction involving real estate is accounted for as a sale only if it qualifies as a sale under the provisions of FAS-66. In addition, FAS-98 prohibits a lease involving real estate from being classified as a sales-type lease unless the lease agreement provides for the title of the leased property to be transferred to the lessee at or shortly after the end of the lease term (FAS-98, par. 5).

Under *sale-leaseback accounting*, the sale portion of the sale-leaseback transaction is recorded as a sale by the seller-lessee, the property sold and all of its related liabilities are eliminated from the seller-lessee's balance sheet, gain or loss on the sale portion of the sale-leaseback transaction is recognized by the seller-lessee in accordance with the provisions of FAS-13 (as amended by FAS-28, FAS-66, and FAS-98), and the lease portion of the sale-leaseback transaction is accounted for in accordance with the provisions of FAS-13 (as amended by FAS-28). Sale-leaseback accounting under FAS-98 is analogous to the full accrual method under FAS-66.

Under FAS-98, a seller-lessee applies sale-leaseback accounting only to those sale-leaseback transactions containing payment terms and provisions that provide for (*a*) a normal leaseback (as defined by FAS-98), (*b*) an adequate initial and continuing investment by the purchaser-lessor (as defined by FAS-66), (*c*) the transfer of all of the other risks and rewards of ownership to the purchaser-lessor, and (*d*) no other continued involvement by the seller-lessee, other than the continued involvement represented by the lease portion of the sale-leaseback transaction (FAS-98, par. 7).

Normal Leaseback

Under FAS-98, a normal leaseback is one in which the seller-lessee actively uses substantially all of the leased property in its trade or business during the lease term. The seller-lessee may sublease a minor portion of the leased property, equal to 10% or less of the reasonable rental value for the entire leased property, and the lease will still qualify as a normal lease. Thus, for the leaseback to qualify as normal under FAS-98, the seller-lessee must actively use substantially all of the leased property in its trade or business in consideration for rent payments, which may include contingent rentals based on the seller-lessee's future operations (FAS-98, par. 8).

If occupancy by the seller-lessee's customers is transient or shortterm, the seller-lessee may provide ancillary services, such as housekeeping, inventory control, entertainment, bookkeeping, and food service. Thus, active use by a seller-lessee in its trade or business includes the use of the leased property as a hotel, bonded warehouse, parking lot, or some other similar business (FAS-98, par. 8).

Adequate Initial and Continuing Investment by the Purchaser-Lessor

To qualify for sale-leaseback accounting under FAS-98, the purchaser-lessor's initial and continuing investment in the property must be adequate as prescribed by FAS-66. In determining whether the purchaser's minimum initial investment is adequate under the provisions of FAS-66, the sales value of the property is used and not the stated sales price that appears in the sales contract.

In addition to an adequate initial investment, FAS-66 requires that the purchaser maintain a continuing investment in the property by increasing the investment each year. The purchaser's total indebtedness for the purchase price of the property must be reduced each year in equal amounts that will extinguish the entire indebtedness (interest and principal) over a specified maximum period. The specified maximum period for land transactions is 20 years. The specified maximum period for all other real estate transactions is no more than that offered at the time of sale for first mortgages by independent financial institutions. (The purchaser's initial investment, continuing investment, and the stated sales price in the property are discussed fully earlier in this chapter.)

Transfer of All Other Risks and Rewards of Ownership

To qualify for sale-leaseback accounting under FAS-98, the sellerlessee must transfer all of the risks and rewards of ownership in the property to the purchaser-lessor.

No Other Continuing Involvement

FAS-98 considers the leaseback portion of a sale-leaseback transaction to be a form of continued involvement with the leased property by the seller-lessee (FAS-98, par. 48). Other than the continued involvement represented by the leaseback portion of the sale-leaseback transaction, a normal leaseback excludes any *other* continuing involvement in the leased property by the seller-lessee. Thus, saleleaseback accounting cannot be used to account for a sale-leaseback transaction in which the seller-lessee has any other continuing involvement in the property besides that represented by the leaseback portion of the transaction. (The continuing involvement of the seller in the property is discussed fully earlier in this chapter.)

An exchange of some stated or unstated rights or privileges is indicated in a sale-leaseback transaction if the terms of the transaction are substantially different from terms that an independent third-party lessor would accept. In this event, the stated or unstated rights or privileges shall be considered in evaluating the continued involvement of the seller-lessee. Terms or conditions indicating stated or unstated rights or privileges may involve the sales price, the interest rate, and terms of any loan from the sellerlessee to the purchaser-lessor (FAS-98, par. 9).

Recognition of Profit by Full Accrual Method

A sale-leaseback transaction must meet the criteria of FAS-98 before the seller-lessee can account for the transaction by the sale-leaseback accounting method (full accrual method). Under the sale-leaseback accounting method, the seller-lessee (*a*) records a sale, (*b*) removes the sold property and its related liabilities from the balance sheet, (*c*) recognizes gain or loss on the sale portion of the transaction in accordance with FAS-66, and (*d*) classifies the lease portion of the transaction as either a capitalized lease or an operating lease, in accordance with the provisions of FAS-13, as amended by FAS-28.

Once a sale-leaseback transaction qualifies for sale-leaseback accounting in accordance with the provisions of FAS-98, the steps below are followed to determine the amount of gain (loss) and the time of recognition of the gain (loss):

Step 1:   Compute the *amount* of gain (loss) on the sale portion of the sale-leaseback transaction in accordance with the provisions of FAS-66. (Disregard the fact that the sale is part of a sale-leaseback transaction.)

   Note: A loss must be recognized immediately on the sale portion of a sale-leaseback transaction if the undepreciated cost of the property sold is more than its fair value. The maximum amount of loss that is recognized immediately cannot exceed the difference between the fair value of the property and its undepreciated cost. If the indicated loss exceeds the difference between the fair value of the property sold and its undepreciated cost, the loss is possibly, in substance, a prepayment of rent. Under this circumstance, it is appropriate to defer the indicated loss and amortize it as prepaid rent (FAS-13, par. 33c, as amended by FAS-28, par. 3).

Step 2:   Classify the lease portion of the sale-leaseback transaction in accordance with the provisions of FAS-13, as amended by FAS-28. [Depending on the percentage amount of the property that the seller-lessee leases back, a lease may be classified under FAS-28 as involving (*a*) substantially all of the property, (*b*) a minor portion of the property, or (*c*) more than a minor portion of the property but less than substantially all.]

   Note: A *minor* portion of the property has been leased back if the present value of the total rents to be paid by the seller-lessee under the terms of the lease agreement is reasonable and is equal to 10% or less of the fair value of the property at the inception of the lease. *Substantially all* of the property has been leased back if the present value of the total rents to be paid by the seller-lessee under the terms of the lease agreement is reasonable and is equal to 90% or more of the fair value of the property at the inception of the lease.

Step 3: Determine whether the lease portion of the sale-leaseback transaction qualifies as a capital lease or an operating lease under the provisions of FAS-13.

Note: Under FAS-13, a lease is classified as a capital lease if it meets one or more of the following criteria:

a. Ownership of the property is transferred to the lessee by the end of the lease term.

b. The lease contains a bargain purchase option.

c. At its inception, the lease term is substantially (75% or more) equal to the estimated economic life of the leased property, including earlier years of use. [This particular criterion cannot be used for a lease that begins within the last 25% of the original estimated economic life of the leased property.]

d. The present value of the minimum lease payments at the beginning of the lease term, excluding executory costs and profits thereon to be paid by the lessor, is 90% or more of the fair value of the property at the inception of the lease, less any investment tax credits retained and expected to be realized by the lessor. [This particular criterion cannot be used for a lease that begins within the last 25% of the original estimated economic life of the leased property.]

Step 4: Recognize the amount of gain (loss) computed in Step 1, based on the percentage amount of the property that the seller-lessee leases back in Step 2 (substantially all of the property, a minor portion of the property, or more than a minor portion of the property but less than substantially all), *and* determine whether, in Step 3, the lease is classified as a capital lease or an operating lease.

If, under Step 2, the lease portion of the sale-leaseback transaction is classified as *substantially all*, any gain (loss) on the sale is deferred and amortized by the seller-lessee, according to whether the lease is classified, under Step 3, as a capital lease or an operating lease, as follows:

Capital lease—if the lease is classified as a capital lease, the gain (loss) on the sale is amortized in proportion to the amortization of the leased property.

Operating lease—if the lease is classified as an operating lease, the gain (loss) on the sale is amortized in proportion to the gross rental charged to expense over the lease term.

If, under Step 2, the lease portion of the sale-leaseback transaction is classified as *minor*, the sale and leaseback are accounted for as two independent transactions based on their separate terms. The lease must provide for a reasonable amount of rent, however, considering prevailing market conditions at the inception of the lease. The seller-lessee must increase or decrease the gain (loss) on the sale of the property by an amount that brings the total rental for the leased property to a reasonable amount. Any amount resulting from a rental adjustment shall be amortized as follows:

Capital lease—the deferred or accrued amount of rental adjustment is amortized in proportion to the amortization of the leased property.

Operating lease—the deferred or accrued amount of rental adjustment is amortized in proportion to the gross rental charged to expense over the lease term.

If, under Step 2, the lease portion of the sale-leaseback transaction is classified as *more than minor but less than substantially all*, the seller-lessee shall recognize any excess gain determined at the date of the sale, according to whether the lease is classified under Step 3 as a capital lease or an operating lease, as follows:

Capital lease—the excess gain (if any) is equal to the amount of gain that exceeds the seller-lessee's recorded amount of the property as determined under the provisions of FAS-13 (the lesser of the fair value of the leased property or the present value of the minimum lease payments). For example, if the seller-lessee's recorded amount of the sale-leaseback property is $100,000 as determined under the provisions of FAS-13, and the amount of gain on the sale portion of the sale-leaseback transaction is $120,000, the excess gain that is recognized by the seller-lessee is $20,000. The balance of the gain ($100,000) is deferred and amortized in proportion to the amortization of the leased property.

Operating lease—the excess gain (if any) on a sale-leaseback transaction is equal to the amount of gain that exceeds the present value of the minimum lease payments over the term of the lease. The amount of gain on the sale portion of the sale-leaseback transaction that is not recognized at the date of the sale is deferred and amortized over the lease term in proportion to the gross rentals charged to expense.

For a complete discussion of sale-leaseback transactions, see the chapter titled "Leases."

Profit Recognition Other Than by the Full Accrual Method

A sale-leaseback transaction must qualify under the provisions of FAS-98 and under most of the provisions of FAS-66 before the full amount of the profit on the sale portion of the transaction can be recognized by the sale-leaseback accounting method (full accrual method).

When one (or more) of the criteria for recognizing the full amount of profit on the sale portion of a sale-leaseback transaction is not met, an alternative method of recognizing revenue from the sale must be used. The alternative method selected may be required by FAS-66 or may be a matter of professional judgment. The four accounting methods recommended by FAS-66 are (1) the deposit method, (2) the cost-recovery method, (3) the installment sales method, and (4) the reduced profit method. (The four alternative methods are discussed earlier in this chapter.)

The collectibility of the receivable should be evaluated periodically. When it becomes apparent that the seller's receivable is reasonably assured of being collected, the seller should change to the full accrual accounting method. (Change to the full accrual method is discussed thoroughly earlier in this chapter.)

Regulated Enterprises—Sale-Leaseback Transactions

FAS-98 applies to regulated enterprises that are subject to FAS-71 (Accounting for the Effects of Certain Types of Regulation). The application of FAS-98 for financial accounting purposes (GAAP) may result in the recognition of income and expense in a different accounting period than that in which the same income and expense are recognized for regulatory purposes (rate-making). Under income tax accounting, this results in a temporary difference. If a temporary difference represents part or all of a phase-in plan as defined by FAS-92 (Regulated Enterprises—Accounting for Phase-In Plans), a specific method of accounting is prescribed by FAS-98. For all other types of temporary differences, a different method of accounting is specified (FAS-98, par. 14).

If a temporary difference represents part or all of a phase-in plan, as defined by FAS-92, it is accounted for in accordance with the provisions of FAS-92. In all other circumstances, a temporary difference is modified to conform with FAS-71. For example, the sale portion of a sale-leaseback transaction may be recognized for regulatory purposes and not recognized for financial accounting purposes because the transaction is accounted for by the deposit method. In this event, amortization of the asset should be modified to equal the total amount of the rental expense and gain or loss allowable for regulatory purposes. Also, the sale portion of a sale-leaseback transaction may be recognized for regulatory purposes and not recognized for financial accounting purposes because the transaction is accounted for as a financing. In this event, amortization of the asset and the total amount of interest imputed under the interest method for the financing should be modified to equal the total rental expense and gain or loss allowable for regulatory purposes (FAS-98, par. 15).

If it is not part of a phase-in plan as defined by FAS-92 and it meets the criteria of FAS-71, a temporary difference between the amount of income or expense allowable for regulatory purposes and the amount of income or expense recognized by the deposit method or as a financing shall be capitalized or accrued as a separate regulatory asset or liability (FAS-98, par. 16).

Financial Statement Disclosure and Presentation

The financial statements of the seller-lessee shall include a description of the terms of the sale-leaseback transaction, including future commitments, obligations, or other provisions that require or result in the seller-lessee's continuing involvement (FAS-98, par. 17).

A seller-lessee that has accounted for a sale-leaseback by the deposit method or as financing shall disclose in the aggregate and for each of the five succeeding fiscal years (FAS-98, par. 18):

- The obligation for future minimum lease payments as of the date of the latest balance sheet presented in the aggregate and for each of the next five years.

- The total of minimum sublease rentals, if any, to be received in the future under noncancelable subleases in the aggregate and for each of the next five years.

Retail Land Sales

The development of a large tract of land, usually over several years, is typical for a company in the retail land sales industry. Master plans are drawn for the improvement of the property, which may include amenities, and all necessary regulatory approvals are obtained. Large advertising campaigns are held at an early stage, frequently resulting in substantial sales before significant development of the property. In most retail land sales, a substantial portion of the sales price is financed by the seller in the form of a long-term receivable secured by the property. Interest and principal are paid by the buyer over an extended number of years. In the event of default, the buyer usually loses his or her entire equity and the property reverts back to the seller. Frequently, the retail land sales contract or existing state law provides for a period in which the purchaser may receive a refund of all or part of any payments made. In addition, the seller may be unable to obtain a deficiency judgment against the buyer because of operation of the law. Finally, many project-wide improvements and amenities are deferred until the later stages of development, when the seller may be faced with financial difficulties.

Because of small down payments, frequent cancellations and refunds, and the possibility that the retail land sales company may not be financially able to complete the project, certain specific conditions must be met before a sale can be recognized.

Profit Recognition

FAS-66 requires that profit on all retail land sales within a project be recognized by a single accounting method. As conditions change for the entire project, the method of profit recognition changes in accordance with the provisions of FAS-66 (FAS-66, par. 44). The provisions of FAS-66 require that the profits on a retail land sales project be recognized by (*a*) the full accrual method, (*b*) the percentage-of-completion method, (*c*) the installment sales method, or (*d*) the deposit method. FAS-66 contains specific criteria that must be met before a particular profit recognition method can be used.

A *retail land sales project* is defined as a "homogeneous, reasonably contiguous area of land that may, for development or marketing, be subdivided in accordance with a master plan" (FAS-66, footnote 17).

Profit Recognition—Full Accrual Method

A retail land sales project must meet all of the following conditions for the full accrual method of accounting to be used for the recognition of profit (FAS-66, par. 45):

- The down payment and all subsequent payments have been made by the buyer, through and including any period of cancellation, and all periods for any refund have expired.

- The buyer has paid a total of 10% or more, in principal or interest, of the total contract sales price.

- The seller's collection experience for the project or for prior projects indicates that at least 90% of the receivables in force for six months after the sale is recorded will be collected in full. A down payment of 20% or more is an acceptable substitute for this experience test.

> **OBSERVATION:** Profit may be recognized before the end of six months if collection experience is based on a prior project. The six-month period is an eligibility test for the full accrual method of accounting.

The collection experience of a prior project may be used if (*a*) the prior project was similar in characteristics to the new project and (*b*) the collection period was long enough to determine collectibility of receivables to maturity dates.

- The seller's receivable for the property sold is not subject to subordination of new loans. However, subordination is allowed for construction of a residence, provided the project's collection experience for such subordinated receivables is approximately the same as that for those receivables that are not subordinated.

- The seller is not obligated to construct amenities or other facilities or to complete any improvements for lots that have been sold.

If all of the above conditions are met for the entire retail land sales project, the seller shall recognize profits by the full accrual method of accounting.

> ☞ **PRACTICE POINTER:**   The actual procedures that must be used to record retail land sales under the full accrual method of accounting are as follows:
>
> - The total contract price of the retail land sale, before any deductions, is recorded as a gross sale. The total contract price includes the total amount of principal and interest that is expected to be received from the sale.
>
> - The down payment on the sale is recorded. The difference between the total contract price of the retail land sale and the down payment is the gross receivable.
>
> - The gross receivable is discounted at the date of sale to yield an amount at which it could be sold on a volume basis without recourse to the seller. The discount on the gross receivable is referred to as a "valuation discount."
>
> - The valuation discount is amortized to income over the life of the retail land sales contract. The interest method should be used to produce a constant rate of amortization.
>
> - An allowance for contract cancellations is established based on estimates of contracts that are not expected to be collected in subsequent periods. Canceled contracts are charged directly to the allowance account.
>
> For the purpose of determining the adequacy of the allowance for contract cancellations in subsequent periods, all receivables that do not conform to the criteria in the following table shall be considered uncollectible and the allowance account adjusted appropriately:

Percentage contract price paid	*Delinquency period*
Less than 25%	90 days
25% but less than 50%	120 days
50% and over	150 days

If a buyer is willing to assume personal liability for his or her debt and apparently has the means and ability to complete all payments, the delinquency periods in the above table may be extended.

- The following items represent deductions from the gross sale to arrive at net sales for the period:
  — Valuation discount
  — Allowance for contract cancellations
  — Deferred portion of gross sale (to be matched with future work or performance of the seller)

- Cost of sales should be computed on net sales for the period.

- A sale that is made and canceled in the same reporting period should be included in, and also deducted from, gross sales or disclosed appropriately in some other manner.

- The unamortized valuation discount (discount on receivables) and the allowance for contract cancellations are shown on the balance sheet as deductions from the related receivables.

- Deferred revenue, less any related costs, is shown on the balance sheet as a liability. Deferred revenue should be recognized in future periods as the work is performed by the seller.

Profit Recognition—Other Than Full Accrual Method

Percentage-of-Completion Method   If the first four criteria for applying the full accrual method of accounting are met for the entire retail land sales project and the fifth criterion is not met (see "Profit Recognition—Full Accrual Method," above), the seller shall recognize profits by the percentage-of-completion method of accounting, provided the following additional criteria are met for the entire project (FAS-66, par. 46):

- Progress on the entire project has passed the preliminary stages and tangible evidence exists to indicate that the project will be completed according to plans. Tangible evidence of such progress includes the following:
  — Funds have actually been expended.
  — Work on project improvements has been initiated.
  — Engineering plans and construction commitments pertaining to lots that have been sold are in existence.
  — Access roads and amenities are substantially completed.
  — There is no evidence of any significant delay to the project, and dependable estimates of costs to complete the project and extent of progress are reasonable.

- At the end of the normal payment period, it is reasonably expected that the property clearly will be useful for its intended purposes as represented by the seller at the time of sale.

If the above criteria are met for the entire project and the first four criteria for applying the full accrual method of accounting are met for the entire project, the seller recognizes profits on retail land sales by the percentage-of-completion method.

Installment Sales Method   If the first two criteria for applying the full accrual method of accounting are met for the entire project and the other three criteria are not met, the seller shall recognize profits by the installment sales method, provided the following additional criteria are met for the entire project (FAS-66, par. 47):

- The current and prospective financial capabilities of the retail land sales company (seller) must reflect with reasonable assurance that the company is capable of completing all of its obligations under the sales contract and master plan.

- Indications of the seller's financial capabilities include (*a*) the sufficiency of equity capital, (*b*) borrowing capacity, and (*c*) positive cash flow from present operations.

If the above criteria are met for the entire project and the first two criteria for applying the full accrual method of accounting are met for the entire project, the seller shall recognize profits on retail land sales by the installment sales method.

Deposit Accounting Method   If a retail land sale does not meet the criteria for accounting by the full accrual method, the percentage-of completion method, or the installment sale method, the seller shall account for all proceeds from retail land sales by the deposit method of-accounting (FAS-66, par. 48). Under the deposit method of ac- counting, the effective date of the sale is deferred and all funds received, including principal and interest, are recorded as deposits on retail land sales.

Change in Accounting Method

If a retail land sales entity has been reporting sales for the entire project by the deposit method and subsequently the criteria for the installment sales method, the percentage-of-completion method, or the full accrual method are met for the entire project, the change to the new method shall be accounted for as a change in accounting estimate (FAS-66, par. 49). Thus, the effects of the change shall be accounted for prospectively in accordance with FAS-154 (Account- ing Changes and Error Corrections). If the effects of the change in an accounting estimate are significant, disclosure of the effects on (*a*) income from continuing operations, (*b*) net income, and (*c*) the related per share data should be made in the financial statements of the period of change.

Initially, retail land sales may be accounted for by the installment sales method, and subsequently the criteria for the percentage-of-completion method may be met for the entire project. In this event, the percentage-of-completion method may be adopted for the entire project. The effects of the change to the percentage-of-completion method are accounted for as a change in accounting estimate and, if material, disclosure of the effects on (*a*) income before extraordinary items, (*b*) net income, and (*c*) related per share data should be made in the financial statements of the period of change.

In reporting the change from the installment sales method to the percentage-of-completion method, the following procedures should be observed:

- If required, the receivables should be discounted to their present values at the date of change in accordance with APB-21 (Interest on Receivables and Payables).

- The liability for the remaining future performance of the seller should be discounted to its present value at the date of the change.

- The amount of discount, if any, on the receivables and the amount of discount, if any, on the liability for remaining future performance by the seller are deducted from the unrealized gross profit on installment sales at the date of the change to arrive at the net credit to income resulting from the change.

Disclosure—Retail Land Sales

Retail land sales companies, diversified entities with significant retail land sales operations, and investors who derive a significant portion of their income from investments involved in retail land sales must disclose specific information in the financial statements, as follows (FAS-66, par. 50):

- The maturities of the receivables from retail land sales for each of the five years following the date of the financial statements

- The amount of delinquent receivables and the method used to determine delinquency

- The weighted average and range of stated interest rates on receivables from retail land sales

- Estimated total costs and anticipated expenditures to improve major areas of the project from which sales are being made, for each of the five years following the date of the financial statements

- The amount of recorded obligations for improvements

- The method of recognizing profit

- The effect of a change in accounting estimate, if the percentage-of-completion method is adopted for a retail land sales project originally reported using the installment method (APB-21)

REAL ESTATE COSTS AND INITIAL RENTAL OPERATIONS

Preacquisition Costs

Costs frequently are incurred before the actual date on which a parcel of real property is acquired. These costs are referred to by FAS-67 as *preacquisition costs*. Practically any type of cost may be classified as a preacquisition cost if it is incurred prior to the date of acquisition of a parcel of real property. For example, the cost of an option to purchase real property at a future date is a preacquisition cost and usually is capitalized. If the option is not exercised on or before its expiration date, however, the option becomes worthless and should be expensed.

All other types of preacquisition costs are expensed when incurred, unless they can be identified specifically to the real property being acquired and (FAS-67, par. 4):

- The preacquisition costs would be capitalized if the property were acquired.

- The acquisition of the property or an option to acquire the property is probable (e.g., the prospective purchaser is actively seeking to acquire the property and can obtain financing).

> **OBSERVATION:** *Probable* implies that the property is available for sale, the purchaser is currently trying to acquire the property, and the necessary financing is reasonably expected to be available.

Thus, preacquisition costs of a real estate project consist of (*a*) unexpired options to purchase real property and (*b*) other costs that meet all of the above conditions. Preacquisition costs that do not qualify for capitalization should be expensed when incurred (FAS-67, par. 5).

After a parcel of real property is acquired, preacquisition costs are reclassified as project costs. In the event that the property is not acquired, capitalized preacquisition costs shall not exceed the amount recoverable, if any, from the sale of options, developmental plans, and other proceeds. Capitalized preacquisition costs in excess of recoverable amounts are charged to expense (FAS-67, par. 5).

Illustration of Preacquisition Costs

Omega Company incurred the following preacquisition costs related to a piece of property:

1. Option to purchase land parcel: $10,000
2. Architectural consultation concerning feasibility of constructing warehouse facility on land parcel: $14,000

Situation 1: At the end of the year in which the above costs were incurred, Omega was actively seeking financing for the land and warehouse facility. Management believes it is probable that financing will be found and the land will be purchased, after which time the warehouse facility will be constructed.

   In this situation, the $10,000 option and the $14,000 feasibility study should be capitalized as preacquisition costs, to be reclassified as project costs when the land purchase and warehouse construction commence.

Situation 2: At the end of the year in which the above costs were incurred, preliminary results of the feasibility study were not optimistic. Omega has suspended its search for financing, pending the final outcome of the feasibility study. The company considers the probability of purchasing the land and constructing the facility as no more than reasonably possible, but is optimistic that it can sell the option for at least its $10,000 cost.

   In this situation, the $10,000 option cost should be carried as an asset, but the $14,000 for the feasibility study should be expensed in the current period.

Project Costs

Project costs of real estate projects may be direct or indirect. Direct costs that are related to the acquisition, development, and construction of a real estate project are capitalized as project costs (FAS-67, par. 7).

   Indirect costs of real estate projects that can be identified clearly to specific projects under development or construction are capitalized as project costs. Indirect costs that are accumulated in one account, but clearly relate to several real estate projects under development or construction, are allocated on a reasonable basis to each of the projects (FAS-67, par. 7).

   Indirect costs on real estate projects not under development or construction are expensed as incurred. In addition, indirect costs that cannot be identified clearly with specific projects such as general and administrative expenses are charged to expense when incurred (FAS-67, par. 7).

Illustration of Direct and Indirect Project Costs

Zeta Co. incurs the following direct and indirect project costs for two major real estate construction projects, identified as L and M:

Direct project costs:	
Project L	$ 150,000
Project M	740,000
Indirect project costs:	
Identified with Projects L and M	270,000
Identified with projects not currently under development	145,000
General and administrative	250,000
Total	$1,555,000

The indirect costs associated with Projects L and M are allocable one-third to Project L and two-thirds to Project M.

Treatment of the $1,555,000 of project costs for the year is as follows (in thousands of dollars):

	Project L	Project M	Current Expense
Direct costs	$150	$740	
Indirect costs:			
Project L ($270 x 1/3)	90		
Project M ($270 x 2/3)		180	
Not allocable ($145 + $250)			$395
	$240	$920	$395

Taxes and Insurance

Property taxes and insurance are capitalized as project costs only during periods in which activities necessary to get the property ready for its intended use are in progress (FAS-67, par. 6).

After real property is substantially completed and ready for its intended use, FAS-67 also requires that property taxes and insurance costs be expensed as incurred (FAS-67, par. 6).

Amenity Costs of Real Property

Golf courses, swimming pools, tennis courts, clubhouses, and other types of amenities frequently are included in the overall plans of a real estate project. The ultimate disposition of an amenity, however, may vary from one real estate project to another. Thus, accounting for the costs of amenities is based on the developer's (management) ulti-mate plans for the disposition of the amenity. In this respect, a devel-oper may decide to retain ownership of the amenity and to either (*a*) operate the amenity or (*b*) eventually sell the amenity. On the other hand, the developer may be required under the terms of the individ-ual sales agreements to sell or otherwise transfer ownership of the amenity to the purchasers of the individual components within the project. In this event, the purchasers of the individual components within the project usually form an association for the purposes of taking title to the amenity and operating the amenity for the common benefit of all owners of individual components within the project.

Accounting for the costs of amenities under the provisions of FAS-67 is as follows:

Ownership Not Retained by Developer   When the ownership of an amenity is to be transferred to the individual components within the real estate project, the net cost of the amenity is accounted for by the developer as a capitalized common cost of the project. The capi-talized common cost of an amenity is allocated to the individual components within the project that are expected to benefit from the use of the amenity. Thus, the total cost of each individual com-ponent in the project that benefits from the amenity will include a proportionate share of the costs of the amenity (FAS-67, par. 8a).

The developer's net cost or gain that is accounted for as a com-mon cost (reduction) of the real estate project may include the sales price, if any, and all other proceeds, if any, from the transfer of the amenity, less the following items:

- Direct costs that clearly are identifiable to the amenity
- Indirect costs that clearly are related to the amenity
- The developer's cost of operating the amenity until the amenity is transferred to the individual components in the project in accor-dance with the sales contract or other contractual agreement
- Common costs of the project that are allocated appropriately to the amenity

If an amenity clearly benefits specific individual components within a real estate project, the common cost (reduction) of the amenity is allocated only to those specific individual components.

Ownership Retained by Developer When a developer retains ownership of an amenity, the total cost of the amenity is capitalized as a separate asset. The total cost of an amenity includes direct costs, indirect costs, and the allocation of common costs, including operating results of the amenity prior to its date of substantial completion and availability for its intended use. Under FAS-67, however, the amount capitalized cannot exceed the estimated fair value of the amenity at its expected date of substantial completion. Any costs in excess of the estimated fair value of the amenity at the expected date of its substantial completion are accounted for as common costs of the real estate project (FAS-67, par. 8b).

After it is substantially completed and ready for its intended use, further revision of the final capitalized cost of an amenity is not permitted. This cost becomes the basis of the amenity for any future sale. The subsequent basis for determining gain or loss on the sale of the amenity is the capitalized cost of the amenity not in excess of its estimated fair value at its date of substantial completion, less any allowable depreciation to the date of the sale.

After its date of substantial completion and availability for its intended use, the operational results of an amenity that is owned by the developer shall be included in the developer's current net income (FAS-67, par. 9).

Incidental Operations of Real Property

Incidental operations of a real estate project usually occur during the holding or development stage of the project and are intended to reduce the cost of the project. Incidental operations do not include activities that result in a profit or return from the proposed development of the real property. For example, revenue received from billboard advertisements placed on the property or miscellaneous concession income would be classified as incidental operations.

If the incremental revenue received from incidental operations exceeds the related incremental costs, the difference is accounted for as a reduction of the capitalized costs of the real estate project. Thus, when incidental operations of a real estate project result in a profit, the capitalized costs of the project are reduced by the amount of profit. Under FAS-67, however, the same does *not* hold true if the incidental operations result in a loss: if the incremental costs of incidental operations exceed the related incremental revenue, the difference is charged to expense when incurred (FAS-67, par. 10). The guidance in FAS-67 on accounting for incidental operations does not apply to real estate time-sharing transactions. Guidance on accounting for incidental operations of real estate time-sharing transactions can be found in SOP 04-2 (Accounting for Real Estate Time-Sharing Transactions) (FAS-152, par. 4).

Allocation of Capitalized Costs

All capitalized costs of a real estate project are allocated to the individual components within the project. If practicable, FAS-67 requires that capitalized costs be allocated by the specific identification method. Under this method, capitalized costs are identified specifically with the individual components within the real estate project. However, if it is impractical to use the specific identification method to allocate capitalized costs, FAS-67 requires that allocations be made as follows (FAS-67, par. 11).

Land Costs Only capitalized costs associated with the land prior to any construction are allocated as land costs. Land costs prior to any construction include capitalized land costs and other preconstruction common costs related to the land, including preconstruction common costs of amenities.

Total capitalized land costs are allocated based on the relative fair value of each land parcel prior to any construction. A land parcel may be identified as a lot, an acre, acreage, a unit, or a tract.

Construction Costs Capitalized construction costs are allocated based on the relative sales value of each individual structure or unit located on a parcel of land. In the event capitalized costs of a real estate project cannot be allocated by the specific identification method or the relative sales value method, the capitalized cost shall be allocated on area methods or other methods appropriate under the circumstances.

Revisions of Estimates

Estimates are used extensively in the acquisition, development, and construction of a real estate project. As a result, revisions of estimated costs occur frequently, and past, present, and future accounting periods may be affected by the revisions.

Revisions of estimates that occur in the acquisition, development, and construction stages of a real estate project are accounted for as changes in accounting estimates (FAS-154). The effects of a change in accounting estimate are accounted for (*a*) in the period of change, if the change affects only that period or (*b*) in the period of change and future periods, if the change affects both. A change in an accounting estimate caused in part or entirely by a change in accounting principle should be reported as a change in accounting estimate. FAS-154 requires that disclosure be made in current period financial statements of the effects of a change in an accounting estimate on (*a*) income from continuing operations, (*b*) net income, and (*c*) related per share data (FAS-154, par. 22). However, ordinary accounting estimates for uncollectible accounts or inventory adjustments, made each period, do not have to be disclosed, unless they are material (FAS-67, par. 12).

Abandonments and Changes in Use

Occasionally a real estate project is partially or completely abandoned, or there is a significant change in the use of the property in the project. Under the provisions of FAS-67, if part or all of a real estate project is abandoned, the related capitalized costs must be expensed immediately. The capitalized costs of an abandoned real estate project should not be allocated to other real estate projects (FAS-67, par. 13).

The cost of land donated to a governmental authority for uses that will benefit the project is not accounted for as abandoned. Under this circumstance, the cost of the donated land is accounted for as a common cost of acquiring the project. Thus, the cost of the donated land is allocated to the other land in the project, based on the relative fair value of each parcel of land prior to construction of any buildings or structures (FAS-67, par. 14).

After significant development and construction costs have been capitalized in a real estate project, there may be a change in the use of part or all of the land within the project. Under the provisions of FAS-67, capitalized costs incurred prior to a change in use of all or part of the land within a real estate project are charged to expense, except in the following circumstance:

> The enterprise has developed a formal plan that indicates that the change in use of the land will result in a higher economic yield than was originally anticipated. In this event, the maximum costs that can be capitalized must not exceed the estimated value of the revised project at the date of substantial completion and availability for its intended use. Capitalized costs in excess of the estimated value of the revised project when substantially completed, if any, are charged to expense (FAS-67, par. 15).

Selling Costs

Costs incurred to sell real estate projects are accounted for as (*a*) project costs, (*b*) prepaid expenses, or (*c*) period costs.

Project Costs

Project costs are capitalized as part of the construction costs of the real estate project provided that both of the following conditions are met (FAS-67, par. 17):

- They are incurred for tangible assets that are used as marketing aids during the marketing period of the real estate project, or for services performed in obtaining regulatory approval for real estate sales in the project.
- The costs incurred are reasonably expected to be recovered from sales.

☞ **PRACTICE POINTER:** Costs to sell real estate that qualify as project costs, less recoverable amounts from incidental operations or salvage value, include legal fees for prospectuses, sales offices, and model units, with or without furnishings.

Costs to sell real estate projects that qualify as project costs become part of the capitalized cost of the project and are allocated to the individual components of the project as common costs.

Prepaid Expenses

Prepaid expenses, which are sometimes called *deferred charges,* are capitalized if:

- They are directly associated with the real estate project;
- The costs are likely to be recoverable from the sales of the project; and
- The full accrual method is not being used to account for sales.

The prepaid expenses are amortized over the period that is expected to benefit from the expenditure (FAS-67, par. 18).

Advances on commissions and unused sales brochures are examples of costs to sell real estate projects that qualify as prepaid expenses.

Period Costs

Period costs are charged to expense in the period incurred because they do not meet the criteria for project costs or prepaid expenses. Costs to sell real estate projects that do not benefit future periods should be expensed in the period incurred as period costs. Grand opening expenses, sales salaries, sales overhead, and advertising costs are examples of period costs (FAS-67, par. 19).

☞ **PRACTICE POINTER:** The guidance in FAS-67 on accounting for costs incurred to sell real estate does not apply to real estate time-sharing transactions. Guidance on accounting for costs incurred to sell real estate in time-sharing transactions can be found in SOP 04-2 (Accounting for Real Estate Time-Sharing Transactions) (FAS-152, par. 4).

Rental Costs of Real Estate Projects

Initial Rental Operations

Initial rental operations commence when a real estate project is substantially completed and available for occupancy. A real estate project is considered *substantially completed and available for occupancy* when tenant improvements have been completed by the developer, but in no event later than one year after major construction activity has been completed, excluding routine maintenance and cleanup (FAS-67, par. 22).

The actual rental operation of a real estate project shall commence when the project is substantially completed and available for occupancy. At this time, rental revenues and related operating costs are recognized on an accrual basis. Operating costs include amortization of deferred rental costs, if any, and depreciation expense (FAS-67, par. 22).

Some portions of a real estate rental project may still require major construction for completion, and other portions of the same project may be substantially completed and available for occupancy. In this event, each portion should be accounted for as a separate project (FAS-67, par. 23).

Operating Leases

Costs incurred to rent real estate projects under operating leases are either chargeable to future periods or chargeable to the current period.

Chargeable to Future Periods If the costs can be identified to, and reasonably expected to be recovered from, specific revenue, such costs are capitalized and amortized to the periods in which the specific revenue is earned. If the costs are for goods not used or services not received, such costs are charged to the future periods in which the goods are used or services are received.

If deferred rental costs can be associated with the revenue from a specific operating lease, such costs are amortized over the lease term. The amortization period commences when the rental project is substantially completed and available for occupancy. If deferred rental costs cannot be identified with the revenue from a specific operating lease, such costs are amortized over the periods benefited. The amortization period commences when the rental project is substantially completed and available for occupancy (FAS-67, par. 21).

> ☛ **PRACTICE POINTER:** Expense unamortized rental costs that subsequently become unrecoverable from future operations when they are determined to be unrecoverable. For example, unamortized rental costs related to specific leases which have been, or will be, terminated should be charged to expense.

Chargeable to the Current Period If the costs to rent real estate projects under operating leases do not qualify as chargeable to future periods, they are accounted for as period costs and expensed as incurred (FAS-67, par. 20).

Recoverability

Real estate projects that are substantially complete and ready for their intended use are to be carried at the lower of carrying amount or fair market value less cost to sell (FAS-144, pars. 34–36). The recognition and measurement principles in FAS-144 (Accounting for Intangible Assets of Motor Carriers) apply to real estate held for development and sale: both property currently being developed and property to be developed in the future (FAS-144, pars. 7–9).

Each individual project is analyzed separately to determine whether a write-down is necessary. An individual project is considered to consist of similar components within the real estate project, such as (*a*) individual residences, (*b*) individual apartments or condominiums, or (*c*) individual lots, acres, or tracts. Thus, a real estate project that includes 50 individual residences, 10 condominium buildings, 20 multifamily buildings, and 100 residential lots would be accounted for as four separate projects for the purposes of determining net realizable values. The net carrying amount of the 100 residential lots may exceed their net realizable value, while the individual net carrying values of the 50 individual residences, 10 condominium buildings, and 20 multifamily buildings may not exceed their individual estimated net realizable values (FAS-67, par. 24).

> **OBSERVATION:** FAS-144 applies to: (1) real estate projects that are substantially complete and that will be sold, (2) real estate held for development, and (3) real estate projects that are substantially complete and that will be held and used (FAS-144, par. C10).

RELATED CHAPTERS IN 2009 *GAAP GUIDE* LEVEL A

Chapter 1, "Accounting Changes"
Chapter 11, "Depreciable Assets and Depreciation"
Chapter 20, "Impairment of Long-Lived Assets"
Chapter 29, "Leases"
Chapter 30, "Long-Term Construction Contracts"
Chapter 41, "Revenue Recognition"
Chapter 54, "Regulated Industries"

RELATED CHAPTERS IN 2009 *GAAP GUIDE* LEVELS B, C, AND D

Chapter 1, "Accounting Changes"
Chapter 19, "Impairment of Long-Lived Assets"

Chapter 26, "Leases"
Chapter 27, "Long-Term Construction Contracts"
Chapter 33, "Real Estate Transactions"
Chapter 36, "Revenue Recognition"

CHAPTER 38
RELATED PARTY DISCLOSURES

CONTENTS

OVERVIEW

Financial statement disclosure of related party transactions is required by GAAP in order for those statements to fairly present financial position, cash flows, and results of operations.

GAAP for related party transactions are presented in the following authoritative pronouncement:

FAS-57   Related Party Disclosures

BACKGROUND

A *related party* is one that can exercise control or significant influence over the management and/or operating policies of another party, to the extent that one of the parties may be prevented from fully pursuing its own separate interests.

Related parties consist of all affiliates of an enterprise, including (a) their management and their immediate families, (b) their principal owners and their immediate families, (c) their investments accounted for by the equity method (absent the election of the fair value option under FAS-159, The Fair Value Option for Financial Assets and Financial Liabilities), (d) beneficial employee trusts that are managed by the management of the enterprise, and (e) any party that may, or does, deal with the enterprise and has ownership of, control over, or can significantly influence the management or operating policies of another party to the extent that an arm's-length transaction may not be achieved (FAS-57, par. 1, as amended by FAS-159, par. C.2.a).

Transactions among related parties generally are accounted for on the same basis as if the parties were not related, unless the *substance* of the transaction is not arm's length. Substance over form is an important consideration when accounting for transactions involving related parties.

Common related party transactions include the following (FAS-57, par. 1):

- Sales, purchases, and transfers of realty and personal property
- Services received or furnished (e.g., accounting, management, engineering, and legal services)
- Use of property and equipment by lease
- Borrowings and lendings
- Maintenance of bank balances as compensating balances for the benefit of another
- Intercompany billings based on allocation of common costs
- Filing of consolidated tax returns

> **OBSERVATION:** The Enron Corp. engaged in a number of related party transactions. These transactions were related to the financial improprieties that caused Enron's failure. Related party transactions are more likely when an entity is dealing with partnerships, particularly when these partnerships are located in tax havens and where there appears to be little economic justification for the partnership's existence. Regulators and standard-setters are focusing more resources on the proper disclosure of related party transactions; auditors and preparers of financial statements need to be aware of this heightened focus.

REPORTING AND DISCLOSURE STANDARDS

FAS-57 (Related Party Disclosures) requires that material related party transactions that are not eliminated in consolidated or combined financial statements be disclosed in the financial statements of the reporting entity. Related party transactions involving compensation arrangements, expense allowances, and similar items incurred in the ordinary course of business, however, do not have to be disclosed (FAS-57, par. 2).

If separate financial statements of an entity that has been consolidated are presented in a financial report that includes the consolidated financial statements, duplicate disclosure of the related party transactions is not necessary. Disclosure of related party transactions is required, however, in separate financial statements of (*a*) a parent company, (*b*) a subsidiary, (*c*) a corporate joint venture, or (*d*) an investee that is 50% owned or less (FAS-57, par. 2).

Information required to be disclosed for material related party transactions is as follows (FAS-57, par. 2):

- The nature of the relationship of the related parties

- A description of the transactions, including amounts and other pertinent information necessary for an understanding of the effects of the related party transactions, for each period in which an income statement is presented (related party transactions of no or nominal amounts must also be disclosed)

- The dollar amount of transactions for each period in which an income statement is presented; also, the effects of any change in terms between the related parties from terms used in prior periods

- If not apparent in the financial statements, (*a*) the terms of related party transactions, (*b*) the manner of settlement of related party transactions, and (*c*) the amount due to or from related parties

If the operating results or financial position of a reporting entity can be altered significantly by the effects of common ownership or management control of the reporting entity and one or more other entities, even if there are no transactions among any of the entities, the nature of the ownership or management control must be disclosed in the financial statements (FAS-57, par. 4).

> ☛ **PRACTICE POINTER:** The amount of detail disclosed for related party transactions must be sufficient for the user of the financial statements to be able to understand the related party transaction and its impact on the financial statements. Thus, all that is necessary may be disclosure of the total amount of a specific type of material related party transaction or of the effects of the relationship between the related parties. In other circumstances, however, more details may be required for the reader of the financial statements to have a clear understanding of the transaction.

One cannot assume that a related party transaction is consummated in the same manner as an arm's-length transaction. Disclosures or other representations of a material related party transaction in financial statements should not imply that the transaction was made on the same basis as an arm's-length transaction, unless the disclosures or representations can be substantiated (FAS-57, par. 3).

Illustrations of Related Party Disclosures

Transaction between company and officers/directors   During 20X5, the company purchased land and buildings adjoining one of its plants from two company directors for $750,000. The board of directors unanimously approved the purchase, with the two directors involved in the transaction abstaining.

Transaction between company and profit-sharing plan   During 20X5, the company purchased land from one of its profit-sharing plans for $750,000. Department of Labor exemption was received prior to the transaction.

Lease between company and officer/owner   Several years ago, the company leased land in upstate New York from John Doe, an officer and principal owner. The company constructed and furnished a residence on the property for use by the company's customers and distributors. The annual lease payment to Doe is $12,500, and the lease continues through December 31, 20X5. At that time, Doe has an option to purchase the residence and furnishings for $50,000 or to renew the lease at $10,000 per year for an additional five years.

Salary advance to officer   During 20X5, the company made a $100,000 salary advance to John Doe, an officer, as part of a new employment contract that required Doe to relocate to Atlanta, Georgia. According to the terms of the contract, Doe is required to repay the loan at $20,000 per year for the next five years, beginning in 20X8.

RELATED CHAPTER IN 2009 *GAAP GUIDE* *LEVEL A*

Chapter 8, "Contingencies, Risks, and Uncertainties"

RELATED CHAPTER IN 2009 *GAAP GUIDE* *LEVELS B, C, AND D*

Chapter 11, "Contingencies, Risks, and Uncertainties"

RELATED CHAPTER IN 2009 *INTERNATIONAL ACCOUNTING/FINANCIAL REPORTING STANDARDS GUIDE*

Chapter 29, "Related Party Disclosures"

CHAPTER 39
RESEARCH AND DEVELOPMENT

CONTENTS

OVERVIEW

Research and development (R&D) cost is carefully defined in the authoritative accounting literature. Once R&D costs are appropriately identified, GAAP require that they be expensed in the period incurred. Some costs related to R&D activities, however, are appropriately capitalized and carried forward as assets if they have alternative future uses. R&D-related assets typically include items of property, plant, and equipment and intangible assets used in the ongoing R&D effort of the enterprise.

The following pronouncements establish the promulgated GAAP for R&D costs:

FAS-2   Accounting for Research and Development Costs

FAS-68   Research and Development Arrangements

FIN-4   Applicability of FASB Statement No. 2 to Business
           Combinations Accounted for by the Purchase Method

2009 TRANSITION GUIDANCE FOR
FAS-141(R) AND FAS-160

The FASB has recently issued FAS-141(R), *Business Combinations*, which is effective for business combinations for which the acquisition date is on or after the beginning of the first annual reporting period beginning on or after December 15, 2008. The FASB has also issued FAS-160, *Noncontrolling Interests in Consolidated Financial Statements, an Amendment of ARB No. 51*, which is effective for fiscal years, and interim periods within those fiscal years, beginning on or after December 15, 2008. Because these standards are not effective for some companies until December 2009, and because early adoption is prohibited, the 2009 *GAAP Guide* reflects the requirements of FAS-141 prior to its revision in December 2007 and does not reflect the requirements of FAS-160. There is a discussion of the changes in the accounting for business combinations under FAS-141(R) in the Appendix to Chapter 4, "Business Combinations." Similarly, the Appendix to Chapter 7, "Consolidated Financial Statements" includes a discussion of the requirements of FAS-160. However, any effects of FAS-141(R) and/or FAS-160 on this chapter have not been reflected in this edition. Therefore, if a company is subject to the requirements of FAS-141(R) and/or FAS-160, the reader is referred to FAS-141(R) and FAS-160 for these new requirements.

BACKGROUND

Research is the planned efforts of a company to discover new information that will help create a new product, service, process, or technique or vastly improve one in current use. *Development* takes the findings generated by research and formulates a plan to create the desired item or to improve an existing one. Development in the context of this area of GAAP does not include normal improvements in existing operations (FAS-2, par. 8). The following specific activities are *not* covered by the provisions of FAS-2:

- Activities that are unique to the extractive industries, such as prospecting, exploration, drilling, mining, and similar functions. Research and development activities of companies in extractive industries that are comparable in nature to other companies, such as the development or improvement of techniques and processes, *are* covered (FAS-2, par. 3).

- Research and development performed under contract for others, including indirect costs that are specifically reimbursable under a contract (FAS-2, par. 2).

☞ **PRACTICE POINTER:**   R&D does not include market research and testing, because these items specifically relate to the selling and marketing operations of a company. In addition, general and administrative expenses not *directly* related to the R&D activities are not included in R&D.

Because of the high degree of uncertainty of any resulting future benefit, the underlying basic principle in accounting for R&D is conservatism. Since at the time of performing R&D there is uncertainty concerning future success, the most conservative approach is to expense the item in the period incurred.

FIN-4 (Applicability of FASB Statement No. 2 to Business Combinations Accounted for by the Purchase Method) provides guidance in applying the provisions of FAS-2 to R&D costs acquired in a business combination accounted for by the purchase method. FIN-6 (Applicability of FASB Statement No. 2 to Computer Software) and FAS-86 (Accounting for the Costs of Computer Software to Be Sold, Leased, or Otherwise Marketed) provide guidance in applying the provisions of FAS-2 to computer software.

ACCOUNTING AND REPORTING RESEARCH AND DEVELOPMENT—GENERAL STANDARDS

All R&D costs covered by GAAP are expensed in the period when they are incurred (FAS-2, par. 12). Assets used in R&D activity, such as machinery, equipment, facilities, and patents that have alternative future uses either in R&D activities or otherwise are capitalized. Depreciation and amortization on such capitalized R&D-related assets is charged to R&D expense. All expenditures in conjunction with an R&D project, including personnel costs, materials, equipment, facilities, and intangibles, for which the company has no alternative future use beyond the specific project for which the items were purchased, are expensed. Indirect costs, including general and administrative expenses, which are *directly* related to the R&D project also are expensed when incurred (FAS-2, par. 11).

Illustration of Determining R&D Expense

Lambert, Inc. develops new products and, therefore, engages in extensive research and development activities. Following is a description of current-period expenditures related to a current Lambert project:

1. Material and labor directly related to the project $150,000

2. Purchase of machinery and equipment required to carry out the project:

a.	Useful only for this project	75,000
b.	Useful for this and other R&D projects over an estimated five-year period	90,000
3.	Contract services acquired	15,000
4.	Overhead and administration allocation	50,000

Assuming the overhead and administration allocation is for activities closely related to the project, and assuming depreciation of machinery and equipment by the straight-line method with no expected salvage value, the R&D expense for the year is:

Material and labor	$150,000
Machinery and equipment	75,000
Depreciation of machinery and equipment ($90,000/5 years)	18,000
Contract services	15,000
Overhead and administration	50,000
R&D expense	$308,000

The machinery and equipment with alternative future uses ($90,000 − $18,000 = $72,000 book value) is considered an asset available for use in future periods.

☛ **PRACTICE POINTER:**   FAS-2 does not require assets related to R&D that have alternative future uses in R&D, production, or other activities to be expensed in the period incurred. Typical assets with alternative future uses include machinery, equipment, facilities, patents, and copyrights. Include amortization and depreciation of these assets in R&D expense as long as the assets are used in R&D activities. No asset described as "research and development" should appear in the balance sheet. Present R&D-related assets that are included in the balance sheet in the normal asset categories they represent—plant assets, intangible assets, etc.

Research and development costs acquired by the purchase method in a business combination are assigned their fair values, if any, in accordance with existing GAAP according to FAS-141 (Business Combinations). The subsequent accounting by the acquirer of these R&D assets is that costs assigned to assets with alternative future uses are capitalized and all others are expensed at the date of consummation of the combination (FIN-4, pars. 4–5).

☛ **PRACTICE POINTER:**   The cost of in-process research and development can constitute a substantial portion of the allocated purchase price when technology companies are purchased. Prior to the issuance of FAS-142, acquirers had a clear incentive to allocate as much of the purchase price as possible to in-process research and development. Because such allocated amounts were charged immediately to expense—rather than recorded as goodwill and amortized over a number of years—the results of future operations would look better. The incentives as to the allocation of purchase price between goodwill and inprocess research and development are not as obvious, now that goodwill is no longer amortized on an annual basis.

Disclosure

The amount of R&D charged to expense for the period must be disclosed in the financial statements for each period presented (FAS-2, par. 13).

RESEARCH AND DEVELOPMENT ARRANGEMENTS

FAS-68 (Research and Development Arrangements) covers an enterprise's research and development arrangements that are partially or completely funded by other parties. In this respect, a typical arrangement is for the parties to set up a limited partnership through which the R&D activities related to a specific project are funded. Although the limited partnership arrangement is used in FAS-68 for illustrative purposes, the legal structure of an R&D arrangement may take a variety of forms and is sometimes influenced by income tax implications and securities regulations (FAS-68, par. 2).

In a typical R&D arrangement, an enterprise that has the basic technology for a particular project is the general partner and manages the R&D activities. The limited partners, who may or may not be related parties, provide all or part of the funds to complete the project. If the funds are not sufficient, the arrangement may allow or require the general partner to either (*a*) sell additional limited partnership interest or (*b*) use its own funds to complete the project. In addition, some funds may be provided in the form of loans or advances to the limited partnership. The repayment of the loans or advances may be guaranteed by the partnership (FAS-68, pars. 17–18).

Contract

The actual R&D activities usually are performed by the enterprise or a related party, under a contract with the limited partnership. The contract price is either fixed or cost plus a fixed or percentage fee and is performed on a *best efforts* basis, with no guarantee of ultimate success. The legal ownership of the results of the project vests with partnership (FAS-68, par. 19). Frequently, the enterprise has an option to acquire the partnership's interest in the project or to obtain exclusive use of the results of the project (FAS-68, par. 20). If the project is a success, the enterprise will usually exercise its option to acquire the project. Under some circumstances, however, even if the project is unsuccessful, the enterprise may still have reason to acquire the project, in spite of the fact that it is not legally required to do so. For example, the enterprise may want to prevent the final results of the project becoming available to a competitor (FAS-68, par. 22).

Many of the liabilities and obligations that an enterprise undertakes in an R&D project that is funded by others are specified in the agreements. Some liabilities and obligations, however, may exist in substance but may not be reduced to writing. For example, future payments by the enterprise to other parties for royalties or the acquisition of the partnership's interest in the project may, in substance, represent (*a*) the repayment of a loan or (*b*) the purchase price of a specific asset (FAS-68, par. 23).

Nature of Obligation

In R&D arrangements that are partially or completely funded by other parties, accounting and reporting for R&D costs depend upon the nature of the obligation that an enterprise incurs in the arrangement. The nature of the obligation in such R&D arrangements can be classified in one of the following categories:

- The obligation is solely to perform contractual services.
- The obligation represents a liability to repay all of the funds provided by the other parties.
- The obligation is partly to perform contractual services and partly a liability to repay some, but not all, of the funds provided by the other parties.

If the nature of the obligation incurred by an enterprise is solely to perform contractual services, all R&D costs are charged to *cost of sales*. If the nature of the obligation represents a liability to repay all of the funds provided by the other parties, all R&D costs are charged to *expense* when incurred.

If the nature of the obligation incurred by an enterprise is partly a liability and partly the performance of contractual services, R&D costs are charged partly to expense and partly to cost of sales. The portion charged to cost of sales is related to the funds provided by the other parties that do not have to be repaid by the enterprise. The portion charged to expense is related to the funds provided by the other parties that *are* likely to be repaid by the enterprise. Under FAS-68, the portion charged to expense is referred to as the enterprise's portion of the R&D costs. Under the provisions of FAS-68, an enterprise shall charge its portion of the R&D costs to expense in the same manner as the liability is incurred. Thus, if the liability arises on a pro rata basis, the enterprise's portion of the R&D costs shall be charged to expense in the same manner. If the liability arises as the initial funds are expended, the enterprise's portion of the R&D costs shall be charged to expense in the same manner (FAS-68, par. 9).

FAS-68 provides guidance in determining the nature of the obligation that an enterprise incurs in R&D arrangements that are partially or completely funded by other parties. FAS-68 requires that an enterprise report in its financial statements the estimated liability, if any, incurred in an R&D arrangement that is partially or completely funded by other parties. The estimated liability shall include any contractually defined obligations and any obligations not contractually defined but otherwise reasonably evident (FAS-68, pars. 5, 7).

An important criterion in determining an enterprise's obligation is whether the financial risk involved in an R&D arrangement has been substantively transferred to other parties. To the extent that the enterprise is committed to repay any of the funds provided by the other parties regardless of the outcome of the research and development, all or part of the risk has not been transferred (FAS-68, par. 6).

Under the provisions of FAS-68, if significant indications exist that the enterprise is *likely* to repay any funds, it is presumed that a liability has been incurred. This presumption can be overcome only by substantial evidence to the contrary. Circumstances in which significant indications exist that the enterprise is likely to repay funds and a liability is presumed are as follows (FAS-68, par. 8):

- Regardless of the success of the R&D project, the enterprise has indicated the intent to repay all or part of the funds provided by other parties.

- If it failed to repay any of the funds, the enterprise would suffer a *severe economic penalty*. Under FAS-68, an economic penalty is *severe* if an enterprise would probably elect, under normal business circumstances, to repay the funds rather than to incur the penalty.

- At the inception of the R&D arrangement, a material related party relationship, as defined in FAS-57 (Related Party Disclosures), exists between the enterprise and any of the parties funding the R&D project.

- At the inception of the R&D arrangement, the project is substantially complete. Under this circumstance, the financial risks involved in the R&D project are already known to all parties.

An obligation may represent a liability whether it is payable in cash, securities, or by some other means (FAS-68, par. 5).

Obligation for Contractual Services

If substantially all of the financial risks of the R&D project are transferred to the other parties and the enterprise is not committed to repay any of the funds provided by the other parties, the enterprise shall account for its obligation as contractual R&D services. If repayment by the enterprise of any of the funds provided by the other parties depends on the availability of a future economic benefit to the enterprise, the enterprise shall also account for its obligation as contractual R&D services. In these circumstances, the financial risks of the R&D arrangement have clearly been transferred to others and the enterprise is only obligated to perform contractual R&D services (FAS-68, par. 10).

Frequently, an enterprise makes a loan or advance to the other parties that is designated to be repaid as a reduction of the purchase price for the results of the project, or as a reduction of future royalty payments from the enterprise. In this event, the portion of the loan or advance that is designated to be repaid as a reduction of the purchase price for the results of the project, or as a reduction of future royalties, shall be accounted for by the enterprise as R&D expense, unless it can be attributed to activities other than R&D, such as marketing or advertising (FAS-68, par. 12).

At or before the completion of the R&D project, the enterprise may elect to exercise its option to purchase the partnership's interest, or to obtain exclusive rights to the results of the project. The enterprise shall account for the purchase of the partnership's interest, or the exclusive rights, in accordance with existing GAAP. Thus, any asset that results from the R&D project shall be assigned its fair value, and intangible assets shall be accounted for in accordance with FAS-142 (Goodwill and Other Intangible Assets) (FAS-68, par. 11).

If an enterprise is required to issue warrants or similar instruments in connection with the R&D arrangement, a portion of the funds provided by the other parties shall be recorded as paid-in capital. The amount capitalized as paid-in capital shall be equal to the fair market value of the warrants or other instruments at the date the R&D arrangement is consummated (FAS-68, par. 13).

Financial Statement Disclosure

Notes to the financial statements shall include the following disclosures for R&D arrangements that are accounted for as contracts to perform R&D services for others (FAS-68, par. 14):

- The terms of the significant agreements relating to the R&D arrangement, including purchase provisions, license agreements, royalty arrangements, and commitments to provide additional funds as of the date of each balance sheet presented

- The amount of R&D costs incurred and compensation earned during the period for such R&D arrangements for each income statement presented

RELATED CHAPTERS IN 2009 *GAAP GUIDE* *LEVEL A*

Chapter 4, "Business Combinations"
Chapter 6, "Computer Software"
Chapter 12, "Development Stage Enterprises"
Chapter 20, "Impairment of Long-Lived Assets"
Chapter 23, "Intangible Assets"
Chapter 38, "Related Party Disclosures"
Chapter 52, "Oil and Gas"

RELATED CHAPTERS IN 2009 *GAAP GUIDE* *LEVELS B, C, AND D*

Chapter 6, "Business Combinations"
Chapter 9, "Computer Software"
Chapter 19, "Impairment of Long-Lived Assets"
Chapter 21, "Intangible Assets"
Chapter 34, "Research and Development"

CHAPTER 40
RESULTS OF OPERATIONS

CONTENTS

OVERVIEW

Reporting the results of operations, primarily determining and presenting net income and comprehensive income, is one of the most important aspects of financial reporting. GAAP provide specific guidance concerning how certain items should be presented in the income statement.

There are several authoritative pronouncements in the area of reporting the results of operations, as follows:

APB-9	Reporting the Results of Operations
APB-30	Reporting the Results of Operations—Reporting the Effects of Disposal of a Segment of a Business, and Extraordinary, Unusual, and Infrequently Occurring Events and Transactions
FAS-16	Prior Period Adjustments
FAS-130	Reporting Comprehensive Income
FAS-144	Accounting for the Impairment or Disposal of Long-Lived Assets
FAS-146	Accounting for Costs Associated with Exit or Disposal Activities
FAS-154	Accounting Changes and Error Corrections
FIN-27	Accounting for a Loss on a Sublease

2009 TRANSITION GUIDANCE FOR FAS-141(R) AND FAS-160

The FASB has recently issued FAS-141(R), *Business Combinations,* which is effective for business combinations for which the acquisition date is on or after the beginning of the first annual reporting period beginning on or after December 15, 2008. The FASB has also issued FAS-160, *Noncontrolling Interests in Consolidated Financial Statements, an Amendment of ARB No. 51,* which is effective for fiscal years, and interim periods within those fiscal years, beginning on or after December 15, 2008. Because these standards are not effective for some companies until December 2009, and because early adoption is prohibited, the 2009 *GAAP Guide* reflects the requirements of

FAS-141 prior to its revision in December 2007 and does not reflect the requirements of FAS-160. There is a discussion of the changes in the accounting for business combinations under FAS-141(R) in the Appendix to Chapter 4, "Business Combinations." Similarly, the Appendix to Chapter 7, "Consolidated Financial Statements" includes a discussion of the requirements of FAS-160. However, any effects of FAS-141(R) and/or FAS-160 on this chapter have not been reflected in this edition. Therefore, if a company is subject to the requirements of FAS-141(R) and/or FAS-160, the reader is referred to FAS-141(R) and FAS-160 for these new requirements.

BACKGROUND

For many years, there were differences of opinion in the accounting profession as to what should be included in net income. Proponents of the *all-inclusive concept* (sometimes called "clean surplus") believed that all items affecting net increases in owners' equity, except dividends and capital transactions, should be included in computing net income. Alternatively, proponents of the *current operating performance concept* (sometimes called "dirty surplus") advocated limiting the determination of net income to normal, recurring items of profit and loss that relate only to the current period and recognizing other items directly in retained earnings. Differences between the two concepts are seen most clearly in the treatment of the following items:

- Unusual or infrequent items
- Extraordinary items
- Changes in accounting principles
- Discontinued operations
- Prior period adjustments
- Certain items that are required by GAAP to be recognized directly in stockholders' equity rather than in net income

Current GAAP (primarily APB-9, APB-30, FAS-16) require the presentation of income in a manner that generally is consistent with the all inclusive concept. Net income includes all items of revenue, expense, gain, and loss during a reporting period, except prior period adjustments, dividends, and capital transactions, and a limited number of items that are required to be recognized directly in equity. Examples of items treated in this manner are certain foreign currency adjustments and certain changes in the value of debt and equity investments.

The FASB first introduced the term "comprehensive income" in its conceptual framework, CON-3 (Elements of Financial Statements), which was replaced subsequently by CON-6 of the same title. According to CON-6, *comprehensive income* is the change in equity of a business enterprise from transactions, other events, and circumstances from nonowner sources during a period. It includes all changes in equity during a period except those resulting from investments by owners and distributions to owners. CON-5 (Recognition and Measurement in Financial Statements of Business Enterprises) concluded that comprehensive income and its components should be reported as part of a full set of financial statements for a period and that earnings (i.e., net income) was a more narrow measurement of performance and, therefore, was a part of comprehensive income. FAS-130 (Reporting Comprehensive Income) requires the presentation of comprehensive income and its components in the financial statements.

IRREGULAR ITEMS REPORTED IN NET INCOME

Extraordinary Items

Extraordinary items are transactions and other events that are (*a*) material in nature, (*b*) unusual in nature, and (*c*) infrequent in occurrence (APB-30, par. 20). Extraordinary items are disclosed separately in the income statement, net of any related income tax effect (APB-30, par. 11). EPS for extraordinary items must be presented on the face of the income statement or in the notes (FAS-128, par. 165b).

Identifying extraordinary items requires informed professional judgment, taking into consideration all the facts involved in a particular situation. Some areas of promulgated GAAP, however, require that an item be treated as extraordinary. The following are the more common items that, if material, should be reported as extraordinary items if they are determined to be unusual in nature, and infrequent in occurrence:

- Most expropriations of property (APB-30, par. 23)
- Gains or losses that are the direct result of a major casualty (APB-30, par. 23)
- Losses resulting from prohibition under a newly enacted law or regulation (APB-30, par. 23)

Discontinued Operations

FAS-144 (Accounting for the Impairment or Disposal of Long-Lived Assets) replaces major portions of APB-30 (Reporting the Results of

Operations—Reporting the Effects of Disposal of a Segment of a Business, and Extraordinary, Unusual, and Infrequently Occurring Events and Transactions) with regard to reporting of discontinued operations. For purposes of applying FAS-144, a component of an entity comprises operations and cash flows that can be clearly distinguished, operationally and for financial reporting purposes, from the rest of the entity. A component may be a reportable segment or an operating segment as those terms are defined in FAS-131 (Disclosures about Segments of an Enterprise and Related Information), a subsidiary, or an asset group (FAS-144, par. 41).

The results of operations of a component that has been disposed of or is classified as held for sale shall be reported in discontinued operations if both of the following conditions are met: (1) the operations and cash flows of the component have been, or will be, eliminated from the ongoing operations of the entity as a result of the disposal, and (2) the entity will have no significant continuing involvement in the operations of the component after the disposal transaction (FAS-144, par. 42).

In a period in which a component of an entity either has been disposed of or is classified as held for sale, the income statement of a business enterprise (statement of activities for a not-for-profit organization) shall report the results of operations of the component, including any gain or loss recognized on the initial or subsequent write-down to fair value, of the component, in discontinued operations. Discontinued operations shall be reported as a separate component, before extraordinary items and the cumulative effect of a change in accounting principle, if any. Any gain or loss recognized on the disposal that is part of the discontinued operations element shall be separately disclosed (FAS-144, par. 43).

The following information is required to be disclosed in conjunction with discontinued operations (FAS-144, par. 47):

- A description of the facts and circumstances leading to the disposal and, if not separately presented on the face of the income statement, the carrying amount(s) of the major classes of assets and liabilities included in the disposal.

- The gain or loss recognized on the initial or subsequent write-down to fair value and, if not separately disclosed on the income statement, the line item where it is included.

- If applicable, the amounts of revenue and pretax profit or loss reported in discontinued operations.

- If applicable, the segment in which the long-lived asset (asset group) is reported under FAS-131.

Illustration of Presentation of Net Income

The following illustrates the presentation of income in accordance with APB-30 and related pronouncements:

Income (loss) from continuing operations before provision for income taxes	$400,000	
Provision for income taxes	(136,000)	
Income (loss) from continuing operations		$264,000
Discontinued operations (Note:_____)		
Income (loss) from operations of discontinued component A (less applicable income taxes $34,000)	$(66,000)	
Loss (gain) on disposal of component A (less applicable income taxes of $17,000)	(33,000)	
Net income (loss) from discontinued operations		(99,000)
Net income (loss) before extraordinary items		$165,000
Extraordinary gain (or loss) (Note:_____) (less applicable income taxes of $41,000)		79,000
Cumulative effect on prior years (to December 31, 20X6) of a change in an accounting principle (less applicable income taxes of $26,000)		(54,000)
Net income		$190,000

Unusual or Infrequent Items

If professional judgment dictates individual treatment of a material event or transaction that does not qualify as an extraordinary item (e.g., unusual or infrequent, but not both), it may be reported separately as a component of income from continuing operations with appropriate footnote disclosure. In this event, however, the separately identified item should not be reported net of its related tax effects or in a manner that implies that the item is an extraordinary item (APB-30, par. 26).

☞ **PRACTICE POINTER:** The FASB does not state precisely what should *not* be done in the presentation of an unusual or infrequent item in order for it to *not* be confused with an extraordinary item. In the presentation of unusual or infrequent items, avoid the following, which are characteristics of the presentation of extraordinary items:

- Net-of-tax presentation
- Presentation of earnings per share on the item
- Presentation of income before and after the item

Prior Period Adjustments

A *prior period adjustment* is defined by FAS-16 (Prior Period Adjustments), amended by FAS-109 (Accounting for Income Taxes), as a correction of an error in a prior period statement. Prior period adjustments are excluded from the determination of net income (FAS-109, par. 288n).

All other items of profit and loss (including accruals for loss contingencies) shall be included in the determination of net income for the period.

In those rare material cases in which prior period adjustments are recorded, the resulting effects should be disclosed in the period in which the adjustments are made by *restating the balance of retained earnings at the beginning of such period* (FAS-16, par. 16).

Both the gross and net effect (of related income taxes) of prior period adjustments on net income should be disclosed in the year of adjustment and all years presented (APB-9, par. 26).

Interim Period Adjustments

An adjustment of prior interim periods of a current fiscal year can include any of the following settlements (FAS-16, par. 13):

- Litigation or similar claims
- Income taxes
- Renegotiation
- Utility revenues governed by rate-making processes

In adjusting interim periods of the current year, any adjustment of prior periods is made to the first interim period of the current year. Adjustments to the other interim periods of the current year are related to the interim period affected (FAS-16, par. 14).

The effects (*a*) on income from continuous operations, (*b*) on net income, and (*c*) on earnings per share of an adjustment to a current interim period must be disclosed fully (FAS-16, par. 15).

Accounting Changes

A change from one generally accepted accounting principle to an-other generally accepted principle is accounted for by retrospec-tively applying the new accounting principle to previous years' financial statements (FAS-154, par. 1). If it is impracticable to deter-mine the effect of the new accounting principle on all prior years affected, the new principle is retrospectively applied to the earliest possible year for which its effects can be determined. Asset and liability balances are adjusted with an offsetting entry to retained earnings as of the earliest year that the effects of retrospectively applying the new principle can be determined (FAS-154, par. 8). If it is impracticable to determine the effect of the change to any prior period, the change is accounted for prospectively (FAS-154, par. 9). A change in the reporting entity also results in retrospective application, such that financial statements of prior years are adjust-ed to reflect the results of the new reporting entity (FAS-154, par. 23).

> ☛ **PRACTICE POINTER:** A change from the FIFO method of in-ventory valuation to the LIFO method often is accounted for prospectively. It may be impracticable to apply the LIFO method retrospectively to prior years that would have been affected (FAS-154, par. 9).

ACCOUNTING FOR COSTS ASSOCIATED WITH EXIT OR DISPOSAL ACTIVITIES

FAS-146 (Accounting for Costs Associated with Exit or Disposal Activities) addresses financial accounting and reporting for costs associated with exit or disposal activities. FAS-146 applies to costs associated with an exit activity that does not involve an entity newly acquired in a business combination or with a disposal activity cov-ered by FAS-144 (Accounting for the Impairment or Disposal of Long-Lived Assets). The costs covered by FAS-146 include, but are not limited to (FAS-146, par. 2):

- Termination benefits provided to current employees that are voluntarily terminated under the terms of a benefit arrange-ment that is, in substance, not an ongoing benefit arrangement or an individual deferred compensation contract.
- Costs to terminate a contract that is not a capital lease.
- Costs to consolidate facilities or relocate employees.

FAS-146 does not apply to costs associated with the retirement of a long-lived asset covered by FAS-143 (Accounting for Asset Retirement Obligations).

> ☛ **PRACTICE POINTER:** Exit activities include, but are not limited to, restructurings. Examples of restructurings are (1) sale or termination of a line of business, (2) closing business activities in a particular location, (3) relocation of business activities, (4) change in management structure, and (5) a reorganization that fundamentally changes the entity's operating nature and focus (FAS-146, footnote 1).

Recognition and Measurement

FAS-146 requires liability recognition for a cost associated with an exit or disposal activity, measured at fair value, in the period in which the liability is incurred (with limited exceptions). In the unusual circumstance in which fair value cannot be reasonably estimated, liability recognition is delayed until such an estimate can reasonably be made (FAS-146, par. 3).

A liability for a cost associated with an exit or disposal activity is incurred when the CON-6 (Elements of Financial Statements) definition of a liability is met:

> Liabilities are probable future sacrifices of economic benefits arising from present obligations of a particular entity to transfer assets or provide services to another entity in the future as a result of past transactions or events.

Only present obligations to others are liabilities under this definition. An obligation becomes a present obligation when a transaction or event occurs that leaves the entity little or no discretion to avoid the future transfer or use of an asset to settle the liability. An exit or disposal plan, in and of itself, does not create a present obligation, although it may lead to one in the future if the criteria for liability recognition are met (FAS-146, par. 4).

The objective of initial measurement of a liability for a cost associated with an exit or disposal activity is fair value. A present value technique is often the best available valuation technique for estimating the fair value of a liability for a cost associated with an exit or disposal activity. For a liability that has uncertainties both in timing and amount, an expected present value technique generally is the appropriate technique. (FAS-135, par. 5, as amended by FAS-157, par. E25, a, b)

> ☛ **PRACTICE POINTER:** In many cases, a quoted market price for the restructuring liability will not be available and the most

appropriate valuation technique will be a present value technique. An expected present value technique is generally preferred to a traditional present value technique. In an expected present value technique, the entity weighs multiple cash flow outcomes, based on their probability of occurrence, and then discounts these cash flows using a credit-adjusted (for the entity's credit standing), risk-free discount rate. The discounted cash flows are then added together to compute the expected present value of the restructuring liability. Conversely, a traditional present value technique subjectively adjusts the discount rate to reflect uncertainty in the amount and timing of the most likely cash flow pattern associated with the restructuring liability. Because a restructuring liability often has uncertainty associated with the amount and timing of the relevant cash flows, FAS-146 expresses a preference for the expected present value technique. CON-7 (Using Cash Flow Information and Present Value in Accounting Measurements) provides a detailed discussion of present value techniques available (FAS-146, par. A4).

Once a liability for an exit or disposal activity has been recognized, in subsequent periods changes in the liability shall be measured using the credit-adjusted, risk-free rate that was used to measure the liability initially. The cumulative effect of a change resulting from a revision to either the timing or the amount of estimated cash flows shall be recognized as an adjustment to the liability in the period of the change and reported in the income statement in the same line item that was used when the related costs were recognized initially and recorded as liabilities. Changes due to the passage of time are recognized as an increase in the carrying amount of the liability and as an expense (e.g., accretion expense) (FAS-146, par. 6).

> **OBSERVATION:**   Accretion expense is not interest cost eligible for capitalization under the provisions of FAS-34 (Capitalization of Interest Cost).

Recognition and Measurement of Certain Costs

One-time termination benefits are benefits provided to current employees who are involuntarily terminated under a one-time benefit arrangement. A one-time benefit arrangement is an arrangement established by a plan or termination that applies for a specified termination event or for a specified future period. A one-time termination benefit arrangement exists at the date the plan termination meets all of the following criteria and has been communicated to employees (FAS-146, par. 8):

- Management commits to a plan of termination.

- The plan identifies the number of employees to be terminated, their job classifications or functions, their locations, and the expected completion date.

- The plan establishes the terms of the benefit arrangement, including the benefits that employees will receive, in sufficient detail to enable employees to determine the type and amount of benefits they will receive if they are involuntarily terminated.

- Actions required to complete the plan indicate that it is unlikely that significant changes to the plan will be made or that the plan will be withdrawn.

The timing of recognition and related measurement of a liability for one-time termination benefits depend on whether employees are required to render service until they are terminated in order to receive the termination benefits and, if so, whether employees will be retained to render services beyond a minimum retention period. The minimum retention period shall not exceed the legal notification period or, if none exists, 60 days (FAS-146, par. 9).

If employees are not required to render service until they are terminated in order to receive the termination benefits or if employees will not be retained to render services beyond the minimum retention period, a liability for the termination benefits shall be recognized (measured at fair value) at the communication date (FAS-146, par. 10).

Illustration of One-Time Termination Benefits—No Future Employee Service Required

On May 1, 20X5, Gardial, Inc., announces plans to close its operations in Bakersfield, California. Gardial, Inc., notifies all of its 300 employees that they will be terminated within 75 days. Each employee will receive a cash payment of $10,000 when that employee ceases providing service during the 75-day period. Because no future employee service is required to receive the one-time termination benefits, Gardial, Inc., will recognize the fair value of its termination liability on the date the plan is communicated to the employees (assuming that the termination benefit plan meets the FAS-146 criteria for recognizing a liability). A liability of $3,000,000 will be recorded on the communication date (given the short discount period, the gross value of the liability is not likely to differ materially from the fair value of the liability).

If employees are required to render service until they are terminated in order to receive the termination benefits and will be retained to render service beyond the minimum retention period, a liability for the termination benefits shall be measured initially at the communication date, based on the fair value of the liability as of the termination date, but recognized ratably over the future service period (FAS-146, par. 11). A change resulting from a revision to either the timing or the amount of estimated cash flows over the future service period shall be measured using the credit-adjusted, risk-free rate that was used initially to measure the liability, and the cumulative effect of the change shall be recognized as an adjustment to the liability in the period of change (FAS-146, par. 12).

Illustration of One-Time Termination Benefits—Future Employee Service Required

On October 1, 20X5, Miller, Inc., announces plans to close its plant in San Antonio, Texas, in 24 months. Employees who remain with Miller until the plant closes will receive a $15,000 cash retention bonus. The bonus will be paid one year after the termination date. An employee who leaves voluntarily before the plant closes will not be eligible for any of the retention bonus.

Miller has 1,000 employees on October 1, 20X5. Miller develops a number of scenarios associated with its likely employee retention over the next 24 months. These are:

- Most likely scenario (70% probability)—600 employees stay with Miller until 9/30/X7
- Optimistic scenario (20% probability)—800 employees stay with Miller until 9/30/X7
- Pessimistic scenario (10% probability)—300 employees stay with Miller until 9/30/X7

Miller announces its restructuring and communicates the employee retention plan to its employees on October 1, 20X5 (assume that Miller meets the FAS-146 criteria for recognizing a liability).

Miller measures what the fair value of the liability will be on the *termination date* (9/30/X7) on the *communication date*. This computation is as follows:

600 employees × $15,000 × 0.70	=	$6,300,000
800 employees × $15,000 × 0.20	=	2,400,000
300 employees × $15,000 × 0.10	=	450,000
Expected payment		$9,150,000

Miller's best estimate on 10/1/X5 (the communication date) of the undiscounted amount of its liability at 9/30/X7 (the termination date) is $9,150,000. Miller's credit-adjusted, risk-free interest rate is 10%. Therefore, the expected present value of Miller's liability on the termination date is computed as follows:

$9,150,000 × .909090
(present value interest factor   = $8,318,174
for $1 at 10% for 1 year)

The expected present value of Miller's termination liability, $8,318,174, is recognized ratably over the next 24 months (i.e., the future service period).

The following journal entry will be made each month for the next 24 months:

Restructuring Expense (8,318,174 / 24)	346,590.48	
Liability for Termination Benefits		346,590.58

During the 12 months from 9/30/X7 (the termination date) until 9/30/X8 (the date of payment of the retention bonus), the liability will increase due to the passage of time and accretion expense will be recognized. The following journal entry will be made each month from 10/1/X7 through 9/30/X8:

Accretion Expense [(9,150,000 – 8,318,174)/12]	69,318.83	
Liability for Termination Benefits		69,318.83

By 9/30/X8, Miller will have a balance of $9,150,000 in the "Liability for Termination Benefits" account. The following journal entry will be recorded on 9/30/X8 for the payment of the retention bonuses:

Liability for Termination Benefits	9,150,000	
Cash		9,150,000

Some termination plans offer both voluntary and involuntary benefits. A voluntary benefit, which is more than the involuntary benefit, is offered to employees who voluntarily terminate their employment. An involuntary benefit is provided to all employees losing their jobs. In this case, a liability for the involuntary benefits is recognized when the restructuring and the benefits under the termination plan are communicated to employees (FAS-146, par. 13). A liability and an expense, for the difference between the voluntary benefit and the involuntary benefit, are recognized when the employee voluntarily resigns (i.e., at that time the employee accepts the employer's offer and a liability exists) (FAS-146, footnote 9). FAS-88 (Employers' Accounting for Settlements and Curtailments of Defined Benefit Pension Plans) provides additional details on the required accounting.

A liability for costs to terminate a lease or other contract before the end of its term shall be recognized and measured at its fair value when the entity terminates the contract in accordance with the contract terms. A liability for costs that will continue to be incurred under a contract for its remaining term without economic benefit to the company shall be recognized and measured at its fair value when the entity ceases using the right conveyed by the contract (e.g., the right to used leased property). If the contract is an operating lease, the fair value of the liability at the cease-use date shall be determined based on the remaining lease rentals, reduced by estimated sublease rentals that could be reasonably obtained for the property, even if the entity does not intend to enter into a sublease. Remaining lease rentals shall not be reduced to an amount less than zero (FAS-146, pars. 14–16).

Illustration of Costs to Terminate an Operating Lease

Ladd, Rentz, and Rush (LRR) lease a facility under an operating lease for $50,000 per year for 15 years. The operating lease began on 1/1/X1. After using the facility for seven years, LRR entered into an exit plan (1/1/X8) where the leased facility will no longer be used beginning on 1/1/X9. Based on market rentals, LRR determines that it could sublease this facility at $35,000 per year for the last seven years of the operating lease. However, LRR, for competitive reasons, decides *not* to sublease this facility beginning on 1/1/X9. LRR's credit-adjusted, risk-free interest rate is 12%.

The fair value of the liability at the cease-use date is computed as follows:

Yearly lease payment	$50,000
Less: Available (market-based) yearly sublease rentals (regardless of whether the property is subleased)	(35,000)
Expected yearly net cash flows	$15,000

The expected present value of LRR's liability on the cease-use date is computed as follows:

$$\begin{array}{l}\$15,000 \times 5.1114 \\ \text{(PVIF for an ordinary annuity of} \qquad = \qquad \$76,761 \\ \$1 \text{ at 12\% for seven years)}\end{array}$$

The following journal entry would be made on the cease-use date to record the liability:

1/1/X9

Restructuring Expense	76,671	
Liability for Restructuring Costs		76,671

The following additional journal entries would be made in years X9 through Y5:

1/1/X9 – 1/1/Y5

Restructuring Expense	35,000	
Liability for Restructuring Costs	15,000	
Cash		50,000

12/31/X9

Accretion Expense	7,401	
Liability for Restructuring Costs		7,401

12/31/Y0

Accretion Expense	6,489	
Liability for Restructuring Costs		6,489

12/31/Y1

Accretion Expense	5,467	
Liability for Restructuring Costs		5,467

12/31/Y2

Accretion Expense	4,323	
Liability for Restructuring Costs		4,323

12/31/Y3

Accretion Expense	3,042	
Liability for Restructuring Costs		3,042

12/31/Y4

Accretion Expense	1,607	
Liability for Restructuring Costs		1,607

Other costs associated with an exit or disposal activity include, but are not limited to, costs to consolidate or close facilities and relocate employees. A liability for costs of this type are recognized and measured at fair value in the period in which the liability is incurred, which generally is when goods or services associated with the activity are received. The liability shall not be recognized before it is incurred, even if the costs are incremental to other operating costs and will be incurred as a direct result of a plan (FAS-146, par. 17).

☞ **PRACTICE POINTER:** Note that many costs associated with a restructuring (e.g., costs of consolidating facilities, closing facilities, and relocating employees) are not recognized until the period when the cost is incurred. Generally, this is the period when the goods or services associated with the restructuring activity are received. This treatment differs from the treatment afforded one-time termination benefits and that afforded the costs associated with terminating a contract. The liability associated with one-time termination benefits is either recorded on the communication date or gradually recognized over the interval between the communication date and the termination date (see the two illustrations of one-time termination benefits, preceding). The liability associated with terminating a contract is recognized on the contract termination date or, in the case of an operating lease, on the cease-use date (see the preceding example on costs to terminate an operating lease). Note that by limiting those costs that can be recognized as a liability before the period when goods or services are received, the judgment required in establishing reserves for restructuring activity is reduced, which is designed to limit management's ability to manage income by establishing overly large restructuring reserves and then reversing these reserves in future periods with the effect of increasing income.

Reporting and Disclosure

Costs associated with an exit or disposal activity that does not involve a discontinued operation shall be included in income from continuing operations before taxes in the income statement of a business enterprise and in income from continuing operations in the statement of activities of a not-for-profit organization. If a subtotal "Income from Operations" is presented, it shall include the amounts of those costs. Costs associated with an exit or disposal activity that is presented as a discontinued operation are included in the results of discontinued operations (FAS-146, par. 18).

If an event or circumstance occurs that discharges an entity's previously recognized liability for an exit or disposal activity, then the liability shall be reversed and the related costs reversed through the same line item in the income statement (statement of activities) used when the liability was previously recognized (FAS-146, par. 19).

The following information shall be disclosed in notes to financial statements in the period in which an exit or disposal activity is initiated, and in future periods until the exit or disposal activity is completed (FAS-146, par. 20):

- A description of the exit or disposal activity, including the facts and circumstances leading to the expected activity and the expected completion date
- For each major type of costs associated with the activity:
  — The total amount expected to be incurred in connection with the activity, the amount incurred in the period, and the cumulative amount incurred to date
  — A reconciliation of the beginning and ending liability balances showing separately the changes during the period attributable to costs incurred and charged to expense, costs paid or otherwise settled, and adjustments to the liability with an explanation of the reasons for those adjustments

- The line item in the income statement (statement of activities) in which the costs described above are aggregated

- For each reportable segment, the total amount of costs expected to be incurred in connection with the activity, the amount incurred in the period, and the cumulative amount incurred to date, net of any adjustments to the liability with an explanation of the reason(s) therefore

- If a liability for a cost associated with the activity is not recognized because fair value cannot be reasonably determined, that fact and the reasons therefore

REPORTING COMPREHENSIVE INCOME

Several accounting standards currently require that certain items that qualify as part of comprehensive income be reported directly in the equity section of the statement of financial position without having been recognized in the determination of net income. Examples of these items include:

- Foreign currency translation adjustments in accordance with FAS-52 (Foreign Currency Translation)

- Unrealized holding gains and losses on available-for-sale securities in accordance with FAS-115 (Accounting for Certain Investments in Debt and Equity Securities)

- The recognition of an asset for an overfunded postretirement benefit plan or a liability for an underfunded postretirement benefit plan in accordance with FAS-158 (Employers' Accounting for Defined Benefit Pension and Other Postretirement Plans). The balance in accumulated other comprehensive income relates to unrecognized gains and losses, unamortized prior service costs or credits, unamortized transition assets or obligations and, in the year of initial adoption of FAS-158, previous years' contributions that exceeded or were less than the net periodic postretirement benefit cost.

- Changes in the fair value of derivative financial instruments classified as cash flow hedges in accordance with FAS-133 (Accounting for Derivative Instruments and Hedging Activities) (That standard also specifies that, for a derivative instrument designated as hedging the foreign currency exposure of a net investment in a foreign operation, the gain or loss from changes in fair value is reported as part of the cumulative translation adjustment.)

Despite the FASB's endorsement of the general concept of comprehensive income and its conclusion that comprehensive income should be included in a full set of financial statements, prior to FAS-130 no authoritative standard required the presentation of comprehensive income or provided guidance on how to present it.

FAS-130 applies to all enterprises that provide a full set of financial statements reporting financial position, results of operations, and cash flows. It does *not* apply to (FAS-130, par. 6):

- Enterprises that have no items of other comprehensive income in any period presented.

- Not-for-profit organizations that must follow FAS-117 (Financial Statements of Not-for-Profit Organizations).

FAS-130 deals with the presentation and display of comprehensive income, but it does not specify when to recognize or how to measure the components of comprehensive income. Those subjects are covered in other current standards or will be covered in future standards (FAS-130, par. 1).

Comprehensive Income Defined

Comprehensive income is a broad concept of an enterprise's financial performance, in that it includes all changes in equity during a period from transactions and events from nonowner sources (e.g., revenue and expense transactions with external parties). The only changes in equity that are excluded from comprehensive income are those resulting from investments by owners and distributions to owners (FAS-130, par. 11).

The term *comprehensive income,* as used in FAS-130, includes net income plus all other components of comprehensive income. The term *other comprehensive income* denotes revenues, expenses, gains, and losses that are included in comprehensive income but not in net income in accordance with GAAP. While the terms *comprehensive income* and *other comprehensive income* are used throughout FAS-130, those precise terms are not required to be used in an enterprise's financial statements (FAS-130, par. 10).

Before FAS-130, some elements of comprehensive income were presented in the income statement and others were reported directly in the equity section of the statement of financial position. All elements were *not* required to be brought together in a single amount of comprehensive income, however.

The FASB believes that information an enterprise provides by reporting comprehensive income—along with related disclosures and other information in the financial statements—will help investors, creditors, and others to assess the enterprise's activities and the timing and magnitude of its future cash flows. Given the diverse nature of the components of other comprehensive income, the FASB indicates that detailed information about each component is important. In fact, the FASB states that information about the components of comprehensive income may be more important than the total of comprehensive income, and the required disclosures are intended to support this stance (FAS-130, pars. 12–13).

Reporting and Display

FAS-130's reporting and display requirements for comprehensive income and other comprehensive income are summarized as follows:

- An amount of net income
- A total amount of comprehensive income in the statement where the components of other comprehensive income are reported
- All components of other comprehensive income, with items classified based on their nature (e.g., foreign currency items, minimum pension liability items, and unrealized gains and losses on investment securities)

☛ **PRACTICE POINTER:** Classifications within net income, such as the following, are *not* affected by FAS-130:

- Continuing operations
- Discontinued operations
- Extraordinary items

If a company has no components of comprehensive income other than net income, it is not required to report comprehensive income.

OBSERVATION: Apparently, the FASB believes that in a situation in which there are no elements of other comprehensive income, to designate a single amount as both net income and comprehensive income is potentially confusing to financial statement users. In this situation, the amount is comparable with net income of an enterprise that presents both net income and comprehensive income, so the FASB determined that no reporting of comprehensive income is appropriate. This should limit the applicability of FAS-130 considerably, because many enterprises do not have transactions that would create a difference between net income and comprehensive income.

Items recognized in other comprehensive income that are later recognized in net income require a reclassification adjustment in order to prevent double counting of transactions in the determination of comprehensive income. Perhaps the easiest example of these transactions is accumulated gains or losses on available-for-sale investment securities that are accumulated in stockholders' equity under FAS-115 until the securities are sold. At the time of the sale, any previously recognized gains or losses that were accumulated in stockholders' equity (i.e., an element of other comprehensive income) are reversed in comprehensive income and then recognized as an element of net income. The reversal of the previous recognition in other comprehensive income offsets the recognition from the previous period and effectively moves the recognition from other comprehensive income to net income when the gain or loss is actually realized in a sale (FAS-130, par. 18).

> ☛ **PRACTICE POINTER:**   Reclassification adjustments may be displayed on the face of the financial statement in which comprehensive income is reported, or they may be disclosed in notes to the financial statements. For all reclassification adjustments, an enterprise may use either a gross display on the face of the financial statement or a net display on the face of the financial statement or in notes to the financial statements.

Illustration of Reclassification Adjustment

A company accounts for its available-for-sale investments in debt and equity securities at fair value in accordance with FAS-115. Information on these investments prior to 20X5—the year in which the investment was sold—is as follows (all numbers in thousands):

	20X3	*20X4*
Purchase	$100	$125
Market value	$120	$260

In 20X3, $20 ($120 – $100) would be recognized by increasing the investment and recording an accumulated unrecognized gain in stockholders' equity. In 20X4, a gain of $15 [$260 – ($125 + $120)] would be recognized in a similar fashion.

Assuming the investments are sold in 20X5 for $260, the accumulated unrecognized gain of $35 ($20 + $15) is offset by the recognition of a $35 reclassification loss in other comprehensive income, and a $35 realized gain is recognized in net income. This transaction results in the following presentation over the three-year period:

	20X3	20X4	20X5
Net income	None	None	$35
Other comprehensive income	$20	$15	($35)
Comprehensive income	$20	$15	None

If the reclassification of ($35) had not been recognized in other comprehensive income in 20X4, a $35 gain would have been recognized in comprehensive income *twice*—once as an element of other comprehensive income and once as an element of net income.

Alternative Display Formats for Comprehensive Income

FAS-130 does not require a single display presentation for elements of comprehensive income and the total of comprehensive income, but it does require that these items be presented in a financial statement that is displayed with the same prominence as other financial statements, which together constitute a full set of financial statements (FAS-130, par. 22).

Three alternative presentation formats are acceptable, either of the first two being preferable to the third. They are:

1. In a single statement of income and comprehensive income that extends a traditional income statement to include (following net income) the elements of other comprehensive income and the total of comprehensive income.

2. In two statements of income. The first is a traditional income statement that ends with an amount of net income. The second begins with net income and includes the elements of other comprehensive income and then a total of comprehensive income.

3. In another financial statement, such as a statement of (changes in) stockholders' equity.

These alternatives are described by example in the following Illustration.

Illustration of Alternative Presentations of Comprehensive Income

Warner, Inc. has revenues of $1,559,231, expenses of $790,000, and two components of other comprehensive income, as follows:

*   Accumulated gains of $100,000 on available-for-sale investments
*   Foreign currency translation adjustments (losses) of $25,000

Net income is $500,000 for 20X5, the current year. Warner's income tax rate is 35%.

Format 1—One Income-Statement Format

Warner, Inc.
Statement of Income and
Comprehensive Income
for Year 20X5

Revenues		$1,559,231
Expenses		790,000
Income before income tax		$769,231
Income tax		269,231
Net income		$500,000
Other comprehensive income, net of income tax:		
Unrealized holding gains	$65,000	
Foreign currency translation	(16,250)	48,750
Comprehensive income		$548,750

Format 2—Two Income-Statement Format*

Warner, Inc.
Statement of Comprehensive
Income
for Year 20X5

Net income		$500,000
Other comprehensive income, net of income tax:		
Unrealized holding gains	$65,000	
Foreign currency translation	(16,250)	48,750
Comprehensive income		$548,750

---

*Statement ending in "net income" unchanged by FAS-130.

Format 3—Statement of Changes in Stockholders' Equity*

Warner, Inc.
Statement of Changes in Stockholders' Equity
for Year 20X5

	Total	Compre- hensive income	Retained earnings	Accumulated other Com- prehensive income	Common stock	Additional paid-in capital
Beginning balances	$XXX		$XXX	$XXX	$XXX	$XXX
Comprehensive income:						
Net income	$500,000	$500,000	$500,000			
Unrealized holding gains	65,000	65,000				
Foreign currency translation	(16,250)	(16,250)				
Other comprehensive income		48,750		$48,750		
Comprehensive income		$548,750				
Common stock issued					$XXX	$XXX
Dividends declared on common stock			($XXX)			
Ending balances	$XXX		$XXX	$XXX	$XXX	$XXX

---

*Income statement unchanged by FAS-130.

Format 3 shows how comprehensive income might be presented in another statement with prominence equal to that of Formats 1 and 2. Appendix B of FAS-130 also illustrates other ways of presenting comprehensive income, as well as the note disclosures that might accompany the presentations.

With any of these alternatives, the components of other comprehensive income may be displayed net of related income taxes, as done in this Illustration, or before related income taxes with one amount shown for the aggregate income-tax effects of all the components of other comprehensive income. Whether the components are displayed net of tax or not, the amounts of income tax expense or benefit allocated to each component of other comprehensive income, including reclassification adjustments, are required to be disclosed.

Equity Section of the Statement of Financial Position

At the end of the reporting period, the total of other comprehensive income is transferred to a separate stockholders' equity account, much like net income is transferred to retained earnings. This separate stockholders' equity account should have an appropriate descriptive title, such as *Accumulated Other Comprehensive Income*. Disclosure of the accumulated balances for each classification of that separate component of equity shall be made on the face of the statement of financial position, in a statement of changes in stockholders' equity, or in notes to the financial statements (FAS-130, par. 26).

The classifications used in the disclosure of the balances of individual components of other comprehensive income must correspond to the classifications used elsewhere in the same financial statements (FAS-130, par. 26).

RELATED CHAPTERS IN 2009 *GAAP GUIDE* LEVEL A

RELATED CHAPTERS IN 2009 *GAAP GUIDE* LEVELS B, C, AND D

RELATED CHAPTER IN 2009 *INTERNATIONAL ACCOUNTING/FINANCIAL REPORTING STANDARDS GUIDE*

Chapter 26, "Non-Current Assets Held for Sale and Discontinued Operations"

CHAPTER 41
REVENUE RECOGNITION

CONTENTS

OVERVIEW

GAAP, as well as recognized industry practices, generally call for revenue recognition at the point of sale. One aspect of a sale that complicates this generally simple rule is a right of return on the part of the buyer. Revenue from sales in which a right of return exists is recognized at the time of sale only if certain specified conditions are met. If those conditions are met, sales revenue and cost of sales are reduced to reflect estimated returns and costs of those returns. If they are not met, revenue recognition is postponed.

A franchise agreement transfers rights owned by the franchisor to a franchisee. The rights transferred for a specified period of time may include the use of patents, secret processes, trademarks, trade names, or other similar assets. The primary accounting problem associated with accounting for franchise fee revenue is the timing of the revenue recognition (i.e., determining when the franchise fee revenue is earned). Accounting standards prescribe specific criteria that must be met for revenue to be recognized.

The authoritative literature dealing with revenue recognition when the right of return exists, as well as franchise revenue, is as follows:

FAS-45   Accounting for Franchise Fee Revenue

FAS-48   Revenue Recognition When Right of Return Exists

> **OBSERVATION:** Much of the existing "Level A" GAAP guidance is highly transaction specific (e.g., franchise fee revenue, revenue recognition when right of return exists). The most generic guidance on revenue recognition currently in force is the Securities and Exchange Commission's Staff Accounting Bulletins on revenue recognition (SAB 101, SAB 104). SAB 101 is largely modeled after the guidance in SOP 97-2 (Software Revenue Recognition). See Chapter 10 of the 2008 *GAAP Guide Levels B, C, and D* for coverage of SOP 97-2. SAB 104 updates the guidance in SAB 101 and reflects changes in the authoritative literature made by the FASB. In addition, a number of EITF consensus positions provide more narrowly focused guidance on revenue recognition (see Chapter 36 of the 2008 *GAAP Guide Levels B, C, and D*). A reader interested in understanding GAAP for recognizing revenue would be well-advised to consult the *GAAP Guide Levels B, C, and D* and, in the context of a public company, to read SAB 101 and SAB 104. SAB-104 is useful as conceptual guidance in areas where no other authoritative literature exists. The FASB has a project on revenue recognition on its agenda and its current plan indicates it will issue a Preliminary Views document sometime in 2008.

2009 TRANSITION GUIDANCE FOR FAS-141(R) AND FAS-160

The FASB has recently issued FAS-141(R), *Business Combinations*, which is effective for business combinations for which the acquisition date is on or after the beginning of the first annual reporting period beginning on or after December 15, 2008. The FASB has also issued FAS-160, *Noncontrolling Interests in Consolidated Financial Statements, an Amendment of ARB No. 51*, which is effective for fiscal years, and interim periods within those fiscal years, beginning on or after December 15, 2008. Because these standards are not effective for some companies until December 2009, and because early adoption is prohibited, the 2009 *GAAP Guide* reflects the requirements of FAS-141 prior to its revision in December 2007 and does not reflect the requirements of FAS-160. There is a discussion of the changes in the accounting for business combinations under FAS-141(R) in the Appendix to Chapter 4, "Business Combinations." Similarly, the Appendix to Chapter 7, "Consolidated Financial Statements" includes a discussion of the requirements of FAS-160. However, any effects of FAS-141(R) and/or FAS-160 on this chapter have not been reflected in this edition. Therefore, if a company is subject to the requirements of FAS-141(R) and/or FAS-160, the reader is referred to FAS-141(R) and FAS-160 for these new requirements.

BACKGROUND

The realization principle requires that revenue be earned before it is recognized. Revenue usually is recognized when the earning process is complete and an exchange has taken place. The earning process is not complete until collection of the sales price is assured reasonably.

In some industries, dealers and distributors of personal property have the right to return unsold merchandise. The right to return merchandise usually is an industry practice but may also occur as a result of a contractual agreement. The return period can last for a few days, as in the perishable food industry, or it can extend for several years, which is not infrequent for some types of publishers. The rate of return of some companies may be high, while in other industries, such as perishable foods, the rate of return may be insignificant.

As long as a right of return exists and the returns could be significant, the seller is exposed to reacquiring the ownership of the property. The risks and rewards of ownership have not, in substance, been passed on to the buyer. Because the earning process is not complete until collection of the sales price is assured reasonably, certain accounting problems arise in recognizing revenue when the right to return exists.

Payment for franchise rights may include an initial franchise fee and/or continuing fees or royalties. The agreement usually also provides for any continuing services that are to be rendered by the franchisor, and any inventory or purchases that may be required of the franchisee. In addition, the franchise agreement typically sets forth the procedure for cancellation, resale, or reacquisition of the franchise by the franchisor.

FAS-48 (Revenue Recognition When Right of Return Exists) contains the specialized accounting and reporting principles and practices that were originally published in AICPA SOP 75-1, titled "Revenue Recognition When Right of Return Exists." FAS-48 does not cover real estate or lease transactions and does not apply to accounting for revenue of service industries.

FAS-45 (Accounting for Franchise Fee Revenue) contains the specialized accounting and reporting principles and practices that were originally published in an AICPA industry accounting guide titled "Accounting for Franchise Fee Revenue." This guide was published in 1973 and covered the accounting problems of the party granting the franchise (franchisor).

REVENUE RECOGNITION FOR RETURNABLE MERCHANDISE

When a buyer has the right to return merchandise purchased, the seller may not recognize income from the sale, unless *all* of the following conditions are met (FAS-48, par. 6):

- The price between the seller and the buyer is substantially fixed, or determinable.

- The seller has received full payment, or the buyer is indebted to the seller and the indebtedness is not contingent on the resale of the merchandise.

- Physical destruction, damage, or theft of the merchandise would not change the buyer's obligation to the seller.

- The buyer has economic substance and is not a front, straw party, or conduit, existing for the benefit of the seller.

- No significant obligations exist for the seller to help the buyer resell the merchandise.

- A reasonable estimate can be made of the amount of future returns.

If all of the above conditions are met, revenue is recognized on sales for which a right of return exists, provided that an appropriate provision is made for costs or losses that may occur in connection with the return of merchandise from the buyer (FAS-48, par. 7).

OBSERVATION: An exchange of one item for a similar item of the same quality and value is not considered a return for the purposes of FAS-48.

If all of the conditions of FAS-48 are met, an appropriate provision for costs or losses that may occur in connection with the return of merchandise from the buyer must be made by the seller. The provision for costs or losses must be in accordance with FAS-5 (Accounting for Contingencies) (FAS-48, par. 7). Under FAS-5, a provision for a loss contingency is accrued, by a charge to income, provided that both of the following conditions exist:

- It is *probable* that at the date of the financial statements, an asset has been impaired or a liability incurred, based on information available prior to the issuance of the financial statements.

- The amount of loss can be estimated reasonably.

The second requirement for the accrual of a loss contingency under FAS-5 is satisfied when all of the conditions of FAS-48 are met. This is because FAS-48 requires that a reasonable estimate can be made of the amount of future returns, which also means that the amount of loss on the returns, if any, should be reasonably estimable. Thus, if returns are *probable* and all of the conditions of FAS-48 are met, an accrual is required by FAS-5. This accrual results in a reduction of sales revenue and a related cost of sales in the income statement, which is consistent with the requirements of FAS-48.

☛ **PRACTICE POINTER:** If all of the conditions of FAS-48 are not met, the seller cannot recognize the sales revenue until the right of return privilege has substantially expired or the provisions of FAS-48 are subsequently met (FAS-48, par. 6). The seller has several alternatives in accounting for these transactions: First, do not record the transaction on the books at all and maintain a **memorandum account** for these types of transactions. Second, record the transaction as a debit to a deferred receivable account and a credit to a deferred sales account. Last, handle the transaction as a consignment. In any event, maintain control for these types of transactions, particularly if they are a part of recurring business activities.

Reasonable Estimates of Returns

Reasonable estimates of returns depend on individual circumstances. An enterprise must take into consideration its individual customers and the types of merchandise involved in determining the estimated amount of returns that may occur. The following factors may impair the ability to make a reasonable estimate of returns (FAS-48, par. 8):

- Possible technological obsolescence or changes in demand for the merchandise
- A long return period
- Little or no past experience in determining returns for similar types of sales of similar merchandise
- An inability to apply past experience due to changing circumstances
- A limited number of similar transactions

☛ **PRACTICE POINTER:** The above factors are to be considered in conjunction with the past experience with a specific customer and the individual product involved in the sale. One or more of these factors may or may not impair the ability of an enterprise to make a reasonable estimate of the amount of future returns.

Illustration of Reasonable Estimates of Returns

The right to return merchandise to a seller may apply to only a portion of a total sale. For example, X Company sells 100,000 widgets to Y Company on January 1 for $1 per widget (cost $0.65). In the sales agreement, X Company grants to Y Company the right to return up to a maximum of 30% of the widgets within six months from the date of sale. Under these circumstances, FAS-48 would only apply to the 30% of the widgets that can be returned by Y Company. Assuming that all of the conditions imposed by FAS-48 are met and it is probable that one-half (50%) of the widgets subject to return will actually be returned and the estimated cost that X Company expects to incur in connection with the returns is $1,000, the computations would be as follows:

Total sale	$100,000
Less: Portion of the sale not subject to FAS-48	70,000
Balance of the sale subject to FAS-48	$ 30,000
Less: Provision for estimated returns (50% of $30,000)	15,000
Balance of sale which is recognized	$ 15,000
Balance of sale not subject to FAS-48	70,000
Total revenue recognized at date of sale	$ 85,000

Under FAS-48, X Company reports $84,000 of revenue on the date the title to the widgets passes to Y Company. X Company also sets up a provision for returnable merchandise and related costs of $16,000. Sales and related cost of sales are reported at their gross amounts in the income statement and the sales and related cost of sales for the *probable* returns are deducted from the gross amounts. The journal entries to record the transactions on the books of X Company are as follows:

Accounts receivable	100,000	
Sales		100,000
(To record the gross sales to Y Company.)		
Cost of sales	65,000	
Inventory		65,000
(To record cost of sales for Y Company order.)		
Estimated sales returns	15,000	
Deferred cost of sales ($0.65 per widget)	9,750	
Cost of sales		9,750
Provision for estimated returns		15,000
(To defer sales of $15,000 and the related cost of sales of $9,750.)		

The provision for estimated returns is a contra accounts to accounts receivable. The deferred cost of sales represents the cost of inventory that is expected to be returned; it is most logically classified as inventory.

FRANCHISE FEE RECOGNITION

Individual Franchise Fees

The two major accounting issues in revenue recognition of initial franchise fees are (1) the time the fee is properly regarded as earned and (2) the assurance of collectibility of any receivable resulting from unpaid portions of the initial fee.

> **OBSERVATION:** These accounting issues are not unique to franchise accounting and merely represent an application of the principle of revenue realization. The realization principle requires that revenue be earned before it is recognized. GAAP require that the realization of revenue be recognized in the accounting period in which the earning process is substantially completed and an exchange has taken place. Revenue usually is recognized at the amount established by the parties to the exchange except for transactions in which collection of the receivable is not reasonably assured.

FAS-45 requires that revenue on individual franchise fees be recognized on the consummation of the transaction, which occurs when all material services or conditions of the sale have been substantially performed. Substantial performance by the franchisor occurs when the following conditions are met (FAS-45, par. 5):

- The franchisor is not obligated in any way (trade practice, law, intent, or agreement) to excuse payment of any unpaid notes or to refund any cash already received.

- The initial services required of the franchisor by contract or otherwise (e.g., training, site selection, etc.) have been substantially performed.

- All other material conditions have been met that affect the consummation of the sale.

The earliest that substantial performance is presumed to occur is when the franchisee actually commences operations of the franchise. This presumption may be overcome, however, if the franchisor can demonstrate that substantial performance occurs at an earlier date (FAS-45, par. 5).

Another accounting issue involved in the recognition of individual franchise fees is the collectibility of any receivable resulting from unpaid portions of the initial franchise fee. An adequate provision for estimated uncollectible amounts from individual franchise fees must be established, if necessary. If the collection of long-term receivables from individual franchise fees is not assured reasonably, the cost recovery or installment sale accounting methods should be used to recognize revenue (FAS-45, par. 6).

Installment Method

Under the installment method of accounting, each payment collected consists of part recovery of cost and part gross profit, in the same ratio that these two elements existed in the original sale. (For a more detailed discussion of the cost recovery and installment methods, see the chapter in this *Guide* titled "Installment Sales.")

Cost Recovery Method

The cost recovery method is used in situations in which recovery of cost is extremely uncertain. Initially, all amounts received are considered recoveries of cost. Once all cost has been recovered, any other collections are recognized as revenue.

Continuing Franchise Fees

Continuing franchise fees are consideration for the continuing rights granted by the franchise agreement and for general and specific services during the life of the franchise agreement. Continuing franchise fees are recognized as revenue when actually earned and receivable from the franchisee. This is true, even if the continuing franchise fee is designated for a specific purpose. If an agency relationship is established by the franchise agreement and a designated portion of the continuing franchise fee is required to be segregated for a specific purpose, however, the designated amounts are recorded as a liability. Any costs incurred for the specific purpose would be charged against the liability. All other costs relating to continuing franchise fees are expensed as incurred (FAS-45, par. 14).

In the event that the continuing franchise fees appear to be insufficient to cover the costs and reasonable profit of the franchisor for the continuing services required by the franchise agreement, a portion of the initial franchise fee, if any, is deferred and amortized over the term of the franchise. The amount deferred should be sufficient to cover all the costs of the continuing services plus a reasonable profit (FAS-45, par. 7).

> **OBSERVATION:** Apparently, FAS-45 assumes that continuing services required by the franchisor coincide with the term of the franchise and amortization should be based on the term of the franchise. An alternate approach would be to relate the amortization period to the period in which the continuing services will be provided by the franchisor, which may not necessarily be the entire term of the franchise.

Area Franchise Fees

Area franchises transfer franchise rights within a geographic area, permitting the opening of a number of franchise outlets. Accounting for revenue recognition from an area franchise is essentially the same as that for individual franchise fees. The only difference is that substantial performance of the franchisor may be more difficult to determine. The terms of the franchise agreement must be used to determine when substantial performance has occurred. In addition, it may be necessary to use the percentage-of-completion method of recognizing revenue in some franchise agreements. For example, an area franchise agreement may require the franchisor to provide specific initial services to any franchise opened in the area. In this event, the franchisor should estimate the number of franchises that are expected to be opened in the area and should recognize a portion of the total area franchise fee as substantial performance occurs for each franchise in the area. Thus, it is necessary to determine the cost of servicing each individual franchise within the area and the total cost of all individual franchises that are expected to be opened in the area. The next step is to determine the percentage of costs that have been substantially performed to the total costs of all individual franchises that are expected to be opened in the area. The resulting percentage is applied to the total initial area franchise revenue to determine the amount of area franchise revenue that can be recognized (FAS-45, pars. 8–9).

☞ **PRACTICE POINTER:**   The percentage-of-completion method of recognizing revenue should be used only in those situations in which costs can be estimated with reasonable reliability.

Estimates of the number of franchises that are expected to be opened in an area franchise are determined by reference to the significant terms and conditions of the franchise agreement (FAS-45, par. 9).

If the franchisor's substantial performance under the terms of the franchise agreement is related to the area franchise, and not to the individual franchises within the area, revenue recognition occurs when all material services and conditions relating to the area franchise have been substantially performed. Thus, this type of area franchise is treated similarly to an individual franchise (FAS-45, par. 8).

Any portion of the franchise revenue that is related to unperformed future services that may have to be refunded is not recognized by the franchisor until the right to refund has expired (FAS-45, par. 8).

Other Franchise Accounting Issues

Franchisee and Franchisor—Unusual Relationships

Unusual relationships may exist between the franchisee and the franchisor, besides those created by the franchise agreement. For example, the franchisor may guarantee debt of the franchisee, or contractually control the franchisee's operations to the extent that an affiliation exists. In all these circumstances, all material services, conditions, or obligations relating to the franchise must be performed substantially by the franchisor before revenue is recognized (FAS-45, par. 10).

> **OBSERVATION:**   The above requirements for unusual relationships between the franchisee and franchisor relate to both individual and area franchises. That is, substantial performance must occur before the franchisor may recognize any revenue.

The initial franchise fee is deferred if it is probable that the franchisor will acquire the franchise back from the franchisee because of an option or other understanding. In this event, the deferred amount is accounted for as a reduction of the cost of reacquiring the franchise when the option or understanding is exercised (FAS-45, par. 11).

Tangible Assets Included in the Franchise Fee

In addition to the initial services of the franchisor, the initial franchise fee may include the sale of specific tangible property, such as inventory, signs, equipment, or real property. Thus, a portion of the initial franchise fee must be allocated to such tangible property. FAS-45 requires that the amount allocated be the fair value of the property. The fair value of the tangible property is recognized as revenue when title to such property passes to the franchisee, even though substantial performance has not occurred for other services included in the franchise agreement (FAS-45, par. 12).

> **OBSERVATION:** FAS-45 does not specify the date on which fair value of the tangible property must be determined. Ordinarily, fair value would be determined at the date of the franchise agreement, which usually establishes the date of the sale.

The franchise agreement may also allocate a portion of the initial franchise fee to specific services that the franchisor will provide. If the various services that the franchisor will provide are interrelated to the extent that objective segregation is impossible, FAS-45 prohibits the recognition of revenue for any specific service until all the services required under the franchise agreement have been substantially performed. If actual prices are available for a specific service through recent sales of the specific service, however, FAS-45 permits recognition of revenue based on substantial performance of that service. In other words, if the franchisor has established objective prices for specific service, a portion of the total franchise fee may be recognized upon completion of substantial performance of the specific services (FAS-45, par. 13).

Continuing Product Sales

If the terms of the franchise agreement allow the franchisee to obtain equipment and supplies from the franchisor at bargain prices, a portion of the initial franchise fee must be deferred. That portion of the fee is either (*a*) the difference between the normal selling price of the equipment and supplies and the bargain purchase price or (*b*) an amount that will enable the franchisor to recover all costs and provide a normal profit. The deferred amount is accounted for as an adjustment of the initial franchise fee and an adjustment of the selling price of the bargain purchase items (FAS-45, par. 15).

> ☞ **PRACTICE POINTER:** The sale of equipment and supplies by the franchisor at normal selling prices, which should include a reasonable profit for the franchisor, is accounted for at the time the sale is complete. Find the amount of sale by reference to the franchise agreement; the cost of the sale is the cost of the equipment or supplies to the franchisor. If it is apparent that the franchisor is not making a reasonable profit on the equipment or supplies, then the rules for "bargain purchases" must be followed.

Agency Sales

Some franchise arrangements in substance establish an agency relationship between the franchisor and the franchisee. The franchisor acts as agent for the franchisee by reselling inventory, equipment, and supplies at no profit. FAS-45 requires that these transactions be accounted for on the franchisor's books as receivables and payables, and not as profit or loss items (FAS-45, par. 16).

Expense Recognition

Direct franchising costs should be matched to their related franchise revenue in accordance with the accrual basis of accounting. This may necessitate the deferral of direct costs incurred prior to revenue recognition and the accrual of direct costs, if any, not yet incurred through the date on which revenue is recognized. Total direct costs that are deferred or accrued must not exceed their estimated related revenue (FAS-45, par. 17).

Selling, general, administrative, and other indirect costs that occur on a regular basis regardless of the sales volume are required to be expensed when incurred (FAS-45, par. 17).

Repossessed Franchises

In repossessing a franchise, the franchisor may or may not refund the consideration previously paid by the franchisee. If a refund is paid by the franchisor, the accounting treatment is equivalent to a cancellation of the original sale. Any revenue previously recognized is treated as a reduction of the revenue of the current period in which the franchise is reacquired (FAS-45, par. 18).

> ☛ **PRACTICE POINTER:** Because substantial performance is required before any revenue is recognized, it is unlikely that a franchisor would grant a refund in the event that the revenue had already been recognized. Instead, it is more likely that the franchisor would enforce collection of any balance due rather than cancel the sale.

If a refund is not paid by the franchisor, the transaction is not considered a cancellation of the sale and no adjustment is made to the previously recorded revenue. If a balance is still owed by the franchisee, however, it may be necessary to review the allowance for uncollectible amounts for the transaction. Also, any deferred revenue on the original sale should be recognized in full (FAS-45, par. 18).

Business Combinations

When a franchisor acquires the operations of one of its own franchises in an arm's-length transaction, FAS-45 requires that the acquisition be accounted for in accordance with FAS-141 (Business Combinations) (see the chapter in this *Guide* titled "Business Combinations").

Purchase Method If the acquisition of an entity's own franchises is accounted for as a purchase, the financial statements of the two entities are combined as of the date of the acquisition and no prior intercompany accounts are eliminated in the combined financial statements. In addition, details of the results of operations for each separate company prior to the date of combination that are included in current combined net income must be disclosed by footnote (FAS-45, par. 19).

Franchise Disclosures

FAS-45 requires that the following disclosures be made in the financial statements or footnotes thereto:

- The nature of all significant commitments and obligations of the franchisor, including a description of the services that have not been substantially performed (FAS-45, par. 20)
- If the installment or cost recovery method is being used to account for franchise fee revenue, the following must be disclosed (FAS-45, par. 21):
  — The sales price of franchises being reported on the installment or cost recovery method
  — The revenue and related deferred costs (currently and cumulative)
  — The periods in which the franchise fees become payable The total revenue that was originally deferred because of uncertainties and then subsequently collected because the uncertainties were resolved
- If significant, separate disclosure for (*a*) initial franchise fees and (*b*) other franchise fee revenue (FAS-45, par. 22)
- Revenue and costs related to non-owned franchises, as opposed to franchises owned and operated by the franchisor (FAS-45, par. 23)
- If significant changes in the ownership of franchises occurs during the period, the following must be disclosed (FAS-45, par. 23):
  — The number of franchises sold during the period
  — The number of franchises purchased during the period

— The number of franchised outlets in operation during the period

— The number of franchisor-owned outlets in operation during the period

The following disclosures, while not required, are considered desirable:

- A statement of whether initial franchise fee revenue will probably decline in the future because sales will reach a saturation point
- If not apparent in the financial statements, the relative contribution to net income of initial franchise fee revenue

---

Illustration of Accounting for Franchise Fee Revenue

Abbott (franchisor) enters into a franchise agreement with Martin (franchisee) that permits Martin to operate a fast-food restaurant under the name of Hot Dog Haven. Abbott operates a large number of restaurants under this name, and via franchises permits others to use the name in geographic areas where Abbott does not have its own operating units.

The initial franchise fee commitment is $10,000. Abbott receives $1,000 from Martin in 20X5 when the agreement is signed. Martin begins operations in 20X6 and is contractually obligated to pay Abbott 25% of the balance of the commitment each year from 20X6 through 20X9. Abbott considers the criteria for substantial performance to have been met in 20X6. Also, Abbott judges collection of the fee to be reasonably assured and makes an adequate allowance for uncollectible commitments based on the aggregate amount of all receivables from commitments to a large number of franchisees.

The agreement between Abbott and Martin also calls for Martin to pay Abbott 2% of total revenues each year as a continuing franchise fee. Abbott expects these amounts to adequately cover its costs of providing continuing service to Martin and to provide a reasonable profit on those costs. Martin reports revenue of $135,000 for 20X6.

General journal entries to record the above for Abbott for 20X5 and 20X6 are as follows:

20X5	Franchise fee receivable	9,000	
	Cash	1,000	
	Unearned franchise fee revenue		10,000
20X6	Unearned franchise fee revenue	10,000	
	Franchise fee revenue		10,000
	Cash ($9,000/4)	2,250	
	Franchise fee receivable		2,250
	Cash ($135,000 × 2%)	2,700	
	Franchise fee revenue		2,700

An entry identical to the second 20X6 entry will be made each year through 20X9. An entry similar to the third 20X6 entry will be made each year for 2% of Martin's revenue.

RELATED CHAPTERS IN 2009 *GAAP GUIDE LEVEL A*

Chapter 2, "Accounting Policies and Standards"
Chapter 22, "Installment Sales"
Chapter 30, "Long-Term Construction Contracts"
Chapter 37, "Real Estate Transactions"

RELATED CHAPTERS IN 2009 *GAAP GUIDE LEVELS B, C, AND D*

Chapter 2, "Accounting Policies and Standards"
Chapter 27, "Long-Term Construction Contracts"
Chapter 33, "Real Estate Transactions"
Chapter 36, "Revenue Recognition"

RELATED CHAPTER IN 2009 *INTERNATIONAL ACCOUNTING/FINANCIAL REPORTING STANDARDS GUIDE*

Chapter 30, "Revenue"

CHAPTER 42
SEGMENT REPORTING

CONTENTS

OVERVIEW

The term *segment reporting* refers to the presentation of information about certain parts of an enterprise, in contrast to information about the entire enterprise. The need for segment information became increasingly apparent in the 1960s and 1970s as enterprises diversified their activities into different industries and product lines, as well as into different geographic areas. Financial analysts and other groups of financial statement users insisted on the importance of disaggregated information—in order for them to assess risk and perform other types of analyses. These needs resulted in the issuance of FAS-14 (Financial Reporting for Segments of a Business Enterprise) and several other pronouncements that amended FAS-14, which together provide the authoritative literature in effect through 1997. That literature was replaced by the following standard, which provides authoritative guidance for segment reporting beginning in 1998:

FAS-131   Disclosures about Segments of an Enterprise and Related Information

BACKGROUND

The objective of presenting disaggregated information about segments of a business enterprise is to produce information about the types of activities in which an enterprise is engaged in and the economic environment in which those activities are carried out. Specifically, the FASB believes that segment information assists financial statement users to (FAS-131, par. 3):

- Understand enterprise performance
- Assess its prospects for future net cash flows
- Make informed decisions about the enterprise

> **OBSERVATION:** The FASB does not specifically discuss the objective of providing information to assist in risk assessment. Risk assessment, however, is an important dimension of financial analysis and underlies, to some extent, the need for segment information. The requirements of FAS-131 (Disclosures about Segments of an Enterprise and Related Information), like its predecessor FAS-14, include information about products and services, information about activities in different geographic areas, and information about reliance on major customers. All relate to areas of significant risk to an enterprise and to areas where risk may vary considerably from situation to situation, including different levels associated with different products, operating in different geographic areas, and differing levels of reliance on major customers.

Since FAS-14 was issued in 1976, various studies and professional groups have emphasized the importance of segment information and described it as essential, fundamental, indispensable, and integral to the investment analysis process (Association of Management and Research). Financial analysts consistently have pointed out two weaknesses of FAS-14: (1) its failure to require an adequate degree of disaggregation and (2) its failure to require segment information in interim financial statements. Both the Canadian Institute of Chartered Accountants and the FASB issued research reports in the early 1990s on the subject. They subsequently decided to jointly pursue a project to improve segment reporting, which resulted in FAS-131 and a comparable standard in Canada.

In 1994, the AICPA's Special Committee on Financial Reporting (the "Jenkins Committee") issued its report, which suggests that for users analyzing a company involved in diverse business segments, information about those segments may be as important as information about the company as a whole. That study suggests that standard setters should give a high priority to improving segment reporting, and that segment information should be reoriented toward the way management operates the business enterprise. In identifying operating segments, FAS-131 requires a management approach that is generally consistent with the AICPA special committee's recommendations.

IDENTIFYING SEGMENTS

Scope

FAS-131 applies to public business enterprises. Any single aspect or combination of the following identifies an enterprise as a public enterprise (FAS-131, par. 9):

- Has issued debt or equity securities that are traded in a public market (a domestic or foreign stock exchange or an over-the-counter market)
- Is required to file financial statements with the Securities and Exchange Commission
- Provides financial statements for the purpose of issuing securities in a public market

FAS-131 does *not* apply in the following situations (FAS-131, par. 9):

- Nonpublic business enterprises
- Not-for-profit enterprises
- The separate financial statements of parents, subsidiaries, joint ventures, or equity method investees if those enterprises' separate statements are consolidated or combined and both the separate company statements and the consolidated or combined statements are included in the same financial report

Although FAS-131 is not required for *nonpublic* business enterprises, FAS-131 encourages them to provide the same information as public business enterprises.

Operating Segments

The concept of operating segments is instrumental to understanding FAS-131. Operating segments are components of an enterprise (FAS-131, par. 10):

- That engage in business activities from which revenues may be earned and in which expenses are incurred.

- Whose operating results are reviewed by the enterprise's chief operating decision maker for purposes of making decisions with regard to resource allocation and performance evaluation.

- For which discrete financial information is available.

FAS-131 includes several guidelines that help implement these general criteria for identifying an enterprise's operating segments, as follows:

- Having earned revenues is not a requirement for a component of a business to be an operating segment (FAS-131, par. 10). For example, a start-up component of the business, which has yet to earn revenue, may be an operating segment.

- Not every component of an enterprise is an operating segment or part of an operating segment (FAS-131, par. 11). For example, corporate headquarters may not be an operating segment.

- Concerning personnel involved in segments (FAS-131, pars. 12–14:

  — The term *chief operating decision maker* is intended to refer to a function, not a specific position title. The intent is to identify that person who performs two functions: (*i*) makes decisions relative to the allocation of resources and (*ii*) evaluates the performance of the segments of the enterprise. The chief operating decision maker could be an individual (e.g., chief executive officer, chief operating officer) or it may be a group of individuals.

☛ **PRACTICE POINTER:** FAS-131 is careful not to use a specific position title that might mean different things in different enterprises. The term *chief operating decision maker* was developed to apply to whatever position within an enterprise that meets certain criteria. A chief operating decision maker makes decisions relative to the allocation of resources and evaluates the performance of segments of the enterprise.

  — The term *segment manager* is intended to refer to the functions having direct accountability to and regular contact with the chief operating decision maker to discuss operating activities, financial results, forecasts, and similar matters. A segment manager may be responsible for more than one segment. The chief operating decision maker also may be a segment manager for one or more operating segments.

- Other factors that may be important in identifying an enterprise's operating segments are (*a*) the nature of the business activities of each component of the enterprise, (*b*) the way the business is organized in terms of managerial responsibility for components of the enterprise, and (c) the manner in which information is presented to the board of directors of the enterprise (FAS-131, par. 13).

- The three primary characteristics of an operating segment may apply to two or more overlapping components of an enterprise (i.e., a matrix organization). For example, one individual may be responsible for each product and service line and another individual may be responsible for each geographic area in which those product and service lines are distributed. The chief operating decision maker may use information both based on products and services and on geographic areas to make decisions about resource allocation and segment performance. In this situation, the components based on products and services are considered operating segments (FAS-131, par. 15).

Reportable Segments

Reportable segments are operating segments that meet the criteria for separate reporting under FAS-131. Essentially, a reportable segment is one that accounts for a sufficient amount of an enterprise's activities to warrant disclosure of separate information.

Quantitative Thresholds

A logical starting point is the quantitative thresholds for identifying reportable segments. These criteria state that an operating segment is a reportable segment if any of the following quantitative criteria is met (FAS-131, par. 18):

- The operating segment's total revenues (both external, such as sales to other enterprises, and intersegment, such as sales between operating segments) make up 10% or more of the combined revenue of all operating segments.

- The absolute amount of the reported profit or loss of the operating segments is 10% or more of the greater (absolute amount) of the total profit of all operating segments reporting a profit or the total loss of all operating segments reporting a loss.

- The operating segment's assets make up 10% or more of the combined assets of all operating segments.

In determining its reportable segments that meet these quantitative criteria, management may combine the activities of two or more operating segments, but only if certain similar economic characteristics are present in both (or all) operating segments. These operating segments' segment characteristics include (FAS-131, par. 17):

- The nature of their products and services
- The nature of their production processes
- The types of their customers
- Their distribution methods
- The nature of their regulatory environment (if applicable).

Another quantitative criterion is that the identified reportable segments must constitute at least 75% of the total consolidated revenue (FAS-131, par. 20). If the operating segments that are initially identified as reportable segments do not meet this threshold, additional operating segments must be identified, even if they do *not* meet the quantitative criteria presented earlier. Information about those operating segments for which separate information is not presented can be combined and presented in the aggregate with an appropriate description (e.g., "all other segments").

Comparability

Comparability among years is an important factor in identifying reportable segments, as evidenced by the following requirements that relate to changes in segments meeting the quantitative criteria from one year to the next (FAS-131, pars. 22–23):

- If a prior year reportable segment fails to meet one of the quantitative criteria but management believes it to be of continuing significance, information about that segment shall continue to be presented.
- If an operating segment meets the criteria as a reportable segment for the first time in the current period, prior-year segment information that is presented for comparative purposes shall be restated to reflect the new reportable segment as a separate segment.

As a practical matter, FAS-131 indicates that ten reportable segments is probably a reasonable maximum number for purposes of disclosing separate segment information (FAS-131, par. 24). While the maximum of ten is not stated as an absolute requirement, management is advised that when the number of reportable segments exceeds ten, consideration should be given to whether a practical limit has been reached.

DISCLOSURE OF INFORMATION ABOUT MULTIPLE REPORTABLE SEGMENTS

Segment information is required in four areas (FAS-131, par. 25):

1. General information

2. Information about segment profit or loss and assets
3. Reconciliation of segment information to aggregate enterprise amounts
4. Interim period information

The information required by FAS-131 must be reported for each period for which an income statement is presented, including prior periods presented for comparative purposes. Reconciliation of segment balance sheet information to enterprise balance sheet amounts is only required when a balance sheet is presented (FAS-131, par. 25, and FAS-135, par. 4x).

The following sections cover the specific disclosure requirements in the four general areas identified above.

General Information

General information is necessary for financial statement users to understand the specific information about segments that is required to be disclosed. The general information logically would precede the information about segment profit or loss and assets and reconciliations, which are identified in the following two sections (FAS-131, par. 26):

1. Factors used to identify the enterprise's reportable segments
2. Types of products and services that are the basis for revenues from each reportable segment

In identifying the enterprise's reportable segments, an explanation of the basis for organization is required. Management may have used the following organizational alternatives, for example:

- Products and services
- Geographic areas
- Regulatory environment
- Combination of factors

Information about Segment Profit or Loss and Assets

The heart of the segment reporting requirements of FAS-131 is information about segments' profit or loss and assets. A measure of profit or loss and total assets is required for each reportable segment. This amount should be based on the information reported to the chief operating decision maker for making decisions about allocating resources to segments and assessing segment performance.

If the chief operating decision maker uses only one measure of segment profit or loss and only one measure of assets, those are the measures that should be reported. On the other hand, if the chief operating decision maker uses multiple measures of segment profit or loss or segment assets in resource allocation decisions and performance evaluation, the information reported to satisfy FAS-131 should be that which management believes is determined most consistently with that used in the determination of the corresponding amounts in the enterprise's consolidated financial statements (FAS-131, par. 30).

In presenting segment profit or loss, the following information is required for each segment if the specific amounts are included in the measure of segment profit or loss reviewed by the chief operating decision maker (FAS-131, par. 27):

- Revenues from external customers
- Revenues from other operating segments
- Interest revenue
- Interest expense
- Depreciation, depletion, and amortization
- Unusual items
- Income recognized on equity-method investments
- Income tax expense or benefit
- Extraordinary items
- Significant noncash items other than depreciation, depletion and amortization

Following are guidelines included in FAS-131 for the determination of the information items listed above:

- In identifying unusual items, APB-30 (Reporting the Results of Operations—Reporting the Effects of Disposal of a Segment of a Business, and Extraordinary, Unusual, and Infrequently Occurring Events and Transactions) is the primary source of authority.
- Interest revenue and expense should be presented separately (i.e., not net) unless the net amount is the figure used by the chief operating decision maker to assess performance and make resource allocation decisions.

Additional information about assets of each reportable segment is required, as follows, if these amounts are considered by the chief operating decision maker in evaluating the assets held by a segment (FAS-131, par. 28):

- The amount of investment in equity method investees
- Total expenditures for additions to long-lived assets (except financial instruments, long-term customer relationships of a financial institution, mortgage and other servicing rights, deferred policy acquisition costs, and deferred income taxes)

In addition to the specific information items about segment profit or loss and segment assets, enterprises are required to present explanatory information that should assist users of the financial statements in better understanding the meaning of that information, as follows (FAS-131, par. 31):

- The basis of accounting for transactions between reportable segments
- Differences in the measurement of the reportable segments' profit or loss and the enterprise's consolidated income before income taxes, extraordinary items, discontinued operations, and cumulative effect of changes in accounting principle
- Differences in the measurement of the reportable segments' assets and the enterprise's consolidated assets
- Any changes from prior years in the measurement of reported segment profit or loss, and the effect, if any, of those changes on the amount of segment profit or loss
- The nature of any asymmetrical allocations to segments

> **OBSERVATION:** In further explaining the second and third requirements above, FAS-131 points out that the required reconciliation information (explained below) may satisfy this requirement. It also indicates that enterprises should consider whether differences in accounting policies with regard to the allocation of centrally incurred costs are necessary for understanding the segment information and, if so, to explain those allocation policies. In further explaining the fifth requirement above, FAS-131 illustrates an "asymmetrical allocation" as an enterprise allocating depreciation to a segment without allocating the related depreciable asset to that segment.

Reconciliations

Reconciliations of certain segment information to the enterprise's consolidated totals are an important part of the disclosure requirements of FAS-131, as indicated in the following table (FAS-131, par. 32):

Segment information	*Reconciled to*	*Consolidated information*
1. Reportable segments' revenues		1. Consolidated revenues
2. Reportable segments' profit or loss		2. Consolidated income before income taxes, extraordinary items, discontinued operations, and cumulative effect of change in accounting principle
3. Reportable segments' assets		3. Consolidated assets
4. Reportable segments' amounts for other significant items		4. Corresponding consolidated amounts

In presenting these reconciliations, all significant reconciling items must be separately identified and described.

> **OBSERVATION:** FAS-131, like many authoritative accounting standards, establishes minimum required disclosures. In the case of segment information, the illustration in paragraph 32d implies that a decision to disclose information beyond the minimum requirements carries with it a responsibility to provide reconciling information about that item for the segments and for the consolidated enterprise. The wording of paragraph 32d is important: "...an enterprise *may choose* to disclose liabilities for its reportable segments, *in which case the enterprise would reconcile* the total of reportable segments' liabilities for each segment to the enterprise's consolidated liabilities if segment liabilities are significant." (Emphasis added.)

Interim Period Information

FAS-131 requires abbreviated segment information in interim financial statements. The following is an abbreviated categorized listing of the information required to be disclosed in condensed interim financial statements (FAS-131, par. 33):

> Revenue
> > From external customers
> > Intersegment
>
> Segment profit or loss
> Material changes from last annual report
> > Total assets

Basis of segmentation
Basis of measuring segment profit or loss
Reconciliation of segment profit or loss to enterprise consolidated income

In meeting the reconciliation of segment profit or loss requirement, enterprises have two alternatives, depending on whether they allocate items such as income taxes and extraordinary items to segments. If they do *not* allocate these items, the reconciliation should be from reportable segments' profit or loss to enterprise consolidated income before income taxes, extraordinary items, discontinued operations, and the cumulative effect of a change in accounting principle. On the other hand, if the items indicated above are allocated to segments, the reconciliation may be from segments' profit or loss to consolidated income after those items. In either case, significant reconciling items are to be separately identified and described in that reconciliation.

> ☛ **PRACTICE POINTER:**   If an enterprise allocates items such as income taxes and extraordinary items to segments, it would be reasonable to expect fewer reconciling items between the total of the reportable segments' profit or loss and the related consolidated totals than would be the case if these same items were *not* allocated to segments and, therefore, were required to be part of the reconciliation. In other words, the more items that are allocated down to the segments in determining their profit or loss, the closer the total of the reportable segments' profit and loss will be to the consolidated enterprise's net income and the fewer the items required to meet the reconciliation requirement.

Restatement of Previously Reported Information

An enterprise may change the structure of its internal organization in a manner that causes information about its reportable segments to lack comparability with previous period information. In this situation, and where practicable, previous period information presented for comparative purposes should be restated in accordance with the revised organization. This requirement applies to both previous interim and annual periods. In addition to restating the financial information presented, an explanation of the change is required, including that previous period information has been restated (FAS-131, par. 34).

Should restatement of previous period information not be practicable in the year of the internal organization change, disclosure is required of current period information under both the previous and the new organizational structure if it is practicable to do so (FAS-131, par. 35).

DISCLOSURE OF ENTERPRISE-WIDE INFORMATION

The previous discussion has focused on disclosure of information about multiple reporting segments. An enterprise is required to report certain disaggregated information, even if it functions as a single operating unit.

Enterprise-wide information is required in the following three areas:

1. Information about products and services
2. Information about geographic areas
3. Information about major customers

Enterprises that are organized around reporting segments may have satisfied these requirements already as a result of satisfying the disclosure requirements for multiple reporting segments. If not, they are required to present the enterprise-wide information, as are enterprises that are not subject to the requirements of those enterprises with multiple reportable segments. Information required in the three areas identified above is as follows:

Products and Services (FAS-131, par. 37)

- Revenues from external customers for each product and service or group of related products and services

Geographic Areas (FAS-131, par. 38)

- Revenues from external customers:
  - Attributable to the enterprise's country of domicile
  - Attributed to all foreign countries in total from which revenue is derived
  - Revenues from individual foreign countries if the amounts are material
  - The basis for attributing revenues from external customers to individual countries

- Long-lived assets (not including financial instruments, long-term customer relationships of a financial institution, mortgage and other servicing rights, deferred policy of acquisition costs, and deferred income taxes:
  - Attributable to the enterprise's country of domicile
  - Attributable to all foreign countries in total where assets are held
  - Assets from individual foreign countries if the amounts are material

Major Customers (FAS-131, par. 39)

- Revenues from a single customer that accounts for 10% or more of revenue
- The segment(s) from which sales to each major customer were made

In preparing the information about products and services and geographic areas, amounts should be based on the same information used to prepare the enterprise's general purpose-financial statements. If this is impracticable, the information is not required, but an explanation should be provided.

In preparing the information about major customers, the following additional guidance is provided:

- Neither the identity of the major customer nor the amount of revenue that each segment reports from that customer is required
- A group of entities under common control is considered a single customer.
- For purposes of identifying major *governmental* customers, the federal government, a state government, a local government, or a foreign government is considered a single customer.

Illustration—Sample Disclosures of Segment Information

FAS-131 requires the disclosure of extensive information about an enterprise's operating segments. Following are brief examples of how some of these requirements might appear in notes to the financial statements. In all cases, dollar figures (in thousands) are assumed for illustrative purposes. For more complete examples, see Appendix B of FAS-131.

Management Policy in Identifying Reportable Segments

Company A's reportable business segments are strategic business units that offer distinctive products and services that are marketed through different channels. They are managed separately because of their unique technology, marketing, and distribution requirements.

Types of Products and Services

Company B has four reportable segments: food processing, apparel manufacturing, insurance, and entertainment. Food processing is a canning operating for sales to regional grocery chains. The apparel segment produces mid-price clothing for distribution through discount department stores. The insurance segment provides primarily property insurance for heavy manufacturing enterprises. The entertainment segment includes several theme parks and multiple-screen theaters.

Segment Profit or Loss

Company C's accounting policies for segments are the same as those described in the summary of significant accounting policies. Management evaluates segment performance based on segment profit or loss before income taxes and nonrecurring gains and losses. Transfers between segments are accounted for at market value.

| | Segments | | | | | Consolidated |
	A	B	C	D	Other	Totals
Revenues from external customers	$200	$200	$300	$400	$100	$1,200
Intersegment revenues		50		60		110
Interest revenue	10	15		40		65
Interest expense	20	10	40	30		100
Depreciation and amortization	50	60	100	120		330
Segment profit	40	75	80	180		375
Segment assets	$180	$220	$280	$450	$250	$1,380
Expenditures for segment assets	20	70	30	80	20	220

Reconciliation of Segment Information to Consolidated Amounts

Information for Company D's reportable segments relates to the enterprise's consolidated totals as follows:

Revenues

Total revenues for reportable segments	$1,800
Other revenues	250
Intersegment revenues	(200)
Total consolidated revenues	$1,850

Profit or Loss

Total profit or loss for reportable segments	$250
Other profit or loss	40
Intersegment profits	(35)
General corporate expenses	(50)
Income before income taxes	$205

Assets

Total assets for reportable segments	$3,000
Assets not attributed to segments	200
Elimination of intersegment receivables	(300)
General corporate assets not attributed to segments	500
Total consolidated assets	$3,400

Geographic Information

Company E attributes revenues and long-lived assets to different geographic areas on the basis of the location of the customer. Revenues and investment in long-lived assets by geographic area are as follows:

	Revenues	Long-lived Assets
United States	$1,200	$ 800
Mexico	500	400
Brazil	450	375
Taiwan	300	200
Other	800	720
Total	$3,250	$2,495

Major Customer Information

Company F has revenue from a single customer that represents $800 of the enterprise's consolidated revenue. This customer is served by the automotive parts operating segment.

RELATED CHAPTERS IN 2009 *GAAP GUIDE* LEVEL A

Chapter 7, "Consolidated Financial Statements"
Chapter 14, "Equity Method"
Chapter 18, "Foreign Operations and Exchange"
Chapter 26, "Interim Financial Reporting"
Chapter 40, "Results of Operations"

RELATED CHAPTERS IN 2009 *GAAP GUIDE* LEVELS B, C, AND D

Chapter 10, "Consolidated Financial Statements"
Chapter 14, "Equity Method"
Chapter 18, "Foreign Operations and Exchange"

Chapter 23, "Interim Financial Reporting"
Chapter 35, "Results of Operations"
Chapter 37, "Segment Reporting"

RELATED CHAPTER IN 2009 *INTERNATIONAL ACCOUNTING/FINANCIAL REPORTING STANDARDS GUIDE*

Chapter 31, "Segment Reporting"

CHAPTER 43
STOCK-BASED PAYMENTS

CONTENTS

OVERVIEW

An entity may pay for goods or services by issuing its stock. Although stock can be issued as compensation for many types of goods or services, the accounting treatment of stock issued in exchange for employee services, especially stock options, has been particularly controversial. In some instances, the stock issued to employees does not include compensation (noncompensatory plan); in other instances, the stock issued to employees includes compensation (compensatory plan). A *compensatory plan* is one in which services rendered by employees are partially compensated for by the issuance of stock. The measurement of compensation expense included in compensatory plans is the primary problem encountered in accounting for stock issued to employees.

GAAP for stock issued as compensation to providers of goods or services are found in the following pronouncement:

FAS-123(R)   Share-Based Payment

2009 TRANSITION GUIDANCE FOR FAS-141(R) AND FAS-160

The FASB has recently issued FAS-141(R), *Business Combinations*, which is effective for business combinations for which the acquisition date is on or after the beginning of the first annual reporting period beginning on or after December 15, 2008. The FASB has also issued FAS-160, *Noncontrolling Interests in Consolidated Financial Statements, an Amendment of ARB No. 51*, which is effective for fiscal years, and interim periods within those fiscal years, beginning on or after December 15, 2008. Because these standards are not effective for some companies until December 2009, and because early adoption is prohibited, the 2009 *GAAP Guide* reflects the requirements of FAS-141 prior to its revision in December 2007 and does not reflect the requirements of FAS-160. There is a discussion of the changes in the accounting for business combinations under FAS-141(R) in the Appendix to Chapter 4, "Business Combinations." Similarly, the Appendix to Chapter 7, "Consolidated Financial Statements" includes a discussion of the requirements of FAS-160. However, any effects of FAS-141(R) and/or FAS-160 on this chapter have not been reflected in this edition. Therefore, if a company is subject to the requirements of FAS-141(R) and/or FAS-160, the reader is referred to FAS-141(R) and FAS-160 for these new requirements.

BACKGROUND

GAAP for issuances of stock as compensation to providers of goods or services is found in FAS-123(R) (Share-Based Payment). FAS-123(R) applies to all share-based payment transactions in which an entity acquires goods or services by issuing its shares, share options, or other equity instruments or by issuing liabilities to an employee or other supplier in amounts based, at least in part, on the price of the entity's shares or other equity instruments or that require or may require settlement by issuing the entity's equity shares or other equity instruments [FAS-123(R), par. 4]. FAS-123(R) does not address shares issued as part of employee share ownership plans (ESOPs). SOP 93-6 remains the primary source of GAAP for ESOPs.

FAS-123(R) provides guidance in accounting for the issuance of employee stock options, restricted stock, performance-based stock issuances, stock appreciation rights, and employee stock purchase plans. Descriptions of the more common types of plans follow.

Employee Stock Option Plan

In a stock option plan, an employee is granted the right to purchase a fixed number of shares at a certain price during a specified period [FAS-123(R), Appendix E].

Restricted Stock Plan

Shares that have been issued under a restricted stock plan cannot be sold for a period of time due to a contractual or governmental restriction. In the case of shares issued to employees, a limitation on the ability to sell the shares typically results from the shares not yet being vested. The employee may be prohibited (restricted) from selling the shares until the employee meets a service or performance condition [FAS-123(R), Appendix E].

Performance-Based Stock Plan

A stock award where a pertinent provision of the award (e.g., vesting, exercisability, exercise price) is affected by whether one or more performance targets are achieved [FAS-123(R), Appendix E].

Stock Appreciation Rights

Under a stock appreciation rights plan, employees receive an amount equal to the increase in the value of a specified number of shares over a specified period of time. This amount usually is paid in cash, although it can be issued in the form of stock.

Employee Stock Purchase Plan

Employee stock purchase plans are a type of employee benefit permitted by the Internal Revenue Code. These types of plans are typically established as either a stock bonus plan or a stock bonus plan combined with a money purchase pension plan and are designed to invest in the employer's stock [FAS-123(R), Appendix E].

> ☞ **PRACTICE POINTER:** In December 2007, the SEC issued SAB 110 on share-based payments, which amended SAB 107, to allow continued use of the "simplified" method of developing an estimate of the expected term of so-called "plain vanilla" stock options accounted for under FS-123(R). When SAB 107 was published, the SEC staff believed that more information

about the employee exercise behavior would become available and, therefore, stated that it would not expect the simplified method to be used for stock option grants after December 31, 2007. SAB 110 extends the use of the simplified method beyond that date based on the fact that such information was not available at December 31, 2007. The SEC staff indicates that it will accept the simplified method beyond December 31, 2007, for "plain vanilla" options in situations such as the following:

- A company does not have sufficient historical exercise data to provide a reasonable basis for estimating expected term due to the limited time its equity shares have been publicly traded.
- A company significantly changes the terms of its share option grants or the types of employees receiving share option grants such that its historical exercise data no longer provides a reasonable basis for estimating expected term.
- A company has or expects to have significant structural changes in its business such that its historical exercise data will no longer provide a reasonable basis for estimating expected term.

NONCOMPENSATORY PLANS

Certain stock purchase plans are not intended to compensate employees. For example, a corporation may intend to raise additional capital or to diversify its ownership to include employees and officers. A plan is *noncompensatory* if the cash received per share is very close to the amount of cash that would be received if the same deal were offered to all shareholders. In these types of transactions, a company generally does not recognize any compensation cost.

An employee share purchase plan that satisfies all of the following criteria does not give rise to recognizable compensation cost:

- The plan satisfies at least one of the following conditions:
  — The terms of the plan are no more favorable than those available to all holders of the same class of shares.
  — Any purchase discount from the market price does not exceed the per-share amount of share issuance costs that would have been incurred to raise a significant amount of capital by a public offering. (A purchase discount of 5% or less from the market price is considered to comply with this condition without justification. A purchase discount greater than 5% that cannot be justified under this condition results in compensation cost for the entire amount of the discount.)

- Substantially all employees that meet limited qualifications may participate on an equitable basis.

- The plan incorporates no option features, other than the following:
  — Employees are permitted a short time (not over 31 days) after the purchase price has been fixed to enroll in the plan.
  — The purchase price is based solely on the market price of the shares at the date of purchase, and employees are permitted to cancel participation before the purchase date and obtain a refund of amounts previously paid [FAS-123(R), par. 12].

A provision that establishes the purchase price as an amount based on the lesser of the equity share's market price at date of grant or its market price at date of purchase is an example of an option feature that causes the plan to be compensatory. Similarly, a plan in which the purchase price is based on the share's market price at the grant date and that permits a participating employee to cancel participation before the purchase date and obtain a refund of amounts previously paid contains an option feature that causes the plan to be compensatory [FAS-123(R), par. 13].

The requisite service period for any compensation cost resulting from an employee share purchase plan is the period over which the employee participates in the plan and pays for the shares [FAS-123(R), par. 14].

The portion of the fair value of an instrument attributed to employee service is net of any amount that an employer pays for that instrument when it is granted. For example, if an employee pays $25 at the grant date for an option with a fair value at that date of $100, the amount attributed to employee service is $75 [FAS-123(R), par. 15].

Illustration of an Employee Share Purchase Plan

Stein Inc. plans to adopt an employee share purchase plan on January 1, 20X6. Stein wants its employee share purchase plan to be noncompensatory. Under the terms of the plan, all employees who have completed six months of service will be eligible to participate in the plan. Employees will be able to purchase up to $8,000 of Stein Inc.'s common stock each year at an eight percent discount from its market price at the date of purchase. The per-share amount of share issuance costs to raise a significant amount of capital by selling stock through a public offering is five percent of Stein's share price. Stein is considering three different alternatives for offering a share discount to existing holders of its common stock.

Alternative 1　Stein Inc. would allow its current common stockholders to purchase up to $8,000 of its stock on a yearly basis at a three percent discount from its market price on the date of purchase. The employee stock purchase plan would be compensatory because the discount offered to employees (eight percent) is larger than the discount offered to existing stockholders (three percent). Therefore, the entire eight percent discount offered to employees would be viewed as compensatory (i.e., compensation expense would be recognized for the full amount of the eight percent discount when employees purchase shares under the plan).

Alternative 2 Stein Inc. would allow its current common stockholders to purchase up to $8,000 of its stock on a yearly basis at an eight percent discount from its market price on the date of purchase. The employee stock purchase plan would be non-compensatory because the discount offered to employees is the same as the discount offered to existing stockholders.

Alternative 3 Stein Inc. would allow its current common stockholders to reinvest dividends received in new shares of common stock. Existing stockholders could buy up to $8,000 of new shares of common stock using dividends received at a discount of eight percent. Since Stein Inc.'s common stock is widely-held, very few existing shareholders would receive dividends equal to $8,000. Therefore, most shareholders would not be able to get the benefit of purchasing $8,000 of stock at an eight percent discount, whereas all employees meeting minimal eligibility requirements would receive this benefit. As a result, this plan would be viewed as compensatory and compensation expense would be recognized for the full amount of the eight percent discount when employees purchase shares under the plan.

COMPENSATORY PLANS

Compensatory plans give rise to compensation, usually out of an offer or agreement by a corporation to issue shares to one or more officers or employees (grantees) at a stated price that is less than the prevailing market price. Under FAS-123(R), the issuance of equity instruments (stock and options) in exchange for goods or services are recognized at the instruments' fair value in an entity's primary financial statements. Although FAS-123(R) applies to the issuance of all equity instruments in exchange for goods or services, its primary focus relates to the accounting for the issuance of equity instruments in exchange for employee services and the resulting recognition of compensation expense.

☞ **PRACTICE POINTER:** The SEC issued Staff Accounting Bulletin No. 107 (SAB 107), *Share-Based Payment,* in March 2005. SAB 107 is designed to provide guidance to public companies in applying FAS-123(R). Although SEC pronouncements typically are not covered in the *GAAP Guide Level A*, this edition is covering selected excerpts of SAB 107 because of the complexity of FAS-123(R) and because SAB 107 provides detailed and specific guidance in applying the provisions of FAS-123(R).

The SEC indicates that it is appropriate to apply FAS-123(R) to share-based payment transactions with nonemployees unless (1) another authoritative accounting pronouncement more clearly applies to the transaction or (2) applying FAS-123(R) would be inconsistent with the instrument issued to the nonemployees. For example, the expected term of an employee share option often is shorter than the option's contractual term because the option is not transferable, it is not hedgeable, and the option's term is truncated if an employee terminates employment after the vesting date but before the end of the contractual term of the option. If an option issued to a nonemployee does not have these restrictions (nontransferability, nonhedgeability, and truncation of the contractual term), it would be inappropriate to value the option using an expected term that is shorter than the contractual term.

Public companies are required to recognize compensation cost for equity instruments based on the grant-date fair value of those instruments. The resulting compensation cost is recognized as an expense over the period that the employee must work in order to be entitled to the award. The grant-date fair value of the equity instrument is estimated using an option-pricing model (e.g., the Black-Scholes model, a binomial model), adjusted to reflect the unique characteristics of the equity instrument. Nonpublic companies also must recognize compensation expense based on the grant-date fair value of the equity instrument issued, though some variation in how this principle is applied may be required due to the inability to determine the fair value of the equity instrument at its date of issuance.

☞ **PRACTICE POINTER:**   SAB 107 indicates that compensation expense for share-based payment arrangements with employees should appear in the same income statement line item as cash-based compensation paid to employees. Some companies might want to highlight the non-cash portion of employee compensation expense (i.e., the expense as a result of a share-based payment arrangement). SAB 107 indicates that companies could make this disclosure as a parenthetical notation to the appropriate income statement line item, in the cash flow statement, in the financial statement notes, or in the MD&A.

Recognition and Measurement Principles

An entity shall recognize the services received or goods acquired in a share-based payment transaction as services are received or when it obtains the goods. The entity shall recognize an increase in equity or a liability, depending on whether the instruments granted satisfy the equity or liability classification criteria [FAS-123(R), par. 5].

A share-based payment transaction with employees shall be measured based on the fair value (or, in some cases, a calculated or intrinsic value) of the equity instrument issued. If the fair value of goods or services received in a share-based payment with non-employees is more reliably measurable than the fair value of the equity instrument issued, the fair value of the goods or services received shall be used to measure the transaction. Conversely, if the fair value of the equity instruments issued in a share-based payment transaction with nonemployees is more reliably measurable than the fair value of the consideration received, the transaction shall be measured at the fair value of the equity instruments issued [FAS-123(R), par. 7].

The cost of services received from employees in exchange for awards of share-based compensation generally shall be measured at the fair value of the equity instruments issued or at the fair value of the liabilities incurred. The fair value of the liabilities incurred in share-based transactions with employees shall be remeasured at the end of each reporting period until settlement [FAS-123(R), par. 10].

Share-based payments awarded to an employee of the reporting entity by a related party or other holder of an economic interest in the entity as compensation for services provided to the entity are share-based transactions to be accounted for under FAS-123(R) unless the transfer is clearly for a purpose other than compensation for services to the reporting entity. The substance of such a transaction is that the economic interest holder makes a capital contribution to the reporting entity and that entity makes a share-based payment to its employee in exchange for services rendered [FAS-123(R), par. 11].

Measurement of Awards Classified as Equity—Public Company

For equity instruments awarded to employees, the measurement objective is to estimate the fair value at the grant date of the equity instruments that the entity is obligated to issue when employees have rendered the required service and have satisfied any other conditions required to earn the right to benefit from the instruments. To satisfy this measurement objective, the restrictions and conditions inherent in equity instruments awarded to employees are treated differently depending on whether they continue in effect after the requisite service period. A restriction that continues in effect (e.g., the inability to transfer vested equity share options to third parties or inability to sell vested shares for a period of time) is considered in estimating the fair value of the instruments at the grant date. For equity share options and similar instruments, the effect of nontransferability is taken into account by reflecting the effects of expected exercise by employees and post-vesting employment termination behavior in estimating the option's expected term, and the option's expected term affects the estimate of the option's fair value [FAS-123(R), pars. 16–17].

In contrast, a restriction that results from the forfeitability of instruments to which employees have not yet earned the right (e.g., the inability to exercise a nonvested equity share option or to sell nonvested shares) is *not* reflected in estimating the fair value of the related instruments at the grant date. Rather, those restrictions are taken into account by recognizing compensation cost only for awards for which employees render the requisite service [FAS-123(R), par. 18].

Ordinarily, awards and share-based employee compensation specify a performance and/or service condition that must be satisfied for an employee to earn the right to benefit from the award. No compensation cost is recognized for instruments that employees forfeit because a service condition or performance condition is not satisfied. Some awards contain a market condition. The effect of a market condition is reflected in the grant-date fair value of the award. Compensation cost is recognized for an award with a market condition provided that the requisite service is rendered, regardless of whether the market condition is satisfied [FAS-123(R), par. 19].

The effects on grant-date fair value of service and performance conditions that apply only during the requisite service period are reflected based on the outcomes of those conditions [FAS-123(R), par. 20].

A nonvested equity share or nonvested equity share unit awarded to an employee shall be measured at its fair value as if it were vested and issued on the grant date. A restricted share awarded to an employee (i.e., a share that will be restricted after the employee has a vested right to it) shall be measured at its fair value, which is the same amount for which a similarly restricted share would be issued to a third party [FAS-123(R), par. 21].

The fair value of an equity share option or similar instrument shall be measured based on the observable market value of an option with the same or similar terms and conditions if one is available. Otherwise, the fair value of an equity share option or similar instrument is estimated using a valuation technique such as an option-pricing model [FAS-123(R), par. 22]. The valuation technique used should possess all of the following characteristics:

- It is applied in a manner consistent with the fair value measurement objective and other requirements of FAS-123(R);

- It is based on established principles of financial economic theory and generally applied in that field; and

- It reflects all substantive characteristics of the instrument [FAS-123(R), par. A8].

The estimated fair value of the instrument at grant date does not take into account the effect on fair value of vesting conditions and other restrictions that apply only during the requisite service period. Under the fair-value-based method required by FAS-123(R), the effect of vesting restrictions that apply only during the requisite service period is reflected by recognizing compensation cost only for instruments for which the requisite service is rendered [FAS-123(R), par. A9].

> ☞ **PRACTICE POINTER:** SAB 107 indicates that only rarely will there be only one acceptable method of determining the fair value of a share-based payment arrangement. SAB 107 also indicates that estimates of fair value are not intended to predict future events. As long as a reasonable and appropriate process was used to estimate fair value, a difference (no matter how significant) between the estimate of fair value and actual future events does not necessarily reflect on the reasonableness of the original estimates.

Valuation Techniques for Share Options and Other Similar Instruments

A lattice model (e.g., a binomial model) and a closed-form model (e.g., the Black-Scholes-Merton formula) are among the valuation techniques that meet the criteria required by FAS-123(R) for estimating the fair values of employee share options and similar instruments. FAS-123(R) does not specify a preference for a particular valuation technique or model for estimating the fair value of employee share options and similar instruments [FAS-123(R), pars. A13–A14].

Illustration of Application of Lattice Model to Valuing an Employee Stock Option

This example illustrates the valuation of stock options using the binomial model, a lattice-based option-pricing model. Aqua Resources Inc. grants fully vested stock options with an exercise price of $25 and a term of five years. The owner of the option can therefore purchase shares of stock for $25 for the next five years until the option expires. There is a 75% probability that the price of the security will increase by 16% each year and a 25% probability that the price will decline by 14% each year. Aqua Resources uses a discount rate of 6%. The bold numbers indicate the expected share prices, and the corresponding numbers below are the option value calculations.

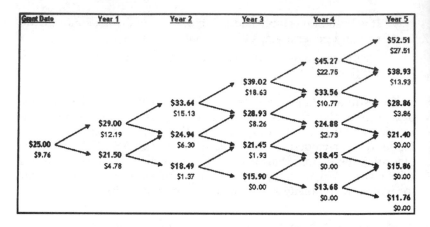

If the share price exceeds $25 by Year 5, the option holder will realize a gain of the net amount upon exercise of the option. For example, if the share price increases all five years, the holder will net $27.51 ($52.51 − $25) upon exercise. If the share price falls below $25 by Year 5, the option holder will not exercise since the share price is less than the exercise price.

To calculate the option value at the time of grant, Entity X first determines the option value at the expiration period and then works backward to the date of the grant. For example, assume that in Year 4, the share price has increased to $45.27 based on the aforementioned estimates. In this case, the option holder has an asset that will either rise to a share price of $52.51 (total five-year net increase of $27.51) or fall to a share price of $38.93 (total five-year net increase of $13.93). The respective probability of these outcomes is 75% and 25%. Using a discount rate of 6%, the value of the option in Year 4 will be $22.75, as calculated below:

Year 4:   [(75% × $27.51)/1.06] + [(25% × $13.93)/1.06] = $22.75

Continuing to work backward, the option value at the grant date is determined as follows:

Year 3: [(75% × $22.75)/1.06] + [(25% × $10.77)/1.06] = $18.63

Year 2: [(75% × $18.63)/1.06] + [(25% × $8.26)/1.06] = $15.13

Year 1: [(75% × $15.13)/1.06] + [(25% × $6.30)/1.06] = $12.19

Grant Date: [(75% × $12.19)/1.06] + [(25% × $4.78)/1.06] = **$ 9.76**

Thus, the value of the option is based on the expected share price at each node of the lattice. Note that when the share price does not exceed the exercise price at Year 5, the option has no value since the option would simply expire unexercised. Accordingly, there is no real risk of loss to the owner; the higher the probability of an increase in stock price, the higher the value of the option. Also note that one of the advantages of the binomial model is that it can use different volatility estimates for different time periods; however, different volatilities are not used in this illustration.

Illustration of Application of Lattice Model—Early Exercise of Fully Vested Options

Using the same information as in the previous example, we allow for the early exercise of the options. Assume that there is an expectation of early exercise when the underlying share price reaches 1.3 times the exercise price. As shown, when the price exceeds $32.50 ($25 × 1.3), employees will exercise their options, stopping the binomial tree from expanding. The underlined share prices indicate where early exercise takes place. The shaded areas represent the portion of the binomial tree that is no longer relevant due to early exercise.

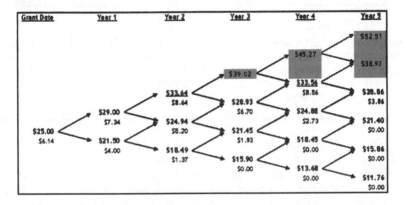

For example, if the share price increases in Years 1 and 2, the value of the option would be $33.64 in Year 2. Because the price now exceeds $32.50, the option holder is assumed to exercise the option early, and no further increases in share value are possible. Therefore, the total net increase is calculated as $8.64 ($33.64 − $25), and the option value at grant date falls from $9.76 to $6.14 as a result of early exercise:

Year 1: [(75% × $8.64)/1.06] + [(25% × $5.2)/1.06] = $7.34

Grant Date: [(75% × $7.34)/1.06] + [(25% × $4.00)/1.06] = **$6.14**

Illustration of Application of Lattice Model—Early Exercise and Cliff Vesting

Using the same information as in the previous examples, we now assume three-year cliff vesting. This extends the life of the option and increases its value from $6.14 to $7.57. Early exercise cannot occur in Year 2 even though the share price may exceed $32.50 by that time, as indicated by the

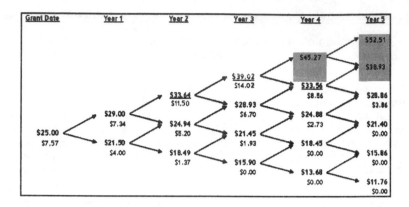

double-underlined share price. The single-underlined share prices indicate where early exercise is allowed and does take place, and the shaded areas represent the portion of the binomial tree that is no longer relevant due to early exercise. The option value at grant date is calculated in the same manner as illustrated previously.

The Black-Scholes-Merton formula assumes that option exercises occur at the end of an option's contractual term and that expected volatility, expected dividends, and risk-free interest rates are constant over the option's term. This formula must be adjusted to take into account certain characteristics of employee share options and similar instruments that are not consistent with the formula's assumptions (e.g., the ability to exercise before the end of the option's contractual term) [FAS-123(R), par. A15].

> **OBSERVATION:** A closed-form model (e.g., Black-Scholes-Merton) is not always appropriate for valuing an employee share option. For example, if an option's exercise is conditional on the entity's stock price rising a certain amount, SAB 107 indicates that a closed-form model would not be appropriate.

Illustration of Application of Black-Scholes-Merton Model to Valuing an Employee Stock Option

Optical Vision Inc. issues 100,000 stock options to its employees on January 1, 20X7. Optical Vision expects its stock price volatility to be relatively constant over time, and it does not expect the risk-free interest rate to fluctuate greatly from its present level. Optical Vision's current dividend yield (d) is 1%, and management plans to maintain a relatively constant dividend yield. Optical Vision will value its issuance of stock options using the Black-Scholes-Merton option pricing method.

Optical Vision's current stock price (S) is $30 per share, and the exercise price (E) of the option is $30 (i.e., as is often the case, the exercise price of the options is set equal to the stock's market price on the date the options are granted). The expected term (T) of the options is 8 years, and the riskfree interest rate (r) is 4%. Optical Vision expects its stock price volatility (σ) (the standard deviation of Optical Vision's daily stock price) to be 50% over the expected term of the option.

The Black-Scholes-Merton formula to value this option is:

$C = (Se^{-dT}N(d1)) - (Ee^{-rT}N(d2))$ where :

C = the computed value of 1 option

e = the base of the natural logarithm (2.7182818)

N(d1 or d2) = the cumulative normal density function – the probability that a particular number falls at or below d1 or d2, respectively

where:

$d1 = \{(\ln (S/E)) + ((r - d + (\sigma^2/2))^*T)\} / (\sigma\sqrt{T})$
$d2 = d1 - (\sigma\sqrt{T})$

ln = the natural logarithm

Therefore, Optical Vision will calculate the value of 1 stock option to be:

$d1 = \{(\ln (\$30 / \$30)) + ((.04 - .01 + (.5^2/2)) * 8)\} / (.5\sqrt{8}) = 0.876812$
$d2 = .876812 - (.5\sqrt{8}) = -0.537401$
$N(d1) = 0.809706$
$N(d2) = 0.295495$
$C = (\$30\ e^{-.01*8}\ 0.809706) - (\$30\ e^{-.04*8}\ 0.295495) = \$15.99$

Therefore, the fair value of the options issued by Optical Vision Inc. on January 1, 20X7 is $1,599,000 ($15.99 × 100,000).

In contrast to the Black-Scholes-Merton formula, a lattice model can be designed to accommodate dynamic assumptions of expected volatility and dividends over the option's contractual term and estimates of expected option exercise patterns during the option's contractual term. This includes the effect of black-out periods. As a result, a lattice model more fully reflects the substantive characteristics of a particular employee share option or similar instrument [FAS-123(R), par. A15].

An entity should change the valuation technique it uses to estimate fair value if it concludes that a different technique is likely to result in a better estimate of fair value [FAS-123(R), par. A17].

☞ **PRACTICE POINTER:** Some entities may not initially use a lattice model because they have not previously captured the data necessary to apply such a model. However, after changing their systems to capture the needed data, such an entity should change to a lattice model from the Black-Scholes-Merton model if the entity concludes that a lattice model provides a better estimate of fair value.

Selecting Assumptions for Use in an Option-Pricing Model

If an observable market price is not available for a share option or similar instrument with the same or similar terms and conditions, the fair value of the instrument shall be estimated using a valuation technique or model that meets the criteria of FAS-123(R) (discussed previously) and takes into account at least the following:

- The exercise price of the option;
- The expected term of the option, considering the option's term and employees' expected exercise behavior and postvesting termination behavior;
- The current price of the underlying share;
- The expected volatility of the price of the underlying share for the expected term of the option;
- The expected dividends on the underlying share for the expected term of the option; and
- The risk-free interest rate(s) for the expected term of the option [FAS-123(R), par. A18].

There may be a range of reasonable estimates of expected volatility, dividends, and term of the option. If no amount within the range is more or less likely than any other amount, the average of the amounts within the range, referred to as the expected value, should be used [FAS-123(R), par. A20].

> **OBSERVATION:** SAB 107 indicates that a company may appropriately conclude that its past experience with the exercise of options by employees is the best estimate of future exercise behavior. In this instance, it is appropriate to use the company's historical exercise experience in estimating the option's expected term.

In certain circumstances, historical information may not be available. If this is the case, the entity might base expectations about future volatility on the average volatilities of similar entities for an appropriate period following their going public [FAS-123(R), par. A22].

The valuation technique an entity selects to estimate fair value for a particular type of instrument should be used consistently and should not be changed unless a different valuation technique is expected to produce a better estimate of fair value. Assumptions used to estimate the fair value of instruments granted to employees also should be determined in a consistent manner from period to period [FAS-123(R), par. A23].

> **OBSERVATION:** SAB 107 indicates that a change in the model or technique used to determine fair value would *not* be considered a change in accounting principle. However, the SEC indicates that companies should not change valuation models or techniques frequently.

A U.S. entity issuing an option on its own shares must use as the risk-free interest rate the implied yields currently available from the U.S. Treasury zero-coupon yield curve over the contractual term of the option if the entity is using a lattice model incorporating the option's contractual term. If the entity is using a closed-form model, the risk-free interest rate is the implied yield currently available on U.S. Treasury zero-coupon issues with a remaining term equal to the expected term used in the model to value the options [FAS-123(R), par. A25].

The expected term of an employee share option or similar instrument is the period of time for which the instrument is expected to be outstanding. In most cases, the expected term is shorter than the option's contractual term because employees typically exercise options before the end of the contractual period [FAS-123(R), par. A26]. The expected term is an assumption in the closed-form model. If an entity uses a lattice model that has been modified to take into account an option's contractual term and employees' expected exercise and post-vesting employment termination behavior, the expected term is estimated based on the resulting output of the lattice [FAS-123(R), par. A27].

> ☞ **PRACTICE POINTER:** SAB 107 indicates that the expected term can be estimated based on (1) the company's historical option exercise experience, (2) exercise patterns of employees in similar industries, or (3) as an output of a lattice model where the expected term can then be used as an input into the Black-Scholes-Merton model. (Note that a lattice model could also be used to value the option itself).

Other factors that may affect expectations about employees' exercise and post-vesting employment termination behavior include:

- The vesting period of the award (the expected term of the award cannot be less than this);

- Employees' historical exercise and post-vesting employment termination behavior for similar grants;
- Expected volatility of the price of the underlying share;
- Blackout periods and other coexisting arrangements, such as agreements that allow for exercise to automatically occur during blackout periods if certain conditions are satisfied; and
- Employees' ages, lengths of service, and home jurisdictions [FAS-123(R), par. A28].

☞ **PRACTICE POINTER:** SAB 107 offers a simplified method of estimating the expected term of "plain-vanilla" options. A plain-vanilla option has the following characteristics: (1) the options are at-the-money when granted, (2) the option can be exercised if service is performed through the vesting date, (3) the options are forfeited if employment is terminated before vesting, and (4) the options can only be exercised for a limited period (30-90 days) if employment is terminated after the options vest. The SEC's simplified method for determining the option's expected term is: [(Vesting period + Original contractual term) / 2]. For example, assume an eight-year contractual term and 25% vesting each year for four years. The vesting period is 2.5 years (10 / 4, determined as follows: the sum of one-year vesting term for the first 25% vested, two-year vesting term for the second 25% vested, three-year vesting term for the third 25% vested, and four-year vesting term for the final 25% vested, divided by four years). The expected term is therefore 5.25 years [(2.5 years + 8 years) / 2]. The use of this simplified method to estimate the expected term of options must be disclosed in the financial statement notes. Finally, the SEC indicates that this simplified method is purely a stop-gap measure until companies develop better data to estimate expected term; the SEC does not expect this simplified method to apply for options granted after December 31, 2007.

Aggregating individual awards into relatively homogeneous groups with respect to exercise and post-vesting employment termination behaviors and estimating the fair value of the options granted to each group separately reduces potential misstatement. An entity shall aggregate individual awards into relatively homogeneous groups with respect to exercise and post-vesting employment termination behaviors regardless of the valuation technique or model used to estimate fair value [FAS-123(R), par. A30].

OBSERVATION: SAB 107 indicates that a reasonable estimate of fair value can be developed using as few as two groups. Groups should be identified based on differences in expected exercise behavior. Two possible groups where exercise behavior will likely differ are executives and non-executives.

Volatility is a measure of the amount by which a financial variable, such as share price, has fluctuated (i.e., historical volatility) or can be expected to fluctuate (i.e., expected volatility) during a period. Option-pricing models require expected volatility as an assumption because an option's value is dependent on potential share returns over the option's term. The higher the volatility, the more the returns on the shares can be expected to vary. An entity's estimate of expected volatility should be reasonable and supportable [FAS-123(R), par. A31].

Factors that should be considered in estimating expected volatility include:

- Volatility in the share price, including potential changes in the entity's share price in the future (e.g., as a result of reversion to the average level of volatility of other similar companies);

- Implied volatility of the share price determined by the market prices of traded options or other traded financial instruments, such as outstanding convertible debt;

- For public companies, the length of time an entity's shares have been publicly traded;

- Appropriate and regular intervals for price observations; and

- Corporate and capital structure, recognizing that entities with greater levels of debt tend to have higher volatility [FAS-123(R), par. A32].

☛ **PRACTICE POINTER:** Some entities have exchange-traded financial instruments (e.g., exchange-traded options) that can be used to derive implied (stock price) volatility. SAB 107 encourages public companies to consider such implied volatility in estimating expected volatility. For example, the SEC indicates that a company with exchange-traded options could rely heavily, possibly even exclusively, on the implied volatility in these options, as evidenced by the option's price, in estimating expected volatility for the purpose of applying FAS-123(R).

OBSERVATION: SAB 107 indicates that daily, weekly, or monthly price observations may provide a sufficient basis to estimate expected volatility. The SEC also indicates that weekly or monthly price observations are more appropriate than daily price observations if the stock is thinly traded. A public company listed on an organized stock exchange would generally use daily price observations to estimate volatility.

Consideration of Market, Performance, and Service Conditions

Analysis of the market, performance, or service conditions that are explicit or implicit in the terms of an award is required to determine the requisite service period over which compensation cost is recognized and whether recognized compensation cost may be reversed if an award fails to vest or become exercisable [FAS-123(R), par. A50].

Vesting or exercisability may be conditional on satisfying two or more types of conditions: a market condition and a performance or service condition. Alternatively, vesting may be conditional on satisfying one of the two or more types of conditions. Regardless of the nature and number of conditions that must be satisfied, the existence of a market condition requires recognition of compensation cost if the requisite service is rendered, even if the market condition is never satisfied [FAS-123(R), par. A51].

Market, performance, and service conditions may affect an award's exercise price, contractual term, quantity, conversion ratio, or other pertinent factors that are relevant in measuring an award's fair value. For instance, an award's quantity may double, or an award's contractual term may be extended, if a company-wide revenue target is achieved. Market conditions that affect an award's fair value are included in the estimate of grant-date fair value. Performance or service conditions that only affect vesting are excluded from the estimate of grant-date fair value, but all other performance or service conditions that affect an award's fair value are included in the estimate of grant-date fair value [FAS-123(R), par. A52].

Illustration of Accounting for a Stock Option with a Market Condition

Beta Company grants share options whose exercise price varies with an index of the share prices of a group of entities in the same industry. This qualifies as a market condition per FAS-123(R). Assume that on January 1, 20X7, Beta grants 50 share options on its common stock with an initial exercise price of $20 to each of 500 employees. The share options have a maximum term of ten years. The exercise price of the share options increases or decreases on December 31 of each year by the same percentage that the index has increased or decreased during the year. For example, if the peer group index increased by 10% in 20X7, the exercise price of the share options during 20X8 would increase to $22 ($20 × 1.10). Assume that, on January 1, 20X7, the peer group index is 500 and the dividend yield on the index is 1%.

Each indexed share option may be analyzed as a share option to exchange 0.04 (20/500) "shares" of the peer group index for a share of Beta stock—that is, to exchange one noncash asset for another. The intrinsic value of a share option to exchange .04 "shares" of the peer group index for a share of Beta stock also equals the difference between the prices of the two assets exchanged.

To illustrate the equivalence of an indexed share option and the share option above, assume that an employee exercises the indexed share option when Beta's share price has increased 100% to $40 and the peer group index has increased 70% from 500 to 850. Thus, the exercise price of the indexed share option is $34 ($20 × 1.70).

Price of Beta share	$40.00
Less: Exercise price of share option	34.00
Intrinsic value of indexed share option	$ 6.00

That is the same as the intrinsic value of a share option to exchange .04 shares of the index for 1 share of Beta stock:

Price of Beta share	$40.00
Less: Price of a share of the peer group index (.04 × $850)	34.00
Intrinsic value at exchange	$ 6.00

Option-pricing models can be extended to value a share option to exchange one asset for another. The volatility of a share option to exchange two noncash assets is based on their cross-volatility, the relationship between the volatilities of the prices of the assets to be exchanged. In a share option with an exercise price payable in cash, the amount of cash to be paid has zero volatility, so only the volatility of the stock needs to be considered in estimating that option's fair value. In contrast, when two noncash assets are involved, the fair value of a share option depends on possible movements in the prices of both assets. In this example, fair value depends on the cross-volatility of a share of the peer group index and a share of Beta stock. Historical cross-volatility can be computed directly based on measures of Beta's share price in shares of the peer group index. For example, Beta's share price was 0.04 shares at the grant date and 0.0471 (40/850) shares at the exercise date. Those share amounts then are used to compute cross-volatility. Cross-volatility can also be computed indirectly based on the respective volatilities of Beta stock and the peer group index and the correlation between them.

In a share option with an exercise price payable in cash, the assumed risk-free interest rate (discount rate) represents the return on cash that will not be paid until exercise. In this example, an equivalent share of the index, rather than cash, is what will not be "paid" until exercise. Therefore, the dividend yield on the peer group index of 1% is used in place of the risk-free interest rate as an input to the option-pricing model.

The initial exercise price for the indexed share option is the value of an equivalent share of the peer group index, which is $20 (0.04 × $500). The fair value of each share option would be based on relevant inputs.

The indexed share options have a three-year explicit service period. The market condition affects the grant-date fair value of the award and its exercisability; however, vesting is based solely on the explicit service period of three years. The at-the-money nature of the award makes the derived service period irrelevant in determining the requisite service period in this example; therefore, the requisite service period of the award is three years based on the explicit service period. The accrual of compensation cost would be based on the number of options for which the requisite service is expected to be rendered, and that cost would be recognized over the requisite service period.

An award may be indexed to a factor in addition to the entity's share price. If that factor is not a market, performance, or service condition, that award is classified as a liability for purposes of FAS-123(R). An example of this is an award of options whose exercise prices are indexed to the market price of a commodity [FAS-123(R), par. A53].

The requisite service period for an award that has only a service condition is presumed to be the vesting period unless there is clear evidence to the contrary. An employee's share-based payment award becomes vested at the date that the employee's right to receive or retain equity shares, other equity instruments, or cash under the award is no longer contingent on satisfaction of either a performance condition or a service condition. Any unrecognized compensation cost shall be recognized when an award becomes vested. If the award includes no market, performance, or service conditions, the entire amount of compensation cost is recognized when the award is granted [FAS-123(R), pars. A55–A56].

A requisite service period may be explicit, implicit, or derived. An explicit service period is one that is stated in the terms of the sharebased payment award. An implicit service period is one that may be inferred from an analysis of an award's terms. A derived service period is based on a market condition in a share-based payment award that affects exercisability, exercise price, or the employee's ability to retain the award. A derived service period is inferred from the application of certain techniques used to estimate fair value [FAS-123(R), pars. A59–A60].

An award with a combination of market, performance, or service conditions may contain multiple explicit, implicit, or derived service periods. For such an award, the estimate of the requisite service period is based on an analysis of (1) all vesting and exercisability conditions; (2) all explicit, implicit, and derived service periods; and (3) the probability that performance or service conditions will be satisfied. For example, if vesting or exercisability is based on satisfying *both* a market condition and a performance or service condition and it is probable that the performance or service condition will be satisfied, an initial estimate of the requisite service period generally is the *longest* of the explicit, implicit, or derived service periods. If vesting or exercisability is based on satisfying *either* a market condition or a performance or service condition and it is probable that the performance or service condition will be satisfied, the initial estimate of the requisite service period generally is the *shortest* of the explicit, implicit, or derived service periods [FAS-123(R), par. A61].

Compensation cost ultimately recognized is equal to the grant-date fair value of the award based on the actual outcome of the performance or service condition. The proper accounting for a change in the initial estimate of the requisite service period depends on whether that change would affect the grant-date fair value of the award that is to be recognized as compensation. For example, if the quantity of instruments for which the requisite service is expected to be rendered changes because a vesting condition becomes probable of satisfaction or if the grant-date fair value of an instrument changes because another performance or service condition becomes probable of satisfaction, the cumulative effect on current and prior periods of those changes in estimates is recognized in the period of change. In contrast, if compensation cost is already being attributed over an initially estimated requisite service period and that period changes because another market, performance, or service condition becomes the basis for the requisite service period, any unrecognized compensation cost at the time of the change is recognized prospectively over the revised requisite service period, if any [FAS-123(R), pars. A65–A66].

Illustration of Accounting for a Stock Option with Performance Conditions

This example illustrates the computation of compensation cost if Alpha Company grants an award of share options with multiple performance conditions. Under the award, employees vest in differing numbers of options depending on the amount by which the market share of one of Alpha's products increases over a three-year period (the options cannot vest before the end of the three-year period).

On January 1, 20X7, Alpha grants to each of its 500 employees an award of up to 150 ten-year-term share options on its common stock. If market share increases by at least 4% by December 31, 20X9, each employee vests in at least 50 share options at that date. If market share increases by at least 8%, another 50 share options vest, for a total of 100. If market share increases by more than 16%, all 150 share options vest. Assume that Alpha's share price on January 1, 20X7, is $20, and the grant-date fair value per share option is $15.

The compensation cost of the award depends on the estimated number of options that will vest. Alpha must determine whether it is probable (probable as defined in FAS-5) that any performance condition will be achieved, that is, whether market share growth will be at least 4% over the three-year period. Accruals of compensation cost are initially based on the probable outcome of the performance conditions—in this case, different levels of market share growth over the three-year vesting period—and adjusted for subsequent changes in the estimated or actual outcome. If Alpha determines that no performance condition is probable of achievement (that is, market share growth is expected to be less than 4%), then no compensation cost is recognized; however, Alpha is required to reassess at each reporting date whether achievement of any performance condition is probable and would begin recognizing compensation cost if and when achievement becomes probable.

Accruals of cost must be based on the probable outcome of performance conditions. Accordingly, Alpha cannot base accruals of compensation cost on an amount that is not a possible outcome (and thus cannot be the probable outcome). For example, if Alpha estimates a 90%, 45%, and 15%

likelihood that market share growth will be at least 4%, 8%, and 16%, respectively, it would not try to determine a weighted average of the possible outcomes because that number of shares is not a possible outcome.

The table below shows the compensation cost that would be recognized in 20X7, 20X8, and 20X9, if Alpha estimates at the grant date that it is probable that market share will increase at least 4 but less than 8% (that is, each employee would receive 50 share options). That estimate remains unchanged until the end of 20X9, when Alpha's market share has actually increased over the three-year period by more than 8%. Thus, each employee vests in 100 share options.

Through 20X7, Alpha's estimated and actual forfeiture rate is 5%. Alpha therefore estimates that 429 employees (500 × .95^3) will remain in service until the vesting date. (If actual forfeiture rates differ from estimated forfeiture rates, Alpha would adjust its estimate of expected forfeiture rates which would affect the recognition of compensation cost.) The compensation cost of the award is initially estimated based on the number of options expected to vest, which in turn is based on the expected level of performance and the fair value of each option. The amount of compensation cost recognized (or attributed) when achievement of a performance condition is probable depends on the relative satisfaction of the performance condition based on performance to date. Alpha determines that recognizing compensation cost ratably over the three-year vesting period is appropriate with one-third of the value of the award recognized each year.

Share Option with Performance Condition—Number of Share Options Varies

Year	Total Value of Award	Pretax Cost for Year	Cumulative Pretax Cost
20X7	$321,750 ($15 × 50 × 429)	$107,250 ($321,750 × 1/3)	$107,250
20X8	$321,750 ($15 × 50 × 429)	$107,250 [($321,750 × 2/3) − $107,250]	$214,500
20X9	$643,500 ($15 × 100 × 429)	$429,000 ($643,500 − $214,500)	$643,500

Reload Options

Some companies issue new options to employees when an employee uses existing shares of the company's stock to exercise a stock option rather than paying in cash. Additional options are issued equal to the number of shares used to pay for the shares purchased under a previous stock option grant [FAS-123(R), Appendix E]. The effect of a reload feature in terms of an award shall not be included in estimating the grant-date fair value of the award. A subsequent grant of reload options shall be accounted for as a separate award when the reload options are granted [FAS-123(R), par. 26].

Measurement of Awards Classified as Equity—Nonpublic Company

As was the case for a public company, stock or options issued by a nonpublic company in exchange for goods or services should be recorded at fair value. In determining the fair value of a stock option, the volatility of the underlying stock needs to be estimated. This can often be difficult for a nonpublic company, given the lack of trading of these shares and their illiquid market. Therefore, a nonpublic entity must exercise judgment in selecting a method to estimate expected volatility and might do so by basing its expected volatility on the average volatilities of similar public entities [FAS-123(R), par. A22].

In other instances, a nonpublic entity may not be able to reasonably estimate the fair value of its equity share options and other instruments because it is not practicable to estimate the expected volatility of its share price. In this circumstance, the entity shall account for the equity share options and similar instruments based on a value calculated using the historical volatility of an appropriate industry sector index. If the complexity of the terms of an equity share option or other equity instrument preclude making a reasonable estimate of fair value, the option or instrument shall be accounted for based on its intrinsic value, remeasured at each reporting date through the date of exercise or other settlement. The intrinsic value method shall continue to be used, even if the entity subsequently concludes that a reasonable estimate of fair value can be made [FAS-123(R), pars. 23-25].

As discussed previously, if it is not practicable for a nonpublic entity to estimate its stock price volatility, the entity may estimate its stock price volatility using an industry-sector index (the calculated value method) [FAS-123(R), par. A44]. For purposes of applying FAS-123(R), it is not practicable for a nonpublic entity to estimate the expected volatility of its share price if it is unable to obtain sufficient historical information about past volatility, or other information on which to base a reasonable and supportable estimate of expected volatility at the grant date of the award without undue cost and effort. In that situation, FAS-123(R) requires the nonpublic entity to estimate a value of its equity share options and similar instruments by substituting the historical volatility of the appropriate industry sector index for the expected share price volatility as an assumption in its valuation model. There are many different indices available to consider in selecting an appropriate industry sector index. An appropriate index is one that is representative of the industry sector in which the nonpublic entity operates and that also reflects, if possible, the size of the entity. In *no* circumstance shall a nonpublic entity use a broad-based market index, such as the S&P 500, Russell 3000®, or Dow Jones Wilshire 5000, because these indices are sufficiently diversified as to be *not* representative of the industry sector(s) in which the nonpublic entity operates [FAS-123(R), pars. A45–A46].

Illustration of Accounting for a Stock Option Award by a Private Company—Company Unable to Estimate Its Expected Stock Price Volatility

Talisman Inc. is a small, private company that develops, markets, and distributes computer software. On January 1, 20X6, Talisman issues 200 stock options to each of its 75 employees. Talisman's share price on January 1, 20X6, is valued at $5, and the exercise price is $5 on that date. The options cliff vest in three years, and the contractual term of the options is seven years. Although the contractual term of the options is seven years, Talisman expects the term of the options to be four years (i.e., Talisman expects the options to be exercised early). Talisman assumes no forfeitures over the next three years (a simplifying assumption for this example), and expects to pay no dividends. We assume away income taxes.

> ☛ **PRACTICE POINTER:**   The AICPA has issued a practice aid, Valuation of Privately-Held-Company Equity Securities Issued as Compensation, that is likely to be helpful in valuing equity securities of privately-held companies where these securities are issued as compensation.

Talisman does not maintain an internal market for its shares, and its shares are rarely traded privately. The last time Talisman issued equity shares was in 20W7, and it has never issued convertible debt securities. In addition, Talisman is unable to identify any similar public companies. As such, Talisman is unable to estimate the expected volatility of its share price—a key input to valuing its employee stock options on January 1, 20X6. Therefore, Talisman will value the options it has issued using the *calculated value method*.

Under the calculated value method, the historical volatility of an appropriate industry sector index is used instead of the company's own stock price volatility. Talisman operates exclusively in the software industry. Using the Dow Jones Indexes Web site and the Industry Classification Benchmark tab on this Web site, Talisman determines that its operations fit within the software subsector of the software and computer services sector. Talisman, based on its share price and contributed capital, would be classified as a small-cap company within the index. Talisman therefore selects the small-cap version of the software index as an appropriate industry sector index. Again, using the Dow Jones Indexes Web site, Talisman obtains the daily closing total return values from the index from January 1, 20X1, through December 31, 20X5 (five years of daily total return values). Using the five years of daily total return values, Talisman computes the annualized historical volatility of the software index to be 30%. This 30% volatility is an input to the option pricing model used by Talisman, and the computed value of the options granted by Talisman is $3.25 per share.

Talisman would make the following journal entries at December 31, 20X6, 20X7, and 20X8:

Compensation cost [(200 × 75 × $3.25) / 3]	16,250	
Additional paid-in capital		16,250

—To recognize compensation cost.

All of the stock options are exercised on December 31, 20X9. Talisman would record the following entry (Talisman issues no-par common stock).

Cash (200 × 75 × $5)	75,000	
Additional paid-in capital	48,750	
Common stock		123,750

—To record the issuance of common stock upon exercise of stock options and to reclassify previously recorded additional paid-in capital.

Recognition of Compensation Cost for an Award Accounted for as an Equity Instrument

Compensation cost associated with an award of share-based employee compensation classified as equity is recognized over the requisite service period with a corresponding credit to equity (usually paid-in capital). The requisite service period is that period during which the employee is required to provide service in exchange for the award (i.e., the vesting period). The service period is estimated based on an analysis of the terms of the share-based payment award. The requisite service period may be explicitly stated or it may be implicit, being inferred from analysis of other terms of the award [FAS-123(R), pars. 39–40].

The total amount of compensation cost recognized at the end of the requisite service period for an award of share-based compensation is based on the number of instruments for which the requisite service has been rendered. An entity shall base initial accruals of compensation cost on the estimated number of instruments for which the requisite service is expected to be rendered. That estimate should be revised if subsequent information indicates that the actual number of instruments is likely to differ from the previous estimate. The cumulative effect on current and prior periods of a change in the estimated number of instruments for which the requisite service is expected to be or has been rendered shall be recognized as compensation cost in the period of the change [FAS-123(R), par. 43].

Accruals of compensation cost for an award with a performance condition shall be based on the probable outcome of that performance condition. Compensation cost is accrued if it is probable that the performance condition will be achieved and is not accrued if it is not probable that the performance condition will be achieved. Previously recognized compensation is not reversed if an employee share option for which the requisite service has been rendered expires unexercised [FAS-123(R), pars. 44–45].

The entity shall make its best estimate of the requisite service period at the grant date and shall base accruals of compensation cost on that period. That initial estimate is adjusted in light of changes in facts and circumstances. If an award requires satisfaction of one or more market, performance, or service conditions (or a combination of these), compensation cost is recognized if the requisite service is rendered. No compensation cost is recognized if the requisite service is not rendered [FAS-123(R), pars. 46–47].

Performance or service conditions that affect vesting are not reflected in estimating the fair value of an award at the grant-date because those conditions are restrictions that result from the forfeitability of instruments to which employees have not yet earned the right. The effect of a market condition is reflected, however, in estimating the fair value of an award at the grant date. Market, performance, and service conditions (or a combination of these) may affect the award's exercise price, contractual term, quantity, conversion ratio, or other factors that are considered in measuring an award's grant-date fair value. That fair value shall be estimated for each possible outcome of such a performance or service condition, and the final measure of compensation shall be based on the amount estimated at the grant date for the condition or outcome that is actually satisfied [FAS-123(R), pars. 48–49].

Modifications of Awards of Equity Instruments

A modification of the terms or conditions of an equity award shall be treated as an exchange of the original award for a new award. The effects of a modification are measured as follows:

- Incremental compensation cost is measured as the excess, if any, of the fair value of the modified award over the fair value of the original award immediately before its terms are modified, based on the share price and other pertinent factors as of that date. The effect of the modification on the number of instruments expected to vest also shall be reflected in determining incremental compensation cost.

- Total recognized compensation cost for an equity award shall at least equal the fair value of the award at the grant-date unless at the date of the modification the performance or service conditions of the original award are not expected to be satisfied. Total compensation cost measured at the date of the modification shall be (1) the portion of the grant-date fair value of the original award for which the requisite service is expected to be rendered at that date plus (2) the incremental cost resulting from the modification.

* A change in compensation cost for an equity award measured at intrinsic value shall be measured by comparing the intrinsic value of the modified award, if any, with the intrinsic value of the original award, if any, immediately before the modification [FAS-123(R), par. 51].

Cancellation of an award accompanied by the concurrent grant of a replacement award or other valuable consideration is accounted for as a modification of the terms of the cancelled award. Incremental compensation cost is measured as the excess of the fair value of the replacement award or other valuable consideration over the fair value of the cancelled award at the cancellation date [FAS-123(R), par. 56].

A cancellation of an award that is not accompanied by the concurrent grant of a replacement award or issuance of other valuable consideration is accounted for as a repurchase for no consideration. Any previously unrecognized compensation cost is recognized at the cancellation date [FAS-123(R), par. 57]. In other circumstances, the entity may pay cash to repurchase an equity award. The cash payment is charged against equity as long as the amount paid does not exceed the fair value of the equity instruments on the date of payment. Additional compensation cost is recognized if the cash payment exceeds the fair value of the equity instruments. Also, any previously unrecognized compensation cost is recognized at the repurchase date [FAS-123(R), par. 55].

Measurement of Awards Classified as Liabilities

In determining whether an instrument shall be classified as a liability or equity, the entity shall apply generally accepted accounting principles applicable to financial instruments issued in transactions that do not involve share-based payments. FAS-150 (Accounting for Certain Financial Instruments with Characteristics of both Liabilities and Equity) provides guidance for making this determination [FAS-123(R), pars. 28–29].

An award may be indexed to a factor in addition to the entity's share price. If the additional factor is not a market, performance, or service condition, the award is classified as a liability for purposes of applying FAS-123(R), and the additional factor shall be reflected in estimating the fair value of the award [FAS-123(R), par. 33].

The determination of whether a share-based payment award should be accounted for as an equity instrument or as a liability shall reflect the substance of the award and any related arrangement.

Generally, the written terms provide the best evidence of the substantive terms of an award, but an entity's past practice may indicate that the substantive terms differ from its written terms [FAS-123(R), par. 34].

The measurement objective for liabilities incurred under share-based compensation arrangements is the same as the measurement objective for equity instruments awarded to employees as described previously. The measurement date for liability instruments, however, is the date of settlement. Liabilities incurred under share-based payment arrangements are remeasured at the end of each reporting period until they are settled [FAS-123(R), par. 36].

A public entity shall measure a liability award under a share-based payment arrangement based on the award's fair value remeasured at each reporting date until settlement. Compensation cost for each period is based on the change in the fair value of the instrument for each reporting period. A nonpublic entity shall make a policy decision regarding whether to measure all of its liabilities incurred under share-based payment arrangements at fair value or measure all such liabilities at intrinsic value. Regardless of the method selected, a nonpublic entity shall remeasure its liabilities under share-based payment arrangements at each reporting date until settlement [FAS-123(R), pars. 37–38].

Changes in the fair value (or intrinsic value for a nonpublic entity that elects that method) of a liability incurred under a share-based payment arrangement that occur during the requisite service period shall be recognized as compensation cost over that period. The percentage of the fair value (or intrinsic value) that is accrued as compensation cost at the end of each period shall equal the percentage of the requisite service that has been rendered to that date. Changes in the fair value (intrinsic value) of a liability that occur after the end of the requisite service period are compensation cost of the period in which the changes occur [FAS-123(R), par. 50].

Illustration of the Accounting for Stock Appreciation Rights to be Settled in Cash—Recognition of a Liability

Ultimate Metrics International is a public company that grants 750,000 share appreciation rights (SARs) to its employees on January 1, 20X8. Each holder of an SAR is to receive in cash the increase in Ultimate Metrics stock price above $15 per share (Ultimate Metrics' stock price on January 1, 20X8). Ultimate Metrics determines the fair value of the SAR grant on January 1, 20X8, in the same manner as if it had issued 750,000 stock options (i.e., an option-pricing model is used). Using an acceptable option-pricing model, Ultimate Metrics computes the fair value of each SAR as $7.50. The SARs cliff vest at the end of three years. Ultimate Metrics expects forfeitures of 7% of the SARs each year, and actual forfeitures equal expected forfeitures. As a result, Ultimate Metrics expects 603,268 (750,000 × .93^3) of the SARs to vest, and the fair value of the

SAR award on January 1, 20X8, is $4,524,510 [(603,268 × $7.50]. Ultimate Metrics' tax rate is 35%.

Because the SARs are to be settled in cash, Ultimate Metrics must record a liability. In addition, FAS-123(R) requires the liability to be remeasured at each reporting date through the date of settlement of the SARs (this period includes the vesting period and any period after the vesting date until the SARs are settled).

The fair value of the SARs is $11.25 at December 31, 20X8, and the resulting fair value of the award is $6,786,765 (603,268 × $11.25). Ultimate Metrics will recognize $2,262,255 ($6,786,765 ÷ 3), one-third of the total fair value, as compensation cost during 20x8. The journal entries recorded at December 31, 20X8, are:

Compensation cost ($6,786,765 ÷ 3)	2,262,255	
Share-based compensation liability		2,262,255
—To recognize compensation cost.		

Deferred tax asset ($2,262,255 × .35)	791,789	
Deferred tax benefit		791,789
—To recognize a deferred tax asset for the temporary difference.		

The fair value of the SARs is $6.75 at December 31, 20X9, and the resulting fair value of the award is $4,072,059 (603,268 × $6.75). Ultimate Metrics will recognize two-thirds of this amount, $2,714,706, as a liability at December 31, 20X9. Compensation cost recognized during 20X9 is $2,714,706 less the amount of compensation cost recognized during 20X8. The journal entries recorded at December 31, 20x9, are:

Compensation cost ($2,714,706 − $2,262,255)	452,451	
Share-based compensation liability		452,451
—To recognize compensation cost.		

Deferred tax asset ($452,451 × .35)	158,358	
Deterred tax benefit		158,358
—To recognize a deferred tax asset for the temporary difference.		

The fair value of the SARs is $12.50 at December 31, 20Y0, and the resulting fair value of the award is $7,540,850 (603,268 × $12.50). The liability at December 31, 20Y0, is this entire amount because the award is now fully vested. Compensation cost recognized during 20Y0 is $7,540,850 less the amounts recognized in 20X8 and 20X9. The journal entries recorded at December 31, 20Y0, are:

Compensation cost ($7,540,850 − $2,262,255 − 452,451)	4,826,144	
Share-based compensation liability		4,826,144
—To recognize compensation cost.		

Deferred tax asset ($4,826,144 × .35)	1,689,150	
Deferred tax benefit		1,689,150
—To recognize a deferred tax asset for the temporary difference.		

All of the SARs are exercised on December 31, 20Y0, and Ultimate Metrics International settles its $7,540,850 liability by making a cash payment. The journal entries are:

Share-based compensation liability		
(2,262,255 + 452,451 + 4,826,144)	7,540,850	
Cash		7,540,850

—To record the cash payment to employees upon the exercise of the SARs.

Deferred tax benefit		
(791,789 + 158,358 + 1,689,150)	2,639,297	
Deferred tax asset		2,639,297

—To write off the deferred tax asset related to the SARs.

Income taxes payable	2,639,297	
Income taxes expense		2,639,297

—To record the current tax benefit provided by the exercise of the SARs.

Accounting for Tax Effects of Share-Based Compensation Awards

Tax deductions generally arise in different amounts and in different periods from compensation costs recognized in financial statements. The cumulative effect of compensation cost recognized for instruments classified as equity that ordinarily would result in a future tax deduction are considered to be deductible temporary differences in applying FAS-109 (Accounting for Income Taxes). FAS-109 requires a deferred tax asset to be evaluated for future realization and to be reduced by a valuation allowance if it is more likely than not that some portion or all of the deferred tax asset will not be realized. Differences between the deductible temporary difference computed pursuant to FAS-123(R) (described previously) and the tax deduction that would result based on the current fair value of the entity's shares shall not be considered in measuring the gross deferred tax asset or determining the need for a valuation allowance for a deferred tax asset recognized under FAS-123(R) [FAS-123(R), pars. 58–59, 61].

If a deduction reported on a tax return for an award of equity instrument exceeds the cumulative compensation cost for those instruments recognized for financial reporting (referred to in FAS-123(R) as the excess tax benefit), any resulting realized tax benefits that exceed the previously recognized deferred tax asset for those instruments are recognized as paid-in capital [FAS-123(R), par. 62].

The amount deductible on the employer's tax return may be less than the cumulative compensation cost recognized for financial reporting purposes. The write-off of a deferred tax asset related to that deficiency, net of any related valuation allowance, is first offset to the extent of any remaining additional paid-in capital from excess tax benefits from previous awards accounted for in accordance with either FAS-123 or FAS-123(R). Entities that continued to apply APB-25 after the original effective date of FAS-123(R) should compute the amount of excess tax benefits that would have been credited to additional paid-in capital if the entity had adopted FAS-123 when it was originally issued. This calculated amount should be used to absorb the tax deficiency (i.e., the remaining balance of the deferred tax asset). Any remaining balance of the write-off of a deferred tax asset related to a tax deficiency shall be recognized in the income statement, regardless of whether FAS-123 had been applied when first issued or whether APB-25 had continued to be used [FAS-123(R), par. 63].

Illustration of Accounting for a Stock Option with a Service Condition—Including Treatment of Income Tax Effects and Presentation in Statement of Cash Flows

Diaz Inc. is a public company that awards 2,000,000 stock options to 4,000 different employees (each employee received 500 options) on January 1, 20X6. The term of the options is seven years, and they vest in full in three years (cliff vesting). These options are not classified as incentive tax options for tax purposes. Diaz Inc.'s tax rate is 35%. Diaz Inc.'s stock price on January 1, 20X6, is $50 per share, and the option's exercise price is also $50. Diaz expects that 5% of the options will be forfeited (due to turnover) in each of the next three years. Using a lattice-based valuation model, the fair value of the options on January 1, 20X6, is $24.75.

Diaz Inc. expects 1,714,750 of the options to vest over the three year period $(2,000,000 \times .95^3)$. Under FAS-123(R) compensation cost is only recognized for those share options where a performance or service condition is met. In this case, the service condition is that each of the 4,000 employees that receive options must work through December 31, 20X8. Estimated total compensation cost is $42,440,062 ($1,714,750 \times 24.75$).

During 20X6 Diaz experienced only a four percent employee turnover rate. However, at 12/31/X6 Diaz still expects the employee turnover rate to average five percent over the X6–X8 period (i.e., the estimate of total compensation cost developed at 1/1/X6 is not changed). Diaz Inc. would prepare the following journal entries at December 31, 20X6:

Compensation cost ($42,440,062 / 3)	14,146,687	
Additional paid-in capital		14,146,687

—To recognize compensation cost in 20X6.

Deferred tax asset ($14,146,687 × .35)	4,951,340	
Deferred tax benefit		4,951,340

—To recognize deferred tax benefit for the temporary difference related to compensation cost.

Note that the net effect of the above entries is that Diaz Inc.'s net income in 20X6 is reduced by $9,195,347 ($14,146,687 − $4,951,340).

During 20X7 employee turnover again runs at a 4% annual rate. Diaz Inc. now expects an average employee turnover of four percent over the X6–X8 period. As such, Diaz computes a new estimate of total compensation cost which is $43,794,432 [(2,000,000 × .96³) × $24.75]. Diaz Inc. will recognize compensation cost in 20X7 so that the sum of compensation cost recognized in 20X6 and 20X7 will equal two-thirds of $43,794,432. Diaz Inc. would prepare the following journal entries at December 31, 20X7:

Compensation cost		
[($43,794,432 × 2/3) − $14,146,687]	15,049,601	
Additional paid-in capital		15,049,601
—To recognize compensation cost in 20X7.		

Deferred tax asset ($15,049,601 × .35)	5,267,360	
Deferred tax benefit		5,267,360

—To recognize deferred tax benefit for the temporary difference related to compensation cost.

   The turnover during 20X8 is 4%. Diaz Inc. would prepare the following journal entries at December 31, 20X8:

Compensation cost ($43,794,432 / 3)	14,598,144	
Additional paid-in capital		14,598,144
—To recognize compensation cost in 20X8.		

Deferred tax asset ($14,598,144 × .35)	5,109,351	
Deferred tax benefit		5,109,351

—To recognize deferred tax benefit for the temporary difference related to compensation cost.

All 1,769,472 (2,000,000 × .96³) vested options are exercised on December 31, 20Y1. Diaz Inc.'s stock price is $120 on December 31, 20Y1. Diaz Inc. would prepare the following journal entry (Diaz issues no par common stock):

Cash (1,769,472 × $50)	88,473,600	
Additional paid-in capital		
($14,146,687 + $15,049,601 + $14,598,144)	43,794,432	
Common stock		132,268,032

—To record the issuance of common stock upon the exercise of the stock options and to reclassify previously recorded additional paid-in capital.

Income Tax Effects

Diaz Inc. is able to deduct the difference between the market price of the stock on the date the options are exercised, $120, and the exercise price of the option, $50, on its federal income tax return. The tax benefits from deductions in excess of compensation cost recognized are recorded as credits to additional paid-in capital. The tax deductible amount is $123,863,040 [($120 − $50) × 1,769,472]. The tax benefit realized by Diaz Inc. is $43,352,064 ($123,863,040 × .35) (assuming sufficient taxable income to fully realize the tax deduction). Diaz Inc. would make the following journal entry at December 31, 20Y1, to record the tax consequences related to the exercise of the stock options:

Deferred tax expense	15,328,051	
($4,951,340 + $5,267,360 + $5,109,351)		
Deferred tax asset		15,328,051

—To write off the deferred tax asset related to stock options exercised.

Income taxes payable ($123,863,040 × .35)	43,352,064	
Income tax expense ($43,794,432 × .35)		15,328,051
Additional paid-in capital		28,024,013
[($123,863,040 − $43,794,432) × .35]		

—To adjust taxes currently payable and current tax expense to recognize the current tax benefit from deductible compensation cost when the options are exercised.

Presentation of Income Tax Effects in Statement of Cash Flows

The tax benefits received as a result of the tax deductible amount exceeding recognized compensation cost is shown as a cash inflow from financing activities. In its 20Y1 Statement of Cash Flows, Diaz Inc. would present a cash inflow of $28,024,013 from excess tax benefits as a result of the exercise of stock options.

Disclosure Requirements

An entity with one or more share-based payment arrangements must disclose information that enables users of the financial statements to understand:

- The nature and terms of such arrangements that existed during the period and the potential effects of those arrangements on shareholders;

- The effect of compensation cost arising from share-based payment arrangements on the income statement;

- The method of estimating the fair value of the goods or services received, or the fair value of the equity instruments granted, during the period; and

- The cash flow effects of share-based payment arrangements [FAS-123(R), par. 64].

Some entities maintain multiple share-based payment arrangements, and these different arrangements may include different types of awards. The above disclosures should be made separately for different share-based payment arrangements if differences in the types of awards make such disclosure necessary [FAS-123(R), par. 65].

The minimum information needed to achieve FAS-123(R)'s disclosure objectives is [FAS-123(R), par. A240]:

- A description of the share-based payment arrangements, including the general terms of the awards under the arrangements. This includes the method used for measuring compensation cost from share-based payments with employees.

- For the most recent year for which an income statement is presented:
  — The number and weighted-average exercise prices for each of the following groups of share options or share units:
    (1) Those outstanding at the beginning of the year.
    (2) Those outstanding at the end of the year.
    (3) Those exercisable or convertible at the end of the year.
    (4) Those granted during the year.
    (5) Those exercised or converted, forfeited, or expired during the year.
  — The number and weighted-average grant-date fair value (or calculated value or intrinsic value for a nonpublic entity that uses either of those approaches) for instruments not covered by the disclosures in the previous paragraph (e.g., nonvested stock). The following disclosures should be made:
    (1) Nonvested shares at the beginning of the year.
    (2) Nonvested shares at the end of the year.
    (3) Shares granted, vested, and forfeited during the year.

- For each year for which an income statement is presented:
  — The weighted-average grant-date fair value (or calculated value or intrinsic value for a nonpublic entity that uses either of those approaches) of equity options or other equity instruments granted during the year.
  — The total intrinsic value of options exercised, share units converted, share-based liabilities paid, and the total fair value of shares vested during the year.

- For fully vested share options (units) and share options (units) expected to vest at the date of the latest balance sheet:
  — The number, weighted-average exercise price (conversion ratio), aggregate intrinsic value, and weighted-average remaining contractual term of options (units) outstanding.

— The number, weighted-average exercise price (conversion ratio), aggregate intrinsic value (only for public companies), and weighted-average remaining contractual term of options (units) currently exercisable (or convertible)

- For each year for which an income statement is presented (these disclosures are not required for a nonpublic company using the intrinsic value method):
  — A description of the method used during the year to estimate the fair value (calculated value) of awards under share-based payment arrangements.
  — A description of the significant assumptions used during the year to estimate the fair value (calculated value) of share-based compensation awards, including:
    (1) Expected term of share options and similar instruments and the method used to incorporate the contractual term for the instruments and employees' expected exercise and post-vesting employment termination behavior into the fair value of the instrument.
    (2) Expected volatility of the entity's shares and the method used to estimate it. A nonpublic company using the calculated value method must disclose why it could not estimate the volatility of its stock, the industry sector index used, why that index was chosen, and how the index was used to calculate volatility.
    (3) Expected dividends.
    (4) Risk-free rate(s).
    (5) Any discount, and how it was estimated, for post-vesting restrictions on the sale of stock received.

- An entity that grants equity or liability instruments under multiple share-based payment arrangements with employees shall provide the information specified above separately for different types of awards to the extent that differences in the characteristics of awards make separate disclosure important for an understanding of the entity's use of share-based compensation.

- For each year for which an income statement is presented:
  — Total compensation cost for share-based payment arrangements recognized in income as well as the total recognized tax benefit related thereto, and the total compensation cost capitalized as part of the cost of an asset.
  — A description of significant modifications, including the terms of the modifications, the number of employees affected, and the total incremental compensation cost resulting from the modifications.

- As of the latest balance sheet date, the total compensation cost related to nonvested awards not yet recognized and the weighted-average period over which this compensation cost is expected to be recognized.

- If not separately disclosed elsewhere, the amount of cash received from the exercise of share options and similar instruments granted under share-based payment arrangements and the tax benefit realized from stock options exercised during the year.

- If not separately disclosed elsewhere, the amount of cash used to settle equity instruments granted under share-based payment arrangements.

- A description of the entity's policy for issuing shares upon share option exercise, including the source of those shares (e.g., newly issued shares or treasury stock). If the entity expects to repurchase shares in the following annual period, the entity shall disclose an estimate of the amount of shares (or range) to be repurchased during that period.

☞ **OBSERVATION:** Given that many companies buy back stock in order to offset the potential earnings per share dilution that would otherwise result from the issuance of stock when options are exercised, the required disclosure of the amount of shares to be repurchased during the next year is likely to be closely followed by financial analysts.

RELATED CHAPTERS IN 2009 *GAAP GUIDE*
LEVEL A

Chapter 13, "Earnings per Share"
Chapter 21, "Income Taxes"
Chapter 26, "Interim Financial Reporting"
Chapter 40, "Results of Operations"
Chapter 44, "Stockholders' Equity"

RELATED CHAPTERS IN 2009 *GAAP GUIDE*
LEVELS B, C, AND D

Chapter 13, "Earnings per Share"
Chapter 20, "Income Taxes"
Chapter 23, "Interim Financial Reporting"
Chapter 35, "Results of Operations"

Chapter 38, "Stock-Based Payments"
Chapter 39, "Stockholders' Equity"

RELATED CHAPTER IN 2009 *INTERNATIONAL ACCOUNTING/FINANCIAL REPORTING STANDARDS GUIDE*

Chapter 32, "Share-Based Payments"

CHAPTER 44
STOCKHOLDERS' EQUITY

CONTENTS

OVERVIEW

The various elements constituting stockholders' equity in the statement of financial position are classified according to source. Stockholders' equity may be classified broadly into four categories: (1) legal capital, (2) additional paid-in capital, (3) minority interests, and (4) retained earnings. Detailed information is presented in the body of the statement, in related notes, or in some combination thereof.

GAAP for stockholders' equity are found in the following pronouncements:

ARB-43	Chapter 1, Prior Opinions
	A. Rules Adopted by Membership
	B. Opinions Issued by Predecessor Committee
	Chapter 7, Capital Accounts
	A. Quasi-Reorganizations
ARB-46	Discontinuance of Dating Earned Surplus
APB-6	Status of Accounting Research Bulletins
	Paragraph 12, Treasury Stock
APB-12	Omnibus Opinion—1967
	Paragraphs 9 and 10, Capital Changes
APB-14	Accounting for Convertible Debt and Debt Issued with Stock Purchase Warrants (Paragraph 16, Debt with Stock Purchase Warrants)
FAS-129	Disclosure of Information about Capital Structure
FAS-160	Noncontrolling Interests in Consolidated Financial Statements

BACKGROUND

Stockholders' equity represents the interest of the owners of a corporation in the corporation's assets. It represents the residual interest in the enterprise's assets, after liabilities have been subtracted, arising from the investment of owners and the retention of earnings over time.

In the balance sheet, stockholders' equity usually is displayed in two broad categories—*paid-in* or *contributed capital* and *retained earnings*. Paid-in or contributed capital represents the amount provided by stockholders in the original purchase of shares of stock or resulting from subsequent transactions with owners, such as treasury stock transactions. Retained earnings represent the amount of previous income of the corporation that has not been distributed to owners as dividends or transferred to paid-in or contributed capital.

Illustration of Balance Sheet Presentation
of Stockholders' Equity
December 31, 20X5

Preferred stock, $50 par value, 10,000 shares authorized, 7,000 shares authorized and outstanding	$ 350,000
Common stock, $25 par value, 100,000 shares authorized, 75,000 shares issued	1,875,000
Paid-in capital in excess of par value on common stock	500,000
Common stock dividend to be distributed	262,500
Total paid-in capital	$2,987,500
Retained earnings	1,000,000
Total paid-in capital and retained earnings	$3,987,500
Treasury stock, 10,000 shares of common stock at cost	(300,000)
Total stockholders' equity	$3,687,500

STOCKHOLDERS' EQUITY TERMINOLOGY
AND RELATIONSHIPS

Legal (or *stated*) *capital* usually is defined by state law. It refers to the amount of capital that must be retained by a corporation for the protection of its creditors. Legal capital may consist of common or preferred shares. Preferred shares may be participating or non-participating as to the earnings of the corporation, may be cumulative or noncumulative as to the payment of dividends, may have a preference claim on assets upon liquidation of the business, and may be callable for redemption at a specified price. Usually, preferred stock does not have voting rights.

Common stock usually has the right to vote, the right to share in earnings, a preemptive right to a proportionate share of any additional common stock issued, and the right to share in assets on liquidation.

Generally, stock is issued with a par value. No-par value stock may or may not have a stated value. *Par* or *stated value* is the amount that is established in the stock account at the time the stock is issued. When stock is issued above or below par value, a premium or discount on the stock is recorded, respectively. A discount reduces paid-in or contributed capital; a premium increases paid-in or contributed capital. A premium on stock is often referred to as "paid-in capital in excess of par value." Because the issuance of stock at a discount is not legal in many jurisdictions, discounts on stock are not frequently encountered.

A corporation's charter contains the types and amounts of stock that it can legally issue, which is called the *authorized capital stock*. When part or all of the authorized capital stock is issued, it is called *issued capital stock*. Since a corporation may own issued capital stock in the form of treasury stock, the amount of issued capital stock in the hands of stockholders is called *outstanding capital stock*.

A corporation may sell its capital stock by subscriptions. An individual subscriber becomes a stockholder upon subscribing to the capital stock; and upon full payment of the subscription, a stock certificate evidencing ownership in the corporation is issued. When the subscription method is used to sell capital stock, a subscription receivable account is debited and a capital stock subscribed account is credited. On payment of the subscription, the subscription receivable account is credited and cash or other assets are debited. On the actual issuance of the stock certificates, the capital stock subscribed account is debited and the regular capital stock account is credited.

Illustration of Capital Stock Relationships

A company has the following capital stock structure: The numbers below represent shares of a particular class of stock (e.g., common stock) and indicate the relationships among the various components of authorized stock. The number of shares authorized is 10,000, of which 8,000 have been issued and 2,000 are unissued. Of the 8,000 issued shares, 7,000 are outstanding (i.e., in the hands of investors) and 1,000 represent treasury shares (i.e., shares that were issued and outstanding at one time, but have been reacquired by the company). Of the 2,000 unissued shares, 500 have been subscribed and 1,500 are unsubscribed. The 500 subscribed shares have been partially paid and are considered unissued until they are fully paid, at which time they will be considered issued and outstanding shares.

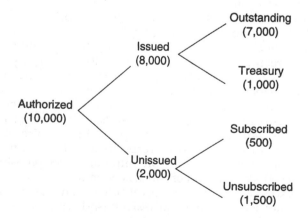

Following are examples of how the numbers of shares change for several independent common capital stock transactions:

1. *Sale of 700 shares of previously unissued stock*—Unsubscribed stock declines by 700 shares, as does the number of unissued shares. Outstanding shares and issued shares both increase by 700. As a result, unissued shares number 1,300 and issued shares number 8,700, of which 7,700 are outstanding.

2. *Sale of 100 shares of treasury stock*—Treasury stock declines to 900 shares and outstanding increases to 7,100 shares. The total number of unissued and issued shares remains unchanged.

3. *Subscribed shares (500) are paid in full*—Subscribed shares become zero, reducing unissued shares to 1,500. Outstanding and issued shares increase to 7,500 and 8,500, respectively.

DISCLOSURE OF INFORMATION ABOUT STOCKHOLDERS' EQUITY

When financial statements are prepared in conformity with GAAP, capital changes must be disclosed in a separate statement(s) or note(s) to the financial statement. This requirement is in addition to disclosure of the changes in retained earnings, although all capital changes may be included in one statement. Capital accounts may have to be disclosed because of changes during the year in capital stock, additional paid-in capital accounts, retained earnings, treasury stock, and other capital accounts (APB-12, pars. 9–10).

FAS-129 (Disclosure of Information about Capital Structure) establishes standards for disclosing information about an entity's capital structure. It consolidates the disclosure requirements that were previously covered in APB-10 (Omnibus Opinion—1966), APB-15 (Earnings per Share), and FAS-47 (Disclosure of Long-Term Obligations). FAS-129 eliminates the exemption for nonpublic entities from certain disclosure requirements about capital structure included in APB-15 as amended by FAS-21 (Suspension of the Reporting of Earnings per Share and Segment Information by Nonpublic Enterprises). It does not change the disclosure requirements for entities for which the reporting requirements of APB-10, APB-15, and FAS-47 were applicable.

Three terms are particularly important in understanding and applying FAS-129—securities, participating rights, and preferred stock (FAS-129, par. 2). These terms are defined as follows:

- **Securities**—evidence of debt or ownership or a related right, including options and warrants as well as debt and stock
- **Participating rights**—contractual rights of security holders to receive dividends or returns from the issuer's profits, cash flows, or returns on investments

- **Preferred stock**—a security that has preferential rights over common stock

FAS-129 requires information about capital structure to be disclosed in three separate categories—information about securities, liquidation preference of preferred stock, and redeemable stock.

Information about Securities

The entity shall provide within its financial statements a summary explanation of the pertinent rights and privileges of the various securities that are outstanding (FAS-129, pars. 4–5). Examples of information that is to be disclosed are:

- Dividend and liquidation preferences
- Participating rights
- Call prices and dates
- Conversion or exercise prices or rates and dates
- Sinking-fund requirements
- Unusual voting rights
- Significant terms of contracts to issue additional shares

In addition to the information about rights and privileges associated with securities, the number of shares issued upon conversion, exercise, or satisfaction of required conditions during the most recent annual fiscal period and any subsequent interim period shall be disclosed.

Liquidation Preference of Preferred Stock

Preferred stock or other senior securities may have a preference in involuntary liquidation that is in excess of the security's par or stated value. In this situation, the issuing entity shall disclose the liquidation preference of the stock (i.e., the relationship of the liquidation preference and the par or stated value of the shares). Under the following guidelines, this disclosure should be (FAS-129, pars. 6–7):

- Presented within the equity section, either parenthetically or "in short" (i.e., included in the body of the financial statement, but not added in the total of stockholders' equity).
- Presented as an aggregate amount.

☞ **PRACTICE POINTER:** Take care not to overlook the requirement that the liquidation preference of preferred stock must be presented in the aggregate and in the body of the equity section of the balance sheet rather than in notes to the financial statements. This is an unusual requirement and could be easily overlooked.

Other disclosures, which may be made either in the financial statements or in related notes, are:

- The aggregate *or* per share amounts at which preferred stock may be called or are subject to redemption through sinking-fund operations or otherwise
- The aggregate *and* per share amounts of cumulative preferred dividends in arrears

Redeemable Stock

Redeemable stock must be repurchased by the issuing entity. In this situation, the issuing entity is required to disclose the amount of redemption requirements, separately by issue or combined, for all issues of stock for which the redemption prices and dates are fixed or determinable. This information is required for each of the next five years following the date of the latest statement of financial position that is presented (FAS-129, par. 8).

Illustration of Capital Structure Disclosures

Following are examples of the disclosures required by FAS-129. Disclosures of information about securities, the liquidation preference of preferred stock, and redeemable stock are the direct result of specific circumstances that exist within the reporting entity. No example can include all possible information that may require disclosure. Care should be taken in relying on these or other examples because of differences that may exist among reporting entities.

Information about Securities

ABC Company's capital structure includes common and preferred stock that is described as follows in its statement of financial position and in the note to the financial statements:

Statement of financial position:

Convertible preferred stock—$40 par value, 5 million shares authorized, 4 million shares and 3.8 million shares issued and outstanding in 20X6 and 20X5, respectively

Common stock—$10 par value, 10 million shares authorized, 6 million shares issued and outstanding in 20X6 and 20X5

Note to the financial statements:

Each share of ABC preferred stock is convertible into four shares of ABC common stock at any time through December 31, 20X9. The preferred stock is entitled to a cumulative annual dividend of $2.50.

Liquidation Preference of Preferred Stock

DEF Company has preferred stock outstanding, as described below in the body of the statement of financial position:

Preferred stock—$10 per share par value, 1 million shares authorized. Issued and outstanding: 20X6 and 20X5—.8 million and .75 million shares, respectively. Aggregate liquidation preference: 20X6 and 20X5—$12 million and $11.25 million, respectively.

Redeemable Stock

GHI Company has redeemable preferred stock outstanding, as described below in notes to the financial statements:

Preferred stock—Each share of GHI preferred stock is convertible into four shares of GHI common stock. On December 31, 20X8, the preferred shares are redeemable at the company's option at $50 per share. Based on the current market price of the stock, the company expects the majority of the preferred shares to be converted into common stock prior to December 31, 20X8.

ADDITIONAL PAID-IN CAPITAL

All stockholders' equity that is not classified as legal capital, minority interests, or retained earnings usually is designated as additional paid-in capital. The common sources of additional paid-in capital are:

- Excess of par or stated value paid for capital stock
- Sale of treasury stock
- The issuance of detachable stock purchase warrants (APB-14, par. 16)
- Donated assets
- Capital created by a corporate readjustment or quasi-reorganization

If capital stock is issued for the acquisition of property and it appears that, at about the same time and pursuant to a previous agreement or understanding, some portion of the stock so issued is donated to the corporation, the par value of the stock is not an appropriate basis for valuing the property. Generally, donated stock should be recorded at fair value at the time it is received. Fair value may be determined by the value of the stock or the value of the asset, services, or other consideration received (ARB-43, Ch. 1A, par. 6).

Charges should not be made to paid-in capital, however created, that are properly chargeable to income accounts of the current or future years (ARB-43, Ch. 1A, par. 2).

NONCONTROLLING INTERESTS

In the presentation of consolidated financial statements, a non-controlling interest (formerly referred to as *minority interest*) is that portion of equity (net assets) in a subsidiary company that is not attributable, directly or indirectly, to the parent company. The noncontrolling interest in the subsidiary is part of the equity of the consolidated group (FAS-160, par, 25).

A noncontrolling interest is reported in the consolidated statement of financial position within equity, clearly labeled as being separate from the parent's equity. For example, the following title might be used: *Noncontrolling interest in subsidiary.* An entity with noncontrolling interests in more than one subsidiary may present those interests in the aggregate in the consolidated statement of financial position (FAS-160, par. 26).

TREASURY STOCK

Treasury stock is a company's own capital stock that has been issued and subsequently reacquired. It is ordinarily presented as a reduction in the amount of stockholders' equity. Treasury stock is not considered an asset, because it is widely held that a corporation cannot own part of itself. The status of treasury stock is similar to that of authorized but unissued capital stock. Dividends on a company's own stock are not considered a part of income (ARB-43, Ch. 1A, par. 4).

If a state law prescribes the manner in which a corporation accounts for the acquisition of treasury stock, the state law is followed, even if the state law is in variance with existing GAAP. Restrictions on the availability of retained earnings for the payment of dividends or any other restrictions required by state law are disclosed in the financial statements (APB-6, par. 13).

Accounting and Reporting

Under GAAP, both the cost method and the par value method of accounting for treasury stock are acceptable. Under the cost method, each acquisition of treasury stock is accounted for at cost. In addition, separate records are maintained to reflect the date of purchase of the treasury stock, the number of shares acquired, and the reacquisition cost per share. Treasury stock may be kept based on an acceptable inventory method, such as FIFO or average cost basis. Upon the sale or other disposition, the treasury stock account is credited for an amount equal to the number of shares sold, multiplied by the cost per share and the difference between this amount and the cash received is treated as paid-in capital in excess of par (stated) value. The cost method of accounting for treasury stock is more commonly used in practice than the par value method.

Under the par value method of accounting for treasury stock, the treasury stock account is increased by the par or stated value of each share reacquired. Any excess paid per share over the par or stated value is debited to paid-in capital in excess of par (stated) value, but only for the amount per share that was originally credited when the stock was issued. Any excess cost per share remaining over the par or stated value per share and the amount per share originally credited to paid-in capital in excess of par (stated) value is charged to retained earnings. If the cost per share of treasury stock is less than the par or stated value per share and the amount per share originally credited to paid-in capital in excess of par (stated) value the difference is credited to paid-in capital from treasury stock transactions. Under the par value method, all of the original capital balances related to the shares reacquired are removed from the books.

When treasury stock is acquired with the intent of retiring the stock (whether or not retirement is actually accomplished), the excess of the price paid for the treasury stock over its par or stated value may be allocated between (a) paid-in capital arising from the same class of stock and (b) retained earnings. The amount of excess that can be allocated to paid-in capital arising from the same class of stock, however, is limited to the sum of (a) any paid-in capital arising from previous retirements and net gains on sales of the same class of treasury stock and (b) the pro rata portion of paid-in capital, voluntary transfers of retained earnings, capitalization of stock dividends, etc., on the same class of stock. For this purpose, any paid-in capital arising from issues of capital stock that are fully retired (formal or constructive) is deemed to be applicable on a pro rata basis to all shares of common stock. As an alternative, the excess of the price paid for the treasury stock over its par or stated value may be charged entirely to retained earnings, based on the fact that a corporation can always capitalize or allocate retained earnings for such a purpose (APB-6, par. 12).

When the price paid for the acquired treasury stock is less than its par or stated value, the difference is credited to paid-in capital.

When treasury stock is acquired for purposes other than retirement, it is disclosed separately in the balance sheet as a deduction from stockholders' equity.

A gain on the sale of treasury stock acquired for purposes other than retirement is credited to paid-in capital from the sale of treasury stock. Losses are charged to paid-in capital, but only to the extent of available net gains from previous sales or retirements of the same class of stock; otherwise, losses are charged to retained earnings (ARB-43, Ch. 1B, par. 7).

If treasury stock is donated to a corporation and then subsequently sold, the entire proceeds shall be credited to paid-in capital from the sale of donated treasury stock (ARB-43, Ch. 1A, par. 6).

☛ **PRACTICE POINTER:** Under the cost and par value methods, adjustments to paid-in capital from treasury stock transactions are recognized at different times and determined in different ways. Under the cost method, base adjustments to paid-in capital on the relationship between the purchase price and the subsequent selling price; they are recognized at the time of the sale of the treasury stock. Under the par value method, base adjustments to paid-in capital on the relationship between the original selling price of the stock and the purchase price; they are recognized at the time of the purchase of the treasury stock.

These relationships are summarized as follows:

	Cost Method	*Par Value Method*
Timing of adjustment to paid-in capital	Point of sale	Point of purchase
Paid-in capital increased	Selling price greater than purchase price	Purchase price less than original selling price
Paid-in capital decreased	Selling price less than purchase price	Purchase price greater than original selling price
Retained earnings decreased	Loss on sale greater than paid-in capital from previous treasury stock transactions	Purchase price is so high that all paid-in capital from previous treasury stock transactions is eliminated

The cost method is much more widely used in practice than the par value method.

Purchase Price of Treasury Stock

If treasury shares are reacquired for a purchase price significantly in excess of their current market price, it is *presumed* that the total purchase price includes amounts for stated or unstated rights or privileges. Under this circumstance, the total purchase price is allocated between the treasury shares and the rights or privileges that are identified with the purchase of the treasury shares based on the fair value of the rights or privileges, or the fair value of the treasury shares, whichever is more clearly evident.

DIVIDENDS

A *dividend* is a pro rata distribution by a corporation, based on shares of a particular class, and usually represents a distribution based on earnings.

Cash Dividends

Cash dividends are the most common type of dividend distribution. Preferred stock usually pays a fixed dividend, expressed in dollars or a percentage.

Three dates usually are involved in a dividend distribution:

1. *Date of declaration*: The date the board of directors formally declares the dividend to the stockholders
2. *Date of record*: The date the board of directors specifies that stockholders of record on that date are entitled to the dividend payment
3. *Date of payment*: The date the dividend is actually disbursed by the corporation or its paying agent

Cash dividends are recorded on the books of the corporation as a liability (dividends payable) on the date of declaration. Dividends are paid only on authorized, issued, and outstanding shares, thereby eliminating any dividend payment on treasury stock.

Stock Dividends

Stock dividends are distributions of a company's own capital stock to its existing stockholders in lieu of cash. Stock dividends are accounted for by transferring an amount equal to the fair market value of the stock from retained earnings to paid-in capital. The dividend is recorded at the date of declaration by reducing retained earnings and establishing a temporary account, such as "Stock Dividend to Be Distributed." Because no asset distribution is required for a stock dividend, that account is part of stockholders' equity, in contrast to a cash dividend payable account, which is a liability. When the stock is distributed, the stock dividend account is eliminated and permanent capital accounts (e.g., common stock and paid-in capital in excess of par [stated] value) are increased (ARB-43, Ch. 7B, par. 10).

Illustration of Stock Dividends

LPS Corporation declares a 5% stock dividend on its 1,000,000 shares of outstanding $10 par common stock (5,000,000 authorized). On the date of declaration, LPS stock is selling for $25 per share.

Total stock dividend (5% of 1,000,000)		50,000 shares
Value of 50,000 shares @ $25 per share (market)		$1,250,000
Date of declaration:		
Retained earnings	1,250,000	
Stock dividend to be distributed		1,250,000
Date of distribution:		
Stock dividend to be distributed	1,250,000	
Common stock (50,000 x $10)		500,000
Paid-in capital in excess of par value		750,000

STOCK SPLITS

When a stock distribution is more than 20% to 25% of the outstanding shares immediately before the distribution, it is considered a stock split, sometimes referred to as a "stock split-up" (ARB-43, Ch. 7B, par. 13). A stock split increases the number of shares of capital stock outstanding, and a reverse stock split decreases the number of shares of capital stock outstanding.

In both straight and reverse stock splits, the total dollar amount of stockholders' equity does not change. The par or stated value per share of capital stock, however, decreases or increases in proportion with the increase or decrease in the number of shares outstanding. For example, in a stock split of 4 for 1 of $40 par value capital stock, the new stock has a par value of $10 and the number of shares outstanding increases to four shares for each share of stock previously outstanding. In a reverse stock split of 1 for 4 of $40 par value capital stock, the new stock has a par value of $160 per share and the number of shares outstanding decreases to one share for each four shares of stock previously outstanding.

A stock split is used by a corporation to reduce the market price of its capital stock to make the market price of the stock more attractive to buyers (ARB-43, Ch. 7B, par. 2). Thus, in a 4 for 1 straight stock split, the new shares would probably sell for about one-fourth of the previous market price of the old shares prior to the split. Reverse stock splits are unusual and are used to increase the market price of a corporation's stock. For example, a reverse stock split of 1 for 4 of stock selling for $3 would probably increase the market price of the new shares to about $12 per share.

No journal entry is required to record a stock split except a memorandum entry in the capital stock account to indicate the new par or stated value of the stock and the number of new shares outstanding after the split. Stock splits should not be referred to as dividends (ARB-43, Ch. 7B, par. 11).

A stock split may, however, be accomplished in the form of a stock dividend. In this case, the distribution of stock is called *a stock split issued in the form of a stock dividend,* and the percentage distribution is large enough (i.e., in excess of 20% to 25% of the outstanding stock) that the market value of the stock reacts accordingly. Accounting in this situation is similar to a stock dividend, except that only the par or stated value of the stock, rather than the market value, is transferred from retained earnings to paid-in capital.

Stock dividends and stock splits are similar in that they result in increased numbers of outstanding shares of stock for which stockholders make no payment. They differ, however, in size, in their impact on the stock's market price, and, most important, in managerial intent. In the case of a stock dividend, management intent usually is to make a distribution to owners while preserving present cash; in the case of a stock split, management intent is to affect (reduce) market price. Accounting for stock dividends and stock splits is summarized in Figure 44-1.

Figure 44-1: Accounting for Stock Dividends and Stock Splits

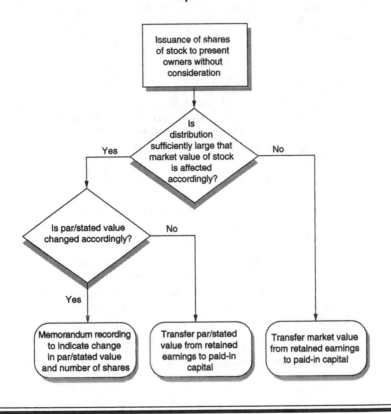

STOCK RIGHTS

No accounting entry is necessary for the entity issuing the stock right or warrant, except for detachable stock purchase warrants or similar rights, which are accounted for separately and assigned a value (see the chapter titled "Convertible Debt and Debt with Warrants").

QUASI-REORGANIZATION

When a struggling business reaches a turnaround point and profitable operations seem likely, a quasi-reorganization may be appropriate to eliminate an accumulated deficit from past unprofitable operations. The resulting financial statements have more credibility and may make it possible for the company to borrow money for its profitable operations. In addition, by eliminating the deficit in retained earnings, the possibility of paying dividends in the foreseeable future becomes more likely.

The specific criteria that must be met for a quasi-reorganization to be appropriate are:

- Assets are overvalued in the balance sheet.

- The company can reasonably expect to be profitable in the future if a restructuring occurs so that future operations are not burdened with the problems of the past.

- Formal shareholder consent is obtained.

Stockholders' equity usually is made up of the following:

- Capital contributed for stock, to the extent of the par or stated value of each class of stock presently outstanding
- Additional paid-in or contributed capital:
  — Capital contributed in excess of par or stated value of each class of stock, whether as a result of original issues, any subsequent reductions of par or stated value, or transactions by the corporation in its own shares
  — Capital received other than for stock, whether from shareholders or others (such as donated capital)
- Retained earnings (or deficit), which represents the accumulated income or loss of the corporation.

Generally, items properly chargeable to current or future years' income accounts may *not* be charged to contributed capital accounts. An exception to this rule occurs in accounting for quasi-reorganizations, in which case a one-time adjustment to contributed capital is appropriate.

Although the corporate entity remains unchanged in a quasi-reorganization, a new basis of accountability is established. Net assets are restated downward to their fair values, and stockholders' equity is reduced. Retained earnings (deficit) is raised to a zero balance by charging any deficit accumulated from operations and the asset adjustments to either (*a*) capital contributed in excess of par or (*b*) capital contributed other than for capital stock. Contributed capital accounts must be large enough to absorb the deficit in retained earnings, including adjustments made as part of the quasi-reorganization.

☞ **PRACTICE POINTER:** Although the capital stock account may not be used to directly absorb a deficit in retained earnings, a corporation may reduce the par value of its existing capital stock and transfer the resulting excess to a capital contributed in excess of par account. This procedure frequently is used in a quasi-reorganization.

Accounting and Reporting

If a corporation restates its assets and stockholders' equity through a quasi-reorganization, it must make a clear report of the proposed restatements to its shareholders and obtain their formal consent (ARB-43, Ch. 7A, par. 3).

Assets are written down to their fair values; if fair values are not readily determinable, conservative estimates are used (ARB-43, Ch. 7A, par. 4). Estimates may also be used to provide for known probable losses prior to the date of the quasi-reorganization, when amounts are indeterminable (ARB-43, Ch. 7A, par. 5).

> ☞ **PRACTICE POINTER:**   Determination of the fair value of assets may be a subjective process, requiring the use of different valuation and appraisal techniques for different asset categories.

If estimates are used and the amounts subsequently are found to be excessive or insufficient, the difference should be charged or credited to the capital account previously charged or credited and not to retained earnings (ARB-43, Ch. 7A, par. 5).

The steps in the accounting procedure are as follows:

Step 1.   All asset amounts to be written off are charged to retained earnings (ARB-43, Ch. 7A, par. 6).

Step 2.   After all amounts to be written off are recognized and charged to retained earnings, the negative (debit) balance is transferred to either (a) capital contributed in excess of par or (b) capital contributed other than for capital stock (ARB-43, Ch. 7A, par. 6).

Capital contributed in excess of par value may have existed prior to the quasi-reorganization, or it may have been created as a result of a reduction of par value in conjunction with the quasi-reorganization.

Step 3.   If a deficit in retained earnings is transferred to an allowable capital account, any subsequent balance sheet must disclose, by dating the retained earnings, that the balance in the retained earnings account has accumulated since the date of reorganization (ARB-43, Ch. 7A, par. 10). For example:

Retained earnings, since July 1, 20X0 $1,234,567

The dating of retained earnings following a quasi-reorganization would rarely, if ever, be of significance after a period of ten years. There may be exceptional circumstances that could justify a period of less than ten years (ARB-46, par. 2).

Step 4. New or additional shares of stock may be issued or exchanged for other shares or existing indebtedness. For example, stockholders may agree to subscribe to additional shares, or bondholders may agree to accept capital stock in lieu of principal or interest in arrears, to provide new cash for future operations. Accounting entries for these types of transactions are handled in accordance with GAAP. Consideration should include whether the issuance of new stock results in a change in control, in which case purchase accounting may be appropriate (ARB-43, Ch. 7A, par. 11).

Step 5. Corporations with subsidiaries should follow the same procedures so that no credit balance remains in consolidated retained earnings after a quasi-reorganization in which losses have been charged to allowable capital accounts (ARB-43, Ch. 7A, par. 6).

In those cases in which losses have been charged to the allowable capital accounts, instead of a credit balance in a subsidiary's retained earnings, the parent company's interest in such retained earnings should be regarded as capitalized by the quasi-reorganization in the same way retained earnings of a subsidiary are capitalized by the parent on the date of its acquisition (ARB-43, Ch. 7A, par. 7).

Step 6. The effective date of the quasi-reorganization from which income of the corporation is thereafter determined should be as close as possible to the date of formal stockholders' consent and preferably at the start of a new fiscal year (ARB-43, Ch. 7A, par. 8).

Adjustments made pursuant to a quasi-reorganization should not be included in the determination of net income for any period.

Accounting for a Tax Benefit

Careful consideration must be given to the proper accounting for any tax attributes in a quasi-reorganization. Under FAS-109 (Accounting for Income Taxes), tax benefits of deductible temporary differences and carryforwards as of the date of the quasi-reorganization ordinarily are reported as a direct addition to capital contributed in excess of par if the tax benefits are recognized in subsequent years. An exception may exist for entities that have previously adopted FAS-96 (Accounting for Income Taxes) and effected a quasi-reorganization; in that instance, subsequent recognition of tax benefits may be included in income and then reclassified from retained earnings to capital contributed in excess of par (FAS-109, par. 39).

Disclosure

Adequate disclosure of all pertinent information should be made in the financial statements. A new retained earnings account dated as of the date of the quasi-reorganization should be established and reflected in subsequent financial statements.

Illustration of Accounting for a Quasi-Reorganization

The Centrex Company experienced losses in each of its first six years of operation. In May 20X5, the company acquired two patents on an advanced solarheating unit, which soon became the standard for the industry. The quarter ended September 30, 20X5, was profitable, and the patent and accompanying licensing agreements indicate that continuing profitability is quite likely.

Centrex is closely held and the stockholders have agreed in principle to a quasi-reorganization. Negotiations have been held with various creditors regarding capitalizing debts.

The balance sheet of Centrex at December 31, 20X5, appears as follows:

Assets:

Cash	$ 25,000
Accounts receivable (net)	410,000
Plant and equipment (net)	1,670,000
Other assets	80,000
Total assets	$2,185,000

Liabilities and Equity:

Accounts payable	$ 840,000
Notes payable—other	300,000
Equipment notes payable	240,000
Common stock	500,000
Paid-in capital in excess of par value—common stock	1,017,000
Retained earnings	(712,000)
Total liabilities and equity	$2,185,000

The stockholders and creditors have approved the following plan of informal reorganization effective January 1, 20X6:

1. The current shareholders will exchange their 100,000 shares of $5 par stock for 100,000 shares of $1 par stock.
2. The creditors have agreed to accept a new issue of 5% preferred stock valued at $300,000 for an equal amount of accounts payable.
3. The plant and equipment will be written down to its fair value of $1,100,000.
4. Accounts receivable of $70,000 will be written off as uncollectible.
5. Other assets will be written down to their fair value of $50,000.

The first step in a quasi-reorganization is to write down all assets to their fair values. In the example, the journal entry would be:

Retained earnings	670,000	
Plant and equipment		
($1,670,000 – $1,100,000)		570,000
Accounts receivable		70,000
Other assets ($80,000 – $50,000)		30,000

Next, the change in the par value of the common stock is recorded:

Common stock	400,000	
Paid-in capital in excess of		
par value—common stock		400,000

The following journal entry records the new preferred stock issued for $300,000 of accounts payable:

Accounts payable	300,000	
5% Preferred stock		300,000

After all the quasi-reorganization adjustments are made, the deficit in retained earnings ($1,382,000) is eliminated against the paid-in capital—common stock—leaving a zero balance in retained earnings:

Paid-in capital—common stock	1,382,000	
Retained earnings		
($712,000 + $670,000)		1,382,000

The Centrex Company balance sheet, after giving effect to the reorganization, appears as follows:

Assets:

Cash	$ 25,000
Accounts receivable (net)	340,000
Plant and equipment (net)	1,100,000
Other assets	50,000
Total assets	$1,515,000

Liabilities and Equity:	
Accounts payable	$ 540,000
Notes payable—other	300,000
Equipment notes payable	240,000
5% Preferred stock	300,000
Common stock ($1 par)	100,000
Paid-in capital in excess of par value—common stock ($1,017,000 + $400,000 –$1,382,000)	35,000
Retained earnings since January 1, 20X5	-0-
Total liabilities and equity	$1,515,000

RELATED CHAPTERS IN 2009 *GAAP GUIDE* *LEVEL A*

Chapter 7, "Consolidated Financial Statements"
Chapter 9, "Convertible Debt and Debt with Warrants"
Chapter 13, "Earnings per Share"
Chapter 21, "Income Taxes"
Chapter 40, "Results of Operations"
Chapter 43, "Stock-Based Payments"

RELATED CHAPTERS IN 2009 *GAAP GUIDE* *LEVELS B, C, AND D*

Chapter 10, "Consolidated Financial Statements"
Chapter 12, "Convertible Debt and Debt with Warrants"
Chapter 13, "Earnings per Share"
Chapter 20, "Income Taxes"
Chapter 35, "Results of Operations"
Chapter 38, "Stock-Based Payments"
Chapter 39, "Stockholders' Equity"

CHAPTER 45
TRANSFER AND SERVICING OF FINANCIAL ASSETS

CONTENTS

OVERVIEW

Transfers of financial assets take many forms and, depending on the nature of the transaction, the transferor may have a continuing interest in the transferred asset. Accounting for transferred assets in which the transferor has no continuing involvement with the transferred asset or with the transferee has been relatively straight forward and not controversial. Transfers of financial assets in which the transferor has some continuing interest, however, have raised issues about the circumstances in which the transfer should be considered a sale of all or part of the assets or a secured borrowing, and how transferors and transferees should account for sales of financial assets and secured borrowings.

GAAP for transactions involving the transfer and servicing of financial assets are primarily established in the following authoritative pronouncements:

FAS-140   Accounting for Transfers and Servicing of Financial
             Assets and Extinguishments of Liabilities
FAS-156   Accounting for Servicing of Financial Assets—An
             Amendment of FASB Statement No. 140

FAS-140 (Accounting for Transfers and Servicing of Financial Assets and Extinguishments of Liabilities) establishes accounting and reporting standards for transfers and servicing of financial assets and extinguishments of liabilities based on the consistent application of the financial-components approach. For each party to a transfer, this approach requires the recognition of financial assets and servicing assets that are controlled by the reporting entity, the derecognition of financial assets when control is surrendered, and the derecognition of liabilities when they are extinguished. Specific criteria are established for determining when control has been surrendered in the transfer of financial assets. FAS-156 (Accounting for Servicing of Financial Assets—An Amendment of FASB Statement No. 140) amends FAS-140 with respect to the accounting for separately recognized servicing assets and servicing liabilities.

> ☞ **PRACTICE POINTER:**   This chapter provides an overview of
> FAS-140. Accounting guidance for transfers of financial assets

also can be found in various EITF issues and a FASB Staff Implementation Guide. In addition, a detailed analysis of relevant accounting guidance for transfers of financial assets can be found in *Financial Instruments*. Because transfers of financial assets can be extremely complex transactions, practitioners encountering these transactions should seek the assistance of experts in analyzing the applicable accounting literature.

BACKGROUND

Definitions

The term *financial asset* is defined in FAS-140 as cash, evidence of an ownership interest in an entity, or a contract that conveys to a second entity a contractual right (a) to receive cash or another financial instrument from a first entity or (b) to exchange other financial instruments on potentially favorable terms with the first entity (FAS-140, par. 364).

The term *financial liability* refers to a contract that imposes a contractual obligation on one entity (a) to deliver cash or another financial instrument to a second entity or (b) to exchange other financial instruments on potentially unfavorable terms with the second entity (FAS-140, par. 364).

The term *transfer* refers to the conveyance of a noncash financial asset to someone other than the issuer of that financial asset. Examples are selling a receivable, putting it into a securitization trust, or posting it as collateral. It excludes the origination of the receivable, the settlement of the receivable, or the restructuring of the receivable into a security in a troubled debt restructuring. The *transferor* is the party that transfers a financial asset (or part of a financial asset or a group of financial assets) that it controls to another entity. The *transferee* is the entity that receives a financial asset from the transferor (FAS-140, par. 364).

The term *servicing asset* is defined in FAS-156 as a contract to service financial assets under which the estimated future revenues from contractually specified servicing fees, late charges, and other ancillary revenues are expected to more than adequately compensate the servicer for performing the servicing. A service contract is either (1) undertaken in conjunction with selling or securitizing the financial assets being serviced or purchased or (2) assumed separately (FAS-156, par. 3).

The term *servicing liability* refers to a contract to service financial assets under which the estimated future revenues from contractually specified servicing fees, late charges, and other ancillary revenues are not expected to adequately compensate the servicer for performing the servicing (FAS-156, par. 3).

Objectives of FAS-140

Transfers of financial assets may take many forms, and accounting for those transfers in which the transferor has no continuing involvement with the transferred asset or with the transferee is uncontroversial. Accounting for transfers of financial assets in which the transferor has a continuing involvement with the assets or with the transferee, however, is less straightforward. Examples of continuing involvement include (FAS-140, par. 2):

- Recourse
- Servicing
- Agreements to reacquire
- Options written or held
- Pledges of collateral

Issues raised by these types of transactions include the circumstances in which the transfers should be considered as sales of part or all of the assets or as secured borrowings and the accounting by transferors and transferees for sales and secured borrowings.

The FASB has stated two broad objectives in establishing standards for the transfer and servicing of financial assets and the extinguishment of liabilities. The first objective is for each party to the transaction to recognize only assets it controls and liabilities it has incurred, to derecognize assets only when control has been surrendered, and to derecognize liabilities only when they have been extinguished. (The term *derecognize* means the opposite of recognize, namely, to remove previously recognized assets or liabilities from the statement of financial position.) For instance, if an entity sells a portion of a financial asset it owns, only the portion sold is derecognized, and the portion that continues to be held by a transferor is still carried as an asset (FAS-140, par. 5).

The second broad objective is that recognition of financial assets and liabilities not be affected by the sequence of transactions that result in their acquisition or incurrence unless the effect of those transactions is to maintain effective control over a transferred financial asset. For example, if a transferor sells financial assets and at the same time writes a put option on those assets, it should recognize the put obligation in the same manner as would an unrelated entity that writes an identical put option on assets it never owned. Certain agreements to repurchase or redeem transferred assets, however, are intended to maintain effective control over the assets and should be accounted for differently than agreements to acquire assets never owned (FAS-140, par. 6).

Objectives of FAS-156

The Board's primary objective in issuing FAS-156 is to achieve more consistent accounting for servicing assets and servicing liabilities and the related derivative financial instruments that entities use to offset the risks associated with changes in the value of the servicing assets and servicing liabilities. Those derivative instruments are required to be accounted for at fair value, with changes in their fair value being reported in current earnings. However, prior to the adoption of FAS-156, unless the derivative meets the "effectiveness" qualification to be classified as a hedge, the change in fair value of the servicing asset or servicing liability is not always reflected in current earnings. FAS-156 is designed to simplify the accounting for servicing assets and servicing liabilities and to provide an opportunity for the changes in fair value of these assets and liabilities and their related derivative instruments to be reflected in earnings in the same period.

CONTROL CRITERIA AND TRANSFEROR ACCOUNTING

FAS-140 specifies three conditions, all of which must be met, for the transferor to have surrendered control over transferred assets (FAS-140, par. 9):

1. The transferred assets have been isolated from the transferor (i.e., they are beyond the reach of the transferor and its creditors).

2. Each transferee (or, if the transferee is a qualifying holder of beneficial interests) has the right to pledge or exchange the assets (or beneficial interests) it received, and no condition both (*a*) constrains the transferee from taking advantage of its right to pledge or exchange and (*b*) provides more than a trivial benefit to the transferor.

3. The transferor does not maintain effective control over the transferred assets either through an agreement that obligates the transferor to repurchase or redeem the assets before their maturity or through the ability to unilaterally cause the holder to return specific assets other than through a cleanup call. (A cleanup call is an option held by the servicer, or its affiliate, to purchase the remaining transferred financial assets, if the amount of outstanding assets or beneficial interests becomes burdensome in relation to the benefits of servicing (FAS-140, par. 364).)

If these conditions are met, the transfer is accounted for as a sale to the extent that consideration other than *beneficial interests* in the transferred assets is received in exchange (FAS-140, par. 9). *Beneficial interests* are defined as rights to receive all or a portion of specified cash inflows to a trust or other entity (including senior and subordinated shares of interest, principal, or other cash inflows to be "passed-through" or "paid-through," premiums due to guarantors, and residual interests) (FAS-140, par. 364).

Transfers of financial assets that meet the above criteria are accounted for as follows (FAS-140, par. 11):

- All assets sold are derecognized.

- All assets obtained and liabilities incurred in consideration as proceeds are recognized. (*Proceeds* refers to cash, derivatives, or other assets that are obtained in a transfer of financial assets, less any liabilities incurred. FAS-156 requires separately recognized servicing assets to be included as part of the proceeds of the sale rather than as an interest that continues to be held by the transferor [FAS-156, par. 4d].)

- Assets obtained and liabilities incurred are measured at fair value, if practicable, and otherwise by alternative measures.

- Any gain or loss on the sale is recognized in income.

After a transfer of financial assets has been recorded in accordance with FAS-140, the transferor shall initially recognize and measure at *fair value*, if practicable, servicing assets and servicing liabilities that are required to be recognized per paragraph 13 of FAS-140. The transferor shall also continue to carry in its statement of financial position any interests that continue to be held in the transferred assets, the amount of which is determined by an allocation of the previous carrying amount based on fair value. Examples of interests that continue to be held by the transferor in the transferred assets are (FAS-140, par. 10, as amended by FAS-156):

- Beneficial interests in assets transferred to a qualified special-purpose entity in a *securitization* (i.e., a process by which financial assets are transformed into securities).

- *Undivided interests* (i.e., partial legal or beneficial ownership of an asset as tenant in common with others).

If the criteria for a sale have not been met, both parties should account for the transaction as a secured borrowing. The transferor should not recognize a gain or loss as a result of the transaction.

SECURITIZATIONS

Securitization refers to the process by which financial assets (such as loans and other receivables) are transformed into securities

(FAS-140, par. 364). Securitizations typically involve a transfer of assets to a special-purpose entity (SPE), through which the characteristics of those assets are changed (e.g., by credit enhancements or derivatives that alter the interest rate or currency characteristics of the original cash flows of the assets). The SPE issues beneficial interests in those assets to third-party investors. Entities enter into securitization transactions for a variety of reasons, for example, to obtain funding more economically or to change the characteristics of the assets transferred to achieve different regulatory or accounting treatment.

Certain types of SPEs, termed *qualifying SPEs* (or *QSPEs*), are given special recognition under FAS-140. Assuming a transfer of assets to a QSPE meets the conditions for a sale under FAS-140, the transferor (and generally all parties involved with the entity) is not required to consolidate the assets and liabilities of the QSPE. This treatment is based on the premise that a QSPE is a very limited, passive vehicle that acts as a conduit to distribute cash flows to investors. In order to be considered a QSPE, an entity must meet four very restrictive conditions (FAS-140, par. 35):

1. The entity is demonstrably distinct from the transferor.
2. The entity's permitted activities are significantly limited and pre-specified by the legal documents establishing the entity.
3. It may hold passive financial instruments, guarantees, servicing rights related to assets held, cash or investments pending distribution to beneficial interest holders, and nonfinancial assets obtained in collection, but only on a temporary basis.
4. It may sell assets only as an automatic response to certain triggering events.

Transfers to a QSPE should be evaluated under the control criteria, taking into consideration the nature of the QSPE, the transferor's rights under the arrangement, and the extent of interests that continue to be held by the transferor. For example, a transferor's right to reacquire specific assets held by the QSPE indicates that the transferor has not relinquished effective control over the assets. Accordingly, the transferor may not account for the transfer of assets as a sale. If the criteria for a sale are not met, then both the transferor and transferee(s) should account for the transaction as a secured borrowing.

In situations where a transfer of assets in a securitization transaction qualifies as a sale, the transferor must recognize any interests it continues to hold (such as subordinated interests or servicing rights). Interest only strips, loans, other receivables, or interests that continue to be held by a transferor in securitizations that can contractually be prepaid or otherwise settled in a manner that the holder would not recover substantially all of its recorded investment are measured like investments in debt securities and classified as either available-for-sale or trading in accordance with FAS-115 (FAS-140, par. 14).

> ☞ **PRACTICE POINTER:** The determination of whether an entity is a QSPE, the evaluation of control criteria for the transfer of assets to a QSPE, and the determination of the gain or loss to be recognized by the transferor are highly technical and much interpreted areas. Practitioners encountering these areas should seek the advice of experts.

Consolidation of QSPEs and Other Securitization Entities

An entity that qualifies as a QSPE is not consolidated by the transferor or its affiliates (FAS-140, par. 46). Further, no other entity consolidates the QSPE unless that entity has the unilateral ability to cause the QSPE to liquidate or change such that it would no longer qualify as a QSPE (FIN-46(R), par. 4(d)). Other entities used to effect securitization transactions must be evaluated under the guidance in FIN-46(R).

FIN-46(R) establishes the term *variable interest entity*, which refers to an entity that has insufficient equity at risk or lack of a controlling financial interest. Specific conditions in FIN-46(R) must be evaluated to establish whether an entity is a variable interest entity and must therefore be consolidated by the entity determined to be the primary beneficiary. Many SPEs are variable interest entities subject to FIN-46 (R); however, the guidance in FIN-46(R) encompasses other types of entities as well. A more detailed discussion of FIN 46(R) can be found in the chapter in this *Guide* titled "Consolidated Financial Statements."

ACCOUNTING FOR SERVICING ASSETS AND LIABILITIES

Initial Measurement of Servicing Assets and Servicing Liabilities

Servicing assets and servicing liabilities that are required to be separately recognized shall be initially measured at fair value, if practicable. An entity is required to recognize a servicing asset or servicing liability each time it undertakes an obligation to service a financial asset by entering into a servicing contract in any of the following situations (FAS-140, par. 13, as amended by FAS-156):

- A transfer of the servicer's financial assets that meets the requirements for sale accounting.

- A transfer of the servicer's financial assets to a qualifying special-purpose entity (SPE) in a guaranteed mortgage securitization in which the transferor retains all of the securities and classifies them as either available-for-sale securities or trading securities in accordance with FAS-115 (Accounting for Certain Investments in Debt and Equity Securities).

- An acquisition or assumption of a servicing obligation that does not relate to financial assets of the servicer or its consolidated affiliates.

An entity that transfers financial assets to a qualifying SPE in a guaranteed mortgage securitization and that classifies its retained securities as debt securities held-to-maturity in accordance with FAS-115 may either separately recognize its servicing assets or servicing liabilities or report those servicing assets or servicing liabilities together with the asset being serviced.

Subsequent Measurement of Servicing Assets and Servicing Liabilities

An entity may choose between two alternative methods of subsequent measurement for each class of separately recognized servicing assets and servicing liabilities—the amortization method and the fair value measurement method. Using the amortization method, servicing assets and servicing liabilities are amortized over the estimated service period and assessed for impairment or increased obligation based on fair value at each reporting period. Using the fair value measurement method, servicing assets and servicing liabilities are measured at their fair value each reporting date with changes in their fair value reported in earnings in the period in which the changes occur.

An entity must separately select, at the beginning of a fiscal year, either the amortization method or the fair value method for subsequent measurement for each class of servicing assets and servicing liabilities and must then apply the selected method to every servicing asset and servicing liability in a class. Classes of servicing assets and servicing liabilities are identified based on (a) the availability of market inputs used in determining the fair values, (b) an entity's method for managing the risks of its servicing assets and servicing liabilities, or (c) both (a) and (b). An election to use the fair value method for subsequent measurement for a class of servicing assets and servicing liabilities cannot be later reversed (FAS-140, par 13, as amended by FAS-156).

One-Time Option to Reclassify Available-for-Sale Securities

FAS-156 permits an entity to make a one-time election to reclassify available-for-sale securities as trading securities without calling into question the treatment of those securities under FAS-115. This election is limited to those available-for-sale securities that an entity intended to use to mitigate the income statement effects of changes in the fair value of servicing assets and servicing liabilities for which the entity has elected the fair value method of subsequent measurement (FAS-156, par. 10). This option can only be exercised as of the beginning of the fiscal year in which the entity adopts FAS-156.

SECURED BORROWINGS AND COLLATERAL

A debtor may grant a security interest in assets to a lender (identified below as the secured party) as collateral for its obligation under a borrowing. If collateral is transferred to the secured party, the arrangement is often referred to as a *pledge*. In some circumstances, a secured party is permitted to sell or repledge collateral it holds under a pledge.

Accounting for collateral by the debtor and the secured party depends on whether the secured party has the right to sell or repledge the collateral and whether the debtor has defaulted under the secured contract.

The following summarizes the accounting by both the debtor and the secured party for collateral transferred in a secured borrowing under several scenarios (FAS-140, par. 15):

Scenario	Accounting Requirements
The secured party is permitted to sell or repledge the collateral.	*Debtor*—Reclassifies the asset and reports it separately from other assets not so encumbered.
	Secured party—Does not recognize the collateral as its asset.
The secured party sells or repledges the collateral.	*Debtor*—Continues to carry the collateral as its asset.
	Secured party—Recognizes the proceeds from the sale of the collateral and records an obligation to return the asset.
The debtor defaults under the contract secured by the collateral and is no longer entitled to the return of the collateral.	*Debtor*—Derecognizes the collateral
	Secured party—Recognizes the collateral as its asset at fair value (or, if the collateral has already been sold, derecognizes the obligation to return the collateral).

EXTINGUISHMENT OF LIABILITIES

A liability is considered extinguished if: (1) the debtor is relieved of its obligations as a result of having paid the creditor or (2) the debtor is legally released from its obligation. A liability must be extinguished before the debtor is permitted to derecognize the liability (FAS-140, par. 16).

DISCLOSURES

FAS-140 includes various disclosure requirements related to transfers and servicing of financial assets and extinguishment of liabilities. These disclosures are summarized as follows (FAS-140, par. 17, as amended by FAS-156):

Disclosures Required in Specified Situations

Condition Requiring Disclosure	Information Required to Be Disclosed
Collateral	
1. Entity has entered into repurchase agreements or securities lending transactions.	Policy for requiring collateral or other security
2. Assets have been pledged and they are not reclassified and separately reported in the balance sheet.	The carrying amounts of the assets and their classification
3. Collateral that can be sold or pledged has been accepted by the entity.	The fair value of the collateral Any amount of the collateral that has been sold or pledged A description of the sources and uses of the collateral
Extinguishment of Debt	
4. Debt was considered extinguished under FAS-76 (Extinguishment of Debt) prior to the effective date of FAS-125 (the predecessor standard to FAS-140).	General description of the transaction and the amount of debt that is considered extinguished at the end of the period so long as that debt is outstanding
5. Assets are set aside after the effective date of FAS-125 (the predecessor standard to FAS-140) solely for satisfying scheduled payments of a specific obligation.	Description of the nature of restrictions placed on such assets

Condition Requiring Disclosure	Information Required to Be Disclosed
Transfers of Assets	
6. It is not practicable to estimate the fair value of certain assets obtained or liabilities incurred in transfers of financial assets during the period.	Description of those items and the reasons why it is not practicable to estimate fair value
Servicing Assets and Liabilities	
7. The entity has servicing assets or servicing liabilities.	Management's basis for determining its classes
	Description of risks and, if applicable, the instruments used to mitigate the income statements effect of changes in their fair value
	Amount of contractually specified servicing fees earned for each period
8. Servicing assets and servicing liabilities are subsequently measured at fair value.	For each class, the activity in the balance of servicing assets and the activity in the balance of servicing liabilities
	Description of the valuation techniques or other methods used to estimate fair value
9. Servicing assets and servicing liabilities are subsequently amortized.	For each class, the activity in the balance of servicing assets and the activity in the balance of servicing liabilities
	For each class, the fair value at the beginning of the period
	Description of the valuation techniques or other methods used to estimate fair value
	Risk characteristics used to stratify for purposes of measuring impairment
	Activity by class in any valuation allowance for impairment of recognized servicing assets

Condition Requiring Disclosure	Information Required to Be Disclosed

Securitizations

10. Financial assets have been securitized and recorded as a sale (disclose separately for each major asset type).

The entity's accounting policy for measuring the intercsts that continue to be held by the transferor and servicing assets or servicing liabilities, including the method used to determine fair value

Characteristics of the securitizations (e.g., a discussion of the transferor's continuing involvement)

Gain or loss from securitizations

Key assumptions used in determining the fair value of interests that continue to be held by the transferor and servicing assets or servicing liabilities (e.g., discount rates, expected prepayments and credit losses, etc.)

Any cash flows, unless repored elsewhere, between the special purpose entity established to consummate the securitization and the sponsoring entity (i.e., the transferor)

Interests That Continue to Be Held

11. Interests that continue to be held by the transferor in financial assets that it has securitized, or servicing assets or servicing liabilities related to assets it has securitized, exist at the balance sheet date (disclose separately for each major asset type).

Accounting policy for subsequently measuring those interests, including how fair value is determined

Key assumptions underlying subsequent measures of fair value (e.g., discount rates, expected prepayments and credit losses.)

Results of sensitivity testing—how the fair value of those interests (including any servicing assets or servicing liabilities) would change given two or more unfavorable variations from the expected level for each key assumptions (see previous disclosure)

Condition Requiring Disclosure	*Information Required to Be Disclosed*
	Total principal amount outstanding, the amount derecognized, the amount still recognized in each category reported in the balance sheet, delinquencies at period end, credit losses during the year for securitized assets, and other financial assets managed with the securitized assets

IMPLEMENTATION GUIDANCE

Appendix A of FAS-140 describes certain provisions of the standard in more detail and describes how they apply to certain types of transactions.

The specific areas for which implementation guidance is provided are as follows:

- Isolation beyond the reach of the transferor and its creditors
- Conditions that constrain a transferee
- Qualifying SPE (special-purpose entity)
- Maintaining effective control over transferred assets
- Changes that result in the transferor's regaining control of assets sold
- Measurement of interests held after a transfer of financial assets
- Interests that continue to be held by a transferor
- Servicing assets and liabilities
- Circumstances in which it is not practicable to estimate fair values
- Securitizations
- Removal-of-accounts provisions
- Sales-type and direct financing lease receivables
- Securities lending transactions

- Repurchase agreements and "wash sales"
- Loan syndications
- Loan participations
- Banker's acceptances and risk participations in them
- Factoring arrangements
- Transfers of receivables with recourse
- Extinguishments of liabilities

The following illustrations highlight two of the most important aspects of FAS-140 for which implementation guidance is provided. These illustrations also provide a flavor of the type of implementation guidance included in Appendix A for all of the areas listed above.

Measurement of Interests Held after a Transfer of Financial Assets

The financial-components approach recognizes that financial assets and liabilities are divisible into a variety of components. The approach requires accounting recognition of these different components, rather than treating a financial asset as an inseparable unit that has been entirely sold or entirely retained. This approach is applied in the following illustration, in which the primary transaction is the sale of loans for cash, but in which separate financial assets are recognized for a call option and an interest rate swap, and a separate financial liability is recognized for the recourse obligation.

Illustration of Recording Transfers with Proceeds of Cash, Derivatives, and Other Liabilities

Fowler Company receives $2,625 in cash by selling loans with a fair value of $2,750 and a carrying amount of $2,500, undertaking no servicing responsibility. Fowler Company obtains from the transferee an option (valued at $160) to purchase loans similar to those sold and assumes a recourse obligation (valued at $120) to purchase delinquent loans. Fowler Company simultaneously enters into an interest rate swap agreement (valued at $100) with the transferee in which it receives fixed interest at an above-market rate and pays a floating rate.

The net proceeds and gain on the sale are determined as follows:

Net proceeds:		
Cash received	$2,625	
Plus: Call option	160	
Interest rate swap	100	
Less: Recourse obligation	(120)	
		$2,765
Carrying amount of loans		(2,500)
Gain on sale	$ 265	

The general journal entry to record the transfer and recognize related assets and liabilities is:

Cash	$2,625	
Call option	160	
Interest rate swap	100	
Loans		$2,500
Recourse obligation		120
Gain on sale		265

Interests That Continue to Be Held by a Transferor

Interests in financial assets that continue to be held by the transfer-or—those that are not included as part of the proceeds from the transfer—are measured at the date of the transfer by allocating the previous carrying amount to the components based on their relative fair values. If no fair value can reasonably be estimated for a compo-nent, it is assigned a zero value. The following illustration demon-strates these procedures in three situations in which a company sells loans with a recourse obligation, acquires a call option to repurchase the loans, agrees to service the loans, and continues to hold an interest in the loans via an interest-only strip receivable: where fair values can be estimated for each component, where the fair value of the servic-ing asset cannot be estimated, and where the fair value of the recourse obligation cannot be estimated.

Illustrations of Recording Transfers with Interests That Continue to Be Held by a Transferor

Anderson Company sells loans with a carrying amount of $2,600 to another entity for cash and a call option to repurchase the loans. Anderson Company agrees to service the transferred loans for the other entity and incurs a recourse obligation to repurchase any delinquent loans. Anderson Company also continues to hold an interest in the loans via an interest-only strip receivable.

Fair values are as follows: servicing asset, $90; call option, $175; recourse obligation, $150; interest-only strip receivable, $100. Anderson received $2,730 in cash.

The net proceeds are determined as follows:

Cash received	$2,730
Plus: Call option	175
Servicing assets	90
Less: Recourse obligation	(150)
Net proceeds	$2,845

This carrying amount is allocated to the loans sold and the servicing asset based on relative fair values as follows:

	Fair Value	Percentage of Total Fair Value	Allocated Carrying Amount
Loans sold	$2,845	97	$2,522
Interest-only strip-receivable	100	3	78
Total	$2,945	100	$2,600

The general journal entry to record the transfer is as follows:

Cash	$2,730	
Servicing asset	90	
Call option	175	
Interest-only strip receivable	78	
Loans		$2,600
Recourse obligation		150
Gain		323

This illustration assumes that fair value can be determined for both the servicing asset and the recourse obligation. If fair value cannot be determined for the servicing asset, it is assigned a zero amount and the gain is reduced from $323 to $233, resulting in the following entry:

Cash	$2,730
Servicing asset	-0-
Call option	175
Interest-only strip receivable	78

Loans	$2,600
Recourse obligation	150
Gain	233

On the other hand, if no fair value is available for the recourse obligation, the gain is eliminated and the recourse obligation is increased from $150 to $473, which is the amount that results in zero gain. The recording entry would be as follows:

Cash	$2,730	
Servicing asset	90	
Call option	175	
Interest-only strip receivable	78	
Loans		$2,600
Recourse obligation		473
Gain		-0-

ACCOUNTING FOR TRANSFERS OF FINANCIAL ASSETS
IMPORTANT NOTICE FOR 2009

As the 2009 *GAAP Guide Level A* goes to press, the FASB has outstanding an Exposure Draft of a Statement of Financial Accounting Standards that may have an important impact on the preparation of financial statements in the future.

The proposed standard clarifies and amends FAS-140 (Accounting for Transfers and Servicing of Financial Assets). The proposed standard changes (1) the requirements for derecognizing financial assets and (2) the initial measurement by the transferor of interests related to transferred financial assets.

Under the proposed standard, the transferor could not derecognize financial assets unless the financial assets are isolated from the transferor and its consolidated affiliates. In evaluating whether the transferred assets are isolated from the transferor, the transferor must consider any arrangement or agreement related to the transfer, even if entered into before or after the transfer. In order to account for a transfer as a sale, the following conditions must be met: (1) the transferred portion of the financial assets and any portion retained by the transferor must be a participating interest and (2) the transferred portion must meet the previously discussed conditions for surrender of control. A participating interest is a portion of a financial asset that (1) conveys proportionate ownership rights where the priority of each participating interest is equal, (2) involves no recourse to or subordination by any participating interest holder, and (3) no participating interest holder is entitled to receive cash before any other participating interest holder. If the above conditions are not met, a sale can be recognized only if an entire financial asset or group of financial assets is transferred to a qualifying SPE or to another entity that is not consolidated with the transferor.

Finally, the proposed standard requires the initial recognition of a transferor's beneficial interests at fair value. The current FASB agenda indicates that a final standard is expected in the fourth quarter of 2008.

RELATED CHAPTERS IN 2009 *GAAP GUIDE*
LEVEL A

Chapter 7, "Consolidated Financial Statements"
Chapter 15, "Extinguishment of Debt"
Chapter 17, "Financial Instruments"
Chapter 28, "Investments in Debt and Equity Securities"

RELATED CHAPTERS IN 2009 *GAAP GUIDE*
LEVELS B, C, AND D

Chapter 10, "Consolidated Financial Statements"
Chapter 15, "Extinguishment of Debt"
Chapter 17, "Financial Instruments"
Chapter 25, "Investments in Debt and Equity Securities"
Chapter 40, "Transfer and Servicing of Financial Assets"

RELATED CHAPTER IN 2009 *INTERNATIONAL ACCOUNTING/FINANCIAL REPORTING STANDARDS GUIDE*

Chapter 16, "Financial Instruments"

CHAPTER 46
TROUBLED DEBT RESTRUCTURING

CONTENTS

OVERVIEW

Debt may be restructured for a variety of reasons. A restructuring of debt is considered a troubled debt restructuring (TDR) if the creditor, for economic or legal reasons related to the debtor's financial difficulties, grants a concession to the debtor that it would not otherwise consider. The concession may stem from an agreement between the creditor and the debtor, or it may be imposed by law or court (FAS-15, par. 2).

A loan is impaired if, based on current information and events, it is probable that the creditor will be unable to collect all amounts due according to the contractual terms of the loan agreement, including both the contractual interest and the principal receivable (FAS-114, par. 8).

GAAP for TDR by both debtors and creditors and for impairments of loans by creditors are included in the following pronouncements:

FAS-15   Accounting by Debtors and Creditors for Troubled Debt Restructurings

FAS-114   Accounting by Creditors for Impairment of a Loan

FAS-118   Accounting by Creditors for Impairment of a Loan-Income Recognition and Disclosures

BACKGROUND

A troubled debt restructuring is one in which the creditor grants the debtor certain concessions that would not normally be considered. The concessions are made because of the debtor's financial difficulty, and the creditor's objective is to maximize recovery of its investment. Troubled debt restructurings are often the result of legal proceedings or of negotiation between the parties (FAS-15, par. 2).

Troubled debt restructurings include situations in which (FAS-15, par. 5):

- The creditor accepts a third-party receivable or other asset(s) of the debtor, in lieu of the receivable from the debtor.

- The creditor accepts an equity interest in the debtor in lieu of the receivable. (This is not to be confused with convertible securities, which are *not* troubled debt restructurings.)

- The creditor accepts modification of the terms of the debt, including but not limited to:
    — Reduction in the stated interest
    — Extension of maturity at an interest rate below the current market rate
    — Reduction in face amount of the debt
    — Reduction in accrued interest

The reductions mentioned in 3(*a*), (*c*), and (*d*) can be either absolute or contingent.

For the purposes of FAS-15 (Accounting by Debtors and Creditors for Troubled Debt Restructuring), troubled debt restructurings do *not* include the following (FAS-15, par. 8):

- Changes in lease agreements

- Employment-related agreements, such as deferred compensation contracts or pension plans
- A debtor's failure to pay trade accounts that do not involve a restructure agreement
- A creditor's legal action to collect accounts that do not involve a restructure agreement

A troubled debt restructuring by a debtor in bankruptcy proceedings is permitted under FAS-15 provided that the restructuring does *not* constitute a *general restatement* of the debtor's liabilities (FAS-15, par. 10 and footnote 4).

FAS-114 (Accounting by Creditors for Impairment of a Loan) was issued by the FASB to address inconsistencies in the measurement and recognition of loan impairment. FAS-114 amends FAS-15 to require a creditor to account for all loans that are restructured as part of a TDR involving a modification of terms as an impaired loan.

Not all debt restructuring is considered troubled, even though the debtor is in financial difficulty. Circumstances in which the restructuring is *not* troubled include (FAS-15, par. 7):

- The debtor satisfies the debt by giving assets or equity with a fair value that at least equals either:
  - — The creditor's recorded receivable, or
  - — The debtor's carrying amount of the payable.
- The creditor reduces the interest rate primarily in response to changes in market rates.
- In exchange for the debtor's debt, the debtor issues new debt securities that have an effective interest rate that is at or near the current market interest rate of debt with similar maturity dates and interest rates issued by nontroubled debtors.

> **OBSERVATION:** If the debtor can obtain funds at current market rates and conditions, this provides evidence that the restructuring is not a troubled debt restructuring.

ACCOUNTING FOR TROUBLED DEBT RESTRUCTURINGS

Debtors and creditors account for troubled debt restructurings by the type of restructuring. Types of restructuring include:

1. Transfer of asset(s) in full settlement.
2. Transfer of an equity interest in full settlement.

3. Modification of terms of the debt.
4. Combinations of the above three types.

Transfer of Asset(s)

The debtor recognizes a gain equal to the excess of the carrying amount of the payable (including accrued interest, premiums, etc.) over the fair value of the asset(s) given up. The difference between the fair value and the carrying amount of the asset(s) given up is the gain or loss on the transfer of asset(s), which is also included in net income in the period the transfer occurs (not presented as an extraordinary item) (FAS-15, pars. 13–14).

> ☛ **PRACTICE POINTER:** Determine fair value either by the assets given up or by the amount payable, whichever is more clearly evident. In the case of a partial settlement, however, use the value of the asset(s) given up. This eliminates the need to allocate the fair value of the payable between the settled portion and the remaining outstanding balance.

When the creditor receives assets as full settlement of a receivable, they are accounted for at their fair value at the time of the restructuring. The fair value of the receivable satisfied can be used if it is more clearly determinable than the fair value of the asset or equity acquired. In partial payments the creditor *must* use the fair value of the asset or equity received (FAS-15, par. 28).

The excess of the recorded receivable over the fair value of the assets received (less cost to sell if a long-lived asset is received) is recognized as a loss (FAS-144, par. C24[b]). The creditor accounts for these assets as if they were acquired for cash (FAS-15, par. 29).

Illustration of Transfer of Assets

A debtor owes $20,000, including accrued interest. The creditor accepts land valued at $17,000 and carried on the debtor's books at its $12,000 cost, in full payment.

Under FAS-15, the debtor recognizes two gains: $5,000 ($17,000 − $12,000) on the transfer of the assets, and $3,000 ($20,000 − $17,000) on the extinguishment of debt.

The creditor recognizes a loss of $3,000 ($20,000 − $17,000).

Transfer of Equity Interest

The difference between the fair value of the equity interest and the carrying amount of the payable is recognized as a gain by the debtor (FAS-15, par. 15).

The creditor records the receipt of an equity interest as any other asset by recording the investment at its fair value and recognizing a loss equal to the difference between the fair value of the equity interest and the amount of the receivable (FAS-15, par. 28).

Illustration of Transfer of Equity Interest

A debtor grants an equity interest valued at $10,000, consisting of 500 shares of $15 par value stock, to retire a payable of $12,000. Under FAS-15, the debtor records the issuance of the stock at $10,000 ($7,500 par value and $2,500 additional paid-in capital) and a gain on the extinguishment of debt of $2,000 ($12,000 − $10,000). The creditor records an investment asset of $10,000 and an ordinary loss of $2,000 ($12,000 − $10,000) on the TDR.

☛ **PRACTICE POINTER:** In applying FAS-15, determining the fair value of an equity interest of a debtor company involved in a troubled debt restructuring may be difficult. In many cases, the company's stock will not be publicly traded, and there may be no recent stock transactions that would be helpful. Even if a recent market price were available, consider whether that price reflects the financially troubled status of the company that exists at the time the troubled debt restructuring takes place.

Modification of Terms

A restructuring that does not involve the transfer of assets or equity often involves the modification of the terms of the debt. The debtor accounts for the effects of the restructuring prospectively and does not change the carrying amount unless the carrying amount exceeds the total future cash payments specified by the new terms. The *total future cash payments* are the principal and interest, including any accrued interest at the time of the restructuring that will be payable by the new terms. *Interest expense* is computed by a method that results in a constant effective rate (such as the interest method). The new effective rate of interest is the discount rate at which the carrying amount of the debt is equal to the present value of the future cash payments (FAS-15, par. 16).

When the total future cash payments are less than the carrying amount, the debtor reduces the carrying amount accordingly and recognizes the difference as a gain. When there are several related accounts (e.g., discount, premium), the reduction may need to be allocated among them. All cash payments after the restructuring go toward reducing the carrying amount, and *no* interest expense is recognized after the date of restructure (FAS-15, par. 17).

When there are indeterminate future payments, or any time the future payments might exceed the carrying amount, the debtor recognizes no gain. The debtor assumes that the future contingent payments will have to be made at least to the extent necessary to obviate any gain. In estimating future cash payments, it is assumed that the maximum amount of periods (and interest) is going to occur (FAS-15, par. 18).

A creditor in a TDR involving a modification of terms accounts for the restructured loan in accordance with FAS-114 (FAS-114, par. 22). FAS-114, as amended by FAS-118 (Accounting by Creditors for Impairment of a Loan—Income Recognition and Disclosures), requires that impaired loans be measured at their present value of expected future cash flows discounted at the loan's contractual interest rate, the loan's observable market price, or the fair value of collateral if the loan is collateral-dependent. (See subsequent section in this chapter for more extensive coverage of FAS-114, as amended by FAS-118.)

> **OBSERVATION:** According to FAS-114, a loan is impaired if it is probable that a creditor will be unable to collect all amounts due according to the contractual terms of the loan agreement. A loan whose terms are modified in a TDR will have already been identified as impaired. For purposes of applying FAS-114, a loan is considered collateral-dependent if repayment is expected to be provided solely by the underlying collateral.

Illustration of Modification of Terms

A debtor has a loan to a creditor, details of which are as follows:

Principal	$10,000
Accrued interest	500
Total	$10,500

They agree on a restructuring in which the total future cash payments, both principal and interest, are $8,000. The present value of these payments is $7,500.

Under FAS-15, the debtor recognizes a gain of $2,500 ($10,500 − $8,000) at the time of the restructuring, and all future payments are specified as principal payments. Under FAS-114, the creditor recognizes a loss of $3,000 ($10,500 − $7,500).

> **OBSERVATION:** The FASB recognized that FAS-114 introduced asymmetry between creditors' and debtors' accounting for TDR involving a modification of terms. The Board determined, however, that FAS-114 should deal only with creditor accounting, because to include debtor accounting would delay issuance of a final Statement. Presumably, at some future date, the asymmetry suggested in the above example will be addressed and resolved.

Combination of Types

When a restructuring involves combinations of asset or equity transfers and modification of terms, the debtor first uses the fair value of any asset or equity to reduce the carrying amount of the payable. The difference between the fair value and the carrying amount of any asset(s) transferred is recognized as gain or loss. The remainder of the restructuring is accounted for as a modification of terms in accordance with FAS-15 (FAS-15, par. 19).

The creditor reduces the recorded investment by the fair value of assets received less cost to sell, including an equity interest in the debtor. Thereafter, the creditor accounts for the TDR in accordance with FAS-114 (FAS-15, par. 33).

Related Issues

Amounts contingently payable in future periods are recognized as payable and as interest expense in accordance with the treatment of other contingencies. The criteria for recognizing a loss contingency are the following:

- It is probable that the liability has been incurred.
- The amount can be reasonably estimable.

If any contingently payable amounts were included in the total future cash payments, they must now be deducted from the carrying amount of the restructured payable to the extent they originally prevented recognition of a gain at the time of the restructuring (FAS-15, par. 22).

In estimating future payments subject to fluctuation, estimates are based on the interest rate in effect at the time of restructure. A change in future rates is treated as a change in accounting estimate. The accounting for these fluctuations cannot result in an immediate gain. Rather, the future payments will reduce the carrying amount, and any residual value is considered gain (FAS-15, par. 23).

If a loss from a troubled debt restructuring has been previously provided in a valuation allowance account, the loss is charged first to the valuation allowance and not directly to net income (FAS-15, par. 35).

Interest rates that fluctuate after a restructuring are accounted for as changes in an accounting estimate in the period they occur. The creditor recognizes a loss and reduces its restructured receivable when fluctuations in interest rates cause the minimum future cash receipts to fall below the recorded investment in the restructured receivable (FAS-15, par. 37).

Legal fees and other direct costs resulting from a TDR are expensed by the creditor when incurred (FAS-15, par. 38).

Legal fees and other direct costs that a debtor incurs in granting an equity interest to a creditor reduce the amount otherwise recorded for that equity interest. All other direct costs that a debtor incurs to effect a TDR are deducted in measuring the gain on restructuring of payables or are included in expense for the period, if no gain on restructuring is recognized (FAS-15, par. 24).

A receivable obtained by a creditor from the sale of assets previously obtained in a TDR is accounted for in accordance with APB-21 (Interest on Receivables and Payables), regardless of whether the assets were obtained in satisfaction of a receivable to which APB-21 was not intended to apply (FAS-15, par. 39).

For creditors, a troubled debt restructuring may involve substituting debt of another business enterprise, individual, or governmental unit for that of a troubled debtor. That kind of restructuring should be accounted for according to its substance (FAS-15, par. 42).

DISCLOSURE REQUIREMENTS FOR TROUBLED DEBT RESTRUCTURINGS

Debtors

The debtor must disclose the following regarding any debt restructuring during a period (FAS-15, par. 25):

- Description of the terms of each restructuring
- Aggregate gain on the restructuring
- Aggregate net gain or loss on asset transfer
- Per share amount of aggregate gain on the restructuring

The debtor also should disclose contingently payable amounts included in the carrying amount of restructured payables and the total of contingently payable amounts and the conditions under which the amounts become payable or are forgiven (FAS-15, par. 26).

Creditors

The creditor shall disclose the following regarding troubled debt restructurings (FAS-15, par. 40; FAS-118, par. 6i):

1. As of the date of each statement of financial position presented, the total recorded investment in the impaired loans at the end of each period, as well as (*a*) the amount of the recorded investment for which there is a related allowance for credit losses, and the amount of that allowance; and (*b*) the amount of the recorded investment for which there is no related allowance for credit losses

2. The creditor's policy for recognizing interest income on impaired loans, including how cash receipts are recorded

3. For each period for which results of operations are presented, the average recorded investment in the impaired loans during each period; the related amount of interest income recognized during the time within that period that the loans were impaired; and, if practicable, the amount of interest income recognized (cash-basis method of accounting) during the time within that period that the loans were impaired

4. Amount(s) of any commitment(s) to lend additional funds to any debtor who is a party to a restructuring

All four disclosures may be made in the aggregate or by major category (FAS-15, par. 41).

IMPAIRMENT OF LOANS

FAS-114 defines a *loan* as "a contractual right to receive money on demand or on fixed or determinable dates that is recognized as an asset in the creditor's statement of financial position." It addresses how allowances for credit losses related to certain loans should be determined. The Statement has wide applicability, establishing standards for all creditors for impairment of loans (FAS-114, par. 4).

FAS-114 does not specify how a creditor should identify loans that are to be evaluated for collectibility. A creditor may apply its normal loan review procedures in making that judgment. Guidance for this decision is found in the AICPA's Audit Procedure Study *Auditing the Allowance for Credit Losses of Banks* and includes the following items (FAS-114, footnote 1):

- Materiality criterion
- Regulatory reports of examination
- Internally generated listings such as "watch lists," past due reports, overdraft listings, and listings of loans to insiders
- Management reports of total loan amounts by borrower
- Historical loss experience by type of loan
- Loan files lacking current financial data related to borrowers and guarantors
- Borrowers experiencing problems such as operating losses, marginal working capital, inadequate cash flow, or business interruptions
- Loans secured by collateral that is not readily marketable or that is subject to deterioration in realizable value
- Loans to borrowers in industries or countries experiencing economic instability
- Loan documentation and compliance exception reports

Direct write-downs of an impaired loan and assessment of overall adequacy of the allowance for credit losses are not covered in FAS-114. FAS-114 applies to all impaired loans except (FAS-114, par. 6):

- A large group of homogeneous loans with small balances where impairment is evaluated on a collective basis (e.g., home mortgage, credit card, consumer installment loans)
- Loans carried at fair value or at the lower of cost or fair value
- Leases
- Debt securities (per FAS-115)

> **OBSERVATION:** The FASB believes that accounting for impaired loans should be consistent among all creditors and types of loans, except those specifically identified above as loans to which FAS-114 does not apply. The Board was unable to identify any compelling reasons why the lending process for consumer, mortgage, commercial, and other loans—whether uncollateralized or collateralized—is fundamentally different. In addition, the Board could not identify any compelling reasons why different types of creditors should account for impaired loans differently, or why financial statement users for a particular industry or size of entity would be better served by accounting that differs from that of other creditors.

Recognition of Impairment

FAS-114 ties accounting for an impairment of a loan directly to the criteria established in FAS-5 (Accounting for Contingencies) for recognizing a loss contingency. Specifically, FAS-114 indicates that a loan is impaired when it is *probable* that a creditor will be unable to collect all amounts due, including principal and interest, according to the contractual terms and schedules of the loan agreement. Normal loan review procedures are to be used in making that judgment. A loan is not considered impaired if (FAS-114, par. 8):

- There is merely an insignificant delay or shortfall in amounts of payments.

- The creditor expects to collect all amounts due, including interest accrued at the contractual interest rate for the period of the delay.

> **OBSERVATION:** Use of the term *probable* in FAS-114 is consistent with its use in FAS-5. FAS-5 indicates a range of probability that must be considered in the decision to accrue a loss contingency, including *probable, reasonably possible,* and *remote.* Virtual certainty is not required before a loss can be accrued. While FAS-114 changes the wording of FAS-5 as it relates to loan impairments that require accrual, it does not change the overall intent of applying FAS-5 standards (FAS-114, par. 10).

Measurement of Impairment

The process of measuring impaired loans requires judgment and estimation, and the eventual outcomes may differ from the estimates. Following is guidance concerning the measurement of impaired loans under FAS-114. Measurement may be on a loan-by-loan or an aggregate basis (FAS-114, par. 12).

- Impairment generally is based on the present value of expected future cash flows discounted at the loan's effective interest rate. As a practical matter, a creditor may measure impairment based on a loan's observable market price or on the fair value of the collateral if the loan is collateral dependent (FAS-114, par. 13).

- A loan is considered collateral dependent when the creditor determines that foreclosure is probable or if the loan is expected to be repaid solely by the underlying collateral (FAS-114, par. 13).

- Estimated costs to sell, on a discounted basis, may be a factor in measuring impairment if those costs are expected to reduce the cash flow available to repay or otherwise satisfy the loan (FAS-114, par. 13).

- If the present value of expected future cash flows (or the loan's observable market price or the collateral's fair value) is less than the recorded investment in the loan (including accrued interest, net deferred loan fees or costs, and unamortized premium or discount), the creditor shall recognize the impairment by creating or adjusting a valuation allowance with a corresponding charge to bad-debt expense (FAS-114, par. 13; FAS-118, par. 6d).

- The present value amount, based on estimated future cash flows of an impaired loan, is discounted at the loan's contractual interest rate. That rate is the rate of return implicit in the loan (FAS-114, par. 14).

  — For a loan restructured in a troubled debt restructuring, present value is based on the original contractual rate, not on the rate specified in the restructuring agreement.

  — If the loan's contractual rate varies based on changes in an independent factor, such as an index or a rate, the loan's effective interest rate may be calculated based on the factor as it changes over the life of the loan, or it may be fixed at the rate that is in effect at the date the loan meets the impairment criteria. (The alternative chosen shall be applied consistently for all loans whose contractual interest rate varies based on subsequent changes in an independent factor.)

- In estimating expected future cash flows, all available evidence should be considered—including the estimated costs to sell if those costs are expected to reduce the cash flows available to repay or otherwise satisfy the loan. The weight given to the evidence should be commensurate with the extent to which the evidence can be objectively verified (FAS-114, par. 15).

- After the initial measurement of impairment, any significant change in the amount or timing of an impaired loan's expected or actual future cash flows should be reflected by a recalculation of the impairment and an adjustment to the allowance account (FAS-114, par. 16).

> **OBSERVATION:** FAS-114 requires that impairment be measured based on the loan's effective interest rate. Alternatively, impairment can be measured based on a new direct measurement of the asset, reflecting the current market rate of interest. The Board concluded that the measurement of impairment should recognize the change in the net carrying amount of the loan based on new information about expected future cash flows, rather than on other factors that may cause a change in the fair value of an impaired loan.

Income Measurement

FAS-118 amends FAS-114 to indicate that guidance is not provided concerning how a creditor should recognize, measure, or display interest income on an impaired loan. Some accounting methods for recognizing income may result in a recorded investment in an impaired loan that is less than the present value of expected future cash flows (or other basis for valuing the loan). In this case, no additional impairment would be recognized. Those accounting methods include recognition of interest income using a cost-recovery method, a cash-basis method, or some combination of those methods. The recorded investment in an impaired loan also may be less than the present value of expected future cash flows (or other basis for valuing the loan) because the creditor has charged off part of the loan (FAS-118, par. 6g).

Disclosures

FAS-118 requires that certain information be disclosed, either in the body of the financial statements or in accompanying notes, for loans that meet the definition of an impaired loan. (See page 47.09 for a discussion of these disclosure requirements.)

In addition, for each period for which results of operations are presented, a creditor shall disclose the activity in the total allowance for credit losses related to loans, including the beginning balances at the beginning and end of the period, additions charged to operations, direct write-downs charged against the allowance, and recoveries of amounts previously charged off (FAS-118, par. 6i).

RELATED CHAPTERS IN 2009 *GAAP GUIDE* *LEVEL A*

Chapter 15, "Extinguishment of Debt"
Chapter 20, "Impairment of Long-Lived Assets"
Chapter 25, "Interest on Receivables and Payables"
Chapter 40, "Results of Operations"

RELATED CHAPTERS IN 2009 *GAAP GUIDE* *LEVELS B, C, AND D*

Chapter 16, "Extinguishment of Debt"
Chapter 19, "Impairment of Long-Lived Assets"
Chapter 22, "Interest on Receivables and Payables"
Chapter 35, "Results of Operations"
Chapter 41, "Troubled Debt Restructuring"

Specialized Industry
Accounting Principles

CHAPTER 47
BANKING AND THRIFT INSTITUTIONS

CONTENTS

OVERVIEW

Specialized industry GAAP for banking and thrift institutions focus on business combinations, with particular emphasis on the determination of goodwill and other assets acquired.

GAAP for banking and thrift institutions are located in the following pronouncements:

FAS-72   Accounting for Certain Acquisitions of Banking or Thrift Institutions

FIN-9   Applying APB Opinions No. 16 and 17 When a Savings and Loan Association or a Similar Institution Is Acquired in a Business Combination Accounted for by the Purchase Method

FAS-147   Acquisitions of Certain Financial Institutions—An Amendment of FASB Statements No. 72 and 144 and FASB Interpretation No. 9

FAS-72 (Accounting for Certain Acquisitions of Banking or Thrift Institutions) amended APB-17 (Intangible Assets) with regard to the amortization of unidentifiable intangible assets (i.e., goodwill) recognized in certain business combinations accounted for by the purchase method. FIN-9 (Applying APB Opinions No. 16 and 17 When a Savings and Loan Association or a Similar Institution Is Acquired in a Business Combination Accounted for by the Purchase Method) concluded that the net-spread method should not be used in determining the amount of goodwill or other intangible assets that are acquired in a business combination accounted for by the purchase method. As a result of FAS-147 (Acquisitions of Certain Financial Institutions—An Amendment of FASB Statements No. 72 and 144 and FASB Interpretation No. 9), the guidance in FAS-72 and FIN-9 now only apply to business combinations involving financial institutions that are mutual enterprises. FAS-147 extends the accounting guidance in FAS-141 (Business Combinations) and FAS-142 (Goodwill and Other Intangible Assets) to most business combinations involving financial institutions.

2009 TRANSITION GUIDANCE FOR FAS-141(R) AND FAS-160

The FASB has recently issued FAS-141(R), *Business Combinations,* which is effective for business combinations for which the acquisition date is on or after the beginning of the first annual reporting period beginning on or after December 15, 2008. The FASB has also issued FAS-160, *Noncontrolling Interests in Consolidated Financial Statements, an Amendment of ARB No. 51,* which is effective for fiscal years, and interim periods within those fiscal years, beginning on or after December 15, 2008. Because these standards are not effective for some companies until December 2009, and because early adoption is prohibited, the 2009 *GAAP Guide* reflects the requirements of FAS-141 prior to its revision in December 2007 and does not reflect the requirements of FAS-160. There is a discussion of the changes in the accounting for business combinations under FAS-141(R) in the Appendix to Chapter 4, "Business Combinations." Similarly, the Appendix to Chapter 7, "Consolidated Financial Statements" includes a discussion of the requirements of FAS-160. However, any effects of FAS-141(R) and/or FAS-160 on this chapter have not been reflected in this edition. Therefore, if a company is subject to the requirements of FAS-141(R) and/or FAS-160, the reader is referred to FAS-141(R) and FAS-160 for these new requirements.

BACKGROUND

FAS-72 was applicable to the acquisition of a financial institution, and specifically to the excess of the fair value of assumed liabilities over the fair value of acquired identifiable assets. Acquisitions of financial institutions where the fair value of assumed liabilities exceeds the fair value of acquired identifiable assets typically arose from the acquisition of a troubled banking or thrift institution. FAS-72 required that any such excess be recognized as an unidentifiable intangible asset (FAS-147, par. A8).

The guidance in FAS-72 conflicted with the guidance in FAS-141 and FAS-142 in two primary ways. First, it is likely that a portion of the unidentifiable intangible asset recognized under FAS-72 was, using the FAS-141 guidance, an identifiable intangible asset. Second, and more substantively, FAS-72 required the amortization of the unidentifiable intangible asset. FAS-142 proscribes the amortization of goodwill; rather, goodwill is periodically evaluated for evidence of impairment (FAS-147, pars. A3, A15). Therefore, prior to the issuance and effective date of FAS-147, business combinations involving troubled banking or thrift institutions were accounted for differently than business combinations in other industries.

FAS-147 applies to business combinations involving financial institutions, except those combinations between mutual enterprises. Financial institutions include commercials banks, savings and loan associations, credit unions, and other depository institutions holding similar types of assets and liabilities. Moreover, the expansion of the scope of FAS-144 to include long-term customer-relationship intangible assets would apply to all types of entities, including mutual enterprises (FAS-147, par. 4 and footnote 1).

BUSINESS COMBINATION ACCOUNTING

An acquisition of a financial institution, or part of a financial institution if the partial acquisition meets the definition of a business combination, is to be accounted for in accordance with FAS-141. In order for a partial acquisition to meet the definition of a business combination, the transferred assets and activities must constitute a business. EITF Issue 98-3 (Determining Whether a Nonmonetary Transaction Involves Receipt of Productive Assets or of a Business), provides guidance on determining whether the transferred assets and activities constitute a business (FAS-147, par. 5).

EITF Issue 98-3 indicates that a business consists of (*a*) inputs, (*b*) processes applied to those inputs, and (*c*) resulting outputs that are used to generate revenues. For a transferred set of activities and assets to be a business, it must contain all of the inputs and processes necessary for it to continue to conduct normal operations after the transferred set is separated from the transferor (see Chapter 28 of the 2008 *GAAP Guide Levels B, C, and D* for additional discussion of EITF Issue 98-3 and the definition of a business). If an acquisition does not meet the definition of a business combination, the purchase price is to be allocated to the individual assets acquired and liabilities assumed based on their relative fair values. Goodwill is not to be recognized.

In the banking industry, it is sometimes uncertain as to whether the acquisition of a branch meets the definition of a business combination. FAS-147 suggests that the acquisition of a branch (the acquisition of less than an entire financial institution) often would not meet the definition of a business combination. Two factors to consider (although neither is determinative) in making this determination is whether the bank's charter is transferred and whether deposit insurance coverage is granted as part of the regulatory approval of the acquisition (FAS-147, pars. A9–A11).

> **OBSERVATION:** As a result of FAS-147, business combinations involving financial institutions (with the exception of business combinations involving mutual enterprises) are treated the same as business combinations in other industries. The applicable accounting guidance for business combinations involving financial institutions is FAS-141 and FAS-142.

Allocating the Cost of an Acquisition

Independent appraisals and/or subsequent sales of acquired assets may provide evidence of fair value. Each identifiable tangible and intangible asset acquired is assigned a portion of the acquisition cost, equal to its fair value at the date of acquisition (FAS-141, par. 35).

The fair value of a long-term interest-bearing asset is the present value of the amount that will be received, less an allowance for uncollectible accounts. The fair value of an assumed liability is its present value at the prevailing interest rates at the date of acquisition (FAS-141, par. 37). A portion of the total acquisition cost is allocated to contingent assets, contingent liabilities, and contingent impairments of assets, if any, provided that (FAS-141, par. 40):

- It is *probable* that the contingent item existed at the consummation date of the business combination accounted for by the purchase method;
- After the consummation date, but prior to the end of the *allocation period*, the facts in item 1 are confirmed; and
- The amount of the asset, liability, or impairment can be *estimated reasonably*.

If the preceding conditions are met, the purchase method requires that a portion of the total cost of acquiring a bank institution be allocated to any contingent items. The allocation period is that which is required by the purchaser to identify and quantify the acquired assets and assumed liabilities for the purposes of allocating the total cost of the acquisition in accordance with FAS-141. The allocation period usually will not exceed one year from the closing date of the purchase transaction (FAS-141, par. F1).

Treatment of an Unidentifiable Intangible Asset

An unidentifiable intangible asset recognized under the provisions of FAS-72 should continue to be amortized *unless the unidentifiable intangible asset arose as part of a business combination*. If the unidentifiable intangible asset arose as part of a business combination, the carrying amount of the unidentifiable intangible asset is to be reclassified as goodwill on the acquisition date (FAS-147, pars. 8–9).

In some cases, however, separate accounting records may have been maintained for intangible assets even though these intangible assets are included in the amount reported as an unidentifiable intangible asset. If these intangible assets arise from contractual or other legal rights, or if they are separable from the entity (see paragraph 39 of FAS-141), they are to be accounted for separately and not reclassified as goodwill. The reclassified goodwill is accounted for prospectively under FAS-142 (FAS-147, par. 9).

IMPAIRMENT GUIDANCE

FAS-147 expands the scope of FAS-144 to include impairments of long-term customer-relationship intangible assets. Examples include depositor- and borrower-relationship intangible assets and credit cardholder intangible assets. Depositor-relationship intangible assets are also referred to as core deposit intangible assets (FAS-147, pars. 15, A16). The expansion of FAS-144 to include impairments of long-term customer-relationship intangible assets applies to all types of financial institutions, including mutual enterprises (FAS-147, par. 4).

Any impairment loss is to be included in determining income in the first period that the FAS-144 impairment loss recognition criteria are applied and met. Any such impairment loss is not to be reported as a cumulative effect adjustment of a change in accounting principle (FAS-147, par. 15).

BUSINESS COMBINATIONS INVOLVING FINANCIAL INSTITUTIONS THAT ARE MUTUAL ENTERPRISES

FAS-147 superseded the accounting guidance in FAS-72 and FIN-9 for business combinations involving financial institutions, except for those combinations between mutual enterprises. Mutual enterprises were excluded from the scope of FAS-147 because the FASB has an ongoing project to provide guidance on accounting and reporting for transactions between mutual enterprises (FAS-147, par. A4). Therefore, the guidance in FAS-72 and FIN-9 continues to apply to business combinations involving financial institutions between mutual enterprises.

At the times that FAS-72 and FIN-9 were issued, many of the business combinations involving financial institutions were between a healthy financial institution and a distressed bank or thrift. As a result, much of the accounting guidance pertains to the acquisition of a troubled bank or thrift.

> **OBSERVATION:** The remaining material in this chapter only applies to mutual enterprises.

Net-Spread Method and Separate-Valuation Method

The two methods available to record the acquisition of a savings and loan association are the *net-spread method* and the *separate-valuation method*.

Under the net-spread method, the spread between interest paid on deposits and interest received on mortgages is used to evaluate whether the difference is normal, subnormal, or above normal for a particular market area. If the spread is normal, the principal assets and liabilities that are being acquired are recorded at the carrying amounts shown on the financial statements of the association being acquired. If the spread is subnormal or above normal, an adjustment is made to compensate for the difference. The acquisition is viewed as the purchase of an entire business and not of separate individual assets. The net-spread method is not acceptable for the purposes of GAAP (FIN-9, par. 4).

The separate-valuation method is based on recording the acquired identifiable assets at fair value at the date of purchase. Any difference between the fair value of assets acquired less liabilities assumed is recorded as purchased goodwill (FIN-9, par. 3).

Fair value of assets is influenced by the ability of the assets to generate future income and/or new business within the territory served. Therefore, if the amount paid for the assets to generate future income or new business can be determined reliably, it is not recorded as goodwill, but the fair value of the separately identifiable intangible asset is recorded and amortized over its estimated life (FAS-141, par. E20e). Any portion of the purchase price that cannot specifically be allocated to identifiable tangible or intangible assets is recorded as goodwill (FIN-9, par. 8).

> **OBSERVATION:** Although FAS-147 supersedes FIN-9 as it relates to business combinations involving financial institutions (with the exception of mutual enterprises), FAS-147 states that the application of the net-spread method is not consistent with the requirements of FAS-141 (FAS-147, par. A21 and footnote 14).

Acquisitions of Troubled Banking Institutions

Upon acquisition of a banking or thrift institution, the excess of the fair value of liabilities assumed over the fair value of the acquired identifiable assets is classified as goodwill (FAS-72, par. 5).

> **OBSERVATION:** Under the purchase method of accounting for a business combination, goodwill is the difference between the cost of the acquisition and the fair value of the net assets acquired. However, FAS-72 does not necessarily apply to the amount of goodwill computed in this manner. FAS-72 applies only to the excess of the fair value of the liabilities assumed over the fair value of the identifiable tangible and intangible assets acquired.

GOODWILL

When a troubled banking or thrift institution is acquired, the excess of the fair value of the liabilities assumed over the fair value of the individual identifiable assets acquired is accounted for as goodwill (FAS-72, par. 5).

Under existing GAAP (FAS-142), goodwill is no longer amortized, but rather is periodically examined for potential impairment. However, goodwill arising from the acquisition of a troubled banking or thrift institution, involving mutual enterprises, still is amortized.

The FASB concluded that goodwill arising in the acquisition of a troubled banking institution should be amortized over a relatively short period because of the uncertainty about the nature and extent of the estimated future benefits related to the goodwill, because (FAS-72, par. 32):

- Goodwill has always been related to the excess future profits a business is likely to earn. It is extremely difficult to justify goodwill in the acquisition of a troubled banking institution that has been incurring large losses.

- CON-3 (Elements of the Financial Statements of Business Enterprises) defines an asset as a probable future economic benefit obtained or controlled by an entity as a result of a past transaction or event. It is doubtful whether goodwill resulting from the acquisition of a troubled banking institution can be classified properly as a *probable future economic benefit*.

> **OBSERVATION:** The preceding factors could lead to the conclusion that any goodwill arising in the acquisition of a troubled banking institution should be written off to expense at the time of acquisition. The FASB prefers a special amortization period and method as a middle ground between the two extremes of (*a*) complete write-off immediately upon acquisition and (*b*) carrying the asset indefinitely, with periodic review for impairment, as provided by FAS-142.

Identifiable Intangible Assets

Identifiable assets include intangible assets at appraised values that can be identified and named, including (FIN-9, par. 6):

- Contracts
- Patents
- Franchises
- Customer lists
- Supplier lists
- Leases

Identifiable intangible assets of a banking or thrift institution may including existing depositor or borrow relationships, such as the capacity of existing savings and loan accounts to generate future income and/or additional business or new business (FIN-9, par. 8). The fair value of these types of identifiable intangible assets must be determined reliably based on existing facts at the date of acquisition without regard to future events (FAS-72, par. 4). If an acquisition of a banking or thrift institution includes any of these types of identifiable intangible assets, a portion of the cost of the acquisition should be assigned to such assets and accounted for similarly to other identifiable intangible assets (see FAS-142).

Maximum Amortization Period

The amount of goodwill and the related periodic amortization, computed in accordance with FAS-72, are calculated at the date of acquisition. The periodic amortization expense is not adjusted in subsequent periods, except as provided by FAS-72 (see below). The maximum period of amortization should not exceed the lesser of 40 years or the estimated remaining life of the long-term interest-bearing assets with maturities in excess of one year, if any, which were acquired in the transaction. If a significant amount of long-term interest-bearing assets with maturities of over one year is not part of the acquisition, goodwill is amortized over the estimated average remaining life of the acquired existing customer deposit base (FAS-72, par. 5).

Method of Amortization

Amortization must be calculated by the use of a constant percentage rate applied to the carrying amount of the long-term interest-bearing assets, which is expected to be outstanding at the beginning of each period. The carrying amount that is expected to be outstanding at the beginning of each period is determined by reference to the terms of the instruments themselves. If any prepayment assumptions are used to calculate the fair value of the acquired long-term interest-bearing assets at the date of acquisition, the same prepayment assumptions must be used to determine the expected carrying amount of long-term interest-bearing assets that will be outstanding in each subsequent period (FAS-72, par. 5).

> **OBSERVATION:** The carrying amount of long-term interest-bearing assets is equal to their face amount, increased or decreased by any related unamortized premium or discount (FAS-72, par. 5).

Subsequent Revision of Amortization

In periods subsequent to the date of acquisition, an enterprise must continually reevaluate the remaining useful life of an intangible asset that is being amortized to determine whether revision of the amortization period is necessary (FAS-72, par. 6; FAS-142, par. D9). If the remaining amortization period is revised, the unamortized cost of the intangible asset must be allocated to the revised period (the total amortization period for an intangible asset can never exceed 40 years from the date of its acquisition). New estimates may indicate the necessity of significantly reducing the carrying amount of an intangible asset (FAS-142, par. 15). Under these circumstances, a charge to net income is made in the applicable year.

If a significant portion of a segment or severable group of the operating assets of an acquired banking or thrift institution is subsequently sold or otherwise disposed of, a proportionate amount of the unamortized goodwill is allocated and charged to the cost of the sale. The sale of acquired long-term interest-bearing assets may result in the loss of the customer base. If the estimated value or benefits of the related unamortized goodwill are significantly reduced as a result of such a sale or liquidation, the reduction must be recognized as a charge to income in the year of sale or liquidation (FAS-72, par. 7).

☞ **PRACTICE POINTER:** The amount of goodwill that results from the application of FAS-72 may not be revised upward (FAS-72, par. 6). If there is a permanent impairment in the value of an unamortized intangible asset, its carrying amount should be reduced to net realizable value by a charge to income in the year in which the impairment is discovered.

Additional Goodwill

In the acquisition of a banking or thrift institution, the amount of goodwill may exceed the difference between the fair value of the liabilities assumed and the fair value of the assets acquired. If so, additional goodwill is recognized and accounted for in accordance with the provisions of FAS-142.

ACCOUNTING FOR REGULATORY ASSISTANCE

An enterprise may receive financial assistance from a regulatory agency such as the Federal Deposit Insurance Corporation (FDIC) or the Federal Savings and Loan Insurance Corporation (FSLIC) for the acquisition of a banking or thrift institution. The assistance may be immediate or granted in periods subsequent to the date of acquisition. Assets and/or liabilities may be transferred to the regulatory agency.

Additional Interest

A regulatory agency often provides periodic financial assistance that is approximately equal to the difference between the average yield on the long-term interest-bearing assets acquired in the acquisition and the current interest cost of carrying such assets (FAS-72, par. 8).

Under FAS-72, the computation of this type of financial assistance is made at the date of acquisition and is based on the difference between the average yield on the long-term interest-bearing assets and the current interest cost of carrying such assets. The amount thus computed is treated as additional interest on the long-term interest-bearing assets. The additional interest is included in determining the present value (fair value) of the long-term interest-bearing assets at the date of acquisition, and is reported in income of the period in which it accrued (FAS-72, par. 8). No other adjustment is made in the carrying amount of the long-term interest-bearing assets for subsequent changes in the estimated amount of financial assistance.

Long-term interest-bearing assets that the acquiring enterprise intends to sell must be reported at an amount not exceeding current market value (FAS-72, par. 8).

Other Types of Financial Assistance

Other types of financial assistance granted by a regulatory agency are accounted for as part of the combination if (*a*) the assistance is *probable* and (*b*) the amount of assistance can be *reasonably estimated*. Under the purchase method, assets that are, or will be, received as a result of regulatory financial assistance must be assigned a portion of the total acquisition cost of the banking or thrift institution (FAS-72, par. 9).

> **OBSERVATION:** FAS-72 does not cover a situation in which the amount of financial assistance by a regulatory agency exceeds the amount of goodwill that would otherwise be recorded in the transaction. In this event, the fair value of the assets acquired will exceed the fair value of the liabilities assumed. Under the purchase method, the excess of acquired assets over assumed liabilities is accounted for as *negative goodwill*. Under FAS-141, the excess is allocated to other acquired assets (through a reduction in their carrying amount) except: (1) financial assets other than equity method investees, (2) assets to be sold, (3) deferred tax assets, (4) prepaid assets

related to pension and postretirement benefit plans, and (5) other current assets. If any excess remains, it is recognized as an extraordinary gain in the period of the combination (FAS-141, par. 44 and par. 45).

Transfer of Assets or Liabilities

Assets and/or liabilities may be transferred to a regulatory agency as part of the plan of financial assistance. The fair value of the assets and/or liabilities that are transferred to the regulatory agency is excluded from the fair market value of the assets and liabilities acquired in the transaction (FAS-72, par. 9).

Financial Assistance after Date of Acquisition

Financial assistance may not be recognized at any time, unless (*a*) it is *probable* and (*b*) the amount of assistance can be *reasonably estimated*. Financial assistance may become *probable* and the amount *reasonably estimable* after the date of acquisition of the banking or thrift institution. Here, the financial assistance is recognized in the financial statements of the period(s) in which it becomes *probable* and the amount *reasonably estimable*. When this occurs, the financial assistance is reported as a reduction of the balance of the unamortized goodwill. Amortization for subsequent periods is adjusted proportionately (FAS-72, par. 9).

☛ **PRACTICE POINTER:** All types of regulatory financial assistance, except assistance in the form of additional interest, must be **probable** and the amount **reasonably estimable** before such assistance is recognized and reported in the financial statements of an enterprise. Financial assistance in the form of additional interest is recognized in accordance with existing GAAP; all other types of financial assistance are recognized only if they are probable and the amounts reasonably estimable.

Under existing GAAP, the accounting recognition of financial assistance depends on the substance of the transaction or the contractual agreement between the parties. Financial assistance may represent (*a*) a bona fide receivable, (*b*) a gain contingency, or (*c*) a contingent asset. A receivable generally is recognized when an exchange takes place, collection of the amount is reasonably assured, and the earning process is complete. A gain contingency should not be recognized prior to its realization, and financial disclosure is necessary (FAS-5). Under the purchase method of accounting, a contingent asset is allocated a portion of the total acquisition cost if certain conditions are met (FAS-141).

Repayment of Financial Assistance

An enterprise may agree to repay (based on the attainment of future profitability levels) all or part of the financial assistance granted by a regulatory agency. Repayment of financial assistance is recognized as a liability and a charge to income of the period in which the repayment is probable and the amounts can be reasonably estimated, in accordance with FAS-5 (FAS-72, par. 10).

Disclosure of Financial Assistance

The nature and amount of financial assistance received by an enterprise from a regulatory agency in connection with the acquisition of a banking or thrift institution must be disclosed in the financial statements (FAS-72, par. 11).

Loan and Commitment Fees

Loan origination and commitment fees and direct loan origination costs are accounted for as prescribed in FAS-91 (Accounting for Nonrefundable Fees and Costs Associated with Originating or Acquiring Loans and Initial Direct Costs of Leases). (**Note:** A discussion of FAS-91 can be found in this *Guide* in the chapter titled "Mortgage Banking.")

RELATED CHAPTERS IN 2009 *GAAP GUIDE* *LEVEL A*

Chapter 4, "Business Combinations"
Chapter 8, "Contingencies, Risks, and Uncertainties"
Chapter 20, "Impairment of Long-Lived Assets"
Chapter 23, "Intangible Assets"
Chapter 29, "Leases"
Chapter 50, "Mortgage Banking"

RELATED CHAPTERS IN 2009 *GAAP GUIDE* *LEVELS B, C, AND D*

Chapter 6, "Business Combinations"
Chapter 13, "Contingencies, Risks, and Uncertainties"
Chapter 19, "Impairment of Long-Lived Assets"
Chapter 21, "Intangible Assets"
Chapter 26, "Leases"

CHAPTER 48
ENTERTAINMENT

CONTENTS

OVERVIEW

Authoritative accounting literature in Level A of the GAAP hierarchy for companies in the entertainment industry are presented in three categories: broadcasters, cable television companies, and records and music. While all of these lines of business have certain things in common, they have unique aspects that are covered in the respective authoritative pronouncements. The FASB literature related to entertainment enterprises draws heavily on former Statements of Position and other work of the AICPA's Accounting Standards Executive Committee.

A *broadcaster* is an entity that transmits radio or television program material. Exhibition rights acquired under a licensing agreement for program material shall be accounted for as a purchase of rights by the licensee (broadcaster); the licensee should record an asset and a liability for the right acquired and the obligation incurred, respectively. The licensee reports the asset and liability for a license agreement when the license period begins and certain other specified conditions are met.

GAAP for all companies generally apply to cable television companies. Certain accounting problems have arisen, however, with regard to the initial recording of assets and the treatment of hookup costs and franchise costs.

Primary sources of revenue include sales of recorded music product (compact discs, cassettes, etc.), the licensing of others to use music, royalties from public performances, revenue from music used in motion pictures, and revenue from the sale of sheet music. If a license agreement is, in substance, a sale and if collectibility of the fee is reasonably assured, GAAP require the licensor to recognize the licensing fee as revenue.

The authoritative literature for the entertainment industry is included in the following pronouncements:

FAS-50	Financial Reporting in the Record and Music Industry
FAS-51	Financial Reporting by Cable Television Companies
FAS-63	Financial Reporting by Broadcasters
FAS-139	Rescission of FASB Statement No. 53 and Amendments to FASB Statements No. 63, 89, and 121

BROADCASTERS

Background

FAS-63 (Financial Reporting by Broadcasters) contains the specialized accounting and reporting principles and practices that were originally published in the AICPA SOP 75-5 (Accounting Practices in the Broadcasting Industry).

A significant change from the specialized accounting principles in SOP 75-5 has been made in FAS-63 concerning the application of APB-21 (Interest on Receivables and Payables) to license agreements for program material rights of broadcasters. Under SOP 75-5, the licensor and licensee were required to apply the provisions of APB-21 to license agreements for program material rights. Under FAS-63, the application of APB-21 is optional (FAS-63, par. 4).

A broadcasting station may be completely independent or may be affiliated with a network. Independent broadcasters purchase or otherwise provide for all of their programming. A network affiliated broadcaster obtains much of its programming from its affiliated network and usually receives an affiliation fee and has lower programming costs than an independent.

Revenues of broadcasters arise from the sale of advertising time. Independent broadcasters sell all of their advertising time, whereas much of an affiliated broadcaster's advertising time is sold by the network. When the broadcaster airs the sponsor's advertising, revenue is recognized. Network-affiliated broadcasters receive revenue from their affiliated networks on a monthly basis. The revenue is based on a formula, and the affiliates submit weekly reports of revenue to their networks.

Advertising rates usually are based on the size of the estimated audience reached by the broadcaster and the quality of the station's programming. Rates vary significantly from market to market. Local and regional rates generally are less than national advertising rates. Rate cards that contain the advertising rates of a broadcaster are determined during rating periods (so called "sweep months") in which the size and demographics of the broadcaster's audience are measured along with the quality of the broadcaster's programming. Rate cards usually are broken down into broadcasting periods called *dayparts* and are revised on a regular basis.

A broadcaster may exchange advertising time for services or products. Such "barter" transactions could result in a broadcaster becoming part of an "ad hoc" network by allowing the programmer to retain a certain number of spots in the telecast. The programmer then sells such spots to a national advertiser. There is no accounting impact to the broadcaster.

Programming costs usually are the largest expense of television broadcasters. Programming costs generally are higher for independent broadcasters, who must obtain all of their programming themselves, than they are for network-affiliated broadcasters. Program material for television broadcasters is purchased under television licenses from producers and distributors. These producers and distributors generally package several films and license the material for one or more exhibitions or for a specified period, at which time the license expires. The license agreement usually provides for installment payments over a period, which is almost always less than the license period. Thus, the producer or distributor receives all of its money for the license prior to the expiration of the license.

Many television broadcasters produce some of their programming material either live or on videotape. Local news broadcasts and local interview shows are popular programs produced by television broadcasters.

Television and radio broadcasters are regulated by the Federal Communications Commission (FCC). Broadcasters are licensed periodically to use frequencies in specific areas, which are assigned by the FCC. In licensing a broadcaster, the FCC may consider the (a) financial position of the broadcaster, (b) advertising policies, (c) quality of the programming, and (d) contribution made to the community in which the broadcaster operates. Advertising rates are not regulated by the FCC, but guidelines have been established for advertising rates by the National Association of Broadcasters.

The major assets of a broadcaster are its FCC license and its network affiliation agreement. Thus, network-affiliated broadcasters usually are more valuable than independent broadcasters.

FAS-63 covers three specific aspects of the broadcasting industry: (1) program material license agreements, (2) barter transactions, and (3) intangible assets.

Program Material License Agreements

FAS-63 requires that broadcasters record the assets and liabilities that are involved in a program material license agreement as a purchase of a right or group of rights (FAS-63, par. 2). The license agreement is reported in the financial statements of the licensee when the license period begins and all of the following conditions are met (FAS-63, par. 3):

- The cost of each license fee for each program is known or is reasonably determinable.

- The broadcaster has accepted the program material in accordance with the terms of the license agreement.

- The program is available for its first showing or telecast under the license agreement.

FAS-63 requires that the balance sheet of broadcasters be classified. Thus, assets and liabilities are classified as current or noncurrent based on the normal operating cycle of the enterprise (FAS-63, par. 3).

The asset and liability that arise from the purchase of program material rights are reported by the licensee or licensor at either (a) the fair value of the liability or (b) the gross amount of the liability. If a present value technique is used to measure fair value, accounting in APB-21 (Interest on Receivables and Payables) shall be applied (FAS-63, par. 4, as amended by FAS-157, par. E9a).

☛ **PRACTICE POINTER:** One purpose of APB-21 is to require that interest be imputed on liabilities that bear an unreasonable rate of interest or no interest at all. Thus, if a reasonable rate of interest is charged on a liability, the provisions of APB-21 would not apply and the liability would be recorded at its gross amount.

APB-21 is based on the pervasive principle of **substance over form**. Allowing the licensee or licensor to report the liability or receivable either **gross** or at **present value** is equivalent to permitting the licensee or licensor to report either the **substance** or the **form** of the transaction.

The cost of rights to a package of programs is allocated to each program right in the package, based on the relative value of each program right to the broadcaster. Amortization of program material rights is computed on the estimated number of times that the program will be aired by the broadcaster. Program rights purchased for unlimited broadcasts may be amortized over the term of the license agreement if the estimated number of future showings is not determinable (FAS-63, par. 5).

Feature programs are amortized on an individual basis. Series programs, however, are amortized on a series basis. An accelerated method of amortization must be used when the first broadcast of a program is more valuable than its reruns, which usually is the case. Thus, the straight-line method of amortization is appropriate only when each broadcast is expected to produce approximately the same amount of revenue (FAS-63, par. 6).

Unamortized program rights shall not exceed their net realizable value or a write-down is required. Program rights are reported in the balance sheet at the lower of their unamortized cost or their estimated net realizable value (FAS-63, par. 7).

☛ **PRACTICE POINTER:** FAS-144 (Accounting for the Impairment or Disposal of Long-Lived Assets) exempts assets covered by certain other FASB pronouncements related to specialized industries, including FAS-63. Therefore, the general standards concerning impairment losses included in FAS-144 do not apply to program rights, and accounting for impairment is based on FAS-63 standards.

Barter Transactions

FAS-63 requires that all barter transactions be recorded at fair value except for barter transactions including the exchange of advertising time for network programming. Revenue from such transactions is recorded at the time the commercials are broadcast, and barter expense is recorded at the time the services are used. If the services or products have not been received at the date the commercial is aired, a receivable is reported. On the other hand, if services or products are received before the date the commercial is aired, a liability is reported (FAS-63, par. 8, as amended by FAS-157, par. E9.4).

☞ **PRACTICE POINTER:** APB-29 requires that nonmonetary exchanges be accounted for at the fair value of the assets or services received or surrendered, whichever is more clearly evident. If fair value is indeterminable, the only valuation available may be the recorded book value of the nonmonetary assets exchanged.

Intangible Assets

FAS-63 requires that intangible assets in the broadcasting industry be accounted for in accordance with FAS-142 (Goodwill and Other Intangible Assets). Thus, intangible assets in the broadcasting industry are only amortized if they are deemed to have a finite life.

If a network affiliation is terminated, any unamortized network affiliation costs are charged to expense unless a replacement agreement exists. In this event, if the fair value of the replacement agreement exceeds the unamortized network affiliation cost of the terminated agreement, no gain is recognized. If the fair value of the replacement agreement is less than the unamortized network affiliation cost of the terminated agreement, however, a loss is recognized to the extent of the difference (FAS-63, par. 9).

Disclosure

Unrecorded program material license agreements that have been executed and do not meet the criteria of FAS-63 must be disclosed in the notes to the financial statements (FAS-63, par. 10).

OBSERVATION: FAS-63 is silent on the extent of note disclosure that is necessary for unrecorded license agreements that have been executed but do not meet the criteria of FAS-63. It appears that the provisions of FAS-47 (Disclosure of Long-Term Obligations), however, may apply to some unrecorded license agreements that have been executed. FAS-47 requires that unrecorded unconditional purchase obligations that (a) are substantially noncancelable, (b) are related to the costs of the specific goods or services in the contract, or are part of the financing arrangement for the facilities that will provide the specified goods or services in the contract, and (c) are for a remaining term in excess of one year must be disclosed by note in the purchaser's financial statements. The disclosures include:

- A description of the nature and term of the obligation.
- The total determinable amount of unrecorded unconditional purchase obligations as of the latest balance sheet date, and for each of the five years after the latest balance sheet date.

- A description of the nature of any variable component of the unrecorded unconditional purchase obligations.
- For each income statement presented, the amounts actually purchased under the unconditional purchase obligations.

OBSERVATION: A broadcaster shall apply the guidance in SOP 00-2 (Accounting by Producers or Distributors of Films) if the broadcaster owns a film that is shown on its cable, network, or local television outlets.

CABLE TELEVISION COMPANIES

Background

FAS-51 contains the specialized accounting and reporting principles and practices that were originally published in the AICPA SOP 79-2 (Accounting by Cable Television Companies).

Cable television (CATV) systems are organized and built to provide uninterrupted program entertainment. The distribution of the television programs by a CATV system usually is made over coaxial or fiber optic cables or satellites to a defined area.

Ordinarily, a cable TV company, which is regulated by the Federal Communications Commission, obtains a franchise from a local governmental authority, which permits the distribution of CATV programs in a specified area. The franchise agreement usually provides for payment of fees to the granting authority and contains, among other provisions, the maximum fees that the company can charge a subscriber. In addition, franchise agreements may include many provisions pertaining to the type and quality of service that must be provided, number of TV channels, type of construction, and duration of the franchise. If all of the terms of the franchise agreement are not met, the governmental authority may retain the right to terminate the contract with the cable TV company.

The operation of a CATV system begins with the purchase of program entertainment. Program entertainment from major suppliers and motion picture studios usually is acquired on a long-term contract. The transmission signals of a cable programming company are picked up by the CATV system by microwave relay, antennas, or satellite, then amplified and distributed to subscribers via coaxial cables. The subscriber usually pays an initial hookup charge and thereafter, a monthly subscription fee.

Key provisions of 1992 federal cable law include use of reasonable subscriber rates, better customer service standards, and sale of program entertainment on a nondiscriminatory basis. A cable operator with more than 12 usable channels must set aside four to carry local commercial TV stations upon demand.

The size of the franchise area and the density of the population usually determine the construction period required to install a CATV system. The type of system being built, however, may also affect the period of construction. For example, if the coaxial cables must be installed underground rather than on utility poles, the period of construction will likely take longer. The construction period is completed when all of the equipment used to receive transmissions (head-end equipment) is installed, all main (head-end) and distribution cables are in place, and most subscriber drops (installation hardware) are installed. The CATV system is *energized* when the first transmission is made to subscribers. It is not unusual to energize part of a CATV system before the entire system is built, because large CATV systems generally are built in sections over several years. When this occurs, a *prematurity period* is established. A prematurity period begins when the first subscriber's revenue is earned and ends when construction of the system is completed or when the first major stage of construction is completed. The prematurity period will vary in direct relation to the size of the franchise area and the density of the population.

The capital investment necessary for even a small CATV system is quite substantial. The acquisition of a franchise and the cost of the physical facilities are expensive, and the operating overhead during the construction period requires a great deal of working capital. Space on utility poles or in underground ducts usually is leased from utility companies.

Initial Recording of Assets

In the construction of a cable TV company, the *prematurity period* begins on the date that subscribers' revenue is earned and ends on the date that the construction of the CATV system is completed or when the first major stage of construction is completed. Some cable TV companies, however, have determined that the prematurity period begins on the date that subscribers' revenue is earned and ends on the date that a predetermined number of subscribers is reached.

The prematurity period must be determined by management prior to the recognition of any earned revenue from the first subscriber. FAS-51 (Financial Reporting by Cable Television Companies) contains a presumption that the prematurity period usually should not exceed two years. Unless very unusual circumstances arise, a prematurity period is not changed after it is established by management (FAS-51, par. 4).

A portion of a CATV system that meets most of the following conditions is in a prematurity period and is accounted for separately from the rest of the system (FAS-51, par. 5):

- It is a separate franchise area or a different geographic area.
- It has separate equipment or facilities.

- It has a separate construction period, break-even point, and/or separate accountability.
- It has a separate budget and/or separate accountability.

FAS-51 distinguishes between capitalized costs attributable to the main cable television plant and other related capitalized costs of a fully operational system, such as the cost of leases on utility poles or underground ducts, leases on satellite or microwave installations, property taxes, and capitalized interest costs. FAS-51 requires that these other related capitalized costs of a fully operational system be amortized over the same period used to depreciate the main cable television plant (FAS-51, par. 10).

All costs of constructing the physical facilities of a CATV system, including materials, direct labor, and construction overhead are capitalized. During the prematurity period, however, some subscribers are receiving service while construction continues on the system. Thus, during the prematurity period a distinction must be made between costs related to (*a*) the current period, (*b*) future periods, and (*c*) both current and future periods (FAS-51, par. 6).

Costs Related to Current Period

Selling, marketing, administrative expenses, and all costs related to current subscribers are accounted for as period costs.

Costs Related to Future Periods

During the prematurity period, all costs of constructing the physical facilities of the CATV system, including materials, direct labor, and construction overhead, continue to be capitalized.

Costs Related to Both Current and Future Periods

Programming costs and other system costs (such as the costs of leases on utility poles or underground ducts, leases on satellite or microwave installations, and property taxes) that are incurred in anticipation of servicing a fully operating system and that will not vary significantly regardless of the number of subscribers should be allocated to both current and future periods.

FAS-51 requires that during the prematurity period, charges for capitalized costs other than those of the main cable television plant are allocated to both current and future periods based on a fraction. The denominator of the fraction is the total expected subscribers at the end of the prematurity period; the numerator of the fraction is the greatest of (1) the average number of actual subscribers, (2) the average number of subscribers expected in a particular month, estimated at the beginning of the prematurity period, and (3) the average number of subscribers that would exist during the month if the expected number of subscribers at the end of the prematurity period were added on a straight-line basis over the prematurity period. The fraction results in the amount of amortization, which is charged to expense in the current period (FAS-51, par. 7).

During the prematurity period, depreciation of the cost of the main cable television plant of the CATV system is allocated by the same fraction. Instead of computing depreciation on the costs incurred to date, however, the total depreciable base of the main cable television plant is estimated, and the total amount of depreciation is determined by applying the depreciation method normally used by the company. After the total amount of depreciation is computed, the fraction described in the previous paragraph is applied to arrive at the amount of depreciation expense that should be charged to the current period (FAS-51, par. 8).

Under the provisions of FAS-34 (Capitalization of Interest Cost) certain interest costs, if material, are capitalized and added to the acquisition cost of assets that require a period of time to get ready for their intended use. The cost of assets to which capitalized interest is allocated includes the cost of both those assets acquired for a company's own use and those acquired for sale in the ordinary course of business (FAS-51, par. 9).

Interest cost is capitalized during the prematurity period on that portion of the CATV system which is undergoing development activities to get it ready for its intended use and is not being used in the earning activities of the system.

☛ **PRACTICE POINTER:** Several requirements of FAS-34 may pose particularly difficult problems for CATV systems. For example, capitalization of interest ceases when the asset being constructed is ready for its intended purpose. This requirement is particularly important in the construction of large CATV systems that are completed and placed into service in phases. Take care to ensure that interest is not capitalized on phases of the project that are complete and ready for service.

FAS-34 also specifies that if the enterprise suspends substantially all activities related to acquisition of the asset, interest capitalization shall cease until activities are resumed. Brief interruptions in activities, interruptions that are externally imposed, and delays that are inherent in the asset acquisition process do not require cessation of interest capitalization. Judge carefully to determine whether delays in CATV system construction require an interruption in the capitalization of interest.

Hookup Revenue and Franchise Costs

Hookup revenue is recognized currently to the extent of direct selling costs. Direct selling costs include those costs that are incurred in obtaining and processing new subscribers. Hookup revenue in excess of direct selling costs is deferred and amortized to revenue over the estimated average subscription period (FAS-51, par. 11).

Initial hookup costs for subscribers are capitalized, and subsequent disconnects and reconnects are charged to expense as incurred. The depreciation period for initial hookup costs for subscribers should not exceed the depreciation period of the main cable television plant (FAS-51, par. 12).

Usually, a CATV company makes a formal franchise application to a local governmental unit to provide cable television service in its geographical area. The costs associated with any successful application may be significant and are accounted for in accordance with FAS-142 (Goodwill and Other Intangible Assets) (FAS-51, par. 13).

The costs associated with unsuccessful franchise applications and abandoned franchises are charged to expense in the period in which it is determined that they cannot benefit any future period (FAS-51, par. 13).

Periodic Review of Recoverability

Capitalized assets not only benefit a future period, but their costs should be recoverable from the expected future revenue. Thus, a periodic review of the capitalized costs of a cable TV company must be made to determine whether the costs are recoverable through future successful operations or future sale of the assets or a write-down to recoverable values is necessary (FAS-51, par. 14).

> **OBSERVATION:** FAS-144 (Accounting for the Impairment or Disposal of Long-Lived Assets) includes a list of pronouncements related to specialized industries that are exempt from the standards of FAS-144. FAS-51 is **not** on that list, and FAS-144 specifically modifies FAS-51 to indicate that capitalized plant and certain identifiable intangible assets of CATV companies are subject to the provisions of FAS-144.

RECORDS AND MUSIC

Background

FAS-50 (Financial Reporting in the Record and Music Industry) contains the specialized accounting and reporting principles and practices that were originally published in the AICPA SOP 76-1 (Accounting Practices in the Record and Music Industry).

Music publishers control the copyrights on their music, which may be owned by an artist-composer. On the other hand, record companies usually depend on an artist who is employed under a personal service contract to produce the record master that is used in manufacturing the ultimate product. The caliber and reputation of the recording artist have a direct effect on the success of any album or individual record.

A record master is produced by an expert sound engineer. Each instrument and voice is first recorded separately on magnetic tape. The sound engineer then combines each instrument and voice, emphasizing and de-emphasizing as he or she deems appropriate. This process is called mixing and is an important phase of manufacturing a record. The mixing process produces a record master, which is used to make acetate discs that are coated with metal. The metal coated disc is used to produce the mold that is eventually used to make the final product. Record masters also are utilized to produce tapes for the manufacturer of tape cartridges, cassettes, and compact discs. The following costs usually are incurred in the production of a record master:

- Costs for the recording studio
- Costs for engineers, mixing experts, directors, and other technical talent
- Costs for musicians, arrangers, vocal background, and other similar talent
- Costs for manufacturing the record master itself

The more successful recording artists are paid a nonrefundable advance against future royalties and bear no cost of producing the record master.

Music publishers license others, on a royalty basis, to use their music. Additional sources of income for music publishers include royalties from public performance, revenue from the music used in motion picture films, and revenue from the sale of sheet music.

Music publishers usually are members of ASCAP (American Society of Composers, Authors, and Publishers), BMI (Broadcast Music Incorporated), or some other society or association. Copyright laws provide that each time music is played publicly, the publisher and/or composer are entitled to a minimum royalty for public performance and mechanical rights, (i.e., rights to reproduce musical composition by any mechanical means—records, tapes, and diskettes). By monitoring radio and TV stations and live performances, ASCAP or BMI collects the royalties due to various publishers and/or composers. After collecting the royalties, ASCAP or BMI make periodic remittances to the publisher and/or composer.

One of the major accounting problems in the record and music industry is the timing of the recognition of a sale. This is because of the return privileges that manufacturers and distributors must make available to their customers. In addition, some manufacturers create discounts by including a certain number of free records in proportion to the size of the order.

> **OBSERVATION:** Accounting and reporting for revenue when a right of return exists is covered by FAS-48 (Revenue Recognition When Right of Return Exists).

Licensor Accounting

Owners of music copyrights or record masters usually enter into license agreements based on a minimum guarantee, which generally is paid in advance by the licensee. The licensor records the receipt of a minimum license guarantee as deferred income (liability), which is recognized as it is earned in accordance with the license agreement. If the license agreement is unclear as to when the guarantee is earned, the only alternative may be to recognize the guarantee over the term of the license agreement (FAS-50, par. 8).

Fees that are not fixed in amount by the terms of the license agreement are not recognized as revenue by the licensor until a reasonable estimate is made of such fees or the license agreement expires (FAS-50, par. 9).

When a licensee receives from the licensor a noncancelable contract for a specified fee granting specific rights to the licensee, who may use these rights at any time without restriction, an outright sale has been consummated. In this event, the earning process is complete and revenue is recognized if collectibility of the balance of the fee, if any, is reasonably assured (FAS-50, par. 7).

> ☞ **PRACTICE POINTER:** GAAP generally prohibit accounting for revenue by installment accounting except where significant doubt exists concerning collectibility. In such cases, a company can use either the cost recovery method or the installment sales method of accounting [(APB-10 (Omnibus Opinion—1966)], depending on the extent of the uncertainty.

Artist Compensation Cost

Royalties earned by artists, adjusted for anticipated returns, are charged to expense in the period in which the related record sale takes place. Royalty advances are recorded as prepaid royalties (an asset) if the past performance and current popularity of the artist to whom the advance is made indicate that the advance will be recoverable from future royalties to be earned by the artist. Advances made to new or previously unsuccessful artists, as well as those not having current popularity, are expensed in the current period. Capitalized advances are charged to expense as subsequent royalties are earned by the artist. If any capitalized advances subsequently appear not to be fully recoverable from future royalties to be earned by the artist, such advances should be charged to expense during the period in which the loss becomes evident. Advance royalties should be classified as current and noncurrent assets, as appropriate (FAS-50, par. 10).

> **OBSERVATION:** FAS-144 (Accounting for the Impairment or Disposal of Long-Lived Assets) exempts assets covered by certain other FASB pronouncements related to specialized industries, including FAS-50. Therefore, the general standards concerning impairment losses included in FAS-144 are not applicable for record and music assets, and accounting for asset impairment is based on FAS-50 standards.

Future royalty guarantees, artist advances payable in the future, and other commitments, if material, should be disclosed in the financial statements (FAS-50, par. 13).

The cost of a record master is recorded as an asset if it is reasonably assured that such cost will be recovered from expected future revenue. This cost should be disclosed separately in the balance sheet. The cost of a record master is amortized to income in proportion to the net revenue that is expected to be realized (FAS-50, par. 11).

Any portion of the cost of a record master that is recoverable from the artist's royalties is accounted for as a royalty advance and disclosed separately in the financial statements (FAS-50, par. 12).

Licensee Accounting

As mentioned previously, license agreements usually are based on a minimum guarantee that generally is paid in advance to the licensor by the licensee. The licensee records this minimum payment as a deferred charge (an asset). The deferred charge is then amortized to expense in accordance with the terms of the license agreement. Any other fees required by the licensing agreement that are not fixed in amount by the terms of the license agreement before the agreement expires must be estimated and accrued on a license-by-license basis by the licensee (FAS-50, par. 15).

RELATED CHAPTERS IN 2009 *GAAP GUIDE* *LEVEL A*

Chapter 1, "Accounting Changes"
Chapter 2, "Accounting Policies and Standards"
Chapter 11, "Depreciable Assets and Depreciation"
Chapter 20, "Impairment of Long-Lived Assets"
Chapter 23, "Intangible Assets"
Chapter 24, "Interest Costs Capitalized"
Chapter 25, "Interest on Receivables and Payables"
Chapter 31, "Long-Term Obligations"
Chapter 41, "Revenue Recognition"

RELATED CHAPTERS IN 2009 *GAAP GUIDE* *LEVELS B, C, AND D*

Chapter 1, "Accounting Changes"
Chapter 2, "Accounting Policies and Standards"
Chapter 19, "Impairment of Long-Lived Assets"
Chapter 21, "Intangible Assets"
Chapter 22, "Interest on Receivables and Payables"
Chapter 36, "Revenue Recognition"

CHAPTER 49
INSURANCE

CONTENTS

OVERVIEW

GAAP for insurance industries contain specialized principles and practices from AICPA Insurance Industry Guides and Statements of Position. They establish financial accounting and reporting standards for insurance enterprises (hereinafter referred to as *insurers*) other than mutual life insurance enterprises, assessable mutuals, and fraternal benefit societies.

An important issue for insurance enterprises is the recognition of revenue on insurance contracts. GAAP require classification of insurance contracts (*policies*) as short-duration and long-duration as follows:

- Short-duration contracts—revenue over the policy period in proportion to coverage
- Long-duration contracts—revenue when premium is due from the policyholder

GAAP for insurers are found in the following pronouncements:

FAS-60	Accounting and Reporting by Insurance Enterprises
FAS-61	Accounting for Title Plant
FAS-91	Accounting for Nonrefundable Fees and Costs Associated with Originating or Acquiring Loans and Initial Direct Costs of Leases
FAS-97	Accounting and Reporting by Insurance Enterprises for Certain Long-Duration Contracts and for Realized Gains and Losses from the Sale of Investments
FAS-113	Accounting and Reporting for Reinsurance of Short-Duration and Long-Duration Contracts
FAS-120	Accounting and Reporting by Mutual Life Insurance Enterprises and by Insurance Enterprises for Certain Long-Duration Participating Contracts
FIN-40	Applicability of Generally Accepted Accounting Principles to Mutual Life Insurance and Other Enterprises

2009 TRANSITION GUIDANCE FOR FAS-141(R) AND FAS-160

The FASB has recently issued FAS-141(R), *Business Combinations*, which is effective for business combinations for which the acquisition date is on or after the beginning of the first annual reporting period beginning on or after December 15, 2008. The FASB has also issued FAS-160, *Noncontrolling Interests in Consolidated Financial Statements, an Amendment of ARB No. 51*, which is effective for fiscal years, and interim periods within those fiscal years, beginning on or after December 15, 2008. Because these standards are not effective for some companies until December 2009, and because early adoption is prohibited, the 2009 *GAAP Guide* reflects the requirements of FAS-141 prior to its revision in December 2007 and does not reflect the requirements of FAS-160. There is a discussion of the changes in the accounting for business combinations under FAS-141(R) in the Appendix to Chapter 4, "Business Combinations." Similarly, the Appendix to Chapter 7, "Consolidated Financial Statements" includes a discussion of the requirements of FAS-160. However, any effects of FAS-141(R) and/or FAS-160 on this chapter have not been reflected in this edition. Therefore, if a company is subject to the requirements of FAS-141(R) and/or FAS-160, the reader is referred to FAS-141(R) and FAS-160 for these new requirements.

BACKGROUND

FAS-60 (Accounting and Reporting by Insurance Enterprises) contains the specialized accounting and reporting principles and practices that were originally published in the following AICPA publications:

- Audits of Stock Life Insurance Companies
- Audits of Fire and Casualty Insurance Companies
- SOP 79-3 (Accounting for Investments of Stock Life Insurance Companies)
- SOP 80-1 (Accounting for Title Insurance Companies)

FAS-60 covers general purpose financial statements for stock life insurance companies and stock and mutual property and liability insurance companies, as well as for reciprocal or interinsurance exchanges. Title insurance companies are covered by FAS-60, except for accounting for a title plant, which is covered by FAS-61 (Accounting for Title Plant). Mortgage guaranty insurance companies are covered by FAS-60, except for premium revenue recognition, claim costs, and acquisition costs. Mutual life insurance companies, assessment enterprises, and fraternal benefit societies are excluded from the provisions of FAS-60.

FAS-91 (Accounting for Nonrefundable Fees and Costs Associated with Originating or Acquiring Loans and Initial Direct Costs of Leases) amended FAS-60 to establish accounting and reporting standards for nonrefundable fees and costs associated with lending, committing, or purchasing a loan or group of loans. FAS-91 specifies accounting for fees and initial direct costs of leasing transactions.

FAS-91 applies to all types of loans and to all types of lenders. (See the chapter titled "Mortgage Banking.")

FAS-97 (Accounting and Reporting by Insurance Enterprises for Certain Long-Duration Contracts and for Realized Gains and Losses from the Sale of Investments) amends FAS-60 to establish accounting and reporting standards for interest-sensitive and flexible premium long-duration insurance contracts, including universal life and certain single premium annuity insurance contracts. The original GAAP for insurance enterprises did not include these recently developed products.

FAS-97 also amends FAS-60 to specify that realized gains and losses of insurance enterprises are to be included as a component of *other income* on a pretax basis. Under FAS-60, realized gains and losses were reported net of taxes in a separate income statement caption after operating income. Under FAS-97, realized gains and losses may not be deferred to future periods.

FAS-97 does not establish accounting and reporting standards for limited-payment and universal-life contracts that address (*a*) loss recognition (premium deficiency), (*b*) accounting for reinsurance, and (*c*) financial statement disclosure. The provisions of FAS-60 that apply to these items also apply to limited-payment and universal-life contracts.

FAS-113 (Accounting and Reporting for Reinsurance of Short-Duration and Long-Duration Contracts) specifies the accounting by insurance enterprises for reinsuring, or ceding, insurance contracts. It amends FAS-60 by eliminating the practice of reporting assets and liabilities related to reinsurance contracts net of the effects of reinsurance. FAS-113 requires reinsurance receivables and prepaid reinsurance premiums to be reported as assets. It establishes the conditions required for a contract with a reinsurer to be accounted for as reinsurance and prescribes accounting and reporting standards for such a contract. It requires ceding companies to disclose the nature, purpose, and effect of reinsurance transactions. It also requires disclosure of concentrations of credit risk associated with reinsurance receivables and prepaid reinsurance premiums in accordance with FAS-133 (Accounting for Derivative Instruments and Hedging Activities).

FAS-120 extends the requirements of FAS-60, FAS-97, and FAS-113 to mutual life insurance companies. FIN-40 (Applicability of Generally Accepted Accounting Principles to Mutual Life Insurance and Other Enterprises) clarifies that enterprises, including mutual life insurance enterprises, that issue financial statements described as being in conformity with GAAP are required to apply all applicable authoritative accounting pronouncements in preparing those statements. While mutual life insurance companies, like many other regulated enterprises, prepare financial statements based on regulatory accounting practices that differ from GAAP, those financial statements should not be described as being prepared in conformity with GAAP.

A primer of insurance terminology is found in the Appendix to this chapter.

CLASSIFICATION OF INSURANCE CONTRACTS

FAS-60 requires that insurance policies be classified as either short-duration contracts or long-duration contracts. In a short-duration contract, the insurance carrier primarily provides insurance protection; in a long-duration contract the insurance company provides services and functions in addition to insurance protection, including loans secured by the insurance policy and various options for the payment of policy benefits.

In determining whether an insurance contract is of short duration or long duration, FAS-60 requires that the following factors be considered (FAS-60, par. 7):

- **Short-duration contracts** The amount of premiums charged, the amount of coverage provided, or other provisions of the contracts can be adjusted or canceled by the insurance companies at the end of any contract period. Short-duration insurance contracts provide insurance protection and are issued for short, fixed periods.

- **Long-duration contracts** The contracts usually are noncancelable, guaranteed renewable, or otherwise not subject to unilateral changes in their provisions. Long-duration insurance contracts provide insurance protection for extended periods and include other services and functions that must be performed.

  Most property and liability insurance contracts and some specialized short-term life insurance contracts are classified as short-duration contracts. Most life insurance contracts, noncancelable disability income policies, and title insurance contracts are classified as long-duration contracts. Accident and health insurance contracts may be of short duration or long duration, according to their expected term of coverage (FAS-60, par. 8).

PREMIUM REVENUE RECOGNITION

Premium revenue recognition is based on short-duration or long-duration contract classification.

Short-Duration Contracts

FAS-60 specifies that premium revenue from short-duration contracts is to be recognized periodically in proportion to the insurance company's performance under the contract. The insurance company's performance under the contract is coverage on the insured risks. In insurance policies in which coverage is provided evenly over the term of the policy, premiums are recognized evenly over the term of the policy. If the period of coverage (risk) is different from the term of the insurance contract, however, the premium is recognized over the period of coverage (the premium income is *matched* to the coverage during which the insurance company is exposed to potential loss). In the event the amount of insurance declines over the term of the policy, the premium is recognized in proportion to the amount of insurance over the term of the policy (FAS-60, par. 13).

In some forms of insurance, such as workers' compensation, the final premium is determined on audit after the termination of coverage. Premiums are based on a rate per $100 of payroll. The insurance company receives a premium deposit at the inception of the policy, and a premium adjustment is made on audit. In this event, an estimate of the final premium adjustment is necessary to recognize the total premium revenue over the term of insurance coverage. If the final total premium cannot be estimated reasonably, the cost recovery method or the deposit method of accounting may be used until the final total premium is known (FAS-60, par. 14).

Over the term of a class of insurance policies, the premiums are expected to pay for losses, if any, and operational expenses and still provide the insurance company with a profit. The amount of losses that a single insurance policy may incur is based on the law of averages. In other words, the loss that a single policy may incur is based on the loss experience of the many policies. As long as an insurance policy is in force, there may be a claim for a loss. The unearned portion of the premiums, at any time, should be sufficient to pay losses, operational expenses, and a margin for profit to the insurer.

In most states, statutory laws provide that insurance companies maintain reserves for possible losses equal to the unearned premiums of all insurance policies outstanding. The most common method used to determine unearned premiums is the *monthly pro rata fractional basis*. This method assumes that the same dollar amount of insurance business is written each day of every month. Thus, the mean of all insurance business written in any month is the middle of the month. One year is divided into 24 periods, and a fraction is assigned to each month as follows: January 1/24, February 3/24, March 5/24, April 7/24, May 9/24, June 11/24, and so forth. The appropriate fraction is then applied to the total original premium to determine the amount of earned and unearned premium.

Most state statutes require that insurance companies maintain their records in a manner in which a determination can be made annually on December 31 of the (*a*) premiums in force on direct insurance business and any reinsurance business and (*b*) premiums in force on insurance policies that have been ceded for reinsurance to other insurance companies.

Long-Duration Contracts

FAS-60 requires that premium revenue from long-duration contracts be recognized when due from the policyholder. Thus, premiums for whole-life, endowment, renewable term, and other long-duration contracts are recognized as revenue when the premiums are due from the policyholders (FAS-97, par. 30).

Title insurance premiums are considered due from policyholders and recognized as revenue when the title insurance company is legally or contractually entitled to the premium. Either the effective date of the title insurance policy or the date of the binder is the likely date on which the title insurance company is legally or contractually entitled to collect the premium (FAS-60, par. 16).

> **OBSERVATION:** The reasoning behind recognizing the entire title insurance premium on the effective date of the policy is that the insurance company has performed all of the acts necessary to earn the revenue.

ACCOUNTING FOR INVESTMENT, LIMITED-PAYMENT, AND UNIVERSAL-LIFE CONTRACTS

The accounting specified by FAS-60 is designed for long-duration insurance contracts that generally provide for (*a*) insurance protection, (*b*) level premium payments, and (*c*) contract terms that are fixed and guaranteed. The long-duration insurance contracts addressed by FAS-97 are referred to as (*a*) investment contracts, (*b*) limited-payment contracts, and (*c*) universal-life contracts (FAS-97, par. 6).

Interest-sensitive and flexible-premium long-duration insurance contracts do not have the fixed and guaranteed terms that are typical of most traditional insurance contracts. Instead, the terms of this type of contract usually allow the insurer to vary the amount of charges and credits made to the policyholder's account, and more often than not, the terms allow the policyholder to vary the amount of premium paid. FAS-97 concludes that the accounting methods established by FAS-60 for the recognition of revenue, based on a percentage of premiums, are not appropriate for insurance contracts in which the insurer has the discretion of varying amounts charged or credited to the policyholder's account or the policyholder has the discretion of varying the amount of premium paid.

An *investment contract* is one that does not subject the insurer to any significant risk of death or disability of the insured. Under FAS-97, investment contracts are accounted for in the same manner as other interest-bearing contracts. Payments received by the insurer are not reported as revenue (FAS-97, par. 15).

A *limited-payment contract* is one that subjects the insurer to risk over a period longer than the premium payment period. Under FAS-97, income from limited-payment insurance contracts is recognized over the period covered by the contract rather than the period that payments are received (FAS-97, par. 16).

A *universal-life contract* is one that contains terms that give the policyholder significant discretion over the amount and timing of premium payments and allows the insurer to vary the amounts charged or credited to the policyholder's account. FAS-97 requires the use of the retrospective deposit method of accounting for universal-life contracts. Under this method, an insurer is required to record a liability for policyholder benefits equal to the amount of the policyholder's account balance. Premiums are not accounted for as revenue under this method (FAS-97, pars. 17, 19).

FAS-97 specifies that when a traditional insurance policy (e.g., whole-life) is surrendered and replaced by an interest-sensitive or flexible-premium insurance contract (e.g., universal-life), the balance of any unamortized deferred policy acquisition costs related to the surrendered policy and any difference between the liability for policyholder benefits and the cash surrender value should be charged to operations (FAS-97, par. 26).

FAS-97 does not establish accounting and reporting standards for limited-payment and universal-life contracts that address loss recognition (premium deficiency), accounting for reinsurance, and financial statement disclosure. The provisions of FAS-60 (premium deficiency and disclosure) and FAS-113 (reinsurance) that apply to these items also apply to limited-payment and universal-life contracts (FAS-113, par. 31).

Investment Contracts

FAS-97 defines an *investment contract* as one that does not expose the insurance enterprise to significant risks arising from policyholders' mortality (death) or morbidity (illness) (FAS-97, par. 7). Since the risk of loss from death or disability is almost nonexistent, an investment contract is viewed more as an investment instrument than as an insurance contract. Under FAS-97, an insurance enterprise shall account for an investment contract in the same way other financial institutions account for most other types of interest-bearing financial instruments. Amounts received by an insurance enterprise as payments for investment contracts shall be reported as liabilities and not reported as revenue (FAS-97, par. 15).

Some long-duration insurance contracts contain terms that permit the policyholder to purchase an annuity at a guaranteed price on settlement of the contract. Under FAS-97, there is no mortality risk involved in this type of contract until the right to purchase the annuity contract has been executed (FAS-97, par. 7).

An insurance enterprise may be required to make annuity payments regardless of whether the beneficiary lives or dies (annuities with a refund feature) and to make additional payments beginning on a specified date if the beneficiary is alive on that date. These types of policies are accounted for as insurance contracts, under both FAS-60 and FAS-97, unless (*a*) there is a remote chance that the beneficiary will be alive on the date that the additional payments begin or (*b*) the present value of the estimated additional payments is immaterial when compared with the present value of all payments that are estimated to be made under the contract (FAS-97, par. 8).

Limited-Payment Contracts

FAS-97 defines a *limited-payment insurance contract* as one in which the terms are fixed and guaranteed, and for which premiums are paid over a period shorter than the period over which benefits are provided. Under FAS-97, the benefit period includes the period during which (*a*) the insurance enterprise is subject to risk from policyholder mortality and morbidity and (*b*) the insurance enterprise is responsible for administration of the contract. The period in which the policyholder or beneficiary elects to have settlement proceeds disbursed is *not* included in the benefit period (FAS-97, par. 9).

The period in which an insurance enterprise is exposed to mortality and morbidity risks in connection with a limited-payment contract extends beyond the period in which premiums are collected. This occurs because premiums are paid over a period shorter than the period over which the insurance enterprise provides benefits. The liability for policyholders' benefits for this type of limited-payment insurance contract is set up and accounted for in accordance with FAS-60 (FAS-97, par. 16).

Here, the earnings process is not completed by the mere collection of premiums. The excess of gross over net premiums received must be deferred and amortized by a constant method over the period that the insurance enterprise provides services. Thus, for life insurance contracts, the deferred premiums are amortized in relationship to the amount of insurance in force. For annuity contracts, the deferred premiums are amortized in relationship to the estimated amount of benefits that are expected to be paid (FAS-97, par. 16).

Universal-Life Contracts

Universal-life insurance contracts do not have fixed and guaranteed terms that are typical of the types of insurance contracts for which the accounting specified in FAS-60 was designed. However, certain types of conventional forms of participating and nonguaranteed-premium contracts may be, in substance, universal-life contracts. Policyholders of universal-life insurance contracts frequently are granted significant discretion over the amount and timing of premium payments. In addition, insurers frequently are granted significant discretion over amounts that accrue to and that are assessed against policyholders. FAS-97 describes as *universal-life insurance contracts* policies that provide death or annuity benefits and have one or more of the following features (FAS-97, par. 10):

- The terms of the contract do not fix and guarantee the amounts assessed by the insurer against the policyholder for mortality coverage, contract administration, initiation, or surrender.

- Interest and other amounts that accrue to the benefit of the policyholder are not fixed and guaranteed by the terms of the contract.

- Without consent of the insurer, the policyholder may change the amount of premium within certain limits set forth in the contract.

FAS-60 prescribed the appropriate accounting for conventional forms of participating and nonguaranteed-premium contracts. However, some conventional forms of participating and nonguaranteed-premium contracts may be, in substance, universal-life contracts, which are accounted for in accordance with the provisions of FAS-97. For the purposes of FAS-97, a *participating contract* is considered a universal-life contract if, without the consent of the insurer, the policyholder can change the amount of the premium, within limits set forth in the contract (FAS-97, par. 12). In addition, both *participating* and *nonguaranteed-premium* insurance contracts are considered universal-life contracts if they contain either of the following features (FAS-97, pars. 12–13):

- Under the terms of the contract, the insurer maintains a stated account balance for the policyholder, which is credited with premiums and interest and assessed for contract administration, mortality coverage, and initiation or surrender fees. The amounts credited to or assessed against the policyholder's account balance are not fixed and guaranteed.

- Changes in interest rates or other market conditions are expected to be the primary cause of changes in any contract element. It is not expected that the primary cause of changes in any contract element will be related to the experience of a group of similar contracts or the enterprise as a whole.

Under FAS-60, a liability for future policy benefits relating to long-duration contracts (except title insurance contracts) is accrued when the insurance enterprise recognizes premium revenue. The liability is based on actuarial assumptions at the time the insurance contracts are executed, and it is presented in the balance sheet at present value. In subsequent periods, changes in the original actuarial assumptions that result in changes in future policy benefits or related costs and expenses are recognized in net income of the period of change (FAS-60, par. 21).

The *liability* for future policy benefits consists of the present value of future policy benefits and related expenses, less the present value of related future net premiums (FAS-60, par. 21). *Gross premium* is the amount the policyholder pays, and it is equal to the net premium plus the profit made by the insurance enterprise. *Net premium* is that portion of the gross premium needed to cover future payments of all policy benefits and related costs and expenses.

Under FAS-97, an insurance enterprise computes its liability for policy benefits for universal-life contracts as the sum of the following (FAS-97, par. 17):

- Any amounts that have been accrued to the benefit of policy-holders at the date of the financial statements

- Any amounts assessed against policyholders to compensate the insurance enterprise for services to be performed over future periods

- Any amounts previously assessed against policyholders that the insurance enterprise must refund if the contract is termi-nated

- Any loss that will probably (likely) occur as a result of premium deficiency (computed in accordance with FAS-60)

In determining its liability for policy benefits, an insurance enter-prise shall not anticipate amounts that may be assessed against policyholders in future periods. In the event that no other amount can be established, the policyholder's cash surrender value in the insurance contract, at the date of the financial statements, represents the insurance enterprise's liability for policy benefits. The liability for policy benefits shall not include a provision for the risk of adverse deviation (FAS-97, par. 18).

An insurance enterprise shall not report premiums collected on universal-life contracts as revenue in its statement of earnings. Rev-enue on universal-life contracts is assessed against policyholders and reported in the period of assessment, unless it is evident that the assessed amount represents compensation to the insurance enter-prise for future services to be provided over more than one period (FAS-97, par. 19).

Amounts assessed against policyholders' balances for future ser-vices to be provided by the insurance enterprise over more than one period are reported as unearned income in the period in which they are assessed. Amounts assessed against policyholders' balances as initiation or front-end fees are also unearned revenue. Unearned revenue shall be amortized to income over the periods benefited based on the same assumptions and factors that are used to amor-tize capitalized acquisition costs (FAS-97, par. 20).

An insurance enterprise shall not report as an expense in its statement of earnings any payments to policyholders that represent a return of policyholders' balances. The cost of contract administration, amortization of capitalized acquisition costs, and benefit claims that exceed related policyholders' balances shall be reported as expenses (FAS-97, par. 21).

Under FAS-97, the amortization of capitalized policy acquisition costs is recognized at a constant rate based on the present value of the gross profit that is expected to be generated by a book (group) of universal-life insurance contracts. The same interest rate used to accrue interest on a policyholder's account shall be used to compute the present value of the gross profit that is expected to be realized on a book of universal-life contracts. In those periods in which material amounts of negative gross profits arise, the present value of estimated gross revenues, gross costs, or the balance of insurance in force shall be used as a substitute allocation base for calculating amortization (FAS-97, par. 22).

Estimated gross profit includes the best estimate of each of the following individual items, over the life of the book of universal-life contracts, without provision for adverse deviation (FAS-97, par. 23):

- Assessments for mortality, less benefit claims in excess of related policyholder balances
- Assessments for contract administration, less costs incurred
- Investment income from, less interest credited to, policyholders' balances
- Assessments against policyholder accounts upon termination
- All other assessed amounts and credits

Under FAS-97, amortization of capitalized acquisition costs is based on the present value of estimated gross profits. Under FAS-60, amortization of capitalized acquisition costs is based on expected premium revenues. Under FAS-60, acquisition costs that are directly related to the production of insurance business include all direct costs and indirect costs, such as underwriting and policy issuance expenses. Collection expenses, professional fees, depreciation, and general and administrative expenses are not directly related to, nor do they vary directly with, the production of new or renewal insurance business; they should be expensed as incurred. Under FAS-97, acquisition costs that vary in a constant relationship to *premiums or insurance in force*, that are recurring in nature, or that tend to be incurred in a level amount from period to period shall be charged to expense in the period incurred (FAS-97, par. 24).

The computation of amortization under FAS-97 includes the accrual of interest on the unamortized balance of capitalized acquisition costs and the balance of any unearned income, at the same interest rate used to discount expected gross profits. Under FAS-97, estimates of expected gross profit must be evaluated periodically; if earlier estimates indicate that revision is necessary, total amortization to date shall be adjusted by a charge or credit to the statement of earnings (FAS-97, par. 25).

To compute the present value of revised estimates of expected gross profits, an insurance enterprise shall use either (a) the rate in effect at the inception of the book of universal-life contracts or (b) the latest revised interest rate applied to the remaining benefit period. The method used to determine the present value of revised estimates of expected gross profit shall be applied consistently in subsequent revisions (FAS-97, par. 25).

Internal Replacement Transactions

A policyholder may use the cash surrender value of an old insurance contract to pay the initial lump-sum premium for a new universal-life contract. This is sometimes referred to as an *internal replacement transaction*. FAS-97 specifies that when a traditional insurance policy is surrendered and replaced by an interest-sensitive or flexible-premium insurance contract, the balance of any unamortized deferred policy acquisition costs related to the surrendered policy and any difference between the liability for policyholder benefits and the cash surrender value should be charged to operations (FAS-97, par. 26).

CLAIM COSTS AND FUTURE POLICY BENEFITS

Property and liability insurance companies must pay claims to policyholders who incur insured losses. At any time, claims may (a) be reported to the insurance company and be in the process of settlement or (b) be incurred but not reported to the insurance company.

A title insurance company insures title to real property. The company scrutinizes the chain of title to prevent losses. In practice, however, claims do occur and the title company incurs losses. Life insurance companies also pay losses.

FAS-60 contains specific GAAP for claim costs and future policy benefits.

Claim Costs

Title insurance companies should accrue estimated claim costs at the time the related insurance premiums are recognized as revenue. Claim costs for other types of insurance contracts are accrued as they occur. A provision for claim costs (liability) should include (*a*) reported losses in the process of settlement and (*b*) estimated losses incurred but not reported (FAS-60, par. 17).

The provision for reported claims in the process of settlement may be made by estimating each reported claim individually. Because there may be a large number of them, however, smaller reported claims may be estimated by an average dollar loss per claim. Thus, the provision for smaller claims frequently is made by multiplying the number of smaller claims by the estimated average loss per claim (FAS-60, par. 18).

Claims incurred but not reported are more difficult to determine and usually are estimated on a formula basis. Formulas use statistics on actual claim experience for prior years, which are then adjusted for current trends and other factors. This is accomplished by examining specific types of insurance policies for a selected period and then relating the loss experience to the premiums in force for the specific type of insurance policies. Formulas are used only for normal losses that are expected to recur. Large losses resulting from catastrophes are not included in the statistics used in determining formulas but are estimated separately, usually on the basis of judgment. Thus, a formula usually will consist of the loss experience determined for a prior period, adjusted for current trends, and a factor for large catastrophic losses.

Statutory Formula Reserves are required by most states for liability and workers' compensation insurance. Several states require minimum reserves for incurred but not reported (IBNR) losses on surety bonds and fidelity policies.

FAS-60 requires that a liability be accrued in the financial statements for reported losses in the process of settlement and unreported losses incurred but not reported. The liability for unpaid losses should include the effects of inflation and other economic factors, and it should be based on the best good faith estimate of the cost of settlement, arrived at by using past loss experience adjusted for current trends. The cost of settlement may be reduced by estimated salvage expected to be recovered from the claim and the exercise of subrogation rights. Amounts of salvage and subrogation should be deducted from the liability for unpaid losses in the balance sheet (FAS-60, par. 18).

Differences in and adjustments to estimates and actual claim payments, which result from periodic reviews, shall be recognized in net income of the period in which the differences or adjustments occur (FAS-60, par. 18).

> **OBSERVATION:** An insurance company may elect to report its liability for unpaid claims and the related claim adjustment expense for short-duration contracts at their present value. Under this method, the amount of the effects of such a presentation must be disclosed in the financial statements.

Title insurance companies and mortgage guaranty companies sometimes acquire real property as a result of settling a claim. Such property should be reported at fair value. Real estate acquired in settling claims shall be separately reported in the balance sheet and shall *not* be classified as an investment. Subsequent reductions in the reported amount and the realized gains and losses on the sale of real estate acquired in settling claims shall be recognized as an adjustment to claims cost incurred. (FAS-60, par. 19, as amended by FAS-157, par. E8.a).

Claim Adjustment Expense

Figuring the liability for reported claims in the process of settlement and for claims incurred but not reported requires an estimation of the amount of the claim. The claims adjustment expenses are the estimated expenses that will be incurred in settling the claims. Claims adjustment expense may be classified as allocated or unallocated (FAS-60, par. 20).

Allocated claims adjustment expenses are those that can be assigned to a specific claim. *Unallocated claims adjustment expenses* are those that cannot be assigned to a specific claim; they include indirect salaries, stationery, postage, rent, travel, and other similar expenses of the claims department.

The liability for the claims adjustment expense is determined by statistical formulas.

FAS-60 requires that a liability for claims adjustment expense for short-duration contracts be accrued for all reported claims in the process of settlement and for all claims incurred but not reported.

Future Policy Benefits

The normal costs of an insurance company include the payment of policy benefits and the expenses of doing business. These costs must be matched to their related premium revenue.

FAS-60 requires that a liability for future policy benefits on long-duration insurance contracts be accrued at the time that premium revenue is recognized. The liability includes the present value of future policy benefits and related expenses, less the present value of related future net premiums. Stated another way, the liability for future policy benefits for a particular group of insurance contracts is the excess of the total amount of net premiums collected over the total amount of related policy benefits paid to date. *Gross premium* is the total cost of the insurance contract to the policyholder. When accumulated with investment income, the gross premium creates a fund that will be sufficient to pay all policy benefits and related costs and expenses and provide a profit for the insurance company. *Net premium* is that portion of the gross premium that is needed to cover all policy benefits and related costs and expenses. Net premium should represent the gross premium, less a profit for the insurance company (FAS-60, par. 21).

Future policy benefits and related expenses are calculated by the use of actuarial assumptions, such as investment yields, mortality and morbidity rates, and estimated terminations or withdrawals. The liability for future policy benefits and related expenses is based on actuarial assumptions existing at the time the insurance contract is executed, and such liability is presented in the balance sheet at its present value (FAS-60, pars. 21–22).

An insurance company pools the risks of many individuals and businesses. Thus, undertaking risks is the primary business of an insurance company. The real risk that an insurance company takes, however, is that actual experience will be worse than the actuarial assumptions used in calculating the premium. This is referred to as the *risk of adverse deviation.*

Changes in the original actuarial assumptions in subsequent periods are recognized in net income of the period of change (FAS-60, par. 21).

OTHER COSTS

Since the matching concept is applied to the recognition of premium revenue, it is logical that the same principle be used in accounting for the costs incurred in obtaining the premium revenue. Thus, variable acquisition costs that are directly or indirectly related to the production of new or renewal premium revenue are deferred and amortized as a charge against income as the related premium revenue is earned. Acquisition costs that are directly related to the production of insurance business include all direct costs and indirect costs, such as underwriting and policy issuance expenses (FAS-60, par. 29).

Deferred acquisition costs are amortized as a charge to income in the same manner the related premium revenue is earned. The method of amortization should be applied consistently from year to year. Unamortized acquisition costs are classified in the balance sheet as assets (FAS-60, pars. 29–30).

Actual acquisition expenses for long-duration contracts should be compared to those used in the actuarial assumptions and, when possible, the actual acquisition expenses should be used in the actuarial assumptions instead of estimates. When estimates are used to determine the acquisition expenses that should be deferred, it is necessary to adjust such estimates to actual amounts if the differences are significant (FAS-60, par. 31).

☛ **PRACTICE POINTER:** Under regulatory accounting practices, charge all acquisition expenses against income in the period incurred. Thus, a significant difference between regulatory accounting practices and GAAP is the deferral and amortization of acquisition expenses. This difference is reflected in stockholders' equity and net income determined under regulatory accounting practices and in stockholders' equity and net income determined under GAAP.

Other expenses of insurance companies are treated in accordance with existing GAAP. Thus, if an expenditure benefits future periods, it may be deferred and charged to the periods benefited. All other expenses, such as investment expenses, general administration, and policy maintenance, that are not directly related to the production of new or renewal insurance business should be charged to operations in the period incurred (FAS-60, par. 27).

DEFICIENCY IN PREMIUMS OR LIABILITY FOR FUTURE POLICY BENEFITS

Insurance companies may incur losses on short-duration and long-duration contracts. For the purposes of FAS-60, premium deficiencies are determined by reasonable grouping of similar insurance policies that are consistent with the company's usual system of acquiring, servicing, and measuring profitability for its insurance business (FAS-60, par. 32). Each of these types of deficiencies is discussed separately below.

Short-Duration Contracts

Premium revenue is intended to be sufficient to cover expected claims, claim adjustment expenses, acquisition costs, policy maintenance costs, estimated dividends to policyholders, and profit. Whenever unearned premiums are less than the total of (a) the related liability for unpaid claim costs and claim adjustment expenses, (b) related unamortized acquisition costs, (c) related estimated policy maintenance costs, and (d) related dividends to policyholders, a premium deficiency exists (FAS-60, par. 33).

Premium deficiencies should be recognized in the financial statements. Recognition should be made by reducing unamortized deferred acquisition costs by a charge to income in the amount of the deficiency. If the unamortized deferred acquisition costs are smaller than the amount of premium deficiency, all of the unamortized deferred acquisition costs should be charged to income, and an additional separate liability for the balance of the premium deficiency should be recorded by a charge to income (FAS-60, par. 34).

☛ **PRACTICE POINTER:** Make a provision for anticipated premium deficiencies when unearned premiums are insufficient to cover all related costs and expenses. Related costs and expenses should include expected claims and claims adjustment expenses, expected policyholder dividends, unamortized deferred acquisition costs, and any anticipated expenses expected to be incurred after the inception date of the policy. If a cost, after the inception date of the policy, is direct or can be attributed to maintaining the policy in force, include it in the determination of the premium deficiency.

If an insurance company includes anticipated investment income in the determination of a premium deficiency, FAS-60 requires that the effects, and the amount of the effects on the financial statements, be disclosed (FAS-60, par. 33).

Long-Duration Contracts

FAS-60 requires that the liability for future policy benefits for long-duration contracts be accrued at the time the premium revenue is recognized. The liability is based on actuarial assumptions at the time the insurance contracts are executed, and it is presented in the balance sheet at present value. In subsequent periods, changes in the original actuarial assumptions that result in changes in future policy benefits or related costs and expenses are recognized in net income of the period of change (FAS-60, par. 21).

The liability for future policy benefits consists of the present value of future policy benefits and related expenses, less the present value of related future net premiums. Net premium is that portion of the gross premium that is needed to cover future payment of all policy benefits and related costs and expenses. Gross premium is the amount the policyholder pays, and it is equal to the net premium plus the profit made by the insurance company.

At any given time, the present value of future gross premiums for a particular group of insurance contracts may be insufficient to cover the present value of future policy benefits and related expenses and the remaining unamortized acquisition costs. In this event, a gross premium deficiency occurs. The gross premium deficiency usually is the result of significant changes in the original actuarial assumptions. The procedures to determine a gross premium deficiency are as follows (FAS-60, par. 35):

1. Compute the present value of future policy benefits and related settlement and maintenance expenses using revised assumptions and updated experience.

2. Compute the present value of future gross premiums using revised assumptions and updated experience.

3. Subtract 1 from 2 to arrive at the new liability for future policy benefits based on revised assumptions and updated experience.

4. Compare the new liability for future policy benefits determined in 3 with the actual recorded liability for future policy benefits, reduced by the actual remaining unamortized acquisition costs. A deficiency exists if the newly computed liability exceeds the actual liability, reduced by the actual remaining unamortized acquisition costs.

A deficiency in the liability for future policy benefits must be recognized in net income by either increasing the liability for future policy benefits, or by decreasing unamortized acquisition costs. The revised assumptions and updated experience shall be used to determine changes in the liability for future policy benefits. A deficiency is not reported if its effect is to create income in future periods (FAS-60, par. 36).

A deficiency in the liability for future policy benefits usually is determined by groups or blocks of similar insurance policies. However, if a group or block of insurance contracts does not indicate a deficiency, but the aggregate liability for an entire line of insurance business does indicate a deficiency, the deficiency should be recognized (FAS-60, par. 37).

ACCOUNTING FOR FINANCIAL GUARANTEE INSURANCE CONTRACTS

The FASB has recently released Statement of Financial Accounting Standards No. 163, *Accounting for Financial Guarantee Insurance Contracts*. FAS-163 applies to financial guarantee insurance and reinsurance contracts issued by life insurance enterprises, property and liability insurance enterprises, title insurance enterprises, mutual life insurance enterprises, assessment enterprises, and fraternal benefit societies (FAS-163, par. 2 and FAS-60, par. 6). FAS-163 does not apply to financial guarantee insurance contracts if they are derivative instruments within the scope of FAS-133, *Accounting for Derivative Instruments and Hedging Activities* (FAS-163, par. 2 and 7). FAS-163 also does not apply to insurance contracts that are similar to financial guarantee insurance contracts (e.g., mortgage guaranty insurance, credit insurance of trade receivables) (FAS-163, par. 6).

A financial guarantee insurance (and reinsurance) contract requires an insurance company to pay the holder of the contract if the insured financial obligation defaults. Examples of financial obligations where financial guarantee insurance may be purchased are municipal bonds and asset-backed securities. The holder of the insured financial obligation (e.g., the party that purchased municipal bonds or asset-backed securities) benefits from the insurance, but this party is not always the purchaser of the insurance. For example, in many cases the issuer of the financial obligation purchases financial guarantee insurance to help market the financial obligation and/or to reduce the interest rate offered on the financial obligation (FAS-163, par. 3 and 5).

Recognition of the Liability for Unearned Premium Revenue

An insurance company issuing a financial guarantee insurance contract is to recognize a liability for unearned premium revenue at the inception of the contract (FAS-163, par. 8). There are generally four possibilities in accounting for the revenue associated with a financial guarantee insurance contract: (1) the full premium is paid in cash at the inception of the contract and the insured financial obligation is not expected to be prepaid before the end of its expected life, (2) the premium is received in installments over the period of the financial guarantee insurance contract and the insured financial obligation is not expected to be prepaid before the end of its expected life, (3) the full premium is paid in cash at the inception of the contract and the insured financial obligation is expected to be prepaid before the end of its expected life, and (4) the premium is received in installments over the period of the financial guarantee insurance contract and the insured financial obligation is expected to be prepaid before the end of its expected life.

If the full premium is paid in cash at the inception of the contract (regardless of whether the insured financial obligation is expected to be prepaid before the end of its expected life), the insurance company shall debit cash for the amount received and credit unearned premium revenue (FAS-163, par. 8 and 9). If the premium is received in installments over the period of the financial guarantee insurance contract and the insured financial obligation is not expected to be prepaid before the end of its expected life, the insurance company shall debit premium receivable and credit unearned premium revenue for the present value of the premiums due over the life of the contract (FAS-163, par. 8 and 10). In this instance, the present value is determined using the risk-free interest rate that corresponds with the contract length determined at the inception of the contract, and the discount on the premium receivable will be amortized (accreted) into earnings over the contract period (FAS-163, par. 11).

If the premium is received in installments over the period of the financial guarantee insurance contract and the insured financial obligation is expected to be prepaid before the end of its expected life, the period that the insurance company is exposed to risk is shorter than the contract life. In this instance, the insurance company shall debit premium receivable and credit unearned premium revenue for the present value of the premiums expected to be collected before the financial obligation being insured is prepaid (FAS-163, par.

8 and 12). The expected collection period, rather than the contractual life of the contract, can only be used if a homogenous pool of assets underlies the financial obligation and the contractual obligation can be contractually prepaid (FAS-163, par. 12). In addition, the prepayments must be probable and the insurance company must be able to reasonably estimate the timing and the amount of the prepayments (FAS-163, par. 12).

Although the recognition and measurement provisions of FAS-163 are to be applied on a contract-by-contract basis (FAS-163, par. 2), the decision to use prepayment assumptions to determine the period over which insurance premiums are expected to be received is an accounting policy decision (i.e., this decision is not to be made on a contract-by-contract basis) (FAS-163, par. 12).

If an entity uses the expected collection period, rather than the contractual period, to measure unearned premium revenue, the entity shall adjust the premium receivable and unearned premium revenue when the prepayment assumptions change. Changes in prepayment assumptions have no effect on earnings. The discount rate is adjusted to the current risk-free rate when prepayment assumptions change (FAS-163, par. 13). In addition, if the unearned premium receivable is measured based on premiums expected to be collected over the contract period, an adjustment to premiums receivable and unearned premium revenue is to be recorded to reflect early principal payments as they occur (FAS-163, par. 15).

An adjustment for uncollectible premiums receivable is to be recorded, with the offset reducing earnings. And, the expected premiums to be collected affects whether a claim liability needs to be recognized (FAS-163, par. 14).

Recognition of Premium Revenue

Revenue is to be recognized over the term of the contract in proportion to the amount of insurance protection provided. As revenue is recognized the unearned premium revenue account is reduced (FAS-163, par. 16). The amount of insurance protection provided is related to the amount outstanding of the insured financial obligation. Revenue recognized in a period is computed using the following formula (FAS-163, par. 17):

> Insured principal amount outstanding during the period X (Present value of premiums due or expected to be collected over the contract period / Sum of all insured principal amounts outstanding during each period of the life of the contract)

Illustration of Premium Revenue Recognition

Sturgeon Inc., an insurance company, agrees to write a financial guarantee insurance contract on a municipal bond on January 1, 20X9. Insured principal payments of $200 million will be made by the municipality over the 10-year life of the bond. The single-premium charged by Sturgeon for writing this contract is $1.125 million. The computation of premium revenue to be recognized in each period is as follows:

Year	Insured Principal Amount Outstanding (beginning of year)	Principal Payments	Premium Revenue Recognized (see below)	Unearned Premium Revenue (beginning of yr balance— revenue recognized)
0				$1,125,000
1	$ 200,000,000	$ 10,000,000	$ 197,368	927,632
2	190,000,000	10,000,000	187,500	740,132
3	180,000,000	20,000,000	177,632	562,500
4	160,000,000	20,000,000	157,895	404,605
5	140,000,000	30,000,000	138,158	266,447
6	110,000,000	30,000,000	108,553	157,895
7	80,000,000	30,000,000	78,947	78,947
8	50,000,000	30,000,000	49,342	29,605
9	20,000,000	10,000,000	19,737	9,868
10	10,000,000	10,000,000	9,868	0
Total	$1,140,000,000	$200,000,000	$1,125,000	

The ratio of: (Present value of premiums due or expected to be collected over the contract period / Sum of all insured principal amounts outstanding during each period of the life of the contract) is:

$1,125,000 / $1,140,000,000 = 0.0009868421

Premium revenue is recognized at a constant rate by multiplying the insured principal amount outstanding at the beginning of each year by 0.0009868.

In some cases, premiums are expected to be received over a shorter period than the contract period (that shorter period is referred to as the *expected period*). The expected period may change because of changes in prepayment assumptions. When prepayment assumptions change, the constant rate used to recognize premium revenue is recalculated. In addition, if a new constant rate is calculated, the entity shall also use the current risk-free rate if insurance premiums are received in installments rather than in a single sum. The new constant rate is applied to the principal amount outstanding in the current and future years (i.e., treated essentially as a change in accounting estimate) (FAS-163, par. 19).

An insured financial obligation is sometimes retired by the issuer before its maturity (a.k.a., a refunding). This often happens when interest rates have decreased, and the issuer replaces the financial obligation being retired with a new financial obligation (FAS-163, par. 20). The financial guarantee insurance contract on a financial obligation is extinguished in a refunding. The insurer shall immediately recognize any nonrefundable unearned premium revenue as premium revenue, and any deferred acquisition costs as an expense (FAS-163, par. 21).

If the insurance enterprise insures the financial obligation issued to replace the instrument that has been refunded, the insurer shall recognize unearned premium revenue based on the premium it would charge to insure the financial obligation issued in a standalone transaction. If the premium charged by the insurer differs from that amount, the insurer shall recognize the difference in current period earnings (FAS-163, par. 21).

Illustration of Early Retirement and Replacement of an Insured Financial Obligation

Kmeta Inc. issues a financial guarantee insurance contract on a 30-year municipal bond for a single premium of $2.5 million. On the seventh anniversary of the bond the bond is retired. Eight hundred thousand of premium revenue has been previously recognized. Kmeta will recognize the remaining unearned premium revenue, $1.7 million, as premium revenue at the time the bond is retired.

The issuer of the municipal bond issues a new bond, at a lower interest rate, to replace the bond being retired. Kmeta issues a financial guarantee insurance contract on the new bond. The premium charged on the new bond is $2 million but the premium would be $3 million in a standalone transaction. Kmeta would recognize unearned premium revenue of $3 million, and $1 million would be charged against earnings in the current period (the difference between the premium charged and the premium that would be charged in a standalone transaction).

Recognition of a Claim Liability

A claim liability is to be recognized when the insurer expects that a claim loss will exceed the unearned premium liability. The claim loss is based on the present value of the net cash outflows expected to be paid under the insurance contract (FAS-163, par. 22). The claim liability is measured based on the present value of the net cash outflows expected to be paid under the insurance contract. The discount rate is the current risk-free rate based on the remaining period of the insurance contract. The remaining period is either the contract period or the expected period (the period that the insured financial obligation is expected to be outstanding (FAS-163, par. 24).

The expected net cash outflows are the cash outflows expected to be paid to the holder of the insured financial obligation, net of potential recoveries. Expected net cash outflows are a probability-weighted amount, reflecting the likelihood of all possible outcomes. This amount is to be based on the insurance enterprise's own assumptions about the likelihood of possible outcomes, and the insurer shall consider relevant market information in developing its assumptions (FAS-163, par. 25).

Illustration of the Determination of Expected Net Cash Outflows

Russell Inc. is an insurer that issues financial guarantee insurance contracts. On 12-31-X9 Russell has a contract with an unearned premium revenue amount of $4 million. The present value of expected net cash outflows on this contract exceeds $4 million so Russell must record a claim liability. The claim liability is developed by Russell by considering the amount, timing, and probability of possible net cash outflows (cash outflows less potential recoveries) to be paid to the holder of the insured financial obligation. Russell Inc. develops the following schedule of present values of possible net cash outflows and their related probabilities.

Discounted Possible Net Cash Outflow	Probability	Probability-Weighted Net Cash Outflow
$40,000,000	5%	$ 2,000,000
30,000,000	15%	4,500,000
25,000,000	25%	6,250,000
15,000,000	45%	6,750,000
5,000,000	10%	500,000
Present value of probability-weighted expected net cash outflows		**$ 20,000,000**

Russell Inc. would record a claim liability of $16 million in the statement of financial position ($20 million less the unearned premium amount of $4 million).

In periods after the initial measurement of a claim liability, the insurer shall update the discount rate of each reporting period. In addition, the claim liability shall be adjusted to reflect changes in the likelihood of default (i.e., changes in the likelihood of the insurer having to perform) and changes in potential recoveries. In no instance is the claim liability to be reduced below zero (FAS-163, par. 27). Changes to the claim liability in subsequent periods affects claim expense in these future periods (FAS-163, par. 28). Finally, as the claim liability grows due to the passage of time, the discount amount on the claim liability is amortized by charges against earnings (FAS-163, par. 27).

Disclosures

Insurance enterprises shall disclose the information necessary for financial statement users to understand the factors affecting the recognition and measurement of financial guarantee insurance contracts (FAS-163, par. 29).

The following disclosures are required in annual periods (and in interim periods if there has been a significant change) (FAS-163, par. 30a):

- For financial guarantee insurance contracts where premiums are received over the contract life rather than all at contract inception:
  — The premium receivable and unearned premium revenue as of the date of the statement of financial position, and the line items on the statement of financial position where these amounts appear
  — The amount of the discount on premium receivable amortized into income during the period, and the line item on the income statement where this amount appears
  — The weighted-average period of the premium receivable
  — The weighted-average risk-free rate used to discount the premium receivable
- A schedule of expected premium receipts related to the outstanding premium receivable balance:
  — Over the next four quarters, and over the next four years (5 years in total)
  — In the remaining periods in 5-year increments
- A rollforward of the premium receivable for the period, including:
  — Beginning balance
  — Premiums received (credits to the premium receivable)
  — New business written (debits to the premium receivable)
  — Adjustments to the premium receivable (e.g., changes to the period of the financial guarantee insurance contract, amortization of the discount on premiums receivable)

    — Ending balance

- A disclosure of the reasons for any acceleration of premium revenue recognition and the related amounts

- A schedule of future expected premium revenue, detailing amounts to be recognized:

    — Over the next four quarters, and over the next four years (5 years in total)

    — In the remaining periods in 5-year increments

- Related to the claim liability

    — Weighted-average risk-free discount rate

    — Description of significant changes to the liability during the period (e.g., change in the discount rate, amortization of the discount on the claim liability, changes in the likelihood of default)

    — The dollar amounts related to the above changes

    — The line items within the income statement that include these amounts

- A description of the entity's risk-management practices for tracking and monitoring deteriorating insured financial obligations. These disclosures are immediately effective upon the issuance of FAS-163 and include:

    — A description of the groupings or categories used to monitor deteriorating insured financial obligations

    — Policies for placing an insured financial obligation in these groupings and categories, and policies related to subsequent monitoring

    — Policies for avoiding or mitigating claim liabilities

    — Expense and liability related to risk mitigation activities (not including reinsurance), and where the expense appears in the income statement and the liability appears in the statement of financial position

Disclosures related to claim liabilities are required at the end of each annual and interim period. These disclosures are to be in the form of a schedule of insured financial obligations, and are immediately effective upon the issuance of FAS-163. The disclosures minimally must include (FAS-163, par. 31):

- Number of issued and outstanding financial guarantee insurance contracts

- Remaining weighted-average contract period

- Contractual payments outstanding subject to insurance, broken out separately by principal and interest
- Gross and net claim liability
- Gross potential recoveries
- Net discount on both the claim liability and on potential recoveries
- Reinsurance recoverables
- Unearned premium revenue

Effective Date and Transition

FAS-163 is effective for financial statements issued for fiscal years beginning after December 15, 2008, and interim periods in those years. However, as discussed previously, certain disclosure requirements are effective immediately upon the issuance of FAS-163. If these required early disclosures are impracticable, the entity needs to state why and indicate its current policy for claim liabilities. Early adoption of FAS-163 is not permitted (FAS-163, par. 32).

FAS-163 applies to existing and future financial guarantee insurance contracts as of the beginning of the year that this statement is first applied. The cumulative effect of applying the statement is recorded as an adjustment to the beginning retained earnings balance, including in the first interim period in which FAS-163 is applied (FAS-163, par. 33). The cumulative effect adjustment is the difference between amounts recognized in the statement of financial position before applying FAS-163 and the amounts recognized in the statement of financial position given the application of this statement. In measuring financial statement amounts, the entity shall use the risk-free interest rate at the time FAS-163 is initially applied (FAS-163, par. 34).

Figure 49-1: Interrelationship among Policyholder, Ceding Company, and Reinsurers

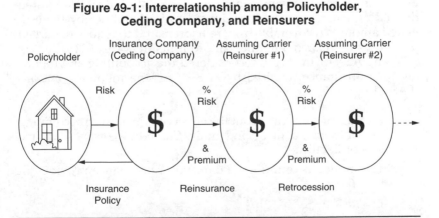

REINSURANCE

An insurance company may obtain indemnification against claims associated with contracts (policies) it has issued by entering into a reinsurance contract with another insurance company, referred to as the *reinsurer* or *assuming carrier*. The insurer, referred to as the *ceding company*, pays an amount to the reinsurer, and the reinsurer agrees to reimburse the insurer for a specified portion of claims paid under the reinsured contracts (policies), as shown in Figure 49-1. Usually, the policyholder is unaware of the reinsurance arrangement. The reinsurer may, in turn, enter into reinsurance contracts with other reinsurers. This process is known as *retrocession* (FAS-113, par. 1).

> **OBSERVATION:** Two particularly important terms are used in the previous paragraph: *insurer* (or ceding company) and *reinsurer* (or assuming company). These are formally defined in the appendix of FAS-113 as follows:
>
> - **Insurer** (ceding company)—the party that pays a reinsurance premium in a reinsurance transaction. The ceding enterprise, or insurer, receives the right to reimbursement from the assuming carrier under the terms of the reinsurance contract.
> - **Reinsurer** (assuming carrier)—the party that receives a reinsurance premium in a reinsurance transaction. The assuming company, or reinsurer, accepts an obligation to reimburse a ceding company under the terms of the reinsurance contract.

FAS-60 specified the accounting by insurance companies for reinsurance contracts. FAS-60 is an extraction of requirements of the AICPA Industry Audit Guides titled "Audits of Fire and Casualty Insurance Companies and Audits of Stock Life Insurance Companies." FAS-60 continued the practice that originated in statutory accounting whereby ceding companies reported insurance activities net of the effects of reinsurance. If the reinsurance contract indemnified the ceding company against loss or liability, FAS-60 required the ceding company to reduce unpaid claim liabilities by the estimated amounts recoverable from reinsurers and to reduce unearned premiums by related amounts paid to reinsurers (FAS-113, par. 2).

With FAS-113, the FASB reconsidered the accounting and reporting for reinsurance required by FAS-60 for the following reasons (FAS-113, par. 5):

- Increasing concerns about the effect of reinsurance accounting for contracts that do not indemnify the ceding company against loss or liability
- The limited accounting guidance on reinsurance provided in FAS-60

- The lack of disclosure requirements for reinsurance transactions
- The established criteria for offsetting

FAS-113 applies to those insurance companies to which FAS-60 applied (FAS-113, par. 6). FAS-60 sets accounting and reporting standards for general-purpose financial statements of (FAS-60, par. 6):

- Stock life insurance companies
- Property and liability insurance companies
- Mortgage guaranty insurance companies (except the sections of FAS-60 on premium revenue and claim cost recognition and acquisition costs)

> **OBSERVATION:** FAS-60 also applies to insurance enterprises that issue guarantee insurance contracts within the scope of FAS-163 (Accounting for Financial Guarantee Insurance Contracts), except for the sections on premium revenue and claim cost recognition (FAS-163, par. C1a).

Some insurance contracts are *fronting arrangements*, wherein the ceding company issues a policy and reinsures all (or substantially all) of the risk with the assuming enterprise. FAS-113 provides guidance for determining whether those contracts meet the conditions for reinsurance accounting. If the conditions for reinsurance accounting are met, FAS-113 is applicable.

The specific accounting provisions in FAS-113 to be followed for reinsurance depend on whether the contract is long-duration or short-duration; if the contract is short-duration, it must be further classified as prospective reinsurance or retroactive reinsurance (FAS-113, par. 6). In *prospective reinsurance*, an assuming company agrees to reimburse a ceding company for losses that may be incurred as a result of future insurable events covered under contracts subject to the reinsurance. In *retroactive reinsurance*, an assuming company agrees to reimburse a ceding company for liabilities incurred as a result of past insurable events covered under contract subject to the reinsurance (FAS-113, Appendix C).

Indemnification

The term *indemnify* means to make whole one who has suffered a loss, or to repair loss or damage already suffered.

Figure 49-2 shows how, when a policyholder suffers a loss, the ceding carrier pays the loss to the policyholder and is indemnified under the reinsurance contract.

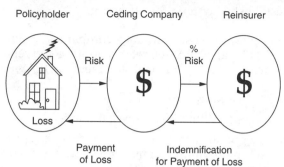

Figure 49-2: Ceding Company Indemnified by Reinsurer

Determining whether a contract with a reinsurer provides indemnification for loss or liability associated with insurance risk requires a careful understanding of the contract and other contracts or agreements between the ceding company and reinsurers. Of particular importance are contractual features that (FAS-113, par. 8):

- Limit the amount of insurance risk that is ceded to the reinsurer
- Delay the timely reimbursement of claims by the reinsurer

The following conditions generally must be met for the reinsurance of short-duration contracts to be considered indemnification contracts (FAS-113, par. 9):

- The reinsurer assumes significant insurance risk.
- It is reasonably possible that the reinsurer may realize a significant loss from the transaction.

A reinsurer is considered not to have assumed significant insurance risk if the probability of significant variation in either the amount or the timing of payments by the reinsurer is remote (e.g., there are contractual provisions in the reinsurance contract that delay timely reimbursement to the ceding company) (FAS-113, par. 9). The ceding company's evaluation of whether it is reasonably possible for a reinsurer to realize a significant loss shall be based on the present value of all cash flows between the ceding and assuming companies under reasonably possible outcomes (FAS-113, par. 10).

> **OBSERVATION:** The terms *remote* and *reasonably possible* used in FAS-113 are borrowed from FAS-5 (Accounting for Contingencies). FAS-5 defines these terms as follows:

- **Remote**—the chance of the future event or events occurring is slight.
- **Reasonably possible**—the chance of the future event or events occurring is more than remote but less than likely.

In evaluating the significance of loss, the present value of all cash flows is compared with the present value of amounts paid or deemed to have been paid to the reinsurer. If the reinsurer is not exposed to the reasonable possibility of significant loss, the ceding company is considered indemnified against loss or liability relating to insurance risk only if the reinsurer has assumed essentially all the risk from the ceding company (FAS-113, par. 11).

For long-duration contracts, indemnification of the ceding company against loss or liability requires the reasonable possibility that the reinsurer may realize significant loss from assuming insurance risk as that concept is contemplated in FAS-60 and FAS-97. FAS-97 defines long-duration contracts that do not subject the insurer to mortality risks (life insurance) or morbidity risks (health insurance) as *investment contracts* (FAS-113, pars. 12–13).

Reporting Assets and Liabilities

Some reinsurance contracts represent legal replacements of one insurer by another. These are often referred to as *assumption* and *novation*. They extinguish the ceding company's liability to the policyholder and logically result in removal of related assets and liabilities from the financial statements of the ceding company, as shown in Figure 49-3 (FAS-113, par. 14).

Other reinsurance contracts do not result in the ceding company being relieved of its legal liability to policyholders and, accordingly, do not result in the removal of the related assets and liabilities from the ceding company's financial statements. Separate assets shall be shown by ceding companies for reinsurance receivables and for amounts paid to the reinsurer relating to the unexpired portion of reinsured contracts (e.g., prepaid reinsurance premiums) (FAS-113, par. 14). Amounts receivable and payable between the ceding company and an individual reinsurer are offset only when a right of setoff exists, as defined in FIN-39 (Offsetting of Amounts Related to Certain Contracts) (FAS-113, par. 15).

The amounts of earned premiums ceded and recoveries recognized under reinsurance contract shall be either (FAS-113, par. 16):

- Reported in the statement of earnings, as separate line items or parenthetically, or
- Disclosed in notes to the financial statements

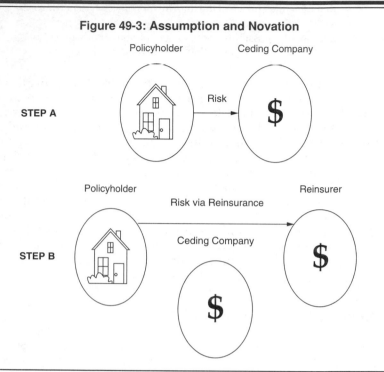

Figure 49-3: Assumption and Novation

Recognition of Revenues and Costs

To apply FAS-113, an entity must first determine whether the contract in question is considered reinsurance. For reinsurance contracts, a further classification must be made into long-duration or short-duration. Short-duration contracts are further classified as prospective or retroactive. This series of decisions is summarized in Figure 49-4 (FAS-113, par. 17).

FAS-113 first prescribes general accounting standards applicable to all reinsurance contracts (pars. 18–20), then discusses standards specifically applicable to short-duration contracts (pars. 21–25), and finally discusses standards specifically applicable to long-duration contracts (par. 26).

For contracts that do not meet the criteria for reinsurance accounting, FAS-113 has little to say, other than to incorporate certain provisions of FAS-60, summarized as follows (FAS-113, par. 18):

- Premiums paid, less the premium to be retained by the reinsurer, are accounted for as a deposit by the ceding company. A net credit resulting from the contract is reported as a liability by

Figure 49-4: Classification of Reinsurance

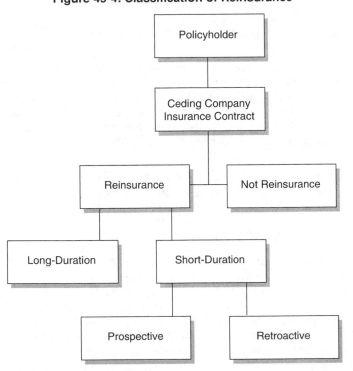

the ceding company. A net charge is reported as an asset by the reinsurer.

- Proceeds from reinsurance transactions that represent recovery of acquisition costs shall reduce applicable unamortized acquisition costs in such a manner that net acquisition costs are capitalized and charged to expense in proportion to net revenue recognized. If the ceding company has agreed to service the related insurance contracts without reasonable compensation, a liability shall be accrued for estimated excess future servicing costs under the contract. The net cost to the assuming company shall be accounted for as an acquisition cost.

Reinsurance contracts do not result in immediate recognition of gains unless the reinsurance contract represents a legal replacement of one insurer by another and, as a result, extinguishes the ceding company's liability to the policyholder (FAS-113, par. 19).

Reinsurance receivables are recognized in a manner consistent with the liability related to the underlying reinsured contracts. The assumptions used to estimate reinsurance receivables are to be consistent with the assumptions used to estimate the related liabilities (FAS-113, par. 20).

Standards for Short-Duration Contracts

Amounts paid for prospective reinsurance contracts are reported as prepaid reinsurance premiums and are amortized over the remaining contract period in proportion to the amount of insurance protection provided. If the amounts paid are subject to adjustment and can be estimated reasonably, the basis for amortization shall be the estimated ultimate amount to be paid (FAS-113, par. 21).

> **OBSERVATION:** FAS-113 defines the *contract period* as the period over which insured events that occur are covered by the reinsured contracts. This is commonly referred to as the *coverage period* or the period during which the contracts are in force (the *policy period*).

For retroactive reinsurance contracts, amounts paid are reported as reinsurance receivables to the extent those amounts do not exceed the recorded liabilities relating to the underlying reinsurance contracts. If the recorded liabilities exceed the amounts paid, reinsurance receivables are increased to reflect the difference, and the resulting gain is deferred. That deferred gain is amortized over the estimated remaining settlement period, applied as follows (FAS-113, par. 22):

- If the amounts and timing of the reinsurance recoveries can be reasonably estimated, the deferred gain is amortized using the effective interest rate inherent in the amount paid to the reinsurer and the estimated timing and amounts of recoveries from the reinsurer (the interest method).

- Otherwise, the proportion of actual recoveries to total estimated recoveries determines the amount of amortization (the recovery method).

If the amounts paid for retroactive reinsurance exceed the recorded liabilities relating to the underlying reinsured contracts, the ceding company shall increase the related liability or reduce the reinsurance receivable, or both. This is done at the time the reinsurance contract is entered into, and the excess is charged to earnings (FAS-113, par. 23).

Fluctuations in liabilities tied to the underlying reinsurance contracts are included in earnings for the relevant period and are reflected in reinsurance receivables. A gain will therefore be adjusted or established and must be deferred and amortized (FAS-113, par. 24).

Changes in the estimated amount of the liabilities affect amounts recoverable from the reinsurer and therefore deferred gains, as shown in Figure 49-5 (FAS-113, par. 24).

When a single reinsurance contract contains both prospective and retroactive provisions, a separate accounting for each should be done when practicable, as shown in Figure 49-6 (FAS-113, par. 25).

Standards for Long-Duration Contracts

Amortization of the estimated cost of reinsurance of long-duration contracts depends on whether the reinsurance contract is long-duration or short-duration. If the reinsurance contract is long-duration, the cost is amortized over the remaining life of the underlying reinsured contracts (policies). (This is in contrast to amortization of the contract period of the reinsurance if the reinsurance contract is short-duration.) Determining whether a contract that reinsures a long-duration insurance contract is long-duration or short-duration in nature is a matter of judgment, requiring consideration of all of the facts and circumstances. The assumptions used in accounting for reinsurance costs should be consistent with those used for the reinsured contracts (policies). Any difference between amounts paid for a reinsurance contract and the amount of the liabilities for policy benefits relating to the underlying reinsurance contracts is part of the estimated cost to be amortized (FAS-113, par. 26).

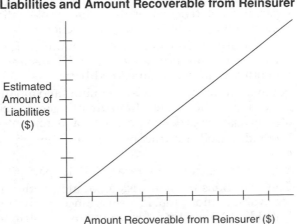

Figure 49-5: Relationship between Estimated Amount of Liabilities and Amount Recoverable from Reinsurer

Estimated Amount of Liabilities ($)

Amount Recoverable from Reinsurer ($)

Figure 49-6: Accounting for Reinsurance Contracts That Combine Prospective and Retroactive Provisions

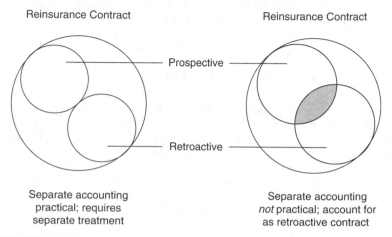

Reinsurance Contract   Reinsurance Contract

Prospective

Retroactive

| Separate accounting practical; requires separate treatment | Separate accounting *not* practical; account for as retroactive contract |

Disclosure

Disclosure requirements for insurance companies are established in FAS-113.

These disclosure requirements can be summarized as follows:

- All insurance companies must disclose (FAS-113, par. 27):
  - The nature, purpose, and effect of ceded reinsurance transactions on the insurance company's operations (In addition, ceding companies shall disclose the fact that the insurer is not relieved of the primary obligation to the policyholder in a reinsurance transaction.)
  - For short-duration contracts, premiums from direct business, reinsurance assumed, and reinsurance ceded, on both a written and an earned basis
  - For long-duration contracts, premiums and amounts assessed against policyholders from direct business, reinsurance assumed and ceded, and premiums and amounts earned
  - Methods used for income recognition on insurance contracts
- Ceding companies must disclose (FAS-113, par. 28):
  - Concentrations of credit risk associated with reinsurance receivables and prepaid reinsurance premiums under FAS-133 (Accounting for Derivative Instruments and Hedging Activities)

POLICYHOLDER DIVIDENDS

Policyholder dividends are accrued reported in the financial statements. If the amount is not known, the use of reasonable estimates is required (FAS-60, par. 41).

The amount of current income allocated to participating insurance contracts is excluded from stockholders' equity by a charge to current operations and a credit to a liability account. The liability account is reduced when dividends subsequently are declared or paid. Dividends declared or paid to participating insurance contracts in excess of the liability also are charged to current operations.

Life insurance companies usually do not pay or declare dividends on participating insurance policies during the first two years, because of the high initial policy acquisition costs. In determining the amount of dividends on participating insurance policies, consideration must be given to any restrictions on such amounts that may be imposed by the terms of the insurance contract, governing law, or company policy. When participating policy dividends are specified in the policy or projected at the time the policy is issued, they should be accrued ratably over the periods in which premiums are collected. Dividends to policyholders are not guaranteed payments, but are subject to a declaration by the insurer's directors. A "guaranteed dividend policy" may actually be a whole-life contract coupled with annually maturing endowments that pay out and appear to be dividends.

CONTINGENT COMMISSIONS

Insurance companies usually agree to pay additional commissions to agents if the business they generate results in a favorable loss experience.

FAS-60 requires that contingent commissions (receivable or payable) be accrued appropriately and appear in the income statement of the periods in which the related profits are recognized (FAS-60, par. 44).

INVESTMENTS

FAS-60 contains specific guidance in the valuation of investments of insurance companies.

Bonds and Other Fixed Income Investments

Bonds are accounted for in accordance with the provisions of FAS-115 (Accounting for Certain Investments in Debt and Equity Secu-

rities) (FAS-115, par. 127a). If the insurance company has the ability
and intent to hold bonds to maturity, the bonds are categorized as a
held-to-maturity security and carried at amortized cost (FAS-115,
par. 7), provided that there has not been an other-than-temporary
decline in the market value of the bonds below amortized cost (FAS-
115, par. 16). If the bonds have suffered an other-than-temporary
decline in market value, the bonds are to be written down to fair
value and the resulting loss included in earnings (FAS-115, par. 16).
Bonds held for speculation are categorized as trading securities and
are to be carried at fair value, and unrealized gains and losses
should be included in earnings (FAS-115, pars. 12–13). Bonds that
are not categorized as either held-to-maturity securities or as trading securities are categorized as available-for-sale securities. Bonds
categorized as available-for-sale securities are carried at fair value,
and unrealized gains and losses are included in the computation of
other comprehensive income (FAS-115, par. 12; FAS-130, par. 33a).

Insurance companies may invest in many other types of fixed
income investments besides bonds (e.g., interest-only strips, retained
interests in securitizations, loans, other receivables). These instruments are categorized by their ability to be contractually prepaid
or otherwise settled, with the investment holder recovering substantially all of its investment. These securities are accounted for either as
available-for-sale or trading securities (FAS-140, par. 14). However,
instruments subject to the provisions of FAS-133 (Accounting for
Derivative Instruments and Hedging Activities) are not subject to
these requirements.

Common and Nonredeemable Preferred Stock

Common and nonredeemable preferred stock with readily determinable fair values are accounted for in accordance with the provisions of
paragraph 127a of FAS-115. Common and nonredeemable preferred
stocks are categorized as either available-for-sale or trading securities
and are carried at fair value (FAS-115, par. 12). Changes in fair value
are included in the determination of income for trading securities
(FAS-115, par. 13), and in the determination of other comprehensive
income for available-for-sale securities (FAS-130, par. 33a).

Investments by insurance companies in equity securities without
readily determinable fair values (per the FAS-115 criteria) are also to
be carried at fair value. Generally, changes in fair value are included
as a component of other comprehensive income, net of related taxes
(FAS-124, par. 107b). The change in fair value is recognized in the
statement of activities for a not-for-profit organization (FAS-124,
par. 107b). However, some or all of the unrealized gain or loss is
to be included in determining income if the security is designated as
being hedged in a fair value hedge (FAS-133, par. 528a).

Mortgages

Mortgages are carried at the balance of the unpaid principal. Mortgages purchased at a discount or premium are carried at amortized cost. An allowance should be used to reduce total mortgages to an expected collectible amount, if necessary, and changes in the allowance account should be included in income (FAS-60, par. 47; FAS-114, par. 23).

Real Estate Investments

Real estate investments are carried at depreciated cost. Amortization, depreciation, and other related costs or credits should be included in the determination of investment income (FAS-60, par. 48).

Loan and Commitment Fees

Loan origination and commitment fees and direct loan origination costs are accounted for as prescribed in FAS-91 (FAS-91, par. 26), as follows:

- Loan origination fees are recognized over the life of the related loan as an adjustment to yield.
- Certain direct loan origination costs are recognized over the life of the related loan as a reduction of the loan's yield.
- With limited exceptions, loan commitment fees are deferred and recognized over the loan commitment period.
- Loan fees, certain direct origination costs, and purchase premiums and discounts on loans are recognized as an adjustment of yield generally by the interest method based on the contractual terms of the loan.

☛ **PRACTICE POINTER:** The straight-line method of amoritization is often used by smaller companies on the basis of materiality.

Reporting Realized Gains and Losses

FAS-97 amends FAS-60 to eliminate the practice of reporting realized investment gains and losses in the statement of earnings, below operating earnings. FAS-97 requires insurance enterprises to report realized gains and losses as a component of other income, on a pretax basis, above earnings from operations in the statement of earnings. In addition, FAS-97 does not permit the direct or indirect deferment of realized investment gains and losses (FAS-97, par. 28).

Permanent declines in security investments, below cost or amortized cost, for those equity securities without readily determinable fair values are recognized as realized losses. These security investments should be written down to their net realizable values, which subsequently become their new cost basis (FAS-60, par. 51; FAS-115, par. 127d). Although FAS-60 provides guidance on accounting for a permanent impairment in investment value for equity securities without readily determinable fair values, for most investments held by insurance enterprises the relevant accounting guidance for permanent impairment in investment values is found in FAS-115. For available-for-sale or held-to-maturity securities, a decline in fair value below amortized cost that is deemed as other-than-temporary should trigger the recognition of a realized loss. The realized loss is the difference between the security's amortized cost and its fair value. This reduced fair value becomes the security's new cost basis (FAS-115, par. 16). Recovery in market value above the new cost basis is not recognized until sale, maturity, or other disposition of the security (FAS-60, par. 51; FAS-115, par. 16).

REAL ESTATE USED IN BUSINESS AND SEPARATE ACCOUNTS

Real estate is classified in accordance with its predominant use either as property used in business or as an investment. Real estate operating expenses, including depreciation, are classified in a manner consistent with the related asset, as either investment expenses or operating expenses (FAS-60, par. 52).

Real estate that the insurance company uses in business should not be accounted for as investment income with a corresponding charge to operations for rental expense. An insurance company cannot include rental income in its financial statements for property it uses in the regular course of business (FAS-60, par. 52).

> **OBSERVATION:** Real estate is always classified as an investment for regulatory accounting purposes, regardless of its use. Rental expense is charged to operations, and rental income is included in investment income for real estate used by the insurance company in its own business.

As a fiduciary, an insurance company may maintain assets and liabilities in separate accounts to fund fixed-benefit plans. In this capacity, the insurance company usually receives a fee and does not assume any investment risk (FAS-60, par. 53).

Except for long-term separate accounts in which the insurance company has guaranteed a specific investment return, investments in separate accounts shall be valued at market. Long-term separate accounts with guaranteed returns shall be valued in the same manner as any other investment of the insurance company. Assets and liabilities of separate accounts shall be reported in the financial statements in summary totals (FAS-60, par. 54).

DEFERRED INCOME TAXES

Insurance companies should generally recognize deferred taxes (assets and liabilities) for the tax consequences of temporary differences (FAS-109, par. 288t). There is one exception to this general requirement. Taxable temporary differences may exist related to "policyholders' surplus." Deferred taxes are not provided for any such taxable temporary differences that arose in fiscal years beginning prior to December 16, 1992 (FAS-109, par. 288t). However, if circumstances dictate that income taxes will be paid because of a reduction in policyholders' surplus, an income tax expense should be accrued on such reductions in the period in which they occur. In effect, these reductions create a temporary difference when they occur, and they should not be accounted for as an extraordinary item (FAS-60, par. 59).

DISCLOSURE

FAS-60 requires the following specific disclosures in the financial statements of insurance companies (FAS-60, par. 60):

- The basis for estimating the following:
  - The liability for unpaid claims
  - The liability for claim adjustment expenses
- The methods and assumptions used in calculating the liability for future policy benefits (In addition, FAS-60 encourages, but does not require, the disclosure of the average rate of assumed investment yields that are in effect for the current period.)
- Capitalized acquisition costs
  - The nature of such costs
  - The method of amortizing such costs
  - The amount of amortization of such costs for the current period
- If the liabilities for unpaid claims and claim adjustment expenses for short-duration contracts are reported at their present values in the financial statements
  - The carrying amount of those liabilities
  - The range of interest rates used to discount those liabilities
- Whether estimated investment income is used in calculating a premium deficiency for short-duration contracts
- Participating insurance of an insurance company
  - The relative percentage of participating insurance

— The method of accounting for participating insurance policyholders' dividends
— The amount of such dividends
— The amount of any additional income allocated to participating insurance policyholders

- Stockholders' equity, statutory capital, and capital surplus
  — The amount of statutory capital and capital surplus
  — The amount of statutory capital and capital surplus required for regulatory purposes, if significant to the enterprise's total statutory capital and capital surplus
  — The nature of statutory restrictions on dividends and the amount of retained earnings not available for dividends to stockholders

MUTUAL LIFE INSURANCE ENTERPRISES

A mutual life insurance enterprise's main product is participating life insurance. These contracts provide certain guaranteed benefits and allow policyholders to share in the profits through dividends. Dividends are paid periodically at the direction of the board of directors, and they reflect the performance of the enterprise for investment activity, mortality experience, and overhead for each particular class of contracts. "Non-participating" contracts pay no dividends (FAS-120, par. 18).

In 1972, the AICPA published an Industry Audit Guide, *Audits of Stock Life Insurance Companies*. That Guide did not apply to mutual life insurance enterprises. Since that time, the FASB has issued three Statements that exempt mutual life insurance enterprises from their requirements:

1. FAS-60 (Accounting and Reporting by Insurance Enterprises)

2. FAS-97 (Accounting and Reporting by Insurance Enterprises for Certain Long-Duration Contracts and for Realized Gains and Losses from the Sale of Investments)

3. FAS-113 (Accounting and Reporting for Reinsurance of Short-Duration and Long-Duration Contracts)

FAS-120 extends the requirements of these Statements to mutual life insurance enterprises, assessment enterprises, and fraternal benefit societies (FAS-120, par. 2). FAS-120 also permits stock life insurance enterprises to apply the provisions of the AICPA's Statement of Position 95-1 (Accounting for Certain Insurance Activities of Mutual Life Insurance Enterprises) to participating life insurance contracts that meet certain specified conditions (FAS-120, par. 2).

OTHER ISSUES

There are significant differences between the accounting principles and practices used in reporting to insurance regulatory agencies and generally accepted accounting principles. The following are some of the more important exceptions to GAAP that are used in regulatory accounting practices:

- Increasing the *policy reserves* account by a direct debit to unassigned surplus (retained earnings) instead of a charge to income
- Charging unassigned surplus with prior service costs of pension plans instead of a charge to income
- Netting liabilities against related assets
- Debiting unassigned surplus for only the par value of certain stock dividends

Nonadmitted Assets

Under regulatory accounting practices, it is not permitted to show certain assets on the balance sheet of an insurance company. Nonadmitted assets are charged to surplus and thus eliminated from the regulatory balance sheet. The more common nonadmitted assets are the following:

- Furniture and equipment
- Automobiles
- Prepaid and deferred expenses
- Goodwill and other intangible assets
- Unauthorized investments
- Investments in excess of authorized amounts
- Receivables from agents (debit balances)
- Receivables from employees and officers
- Accrued income on investments in default
- Receivables from unauthorized reinsurers

In presenting financial statements in conformity with GAAP, nonadmitted assets must be restored. This is accomplished by debiting the various assets and crediting retained earnings (surplus). However, care must be exercised in determining the collectibility of receivables that are restored.

Stockholders' Equity

For financial statements to be presented in conformity with GAAP, it may be necessary to reclassify an insurance company's equity account. As mentioned previously, nonadmitted assets must be restored by a credit to retained earnings. If an insurance company has increased its policy reserves by a direct charge to surplus, the transaction will have to be redone to be in conformity with GAAP. Care must also be exercised in segregating appropriated surplus from unassigned surplus for financial statement purposes.

TITLE PLANT

Background

A title insurance company issues title insurance policies. Title insurance provides protection against losses incurred by a buyer or lender resulting from liens or other title defects on property purchased or secured. If a buyer obtains title insurance on real estate that is being purchased and subsequently a loss is incurred because of a lien or defect in the title to the property, the title insurance company will pay the loss up to the policy limit, or if so endorsed, up to the market value of the property. There are two types of policies: the owner's form and the lender's form. The owner's form protects the owner's equity interest in the property. The lender's form protects the lender for the amount loaned against the property. Lenders require an amount of insurance at least equal to the amount loaned in order to cover their interest.

A title insurance policy is unique because the premiums are not refundable and the term of the policy is indefinite. The amount of insurance and the date of title search are stated in the policy. Any loss in excess of the amount of title insurance and any loss that occurs because of a lien or defect which did not exist up to the date of the title search are not covered.

When a title insurer receives an application for title insurance, a title search is made. The search consists of reviewing and scrutinizing the chain of ownership of the property up to the date of the search. Each change of ownership is examined to make sure it was properly made and that no defects or unpaid liens exist against the title to the property. If a lien or defect is discovered, the title insurance policy is issued with the discovered lien or defect cited in the policy and not covered. The buyer may be able to cancel the purchase of the property or compel the seller to cure the existing lien or defect. Most contracts for the sale of real property contain a provision to the effect that the property is being sold free of any liens and/or defects, and that the buyer has a specified period to determine whether any liens or defects do exist against the property being purchased. The seller is given time up to the day of closing to cure the defect.

The records that a title insurance company uses to search the chain of ownership of a parcel of real estate are called the *title plant*. The title plant consists of the public records of a specific geographic area (e.g., town, city, county) that have been indexed and integrated so that an individual parcel of real property may be located easily. The title insurer or an abstractor prepares an abstract from the title plant records. An abstract is a short summary of the ownership history of a specific parcel of real property.

A title plant usually is revised on a daily basis. A well-maintained title plant usually will increase in value over time. The estimated useful life of a title plant generally is indefinite.

Accounting for Title Plant

Capitalization of Title Plant

Until a title plant is ready for use, all direct costs incurred to acquire, organize, or construct the title plant are capitalized (FAS-61, par. 3).

> ☛ **PRACTICE POINTER:** A title plant may be constructed or purchased by an enterprise. In either case, capitalize costs directly identified with the title plant. A purchase may consist of (a) a copy of the title plant, (b) an undivided interest in the title plant, or (c) the exclusive ownership (outright purchase) of the title plant (FAS-61, par. 4).

A title plant that is constructed or otherwise acquired will cover a definite period of time. For example, an enterprise may purchase a title plant of a particular geographic area that covers the period January 1, 1940, through December 31, 2001. Subsequently, the enterprise may construct or otherwise acquire a title plant for the same geographic area that covers the period from January 1, 1900, through December 31, 1939. This type of title plant is sometimes referred to as an *antecedent title plant* or *backplant*. The same rules for capitalization of direct costs apply. Thus, costs incurred to construct or otherwise acquire a backplant are capitalized if they can be identified directly with the acquisition of the backplant (FAS-61, par. 5).

FAS-61 states that capitalized costs of a title plant should not ordinarily be depreciated or otherwise charged to income. Unless there is an impairment in the carrying amount of the title plant, the undepreciated capitalized costs are reported as an asset indefinitely on the balance sheet. The impairment of a title plant below its carrying amount is recognized in the income of the period in which the impairment is discovered (FAS-61, par. 6).

☛ **PRACTICE POINTER:** The carrying amount of a title plant may become impaired if:

- The title plant is not properly maintained on a current basis.
- The title plant becomes partially or completely obsolete.
- The title plant is abandoned or severely neglected.
- Economics, competition, or legal factors result in a decline in the value of the title plant.

Maintenance and Operating Expenses

Costs incurred to revise a title plant may be expensed or capitalized separately, but may not be added to the carrying amount of the title plant. If such costs are capitalized separately, they are amortized over their estimated useful lives in a systematic manner (FAS-61, par. 8).

FAS-61 requires that all title plant maintenance and operational costs be expensed in the period incurred. The cost to update or maintain the title plant on a current basis and the cost of performing title searches to issue title policies are expensed as they are incurred (FAS-61, par. 7).

Sale of Title Plant

A sale of a title plant may consist of (*a*) an outright sale, (*b*) a sale of an undivided interest, or (*c*) a sale of a copy, or the right to use, the title plant. FAS-61 requires that gain or loss on any sale of a title plant be reported separately in the financial statements (FAS-61, par. 9).

Gain or loss on the sale of a title plant depends on the type of sale executed by the seller. In the event of an outright sale of the title plant, gain or loss is the difference between the selling price and the net carrying amount of the title plant on the date of sale (FAS-61, par. 9a).

In the event of the sale of an undivided interest in a title plant, gain or loss is the difference between the selling price and the pro rata portion of the title plant that is attributable to the sale of the undivided interest (FAS-61, par. 9b).

In a sale of a copy, or the right to use the title plant, no cost is allocated to the sale unless the value of the title plant decreases as a result of the sale. In the sale of a copy or the right to use the title plant, the sales price usually represents the gain on the sale (FAS-61, par. 9c).

Illustration of Accounting for Expenditures Related to Title Plant

Beta Co. engaged in the following activities related to the establishment of a title plant. It paid $50,000 of direct costs to construct and organize the title plant, $12,500 to perform title searches to support the issuance of title policies, and $10,000 to update the title plant. Beta Co. determined that the title plant had experienced a $7,000 impairment in value. Beta Co. sold the title plant for $52,000.

The $10,000 paid to update the title plant is to be capitalized separately and amortized over its estimated useful life of five years. The sale of the title plant occurred two years after the updating had been done.

Entries to record the above transaction are as follows:

To record the construction and organization of the title plant:

Title plant	50,000	
Cash		50,000

To record the cost of performing title searches:

Title search expense	12,500	
Cash		12,500

To record the cost of updating the title plant:

Deferred title plant updating cost	10,000	
Cash		10,000

To record amortization of the cost of updating the title plant:

Amortization expense ($10,000 / 5)	2,000	
Cash		2,000

(A similar entry is made each year until the updating cost is fully amortized.)

To record the impairment in value of the title plant:

Impairment loss on title plant	7,000	
Title plant		7,000

To record sale of title plant:

Cash	52,000	
Title plant ($50,000 –$7,000)		43,000
Deferred title plant updating cost ($10,000 – $4,000)		6,000
Gain on sale of title plant		3,000

INSURANCE
IMPORTANT NOTICE FOR 2009

As the 2009 *GAAP Guide Level A* goes to press, the FASB has outstanding an Exposure Draft of a proposed Interpretation titled, "Accounting for Financial Guarantee Insurance Contracts: An Interpretation of FASB Standard No. 60." A financial guarantee insurance contract is issued by an insurer to a party holding a financial asset (e.g., a municipal bond), and promises payment to the holder of the guarantee contract if the issuer of the financial asset fails to pay required principal or interest payments (i.e., default).

FAS-60, *Accounting and Reporting by Insurance Enterprises*, issued in 1982, is the primary source of accounting and reporting guidance for insurance enterprises. Financial guarantors contend that FAS-60 does not sufficiently address the unique aspects of financial guarantee insurance contracts, primarily because such contracts did not exist at the time FAS-60 was issued. This contention has led to diversity in practice for financial guarantee insurance contracts. The FASB added a project on this subject to its agenda in June 2005.

The objective of the Financial Guarantee Insurance project is to improve the comparability of financial reporting by insurance enterprises by establishing a single approach for recognition and measurement of financial guarantee insurance contracts under FAS-60. The focus is on premium revenue and claim liabilities. In addition, the Exposure Draft would require additional disclosures about financial guarantee insurance contracts that would improve the usefulness of information provided to financial statement users.

Several of the major decisions made to date are summarized as follows:

- An insurance enterprise would recognize a claim liability on a financial guarantee insurance contract when it expects a claim loss will exceed the unearned premium revenue for that contract based on expected cash flows. The discount rate used to measure the claim liability would be on the risk-free market rate and updated each quarter.

- Premium revenue recognition guidance will be provided based on applying a fixed percentage of the premium to the amount of outstanding exposure at each reporting date.

- An asset would be recognized for the premium receivable and a liability for the unearned premium revenue at inception of a financial guarantee insurance contract where premiums are received in installments.

- Extensive additional disclosures would be required.

The revised proposed effective date of the Exposure Draft is for financial statements in fiscal years beginning after December 15, 2008. The current FASB project plan shows an expected issuance date of a final standard in the second quarter of 2008.

RELATED CHAPTER IN 2009 *INTERNATIONAL ACCOUNTING/FINANCIAL REPORTING STANDARDS GUIDE*

Chapter 34, "Insurance Contracts"

APPENDIX: INSURANCE PRIMER

PROPERTY AND LIABILITY INSURANCE COMPANIES

Other than the different products sold, property and liability companies (property and casualty companies) and life insurance companies are similar in that they are structured as:

- A mutual company (assessable or nonassessable, participating or nonparticipating)
- A capital stock company
- A reciprocal or interinsurance exchange

Regardless of the structure of the company, reinsurance typically is sought from other insurance companies or specialty reinsurers to spread the burden of losses.

The principal differences among mutual and stock insurance companies relate to ownership and the distribution of profits and losses.

Mutual vs. Stock Companies

	Ownership	Profits	Losses
Nonparticipating assessable mutual	Policyholders	Rates adjusted	Policyholders assessed and reinsurance
Nonparticipating nonassessable mutual	Policyholders	Rates adjusted downward	Rates adjusted upward and reinsurance
Participating assessable mutual	Policyholders	Dividends to policyholders	Policyholders assessed and reinsurance
Participating nonassessable mutual	Policyholders	Dividends to policyholders	Rates adjusted upward and reinsurance
Stock company (corporate form)	Shareholders	Shareholders	Reinsurance

RECIPROCALS AND INTERINSURANCE EXCHANGES

Reciprocals and interinsurance exchanges are unincorporated forms of cooperative insurance facilities. Such organizations hold approximately 2.4% of the insurance market. They are not insurance companies, but are organizations created by entities (factories, municipalities, etc.) that share similar risks of loss.

Each member agrees to pay its share of the losses of the entire group from its own assets (limited to an amount specified in the agreement among the members).

Most property and liability insurance companies sell multiple lines of insurance. The lines of property and liability insurance usually are grouped as the following:

- Property coverage
- Business liability
- Business auto policies
- Package policies
- Crime insurance
- Bonding
- Workers' compensation and disability benefits coverage
- Personal lines policies
  — Auto
  — Homeowners

- Boiler and equipment policies
- Inland marine (floaters) coverage
- Ocean marine (ships, cargo, yacht) coverage

From an economic standpoint, insurance is a method used to spread a specific risk among policyholders. The insurance company assumes the specific risk and charges a premium based on past loss experiences for the specific risk. The premiums collected by the insurance company are used to pay current losses and operational costs, and the balance is invested. Thus, the two main sources of income for a property and liability insurance company are (1) premiums and (2) investment income.

INSURABLE INTEREST

An owner of an insurance contract must have an insurable interest in the subject matter of the policy for the contract to be valid. An insurable interest in life insurance need only exist at the time the policy is issued, while an insurable interest in property insurance must exist at the time of the loss.

An insurable interest is a test of financial relationship. A husband may insure the life of his wife, an employer the life of an employee, a creditor the life of his or her debtor, and a partner the life of his or her co-partners. In life insurance the insurable interest must exist only at the time the policy is issued, and if the relationship is subsequently broken (e.g., divorce, dissolution of a partnership) the owner may still collect the benefits of the insurance contract.

In property insurance, the insurable interest must exist at the time a loss is incurred. If a landlord sells a piece of property, he or she has no further insurable interest on the property and is not entitled to collect for any losses on it.

DEPARTMENTAL FUNCTIONS

The departmental functions of a typical property and liability insurance company would consist of (a) an agency department, (b) an underwriting department, (c) a policy service department, (d) an investment department, and (e) a claims department.

The agency department is responsible for the marketing functions of the insurance company. Supervision and training of sales personnel, sales promotion, and other selling activities are handled by the agency department. Most property and liability companies market their policies through independent agents under a franchise arrangement.

The underwriting department is responsible for evaluating the risks that are submitted to the insurance company, and it controls the issuance of policies.

The policy service department is responsible for bookkeeping activities, such as premium notices and collection, changes in address, beneficiary and similar changes, and the payment of loss claims.

The investment department manages the insurance company's investments.

The claims department is responsible for assessing and approving claims.

CASH BASIS

Usually, insurance companies keep their general ledgers on a cash basis. Some reports required by regulatory agencies must be prepared on a cash basis, particularly details of income and expense. Assets that have been recorded on the books of an insurance company are called *ledger assets*. Others are called *nonledger assets*. Nonledger assets arise from the adjusting journal entries necessary to convert the cash basis trial balance to the accrual basis. Liabilities are referred to in the same manner, so those recorded on the books are called *ledger liabilities* and others are called *nonledger liabilities*.

Because insurance companies use the cash basis, most liabilities are nonledger. An insurance company will have few nonledger assets, because most of its assets arise from cash transactions.

When adjusting journal entries are made for workpapers to convert the cash basis trial balance to the accrual basis, they are not posted to the books. Therefore, the books of insurance companies are on the cash basis. The insurance company will keep other records, such as a *claims register*, so that information is available to adjust easily to the accrual basis.

The claims register keeps track of claims pending, paid, negotiated, and rejected, while the cash basis trial balance reflects only the claims actually paid. The claims register is used to prepare some of the adjusting journal entries necessary for conversion to the accrual basis.

REINSURANCE

When an insurance company issues a policy (contract), it assumes the risk of loss from the policyholder in exchange for a premium. The policyholder, unable to bear the risk alone, passes it to the insurance company.

The insurer may hold the risk for the duration of the contract, or may itself seek to pass along all or a portion of the risk to another professional risk bearer, in exchange for a portion of the premium collected from the policyholder.

In the practice of reinsurance, the insurers are labeled:

- *Ceding carrier*   The company that issues the policy to the policyholder
- *Assuming carrier*   The reinsurance company

Reinsurance is arranged between the ceding and assuming carriers under the following types of contracts:

- *Quota share reinsurance*   Each company pays a predetermined percentage of every loss.
- *Excess cover reinsurance*   The ceding carrier agrees to pay all losses up to a specified dollar amount over which the reinsurer pays all amounts.
- *Facultative reinsurance*   A single reinsurance contract for a specific policy or policyholder.
- *Blanket reinsurance*   The assuming carrier agrees to automatically reinsure the policies issued by the ceding carrier subject to

prearranged conditions, costs, and limitations. The ceding carrier submits a monthly report of all policies issued under the agreement with payment of the premiums due.

REGULATION OF THE INDUSTRY

The insurance industry is state-regulated. The insurance department of each state monitors the solvency, dealings, and investments of insurance companies. The companies make mandatory periodic reports to the insurance departments.

The National Association of Insurance Commissioners (NAIC) is an organization composed of the insurance commissioners from each state. It meets semiannually and makes recommendations for new rules and procedures, which are almost always adopted by the states. NAIC is concerned with financial reporting and auditing of insurance companies, and has assisted in the development of uniform annual reports and an examiner's manual written in the form of an audit program for insurance companies.

MARKETING

Insurance companies market their policies through:

- Company agents
- Captive agents
- Brokers
- Independent agents
- General agents

Company Agents

Company agents are employees of the insurer. They are paid a salary or a combination of salary and commissions on the policies they sell. A company agent may bind the insurer to a contract for insurance.

Captive Agents

Captive agents are independent contractors who have agreed to represent one ins urer exclusively and sell only its products (some exceptions are made for risks the insurer will not accept). A captive agency carries all its own expenses, but it does not own the list of policyholders it produces. A captive agent may bind the insurer to a contract for insurance.

Brokers

Brokers are independent enterprises. A broker's function is to represent a client, not the insurer. The broker presents the client's proposal for insurance to any insurer willing to consider business from the broker. A broker has no powers of agency with the insurers, and coverage is effective only when deemed so by the insurer. A broker also may solicit coverage for a client from an agent of the insurer.

Independent Agents

Independent agents are independent contractors who are free to represent several insurers. The independent agent has the power to bind the insurers to insurance contracts within the prearranged limits and guidelines. The agency carries all its own expenses and typically also acts as a broker if so licensed and when required.

General Agents

General agents are independent contractors who have been given virtually all the powers and functions of the insurer itself, including:

- Binding the insurer on contracts of insurance
- Appointing agents
- Managing the insurer's business in a given exclusive territory
- Paying claims
- Issuing policies

CLAIM SERVICE

Insurance companies may handle their policy claims through salaried employees who investigate a claim and propose a settlement with the claimant. They also may use adjustment bureaus to investigate, adjust, and settle claims. Adjustment bureaus are sponsored by member insurance companies. The expenses of a bureau are paid by the members, usually based on the number of claims handled or the dollar value of the claims. Usually the right of final approval of all settlements made by an adjustment bureau is exercised by the insurance company. Members are not obligated to use the bureau.

Independent insurance adjustors, who work on a fee basis, are another alternative an insurance company may use.

Most of the accounting and statistical data used by a property and liability insurance company appears in the daily reports. A *daily report* is a copy of the front of the insurance policy that contains practically all the accounting and statistical data necessary to record the transaction. Copies of the daily reports are distributed to several departments at the home office of the insurance company.

STOCK LIFE INSURANCE COMPANIES

The proceeds of a life insurance policy are intended to provide financial security to one or more beneficiaries named in the policy. Upon death of the insured, the insurance company pays the beneficiary the face amount of the policy, less any outstanding indebtedness. The proceeds of the insurance policy are not always paid in a lump sum. One alternative, for example, is an election made by a policyholder for the insurance company to pay the beneficiary certain periodic amounts, or to pay the proceeds when the beneficiary reaches a specified age. In this event, the proceeds are held by the insurance company and usually will earn interest. Almost any type of arrangement can be made with a life insurance company for the payment of a policy's proceeds.

From an economic standpoint, insurance is a method of spreading a specific risk among many individuals. The insurance company assumes the specific risk, such as death, and charges a premium based on actuarial calculations.

In the case of death, mortality tables reflecting the frequency of deaths of individuals in various age groups are used to predict the life expectancy of the insured.

Illustration of Use of Mortality Tables

Note: The mortality figures and other detailed information in this example are included for illustration only and should not be relied upon to represent accurate amounts at a specific point in time.

- For a group of 100,000 males, age 20, the death rate in a year is 179.
- Therefore, the rate per $1,000 of life insurance for one year for a 20-year-old male is $1.79.
- The insurance company then loads the rate to cover:
  — Costs of processing
  — Commissions
  — Profit

- A final rate per $1,000 of life insurance for a 20-year-old male would be approximately $2.14.
- The annual premium for pure life insurance of $100,000 for the 20-year-old male would be $214.

The premiums collected by the insurance company are used to pay current benefits and costs, and the balance is invested to yield investment income. Theoretically, if an individual dies in the year that the mortality tables predict, the accumulated net premiums collected by the insurance company, plus the investment earned on the accumulated premiums, should be sufficient to pay the face amount of the policy and still leave a profit. These accumulated premiums and investment income are reflected on the balance sheet of an insurance company as *policy reserves.*

Annuities

The function of an annuity contract is to pay out accumulated cash systematically to the beneficiary (*annuitant*). An annuity can be:

- A temporary annuity—payable for a fixed number of years.
- A whole-life annuity—payable for the life of the annuitant.

In its elemental form, the contract pays the annuitant only while he or she is alive. If the annuitant dies while collecting annuity benefits, the insurance company keeps the funds and uses them to pay other annuitants who are living beyond their predicted life expectancies.

Modern annuities have a refund option whereby a cash refund of unused money is paid to a contingent beneficiary upon the death of the annuitant. There are two types of annuities:

1. A *joint and survivorship contract* involves two or more annuitants and provides for guaranteed periodic payments to any surviving annuitant.

2. The periodic annuity payment from a *variable annuity* fluctuates in accordance with investment experience. Investments for variable annuities are kept in a separate fund, and the amount of the periodic annuity is based on the performance of the investments. Variable annuities may or may not include a minimum death benefit during the accumulation period.

Accident and health insurance policies are issued on an individual or group basis. The policies pay for hospital and medical care, and sometimes for the loss of income during periods that the insured is incapacitated.

Generally, life insurance companies are exempt from registration under the Securities Exchange Act of 1934. Many insurance companies have established holding companies, however, that are not considered life insurance companies and, thus, must be registered under the 1934 Act. In addition, some insurance companies have registered their shares under the 1934 Act so that the shares can be listed and traded on a national stock exchange. Public offerings of life insurance companies' stock must be registered under the Securities Act of 1933.

If an insurance company has registered under either of the securities acts, it must comply with annual and periodic reporting requirements and proxy solicitation rules.

An insurance company receives its revenues from premiums and investment income. Premium income may be derived directly from the owner of the policy or from reinsurance agreements with other insurance companies. Investment income is regulated by insurance statutes that set forth the types of investments that may be made.

Life insurance companies generally sell (*a*) life insurance, (*b*) annuity contracts, and (*c*) accident and health contracts. The more common policies are discussed below.

Whole-Life Policies

Benefits, which are paid upon death of the insured, are equal to the face amount of the policy, less cash value borrowed from the policy by the policyholder. Whole-life policies usually accumulate a cash surrender value, which increases over time. The owner of the policy can borrow from the insurance policy. The accumulated cash value can be used as collateral to secure a bank loan.

Premiums for whole-life insurance generally are level; that is, they are the same amount each year. They are payable annually, but more frequent payments can be made by payment of a small service fee. A whole-life policy can be paid in one lump-sum payment at the beginning of the policy term. Most policies are paid quarterly, semiannually, or annually. A *straight-life* policy (also called *ordinary life*) requires that premiums be paid during the entire life of the insured (to age 100). A limited-payment policy requires that premiums be paid over a specified period, usually 10, 20, or 30 years. As a result, the premiums on a limited-payment policy are always higher than those of a straight-life policy, but the total cost of the policy usually is less. Coverage remains in force for the entire life of the insured.

Limited-Payment Life Contracts

A limited-payment plan is a modified form of whole-life insurance, made up of elements of whole-life and term insurance. Premiums are used to provide term insurance coverage and simultaneously accrue a cash reserve. At a specified date, the policyholder stops paying premiums and the accrued cash is used to purchase term coverage on the policyholder's life to an age of 61 or 70.

Universal-Life Contracts

In the late 1970s, interest rates soared (as high as 21% prime rate). Whole-life policyholders who were realizing 3% to 4% on the cash reserve in their policies found it beneficial to cancel the whole-life contract and invest the cash surrender value in a money market instrument.

In response to mass cancellations, insurers developed the universal-life contract, which mated life insurance coverage with money market returns.

Projections of earnings are based on interest rates at the time of the inception of the policy; however, three factors inherent in the contract will affect the real net result:

1. The mortality rate upon which the contract price was quoted can be adjusted by the insurance company. If it is adjusted upward, more of the premium is used to provide life coverage, and less is used to accumulate a cash reserve.

2. The insurer can charge fees against the policy that may be subject to change at the insurer's option.

3. Interest rates are adjusted throughout the policy term.

Term Insurance Policies

Term insurance policies are issued for a specific period, and death benefits are paid only if the insured dies during the specified period. Benefits are equal to the face amount of the policy. Term insurance policies do not accumulate any cash surrender value.

Term insurance policies are written for short periods, usually one to five years. In most cases, however, the policyholder is granted the right to renew a term insurance policy up to a maximum age (60 or 65) without having to submit additional evidence of insurability. The term policy also may grant the policyholder the right to convert the term insurance to whole-life or some other type of coverage.

Premiums for term insurance policies usually increase with the age of the insured. Payments must be made annually, but they may be made at interim periods during the year for an additional service charge.

Since term insurance does not accumulate any cash value, the premiums constitute payment for insurance protection only. Thus, most people feel that term insurance is best when pure protection is sought.

An insurance company may issue group term life insurance policies. A group term policy insures a specific group of individuals under a single master contract, usually for one year. Premiums are calculated on the basis of the ages of the individuals in the group.

Endowment Insurance Policies

Endowment policies are issued for a specific time, called the *endowment period*, and they have a maturity date on which the insured receives the face amount of the policy, less any indebtedness to the insurance company. If the insured dies during the endowment period, however, the insurance company pays the face amount, less any indebtedness, to the beneficiary of the policy. Thus, the insured has insurance protection during the endowment period and, if living at the maturity date, receives the face amount of the policy, less any indebtedness to the insurance company. Endowment policies accumulate a cash value, which increases with time and may be used as collateral for a loan.

Premiums for endowment policies can be a single lump-sum payment or a limited-payment basis, but generally they are payable over the endowment period specified in the policy.

Basic insurance policies can be expanded by the use of riders that are attached to, and made part of, the insurance contract.

Nonforfeiture Benefits in Whole-Life Insurance

The standard nonforfeiture law of 1948 protects policyholders who allow their whole-life policy to lapse. The insurance company must offer the policyholder:

- The cash surrender value of the policy in cash payment to the insured.

- A reduced paid-up life policy to death (accumulated cash in the policy is used to purchase a lesser amount of permanent coverage).

- Extended term coverage (the accumulated cash in the policy is used to purchase term insurance expiring at age 65 or 70).

Waiver of Premium Rider

This rider provides for the waiver of all premiums during periods of disability of the insured. An accidental death benefit rider (double indemnity) provides that, if the insured dies by accidental means, the insurance company will pay multiples (usually two or three times) of the face amount of the policy. An additional premium is charged for each rider.

Health Insurance

Health insurance typically is offered in these forms:

- Basic hospital benefits
  — Providing scheduled coverage [a specified amount per day for room and board for a certain maximum number of days (no deductible)]
- Basic doctor/surgical benefits
  — Providing scheduled coverage (a specified amount for certain listed procedures)
- Major medical coverage
  — Providing coverage that applies in addition to the basic coverages when those coverages have been exhausted by a claim
  — Coverage for all other medical expenses not included in the basic coverages
  — The major medical coverage is payable after a deductible, either after the basic coverage is exhausted or before any payment for uncovered medical expenses.
  — After the deductible, the major medical coverage pays only 80% of the covered claim up to a specified dollar limit. Thereafter, the claim is covered 100% to the limit (if one exists) of the major medical policy (coinsurance).

CHAPTER 50
MORTGAGE BANKING

CONTENTS

OVERVIEW

Mortgage banking activities primarily consist of three separate but interrelated activities: (1) the origination or acquisition of mortgage loans, (2) the sale of the loans to permanent investors, and (3) the subsequent long-term servicing of the loans. GAAP for mortgage banking activities, which prescribe principles in these and other related areas of accounting, are found in the following pronouncements:

FAS-65   Accounting for Certain Mortgage Banking Activities

FAS-91   Accounting for Nonrefundable Fees and Costs Associated with Originating or Acquiring Loans and Initial Direct Costs of Leases

FAS-134   Accounting for Mortgage-Backed Securities Retained after the Securitization of Mortgage Loans Held for Sale by a Mortgage Banking Enterprise

BACKGROUND

FAS-65 (Accounting for Certain Mortgage Banking Activities) contains the specialized accounting and reporting principles and practices that were originally published in SOP 74-12 (Accounting Practices in the Mortgage Banking Industry) and SOP 76-2 (Accounting for Origination Costs and Loan and Commitment Fees in the Mortgage Banking Industry).

FAS-65 establishes GAAP for an enterprise or that portion of an enterprise's operations engaged primarily in originating, marketing, and servicing mortgage loans for other than its own account. A financial institution or other enterprise that has operations that consist of originating, marketing, and servicing mortgage loans for others must apply the provisions of FAS-65 to those operations. FAS-65 was amended by FAS-91 (Accounting for Nonrefundable Fees and Costs Associated with Originating or Acquiring Loans and Direct Costs of Leases) and FAS-122 (Accounting for Mortgage Service Rights), which subsequently was amended by FAS-125 (Accounting for Transfers and Servicing of Financial Assets and Extinguishments of Liabilities), which was superseded by FAS-140 (Accounting for Transfers and Servicing of Financial Assets and Extinguishments of Liabilities—A Replacement of FASB Statement No. 125).

MORTGAGE LOANS

One of the more difficult problems in accounting for mortgage loans receivable and mortgage-backed securities of an enterprise engaged in mortgage banking activity is the valuation for reporting purposes.

The valuation of mortgage loans receivable and mortgage-backed securities depends upon whether they are held for sale or for longterm investment. Most mortgage loans and mortgage-backed securities are held for sale in the ordinary course of business of a mortgage banker. Valuation of mortgage loans receivable and mortgage-backed securities for reporting purposes is determined as of the balance sheet date.

FAS-65, as amended by FAS-115 (Accounting for Certain Investments in Debt and Equity Securities) and FAS-125, which was superseded by FAS-140, requires that after the securitization of a mortgage loan held for resale, a mortgage banking enterprise must classify the resulting mortgage-backed security as a trading security. FAS-134 (Accounting for Mortgage-Backed Securities Retained after the Securitization of Mortgage Loans Held for Sale by a Mortgage Banking Enterprise) amends this requirement so that, after the securitization of a mortgage loan held for sale, any retained mortgage-backed securities are to be classified as trading, available-for-sale, or held-to-maturity in accordance with FAS-115 (FAS-134, par. 3).

Held for Long-Term Investment

For a mortgage loan or mortgage-backed security to be classified as a long-term investment, the banking enterprise must have the requisite intent and ability to hold the loan to maturity or for an extended period. When a mortgage loan receivable is reclassified as a long-term investment, the transfer must be made at the lower of cost or market on the date of transfer (FAS-65, par. 6). In the event of a permanent impairment in the value of a mortgage loan classified as a long-term investment, its carrying value is further reduced to net realizable value. The amount of reduction is reported in net income of the period in which the impairment is discovered. In subsequent periods, any market recovery from the net realizable value is realized only at the time of sale, maturity, or other disposition of the mortgage loan (FAS-65, par. 7).

Any difference between the carrying amount of the loan and its outstanding principal balance is recognized as an adjustment to yield and amortized to income by the interest method over the estimated life of the loan. The interest method is applied in accordance with paragraphs 18 and 19 of FAS-91 (FAS-91, par. 27).

Held for Sale

All mortgage loans receivable held for sale are valued at the lower of cost or market (as defined by FAS-65), according to the type of mortgage loan. Write-downs of a mortgage loan to the lower of cost or market are included in net income of the period in which the adjustment occurs (FAS-65, par. 4). If a mortgage loan has been the hedged item in a fair value hedge, the loan's cost basis used in lower-of-cost-or-market accounting should reflect the effect of the adjustment of its carrying amount to fair value in accordance with FAS-133 (Accounting for Derivative Instruments and Hedging Activities) (FAS-133, par. 529a).

After write-down, write-ups to market values in subsequent periods are recorded, but total recorded market value is not permitted to exceed cost. The journal entry to record the recovery of market value is a debit to mortgage loans (valuation allowance) and a credit to an income account.

For the purposes of disclosure, mortgage loans and mortgage-backed securities are classified in at least the following two categories: (1) residential (one to four units) and (2) commercial. Lower of cost or market can be determined on the total of all mortgage loans in a particular category or for each individual mortgage loan or mortgage-backed security (FAS-65, par. 9).

Discounts resulting from the purchase of mortgage loans that are held for sale are not realized as income until the loans are actually sold.

Lower of cost or market is determined in accordance with the type of mortgage loan receivable or mortgage-based security, as follows (FAS-65, par. 9):

- *Loans and Securities Covered by Commitments* Mortgage loans and mortgage-backed securities are based on fair values (FAS-65, par. 9 and FAS-133, par. 529b).

  Mortgage loans that do not conform to the required specifications in the commitments, or where reasonable doubts exist about the acceptance of the commitment, are viewed as uncommitted (FAS-65, footnote 3).

- *Loans Not Covered by Commitments* Market value for loans not covered by commitments is the market value of the loans as determined by reference to the normal market in which the mortgage banker operates (FAS-65, par. 9).

  Quotations supplied by GNMA or by the FNMA Free Market System or other public markets should be used when appropriate. If no established market quotations are available, market prices should be determined by the enterprise's normal market outlets.

- *Mortgage-Backed Securities Not Covered by Commitments* The fair value of mortgage-backed securities not covered by commitments that are collateralized by the mortgage bank's own loans is typically based on the securities' market value. In some cases, the trust holding the loans can be readily terminated and the loans sold directly. In these cases, the securities' fair value is based on the market value of the loans or securities, depending on the mortgage bank's sales intent. In other cases, fair value is based on the published mortgage-backed securities yields (FAS-65, par. 9; FAS-115, par. 128[g]).

Costs of Purchasing Mortgage Loans

Certain costs may be capitalized in acquiring the rights to service mortgage loans. These costs are not included in determining the loan's cost in valuing the loan at lower of cost or market (FAS-65, par. 10).

Repurchase Agreements

Frequently, a mortgage banking enterprise will enter into formal or informal repurchase agreements (repos) with a lending institution. In a repurchase agreement, the mortgage banking enterprise will give the lending institution a block of mortgage loans and/or mortgage-backed securities as collateral for a loan. On the surface, the transaction may appear as a sale of the mortgage loans and/or mortgage-backed securities to the lending institution, with an agreement, formal or otherwise, that the mortgage banking enterprise will repurchase the loans and/or securities at an agreed-upon price, usually equal to the amount of the loan. If the mortgage banking enterprise fails to repurchase the mortgage loans and/or mortgage-backed securities in accordance with the agreement, the lending institution exercises ownership of the loans and/or securities. The mortgage banking enterprise pays an agreed-upon rate of interest for the use of the funds.

Formal and informal repurchase agreements are accounted for by the mortgage banking enterprise as a financing, and no sale is recorded.

Historically, short-term interest rates have always been less than long-term interest rates. Thus, when a mortgage banker paid interest on short-term warehouse loans, the interest received on the pledged mortgage loans always exceeded the amount paid to carry them on a short-term basis. The difference between the short-term and long-term interest rates creates a *positive spread* for the mortgage banker. Sometimes interest rates reverse, however, and short-term rates exceed long-term rates. This results in a *negative spread*. Since the cost of warehousing mortgage loans by a mortgage banker is primarily a financing activity, negative spreads in interest rates should be charged to current operations as they are incurred.

Mortgage Servicing Fees

Mortgage loans require servicing, including collecting, sending notices, maintaining mortgage records, and other related chores. The owner of a loan or portfolio of loans may perform the servicing function, or it may contract with someone else to perform such services. Servicing fees are based on a percentage of the unpaid principal balance of the loans. Servicing revenue can be substantial.

OBSERVATION: Accounting for servicing assets and liabilities was previously covered in FAS-65, but is now found in FAS-140 (Accounting for Transfers and Servicing of Financial Assets and Extinguishments of Liabilities). The reader is encouraged to consult "Transfer and Servicing of Financial Assets," of this *Guide* for coverage of this topic.

Normal Servicing Fees

Under FAS-65, a current (normal) servicing fee rate is representative of servicing fee rates most commonly used in comparable servicing agreements covering similar types of mortgage loans (FAS-65, par. 34). Federally sponsored secondary market makers for mortgage loans, such as Government National Mortgage Association (GNMA), Federal Home Loan Mortgage Corporation (FHLMC), and Federal National Mortgage Association (FNMA), set minimum servicing fee rates. For purposes of determining gain or loss on mortgage loans sold to those agencies with servicing retained, servicing fee rates that are specified in servicing agreements with GNMA, FHLMC, and FNMA generally are considered *normal servicing fee rates*, as that term is used in FAS-65.

If a seller-servicer sells mortgage loans directly to private-sector investors and retains the servicing of those loans, the seller-servicer should charge the private-sector investors a *current (normal) servicing fee rate* as defined in FAS-65. The seller-servicer should consider the normal servicing fee rates currently being charged by federally sponsored secondary market makers in comparable servicing agreements for similar types of mortgage loans.

If the servicing fee rate charged by the seller-servicer is not a normal servicing fee rate, an adjustment must be made to the sales price of the mortgage loans to the private-sector investors. In this event, gain or loss on the sale of the mortgage loans is adjusted to provide a normal profit on future servicing income, based on estimated prevailing normal servicing fee rates. The amount of adjustment is calculated on the date of sale and is equal to the difference between total servicing fee income based on current prevailing normal servicing fee rates and total servicing fee income based on the contractually agreed-upon servicing fee rate.

Prepayments of mortgage loans generally are taken into consideration at the time servicing rights are recorded on the books of a servicer of mortgage loans. The servicer sets up an allowance for future prepayments that may occur from refinancings or other sources. In this event, when there is a prepayment, no adjustment to the recorded amount of the servicing right is necessary. If the mortgage loan servicer did not set up an allowance for prepayments at the time the servicing right was originally recorded, however, an adjustment to the servicing right asset would be required when a prepayment is made.

Transactions with Affiliates

In separate financial statements of mortgage banking enterprises, special treatment is afforded sales of mortgage loans that are made to affiliated enterprises. The selling affiliate must first adjust the carrying amount of the mortgage loans to the lower of cost or market before computing gain or loss on the sale. Any adjustment is charged or credited to income by the selling affiliate. The gain or loss on the sale of mortgage loans to an affiliated enterprise is the difference between the sales price and the lower of cost or market of the loans (FAS-65, par. 12).

Gain or loss on the sale or mortgage loans is determined as of the measurement date, which is the first date that management decides that the sale shall take place. The measurement date must be supported by formal approval of the sale by the purchasing affiliate and the issuance of a binding commitment. The binding commitment must be approved and accepted by the selling mortgage banker (FAS-65, par. 12).

A mortgage banker may act as an agent for an affiliated company. The affiliated company is principal and retains all risks of ownership. In its capacity as an agent, the mortgage banker will originate certain specified types of loans for, and authorized by, the affiliated company. Under these circumstances, the mortgage banker may charge an origination fee for services rendered in acquiring the loans. The affiliated company should record the loans acquired at the mortgage banker's acquisition cost (FAS-65, par. 13).

Agreements or arrangements that do not bind the affiliated company to purchase the loans originated by the affiliated mortgage banker, such as *right of first refusal* contracts, do not establish a principal–agency relationship (FAS-65, par. 13).

> **OBSERVATION:**   This section on transactions with affiliates is applicable only to the separate financial statements of mortgage banking enterprises. Also, in separate financial statements of mortgage banking enterprises, material transactions with affiliates are subject to the disclosure provisions of FAS-57 (Related Party Disclosures).

Issuance Costs for GNMA Securities

A mortgage banking enterprise may use either the concurrent dates method (15 days) or the internal reserve method (45 days) to pay the holder(s) of GNMA mortgage-backed securities. Only under the internal reserve method is the mortgage banking enterprise required to deposit one month's interest on the mortgage loans with a trustee (FAS-65, par. 15).

Under the provisions of FAS-65, the one month's interest required by the internal reserve method is capitalized and amortized by a mortgage banking enterprise. Amortization of any amount deferred is over the period of, and in proportion to, the estimated net servicing income expected to be earned from the related underlying mortgage loans.

The total amount deferred by a mortgage banking enterprise for issuance costs or under any other provision of FAS-65 may not exceed the present value of the future net servicing income (FAS-65, par. 15). Future net servicing income is the difference between estimated future servicing revenue and the estimated future related servicing costs.

LOAN AND COMMITMENT FEES

Nonrefundable loan and commitment fees representing compensation for a variety of services may be received or paid by a mortgage banking enterprise. Examples of fees received are fees for designating funds for the borrower, fees for services rendered by a third party, and fees received for arranging a loan between a permanent investor and a borrower (FAS-65, par. 20).

Fees received for services rendered by a third party relating to loan origination costs, such as appraisal fees, are recognized when the services are performed (FAS-65, par. 22).

When a mortgage banking institution arranges a loan commitment between a permanent investor and a borrower, the loan placement fee received is recognized as revenue when all significant services have been performed. Loan placement fees also include transactions in which a commitment is obtained from an investor before or at the time a related commitment is made to a borrower, and the commitment from the borrower requires the simultaneous assignment of the commitment to the investor and the transfer to the borrower of the funds received from the investor (FAS-65, par. 24).

Certain fees ordinarily relate to blocks of loans, such as residential loan fees. In such a case, the fee recognized for an individual loan transaction is based on the ratio of the individual loan amount to the total commitment amount (FAS-65, par. 23).

FAS-91 provides additional guidance in accounting for loan and commitment fees.

FINANCIAL STATEMENT DISCLOSURE

Balance sheet presentations of mortgage banking enterprises for reporting purposes may be classified or unclassified. Mortgage loans receivable must be disclosed separately as to: (*a*) those held for sale and (*b*) those held for long-term investment (FAS-65, par. 28). In addition, disclosure must be made of the method used to determine the lower of cost or market value of mortgage loans receivable and mortgage-backed securities (FAS-65, par. 29).

NONREFUNDABLE FEES AND COSTS ASSOCIATED WITH ORIGINATING OR ACQUIRING LOANS

Loan origination fees and commitment fees represent a primary source of revenue to a mortgage banking enterprise. In addition, a mortgage banker may pay a fee to a permanent investor for that permanent investor's commitment to purchase certain specified mortgage loans from the mortgage banker during a specified term.

FAS-91 establishes accounting and reporting standards for nonrefundable fees and costs associated with lending, committing to lend, or purchasing a loan or a group of loans. FAS-91 also specifies the appropriate accounting for fees and initial direct costs associated with leasing transactions.

FAS-91 applies to all types of loans, including debt securities, and to all types of lenders, including banks, thrift institutions, insurance companies, mortgage bankers, and other financial and nonfinancial institutions. FAS-91 does *not* apply to nonrefundable fees and costs associated with originating or acquiring loans carried at market value (FAS-91, par. 34).

Appendix C of FAS-91 contains the following definitions of terms used in FAS-91:

- **Commitment fees** Fees charged for entering into an agreement that obligates the enterprise to make or acquire a loan or to satisfy an obligation of the other party under a specified condition. For purposes of this Statement [FAS-91], the term *commitment fees* includes fees for letters of credit and obligations to purchase a loan or group of loans and pass-through certificates.

- **Credit card fees** The periodic uniform fees that entitle cardholders to use credit cards. The amount of such fees generally is not dependent upon the level of credit available or frequency of usage. Typically the use of credit cards facilitates the cardholder's payment for the purchase of goods and services on a periodic, as-billed basis (usually monthly), involves the extension of credit, and, if payment is not made when billed, involves imposition of interest or finance charges. For the purposes of this Statement [FAS-91], the term *credit card fees* includes fees received in similar arrangements, such as charge card and cash card fees.

- **Incremental direct costs** Costs to originate a loan that (*a*) result directly from and are essential to the lending transaction and (*b*) would not have been incurred by the lender had that lending transaction not occurred.

- **Origination fees** Fees charged to the borrower in connection with the process of originating, refinancing, or restructuring a loan. This term includes, but is not limited to, points, management, arrangement, placement, application, underwriting, and other fees pursuant to a lending or leasing transaction and also includes syndication and participation fees to the extent they are associated with the portion of the loan retained by the lender.

Direct Loan Origination Costs

Under FAS-91, there are only two categories of direct loan origination costs on completed loans that may be offset against any related loan origination fees or any related commitment fees. The first category includes those incremental direct costs that are incurred in originating loan transactions with independent third parties. *Incremental direct costs* are costs that are incurred to originate loans that (*a*) result directly from and are essential to the lending transaction and (*b*) would not have been incurred by the lender if that lending transaction had not occurred (FAS-65, pars. 5–6).

The second category includes certain costs that are directly related to the following activities performed by the lender in connection with a loan or a loan commitment:

- Evaluating the prospective borrower's financial condition
- Evaluating and recording guarantees, collateral, and other security arrangements
- Negotiating the terms of the loan
- Preparing and processing loan documents
- Closing the transaction

Direct loan origination costs include only that portion of the lender's total employee compensation (including payroll-related fringe benefits) that is directly related to time spent performing the above activities for a specific loan and other costs related to those activities that would not have been incurred if not for that specific loan (FAS-91, par. 6).

All other lending-related costs are expensed by the lender as incurred. Costs related to activities performed by the lender for advertising, soliciting potential borrowers, servicing existing loans, and performing other ancillary activities related to establishing and monitoring credit policies, supervision, and administration are charged to expense as incurred. Employees' compensation and fringe benefits related to those activities, unsuccessful loan origination efforts, and idle time are charged to expense as incurred. Administrative costs, rent, depreciation, and all other occupancy and equipment costs are considered indirect costs and are charged to expense as incurred (FAS-91, par. 7).

Loan Origination Fees

An enterprise may acquire an individual loan contract by originating a loan directly with the borrower or by purchasing a loan from a party other than the borrower. Although the provisions of FAS-91 generally must be applied to each individual loan contract, similar individual loan contracts may be grouped together for the purpose of recognizing net fees or costs and purchase premiums or discounts, provided the amounts do not differ materially from the amounts that would have been recognized on an individual loan-by-loan basis (FAS-91, par. 4).

> **OBSERVATION:** Individual loan contracts that are grouped together must have sufficiently similar characteristics and approximately the same level of net fees or costs to permit the recalculation of the carrying amount of individual loan contracts. Thus, if an individual loan contract in the group is sold, its carrying amount must be recalculable.

Loan origination fees and direct loan origination costs that are incurred on a specific loan are offset against each other and accounted for as follows (FAS-91, par. 27c):

- *If Loan Is Held for Resale*   The loan origination fee and the related direct loan origination costs are deferred and recognized at the time the loan is sold.

- *If Loan Is Held for Investment*   The net difference between the loan origination fee and the related direct loan origination cost is deferred and recognized over the life of the loan as an adjustment of the yield on the loan. The interest method is used to amortize the net fee or cost over the life of the loan.

Commitment Fees

A loan commitment is a written offer from a lender to a borrower to lend funds for a specific purpose and term. A commitment term may be as short as one week, as long as one year, or longer. A floating rate commitment is one in which the interest rate to be charged on the loan is determined by the prevailing rate of interest at the time the loan is drawn upon. A fixed rate commitment is one in which the interest rate is specified in the commitment.

The recognition of revenue from loan commitment fees varies with the type and substance of the commitment. Income is recognized on all commitments if the loan is not made and the term of the commitment expires. In this event, the lender has no further obligation to perform, and the loan commitment fee is earned (FAS-91, par. 8).

If a loan commitment is exercised before the expiration of the commitment period, the related commitment fee and direct loan origination cost are deferred and recognized over the life of the loan as an adjustment of the yield on the loan. The interest method is used to amortize the net fee or cost over the life of the loan (FAS-91, par. 8).

If only a *remote* (unlikely) possibility exists that a commitment will be exercised based on an enterprise's past experience with similar types of commitments, the commitment fee is recognized as service fee income on a straight-line basis over the commitment period. If the commitment is exercised before the end of the commitment period, the balance of the remaining unamortized commitment fee on the date the commitment is exercised is recognized over the life of the loan as an adjustment of the yield on the loan (FAS-91, par. 8a).

The commitment fee is recognized as service fee income as of the determination date if (*a*) the amount of a commitment fee is determined retrospectively as a percentage of an available line of credit unused in a previous period, (*b*) the percentage is nominal in relation to the stated interest rate on any related borrowing, and (*c*) borrowing will bear a market interest rate at the date the loan is made (FAS-91, par. 8b).

Credit Card Fees

Credit card fees that are charged periodically to cardholders' accounts are considered loan commitments. Under FAS-91, credit card fees are deferred and recognized on a straight-line basis over the period in which the cardholder is entitled to use the card. Other similar card arrangements that involve the extension of credit by a card issuer are accounted for in the same manner (FAS-91, par. 10).

Syndication Fees

Loan syndication fees are recognized upon completion of the syndication loan, unless a portion of the syndication loan is retained by the syndication manager. The yield on the portion of the syndication loan retained by the syndication manager shall not be less than the average yield of all syndication loans, including fees, that are held by the other syndication participants (FAS-91, par. 11).

If the yield on the portion of the loan retained by the syndication manager is less than the average yield to the other syndication participants, the syndication manager shall defer a portion of the syndication fee in an amount that will produce a yield on the portion of the loan retained that is not less than the average yield of the loans held by the other syndication participants (FAS-91, par. 11).

Fees and Costs in Refinancings or Restructurings

A refinanced loan, other than a troubled debt restructuring, as discussed in FAS-15 (Accounting by Debtors and Creditors for Troubled Debt Restructurings), is accounted for as a new loan if its terms are at least as favorable to the *lender* as the terms for comparable loans to other customers with similar collection risks who are not refinancing or restructuring a loan with the lender. This means that the effective yield of the new loan should be at least equal to the effective yield of comparable loans of other customers with similar collection risks who are not refinancing (FAS-91, par. 12).

> **OBSERVATION:** The comparison of effective yields takes into consideration the level of nominal interest rate, commitment and origination fees, and direct loan origination costs. In addition, the comparison of other factors, such as compensating balance arrangements, should be considered when appropriate.

Any unamortized net fees or costs and any prepayment penalties from the original loan are recognized in interest income when the new loan is granted (FAS-91, par. 12).

If the terms of a refinancing or restructuring are not at least as favorable to the lender as the terms for comparable loans to other customers with similar collection risks who are not refinancing or restructuring loans with the lender, or if only minor modifications are made to the original loan contract, the unamortized net fees or costs from the original loan and any prepayment penalties are carried forward as a part of the net investment in the new loan. The investment in the new loan consists of (*a*) the remaining net investment in the original loan, (*b*) any additional amounts loaned, (*c*) any fees received, and (*d*) any direct loan origination costs that are associated with the refinancing or restructuring. The remaining net investment in the original loan consists of the unpaid loan principal, any remaining unamortized net fees or costs, any remaining unamortized purchase premium or discount, and any accrued interest receivable (FAS-91, par. 13).

Fees received in connection with a modification of terms of a troubled debt restructuring shall be applied as a reduction of the recorded investment in the loan. All related costs, including direct loan origination costs, are charged to expense as incurred (FAS-91, par. 14).

Purchase of a Loan or Group of Loans

The initial investment in a purchased loan or group of loans shall include the amount paid to the seller plus any fees paid or less any fees received. The difference between the initial investment in a purchased loan or group of loans and the principal amount at the date of purchase is recognized as an adjustment of the yield over the life of the loan or group of loans. All other costs incurred in connection with acquiring purchased loans or committing to purchase loans are charged to expense as incurred (FAS-91, par. 15).

For the purposes of FAS-91, the initial investment made for loans purchased as a group may be accounted for in the aggregate or may be allocated to the individual loans in the group. The cash flows generated by the payment terms of the underlying loan contracts are used to calculate the constant effective yield necessary to apply the interest method. Prepayments of principal are not anticipated in calculating the constant effective yield, unless the conditions specified by FAS-91 are met. If prepayments of principal are not anticipated and prepayments occur or a portion of the purchased loans is sold, a proportionate amount of the related deferred fees and purchase premium or discount is recognized in income so that the effective interest rate on the remaining portion of loans continues unchanged (FAS-91, par. 16).

Application of the Interest Method

Except for demand loans and revolving lines of credit (see following discussion), the interest method is used to amortize net fees or costs that are required under FAS-91 to be recognized as yield adjustments over the life of their related loans. The interest method produces a constant effective rate of interest income on the remaining net investment in the loan receivable. The net investment in the loan receivable consists of the principal amount of the loan receivable adjusted for any unamortized fees or costs and purchase premium or discount. The amount of periodic amortization is equal to the difference between the stated interest on the outstanding principal amount of the loan receivable and the amount of periodic interest income calculated by the interest method (FAS-91, par. 18).

During those periods in which interest income on a loan is not being recognized because of concerns about realization of the loan principal or interest, deferred net fees or costs are not amortized (FAS-91, par. 17).

Under FAS-91, when the stated interest rate is not constant throughout the term of a loan, the interest method is applied as follows (FAS-91, par. 18):

- *Interest Rate Increases*   If the stated interest rate increases during the term of the loan, the amount of interest accrued in the early periods under the interest method will exceed the stated amount of interest for the same periods. In this event, the net investment in the loan could increase to an amount greater than the amount at which the borrower could settle the obligation. Under FAS-91, no interest income is recognized during any period in which the borrower can settle the obligation for less than the amount of the net investment in the loan. In determining the amount at which the borrower can settle the obligation, prepayment penalties are considered only to the extent that such penalties are imposed throughout the loan term.

- *Interest Rate Decreases*   If the stated interest rate decreases during the term of the loan, the amount of periodic interest accrued in the early periods under the interest method will be less than the stated amount of interest received for the same periods. In that circumstance, the excess stated interest received during the early periods of the loan is deferred and recognized in those future periods when the constant effective yield under the interest method exceeds the stated interest rate.

- *Interest Rate Varies*   The stated interest rate on a loan may be based on the future changes that occur in an independent factor, such as the prime interest rate, the London Interbank Offered Rate (LIBOR), or the U.S. Treasury bill weekly average rate. In this event, the calculation of the constant effective yield necessary to recognize fees and costs is based either on the independent factor in effect at the inception of the loan or on the independent factor as it changes over the life of the loan.

Prepayments of Principal Anticipated

The cash flows generated by the payment terms of the underlying loan contracts are used to calculate the constant effective yield necessary to apply the interest method, and prepayments of principal are not anticipated to shorten the loan term. If an enterprise holds a large number of similar loans for which prepayments are *probable* (likely) and the timing and amount of prepayments can be estimated reasonably, an enterprise may consider estimates of future principal prepayments in calculating the constant effective yield necessary to apply the interest method (FAS-91, par. 19).

> ☞ **PRACTICE POINTER:** To permit the recalculation of their carrying amounts, individual loan contracts that are grouped together must have sufficiently similar characteristics and have approximately the same levels of net fees or costs. Thus, if an individual loan contract in the group is sold, that loan's carrying amount must be recalculable.

If the enterprise anticipates prepayments in applying the interest method and a difference arises between the prepayments anticipated and actual prepayments received, the enterprise shall recalculate the effective yield to reflect the actual payments received to date and the remaining anticipated future payments. In this event, the net investment in the loans is adjusted to the amount that would have existed if the new effective yield had been applied since the acquisition of the loans. The investment in the loans is adjusted to the new balance with a corresponding charge or credit to interest income (FAS-91, par. 19).

Enterprises that anticipate prepayments shall disclose that policy and the significant assumptions underlying the prepayment estimates. The practice of recognizing net fees over the estimated average life of a group of loans shall no longer be acceptable (FAS-91, par. 19).

> **OBSERVATION:** Most of the above information is included in paragraph 19 of FAS-91, which sets forth the conditions that must exist for an enterprise to anticipate prepayments of principal in calculating the constant effective yield necessary to apply the interest method. Absent a reasonably large number of loans with similar characteristics, the FASB believes the reliability of reasonably projecting cash flows is diminished to an unacceptable level (FAS-91, par. 58). When the conditions of paragraph 19 are not met, the FASB concluded that anticipation of prepayments is not appropriate and that recognition of fees and costs and purchase premiums or discounts should be in accordance with the repayment terms provided in the loan contract, with any unamortized amount recognized in income if and when prepayment occurs. In this respect, the practice of recognizing net fees over the estimated average life of a group of loans shall no longer be acceptable (FAS-91, par. 19).

Demand Loans and Revolving Lines of Credit

A demand loan does not have scheduled repayment terms, because it is payable on demand. A revolving line of credit usually grants the borrower the option of making multiple borrowings up to a specified maximum to repay portions of previous borrowings, and then to reborrow more funds under the same contract. As mentioned above, net fees or costs that are incurred in connection with demand loans and revolving lines of credit are not recognized by the interest method, but are recognized as follows (FAS-91, par. 20):

- *Demand Loans* Net fees or costs on demand loans may be recognized as an adjustment of yield on a straight-line basis over a period that is consistent with (*a*) the understanding between the borrower and lender and (*b*) if no understanding exists, the lender's estimate of the period in which the loan will remain outstanding. At the time the loan is paid in full, any unamortized balance of net fees or costs shall also be recognized in full.

* *Revolving Lines of Credit*   Net fees or costs on revolving lines of credit or similar arrangements are recognized in income on a straight-line basis over the period in which the revolving line of credit is active, provided that borrowings are outstanding for the maximum term specified in the loan agreement.

   At the time all borrowings are repaid in full by the borrower, and no additional funds can be borrowed under the terms of the loan agreement, the balance of any unamortized net fees or costs are recognized in income.

   When the loan agreement specifies a repayment schedule for the funds borrowed and no additional funds can be borrowed under the terms of the loan agreement, the interest method is used to recognize any net unamortized fees or costs.

Balance Sheet and Income Statement Classifications

The unamortized balance of loan origination, commitment, and other fees and costs and purchase premiums and discounts that are being recognized as an adjustment of yield is reported on the balance sheet of an enterprise as part of the related loan receivable balance (FAS-91, par. 21).

Amortization of loan origination, commitment, and other fees and costs recognized as an adjustment of yield is reported as part of interest income. For commitment fees and other fees that are being amortized on a straight-line basis over the commitment period or included in income when the commitment expires, amortization is reported in the income statement as service fee income (FAS-91, par. 22).

RELATED CHAPTERS IN 2009 *GAAP GUIDE* *LEVEL A*

Chapter 17, "Financial Instruments"
Chapter 23, "Intangible Assets"
Chapter 28, "Investments in Debt and Equity Securities"
Chapter 46, "Troubled Debt Restructuring"
Chapter 47, "Banking and Thrift Institutions"

RELATED CHAPTERS IN 2009 *GAAP GUIDE LEVELS B, C, AND D*

Chapter 17, "Financial Instruments"
Chapter 21, "Intangible Assets"
Chapter 25, "Investments in Debt and Equity Securities"
Chapter 41, "Troubled Debt Restructuring"

CHAPTER 51
NOT-FOR-PROFIT ORGANIZATIONS

CONTENTS

OVERVIEW

Historically, accounting principles for not-for-profit organizations have been fragmented into industry-specific pronouncements prepared by the AICPA and other groups. The result of this fragmentation is that the practices followed by the various types of organizations were inconsistent. The FASB has undertaken a broad project to address many of these inconsistencies and to attempt to improve the accounting and reporting of not-for-profit entities.

GAAP for not-for-profit organizations are found in the following pronouncements:

FAS-87	Employers' Accounting for Pensions
FAS-88	Employers' Accounting for Settlements and Curtailments of Defined Benefit Pension Plans and for Termination Benefits
FAS-93	Recognition of Depreciation by Not-for-Profit Organizations
FAS-99	Deferral of the Effective Date of Recognition of Depreciation by Not-for-Profit Organizations
FAS-106	Employers' Accounting for Postretirement Benefits Other Than Pensions
FAS-116	Accounting for Contributions Received and Contributions Made
FAS-117	Financial Statements of Not-for-Profit Organizations
FAS-124	Accounting for Certain Investments Held by Not-for-Profit Organizations
FAS-136	Transfer of Assets to a Not-for-Profit Organization or Charitable Trust That Raises or Holds Contributions for Others
FAS-158	Employers' Accounting for Defined Benefit Pension and Other Postretirement Plans

BACKGROUND

Prior to the issuance of FAS-93 (Recognition of Depreciation by Not-for-Profit Organizations), the FASB and its predecessors did not provide guidance on the subject of accounting for not-for-profit organizations. The primary sources of GAAP for these entities were contained in the following AICPA Audit Guides and Statements of Position, such as the following:

- Audits of Colleges and Universities
- Audits of Voluntary Health and Welfare Organizations (1974)
- SOP 78-10 (Accounting Principles and Reporting Practices of Certain Non-Profit Organizations) (1978)
- Audits of Providers of Health Care Services (1990)

FAS-93 extends the provisions of paragraph 5 of APB-12 (Omnibus Opinion—1967) to not-for-profit organizations, requiring disclosure of information about depreciable assets and depreciation (FAS-93, par. 2). FAS-93 also supersedes (*a*) those sections of the College and University Audit Guide that made depreciation optional and (*b*) SOP 78-10, which exempted certain long-lived tangible assets from depreciation (FAS-93, par. 3).

FAS-116 (Accounting for Contributions Received and Contributions Made) and FAS-117 (Financial Statements of Not-for-Profit Organizations) provide for significant changes in the standards for accounting for contributions received and made by all entities, as well as for the format and content of financial statements of all not-for-profit organizations. Accordingly, these two Statements supersede all inconsistent portions of the above AICPA Audit Guides and SOP 78-10. FAS-124 (Accounting for Certain Investments Held by Not-for-Profit Organizations) establishes standards of financial accounting and reporting for equity investments with readily determinable fair values and for all investments in debt securities.

FINANCIAL STATEMENTS OF NOT-FOR-PROFIT ORGANIZATIONS

FAS-117 establishes standards for external financial statements of not-for-profit organizations. It requires not-for-profits to present a statement of financial position, a statement of activities, and a statement of cash flows. Operating cash flows of (*a*) unrestricted net assets, (*b*) temporarily restricted net assets, and (*c*) permanently restricted net assets must be disclosed separately in the statement of activities, and the statement of financial position must distinguish among these three classes of net assets. FAS-117 amends FAS-95 (Statement of Cash Flows), extending its provisions to not-for-profit entities (FAS-117, par. 1). Not-for-profit entities are also required to disclose expenses by functional classification. Voluntary Health and Welfare Organizations (VHWO) are required, and Other Not-for-Profit Organizations (ONPO) are encouraged, to disclose expenses by natural classification as well (FAS-117, par. 1).

Financial Statements Required

FAS-117 (*a*) specifies three financial statements that must be present in external financial reports and (*b*) standardizes the approach to the disclosure of operating cash flows from unrestricted, temporarily restricted, and permanently restricted net assets. FAS-117 reviews and discusses the fundamental concepts governing financial reporting; it emphasizes that general-purpose financial statements can be prepared to serve a wide range of user needs, including an assessment of management's stewardship responsibilities to safeguard entity assets and use them for authorized activities. FAS-117 further specifies that the user's primary informational needs include (FAS-117, par. 5):

- Information about assets and liabilities
- Inflows and outflows of resources
- Cash flows
- Service efforts of the organization

Three financial statements are necessary to provide this information (FAS-117, par. 6):

- Statement of financial position
- Statement of activities
- Statement of cash flows

FAS-117 also requires specific notes to the financial statements which complete the disclosures relevant to the information needs listed above.

FAS-117 also emphasizes that the disclosure requirements contained in all authoritative literature that do not specifically exempt not-for-profit entities remain in effect (FAS-117, par. 7). Another noteworthy aspect of FAS-117 is that the degree of disaggregated fund information is not limited. Preparers have flexibility regarding the amount of detail provided, the order of line items, and the grouping of assets, liabilities, revenues, expenses, and gains. However, it is expected that the exercise of this flexibility will be similar to that used by business enterprises (FAS-117, par. 8).

FAS-117 does not address issues related to measurement focus, basis of accounting, or measurement methods (FAS-117, par. 8).

Statement of Financial Position

According to FAS-117, the objective of the statement of financial position is to present information about assets, liabilities, and net assets to facilitate analysis of credit, liquidity, ability to meet obligations, and the need to obtain external financing (FAS-117, par. 9). In particular, FAS-117 emphasizes the need to distinguish between unrestricted assets and permanently or temporarily restricted assets. However, the focus of FAS-117 is on the organization as a whole, and therefore, the total amounts for assets, liabilities, and net assets must be reported (FAS-117, par. 10).

The statement of financial position must provide information about the entity's liquidity. This disclosure can be accomplished (*a*) by sequencing assets in the order of diminishing liquidity or by current/noncurrent classification or (*b*) by sequencing liabilities according to their nearness to maturity (FAS-117, par. 12).

Particular attention should be paid to disclosing which elements of the statement of financial position have donor-imposed restrictions on their use. Restrictions exist because assets cannot be used until a future period, because they may be used only for certain types of expenditures, or because only the investment income from the assetsmay be used. Internally imposed restrictions made by the governing board of an entity must also be disclosed. Preparers are given flexibility about where to show disclosures about restrictions: on the face of the statements or in notes to the statements (FAS-117, pars. 14 and 15).

FAS-117 requires a not-for-profit entity to prepare a single, combined balance sheet with a net assets section distinguishing between classes of asset restrictions (FAS-117, par. 13):

Net assets:

Unrestricted	$ xxx
Temporarily restricted	xxx
Permanently restricted	xxx
Total net assets	$ xxx
Total liabilities and net assets	$ xxx

While accounts may be maintained on a fund basis, the above example emphasizes that the reporting focuses on the nature of the restrictions and not on the particular fund in which an asset is carried.

> ☞ **PRACTICE POINTER:** FAS-117 makes no recommendations about whether the statement of financial position should show assets and liabilities by fund. Indeed, the terms fund and fund balance are not used in FAS-117. In its discussion of the statement of activities, FAS-117 explicitly states that reporting by fund groups is not precluded, but is not a necessary part of external reporting. Accordingly, it seems clear that entities may prepare a statement of financial position that includes disaggregated fund groups, as long as those groups aggregate with net asset classes. It is also important to note that the statement of activities change in net asset class must articulate with the net assets shown on the statement of financial position. FAS-117 emphasizes that information should be simplified, condensed, and aggregated into meaningful totals, and that the statements should not be obscured by unnecessary fund or line item details.

FAS-117 requires that either the statements or the notes thereto give information describing the amount and nature of the various types of restrictions that exist within the major categories of *temporarily restricted* or *permanently restricted* assets. For example, disclosures must be made to show the amount of assets temporarily restricted as to time of availability or as to type of use allowed. Within the category of permanently restricted assets, differentiation should be made regarding assets of an endowment nature, which earn income, and assets that may be part of a collection (of art objects, historical treasures, etc.) (FAS-117, par. 14). Entities may disclose board designations on unrestricted assets either on the face of the statements or in notes (FAS-117, par. 16).

Statement of Activities

The statement of activities is the operating statement for a not-for-profit entity, analogous to an income statement for a business. This statement combines the revenues, expenses, gains, and losses with the changes in equities. The statement should use the term *changes in net assets* or *changes in equities* to describe equity (FAS-117, par. 18). FAS-117 sees net assets or equities as encompassing the whole of the net assets of the entity. The statement of activities must report the changes in total net assets and the change in each net asset class (FAS-117, par. 19). Thus, an important dimension of reporting operations for not-for-profit entities by FAS-117 is the use of net asset classes. The requirement is to report changes in unrestricted, temporarily restricted, and permanently restricted net assets in the statement of activities. Therefore, the statement will contain sections for changes in unrestricted net assets (which includes revenues and gains), changes in temporarily restricted net assets (both inflows and outflows), and a line for total changes in net assets.

Illustration of Format of Statement of Financial Position

NFP Organization #1
Statement of Financial Position
December 31, 20X5
(in thousands)

Assets:

Cash and cash equivalents	$ 15
Accounts and interest receivable	425
Inventories and prepaid expenses	120
Contributions receivable	600
Short-term investments	300

Assets restricted to investment in land, buildings, and equipment	1,050
Land, buildings, and equipment	12,300
Long-term investments	43,600
Total assets	$58,410

Liabilities and net assets:	
Accounts payable	$ 500
Refundable advance	75
Grants payable	100
Notes payable	200
Annuity obligations	330
Long-term debt	900
Total liabilities	$ 2,105
Net assets:	
Unrestricted	$23,010
Temporarily restricted (Note B)	4,800
Permanently restricted (Note C)	28,495
Total net assets	56,305
Total liabilities and net assets	$58,410

═══════════════════════════════════════

═══════════════════════════════════════

Illustration of Format of the Statement of Activities

NFP Organization #2
Statement of Activities for Year Ending June 30, 20X8
(in thousands)

Changes in unrestricted net assets:	
Revenues and gains:	
Contributions	$ 900
Fees	450
Investment income	25
Other	10
Total unrestricted income	$ 1,385
Net assets released from restrictions:	
Program restrictions satisfied	$ 250
Equipment acquisition restrictions satisfied	200
Time restrictions expired	100
Total assets released from restrictions	550
Total support	1,935

Less: Expenses and losses:	
Program A	600
Program B	750
Management and administrative	400
Fund-raising expenses	100
Total expenses and losses	1,850
Increase in unrestricted net assets	85
Changes in temporarily restricted net assets:	
Contributions	650
Investment income	250
Net assets released from restrictions	(110)
Increase in temporarily restricted net assets	790
Changes in permanently restricted net assets:	
Contributions	310
Investment income	80
Net realized and unrealized losses on investments	(550)
Decrease in permanently restricted net assets	(160)
Increase in net assets	715
Net assets, beginning of the year	2,600
Net assets, end of the year	$ 3,315

FAS-117 states that the term *changes in net assets* or *change in equity* should be used in the statement (FAS-117, par. 18).

> ☞ **PRACTICE POINTER:** FAS-117 does not specifically state that the operating statement must be titled "Statement of Activities." The operating statement may be disaggregated into a "Statement of Unrestricted Revenues, Expenses, and Other Changes in Unrestricted Net Assets" (changes in unrestricted net assets in the previous illustration) together with a second statement, "Statement of Changes in Net Assets" (changes in temporarily and permanently restricted net assets in the previous illustration). FAS-117 unequivocally states, however, that the focus must be on net assets and the three major classes of restrictions: unrestricted, temporarily restricted, and permanently restricted.

The reporting of restricted resources is straightforward under FAS-117. When donor-restricted assets are received, they normally are reported as restricted revenues or gains. In cases in which the restrictions are met in the same period the resources are received, it is permissible to classify the receipts as unrestricted, provided the policy is disclosed and applied consistently (FAS-117, par. 21). In addition, gains and losses on investments are unrestricted, regardless of the nature of the restrictions on the investment assets, unless the governing board determines that the law requires that such gains and losses be restricted (FAS-117, par. 22). Finally, FAS-117 allows reporting of subtotals for operating and nonoperating items, expendable and nonexpendable items, or other terms as desired to provide additional detail within the three classes of net assets. This additional detail is not required, but preparers can make such distinctions as they deem necessary (FAS-117, par. 23).

FAS-117 allows the reporting of gains and losses as net amounts if they result from peripheral transactions, such as disposal of assets. In its basis for conclusion, the FASB clearly states that this approach should not be used for special events that are ongoing major activities (FAS-117, par. 25).

Service Efforts One of the most important disclosures for not-for-profit organizations is information about service efforts. In health care entities, colleges and universities, and ONPOs, this disclosure is accomplished by arranging the statement of activities along functional lines. For VHWOs, this information traditionally has been contained in the Statement of Functional Expenses. Functional expense disclosure involves informing the statement users of the different types of expenses (e.g., salaries, rent, professional fees) incurred for the major types of programs or functions the entity conducts.

FAS-117 requires all not-for-profits to report expenditures by functional classification and encourages ONPOs, health care providers, and colleges and universities to also provide disclosure of expenses by natural classification (FAS-117, par. 26).

Health care providers, colleges and universities, and ONPOs can comply with the functional expense disclosure standards by reporting expenses by function in the statement of activities. VHWOs are required to show expenses by both functional and natural classifications (FAS-117, par. 26). This must be done by showing, in a matrix-formatted statement, the amounts and types of expenses allocated to programs compared with the amounts spent on administration and fund-raising. The matrix format is accomplished by using multiple columns for each type of program or support expenditure while retaining line item expense categories in vertical format. This approach enables statement users to understand the basis of program expenditures and total expenditures and to compare the amounts of expenditures for programs with those for support.

> **OBSERVATION:** Although an ONPO's disclosure of expenses in a functional-natural matrix is **not required** by FAS-117, any ONPO whose primary mission is to conduct public service, educational, research, or similar programs will have to disclose these data to fulfill the concept of full disclosure. FAS-117 has

an expressed goal of describing the minimum disclosures necessary. Preparers are expected to exercise their professional judgment and go beyond the minimum disclosures as needed.

Proper classification of expenditures between program and support is a fundamental disclosure principle. FAS-117 provides detailed guidance about the appropriate classification of items of a support nature. Supporting activities are divided into three categories: (1) management and general, (2) fund-raising, and (3) membership development (FAS-117, par. 28).

> **OBSERVATION:** FAS-117 specifies that membership development is an element of support activity and should be so reported.
>
> Also, it is important to emphasize that much information about service efforts may not be presentable in the body of the financial statements. Accordingly, preparers should ensure that notes provide full disclosure of information describing service accomplishments, including program descriptions, statistical data relevant to program inputs and outputs, and narratives about accomplishments.

Statement of Cash Flows

FAS-117 amends several sections of FAS-95 to require that not-for-profit organizations include a statement of cash flows in their financial statement package (FAS-117, par. 30). All these changes involve minor wording changes or additions to FAS-95 to clarify that FAS-95 is applicable to not-forprofit entities. As is the case for business entities, either the direct or indirect method may be used to present the cash flow information. The cash flow statement is best presented on an aggregated basis for the three classes of net assets; to do otherwise would result in a very detailed statement.

> ☞ **PRACTICE POINTER:** The statement of cash flows as required by FAS-117 is essentially the same as that required by FAS-95 for business enterprises. The only substantive difference is the substitution of "change in net assets" of the not-for-profit organization for "net income" of the business organization. For that reason, an illustration of the statement of cash flows is not presented here; see the chapter in this *Guide* titled "Cash Flow Statement."

DEPRECIATION

FAS-93 requires that not-for-profit entities recognize the cost of using up the future economic benefits or service potential of longlived tangible assets by reporting depreciation on those assets. In addition, disclosure of the following items is required for those assets (FAS-93, par. 5):

- Depreciation expense for the period
- Balances of major classes of depreciable assets by nature or function
- Accumulated depreciation by major class or in total
- A description of the methods of depreciation used

Depreciation is not required to be taken on works of art or historical treasures considered to have an indefinite service potential or an extraordinarily long useful life. Verifiable evidence should exist which indicates that (*a*) the historical treasures or works of art are of such value that they are worth preserving perpetually and (*b*) the entity has the capacity to preserve the undiminished service potential of the asset for an indefinite period, and is doing so (FAS-93, par. 6).

CONTRIBUTIONS RECEIVED AND MADE

FAS-116 provides guidance in accounting for contributions received and contributions given, promises to give cash or other assets, contributed services, collections of works of art, and gifts with donor-stipulated conditions. FAS-116 also specifies when to recognize the expirations of donor-imposed restrictions. FAS-116 standardizes the terminology used to describe the contributions and in the timing of recognition of income for the contributions received and expense for contributions given.

> **OBSERVATION:** FAS-116 is consistent with the general trend toward a full accrual approach to the recognition of revenue and expenses, as well as an emphasis on fair market value as a basis for measuring nonmonetary transactions.

FAS-116 applies to contributions of cash, nonmonetary assets, and services, and to promises to give the same. It applies to exchange transactions in which the value received is substantially different from the value given. It does *not* apply to (*a*) bargained arm's-length transactions without a gift element or (*b*) transactions in which the entity is an intermediary or is acting in some form of agency capacity (FAS-116, par. 4).

> **OBSERVATION:** Transfers of assets in which the reporting en-
> tity acts as an agent are not contributions. Accordingly, the
> guidance in AICPA Audit Guides for agency funds continues
> to be authoritative. However, FAS-116's basis for conclusion
> provides an analysis that differentiates between receipt of
> funds by an agent or intermediary and receipt of funds by an
> entity as a donee. This analysis indicates that the United Way
> organizations and other federated fund-raising entities are
> donees, not agents. In instances in which a donor uses an inter-
> mediary that acts as an agent to transfer assets to a third-party
> donee, neither the receipt nor the disbursement by the agent is a
> contribution received or made. Furthermore, a recipient of
> funds that makes disbursements in accordance with strict
> donor instructions (i.e., the recipient has discretion regarding
> the use made of those funds) is also an agent.

Also expressly excluded from the scope of FAS-116 are transactions
that convey only contingent or indirect benefits, such as tax abate-
ments. Transfers of assets from governments to businesses also are
not covered by the Statement. The FASB concluded that these transactions pose specific complexities that may require further study, and so
excluded them from the scope of the Statement (FAS-116, par. 4).

Contributions in FAS-116 include cash, assets, or services—or unconditional promises to give these in the future (FAS-116, par. 5). The
Statement emphasizes the word *promise* and requires verifiable doc-
umentary evidence that a promise has been made (FAS-116, par. 6). It
also distinguishes between donor-imposed *conditions* and donor-
imposed *restrictions* to provide a basis for differentiating the way
these items are reported (FAS-116, par. 7). Imposing restrictions on
how a gift is to be used does not delay recognition of income or expense. However, recognition of conditional gifts is delayed until the
conditions are substantially met.

Contributions Received

FAS-116 generally requires that all unconditional contributions—
whether assets, services, or reductions of liabilities—be measured
at fair market value on the date received and be recognized currently
as revenue or gains (FAS-116, par. 8). FAS-116 takes the current recognition, fair value approach, which embraces the characteristics of
relevance and reliability and the qualities of comparability and consistency that are discussed in FASB Concepts Statement No. 2 (Qualitative Characteristics of Accounting Information).

> **OBSERVATION:** The FASB Statements of Financial Account-
> ing Concepts are intended to provide conceptual guidance in
> selecting the economic events recognized and reported in

financial statements. Concepts Statement No. 2 examines the characteristics of accounting information and is useful as a reference to understanding the importance attached to various concepts that are emphasized in the FASB Standards.

FAS-116 also provides guidance in accounting for donated services. In particular, it holds that donated services must create or enhance nonfinancial assets, or must be of a specialized nature, must be provided by individuals possessing those skills, and typically need to be purchased, before they can be included as revenue or gains in the operating statement (FAS-116, par. 9). Thus, routine volunteer services requiring no particular expertise may not be reported as contribution revenue. Finally, FAS-116 requires explanatory footnotes that describe the programs or activities for which contributed services are used and other information that aids in assessing the success or viability of the entity (FAS-116, par. 10).

Assets to be included in a collection are recognized as revenue or gains if they are capitalized, but may not be included in revenue or gains if they are not capitalized (FAS-116, par. 13). To be part of a collection, the assets must be (FAS-116, par. 11):

- Held for public exhibition, education, or research rather than held for financial gain
- Protected, preserved, and not used as collateral or otherwise encumbered
- Subject to a policy that requires the proceeds of collection items sold to be reinvested in collections

Entities are encouraged by FAS-116 to capitalize collections retroactively or on a prospective basis; however, capitalization is *optional*. Capitalization of selected items is not permitted (FAS-116, par. 12). An entity that does not capitalize collections is required to disclose additional information as described later in this chapter.

Contribution Standards Applicable Only to Not-for-Profit Entities

FAS-116 requires that not-for-profit organizations distinguish the use of assets and support as *unrestricted, temporarily restricted,* or *permanently restricted* (FAS-116, par. 14). This separation could be accomplished through fund accounting by having a different fund for each of the three classes of net assets. Support that is restricted by donors as being available only in future accounting periods is reported as restricted support (FAS-116, par. 15).

Expiration of donor-imposed restrictions requires reclassification of net assets from restricted to unrestricted, or from a restricted to an unrestricted fund. FAS-117 provides guidance on financial statement format. Since restricted contributions are reported as support in the temporarily restricted class of net assets when first received, they are reclassified in the operating statement when restrictions lapse. FAS-116 requires that contributions to acquire fixed assets or contributions of plant assets be reported as restricted support over the life of the asset if (a) the donor restricts the use and disposition of the asset or (b) the donee has a policy of imposing a time restriction that expires over the life of the donated assets or the life of assets acquired with donated money (FAS-116, par. 16).

When restrictions lapse, recognition is required in the statement of activities. In general, a restriction expires when the period of the restriction has lapsed or when an expenditure for an authorized purpose is made. If an expense is incurred for a purpose for which both unrestricted and temporarily restricted net assets are available, the donor-imposed restriction is met (FAS-116, par. 17).

Contributions Made

FAS-116 continues the emphasis on full accrual and fair market value in providing guidance for contributions made. The fair market value emphasis is particularly evident in the directions given for accounting for contributions of nonmonetary assets. Contributions of nonmonetary assets are recognized as expenses and decreases in assets (or increases in liabilities) in the period made. Donors should find the most objective way possible to determine the fair market value of nonmonetary assets (FAS-116, par. 18).

> **OBSERVATION:** Absence of a definite valuation does not justify use of historical cost as a basis for recording the transaction.

FAS-116 states that appraisals, present value of estimated cash flows, net realizable value, and quoted market prices are all acceptable ways of determining the fair market value of donated nonmonetary assets (FAS-116, par. 19). If a present value technique is used to measure fair value of unconditional promises to give cash, subsequent accruals of the interest element shall be accounted for as contribution income by donees and contribution expense by donors. Not-for-profit organizations shall report the contribution increase as an increase in either temporarily or permanently restricted net assets if the underlying promise to give is donor restricted (FAS-116, par. 20, as amended by FAS-157, par. E16, b).

Conditional Promises

Material gifts or promises subject to conditions present accounting problems regarding the appropriate time to recognize the gift revenue or expense. They may also create the need for additional note disclosures describing the nature of the conditions. FAS-116 requires that a promise to give be recognized when the conditions of the promise are substantially met (FAS-116, par. 22). Conditional promises are essentially contingent events. If the contingent event (condition) is remote, it may be ignored and the promise accounted for as an unconditional promise. Otherwise, the gift is not recognized until the conditions have been substantially met. Although FAS-116 requires note disclosure by recipients of conditional promises, there is no similar requirement for the promisor.

Recognition problems also occur for donees when ambiguous wording makes it difficult to determine if conditions for recognition exist. Conditional promises are essentially contingent revenue for the donee. FAS-5 (Accounting for Contingencies) prohibits recognition of contingent gains, and FAS-116 is consistent with FAS-5 in that regard (FAS-116, par. 23). The donee need only prepare a note to the financial statements describing the nature and conditions of the promise and the amounts promised (FAS-116, par. 25). Accrual of conditional promises is not permitted unless the probability that the condition will not lapse is remote. For unconditional promises, the notes to the financial statements should indicate the timing of the cash flows as well as amounts, and should disclose the balances in any allowances for uncollectibles (FAS-116, par. 24).

Additional Disclosures for Collections

As described previously, capitalization of collections by donees is optional. FAS-116 requires that the financial statements disclose the cash flows associated with collections *whether the collection is capitalized or not*. The choice of capitalization policy affects the way that these cash flows are disclosed. If collections are capitalized, the cash consequences of collection activities are a result of routine transactions recorded in the ledger, and would appear in the statement of activities (FAS-116, par. 26).

If collections are *not* capitalized, the cash consequences of collection activities appear in the statement of activities within a separate category called "changes in permanently restricted net assets." This category follows the revenue and expense categories. Substantial descriptive notes regarding the collections are required when collections are not capitalized. These disclosures must include the relative significance of the collection, along with the accounting and stewardship policies followed. In addition, the notes should indicate the values of items sold, lost, or destroyed. A line in the financial statements must refer to the collections note (FAS-116, par. 27).

> **OBSERVATION:** The note disclosures required for uncapitalized collections are extensive. They emphasize that readers of the financial statements must be made aware of the details of all significant changes in the collection. In particular, statement users must be advised regarding casualty losses, insurance recoveries, accounting policies, and managerial controls in place. The concept of *full disclosure* is very much in evidence in this standard.

ACCOUNTING FOR INVESTMENTS

Definitions and Applicability

FAS-124 establishes standards for certain investments in debt and equity securities. The term *securities* is defined in FAS-124 as a share, participation, or other interest in property or in an enterprise of the issuer or an obligation of the issuer that has the following characteristics (FAS-124, par. 112):

- It is represented by an instrument issued in bearer or registered form, or it is registered in books maintained to record transfers by or on behalf of the issuer.

- It is of a type that is commonly dealt in on securities exchanges or markets or, when it is represented by an instrument, commonly recognized as a medium for investment in any area in which it is issued or dealt in.

- It is one of a class or series, or by its terms is divisible into a class or series of shares, participations, interests, or obligations.

Generally accepted accounting principles other than those discussed in FAS-124 also apply to investments held by not-for-profit organizations. For example, not-for-profit organizations must disclose information required by FAS-107 (*Disclosures about Fair Value of Financial Instruments*) and FAS-159 (*The Fair Value Option for Financial Assets and Financial Liabilities*) (FAS 124, par. 6, as amended by FAS-159, par. C6, a).

Equity securities represent an ownership interest in an enterprise (e.g., common and preferred stock) or the right to acquire (e.g., warrants, rights, call options) or dispose of (e.g., put options) an ownership interest at fixed or determinable prices. Convertible debt and preferred stock that by their terms either must be redeemed by the issuing enterprise or are redeemable at the option of the investor are not considered equity securities (FAS-124, par. 112).

Debt securities represent a creditor relationship with an enterprise. Debt securities include U.S. Treasury securities, U.S. government agency securities, municipal securities, corporate bonds, convertible debt, commercial paper, securitized debt instruments and interest-only and principal-only strips. Preferred stock that must be redeemed by the issuing enterprise or that is redeemable at the option of the investor, as well as collateralized mortgage obligations that are issued in equity form but are required to be accounted for as nonequity instruments regardless of how the instruments are classified, are considered debt securities. The term excludes option contracts, financial futures contracts, forward contracts, lease contracts, and swap contracts (FAS-124, par. 112).

An equity security is deemed to have a readily determinable fair value if one of the following criteria is met:

1. Sales prices or bid-and-asked quotations for the security are available on a securities exchange registered with the Securities and Exchange Commission (SEC) or in the over-the-counter market. For over-the-counter market prices to qualify, they must be publicly reported by the National Association of Securities Dealers Automated Quotation (NASDAQ) system or by the National Quotation Bureau.

    OBSERVATION: Restricted stock does not meet this criterion. The term *restricted stock* refers to equity securities for which sale is restricted at acquisition by governmental or contractual requirement, other than in connection with being pledged as collateral, except if that requirement terminates within one year or if the holder has the power by contract or otherwise to cause the requirement to be met within one year. Any portion of the security that can be reasonably expected to qualify for sale within one year is not considered restricted.

2. For an equity security traded only in a foreign market, that market is of a breadth and scope comparable to a U.S. market referred to in 1 above.

3. For an investment in a mutual fund, the fair value per share or unit is determined and published and is the basis for current transactions.

Measurement and Recognition Standards

The most important measurement and recognition requirement is that qualifying investments in equity securities (i.e., investments that have readily determinable fair values and are not accounted for by the equity method or consolidation) and all investments in debt securities are to be accounted for at fair value in the statement of financial position (FAS-124, par. 7).

> **OBSERVATION:** FAS-115, which specifies requirements for debt and equity investments for business enterprises, includes a category of investments labeled "held to maturity," which includes only certain debt securities that are accounted for at amortized cost. While the requirements of FAS-115 for business organizations and FAS-124 for not-for-profit organizations are comparable in many respects, an important difference is that FAS-124 does not include a category of investment for debt securities that are **not** measured at fair value as FAS-115 does for business enterprises.

Building on the general reporting requirements of FAS-117, FAS-124 provides the following guidance for the income effects of measuring investments at fair value (FAS-124, pars. 8–10):

- Gains and losses on investments resulting from their measurement at fair value are to be reported in the statement of activities as increases or decreases in unrestricted net assets, unless their use is temporarily or permanently restricted by donor stipulation or by law.

- Dividend, interest, and other investment income is to be reported in the period earned as increases in unrestricted net assets, unless the use of the assets received is limited by donor restrictions.

- Donor-restricted investment income is to be reported as an increase in temporarily restricted net assets or permanently restricted net assets, depending on the nature of the donor restriction.

- Gains and investment income that are limited to specific uses by donor restriction may be reported as increases in unrestricted net assets if the restrictions are met in the same reporting period as the gains and income are recognized (provided the organization has a similar policy for reporting contributions received, applies that policy consistently, and discloses that policy).

FAS-124 also deals with accounting for a *donor-restricted* endowment fund, which is an endowment fund created by a donor stipulating that the gift be invested in perpetuity or for a specified term. Gains and losses on investments in a donor-restricted endowment fund are classified as changes in unrestricted net assets, unless they are temporarily or permanently restricted by a donor's stipulation or by law that extends the donor's restriction to them (FAS-124, par. 11).

> **OBSERVATION:** FAS-117 states that gains and losses on restricted net assets are unrestricted unless the donor stipulates otherwise. Thus, in a permanent endowment, three possibilities exist:
>
> 1. Neither the donor nor law stipulates that the endowment restriction extends to gains and losses, in which case the gains and losses are unrestricted income.
> 2. The donor stipulates that gains and losses are to be used for some restricted purpose, often the same purpose for which the endowment income is restricted. In this case, the gains and losses are temporarily restricted income.
> 3. Either the donor or law stipulates that gains and losses become part of the endowment principal. In this case, the gains and losses are permanently restricted income. FAS-124 mentions the situation in which an endowment cannot be sold (i.e., must be held in perpetuity), in which case gains and losses on that security would be permanently restricted income.

As a general rule (i.e., unless otherwise restricted by donor stipulation or law), losses on investments in a donor-restricted endowment reduce temporarily restricted net assets to the extent that donor-imposed temporary restrictions on net appreciation of the fund have not been met before the loss occurs. Further losses reduce unrestricted net assets (FAS-124, par. 12). If losses reduce the assets of a donor-restricted endowment fund below the level required by donor stipulation or law, gains that restore the fair value of the assets to the required level are classified as increases in unrestricted net assets (FAS-124, par. 13).

Disclosure Standards

The FAS-124 disclosure requirements can be separated into three classifications.

First, the following information related to the statement of activities is required (FAS-124, par. 14):

- Composition of investment return, including at least the following components:
  - Investment income (e.g., dividends, interest)
  - Net realized gains or losses on investments reported at other than fair value
  - Net gains or losses on investments reported at fair value

- A reconciliation of investment return to amounts reported in the statement of activities, if the investment is separated into operating and nonoperating amounts and an explanation of how the amount included in operations is computed, including any changes in policy, used to make that classification

Second, the following information related to the statement of financial position is required (FAS-124, par. 15):

- Aggregate carrying amount of investments by major type
- Basis for determining the carrying amount for investments other than equity securities with readily determinable fair values and all debt securities
- The method(s) and significant assumptions used to determine fair values (related to the FAS-107 requirement)
- The aggregate amount of the deficiencies for all donor-restricted endowment funds for which the fair value of the assets at the reporting date is less than the level required by donor stipulations or law

Third, for the most recent period for which a statement of financial position is presented, the nature of and carrying amount for each individual investment or group of investments that represents a significant concentration of market risk are required (FAS-124, par. 16).

ACCOUNTING FOR TRANSFERS OF ASSETS

FAS-116 includes the following statement (par. 4):

> This Statement does not apply to transfers of assets in which the reporting entity acts as an agent, trustee, or intermediary, rather than as a donor or donee.

FAS-136 (Transfer of Assets to a Not-for-Profit Organization or Charitable Trust That Raises or Holds Contributions for Others) amends FAS-114 by requiring a recipient organization to recognize at fair value an asset and liability instead of contribution revenue if the recipient organization accepts cash or other financial assets from a donor and agrees to use those assets, or disburse them and the return from investing the assets, or both, to a specified beneficiary (FAS-136, par. 11). The specified beneficiary reports its interest in the assets held by the recipient organization as an asset and as contribution revenue (FAS-136, par. 15). Exceptions to the above are situations in which the recipient organization is granted variance power (i.e., can redirect the use of funds) and in which the recipient and beneficiary organizations are interrelated (FAS-136, pars. 12–14).

FAS-136 also specifies criteria for determining when the recipient organization and the specified beneficiary are considered interrelated organizations. These criteria are typically met by a not-for-profit organization and a related foundation (FAS-136, pars. 13–14).

ACCOUNTING FOR DEFINED BENEFIT POSTRETIREMENT PLANS

A not-for-profit entity may sponsor a defined benefit postretirement plan for its employees. The accounting requirements for these plans generally parallel those for business entities. The not-for-profit entity shall recognize in its statement of financial position the funded status of the benefit plan as the difference between the fair value of the plan assets and its benefit obligation (FAS-158, par. 8a). The aggregate status of all overfunded plans is recognized as an asset in the statement of financial position. The aggregate status of all underfunded plans is recognized as a liability in the statement of financial position. The asset is presented as a noncurrent asset. The liability is presented as a current liability, noncurrent liability, or a combination. The current portion is the amount by which the actuarial present value of benefits included in the benefit obligation payable in the next 12 months, or operating cycle if longer, exceeds the fair value of plan assets (FAS-158, par. 8b).

A not-for-profit entity shall recognize the gains or losses and the prior service costs or credits that arise during the period but are not recognized as components of net periodic benefit cost in accordance with FAS-87 (Employers' Accounting for Pensions) and FAS-106 (Employers' Accounting for Postretirement Benefits Other Than Pensions). This disclosure shall be a separate line item or items in the changes in unrestricted net assets, apart from expenses. There is no requirement as to whether the separate line items are to be included within or outside the intermediate measure of operations or performance indicator, if one is presented (FAS-87, par. 74A, and FAS-106, par. 103A, as amended by FAS-158, par. C2s and D2u).

> ☞ **PRACTICE POINTER:** AICPA guidance for certain types of health care organizations requires that certain items of other comprehensive income are reported outside the performance indicator.

The entity is required to reclassify to net periodic benefit cost a portion of the net gain or loss and prior service costs and credits previously recognized as a separate line item or items, and a portion of the transition asset or obligation remaining from the initial application of FAS-87 and FAS-106 and the recognition and amortization provisions of FAS-87, FAS-88 (Employers' Accounting for Settlements and Curtailments of Defined Benefit Pension Plans and for Termination Benefits), and FAS-106. The contra adjustments are reported in the same line item or items within changes in unrestricted net assets, apart from expenses, as the initially recognized amounts. Net periodic benefit cost is reported by functional classification as required by FAS-117 (FAS-87, par. 74B, and FAS-106, par. 103B, as amended by FAS-158, pars. C2s and D2u).

References throughout FAS-158 to accumulated other comprehensive income relate to unrestricted net assets for a not-for-profit entity (FAS-87, par. 74C, and FAS-106, par. 103C, as amended by FAS-158, pars. C2s and D2u). Any income tax effects are to be determined in accordance with the guidance in FAS-109, Accounting for Income Taxes (FAS-158, par. 8e).

Not-for-profit entities shall measure plan assets and benefit obligations as of the date of the fiscal year-end statement of financial position unless the exceptions described in the chapters on pension and other postretirement benefit plans apply (i.e., a consolidated subsidiary or an equity method investee) (FAS-158, par. 9).

Illustration of Application of FAS-158 by a Not-for-Profit Entity

Our Sisters of Mercy Health System adopts the recognition provisions of FAS-158 at the end of its fiscal year, June 30, 20X7. Relevant pension-related data at June 30, 20X7 are:

	6/30/X7 (in thousands)
Projected benefit obligation	$(1,900)
Plan assets at fair value	1,250
Funded status	(650)
Items not yet recognized as a component of net periodic pension cost:	
Transition obligation	(125)
Prior service cost	(140)
Net loss	(175)
Total	(440)

The Health System is not subject to income taxes. The Health System's balance in the accrued pension cost account at June 30, 20X7, is $210,000. The Health System would make the following entry at June 30, 20X7, to adopt FAS-158:

To recognize the underfunded status of the pension plan at June 30, 20X7, and to adjust the ending balance of unrestricted net assets for the transition obligation, prior service cost, and net loss that have not yet been included as a component of net periodic benefit cost (in thousands):

Change in unrestricted net assets to initially apply FAS-158 recognition provisions	440	
Liability for pension benefits		440
($125 + $140 + $175)		

The $440,000 reduction in unrestricted net assets is included in the 20X7 Statement of Activities apart from expenses and outside its intermediate measure of operations. Relevant pension-related data at June 30, 20X8 are:

	6/30/X7 (in thousands)	6/30/X8 (in thousands)
Projected benefit obligation	$(1,900)	$(1,800)
Plan assets at fair value	1,250	1,200
Funded status	(650)	(600)
Items not yet recognized as a component of net periodic benefit cost:		
Transition obligation	(125)	(105)
Prior service cost	(140)	(90)
Net loss	(175)	(75)
Total	(440)	(270)

The plan assets declined in value by $50,000 during 2008, and as the expected return on plan assets is $65,000, there is an unexpected loss of $115,000 during 20X7. In addition, there is an actuarial gain during the year of $215,000. The unexpected loss on pension plan assets of $115,000, when combined with the actuarial gain of $215,000, results in a decrease in the net loss account of $100,000 during the year. There were no pension plan contributions during the year.

Data on the components of net periodic benefit cost for 20X8 is (in thousands):

Service cost	$55
Interest cost	60
Expected return on plan assets	(65)
Amortization of transition obligation	20
Amortization of prior service cost	50
Amortization of net (gain) loss	0
Net periodic benefit cost	$120

The Health System would make the following journal entries during 20X8 (in thousands):

To recognize service cost, interest cost, and the expected return on plan assets in net periodic benefit cost:

Net periodic benefit cost (by functional category)	50	
(55 + 60 − 65)		
Liability for pension benefits		50

To recognize the reduction in the net loss as an increase in unrestricted net assets:

Liability for pension benefits	100	
Net loss not yet recognized in net periodic benefit cost		100

To recognize the amortization of the transition obligation in net periodic benefit cost:

Net periodic benefit cost (by functional category)	20	
Transition obligation not yet recognized in net periodic benefit cost		20

To recognize the amortization of prior service cost in net periodic benefit cost:

Net periodic benefit cost (by functional category)	50	
Prior service cost not yet recognized in net periodic benefit cost		50

Disclosures

Not-for-profit entities that sponsor defined benefit pension or other postretirement benefit plans need to disclose the following (FAS-158, par. 10):

- For each annual statement of activities presented, the net gain or loss and the net prior service cost or credit recognized in the statement of activities apart from expenses
- Separate disclosure is required for amounts arising during the period and amounts reclassified as components of net periodic benefit cost during the period
- For each annual statement of activities presented, the net transition asset or obligation recognized as components of net periodic benefit cost for the period
- For each annual statement of financial position presented, the amounts that have not yet been recognized as components of net periodic benefit cost, with separate disclosure of the net gain or loss, net prior service cost or credit, and net transition asset or obligation

- The amounts of net gain or loss, net prior service cost or credit, and net transition asset or obligation that arose previously and are expected to be recognized as components of net periodic benefit cost over the fiscal year that follows the most recent annual statement of financial position presented

- The amount and timing of any plan assets expected to be returned to the plan sponsor during the 12-month period, or operating cycle if longer, that follows the most recent annual statement of financial position presented

The above-mentioned disclosures are to be made separately for pension plans and other postretirement benefit plans.

NOT-FOR-PROFIT ORGANIZATIONS
IMPORTANT NOTICE FOR 2009

As the 2009 *GAAP Guide Level A* goes to press, the FASB has outstanding two related exposure drafts or proposed standards that would significantly affect not-for-profit organizations. The titles of the two proposed standards are *Not-for-Profit Organizations: Mergers and Acquisitions* and *Not-for-Profit Organizations: Goodwill and Other Intangible Assets Acquired in a Merger or Acquisition*. The objective of the project is to develop standards of accounting and reporting that will improve the completeness, relevance, and comparability of financial information about mergers and acquisitions by not-for-profit organizations. A related objective is to assist NFP organizations in applying FAS-142, *Goodwill and Other Intangible Assets*.

At the inception of the project, the FASB affirmed its view that similar transactions and circumstances should be accounted for similarly. This led to the conclusion that acquisitions and mergers by NFP organizations are similar in many respects to acquisitions and mergers by business entities, thus the overall approach should be the same. The presumption was made that FAS-141(R) (*Business Combinations*) standards for business organizations should be applied by NFP organizations unless a difference is identified that justifies a different accounting treatment.

Two Exposure Drafts were issued in October 2006. Since that time, extensive discussion has occurred and the FASB has completed its project on business combinations and consolidated financial statements for business enterprises.

As part of the deliberations of the October 2006 Exposure Drafts for NFP organizations, the FASB has reached the following decisions:

- A merger is different from an acquisition and justifies a different accounting treatment. The feature that distinguishes a merger is control; that is, in a merger the governing bodies of two or more NFP organizations cede control of those organizations to create a new organization. One organization obtains control over the net assets of another organization or business.

- The acquisition method should be required for acquisitions by NFP organizations. The carryover method of accounting should be retained for mergers between NFP organizations. The FASB considered, but rejected, suggestions that it permit use of the carryover method of accounting for acquisitions by smaller NFP organizations.

The current FASB agenda and project plan indicates its plan to issue final standards on mergers and acquisitions and goodwill and other intangible assets in the fourth quarter of 2008.

RELATED CHAPTERS IN 2009 *GAAP GUIDE* *LEVEL A*

Chapter 5, "Cash Flow Statement"
Chapter 11, "Depreciable Assets and Depreciation"
Chapter 28, "Investments in Debt and Equity Securities"
Chapter 32, "Nonmonetary Transactions"
Chapter 33, "Pension Plans"
Chapter 34, "Postemployment and Postretirement Benefits Other Than Pensions"

RELATED CHAPTERS IN 2009 *GAAP GUIDE* *LEVELS B, C, AND D*

Chapter 8, "Cash Flow Statement"
Chapter 25, "Investments in Debt and Equity Securities"
Chapter 28, "Nonmonetary Transactions"
Chapter 29, "Pension Plans—Employers"
Chapter 30, "Pension Plans—Settlements and Curtailments"
Chapter 32, "Postemployment and Postretirement Benefits Other Than Pensions"

CHAPTER 52
OIL AND GAS

CONTENTS

OVERVIEW

Oil and gas producing activities of a business enterprise include the acquisition of mineral interests in properties, exploration, development, and production of crude oil, including condensate and natural gas liquids, and natural gas. These are referred to collectively as oil and gas producing activities in the authoritative accounting literature.

GAAP for oil and gas producing activities are established in the following pronouncements:

FAS-19	Financial Accounting and Reporting by Oil and Gas Producing Companies
FAS-25	Suspension of Certain Accounting Requirements for Oil and Gas Producing Companies
FAS-69	Disclosures about Oil and Gas Producing Activities
FAS-89	Financial Reporting and Changing Prices
FIN-33	Applying FASB Statement No. 34 to Oil and Gas Producing Operations Accounted for by the Full Cost Method
FIN-36	Accounting for Exploratory Wells in Progress at the End of a Period

BACKGROUND

GAAP concerning accounting and reporting by oil and gas producing companies are specified in FAS-19 (Financial Accounting and Reporting by Oil and Gas Producing Companies), which was to be effective for fiscal years beginning after December 15, 1978. Because the SEC rejected the successful-efforts accounting method, FAS-19 was amended in February 1979 by FAS-25 (Suspension of Certain Accounting Requirements for Oil and Gas Producing Companies), which suspended FAS-19 by eliminating its effective date for requiring certain FAS-19 provisions related to the successful efforts method of accounting. Nonpromulgated GAAP, in the form of industry practices, exist for alternative methods (full-cost, current-value, and discovery-value accounting methods).

FAS-69 (Disclosures about Oil and Gas Producing Activities) establishes comprehensive financial statement disclosures for oil and gas producing companies. FAS-89 (Financial Reporting and Changing Prices) amends FAS-69, eliminating the required disclosure of supplementary current cost information by oil and gas producing companies. FAS-19 covers only producing activities and specifically excludes the transporting, refining, and marketing of oil and/or gas. In addition, the promulgated GAAP do *not* cover the following (FAS-19, par. 6):

- Production of other wasting (nonregenerative) natural resources
- Production of geothermal steam

- Extraction of hydrocarbons as a by-product of the production of geothermal steam (Geothermal Steam Act of 1970)
- Extraction of hydrocarbons from shale, tar sands, or coal
- Accounting for interest on funds borrowed to finance oil and/ or gas producing activities.

FAS-25 specifically states that for the purposes of the promulgated GAAP on accounting changes the provisions of FAS-19 pertaining to the successful-efforts method remain in effect (FAS-25, par. 4). Since FAS-19 expresses a preference for the successful-efforts method of accounting and rejects other methods, an enterprise that changes to any method other than the successful-efforts method will have the burden of justifying such change [FAS-154 (Accounting Changes and Error Corrections)].

OIL AND GAS ACCOUNTING TERMINOLOGY

A major challenge in understanding the activities pertaining to the oil and gas producing industry is understanding the specialized terminology that is used. Following is a discussion of several of the key terms that must be understood.

Properties

Properties include any ownership in, or an interest representing the right to, or the participation in, the extraction of oil and/or gas. The term *properties* also includes a nonoperating interest, such as royalty interests, or production interests payable in oil and/or gas. Properties exclude contracts representing the right to purchase oil and/or gas (supply contracts).

Reservoir

Reservoir refers to a separate confined underground formation containing a natural accumulation of producible oil and/or gas (FAS-19, par. 273).

Field

Field refers to one or more reservoirs related to the same individual geological structural feature and/or stratigraphic condition (FAS-19, par. 272).

Proved Area

A *proved area* is that part of the property in which proved reserves have been attributed specifically (FAS-19, par. 275).

Proved Reserves

The following definitions of *proved reserves* are those that were adopted by the SEC on December 19, 1978 (ASR-257), and were current at the date of publication. These definitions were developed by the Department of Energy for its financial reporting purposes.

Proved Oil and Gas Reserves

Proved oil and gas reserves are the estimated quantities of crude oil, natural gas, and natural gas liquids, which geological and engineering data demonstrate with reasonable certainty to be recoverable in future years from known reservoirs under existing economic and operating conditions; that is, prices and costs as of the date the estimate is made. Prices include consideration of changes in existing prices provided only by contractual arrangements, but not on escalations based upon future conditions (FAS-25, par. 34).

Reservoirs are considered proved if economic productibility is supported by either actual production or conclusive formation test. The area of a reservoir considered proved includes (*a*) that portion delineated by drilling and defined by gas–oil and/or oil–water contacts, if any, and (*b*) the immediately adjoining portions not yet drilled, but which can be reasonably judged as economically productive based on available geological and engineering data. In the absence of information on fluid contacts, the lowest known structural occurrence of hydrocarbons controls the lower proved limit of the reservoir.

Reserves which can be produced economically through application of improved recovery techniques (such as fluid injection) are included in the *proved* classification when successful testing by a pilot project, or the operation of an installed program in the reservoir, provides support for the engineering analysis on which the project or program is based.

Estimates of proved reserves do *not* include the following: (*a*) oil that may become available from known reservoirs but is classified separately as *indicated additional reserve*; (*b*) crude oil, natural gas, and natural gas liquids, the recovery of which is subject to reasonable doubt because of uncertainty as to geology, reservoir characteristics, or economic factors; (*c*) crude oil, natural gas, and natural gas liquids that may occur in undrilled prospects; and (*d*) crude oil, natural gas, and natural gas liquids that may be recovered from oil shales, coal, gilsonite and other such sources.

Proved Developed Oil and Gas Reserves

Proved developed oil and gas reserves are reserves that can be expected to be recovered through existing wells with existing equipment and operating methods. Additional oil and gas expected to be obtained through the application of fluid injection or other improved recovery techniques for supplementing the natural forces and mechanisms of primary recovery should be included as *proved developed reserves* only after testing by a pilot project or after the operation of an installed program has confirmed through production response that increased recovery will be achieved (FAS-25, par. 34).

Proved Undeveloped Reserves

Proved undeveloped oil and gas reserves are reserves that are expected to be recovered from new wells on undrilled acreage, or from existing wells where a relatively major expenditure is required for recompletion. Reserves on undrilled acreage shall be limited to those drilling units offsetting productive units that are reasonably certain of production when drilled. Proved reserves for other undrilled units can be claimed only where it can be demonstrated with certainty that there is continuity of production from the existing productive formation. Under no circumstances should estimates for proved undeveloped reserves be attributable to any acreage for which an application of fluid injection or other improved recovery technique is contemplated, unless such techniques have been proved effective by actual tests in the area and in the same reservoir (FAS-25, par. 34).

Wells, Related Equipment, and Facilities

These include the cost of drilling and equipping *completed* wells, access to proved reserves, and facilities for extracting, treating, gathering, and storing the oil and/or gas (FAS-19, par. 11b).

Uncompleted Wells, Equipment, and Facilities

These include the costs of all uncompleted wells, equipment, and facilities (FAS-19, par. 11d).

Support Equipment and Facilities

These include the cost of support equipment and facilities used in producing oil and/or gas. Examples are construction and grading equipment, seismic equipment, vehicles, repair shops, warehouses, camps, and division, district, or field offices (FAS-19, par. 11c).

Stratigraphic Test Wells (Expendable Wells)

These wells generally are drilled without the intention of being completed for production, and are a geological drilling effort to gather information about specific geologic conditions. Core tests and other expendable holes are classified as stratigraphic test wells.

A stratigraphic test well drilled in a proved area is called a *development-type stratigraphic test well*. When drilled on an unproved area, these wells are called exploratory-type stratigraphic test wells.

Service Wells

These are wells drilled to service or support production in an existing field. Examples are injection wells (gas, water, steam, air) and observation wells (FAS-19, par. 274).

Development Wells

These are wells drilled for producing oil and/or gas in a proved area known to be productive (FAS-19, par. 274).

Exploratory Wells

These are wells drilled for exploration or discovery, usually on unproved areas. If a well is classified as a development, service, or stratigraphic test well, it cannot be an exploratory well (FAS-19, par. 274).

Supply Agreements

These are long-term contracts or similar agreements that represent the right to purchase oil and/or gas, including agreements with foreign governments.

Discovery-Value Accounting

This refers to estimated methods used to determine the value of oil and/or gas reserves, either when discovered or when developed at a later date. The most common estimated valuation methods are:

- *Current cost*—the amount of cash that currently would have to be paid to acquire the same asset. Similar to current reproduction cost or current replacement cost.

- *Current exit value in orderly liquidation*—the net amount of cash that would be received in the current orderly liquidation of the asset.

- *Expected exit value in due course of business*—the nondiscounted amount of cash the asset is expected to bring in the due course of business, less any direct costs incurred in its disposal (net realizable value). Under this method, the oil and/or gas reserves would be valued at an amount equal to the estimated net cash flow from the reserves.

- *Present value of expected cash flow*—the present value of the expected cash inflows from the reserves, less the present value of the expected related cash outflows to produce the cash inflows. Various different discount rates have been recommended, such as the prime rate, company's cost of capital, and the rate on long-term government bonds.

Under the discovery-value accounting method, property acquisition and other prediscovery expenditures would be deferred and written off when the areas to which the costs apply have been explored and the reserves, if any, determined and valued.

Under FAS-19, the discovery-value accounting method is unacceptable.

Current-Value Accounting

One of the four valuation methods mentioned above in discovery-value accounting is applied on a continuous basis, and oil and/or gas reserves are revalued at each financial statement date using the most current information available. Property acquisition and other prediscovery expenditures are deferred and written off when the areas to which the costs apply have been explored and the oil and/or gas reserves, if any, determined and valued.

The uncertainties and inherent unreliability in using estimates to value oil and/or gas reserves render the discovery-value and current-value methods undesirable.

Under FAS-19, the current-value method is unacceptable (FAS-19, par. 4).

Full-Cost Accounting

Full-cost accounting considers all costs of unsuccessful and successful property acquisition and exploration activities as a cost of discovering reserves. Thus, all costs are considered an integral part of the acquisition, discovery, and development of oil and/or gas reserves; and costs that cannot be directly related to the discovery of specific reserves are capitalized nonetheless.

In full costing, a country usually is selected as a cost center, and all costs incurred within the cost center are capitalized and subsequently amortized against the proved oil and/or gas reserves produced within the cost center by either the units of production or gross revenue methods. There is a limitation that capitalized costs of a cost center should not exceed the present value of the oil and/or gas reserves of the same cost center.

Under FAS-19, the full-cost accounting method is unacceptable. Because FAS-25 suspended the effective date of FAS-19, however, many companies continue to apply the full-cost method.

The promulgated rules for the full cost accounting method are contained in Rule 4-10 of Regulation S-X of the Securities and Exchange Commission (SEC). The Rule is titled "Financial Accounting and Reporting for Oil and Gas Producing Activities Pursuant to the Federal Securities Laws and the Energy Policy and Conservation Act of 1975." Additional interpretations of the rules are contained in "Topic 12: Oil and Gas Producing Activities" of the SEC's Staff Accounting Bulletins and Sections 405 and 406 of the SEC's Codification of Financial Reporting Releases.

Successful-Efforts Costing

A cause-and-effect relationship between costs incurred and the discovery of specific reserves is required. The incurrence of a cost with no identifiable future benefit usually is expensed under the successful-efforts method.

Under the successful-efforts method of accounting, certain costs are capitalized while others are expensed when incurred. The types of costs capitalized include:

- Mineral interests in properties, which include fee ownership or a lease, concession, or other interest representing the right to extract oil or gas, including royalty interests, production payments payable in oil and gas, and other nonoperating interests in properties operated by others

- Wells and related equipment and facilities, the costs of which include those incurred to:
  — Obtain access to proved reserves and provide facilities for extracting, treating, gathering, and storing the oil and gas, including the drilling and equipping of development wells (whether those wells are successful or unsuccessful), and service wells

— Drill and equip exploratory wells that have found proved reserves

- Support equipment and facilities used in oil and gas producing activities
- Uncompleted wells, equipment, and facilities

Costs other than the above incurred in oil and gas producing activities are charged to expense. Examples include geological and geophysical costs, the costs of carrying and retaining undeveloped properties, and the costs of drilling exploratory wells that do not find proved reserves.

Under successful-efforts costing, all property acquisition costs are capitalized when incurred, though different methods subsequently may be used to dispose of these costs by independent oil and gas exploration companies but not by integrated companies.

Under present tax law, intangible drilling costs generally are deductible as an expense in the year incurred.

FAS-19 generally is based on the successful-efforts costing method.

LEGAL BACKGROUND

In 1975, Congress enacted the Energy Policy and Conservation Act. Title V, Section 503, of the act grants the following powers to the Securities and Exchange Commission:

> ... to prescribe rules applicable to persons engaged in the production of crude oil or natural gas, or make effective by recognition, or by other appropriate means indicating a determination to rely on, accounting practices developed by the Financial Accounting Standards Board, if the Securities and Exchange Commission is assured that such practice will be observed by persons engaged in the production of crude oil or natural gas to the same extent as would result if the Securities and Exchange Commission had prescribed such practices by rule.

In addition, the act requires that certain information about national energy be compiled for both domestic and foreign operations, and consist of the following data:

- The separate calculation of capital, revenue, and operating cost information pertaining to:
  - Prospecting
  - Acquisition
  - Exploration
  - Development
  - Production

The calculation of capital, revenue, and operating cost information includes geological and geophysical costs, carrying costs, unsuccessful exploratory drilling costs, intangible drilling and development costs on productive wells, the cost of unsuccessful development wells, and the cost of acquiring oil and gas reserves by means other than development. Any such calculation shall take into account disposition of capitalized costs, contractual arrangements involving special conveyance of rights and joint operations, differences between book and tax income, and prices used in the transfer of products or other assets from one person to any other person, including a person controlled by, controlling, or under common control with such person.

- The full presentation of the financial information of persons engaged in the production of crude oil or natural gas, including:
  — Disclosure of reserves and operating activities, both domestic and foreign, to facilitate evaluation of financial effort and result
  — Classification of financial information by function to facilitate correlation with reserve and operating statistics, both domestic and foreign
- Such other information, projections, and relationships of collected data as shall be necessary to facilitate the compilation of such base data

Securities Act Release No. 5706, issued on May 12, 1976, requires that certain information relating to oil and/or gas properties, reserves, and production be disclosed in registration statements, proxy statements, and reports filed with the Commission.

Securities Act Release No. 5801, issued on January 31, 1977, states that the Commission, consistent with its policy established in Accounting Series Release No. 150, will look to the FASB to provide leadership in setting forth accounting standards and principles for the producers of oil and/or gas.

Securities Act Release No. 5837, issued on June 30, 1977, solicits comments from interested parties with respect to the Commission's responsibility under the Energy Policy and Conservation Act of 1975. The release also states that the Commission will attempt to coordinate the reporting requirements promulgated by the FASB in its own disclosure and reporting requirements.

Securities Release No. 5861 and Securities Release No. 5877, issued on August 31, 1977, and October 26, 1977, respectively, generally adopt as a Commission regulation the accounting standards and disclosures that are contained in FAS-19. These releases apply to filings with the SEC and to reports filed with the Department of Energy.

Securities Release No. 5878, also issued on October 26, 1977, deals with replacement cost information (ASR-190) for certain registrants. In lieu of replacement cost information, the release requires the disclosure of the present value of future net revenues estimated to be received in the future from the production of proved oil and/or gas reserves. This release becomes effective for filings covering fiscal years ending after December 24, 1978.

On August 31, 1978, the SEC issued ASR-253 which included the following:

- Adopted the successful-efforts accounting method and disclosure requirements of FAS-19

- Indicated that a form of full-cost accounting for oil and gas producing companies will be developed by the SEC as an acceptable reportable alternative for the SEC

- Concluded that the full-cost and successful-efforts methods based upon historical costs fail to provide sufficient information for gas and oil producing companies, and that the SEC would take steps to develop an accounting method based on current valuation of proved oil and gas reserves

- Adopted disclosure rules for certain information regardless of the accounting method used

- Adopted the definition of *proved reserves*, which differed from that prescribed by FAS-19

On December 19, 1978, the SEC issued ASR-257 and ASR-258, which included the following:

- Reaffirmed the conclusions the SEC prescribed in ASR-253 (enumerated above)

- Adopted definitions of proved reserves developed by the Department of Energy for its reporting purposes

- Described the form of full-cost accounting for gas and oil producing companies that would be acceptable as an alternative to the successful-efforts method for reporting to the SEC

In 1982, the SEC issued ASR-300, adopting the disclosure requirements of FAS-69, discussed later in this chapter. The SEC issued Financial Reporting Release (FRR) 14 in 1983 and FRR-17 in 1984, clarifying the full-cost method of accounting.

ACCOUNTING PRINCIPLES—BASIC CONCEPTS

FAS-19 does not address the transporting, refining, and marketing aspects of oil and/or gas production. The functions covered by the promulgated GAAP are (*a*) acquisition of properties, (*b*) exploration, (*c*) development, and (*d*) production (FAS-19, par. 1).

Generally, the incurrence of a cost that results in the acquisition of an asset is capitalized and subsequently amortized, unless the asset becomes impaired or worthless, in which case it is reduced in value or written off (FAS-19, par. 12). Costs that do not result in the acquisition of an asset, such as carrying costs of undeveloped properties, geological and geophysical (G&G) costs, and the costs of drilling exploratory wells that do not find proved reserves, are charged to expense when incurred (FAS-19, par. 13).

Costs incurred to operate and maintain producing wells, related equipment, and facilities become part of the total production costs (also known as *lifting costs*). The other part of production costs comprise depreciation, depletion, and amortization of the costs capitalized as property acquisition, exploration, and development costs.

Before the accounting treatment of a cost can be determined, it must be first classified as a cost of acquiring properties, exploring, developing, or producing. For example, support equipment and labor can be classified as any of the functional activities in the oil and gas industry. Labor used in developing a producing well is capitalized and subsequently amortized, whereas labor costs incurred in operating producing wells become part of production costs.

The following is a brief discussion of the accounting principles and basic concepts involved in each function of the oil and gas industry.

Acquisition of Properties

Acquisition of properties includes all costs to purchase, lease, or otherwise acquire a proved or unproved property, including brokers' fees, legal fees, and recording fees, and other costs incurred in acquiring properties (FAS-19, par. 15). The acquisition of properties may include the transfer of all or part of the rights and responsibilities of operating the properties (operating interest) or none of the rights or responsibilities of operating (nonoperating interest).

If the interest in the property acquired is in substance a borrowing repayable in cash or its equivalent, it is treated as a borrowing and not as the acquisition of an interest in the property.

If part or all of an interest in a property is sold and substantial uncertainty exists in the recovery of the applicable costs involved or if the seller has a substantial future performance obligation to drill a well or to operate the property without reimbursement, no gain is recognized on these types of conveyances.

As in all nonmonetary exchanges of like property, gain or loss is recognized only to the extent of any *boot* received, as follows:

- Exchange of assets used in oil and gas producing activities for other assets used in oil and gas producing activities

- A joint pooling of assets to find, develop, or produce oil and/or gas from a particular property

Unproved properties are reclassified to proved properties when proved reserves are attributed to the property. Periodic assessment of unproved properties is made to determine whether they have been impaired. Impairment is likely if a dry hole has been drilled and there are no future plans to continue drilling, or if the end of a lease approaches and drilling has not commenced on the property. Losses for impairment of unproved properties are made by a charge to income and a credit to a valuation account in the year the impairment occurs (FAS-19, par. 28).

If an unproved property is abandoned or becomes worthless, all related capitalized costs are charged first against any related allowance for impairment account, and any excess charged to income of the period that the unproved property is abandoned or becomes worthless (FAS-19, par. 40). If only a small portion of an amortization base is abandoned or becomes worthless, then that portion is considered fully amortized and its cost charged to the accumulated depreciation, depletion, or amortization account, and no gain or loss is recognized (FAS-19, par. 41).

The unit-of-production method is used to amortize (deplete) all capitalized property acquisition costs of proved properties. As stated previously, this amortization (depletion) becomes part of the production costs (lifting costs). Amortization rates should be reviewed at least annually and revisions should be accounted for prospectively as changes in accounting estimates as described by FAS-154 (FAS-19, par. 30).

In proved properties that contain both oil and gas reserves, a common unit of measure based on the approximate relative energy content of the oil and gas should be used as the unit of production in the current period. Amortization is then based on the converted common unit of measure. In the event that either oil or gas dominates the content of both reserves and current production, unit-of-production amortization may be computed on the dominant mineral only (FAS-19, par. 38).

Exploration

Exploration includes all costs relating to the search for oil and/or gas reserves, including depreciation and applicable costs of support equipment and facilities, drilling exploratory wells, and exploratory-type stratigraphic test wells. Exploration costs may be incurred before the actual acquisition of the property, and in this sense they are sometimes referred to as *prospecting costs* (FAS-19, par. 16).

Some exploration costs do not represent the acquisition of an identifiable asset, and are therefore charged directly to expense when incurred. The cost of carrying and maintaining undeveloped properties is an expense, because such costs do not increase the potential that the properties will contain proved reserves. Examples of these types of expenses are delay rentals, taxes on properties, legal costs, and loan maintenance (FAS-19, pars. 17–18).

Geological, topographical, and geophysical studies (G&G costs) and related salaries and other expenses also are expensed, because they do not represent the acquisition of an identifiable asset. The studies frequently are made before the acquisition of the property and represent research or information costs. More often than not, G&G costs are incurred and the properties are never acquired (FAS-19, par. 18).

Pending the determination of whether a well has proved reserves, all costs of drilling exploratory wells are capitalized and are classified as uncompleted wells, equipment and facilities. The disposition of exploratory wells and their related costs usually is made shortly after completion, and if the well has proved reserves, the costs are capitalized and reclassified as wells, related equipment and facilities. If no proved reserves are found, however, the capitalized costs of drilling the well, less any salvage value, are charged to expense (FAS-19, par. 19). If an exploratory well is in progress at the end of an accounting period and the well is determined not to have found proved reserves before the financial statements for the period are issued, the costs incurred through the end of the period, net of any salvage value, should be charged to expense for that period (FAS-19, par. 33). However, previously issued financial statements are not restated retroactively to account for subsequently learned information (FIN-36, par. 2).

Sometimes an exploratory well cannot be classified as having found proved reserves on completion of drilling, because justification for major capital expenditures, such as a trunk pipeline, must be made, which may depend on the success of additional exploratory wells in the same area. In this event, the exploratory well and its related costs may be carried on the books as an asset for a period not exceeding one year, providing both of the following conditions are met (FAS-19, par. 31):

- A sufficient quantity of reserves was found to justify the completion as a producing well if the required capital expenditures are made.

- Drilling of other exploratory wells has commenced or is firmly planned for the near future.

If the above conditions are not met, the exploratory well and all its related costs are charged to expense.

Costs incurred for an exploratory well or stratigraphic test well, net of salvage value, are charged to expense for the period, if the following conditions exist (FAS-19, par. 34):

- The well is in progress (uncompleted) at the end of the period.

- A determination has been made prior to the issuance of the financial statements that the well has not located any proved reserves. In other words, the well has proved to be dry.

FIN-36 (Accounting for Exploratory Wells in Progress at the End of a Period) requires that only the costs incurred through the end of the reporting period, net of any salvage value, need be charged to expense. The amount charged to expense should include costs incurred during the current period, as well as costs that were incurred and capitalized in prior periods (FIN-36, par. 2). Thus, estimated costs to complete the uncompleted "dry well," if necessary, should not be accrued, since they will be charged to expense when incurred in subsequent periods.

The unit-of-production method is used to amortize all capitalized exploration costs, including support equipment and facilities. As stated previously, this amortization becomes part of the cost of production (lifting costs) (FAS-19, par. 35).

An enterprise may conduct G&G studies and other exploration activities on a property owned by another party. In exchange, the enterprise is contractually entitled to receive an interest in the property if proved reserves are found or to be reimbursed by the owner for the G&G and other costs incurred if provided reserves are not found. The enterprise conducting the G&G studies and other exploration activities shall account for those costs as a receivable when they are incurred. If proved reserves are found, the receivable then becomes the cost of the proved property acquired (FAS-19, par. 20).

Development

Development includes all costs incurred in creating a production system of wells, related equipment, and facilities on proved reserves so that the oil and/or gas can be produced (lifted). Development costs are associated with specific proved reserves; exploration costs are associated with unproved reserves. The cost of building a road to gain access to proved reserves is a development cost, as is the cost of providing facilities for extracting, treating, gathering, and storing the oil and/or gas. Development costs also include depreciation and operating costs of support equipment and facilities used in development activities (FAS-19, par. 21).

Development costs are associated with previously discovered proved reserves with known future benefits. Therefore, under promulgated GAAP, unsuccessful development wells (dry holes) are capitalized as a cost of creating the overall production system for proved reserves (FAS-19, par. 22).

The unit-of-production method is used to amortize (deplete) all capitalized development costs. As stated previously, this amortization (depletion) becomes part of the production costs (lifting costs). Amortization rates should be reviewed at least annually, and revisions should be accounted for prospectively as changes in accounting estimates (FAS-19, par. 35).

In proved properties that contain both oil and gas, a common unit of measure based on the approximate relative energy content of the oil and gas should be used as the unit of production for the purpose of determining the number of units produced in the current period. Amortization is then based on the converted common unit of measure. In the event that either oil or gas dominates the content of both reserves and current production, unit-of-production amortization may be computed on the dominant mineral only (FAS-19, par. 38).

Production

Production includes all costs incurred in lifting the oil and/or gas to the surface, and gathering, treating, field processing, and field storage. FAS-19 provides that the production function terminates at the outlet valve on the leased property or the field production storage tank, or under unusual circumstances, at the first point at which the oil and/or gas is delivered to a main pipeline, refinery, marine terminal, or a common carrier (FAS-19, par. 23).

Production costs include labor, fuel, and supplies needed to operate the developed wells and related equipment, repairs, property taxes, and insurance on proved properties, and wells, related equipment, and facilities (FAS-19, par. 24).

Costs incurred to operate and maintain the production system become part of the total production costs (lifting costs). The other part of the production costs consists of the depreciation, depletion, and amortization of the costs capitalized as property acquisition, exploration, and development costs (FAS-19, par. 25).

Support Equipment and Facilities

Costs for support equipment and facilities may be incurred for exploration, development, or production activities. Generally, these costs are capitalized and depreciated over their estimated useful lives or the life of the lease, whichever is appropriate. The depreciation expense and related costs of operating the support equipment and facilities are charged to the related activity (exploration, development, or production). When support equipment and facilities are utilized for more than one activity, the depreciation expense and operating costs should be allocated between the activities on a reasonable basis (FAS-19, par. 26).

Residual salvage values should be considered in determining depreciation and amortization rates (FAS-19, par. 37). The estimated costs associated with obligations for dismantlement, restoration, and abandonment should be accounted for in accordance with FAS-143 (Accounting for Asset Retirement Obligations) (FAS-143, par. 23).

Balance Sheet—Subsequent Information

GAAP require that information that becomes available subsequent to the balance sheet date and prior to the issuance of the financial statements should be taken into consideration in determining conditions that existed at the balance sheet date. The determination at the balance sheet date of whether an exploratory well has found proved reserves, the impairment of unproved properties, and similar conditions may be based on information that becomes available subsequent to the balance sheet date and prior to the issuance of the financial statements (FAS-19, par. 39).

MINERAL CONVEYANCES AND RELATED TRANSACTIONS

Mineral interests in properties frequently are conveyed to others. Conveyances of those interests may involve the transfer of all or part of the rights and responsibilities of operating a property. The transferer may or may not retain an interest in the oil and gas produced that is free of the responsibilities and costs of operating the property (i.e., a nonoperating interest). A transaction may involve the transfer of a nonoperating interest to another party and the retention of the operating interest (FAS-19, par. 42).

An entity may convey an interest in mineral properties or other similar assets. FAS-19, as amended by FAS-145, indicates that gain or loss should not be recognized at the time of conveyance for certain types of conveyances. These are (FAS-145, par. 9d):

- The transfer of either proved or unproved properties used in oil and gas producing activities for other assets also used in oil and gas producing activities, except if proved properties are transferred where an impairment loss is indicated. In that instance, the impairment loss would be recognized in accordance with the provision of FAS-144 (Accounting for the Impairment or Disposal of Long-Lived Assets).

- Assets are pooled in a joint initiative to find, develop, or produce oil and gas.

In the following types of conveyances, gain shall not be recognized at the time of the conveyance (FAS-19, par. 45):

- A part of an interest owned is sold and substantial uncertainty exists about recovery of the costs applicable to the retained interest.

- A part of an interest is sold and the seller has a substantial obligation for future performance, such as an obligation to drill a well or to operate the property without proportional reimbursement for that portion of the drilling or operating costs applicable to the interest sold.

For conveyances other than the types listed in the previous two paragraphs, gain or loss shall be recognized at the time of the conveyance unless there are other aspects of the transaction that would prohibit such recognition under generally accepted accounting principles for all enterprises (FAS-19, par. 46).

INCOME TAX CONSIDERATIONS

Deferred income taxes should be recognized for items that enter into the determination of pretax accounting income and taxable income in different periods (temporary differences). A future tax benefit arising from an excess of statutory depletion over cost depletion should not be recognized until the period where this excess is deducted for tax purposes (FAS-19, par. 62; FAS-109, par. 288o).

As discussed in FAS-109 (Accounting for Income Taxes), deferred tax liabilities and assets are required to be recognized for the expected future tax consequences of events that have been included in the financial statements or tax returns. Deferred tax liabilities and assets are established to reflect the future tax consequences of carryforwards and credits as well as differences between the financial statements and tax bases of assets and liabilities using the provisions of enacted tax laws and rates in effect for the year in which the differences are expected to reverse.

DISCLOSURES

Most of the disclosure requirements of FAS-69 pertain to *publicly held enterprises*. A *public enterprise* is defined as "a business enterprise (*a*) whose debt or equity securities are traded in a public market on a domestic stock exchange or in a domestic over-the-counter market (including securities quoted only locally or regionally), or (*b*) that is required to file financial statements with a regulatory agency in the preparation for the sale of securities domestically" (FAS-69, par. 1).

General Disclosures

Interim financial reports are not required to contain the disclosures mandated by FAS-69. However, interim financial reports are required to contain disclosure of favorable or adverse events concerning an enterprise's proved oil and gas reserves. A major oil or gas discovery is the type of favorable event that must be disclosed in interim financial reports. A major accident, such as a fire, that consumes significant quantities of proved oil and gas reserves is the type of adverse event that must be disclosed in interim financial reports (FAS-69, par. 9).

The method of accounting for costs incurred in oil and gas producing activities and the manner of disposing of capitalized costs must be disclosed fully by both public and nonpublic enterprises that are engaged in oil and gas producing activities (FAS-69, par. 6).

> ☞ **PRACTICE POINTER:** Disclosure of accounting policies is required by APB-22 (Disclosure of Accounting Policies). Both the accounting principle and the method of applying the principle should be disclosed, but accounting principles and their methods of application in the following areas are considered particularly important:
>
> - A selection from existing acceptable alternatives
> - The areas that are peculiar to a specific industry in which the entity operates
> - Unusual and innovative applications of GAAP
>
> Any, or all, of these may come into play in applying APB-22 by oil and gas producing companies.

When a complete set of annual financial statements is presented, publicly held enterprises that have significant oil and gas producing activities shall also disclose, as supplementary information to the financial statements, the following information relating to gas and oil producing activities (FAS-69, par. 7):

- Proved oil and gas reserve quantities
- Capitalized costs
- Costs incurred for property acquisition, exploration, and development activities
- Results of operations
- A standardized measure of discounted future net cash flows

The above supplementary information should be disclosed in complete sets of annual financial statements by publicly traded enterprises that have significant oil and gas producing activities. The test of whether an enterprise has significant oil and gas producing activities must be applied separately for each year that a complete set of annual financial statements is presented (FAS-69, par. 8).

If an enterprise satisfies one or more of the following tests, it is considered as having significant oil and gas producing activities (FAS-69, par. 8):

- Its *revenue* from oil and gas producing activities (defined below) is at least 10% of the total revenue from all of the enterprise's *industry segments* (defined below).
- The greater of (excluding income taxes):
  - Its operating profit from oil and gas producing activities is at least 10% of the total operating profit of all of the enterprise's industry segments that reflect operating profits.

— Its operating loss from oil and gas producing activities is at least 10% of the total operating losses of all of the enterprise's industry segments which reflect operating losses.

- Its *identifiable assets* (defined below) relating to oil and gas producing activities are at least 10% of all of the identifiable assets of all of the enterprise's industry segments (FAS-131, par. 133b).

The following definitions are used in applying the above tests for significant oil and gas producing activities:

Revenue

Revenue includes sales to unaffiliated organizations in connection with (a) networking interests, (b) royalty interests, (c) oil payment interests, and (d) net profit interests of the reporting enterprise. Intercompany sales or transfers are also included as revenue, based on appropriate market prices, which are equivalent to an arm's length transaction at the point of delivery from the producing unit. Excluded from gross revenue are (a) royalty payments and (b) net profit disbursements. Production or severance taxes are included as part of production costs and are not deducted in determining gross revenue (FAS-69, par. 25).

Industry Segment

An *industry segment* is a component of an enterprise that sells its products or services primarily to outsiders for a profit (FAS-131, par. 133a).

Identifiable Assets

Identifiable Assets are tangible and intangible assets used exclusively by a segment of an enterprise, or the allocated portion of assets used jointly by more than one segment. General corporate assets are not allocated to segments (FAS-131, par. 133b).

Goodwill is included in an industry segment's identifiable assets. An industry segment's identifiable assets are computed net of any valuation account, such as allowance for doubtful accounts, accumulated depreciation, etc.

Loans and advances between industry segments whose principal operations are financial (e.g., banking, leasing, insurance) and whose income is derived from such loans and advances, should be included as an identifiable industry segment asset.

Disclosures—Proved Oil and Gas Reserve Quantities

Publicly held enterprises disclose, as supplementary information to each of their annual financial statements presented, the net quantities of proved reserves and proved developed reserves of crude oil and natural gas (FAS-69, par. 10).

The net quantities of crude oil, which includes condensate and natural gas liquids, are stated in barrels. The net quantities of natural gas are stated in cubic feet (FAS-69, par. 15). Net quantities of crude oil and gas, if significant, are reported for the company's home country and each foreign geographic area (country or group of countries) in which significant reserves are located (FAS-69, par. 12).

In determining net quantities, the following rules apply:

- Net quantities exclude oil and gas subject to purchase under long-term supply, purchase, or similar agreements including those with governments. If the company participates in the operation of the oil and/or gas producing properties or otherwise acts as a producer, however, this information is reported separately (see below) (FAS-69, par. 13).

- Companies issuing consolidated financial statements include all the net quantities attributable to the parent company and all the net quantities attributable to the consolidated subsidiaries, whether or not wholly owned (FAS-69, par. 14).

  A significant portion of the net quantities at the end of the year may be attributable to a consolidated subsidiary that has a significant minority interest. In this event, disclosure of these facts and the approximate portion attributable to the consolidated subsidiary is required by FAS-69.

- Net quantities of investments that are proportionately consolidated include the proportionate share of the investee's net quantities of oil and gas reserves (FAS-69, par. 14).

- Net quantities of investments that are accounted for by the equity method are excluded. (This information is reported separately; see below) (FAS-69, par. 14).

- Net quantities include any from royalty interest owned if the information is available. If the information is not available, a statement of that fact must be made and net quantities *produced* attributable to the royalty interest must be disclosed for each period presented (FAS-69, par. 10).

- Net quantities include operating and nonoperating interest in properties (FAS-69, par. 10).

- Net quantities do not include interest of others in properties (FAS-69, par. 10).

Beginning and ending net quantities in proved reserves and proved developed reserves of crude oil (including condensate and natural gas liquids) and natural gas and net changes during the year must be reported at the end of each year in which a complete set of financial statements is presented.

Illustration of Disclosing Net Quantities

(Oil in thousands of barrels, natural gas in millions of cubic feet)	Total Worldwide		United States		Foreign Geographic Area A		Foreign Geographic Area B		Other Foreign Geographic Areas	
	Oil	Gas	Oil	Gas	Oil	Gas	Oil	Gas	Oil	Gas
Proved developed and undeveloped reserve:										
1. Beginning of year	765	4,096	500	2,300	120	1,416	125	360	20	20
2. Revisions of previous estimates	10	(33)	(32)	25	25	(16)	20	(45)	(3)	3
3. Improved recovery	5	10	3	10	2	0	0	0	0	0
4. Purchases of minerals-in-place	7	5	5	5	2	0	0	0	0	0
5. Extensions, discoveries, and other additions	77	305	65	185	10	80	1	35	1	5
6. Production	(109)	(433)	(76)	(250)	(12)	(135)	(18)	(40)	(3)	(8)
7. Sales of minerals-in-place	(4)	(3)	(4)	(3)	0	0	0	0	0	0
8. End of year	751	3,947	461	2,272	147	1,345	128	310	15	20
9. Proved developed reserves:										
Beginning of year	693	3,320	500	1,800	80	1,200	105	300	8	20
End of year	668	3,295	475	1,875	78	1,150	110	250	5	20

	Total Worldwide		United States		Foreign Geographic Area A		Foreign Geographic Area B		Other Foreign Geographic Areas	
	Oil	Gas	Oil	Gas	Oil	Gas	Oil	Gas	Oil	Gas
Oil and gas applicable to long-term supply agreements with governments or authorities in which the company acts as producer:										
10. Proved reserves at end of year	—	—	—	—	—	—	—	—	125	—
11. Received during the year	—	—	—	—	—	—	—	—	25	—
12. Company's proportionate interest in reserves of investees accounted for by the equity method, end of year	—	—	—	—	6	90	—	—	—	—

An explanation of each item in the chart follows:

1. **Beginning of year** The total net quantities at the beginning of the year

2. **Revisions of previous estimates** Upward or downward revision of proved reserves resulting from new information or changes in economic factors

3. **Improved recovery** Changes during the year resulting from new recovery techniques

4. **Purchases of minerals-in-place** Purchases during the year of proved developed and undeveloped reserves

5. **Extensions, discoveries, and other additions** Proved reserves resulting from the extension of previously discovered reservoirs, discovery of new fields or new reservoirs in old fields, and other additions

6. **Production** The total amount of net quantities produced for the year

7. **Sales of minerals-in-place** Sales during the year of proved developed and undeveloped reserves

8. **End of year** The total net quantities at the end of the year (All items above this item should add up to this item.)

9. **Proved developed reserves** Net quantities of proved developed reserves only for the beginning and ending of the year (Proved developed reserves include oil and/or gas expected to be recovered through existing wells using existing equipment and operation methods. Proved undeveloped reserves are those in which oil and/or gas is expected to be recovered from new wells on undrilled acreage or from existing wells that require major expenditures for completion.)

Net quantities subject to purchase under long-term supply agreements with governments or authorities and net quantities received during the year under such agreements must be disclosed separately (FAS-69, par. 28).

An investor's share of net quantities of an investment accounted for by the equity method shall be disclosed separately at the end of the year (FAS-69, par. 20).

If important economic factors or significant uncertainties are involved in any of the net quantities reported by an enterprise, an explanatory note should accompany the supplementary oil and gas information. Important economic factors or significant uncertainties would include (a) exceptionally high future development or lifting expenditures and (b) contractual obligations requiring the enterprise to sell significant quantities of oil or gas at substantially lower prices than the expected market price at the time of production (FAS-69, par. 16).

If a government restricts or prohibits the disclosure of any of the net quantities of oil and gas reserves required by FAS-69, or requires disclosure of a different nature than required by FAS-69, an enterprise must disclose the fact that (a) the net quantity reserves from that particular country are excluded from the supplementary information, or (b) the net quantity reserves from that particular country are other than proved (FAS-69, par. 17).

Disclosures—Capitalized Costs

Publicly held enterprises shall disclose in each of their annual financial statements presented the total amount of capitalized costs and related accumulated depreciation (depletion) (amortization) and valuation allowances relating to oil and gas producing activities. Under FAS-19, capitalized costs are classified as follows (FAS-19, par. 11):

- Mineral interest in properties which must be classified as (*a*) proved properties or (*b*) unproved properties
- Wells, related equipment and facilities
- Support equipment and facilities used in oil and gas producing activities
- Uncompleted wells, equipment and facilities

Existing GAAP (APB-12 (Omnibus Opinion—1967)) require that the balances of major classes of depreciable assets, by nature or function, be disclosed in the financial statements of an enterprise. Thus, to comply with existing GAAP, it would appear appropriate to use the above classifications for capitalized costs relating to oil and gas producing activities. However, FAS-69 states that it often may be appropriate to combine one or more, or two or more, of the classifications of capitalized costs and offers the following illustration:

	Total (in thousands of dollars)
Unproved oil and gas properties	$ 300,000
Proved oil and gas properties	2,972,000
	$3,272,000
Less: Accumulated depreciation, depletion amortization, and valuation allowances	515,000
Net capitalized costs	$2,757,000
Proportionate share of capitalized costs of investments accounted for by the equity method	$ 125,000

FAS-69 expressly requires that capitalized costs of unproved properties, if significant, be disclosed separately (FAS-69, par. 19).

Under the provisions of FAS-69, capitalized costs of support equipment and facilities may be disclosed separately or included as appropriate with capitalized costs of proved and unproved properties (FAS-69, par. 19).

An enterprise's proportionate share of the total capitalized costs relating to oil and gas producing activities of an investment accounted for by the equity method must be disclosed separately in each annual financial statement presented (FAS-69, par. 20).

Disclosures—Incurred Functional Costs

Publicly held enterprises shall disclose in each of their annual financial statements presented the total capitalized or expensed costs for the following functional activities of oil and gas producing companies (FAS-69, par. 21):

- Property acquisition costs
- Exploration costs
- Development costs

Exploration and development costs include the depreciation expense of support equipment and facilities, but exclude the expenditures to acquire such equipment and facilities. Any of these functional costs that are incurred in a foreign country are disclosed separately by geographic areas in the same manner that net quantities of oil and gas are disclosed (FAS-69, par. 22).

Illustration of Disclosure of Property Acquisition, Exploration, and Development Costs Required by FAS-69

(in millions)	Total Worldwide	United States	Foreign Geographic Area A	Foreign Geographic Area B	Other Foreign Geographic Areas
Property acquisition costs:					
Proved	$ 15	$ 3	$ 2	$ 2	$ 8
Unproved	5	5	—	—	—
Exploration costs	250	150	50	40	10
Development costs	660	420	110	80	50
Proportionate share of the property, acquisition, exploration, and development costs from investments accounted for by the equity method	10	—	10	—	—

An enterprise's proportionate share of the total property acquisition, exploration, and development costs relating to oil and gas producing activities of an investment accounted for by the equity method must be disclosed separately, in total and by geographic area, in each annual financial statement presented (FAS-69, par. 23).

If costs to acquire a mineral interest in proved reserves are significant, FAS-69 requires that they be disclosed separately from costs to acquire interests in unproved reserves (FAS-69, par. 22).

Disclosures—Results of Operations

Publicly held enterprises shall disclose in each of their annual financial statements presented the results of operations (as defined below) for oil and gas producing activities. If the enterprise is subject to the segmentation provisions of FAS-131, however, the results of operations shall be included with the other segment information required by FAS-131.

Results of operations include an enterprise's interest in proved oil and gas reserves and oil and gas subject to purchase under long-term supply contracts and similar agreements.

Under FAS-69, results of operations for oil and gas producing activities are disclosed in total and for each geographic area for which related reserve quantities are disclosed (FAS-69, par. 24).

The following information is disclosed for results of operations for oil and gas producing activities (FAS-69, par. 24):

Revenue

Revenue includes sales to unaffiliated organizations in connection with (a) net working interests, (b) royalty interests, (c) oil payment interests, and (d) net profit interests of the reporting enterprise (FAS-69, par. 25).

Regarding gas sales, production is not always sold in accordance with the respective joint revenue interest of the owners of the well for various reasons. In these situations, revenue is recorded on either the entitlements method or the sales method. Under the entitlements method, each unit of gas sold is assumed to be jointly owned by the owners of the well, and each joint revenue interest owner records a proportionate share of the gas sold from the well, regardless of whose customer the gas is sold to or who collects the revenue from the sale. Normally, a receivable or payable is recorded under these circumstances to reflect the imbalance. Receivables should be net of selling expenses. Under the sales method of accounting, an owner of a revenue interest in a well records only the gas it sells to its customers for which it collects the revenue. The method of accounting for gas imbalances should be disclosed in the footnotes to the financial statements.

Intercompany sales or transfers also are included as revenue, based on appropriate market prices, which are equivalent to arm's-length transactions at the point of delivery from the producing unit (FAS-69, par. 25).

Excluded from gross revenue are royalty payments and net profit disbursements. Production or severance taxes are included as part of production costs and are not deducted in determining gross revenue (FAS-69, par. 25).

Production

Includes all costs incurred in lifting the oil and/or gas to the surface, and gathering, treating, field processing, and field storage. The production function terminates at the outlet valve on the leased property or the field production storage tank, or under unusual circumstances, at the first point at which the oil and/or gas is delivered to a main pipeline, refinery, marine terminal, or a common carrier (FAS-19, par. 23).

Production costs include labor, fuel, and supplies needed to operate the developed wells and related equipment, repairs, property taxes, and insurance on proved properties, and wells, related equipment, and facilities (FAS-19, par. 24).

Costs incurred to operate and maintain the production system become part of the total production costs (lifting costs) (FAS-19, par. 24).

Depreciation, depletion, amortization, and valuation allowances related to capitalized costs are excluded from production costs and disclosed under a separate caption (see below) (FAS-19, par. 25).

Exploration

Exploration includes all costs relating to the search for oil and/or gas reserves, including applicable costs of support equipment and facilities, drilling exploratory wells, and exploratory-type stratigraphic test wells. Exploration costs may be incurred before the actual acquisition of the property, and in this sense they are sometimes referred to as prospecting costs (FAS-19, par. 16).

Some exploration costs do not represent the acquisition of an identifiable asset, and are therefore charged directly to expense when incurred. The cost of carrying and maintaining undeveloped properties is an expense, because such costs do not increase the potential that the properties will contain proved reserves. Examples of these types of expenses are delay rentals, taxes on properties, legal costs, and land maintenance (FAS-19, pars. 17–18).

Geological, topographical, and geophysical studies (G&G costs) and related salary and other expenses also are expensed, because they do not represent the acquisition of an identifiable asset. The studies frequently are made before the acquisition of the property and represent research or information costs. More often than not, G&G costs are incurred and the properties are never acquired (FAS-19, par. 18).

Depreciation, depletion, amortization, and valuation allowances related to capitalized costs are excluded from exploration expenses and disclosed under a separate caption (see below).

Depreciation, Depletion, Amortization, and Valuation Allowances

Depreciation, depletion, amortization, and valuation allowances related to oil and gas producing activities, except those which are part of general overhead and financing costs, are disclosed separately under this caption.

> ☞ **PRACTICE POINTER:** Interest capitalized under the provisions
> of FAS-34 on qualifying assets used in oil and gas producing
> activities is charged to net income as depreciation, depletion,
> or amortization of the cost of the related asset.

Income Tax Expense

The determination of *income tax expense* reflects any permanent differences relating to oil and gas activities, provided that such permanent differences are reflected appropriately in the enterprise's consolidated income tax expense for the period (FAS-69, par. 26).

Results of Operations

Results of operations are equal to revenues, less (*a*) production costs, (*b*) exploration expenses, (*c*) depreciation, depletion, amortization, and valuation allowances, and (*d*) income tax expense. Results of operations for oil and gas producing activities do not include general corporate overhead and financing costs. However, corporate overhead or expenses incurred at a central administrative office may include operating expenses of oil and gas producing activities and should be accounted for as such. In determining whether an expenditure is or is not an operating expense of oil and gas producing activities, the nature of the expense governs. The location in which the expense is recorded or paid is irrelevant (FAS-69, par. 27).

Illustration of Disclosure of Results of Operations
(as Defined Herein)

(in millions)	Total Worldwide	United States	Foreign Geographic Area A	Foreign Geographic Area B	Other Foreign Geographic Areas
Revenues	$1,800	$1,200	$450	$100	$ 50
Production costs	(630)	(380)	(210)	(25)	(15)
Exploration expenses	(250)	(150)	(50)	(40)	(10)
Depreciation, depletion, amortization, and valuation provisions	(700)	(475)	(175)	(40)	(10)
	220	195	15	(5)	15
Income tax expense	(81)	(66)	(6)	(2)	(7)
Results of operations for producing activities (excluding corporate overhead and financing costs)	$ 139	$ 129	$ 9	$ (7)	$ 8
Enterprise's share of equity method investees' results of operations for producing activities (excluding corporate overhead and financing costs)	$ 10	$ —	$ 10	$ —	$ —

Results of operations do not include an enterprise's proportionate share of the results of operations (as defined herein) of oil and gas producing activities from investments accounted for by the equity method. An enterprise's proportionate share of the results of operations (as defined herein) from an investment accounted for by the equity method must be disclosed separately, in total and by geographic area, in each annual financial statement presented (FAS-69, par. 29).

Disclosures—Discounted Future Net Cash Flows

Publicly held enterprises disclose, in each of their annual financial statements presented, a statement of the present value of future net cash flows, in total and by geographic area, from (*a*) the net quantities of proved reserves and proved developed reserves of crude oil and natural gas and (*b*) the net quantities of oil and gas subject to purchase under long-term supply contracts and similar agreements, and contracts in which the enterprise participates in the operation of the oil or gas producing properties or otherwise acts as a producer. Items (*a*) and (*b*) may be combined into one statement of the present value of future net cash flows (FAS-69, par. 30).

Under the provisions of FAS-69, a standardized measure of discounted future net cash flows is achieved by utilizing a 10% discount rate. The statement of the present value of future net cash flows must include the following detail (FAS-69, par. 30):

Future Cash Inflows

Future cash inflows are calculated by multiplying the current year end net quantities of oil and gas reserves (items (*a*) and (*b*) above) by their respective current year-end prices. Future price changes are considered, but only to the extent of existing contractual agreements. In other words, prices that appear in existing agreements may be used, but only to the extent of the quantities involved in the agreement.

Future Development and Production Costs

Future development and production costs are estimated expenditures which should be incurred in producing the future cash inflows. Future development and production costs are estimated based on current year-end costs and existing economic environment. If significant, future development costs are disclosed separately.

Future Income Tax Expenses

Future income tax expenses are calculated by applying the current year-end statutory income tax rates, and giving consideration to new rates already enacted, to the total pretax future cash flows from the net quantities of oil and gas reserves, less (*a*) the tax basis of the properties involved and (*b*) allowable tax deductions, credits, and allowances (FAS-109, par. 288u).

Future Net Cash Flows

Future net cash flows are calculated by deducting future development and production costs and future income tax expenses from the future cash inflows.

Discount

Discount is calculated by applying a standardized 10% rate per year, which shall reflect the timing of the receipts of the future net cash flows from the net quantities of oil and gas reserves.

Standardized Measure of Discounted Future Net Cash Flows

The *standardized measure of discounted future net cash flows* is calculated by deducting the discount from the future net cash flows.

A significant portion of the consolidated standardized measure of discounted future net cash flows may be attributable to a consolidated subsidiary that has a significant minority interest. In this event, disclosure of these facts and the approximate portion attributed to the consolidated subsidiary is required (FAS-69, par. 31).

The standardized measure of discounted future net cash flows does not include an enterprise's proportionate share of the standardized measure of discounted future net cash flows from investments accounted for by the equity method. An enterprise's proportionate share of the standardized measure of discounted future net cash flows from investments accounted for by the equity method must be disclosed separately, in total and by geographic area, in each annual financial statement presented (FAS-69, par. 32).

An enterprise shall disclose, in each annual financial statement it presents, a statement of the changes in the standardized measure of discounted future net cash flows, in total and by geographic area. The factors that cause these changes shall be disclosed separately, if significant, under the following categories (FAS-69, par. 33):

1. Sales and transfers of oil and gas produced during the period, net of production costs

2. Net changes in sales and transfer prices, and changes in future development and production (lifting) costs

3. Previously estimated future development costs incurred during the period

4. Net changes for extensions, discoveries, additions, and improved recovery, less related future development and production costs

5. Net changes for revisions in quantity estimates

6. Net changes because of purchases and sales of minerals in place

7. Accretion of discount

8. Net changes in income taxes

9. Other (including the effect of changes in estimated rates of production)

> **OBSERVATION:** *Accretion of discount* (item 7 above) is a term the SEC uses to refer to the annual amount of imputed interest that is calculated on the standardized measure of discounted future net cash flows (see Illustration below).

Illustration of Standardized Measure of
Discounted Future Net Cash Flows

A newly formed oil company spends $200,000 to drill for oil and discovers a commercially exploitable well. At year-end it is estimated that this well will produce 10,000 barrels of oil for the next three years, for a total of 30,000 barrels. The year-end price of oil is $35 per barrel, and future development and production costs and future income tax expenses are estimated, at year-end prices, to be $5 per barrel. The standardized measure of discounted future net cash flows at 10% is $30 ($35 – $5) × 10,000 = $300,000 × 2.48685 (present value of an ordinary annuity at 10% for 3 periods) = $746,055. The amortization table for the three-year period is as follows:

Year	Present Value (A)	Interest (B)	Total	Net Cash Flow	Present Value Balance
1	$746,055	$74,606	$820,661	$300,000	$520,661
2	520,661	52,066	572,727	300,000	272,727
3	272,727	27,273	300,000	300,000	-0-

(A) = Standardized measure of discounted future net cash flows
(B) = Accretion of discount

In computing the changes in the standardized measure of discounted future net cash flows, the effects of price changes are calculated before the effects of quantity changes, so the latter will be priced at year-end prices. The effect of changes in income taxes includes the effect of the income taxes incurred during the period and the effect of changes in future income tax expenses. All other changes except the accretion of discount and income taxes shall be reported pretax (FAS-69, par. 33).

Footnotes are required for any additional information that is needed to prevent the disclosures from being misleading (FAS-69, par. 34).

> ☞ **PRACTICE POINTER:** FAS-19 requires information that becomes available after the balance sheet date and before the issuance of the financial statements to be taken into consideration in determining conditions that existed at the balance sheet date. The determination at the balance sheet date of whether an exploratory well contains proved reserves, the impairment of unproved properties, and similar factors may be based on information that becomes available after the balance sheet date and before the issuance of the financial statements.

Illustration of Disclosure of Standardized Measure of Discounted Future Net Cash Flows and Changes Therein

(in millions)	Total Worldwide	United States	Foreign Geographic Area A	Foreign Geographic Area B	Other Foreign Geographic Areas
Future cash inflows*	$ 19,890	$ 11,340	$ 6,800	$ 1,500	$ 250
Future production and development costs*	(8,725)	(5,200)	(2,800)	(600)	(125)
Future income tax expenses*	(4,835)	(2,835)	(1,600)	(325)	(75)
Future net cash flows	6,330	3,305	2,400	575	50
10% annual discount for estimated timing of cash flows	(3,000)	(1,635)	(1,100)	(250)	(25)
Standardized measure of discounted future net cash flows relating to proved oil and gas reserves	$ 3,330	$ 1,670	$ 1,300	$ 325	$ 25
Enterprise's share of equity method investees' standardized measure of discounted future net cash flows relating to proved oil and gas reserves	$ 100	$ —	$ 100	$ —	$ —

Beginning of year	$ 3,700
Changes resulting from: Sales and transfers of oil and gas produced, net of production costs	(1,170)
Net changes in prices, and production costs	(450)
Extensions, discoveries, additions, and improved recovery, less related costs	500
Development costs incurred during the period	535
Net changes in future development costs	25
Revisions of previous quantity estimates	55
Net change in purchases and sales of minerals-in-place	25
Accretion of discount	375
Net change in income taxes	(215)
Other	(50)
End of year	$ 3,330

*Future net cash flows were computed using year-end prices and costs and year-end statutory tax rates that relate to existing proved oil and gas reserves in which the enterprise has mineral interests, or for which the enterprise has long-term supply, purchase, or similar agreements where the enterprise serves as the producer of the reserves.

RELATED CHAPTERS IN 2009 *GAAP GUIDE* *LEVEL A*

Chapter 11, "Depreciable Assets and Depreciation"
Chapter 16, "Fair Value"
Chapter 21, "Income Taxes"
Chapter 26, "Interim Financial Reporting"
Chapter 42, "Segment Reporting"

RELATED CHAPTERS IN 2009 *GAAP GUIDE* *LEVELS B, C, AND D*

Chapter 16, "Fair Value"
Chapter 20, "Income Taxes"
Chapter 23, "Interim Financial Reporting"
Chapter 37, "Segment Reporting"

CHAPTER 53
PENSION PLANS

CONTENTS

OVERVIEW

GAAP for pensions encompass accounting and reporting for pension plans for employers and, in addition, financial reporting for pension plans as separate reporting units. The subject of this section is pension plan financial statements. Disclosure of the following information, either in statement form or otherwise, is required (FAS-35, par. 6):

- Net assets available for benefits
- Changes in net assets available for benefits
- Actuarial present value of accumulated plan benefits
- Effects of certain factors affecting the year-to-year change in the actuarial present value of accumulated plan benefits

GAAP establishing accounting and reporting standards for defined benefit pension plans are included in the following pronouncements:

FAS-35	Accounting and Reporting by Defined Benefit Pension Plans
FAS-110	Reporting by Defined Benefit Pension Plans of Investment Contracts
FAS-135	Rescission of FASB Statement No. 75 and Technical Corrections

BACKGROUND

A defined benefit plan is a plan that provides for a determinable pension benefit to be paid on retirement or the occurrence of certain other events. Based on the benefits expected to be paid, the employer's contributions can be computed actuarially. A plan that specifies a fixed rate of employers' contributions is considered to be a defined benefit pension plan for the purposes of FAS-35 (Accounting and Reporting by Defined Benefit Pension Plans), if employers' contributions are periodically adjusted to allow for payment of defined benefits that are described in the plan.

The main objective of the financial statements of defined benefit pension plans is to provide financial information that may be utilized to assess the present and future ability of the pension plan to pay benefits as they become due. The financial statements contain information about (*a*) the resources of the pension plan, (*b*) the accumulated plan benefits of participants, (*c*) the transactions affecting the plan's resources and benefits, and (*d*) other additional information, as necessary to provide clarity to the financial statement presentation (FAS-35, par. 5).

> ☛ **PRACTICE POINTER:**   FAS-35 does not require that financial statements be prepared and distributed for defined benefit plans. When financial statements of defined benefit plans *are* prepared and presented, however, they must comply with the provisions of FAS-35 to be in conformity with GAAP.

All financial statements and information should be prepared and presented for the same fiscal or calendar period. Thus, net assets available for benefits and the actuarial present value of accumulated plan benefits are presented as of the same date and the changes in both are presented for the same period. Financial statements for the most recent year-end period are preferred by FAS-35. If the information on the actuarial present value of accumulated plan benefits is not available or cannot be determined reasonably for the most recent year-end period, however, then such information shall be presented as of the beginning of the year. In this event, all other financial statements and changes in financial statements must be presented for the same period (i.e., all financial statements must be in comparative form) (FAS-35, par. 7).

The information concerning the actuarial present value of accumulated plan benefits and its year-to-year changes may be presented on the face of the statement of net assets, as a separate statement, or in notes to the financial statements. However, each category of information must be presented in its entirety in the same location on the financial statements regardless of the format in which it is presented (FAS-35, par. 8).

Benefit information may become available during a fiscal year and not at the beginning or end of the year. In this event, FAS-35 allows the use of averages or approximations in determining benefit information at the beginning or end of the fiscal year. However, the method used to estimate benefit information must produce results similar to those required by FAS-35 (FAS-35, par. 29).

FAS-75 (Deferral of the Effective Date of Certain Accounting Requirements of Pension Plans of State and Local Governmental Units) indefinitely deferred the effective date of FAS-35 for plans sponsored by and providing benefits for employees of state and local governments. In 1994, the GASB issued a standard that established financial reporting standards for pension plans of state and local governmental entities. As a result, the provisions of FAS-35, deferred by FAS-75, were no longer applicable for plans of state and local governmental entities. In 1999, the FASB issued FAS-135 (Rescission of FASB Statement No. 75 and Technical Corrections), which removed FAS-75 from the authoritative literature because it was no longer required.

PENSION PLAN INFORMATION

Net Assets Available for Benefits

The pension plan's resources should be identified in reasonable detail and presented on the accrual basis of accounting (FAS-35, par. 9).

> ☞ **PRACTICE POINTER:** Comparison of the current year and the immediate prior year is used in FAS-35 only when the benefit information date is at the beginning of the current year. If the benefit information date is at the end of the current year, only

the current year is presented. In footnote 1 of FAS-35, however, it is suggested that comparative financial statements for several plan years are more useful in assessing a plan's ability to provide future benefits. In addition, financial reporting required by the Employee Retirement Income Security Act (ERISA) requires that the statement of net assets be in comparative form.

Investments

All pension plan investments that are held to provide benefits for the plan's participants, excluding insurance contracts, must be identified in reasonable detail and presented at fair value in the financial statements. FAS-35 defines *fair value* as the amount that could reasonably be expected to be received in a current sale between a willing buyer and a willing seller, neither of whom is compelled to buy or sell. Plan investments include debt or equity securities, real estate, and other types of investments held to provide benefits for the plan's participants. Quoted market values, in an active market, are used as fair value when available (FAS-35, par. 11). If fair value is determined by some other method, the method should be disclosed adequately in the financial statements or footnotes thereto (FAS-35, par. 13).

In addition, an investment contract issued by an insurance company must be recorded at fair value (FAS-110, par. 4). An exception exists for deposit administration and immediate participation guarantee contracts entered into before December 15, 1992. These contracts can continue to be accounted for at contract value (FAS-110, par. 8).

Insurance Contracts

FAS-110 requires insurance contracts to be presented in the same manner as specified in the annual report filed with certain governmental agencies pursuant to ERISA. Such contracts are presented either at fair value or at amounts determined by the insurance enterprise (contract value). A plan not subject to ERISA presents its insurance contracts as if the plan were subject to the reporting requirements of ERISA (FAS-110, par. 4).

Insurance contracts generally are characterized by the following (FAS-110, par. 5):

- The purchaser of the insurance contract makes an initial payment or deposit to the insurance enterprise in advance of the possible occurrence or discovery of an insured event.
- When the insurance contract is made, the insurance enterprise ordinarily does not know if, how much, or when amounts will be paid under the contract.

Contracts that do not subject the insurance enterprise to risks arising from policyholders' mortality or morbidity are investment, rather than insurance, contracts. A *mortality or morbidity risk* is present

Illustration of Presentation Suggested by FAS-35

Statement of Net Assets Available for Benefits

	December 31	
	20X7	*20X6*
Assets:		
Investments at quoted market values (Note:————)		
Federal and state debt securities	$ 500,000	$ 1,000,000
Corporate debt securities	3,500,000	3,000,000
Common stock	6,000,000	5,500,000
	$10,000,000	$ 9,500,000
Investments at estimated fair value (Note:————)		
Corporate debt securities	$ 500,000	$ 600,000
Preferred stock	400,000	400,000
Mortgages	1,100,000	1,000,000
Real estate	500,000	600,000
	$ 2,500,000	$ 2,600,000
Deposit administrative contract at contract value* (Note:————)	1,100,000	1,050,000
Total investments	$13,600,000	$13,150,000
Cash	100,000	110,000
Contributions receivable— employers	600,000	500,000
Accrued interest and dividends	90,000	80,000
Total assets	$14,390,000	$13,840,000
Liabilities:		
Accounts payable and accrued	(80,000)	(75,000)
Net assets available for benefits	$14,310,000	$13,765,000

*If issued prior to 3/20/92.

if the insurance enterprise is required to make payments or forego required premiums contingent upon the death or disability (life insurance contracts) or the continued survival (annuity contracts) of a specific individual or group of individuals (FAS-110, par. 6).

Contributions Receivable

Contributions receivable from employees, employers, state or federal grants, and other sources should be identified separately in the financial statements. Contributions receivable should be reported on the accrual basis pursuant to actual legal or contractual obligations or formal commitments (FAS-35, par. 10). The fact that an employer accrues a liability to a pension plan does not, by itself, provide a basis for a pension plan to record a corresponding receivable.

In order for a pension plan to record an employer's contribution receivable, the receivable must be supported by a formal commitment or an actual legal or contractual obligation. However, FAS-35 states that evidence of a formal commitment may include (*a*) the formal approval of a specified contribution, (*b*) a consistent pattern of payments made after the pension plan's year-end pursuant to an established funding policy that attributes the payments to the preceding plan year, and (*c*) a federal tax deduction taken for the contribution by the employer for periods ending on or before the reporting date for the pension plan (FAS-35, par. 10).

☛ **PRACTICE POINTER:** Many pension plans allow a company, at its discretion, to discontinue contributions and/or the plan itself. The resulting legal position is that the company has no legal liability for future pension fund contributions, and employees have no rights to any benefits beyond those already provided for in the pension fund. However, the position of GAAP is one of substance over form and that a business is viewed as an entity that will continue to exist (going-concern concept). Therefore, GAAP require that the "no future legal liability clauses" of a pension plan be ignored for the purposes of determining the annual pension costs of employers.

Operating Assets

Assets that are used in the actual operation of a pension plan are reported at amortized cost on the financial statements. For example, buildings, leasehold improvements, furniture, equipment, and fixtures that are used in the everyday operation of a pension plan are presented at historical cost, less accumulated depreciation or amortization (FAS-35, par. 14).

Changes in Net Assets Available for Benefits

Significant changes in net assets available for benefits should be identified in reasonable detail in the Statement of Changes in Net Assets Available for Benefits.

Illustration of Presentation Suggested by FAS-35

Statement of Changes in Net Assets Available for Benefits
Year Ended December 31

	20X7
Investment Income:	
Interest	$ 315,000
Dividend	475,000
Rental	50,000
Increase (decrease) in investments at quoted market values (Note:———)	145,000
Increase (decrease) in investments at estimated fair values (Note:———)	(210,000)
	$ 775,000
Less: Investment expenses	120,000
	$ 655,000
Contributions from employers (Note:———)	800,000
Total	$ 1,455,000
Less: Direct benefit payments to participants	$ 460,000
Less: Annuity contracts purchased (Note:———)	400,000
Less: Expenses of administration	50,000
Total	910,000
Net increase in net assets	$ 545,000
Net assets available for benefits:	
Beginning of year	13,765,000
End of year	$14,310,000

The minimum disclosures required by FAS-35 that appear in the Statement of Changes in Net Assets Available for Benefits or its related footnotes are as follows (FAS-35, par. 15):

- Investment income, other than from realized or unrealized gains or losses on investments.

- Total realized and unrealized gains or losses on investments presented at quoted market values are reported separately from those of investments presented at estimated fair value.

- Contributions from employers, participants, and others are reported separately. Cash and noncash contributions from employers are disclosed. Noncash contributions are recorded at their fair value on the date of receipt and, if significant, are fully described in the financial statements or footnotes thereto.

- Direct benefit payments to participants are reported separately.

- Purchases of insurance contracts that are excluded from the plan's assets are reported separately. Dividend income on insurance contracts that are excluded from the plan's assets may be netted against the purchase of such contracts. The dividend income policy on insurance contracts should be disclosed in a footnote to the financial statements.

- Expenses of administering the plan are reported separately.

Accumulated Plan Benefits of Participants

FAS-35 requires that certain specified information regarding the actuarial present value of accumulated plan benefits of participants be disclosed as part of the financial statements. The present value of the accumulated plan benefits must be determined as of the plan benefit information date. Thus, if the plan benefit information date is the beginning of the year, the present value of the accumulated plan benefits must be determined as of the beginning of the year (FAS-35, par. 6).

In addition, financial statements as of the beginning of the year must also be included in the presentation. On the other hand, if the plan benefit information is dated as of the end of the year, the present value of the accumulated plan benefits must be determined as of the same date, and financial statements as of the end of the year must also be included in the presentation. FAS-35 states a preference for the use of end-of-year benefit information (FAS-35, par. 7).

FAS-35 allows considerable flexibility in presenting the actuarial present value of accumulated plan benefits and the changes therein from year to year (FAS-35, par. 8).

FAS-35 requires that the total actuarial present value of accumulated plan benefits be separated into at least three categories: (1) vested benefits of participants currently receiving payments, (2) vested benefits of other participants, and (3) nonvested benefits. Vested benefits of participants currently receiving payments include benefits due and payable as of the benefit information date. Disclosure of the accumulated contributions of present employees, including interest, if any, as of the benefit information date should be made in a footnote to the financial statements. In addition, the rate of interest, if any, should also be disclosed (FAS-35, par. 22).

For the purposes of FAS-35, the assumption is made that a pension plan will continue to exist (going-concern concept). The best estimates should be used in each actuarial assumption to reflect the pension plan's most likely expectations. The following specific assumptions must be applied (FAS-35, par. 20):

- Assumed rates of return shall reflect the expected rates of return during the periods for which payment of benefits is deferred and shall be consistent with returns realistically achievable on the types of assets held by the plan and the plan's investment policy. To the extent that assumed rates of return are based on values of existing plan assets, the values used in determining assumed rates of return shall be the values presented in the plan's financial statements pursuant to the requirements of FAS-35.

- Expected rates of inflation assumed in estimating automatic cost-of-living adjustments shall be consistent with the assumed rates of return.

- Administrative expenses expected to be paid by the plan (not those paid by the sponsor) that are associated with providing accumulated plan benefits shall be reflected either by adjusting appropriately the assumed rates of return or by assigning those expenses to future periods and discounting them to the benefit information date. If the former method is used, the adjustment of the assumed rates of return shall be disclosed separately.

Illustration of Presentation Suggested by FAS-35

Statement of Accumulated Plan Benefits
Year Ended December 31

	20X7
Actuarial present value of accumulated plan benefits (Note:————)	
Vested benefits	
Participants currently receiving payments	$ 4,650,000
Other participants	7,100,000
	$11,750,000
Nonvested benefits	1,100,000
Total actuarial present value of accumulated plan benefits	$12,850,000

An acceptable alternative in determining the actuarial present value of accumulated plan benefits as of the benefit information date is to use the same assumptions an insurance company would use if it were to issue an insurance contract providing the same accumulated plan benefits to the same participants (FAS-35, par. 21).

Accumulated plan benefits are determined at the benefit information date in accordance with the provisions of the pension plan. Accumulated plan benefits include those expected to be paid to (*a*) retired or terminated employees or their beneficiaries, (*b*) beneficiaries of deceased employees, and (*c*) present employees or their beneficiaries (FAS-35, par. 16).

Pension plan benefits usually can be determined by reference to the provisions in the plan. In most pension plans, benefits usually are based on each year of service (employment) rendered by the employee. If the benefits are not clearly determinable from the provisions of the plan, FAS-35 requires the following computation to determine the accumulated benefits (FAS-35, par. 17):

Benefits Includable in Vested Benefits

$$\frac{\text{Number of years of service completed to the benefit information date}}{\text{Number of years of service that will have been completed when the benefits will first be fully vested}} = \begin{array}{c}\text{Percentage}\\\text{of plan benefits}\\\text{accumulated}\end{array}$$

The above computation is used to determine the amount of plan benefits that have been accumulated to the benefit information date; it is used for plan benefits that are classified as vested benefits.

The following computation is used to determine the amount of plan benefits that are not includable in vested benefits that have been accumulated to the benefit information date. This type of plan benefit includes death or disability benefits that are payable only if death or disability occurs during active service (FAS-35, par. 17).

Benefits Not Includable in Vested Benefits

$$\frac{\text{Number of years of service completed to the date benefit information date}}{\text{Estimated number of years' service upon anticipated separation from covered employment}} = \begin{array}{c}\text{Percentage}\\\text{of plan benefits}\\\text{accumulated}\end{array}$$

FAS-35 requires that the following procedures be applied in determining accumulated plan benefits (FAS-35, par. 18):

- Accumulated plan benefits shall be determined as of the benefit information date based on employees' history of earnings and service, and other appropriate factors.

- In the case of periodic benefit increases, death benefits, early retirement benefits, and disability benefits, accumulated plan benefits should be based on employees' projected years of service.

- All automatic benefit increases that are specified in the plan, such as cost-of-living increases, which are expected to occur subsequent to the benefit information date, shall be recognized in determining accumulated plan benefits.

- Benefits that are covered by allocated insurance contracts that are not included as plan assets (in accordance with FAS-35) are not included in determining accumulated plan benefits, provided that payment for the allocated insurance contract has been made to the insurance company.

- Benefits arising from plan amendments adopted subsequent to the benefit information date shall not be included in determining accumulated plan benefits.

- In computing Social Security benefits, employees' earnings as of the benefit information date shall be used to determine future compensation. Increases in Social Security benefits or in compensation base arising from present or future Social Security laws shall be excluded in determining future compensation.

Changes in Accumulated Plan Benefits

Certain factors that cause changes in the actuarial present value of accumulated plan benefits between the current and prior benefit information dates, if significant either individually or in the aggregate, shall be identified in the financial statements or the footnotes thereto. Significant changes that are caused by individual factors shall be identified separately. The minimum disclosure required by FAS-35 includes the effects of the following factors, if significant (FAS-35, par. 25):

- Plan amendments
- Changes in the nature of the plan, such as a merger with another plan, or a spin-off of a plan
- Changes in actuarial assumptions

> **OBSERVATION:** An acceptable alternative permitted by FAS-35 to determine the actuarial present value of accumulated plan benefits as of the benefit information date, is to use the same assumptions an insurance company would use if it were to issue an insurance contract to provide the same accumulated plan benefits to the same participants. If a pension plan uses this method, it should disclose, if practical, the effects of changes in the actuarial present value of accumulated plan benefits that are caused by changes in actuarial assumptions. If the effects cannot be disclosed separately, they should be included in determining accumulated benefits.

Other factors that may cause significant changes in the actuarial present value of accumulated plan benefits are events and transactions that affect (*a*) the amount of accumulated benefits, (*b*) the discount period, and (*c*) the amount of benefits paid. These factors may be identified in the financial statements. Actuarial gains and losses may be disclosed separately, or included with the effect of additional accumulated benefits (FAS-35, par. 25).

Amounts paid to an insurance company for the purchase of insurance contracts are included in determining the amount of benefits paid. However, amounts paid by an insurance company for benefits, in accordance with an insurance contract that has been excluded from the plan's assets (in accordance with FAS-35), are not included in determining the amount of benefits paid (FAS-35, par. 25).

Changes in actuarial assumptions that result from changes in a plan's expected experience are treated as changes in accounting estimates. Accounting estimates are accounted for in the year of change and, if necessary, future years. Prior years' financial statements are not restated in accounting for a change in an accounting estimate in accordance with FAS-154 (Accounting Changes and Error Corrections) (FAS-35, par. 23).

Changes in the actuarial present value of accumulated plan benefits may be presented in the form of a separate reconciliation statement, or elsewhere in the financial statements. If the reconciliation statement is used, it should reflect the actuarial present value of accumulated plan benefits at both the beginning and the end of the year. The amount of detail between the beginning and end of year depends on whether a full presentation is made, or only the required minimum disclosures. If a full presentation is made, then all changes are identified and disclosed. If only the required minimum disclosures are made, however, it is necessary to include all other changes on one line to reconcile the beginning and ending balances (FAS-35, par. 26).

Illustration of Presentation Suggested by FAS-35

Statement of Changes in Accumulated
Plan Benefits

	Year ended December 31, 20X7 *Increase (Decrease)*
Actuarial present value of accumulated plan benefits, at beginning of year	$12,705,000
Plan amendment	370,000
Changes in actuarial assumptions	(210,000)
Other factors	(15,000)
Actuarial present value of accumulated plan benefits, at end of the year	$12,850,000

If the minimum required disclosures pertaining to the changes in the actuarial present value of accumulated plan benefits are made elsewhere in the financial statements and not in a reconciliation statement format, FAS-35 requires that the actuarial present value of accumulated plan benefits, as of the preceding benefit information date, also be disclosed (FAS-35, par. 25).

Other Financial Statement Disclosures

In addition to the financial statement and footnote disclosures mentioned previously, FAS-35 requires two specific, additional note disclosures and several other disclosures if they are applicable. The two required note disclosures appear in the plan's significant accounting policies in accordance with APB-22 (Disclosure of Accounting Policies). They are as follows (FAS-35, par. 27):

- The significant assumptions and method used to determine fair value of investments and the value of reported insurance contracts must be described adequately.

- The significant assumptions and method used to determine the actuarial present value of accumulated plan benefits must be described adequately. In addition, any significant changes in assumptions or methods that occur during the reporting period must be described.

Other required financial statement disclosures (if applicable) are as follows (FAS-35, par. 28):

- A brief description of the important provisions of the pension plan agreement. If this information is made generally available from sources other than the financial statements, however, reference to such sources may be made in the financial statements, instead of providing the brief description.

- Significant amendments to the pension plan that are adopted on or before the latest benefit information date should be described. In the event that significant plan amendments are adopted between the latest benefit information date and the end of the plan's year, disclosure should be made to the effect that the present value of accumulated plan benefits does not include the effects of those amendments.

- The order of priority for plan participants' claims to the assets of the plan upon termination of the plan should be described generally. In addition, a description of any benefits guaranteed by the Pension Benefit Guaranty Corporation (PBGC) and a description of the applicability of any PBGC guaranty to any recent plan amendment should be included.

  If the information required above is made generally available from sources other than the financial statements, reference to such sources may be made in the financial statements, provided that the following (or similar) disclosure is made in the financial statements:

  > "Should the pension plan terminate at some future time, its net assets generally will not be available on a pro rata basis to provide participants' benefits. Whether a particular participant's accumulated plan benefits will be paid depends on both the priority of those benefits and the level of benefits guaranteed by the Pension Benefit Guaranty Corporation at that time. Some benefits may be fully or partially provided for by the then existing assets and the Pension Benefit Guaranty Corporation, while other benefits may not be provided for at all."

- Significant plan administration costs that are being absorbed by the employer should be disclosed.

- The policy for funding the pension plan and any changes in policy during the plan's year should be described. The method for determining participants' contributions, if any, should be described and plans subject to ERISA must disclose whether ERISA minimum funding requirements have been met. The status of minimum funding waivers should be disclosed, if applicable.

- The pension plan's policy concerning purchased insurance contracts that are excluded from the pension plan's assets should be disclosed.

- Disclosure of whether or not a favorable "determination letter" has been obtained for federal income tax purposes should be made. And, if such a favorable tax determination letter has not been obtained, the federal income tax status of the plan.

- Disclosure of any plan investments that represent 5% or more of the net assets available for benefits should be made.

- Disclosure of any significant real estate or other transactions between the plan and the (*a*) employer, (*b*) sponsor, or (*c*) employee organization should be made.

- Unusual or infrequent events and the effects of such events that occur subsequent to the latest benefit information date but prior to the issuance of the financial statements and that may significantly affect the plan's present and future ability to pay benefits should be disclosed. In the event that the effects of such events are not reasonably determinable, all substantive reasons should be disclosed.

Illustration of Financial Statement Notes Required or Applicable under FAS-35

Summary of Significant Accounting Policies

Description of Pension Plan This pension plan is called the ABC Company Defined Benefit Pension Plan and covers substantially all of the employees of the ABC Company. The Plan is subject to the provisions of the Employee Retirement Income Security Act of 1974 (ERISA).

Annual pension benefits begin at the normal retirement age (65) for employees with five or more years of service to the company. The amount received at age 65 is equal to 1 1/2% of the final five-year average annual compensation for each year of service. Employees may elect to retire early from ages 55 to 64. The portion of the accumulated plan benefits attributable to the Company's contributions to an employee is forfeited if an employee discontinues employment before rendering five years of service. Several elections are available to employees for the distribution of pension benefits. Employees may elect to receive their pension benefits in the form of a joint and survivor annuity, single life annuity, or as a lump-sum distribution upon termination or retirement. The minimum amount that an employee may receive upon electing a life annuity is the greater of the annuity for five years or the employee's accumulated contributions to the plan, plus interest.

Death benefits are paid to the beneficiary equal to the value of the employee's accumulated pension benefits if the active employee was 55 years or older. Annual disability benefits are paid to an active employee who has become disabled, equal to the normal retirement benefits that have been accumulated at the time of disability. At normal retirement age, the disabled employee would begin receiving normal retirement benefits computed as if he or she had retired at the date of disability.

Investment Valuation Investments are valued at quoted market prices when available. Securities for which no quoted market price is available are valued at a fair value. Fair value is based upon a combination of different factors. In most cases, corporate bonds are valued through comparison of similar securities' yields. Restricted common stock usually is valued at the quoted price of the issuer's unrestricted stock, reduced by a discount to reflect the restriction. If neither a quoted market price is available nor an unrestricted stock of the issuer exists, then a value is determined on a multiple of current earnings reduced by comparison of similar companies' earnings with a quoted price.

Mortgages are valued at their present values based on prevailing interest rates applied to the future principal and interest payments. Real estate leased to third parties is valued at the present value of all future rental receipts and estimated residual values. The interest rate used to discount future values varies with the risks inherent in each real estate investment.

The value of the Plan's deposit administration contract with American Insurance Company, dated October 2, 19X1, is contract value. Contract value is determined by the contributions made plus interest at the rate specified in the contract less funds used to purchase annuities and pay expenses. The Plan's assets do not include those funds used to purchase annuities. When an annuity is purchased, American Insurance Company is required to pay all related pension benefits to a particular employee.

Actuarial Present Value of Accumulated Plan Benefits All future periodic benefit payments, including any lump-sum distributions provided for under the provisions of the Plan, are included in Accumulated Plan Benefits. Accumulated plan benefits include all benefits that may be paid to present employees or beneficiaries, retired or terminated employees or beneficiaries, and beneficiaries of employees who have died. The plan provides for benefits that are based on the employee's compensation during the last five years of eligible service. The basis of the accumulated plan benefits for active employees is the average compensation during the last five years of service. All benefits are included, up to the valuation date, providing that they are related to services rendered by the employee. Any benefits that are provided from assets that are excluded from the Plan's assets, are excluded from accumulated plan benefits.

The actuarial present value for the accumulated plan benefits is computed by American Appraisal Inc. Certain assumptions are utilized to adjust the accumulated plan benefits to reflect the present value of money and the probability of payment. Significant actuarial assumptions utilized in the valuations presented as of December 31, 20X9, and December 20X8 are as follows: Participants' life expectancy based on mortality tables (), average retirement age of 62.

Termination of the Plan In the event of termination, the net assets of the plan will be allocated, in accordance with ERISA and its related regulations. The order of priority is as follows:

1. Any benefits related to the contributions of the employees
2. Any annuity benefits that have been received for at least the past three years by former employees or their beneficiaries or that employees eligible to retire for that three-year period would have received if they had retired with benefits under the Plan. (The priority amount is the lowest benefit payable or paid during the five-year period before termination of the Plan.)
3. Insured vested benefits by the Pension Benefit Guaranty Corporation (PBGC) up to certain limitations
4. All uninsured vested benefits
5. All nonvested benefits

Annuity contracts for which the American Insurance Company is obligated to pay benefits are not included in the above priority schedule.

PBGC insurance benefits include most vested normal age retirement benefits, early retirement benefits, and certain disability and survivor's pensions. However, not all benefits under the Plan are guaranteed by PBGC and certain limitations are placed on some of the benefits guaranteed. Vested benefits are guaranteed at the level in effect at the Plan termination date, but are subject to a statutory ceiling that limits individual monthly benefits. The ceiling in 20X9 and 20X8 was XXX,XXX and XXX,XXX, respectively, for employees who are 65 years old and elect a single life annuity. All other annuitants are subject to a downward adjustment. Benefit improvements as a result of a Plan amendment are not automatically fully guaranteed by PBGC. PBGC guarantees the greater of 20% or $20 for each year following the effective date of an amendment. Thus, the full increase in benefits would be completely guaranteed within five years after an amendment assuming primary ceilings are in effect.

Investments Other Than Insurance Company Contract   All of the Plan's investments are held by a bank-administered trust fund, except for the deposit administration contract. The fair values of those investments for 20X9 and 20X8 were XXX,XXX and XXX,XXX, respectively.

Insurance Contract   The company entered into a deposit administration contract with the American Insurance Company in 19X1. The Plan deposits a minimum of $100,000 annually, which is placed in an unallocated fund. American adds interest to the fund at a stated rate of 7%. The interest rate can be changed after 19X9, but the different rate only affects deposits made after the date of change. Withdrawals are made from the fund under the direction of the Plan's administration to purchase an annuity. American Insurance Company premiums on purchased annuities are fixed for the term of the contract. Periodic dividends, if any, increase the unallocated fund. Dividends received in 20X9 and 20X8 were XXX and XXX, respectively. These dividends are deducted from the purchased annuity contract payments on the Statement of Changes in Net Assets.

Plan Amendment   There is an amendment to the plan expected in 20Y0, which will increase the annual pension benefits for each year of service.

RELATED CHAPTERS IN 2009 *GAAP GUIDE LEVEL A*

Chapter 33, "Pension Plans"
Chapter 34, "Postemployment and Postretirement Benefits Other Than Pensions"

RELATED CHAPTERS IN 2009 *GAAP GUIDE LEVELS B, C, AND D*

Chapter 29, "Pension Plans—Employers"
Chapter 30, "Pension Plans—Settlements and Curtailments"
Chapter 32, "Postemployment and Postretirement Benefits Other Than Pensions"

RELATED CHAPTER IN 2009 *INTERNATIONAL ACCOUNTING/FINANCIAL REPORTING STANDARDS GUIDE*

Chapter 13, "Employer Benefits"

CHAPTER 54
REGULATED INDUSTRIES

CONTENTS

OVERVIEW

GAAP include specific coverage of regulated enterprises, indicating the applicability of GAAP to those enterprises and, in some instances, providing alternative procedures for them. In general, the type of regulation discussed is that which permits rates or prices to be set at levels intended to recover the estimated costs of providing regulated services and products.

An important accounting issue for regulated enterprises is the capitalization of costs and their associated recovery. Generally, if regulation provides assurance that incurred costs will be recovered, those costs should be capitalized. If current recovery is provided for costs that will be incurred in the future, regulated enterprises should recognize those costs as liabilities.

GAAP for regulated enterprises are found in the following pronouncements:

FAS-71	Accounting for the Effects of Certain Types of Regulation
FAS-90	Regulated Enterprises—Accounting for Abandonments and Disallowances of Plant Costs
FAS-92	Regulated Enterprises—Accounting for Phase-in Plans
FAS-101	Regulated Enterprises—Accounting for the Discontinuation of Application of FASB Statement No. 71
FAS-106	Employers' Accounting for Postretirement Benefits Other Than Pensions
FAS-109	Accounting for Income Taxes
FAS-144	Accounting for the Impairment or Disposal of Long-Lived Assets

BACKGROUND

Over the years, state and federal regulatory agencies have been established by governmental authorities to regulate certain industries that provide essential services to the general public (i.e., public utilities, railroads, insurance companies, and cable television). One of the primary functions of regulatory agencies is to establish rates that the regulated enterprise can charge for its services or products. In connection with their regulatory authority, most agencies prescribe the types of accounting records and reports that the regulated enterprise must maintain. Frequently, these prescribed accounting rules conflict with GAAP.

The Addendum to APB-2 (Accounting Principles for Regulated Industries) required that financial statements of a regulated business intended for public use be based on existing GAAP, with appropriate recognition given to the rate-making process established by the regulatory agency. Under GAAS, an independent auditor must comply with the reporting standard that financial statements be presented in accordance with GAAP.

Different methods are used by regulatory agencies to set rates for regulated enterprises. The many different methods can be classified into (*a*) individual cost-of-service, (*b*) group rate-setting, and (*c*) a combination of both individual cost-of-service and group rate-setting.

Under the individual cost-of-service method of rate setting, the *allowable costs* that an enterprise usually is permitted to recover are all actual and/or estimated costs that are required to provide the service to the public, including a return on investment to compensate sources of long-term debt and equity capital. The rate or rates charged to different classes of customers are designed, but not guaranteed, to produce total revenue for the enterprise equal to the allowable costs. The individual cost-of-service method usually is used in setting rates for public utilities. An enterprise is more ensured of cost recovery under the individual cost-of-service method than any other method.

Under the group rate-setting method, the allowable costs that an enterprise may recover are based on rates established on an industry-wide, area-wide, or some other aggregate basis. Group rate-setting usually is utilized in more competitive industries, such as airlines, motor carriers, railroads, and insurance companies, than those in which the individual cost-of-service method is used.

Under the combination of individual cost-of-service and group rate-setting methods, the allowable costs that an enterprise can recover are based on some combination of both methods. Under the combination method, however, allowable costs usually do not include a provision for a return on investment, but may include an allowance for inflation or working capital.

Through the regulatory process, an enterprise is substantially assured of recovering its allowable costs by the collection of revenue from its customers. It must be noted that under some methods of rate-setting, allowable costs include a return on investment for the regulated enterprise. The economic effect of regulation is the substantiation that an asset exists or does not exist. As allowable costs are incurred by a regulated enterprise, they should be capitalized as assets. Costs that are not allowable under the regulatory process, however, are not substantially assured of being recovered and should be expensed as incurred.

FAS-71 (Accounting for the Effects of Certain Types of Regulation) establishes GAAP for enterprises whose regulators have the power to approve and/or regulate the rates that enterprises may charge customers for services or products. It contains the criteria that an enterprise must meet to be classified as a *regulated enterprise* and also establishes GAAP for the capitalization of allowable costs. FAS-90 (Regulated Enterprises—Accounting for Abandonments and Disallowances of Plant Costs) amends FAS-71 to specify the appropriate accounting for abandonments of plants and the disallowances of costs of recently completed plants.

FAS-90 also amends FAS-71 to provide that an allowance for interest on funds used during the construction stage of an asset should be capitalized only if it is *probable* (likely) that such an allowance will be included subsequently by the governing regulatory authorities as an allowable cost of the constructed asset.

FAS-92 (Regulated Enterprises—Accounting for Phase-in Plans) amends FAS-71 to specify the accounting for phase-in plans. FAS-92 specifically addresses those phase-in plans ordered by a regulator in connection with a plant on which construction was started before January 1, 1988.

FAS-101 (Regulated Enterprises—Accounting for the Discontinuation of Application of FASB Statement No. 71) establishes the appropriate accounting for situations in which an enterprise discontinues the application of the provisions of FAS-71.

FAS-144 (Accounting for the Impairment or Disposal of Long-Lived Assets) amends FAS-71 and FAS-101 to establish accounting standards for the impairment of long-lived and certain other assets, except that impairment of (1) regulatory assets will continue to be governed by paragraph 9 of FAS-71 and (2) costs of recently complete plants will continue to be addressed by paragraph 7 of FAS-90.

For the purposes of FAS-71, a regulator may be an independent third party, or a governing board of the regulated enterprise empowered by statute or contract. FAS-71 supersedes the Addendum to APB-2. Paragraph 108 of FAS-71 amends APB-30 (Reporting the Results of Operations) to specify that utility refunds to customers be disclosed net of their tax effects, as a separate line item in the income statement. APB-30 generally prohibits net-of-tax disclosure of unusual or infrequently occurring items that do not qualify as extraordinary items.

FAS-71 does not identify any specific industry as *regulated*. Instead, the focus of FAS-71 is on the nature of regulation and its resulting financial effects on a specific enterprise. Thus, any enterprise in any industry that meets all of the criteria of FAS-71 must comply with its provisions.

FAS-71 does not change the fact that companies in regulated industries must comply with all existing and future authoritative accounting pronouncements. If a conflict arises between an authoritative accounting pronouncement and FAS-71, however, a regulated enterprise shall apply the provisions of FAS-71 instead of the conflicting pronouncement. The following conditions govern the application of FAS-71 (FAS-71, pars. 5–8):

- FAS-71 applies only to financial statements issued for external general purposes, not to financial statements submitted to a regulatory agency.
- FAS-71 shall be applied only to regulated enterprises or those portions of the operations of a regulated enterprise that meet the specific criteria established by FAS-71.
- FAS-71 does not apply to emergency governmental actions that are imposed under unusual circumstances, such as price controls during periods of high inflation.

CRITERIA FOR REGULATED OPERATIONS

FAS-71 applies to financial statements issued for general purposes by an enterprise that has regulated operations and meets all of the following criteria (FAS-71, par. 5):

- An independent third-party regulator or a governing board of the regulated enterprise that has been empowered by statute or contract establishes or approves the rates the enterprise can charge its customers for its services or products.
- The established or approved rates of the independent third-party regulator or governing board of the regulated enterprise are intended to recover the specific costs of the regulated services or products.
- The rates set by the independent third-party regulator or governing board of the regulated enterprise to recover the costs of the regulated enterprise are reasonable and likely to be collected. (In applying this criterion, consideration must be given to the demand for the services or products and the level of direct and indirect competition.)

The thrust of FAS-71 is that the regulatory process can provide a basis for the regulated enterprise to recognize a specific asset. In this respect, FAS-71 requires that the following conditions be met for a regulated enterprise to recognize an incurred cost as a regulatory asset (FAS-71, par. 9):

- The regulator's intent to provide recovery of a specific incurred cost must be clear, if the revenue is to be provided through an automatic rate-adjustment clause.

- Based on available evidence, it is expected that the regulated rates will produce revenue about equal to the specific incurred cost.

An enterprise must first qualify as a regulated enterprise by meeting the specified criteria of FAS-71, and then both of the above conditions must be met before an incurred cost can be capitalized as an asset. In addition, if an incurred cost ceases to meet these two criteria, the cost should be charged to earnings (FAS-144, par. C32a).

The essence of the first criterion in FAS-71 is the existence of a regulator that can approve and/or regulate the rates that the enterprise can charge its customers for its services or products. The regulator may be an independent third party or a governing board of the enterprise empowered by statute or contract. A contractual arrangement between an enterprise and its sole or principal customer may create the appearance of *regulation*. However, the sole or principal customer of the enterprise is also responsible for payment of the services or products and thus is not, in a strict sense, an independent third-party regulator or governing board empowered by statute or contract. Therefore, Medicare, Medicaid, and similar contractual arrangements are excluded from the scope of FAS-71 (FAS-71, par. 62).

The principal economic effect of the regulatory process covered by FAS-71 is that it can provide substantiation that an asset does or does not exist at the time a regulated enterprise incurs costs to provide services or products (FAS-71, par. 9).

Under the provisions of FAS-71 the regulated rates must be designed to recover the specific costs of the regulated services or products. This usually is best accomplished by the individual cost-of-service method of rate-setting. Thus, the second criterion of FAS-71 requires that there be a cause-and-effect relationship between costs and revenues (FAS-71, par. 61).

A cause-and-effect relationship usually does not exist if regulated rates are based on industry-wide costs. The cause-and-effect relationship is intended to be applied to the substance and not the form of the regulation. If regulated rates are based on the costs of a particular group of companies and there is a dominant company within the group, the costs of the dominant company may represent the costs of the entire group. Here, the second criterion of FAS-71 would be met (FAS-71, par. 65).

The third criterion requires that the rates sufficient to recover incurred costs be reasonable to the ultimate consumer and likely to be collected (FAS-71, par. 66).

If the regulatory process is based on the recovery of future costs and not specific incurred costs, the provisions of FAS-71 are not met. If a *rate order* authorizing regulated rates for an enterprise does not specify clearly the recovery of specific incurred costs, the provisions of FAS-71 are not met. The rate order must indicate clearly the specific incurred costs that are designated for recovery. These specific incurred costs are referred to as *allowable costs,* in accordance with FAS-144 and consistent with GAAP applicable to other enterprises in general (FAS-71, par. 78).

In addition, if a regulator subsequently allows recovery through rates of costs previously excluded from allowable costs and written off, that action shall result in recognition of a new asset. The classification of that asset shall be consistent with the classification that would have resulted if those costs had been included initially in allowable costs. This provision to reinstate costs previously written off under FAS-144 is unique to rate-regulated industries.

Sometimes the nature of an incurred cost, such as the abandonment of part or all of a particular facility, cannot be anticipated by the regulated enterprise or the regulator. Under these circumstances, the intent of the regulator may be inferred based on available evidence or regulatory precedent, and, as a result, it may be probable that the future rate increases will be provided by the regulator for the specific recovery of the unanticipated future cost (FAS-90, par. 3).

On the other hand, the regulatory process may indicate the reduction or elimination of an existing asset or substantiate the existence of a liability (FAS-71, pars. 10 and 11). If a regulator subsequently excludes some or all of the cost from allowable costs, the asset's carrying amount should be reduced by the amount of the excluded cost (FAS-144, par. C32b). Here, the cost or related asset must be accounted for under existing GAAP, which are applied to other enterprises in general (FAS-71, par. 10).

> **OBSERVATION:** If the regulatory process can create an asset, it appears that deregulation may result in the permanent impairment of an asset that owes its existence to regulation. Additionally, as competition becomes more pervasive in the rate-regulated industries, costs (particularly plant costs) may become "stranded" in that the utility is unable to recover its cost or plant investment because the customer has changed the nature of the services it has historically received from the utility.

A regulated enterprise may be required by the regulator to refund revenue that was collected in prior periods; or the regulator may include in its regulated rates amounts that are intended to recover specific costs that may be incurred in the future, with the understanding that if the costs are not incurred, an adjustment will be made to future regulated rates. In either instance, the regulator has substantiated the existence of a liability (FAS-71, par. 11). In the event of customer refunds, FAS-71 requires that they be recorded as liabilities if they can be estimated reasonably and either (a) were ordered by the regulator and are unpaid or (b) are likely to occur and are not yet recorded.

If the regulator includes amounts in its rates that are intended to recover expected future costs that must be accounted for, a liability is created equal to the amount of revenue collected for the expected future costs (FAS-71, par. 11b).

The amount of revenue collected for the expected future costs is recorded as unearned revenue until those costs are actually incurred or an adjustment is made by the regulator. For example, a regulator may include in its regulated rates an amount for expected future uninsured storm damages. In this respect, the regulator may require that any amounts not actually incurred in the future for storm damages must be refunded to customers in the form of a future adjustment in the regulated rates. As the revenue attributable to the future storm damage is collected, FAS-71 requires that it be recorded as a liability and included in income only when the actual storm damage costs are incurred (FAS-71, par. 11b).

A regulator can substantiate the existence of another type of liability by requiring the regulated enterprise to credit customers over a future period for gains or other reductions of net allowable costs. The gains or other reductions in net allowable costs usually are amortized over the related future periods by a corresponding reduction in the approved regulated rates. In this event, FAS-71 requires that a liability be recorded in the amount of the future amortization (FAS-71, par. 11c). If a liability is recorded because of the regulatory process, it can only be reduced or eliminated by the regulatory process (FAS-71, par. 12).

An enterprise subject to FAS-71 must comply with all of its provisions. If there is a conflict between FAS-71 and existing GAAP, the provisions of FAS-71 must be applied (FAS-71, par. 7). In all other circumstances, however, existing GAAP must be followed and applied by a regulated enterprise. If a regulated enterprise is required by court order (affirmative injunction) to capitalize and amortize a particular cost and the cost does not qualify for capitalization under existing GAAP or FAS-71, the regulated enterprise cannot capitalize the cost in financial statements purported to be presented in accordance with GAAP.

ACCOUNTING FOR ABANDONMENTS

Historically, utilities have abandoned plants in early stages of construction, rather than after incurring major construction costs. Prior to the issuance of FAS-71, most regulated enterprises accounted for the costs of abandoned plants on a cost-recovery basis (no loss was recorded if revenues promised by a regulator were expected to recover the recorded costs).

The cost-recovery approach of accounting for abandonments is based on the view that the regulator is disallowing future earnings, rather than disallowing a portion of the cost of the abandoned plant. Thus, the effect of the cost-recovery approach is to delay the recognition of losses that are known to have been incurred.

Originally, FAS-71 required that an abandoned plant be reported at the lesser of its cost or the probable *gross revenue* expected to be allowed on the portion of the cost of the abandoned plant that the regulator included in allowable costs for rate-making purposes. Thus, FAS-71 did not change the practice of accounting for the cost of an abandoned plant on a cost-recovery basis.

FAS-90 amended FAS-71 to require that the future revenue that is expected to result from the regulator's inclusion of the cost of an abandoned plant in allowable costs for rate-making purposes be reported at its *present value* when the abandonment becomes *probable*. If the carrying amount of the abandoned plant exceeds that present value, a loss is recognized.

FAS-90 further amended FAS-71 by requiring the definition of *probable* to be consistent with the use of the term in FAS-5 (Accounting for Contingencies), namely, that a transaction or event is likely to occur (FAS-90, footnote 1). Under FAS-90, the probability that an enterprise will abandon an asset may be classified as (*a*) probable, (*b*) reasonably possible, or (*c*) remote. For purposes of FAS-90, *probable* means that the abandonment is likely to occur, *remote* means that the abandonment is not likely to occur, and *reasonably possible* means that the probability of the abandonment occurring is somewhere between probable and remote.

On the date it becomes probable that an enterprise will abandon an operating asset or an asset under construction, the total cost of that asset is removed from the books of account (plant-in-service or construction work-in-process) and reclassified as a new asset (e.g., a regulatory asset). The amount of cost assigned to the new asset depends on the amount of the total cost of the abandoned plant that the enterprise estimates will be allowed by the governing regulatory authorities. Another factor is whether recovery of the allowed cost is likely to be provided with a full return on investment, or with partial or no return on investment from the date the abandonment becomes probable through the date recovery is completed.

If it is probable (likely) that all or part of the cost of the abandoned plant will be disallowed by the governing regulatory authorities and the amount of the disallowed cost can be estimated reasonably, the disallowed cost is recognized as a current loss and deducted from the total cost of the abandoned plant.

If Full Return on Investment Is Expected

The total cost of the abandoned plant, less the amount of the probable disallowed cost that is recognized as a loss, is recorded and reported as a separate asset (FAS-90, par. 3a).

If Partial or No Return on Investment Is Expected

The present value of the expected future revenue to be generated from the allowable cost of the abandoned plant, plus any return on investment, is reported as a separate new asset. Any excess of the total cost of the abandoned plant reduced by the amount of disallowed cost reported as a loss, *over* the amount of the separate new asset, is reported as an additional loss (FAS-90, par. 3b).

An enterprise shall use its incremental borrowing rate to compute the present value of the expected future revenue to be generated from the allowable cost of the abandoned plant. An enterprise's incremental borrowing rate is the rate that an enterprise would have to pay to borrow an equivalent amount for a period equal to the expected recovery period (FAS-90, par. 3b).

To compute the present value of expected future revenue to be generated from the allowable cost of the abandoned plant, an enterprise may be required to estimate the probable period before recovery is expected to begin and the probable period over which recovery is expected to be provided (FAS-90, par. 3b). If the estimate of either of these periods is a range (similar to a minimum-maximum), the present value is based on the minimum amount in the range, unless some other amount within the range appears to be a better estimate (FIN-14, par. 3).

Subsequent Period Adjustments to the Separate New Asset

In accounting for the abandonment of a plant, estimates that may be used by an enterprise to calculate and record the amount of the separate new asset include (FAS-90, par. 4):

- The amount of any probable disallowed cost of the abandoned plant that can be estimated reasonably
- Whether recovery of the allowed cost of the abandoned plant is likely to be provided with a full return on investment, a partial return on investment, or no return on investment
- The period from the date the abandonment becomes *probable* through the date recovery is completed
- The probable period before recovery is expected to begin and the probable period over which recovery is expected to be provided

FAS-90 requires that an adjustment be made to the recorded amount of the new asset if new information indicates that the estimates used by an enterprise to record the amount of the separate new asset have changed. The amount of the adjustment is recognized as a gain or loss in the net income of the period in which the adjustment arises. However, no adjustment is made to the recorded amount of the separate new asset for changes in the enterprise's incremental borrowing rate (FAS-90, par. 4).

Accrued Carrying Charges on the Separate New Asset

A carrying charge is accrued and added to the carrying amount of the recorded separate new asset during the period between the date on which the new asset is recognized by an enterprise and the date on which recovery begins (FAS-90, par. 5).

The rate of the carrying charge is based on whether a full return on investment is likely to be provided, or a partial or no return on investment is likely to be provided (FAS-90, par. 5).

If Full Return on Investment Is Expected

A rate equal to the allowed overall cost of capital in the jurisdiction in which recovery is expected to be provided is used to calculate the amount of the accrued carrying charge.

If Partial or No Return on Investment Is Expected

The same rate that was used to compute the present value of the expected future revenue to be generated from the allowable cost of the abandoned plant is used to calculate the amount of the accrued carrying charge.

Amortization of Separate New Asset During Recovery Period

The separate new asset is amortized during the recovery period, based on whether a full return on investment is likely to be provided, or a partial or no return on investment is likely to be provided (FAS-90, par. 6).

If Full Return on Investment Is Expected

The separate new asset is amortized during the recovery period in the same manner as that used for rate-making purposes.

If Partial or No Return on Investment Is Expected

The separate new asset is amortized during the recovery period at the same rate that was used to compute the present value of the expected future revenue to be generated from the allowable cost of the abandoned plant. (**Note:** This method of amortization will produce a constant return on the unamortized investment in the new asset equal to the rate at which the expected revenues were discounted.)

Accounting for Disallowances of Plant Costs

FAS-71 addresses the disallowance of costs by a regulator, indicating that when a disallowance occurs, "the carrying amount of any related asset shall be reduced to the extent of the excluded cost. Whether other assets have been impaired shall be judged the same as for enterprises in general" (FAS-71, par. 10; FAS-121, as amended by FAS-144, par. C32b).

An enterprise's estimate of the cost of the abandoned plant that will be allowed should be based on the facts and circumstances related to the specific abandonment and should consider the past practice and current policies of the governing regulatory authorities (FAS-90, par. 3).

Under FAS-90, if it becomes probable that part of the cost of a recently completed plant will be disallowed by the governing regulatory authorities and the amount of the disallowed cost can be estimated reasonably, the disallowed cost is recognized as a current loss and deducted from the total cost of the recently completed plant (FAS-90, par. 7).

☞ **PRACTICE POINTER:** If only a range of the amount of the disallowed cost (similar to the minimum or maximum) can be established, then use the minimum amount in the range, unless some other amount within the range appears to be a better estimate (FIN-14, par. 3).

If part of the cost of the recently completed plant is explicitly, but indirectly, disallowed, such as an explicit disallowance of return on investment on a portion of the plant, an equivalent amount of cost is deducted from the reported cost of the recently completed plant and recognized as a loss (FAS-90, par. 7).

ACCOUNTING FOR PHASE-IN PLANS

Under traditional rate-making procedures, a utility is granted an increase in rates to provide for the recovery of the allowable costs of a newly completed utility plant that is placed in service. However, the impact of significantly increased costs such as those associated with nuclear plants and the high cost of capital has resulted in rate spikes. A *rate spike* is an unusually high, one-time increase in the rates of a regulated enterprise. To reduce the effect of such spikes, regulatory authorities and utilities have developed phase-in plans that allow for a gradual increase in rates.

Several different types of phase-in plans have been developed, all of which are designed to reduce the impact of rate spikes by (*a*) deferring a portion of the initial rate increase to future years and (*b*) providing the regulated enterprise with a return on the amounts deferred. Instead of the traditional pattern of an increase in allowable costs followed by a decrease in allowable costs for utility plants after the plants are placed in service, phase-in plans create a pattern of gradually increasing allowable costs for the initial years of the plant's service life.

The *allowable costs* that a regulatory authority usually permits a regulated enterprise to recover from the rates it charges to its customers include actual and/or estimated costs that are incurred to provide a product or service to the public, including a return on investment to compensate sources of long-term debt and equity capital. The rates that are approved by a regulatory authority are designed, but not guaranteed, to produce total revenue for a regulated enterprise that is approximately equal to its allowable costs.

Under the provisions of FAS-92, a phase-in plan is any method used to recognize allowable costs in the rates charged by a regulated enterprise to its customers that also meets all of the following criteria (FAS-92, par. 3):

- The phase-in plan was adopted by the regulator in connection with a major plant of the regulated enterprise (or of one of its suppliers) that is newly completed or scheduled for completion in the near future.

- The method defers the rates approved to recover the allowable costs of the regulated enterprise beyond the period in which those allowable costs would have been charged to expense under GAAP applicable to enterprises in general.

- The method defers the rates approved to recover the allowable costs of the regulated enterprise beyond the period in which those rates would have been ordered by the enterprise's regulator under the rate-making method routinely used prior to 1982 for similar allowable costs of the same regulated enterprise.

> **OBSERVATION:** The definition of a *phase-in plan* under FAS-92 focuses on methods of rate-making that defer recognition of allowable costs (a) that would not be deferred under GAAP applicable to enterprises in general and (b) that would not have been deferred in the past under the methods of rate-making used by a regulated enterprise's regulator (FAS-92, par. 47).

Under FAS-92, accounting for the deferment of the allowable costs of a plant in connection with a phase-in plan ordered by a regulator depends on whether the physical construction of the plant was substantially completed *before* January 1, 1988.

> **OBSERVATION:** Paragraph 4 of FAS-92 addresses those phase-in plans ordered by a regulator in connection with a plant on which no substantial physical construction had been performed before January 1, 1988, while paragraph 5 of FAS-92 addresses those phase-in plans ordered by a regulator in connection with a plant on which substantial physical construction had been performed before January 1, 1988. Other than by implication, neither paragraph appears to address phase-in plans ordered by a regulator in connection with a plant on which construction was started after January 1, 1988.

Plant Not Substantially Completed before January 1, 1988

If no substantial physical construction had been performed on a plant before January 1, 1988, *none* of the allowable costs that are deferred for future recovery under any phase-in plan ordered by a regulator may be capitalized for *financial reporting purposes* (FAS-92, par. 4). (**Note:** In this context, allowable costs that are deferred for future recovery are those that are deferred beyond the period in which they would otherwise be charged to expense under GAAP applicable to enterprises in general.)

Plant Completed or Substantially Completed before January 1, 1988

If a plant had been completed or substantially completed before January 1, 1988, *all* allowable costs that are deferred for future recovery under any phase-in plan ordered by a regulator are capitalized as a separate asset (a deferred charge) for *financial reporting purposes* (FAS-92, par. 5). All of the following criteria must be met (**Note:** Under FAS-92, these criteria are used to determine whether capitalization is appropriate.):

- The regulator has agreed, in a formal plan, to the deferral of the allowable costs.

- The timing of the recovery of all allowable costs that are deferred to future periods is specified in the formal plan agreed to by the regulator.

- The recovery of all allowable costs deferred to future periods is scheduled to occur within ten years of the date on which the deferrals began.

- The percentage increase in rates scheduled under the phase-in plan for each year cannot exceed the percentage increase of the immediately preceding year. The percentage increase in rates for year two of the phase-in plan cannot exceed the percentage increase in rates for year one of the phase-in plan, and the percentage increase in rates for year three cannot exceed the percentage increase for year two, and so forth.

If *all* of the above criteria are not met, *none* of the allowable costs that are deferred for future recovery under the regulator's formal plan shall be capitalized for *financial reporting purposes* (FAS-92, par. 5). (**Note:** In this context, allowable costs that are deferred for future recovery are those that are deferred beyond the period in which they would otherwise be charged to expense under GAAP applicable to enterprises in general.)

Modification, Replacement, or Supplement of an Existing Phase-In Plan

When an existing phase-in plan is modified or a new plan is ordered to replace or supplement an existing plan, the specific criteria required by FAS-92 to determine whether capitalization of allowable costs is appropriate for *financial reporting purposes* (discussed above) are applied to the combination of both the original plan and the new plan. The date at which deferrals begin, for the purpose of recovering all deferred allowable costs within ten years (criterion 3, above), is the date of the earliest deferral under either the new or the old plan. The final recovery date is the date of the last recovery of all amounts deferred under the plan (FAS-92, par. 6).

ALLOWANCE FOR FUNDS USED DURING CONSTRUCTION (AFUDC)

FAS-71 requires that an enterprise capitalize an allowance for the funds used during the construction stage of an asset in lieu of capitalizing interest in accordance with FAS-34 (Capitalization of Interest Cost). AFUDC usually included interest costs on borrowing, or interest costs on a designated portion of equity funds, or both. The cost of the constructed asset is increased by the amount of AFUDC (FAS-71, par. 15). This increased cost is recovered through higher depreciation charges included in allowable costs over the life of the asset. The offsetting entry when this increase is recorded in the asset account is generally to increase "other income" for interest cost on equity funds and to reduce interest expense for interest costs on borrowings.

FAS-90 amends FAS-71 to specify that an allowance for funds used during the construction stage of an asset should be capitalized only if it is *probable* (likely) that the allowance for funds will be included subsequently by the governing regulatory authorities as an allowable cost of the constructed asset (FAS-90, par. 8). If it is *not probable* (not likely) that the allowance for funds used during the construction stage of an asset will be included as an allowable cost for rate-making purposes, a regulated enterprise may not alternatively capitalize interest cost in accordance with FAS-34 (FAS-90, par. 66).

A disallowance of a cost is the result of a rate-making action that prevents a regulated enterprise from recovering either some amount of its investment or some amount of return on its investment. Some existing phase-in plans have deferred allowable costs for recovery in future periods for rate-making purposes and have not provided a return on the investment on those deferred costs during the deferral period. This type of phase-in plan is in substance partially a deferral and partially a disallowance, and any disallowance should be accounted for in accordance with FAS-90.

After the initial application of FAS-92, any allowance for earnings on shareholders' investment that is capitalized for rate-making purposes other than for an asset during its construction stage or as part of a phase-in plan may not be capitalized for *financial reporting purposes* (FAS-92, par. 9).

CAPITALIZED AMOUNTS—
CLASSIFICATION AND DISCLOSURE

Cumulative amounts that are capitalized under phase-in plans are reported as a separate asset in the balance sheet. The net amount that has been capitalized in each period or the net amount of previously capitalized allowable costs that are recovered during each period is reported as a separate item of other income or expense in the income statement. Allowable costs that have been capitalized are not reported as reductions of other expenses (FAS-92, par. 10).

The terms of any phase-in plans in effect during the year or ordered for future years are disclosed in the financial statements. If allowable costs have been deferred for future recovery by a regulator for rate-making purposes, but not for *financial reporting purposes*, FAS-92 requires the financial statement disclosure of the net amount of such allowable costs that have been deferred for future recovery, and in addition, the disclosure of the net change in the related deferrals for those plans during the year (FAS-92, par. 11). FAS-92 also requires the financial statement disclosure of the nature and amounts of any allowance for earnings on shareholders' investment that has been capitalized for rate-making purposes but not capitalized for *financial reporting purposes* (FAS-92, par. 12).

SPECIFIC STANDARDS FOR
REGULATED ENTERPRISES

In addition to the items discussed above, regulated enterprises subject to the provisions of FAS-71 must comply with the following specific standards.

Intercompany Profits

Under existing GAAP, 100% of any intercompany profits must be eliminated in consolidated financial statements (ARB-51 (Consolidated Financial Statements)) and investments accounted for by the equity method (APB-18 (The Equity Method of Accounting for

Investments in Common Stock)). Under the provisions of FAS-71, however, a regulated enterprise shall not eliminate intercompany profits on sales to regulated affiliates if (FAS-71, par. 16):

- The sales price is reasonable (as evidenced by the acceptance of the sales price by the enterprise's regulator, or in light of the specific circumstance).

- It is expected (based on available evidence) that the approximate sales price which resulted in the intercompany profit will be recovered as an allowable cost.

If the above conditions are met, the realization of the intercompany profits are reasonably substantiated by the regulatory process. The intercompany profits shall not be eliminated because they are assured reasonably of being realized.

Deferred Income Taxes

Regulated enterprises (as defined by FAS-71) must comply with the following provisions of FAS-109:

- The use of the net-of-tax accounting and reporting method is prohibited.

- A deferred tax liability is required to be recognized for (*a*) the tax benefits of originating temporary differences that are passed on to customers and (*b*) the equity component of the allowance for funds used during construction.

- A deferred tax liability or asset is adjusted for any enacted change in the tax laws or rates.

An asset is recognized by a regulated enterprise in the amount of the probable future revenue that will be received from customers if it is *probable* that the regulator will allow a future increase in rates (FAS-71, par. 9). On the other hand, if it is probable that there will be a future decrease in rates, a regulated enterprise shall recognize a liability in the amount of the probable reduction in future revenue in accordance with FAS-71 (FAS-71, par. 11). Here, the asset or liability recognized by the regulated enterprise also is a temporary difference, and a deferred tax liability or asset shall be recognized for the deferred tax effects of that temporary difference [FAS-109 (Accounting for Income Taxes), par. 58].

Disclosure of Customer Refunds

Disclosure shall be made of any refunds that have a material effect on net income and that are not recognized in the same period as the related revenue. Disclosure shall include the effect on net income and indicate the years that the related revenue was recognized. The material effect on net income, net of related income taxes, may be disclosed as a separate line item in the income statement, but may not be presented as an extraordinary item (FAS-71, par. 19).

Disclosure of Certain Unamortized Costs

A regulator may exclude a specific cost in calculating the return on equity for a regulated enterprise, but may allow recovery of the actual cost over the current and future periods. For example, severe storm damage may be incurred for which the regulator allows the recovery over the current and future periods. The storm damage is not allowed to be included in determining the rate of return on equity for the regulated enterprise. The regulator allows recovery of the actual cost, but no profit is made on the incurred storm damage cost. The following disclosures are required by FAS-71 for major costs that do not provide a return on investment and are required to be amortized over the current and future periods (FAS-71, par. 20):

- The unamortized amount of such costs
- The remaining period of amortization

    ☛ **PRACTICE POINTER:** The result of the above disclosure requirements of FAS-71 is that if a cost is recoverable over an extended period and the regulator does not allow a return on investment (profit) for that specific cost, the unamortized balance of such costs must be disclosed along with the remaining amortization period.

Accounting for Postretirement Benefit Costs

FAS-106 requires most enterprises, including rate-regulated entities, to recognize postretirement benefit costs (OPEB costs) over the service periods of their employees rather than on a pay-as-you-go or terminal accrual basis. The predominant practice by rate-regulated companies before the adoption of FAS-106 was to include OPEB costs as an allowable cost on the pay-as-you-go basis (e.g., as the benefits were paid to retired employees). Regulators generally did not object to this treatment in rates. However, with the adoption of accrual accounting for these benefits costs, utilities were faced with the issue of how to account for the difference between the pay-as-you-go amount historically being recovered in rates and the incremental increase resulting from accrual under FAS-106.

If the FAS-71 criteria are met for a regulated enterprise to recognize an incurred cost as a regulatory asset (see "Criteria for Regulated Operations," earlier in this chapter), the entity would recognize the difference between net periodic postretirement benefit cost and the amount of such costs currently allowable for rate-making purposes as an asset (FAS-106, par. 364).

GOING OFF FAS-71

The rate-regulated industry continues to undergo significant changes. Competition, deregulation, regulatory disallowances, and market-sensitive rate structures are driving these changes. Most of the regional telephone holding companies created upon the breakup of AT&T in 1984 no longer follow FAS-71. Many other companies in rate-regulated industries are evaluating the applicability of FAS-71 as these changes evolve.

Discontinuing Application of FAS-71

FAS-101 establishes the appropriate accounting that should be applied when an enterprise discontinues the application of the provisions of FAS-71. Under FAS-101, an enterprise shall discontinue the application of the provisions of FAS-71 as of the date it determines that its "regulatory" operations in a particular regulatory jurisdiction cease to meet the criteria of FAS-71 (FAS-101, par. 5).

If the application of FAS-71 is discontinued for one separable portion of "regulatory" operations in a particular regulatory jurisdiction, there is a presumption that the application of FAS-71 should be discontinued for all other "regulatory" operations within that same particular regulatory jurisdiction. However, an enterprise shall continue to apply the provisions of FAS-71 to any separable portion of "regulatory" operations that continues to meet the criteria of FAS-71, regardless of whether or not the other separable portions within the same particular regulatory jurisdiction meet the criteria of FAS-71 (FAS-101, par. 5).

Reporting the Discontinuance of FAS-71

FAS-101 requires an enterprise to record the net effects of discontinuing the application of the provisions of FAS-71. At the time an enterprise ceases to meet the criteria for applying FAS-71, assets or liabilities that were recognized as a result of the actions of a regulator must be removed from the enterprise's statement of financial position. Carrying amounts of plant, equipment, and inventory as reported under the provisions of FAS-71 shall not be adjusted for (*a*) an allowance for funds used during construction of an asset, (*b*) intercompany profits on sales to regulated affiliates, and (*c*) disallowances of costs of recently completed plants. On the other hand, carrying amounts of plant, equipment, and inventory shall be adjusted if those assets are impaired, with impairment being accounted for in the same manner as for enterprises in general (FAS-101, par. 6).

FAS-144 requires enterprises in general to evaluate as asset for impairment when events occur or conditions exist that indicate that the carrying amount of the asset may not be recoverable. Many of those conditions exist today for regulated enterprises. One example of such a condition, described in FAS-144, is a change in business climate that affects the value of an asset. As indicated above, competition and the introduction of new forms of rate-making are definitely changing the business climate in which regulated enterprises operate and may affect the value of their assets.

Once management determines that an asset should be evaluated for impairment, an enterprise is required to estimate the future undiscounted cash flows expected to be generated from the use of the asset and its eventual disposition less the future cash outflows expected to be necessary to obtain those inflows. If the carrying amount of the asset is greater than the estimated undiscounted cash flows, an impairment loss should be recognized. Assets should be grouped at the lowest level for which there are identified cash flows from the asset or group of assets that are largely independent of the cash flows of other assets or groups of assets (FAS-144, par. 10).

After all adjustments required by FAS-101 are recorded, the net effect of these adjustments shall be included in the income of the period in which the application of FAS-71 is discontinued, and the net amount shall be reported in the financial statements as an extraordinary item in accordance with APB-30 (Reporting the Results of Operations) (FAS-101, par. 6).

Disclosures and Amendment to APB-30

The following financial statement disclosures shall be made in the period in which an enterprise discontinues the application of FAS-71 to all or any portion of its regulated operations (FAS-101, pars. 8–9):

- The reason(s) for the discontinuation of applying FAS-71
- The identification of the portion(s) of operations to which the application of FAS-71 is being discontinued
- Separate disclosure of the net adjustment, less related taxes, resulting from the discontinuation of applying FAS-71, as an extraordinary item in the statement of operations

APB-30 contains the criteria for classifying an amount as an extraordinary item in the financial statements of an enterprise. FAS-101 amends APB-30 by requiring the net adjustment resulting from the discontinuation of FAS-71 to be classified as an extraordinary item regardless of the criteria in paragraph 20 of APB-30 for classifying an extraordinary item (FAS-101, par. 10).

RELATED CHAPTERS IN 2009
GAAP GUIDE LEVEL A

Chapter 7, "Consolidated Financial Statements"
Chapter 20, "Impairment of Long-Lived Assets"
Chapter 21, "Income Taxes"
Chapter 24, "Interest Costs Capitalized"
Chapter 34, "Postemployment and Postretirement Benefits Other
   Than Pensions"
Chapter 40, "Results of Operations"

RELATED CHAPTERS IN 2009
GAAP GUIDE LEVELS B, C, AND D

Chapter 10, "Consolidated Financial Statements"
Chapter 19, "Impairment of Long-Lived Assets"
Chapter 20, "Income Taxes"
Chapter 32, "Postemployment and Postretirement Benefits Other
   Than Pensions"
Chapter 35, "Results of Operations"

Accounting Resources on the Web

The following World Wide Web addresses are just a few of the resources on the Internet that are available to practitioners. Because of the evolving nature of the Internet, some addresses may change. In such a case, refer to one of the many Internet search engines, such as Google (http://www.google.com) or Yahoo (http://www.yahoo.com).

Accounting Research Manager
   http://www.accountingresearchmanager.com

AICPA   http://www.aicpa.org

American Accounting Association
   http://aaahq.org

CCH Integrated Solutions   http://cchgroup.com/

CCH Learning Center   http://cch.learningcenter.com

FASAB   http://www.fasab.gov

FASB   http://www.fasb.org

Federal Tax Law   http://www.taxsites.com/Federal.html

FedWorld   http://www.fedworld.gov

GASB   http://www.gasb.org

Government Accountability Office   http://www.gao.gov

House of Representatives   http://www.house.gov

International Accounting Standards Board
   http://www.iasb.org/Home.htm

IRS Digital Daily   http://www.irs.gov/

Library of Congress   http://www.loc.gov

National Association of State Boards of Accountancy
   http://www.nasba.org

Office of Management and Budget   http://www.whitehouse
.gov/omb/

ProSystem *fx* **Engagement**   http://www.tax.cchgroup.com/Engage-
ment/default

Public Company Accounting Oversight Board
http://www.pcaobus.org

Securities and Exchange Commission   http://www.sec.gov

Thomas Legislative Research   http://thomas.loc.gov

Cross-Reference

ORIGINAL PRONOUNCEMENTS TO
2009 *GAAP GUIDE LEVEL A CHAPTERS*

This locator provides instant cross-reference between an original pronouncement and the chapter(s) in this publication in which a pronouncement is covered. Original pronouncements are listed chronologically on the left and the chapter(s) in which they appear in the 2009 *GAAP Guide Level A* in the center column. When an original pronouncement has been superseded, cross-reference is made to the succeeding pronouncement.

The FASB is requesting accountants and auditors to experiment with a codification of all authoritative accounting literature which is expected to replace all outstanding pronouncements. The codification is available without charge from the FASB web site. As a service to users of the 2009 *GAAP Guide Level A*, and 2009 *GAAP Guide Levels B, C and D*, the following cross-reference section includes, for the first time, cross-references to the FASB's codification.

Pronouncements for which no sections in the FASB codification are indicated result from the fact that the pronouncement has been superseded, is not currently in the codification due to the incomplete status of the project, or has been issued so recently that it is not yet incorporated into the codification.

Many pronouncements appear in the more than one place. In this cross-reference, the primary coverage is found in the section(s) indicated, but for an identification of all sections in the codification affected by a pronouncement, the user is encouraged to consult the "Cross-Reference" search function in the codification.

ACCOUNTING RESEARCH BULLETINS (ARBs)

(Accounting Research Bulletins 1–42 were revised, restated, or withdrawn at the time ARB No. 43 was issued.)

ORIGINAL PRONOUNCEMENT	2009 *GAAP GUIDE LEVEL A* REFERENCE	FASB ACCOUNTING STANDARDS CODIFICATION (ASC) TOPIC
ARB No. 43 Restatement and Revision of Accounting Research Bulletins		
Chapter 1—Prior Opinions		
1-A: Rules Adopted by Membership	Portions amended or superseded by FAS-111 and 141(R).	310, Receivables 505, Equity 605, Revenue Recognition
	Balance Sheet Classification and Related Display Issues, ch. 3	850, Related Party Disclosures
	Consolidated Financial Statements, ch. 7	
	Installment Sales, ch. 22	
	Stockholders' Equity, ch. 44	

1-B: Opinion Issued by Predecessor Committee	Portions amended or superseded by APB-6.	505, Equity
	Stockholders' Equity, ch. **44**	

Chapter 2—Form of Statements

2-A: Comparative Financial Statements	Portions amended or superseded by APB-20 and FAS-154.	205, Presentation of Financial Statements
	Consolidated Financial Statements, ch. **7**	
2-B: Combined Statement of Income and Earned Surplus	Superseded by APB-9.	—

Chapter 3—Working Capital

3-A: Current Assets and Current Liabilities	Portions amended or superseded by APB-6, APB-21, FAS-6, 78, 154, and 158.	210, Balance Sheet 310, Receivables 340, Deferred Costs and Other Assets
	Balance Sheet Classification and Related Display Issues, ch. **3**	470, Debt
3-B: Application of United States Government Securities Against Liabilities for Federal Taxes on Income	Superseded by APB-10.	—

Chapter 4

Inventory Pricing	Inventory, ch. **27**	330, Inventory

Chapter 5

Intangible Assets	Superseded by APB-16, APB-17, and FAS 142.	—

Chapter 6

Contingency Reserves	Superseded by FAS-5.	—

Chapter 7—Capital Accounts

7-A: Quasi-Reorganization or Corporate Readjustment	Portions amended or superseded by FAS-111.	852, Reorganizations
	Stockholders' Equity, ch. **44**	
7-B: Stock Dividends and Stock Split-Ups	Portions amended or superseded by APB-6.	505, Equity
	Stockholders' Equity, ch. **44**	
7-C: Business Combinations	Superseded by ARB-48.	—

Chapter 8

Income and Earned Surplus	Superseded by APB-9.	—

Chapter 9—Depreciation

9-A: Depreciation and High Costs	Depreciable Assets and Depreciation, ch. **11**	360, Property, Plant, and Equipment
9-B: Depreciation on Appreciation	Superseded by APB-6.	—
9-C: Emergency Facilities—Depreciation, Amortization, and Income Taxes	Portions amended or superseded by APB-6 and 11, FAS-96 and 109. Depreciable Assets and Depreciation, ch. **11**	—

Chapter 10—Taxes

10-A: Real and Personal Property Taxes	Portions amended or superseded by APB-9 and FAS-111.	720, Other Expenses
	Property Taxes, ch. **36**	
10-B: Income Taxes	Superseded by APB-11, FAS-96 and 109.	—

Chapter 11—Government Contracts

11-A: Cost-Plus-Fixed-Fee Contracts	Government Contracts, ch. **19**	912, Contractors—Federal Government
11-B: Renegotiation	Portions amended or superseded by APB-9, 11, FAS-96, 109, and 111.	912, Contractors—Federal Government
	Government Contracts, ch. **19**	
11-C: Terminated War and Defense Contracts	Government Contracts, ch. **19**	912, Contractors—Federal Government

Chapter 12

Foreign Operations and Foreign Exchange	Superseded by FAS-52 and 94.	—

Chapter 13—Compensation

13-A: Pension Plans—Annuity Costs Based on Past Service	Superseded by APB-8.	—
13-B: Compensation Involved in Stock Option and Stock Purchase Plans	Superseded by APB-25 and FAS-123.	—

Chapter 14

Disclosures of Long-Term Leases in Financial Statements of Lessees	Superseded by APB-5.	—

Chapter 15

Unamortized Discount, Issue Cost, and Redemption Premium on Bonds Refunded	Superseded by APB-26.	—

ARB No. 44

Declining-Balance Depreciation	Superseded by ARB-44 (Revised).	—

ARB No. 44 (Revised)

Declining-Balance Depreciation	Superseded by FAS-96 and FAS-109.	—

ARB No. 45

Long-Term Construction-Type Contracts	Long-Term Construction Contracts, ch. **30**	605, Revenue Recognition

ARB No. 46

Discontinuance of Dating Earned Surplus	Stockholders' Equity, ch. **44**	—

ARB No. 47

Accounting for Costs of Pension Plans	Superseded by APB-8.	—

ARB No. 48

Business Combinations	Superseded by APB-16.	—

ARB No. 49

Earnings per Share	Superseded by APB-9.	—

ARB No. 50

Contingencies	Superseded by FAS-5.	—

ARB No. 51

Consolidated Financial Statements	Portions amended or superseded by APB-10, 11, 16, 18, 23, FAS-58, 71, 94, 96, 109, 111, and 144.	810, Consolidation
	Consolidated Financial Statements, ch. **7**	

ACCOUNTING PRINCIPLES BOARD OPINIONS (APBs)

ORIGINAL PRONOUNCEMENT	2009 *GAAP GUIDE LEVEL A* REFERENCE	FASB ACCOUNTING STANDARDS CODIFICATION (ASC) TOPIC
APB Opinion No. 1		
New Depreciation Guidelines and Rules	Superseded by FAS-96 and 109.	—
APB Opinion No. 2		
Accounting for the "Investment Credit"	Portions amended or superseded by APB-4, FAS-71 and 109.	740, Income Taxes
	Income Taxes, ch. **21**	
APB Opinion No. 2—Addendum		
Accounting Principles for Regulated Industries	Superseded by FAS-71.	740, Income Taxes
APB Opinion No. 3		
The Statement of Source and Application of Funds	Superseded by APB-19.	—
APB Opinion No. 4		
Accounting for the "Investment Credit"	Income Taxes, ch. **21**	740, Income Taxes
APB Opinion No. 5		
Reporting of Leases in Financial Statements of Lessee	Superseded by FAS-13.	—
APB Opinion No. 6		
Status of Accounting Research Bulletins	Portions amended or superseded by APB-11, 16, 17, 26, 28, FAS-8, 52, 71, 96, 109, and 111.	—
	Depreciable Assets and Depreciation, ch. **11**	
	Stockholders' Equity, ch. **44**	
APB Opinion No. 7		
Accounting for Leases in Financial Statements of Lessors	Superseded by FAS-13.	—
APB Opinion No. 8		
Accounting for the Cost of Pension Plans	Superseded by FAS-87.	—

APB Opinion No. 19

Reporting Changes in Financial Position · Superseded by FAS-95. · —

APB Opinion No. 20

Accounting Changes · Superseded by FAS-154. · —

APB Opinion No. 21

Interest on Receivables and Payables · Portions amended or superseded by FAS-34, 96, 109, 157, and 159. · 835, Interest

Interest on Receivables and Payables, ch. **25**

APB Opinion No. 22

Disclosure of Accounting Policies · Portions amended by FAS-2, 8, 52, 95, 111, and 154. · 235, Notes to Financial Statements

Accounting Policies and Standards, ch. **2**

APB Opinion No. 23

Accounting for Income Taxes— Special Areas · Portions amended or superseded by FAS-9, 60, 71, 96, and 109. · 740, Income Taxes

Income Taxes, ch. **21**

APB Opinion No. 24

Accounting for Income Taxes— Investments in Common Stock Accounted for by the Equity Method (Other Than Subsidiaries and Corporate Joint Ventures) · Superseded by FAS-96 and 109. · —

APB Opinion No. 25

Accounting for Stock Issued to Employees · Portions amended or superseded by FAS-96, 109, and 123. · —

Stock-Based Payments, ch. **43**

APB Opinion No. 26

Early Extinguishment of Debt · Portions amended or superseded by APB-30, FAS-4, 13, 15, 71, 76, 84, and 125. · 470, Debt

Extinguishment of Debt, ch. **15**

APB Opinion No. 27

Accounting for Lease Transactions by Manufacturer or Dealer Lessors · Superseded by FAS-13. · —

APB Opinion No. 28

Interim Financial Reporting · Portions amended or superseded by FAS-3, 95, 96, 109, 123(R), 128, 141(R), 144, 145, 148, 154, 157, 158, and 161. · 270, Interim Reporting

Interim Financial Reporting, ch. **26**

Inventory, ch. **27**

APB Opinion No. 29

Accounting for Nonmonetary Transactions	Portions amended or superseded by FAS-71, 96, 109, 123, 141(R), 144, 157, and 160.	845, Nonmonetary Transactions
	Nonmonetary Transactions, ch. **32**	

APB Opinion No. 30

Reporting the Results of Operations—

Reporting the Effects of Disposal of a Segment of a Business, and Extraordinary, Unusual, and Infrequently Occurring Events and Transactions	Portions amended or superseded by FAS-4, 16, 60, 83, 96, 97, 101, 109, 128, 141(R), 144, 145, and 154.	225, Income Statement
	Results of Operations, ch. **40**	

APB Opinion No. 31

Disclosure of Lease Commitments by Lessees	Superseded by FAS-13.	—

FINANCIAL ACCOUNTING STANDARDS BOARD STATEMENTS (FASs)

ORIGINAL PRONOUNCEMENT	2009 *GAAP GUIDE* *LEVEL A* REFERENCE	FASB ACCOUNTING STANDARDS CODIFICATION (ASC) TOPIC
FASB Statement No. 1		
Disclosure of Foreign Currency Translation Information	Superseded by FAS-8 and 52.	—
FASB Statement No. 2		
Accounting for Research and Development Costs	Portions amended or superseded by FAS-71, 86, and 141(R).	730, Research and Development
	Inventory, ch. **27**	
	Research and Development, ch. **39**	
FASB Statement No. 3		
Reporting Accounting Changes in Interim Financial Statements	Superseded by FAS-154. Accounting Changes, ch.**1**	—
FASB Statement No. 4		
Reporting Gains and Losses from Extinguishment of Debt	Superseded by FAS-145.	—
FASB Statement No. 5		
Accounting for Contingencies	Portions amended or superseded by FAS-11, 16, 60, 71, 87, 111, 112, 113, 114, 123, and 141(R).	450, Contingencies
	Contingencies, Risks, and Uncertainties, ch. **8**	

FASB Statement No. 6

Classification of Short-Term Obligations Expected to Be Refinanced	Balance Sheet Classification and Related Display Issues, ch. **3**	210, Balance Sheet 470, Debt

FASB Statement No. 7

Accounting and Reporting by Development Stage Enterprises	Portions amended or superseded by FAS-71 and 95. Development Stage Enterprises, ch. **12**	915, Development Stage Entities

FASB Statement No. 8

Accounting for the Translation of Foreign Currency Transactions and Foreign Currency Financial Statements	Superseded by FAS-52.	—

FASB Statement No. 9

Accounting for Income Taxes—Oil and Gas Producing Companies	Superseded by FAS-19.	—

FASB Statement No. 10

Extension of "Grandfather" Provisions for Business Combinations	Superseded by FAS-141. Business Combinations, ch. **4**	—

FASB Statement No. 11

Accounting for Contingencies—Transition Method	No longer relevant.	—

FASB Statement No. 12

Accounting for Certain Marketable Securities	Superseded by FAS-115.	—

FASB Statement No. 13

Accounting for Leases	Portions amended or superseded by FAS-17, 22, 23, 26, 27, 28, 29, 34, 71, 77, 91, 96, 98, 109, 125, 140, and 157. Leases, ch. **29**	840, Leases

FASB Statement No. 14

Financial Reporting for Segments of a Business Enterprise	Superseded by FAS-131.	—

FASB Statement No. 15

Accounting by Debtors and Creditors for Troubled Debt Restructurings	Portions amended or superseded by FAS-71, 111, 114, 121, 141(R), 145, and 157. Troubled Debt Restructuring, ch. **46**	310, Receivables 470, Debt

FASB Statement No. 16

Prior Period Adjustments	Portions amended or superseded by FAS-71, 96, 109, 141, and 154. Results of Operations, ch. **40**	250, Accounting Changes and Error Corrections 270, Interim Reporting

FASB Statement No. 17

Accounting for Leases—Initial Direct Costs	Superseded by FAS-91.	—

FASB Statement No. 18

| Financial Reporting for Segments of a Business Enterprise—Interim Financial Statements | Superseded by FAS-131. | — |

FASB Statement No. 19

| Financial Accounting and Reporting by Oil and Gas Producing Companies | Portions amended or superseded by FAS-25, 69, 71, 96, 109, 121, 143, 144, 145, 154, and 157. | 932, Extractive Industries—Oil and Gas |
| | Oil and Gas, ch. **52** | |

FASB Statement No. 20

| Accounting for Forward Exchange Contracts | Superseded by FAS-52. | — |

FASB Statement No. 21

| Suspension of the Reporting of Earnings per Share and Segment Information by Nonpublic Enterprises | Superseded by FAS-131. | — |

FASB Statement No. 22

Changes in the Provisions of Lease Agreements Resulting from Refundings of Tax-Exempt Debt	Portions amended or superseded by FAS-71, 76, 95, 123, 125, 128, 140, and 145.	840, Leases
	Extinguishment of Debt, ch. **16**	
	Leases, ch. **29**	

FASB Statement No. 23

| Inception of the Lease | Leases, ch. **29** | 840, Leases |

FASB Statement No. 24

| Reporting Segment Information in Financial Statements That Are Presented in Another Enterprise's Financial Report | Superseded by FAS-131. | — |

FASB Statement No. 25

| Suspension of Certain Accounting Requirements for Oil and Gas Producing Companies | Portions amended or superseded by FAS-111 and 154. | — |

FASB Statement No. 26

| Profit Recognition on Sales-Type Leases of Real Estate | Superseded by FAS-98. | — |

FASB Statement No. 27

| Classification of Renewals or Extensions of Existing Sales-Type or Direct Financing Leases | Leases, ch. **29** | 840, Leases |

FASB Statement No. 28

| Accounting for Sales with Leasebacks | Portions amended or superseded by FAS-66. | 840, Leases |
| | Leases, ch. **29** | |

FASB Statement No. 29

| Determining Contingent Rentals | Portions amended by FAS-98. | 840, Leases |
| | Leases, ch. **29** | |

FASB Statement No. 30

Disclosure of Information About Major Customers

Superseded by FAS-131.

—

FASB Statement No. 31

Accounting for Tax Benefits Related to U.K. Tax Legislation Concerning Stock Relief

Superseded by FAS-96 and 109.

—

FASB Statement No. 32

Specialized Accounting and Reporting Principles and Practices in AICPA Statements of Position and Guides on Accounting and Auditing Matters

Superseded by FAS-111.

—

FASB Statement No. 33

Financial Reporting and Changing Prices

Superseded by FAS-89.

—

FASB Statement No. 34

Capitalization of Interest Cost

Portions amended or superseded by FAS-42, 58, 62, 71, 75, and 121.

Interest Costs Capitalized, ch. **24**

835, Interest

FASB Statement No. 35

Accounting and Reporting by Defined Benefit Pension Plans

Portions amended or superseded by FAS-59, 75, 110, and 157.

Pension Plans, ch. **53**

960, Plan Accounting— Defined Benefit Pension Plans

FASB Statement No. 36

Disclosure of Pension Information

Superseded by FAS-87.

—

FASB Statement No. 37

Balance Sheet Classification of Deferred Income Taxes

Income Taxes, ch. **21**

740, Income Taxes

FASB Statement No. 38

Accounting for Preacquisition Contingencies of Purchased Enterprises

Superseded by FAS-141.

—

FASB Statement No. 39

Financial Reporting and Changing Prices: Specialized Assets—Mining and Oil and Gas

Superseded by FAS-89.

—

FASB Statement No. 40

Financial Reporting and Changing Prices: Specialized Assets—Timberlands and Growing Timber

Superseded by FAS-89.

—

FASB Statement No. 41

Financial Reporting and Changing Prices: Specialized Assets— Income-Producing Real Estate

Superseded by FAS-89.

—

FASB Statement No. 42

Determining Materiality for Capitalization of Interest Cost

Interest Costs Capitalized, ch. **24**

835, Interest

FASB Statement No. 43

Accounting for Compensated Absences	Portions amended or superseded by FAS-71, 112, and 123.	420, Exit or Disposal Cost Obligations 710, Compensation— General
	Balance Sheet Classification and Related Display Issues, ch.3	

FASB Statement No. 44

Accounting for Intangible Assets of Motor Carriers	Superseded by FAS-145.	—

FASB Statement No. 45

Accounting for Franchise Fee Revenue	Portions amended by FAS-141(R).	952, Franchisors
	Revenue Recognition, ch. **41**	

FASB Statement No. 46

Financial Reporting and Changing Prices: Motion Picture Films	Superseded by FAS-89.	—

FASB Statement No. 47

Disclosure of Long-Term Obligations	Portions superseded by FAS-129.	440, Commitments
	Long-Term Obligations, ch. **31**	

FASB Statement No. 48

Revenue Recognition When Right of Return Exists	Revenue Recognition, ch. **41**	605, Revenue Recognition

FASB Statement No. 49

Accounting for Product Financing Arrangements	Portions superseded by FAS-71.	470, Debt
	Product Financing Arrangements, ch. **35**	

FASB Statement No. 50

Financial Reporting in the Record and Music Industry	Entertainment, ch. **48**	928, Entertainment— Music

FASB Statement No. 51

Financial Reporting by Cable Television Companies	Portions amended or superseded by FAS-71, and 142.	922, Entertainment— Cable Television
	Entertainment, ch. **48**	

FASB Statement No. 52

Foreign Currency Translation	Portions amended or superseded by FAS-109, 141(R), 142, and 154.	830, Foreign Currency Matters
	Foreign Operations and Exchange, ch. **18**	

FASB Statement No. 53

Financial Reporting by Producers and Distributors of Motion Picture Films	Rescinded and replaced by SOP 00-2.	—

FASB Statement No. 54

Financial Reporting and Changing Prices: Investment Companies	Superseded by FAS-89.	—

FASB Statement No. 55

Determining Whether a Convertible Security Is a Common Stock Equivalent	Superseded by FAS-111.	—

FASB Statement No. 56

Designation of AICPA Guide and Statement of Position (SOP) 81-1 on Contractor Accounting and SOP 81-2 Concerning Hospital-Related Organizations as Preferable for Purposes of Applying APB Opinion 20	Superseded by FAS-111.	—

FASB Statement No. 57

Related Party Disclosures	Portions amended or superseded by FAS-95, 96, 109, and 159.	850, Related Party Disclosures
	Related Party Disclosures, ch. **38**	

FASB Statement No. 58

Capitalization of Interest Cost in Financial Statements That Include Investments Accounted For by the Equity Method	Interest Costs Capitalized, ch. **24**	835, Interest

FASB Statement No. 59

Deferral of the Effective Date of Certain Accounting Requirements for Pension Plans of State and Local Governmental Units	Superseded by FAS-75.	—

FASB Statement No. 60

Accounting and Reporting by Insurance Enterprises	Portions amended or superseded by FAS-91, 96, 97, 109, 113, 114, 115, 120, 121, 124, 141(R), 145, 157, 160, and 163.	325, Investments—Other
	Insurance, ch. **49**	

FASB Statement No. 61

Accounting for Title Plant	Portions amended by FAS-121.	950, Financial Services—Title Plant
	Insurance, ch. **49**	

FASB Statement No. 62

Capitalization of Interest Cost in Situations Involving Certain Tax-Exempt Borrowings and Certain Gifts and Grants	Interest Costs Capitalized, ch. **24**	835, Interest

FASB Statement No. 63

Financial Reporting by Broadcasters	Portions amended or superseded by FAS-157.	920, Entertainment—Broadcasters
	Entertainment, ch. **48**	

FASB Statement No. 64

Extinguishments of Debt Made to Satisfy Sinking-Fund Requirements	Superseded by FAS-145.	—

FASB Statement No. 76

Extinguishment of Debt — Superseded by FAS-125. — —

FASB Statement No. 77

Reporting by Transferors for Transfers of Receivables with Recourse — Superseded by FAS-125. — —

FASB Statement No. 78

Classification of Obligations That Are Callable by the Creditor — Balance Sheet Classification and Related Display Issues, ch. **3** — 470, Debt

FASB Statement No. 79

Elimination of Certain Disclosures for Business Combinations by Nonpublic Enterprises — Superseded by FAS-141.

Business Combinations, ch. **4** — —

FASB Statement No. 80

Accounting for Futures Contracts — Superseded by FAS-133. — —

FASB Statement No. 81

Disclosure of Postretirement Health Care and Life Insurance Benefits — Superseded by FAS-106. — —

FASB Statement No. 82

Financial Reporting and Changing Prices: Elimination of Certain Disclosures — Superseded by FAS-89. — —

FASB Statement No. 83

Designation of AICPA Guides and Statement of Position on Accounting by Brokers and Dealers in Securities, by Employee Benefit Plans, and by Banks as Preferable for Purposes of Applying APB Opinion 20 — Superseded. — —

FASB Statement No. 84

Induced Conversions of Convertible Debt — Convertible Debt and Debt with Warrants, ch. **9** — 470, Debt

FASB Statement No. 85

Yield Test for Determining whether a Convertible Security Is a Common Stock Equivalent — Superseded by FAS-128. — —

FASB Statement No. 86

Accounting for the Costs of Computer Software to Be Sold, Leased, or Otherwise Marketed — Portions amended by FAS-141(R).
Computer Software, ch. **6** — 985, Software

FASB Statement No. 87

Employers' Accounting for Pensions — Portions amended or superseded by FAS-96, 106, 109, 141(R), 157, and 158.

Pension Plans, ch. **33** — 715, Compensation—Retirement Benefits

FASB Statement No. 88

Employers' Accounting for Settlements and Curtailments of Defined Benefit Pension Plans and for Termination Benefits — Portions amended or superseded by FAS-144 and 158. — 715, Compensation—Retirement Benefits

FASB Statement No. 89

Financial Reporting and Changing Prices	Portions amended or superseded by FAS-96, 109, and 160.	255, Changing Prices
	Oil and Gas, ch. **52**	

FASB Statement No. 90

Regulated Enterprises—Accounting for Abandonments and Disallowances of Plant Costs	Portions amended or superseded by FAS-92, 96, and 109.	980, Regulated Operations
	Regulated Industries, ch. **54**	

FASB Statement No. 91

Accounting for Nonrefundable Fees and Costs Associated with Originating or Acquiring Loans and Initial Direct Costs of Leases	Portions amended or superseded by FAS-98, 114, 115, and 124.	310, Receivables
	Leases, ch. **29**	
	Banking and Thrift Institutions, ch. **47**	
	Insurance, ch. **49**	
	Mortgage Banking, ch.**50**	

FASB Statement No. 92

Regulated Enterprises—Accounting for Phase-in Plans	Regulated Industries, ch. **54**	—

FASB Statement No. 93

Recognition of Depreciation by Not-for-Profit Organizations	Portions amended or superseded by FAS-99.	958, Not-for-Profit Entities
	Not-for-Profit Organizations, ch. **51**	

FASB Statement No. 94

Consolidation of All Majority-Owned Subsidiaries	Consolidated Financial Statements, ch. **7**	810, Consolidation
	Equity Method, ch. **14**	

FASB Statement No. 95

Statement of Cash Flows	Portions amended or superseded by FAS-102, 104, 117, 141(R), 145, and 159.	230, Statement of Cash Flows
	Cash Flow Statement, ch.**5**	

FASB Statement No. 96

Accounting for Income Taxes	Superseded by FAS-109.	—

FASB Statement No. 97

Accounting and Reporting by Insurance Enterprises for Certain Long-Duration Contracts and for Realized Gains and Losses from the Sale of Investments	Portions amended or superseded by FAS-113, 115, and 120.	325, Investments—Other
	Insurance, ch. **49**	

FASB Statement No. 98

Accounting for Leases: • Sale-Leaseback Transactions Involving Real Estate • Sales-Type Leases of Real Estate • Definition of the Lease Term	Leases, ch. **29** Real Estate Transactions, ch. **37**	840, Leases

- Initial Direct Costs of
  Direct Financing Leases

FASB Statement No. 99

Deferral of the Effective Date of Recognition of Depreciation by Not-for-Profit Organizations	Not-for-Profit Organizations, ch. **51**	958, Not-for-Profit Entities

FASB Statement No. 100

Accounting for Income Taxes—Deferral of the Effective Date of FASB Statement No. 96	Superseded by FAS-103, 108, and 109.	—

FASB Statement No. 101

Regulated Enterprises—Accounting for the Discontinuation of Application of FASB Statement No. 71	Portions amended by FAS-121.	980, Regulated Operations
	Regulated Industries, ch. **54**	

FASB Statement No. 102

Statement of Cash Flows—Exemption of Certain Enterprises and Classification of Cash Flows from Certain Securities Acquired for Resale	Portions amended or superseded by FAS-115, 145 and 159.	230, Statement of Cash Flows
	Cash Flow Statement, ch. **5**	960, Plan Accounting—Defined Benefit Pension Plans

FASB Statement No. 103

Accounting for Income Taxes—Deferral of the Effective Date of FASB Statement No. 96	Superseded by FAS-108 and 109.	—

FASB Statement No. 104

Statement of Cash Flows—Net Reporting of Certain Cash Receipts and Cash Payments and Classification of Cash Flows from Hedging Transactions	Cash Flow Statement, ch. **5**	230, Statement of Cash Flows

FASB Statement No. 105

Disclosure of Information About Financial Instruments with Off-Balance-Sheet Risk and Financial Instruments with Concentrations of Credit Risk	Superseded by FAS-133.	—

FASB Statement No. 106

Employers' Accounting for Postretirement Benefits Other Than Pensions	Portions amended or superseded by FAS-141, 144, 157, and 158.	715, Compensation—Retirement Benefits
	Deferred Compensation Contracts, ch. **10**	
	Postemployment and Postretirement Benefits Other Than Pensions, ch. **34**	
	Regulated Industries, ch. **54**	

FASB Statement No. 107

Disclosures about Fair Value of Financial Instruments	Portions amended or superseded by FAS-112, 119, 123, 126, 133, 140, 157, 161, and 163.	825, Financial Instruments
	Financial Instruments, ch. **17**	

FASB Statement No. 108

Accounting for Income Taxes—Deferral of the Effective Date of FASB Statement No. 96	Superseded by FAS-109.	—

FASB Statement No. 109

Accounting for Income Taxes	Portions amended or superseded by FAS-115, 123, and 141(R). Depreciable Assets and Depreciation, ch. **11** Income Taxes, ch. **21**	740, Income Taxes

FASB Statement No. 110

Reporting by Defined Benefit Pension Plans of Investment Contracts	Pension Plans, ch. **53**	960, Plan Accounting—Defined Benefit Pension Plans

FASB Statement No. 111

Rescission of FASB Statement No. 32 and Technical Corrections	Accounting Changes, ch. **1**	—

FASB Statement No. 112

Employers' Accounting for Postemployment Benefits	Portions amended or superseded by FAS-123. Postemployment and Postretirement Benefits Other Than Pensions, ch. **34**	712, Compensation—Nonretirement Postemployment Benefits

FASB Statement No. 113

Accounting and Reporting for Reinsurance of Short-Duration and Long-Duration Contracts	Portions amended or superseded by FAS-120 and 141(R). Insurance, ch. **49**	310, Receivables

FASB Statement No. 114

Accounting by Creditors for Impairment of a Loan	Portions amended or superseded by FAS-118. Impairment of Long-Lived Assets, ch.**20** Troubled Debt Restructuring, ch. **46**	310, Receivables

FASB Statement No. 115

Accounting for Certain Investments in Debt and Equity Securities	Portions amended by FAS-124, 125, 145, 157, and 159. Investments in Debt and Equity Securities, ch. **28**	320, Investments—Debt and Equity Securities

FASB Statement No. 116

Accounting for Contributions Received and Contributions Made	Portions amended or superseded by FAS-157. Not-for-Profit Organizations, ch. **51**	720, Other Expenses 958, Not-for-Profit Entities

FASB Statement No. 117

Financial Statements of Not-for-Profit Organizations	Portions amended by FAS-124. Not-for-Profit Organizations, ch. **52**	958, Not-for-Profit Entities

FASB Statement No. 118

Accounting by Creditors for Impairment of a Loan—Income Recognition and Disclosures	Impairment of Long-Lived Assets, ch. **20**	310, Receivables

FASB Statement No. 119

Disclosure about Derivative Financial Instruments and Fair Value of Financial Instruments	Superseded by FAS-133.	—

FASB Statement No. 120

Accounting and Reporting by Mutual Life Insurance Enterprises and by Insurance Enterprises for Certain Long-Duration Participating Contracts	Portions amended by FAS-141(R) and 162. Insurance, ch. **49**	325, Investments—Other

FASB Statement No. 121

Accounting for the Impairment of Long-Lived Assets and for Long-Lived Assets to Be Disposed Of	Superseded by FAS-144.	—

FASB Statement No. 122

Accounting for Mortgage Servicing Rights	Superseded by FAS-125.	—

FASB Statement No. 123

Accounting for Stock-Based Compensation	Superseded by FAS-123 (revised 2004).	—

FASB Statement No. 123 (revised 2004)

Share-Based Payment	Portions amended by FAS-141(R) and 154. Stock-Based Payments, ch. **43**	505, Equity 718, Compensation—Stock Compensation

FASB Statement No. 124

Accounting for Certain Investments Held by Not-for-Profit Organizations	Portions amended or superseded by FAS-157 and 159. Not-for-Profit Organizations, ch. **51**	958, Not-for-Profit Entities

FASB Statement No. 125

Accounting for Transfers and Servicing of Financial Assets and Extinguishments of Liabilities	Superseded by FAS-140.	—

FASB Statement No. 126

Exemption from Certain Required Disclosures about Financial Instruments for Certain Nonpublic Entities	Financial Instruments, ch. **17**	825, Financial Instruments

FASB Statement No. 127

Deferral of the Effective Date of Certain Provisions of FASB Statement No. 125	Transfer and Servicing of Financial Assets, ch. **45**	860, Transfers and Servicing

FASB Statement No. 128

Earnings per Share	Portions amended or superseded by FAS-123(R), 141, 145, and 150. Earnings per Share, ch. **13**	260, Earnings per Share

FASB Statement No. 139

Rescission of FASB Statement No. 53 and amendments to FASB Statements No. 63, 89, and 121

Financial Instruments, ch. **17**

255, Changing Prices
920, Entertainment—Broadcasters

FASB Statement No. 140

Accounting for Transfers and Servicing of Financial Assets and Extinguishments of Debt

Portions amended or superseded by FTB 01-1, FAS-156, and 157.

Transfer and Servicing of Financial Assets, ch. **45**

860, Transfers and Servicing

FASB Statement No. 141

Business Combinations

Superseded by FAS-141(R).

—

FASB Statement No. 141(R)

Business Combinations

Business Combinations, ch. **4**

—

FASB Statement No. 142

Goodwill and Other Intangible Assets

Portions amended or superseded by FAS-141(R), 145, 147, 157, and 160.

Intangible Assets, ch. **23**

350, Intangibles—Goodwill and Other

FASB Statement No. 143

Accounting for Asset Retirement Obligations

Portions amended or superseded by FAS-144, 154, and 157.

Depreciable Assets and Deprecations, ch. **11**

410, Asset Retirement and Environmental Obligations

FASB Statement No. 144

Accounting for the Impairment or Disposal of Long-Lived Assets

Portions amended or superseded by FAS-141(R), 145, 147, 154, and 157.

Impairment of Long-Lived Assets, ch. **20**

205, Presentation of Financial Statements
360, Property, Plant, and Equipment

FASB Statement No. 145

Rescission of FASB Statements No. 4, 44, and 64, Amendment of FASB Statement No. 13, and Technical Corrections

Extinguishment of Debt, ch. **15**

Leases, ch. **29**

470, Debt

FASB Statement No. 146

Accounting for Costs Associated with Exit or Disposal Activities

Portions amended or superseded by FAS-141(R) and 157.

Results of Operations, ch. **40**

420, Exit or Disposal Cost Obligations

FASB Statement No. 147

Acquisitions of Certain Financial Institutions

Superseded by FAS-141(R).

—

FASB Statement No. 148

Accounting for Stock-Based Compensation—Transition and Disclosure

Stock-Based Payments, ch. **43**

505, Equity
718, Compensation—Stock Compensation

FASB Statement No. 161

Disclosures about Derivative Instruments and Hedging Activities	Portions amended by FAS-162.	—
	Financial Instruments, ch. **17**	

FASB Statement No. 162

The Hierarchy of Generally Accepted Accounting Principles	About the GAAP Hierarchy (page)	—

FASB Statement No. 163

Accounting for Financial Guarantee Insurance Contracts	Insurance, ch. **49**	—

FINANCIAL ACCOUNTING STANDARDS BOARD INTERPRETATIONS (FINs)

ORIGINAL PRONOUNCEMENT	2009 *GAAP GUIDE* *LEVEL A* REFERENCE	FASB ACCOUNTING STANDARDS CODIFICATION (ASC) TOPIC
FASB Interpretation No. 1		
Accounting Changes Related to the Cost of Inventory	Portions amended by FAS-154.	250, Accounting Changes and Error Corrections 330, Inventory
	Accounting Changes, ch.1	
	Inventory, ch. **27**	
FASB Interpretation No. 2		
Imputing Interest on Debt Arrangements Made under the Federal Bankruptcy Act	Superseded by FAS-15.	—
FASB Interpretation No. 3		
Accounting for the Cost of Pension Plans Subject to the Employee Retirement Income Security Act of 1974	Superseded by FAS-87.	—
FASB Interpretation No. 4		
Applicability of FASB Statement No. 2 to Business Combinations Accounted for by the Purchase Method	Superseded by FAS-141(R).	—
FASB Interpretation No. 5		
Applicability of FASB Statement No. 2 to Development Stage Enterprises	Superseded by FAS-7.	—
FASB Interpretation No. 6		
Applicability of FASB Statement No. 2 to Computer Software	Portions amended or superseded by FAS-86.	730, Research and Development
	Research and Development, ch. **40**	
FASB Interpretation No. 7		
Applying FASB Statement No. 7 in Financial Statements of Established Operating Enterprises	Portions amended by FAS-154.	915, Development Stage Entities
	Development Stage Enterprises, ch. **13**	

FASB Interpretation No. 21

Accounting for Leases in a Business Combination	Portions amended by FAS-141(R) and 145.	840, Leases
	Leases, ch. **29**	

FASB Interpretation No. 22

Applicability of Indefinite Reversal Criteria To Timing Differences	Superseded by FAS-109.	—

FASB Interpretation No. 23

Leases of Certain Property Owned by a Governmental Unit or Authority	Leases, ch. **29**	840, Leases

FASB Interpretation No. 24

Leases Involving Only Part of a Building	Leases, ch. **29**	840, Leases

FASB Interpretation No. 25

Accounting for an Unused Investment Tax Credit	Superseded by FAS-96 and 109.	—

FASB Interpretation No. 26

Accounting for Purchase of a Leased Asset by the Lessee during the Term of the Lease	Portions amended by FAS-141(R).	840, Leases
	Leases, ch. **29**	

FASB Interpretation No. 27

Accounting for a Loss on a Sublease	Leases, ch. **29**	—
	Results of Operations, ch.41	

FASB Interpretation No. 28

Accounting for Stock Appreciation Rights and Other Variable Stock Option or Award Plans	Portions amended or superseded by FAS-123 and 128, and FIN-31.	505, Equity 718, Compensation, Stock Compensation
	Stock-Based Payments, ch. **44**	

FASB Interpretation No. 29

Reporting Tax Benefits Realized on Disposition of Investments in Certain Subsidiaries and Other Investees	Superseded by FAS-96 and 109.	—

FASB Interpretation No. 30

Accounting for Involuntary Conversions of Nonmonetary Assets to Monetary Assets	Portions amended or superseded by FAS-96, 109, and 125.	605, Revenue Recognition
	Nonmonetary Transactions, ch. **32**	

FASB Interpretation No. 31

Treatment of Stock Compensation Plans in EPS Computations	Superseded by FAS-128.	—

FASB Interpretation No. 32

Application of Percentage Limitations in Recognizing Investment Tax Credit	Superseded by FAS-96 and 109.	—

FASB Interpretation No. 43

| Real Estate Sales | Portions amended or superseded by FAS-140.

Real Estate Transactions, ch. **38** | 360, Property, Plant, and Equipment |

FASB Interpretation No. 44

| Accounting for Certain Transactions Involving Stock Compensation | Portions amended or superseded by FAS-141.

Stock-Based Payments, ch. **44** | 505, Equity
718, Compensation, Stock Compensation |

FASB Interpretation No. 45

| Guarantor's Accounting and Disclosure Requirements for Guarantees, Including Indirect Guarantees of Indebtedness of Others | Portions amended by FAS-157, 162, and 163.

Contingencies, Risks, and Uncertainties, ch. **9** | 460, Guarantees |

FASB Interpretation No. 46

| Consolidation of Variable Interest Entities | Superseded by FAS-46 (revised December 2003) | — |

FASB Interpretation No. 46 (revised December 2003)

| Consolidation of Variable Interest Entities | Portions amended by FAS-141(R) and 160.

Consolidated Financial Statements, ch. **8** | 810, Consolidations |

FASB Interpretation No. 47

| Accounting for Conditional Asset Retirement Obligations | Depreciable Assets and Depreciation, ch. **12** | 410, Asset Retirement and Environmental Obligations |

FASB Interpretation No. 48

| Accounting for Uncertainty in Income Taxes | Portions amended by FAS-141(R) and 160.

Income Taxes, ch. **21** | 740, Income Taxes |

ORIGINAL PRONOUNCEMENTS TO
2009 GAAP GUIDE LEVELS B, C, AND D CHAPTERS

This locator provides instant cross-reference between an original pronouncement and the chapter(s) in this publication in which a pronouncement is covered. Original pronouncements are listed chronologically on the left and the chapter(s) in which they appear in the 2009 *GAAP Guide Levels B, C, and D* on the right. When an original pronouncement has been superseded, cross-reference is made to the succeeding pronouncement.

The FASB is requesting accountants and auditors to experiment with a codification of all authoritative accounting literature which is expected to replace all outstanding pronouncements. The codification is available without charge from the FASB web site. As a service to users of the 2009 *GAAP Guide Level A*, and 2009 *GAAP Guide Levels B, C and D*, the following cross-reference section include, for the first time, cross-references to the FASB's codification.

Pronouncements for which no section in the FASB codification are indicated result from the fact that the pronouncement has been superseded, is not currently in the codification due to the incomplete status of the project, or has been issued so recently that it is not yet incorporated into the codification.

Many pronouncements appear in the more than one place. In this cross-reference, the primary coverage is found in the section(s) indicated, but for an identification of all sections in the codification affected by a pronouncement, the user is encouraged to consult the "Cross-Reference" search function in the codification.

FASB TECHNICAL BULLETINS

ORIGINAL PRONOUNCEMENT	2009 *GAAP GUIDE LEVELS B, C, AND D* REFERENCE	FASB ACCOUNTING STANDARDS CODIFICATION (ASC) TOPIC
FTB 79-1 (R)		
Purpose and Scope of FASB Technical Bulletins and Procedures for Issuance	Accounting Policies and Standards, ch. **2**	—
FTB 79-3		
Subjective Acceleration Clauses in Long-Term Debt Agreements	Balance Sheet Classification and Related Display Issues, ch. **4**	470, Debt
FTB 79-4		
Segment Reporting of Puerto Rican Operations	Segment Reporting, ch. **37**	280, Segment Reporting
FTB 79-5		
Meaning of the Term "Customer" as It Applies to Health Care Facilities under FASB Statement No. 14	Segment Reporting, ch. **37**	954, Health Care Entities
FTB 79-8		
Applicability of FASB Statements 21 and 33 to Certain Brokers and Dealers in Securities	Superseded by FAS-131, paragraph 128(f).	—
FTB 79-9		
Accounting for Interim Periods for Changes in Income Tax Rates	Interim Financial Reporting, ch. **23**	740, Income Taxes
FTB 79-10		
Fiscal Funding Clauses in Lease Agreements	Leases, ch. **26**	840, Leases

FTB 79-12

Interest Rate Used in Calculating the Present Value of Minimum Lease Payments	Leases, ch. **26**	—

FTB 79-13

Applicability of FASB Statement No. 13 to Current Value Financial Statements	Changing Prices, ch. **9**	840, Leases

FTB 79-14

Upward Adjustment of Guaranteed Residual Values	Leases, ch. **26**	460, Guarantees 840, Leases

FTB 79-15

Accounting for Loss on a Sublease Not Involving the Disposal of a Segment	Leases, ch. **26**	840, Leases

FTB 79-16 (R)

Effect of a Change in Income Tax Rate on the Accounting for Leveraged Leases	Leases, ch. **26**	840, Leases

FTB 79-17

Reporting Cumulative Effect Adjustment from Retroactive Application of FASB Statement No. 13	Leases, ch. **26**	—

FTB 79-18

Transition Requirement of Certain FASB Amendments and Interpretations of FASB Statement No. 13	Leases, ch. **26**	—

FTB 79-19

Investor's Accounting for Unrealized Losses on Marketable Securities Owned by an Equity Method Investee	Paragraph 1 amended by Paragraph 135(a) of FAS-115 and Paragraph 6 replaced by Paragraph 135(b) of FAS-113. Equity Method, ch. **15**	—

FTB 80-1

Early Extinguishment of Debt through Exchange for Common or Preferred Stock	Portions amended by FAS-111 and FAS-145. Extinguishment of Debt, ch. **16**	470, Debt

FTB 80-2

Classification of Debt Restructurings by Debtors and Creditors	Troubled Debt Restructuring, ch. **41**	310, Receivables 470, Debt

FTB 81-6

Applicability of Statement 15 to Debtors in Bankruptcy Situations	Troubled Debt Restructuring, ch. **41**	470, Debt

FTB 82-1

Disclosure of the Sale or Purchase of Tax Benefits through Tax Leases	Portions amended by FAS-95, 96, and 145. Accounting Policies and Standards, ch. **2**	—

FTB 84-1

| Accounting for Stock Issued to Acquire the Results of a Research and Development Arrangement | Portions amended by FAS-141. | — |
| | Research and Development, ch. **34** | |

FTB 85-1

| Accounting for the Receipt of Federal Home Loan Mortgage Corporation Participating Preferred Stock | Nonmonetary Transactions, ch. **28** | — |

FTB 85-3

| Accounting for Operating Leases with Scheduled Rent Increases | Leases, ch. **26** | 840, Leases |

FTB 85-4

| Accounting for Purchases of Life Insurance | Balance Sheet Classification and Related Display Issues, ch. **4** | 325, Investments—Other |

FTB 85-5

| Issues Relating to Accounting for Business Combinations | Portions amended by FAS-141. | — |
| | Business Combinations, ch. **6** | |

FTB 85-6

| Accounting for a Purchase of Treasury Shares at a Price Significantly in Excess of the Current Market Price of the Shares and the Income Statement Classification of Costs Incurred in Defending against a Takeover Attempt | Stockholders' Equity, ch. **39** | 225, Income Statement 505, Equity |

FTB 86-2

| Accounting for an Interest in the Residual Value of a Leased Asset | Portions amended by FAS-140. | 360, Property, Plant, and Equipment |
| | Leases, ch. **26** | 460, Guarantees 840, Leases |

FTB 88-1

| Issues Related to Accounting for Leases | Leases, ch. **26** | 840, Leases |

FTB 90-1

| Accounting for Separately Priced Extended Warranty and Product Maintenance Contracts | Revenue Recognition, ch. **36** | 460, Guarantees 605, Revenue Recognition |

FTB 94-1

| Application of Statement 115 to Debt Securities Restructured in a Troubled Debt Restructuring | Troubled Debt Restructuring, ch. **41** | 320, Investments—Debt and Equity Securities |

FTB 97-1

| Accounting under Statement 123 for Certain Employee Stock Purchase Plans with a Look-Back Option | Stock-Based Payments, ch. **38** | 718, Compensation—Stock Compensation |

FTB 01-1

| Effective Date for Certain Financial Institutions of Certain Provisions of Statement 140 Related to the Isolation of Transferred Assets | Transfer and Servicing of Financial Assets, ch. **40** | — |

AICPA STATEMENTS OF POSITION

ORIGINAL PRONOUNCEMENT	2009 *GAAP GUIDE LEVELS B, C, AND D* REFERENCE	FASB ACCOUNTING STANDARDS CODIFICATION (ASC) TOPIC
SOP 76-3		
Accounting Practices for Certain Employee Stock Ownership Plans	Stock-Based Payments, ch. **38**	—
SOP 81-1		
Accounting for Performance of Construction-Type and Certain Production-Type Contracts	Long-Term Construction Contracts, ch. **27**	605, Revenue Recognition
SOP 82-1		
Accounting and Financial Reporting for Personal Financial Statements	Personal Financial Statements, ch. **31**	—
SOP 90-3		
Definition of the term *Substantially the Same for Holders of Debt Instruments*, as Used in Certain Audit Guides and a Statement of Position	Investments in Debt and Equity Securities, ch. **25**	860, Transfers and Servicing
SOP 90-7		
Financial Reporting by Entities in Reorganization under the Bankruptcy Code	Bankruptcy and Reorganization, ch. **5**	852, Reorganizations
SOP 93-3		
Rescission of Accounting Principles Board Statements	Accounting Policies and Standards, ch. **2**	225, Changing Prices
SOP 93-4		
Foreign Currency Accounting and Financial Statement Presentation for Investment Companies	Foreign Operations and Exchange, ch. **18**	946, Financial Services— Investment Companies
SOP 93-6		
Employers' Accounting for Employee Stock Ownership Plans	Stock-Based Payments, ch. **38**	460, Guarantees 718, Compensation
SOP 93-7		
Reporting on Advertising Costs	Advertising, ch. **3**	340, Deferred Costs 720, Other Expenses 958, Not for Profit Entities
SOP 94-6		
Disclosure of Certain Significant Risks and Uncertainties	Contingencies, Risks, and Uncertainties, ch. **12**	205, 275, 330, 410, 450, 460, 605, 740, 932, 958, 985
SOP 96-1		
Environmental Remediation Liabilities	Contingencies, Risks, and Uncertainties, ch. **12**	410, Asset Retirement and Environmental Obligations
SOP 97-2		
Software Revenue Recognition	Computer Software, ch. **10**	450, Contingencies 605, Revenue Recognition 730, Research and Development 985, Software

SOP 98-1

Accounting for Costs of Computer Software Developed or Obtained for Internal Use

Computer Software, ch. **10**

350, Intangibles—Goodwill and Other
730, Research and Development
985, Software

SOP 98-5

Reporting on the Costs of Start-Up Activities

Results of Operations, ch. **35**

720, Other Expenses

SOP 98-9

Modification of SOP 97-2, Software Revenue Recognition, With Respect to Certain Transactions

Computer Software, ch. **10**

—

SOP 01-6

Accounting for Certain Entities (Including Entities with Trade Receivables) That Lend To or Finance the Activities of Others

Contingencies, Risks, and Uncertainties, ch. **12**

310, 460, 605, 825, 860, 942, 948

SOP 03-3

Accounting for Certain Loans or Debt Securities Acquired in a Transfer

Transfer of Financial Assets, ch. **40**

310, Receivables
835, Interest

SOP 04-2

Accounting for Real Estate Time-Sharing Transactions

Real Estate Transactions, ch. **34**

978, Real Estate—Time Sharing Activities

SOP 07-1

Clarification of the Scope of the Audit and Accounting Guide "Investment Companies" and Accounting by Parent Companies and Equity Method Investors for Investments in Investment Companies

Financial Investments, ch. **17**

946, Investment Companies

FASB STAFF POSITIONS

ORIGINAL PRONOUNCEMENT	2009 *GAAP GUIDE LEVELS B, C, AND D* REFERENCE	FASB ACCOUNTING STANDARDS CODIFICATION (ASC) TOPIC
FAS 13-1		
Accounting for Rental Costs Incurred during a Construction Period	Real Estate Transactions, ch. **34**	840, Leases
FAS 13-2		
Accounting for a Change in the Timing of Cash Flows Relating to Income Taxes Generated by a Leveraged Transaction	Leases, ch. **26**	—
FAS 19-1		
Accounting for Suspended Well Costs	Capitalization and Expense Recognition Concepts, ch. **7**	932, Extractive Activities—Oil and Gas

FAS 97-1

Situations in Which Paragraphs 17 (b) and 20 of FASB Statement No. 97, "Accounting and Reporting by Insurance Enterprises for Certain Long-Duration Contracts and for Realized Gains and Losses from the Sale of Investments," Permit or Require Accrual of an Unearned Revenue Liability

Revenue Recognition, ch. **36**

—

FAS 106-1

Accounting and Disclosure Requirements Related to the Medicare Prescription Drug Improvement and Modernization Act of 2003

Superseded by FSP FAS 106-2.

—

FAS 106-2

Accounting and Disclosure Requirements Related to the Medicare Prescription Drug, Improvement and Modernization Act of 2003

Postemployment and Retirement Benefits Other Than Pensions, ch. **32**

715, Compensation—Retirement Benefits
740, Income Taxes

FAS 109-1

Application of FASB Statement No. 109, "Accounting for Income Taxes," to the Tax Deduction on Qualified Production Activities Provided by the American Jobs Creation Act of 2004

Income Taxes, ch. **20**

740, Income Taxes

FAS 109-2

Accounting and Disclosure Guidance for the Foreign Earnings Repatriation Provision within the American Jobs Creation Act of 2004

Income Taxes, ch. **20**

—

FAS 115-1 and FAS 124-1

The Meaning of Other-Than-Temporary Impairment and Its Application to Certain Investments

Investments in Debt and Equity Securities, ch., **25**

Investments—320, Debt and Equity Securities
325, Investments—Other
958, Not-for-Profit Entities

FAS 123(R)-1

Classification and Measurement of Freestanding Financial Instruments Originally Issued in Exchange for Employee Services under FASB Statement No. 123(R)

Stock-Based Payments, ch. **38**

718, Compensation—Stock Compensation

FAS 123(R)-2

Practical Accommodation to the Application of Grant Date as Defined in FASB Statement No. 123(R)

Stock-Based Payments, ch. **38**

718, Compensation—Stock Compensation

FAS 123(R)-3

Transition Election Related to Accounting for the Tax Effects of Share-Based Payment Awards

Stock-Based Payments, ch. **38**

—

FAS 123(R)-4

Classification of Options and Similar Instruments Issued as Employee Compensation That Allow for Cash Settlement upon the Occurrence of a Contingent Event

Stock-Based Payments, ch. **38**

718, Compensation—Stock Compensation

FAS 123(R)-5

Amendment of FASB Staff Position 123(R)-1   Stock-Based Payments, ch. **38**   —

FAS 123(R)-6

Technical Corrections of FASB Statement No. 123(R)   Stock-Based Payments, ch. **38**   —

FAS 126-1

Applicability of Certain Disclosure and Interim Reporting Requirements for Obligors for Conduit Debt Securities   Financial Instruments, ch. **17**   —

FAS 129-1

Disclosure Requirements under FASB Statement No. 129, "Disclosure of Information about Capital Structure, Relating to Contingently Convertible Securities"   Stockholders' Equity, ch. **39**   470, Debit 505, Equity

FAS 140-1

Accounting for Accrued Interest Receivable Related to Securitized and Sold Receivables under Statement No. 140   Transfer and Servicing of Financial Assets, ch. **40**   860, Transfers and Servicing

FAS 140-2

Clarification of the Application of Paragraphs 40(b) and 40(c) of FASB Statement No. 140   Transfer and Servicing of Financial Assets, ch. **40**   860, Transfers and Servicing

FAS 140-3

Accounting for Transfers of Financial Assets and Repurchase Financing Transactions   Transfers of Financial Assets, ch. **40**   —

FAS 141-1 and FAS 142-1

Interaction of FASB Statements No. 141, "Business Combinations," and No. 142, "Goodwill and Other Intangible Assets," and EITF Issue No. 04-2, "Whether Mineral Rights Are Tangible or Intangible Assets"   Intangible Assets, ch. **21**   —

FAS 142-2

Application of FASB Statement No. 142, "Goodwill and Other Intangible Assets," to Oil- and Gas-Producing Entities   Intangible Assets, ch. **21**   932, Extractive Activities— Oil and Gas

FAS 142-3

Determination of the Useful Life of Intangible Assets   Intangible Assets, ch. **21**   —

FAS 143-1

Accounting for Electronic Equipment Waste Obligations   Capitalization and Expense Recognition Concepts, ch. **7**   410, Asset Retirement and Environmental Obligations 720, Other Expenses

FAS 144-1

Determination of Cost Basis for Foreclosed Assets under FASB Statement No. 15, "Accounting by Debtors and Creditors for Troubled Debt Restructurings," and the Measurement of Cumulative Losses Previously Recognized under Paragraph 37 of FASB Statement No. 144, "Accounting for the Impairment or Disposal of Long-Lived Assets"	Impairment of Long-Lived Assets, ch. **19**	310, Receivables

FAS 146-1

Determining Whether a One-Time Termination Benefit Offered in Connection with an Exit or Disposal Activity Is, in Substance, an Enhancement to an Ongoing Benefit Arrangement	Pension Plans—Settlements and Curtailments, ch. **30**	420, Exit and Disposel Cost Obligations 715, Compensation— Retirement Benefits

FAS 150-1

Issuer's Accounting for Freestanding Financial Instruments Composed of More Than One Option or Forward Contract Embodying Obligations under FASB Statement No. 150, "Accounting for Certain Financial Instruments with Characteristics of both Liabilities and Equity"	Financial Instruments, ch. **17**	480, Distinguishing Liabilities and Equity

FAS 150-2

Accounting for Mandatorily Redeemable Shares Requiring Redemption by Payment of an Amount That Differs from the Book Value of Those Shares, under FASB Statement No. 150, "Accounting for Certain Financial Instruments with Characteristics of both Liabilities and Equity"	Financial Instruments, ch. **17**	—

FAS 150-3

Effective Date and Transition for Mandatorily Redeemable Financial Instruments of Certain Nonpublic Entities of FASB Statement No. 150, "Accounting for Certain Financial Instruments with Characteristics of both Liabilities and Equity"	Financial Instruments, ch. **17**	480, Distinguishing Liabilities and Equity

FAS 150-4

Issuers' Accounting for Employee Stock Ownership Plans under FASB Statement No. 150, "Accounting for Certain Financial Instruments with Characteristics of both Liabilities and Equity"	Financial Instruments, ch. **17**	480, Distinguishing Liabilities and Equity

FAS 150-5

Issuer's Accounting under FASB Statement No.150 for Freestanding Warrants and Other Similar Instruments on Shares That Are Redeemable	Financial Instruments, ch. **17**	480, Distinguishing Liabilities and Equity

FAS 157-1

Application of FASB Statement No. 157 to FASB Statement No. 13 and Other Accounting Pronouncements That Address Fair Value Measurements for Purposes of Lease Classification or Measurement under Statement 13	Leases, ch. **26**	—

FAS 157-2

Effective Date of FASB Statement No. 157	Fair Value, ch. **16**	—

FAS 158-1

Conforming Amendments to the Illustrations in FASB Statements No. 87, No. 88, and No. 106 and to Related Staff Implementation Guides	Pension Plans-Employers, ch. **29** Pension Plans-Settlements and Curtailments, ch. **30** Postemployment and Postretiremnt Benefits Other Than Pensions, ch. **32**	330, Inventory 715, Compensation— Retirement Benefits

FIN 39-1

Amendment of FASB Interpretation No. 39	Financial Instruments, ch. **17**	—

FIN 45-1

Accounting for Intellectual Property Infringement Indemnification under FIN-45	Contingencies, Risks, and Uncertainties, ch. **12**	460, Guarantees

FIN 45-2

Whether FASB Interpretation No. 45, "Guarantor's Accounting and Disclosure Requirements for Guarantees, Including Indirect Guarantees of Indebtedness of Others," Provides Support for Subsequently Accounting for a Guarantor's Liability at Fair Value	Contingencies, Risks, and Uncertainties, ch. **12**	460, Guarantees

FIN 45-3

Application of FASB Interpretation No. 45 to Minimum Revenue Guarantees Granted to a Business or Its Owners	Contingencies, Risks, and Uncertainties, ch. **12**	460, Guarantees

FIN 46(R)-1

Reporting Variable Interests in Specified Assets of Variable Interest Entities under Paragraph 13 of FASB Interpretation No. 46 (Revised December 2003), "Consolidation of Variable Interest Entities"	Consolidated Financial Statements, ch. **11**	801, Consolidation

FIN 46(R)-2

Calculation of Expected Losses under FASB Interpretation No. 46 (Revised December 2003), "Consolidation of Variable Interest Entities"	Consolidated Financial Statements, ch. **11**	801, Consolidation

FIN 46(R)-3

Evaluating Whether As a Group the Holders of the Equity Investments at Risk Lack the Direct or Indirect Ability to Make Decisions about an Entity's Activities through Voting Rights or Similar Rights under FASB Interpretation No. 46 (Revised December 2003), "Consolidation of Variable Interest Entities"	Consolidated Financial Statements, ch. **11**	801, Consolidation 952, Franchisors

FIN 46(R)-4

Technical Correction of FASB Interpretation No. 46 (revised December 2003), Consolidation of Variable Interest Entities, Relating to Its Effects on Question No. 12 of EITF Issue No. 96-21, "Implementation Issues in Accounting for Leasing Transactions Involving Special-Purpose Entities"	Consolidated Financial Statements, ch. **11**	—

FIN 46(R)-5

Implicit Variable Interests under FASB Interpretation No. 46 (revised December 2003), "Consolidation of Variable Interest"	Consolidated Financial Statements, ch. **11**	801, Consolidation

FIN 46(R)-6

Determining the Variability to Be Considered in Applying FASB Interpretation No. 46(R)	Consolidated Financial Statements, ch. **11**	801, Consolidation

FIN 46(R)-7

Application of FASB Interpretation No. 46(R) to Investment Companies	Consolidated Financial Statements, ch. **11**	—

FIN 48-1

Definition of *Settlement* in FASB Interpretation No. 48	Income Taxes, ch. **20**	740, Income Taxes

FIN 48-2

Effective Date of FASB Interpretation No. 48 for Nonpublic Enterprises	Income Taxes, ch. **20**	—

APB 14-1

Accounting for Convertible Debt Instruments That May Be Settled in Cash upon Conversion (Including Partial Cash Settlement)	Convertible Debt and Debt with Warrants, ch. **13**	—

APB 18-1

Accounting by an Investor for Its Proportionate Share of Accumulated Other Comprehensive Income of an Investee Accounted for under the Equity Method in Accordance with APB Opinion No. 18 upon Loss of Significant Influence	Equity Method, ch. **15**	323, Investments—Equity Method and Joint Ventures

FTB 85-4-1

Accounting for Life Settlement Contracts by Third-Party Providers	Results of Operations, ch. **35**	325, Investments—Other

SOP 78-9-1

Interaction of AICPA Statement of Position 78-9 and EITF Issue No. 04-5	Consolidated Financial Statements, ch. **11**	970, Real Estate—General

SOP 90-7-1

An Amendment of AICPA Statement of Position 90-7	Bankruptcy and Reorganization, ch. **5**	—

SOP-94-6-1

Terms of Loan Products That May Give Rise to a Concentration of Credit Risk	Contingencies, Risks, and Uncertainties, ch. **12**	310, Receivables 825, Financial Instruments

SOP 07-1-1

Effective Date of AICPA Statement of Position 07-1	Consolidated Financial Statements, ch. **10**	—

FSP AAG INV-1 and SOP 94-4-1

Reporting of Fully Benefit-Responsive Investment Contracts Held by Certain Investment Companies Subject to the AICPA Investment Company Guide and Defined-Contribution Health and Welfare and Pension Plans	Not discussed in this Guide.	946, Investment Companies

FSP AUG AIR-1

Accounting for Planned Major Maintenance Activities	Capitalization and Expense Recognition Concepts, ch. **7**	360, Property, Plant, and Equipment 908, Airlines

EITF 85-24-1

Application of EITF Issue No. 85-24, "Distribution Fees by Distributors of Mutual Funds That Do Not Have a Front-End Sales Charge," When Cash for the Right to Future Distribution Fees for Shares Previously Sold Is Received from Third Parties	Revenue Recognition, ch. **36**	946, Investment Companies

EITF 00-19-1

Application of EITF Issue No. 00-19 to Freestanding Financial Instruments Originally Issued as Employee Compensation	Superseded by FSP FAS 123 (R)-1.	—

EITF 00-19-2

Accounting for Registration Payment Arrangements	Financial Instruments, ch. **17**	470, Debt 815, Derivatives and Hedging 825, Financial Investments

EITF 03-1-1

Effective Date of Paragraphs 10–20 of EITF Issue No. 03-1, "The Meaning of Other-Than-Temporary Impairment and Its Application to Certain Investments"	Superseded by FSP FAS 115-1 and FSP FAS 124-1.	—

CONSENSUS POSITIONS OF THE
EMERGING ISSUES TASK FORCE (EITF)

ORIGINAL PRONOUNCEMENT	2009 *GAAP GUIDE LEVELS B, C, AND D* REFERENCE	FASB ACCOUNTING STANDARDS CODIFICATION (ASC) TOPIC
84-1		
Tax Reform Act of 1984: Deferred Income Taxes of Stock Life Insurance Companies	Resolved by FTB 84-3, which was superseded by FAS-96 and FAS-109.	—
84-2		
Tax Reform Act of 1984: Deferred Income Taxes Relating to Domestic International Sales Corporations	No consensus. Resolved by FTB 84-2, which was superseded by FAS-96 and FAS-109.	—
84-3		
Convertible Debt "Sweeteners"	Resolved by FAS-84.	—
84-4		
Acquisition, Development, and Construction Loans	Resolved by PB-1, Exhibit I.	810, Consolidation 815, Derivatives and Hedging
84-5		
Sale of Marketable Securities with a Put Option	Included in discussion of Issue 85-40.	460, Guarantees 860, Transfers and Servicing
84-6		
Termination of Defined Benefit Pension Plans	Superseded by FAS-88.	—
84-7		
Termination of Interest Rate Swaps	Nullified by FAS-133.	—
84-8		
Variable Stock Purchase Warrants Given by Suppliers to Customers	Resolved by FAS-123(R).	—
84-9		
Deposit Float of Banks	Accounting Changes, ch. **1**	—
84-10		
LIFO Conformity of Companies Relying on Insilco Tax Court Decision	No consensus.	—
84-11		
Offsetting Installment Note Receivables and Bank Debt ("Note Monetization")	Resolved by SAB-70, FTB 86-2, and FIN-39.	—
84-12		
Operating Leases with Scheduled Rent Increases	Consensus nullified by FTB 85-3. FTB 88-1 provides additional guidance.	—
84-13		
Purchase of Stock Options and Stock Appreciation Rights in a Leveraged Buyout	Nullified by FAS-123(R).	—
84-14		
Deferred Interest Rate Setting	Nullified by FAS-133.	—

84-15

Grantor Trusts Consolidation	No consensus. Addressed in FTB 85-2, which was superseded by FAS-125.	—

84-16

Earnings-per-Share Cash-Yield Test for Zero Coupon Bonds	Resolved by FAS-85.	—

84-17

Profit Recognition on Sales of Real Estate with Graduated Payment Mortgages or Insured Mortgages	Real Estate Transactions, ch. **33**	360, Property, Plant, and Equipment

84-18

Stock Option Pyramiding	Nullified by FAS-123(R).	—

84-19

Mortgage Loan Payment Modifications	Financial Instruments, ch. **17**	310, Receivables

84-20

GMNA Dollar Rolls	Partially resolved by guidance in paragraphs 9, 27-30-,68, and 70 of FAS-125.	815, Derivatives and Hedging 860, Transfers and Servicing

84-21

Sale of a Loan with a Partial Participation Retained	Resolved by FAS-125, paragraphs 10 and 39.	—

84-22

Prior Years' Earnings per Share Following a Savings and Loan Association Conversion and Pooling	No consensus. Resolved by FAS-141.	—

84-23

Leveraged Buyout Holding Company Debt	No consensus. Guidance provided by SAB-73 and FAS-105.	—

84-24

LIFO Accounting Issues	No consensus. SAB-58 provides guidance.	—

84-25

Offsetting Nonrecourse Debt with Sales-Type or Direct Financing Lease Receivables	Resolved by FTB 86-2 and SEC Staff Accounting Bulletin No. 70.	—

84-26

Defeasance of Special-Purpose Borrowings	Resolved by FAS-125.	—

84-27

Deferred Taxes on Subsidiary Stock Sales	No consensus. Resolved by FAS-96, which was superseded by FAS-109.	—

84-28

Impairment of Long-Lived Assets	No consensus. Resolved by FAS-121.	—

84-29

Gain and Los Recognition on Exchanges of Productive Assets and the Effect of Boot	No consensus. Resolved by EITF Issues 86-29 and 87-29.	—

84-30

Sales of Loans to Special-Purpose Entities	Resolved by FIN-46 and FIN-46(R) for entities under the scope of those pronouncements.	—

84-31

Equity Certificates of Deposit	Resolved by FAS-133.	—

84-32

	Not used. —

84-33

Acquisition of a Tax Loss Carryforward— Temporary Parent-Subsidiary Relationship	Resolved by FAS-144.	—

84-34

Permanent Discount Restricted Stock Purchase Plans	Nullified by FAS-123(R), except for nonpublic entities under the scope of paragraph 83 of FAS-123(R).	—

84-35

Business Combinations: Sale of Duplicate Facilities and Accrual of Liabilities	Nullified by FAS-141(R).	—

84-36

Interest Rate Swap Transactions	Nullified by FAS-133.	—

84-37

Sale-Leaseback Transaction with Repurchase Option	No consensus. See FAS-98.	840, Leases

84-38

Identical Common Shares for a Pooling Of Interests	Nullified by FTB 85-5.	—

84-39

Transfers of Monetary and Nonmonetary Assets among Individuals and Entities Under Common Control	No consensus.	—

84-40

Long-Term Debt Repayable by a Capital Stock Transaction	Issue 1 nullified by FIN-46 and FIN-46 (R) and Issue 2 resolved by FAS-150.	—

84-41

Consolidation of Subsidiary Instantaneous Defeasance	Resolved by FAS-94.	—

84-42

Push-Down of Parent Company Debt to a Subsidiary	No consensus. See SAB 43.	—

84-43

Income Tax Effects of Asset Evaluation in Certain Foreign Countries	Nullified by FAS-109.	—

84-44

Partial Termination of a Defined Benefit Pension Plan	Resolved by FAS-88.	—

85-1

Classifying Notes Received for Capital Stock	Balance Sheet Classification and Related Display Issues, ch. 4	310, Receivables 505, Equity 850, Related Party Disclosures

85-2

Classification of Costs Incurred in a Takeover Defense	Nullified by TB 85-6.	—

85-3

Tax Benefits Relating to Asset Dispositions Following an Acquisition of a Financial Institution	Consensus nullified by FAS-96, which was superseded by FAS-109.	—

85-4

Downstream Mergers and Other Stock Transactions between Companies under Common Control	No consensus. Resolved by FTB 85-5.	—

85-5

Restoration of Deferred Taxes Previously Eliminated by Net Operating Loss Recognition	No consensus. Resolved by FAS-96, which was superseded by FAS-109.	—

85-6

Futures Implementation Questions	Resolved by Q and A to FAS-80.	—

85-7

Federal Home Loan Mortgage Corporation Stock	No consensus. Resolved by FTB 85-1.	—

85-8

Amortization of Thrift Intangibles	Nullified by FAS-141(R).	—

85-9

Revenue Recognition on Options to Purchase Stock of Another Entity	Convertible Debt and Debt with Warrants, ch. 13	—

85-10

Employee Stock Ownership Plan Contribution Funded by a Pension Plan Termination	Nullified by FAS-88.	—

85-11

Use of an Employee Stock Ownership Plan in a Leveraged Buyout	No consensus. See SOP 93-6.	—

85-12

Retention of Specialized Accounting for Investments in Consolidation	Consolidated Financial Statements, ch. 11	810, Consolidation

85-13

Sale of Mortgage Service Rights on Mortgages Owned by Others	Transfer and Servicing of Financial Assets, ch. 40	860, Transfers and Servicing

85-14

Securities That Can Be Acquired for Cash in a Pooling of Interests	Nullified by FAS-141.	—

85-15

Recognizing Benefits of Purchased Net Operating Loss Carryforwards	Consensus nullified by FAS-96, which was superseded by FAS-109.	—

85-16

Leveraged Leases: Real Estate Leases and Sale-Leaseback Transactions, Delayed Equity Contributions by Lessors	Leases, ch. **26**	840, Leases

85-17

Accrued Interest upon Conversion of Convertible Debt	Convertible Debt and Debt with Warrants, ch. **13**	470, Debt 835, Interest

85-18

Earnings-per-Share Effect of Equity Commitment Notes	Superseded by FAS-128.	—

85-19

	Not used.	—

85-20

Recognition of Fees for Guaranteeing a Loan	Contingencies, Risks, and Uncertainties, ch. **12**	310, Receivables 460, Guarantees 605, Revenue Recognition

85-21

Changes of Ownership Resulting in a New Basis of Accounting	Business Combinations, ch. **6**	—

85-22

Retroactive Application of FASB Technical Bulletins	No longer relevant.	—

85-23

Effect of a Redemption Agreement on Carrying Value of a Security	Investments in Debt and Equity Securities, ch. **25**	—

85-24

Distribution Fees by Distributors of Mutual Funds That Do Not Have a Front-End Sales Charge	Revenue Recognition, ch. **36**	605, Revenue Recognition

85-25

Sale of Preferred Stocks with a Put Option	Included in discussion of Issue 85-40.	460, Guarantees 860, Transfers and Servicing

85-26

Measurement of Servicing Fee under FASB Statement No. 65 When a Loan Is Sold with Servicing Retained	No consensus. Resolved by FTB 87-3 and FAS-125.	—

85-27

Recognition of Receipts from Made-Up Rental Shortfalls	Real Estate Transactions, ch. **33**	360, Property, Plant, and Equipment

85-28

Consolidation Issues Relating to Collateralized Mortgage Obligations	Resolved by FAS-94.	—

85-29

Convertible Bonds with a "Premium Put"	Convertible Debt and Debt with Warrants, ch. **13**	—

85-30

Sale of Marketable Securities at a Gain with a Put Option	No consensus. Resolved by FAS-125.	—

85-31

Comptroller of the Currency's Rule on Deferred Tax Debits	Not discussed in this Guide.	942, Financial Services

85-32

Purchased Lease Residuals	Nullified by FTB 86-2.	—

85-33

Disallowance of Income Tax Deduction	Nullified by FAS-109.	—

85-34

Banker's Acceptances and Risk Participations	Resolved by FAS-125.	—

85-35

Transition and Implementation Issues for FASB Statement No. 86	No longer useful.	—

85-36

Discontinued Operations with Expected Gain and Interim Operating Losses	Nullified by FAS-144.	—

85-37

Recognition of Note Received for Real Estate Syndication Activities	Resolved by SOP 92-1.	—

85-38

Negative Amortizing Loans	No longer useful.	—

85-39

Implications of SEC Staff Accounting Bulletin No. 59 on Noncurrent Marketable Equity Securities	Investments in Debt and Equity Securities, ch. **25**	—

85-40

Comprehensive Review of Sales of Marketable Securities with Put Arrangements	Transfer and Servicing of Financial Assets, ch. **40**	—

85-41

Accounting for Savings and Loan Associations and FSLIC Management Consignment Program	Not discussed in this Guide.	—

85-42

Amortization of Goodwill Resulting from Recording Time Savings Deposits at Fair Value	Nullified by FAS-141(R).	—

85-43

Sale of Subsidiary for Equity Interest in Buyer	Resolved by Issue 86-29.	—

85-44

Differences between Loan Loss Allowances	Not discussed in this Guide.	—

85-45

Business Combinations: Settlement of Stock Options and Awards	Nullified by FAS-123(R).	—

85-46

| Partnership's Purchase of Withdrawing Partner's Equity | No consensus. | — |

86-1

| Recognizing Net Operating Loss Carryforwards | Nullified by FAS-109. | — |

86-2

| Retroactive Wage Adjustments Affecting Medicare Payments | No longer relevant. | |

86-3

| Retroactive Regulations Regarding IRC Section 338 Purchase Price Allocations | The consensus on Issue 1 is no longer relevant. The consensus on Issue 2 was superseded by FAS-109. | — |

86-4

| Income Statement Treatment of Income Tax Benefit for Employee Stock Ownership Plan Dividends | Consensus nullified by FAS-96, which was superseded by FAS-109. | — |

86-5

| Classifying Demand Notes with Repayment Terms | Balance Sheet Classification and Related Display Issues, ch. **4** | 470, Debt |

86-6

| Antispeculation Clauses in Real Estate Sales Contracts | Real Estate Transactions, ch. **33** | 360, Plant, Property, and Equipment |

86-7

| Recognition by Homebuilders of Profit from Sales of Land and Related Construction Contracts | Real Estate Transactions, ch. **33** | 970, Real Estate—General |

86-8

| Sale of Bad-Debt Recovery Rights | Financial Instruments, ch. **17** | 860, Transfers and Servicing |

86-9

| IRC Section 338 and Push-Down Accounting | Income Taxes, ch. **20** | — |
| | Also see Issue 94-10. | |

86-10

| Pooling with 10 Percent Cash Payout Determined by Lottery | Nullified by FAS-141. | — |

86-11

| Recognition of Possible 1986 Tax Law Changes | Resolved by FTB 86-1, which was superseded by FAS-96 and FAS-109. | — |

86-12

| Accounting by Insureds for Claims-Made Insurance Policies | Codified in Issue 03-8. | — |
| | Contingencies, Risks, and Uncertainties, ch. **12** | |

86-13

| Recognition of Inventory Market Declines at Interim Reporting Dates | Interim Financial Reporting, ch. **23** | 330, Inventory |

86-14

| Purchased Research and Development Projects in a Business Combination | Nullified by FAS-141(R). | — |

86-15

| Increasing-Rate Debt | Balance Sheet Classification and Related Display Issues, ch. **4** | 470, Debt
835, Interest |
| | Interest on Receivables and Payables, ch. **22** | |

86-16

| Carryover of Predecessor Cost in Leveraged Buyout Transactions | Superseded by Issue 88-16. | — |

86-17

| Deferred Profit on Sale-Leaseback Transaction with Lessee Guarantee of Residual Value | Leases, ch. **26** | 460, Guarantees
840, Leases |

86-18

| Debtor's Accounting for a Modification of Debt Terms | Superseded by Issue 96-19 and resolved by FIN-39. | — |

86-19

| Change in Accounting for Other Postemployment Benefits | Resolved by FAS-106. | — |

86-20

| Accounting for Other Postemployment Benefits Of an Acquired Company | Nullified by FAS-106. | — |

86-21

| Application of the AICPA Notice to Practitioners regarding Acquisition, Development, and Construction Arrangements to Acquisition of an Operating Property | Real Estate Transactions, ch. **33** | 310, Receivables
815, Derivatives and Hedging |

86-22

| Display of Business Restructuring Provisions in the Income Statement | No consensus. See SAB 67 and FAS-144. | — |

86-23 | Not used. |

86-24

| Third-Party Establishment of Collateralized Mortgage Obligations | No longer relevant because of the issuance of FAS-125 and FAS-140. | — |

86-25

| Offsetting Foreign Currency Swaps | Foreign Operations and Exchange, ch. **18** | 815, Derivatives and Hedging |

86-26

| Using Forward Commitments as a Surrogate for Deferred Rate Setting | Resolved by FAS-133. | — |

86-27

| Measurement of Excess Contributions to a Defined Contribution Plan or Employee Stock Ownership Plan | Stock-Based Payments, ch. **38** | 715, Compensation—Retirement Benefits |

86-28

Accounting Implications of Indexed Debt Instruments	Financial Instruments, ch. **17**	—

86-29

Nonmonetary Transactions: Magnitude of Boot and the Exceptions to the Use of Fair Value	Codified in Issue 01-2.	—

86-30

Classification of Obligations When a Violation Is Waived by the Creditor	Balance Sheet Classification and Related Display Issues, ch. **4**	470, Debt

86-31

Reporting the Tax Implications of a Pooling of a Bank and a Savings and Loan Association	Nullified by FAS-141.	—

86-32

Early Extinguishment of a Subsidiary's Mandatorily Redeemable Preferred Stock	Stockholders' Equity, ch. **39**	505, Equity 810, Consolidation

86-33

Tax Indemnifications in Lease Agreements	Leases, ch. **26**	840, Leases

86-34

Futures Contracts Used as Hedges of Anticipated Reverse Repurchase Transactions	Nullified by FAS-133.	—

86-35

Debentures with Detachable Stock Purchase Warrants	Superseded by Issue 96-13, which has been codified in Issue 00-19.	—
	Financial Instruments, ch. **17**	

86-36

Invasion of a Defeasance Trust	Extinguishment of Debt, ch. **16**	—

86-37

Recognition of Tax Benefit of Discounting Loss Reserves of Insurance Companies	Consensus nullified by FAS-96, which was superseded by FAS-109.	—

86-38

Implications of Mortgage Prepayments on Amortization of Servicing Rights	Consensus in Section A nullified by FAS-122.	—
	Consensus in Section B nullified by FAS-125.	
	Consensus in Section C superseded by Issue 89-4.	

86-39

Gains from the Sale of Mortgage Loans with Servicing Rights Retained	Nullified by FAS-125, which supersedes FAS-122. See paragraphs 10 and 39 of FAS-125 for guidance.	—

86-40

Investments in Open-End Mutual Funds That Invest in U.S. Government Securities	Consensus no longer applies. Resolved by FAS-115.	320, Investments—Debt and Equity Securities

86-41

Carryforward of the Corporate Alternative Minimum Tax Credit	Consensus nullified by FAS-96, which was superseded by FAS-109.	—

86-42

Effect of a Change in Tax Rates on Assets and Liabilities Recorded Not-of-Tax in a Purchase Business Combination	Consensus nullified by FAS-96, which was superseded by FAS-109.	—

86-43

Effect of a Change in Tax Law or Rates on Leveraged Leases	Leases, ch. **26**	840, Leases

86-44

Effect of a Change in Tax Law on Investments in Safe Harbor Leases	Leases, ch. **26**	—

86-45

Imputation of Dividends on Preferred Stock Redeemable at the Issuer's Option with Initial Below-Market Dividend Rate	No consensus.	—

86-46

Uniform Capitalization Rules for Inventory under the Tax Reform Act of 1986	Inventory, ch. **24**	330, Inventory

87-1

Deferral Accounting for Cash Securities That Are Used to Hedge Rate or Price Risk	Resolved by FAS-133.	—

87-2

Net Present Value Method of Valuing Speculative Foreign Exchange Contracts	Resolved by FAS-133.	—

87-3

	Not used.

87-4

Restructuring of Operations: Implications of SEC Staff Accounting Bulletin No. 67	Results of Operations, ch. **35**	—

87-5

Troubled Debt Restructurings: Interrelationship Between FASB Statement No. 15 and the AICPA Savings and Loan Guide	Nullified by FAS-114.	—

87-6

Adjustments Relating to Stock Compensation Plans	Nullified by FIN-44.	—

87-7

Sale of an Asset Subject to a Lease and Nonrecourse Financing: "Wrap Lease Transactions"	Leases, ch. **26**	—

87-8

Tax Reform Act of 1986: Issues Related to the Alternative Minimum Tax	Income Taxes, ch. **20** Leases, ch. **26** Consensuses on Issues 2–9 and 11 were nullified by FAS-109.	740, Income Taxes 840, Leases

87-9

Profit Recognition on Sales of Real Estate with Insured Mortgages or Surety Bonds	Real Estate Transactions, ch. **33**	360, Property, Plant, and Equipment

87-10

Revenue Recognition by Television "Barter" Syndicators	Revenue Recognition, ch. **36**	—

87-11

Allocation of Purchase Price to Assets to Be Sold	Nullified by FAS-144.	—

87-12

Foreign Debt-for-Equity Swaps	Foreign Operations and Exchange, ch. **18**	830, Foreign Currency Matters

87-13

Amortization of Prior Service Cost for a Defined Benefit Plan When There Is a History of Plan Amendments	No consensus. Resolved by Question and Answer No. 20 of FASB Special Report on FAS-87.	—

87-14

	Not used.	—

87-15

Effect of a Standstill Agreement on Pooling-of-Interests Accounting	Nullified by FAS-141.	—

87-16

Whether the 90 Percent Test for a Pooling of Interests Is Applied Separately to Each Company or on a Combined Basis	Nullified by FAS-141.	—

87-17

Spinoffs or Other Distributions of Loans Receivable to Shareholders	Codified in Issue 01-2.	—

87-18

Use of Zero Coupon Bonds in a Troubled Debt Restructuring	Troubled Debt Restructuring, ch. **41**	310, Receivables

87-19

Substituted Debtors in a Troubled Debt Restructuring	Troubled Debt Restructuring, ch. **41**	310, Receivables

87-20

Offsetting Certificates of Deposit against High-Coupon Debt	Issue 1 resolved by FAS-125. Issue 2 superseded by Issue 96-19.	—

87-21

Change of Accounting Basis in Master Limited Partnership Transactions

Business Combinations, ch. **6**

—

87-22

Prepayments to the Secondary Reserve of the FSLIC

No longer relevant. See Topics D-47 and D-57.

—

87-23

Book Value Stock Purchase Plans

Nullified by FAS-123(R), except for nonpublic entities under the scope of paragraph 83 of FAS-123(R); Issue 3 nullified by SOP 93-6.

—

87-24

Allocation of Interest to Discontinued Operations

Results of Operations, ch. **35**

205, Presentation of Financial Statements

87-25

Sale of Convertible, Adjustable-Rate Mortgages with Contingent Repayment Agreement

No consensus. Resolved by FAS-125 and FAS-140.

—

87-26

Hedging of a Foreign Currency Exposure with a Tandem Currency

Nullified by FAS-133.

—

87-27

Poolings of Companies That Do Not Have a Controlling Class of Common Stock

Nullified by FAS-141.

—

87-28

Provision for Deferred Taxes on Increases in Cash Surrender Value of Key-Person Life Insurance

Resolved by FAS-109.

—

87-29

Exchange of Real Estate Involving Boot

Codified in Issue 01-2.

—

87-30

Sale of a Short-Term Loan Made under a Long-Term Credit Commitment

Transfer and Servicing of Financial Assets, ch. **40**

860, Transfers and Servicing

87-31

Sale of Put Options on Issuer's Stock

Codified in Issue 00-19.

—

87-32

Not used.

—

87-33

Stock Compensation Issues Related to Market Decline

Nullified by FIN-44.

—

87-34

Sale of Mortgage Servicing Rights with a Subservicing Agreement

Not discussed.

860, Transfers and Servicing

88-1

Determination of Vested Benefit Obligation for a Defined Benefit Pension Plan

Pension Plans—Employers, ch. **29**

715, Compensation—Retirement Benefits

88-2	Not used.	—
88-3		
Rental Concessions Provided by Landlord	Resolved by FTB 88-1 and Issues 88-10 and 94-3.	—
88-4		
Classification of Payment Made to IRS to Retain Fiscal Year	Capitalization and Expense Recognition Concepts, ch. **7**	740, Income Taxes
88-5		
Recognition of Insurance Death Benefits	Revenue Recognition, ch. **36**	325, Investments—Other
	No consensus on Issue 2, but FAS-109 provides guidance.	
88-6		
Book Value Stock Plans in an Initial Public Offering	Nullified by FAS-123(R), except for nonpublic entities under the scope of paragraph 83 of FAS-123(R).	—
88-7	Not used.	—
88-8	Partially nullified and partially resolved by FAS-133.	—
88-9		
Put Warrants	Nullified by FAS-128, FAS-133, and FAS-150 and superseded by Issue 96-13.	—
88-10		
Costs Associated with Lease Modification or Termination	FAS-146 resolves Issue 1 and nullifies Issues 2 and 3.	—
88-11		
Allocation of Recorded Investment When a Loan or Part of a Loan Is Sold	Nullified by FAS-156.	—
88-12		
Transfer of Ownership Interest as Part of Down Payment under FASB Statement No. 66	Real Estate Transactions, ch. **33**	360, Property, Plant, and Equipment
88-13	Not used.	—
88-14		
Settlement of Fees with Extra Units to a General Partner in a Master Limited Partnership	No consensus. Resolved by SOP 92-1.	—
88-15		
Classification of Subsidiary's Loan Payable in Consolidated Balance Sheet When Subsidiary's and Parent's Fiscal Years Differ	Balance Sheet Classification and Related Display Issues, ch. **4**	470, Debt 810, Consolidation
88-16		
Basis in Leveraged Buyout Transactions	Nullified by FAS-141(R).	—

88-17

Accounting for Fees and Costs Associated with Loan Syndications and Loan Participations — Partially nullified by FAS-125 and superseded by Issue 97-3. — —

88-18

Sales of Future Revenues — Balance Sheet Classification and Related Display Issues, ch. **4** — 470, Debt

Foreign Operations and Exchange, ch. **18**

Revenue Recognition, ch. **36**

88-19

FSLIC-Assisted Acquisitions of Thrifts — Nullified by FAS-141(R). — —

88-20

Difference between Initial Investment and Principal Amount of Loans in a Purchased Credit Card Portfolio — Intangible Assets, ch. **21** — 310, Receivables

88-21

Accounting for the Sale of Property Subject to the Seller's Preexisting Lease — Leases, ch. **26** — 840, Leases

88-22

Securitization of Credit Card and Other Receivable Portfolios — Transfer and Servicing of Financial Assets, ch. **40** — 860, Transfers and Servicing

88-23

Lump-Sum Payments under Union Contracts — Capitalization and Expense Recognition Concepts, ch. **7** — 710, Compensation— General

88-24

Effect of Various Forms of Financing under FASB Statement No. 66 — Real Estate Transactions, ch. **33** — 360, Property, Plant, and Equipment

88-25

Ongoing Accounting and Reporting for a Newly Created Liquidating Bank — Not discussed in this Guide. — 942, Financial Services

88-26

Controlling Preferred Stock in a Pooling of Interests — Nullified by FAS-141. — 852, Reorganizations

88-27

Effect of Unlocated Shares in an Employee Stock Ownership Plan on Accounting for Business Combinations — Nullified by FAS-141. — —

89-1

Accounting by a Pension Plan for Bank Investment Contracts and Guaranteed Investment Contracts — Resolved by FAS-110 and SOP 94-4. — —

89-2

Maximum Maturity Guarantees on Transfers of Receivables with Recourse — See FAS-140 and FIN-45 for guidance. — —

89-3

Balance Sheet Presentation of Savings Accounts in Financial Statements of Credit Unions	Not discussed.	942, Financial Services— Depository and Lending

89-4

Accounting for a Purchased Investment in a Collateralized Mortgage Obligation Instrument or in a Mortgage-Backed Interest-Only Certificate	Superseded by Issue 99-20.	—

89-5

Sale of Mortgage Loan Servicing Rights	Superseded by Issue 95-5.	—

89-6

	Not used.	—

89-7

Exchange of Assets or Interest in a Subsidiary for a Noncontrolling Equity Interest in a New Entity	Codified in Issue 01-2.	—

89-8

Expense Recognition for Employee Stock Ownership Plans	Stock-Based Payments, ch. **38**	—

89-9

Accounting for In-Substance Foreclosures	Nullified by FAS-114.	—

89-10

Sponsor's Recognition of Employee Stock Ownership Plan Debt	Nullified by SOP 93-6.	—

89-11

Sponsor's Balance Sheet Classification of Capital Stock with a Put Option Held by an Employee Stock Ownership Plan	Balance Sheet Classification and Related Display Issues, ch. **4**	480, Distinguishing Liabilities and Equity

89-12

Earnings-per-Share Issues Related to Convertible Preferred Stock Held by an Employee Stock Ownership Plan	Stock-Based Payments, ch. **38**	—

89-13

Accounting for the Cost of Asbestos Removal	Capitalization and Expense Recognition Concepts, ch. **7** Results of Operations, ch. **35**	410, Asset Retirement and Environmental Obligations

89-14

Valuation of Repossessed Real Estate	Real Estate Transactions, ch. **33**	310, Receivables

89-15

Accounting for a Modification of Debt Terms When the Debtor Is Experiencing Financial Difficulties	Superseded by Issue 02-4.	—

89-16

Consideration of Executory Costs in Sale-Leaseback Transactions	Leases, ch. **26**	840, Leases

89-17

Accounting for the Retail Sale of an Extended Warranty Contract in Connection with the Sale of a Product — Nullified by FTB 90-1. — —

89-18

Divestitures of Certain Investment Securities to an Unregulated Commonly Controlled Entity under F IRREA — Consensus no longer applies. Resolved by FAS-115. — —

89-19

Accounting for a Change in Goodwill Amortization for Business Combinations Initiated Prior to the Effective Date of FASB Statement No. 72 — Nullified by FAS-141(R). — —

89-20

Accounting for Cross Border Tax Benefit Leases — Leases, ch. **26** — 840, Leases

90-1 — Not used. — —

90-2

Exchange of Interest-Only and Principal-Only Securities for a Mortgage-Backed Security — Nullified by FAS-125. — —

90-3

Accounting for Employers' Obligations for Future Contributions to a Multiemployer Pension Plan — Pension Plans—Employers, ch. **29** — 715, Compensation—Retirement Benefits

90-4

Earnings-per-Share Treatment of Tax Benefits for Dividends on Stock Held by an Employee Stock Ownership Plan — Issue 1 nullified by FAS-128. (See Appendix F of FAS-128 for discussion on deduction of dividends.) Issue 2 addressed in Issue 92-3. — 718, Compensation—Stock Compensation

90-5

Exchanges of Ownership Interests between Entities under Common Control — Business Combinations, ch. **6** Issue 1 nullified by FAS-141(R). Issue 2 nullified by FAS-160. — —

90-6

Accounting for Certain Events Not Addressed in Issue No. 87-11 Relating to an Acquired Operating Unit to Be Sold — Nullified by FAS-144. — —

90-7

Accounting for a Reload Stock Option — Nullified by FAS-123(R), except for nonpublic entities under the scope of paragraph 83 of FAS-123(R). — —

90-8

Capitalization of Costs to Treat Environmental Contamination	Capitalization and Expense Recognition Concepts, ch. **7**	410, Asset Retirement and Environmental Obligations

90-9

Changes to Fixed Employee Stock Option Plans as a Result of Equity Restructuring	Nullified by FIN-44.	—

90-10

Accounting for a Business Combination Involving a Majority-Owned Investee of a Venture Capital Company	Resolved by FAS-141.	—

90-11

Accounting for Exit and Entrance Fees Incurred in a Conversion from the Savings Association Insurance Fund to the Bank Insurance Fund	No longer useful.	—

90-12

Allocating Basis to Individual Assets and Liabilities for Transactions within the Scope of Issue No. 88-16	Nullified by FAS-141(R).	—

90-13

Accounting for Simultaneous Common Control Mergers	Business Combinations, ch. **6** Issue 1 nullified by FAS-141(R). Issue 2 nullified by FAS-160.	—

90-14

Unsecured Guarantee by Parent of Subsidiary's Lease Payments in a Sale-Leaseback Transaction	Leases, ch. **26**	460, Guarantees 840, Leases

90-15

Impact of Nonsubstantive Lessors, Residual Value Guarantees, and Other Provisions in Leasing Transactions	Nullified by FIN-46 and FIN-46(R) for entities under their scope.	—

90-16

Accounting for Discontinued Operations Subsequently Retained	Nullified by FAS-144.	—

90-17

Hedging Foreign Currency Risk with Purchased Options	Affirmed by FAS-133.	—

90-18

Effect of a "Removal of Accounts" Provision on the Accounting for a Credit Card Securitization	Transfer and Servicing of Financial Assets, ch. **40**	—

90-19

Convertible Bonds with Issuer Option to Settle for Cash upon Conversion	Nullified by FSP APB-14-1.	—

90-20

Impact of an Uncollateralized Irrevocable Letter of Credit on a Real Estate Sale-Leaseback Transaction	Leases, ch. **26**	460, Guarantees 840, Leases

90-21

Balance Sheet Treatment of a Sale of Mortgage Servicing Rights with a Subservicing Agreement	Transfer and Servicing of Financial Assets, ch. **40**	460, Guarantees 860, Reorganizations

90-22

Accounting for Gas-Balancing Arrangements	Revenue Recognition, ch. **36**	932, Extractive Activities—Oil and Gas

91-1

Hedging Intercompany Foreign Currency Risks	Nullified by FAS-133.	—

91-2

Debtor's Accounting for Forfeiture of Real Estate Subject to a Nonrecourse Mortgage	No consensus. SEC and FASB staffs agree that FAS-15 applies.	—

91-3

Accounting for Income Tax Benefits from Bad Debts of a Savings and Loan Association	No consensus. Resolved by FAS-109 with additional guidance in SEC SAB-91.	—

91-4

Hedging Foreign Currency Risks with Complex Options and Similar Transactions	Resolved by FAS-133.	—

91-5

Nonmonetary Exchange of Cost-Method Investments	Business Combinations, ch. **6**	325, Investments—Other

91-6

Revenue Recognition of Long-Term Power Sales Contracts	Revenue Recognition, ch. **36**	440, Commitments 980, Regulated Operations

91-7

Accounting for Pension Benefits Paid by Employers after Insurance Companies Fail to Provide Annuity Benefits	Pension Plans—Settlements and Curtailments, ch. **30**	715, Compensation—Retirement Benefits

91-8

Application of FASB Statement No. 96 to a State Tax Based on the Greater of a Franchise Tax or an Income Tax	Income Taxes, ch. **20**	740, Income Taxes

91-9

Revenue and Expense Recognition for Freight Services in Process	Revenue Recognition, ch. **36**	605, Revenue Recognition

91-10

Accounting for Special Assessments and Tax Increment Financing Entities	Contingencies, Risks, and Uncertainties, ch. **12**	970, Real Estate—General

92-1

Allocation of Residual Value or First-Loss Guarantee to Minimum Lease Payments in Leases Involving Land and Building(s)	Leases, ch. **26**	460, Guarantees 840, Leases

92-2

Measuring Loss Accruals by Transferors for Transfers of Receivables with Recourse	Transfer and Servicing of Financial Assets, ch. **40**	—

92-3

Earnings-per-Share Treatment of Tax Benefits for Dividends on Unlocated Stock Held by an Employee Stock Ownership Plan (Consideration of the Implications of FASB Statement No. 109 on Issue 2 of EITF Issue No. 90-4)	Stock-Based Payments, ch. **38**	—

92-4

Accounting for a Change in Functional Currency When an Economy Ceases to Be Considered Highly Inflationary	Foreign Operations and Exchange, ch. **18**	830, Foreign Currency Matters

92-5

Amortization Period for Net Deferred Credit Card Origination Costs	Financial Instruments, ch. **17**	—

92-6

	Not used.

92-7

Accounting by Rate-Regulated Utilities for the Effects of Certain Alternative Revenue Programs	Revenue Recognition, ch. **36**	980, Regulated Operations

92-8

Accounting for the Income Tax Effects under FASB Statement No. 109 of a Change in Functional Currency When an Economy Ceases to Be Considered Highly Inflationary	Foreign Operations and Exchange, ch. **18**	830, Foreign Currency Matters

92-9

Accounting for the Present Value of Future Profits Resulting from the Acquisition of a Life Insurance Company	Nullified by FAS-141(R).	—

92-10

Loan Acquisitions Involving Table Funding Arrangements	Nullified by FAS-125.	—

92-11

	Not used.	—

92-12

Accounting for OPEB Costs by Rate-Regulated Enterprises	Postemployment and Postretirement Benefits Other Than Pensions, ch. **32**	715, Compensation— Retirement Benefits 980, Regulated Operations

92-13

Accounting for Estimated Payments in Connection with the Coal Industry Retiree Health Benefit Act of 1992	Contingencies, Risks, and Uncertainties, ch. **12**	450, Contingencies 715, Compensation— Retirement Benefits 930, Extractive Activities— Oil and Gas

93-1

Accounting for Individual Credit Card Acquisitions	Financial Instruments, ch. 17	310, Receivables

93-2

Effect of Acquisition of Employer Shares for/by an Employee Benefit Trust on Accounting for Business Combinations	Resolved by FAS-141.	—

93-3

Plan Assets under FASB Statement No. 106	Postemployment and Postretirement Benefits Other Than Pensions, ch. 32	710, Compensation— General 715, Compensation— Retirement Benefits

93-4

Accounting for Regulatory Assets	See Subsequent Development in Issue 92-12. Postemployment and Postretirement Benefits Other Than Pensions, ch. 32.	980, Regulated Operations

93-5

Accounting for Environmental Liabilities	Incorporated in and nullified by SOP 96-1.	—

93-6

Accounting for Multiple-Year Retrospectively Rated Contracts by Ceding and Assuming Enterprises	Not discussed in this Guide.	—

93-7

Uncertainties Related to Income Taxes in a Purchase Business Combination	Nullified by FAS-141(R).	—

93-8

Accounting for the Sale and Leaseback of an Asset That Is Leased to Another Party	Leases, ch. 26	840, Leases

93-9

Application of FASB Statement No. 109 in Foreign Financial Statements Restated for General Price-Level Changes	Income Taxes, ch. 20	830, Foreign Currency Matters

93-10

Accounting for Dual Currency Bonds	Resolved by FAS-133.	—

93-11

Accounting for Barter Transactions Involving Barter Credits	Nonmonetary Transactions, ch. 28	845, Nonmonetary Transactions

93-12

Recognition and Measurement of the Tax Benefit of Excess Tax-Deductible Goodwill Resulting from a Retroactive Change in Tax Law	Income Taxes, ch. 20	—

93-13

Effect of a Retroactive Change in Enacted Tax Rates That Is Included in Income from Continuing Operations	Income Taxes, ch. **20**	740, Income Taxes

93-14

Accounting for Multiple-Year Retrospectively Rated Insurance Contracts by Insurance Enterprises and Other Enterprises	Not discussed in this Guide.	450, Contingencies 720, Other Expenses

93-15 Not used. —

93-16

Application of FASB Statement No. 109 to Basis Differences within Foreign Subsidiaries That Meet the Indefinite Reversal Criterion of APB Opinion No. 23	Income Taxes, ch. **20**	740, Income Taxes 830, Foreign Currency Matters

93-17

Recognition of Deferred Tax Assets for a Parent Company's Excess Tax Basis in the Stock of a Subsidiary That Is Accounted for as a Discontinued Operation	Income Taxes, ch. **20**	740, Income Taxes

93-18

Recognition of Impairment for an Investment in a Collateralized Mortgage Obligation Instrument or in a Mortgage-Backed Interest-Only Certificate	Superseded by Issue 99-20.	—

94-1

Accounting for Tax Benefits Resulting from Investments in Affordable Housing Projects	Real Estate Transactions, ch. **33**	323, Investments—Debt and Securities

94-2

Treatment of Minority Interests in Certain Real Estate Investment Trusts	Nullified by FAS-160.	323, Investments—Debt and Securities

94-3

Liability Recognition for Certain Employee Termination Benefits and Other Costs to Exit an Activity (including Certain Costs Incurred in a Restructuring)	Nullified by FAS-146.	—

94-4

Classification of an Investment in a Mortgage-Backed Interest-Only Certificate as Held-to-Maturity	Resolved by FAS-125.	—

94-5

Determination of What Constitutes All Risks and Rewards and No Significant Unresolved Contingencies in a Sale of Mortgage Loan Servicing Rights under Issue No. 89-5	Superseded by Issue 95-5.	—

95-8

Accounting for Contingent Consideration Paid to the Shareholders of an Acquired Enterprise in a Purchase Business Combination	Nullified by FAS-141(R).	—

95-9

Accounting for Tax Effects of Dividends in France in Accordance with FASB Statement No. 109	Income Taxes, ch. 20	740, Income Taxes

95-10

Accounting for Tax Credits Related to Dividend Payments in Accordance with FASB Statement No. 109	Income Taxes, ch. 20	740, Income Taxes

95-11

Accounting for Derivative Instruments Containing both a Written Option-Based Component and a Forward-Based Component	Resolved by FAS-133.	—

95-12

Pooling of Interests with a Common Investment in a Joint Venture	Nullified by FAS-141.	—

95-13

Classification of Debt Issue Costs in the Statement of Cash Flows	Cash Flow Statement, ch. 8	230, Statement of Cash Flows

95-14

Recognition of Liabilities in Anticipation of a Business Combination	Nullified by FAS-146.	—

95-15

Recognition of Gain or Loss When a Binding Contract Requires a Debt Extinguishment to Occur at a Future Date for a Specified Amount	Superseded by Issue 96-19.	—

95-16

Accounting for Stock Compensation Arrangements with Employer Loan Features under APB Opinion No. 25	Nullified by FAS-123(R), except for nonpublic entities under the scope of paragraph 83 of FAS-123(R).	—

95-17

Accounting for Modifications to an Operating Lease That Do Not Change the Lease Classification	Leases, ch. 26	840, Leases

95-18

Accounting and Reporting for a Discontinued Business Segment When the Measurement Date Occurs after the Balance Sheet Date but before the Issuance of Financial Statements	Nullified by FAS-144.	—

95-19

Determination of the Measurement Date for the Market Price of Securities Issued in Purchase Business Combination	Codified in Issue 99-12.	—

95-20

Measurement in the Consolidated Financial Statements of a Parent of the Tax Effects Related to the Operations of a Foreign Subsidiary That Receives Tax Credits Related to Dividend Payments	Income Taxes, ch. 20	740, Income Taxes

95-21

Accounting for Assets to Be Disposed of Acquired in a Purchase Business Combination	Resolved by FAS-144.	—

95-22

Balance Sheet Classification of Borrowings Outstanding under Revolving Credit Agreements That Include both a Subjective Acceleration Clause and a Lock-Box Arrangement	Balance Sheet Classification and Related Display Issues, ch. **4**	470, Debt

95-23

The Treatment of Certain Site Restoration/Environmental Exit Costs When Testing a Long-Lived Asset for Impairment	Impairment of Long-Lived Assets, ch. **19**	360, Property, Plant, and Equipment

96-1

Sale of Put Options on Issuer's Stock That Require Or Permit Cash Settlement	Codified in Issue 00-19.	—

96-2

Impairment Recognition When a Nonmonetary Asset Is Exchanged or Is Distributed to Owners and Is Accounted for at the Asset's Recorded Amount	Codified in Issue 01-2.	—

96-3

Accounting for Equity Instruments That Are Issued for Consideration Other Than Employee Services under FASB Statement No. 123	Superseded by Issue 96-18.	—

96-4

Accounting for Reorganizations Involving a Non–Pro Rata Split-off of Certain Nonmonetary Assets to Owners	Codified in Issue 01-2.	—

96-5

Recognition of Liabilities for Contractual Termination Benefits or Changing Benefit Plan Assumptions in Anticipation of a Business Combination	Business Combinations, ch. **6**	420, Exit or Disposal Cost Obligations 450, Contingencies 710, Compensation—General

		712, Compensation—Nonretirement Postemployment Benefits 715, Retirement Benefits
96-6		
Accounting for the Film and Software Costs Associated with Developing Entertainment and Educational Software Products	Computer Software, ch. **10**	985, Software
96-7		
Accounting for Deferred Taxes on In-Process Research and Development Activities Acquired in a Purchase Business Combination	Nullified by FAS-141(R).	—
96-8		
Accounting for a Business Combination When the Issuing Company Has Targeted Stock	Nullified by FAS-141.	—
96-9		
Classification of Inventory Markdowns and Other Costs Associated with a Restructuring	Results of Operations, ch. **35**	330, Inventory 420, Exit or Disposal Cost Obligations
96-10		
Impact of Certain Transactions on the Held-to-Maturity Classification under FASB Statement No. 115	Investments in Debt and Equity Securities, ch. **25**	320, Investments—Debt and Equity Securities
96-11		
Accounting for Forward Contracts and Purchased Options to Acquire Securities Covered by FASB Statement No. 115	Investments in Debt and Equity Securities, ch. **25**	320, Investments—Debt and Equity Securities 815, Derivatives and Hedging
96-12		
Recognition of Interest Income and Balance Sheet Classification of Structured Notes	Financial Instruments, ch. **17**	320, Investments—Debt and Equity Securities 835, Interest
96-13		
Accounting for Derivative Financial Instruments Indexed to, and Potentially Settled in, a Company's Own Stock	Codified in Issue 00-19.	—
96-14		
Accounting for the Costs Associated with Modifying Computer Software for the Year 2000	No longer useful.	—
96-15		
Accounting for the Effects of Changes in Foreign Currency Exchange Rates on Foreign-Currency-Denominated Available-for-Sale Debt Securities	Foreign Operations and Exchange, ch. **18**	320, Investments—Debt and Equity Securities 830, Foreign Currency Matters

97-3

Accounting for Fees and Costs Associated with Loan Syndications and Loan Participations after the Issuance of FASB Statement No. 125	Transfer and Servicing of Financial Assets, ch. **40**	310, Receivables 860, Transfers and Servicing

97-4

Deregulation of the Pricing of Electricity— Issues Related to the Application of FASB Statements No. 71 and 101	Not discussed.	980, Regulated Operations

97-5

Accounting for the Delayed Receipt of Option Shares upon Exercise under APB Opinion No. 25	Nullified by FAS-123(R), except for entities under the scope of paragraph 83 of FAS-123(R).	—

97-6

Application of Issue No. 96-20 to Qualifying Special-Purpose Entities Receiving Transferred Financial Assets Prior to the Effective Date of FASB Statement No. 125	Nullified by FAS-140.	—

97-7

Accounting for Hedges of the Foreign Currency Risk Inherent in an Available for-Sale Marketable Equity Security	Foreign Operations and Exchange, ch. **18**	—

97-8

Accounting for Contingent Consideration Issued in a Purchase Business Combination	Nullified by FAS-141(R).	—

97-9

Effect on Pooling-of-Interests Accounting of Certain Contingently Exercisable Options or Other Equity Instruments	Nullified by FAS-141.	—

97-10

The Effect of Lessee Involvement in Asset Construction	Leases, ch. **26**	840, Leases

97-11

Accounting for Internal Costs Relating to Real Estate Property Acquisitions	Capitalization and Expense Recognition Concepts, ch. **7**	970, Real Estate—General

97-12

Accounting for Increased Share Authorizations in an IRS Section 423 Employee Stock Purchase Plan under APB Opinion No. 25	Nullified by FAS-123(R), except for nonpublic entities under the scope of paragraph 83 of FAS-123(R).	—

97-13

Accounting for Costs Incurred in Connection with a Consulting Contract or an Internal Project That Combines Business Process Reengineering and Information Technology Transformation	Capitalization and Expense Recognition Concepts, ch. **7**	720, Other Expenses

97-14

Accounting for Deferred Compensation Arrangements Where Amounts Earned Are Held in a Rabbi Trust and Invested	Consolidated Financial Statements, ch. **11**	710, Compensation— General 810, Consolidation

97-15

Accounting for Contingency Arrangements Based on Security Prices in a Purchase Business Combination	Nullified by FAS-141(R).	—

98-1

Valuation of Debt Assumed in a Purchase Business Combination	Nullified by FAS-141(R).	—

98-2

Accounting by a Subsidiary or Joint Venture for an Investment in the Stock of Its Parent Company or Joint Venture Partner	Stockholders' Equity, ch. **39**	—

98-3

Determining Whether a Nonmonetary Transaction Involves Receipt of Productive Assets or of a Business	Nullified by FAS-141(R).	—

98-4

Accounting by a Joint Venture for Business Received at Its Formation	Removed from EITF agenda; to be addressed in FASB's New Basis project.	845, Nonmonetary Transactions

98-5

Accounting for Convertible Securities with Beneficial Conversion Features or Contingently Adjustable Conversion Ratios	Convertible Debt and Debt with Warrants, ch. **13**	470, Debt 505, Equity

98-6

Investor's Accounting for an Investment in a Limited Partnership When the Investor Is the Sole General Partner and the Limited Partners Have Certain Approval or Veto Rights	No consensus.	—

98-7

Accounting for Exchanges of Similar Equity Method Investments	Codified in Issue 01-2.	—

98-8

Accounting for Transfers of Investments That Are in Substance Real Estate	Real Estate Transactions, ch. **33**	360, Property, Plant, and Equipment

98-9

Accounting for Contingent Rent	Leases, ch. **26**	450, Contingencies 840, Leases

98-10

Accounting for Contracts Involved in Energy Trading and Risk Management Activities	Superseded by Issue 02-3.	—

98-11

Accounting for Acquired Temporary Differences in Certain Purchase Transactions That Are Not Accounted for as Business Combinations	Income Taxes, ch. **20**	740, Income Taxes

98-12

Application of Issue No. 96-13 to Forward Equity Sales Transactions	Nullified by FAS-150.	—

98-13

Accounting by an Equity Method Investor for Investee Losses When the Investor Has Loans to and Investments in Other Securities of the Investee	Equity Method, ch. **15**	320, Investments—Debt and Equity Securities 323, Investments—Equity Method and Joint Ventures

98-14

Debtor's Accounting for Changes in Line-of-Credit or Revolving-Debt Arrangements	Extinguishment of Debt, ch. **16**	470, Debt

98-15

Structured Notes Acquired for a Specified Investment Strategy	Financial Instruments, ch. **17**	320, Investments—Debt and Equity Securities

99-1

Accounting for Debt Convertible into the Stock of a Consolidated Subsidiary	Convertible Debt and Debt with Warrants, ch. **13**	470, Debt

99-2

Accounting for Weather Derivatives	Financial Instruments, ch. **17**	460, Guarantees 815, Derivatives and Hedging

99-3

Application of Issue No. 96-13 to Derivative Instruments with Multiple Settlement Alternatives	Codified in Issue 00-19.	—

99-4

Accounting for Stock Received from the Demutualization of a Mutual Insurance Company	Nonmonetary Transactions, ch. **28**	325, Investments—Other

99-5

Accounting for Pre-Production Costs Related to Long-Term Supply Arrangements	Capitalization and Expense Recognition Concepts, ch. **7**	340, Deferred Costs and Other Assets 460, Guarantees 730, Research and Development

99-6

Impact of Acceleration Provisions in Grants Made between Initiation and Consummation of a Pooling-of-Interests Business Combination	Nullified by FAS-141.	—

99-7

Accounting for an Accelerated Share Repurchase Program	Stockholders' Equity, ch. **39**	260, Earnings per Share 505, Equity

99-8

| Accounting for Transfers of Assets That Are Derivative Instruments but That Are Not Financial Assets | Transfer and Servicing of Financial Assets, ch. **40** | 815, Derivatives and Hedging 860, Transfers and Servicing |

99-9

| Effect of Derivative Gains and Losses on the Capitalization of Interest | Financial Instruments, ch. **17** | 815, Derivatives and Hedging |

99-10

| Percentage Used to Determine the Amount of Equity Method Losses | Equity Method, ch. **15** | 323, Investments—Equity Method and Joint Ventures |

99-11

| Subsequent Events Caused by Year 2000 | No longer relevant. | — |

99-12

| Determination of the Measurement Date for the Market Price of Acquirer Securities Issued in a Purchase Business Combination | Nullified by FAS-141(R). | — |

99-13

| Application of Issue No. 97-10 and FASB Interpretation No. 23 to Entities That Enter into Leases with Governmental Entities | Leases, ch. **26** | 840, Leases |

99-14

| Recognition of Losses on Firmly Committed Executory Contracts | Removed from EITF agenda. | — |

99-15

| Accounting for Decreases in Deferred Tax Asset Valuation Allowances Established in a Purchase Business Combination As a Result of a Change in Tax Regulations | Nullified by FAS-141(R). | — |

99-16

| Accounting for Transactions with Elements of Research and Development Arrangements | Research and Development, ch. **34** | 810, Consolidation |

99-17

| Accounting for Advertising Barter Transactions | Nonmonetary Transactions, ch. **28** | 605, Revenue Recognition |

99-18

| Effect on Pooling-of-Interests Accounting of Contracts Indexed to a Company's Own Stock | Resolved by FAS-141. | — |

99-19

| Reporting Revenue Gross as a Principal versus Net as an Agent | Revenue Recognition, ch. **36** | 605, Revenue Recognition |

99-20

Recognition of Interest Income and Impairment on Certain Investments	Transfer and Servicing of Financial Assets, ch. **40**	310, Receivables 320, Investments—Debt and Equity Securities 325, Investments—Other 835, Interest

00-1

Balance Sheet and Income Statement Display under the Equity Method for Investments in Certain Partnerships and Other Unincorporated Noncontrolled Ventures	Equity Method, ch. **15**	323, Investments—Equity Method and Joint Ventures 810, Consolidation 910, Contractors—Construction 930, Extractive Activities—Mining 932, Extractive Activities—Oil and Gas

00-2

Accounting for Web Site Development Costs Capitalization or Expense Recognition	Capitalization and Expense Recognition Concepts, ch. **7**	350, Intangibles—Goodwill and Other

00-3

Application of AICPA Statement of Position 97-2 to Arrangements That Include the Right to Use Software Stored on Another Entity's Hardware	Computer Software, ch. **10**	985, Software

00-4

Majority Owner's Accounting for the Minority Interest in a Subsidiary and a Derivative	Financial Instruments, ch. **17**	460, Guarantees 480, Distinguishing Liabilities from Equity

00-5

Determining Whether a Nonmonetary Transaction Is an Exchange of Similar Productive Assets	Codified in Issue 01-2.	—

00-6

Accounting for Freestanding Derivative Financial Instruments Indexed to, and Potentially Settled in, the Stock of a Consolidated Subsidiary	Financial Instruments, ch. **17**	460, Guarantees 810, Consolidation 815, Derivatives and Hedging

00-7

Application of Issue No. 96-13 to Equity Derivative Transactions That Contain Certain Provisions That Require Net Cash Settlement If Certain Events outside the Control of the Issuer Occur	Codified in Issue 00-19.	—

00-8

Accounting by a Grantee for an Equity Instrument to Be Received in Conjunction with Providing Goods or Services	Stock-Based Payments, ch. **38**	505, Equity 845, Nonmonetary Transactions

00-9

Classification of a Gain or Loss from a Hedge of Debt That Is Extinguished	Extinguishment of Debt, ch. **16**	815, Derivatives and Hedging

00-10

Accounting for Shipping and Handling Fees and Costs	Revenue Recognition, ch. **36**	605, Revenue Recognition

00-11

Meeting the Ownership Transfer Requirements of FASB Statement No. 13 for Leases of Real Estate	Leases, ch. **26**	840, Leases

00-12

Accounting for Stock-Based Compensation Granted by an Investor to Employees of an Equity Method Investee	Equity Method, ch. **15**	323, Investments—Equity Method and Joint Ventures 505, Equity 718, Compensation—Stock Compensation

00-13

Determining Whether Equipment Is "Integral Equipment" Subject to FASB Statements No. 66 and No. 98	Real Estate Transactions, ch. **33**	360, Property, Plant, and Equipment

00-14

Accounting for Certain Sales Incentives	Codified in Issue 01-9.	—

00-15

Classification in the Statement of Cash Flows of the Income Tax Benefit Received by a Company upon Exercise of a Nonqualified Employee Stock Options	Nullified by FAS-123(R), except for nonpublic entities under the scope of paragraph 83 of FAS-123(R).	—

00-16

Recognition and Measurement of Employer Payroll Taxes on Employee Stock-Based Compensation	Stock-Based Payments, ch. **38**	718, Compensation—Stock Compensation

00-17

Measuring the Fair Value of Energy-Related Contracts in Applying EITF Issue No. 98-10, "Accounting for Contracts Involved in EnergyTrading and Risk Management Activities"	Superseded by Issue 02-3.	—

00-18

Accounting Recognition for Certain Transactions Involving Equity Instruments Granted to Other Than Employees	Stock-Based Payments, ch. **38**	505, Equity

00-19

Determination of Whether Share Settlement is within the Control of the Issuer for Purposes of Applying Issue 96-13	Earnings per Share, ch. **14** Financial Instruments, ch. **17**	460, Guarantees 480, Distinguishing Liabilities from Equity 505, Equity 815, Derivatives and Hedging

00-20

Accounting for Costs incurred to Acquire or Originate Information for Database Content and Other Collections Information	No longer relevant.	—

00-21

Accounting for Revenue Arrangements with Multiple Elements	Removed from the EITF agenda.	605, Revenue Recognition

00-22

Accounting for "Points" and Certain Other Time-Based Sales Incentive Offers, and Offers for Free Products or Services to Be Delivered in the Future	Removed from EITF agenda.	—

00-23

Issues Related to the Accounting for Stock Compensation under APB Opinion No. 25, *Accounting for Stock Issued to Employees*, and FASB Interpretation No. 44, *Accounting for Certain Transactions Involving Stock Compensation*	Nullified by FAS-123(R), except for nonpublic entities under the scope of paragraph 83 of FAS-123(R).	—

00-24

Revenue Recognition: Sales Arrangements That Include Specified-Price Trade-in Rights	Removed from EITF agenda.	—

00-25

Vendor Income Statement Consideration from a Vendor to a Retailer	Codified in Issue 01-9.	—

00-26

Recognition by a Seller of Losses on Firmly Committed Executory Contracts	Removed from EITF agenda.	—

00-27

Application of Issue No. 98-5 to Certain Convertible Instruments	Convertible Debt and Debt with Warrants, ch. **13**	260, Earnings per Share 470, Debt 505, Equity

01-1

Accounting for Convertible Instrument Granted or Issued to a Nonemployee for Goods or Services and Cash	Stock-Based Payments, ch. **38**	470, Debt

01-2

Interpretations of APB Opinion No. 29, Accounting for Nonmonetary Transactions	Nonmonetary Transactions, ch. **28**	845, Nonmonetary Transactions

01-3

Accounting in a Purchase Business Combination for Deferred Revenue of an Acquiree	Nullified by FAS-141(R).	—

01-4

Accounting for Sales of Fractional Interests in Equipment	Removed from EITF agenda.	—

01-5

Application of FASB Statement No. 52, *Foreign Currency Translation,* to an Investment Being Evaluated for Impairment That Will Be Disposed Of	Foreign Operations and Exchange, ch. **18**	830, Foreign Currency Matters

01-6

The Meaning of "Indexed to a Company's Own Stock"	Financial Instruments, ch. **17**	815, Derivatives and Hedging

01-7

Creditor's Accounting for a Modification or Exchange of Debt Instruments	Extinguishment of Debt, ch. **16**	310, Receivables

01-8

Determining Whether an Arrangement Is a Lease	Leases, ch. **26**	440, Commitments 815, Derivatives and Hedging 840, Leases

01-9

Accounting for Consideration Given by a Vendor to a Customer or a Reseller of the Vendor's Products	Revenue Recognition, ch. **36**	330, Inventory 605, Revenue Recognition

01-10

Accounting for the Impact of the Terrorist Attacks of September 11, 2001	Results of Operations, ch. **35**	—

01-11

Application of EITF Issue No. 00-19, "Accounting for Derivative Financial Instruments Indexed to, and Potentially Settled in, a Company's Own Stock," to a Contemporaneous Forward Purchase Contract and Written Put Option	Resolved by FAS-150.	—

01-12

The Impact of the Requirements of FASB Statement No. 133, *Accounting for Derivative Instruments and Hedging Activities,* on Residual Value Guarantees in Connection with a Lease	Leases, ch. **26**	460, Guarantees 815, Derivatives and Hedging 840, Leases

01-13

Income Statement Display of Business Interruption Insurance Recoveries	Results of Operations, ch. **35**	225, Income Statement 450, Contingencies

01-14

Income Statement Characterization of Reimbursements Received for "Out-of-Pocket" Expenses Incurred	Results of Operations, ch. **35**	605, Revenue Recognition

02-2

| When Certain Contracts That Meet the Definition of Financial Instruments Should Be Combined for Accounting Purposes | Removed from EITF agenda. Partially resolved by FAS-150. | — |

02-3

| Issues Involved in Accounting for Derivative Contracts Held for Trading Purposes and Contracts Involved in Energy Trading and Risk Management | Financial Instruments, ch. **17** | 815, Derivatives and Hedging 932, Extractive Activities— Oil and Gas |

02-4

| Debtor's Accounting for a Modification or an Exchange of Debt Instruments in accordance with FASB Statement No. 15, *Accounting by Debtors and Creditors for Troubled Debt Restructurings* | No consensus. | 470, Debt |

02-5

| Definition of "Common Control" in Relation to FASB Statement No. 141, *Business Combinations* | Business Combinations, ch. **6** | — |

02-6

| Classification of Cash Flows of Payments Made to Settle an Asset Retirement Obligation within the Scope of FASB Statement No. 143, *Accounting for Asset Retirement Obligations* | Cash Flow Statement, ch. **8** | 230, Statement of Cash Flows |

02-7

| Unit of Accounting for Testing Impairment of Indefinite-Lived Intangible Assets | Impairment of Long-Lived Assets, ch. **19** | 350, Intangibles— Goodwill and Other |

02-8

| Accounting for Options Granted to Employees in Unrestricted, Publicly Traded Shares of an Unrelated Entity | Stock-Based Payments, ch. **38** | 815, Derivatives and Hedging |

02-9

| Accounting for Changes That Result in a Transferor Regaining Control of Financial Assets Sold | Transfer and Servicing of Financial Assets, ch. **40** | 860, Transfers and Servicing |

02-10

| Determining Whether a Debtor Is Legally Released as Primary Obligor When the Debtor Becomes Secondarily Liable Under the Original Obligation | Removed from EITF agenda. | — |

02-11

| Accounting for Reverse Spinoffs | Stockholders' Equity, ch. **39** | 505, Equity |

02-12

| Permitted Activities of a Qualifying Special-Purpose Entity in Issuing Beneficial Interests under FASB Statement No. 140, | Removed from EITF agenda. | — |

03-5

Applicability of AICPA Statement of Position 97-2, *Software Revenue Recognition,* to Non-Software Deliverables in an Arrangement Containing More-Than-Incidental Software	Computer Software, ch. **10**	985, Software

03-6

Participating Securities and the Two-Class Method under FASB Statement No. 128, *Earnings per Share*	Earnings per Share, ch. **14**	260, Earnings per Share

03-7

Accounting for the Settlement of the Equity-Settled Portion of a Convertible Debt Instrument That Permits or Requires the Conversion Spread to Be Settled in Stock (Instrument C of Issue 90-19)	Nullified by FSP APB-14-1.	—

03-8

Accounting for Claims-Made Insurance and Retroactive Insurance Contracts by the Insured Entity	Contingencies, Risks, and Uncertainties, ch. **12**	720, Other Expenses

03-9

Determination of the Useful Life of Renewable Intangible Assets under FASB Statement No. 142	Removed from EITF agenda.	—

03-10

Application EITF Issue No. 02-16, "Accounting By a Customer (Including a Reseller) for Certain Consideration Received from a Vender," by Resellers to Sales Incentives Offered to Consumers by Manufacturers	Revenue Recognition, ch. **36**	605, Revenue Recognition

03-11

Reporting Realized Gains and Losses on Derivative Instruments That Are Subject to FASB Statement No. 133, *Accounting for Derivative Instruments and Hedging Activities,* and Not "Held for Trading Purposes" as Defined in EITF Issue No. 02-3, "Issues Involved in Accounting for Derivative Contracts Held for Trading Purposes and Contracts Involved in Energy Trading and Risk Management Activities"	Financial Instruments, ch. **17**	815, Derivatives and Hedging

03-12

Impact of FASB Interpretation No. 45 on Issue No. 95-1	Revenue Recognition, ch. **36**	460, Guarantees

03-13

Applying the conditions in Paragraph 42 of FASB Statement No. 144 in Determining Whether to Report Discontinued Operations	Results of Operations, ch. **35**	205, Presentation of Financial Statements

03-14

| Participants' Accounting for Emissions Allowances under a "Cap and Trade" Program | Removed from EITF agenda. | — |

03-15 — Not used. —

03-16

| Accounting for Investments in Limited Liability Companies | Equity Method, ch. **15** | 323, Investments—Equity Method and Joint Ventures 956, Limited Liability Entities |

03-17

| Subsequent Accounting for Executory Contracts That Have Been Recognized on an Entity's Balance Sheet | Removed from EITF agenda. | — |

04-1

| Accounting for Pre-existing Contractual Relationships between the Parties to a Purchase Business Combination | Nullified by FAS-141(R). | — |

04-2

| Whether Mineral Rights Are Tangible or Intangible Assets and Related Issues | Nullified by FAS-141(R). | — |

04-3

| Mining Assets: Impairment and Business Combinations | Business Combinations, ch. **6** | 930, Extractive Activities—Mining |

04-4

| Allocation of Goodwill to Reporting Units for a Mining Enterprise | Removed from EITF agenda. | — |

04-5

| Investor's Accounting for an Investment in a Limited Partnership When the Investor Is the Sole General Partner and the Limited Partners Have Certain Rights | Consolidated Financial Statements, ch. **11** | 810, Consolidation |

04-6

| Accounting for Stripping Costs Incurred during Production in the Mining Industry | Inventory, ch. **24** | 930, Extractive Activities—Mining |

04-7

| Determining Whether an Interest Is a Variable Interest In a Potential Variable Interest Entity | Removed from EITF agenda. | — |

See FSP FIN-46(R)-6.

04-8

| The Effect of Contingently Convertible Debt on Diluted Earnings per Share | Earnings per Share, ch. **14** | 260, Earnings per Share |

04-9

Accounting for Suspended Well Costs	Resolved by FSP FAS 19-1.	—

04-10

Determining Whether to Aggregate Operating Segments That Do Not Meet the Quantitative Thresholds	Segment Reporting, ch. **37**	280, Segment Reporting

04-11

Accounting in a Business Combination for Deferred Postcontract Customer Support Revenue of a Software Vendor	Removed from EITF agenda.	—

04-12

Determining Whether Equity-Based Compensation Awards Are Participating Securities	Removed from EITF agenda.	—

04-13

Accounting for Purchases and Sales of Inventory with the Same Counterparty	Nonmonetary Transactions, ch. **28**	845, Nonmonetary Transactions

05-1

Accounting for the Conversion of an Instrument That Becomes Convertible upon the Issuer's Exercise of a Call Option	Convertible Debt and Debt with Warrants, ch. **13**	470, Debt

05-2

The Meaning of "Conventional Convertible Debt Instrument" in EITF Issue 00-19, "Accounting for Derivative Financial Instruments Indexed to and Potentially Settled in, a Company's Own Stock"	Financial Instruments, ch. **18**	815, Derivatives and Hedging

05-3

Accounting for Rental Costs Incurred During the Construction Period	Removed from EITF agenda. See FSP FAS 13-1.	—

05-4

The Effect of a Liquidated Damages Clause on a Freestanding Financial Instrument Subject to EITF Issue No. 00-19, "Accounting for Derivative Financial Instruments Indexed to, and Potentially Settled in, a Company's Own Stock"	Removed from EITF's agenda.	—

05-5

Accounting for Early Retirement or Postemployment Programs with Specific Features (such as Term Specified in Altersteilzeit [ATZ] Early Retirement Arrangements)	Pension Plans—Employers ch. **29**	715, Compensation—Retirement Benefits

05-6

Determining the Amortization Period for Leasehold Improvements	Leases, ch. **26**	840, Leases

05-7

Accounting for Modifications to Conversion Options Embedded in Debt Instruments and Related Issues	Superseded by Issue 06-6.	—

05-8

Income Tax Consequences of Issuing Convertible Debt with a Beneficial Conversion Feature	Income Taxes, ch. **20**	740, Income Taxes

06-1

Accounting for Consideration Given by a Service Provider to Manufacturers or Resellers of Equipment Necessary for an End-Customer to Receive Service from the Service Provider	Revenue Recognition, ch. **36**	605, Revenue Recognition

06-2

Accounting for Sabbatical Leave and Other Similar Benefits Pursuant to FASB Statement No. 43,"Accounting for Compensated Absences"	Results of Operations, ch. **35**	710, Compensation—General

06-3

How Taxes Collected from Customers and Remitted to Governmental Authorities Should be Presented in the Income Statement (That Is, Gross versus Net Presentation)	Results of Operations, ch. **35**	605, Revenue Recognition

06-4

Accounting for Deferred Compensation and Postretirement Benefit Aspects of Endorsement Split-Dollar Life Insurance Arrangements	Postemployment and Postretirement Benefits Other Than Pensions, ch. **32**	715, Compensation—Retirement Benefits

06-5

Accounting for Purchases of Life Insurance—Determining the Amount That Could Be Realized in Accordance with FASB Technical Bulletin No. 85-4	Balance Sheet Classification, ch. **4**	325, Investments—Other

06-6

Debtor's Accounting for a Modification (or Exchange) of Convertible Debt	Extinguishment of Debt, ch. **16**	470, Debt

06-7

Issuer's Accounting for a Previously Bifurcated Conversion Option in a Convertible Debt Instrument When the Conversion Option No Longer Meets the Bifurcation Criteria in FASB Statement No. 133, *Accounting for Derivative Instruments and Hedging Activities*	Convertible Debt and Debt with Warrants, ch. **13**	470, Debt 815, Derivatives and Hedging

06-8

Applicability of the Assessment of a Buyer's Continuing Investment under FASB Statement No. 66, *Accounting for Sales of Real Estate,* for Sales of Condominiums	Real Estate Transactions, ch. 33	360, Property, Plant, and Equipment

06-9

Reporting a Change in (or the Elimination of) a Previously Existing Difference between the Fiscal Year-End of a Parent Company and That of a Consolidated Entity or between the Reporting Period of an Investor and That of an Equity Method Investee	Accounting Changes, ch. 1	810, Consolidation

06-10

Accounting for Deferred Compensation and Postretirement Benefit Aspects of Collateral Assignment Split-Dollar Life Insurance Arrangements	Postemployment and Postretirement Benefits Other Than Pensions ch. 32	715, Compensation—Retirement Benefits

06-11

Accounting for Income Tax Benefits of Dividends on Share-Based Payment Awards	Income Taxes, ch. **20**	—

06-12

Accounting for Physical Commodity Inventories for Entities within the Scope of the AICPA Audit and Accounting Guide, *Brokers and Dealers in Securities*	Under discussion.	—

07-1

Accounting for Collaborative Arrangements Related to the Development and Commercialization of Intellectual Property	Results of Operations, ch. **35**	—

07-2

Accounting for Convertible Debt Instruments That Require or Permit Partial Cash Settlement upon Conversion	Removed from EITF's agenda.	—

07-3

Accounting for Advance Payments for Goods or Services to Be Used in Future Research and Development Activities	Research and Development, ch. **34**	—

07-4

Application of the Two-Class Method under FASB Statement No. 128, *Earnings per Share,* to Master Limited Partnerships	Earnings per Share, ch. **13**	—

07-5

| Determining Whether an Instrument (or Embedded Features) Is Indexed to an Entity's Own Stock | Financial Instruments, ch. **17** | — |

07-6

| Accounting for the Sale of Real Estate Subject to the Requirements of FASB Statement No. 66, *Accounting for Sales of Real Estate,* When the Agreement Includes a Buy-Sell Clause | Real Estate Transactions, ch. **33** | — |

08-1

| Revenue Recognition for a Single Unit of Accounting | Under discussion. | — |

08-2

| Lessor Revenue Recognition for Maintenance Services | Removed from the EITF's agenda. | — |

08-3

| Accounting by Lessees for Maintenance Deposits under Lease Arrangements | Leases, ch. **26** | — |

08-4

| Transition Guidance for Conforming Changes to Issue No. 98-5 | Convertible Debt and Debt with Warrants, ch. **13** | — |

08-5

| Issuer's Accounting for Liabilities Measured at Fair Value with a Third-Party Guarantee | Fair Value, ch. **16** | — |

EITF/FASB/SEC STAFF ANNOUNCEMENTS

ORIGINAL PRONOUNCEMENT	2009 *GAAP GUIDE LEVELS B, C, AND D* REFERENCE	FASB ACCOUNTING STANDARDS CODIFICATION (ASC) TOPIC
D-1		
Implications and Implementation of an EITF Consensus	Accounting Changes, ch. **1**	—
D-2		
Applicability of FASB Statement No. 65 to Savings and Loan Associations	Not discussed in this Guide.	—
D-3		
International Loan Swaps	No longer relevant.	—
D-4		
Argentine Government Guarantee of U.S. Dollar-Denominated Loans to the Argentine Private Sector	Not discussed.	—

D-5

Extraordinary Treatment Related to Abandoned Nuclear Power Plants	Resolved by FAS-90.	—

D-6

Income Capital Certificates and Permanent Income Capital Certificates	No longer relevant.	—

D-7

Adjustment of Deferred Taxes to Reflect Change in Income Tax Rate	Resolved by FAS-109.	—

D-8

Accruing Bad-Debt Expense at Inception of a Lease	Leases, ch. **26**	—

D-9

Lessor Accounting under FASB Statement No. 91	Resolved by FAS-98.	—

D-10

Required Use of Interest Method in Recognizing Interest Income	Financial Instruments, ch. **17**	835, Interest

D-11

Impact of Stock Market Decline	Investments in Debt and Equity Securities, ch. **25**	—

D-12

Foreign Currency Translation—Selection of Exchange Rate When Trading Is Temporarily Suspended	Foreign Operations and Exchange, ch. **18**	830, Foreign Currency Matters

D-13

Transfers of Receivables in Which Risk of Foreign Currency Fluctuation is Retained	Superseded by FAS-125.	—

D-14

Transactions Involving Special-Purpose Entities	Nullified by FIN-46 and FIN-46(R).	—

D-15

Earnings-per-Share Presentation for Securities Not Specifically Covered by APB Opinion No. 15	Rescinded by SEC staff because FAS-128 issued.	—

D-16

Hedging Foreign Currency Risks of Future Net Income, Revenues, or Costs	Nullified by FAS-133.	—

D-17

Continued Applicability of the FASB Special Report on Implementation of Statement 96	Nullified by FAS-109.	—

D-18

Accounting for Compensation Expense If Stock Appreciation Rights Are Cancelled	Nullified by FAS-123(R).	—

D-19

| Impact on Pooling-of-Interests Accounting of Treasury Shares Acquired to Satisfy Conversions in a Leveraged Preferred Stock ESOP | Nullified by FAS-141. | — |

D-20

Disclosure of Components of Deferred Tax Expense — No longer relevant. —

D-21

Phase-in Plans When Two Plants Are Completed at Different Times but Share Common Facilities — Not discussed in this Guide. — 980, Regulated Operations

D-22

Questions Related to the Implementation of FASB Statement No. 105 — Nullified by FAS-133. —

D-23

Subjective Acceleration Clauses and Debt Classification — Balance Sheet Classification and Related Display Issues, ch. **4** — 470, Debt

D-24

Sale-Leaseback Transactions with Continuing Involvement — Leases, ch. **26** — 840, Leases

D-25

Application of APB Opinion No. 10, Paragraph 7, to Market Values Recognized for Off-Balance-Sheet Financial Instruments — Superseded by FIN 39. —

D-26

SEC Disclosure Requirements Prior to Adoption of Standard on Accounting for Postretirement Benefits Other Than Pensions — No longer relevant. —

D-27

Accounting for the Transfer of Excess Pension Assets to a Retiree Health Care Benefits Account — Pension Plans—Employers, ch. **29** — 715, Compensation—Retirement Benefits

D-28

SEC Disclosure Requirements prior to Adoption of Standard on Accounting for Income Taxes — No longer relevant. —

D-29

Implementation of FASB Statement No. 107. — No longer relevant. —

D-30

Adjustment Due to Effect of a Change in Tax Laws or Rates — Income Taxes, ch. **20** — 740, Income Taxes

D-31

Temporary Differences Related to LIFO Inventory and Tax-to-Tax Differences — Income Taxes, ch. **20** — 740, Income Taxes

D-32

Intraperiod Tax Allocation of the TaxEffect of Pretax Income from Continuing Operations	Income Taxes, ch. **20**	740, Income Taxes

D-33

Timing of Recognition of Tax Benefits for Pre-reorganization Temporary Differences and Carryforwards	Income Taxes, ch. **20**	852, Reorganizations

D-34

Accounting for Reinsurance: Questions and Answers about FASB Statement No. 113	Not discussed in this Guide.	—

D-35

FASB Staff Views on Issue No. 93-6, "Accounting for Multiple-Year Retrospectively Rated Contracts by Ceding and Assuming Enterprises"	Not discussed in this Guide.	450, Contingencies

D-36

Selection of Discount Rates Used for Measuring Defined Benefit Pension Obligations and Obligations of Postretirement Benefit Plans Other Than Pensions	Pension Plans—Employers, ch. **29**	715, Compensation— Retirement Benefits

D-37

Classification of In-Substance Foreclosed Assets	Nullified by FAS-114.	—

D-38

Reclassification of Securities in Anticipation of Adoption of FASB Statement No. 115	No longer relevant.	—

D-39

Questions Related to the Implementation of FASB Statement No. 115	Investments in Debt and Equity Securities, ch. **25**	942, Financial Services— Depository and Lending

D-40

Planned Sale of Securities following a Business Combination Expected to Be Accounted for as a Pooling of Interests	Superseded by FAS-141.	—

D-41

Adjustments in Assets and Liabilities for Holding Gains and Losses as Related to the Implementation of FASB Statement No. 115	Investments in Debt and Equity Securities, ch. **25**	320, Investments—Debt and Equity Securities

D-42

The Effect on the Calculation of Earnings per Share for the Redemption or Induced Conversion of Preferred Stock	Earnings per Share, ch. **14**	260, Earnings per Share

D-43

Assurance That a Right of Setoff Is Enforceable in a Bankruptcy under FASB Interpretation No. 39	Results of Operations, ch. **35**	210, Balance Sheet

D-44

Recognition of Other-Than-Temporary Impairment upon the Planned Sale of a Security Whose Cost Exceeds Fair Value	Nullified by FSP FAS 115-1 and FSP FAS 124-1.	—

D-45

Implementation of FASB Statement No. 121 for Assets to Be Disposed Of	Superseded by FAS-144.	—

D-46

Accounting for Limited Partnership Investments	Equity Method, ch. **15**	323, Investments—Equity Method and Joint Ventures

D-47

Accounting for the Refund of Bank Insurance Fund and Savings Association Insurance Fund Premiums	Not discussed in this Guide.	—

D-48

The Applicability of FASB Statement No. 65 to Mortgage-Backed Securities That Are Held to Maturity	Superseded by FAS-125.	—

D-49

Classifying Net Appreciation on Investments of a Donor-Related Endowment Fund	Not discussed in this Guide.	958, Not-for-Profit Entities

D-50

Classification of Gains and Losses from the Termination of an Interest Rate Swap Designated to Commercial Paper	Financial Instruments, ch. **17**	815, Derivatives and Hedging

D-51

The Applicability of FASB Statement No. 115 to Desecuritizations of Financial Assets	Investments in Debt and Equity Securities, ch. **25**	320, Investments—Debt and Equity Securities 860, Transfers and Servicing

D-52

Impact of FASB Statement No. 125 on EITF Issues	No longer necessary.	—

D-53

Computation of Earnings per Share for a Period That Includes a Redemption or an Induced Conversion of a Portion of a Class of Preferred Stock	Earnings per Share, ch. **14**	260, Earnings per Share

D-65

| Maintaining Collateral in Repurchase Agreements and Similar Transactions under FASB Statement No. 125 | Transfer and Servicing of Financial Assets, ch. **40** | — |

D-66

| Effect of a Special-Purpose Entity's Powers to Sell, Exchange, Repledge, or Distribute Transferred Financial Assets under FASB Statement No. 125 | Transfer and Servicing of Financial Assets, ch. **40** | 860, Transfers and Servicing |

D-67

| Isolation of Assets Transferred by Financial Institutions under FASB Statement No. 125 | No longer applies. | — |

D-68

| Accounting by an Equity Method Investor for Investee Losses When the Investor Has Loans to and Investments in Other Securities of an Investee | Equity Method, ch. **15** | 323, Investments—Method and Joint Ventures |

D-69

| Gain Recognition on Transfers of Financial Assets under FASB Statement No. 125 | Transfer and Servicing of Financial Assets, ch. **40** | — |

D-70

| Questions Related to the Implementation of FASB Statement No. 131 | Results of Operations, ch. **35** | 280, Segment Reporting |

D-71

| Accounting Issues Relating to the Introduction of the European Economic and Monetary Union (EMU) | Foreign Operations and Exchange, ch. **18** | — |

D-72

| Effect of Contracts That May Be Settled in Stock or Cash on the Computation of Diluted Earnings per Share | Earnings per Share, ch. **14** | 260, Earnings per Share |

D-73

| Reclassification and Subsequent Sales of Securities in Connection with the Adoption of FASB Statement No. 133 | Resolved by FAS-133. | — |

D-74

| Issues Concerning the Scope of the AICPA Guide on Investment Companies | Not discussed in this Guide. | — |

D-75

| When to Recognize Gains and Losses on Assets Transferred to a Qualifying Special-Purpose Entity | Superseded by FAS-140. | — |

D-76

Accounting by Advisors for Offering Costs Paid on Behalf of Funds, When the Advisor Does Not Receive both 12b-1 Fees and Contingent Deferred Sales Charges	Not discussed in this Guide.	946, Financial Services—Investment Companies

D-77

Accounting for Legal Costs Expected to Be Incurred in Connection with a Loss Contingency	Capitalization and Expense Recognition Concepts, ch. **7**	450, Contingencies

D-78

Accounting for Supervisory Goodwill Litigation Awards and Settlements	Not discussed in this Guide.	—

D-79

Accounting for Retroactive Insurance Contracts Purchased by Entities Other Than Insurance Enterprises	Codified in Issue 03-8.	—

D-80

Application of FASB Statements No. 5 and No. 114 to a Loan Portfolio	Troubled Debt Restructuring, ch. **41**	310, Receivables 450, Contingencies

D-81

Accounting for the Aquisition of Consolidated Businesses	Rescinded by the SEC staff.	—

D-82

Effect of Preferred Stock Dividends Payable in Common Shares on Computation of Income Available to Common Stockholders	Earnings per Share, ch. **14**	260, Earnings per Share

D-83

Accounting for Payroll Taxes Associated with Stock Option Exercises	Stock-Based Payments, ch. **38**	718, Compensation—Stock Compensation

D-84

Accounting for Subsequent Investments in an Investee After Suspension of Equity Method Loss Recognition When an Investor Increases Its Ownership Interest from Significant Influence to Control through a Market Purchase of Voting Securities	Equity Method, ch. **15**	323, Investments—Equity Method and Joint Ventures

D-85

Application of Certain Transition Provisions in SEC Staff Accounting Bulletin No. 101	Revenue Recognition, ch. **36**	—

D-86

Issuance of Financial Statements	Results of Operations, ch. **35**	855, Subsequent Events

D-87

| Determination of the Measurement Date for Consideration Given by the Acquirer in a Business Combination When That Consideration Is Securities Other Than Those Issued by the Acquirer | Nullified by FAS-141(R). | — |

D-88

| Planned Major Maintenance Activities | Resolved by FSP AUG AIR-1. | — |

D-89

| Accounting for Costs of Future Medicare Compliance Audits | Capitalization and Expense Recognition Concepts, ch. 7 | 954, Health Care Entities 958, Not-for-Profit Entities |

D-90

| Grantor Balance Sheet Presentation of Unvested, Forfeitable Equity Instruments Granted to a Nonemployee | Stock-Based Payments, ch. 38 | 505, Equity |

D-91

| Application of APB Opinion No. 25, *Accounting for Stock Issued to Employees*, and FASB Interpretation No. 44, *Accounting for Certain Transaction Involving Stock Compensation*, to an Indirect Repricing of of a Stock Option | Nullified by FAS-123(R). | — |

D-92

| The Effect of FASB Statement No. 135, *Rescission of FASB Statement No. 75 and Technical Corrections*, on the Measurement and Recognition of Net Period Benefit Cost under FASB Statements No. 87, *Employers' Accounting for Pensions*, and No. 106, *Employers' Accounting for Postretirement Benefits Other Than Pensions* | Nullified by FAS-145. | — |

D-93

| Accounting for the Rescission of the Exercise of Employee Stock Options | Nullified by FAS-123(R). | — |

D-94

| Questions and Answers Related to the Implementation of FASB Statement No. 140 | Superseded by FTB 01-1 | — |

D-95

| Effect of Participating Convertible Securities on the Computation of Basic Earnings per Share | Nullified by Issue 03-6. | — |

D-96

| Accounting for Management Fees Based on a Formula | Revenue Recognition, ch. 36 | 605, Revenue Recognition |

D-97

| Push Down Accounting | Consolidated Financial Statements, ch. 11 | — |

D-98

| Classification and Measurement of Redeemable Securities | Financial Instruments, ch. **17** | 260, Earnings per Share 480, Distinguishing Liabilities from Equity 718, Compensation—Stock Compensation |

D-99

| Questions and Answers Related to Servicing Activities in a Qualifying Special-Purpose Entity under FASB Statement No. 140 | Incorporated in *FASB Staff Implementation Guides,* Questions 22A, 24A, 25A-B, and 28A-D in Q&A 140. | — |

D-100

| Clarification of Paragraph 61(b) of FASB Statement No. 141 and Paragraph 49(b) of FASB Statement No. 142 | Nullified by FAS-141(R). | — |

D-101

| Clarification of Reporting Unit Guidance in Paragraph 30 of FASB Statement No. 142 | Segment Reporting, ch. **37** | 350, Intangibles—Goodwill and Other |

D-102

| Documentation of the Methods Used to Measure Hedge Ineffectiveness under FASB Statement No. 133 | Financial Instruments, ch. **17** | 815, Derivatives and Hedging |

D-103

| Income Statement Characterization of Reimbursements Received for "Out-of-Pocket" Expenses Incurred | Renumbered as Issue 01-14 | — |
| | Results of Operations, ch. **35** | |

D-104

| Clarification of Transition Guidance in Paragraph 51 of FASB Statement No. 144 | Impairment of Long-Lived Assets, ch. **19** | — |

D-105

| Accounting in Consolidation for Energy Trading Contracts between Affiliated Entities When the Activities of One but Not Both Affiliates Are within the Scope of EITF Issue No. 98-10, "Accounting for Contracts Involved in Energy Trading and Risk Management Activities" | Superseded by Issue 02-3. | — |

D-106

| Clarification of Q&A No. 37 of FASB Special Report, *A Guide to Implementation of Statement 87 on Employers' Accounting for Pensions* | Superseded by FAS-158. | — |

D-107

| Lessor Consideration of Third-Party Residual Value Guarantees | Leases, ch. **26** | 840, Leases |

D-108

Use of the Residual Method to Value Acquired Assets Other Than Goodwill	Business Combinations, ch. **6**	350, Intangibles— Goodwill and Other

D-109

Determining the Nature of a Host Contract Related to a Hybrid Financial Instrument Issued In the Form of a Share under FASB Statement No. 133.	Financial Instruments, ch. **17**	815, Derivatives and Hedging

AICPA ACSEC PRACTICE BULLETINS

ORIGINAL PRONOUNCEMENT	2009 *GAAP GUIDE* *LEVELS B, C, AND D* REFERENCE	FASB ACCOUNTING STANDARDS CODIFICATION (ASC) TOPIC
PB-1		
Purpose and Scope of AcSEC Practice Bulletins and Procedures for Their Issuance	Accounting Policies and Standards, ch. **2**	310, Receivables 360, Property, Plant, and Equipment
PB-2		
Elimination of Profits Resulting from Intercompany Transfers of LIFO Inventories	Inventory, ch. **24**	810, Consolidation
PB-4		
Accounting for Foreign Debt/ Equity Swaps	Financial Instruments, ch. **17**	942, Financial Services— Depository and Lending
PB-5		
Income Recognition on Loans to Financially Troubled Countries	Troubled Debt Restructuring, ch. **41**	942, Financial Services— Depository and Lending
PB-11		
Accounting for Preconfirmation Contingencies in Fresh-Start Reporting	Nullified by FSP SOP 90-7-1.	—
PB-13		
Direct-Response Advertising and Probable Future Benefits	Advertising, ch. **3**	340, Deferred Costs and Other Assets
PB-14		
Accounting and Reporting by Limited Liability Companies and Limited Liability Partnerships	Stockholders' Equity, ch. **39**	850, Related Party Disclosures 956, Limited Liability Entities

AICPA ACCOUNTING INTERPRETATIONS

ORIGINAL PRONOUNCEMENT	2009 *GAAP GUIDE* *LEVELS B, C, AND D* REFERENCE	FASB ACCOUNTING STANDARDS CODIFICATION (ASC) TOPIC
AIN-APB 4		
Accounting for the Investment Tax Credit: Accounting Interpretations of APB Opinion No. 4	Income Taxes, ch. **20**	—

AIN-APB-9

Reporting the Results of Operations: Unofficial Accounting Interpretations of APB Opinion No. 9	Results of Operations, ch. **35**	225, Income Statement

AIN-APB 16

Business Combinations: Accounting Interpretations of APB Opinion No. 16	Superseded by FAS-141 for business combinations initiated after June 30, 2001.	—

AIN-APB 17

Intangible Assets: Unofficial Accounting Interpretations of APB Opinion No. 17	Superseded by FAS-142 for fiscal years beginning after December 15, 2001.	—

AIN-APB 18

The Equity Method of Accounting for Investments in Common Stock: Accounting Interpretations of APB Opinion No. 18	Equity Method, ch. **15**	323, Investments—Equity Method and Joint Ventures 810, Consolidation

AIN-APB 21

Interest on Receivables and Payables: Accounting Interpretations of APB Opinion No. 21	Interest on Receivables and Payables, ch. **22**	932, Extractive Activities— Oil and Gas

AIN-APB 25

Accounting for Stock Issued to Employees: Accounting Interpretations of APB Opinion No. 25	Stock-Based Payments, ch. **38**	—

AIN-APB 26

Early Extinguishment of Debt: Accounting Interpretations of APB Opinion No. 26	Extinguishment of Debt, ch. **16**	470, Debt

AIN-APB-30

Reporting the Results of Operations: Accounting Interpretations of APB Opinion No. 30	Results of Operations, ch. **35**	225, Income Statement

FASB IMPLEMENTATION GUIDES

ORIGINAL PRONOUNCEMENT	2009 *GAAP GUIDE* *LEVELS B, C, AND D* REFERENCE	FASB ACCOUNTING STANDARDS CODIFICATION (ASC) TOPIC
FIG-FAS 109		
A Guide to Implementation of Statement 109 on Accounting for Income Taxes	Income Taxes, ch. **20**	740, Income Taxes 852, Reorganizations 855, Subsequent Events 942, Financial Services— Depository and Lending
FIG-FAS 5, 114		
Application of FASB Statements 5 and 114 to a Loan Portfolio	Troubled Debt Restructuring, ch. **41**	—

FIG-FAS 115

A Guide to Implementation of Statement 115 on Accounting for Certain Investments in Debt and Equity Securities	Investments in Debt and Equity Securities, ch. **25**	320, Investments—Debt and Equity Securities 323, Investments—Equity Method and Joint Ventures 958, Not-for-Profit Entities

FIG-FAS 131

Guidance on Applying Statement 31	Segment Reporting, ch. **37**	280, Segment Reporting

FIG-FAS 140

A Guide to Implementation of Statement 140 on Accounting for Transfers and Servicing of Financial Assets and Extinguishments of Liabilities	Transfer and Servicing of Financial Assets, ch. **40**	405, Liabilities 860, Transfers and Servicing

AICPA STAFF GUIDANCE

ORIGINAL PRONOUNCEMENT	2009 *GAAP GUIDE* *LEVELS B, C, AND D* REFERENCE	FASB ACCOUNTING STANDARDS CODIFICATION (ASC) TOPIC
AICPA Staff Guidance on Implementing SOP 97-2		
Software Revenue Recognition	Computer Software, ch. **10**	—

INDEX

C

E